The Common European
Law of Torts

The Common European Law of Torts

Volume One

The Core Areas of Tort Law, its Approximation in Europe, and its Accommodation in the Legal System

by

CHRISTIAN VON BAR

Dr. jur., Professor of Law and Director of the Institute of Private International and Comparative Law of the University of Osnabrück, Honorary Bencher of Gray's Inn

CLARENDON PRESS · OXFORD

OXFORD
UNIVERSITY PRESS

Great Clarendon Street, Oxford OX2 6DP

Oxford University Press is a department of the University of Oxford.
It furthers the University's objective of excellence in research, scholarship,
and education by publishing worldwide in

Oxford New York

Auckland Bangkok Buenos Aires Cape Town Chennai
Dar es Salaam Delhi Hong Kong Istanbul Karachi Kolkata
Kuala Lumpur Madrid Melbourne Mexico City Mumbai Nairobi
São Paulo Shanghai Taipei Tokyo Toronto

Oxford is a registered trade mark of Oxford University Press
in the UK and in certain other countries

Published in the United States
by Oxford University Press Inc., New York

Printed in Great Britain by

Antony Rowe Ltd., Eastbourne

As wine and oyl are Imported to us from abroad: so must ripe Understanding, and many civil Vertues, be imported into our minds from Foreign Writings, and examples of best Ages, we shall else miscarry still, and come short in the attempts of great Enterprise.

John Milton, The Character of the Long Parliament (1641) (*The Works of John Milton*, Vol. XVIII, New York 1938)

Es gehört wesentlich zur Bildung jener grosen Völkerfamilie des westlichen Europa, daß sie nicht blos durch Politik, sondern durch Gleichheit der Cultur und Uebereinstimmung der Gesetzgebung unter einander verknüpft sey.

Karl Ernst *Schmid, Kritische Einleitung in das bürgerliche Recht des französischen Reichs*, Vol. I, 2. Abt., Hildburghausen 1809

Charlemagne nous rappelle que l'Europe est plus ancienne que les états qui la composent. Avec notre communauté, nous redécouvrons l'Europe dans sa totalité.

Jacques Delors on the occasion of his receipt of the International Charlemagne Prize, Aachen 1992

Outline Table of Contents

Detailed Table of Contents

Foreword

I am greatly honoured to be invited to write a Foreword to the English edition of Professor Christian von Bar's book entitled *The Common European Law of Torts*.

Comparative Lawyers in this country have been eagerly looking forward to the publication of this book in English. They will not be disappointed. Here is surely one of the most remarkable, and significant, books on comparative law ever to have seen the light of day.

The book is based on a study of the Law of Torts in all sixteen countries of the European Union. The logistics alone are formidable. Thousands of cases, from all these countries, have been translated into the German language and, as Professor von Bar tells us in his Preface, subjected to examination in a Permanent Seminar on the European Common Law of Torts. But the tasks of distillation, collation and synthesis of these many cases, as well as of the relevant statutes, have been performed by one man, as of course has been the creation of the text of this book. Professor von Bar states in his Preface:

'The person who looks, not only at his own, but also at surrounding laws, broadens the range of possible debate. In writing about different laws he undertakes work which is fundamentally no different from that on his own legal system, so long as the systems are equal in their basic values, in the quality of their legal method, and have continuously learned from each other.'

I cannot help feeling that this statement, while no doubt true in itself, conceals the scale of the operation, and fails to reveal the extraordinary knowledge and skill required to undertake so sophisticated an enterprise. The timeworn expression 'magnum opus' is scarcely adequate to describe this work.

As the reader will discover, a fundamental division is made between on the one hand the Codified Law of Delict of Continental Europe, and on the other hand Scandinavian Liability Laws and the Common Law of Torts. Two substantial sections are devoted to the description and exposition of these two subjects. Both are of profound interest. It is most enlightening for an English common lawyer to read a description of his own law as seen through they eyes of a German comparative lawyer. But it is also educative for him to discover the remarkable differences which exist between the codified systems themselves.

However the story does not stop there. There follow three more substantial sections, concerned with (1) Unification and Approximation of the Law of Delict within the European Union; (2) The Law of Delict in the Context of Private Law—i.e., in relation to Contract, Property Law, and what we call Restitution; and (3) Delict, Constitutional, and Criminal Law. Of these three, I found most interesting the first. It is plain where Professor von Bar's heart lies. His hope, and his aspiration, is that there should evolve (though not through imposition) a truly Common European Law of Torts, applicable throughout the European Union, including the common law countries. He must see his book as a first step along the road to unification. Such a goal is, of course, not easy for a common lawyer to accept, since it must ultimately involve the adoption of a codified system and, it would seem, the abandonment of a case method founded upon the common law's cherished concept of the working hypothesis drawn from the facts of decided cases.

But we must recognise that we live, and work, in an age in which comparative law is becoming a reality. We must all welcome the extension of our legal experience which comes from the study of other systems of law; and we, the judges and scholars of the common law countries, must struggle to ensure that the development of our own system of law, to which we are dedicated, should benefit from that study. Experience has shown that this is not an easy exercise; but, in the end, the rewards will surely be great indeed, and not only for our own legal system, for the common law itself has much to offer. For us, Professor von Bar's remarkable book is both an education and a challenge. Let us profit from the first, and accept the second, in a spirit of willing cooperation and enterprise. And, judging from my own experience of working with distinguished European lawyers, both judges and professors, from civil law countries, this will not only be profoundly interesting, but also most enjoyable.

House of Lords   Robert Goff
London

Preface

This attempt to draw up a system of a common European law of torts is an orthodox treatise on the non-contractual law of obligations. This book displays distinctive features only in so far as its material stems from all the laws of tort within the European Union. It seemed possible to understand and portray each tort law as merely a national manifestation of a single discipline. For, although different legal practices which have each grown naturally in their own environment do occasionally lead to different results, they can be dealt with in the same way as a single legal system in which a lawyer has to find his way through a variety of opinions. The person who looks, not only at his own, but also at surrounding laws, broadens the range of possible debate. In writing about different laws he undertakes work which is fundamentally no different from that on his own legal system, so long as the systems are equal in their basic values, in the quality of their legal method, and have continuously learned from each other. This is the case in the countries of the European Union, and it is therefore possible to condense their different national laws to a *common* European law of torts, or delict. To try to understand its structures does not mean leaving distinctive features of individual national laws out of consideration. Without an understanding of their effectiveness and their elegance, the treasure of judicial knowledge, which distinguishes European private law, will not be appreciated. However, to think in a European fashion means first to stress the common characteristics, secondly, to understand national laws as reactions to developments in neighbouring countries, and thirdly, to tackle historical coincidences and rough edges, which, in view of the process of European unification, can be ground down without substantial loss.

European legal politics is not our primary concern, and the question whether reflections on common European private law can flow into a 'general' law, that is to say into an extensive unification of law in the fashion of a Civil Code, is altogether a *cura posterior*. The challenge is to identify how the sixteen systems actually function, not how they would function if they were united in one system. In our Permanent Seminar on the European Common Law of Torts we tried to master the wealth of material. I have portrayed its methods in another place (in: v. Bar, *A Common European Law of Tort*, Rome 1996, Centro di studi e ricerche di diritto comparato e straniero, saggi, conferenze e seminari). The participants—splendid young lawyers from all parts of the European Union—helped me not only with the investigation of the judgments, but also corrected my drafts and helped with the collection of the latest publications. Despite their invaluable help the danger of my drawing false

xxiii

conclusions remained. For all mistakes, I alone am responsible. I will also not always have succeeded in completely shedding my German skin: however, I hope that is not really important. What counts is the change of approach: we are not portraying here a single national law in comparison with other laws, rather we have chosen from the start a European standpoint, 'European' meaning the states of the European Union.

The analysis of a whole area of law on the basis of sixteen jurisdictions (not counting some additional local peculiarities) places comparative law before new and hitherto little-considered problems. The level of abstraction must change from subject to subject. It is necessary to register how the different systems work, without proceeding on a country-by-country basis. Sometimes methodological questions form the *tertium comparationis*, at other times practical cases. If one does not wish to drown in a sea of material—we have translated several thousand decisions—one must seize the functions of certain legal concepts, and connect them. In addition, it has proved to be particularly important (and difficult) to understand in what way the law of torts is related to its respective neighbouring disciplines. For the parameters of tort law vary from country to country. The more I learn of the achievements of other countries and former generations of lawyers, the greater the respect I feel for both. Might not the idea of a 'national private law' be a contradiction in itself?

I have been forced to resist the temptation to incorporate into the English translation developments which have taken place since publication of the German edition. Given the volume of material involved, to do so would have been tantamount to producing a revised edition. It would also have resulted in considerable differences between this work and the recently published Japanese and almost complete Italian translations. Accordingly, this edition is correct as at summer 1996; subsequent events are taken into account in Volume Two.

The table of abbreviations is the work of Kerstin Hölter. The bibliographical details involved are based, wherever possible, on the *Verzeichnis rechtswissenschaftlicher Zeitschriften und Serien in ausgewählten Bibliotheken der Bundesrepublik Deutschland einschließlich Berlin (West)* (Munich, New York *et al.*, 3rd edn. 1990). I thank Rüdiger Baatz, librarian of the Hamburg Max Planck Institute, for many references. In the choice of abbreviations I have relied as far as possible on the list of suggestions provided in *RabelsZ*. Nicola Everitt and Björn Fasterling identified a series of Irish, Finnish, and Swedish decisions. In the construction of a specialized library, I was supported by the commitment of Hella Zuther. I thank the Beck Publishing House, which produced the German version of this book, for allowing this English publication.

Preface

I had the privilege of finding in the *Fritz Thyssen* Foundation in Cologne a generous and perfectly unbureaucratic sponsor, who had no guarantee of the project's success. The Foundation provided incentive and encouragement. My replacement during two sabbatical semesters was financed, as were other things, by the Leibniz Prize of the *Deutsche Forschungsgemeinschaft*. This gave me the academic's most valuable asset: time.

While translating this book we had to remember that it should be comprehensible to British lawyers and to those of other countries who read English. This caused great difficulties. We began with an initial translation, primarily the work of Frau Doris Paterson-Czech, but also of Sean Middleton and Benedict Knightley Leonard to a more limited extent. Thereafter, Catherine Hughes, Jenny Sweetnam, Benedict Leonard and I attempted to refine the initial work. I worked closely with all involved. Even then, extensive polishing was required by Anna Rayne who looked after me with her great experience of the Oxford University Press. Finally, that this translation has actually materialized is thanks once again to the financial support of the *Deutsche Forschungsgemeinschaft*.

God willing, the second volume of this book will appear in German in about one year. Its translation in English will occupy a further year. It will concern damage and damages, liability for fault and for risk, causation and remoteness of damage, the defendant's defences, and the relationship between liability and insurance.

Osnabrück, July 1998
Christian v. Bar

Acknowledgements

This book presents the results of about 130 sittings of my Permanent Seminar on the Common European Law of Torts supported by the *Fritz Thyssen* Foundation in Cologne. For the Seminar I was also able to rely to a considerable extent upon the funds of my Leibniz Prize of 1993. Without the support of the Foundation and the *Deutsche Forschungsgemeinschaft* the Seminar would not have taken place, and without the Seminar the book would not have resulted. Much of the material used in the book was summarized by the Seminar participants. So my special thanks go to:

Mr Jeroen Antonides, LL M (Dutch law)
lic. jur. Hilde Billiet (Belgian, French and Luxembourgeois law)
lic. jur. Evlalia Eleftheriadou, LL M (Greek law)
lic. jur. Elena Garrido Martín, LL M (Spanish law)
Benedict Knightley Leonard, Barrister (English law 1995–6)
Sean Middleton, LL M, Barrister (English law 1993–5)
Wiss. Mitarbeiter Franz Nieper (Austrian law)
Dott. Karl Pfeifer, LL M (Italian law 1993 and 1995–6)
lic. jur. Elena Rodríguez Mariscal (Portuguese law)
Wiss. Mitarbeiter Assessor Ingo Rogge (Scottish law)
cand. jur. Malene Stein Poulsen, LL M (Danish law)
Mr Arjen Westerdijk (Italian law 1994, Belgian law 1995–6)

Table of Literature Cited in Abbreviated Form

This table contains literature cited frequently and therefore only in an abbreviated form. Unless otherwise indicated this literature does not reappear in the bibliographies preceeding each part or section. For clarity the names of Portuguese authors are listed under the first surname of the author, contrary to the national habit.

Albaladejo, *Derecho civil* vol. ii (2) 8th edn.
Manuel Albaladejo, *Derecho civil*, vol. ii: *Derecho de obligaciones*, book 2: *Contratos en particular y las obligaciones no contractuales* (8th edn. Barcelona 1989)

Almeida Costa, *Obrigações* 5th edn.
Mário Júlio de Almeida Costa, *Direito das Obrigações* (5th edn. Coimbra 1991) (partly quoted here from the 4th edn. 1984)

Alpa, *Responsabilità civile*
Guido Alpa, *Responsabilità civile e danno. Lineamenti e questioni* (Bologna 1991)

Alpa/Bessone, *Atipicità* vol. i, 2nd edn., vol. ii (1) and (2) 2nd edn.
Guido Alpa and Mario Bessone, *Atipicità dell'illecito*, vol. i: *I Profili dottrinali*, vol. ii (in two parts): *Orientamenti della giurisprudenza* (2nd edn. Milan 1981)

Alpa/Bessone, *Responsabilità civile* vol. i and vol. ii 2nd edn.
Guido Alpa and Mario Bessone, La responsabilità civile, vol. i: *Prospettiva storica, colpa aquiliana, illecito contrattuale*; vol. ii: *Rischio d'impresa, assicurazione, analisi economica del diritto* (2nd edn. Milan 1980)

Alpa/Bessone, *Trattato* vol. xiv 2nd edn.
Pietro Rescigno (ed.), *Trattato di Diritto privato*, vol. xiv: *Obbligazioni e Contratti VI* by Guido Alpa and Mario Bessone (2nd [unaltered] edn. Turin 1990)

Andersen *et al.* (-author), *Dansk Privatret* 6th edn.
Paul Krüger Andersen, Halfdan Krag Jespersen, Aage Michelsen, Jørgen Nørgaard, Hardy Rechnagel, and Niels Ørgaard, *Dansk Privatret* (2nd impression of the 6th edn., Copenhagen 1989)

Andersen/Madsen/Nørgaard, *Aftaler og mellemmænd* 2nd edn.
Lennart Lynge Andersen, Palle Bo Madsen and Jørgen Nørgaard, *Aftaler og mellemmænd* (2nd edn. Copenhagen 1991)

André, *Responsabilités*
Robert André, *Les Responsabilités* (typescript Brussels 1981)

Antolisei, *Diritto Penale* 10th edn.

Francesco Antolisei, *Manuale di Diritto Penale. Parte Generale* (10th edn. Milan 1985)

Antunes Varela, *Do Projectol ao Código Civil*

João de Matos Antunes Varela, *Do Projecto ao Código Civil, Comunicação feita na Assembleia Nacional no dia 26 de Novembro de 1966* (Lisbon 1966) (quoted here from the reproduction in *BolMinJust* 161 [1966] pp. 1–85)

Antunes Varela, *Obrigações em Geral* vol. i 7th edn.

João de Matos Antunes Varela, *Das Obrigações em Geral*, vol. i (7th edn. Coimbra 1991)

Asser (-Hartkamp), *Verbintenissenrecht* vol i, 9th edn. vol. ii, 8th edn., and vol iii, 9th edn.

C. Asser's *Handleiding tot de beoefening van het Nederlands burgerlijk recht. Verbintenissenrecht.* Vol. i: *De verbintenis in het algemeen* (9th edn. Zwolle 1992), vol. ii: *Algemene leer der overeenkomsten* (8th edn. Zwolle 1989) and vol. iii: *De verbintenis uit de wet* (9th edn. Zwolle 1994, also quoted partly from the 8th edn. Zwolle 1990) by A. S. Hartkamp

Atiyah (-Cane), *Accidents* 4th edn.

P. S. Atiyah, *Accidents, Compensation and the Law* (5th edn. London *et al.* 1993) by Peter Cane

Aubry/Rau (-Dejean de la Batie) vol. vi, 7th edn.

Charles Aubry and Charles-Frédéric Rau, *Droit civil français*, vol. vi: André Ponsard and Noël Dejean de la Batie, *Contrats civils divers, quasi-contrats, responsabilité civile* (7th edn. Paris 1975)

Bajo Fernández/Díaz-Maroto y Villarejo, *Derecho Penal* 2nd edn.

Miguel Bajo Fernández and Julio Díaz-Maroto y Villarejo, *Manual de Derecho Penal. Parte Especial: Delitos contra la libertad y seguridad, libertad sexual, honor y estado civil* (2nd edn. Madrid 1991)

Baker, *Tort* 5th edn.

C. D. Baker, *Tort* (5th edn. London 1991)

Balis, *Enochikon Dikaion, Genikon Meros* 3rd edn.

Georg Balis, *Enochikon Dikaion Geniko meros* (3rd edn. [New impression] Athens 1969) (Law of Obligations, general part)

Balis, *Genikai Archai tou Astikou Dikaiou* 8th edn.

Georg Balis, *Genikai Archai tou Astikou Dikaiou* (8th edn. Athens 1961) (General Principles of Civil Law)

v. Bar, *Verkehrspflichten*

Christian v. Bar, *Verkehrspflichten. Richter-*

	liche Gefahrsteuerungsgebote im deutschen Deliktsrecht (Cologne *et al.* 1980)
v. Bar (-author), *DeliktsR in Europa*	Christian v. Bar (ed.), *Deliktsrecht in Europa*. With country reports by Jørgen Nørgaard und Hans Henrik Vagner (Denmark), Josephine Shaw (England and Wales), Peter Gotthardt (France), Spyridon Vrellis (Greece), Francesco D. Busnelli (Italy), Ewoud Hondius and Cees van Dam (Netherlands), Peter Lødrup and Viggo Hagstrøm (Norway), Bernd Schilcher and Wolfgang Kleewein (Austria), Jerzy Poczobut (Poland), Jorge Sinde Monteiro, Rui Moura Ramos and Heinrich Ewald Hörster (Portugal, published 1994), Henning Witte (Sweden), Alfred Keller (Switzerland), Josep Santdiumenge (Spain), and Seref Ertas (Turkey) (Cologne *et al.* 1993)
Bénabent, *Obligations* 3rd edn.	Alain Bénabent, *Droit civil. Les obligations* (3rd edn. Paris 1991)
Bengtsson, *Allmännas ansvar*	Bertil Bengtsson, *Det allmännas ansvar enligt skadeståndslagen* (Stockholm 1990)
Bengtsson/Nordenson/ Strömbäck, *Skadestånd* 3rd edn.	Bertil Bengtsson, Ulf Nordenson and Erland Strömbäck, *Skadestånd, Lagstiftning och Praxis med kommentarer* (3rd edn. Uddevalla 1985)
Benucci, *Responsabilità civile*	Eduardo Bonasi Benucci, *La responsabilità civile. Esposizione critica e sistematica della giurisprudenza* (Milan 1955)
BGB-RGRK (-author) 12th edn.	*Das Bürgerliche Gesetzbuch mit besonderer Berücksichtigung der Rechtsprechung des Reichgerichts und des Bundesgerichtshofes* (12th edn. Berlin and New York 1989) (quoted here with the commentary of Friedrich Kreft, Karl Nüßgens, and Erich Steffen) (formerly 'Reichsgerichts-räte-Kommentar')
Bianca, *Diritto civile* vols. iii and iv	C. Massimo Bianca, *Diritto civile*, vol. iii: *Il contratto* (New impression of the 1st edn. 1984 Milan 1987); vol. iv: *L'obbligazione* (altered reprint of the 1st edn. 1990 Milan 1992)

Bloembergen (-author), *Onrechtmatige daad* vols. i and ii

A. R. Bloembergen (ed.), *Onrechtmatige daad*, vols. i and ii (loose-leaf collection, Deventer, Oct. 1994) (quoted here with the commentaries of A. R. Bloembergen, C. H. M. Jansen, G. E. van Maanen, J. P. Michiels van Kessenich-Hoogendam, C. J. J. C. van Nispen, and F. T. Oldenhuis)

Bloembergen (-author), *Schadevergoeding*

A. R. Bloembergen (ed.), *Schadevergoeding* (loose-leaf collection, Deventer, as of June 1994) (quoted here with the commentaries of A. R. Bloembergen, A. T. Bolt, R. J. B. Boonekamp and T. E. Deurvorst)

Brüggemeier, *Deliktsrecht*

Gert Brüggemeier, *Deliktsrecht: Ein Hand-und Lehrbuch* (Baden-Baden 1986)

Burrows, *Remedies*

A. S. Burrows, *Remedies for Torts and Breach of Contract* (London 1987)

Bussani, *Colpa soggettiva*

Mauro Bussani, *La colpa soggettiva* (Padua 1991)

Capitant (-*Terré/Lequette*), *Grands arrêts* 9th edn.

Henri Capitant, *Les grands arrêts de la jurisprudence civile*. François Terré and Yves Lequette (edd.). (9th edn. Paris 1991)

Carbonnier, *Droit Civil* vol. i, 16th edn. vol. iii, 15th edn. and vol. iv, 14th edn.

Jean Carbonnier, *Droit Civil*, vol. i: *Introduction, Les Personnes* (16th edn. Paris 1987), vol. iii: *Les Biens* (15th edn. Paris 1992; also quoted partly from the 14th edn. Paris 1990), vol. iv: *Les Obligations* (14th edn. Paris 1990)

Castán Tobeñas, *Derecho civil* vol. iv, 12th edn.

José Castán Tobeñas, *Derecho civil español, común y foral*, vol. iv: *Derecho de obligaciones. Las particulares relaciones obligatorias* (12th edn. Madrid 1985)

Cavanillas Múgica, *Transformación*

Santiago Cavanillas Múgica, *La transformación de la responsabilidad civil en la jurisprudencia* (Pamplona 1987)

Cavanillas Múgica/Tapia Fernández, *Concurrencia de responsabilidad*

Santiago Cavanillas Múgica and Isabel Tapia Fernández, *La concurrencia de responsabilidad contractual y extracontractual*. Tratamiento sustantivo y procesal (Madrid 1992)

Cendon (-author) vol. iv

Paolo Cendon (ed.), *Commentario al Codice Civile*, vol. iv (in two books,

Arts. 1173–1654 and Arts. 1655–2059), quoted here with the commentaries of Guido Santoro (Arts. 1218–1222), Saverio Schiavone (Arts. 1483–1499), Umberto Breccia (Art. 2031), Luigi Gaudino (Arts. 2043, 2049, and 2056), Angelo Venchiarutti (Arts. 2044–2048), Patrizia Ziviz (Arts. 2050–2052, 2059), Mauro Bussani (Art. 2053), Flavio Peccenini (Art. 2054), Fabrizio Devescovi, and Mariarosa Gambi (Art. 2055), Pier Giuseppe Monateri (Art. 2057) and Enrico Tomasi (Art. 2058) (new impression of the 1991 Turin edition, Turin 1992)

Cendon (ed.), *Responsabilità civile*
La Responsabilià civile. Saggi critici e rassegne di giurisprudenza, Paolo Cendon (ed.) with contributions by M. Bussani, G. Caselli, P. Cendon, L. Gaudino, A. Venchiarutti, and P. Ziviz (the precise titles of which are listed in the relevant bibliography) (Milan 1988)

Charlesworth & Percy (-*Percy*), *Negligence* 8th edn.
John Charlesworth, *On Negligence* (8th edn. London 1990 [supplement 1993]) by R. A. Percy (The Common Law Library No. 6)

Cian/Trabucchi, *Commentario breve* 4th edn.
Giorgio Cian and Alberto Trabucchi, *Commentario breve al Codice Civile* (4th edn. Padua 1992)

Clerk & Lindsell (-author), *Torts* 16th edn.
Clerk & Lindsell on Torts, edited and written by M. R. Brazier, A. S. Burrows, H. F. Carty, R. W. M. Dias (general editor), J. Jeffs, A. Tettenborn, Lord Wedderburn, and D. E. C. Yale (16th edn. London 1989 [supplement 1993])

Código civil, Debates parlamentarios vols. i and ii
El Código civil. Debates parlamentarios 1885–1889 Provisional studies by José Luis de los Mozos, edited by Rosario Herrero Gutiérrez and María Ángeles Vallejo Úbeda (reprint Madrid 1989)

Cooke, *Tort*
John Cooke, *Law of Tort* (London 1992)

Cooke/Oughton, *Obligations*
P. J. Cooke and D. W. Oughton, *The Common Law of Obligations* (London 1989)

Cornelis, *Buitencontractueel aansprakelijkheidsrecht/ Responsabilité extra-contractuelle*

Ludo Cornelis, *Beginselen van het Belgische buitencontractuele aansprakelijkheidsrecht*, vol. i: *De onrechtmatige daad* (Antwerp *et al.* 1989); appearing in French under the title: *Principes du droit belge de la responsabilité extra-contractuelle*, vol. i: *L'acte illicite* (Brussels *et al.* 1991)

de Cupis, *Il danno* vol. i, 3rd edn. and vol. ii, 3rd edn.

Adriano de Cupis, *Il danno. Teoria generale della responsabilità civile*, 2 vols. (3rd edn. Milan 1979)

Dahl *et al. Obligationsretlig Domssamling* 6th edn.

Børge Dahl, Bo von Eyben, Bernhard Gomard, Joseph Lookofsky, Peter Møgelvang-Hansen, and Jørgen Nørgaard, *Obligationsretlig Domssamling* (6th edn. Copenhagen 1988)

Dalcq, *Responsabilité civile* vol. i, 2nd edn. and vol. ii

Roger O. Dalcq, *Traité de la responsabilité civile*, vol. i: *Les causes de responsabilité.* Vol. ii: *Le lien de causalité. Le dommage et sa réparation* (=*Les Novelles Corpus Juris Belgici*, established by Léon Hennebicq, Droit Civil, 5 vols, vol. i [2nd edn.] and vol. ii) (Brussels 1967 and 1962 respectively)

De Ángel Yáguez, *Responsabilidad civil* 3rd edn.

Ricardo de Ángel Yáguez, *Tratado de Responsabilidad civil* (3rd edn. Madrid 1993)

Deliyannis/Kornilakis, Eidiko Enochiko Dikaio vols. i, ii, and iii

Johannes Deliyannis and Panos Kornilakis, *Eidiko Enochiko Dikaio* (in particular, The Law of Obligations), 3 vols. (Thessalonika 1992)

Deutsch, *Haftungsrecht* vol. i

Erwin Deutsch, *Haftungsrecht*, vol. i: *Allgemeine Lehren* (Cologne 1976)

Deutsch, *Unerlaubte Handlungen* 2nd edn.

Erwin Deutsch, *Unerlaubte Handlungen, Schadensersatz und Schmerzensgeld* (2nd edn. Cologne *et al.* 1993)

Dias/Markesinis, *English Law of Torts*

R. W. M. Dias and B. S. Markesinis, *The English Law of Torts* (Brussels 1976)

Dias/Markesinis, *Tort Law* 2nd edn.

R. W. M. Dias and B. S. Markesinis, *Tort Law* (2nd edn. Oxford 1989)

Díez-Picazo, *Fundamentos* vol. i, 4th edn., vol. ii, 4th edn., and vol. iii, 4th edn.

Luis Díez-Picazo, *Fundamentos del Derecho civil patrimonial*, vol. i: *Introducción. Teoría del contrato* (4th edn. Madrid

1993); vol. ii: *Las relaciones obligatorias* (4th edn. Madrid 1993) and vol. iii: *Las relaciones jurídico-reales. El registro de la propiedad. La posesión* (4th edn. Madrid 1995)

Díez-Picazo/Gullón, *Sistema* vol. i, 7th edn., vol. ii, 6th edn., and vol. iii, 4th edn.

Luis Díez-Picazo and Antonio Gullón, *Sistema de Derecho Civil*, vol. i (7th edn. Madrid 1989) and vol. ii (6th edn. Madrid 1989; also partly quoted from the 5th edn. 1987) and vol. iii (new impression 1989 of the 4th edn. Madrid 1988)

Dufwa, *Flera Skadeståndssky-ldiga* vols. i, ii, and iii

Bill W. Dufwa, *Flera Skadeståndsskyldiga*, 3 vols, (Stockholm 1993)

Dugdale/Stanton, *Professional Negligence*

A. M. Dugdale and K. M. Stanton, *Professional Negligence* (London 1982)

van Dunné, *Verbintenissenrecht* vol. i, 2nd edn. and vol. ii, 2nd edn.

J. M. van Dunné, *Verbintenissenrecht*, vol. i: *Contractenrecht*, pt. 1: *Totstandkoming van overeenkomsten, inhoud, contractsvoorwaarden, gebreken*, vol. ii: *Contractenrecht*, pt. 2; *Onrechtmatige daad, overige verbintenissen* (2nd edn. Deventer 1993)

Encyclopédie Dalloz (-author), *Rép. Dr. Civ.* vols. ii and viii

Encyclopédie Dalloz, Répertoire de droit civil, vols. ii and viii (Paris, updated 1995), including: Françoise Bénac-Schmidt and Christian Larroumet, *Responsabilité du fait des choses inanimées, Responsabilité du fait des animaux, Responsabilité du fait des bâtiments* and *Responsabilité du fait d'autrui*; Philippe Conte, *Responsabilité du fait personnel*; Marie-Claire Lambert-Piéri, *Responsabilité—Régime des accidents de la circulation*; Gérard Légier, *Responsabilité contractuelle*; Rodière, *Responsabilité du fait personnel*; and André Tunc, *Responsabilité (en général)*

ErmAK (-author)

Ermineia tou Astikou Kodikos (Athens 1949ff.) (Commentary on Cc; not fully published, quoted here with the commentaries of Litzeropoulos, Michaelides-Nouaros and Sourlas)

Erman (-*Schiemann*) vol. i, 9th edn.
Handkommentar zum Bürgerlichen Gesetzbuch in zwei Bänden. Until the 4th edn. edited by Walter Erman; quoted here with the commentary of §§ 823–838, 840–853 by Gottfried Schiemann (9th edn. Munster 1993)

Espín Cánovas, *Manual de Derecho civil* vol. iii, 6th edn.
Diego Espín Cánovas, *Manual de Derecho civil español* vol. iii: *Obligaciones y contratos* (6th edn. Madrid 1983)

Esser/Schmidt, *Schuldrecht* vol. i (2) 7th edn.
Schuldrecht, vol. i: *Allgemeiner Teil*, vol. ii: *Durchführungshindernisse und Vertragshaftung, Schadensausgleich und Mehrseitigkeit beim Schuldverhältnis*. Started by Josef Esser, continued by Eike Schmidt (7th edn. Heidelberg 1993)

Esser/Weyers, *Schuldrecht* vol. ii, 7th edn.
Schuldrecht, vol. ii: *Besonderer Teil*. Started by Josef Esser, continued by Hans-Leo Weyers (7th edn. Heidelberg 1991)

von Eyben, *Patientforsikring*
Bo von Eyben, *Patientforsikring* (Copenhagen 1993)

von Eyben/Nørgaard/Vagner, *Erstatningsret* 2nd edn.
Bo von Eyben, Jørgen Nørgaard, and Hans Henrik Vagner, *Lærebog i erstatningsret* (2nd edn. Copenhagen 1993)

Ferid/Sonnenberger, *Frz. Zivilrecht* vol. ii, 2nd edn.
Murad Ferid and Hans Jürgen Sonnenberger, *Das französische Zivilrecht*, vol. ii: *Schuldrecht: Die einzelnen Schuldverhältnisse. Sachenrecht.* (2nd edn. Heidelberg 1986)

Ferrari, *Atipicità*
Franco Ferrari, *Atipicità dell'illecito civile* (Milan 1992)

Fikentscher, *Schuldrecht* 8th edn.
Wolfgang Fikentscher, *Schuldrecht* (8th edn. Berlin 1991)

Filios, *Enochiko Dikaio* vol. ii (2) 3rd edn.
Pavlos Filios, *Enochiko Dikaio*, vol. ii: *Eidiko Meros*, 2nd book (3rd edn. Athens 1992) (Law of Obligations, special part, 2nd book; dealing with Tort)

Fleming, *Torts* 8th edn.
John Gunther Fleming, *The Law of Torts* (8th edn. North Ryde, N S W, 1993)

Flour/Aubert, *Obligations* vol. ii, 5th edn.
Jacques Flour and Jean-Luc Aubert, *Droit Civil. Les Obligations*, vol. ii: *Le Fait Juridique* (5th edn. Paris 1991)

Forchielli, *Responsabilità civile*
Paolo Forchielli, *Responsabilità civile* (Padua 1983)

Franzoni, *Fatti illeciti*

Massimo Franzoni, *Dei fatti illeciti*. Arts. 2043–2059 of the commentary to the Codice civile by Scialoja-Branca. Francesco Galgano (ed.) (Bologna and Rome 1993)

Galgano, *Diritto civile e commerciale* vol. ii (1) and (2) 2nd edn.

Francesco Galgano, *Diritto civile e commerciale*, vol. ii: *Le obbligazioni e i contratti*, pt. 1: *Obbligazioni in generale, contratti in generale* (2nd edn. Milan 1993); pt. 2: *I singoli contratti, gli atti unilaterali e titoli di credito, i fatti illeciti e gli altri fatti fonte di obbligazione, la tutela del credito* (reprint 1992 of the 2nd edn. Milan 1990)

Galvão Telles, *Obrigações* 6th edn.

Inocêncio Galvão Telles, *Direito das Obrigações* (6th edn. Coimbra 1989)

Geigel (-author), *Haftpflichtprozeß* 21st edn.

Robert Geigel, *Der Haftpflichtprozeß*, edited by Günter Schlegelmilch, revised by Kurt Haag, Hans-Ulrich Kolb, Adalbert Kunschert, Hermann Plagemann, Roland Rixecker, Günter Schlegelmilch, and Erich Schönwerth (21st edn. Munich 1993)

Gentile/Guerreri/Guerreri, *La responsabilità* vols. i—ix

La responsabilità. Rassegna di bibliografia e giurisprudenza Guido Gentile (ed.) (†), Dante e Gigliola Guerreri with contributions from Augusta Lagostena Bassi (loose-leaf edition in 9 vols. as of 31 Dec. 1991) (Milan 1992) (cited by key words, sections [1–946], and numbers; e.g. 'voce Responsabilità civile—cose in custodia 69 [223]')

Georgiades, *Sitimata astikis evthinis*

Apostolos Georgiades, *Sitimata astikis evthinis* (Athens 1972) (Problems of Civil Liability)

Georgiades/Stathopoulos (-author), *Greek Cc* vols. i, ii, iv, and v

Apostolos Georgiades and Michael Stathopoulos, *Astikos Kodikas (erminia kat'arthro)*, vol. i: *Genikai Archai* (Athens 1978); vol. ii: *Geniko Enochiko* (Athens 1979); vol. iv: *Eidiko Enochiko* (Athens 1982); and vol. v: *Empragmato Dikaio* (Athens 1985); (Commentary on Greek Cc, vol. i: General Principles; vol. ii: Law of Obligations, general part; vol.

iv: Law of Obligations, special part; and vol. v: Property Law)

Geri/Breccia/Busnelli/Natoli, *Diritto civile* vol. iii
Lina Bigliazzi Geri, Umberto Breccia, Francesco D. Busnelli, and Ugo Natoli, *Diritto civile*, vol. iii: *Obbligazioni e contratti* (new impression of the 1989 Turin edition, Turin 1990) (*Il sistema giuridico italiano*)

Van Gerven, *Verbintenissenrecht* vol. ii, 3rd edn.
Walter Van Gerven, *Verbintenissenrecht*, book 2 (3rd edn. Leuven 1988)

Giur. sist. Bigiavi (-author) vols. i–iv
La responsabilità civile. Una rassegna di dottrina e giurisprudenza, directed by Guido Alpa and Mario Bessone (*Giurisprudenza sistematica di diritto civile e commerciale, fondata da Walter Bigiavi*) (6 vols., Turin 1987)

Gloag/Henderson (-author), *Introduction* 9th edn.
W. M. Gloag and R. Candlish Henderson, *Introduction to the Law of Scotland*, A. B. Wilkinson and W. A. Wilson (edd.) assisted by J. A. D. Hope, A. F. Rodger, and Ann Paton (9th edn. Edinburgh 1987)

Gomard, *Almindelig kontraktsret*
Bernhard Gomard, *Almindelig kontraktsret* (Copenhagen 1988)

Gomard, *Civilprocessen* 2nd edn.
Bernhard Gomard, *Civilprocessen* (2nd edn. Copenhagen 1984)

Gomard, *Erstatningsregler*
Bernhard Gomard, *Forholdet mellem Erstatningsregler i og uden for Kontraktsforhold* (reprint of the 1958 issue, Copenhagen 1990)

Gomard, *Obligationsret* vol. i, 2nd edn., vols. ii and iii
Bernhard Gomard, *Obligationsret*; vol. i (2nd issue of the 2nd edn., Copenhagen 1990); vol. ii (2nd issue of the 1st edn., Copenhagen 1993) and vol. iii (Copenhagen 1993)

Gomard, *Obligationsretten i en nøddeskal* vol. i, vol. ii, vol. iii, 6th edn., and vol. iv
Bernhard Gomard, *Obligationsretten i en nøddeskal* (in 3 vols. and a supplement) (Copenhagen 1972/73 vols. i and ii, 1989 vol. iii, 6th edn., and 1977 vol. iv)

Gschnitzer/Faistenberger/ Barta/ Eccher, *Schuldrecht* BT 2nd edn.
Franz Gschnitzer, *Österreichisches Schuldrecht. Besonderer Teil und Schadenersatz*, 2nd edn. by Christoph Faistenberger,

Heinz Barta, and Bernhard Eccher (Vienna and New York 1988)

Hagstrøm, *Culpanormen* 4th edn.
Viggo Hagstrøm, *Culpanormen* (4th edn. Oslo 1983)

Halsbury's Laws of England (-author) 4th edn.
Lord Hailsham of St Marylebone (ed.), *Halsbury's Laws of England*, 56 vols. including supplements (4th edn. London, last supplement vol. 1994)

Harpwood, *Tort*
Vivienne Harpwood, *Law of Tort* (London 1994)

Hellner, *Skadeståndsrätt* 4th edn.
Jan Hellner, *Skadeståndsrätt* (4th edn. Stockholm 1985 with supplement 1987)

Hepple & Matthews, *Tort* 3rd edn.
B. A. Hepple and M. H. Matthews, *Tort: Cases and Materials* (4th edn. London 1991)

Hijma/Olthof, *Compendium* 4th edn.
Jac. Hijma and M. M. Olthof, *Compendium van het Nederlands vermogensrecht. Leidraad voor het NBW met verwijzingen naar het BW* (4th edn. Deventer 1990)

Hörster, *Parte Geral*
Heinrich Ewald Hörster, *A Parte Geral do Código Civil Português* (Coimbra 1992)

Jackson & Powell, *Professional Negligence* 3rd edn.
Rupert Jackson and John L. Powell, *On Professional Negligence* (3rd edn. London 1992) (with contributions from Mark R. N. Cannon, Hugh L. Evans, Iain H. D. Hughes, Roger P. D. Stewart and Jalil A. Asif) (The Common Law Library No. 12)

Jakobs/Schubert, *Beratung des BGB*
Horst Heinrich Jakobs and Werner-Schubert, *Die Beratung des Bürgerlichen Gesetzbuchs in systematischer Zusammenstellung der unveröffentlichten Quellen. Recht der Schuldverhältnisse III, §§ 652 bis 853* (Berlin 1983)

James/Brown, *Principles* 4th edn.
Philip James and D. J. Latham Brown, General Principles of the Law of Torts (4th edn. London 1978)

Jansen, *Onrechtmatige daad*
C. H. M. Jansen, *Onrechtmatige daad: algemene bepalingen* (Monografieën Nieuw BW; B series vol. 45) (Deventer 1986)

JClCiv (-author)
Collection des Juris-Classeurs. Juris-Classeur Civil. Directeurs à partir de 1980 Pierre

Catala and Philippe Simler. (Loose-leaf, Paris 1962 ff., as of 1995) (cited by author, keyword, article, and if neccesary fasc.)

Jones, *Torts* 3rd edn.

Michael Jones, *Textbook on Torts* (4th edn. London 1994)

Jørgensen, *Erstatningsret* 2nd edn.

Stig Jørgensen, *Erstatningsret* (reprint [containing no year] of the 2nd edn., Copenhagen 1971)

Jørgensen/Nørgaard, *Erstatningsret*

Stig Jørgensen and Jørgen Nørgaard, *Erstatningsret* (Copenhagen 1976)

Jourdain, *Principes*

Patrice Jourdain, *Les principes de la responsabilité civile* (Paris 1992)

Karlgren, *Skadeståndsrätt* 5th edn.

Hjalmar Karlgren, *Skadeståndsrätt* (5th edn. Stockholm 1972)

Karnov (-author), vol. i 13th edn.–vol. vii 13th edn.

Karnovs Lovsamling, Claus Gulmann, W. E. von Eyben Jørgen Nørgaard (edd.) (13th edn. Copenhagen 1992 [vols. i to iii] and 1993 [vols. iv and v] and 1994 [vols. vi and vii])

Kavkas/Kavkas, *Enochikon Dikaion* vol. ii 6th edn.

Konstantin Kavkas and Dimitrios Kavkas, *Enochikon Dikaion (Erminia kata arthron), Eidiko meros*, vol. ii (Arts. 730–944 Cc) (6th edn. Athens 1982) (Law of Obligations special part, commentary)

Kötz, *Deliktsrecht* 7th edn.

Hein Kötz, *Deliktsrecht* (7th edn. Neuwied 1996; occasionally also quoted here from the 6th edn. Neuwied 1994)

Koziol, *Österr. Haftpflichtrecht* vol. i, 2nd edn. and if necessary as Koziol (-*Rummel*)—vol. ii, 2nd edn.

Helmut Koziol, *Österreichisches Haftpflichtrecht*, vol. i: general part (2nd edn. Vienna 1980), vol. ii: special part (2nd edn. Vienna 1984; with a section on unfair competition by Peter Rummel)

Koziol/Welser, *Grundriß* vol. i, 9th edn.

Helmut Koziol and Rudolf Welser, *Grundriß des bürgerlichen Rechts*, vol. i: *Allgemeiner Teil und Schuldrecht* (10th edn. Vienna 1995; occasionally also quoted from the 9th edn. Vienna 1992)

Kruse, *Erstatningsretten* 5th edn.

Anders Vinding Kruse, *Erstatningsretten* (5th edn. Copenhagen 1989)

Kruse/Møller, *Erstatningsansvarsloven* 3rd edn.

Anders Vinding Kruse and Jens Møller, *Erstatningsansvarsloven med kommentarer* (3rd edn. Copenhagen 1993)

Lambert-Faivre, *Droit des assurances* 8th edn.

Yvonne Lambert-Faivre, *Droit des assurances* (8th edn. Paris 1992)

Larenz/Canaris, *Schuldrecht* vol. ii (2) 13th edn.

Karl Larenz, *Lehrbuch des Schuldrechts*, vol. ii: *Besonderer Teil*. 2nd book continued by Claus-Wilhelm Canaris (13th edn. Munich 1994)

The Laws of Scotland (-author)

The Law Society of Scotland, Thomas Smith (general editor), *The Laws of Scotland*. Stair Memorial Encyclopaedia (25 vols., Edinburgh, vol. i 1987 ff.)

Lawson/Markesinis, *Tortious Liability* vols. i and ii

F. H. Lawson and B. S. Markesinis, *Tortious Liability for Unintentional Harm in the Common Law and the Civil Law*, vol. i: text; vol. ii: Materials (Cambridge [UK] *et al.* 1982)

Lete del Río, *Obligaciones* vol. ii

José Manuel Lete del Río, *Derecho de Obligaciones*, vol. ii: *El contrato en general. Cuasicontratos. Enriquecimiento sin causa. Responsabilidad extracontractual* (Madrid 1989)

Levi, *Responsabilità civile e responsabilità oggettiva*

Giulio Levi, *Responsabilità civile e responsabilità oggettiva. Diversi modi di introduzione della responsabilità oggettiva e loro influenza sulla legislazione italiana* (Milan 1986)

Litzeropoulos, *Stoicheia Enochikou Dikaiou ii*

Alexandros Litzeropoulos, *Stoicheia Enochikou Dikaiou* (Paradoseis) (Athens 1960, reprint 1968) (Elements of the Law of Obligations, lectures)

Locré, vol. vi

M. le baron de Locré (ed.), *Législation Civile, Commerciale et Criminelle ou Commentaire et Complément des Codes Français*, vol. vi. New impression of the 1836 Brussels edition (Frankfurt am Main 1990)

Lødrup, *Erstatningsrett* 2nd edn.

Peter Lødrup, *Lærebok i erstatningsrett* (2nd edn. Oslo 1987)

López Garrido/García Arán, *Código Penal de 1995*

Diego López Garrido and Mercedes García Arán, *El Código Penal de 1995 y la voluntad del legislador. Comentario al texto y al debate parlamentario* (Madrid 1995)

Lyngsø, *Dansk Forsikringsret* 6th edn.

Preben Lyngsø, *Dansk Forsikringsret* (6th edn. Copenhagen 1990) van Maanen, *Onrechtmatige Daad*

G. E. van Maanen, *Onrechtmatige Daad. Aspekten van de ontwikkeling van een omstreden leerstuk* (Deventer 1986)

Malaurie/Aynès, *Droit civil* 3rd edn.

Philippe Malaurie and Laurent Aynès, *Cours de droit civil. Les obligations* (3rd edn. Paris 1992)

Markesinis, *German Law of Torts* 3rd edn.

Basil S. Markesinis, *The German Law of Torts: A Comparative Introduction* (3rd edn. Oxford 1994)

Markesinis/Deakin, *Tort Law* 3rd edn.

Basil S. Markesinis and Simon F. Deakin, *Tort Law* (3rd edn. Oxford 1994)

De Martini, *Fatti produttivi di danno*

Demetrio de Martini, *I fatti produttivi di danno risarcibile* (Padua 1983)

Martins de Almeida, *Manual de Acidentes* 3rd edn.

Dario Martins de Almeida, *Manual de Acidentes de Viação* (3rd edn. Coimbra 1987)

Marty/Raynaud, *Droit Civil* vol. i, 2nd edn., and vol. ii (1) 2nd edn.

Gabriel Marty and Pierre Raynaud, *Droit Civil*, vol. i: *Introduction générale à l'étude du droit* (2nd edn. Paris 1972) and vol. ii: *Les Obligations*. Book 1: *Les sources* (2nd edn. Paris 1988)

Mazeaud/Chabas, *Obligations* 8th edn.

Established by Henri, Léon, and Jean Mazeaud; François Chabas, *Leçons de droit civil*, vol. ii, book 1: *Obligations, théorie générale* (8th edn. Paris 1991)

Mazeaud/Tunc, *Responsabilité civile* vol. i, 6th edn. Mazeaud /Mazeaud, *Responsabilité civile* vol. ii, 6th edn. or Mazeaud /Mazeaud/Chabas, *Responsabilité civile* vol. iii (1) 6th edn.

Henri and Léon Mazeaud and André Tunc, *Traité théorique et pratique de la Responsabilité civile délictuelle et contractuelle*, vol. i (6th edn. Paris 1965) Henri, Léon, and Jean Mazeaud, *Traité théorique et pratique de la responsabilité civile délictuelle et contractuelle*, vol. ii (6th edn. Paris 1970) or Henri, Leon and Jean Mazeaud and François Chabas, *Traité théorique et pratique de la responsabilité civile délictuelle et contractuelle*, vol. iii, pt. 1 (Paris 1978)

McMahon/Binchy, *Casebook* 2nd edn.

Bryan M. E. McMahon and William Binchy, *A Casebook on the Irish Law of Torts* (2nd edn. Dublin 1992)

McMahon/Binchy, *Irish Law of Torts* 2nd edn.

Bryan M. E. McMahon and William Binchy, *Irish Law of Torts* (2nd edn. Dublin 1990)

Menezes Cordeiro, *Obrigações* vols. i and ii   A. M. R. Menezes Cordeiro, *Direito das Obrigações*, vols. i and ii (Lisbon 1980)

Michaelides-Nouaros, *Enochikon Dikaion*   Georg Michaelides-Nouaros, *Enochikon Dikaion* (Law of Obligations) (Thessaloika, containing no year, probably 1959)

Morillas Cueva, *Consecuencias del delito*   Lorenzo Morillas Cueva, *Teoría de las consecuencias jurídicas del delito* (Madrid 1991)

Mot vol. ii   *Motive zu dem Entwurfe eines Bürgerlichen Gesetzbuches für das Deutsche Reich*, vol. ii: *Recht der Schuldverhältnisse* (Berlin and Leipzig 1888)

Mullis/Oliphant, *Torts*   Alistair Mullis and Ken Oliphant, *Torts* (Basingstoke and London 1993)

MünchKomm (-author) 2nd and 3rd edns.   *Münchener Kommentar zum Bürgerlichen Gesetzbuch*, edited by Kurt Rebmann and Franz Jürgen Säcker, 7 vols. (2nd edn. Munich 1984–90, 3rd edn. from 1992); quoted here with the commentaries of Dieter Medicus, Wolfgang Grunsky, Hans-Joachim Mertens, and Peter Schwerdtner

Neto/Martins, *Código civil* 7th edn.   Abílio Neto and Herlander A. Martins, *Código civil anotado* (7th edn. Lisbon 1990)

Nygaard, *Skade og ansvar* 2nd edn.   Nils Nygaard, *Skade og ansvar* (4th issue of the 2nd edn. Oslo 1994)

Oliveira Matos, *Código da Estrada* 7th edn.   Manuel de Oliveira Matos, *Código da Estrada Anotado* (7th edn. Coimbra 1991)

de Page, *Droit Civil Belge* vol. ii, 3rd edn., and vol. iii, 3rd edn.   Henri de Page, *Traité élémentaire de droit civil belge*, vol. ii, *Les incapables, les obligations (première partie)* (3rd edn. Brussels 1964); vol. iii, *Les obligations (seconde partie)* (3rd edn. Brussels 1967)

Palandt (-author) 54th edn.   Palandt, *Bürgerliches Gesetzbuch*, revised by Peter Bassenge, Uwe Diederichsen, Wolfgang Edenhofer, Helmut Heinrichs, Andreas Heldrich, and Hans Putzo (54th edn. Munich 1995)

Pandolfelli *et al.*, *Codice civile*   G. Pandolfelli, G. Scarpello, M. Stella Richter, and G. Dallari, *Codice Civile. Libro delle obbligazioni. Illustrato con i lavori preparatori e disposizioni di attua-zione e transitorie* (Milan 1942)

Pannett, *Torts* 6th edn. — A. J. Pannett, *Law of Torts* (6th edn. London 1994)

Papantoniou, *Genikes Arches* 3rd edn. — Nikolaus Papantoniou, *Genikes Arches tou Astikou Dikaiou* (3rd edn. Athens 1983) (General Principles of Civil Law)

Parlementaire Geschiedenis vol. vi — *Parlementaire Geschiedenis van het Nieuwe Burgerlijk Wetboek. Parlementaire Stukken systematisch gerangschikt en van Noten voorzien* by C. J. van Zeben and W. du Pon with contributions from M. M. Olthof. Boek 6: *Algemeen Gedeelte van het Verbintenissenrecht* (Deventer 1981)

Parlementaire Geschiedenis vol. vi (Inv.) — *Parlementaire Geschiedenis van het Nieuwe Burgerlijk Wetboek*, Boek 6 (Invoering). Invoering Boeken 3, 5 en 6. Boek 6: *Algemeen gedeelte van het verbintenissen-recht* by W. H. M. Reehuis and E. E. Slob (Deventer 1990)

Pascual Estevill, *Responsabilidad civil* vols. i, ii (1) and ii (2) — Luis Pascual Estevill, *Responsabilidad civil*, vol. i: *Hacia un concepto actual de la responsabilidad civil (Parte General)* (Barcelona 1989); vol. ii, book 1: *Respon-sabilidad contractual (Parte especial)* (Bar-celona 1992); vol. ii, book 2: *La responsabilidad extracontractual aquiliana o delictual (Parte especial cont.)* (Barcelona 1990)

Patti, *Famiglia e responsabilità civile* — Salvatore Patti, *Famiglia e responsabilità civile* (Milan 1984)

Paz-Ares/Díez-Picazo/ Bercovitz/Salvador (-author), *Código Civil* vol. i, 2nd edn., and vol. ii, 2nd edn. — Cándido Paz-Ares, Luis Díez-Picazo, Rodrigo Bercovitz, and Pablo Salvador, *Comentario del Código Civil*, 2 vols., pub-lished by the Ministerio de Justicia (2nd edn. Madrid 1993)

Pereira Coelho, *Obrigações* — Francisco Manuel Pereira Coelho, *Obri-gações (sumários das lições ao curso de 1966–1967)* (Coimbra 1967, typescript)

Perlingieri (-author), *Codice civile* vol. iv (2), 2nd edn. — Pietro Perlingieri (ed.), *Codice civile annotato con la dottrina e la giurispru-denza*, vol. iv, 2nd book: Arts. 1470–2059 (2nd edn. Naples 1991). Quoted here with the commentaries of Concetta Maglione and Antonio Flamini

Pessoa Jorge, *Pressupostos da Responsabilidade civil* — Fernando de Sandy Lopes Pessoa Jorge, *Ensaio sobre os Pressupostos da Responsabilidade civil* (Lisbon 1968)

Pires de Lima/Antunes Varela, *Cc anotado* vol. i, 4th edn. and vol. ii, 4th edn. — Pires de Lima and Antunes Varela, *Código civil anotado*, vols. i and ii (4th edn. Coimbra 1987)

Pitchfork, *Tort* 8th edn. — E. D. Pitchfork, *Tort Textbook* (8th edn. London 1994)

Planiol/Ripert (-*Esmein*) vol. vi (1), 2nd edn. — Marcel Planiol and Georges Ripert, *Droit Civil Français*, vol. vi: *Obligations*. First part by Paul Esmein (2nd edn. Paris 1952)

Prata, *Dicionário Jurídico* 3rd edn. — Ana Prata, *Dicionário Jurídico. Direito civil, direito processual civil, organização judiciária* (3rd edn. Coimbra 1992)

Prot. vol. ii — *Protokolle der Kommission für die zweite Lesung des Entwurfs des Bürgerlichen Gesetzbuchs*, revised under commission of the German Reich Justice Ministry by von Achilles, Gebhard, and Spahn, vol. ii: *Recht der Schuldverhältnisse* (Berlin 1898)

Puig Brutau, *Compendio* vol. ii, 2nd edn. — José Puig Brutau, *Compendio de Derecho Civil*, vol. ii: *Obligaciones derivadas de actos ilícitos* (2nd edn. Barcelona 1994 quoted here, quoted also here from the 1st edn. Barcelona 1987)

Puig Brutau, *Fundamentos* vol. ii (3) — José Puig Brutau, *Fundamentos de Derecho civil*, vol. ii, book 3: *Enriquecimiento injusto, Responsabilidad extracontractual, Derecho a la intimidad* (Barcelona 1983)

Rescigno, *Manuale* — Pietro Rescigno, *Manuale del diritto privato italiano* (Naples 1973)

Rodotà, *Problema della responsabilità civile* — Stefano Rodotà, *Il problema della responsabilità civile* (Milan 1964)

Rogers, *Tort* 2nd edn. — W. V. R. Rogers, *The Law of Tort* (London 1994) (Fundamental Principles of Law)

Ronse, *Schade en schadeloosstelling* vol. i, 2nd end. — Jan Ronse, *Schade en schadeloosstelling*; vol. i, 2nd edn.; Lode de Wilde, Antoon Claeys, and Ingrid Mallems (edd.) (Ghent 1988)

Roos, *Ersättningsrätt*

Carl Martin Roos, *Ersättningsrätt och Ersättningssystem* (Stockholm 1990)

Ruiz Serramalera, *Obligaciones* vol. ii

Ricardo Ruiz Serramalera, *Derecho civil. Derecho de obligaciones* vol. ii: *Los contratos y los actos ilítos* (Madrid 1992)

Rummel (*-Reischauer*), *ABGB* vol. ii, 2nd edn.

Peter Rummel (ed.), *Commentary on the general civil code in two volumes* (2nd edn. Vienna 1992), quoted here with the commentary of Rudolf Reischauer

Salmond/Heuston (-Heuston and Buckley), *Torts* 20th edn.

William Guthrie Salmond and R. F. V. Heuston on the Law of Torts, R. F. V. Heuston and R. A. Buckley (edd.) (20th edn. London 1994)

Saxén, *Skadeståndsrätt*

Hans Saxén, *Skadeståndsrätt* (Åbo 1975) (Acta Academiae Aboensis, Series A, vol. 50, no. 3) with appendix (Tiillläg till Skadeståndsrätt) (Åbo 1983) (Acta Academiae Aboensis, Series A, vol. 62, no 2)

Santos Briz, *Responsabilidad civil* vol. i, 6th edn., and vol. ii, 6th edn.

Jaime Santos Briz, *La responsabilidad civil. Derecho sustantivo y Derecho procesal*, 2 vols. (6th edn. Madrid 1991)

Schedion *Astikou Kodikos*

Ipourgeion Dikaiosinis, *Sintaktiki epitropi Astikou Kodikos, Schedion Astikou Kodikos,Genikai Archai* (General Foundations)(Athens 1936), vol. ii: *Enochikon Dikaion* (Law of Obligations) (Athens 1935), Dikaion ton Prosopon (Right of the Individual) (Athens 1936) (Motives and Materials of the Greek Civil Code)

Schlesinger (-author), *Commentario*

Il Codice Civile. Commentario diretto da Pietro Schlesinger (Milan 1993). Quoted here with the commentaries of Guido Patti and Salvatore Patti

Schoordijk, *Verbintenissenrecht*

H. C. F. Schoordijk, *Het Algemeen Gedeelte van het Verbintenissenrecht naar het Nieuw Burgerlijk Wetboek* (Deventer 1979)

Schut, *Onrechtmatige daad* 4th edn.

G. H. A. Schut, *Onrechtmatige Daad. Volgens BW en NBW* (4th edn. Zwolle 1990)

Schwimann (-author), *ABGB* vols. i–v

Michael Schwimann (ed.), *Praxiskommentar zum Bürgerlichen Gesetzbuch samt Nebengesetzen in fünf Bänden*, vol. i §§ 1–

	284 ABGB, EheG, 1. DVEheG (Vienna 1990); vol. ii §§ 285–530 ABGB (Vienna 1987); vol. iii §§ 531–858 (Vienna 1989); vol. iv/book 1 §§ 859–1089 ABGB (Vienna 1988); vol. iv/book 2 §§ 1090–1292 ABGB, KSchG, UN-Kaufrecht (Vienna 1988); vol. v §§ 1293–1502 ABGB (Vienna 1987); quoted here with the commentaries of Friedrich Harrer, Peter Jabornegg, and Herbert Pimmer
Sinde Monteiro, *Estudos*	Jorge Ferreira Sinde Monteiro, *Estudos sobre a responsabilidade civil* (Coimbra 1983)
Sinde Monteiro, *Responsabilidade por conselhos*	Jorge Ferreira Sinde Monteiro, *Responsabilidade por conselhos, recomendações ou informações* (Coimbra 1989)
Soergel (-author), *BGB* 11th and 12th edns.	*Bürgerliches Gesetzbuch mit Einführungsgesetz und Nebengesetzen*, Commentary in 10 vols. started by Hs. Th. Soergel, vol. i (*General Part*) §§ 1–240 (1988), vol. ii (*Law of Obligations I*) §§ 241–432 (1990) (all 12th edn.) as well as vol. iv (*Law of Obligations III*) §§ 705–853 (1985) (11th edn. Stuttgart, Berlin, Cologne, Mainz); quoted here with the commentaries of Hermann Fahse, Günther Hönn, Hans-Joachim Mertens, Arndt Teichmann, and Albrecht Zeuner
Spier, *Schadevergoeding*	Jaap Spier, *Schadevergoeding: algemeen*, vol. iii (Monografieën Nieuw BW, B-36) (Deventer 1992)
Spyridakis, *Genikes Arches* vol. i	Johannes Spyridakis, *Genikes Arches*, vol. i (Athens 1985) (General Foundations)
Stanton, *Tort*	K. Stanton, *The Modern Law of Tort* (London 1994)
Starck (-*Roland/Boyer*), *Obligations* vols. i and ii, both 4th edn.	Boris Starck, *Obligations. 1. Responsabilité délictuelle* (4th edn. Paris 1991); 2: *Contrat* (4th edn. Paris 1993) Henri Roland and Laurent Boyer (edd.).
Stathopoulos, *Geniko Enochiko Dikaio* vols. i and ii	Michael Stathopoulos, *Geniko Enochiko Dikaio*, vols. i and ii (Athens 1979 and 1983) (General Law of Obligations, 2 vols.)

Stathopoulos, *Geniko Enochiko Dikaio* vol. Ai, 2nd edn. Micheal Stathopoulos, *Geniko Enochiko Dikaio* vol. Ai (General Law of Obligations) (2nd edn. Athens 1993)

Staudinger (-author), *BGB* 12th and 13th edns. *J. v. Staudinger's Kommentar zum Bürgerlichen Gesetzbuch mit Einführungsgesetz und Nebengesetzen* (if no other specified, then 12th edn., partly also 13th revision, Berlin), containing: Staudinger (-Merten/Kirchhof), EGBGB, Arts. 1–5 (1985); (-Medicus), *Law of Obligations*, §§ 243, 249–254 (1983); (-Schäfer) §§ 823–832 and §§ 833–853 (1986) and (-Gursky), *Property Law*, §§ 951–1011 (1989, §§ 985–1011 in 13th edn. 1993)

Stewart, *Casebook* William J. Stewart, *A Casebook on Delict* (Edinburgh 1991)

Stewart, *Introduction* 2nd end. William J. Stewart, *An Introduction to the Scots Law of Delict* (2nd edn. Edinburgh 1993)

Stoll, *Haftungsfolgen* Hans Stoll, *Haftungsfolgen im bürgerlichen Recht. Eine Darstellung auf rechtsvergleichender Grundlage* (Heidelberg 1993) (Freiburger Rechts- und Staatswissenschaftliche Abhandlungen vol. 58)

Street(-*Brazier*), *Torts* 9th edn *Street on Torts, The Law of Torts* (9th edn. London *et al.* 1993); Margaret Brazier (ed.)

T&C (-author) 2nd edn J. H. Nieuwenhuis, C. J. J. M. Stolker, W. L. Valk (edd.), *Nieuw Burgerlijk Wetboek. Tekst & Commentaar* (2nd edn. Deventer 1994, quoted partly from the 1st edn. Deventer 1990); quoted here with the commentaries of G. H. Lankhorst, W. J. G. Oosterveen, F. A. Steketee, and C. J. J. M. Stolker

Terré/Simler/Lequette, *Obligations* 5th edn. François Terré, Philippe Simler, and Yves Lequette, *Droit civil. Les Obligations* (5th edn., Paris 1993; partly quoted here from the Weill and Terré 4th edn., see under Weil/Terré)

Thomson, *Delictual Liability* J. M. Thomson, *Delictual Liability* (Edinburgh 1994)

Tjomsland/Stray Ryssdal, Steinar Tjomsland, and Anders Chr.

Dommer i erstatningsrett 2nd edn.
Stray Rysdal (edd.), *Dommer i erstatningsrett* (2nd edn., 3rd impression Oslo 1992)

le Tourneau, *Responsabilité civile* 3rd edn.
Phillippe le Tourneau, *La responsabilité civile* (3rd edn. Paris 1982)

Trabucchi, *Istituzioni* 33rd edn.
Alberto Trabucchi, *Istituzioni di Diritto Civile* (33rd edn. Padua 1992)

Trolle, *Risiko og Skyld* 2nd edn.
Jørgen Trolle, *Risiko og skyld i erstatningspraksis* (2nd edn. Copenhagen 1969)

Tunc, *Responsabilité civile* 2nd edn.
André Tunc, *La Responsabilité civile* (2nd edn. Paris 1989)

Ussing (-*Kruse*), *Obligationsretten* vol. i, 4th edn.
Henry Ussing, *Obligationsretten Almindelig Del (4th edn. revised by A. Vinding Kruse) (Aarhus 1967)*

Viney, *Introduction* 2nd edn.
Geneviève Viney, *Traité de droit civil* (sous la direction de Jacques Ghestin). *Les Obligations. Introduction à la responsabilité* (2nd edn. Paris 1995)

Viney, *La responsabilité: conditions*
Geneviève Viney, *Traité de droit civil* (sous la direction de Jacques Ghestin). *Les obligations. La responsabilité: conditions* (Paris 1982)

Viney, *La responsabilité: effets*
Geneviève Viney, *Traité de droit civil* (sous la direction de Jacques Ghestin). *Les obligations. La responsabilité: effets* (Paris 1988)

Visintini, *Fatti illeciti* vols. i and ii
Giovanna Visintini, *I fatti illeciti*, 2 vols.: vol. i: *Ingiustizia del danno. Imputabilità* (Padua 1987), vol. ii: *La colpa in rapporto agli altri criteri di imputazione della responsabilità* (Padua 1990)

Visintini, *Responsabilità civile*
Giovanna Visintini, *La responsabilità civile nella giurisprudenza* (Padua 1967)

Walker, *Delict* 2nd edn.
David M. Walker, *The Law of Delict in Scotland* (2nd edn. Edinburgh 1981)

Walker, *Principles* vols. i and ii, both 4th edn.
David M. Walker, *Principles of Scottish Private Law*, vol. i (books I—III) and vol. ii (book IV: *Law of Obligations*) (4th edn. Oxford 1988)

Weill/Terré, *Obligations* 4th edn.
Alex Weill and François Terré, *Droit Civil. Les Obligations* (4th edn. Paris 1986; for the 5th edn. 1993 see Terré/Simler/Lequette)

Weir, *Casebook* 7th edn.

Tony Weir, *A Casebook on Tort* (7th edn. London 1992)

White, *Irish Law of Damages* vols. i and ii

John P. M. White, *Irish Law of Damages for Personal Injuries and Death* (2 vols., Dublin 1989)

Williams/Hepple, *Foundations* 2nd edn.

Glanville Williams and B. A. Hepple, *Foundations of the Law of Tort* (2nd edn. London 1984)

Winfield/Jolowicz (-*Rogers*), *Tort* 14th ed.

Percy Harry Winfield and John Anthony Jolowicz on Tort William Vaughan Horton Rogers (ed.) (14th edn. London 1994)

Yzquierdo Tolsada, *Responsabilidad civil*

Mariano Yzquierdo Tolsada, *Responsabilidad civil. Contractual y extracontractual,* vol. i (Madrid 1993)

Zepos, *Enochikon Dikaion* vols. i and ii (2), both 2nd edn.

Panagiotis Zepos, *Enochikon Dikaion,* vol. i: *Genikon Meros* (2nd edn. Athens 1955) (Law of Obligations, general part) and vol. ii: book 2: *Eidikon Meros,* (2nd edn. Athens 1965) (Law of Obligations, special part)

Zweigert/Kötz, *Rechtsvergleichung* 3rd edn.

Konrad Zweigert and Hein Kötz, *Eim führung in die Rechtsvergleichung auf dem Gebiete des Privatrechts* (3nd edn. Tübingen 1996, partly quoted here also from the 2nd edition 1984)

Table of Chronicles on Judgments Cited Repeatedly

The following table contains the chronicles on judgments which have been cited repeatedly and therefore only by stating their source. These chronicles are *not* listed in the bibliographies heading the individual sections of the book.

Byrne & Binchy, *Annual Review(s) of Irish Law* 1987–1992 — Raymond Byrne and William Binchy, *Annual Review of Irish Law* 1987 (Dublin 1988); 1988 (1989); 1989 (1990); 1990 (1993); 1992 (1994)

Dalcq, *Rev.crit.jur.belge* 1980 pp. 355–416 and 1981 pp. 87–172 — Roger O. Dalcq, 'Examen de jurisprudence (1973 à 1979). La responsabilité délictuelle et quasi-délictuelle'

Dalcq, *Rev.crit.jur.belge* 1987 pp. 601–672 and 1988 pp. 391–493 — Roger O. Dalcq, 'Examen de jurisprudence (1980 à 1986). La responsabilité délictuelle et quasi-délictuelle'

Dalcq/Schamps, *Rev.crit.jur.belge* 1995 pp. 525–638 — Roger O. Dalcq and Geneviève Schamps, 'Examen de jurisprudence (1987 à 1993). La responsabilité délictuelle et quasi-délictuelle'

Durry, *Rev.trim.dr.civ.* 66 (1968) pp. 711–731, 71 (1973) pp. 773–785 and 82 (1984) pp. 315–324 — Georges Durry, 'Jurisprudence française en matière de droit civil (responsabilité civile)'

Fagnart, *JT* 1976 pp. 569–633 — Jean-Luc Fagnart, 'Chronique de jurisprudence. La responsabilité civile (1968–1975)'

Fagnart/Denève, *JT* 1986 pp. 297–316 — Jean-Luc Fagnart and Myriam Denève, 'La responsabilité civile (1976–1984)'

Jourdain, *Rev.trim.dr.civ.* 90 (1991) pp. 119–133 and 539–559 — Patrice Jourdain, 'Jurisprudence française en matière de droit civil—Responsabilité civile'

Van Ommeslaghe, *Rev.crit.jur.belge* 1986, pp. 33–259 — Pierre Van Ommeslaghe, 'Examen de Jurisprudence (1974 à 1982). Les Obligations'

Schuermans/Van Oevelen/Persyn/Ernst/Schuermans, *TPR* 1994 pp. 851–1430 — Luc Schuermans, Aloïs Van Oevelen, Chris Persyn, Philippe Ernst, and Jean-Luc Schuermans, 'Overzicht van rechtspraak. Onrechtmatige daad,

	schade en schadeloosstelling 1983–1992'.
Schuermans/Schryvers/ Simoens/Van Oevelen/ Schamp, *TPR* 1984 pp. 511–878	Luc Schuermans, Jacques Schryvers, Dries Simoens, Aloïs Van Oevelen and Hugo Schamp, 'Overzicht van rechtspraak onrechtmatige daad, schade en schadeloosstelling (1977–1982)'
Vandenberghe/Van Quickenborne/Geelen/De Coster, *TPR* 1987 pp. 1255–1615	Hugo Vandenberghe, Marc Van Quickenborne, Koen Geelen, and Steven De Coster, 'Overzicht van rechtspraak. Aansprakelijkheid uit onrechtmatige daad 1979–1984'
Vandenberghe/Van Quickenborne/Hamelink, *TPR* 1980 pp. 1139–1475	Hugo Vandenberghe, Marc Van Quickenborne, and P. Hamelink, 'Overzicht van rechtspraak. Aansprakelijkheid uit onrechtmatige daad 1964–1978'
Viney, *Sem.Jur.* 1993 Doctr. 3664, pp. 144–150	Geneviève Viney, 'Responsabilité civile'
Viney, *Sem.Jur.* 1994 Doctr. 3773, pp. 304–314	Geneviève Viney, 'Responsabilité civile'
Viney, *Sem.Jur.* 1994 Doctr. 3809, pp. 550–560	Geneviève Viney, 'Responsabilité civile'

Table of Translations of Codes and Tort Law Statutes into the English and German Languages used without Special Indication of Sources

A. Foreign legal texts translated into the English language

I. Belgium
Code Civil: Crabb, John H., *The Constitution of Belgium and the Belgian Civil Code*, Littleton, Colorado, 1982

II. Denmark
1. Damages Lability Act no. 228, 23 May 1984, Working draft of the Danish Justice Ministry (unpublished)
2. Product Liability Act no. 371, 7 June 1989, Working draft of the Danish Justice Ministry (unpublished)
3. The Constitution of the Kingdom of Denmark Act, 5 June 1953, Working draft of the Danish Justice Ministry (unpublished)
4. The Succession to the Throne Act, 27 March 1953, Working draft of the Danish Justice Ministry (unpublished)

III. France
Code Civil: *The French Civil Code* (as amended on 1 July 1994). Translated with an introduction by John H. Crabb, The Hague 1995

IV. Germany
1. Forrester, Ian, *The German Civil Code*, Amsterdam 1975
2. §§ 226–231, 249–255, 276–278, 328–331, 676, 904, 906, 907, 1004, 823–840, 842–847, 851, 852 BGB; Markesinis, Basil S., *The German Law of Torts*, 3rd edn., Oxford 1994
3. Arts. 1–19 of the German Constitution: Markesinis op. cit.
4. Product Liability Act: Lipstein, Kurt in: Markesinis op. cit.
5. §§ 7–20 Road Traffic Act: Markesinis op. cit.
6. Liability Act: Markesinis op. cit.
7. Rothmann, F. B., *The German Code of Criminal Procedure*, 1973

V. Greece
The Greek Civil Code, translated by Constantine Taliadouros, Athens 1982; Supplement to the Greek Civil Code (Law no. 1329, 18 February 1983, amending the provisions of the Civil Code which govern family relationships), translated by Constantine Taliadoros, Athens 1983

VI. Italy
Codice Civile: *The Italian Civil Code*, translated by Beltramo, Mario/

Longo, Giovanni E./ Merryman, John Henry, 2nd edn., Dobbs Ferry, NY 1993

VII. The Netherlands

Books 3, 5, 6 Netherlands Civil Code: *The New Netherlands Civil Code*, Patrimonial Law (property, obligations, and special contracts), translated by P. P. C. Haanappel and Ejan Mackaay, Deventer, Boston 1990

VIII. Spain

1. Código Civil: *The Civil Code of Spain*, translated by Julio Romanach, Baton Rouge, LA 1994
2. Secs. 25–28 General Act 26/1984, 19 July 1984 on Consumer and User Protection: Pemán Domecq, Paloma, *Product Liability in Spain, Comp-LYB* 15 (1993), pp. 137–161

B. Foreign legal texts translated into the German language

I. Belgium

1. The Constitution of the Kingdom of Belgium Act, 7 February 1831 (as amended on 16 February 1993): Verfassung des Königreichs Belgien v. 7. Februar 1831, i.d.F. v. 16. Februar 1993: Kimmel, Adolf, in: *Die Verfassungen der EG-Mitgliedstaaten*, as of 1 July 1993, 3rd edn., Munich 1993, pp. 1–25
2. Product Liability Act, 25 February 1991: Produkthaftungsgesetz v. 25. Februar 1991: BfAI (ed.), *Europäische Gemeinschaften, EG-Produkthaftung*, 2nd edn., Cologne, Berlin 1992, AWSt-A 3/92, pp. 77–81 = *PHI* 1991, pp. 132–134

II. Denmark

1. Damages Liability Act no. 228, 23 May 1984, with later amendments: Gesetz Nr. 228 vom 23. Mai 1984 über die Verpflichtung zum Schadensersatz mit späteren Änderungen: Nørgaard, Jørgen/Vagner, Hans Henrik, 'Landesbericht Dänemark', in: Bar, Christian v. (ed.), *Deliktsrecht in Europa*, Cologne 1993
2. Book 3–19–2 of the Danish Code Christan V, 15 April 1683: dänisches Gesetzbuch Christian V v. 15. April 1683: Nørgaard/Vagner op. cit.; Woellert, Kai, *Die außervertragliche Haftung für schädigendes Verhalten von Hilfspersonen im Nordischen Recht*, diss. Kiel 1972; Schmahl, Hans Ludwig, *Das Adhäsionsverfahren im dänischen Recht*, Itzehoe 1980
3. §§ 63, 64 Act no. 443, 3 October 1985, on Minors and Guardianship: Nørgaard/Vagner op. cit.
4. §§ 101–108 Road Traffic Act, 17 Feb. 1986: Straßenverkehrsgesetz v. 10.6.1976: Nørgaard/Vagner op. cit.
5. §§ 101–116 Road Traffic Act, 27 June 1961: Straßenverkehrsgesetz v. 10.6.1976: Schmahl op. cit.

6. § 65 I s.1, II, V Road Traffic Act, 27 June 1961: Straßenverkehrsgesetz v. 10.6.1976: Woellert op. cit.
7. Act no. 31, 7 June 1989 on Product Liability: BfAI (ed.), *Europäische Gemeinschaften, EG-Produkthaftung*, 2nd edn., Cologne, Berlin 1992, AWSt-A 3/92, pp. 125–129 = *PHI* 1989, pp. 175–177
8. The Constitution of the Kingdom of Denmark Act, 5 June 1953: Verfassung des Königreichs Dänemark v. 5. Juni 1953: Mayer-Tasch, Peter Cornelius / Kimmel, Adolf (responsible for the technical translation), in: *Die Verfassungen der EG-Mitgliedstaaten*, as of 1st July 1993, 3rd edn., Munich 1993, pp. 26–97
9. § 1 Act on the Liability of Employers for Damage Inflicted by Employees: Gesetz über die Haftung des Arbeitsgebers für Schadenshandlungen der Angestellten: Woellert op. cit.
10. §§ 1, 9 Act on the Liability for Damages Arising from the Operation of the Railways, 11 March 1921: Gesetz über die Haftung für Schäden beim Betrieb von Eisenbahnen v. 11. March 1921: Woellert op. cit.
11. § 127 I Air Traffic Act, 10 June 1960: Luftverkehrsgesetz v. 10. Juni 1960: Woellert op. cit.
12. § 4 I Accident Insurance Act, 12 April 1949: Unfallversicherungsgesetz v. 12. April 1949: Woellert op. cit.
13. § 25 Insurance Contract Act no. 129, 15 April 1930: Versicherungsvertragsgesetz Nr. 129 v.15. April 1930: Woellert op. cit.; Schmahl op. cit.
14. Act no. 367, 27 May 1991 on Patient Insurance: Gesetz Nr. 367 v. 27. Mai 1991 über die Patientenversicherung: Stein-Poulsen, Malene, 'Das dänische Patientenversicherungsgesetz', *VersRAI* 1995, pp. 19–25
15. §§ 267–275a Criminal Code, 8 February 1974: Strafgesetz v. 8.2.1974: Schmahl op. cit.

III. England and Wales
 1. The Constitution of the United Kingdom of Great Britain and Northern Ireland: Verfassungstexte des Vereinigten Königreiches von Großbritannien und Nordirland: Mayer-Tasch, Peter Cornelius, in: *Die Verfassungen der EG-Mitgliedstaaten*, as of 1 July 1993, 3rd edn., Munich 1993, pp. 416–434
 2. Secs. 1–9, 45, 46, 49, 50 Consumer Protection Act 1987: BfAI (ed.), *Europäische Gemeinschaften, EG-Produkthaftung*, 2nd edn., Cologne, Berlin 1992, AWSt-A 3/92, pp. 104–114 = *PHI* 1989, pp. 18–25

IV. Finland
 1. Damages Act no. 412, 31 May 1974: Schadensersatzgesetz Nr. 412 v. 31.5.1974: Fasterling, Björn, *VersRAI* 1995, pp. 14–16

2. § 1 Act on Employer Liability: Gesetz über die Haftung des Arbeits-gebers: Woellert, Kai, *Die außervertragliche Haftung für schädigendes Verhalten von Hilfspersonen im nordischen Recht*, diss. Kiel 1972
3. § 11 Sea Act, 9 June 1939: Seegesetz v. 9. Juni 1939: Woellert op. cit.
4. § 1 s. 1, § 4, § 8 I Vehicle Insurance Act, 26 June 1959: Verkehrsver-sicherungsgesetz v. 26. Juni 1959: Woellert op. cit.
5. §§ 2, 3 Act on the Liability for Damages Arising from the Operation of the Railway, 19 February 1898: Gesetz über die Haftung für Schäden beim Betrieb von Eisenbahnen v. 19. Februar 1898: Woellert op. cit.
6. §§ 6 I, 8 Air Traffic Act, 25 May 1923: Luftverkehrsgesetz v. 25. Mai 1923: Woellert op. cit.
7. §§ 1 I s. 1, 8 I, 61 Accident Insurance Act, 20 August 1948: Gesetz über die Unfallversicherung v. 20. August 1948: Woellert op. cit.
8. § 25 Insurance Contract Act, 12 May 1933: Versicherungsvertragsge-setz v. 12. Mai 1933: Woellert op. cit.
9. Act no. 694, 17 August 1990 (Product Liability Act): Gesetz Nr. 694 v. 17. August 1990 (Produkthaftungsgesetz): *PHI* 1991, pp. 53–55

V. France
1. Code Civil: The French Civil Code, as of 1 June 1939: Das französische bürgerliche Gesetzbuch, Nach dem Stand vom 1. Juni 1939; Part I, Arts. 1–1130; Part II, Arts. 1131–2281; in: *Französische Gesetzestexte in deutscher Übersetzung*, vol. iv, Leipzig, Strasbourg, Zurich 1939
2. Arts. 489–2, 1382–1386 Code Civil: Gotthardt, Peter, 'Landesbericht Frankreich', in: Bar, Christian v. (ed.), *Deliktsrecht in Europa*, Cologne 1993
3. Act, 5 July 1985: Gesetz vom 5. Juli 1985: Gotthardt op. cit.
4. The Constitution of the Republic of France, 4 October 1958 (as amended on 25 June 1992) including a declaration concerning human and civil rights, 26 August 1789 and the preamble to the constitution, 27 October 1946: Verfassung der Republik Frankreich v. 4. Oktober 1958, i.d.F. v. 25. Juni 1992 mit der Erklärung der Menschen- und Bürgerrechte v. 26. Aug 1789 und der Präambel der Verfassung v. 27. Oktober 1946: Kimmel, Adolf, in: *Die Verfassungen der EG-Mitglied-staaten*, as of 1 July 1993, 3rd edn., Munich 1993, pp. 98–121

VI. Greece
1. Civil Code: Gogos, Demetrius, *Das Zivilgesetzbuch von Griechenland*, Berlin, Tübingen 1951
2. Arts. 26, 71, 914–938 Civil Code: Vrellis, Spyridon, 'Landesbericht Griechenland', in: Bar, Christian v. (ed.), *Deliktsrecht in Europa*, Cologne 1993
3. Arts. 57–59, 932, 933, 1453 Civil Code: Zepos, Pan J., 'Der Schutz der Persönlichkeit nach dem griechischen Zivilgesetzbuch', in: *Festschrift*

für Ernst v. Caemmerer; Ficker, Hans Claudius/König, Detlef/ Kreuzer, Karl F *et al.* (edd.); Tübingen 1978, pp. 1131–1139

4. Arts. 57, 58, 198, 298–300, 330–336, 914, 915, 917, 919, 924–926, 932, 1003–1005, 1108, 1453 Civil Code: Rodopoulos, George, 'Eingetretene Modifikationen im griechischen Haftpflichtrecht', in: *AID*, Landesreferate, Thema I: Wandel im Haftpflichtrecht unserer Zeit—zugleich eine Herausforderung der Versicherung, Budapest 1986, pp. 277–283

5. Arts. 298, 332, 914, 925, 928, 932 Civil Code: Karakostas, Ioannis, 'Grundzüge der Produkthaftung in Griechenland', *PHI* 1988, pp. 157–161

6. Arts. 3, 4, 323, 903, 905, 906 Code of Civil Procedure: Zivilprozeßordnung: Vrellis op. cit.

7. Art. 2 Code of Criminal Procedure: Strafprozeßordnung: Vrellis op. cit.

8. Arts. 4, 5, 7 and 9 of the Acts ΓΝ/1911 'on the Criminal Liability for Delict and the Third Party Liability for Motor Vehicles': Artt. 4, 5, und 9 des Gesetz ΓΝ/1911 'über die strafrechtliche Deliktshaftung und die Haftpflicht aus Kraftfahrzeugen': Rodopoulos op. cit., pp. 284–285; Vrellis op. cit.

9. Arts. 300, 482, 487, 932 Civil Code; Arts. 8, 10, 15: Act no. 1961, 3 September 1991 on Consumer Protection: Gesetz Nr. 1961/3.9.1991 zum Schutz des Verbrauchers: Schinas, Georgios M., 'Konsumentenschutz in Griechenland', *JBl* 1992, pp. 682–694

10. Arts. 1–6, 8–11, 13–14, 16, 17, 19, 25–30, 30a, 33–35 Act 489, 31 December 1914/8 January 1915 'on the Liability for Damages for Accidents of Employees at Work': Gesetz 489 v. 31.12.1914/8.1.1915: 'über die Schadensersatzhaftung für von den Arbeitern während der Arbeit erlittene Unfälle': Vrellis op. cit.

11. Emergency Act 1846, 14–21 June 1951 'on Social Insurances': Notgesetz 1846 v. 14/21.6.1951 'über Sozialversicherungen': Vrellis op. cit.

12. Arts. 85, 86 Presidential Decree 611/1977 'On the Codification of Valid Regulations Concerning the Position of Civil Servants and Legal Persons under Public Law in a Uniform Text with the Title "Beamten Kodex"': Präsidialverordnung 611/1977 'über die Kodifizierung der sich auf den Stand der Beamten des Staates und der juristischen Personen des öffentlichen Rechts beziehenden geltenden Vorschriften in einem einheitlichen Text mit dem Titel "Beamten-Kodex"': Vrellis op. cit.

13. Arts. 84, 289, 291 Act on Civil Maritime Law: Gesetz über das private Seerecht: Vrellis op. cit.

14. Product Liability Order: Produkthaftungsverordnung: Schmidt-Salzer, Joachim/Hollmann, Hermann H., 'Griechische Produkthaftungsverordnung', in: *Kommentar EG-Produkthaftung*, vol. ii,

Produkthaftungsgesetze im Ausland, pamphlet 3, pp. 2–10, Heidelberg 1990; *PHI* 1988, pp. 162–164

15. Act no. 1961, 3 September 1991 on Consumer Protection and other Provisions: Gesetz Nr. 1961 v. 3.9.1991 über den Schütz des Verbrauchers und andere Bestimmungen: BfAI (ed.), *Internationales und ausländisches Wirtschafts- und Steuerrecht, Griechenland, Verbraucherschutz*, Cologne, Berlin 1994

16. Arts. 7–17, 50 Act no. 1961/1991 on Consumer Protection and other Provisions: Gesetz Nr. 1961/1991 über den Schutz des Verbrauchers und andere Bestimmungen BfAI (ed.), *Europäische Gemeinschaften, EG-Produkthaftung*, 2nd edn., Cologne, Berlin 1992, AWSt-A 3/92, pp. 200–204

17. Arts. 27–29 (Chapter 4, Consumer Protection) Act no. 2000, 24 Dec 1991: BfAI (ed.), 'Internationales und ausländisches Wirtschafts- und Steuerrecht, Griechenland, Verbraucherschutz', Cologne, Berlin 1994 = *GRUR Int.* 1992, pp. 824

18. The Constitution of the Republic of Greece 9–11 June 1975 (as amended on 12 March 1986): Verfassung der Republik Griechenland v. 9./11. Juni 1975, i.d.F. v. 12. März 1986: Dagtoglou, Prodomos, *JöR* 1983, pp. 360–393; also: revised by Maria Karajanni, *Die Verfassungen der EG-Mitgliedstaaten*, as of 1 July 1993, 3rd edn., Munich 1993, pp. 122–175

VII. Ireland

1. The Constitution of the Republic of Ireland, 1 July 1937 (as amended on 26 November 1992: Verfassung der Republik Irland v. 1. Juli 1937, i.d.F. v. 26. November 1992: Mayer-Tasch, Peter Cornelius/Kimmel, Adolf, in: *Die Verfassungen der EG-Mitgliedstaaten*, as of 1 July 1993, 3rd edn., Munich 1993, pp. 176–210

2. Product Liability Act: Produkthaftungsgesetz: *PHI* 1992, pp. 64–67

VIII. Italy

1. Codice civile: Civil Code: Bauer, Max W./Eccher, Bernhard/König, Bernhard/Kreuzer, Josef/Zanon, Heinz, *Italienisches Zivilgesetzbuch / Codice civile*, Bilingual work, Bozen 1987

2. Codice civile: Italian Civil Code (1942) inclusive introductory, procedural, and transitionary provisions: Italienisches Zivilgesetzbuch (1942) nebst Einführungs-, Durchführungs- und Übergangsvorschriften. Introduction by Gerhard Luther, translation of legal text by Hans Lackner, Erwin Langer, Mariano San Nicolò, Josef Raffeiner, and Otto Vinatzer, 2nd edn., Berlin, Tübingen 1968

3. Arts. 25 II, 28, 29, 2043–2059, 2947 Codice civile: Busnelli, Francesco D. 'Landesbericht Italien', in: Bar, Christian v. (ed.), *Deliktsrecht in Europa*, Cologne 1993

4. Arts. 2, 10, 11, 66 Order on the Unified Version of the Regulation on Compulsory Insurance against Accidents at Work and Work Related Illnesses: Verordnung über die einheitliche Fassung der Regelung zur Pflichtversicherung gegen Arbeitsunfälle und Berufskrankheiten: Busnelli op. cit.

5. Arts. 18, 19 Act on Third Party Insurance for Motor Vehicles and Water Craft: Gesetz über die Haftpflichtversicherung für den Verkehr mit Kraftfahrzeugen und Wasserfahrzeugen: Busnelli op. cit.

6. Arts. 15, 18–20, 22, 23 Act on the Peaceful Use of Nuclear Energy: Gesetz über die friedliche Nutzung von Kernenergie: Busnelli op. cit.

7. Art. 18 Act on the Establishment of a Ministry of the Environment and Regulations for Environmental Protection: Gesetz über die Einrichtung eines Umweltministeriums und Regelungen zum Umweltschutz: Busnelli op. cit.

8. Arts. 2, 3, 5, 7–9, 13, 14: Damages Act based on the Execution of the Authority of a Judge and the Liability of Judges: Gesetz über den Ersatz für Schäden aufgrund der Ausübung richterlicher Befugnisse und die Haftung der Richter: Busnelli op. cit.

9. Product Liability Order (Order of the President of the Republic, 24 May 1988, no. 224): Produkthaftungsverordnung (Verordnung des Präsidenten der Republik v. 24 Mai 1988, Nr. 224): Busnelli op. cit.; Schmidt-Salzer, Joachim/Hollmann, Hermann H., 'Italienische Produkthaftungsverordnung', in: *Kommentar EG-Produkthaftung*, vol. ii, *Produkthaftungsgesetze im Ausland*, pamphlet 3, pp. 11–27, Heidelberg 1990; BfAI (ed.), *Europäische Gemeinschaften, EG-Produkthaftung*, 2nd edn., Cologne, Berlin 1992, AWSt-A 3/92, pp. 188–193 = *PHI* 1988, pp. 125–128

10. Arts. 2, 3, 9, 32, 41: Italian Constitution: ital. Verfassung: Dinter-Huzel, Eva, *Italien, Haftung für Umweltschäden*, BfAI (ed.) 1989, AWSt-A 9/89, Cologne 1989

11. Art. 132 Criminal Code: Strafgesetzbuch: Dinter-Huzel op. cit.

12. Code of Criminal Procedure with supplementary statutes, as of 31 January 1991: Strafprozeßordnung mit Nebengesetzen, Stand 31.1.1991: Bauer, Max W./König, Bernhard/Kreuzer, Josef/Riz, Roland/Zanon, Heinz (editor and translator), *Italienische Strafprozeßordnung mit Nebengesetzen / Codice di procedura penale con leggi complementari*, bilingual publication, Bozen 1991

13. Arts. 13, 18 Act, 8 July 1986, on the Establishment of a Ministry of the Environment and Provisions in the Area of Damage to the Environment: Gesetz v. 8.7.1986 über die Einrichtung eines Umweltministeriums und Vorschriften auf dem Gebiet des Umweltschadens: Dinter-Huzel op. cit.

14. Constitution of the Republic of Italy, 27 December 1947 (as amended

on 22 November 1967) Verfassung der Republik Italien v. 27. Dezember 1947, i.d.F. v. 22. November 1967: Kimmel, Adolf, in: *Die Verfassungen der EG-Mitgliedstaaten*, as of 1 July 1993, 3rd edn., Munich 1993, pp. 211–238

IX. Luxembourg
1. The Constitution of the Grand Duchy of Luxembourg, 17 October 1868 (as amended on 25 November 1983): Verfassung des Großherzogtums Luxemburg v. 17. Oktober 1868, i.d.F. v. 25. November 1983: Kimmel, Adolf, in: *Die Verfassungen der EG-Mitgliedstaaten*, as of 1 July 1993, 3rd edn., Munich 1993, pp. 239–253
2 Product Liability Act (Act on the Civil Liability for Defective Products, 21 April 1989): Produkthaftungsgesetz (Gesetz v. 21. April 1989 über die zivilrechtliche Haftung für fehlerhafte Produkte): Schmidt-Salzer, Joachim/Hollmann, Hermann H., 'Luxemburgisches Produkthaftungsgesetz', in: *Kommentar EG-Produkthaftung*, vol. ii, *Produkthaftungsgesetze im Ausland*, pamphlet 3, pp. 28–36, Heidelberg 1990; BfAI (ed.), *Europäische Gemeinschaften, EG-Produkthaftung*, 2nd edn., Cologne, Berlin 1992, AWSt-A 3/92, pp. 85–87 = *PHI* 1989, pp. 126–127

X. The Netherlands
1. Book 6, 7, 7A BW: Nieper, Franz/Westerdijk, Arjen S. (ed.), *Niederländisches Bürgerliches Gesetzbuch, Buch 6 Allgemeiner Teils des Schuldrechts, Buch 7 und 7A Besondere Verträge*, Munich, The Hague, London, Boston 1995
2. Book 3, 4, 5 BW: Nieper, Franz/Westerdijk, Arjen S. (ed.), *Niederländisches Bürgerliches Gesetzbuch, Buch 3 Allgemeines Vermögensrecht, Buch 4 Erbrecht und Buch 5 Sachenrecht*, Munich, The Hague, London, Boston 1996
3. Arts. 6: 95–110, 162–193, 197 BW: Hondius, Ewoud/van Dam, Cees, 'Landesbericht Niederlande', in: Bar, Christian v. (ed.), *Deliktsrecht in Europa*, Cologne 1993
4. Arts. 6: 95, 162, 163, 194–196, 7A: 1638 aa lid 3 BW: Mertz, Jürgen, *Der Schutz primärer Vermögensinteressen im niederländischen Deliktsrecht im Vergleich zur deutschen Rechtsprechung*, diss. Osnabrück 1993
5. Art. 6: 162, 173, 174, 179, 181 BW: Hondius, Ewoud/Braams, Wilhelm, *Auf dem Weg zu einem europäischen Haftungsrecht* (Europainstitut des Saarlandes Nr. 162), Saarbrücken 1989
6. Arts. 6: 173, 174, 179, 180, 181, 183 BW: Jonas, Johannes Gerhart, *Die verschuldensunabhängige außervertragliche Haftung für Sachen im Entwurf zum Nieuw Burgerlijk Wetboek der Niederlande*, Munich 1987
7. Art. 1407 a–j BW (old) (Product Liability Act): (Produkthaftungsgesetz): BfAI (ed.), Europäische Gemeinschaften, EG-Produkthaftung,

2nd edn., Cologne, Berlin 1992, AWSt-A 3/92, pp. 143–146 = *PHI* 1991, pp. 27–29
8. Art. 31 Road Traffic Act: Straßenverkehrsgesetz (old version): Hondius/van Dam op. cit.
9. Arts. 1–16, 22–27 Act on Third Party Insurance for Motor Vehicles: Gesetz über die Haftpflichtversicherung für Kraftfahrzeuge: Hondius/van Dam op. cit.
10. Arts. 61ae–61ai Act on General Environmental Matters: Gesetz über allgemeine Umweltbestimmungen, Titel 5 Luftverunreinigungsfonds: Bar, Christian v./van Veldhuizen, Onno, 'Der niederländische Luftverunreinigungsfonds', *UTR*, vol xii (1990), pp. 367–380
11. The Constitution of the Kingdom of the Netherlands, 17 February 1983: Verfassung des Königreiches der Niederlande v. 17. Februar 1983: 'Übersetzung des Ministeriums des Innern, Stabsabteilung Verfassungs- und Gesetzgebungsangelegenheiten, in Zusammenarbeit mit dem Sprachendienst des Ministeriums für Auswärtige Angelegenheiten', in: *Die Verfassungen der EG-Mitgliedstaaten*, as of 1 July 1993, 3rd edn., Munich 1993, pp. 254–283

XI. Portugal
1. Arts. 9, 10, 66–68, 70–81, 334–340, 402, 483–510, 512, 513, 516, 528, 534, 562–572 Código Civil, 25 November 1966: Lillienskiold, Mark v., *Aktuelle Probleme des portugiesischen Delikts- und Schadensersatzrechts*, Bonn 1975
2. Arts. 45, 70, 71, 79–81, 227, 334–340, 483–510, 562–572, 799 Código Civil: Sinde Monteiro, Jorge/Moura Ramos, Rui/Hörster, Heinrich Ewald, 'Landesbericht Portugal', in: Bar, Christian v. (ed.), *Deliktsrecht in Europa*, Cologne 1994
3. Arts. 65, 65–A, 74, 99, 100, 1094–1096 Code of Civil Procedure: Zivilprozeßgesetzbuch: Sinde Monteiro/Moura Ramos/Hörster op. cit.
4. Product Liability Act (Decree Act no. 383/89, 6 November 1989): Produkthaftungsgesetz (Dekretgesetz Nr. 383/89 v. 6. November 1989): BfAI (ed.), *Europäische Gemeinschaften, EG-Produkthaftung*, 2nd edn., Cologne, Berlin 1992, AWSt-A 3/92, S. 174–176 = *PHI* 1990, pp. 10–11
5. Arts. 8, 9 Product Liability Act, regulation no. 383/89, 6 November 1989: Produckthaftungsgesetz, Gesetesverordnung Nr. 383/89 v. 6.11.1989: Sinde Monteiro/Moura Ramos/Hörster op. cit.
6. Arts. 11, 12, 16 Labour Court Procedural Code: Arbeitsgerichtsgesetzbuch: Sinde Monteiro/Moura Ramos/Hörster op. cit.
7. Arts. 391–394, 400 Criminal Code, 16 September 1886: Strafgesetzbuch v. 16. September 1886: v. Lillienskiold op. cit.

8. Arts. 29, 34, 690 Code of Criminal Procedure, 15 February 1929: Strafprozeßordnung v. 15. Februar 1929: v. Lillienskiold op. cit.

9. Basis LIII, LIV Hunting Act, 28 May 1967: Jagdgesetz v. 28. Mai 1967: v. Lillienskiold op. cit.

10. Art. 33 Hunting Act, Act no. 30/86, 27 August 1986: Jagdgesetz, Gesetz Nr. 30/86 v. 27.8.1986: Sinde Monteiro/Moura Ramos/Hörster op. cit.

11. Arts. 233, 234 Implementing Regulation on Hunting, 14 August 1967: Jagd-Ausführungsverordnung v. 14. August 1967: v. Lillienskiold op. cit.

12. Arts. 96, 97 Implementing Regulation for Hunting Law, regulation no. 251/92, 12 November 1992: Durchführungsverordnung zum Jagdgesetz, Gesetzesverordnung Nr. 251/92 v. 12.11.1992: Sinde Monteiro/Moura Ramos/Hörster op. cit.

13. Arts. 40, 41 Foundation Act on the Environment, Act no. 11/87, 7 April 1990: Grundlagengesetz über die Umwelt, Gesetz Nr. 11/87 v. 7.4.1990: Sinde Monteiro/Moura Ramos/Hörster op. cit.

14. Art. 48 Water Quality Act, regulation no. 74/90, 7 March 1990: Wasserqualitätsgesetz, Gesetzesverordnung Nr. 74/90 v. 7.3.1990: Sinde Monteiro/Moura Ramos/Hörster op. cit.

15. Arts. 10, 11 Air Transport Act, regulation no. 321/89, 25 September 1989: Luftbeförderungsgesetz, Gesetzesverordnung Nr. 321/89 v. 25.9.1989: Sinde Monteiro/Moura Ramos/Hörster op. cit.

16. Art. 14 Light Aircraft Legislation, regulation no. 71/90, 2 March 1990: Gesetzgebung über Ultraleichtflugzeuge, Gesetzesverordnung Nr. 71/90 v. 2.3.1990: Sinde Monteiro/Moura Ramos/Hörster op. cit.

17. Art. 10 Radiation Protection Act, regulation no. 348/89, 12 October 1989: Strahlenschutzgesetz, Gesetzesverordnung Nr. 348/89 v. 12.10.1989: Sinde Monteiro/Moura Ramos/Hörster op. cit.

18. Art. 9 Act on the Removal and the Transplantation of Human Organs and Tissue, Act no. 12/93, 22 April 1993: Gesetz über die Entnahme und die Transplantation menschlicher Organe und Gewebeteile, Gesetz Nr. 12/93 v. 22.4.1993: Sinde Monteiro/Moura Ramos/Hörster op. cit.

19. Art. 29 Compulsory Motor Insurance Act, regulation no. 522/85, 31 December 1985: Kraftfahrzeugpflichtversicherungsgesetz, Gesetzesverordnung Nr. 522/85 v. 31.12.1985: Sinde Monteiro/Moura Ramos/Hörster op. cit.

20. The Constitution of the Republic of Portugal, 2 April 1976 (as amended on 25 November 1992): Verfassung der Republik Portugal v. 2. April 1976, i.d.F. v. 25. November 1992: Thomashausen, André, *JöR* 1983, pp. 446–501; also: revised by Heike Buss and Adolf

Kimmel, *Die Verfassungen der EG-Mitgliedstaaten*, as of 1 July 1993, 3rd edn., Munich 1993, pp. 284–369

XII. Scotland

1. The Constitution of the United Kingdom of Great Britain and Northern Ireland: Verfassungstexte des Vereinigten Königreiches von Großbritannien und Nordirland: Mayer-Tasch, Peter Cornelius, in: *Die Verfassungen der EG-Mitgliedstaaten*, as of 1 July 1993, 3rd edn., Munich 1993, pp. 416–434

2. Secs. 1–9, 45, 46, 49, 50 Consumer Protection Act 1987: BfAI (ed.), *Europäische Gemeinschaften, EG-Produkthaftung*, 2nd edn., Cologne, Berlin, AWSt-A 3/92, pp. 104–114 = *PHI* 1989, pp. 18–25

XIV. Spain

1. Código Civil: Peuster, Witold, *Das spanische Zivilgesetzbuch*, Cologne 1979

2. Arts. 10 no. 9 I & nos. 10, 12, 16, 391, 590, 1089, 1092, 1093, 1101, 1104, 1106, 1108, 1591, 1784, 1903–1910 Código Civil: Santdiumenge, Josep, 'Landesbericht Spanien', in: Bar, Christian v. (ed.), *Deliktsrecht in Europa*, Cologne 1993

3. Art. 51 of the Spanish Constitution: Birke, Albrecht, *Das neue spanische Konsumenten-Schutzgesetz*, *PHI* 1985, pp. 8–14

4. Arts. 362 I, 903, 951–958 Code of Civil Procedure: Zivilprozeßordnung: Santdiumenge op. cit.

5. Arts. 19–22, 101–108, 115, 117, 347–*bis*, 534–*ter* Criminal Code: Strafgesetzbuch: Santdiumenge op. cit.

6. Arts. 100, 110–112, 114–117 Code of Criminal Procedure: Strafprozeßordnung: Santdiumenge op. cit.

7. Art. 488 II Compilation of the Civil Foral Law of Navarra: Santdiumenge op. cit.

8. Art. 65 Press Act: Pressegesetz: Santdiumenge op. cit.

9. Arts. 120–122, 133 Compulsory Purchase Act: Enteignungsgesetz: Santdiumenge op. cit.

10. Art. 123 I Air Traffic Act: Luftfahrtgesetz: Santdiumenge op. cit.

11. Arts. 45 I, 49, 52 Atomic Energy Act: Atomenergiegesetz: Santdiumenge op. cit.

12. Arts. 1, 2, 10, 25–31 Consumer Protection Act: Verbraucherschutzgesetz: Birke, Albrecht, 'Das neue spanische Konsumenten-Schutzgesetz', *PHI* 1985, pp. 8–14

13. Arts. 1 nos. 2 and 3, 25–29 Consumer Protection Act: Verbraucherschutzgesetz: Santdiumenge op. cit.

14. Consumer Protection Act (draft): Verbraucherschutzgesetz (Entwurf): *PHI* 1993, pp. 154–156; Rodríguez Buján, J., *VersRAI* 1993, pp. 62–64

15. Art. 33 V Federal Spanish Hunting Law: Gemeinspanisches Jagdgesetz: Santdiumenge op. cit.
16. Arts. 225, 229 Land Act: Bodengesetz: Santdiumenge op. cit.
17. Art. 296 Mortgage Act: Hypothekengesetz: Santdiumenge op. cit.
18. Art. 97 II Commercial Code: Handelsgesetzbuch: Santdiumenge op. cit.
19. Arts. 40, 41, 43 Act on the Order of Public Administration: Gesetz über die Ordnung der Staatsverwaltung: Santdiumenge op. cit.
20. Arts. 93 no. 3, 125 no. 2 General Social Insurance Act: Allgemeines Gesetz über die Sozialversicherung: Santdiumenge op. cit.
21. Arts. 30 no. 3, 57, 62, 72 Catalonian Housing Act: Katalanisches Wohnungsgesetz v. 29.11.1991: Santdiumenge op. cit.
22. Art. 12 Catalonian Consumer Protection Act, 8 January 1990: Katalanisches Konsumentenschutzgesetz v. 8.1.1990: Santdiumenge op. cit.
23. Art. 54 Municipal Administration Act, 2 April 1985: Kommunalverwaltungsgesetz v. 2.4.1985: Santdiumenge op. cit.
24. Arts. 224, 225 Royal Decree 2568/1986 on the Promulgation of the Regulations Concerning the Organisation, Functions and the Legal Status of Local Corporations, 28 November 1986: Königliches Dekret 2568/1986 zur Verkündung des Reglements über die Organisation, das Funktionieren und die Rechtsstellung der örtlichen Körperschaften v. 28.11.1986: Santdiumenge op. cit.
25. Art. 133 Company Shares Act: Aktiengesetz: Santdiumenge op. cit.
26. Arts. 1, 4, 5, 13, 14 Royal Decree 673/92, which regulates the compensation claims of victims of armed gangs and terrorist elements, 19 June 1992: Königliches Dekret 673/92, durch welches die Entschädigungsansprüche der Opfer von bewaffneten Banden und terroristischen Elementen geregelt werden, v. 19.6.1992: Santdiumenge op. cit.
27. Arts. 73, 75, 76, 107–109 Act on Insurance Contracts: Gesetz über den Versicherungsvertrag: Santdiumenge op. cit.
28. Arts. 1–7, 11, 12, 14, 16 Royal Decree 2641/1986, through which the insurance regulation for civil liability, referring to the use and traffic of motor vehicles with compulsory insurance, is accepted, 30 December 1986: Königliches Dekret 2641/1986, durch welches das Versicherungsreglement für die zivilrechtliche Haftung, bezogen auf den Gebrauch und den Verkehr von Motorfahrzeugen mit obligatorischer Versicherung, gebilligt wird, v. 30.12.1986: Santdiumenge op. cit.
29. Arts. 1 no. 2, 2 no. 3, 9 Act, 1/1982 on the Civil Law Protection of the Right to Honour, to Privacy, and to One's Own Picture, 5 May 1982: Organgesetz 1/1982 über den zivilrechtlichen Schutz des Rechts auf

Ehre, auf persönliche und familiäre Privatsphäre und auf das eigene Bild, v. 5.5.1982: Santdiumenge op. cit.

30. Art. 3 Act 13/1990 (Catalonia) on the Claim to Compel Someone to Refrain from Doing Something, Nuisance, Limited Personal Servitudes, and Neigbourhood Relations: Gesetz 13/1990 (Katalonien) über den Unterlassungsanspruch, die Immissionen, die Dienstbarkeiten und Nachbarschaftsbeziehungen: Santdiumenge op. cit.

31. Arts. 237–241 Royal Decree 1/92, through which the revised text of the Acts on land and town planning is accepted, 26 June 1992: Königliches Gesetzliches Dekret 1/92, durch welches der überarbeitete Text des Gesetzes über den Boden und die Stadtplanung gebilligt wird, v. 26.6.1992: Santdiumenge op. cit.

32. Arts. 123, 125 Act on Intellectual Propery: Gesetz über intellektuelles Eigentum: Santdiumenge op. cit.

33. Additional provision no. 3 to the Act 3/89 on the Adjusting Reform of the Criminal Code: Zusatzbestimmung Nr. 3 zum Organgesetz 3/89 über die Anpassungsreform des Strafgesetzbuches: Santdiumenge op. cit.

34. Arts. 1, 3–5 Royal Decree 1301/86, which adjusts the revised texts of the acts on the use and traffic of motor vehicles to the EC Directive, 28 June 1986: Königliches Gesetzliches Dekret 1301/86, welches den neugefaßten Text des Gesetzes über den Gebrauch und den Verkehr von Motorfahrzeugen an die Rechtsordnung der Europäischen Gemeinschaft anpaßt, v. 28.6.1986: Santdiumenge op. cit.

35. Arts. 11, 12 Decree 632/68, by which the revised text of the Acts 122/62, 24 December 1962, on the use and traffic of motor vehicles is passed, 21 March 1968: Dekret 632/68, durch welches der überarbeitete Text des Gesetzes 122/62 v. 24.12.1962 über den Gebrauch und den Verkehr von Motorfahrzeugen angenommen wird, v. 21.3.1968: Santdiumenge op cit:

36. Art. 11 Act 21/90, 19 December 1990, by which Spanish law is aligned to EEC Directive 88/357 on the freedom of insurance services with the exception of life assurance and which updates the legislation on private insurance: Gesetz 21/90 v. 19.12.1990, welches das spanische Recht an die Richtlinie 88/357 EWG über die Freizügigkeit von Dienstleistungen bei Versicherungen mit Ausnahme der Lebensversicherung angleicht und die Gesetzgebung über Privatversicherungen aktualisiert: Santdiumenge op. cit.

37. Arts. 1, 2 Directive on the compensation limit for bodily damage, 16 March 1987: Anweisung über Entschädigungsgrenzen wegen körperlicher Schäden v. 16.3.1987: Santdiumenge op. cit.

38. Art. 53 Decree, 22 June 1956, through which the revised version of the legislation on accidents at work is accepted: Dekret v. 22.6.1956,

durch welches die überarbeitete Fassung der Gesetzgebung über Arbeitsunfälle gebilligt wird: Santdiumenge op cit.

39. Art. 189 Order on accidents at work, 22 June 1956: Verordnung über Arbeitsunfälle v. 22.6.1956: Santdiumenge op. cit.

40. Arts. 51 no. 1, 58 Royal Decree 2187/78, through which the order concerning the discipline of town planning on the implementation and carrying out of the Land Acts is promulgated: Königliches Dekret 2187/78, durch welches die Verordnung über Disziplin der Stadtplanung zur Durchführung und Anwendung des Bodengesetzes verkündet wird: Santdiumenge op. cit.

41. Arts. 102–106 Royal Decree 2090/82, through which the general statute of the legal profession is accepted, 24 July 1982: Königliches Dekret 2090/82, durch welches das Allgemeine Statut der Rechtsanwaltschaft gebilligt wird, v. 24.7.1982: Santdiumenge op. cit.

42. Art. 27 Royal Decree 2046/82, through which the general statute of the status of the court is accepted, 30 July 1982: Königliches Dekret 2046/82, durch welches das Allgemeine Statut der Gerichtsprokuratoren gebilligt wird, v. 30.7.1982: Santdiumenge op. cit.

43. The Constitution of the Kingdom of Spain, 29 December 1978 (as amended on 27 August 1992): Verfassung des Königreiches Spanien v. 29 Dezember 1978, i.d.F. v. 27. August 1992: Kimmel, Adolf, in: *Die Verfassungen der EG-Mitgliedstaaten*, as of 1 July 1993, 3rd edn., Munich 1993, pp. 371–415

44. Product Liability Act: Gesetz Nr. 22/1994 v. 8.7.1994 (Produkthaftungsgesetz): Rodríguez Buján, J., 'Das spanische Produkthaftungsgesetz', *VersRAI* 1995, pp. 45–46

XIII. Sweden

1. Damages Act, 2 June 1972: Schadensersatzgesetz v. 2. Juni 1972 (SFS 1972: 207/1975: 404): Witte, Henning, 'Landesbericht Schweden', in: Bar, Christian v., *Deliktsrecht in Europa*, Cologne 1993

2. Chapter 3, 1 § Damages Act, (cited here from the version of 19 March 1971): Schadensersatzgesetz v. 19. März 1971: Woellert, Kai, *Die außervertragliche Haftung für schädigendes Verhalten von Hilfspersonen im nordischen Recht*, diss. Kiel 1972

3. 1 §, 8 §-29 § Traffic Damage Act: Verkehrsschadensgesetz (SFS 1975: 1410): Witte op. cit.

4. 14 § Road Traffic Order: Straßenverkehrsordnung (SFS 1972: 603): Witte op. cit.

5. 39 § Road Traffic Order, 28 September 1951: Straßenverkehrsordnung v. 28. September 1951: Woellert op. cit.

6. Product Liability Act: Produkthaftungsgesetz (SFS 1992: 18): Witte op. cit. = *PHI* 1992, p. 159 f.

7. Environmental Liability Act: Umwelthaftungsgesetz (SFS 1986: 225): Witte op. cit.

8. 1 § Act on Liability for Damages of Employers and Employees: Gesetz über die Schadensersatzpflicht des Arbeitgebers und Arbeitnehmers: Woellert op. cit.

9. 2 § I, and 3 § Act on the Liability for Damages arising from the Use of Motor Vehicles, 30 June 1916: Gesetz über die Haftung für Schäden beim Betrieb von Kraftfahrzeugen v. 30. Juni 1916: Woellert op. cit.

10. 2 §, 6 § I Act on the Liability for Damages Arising from the Operation of the Railways, 12 March 1886: Gesetz über die Haftung für Schäden beim Betrieb von Eisenbahnen v. 12. März 1886: Woellert op. cit.

11. 1 § I Act on the Liability for Damages Arising in Air Traffic, 26 May 1922: Gesetz über die Haftung für Schäden im Luftverkehr v. 26. Mai 1922: Woellert op. cit.

12. Chapter 1, 1 §, chapter 20, 7 § Act on General Insurance, 25 March 1962: Gesetz über die allgemeine Versicherung v. 25. März 1962: Woellert op. cit.

13. 51 § Act on Insurance for Work Related Damages, 14 May 1954 (as amended on 15 December 1967): Gesetz über die Berufsschadenversicherung v. 14. Mai 1954 i.d.F. v. 15. Dezember 1967: Woellert op. cit.

14. 25 § Insurance Contract Act, 8 April 1927: Versicherungsvertragsgesetz v. 8. April 1927: Woellert op. cit.

15. 7 § I Work Protection Act, 3 January 1949: Arbeitsschutzgesetz v. 3. Januar 1949: Woellert op. cit.

Table of Codes and Statutes

cited by margin number; references to footnotes are in brackets

Table of Treaties and Enactments of the European Union

cited by margin number; references o footnotes are in brackets

Basel Convention of 22 Mar. 1989 on the Control of Transboundary Movements of Hazardous Wastes and their Disposal (BGBl. 1994 II p. 2704)
– Art. 12: 381

BMW (Beneluxverdrag met eenvormige wet inzake de warenmerken of 19 Mar. 1962; Stb. 1963 no. 221; Monit.belg., 14 Oct. 1969)
– Art. 13: 369 (6)

Brussels International Convention on Tourists Travel Contract of 23 Apr. 1970 (BT-Drucks. 8 /786)
– Art. 15: 377

BTMW (Beneluxverdrag inzake tekeningen of modellen met eenvormige Beneluxwet inzake tekeningen of modellen of 25 Oct. 1966; Trb. no. 292; Monit.-belg., 29 Dec. 1973)
– Art. 14 subsec. 5: 369 (6)

CIM (Convention internationale concernant le transport des marchandises par chemins de fer of 7 Feb. 1970; International agreement on rail freight; BGBl. 1974 II p. 381)
– Art. 51 subsec. 1: 377

CIV (Convention internationale concernant le transport des voyageurs et des baggages par chemins de fer; International

Convention of 7 Feb. 1970 on Railway Transport of Passengers and Luggage; BGBl. 1974 II p. 359)
– Art. 46 subsec. 1: 377

CMR (Geneva Convention of 19 May 1956 on the Contract for the International Carriage of Goods by Road; UNTS 399 p. 189; BGBl. 1961 II p. 1119
– Art. 17 subsec. 1: 447 (224)
– Art. 17 subsec. 2: 447 (224)
– Art. 28: 377

(First) Council Directive 72/166/ EEC of 24 Apr. 1972 on the Approximation of the Laws of the Member States Relating to Insurance against Civil Liability in Respect of the Use of Motor Vehicles, and to the Enforcement of the Obligation to Insure Against Such Liability (OJ L 103, 2 May 1972 p. 1; with amendment by Dir. 72/430/EEC of 19 Dec. 1972; OJ L 291, 28 Dec. 1972 p. 162)
– Art. 1 no. 5: 378 (73)

Council Directive 76/207/EEC on the Implementation of the Principle of Equal Treatment for Men and Women as Regards Access to Employment, Vocational Training, Promotion, and Working Conditions of 9 Dec. 1976 (OJ L 39 p. 40)

Table of UK and Irish Cases

cited by margin number, references to footnotes are in brackets

Abbreviations

AB	*Wet algemeene bepalingen*. Act of 15 May 1829 on the general provisions for the legislation of the kingdom (Stb. 28) (Netherlands)
ABGB	*Allgemeines Bürgerliches Gesetzbuch*, 1 June 1811 (JGS 946) (Austrian Civil Code)
AC	Law Reports, Appeal Cases (House of Lords; London 1.1875/76 ff.; the collection up to 1890 cited as Appeal Cases; from 1891 the abbreviation AC is used; cited by year, book, and page)
AcP	*Archiv für die civilistische Praxis* (Tübingen, vol. 1 [1818]–vol. 149 [1944]); vol. 150 (1948/49) ff.; incorporating *Archiv für bürgerliches Recht*; cited by volume, year, and page)
Acta Jur.	*Acta Juridica* (Kapstadt 1.1958 [1959] ff.; cited by year and page)
AG	Amtsgericht (Local Court, Germany); *Aktiengesellschaft* (PLC)
A-G	*Advocaat-Generaal* (Netherlands); Attorney-General (England); *Avocat-Général* (Belgium; France)
AID	*Archeion Idiotiku Dikaiu (Triminiaia nomiki epitheorisis*; Athens 1.1934–17.1954/59; cited by volume, year, and page)
All ER	All England Law Reports (London 1.1936 ff.; cited by year, book, and page).
ALR	*Allgemeines Landrecht für die preußischen Staaten*, 1 June 1794 (General Land Law for the Prussian States)
A.L.R.	Australian Law Reports (Sydney 1.1973 ff.; cited by volume, year, and page)
alt.	alternative
AMG	*Arzneimittelgesetz. Gesetz zur Neuordnung des Arzneimittelrechts* v. 24.08.1976 (Act on Medication Reform, 24 Aug. 1976) (BGBl. 1976 I p. 2995) (Germany)
AmJCompL	*American Journal of Comparative Law* (Baltimore 1.1952 ff.; cited by volume, year, and page)
AN	*Anagastikos Nomos* (Emergency laws) (Greece)
An. Der. Civ.	*Anuario de Derecho Civil* (Madrid 1.1948 ff.; cited by volume, year, and page)
Ann. Louv.	*Annales de Droit de Louvain* (Brussels 41.1981 ff.;

	previously Annales de droit et de sciences politiques; cited by year and page)
Annal. prop. ind.	*Annales de la propriété industrielle, artistique et littéraire* (Paris 1.1855 ff.; cited by year and page)
App.	Corte d'Appello (Court of Appeal) (Italy)
App. Cas.	Appeal Cases: see AC
Arch. civ.	*Archivio civile* (Piacenza, 4th Series 1.1958 ff.; cited by year and page)
Arch. Giur. circolaz.	*Archivio Giuridico della circolazione e dei sinistri stradali* (Piacenza, 4th Series 1.1955–22.1976 ff.; cited by year and page)
ArchN	*Archeion Nomologicas* (Athens 1.1949 ff.; cited by volume, year, and page)
Arch. resp. civ.	*Archivio della responsabilità civile e dei problemi del danno* (Piacenza 1.1958 ff.; cited by year and page)
Arm.	*Armenopoulos miniaia nomiki epitheorisis* (Thessalonika 1.1946/47 ff.; cited by year and page)
Art., Arts.	Article(s)
ASVG	Allgemeines Sozialversicherungsrecht (General Social Insurance Act) (BGBl. 1955/189) (Austria)
AtomHG	Atomhaftpflichtgesetz (Nuclear Liability Act) (BGBl. 1964/117) (Austria)
A & V	*Aansprakelijkheid en Verzekering* (Deventer 1.1993 ff.; cited by year and page)
AWSt-A	Reference term used in the publications of the BfAI (q.V.)
B.	Baron
B & Ad.	Barnewall & Adolphus' King's Bench Reports (109–110 *ER*) (London 1.1830–11.1840; cited by volume and page)
BAG	Bundesarbeitsgericht (Federal Labour Court) (Germany)
BAGE	Entscheidungen des Bundesarbeitsgericht (Decisions of the Federal Labour Court) (Berlin 1.1955 ff.; cited by volume and page)
BB	*Banca, borsa e titoli di credito* = rivista di dottrina e giurisprudenza (Milan 1.1934–8.1941, 11.1948 ff.; cited by year, book, and column)
BB	*Betriebs-Berater* (Heidelberg 1.1946 ff.; cited by year and page)
BD	Byretsdom (local court judgment) (Denmark)
BfAI	Bundesstelle für Außenhandelsinformation

	(Federal Office for Information on Foreign Trade) (Cologne)
BG	Bundesgericht (Supreme Court, Switzerland); Bezirksgericht (Court of Appeal, former GDR; partly also Germany); Bezirksgericht (Court of First Instance, general jurisdiction, Austria)
BGB	Bürgerliches Gesetzbuch (German Civil Code), 18 Aug. 1896 (RGBl. p. 195) (Germany)
BGBl.	Bundesgesetzblatt (Government Gazette, Germany) 1950; then in parts: BGBl. part I (1951 ff.) BGBl. part II (1951 ff.) BGBl. part III = Sammlung des Bundesrechts (Collection of Federal Statutes) (Cologne, Bonn 1.1958 ff.)
BGE	Entscheidungen des schweizerischen Bundesgerichtes (Decisions of the Swiss Federal [Supreme] Court; also referred to as Arrêts du Tribunal Fédéral Suisse) (Lausanne 1.1875 ff.; from 23.1897 2 books without special titles; separation from 40.1914; cited by volume, book, and page)
BGH	Bundesgerichtshof (Federal [Supreme] Court, Germany–before 1990 for West Germany only)
BGHZ	Amtliche Sammlung der Entscheidungen des Bundesgerichtshofes in Zivilsachen (Decisions of the German Federal Court in civil matters) (Cologne, Berlin 1.1951 ff.; cited by volume and page)
BinnSchG	Binnenschiffahrtsgesetz (Inland Waterways Act) (RGBl. 1898, 369, 868) (Austria); Gesetz über den gewerblichen Binnenschiffsverkehr (Act on Industrial Inland Waterway Traffic) (as amended on 8 Jan. 1969) (BGBl. I p. 66) (Germany)
BJagdG	Bundesjagdgesetz (Federal Hunting Act) (as amended on 29 Sep. 1976) (BGBl. I 2849) (Germany)
BJC	Boletín de Jurisprudencia Constitucional (Bulletin of the Constitutional Court) (Spain) (Madrid 1.1981 ff.; cited by volume, year, and page)
BOE	Boletín Oficial del Estado (Official Gazette, Spain) (Madrid 1.1936 ff.; cited by year, number, and date)
BolMinJust	*Boletim do Ministério da Justiça* (Bulletin of the Ministry of Justice) (Lisbon 1.1940/41 ff.; cited by volume, year, and page)

Brussels Convention	Brussels Convention on Jurisdiction and Enforcement of Judgments in Civil and Commercial Matters, 27 Sep. 1968 (OJ 1978 L304, p. 77)
BS	Belgisch Staatsblad; see Monit. belge
B & S	Best & Smith Queen's Bench Reports (London 1.1861—5.1865; cited by year, volume, and page)
Bull.Ass.	*Bulletin des Assurances* (Brussels 1.1921 ff.; cited by year and page)
Bull.civ.	Bulletin des arrêts de la Cour de Cassation rendus en matière civile (Bulletin of the decisions of the Court of Cassation in civil matters) (France) (Paris 12.1804/05, 128.1926 ff.; cited by year, book, and number)
Bull.crim.	Bulletin des arrêts de la Cour de Cassation rendus en matière criminelle (Bulletin of the decisions of the Court of Cassation in criminal matters) (France) (Paris 9.1804 ff.; cited by year, book, and number)
Bull.EU	Bulletin of the European Union; (before 1993, Bulletin of the European Communities) (Luxembourg 1.1968 ff.; cited by year and number)
BVerfG	Bundesverfassungsgericht (Federal Constitutional Court) (Germany)
BVerfGE	Amtliche Sammlung der Entscheidungen des Bundesverfassungsgerichts (Decisions of the Federal Constitutional Court) (Tübingen 1.1952 ff.; cited by volume and page)
BVerfGG	Bundesverfassungsgerichtsgesetz (Statute of the Constitutional Court of the Federal Republic of Germany) as amended on the announcement of 12 Dec. 1985 (BGBl. I p. 2229)
BW	Nieuw Burgerlijk Wetboek, 1 Jan. 1992 (Boek 1, 1 Jan. 1970: Stb. 1969, no. 167 in conjunction with KB, 4 June 1969 Stb. 1969 no. 259) (Boek 2, 26 July 1976: Stb. 1976 no. 228 in conjunction with KB, 12 June 1976, Stb. 1976 no. 342) (Boek 3, 4, 5, 6, 7, 7A, 1 Jan. 1992: Stb. 1989 no. 61 b in conjunction with KB 20 Feb. 1990, Stb. 1990 no. 90) (Boek 8, 1 April 1991: Stb. 1991 no. 126) (Dutch Civil Code)
BW (old)	Burgerlijk Wetboek, 1 Oct. 1838 (Stb. 1831 nos. 1 and 6 in conjunction with KB, 10 Apr. 1838, Stb. 1838 no. 12) (old Dutch Civil Code)
CA	Court of Appeal (England)

Cass.	Cour de Cassation (France, Belgium); Corte di Cassazione (Italy, when none other specified: sezione civile) (Court of Cassation)
Cass.ass.plén.	Cour de cassation, assemblée plénière (France)
Cass.civ.	Cour de cassation, chambre civile (France)
Cass.com.	Cour de cassation, chambre commerciale (France)
Cass.crim.	Cour de cassation, chambre criminelle (France)
Cass.mixte	Cour de cassation, chambre mixte (France)
Cass.req.	Cour de cassation, chambre des requêtes (abolished) (France)
Cass.sez.pen.	Corte di Cassazione, sezione penale (Italy)
Cass.sez.un.	Corte di Cassazione, sezione unite (Italy)
Cass.soc.	Cour de cassation, Chambre sociale (France)
Cc	Code Civil (Civil Code) (France: 21 Mar. 1804; Belgium, Luxembourg: 5 Mar. 1803 [15 Mar. 1803]); (Greece: Astikos Kodikas 23 Feb. 1946 [AN 2250/1940; FEK A 91/1940 p. 597]); (Switzerland: 10 Dec. 1907 [SR 210]); (GDR) Codice Civile (Italy [Gaz.Uff., 4 Apr. 1942, no. 79 and 79 bis; edizione straordinaria]); Código Civil (Spain: 24 July 1889 [Gaceta de Madrid no. 206, 25 July 1889]); (Portugal: [Decreto-Lei no. 47–344, 25 Nov. 1966])
Cc Introd. Act	Civil Code Introductory Act (Eisagogikos nomos) (AN 2783/1941 FEK A 29/1941 p. 145) (Greece)
C.com.	Código de comercio (Commercial Code), 22 Aug. 1885 (Gaceta no. 289–328, 16 Oct.–24 Nov. 1885) (Spain); Code de commerce, 1808 (France); Wetboek van Koophandel (Commercial Code), 10 Sep. 1807 (Belgium)
CE	Constitución Española (Spanish Constitution) 27 Dec. 1987, altered, 27 Aug. 1992 (BOE no. 311.1., 29 Dec. 1978) (Spain)
CFI	Court of First Instance
Ch.	The Chancery Division Law Reports (London 1.1875/76 ff.; cited by year, book, and page)
CIM	Convention Internationale Concernant le Transport des Marchandises par Chemins de Fer. International agreement of 7 Feb. 1970 on rail freight (BGB1. 1974 II p. 381).
CIV	Convention Internationale Concernant le Transport des Voyageurs et des Bagages par Chemins de Fer. International agreement of 7 Feb. 1970 on

the movement of people and baggage by rail (BGB1. 1974 II pp. 359, 580)

CJ	*Colectânea de Jurisprudência* (Coimbra 1.1976 ff.; cited by volume, year, part, and page)
CJ (ST)	*Colectânea de Jurisprudência: Acórdãos do Supremo Tribunal de Justiça* (Coimbra 1.1993 ff.; cited by volume, year, part, and page)
CLJ	*Cambridge Law Journal* (Cambridge 1.1921/23 ff., parts without volume numbers; cited, as far as possible, by volume, year, and page)
CML Rep.	Common Market Law Reports (London 1.1963 ff.; cited by volume, year, and page)
CMR	Convention relative au Contrat de Transport International de Marchandises par Route. Convention on the Contract for the International Carriage of Goods by Road, 19 May 1956 (UNTS vol. 399 p. 189; BGBl. 1961 II p. 1119, 1962 II p. 12)
Code jud.	Code judiciaire (Code of civil procedure), 10 Oct. 1967 (Monit. belge, 31 Oct. 1967) (Belgium)
col.	colona
Col. Leg. Esp.	*Colección Legislativa de España.* First series, third part: Jurisprudencia civil (Madrid 1.1889 ff.; cited by volume, year, book, number, and page)
COM	Publications of the EU Commission (Brussels 1.1968 ff.)
Comp. LYB	*Comparative Law Yearbook* (The Hague 1.1977 ff.; cited by year and page)
Contratto e Impresa	*Contratto e Impresa* (Padua 1.1985 ff.; cited by year and page)
Corr.	Correctionnel (Court of First Instance in Criminal Matters) (Belgium)
Corr. giur.	*Corriere giuridico* (Milan 1.1984 ff.; cited by year and page)
Corte Cost.	Corte Costituzionale (Constitutional Court) (Italy)
Cour	Cour Supérieure de Justice (in its function as Cour d'assises, Cour de cassation, or Cour d'appel) (Luxembourg)
CP	Code Pénal (Penal Code) (France; Luxembourg, 16 June 1879 [Mémorial, 1879 p. 589]); Strafwetboek (Penal Code) (Belgium, 8 June 1867 [Monit. belge, 9 June 1867]); Codice Penale (Italy no. 1938, 19 Sep. 1930 [Gaz.Uff. no. 253 suppl. 28

	Sep. 1930]); Código Penal (Spain; 14 Sep. 1973 [BOE no. 297–300, 12–15 Dec. 1973]) (Portugal [Decreto 16 Sep. 1886])
C.proc.civ.	(Nouveau) Code de procédure civile (France); Codice di procedura civile (Italy, 21 Apr. 1942 [RD, 28 Oct. 1940, no. 1443 Gaz.Uff. no. 253, 28 Oct. 1940]); Código de Processo Civil (Portugal, 28 Dec. 1961 [Dec. Lei no. 44129]) (Code of civil procedure)
C.proc.crim.	Code de procédure criminelle (Wetboek van Strafvordering) (17 Apr. 1878 [Monit.belge, 25 Apr. 1878]) (Belgium)
C. proc. pen.	Code de procédure pénale (France); Codice di procedura penale (Italy, 1 July 1931 [RD, 19 Oct. 1930 no. 1399: Gaz.Uff. 28 Oct. 1930 no. 253 Suppl.]); Código de processo penal (Portugal [Decreto Lei no. 16489, 15 Feb.1929 Diário do Governo]). (Code of criminal procedure)
Cuad. Civ. Jur.	*Cuadernos Civitas de Jurisprudencia Civil* (Madrid 1.1983 ff.; cited by year and page)
D.	*Recueil de jurisprudence Dalloz* (Paris; also *Recueil général des lois et arrêts* or *Recueil Sirey*; 1801/02 ff.; with different forms and titles: *DA* (*Recueil analytique Dalloz* [1941–1944]); *DC* (*Recueil critique Dalloz* [1941–1944]); *DH* (*Recueil hebdomadaire Dalloz* [1924–1940]); *DP* (*Recueil périodique et critique Dalloz* [1924–1940]); *Recueil Dalloz, Recueil Sirey,* combined since 1955; *Recueil Dalloz et Recueil Sirey*; from 1965: *Recueil Dalloz-Sirey*; appearing in parts: *D. Chron./Jur.* [Chronique/Jurisprudence], *D. IR/Légis.* [Informations Rapides/Législation], *D. Somm.* [Sommaires Commentés]; cited by year, book, and page)
D.	décret (decree) (France)
DAR	*Deutsches Autorecht* (Munich 1.1926 ff.; cited by year and page)
DB	*Der Betrieb* Wochenschrift für Betriebswirtshaft, Steuerrecht, Wirtschaftsrecht, Arbeitsrecht (Düsseldorf, 1.1948 ff.; cited by year and page)
DC	see *D.*
DH	see *D.*
Diário Rep.	Diário da República. Portugese Government Gazette (Lisbon 1.1976 ff.; cited by year and number)

Dig.	Digest of Justinian (Pandects)
Dir. fam. pers.	*Diritto di famiglia e delle persone* (Milan 1.1972 ff.; cited by year, and if necessary by part and page)
Dir. inf.	*Diritto dell'informazione e dell'informatica* (Milan 1.1985 ff.; cited by year and page)
diss.	dissertation
DJ	*Deutsche Justiz* (Berlin 1.1933–13.1945; cited by year and page)
DJT	Deutscher Juristentag (German Lawyers' Association)
DL	Danske Lov, 15 Apr. 1683 (Danish Civil Code)
DLR (3rd)	Dominion Law Reports (Ontario 3rd Series 1.1969–150.1984; cited by volume, year, and page)
DNotZ	*Deutsche Notarzeitschrift* (Munich, Berlin 1.1901–33.1933 Magazine of the German Association of Public Notaries; 33.1933 ff.; cited by year and page)
DPR	Decreto Presidente della Repubblica (Presidential decree) (Italy)
Droit soc.	*Droit social* (Paris 1.1938 ff.; cited by year and page)
Dr. prat. com. int.	*Droit et pratique du commerce international* (Paris 1.1975 ff.; cited by year and page)
EAL	Erstatningsansvarsloven; Damages Liability Act, no. 228, 23 May 1984 (Lovtidende A 1984 p. 742) (Denmark)
E B & E	Ellis, Blackburn & Ellis' Queen's Bench Reports (120 ER) (London 1.1858–4.1861; cited by year, volume, and page)
EC	European Community
ECE	Economic Commission for Europe
ECHR	European Convention Human Rights
ECJ	Court of Justice of the European Communities (Luxembourg)
ECLR	*European Competition Law Review* (Oxford 1.1980 ff.; cited by volume, year, and page)
ECR	European court reports. Reports of cases before the Court of Justice and the Court of First Instance / Court of Justice of the European Communities (Luxembourg 1.1954 ff.) (until 1989 Reports of cases before the Court) (cited by volume, year, and page)

ed(d).	editor(s)
edn.	edition
EED	*Epitheorissis Egatikou Dikaiou* (Athens 1.1941 ff.; cited by volume, year, and page)
EEN	*Ephimeris Ellinon Nomikon* (Athens 1.1934 ff.; cited by volume, year, and page)
EFSlg	*Sammlung ehe- und familienrechtlicher Entscheidungen* (Decisions on marriage and family law) (Vienna 1.1965 ff.; cited by the number of the decision)
e.g.	*exempli gratia* (for example)
EGBGB	Einführungsgesetz zum Bürgerlichen Gesetzbuche (BGB Introductory Act), 18 Aug. 1896 (RGBl. p. 604) (Germany)
Eis.	Eisagogi, introduction.
EKHG	Eisenbahn- und Kraftfahrzeughaftpflichtgesetz (Rail and Road Traffic Liability Act) 21 Jan. 1959 (BGBl. 1959/48) (Austria)
El. & Bl.	Ellis & Blackburn's Queen's Bench Reports; see E B & E
EllDik	*Elliniki Dikeosini* (Athens 1.1960 ff.; cited by volume, year, and page)
ER	*The English Reports* (London 1.1900–178.1932; cited by volume and page)
ERPL	*European Review of Private Law* (Deventer 1.1994 ff.; cited by volume, year, and page)
et al.	*et alii* (and others)
ETS	European Treaty Series (Strasbourg 1.1949–3.1949, 4.1950 ff.; cited by volume and number)
EU	European Union
EuGRZ	*Europäische Grundrechte-Zeitschrift* (Strasbourg 1.1974 ff.; cited by year and page)
Eur.Conv.Hum.Rt.	European Convention on the Protection of Human Rights, 4 Nov. 1950
Eur. Transp. L	*European Transport Law* (Antwerp 1.1966 ff.; cited by volume, year, and page)
EuZW	*Europäische Zeitschrift für Wirtschaftsrecht* (Munich, Frankfurt/Main 1.1990 ff.; cited by year and page)
EvBl	*Evidenzblatt der Rechtsmittelentscheidungen* (Vienna 1.1934 ff.; included in the ÖJZ (since 1946); see there; cited by year and page)
EWiR	*Entscheidungen zum Wirtschaftsrecht* (Cologne 1.1985 ff.; cited by §, number, year, and page)

EWS	*Europäisches Wirtschafts- und Steuerrecht* (Munich 1.1990 ff.; cited by year and page)
F.	Federal Reporter (St. Paul/Minnesota, 1st Series: 1.1880–300.1925; cited by volume, year, and page)
F. 2d.	Federal Reporter (St. Paul/Minnesota, 2nd series: 1.1924/5 (1925) ff.; cited by volume, year, and page)
FamRZ	*Zeitschrift für das gesamte Familienrecht* (Bielefeld 1.1954 ff.; until 9.1962: *Ehe und Familie im privaten und öffentlichen Recht*; cited by year and page)
fasc.	fascicule
FEK	*Fyllo Ephimeridas Kyberniseos* (Greek Government Gazette; cited by year, volume, and if necessary, book, and number)
f(f).	following page(s)
FFS	Finlands Författningssamling (Finnish Official Gazette) (Helsingfors 1.1860 ff.; cited by year, number, and page)
FL	Færdselsloven; Act no. 149, 20 Mar. 1918 (Lovtidende A 1918 pp. 578–592) on road traffic (Denmark)
fn.	footnote
Foro.it.	*Il Foro italiano: raccolta di giurisprudenza civile, commerciale, penale, amministrativa* (Rome 1.1876 ff.; cited by year, book, and column)
Foro.it.Mass.	*Massimario del Foro italiano* (Rome 1.1930 ff.; cited by volume, year, number, and column)
Foro.pad.	*Il Foro padano* (Milan 1.1946 ff.; cited by year, book, and column)
FS	Festschrift
FSR	Fleet Street Patent Law Reports (London 1.1963 ff.; cited by year and page)
F.Supp.	Federal Supplement (St. Paul/Minnesota 1.1932/33 ff.; cited by volume and page)
FuR	*Familie und Recht* (Neuwied 1.1990 ff.; cited by year and page)
Gai.	Gaius
Gaz. Pal.	*Gazette du Palais* (Paris 1.1881/82 ff.; cited by year, book, and page)
Gaz. Uff.	Gazzetta Ufficiale della Repubblica italiana (Italian Official Gazette) (Rome 1.1860 ff.; cited by year, number, and page)

GenTG	Gentechnikgesetz. Gesetz zur Regelung der Gentechnik v. 20.06.1990 (Act on the Regulation of Genetic Engineering, 20 June 1990) (BGB1. I p. 1080) (Germany)
Giur. cost.	*Giurisprudenza costituzionale* (Milan 1.1956–20.1975; then: Parte 1 = Corte costituzionale 21.1976 ff.; Parte 2 = Ordinanza di rinvio ed i ricorsi 21.1976 ff.; Parte 3 = Quaderni della giurisprudenza costituzionale 1.1964–7.1968; NS 1.1972 ff.)
Giur.it.	*Giurisprudenza italiana* (Turin 14.1862 ff.; cited by year, part, and if necessary, section, and column)
Giur.it.Mass.	*Massimario della Giurisprudenza italiana* (Turin 1.1931 ff.; cited by year, number, and page)
Giur.mer.	*Giurisprudenza di merito* (Milan 1.1969 ff.; cited by year, book, and page)
Giur.tosc.	*Giurisprudenza toscana* (Milan *et al.* 1.1950 ff.; cited by year and page)
Giust.civ.	*Giustizia civile: Rivista bimestrale di giurisprudenza* (Milan 1.1951 ff.; cited by year, book, and page)
Giust.civ.Mass.	*Giustizia civile: Massimario annotato della cassazione* (Milan 1.1955–7.1957 (1957/58), 1958 ff.; cited by year, number, and page)
GRUR	*Gewerblicher Rechtsschutz und Urheberrecht* (Weinham 1.1896–49.1944, 50.1948 ff.; cited by year and page)
GRUR Int.	*Gewerblicher Rechtsschutz und Urheberrecht, Internationaler Teil* (Weinheim 1.1980 ff.; from 1966 to 1980 *Auslands- und internationaler Teil*; cited by year and page)
GrW	Grondwet (Dutch Constitution, 17 Feb. 1983) (Stb. p. 70)
GWB	Gesetz gegen Wettbewerbsbeschränkungen (Act against Restrictions to Competition), 27 July 1957 (BGBl. I p. 1081) (Germany)
HC	High Court (Eire)
HD	Højesteretsdom (Denmark); Høyesterettsdom (Norway); Högsta domstolens domar (Sweden, Finland) (Judgment of the Supreme Court)
HD	Redogörelser och meddelanden angående högsta domstolens avgöranden (Decisions of the Finnish Supreme Court) (Helsinki 1.1926 ff.; cited by year, section, and page)

HGB	Handelsgesetzbuch (German Commercial Code), 10 May 1897 (RGBl. p. 219)
HK	Højesterets kendelse (Supreme Court Decisions, Denmark)
HL	House of Lords (England)
HL Cas.	Clark's House of Lords Cases (London 1.1847–10.1866; cited by volume, year, and page)
HLR	Housing Law Reports (London 1.1967 ff.; cited by year, volume, and page)
HovR	Hovrätt (Court of Appeal; Finland, Sweden)
HPflG	Haftpflichtgesetz (Liability Act), 4 Jan. 1978 (BGBl. I p. 145) (Germany)
HR	Hoge Raad (Supreme Court, Netherlands)
ICR	Industrial Cases Reports (London 1.1975 ff.; cited by year and page)
i.e.	*id est* (that is to say)
ILRM	Irish Law Reports Monthly (Dublin 1.1981 ff.; cited by year and page)
ILT	*Irish Law Times* (NS Dublin 1.1983 ff.; cited by year and page)
Inf. AuslR	*Informationsbrief Ausländerrecht* (Frankfurt/Main 1.1979 ff.; cited by year and page)
Inst.	Institutions of Justinian
Int. Bus. Lawyer	*International Business Lawyer* (London 1.1973 ff.; cited by year and page)
Int.Comp.LQ	*International and Comparative Law Quarterly* (London 1.1952 ff.; cited by volume, year, and page)
Int.Enc.Comp.L	*International Encyclopedia of Comparative Law* (Tübingen, New York 1.1970 ff.; cited by volume, chapter, and margin number)
IR	Irish Reports (Dublin 1.1894 ff; including the subseries Common Law Series [1.1867 (1868)–11.1877 (1878)] as well as Equity Series [1.1867 (1868) ff.]; cited by year, book, and page)
Ir. LR	Irish Law Reports, 1st series (Dublin 1.1838–12.1850; cited by year, book, and page)
IRLR	Industrial Relations Law Reports(London 1.1972 ff.; cited by year and page)
J	*Juristen* (Copenhagen 1.1919 ff.; cited by year and page)
J	Judge (High Court) (UK)
JA	*Juristische Arbeitsblätter* (Bielefeld 1.1969 ff.; cited by year and page)

JBl	*Juristische Blätter* (Vienna 1.1872 ff.; cited by year and page)
JC	High Court of Justiciary (Scotland)
JClCiv	see Table of Literature Cited in Abbreviated Form
JCP	*Juris-Classeur Périodique*; see *Sem.Jur.*
J de Paix	Justice de Paix (Luxembourg); Justice de Paix (Vredegerecht) (Belgium) (Justice of the Peace)
J. Environ. L	*Journal of Environmental Law* (New York 1.1974/75 ff; cited by volume, year, and page)
JFT	*Tidskrift utgiven av Juridiska Föreningen i Finnland* (Helsingfors 1.1936 ff; cited by year and page)
JGG	Jugendgerichtsgesetz (Juvenile Court Act), 4 Aug. 1953 (BGBl. I p. 751) (Germany)
JGS	Justizgesetzsammlung. Gesetze und Verordnungen in Justizsachen (Collection of Statutes) (Vienna 1780–1848; cited by year and number) (Austria)
JhJb	*Jherings Jahrbücher für die Dogmatik des bürgerlichen Rechts* (Jena 1.1857–90.1943; until 37.1897 *Jahrbuch für die Dogmatik des heutigen römischen Rechts und deutschen Privatrechts*; cited by volume, year, and page)
JO	Journal Officiel de la République Française. Lois et Décrets. Official Gazette of the French Republic. Acts and Decrees (Paris 1.1869 ff.; cited by year, date, and page).
JöR	*Jahrbuch des öffentlichen Rechts der Gegenwart* (Tübingen 1.1907–25.1938; NS 1.1951 ff.; cited by volume, year, and page)
JP	Juge de Paix (Luxembourg); Juge de Paix or Vrederechter (Belgium) (Justice of the Peace)
JR	*Juristische Rundschau* (Berlin 1.1947 ff; cited by year and page)
JT	*Journal des Tribunaux* (Brussels 1.1881–96.1981; 101.1982 ff.; 97–100 not produced; cited by year and page)
Jura	*Jura. Juristische Ausbildung* (Berlin *et al.* 1.1979 ff.; cited by year and page)
Jurid. Rev.	*Juridical Review* (Edinburgh, London 1.1889–67.1955; NS 1.1956 ff.; cited by year and page)
JuS	*Juristische Schulung* (Munich, Frankfurt/Main 1.1961 ff.; cited by year and page)
JUS	*Rivista di scienze giuridiche* (Milan 1.1940–4.1943;

	NS 1.1950–20.1969; 21.1974 ff.; cited by year and page)
JZ	*Juristenzeitung* (Tübingen 1.1945 ff.; Continuation of the German *Rechtszeitschrift* and the south German *Juristenzeitung*, 6.1951 ff.; cited by year and page)
KB	Law Reports, King's Bench Division (London 1.1875/76 ff.; cited by year, book, and page)
KB	Koninklijk Besluit (Royal decree, Netherlands)
KF	*Karlsruher Forum*, supplement to *VersR* (Karlsruhe 1.1959 ff.; cited by year and page)
KG	*Kort Geding* (from 1.1981 contained in *Rechtspraak van de Week*; see *RvdW*)
KG	Kammergericht (Berlin Court of Appeal, Germany)
KG	Kommanditgesellschaft
KIR	Knight's Industrial Reports (London 1.1966–10.1975; cited by year, volume, and page
KPD	Kodikas Pinikis Dikonomias (Code of Criminal Procedure) (Act no. 1493, 17 Aug. 1950, FEK 182/1950 pp. 1004–1074) (Greece)
KPolDik	Kodikas Politikis Dikonomias (Code of Civil Procedure) (Royal Decree 657/1971 FEK 219/1 Jan. 1971 p. 75) (Greece)
Ktg.	Kantongerecht (Local Court, Netherlands)
KTS	*Konkurs-, Treuhand- und Schiedsgerichtswesen* (Cologne *et al.* 1.1939–52.1991; cited by year and page)
L	Loi (France); Lov (Scandinavia); Lag (Finland, Sweden) (Act)
La Ley	*Revista jurídica española de doctrina, jurisprudencia y bibliografía* (Madrid 1.1980 ff.; cited by year, book, and page)
Lavoro 80	*Lavoro 80—Rivista di diritto del lavoro pubblico e privato* (Milan 1.1981 ff.; cited by year and page)
Lav. prev. oggi	*Lavoro e previdenza oggi* (Milan 1.1974 ff.; cited by year and page)
LC	Lord Chancellor (UK)
LEC	Ley de Enjuiciamiento Civil, 3 Feb. 1881 (Code of Civil Procedure. Gaceta de Madrid no. 36–53, 5–22 Feb. 1881) (Spain)
LECr	Ley de Enjuiciamiento Criminal, 14 July 1882 (Code of Criminal Procedure. Gaceta de Madrid no. 260–283, 17 Sep.–10 Oct. 1882) (Spain)

LG	Landgericht (Germany); Landesgericht (Austria) (Court of the First Instance, general jurisdiction, also Court of Appeal for Local Courts)
LGR	Local Government Reports (London 1.1911 ff.; cited by volume, year, and page)
Limb. Rechtsl.	*Limburgs Rechtsleven* (Beringen 1.1958 ff.; cited by year and page)
LJ	Lord Justice (Court of Appeal judge, UK)
Lloyd's List Law Rep.	Lloyd's List Law Reports (London 1.1919–32.1950; cited by volume, year, and page)
Lloyd's Rep.	*Lloyd's Law Reports* (London 1.1968 ff.; cited by volume, year, and page)
LM	*Lindenmaier-Möhring, Nachschlagwerk des Bundesgerichtshofs* (in civil cases, Munich 1.1951 ff.; cited by act, paragraph, and number)
LNTS	League of Nations Treaty Series (Geneva 1.1920–205.1944/46; cited by volume and page)
LOTC	Ley Orgánica del Tribunal Constitucional, 3 Oct. 1979 (BOE no. 239, 5 Oct. 1979) (Statute of the Constitutional Court, Spain)
LP	Lord President (Scotland)
LQR	*Law Quarterly Review* (London 1.1885 ff.; cited by volume, year, and page)
LR Ex.	Law Reports, Exchequer Division (London 1.1875/76–5.1879/80; cited by year, book, and page)
LuftVG	Luftverkehrsgesetz (Air Traffic Act) 14 Jan. 1981 (BGBl. I p. 61) (Germany); (RGBl. 1936 I p. 653) (Austria)
McGill LJ	*McGill Law Journal* (Montreal 1.1952/55 (1954); cited by volume, year, and page)
MedienG	Mediengesetz (Media Act) (BGBl. 1981/314) (Austria)
MJ	*Maastricht Journal of European and Comparative Law* (Antwerp, Baden-Baden 1.1994; cited by volume, year, and page)
ML	Myndighedsloven. Act, 30 June 1922 no. 277 (Lovtidende A p. 1379–1389) on minors and guardianship (Denmark)
ModLRev	*Modern Law Review* (London 1.1937/38 ff.; cited by year and page)
Monit. belge	Moniteur belge des arrêtés des secrétaires généraux: journal officiel (Official Gazette, Belgium) (Brussels 1.1831 ff.; cited by date)

MR	Master of the Rolls (Member and President of the Civil Division of the Court of Appeal, UK)
MuSchG	Gesetz zum Schutz der erwerbstätigen Mutter (Act on the protection of working mothers) (18 Apr. 1968; BGBl. I p. 315) (Germany)
M & W	Meeson and Welsby's Reports, Exchequer (London 1.1836–16.1847; cited by volume and page)
n.	number (in Italian decisions and acts)
NCP	Nuevo Código Penal, 23 November 1995 (New Penal Code) (Ley Orgánica 10/1995, 23 November 1995, BOE no. 281, 24 November 1995) (Spain)
NDS	*Nordisk Domssamling* (Oslo 1.1958 ff; cited by year and page)
Nds. Rpflege	*Niedersächsische Rechtspflege* (Celle 1.1947 ff.; cited by year and page)
NedJur	*Nederlandse jurisprudentie* (Zwolle 1913 ff.; until 1935 cited by year and page, then by year, number, and page)
Ned. Rechtspraak	*Nederlandsche Rechtspraak of verzameling van arresten en gewijsden van den Hoogen Raad der Nederlanden en verdere rechtscollegien* (The Hague 1.1838 ff.; cited by volume, year, and page)
New LJ	*New Law Journal* (London 1.1850 ff.; cited by volume, year, and page)
NGCC	*Nuova Giurisprudenza Civile Commentata* (Padua 1.1984 ff.; cited by year, book, and page)
NILQ	*Northern Ireland Legal Quarterly* (Belfast 1.1936/ 37–14.1960/61; NS 1 = 15.1964 ff.; cited by volume, year, and page)
NJ	*Neue Justiz* (Berlin 1.1947 ff.; cited by year and page)
NJA	*Nytt juridiskt arkiv* (Stockholm 1.1874 ff.; from 1876 in parts: part 1: Rätsfall fråm högsta domstolen [until 1 Oct. 1983: Tidskrift för lagskippning], cited by year, number and page; part 2: Tidskrift för lagstiftning: cited by year, part, and page)
NJB	*Nederlands Juristenblad* (Zwolle 1.1926 ff.; 1936–1943 same contents as *Weekblad van het recht*; cited by year and page)
NJW	*Neue Juristische Wochenschrift* (Munich *et al.* 1.1947 ff.; previously: *JW*; cited by year and page)
NJW-RR	*NJW-Rechtsprechungsreport* (Munich 1.1986 ff.; cited by year and page)

no(s).	number(s); margin number(s)
NoB	*Nomiko Bima; miniaion nomikon periodikon* (Athens 1.1953 ff.; cited by volume, year, and page)
NRt.	*Norsk Retstidende*: see Rt
NS	New Series
NTBR	*Nederlands Tijdschrift voor Burgerlijk Recht* (Deventer 1.1984 ff; cited by year and page)
NuR	*Natur und Recht* (Hamburg, Berlin 1.1979 ff.; cited by year and page)
NVwZ	*Neue Zeitschrift für Verwaltungsrecht* (Munich, Frankfurt/Main 1.1988 ff.; cited by year and page)
NZLR	New Zealand Law Reports (Wellington 1.1883 ff.; cited by year, book, and page)
NZV	*Neue Zeitschrift für Verkehrsrecht* (Munich and Frankfurt/Main 1.1988 ff.; cited by year and page)
ObGerBritZ	Oberster Gerichtshof für die Britische Zone (Supreme Court for the British Zone, Germany)
ÖBl	*Österreichische Blätter für gewerblichen Rechtsschutz und Urheberrecht* (Vienna 1.1952 ff.; cited by year and page)
obs.	observations
ÖJZ	*Österreichische Juristenzeitung* (Vienna 1.1946 ff.; cited by year and page)
ØLD	Østre Landsrets Dom (Judgments of the Eastern High Court, Denmark)
ØLK	Østre Landsrets Kendelse (Decisions of the Eastern High Court; Denmark)
OG	Oberstes Gericht (Supreme Court, former GDR)
OGH	Oberster Gerichtshof (Supreme Court, Austria)
OGZ	Entscheidungen des Obersten Gerichts der Deutschen Demokratischen Republik in Zivilsachen (former GDR Supreme Court decisions in civil matters) (Berlin 13.1974–16.1983; cited by volume and page)
OJ	Official Journal of the European Communities (Brussels 1.1958 ff.; from 11.1968 ff.: issue C [Communication]: Information and Notices; from 1.1958 ff.: Issue L [Législation]: Legislation) (cited by issue, number, date, and page)
OLG	Oberlandesgericht (Court of Appeal, Austria; Germany)

OLGZ	Entscheidungen der Oberlandesgerichte in Zivilsachen einschließlich der freiwilligen Gerichtsbarkeit (Decisions of the Court of Appeal in civil matters including jurisdiction over non-contentious matters) (Munich, Berlin 1.1965 ff; cited by year and page)
op. cit	*opere citato* (in the place cited)
OR	Obligationenrecht (Bundesgesetz betreffend die Ergänzung des Schweizerischen Zivilgesetzbuches: 5th Part: Obligationenrecht, vom 30.3.1911 [SR 220]) (Swiss Code of Obligations, 30 Mar. 1911)
Ow.	(Rijks-) Octrooiwet (Patent Act), 7 Nov. 1910 (Stb. 313) and 15 Dec. 1995 (Stb. 51) (Netherlands)
p(p).	page(s)
P. 2d	Pacific Reporter, Second Series (St. Paul, Minn. 1.1931 ff.; cited by year, volume, and page)
Pas. belge	*Pasicrisie belge (Recueil général de la jurisprudence des cours et tribunaux de Belgique.* Part 1 = Arrêts de la Cour de Cassation 3rd Series 1865–1924; 112.1925 ff.; part 2 = Arrêts de la Cour d'Appel 3rd Series 1865–1924; 112.1925 ff.; part 3 = Jugements des tribunaux 3rd Series 1865–1924; 112.1925 ff.; part 4 = Jurisprudence étrangère 3rd Series 1893–1924; 112.1925 ff.; part 5 = Revue de droit belge 3rd Series 1893 ff.; cited by year, book, and page)
Pasin. belge	*Pasinomie belge ou Collection complète des lois, décrets, arrêtés et règlements généraux qui peuvent être invoqués en Belgique* (Brussels 1.1788 ff; cited by year and page)
Pas. luxemb.	*Pasicrisie luxembourgeoise (Recueil de la jurisprudence luxembourgeoise en matière civile, commerciale, criminale, de droit public, fiscal, administratif et notariel;* Luxembourg 1.1881 ff.; cited by volume, year, and page)
PC	Privy Council (England)
PflVG	Gesetz über die Pflichtversicherung für KfZ-Halter (Act on compulsory insurance for the keeper of a motor vehicle) (5 Apr. 1965 BGBl. I p. 213; BGBl. III p. 925–1) (Germany)
PHI	*Produkthaftung International* (Karlsruhe 1.1981 ff.; cited by year and page)

PK	Penikos Kodikas (Criminal Code. Act no. 1492/1950. FEK 182/1950 pp. 963—1003) (Greece)
PLC	Public Limited Company
Poder Judicial	*Consejo General del Poder Judicial* (Madrid 1.1981 ff; cited by year and page)
pr.	principium
Pret.	Pretura (Local Court, Italy)
PrObTrE	Entscheidungen des königlich preußischen Obertribunals (Decisions of the royal Prussian higher tribunal) (Berlin 1.1837 ff.; cited by volume and page)
ProdHG	Gesetz über die Haftung für fehlerhafte Produkte (Product Liability Act, 15 Dec. 1989; BGBl. I p. 2198) (Germany)
QB	Law Reports, Queen's Bench Division (London 1.1875/76 ff.; cited by year, book, and page)
R.	Règlement (order, France)
RabelsZ	*Zeitschrift für ausländisches und internationales Privatrecht* (Berlin, Tübingen 1.1927 ff.; from 26.1961: *Rabels Zeitschrift für ausländisches und internationales Privatrecht*; cited by volume, year, and page)
RaDC	*Rassegna di diritto civile* (Naples 1.1980 ff.; cited by year and page)
RAJ	*Repertorio Aranzadi de Jurisprudencia* (Pamplona 1.1930/31 2.1934 ff.; cited by year, number, and page)
Rass. Avv. Stato	*Rassegna mensile dell' Avvocatura dello Stato* (Rome 1.1948 ff.; cited by year, book, and page)
Rass. dir. civ.	*Rassegna di diritto civile* (Naples 1.1980 ff.; cited by year and page)
Rb.	Arrondissementsrechtbank (District Court, Court of First Instance, general jurisdiction, Netherlands)
RC	Relação (Court of Appeal) de Coimbra (Portugal)
RCR	Relazione della Commissione Reale al progetto del libro 'obbligazioni e contratti' (see Pandolfelli *et al.*, *Codice civile*, in the Table of Literature Cited in an Abbreviated Form)
RD	Regio Decreto (Royal decree, Italy)
RdA	*Recht der Arbeit* (Munich 1.1948 ff.; cited by year and page)
RdS	*Recht der Schule* (Vienna 1.1979 ff.; cited by year and page)

recht	*Recht, Zeitschrift für juristische Ausbildung* (Berne 1.1983 ff.; cited by year and page)
RE	Relação (Court of Appeal) de Évora (Portugal)
ref.	reference
Rep.Foro.it.	*Repertorio del Foro italiano (legislazione, bibliografia, giurisprudenza*; Rome 1.1878 ff.; previously: *Repertorio generale annuale di giurisprudenza, bibliografia e legislazione*; cited by volume, year, and column)
Rep. gen.	*Repertorio generale della Giurisprudenza italiana* (Turin 1.1890 ff.; previously: *Repertorio generale annuale della Giurisprudenza italiana*; cited by year, number, and column)
Rep. Giur. it.	*Repertorio generale della giurisprudenza italiana* (Turin 1.1848 ff.; cited by year, key word, and number)
resp.	respectively
Resp. Civ. e Prev.	*Responsabilità Civile e Previdenza* (Milan 1.1930 ff.; cited by year and page)
Resp. civ. assur.	*Responsabilité civile et assurances.* Monthly review . (Paris 1.1988 ff.; cited by year and page)
Rev.crit.jur.belge	*Revue critique de jurisprudence belge* (Brussels 1.1947 ff.; cited by year and page)
Rev.crit.légis. et juris.	*Revue critique de législation et de jurisprudence* (Paris 1.1851 ff.; cited by year and page)
Rev.dr.int.dr.comp.	*Revue de droit international et de droit comparé* (Brussels 1.1924 ff.; 1940–48 not published; cited by volume, year, and page)
Rev.dr.publ.	*Revue de droit public et de la science politique en France et à l'étranger* (Paris 1.1894 ff.; cited by volume, year, and page)
Rev.dr.sanit.soc.	*Revue de droit sanitaire et social* (Paris 1.1965 ff.; cited by year and page)
Rev.dr.uniforme	*Revue de droit uniforme. Uniform Law Review* (Rome 1.1973 ff.; cited by year, part, and page)
Rev.gén.dr.	*Revue générale du droit, de la législation et de jurisprudence en France et à l'étranger* (Paris 1.1877–62.1938; cited by year and page)
Rev.Hell.	*Revue Hellénique de droit international* (Athens 1.1948 ff.; cited by volume, year, and page)
Rev.int.dr.comp.	*Revue internationale de droit comparé* (1.1869/72–71.1947/48; previously: *Bulletin de la Société de Législation Comparée*; Paris 1.1949 ff.; cited by volume, year, and page)

Rev.jur.pol.Ind.Coop.	*Revue juridique et politique, Indépendance et Coopération* (Paris NS 1.1946 ff.; cited by volume, year, and page)
Rev.trim.dr.civ.	*Revue trimestrielle de droit civil* (Paris 1.1902–38.1939, 39/40.1940/41–78.1979 = vol. 39–77, 79.1980 ff.; cited by volume, year, and page)
RFDA	*Revue Française de Droit Aérien* (Paris 1.1946/47 (1947) ff.; cited by year and page)
RG	Relazione del Guardasigilli al progetto ministeriale delle obbligazioni (see Pandolfelli *et al.*, *Codice civile*, in the Table of Literature Cited in an Abbreviated Form)
RG	Reichsgericht (Supreme Court of the German Reich)
RGAR	*Révue générale des assurances et des responsabilités* (Brussels 1.1927 ff.; cited by year and number)
RGBl.	Reichsgesetzblatt (Government Gazette of the German Reich) (Berlin 1871–1945; from 1922 divided into parts I and II)
RGZ	Amtliche Sammlung der Entscheidungen des Reichsgerichtes in Zivilsachen (Decisions of the German Imperial Court in civil matters) (Berlin 1.1872–172.1945; cited by volume and page)
RHG	Reichshaftpflichtgesetz (Imperial Third Party Liability Act, Austria) (RGBl. 1871 p. 201)
Riv. crit. dir. priv.	*Rivista critica del diritto privato* (Bologna 1.1989 ff.; cited by year and page)
Riv. Dir. Civ.	*Rivista di Diritto Civile* (Padua 1.1955 ff.; cited by year, book, and page)
Riv. Dir. Com.	*Rivista del Diritto Commerciale e del Diritto generale delle obbligazioni* (Milan 1.1903 ff.; cited by year, book, and page)
Riv. dir. eur.	*Rivista di diritto europeo* (Rome 1.1961 ff.; cited by year and page)
Riv. dir. lav.	*Rivista di diritto del lavoro* (Milan 1.1949–32.1980; cited by year and page)
Riv. giur. circ. trasp.	*Rivista giuridica della circolazione e dei trasporti* (Rome 1.1947 ff.; cited by year and page)
Riv. giur. lav.	*Rivista giuridica del lavoro e della previdenza sociale* (Rome 1.1954 ff; part 1: Dottrina; part 2: Giurisprudenza; part 3: Previdenza; part 4: Diritto penale del lavoro; cited by year, book, and page)
Riv. trim. dir. proc. civ.	*Rivista trimestrale di diritto e procedura civile* (Milan 1.1947 ff.; cited by year and page)

RIW	*Recht der Internationalen Wirtschaft* (Heidelberg 1954–1957 and 1975 ff.; from 1958 to 1974 *Außenwirtschaftdienst des Betriebsberaters [AWD]*; cited by year and page)
RJDA	*Revue de jurisprudence du droit des affaires* (Paris 1.1991 ff.; cited by year and page)
RL	Relação (Court of Appeal) de Lisboa (Portugal)
RLJ	*Revista de Legislação e Jurisprudência* (Coimbra 1.1868/69 ff.; cited by volume, year, and page)
RM	*Rechtsgeleerd magazijn: tijdschrift voor binnen- en buitenlandsche rechtsstudie* (Haarlem 1.1882–58.1939; cited by year and page)
RM-Themis	*Rechtsgeleerd magazijn Themis. Tijdschrift voor publiek- en privaatrecht* (Zwolle 1.1939 ff.; cited by year and page)
RP	Relação (Court of Appeal) do Porto (Portugal)
RPC	Reports of Patents, Design and Trade Mark Cases (London 1.1884 ff.; cited by year and page)
RPL	Retsplejeloven (Rules of Procedure no. 90, 11 Apr. 1916 [Lovtidende A 1916 p. 417–675]) (Denmark)
RR	Relazione al Re Imperatore sul libro 'delle obbligazioni' (see Pandolfelli *et al.*, *Codice civile*, in the Table of Literature Cited in an Abbreviated Form)
RRJ	*Revue de la Recherche Juridique. Droit Prospectif* (Aix-en-Provence 1.1974/75 ff.; cited by year and page)
r+s	*Recht und Schaden* (Kippenheim 1.1974 ff.; cited by year and page)
Rt.	*Norsk Retstidende* (Oslo 1.1836 ff.; cited by year and page)
Rv	Wetboek van Burgerlijke Rechtsvordering (Stb. 1828 no. 14) (Code of civil procedure, Netherlands)
RvdW	*Rechtspraak van de Week* (Zwolle 1.1939 ff.; cited by year and number)
RVO	Reichsversicherungsordnung, 19 July 1911 (Imperial Social Insurance Act) (RGBl. p. 509) (Germany)
RW	*Rechtskundig Weekblad* (Antwerp 1.1931/32 ff.; cited by year and page)
s.	sentencenumber (as in: §3 II s.1); section number of UK statutes
S.	*Recueil Sirey*; see *D.*

SavZ Rom.Abt.	*Zeitschrift der Savigny-Stiftung für Rechtsgeschichte* (until vol. 31 divided into *Germanist.Abt., Romanist.Abt.,* and *Kanonist.Abt.* each department has its own system of numbering volumes. Rom.Abt.: 1. = 14.1880–65 = 78.1947 ff.; cited by volume, year, and page)
SC	Session Cases. New Series. Scottish cases decided in the Court of Session, and also in the Court of Justiciary (JC) and House of Lords (HL); Edinburgh 1.1907 ff.; cited by year and page)
Scan.Stud.L.	*Scandinavian Studies in Law* (Stockholm 1.1957 ff.); cited by volume, year, and page
SCR	Supreme Court Reports or Rapports judiciaires du Canada, Supreme Court (Ottawa 1.1923 ff.; cited by year and page)
Scientia jurídica	*Scientia jurídica* (Braga 1.1951/52 ff.; cited by volume, year, and page)
sec.	section number (as in: §3 II sec. 1)
SEK	Reference of the Commission General Secretary's Office and of the Council of the European Union
Sem.Jur.	*La Semaine Juridique, Edition Générale.* (also *Juris Classeur Périodique*; Paris 1.1927 ff.; cited by year, book, and number)
Sem.Jur., Ed.E.	*La Semaine Juridique, Edition Entreprise. Cahiers de Droit de l'entreprise* (Paris 1. 1966 ff; cited by year, part, and number)
SDR	Special Drawing Right
SFS	Svensk författningssamling (Official Gazette, Sweden) (Stockholm 1.1825 ff; cited by year and number)
SGB	Sozialgesetzbuch (Social Security Code, Germany) 11 Dec. 1975 (BGBl. I p. 3015)
SHD	Sø- og Handelsretsdom. Judgement of the Maritime and Commercial Court Copenhagen (Denmark)
Sh. Ct.	Sheriff Court (Scotland)
SJT	*Svensk Juristtidning* (Stockholm 1.1916 ff.; cited by year and page)
SJZ	*Schweizerische Juristenzeitung* (Zürich 1.1904/1905 ff; cited by year and page)
Skl.	Skadeerstatningsloven. Damages Act (Norway: Norsk lovtidend II 1969 p. 419)
SKL	Skadeståndslag. Damages Act (Sweden: 2 June

	1972 [SFS 1972: 207]; Finland: 31 May 1974 [FFS 1974, no. 412, p. 705])
SLT	*Scots Law Times* (reports; Edinburgh 1.1893/94 ff; Sheriff Court reports 1.1922 ff.; cited by year and page)
Sr	Wetboek van Strafrecht (Stb. 1881, p. 40 [Nr. 35]) (Penal Code, Netherlands)
SR	Systematische Sammlung des Bundesrechts (since 1970; cited by number) (Switzerland)
STA	Supremo Tribunal Administrativo (Supreme Court in Administrative Matters) (Portugal)
Stb.	Staatsblad van het Koninkrijk der Nederlanden (Official Gazette, Netherlands) (Zwolle 1.1813 ff.; cited by year and number)
StGB	Strafgesetzbuch 15 May 1871 (RGBl. p. 127) (Penal Code, Germany); Bundesgesetz vom 23.1.1974 über die mit gerichtlicher Strafe bedrohten Handlungen 23 Jan. 1974 (BGBl. no. 60) (Penal Code, Austria)
STJ	Supremo Tribunal de Justiça (Supreme Court, Portugal)
STRFL	Bogerlig Straffelov (Civil Penal Code, Denmark) (Act no. 126, 15 Apr. 1930 [Lovtidende A 1930, pp. 697–752])
StVG	Straßenverkehrsgesetz (Road Traffic Act, Germany) 19 Dec. 1952 (BGBl. I p. 832)
Sup. Ct.	Supreme Court (Eire)
Sv	Wetboek van Strafvordering (Code of Criminal Procedure, Netherlands) (Stb. 15.1.1921, no. 14)
SW 2d	South Western Reporter, second series (St. Paul, Minn. 1.1928 ff.; cited by volume and page)
SZ	Entscheidungen des österreichischen Obersten Gerichtshofs in Zivilsachen (Vienna 1.1919–20.1938; 21.1946 ff.; with changing titles; until vol. 34.1961: Entscheidungen des österreichischen Obersten Gerichtshofs in Zivil- und Justizverwaltungssachen; cited by volume, number, and page)
tab.	tabulae
TBP	*Tijdschrift voor Bestuurswetenschappen en Publiekrecht* (Brussels 1.1946 ff., from 1.1946 to 6.1951 under the title *Tijdschrift voor Bestuurswetenschappen*; cited by year and page)

TC	Tribunal Constitucional (Constitutional Court, Spain)
Tel Aviv Univ. Stud. L.	*Tel Aviv University Studies in Law* (Tel Aviv 1.1975 ff.; cited by volume, year, and page)
Temi	*Il Temi. Rivista di giurisprudenza Italiana* (Parma, Milan *et al.* NS 1 = 22.1946 ff; cited by year and page)
Temi nap.	*Il Temi napoletana* (Milan 1.1958 ff.; cited by year and page)
Themis	*Hebdomacliaia dikastike ephemeris ekdiclomene en Athenais* (Athens 1.1890/91 (1930)–65.1954/55; cited by volume, year, and page)
TLR	Times Law Reports (London 1.1884 ff.; cited by volume, year, and page)
TMA	*Tweemaandelijks tijdschrift voor milieu aansprakelijkheid. Environmental Liability Law Review* (Lelystad 1.1987 ff.; cited by year and page)
To Σ	*To Syntagma* (Athens 1.1975 ff.; cited by volume, year, and page)
TPR	*Tijdschrift voor Privaatrecht* (Ghent 1.1964 ff.; cited by year and page)
TranspR	*Transportrecht* (Frankfurt/Main 1.1978 ff.; cited by year and page)
Trb.	Tractatenblad van het Kononkrijk der Nederlanden (Official Gazette recording treaties in force in the Netherlands) (The Hague 1.1951 ff.; cited by year and page)
Treaty of Rome	Treaty establishing the European Community, 25 Mar. 1957
Trib.	Tribunale (Court of First Instance, general jurisdiction, Italy)
Trib.Com.	Tribunal de Commerce (Commercial Court, Belgium and France)
Trib.Diek.	Tribunal d'arrondissement à Diekirch (Court of First Instance, general jurisdiction, Luxembourg)
Trib.enfants	Tribunal pour enfants (Juvenile Court, France)
Trib.gr.inst.	Tribunal de grande instance (Court of First Instance, general jurisdiction, France)
Trib.Lux.	Tribunal d'arrondissement à Luxembourg (Court of First Instance, general jurisdiction, Luxembourg)
TS	Tribunal Supremo (Supreme Court, Spain)
Tul. Civ. Law Forum	*Tulane Civil Law Forum* (New Orleans, 1.1973–

	1977; NS 1.1987 ff.; cited by volume, year, and page)
TulLRev	*Tulane Law Review* (New Orleans, 1.1916 ff.; cited by volume, year, and page)
UfR	*Ugeskrift for Retsvæsen* (Copenhagen 1.1867 ff.; from 1902 split into parts: A = Dansk domssamling; B = Juridiske afhandlinger, meddelelser; C = Abstracts; cited by year, part, and page)
Ulp.	Ulpian
UmweltHG	Umwelthaftungsgesetz (Environmental Liability Act), 10 Dec. 1990 (BGBl. I p. 2634) (Germany)
Unif. L. Rev	*Uniform Law Review = Revue de droit uniforme*; see *Rev. dr. uniforme*
UNTS	United Nations Treaty Series (Washington DC 1.1946/47 ff.; cited by volume and page)
US	United States Supreme Court Reports (Rochester, New York 1.1875 ff., cited by volume, year, and page)
UTR	*Umwelt- und Technikrecht* (Düsseldorf 1.1986 ff.; cited by volume, year, and page)
UWG	Gesetz gegen den unlauteren Wettbewerb (Act against unfair competition, Germany) 7 June 1909 (RGBl. p. 499)
v.	*versus*
VC	Vice-Chancellor, the head of the Chancery Division of the UK High Court
VersR	*Versicherungsrecht* (*Juristische Rundschau* für die Individualversicherung; Karlsruhe 1.1950 ff.; cited by year and page)
VersRAI	*Versicherungsrecht Beilage Ausland* (Karlsruhe 1.1959/60, 2.1961 ff.; cited by year and page)
VfGH	Verfassungsgerichtshof (Constitutional Court, Austria)
VfSlg.	Verfassungssammlung. Sammlung der Erkenntnisse und wichtigsten Beschlüsse des Verfassungsgerichtshofes (Collection of cases before the Austrian Constitutional Court) (Vienna 1.1919 ff., New Series 33.1968 ff.; cited by the no. of the decision)
VLD	Vestre Landsrets dom (Judgments of Western High Court, Denmark)
VLK	Vestre Landsrets kendelse (Decisions of Western High Court; Denmark)

vol.	volume
VR	*Verkeersrecht* (The Hague 1.1953/54 ff.; cited by year and number)
Vrb	*Verzekeringsrechtelijke berichten* (Zwolle 1. 1989 ff.; cited by year and page)
Vred.	Vredegerecht (Justice of the Peace, Belgium)
VVDStRL	*Veröffentlichungen der Vereinigung Deutscher Staatsrechtslehrer* (Berlin 1.1924 ff.; cited by volume, year, and page)
VVG	Gesetz über den Versicherungsvertrag (Act on insurance contracts, Germany) 30 May 1908 (RGBl. p. 263)
Vw	*Versicherungswirtschaft* (Karlsruhe 1.1946 ff.; cited by year and page)
VwGH	Verwaltungsgerichtshof (Supreme Administrative Court, Austria)
W	*Weekblad van het Recht* (Zwolle *et al.* 1.1839–105.1943; from 1936 contents the same as *Nederlands Juristenblad (NJB)*; cited by year, number, and page)
Warsaw Convention	Convention for the Unification of Certain Rules Relating to International Carriage by Air 12 October 1929 (first convention relating to the unification of private air law, RGB1. 1933 II p. 1039; The Hague version, 28 Sep. 1955, BGB1. 1958 II pp. 291, 312, 1964 II p. 1295)
WBl	*Wirtschaftsrechtliche Blätter* (Vienna, 1.1987 ff.; cited by year and page)
WHG	Wasserhaushaltsgesetz (Gesetz zur Ordnung des Wasserhaushalts 23 September 1986; BGB1. III 753–1) (German Water Budget Act)
WiB	*Wirtschaftsrechtliche Beratung* (Munich, Frankfurt/Main 1.1994 ff.; cited by year and page)
WLR	Weekly Law Reports (containing descisions in the House of Lords, the Privy Council, the Supreme Court of Judicature, Assize Courts; London 1.1953 ff.; cited by year, book, and page)
WM	*Wertpapier-Mitteilungen*: Zeitschrift für Wirtschafts- und Bankrecht (Frankfurt/Main *et al.* 1.1947 ff.; cited by year and page)
WPNR	*Weekblad voor privaatrecht, notariaat en registratie* (The Hague 1.1870 ff.; cited by year, number, and page)

WRG	Wasserrechtsgesetz, (Water Act, Austria) 1959 (BGBl. p. 215)
WVW	Wegenverkeerswet (Road Traffic Act, Netherlands) 13 Sep. 1935 (Stb. 554) and 21 Apr. 1994 (Stb 475)
WWR	Western Weekly Reports (Calgary 1.1911/12 (1912)–10.1916; 1917–1950; NS 1.1951 ff.; cited by year, book, and page)
ZBernJV	*Zeitschrift des Bernischen Juristenvereins* (Revue de la société des juristes bernois; Berne 1.1864/65 ff.; cited by volume, year, and page)
ZEuP	*Zeitschrift für Europäisches Privatrecht* (Munich 1.1993 ff.; cited by year and page)
ZEV	*Zeitschrift für Erbrecht und Vermögensnachfolge* (Munich, Frankfurt/Main 1.1994 ff; cited by year and page)
ZfRV	*Zeitschrift für Rechtsvergleichung* (Vienna 1.1960 ff; cited by year and page)
ZfS	*Zeitschrift für Schadensrecht* (Essen 1.1980 ff.; cited by year and page)
ZfU	*Zeitschrift für Umweltpolitik und Umweltrecht. Journal of Environmental Law and Policy. Revue de la politique et du droit d'environnement* (Frankfurt/Main 1.1978 ff.; cited by year and page)
ZfVB	*Zeitschrift für Verwaltung,* inserted: Judgments (Vienna 1.1976 ff.; cited by year and page)
ZHR	*Zeitschrift für das gesamte Handels- und Wirtschaftsrecht* (Heidelberg 1.1858–110.1944, 111.1948 under different titles: until vol. 60: *Zeitschrift für das gesamte Handelsrecht,* until vol. 124 (1962): *Zeitschrift für das gesamte Handels- und Wirtschaftsrecht;* cited by volume, year, and page)
ZIP	*Zeitschrift für Wirtschaftsrecht und Insolvenzpraxis* (previously *Insolvenzrecht;* Cologne 1.1980 ff.; cited by year and page)
ZRP	*Zeitschrift für Rechtspolitik* (Munich 1.1968 ff.; cited by year and page)
ZSR	*Zeitschrift für Schweizerisches Recht* (Basle NS 1.1882 ff.; cited by volume, year, and page)
ZVersWiss	*Zeitschrift für die gesamte Versicherungswissenschaft* (Karlsruhe 1.1901 ff.; 43.1943, 56.1967 ff.; cited by year and page)
ZVglRWiss	*Zeitschrift für vergleichende Rechtswissenschaft*

(Heidelberg 1.1878 ff.; cited by volume, year, and page)

ZVR   *Zeitschrift für Verkehrsrecht* (Vienna 1.1956 ff.; cited by year, number of the decision, and page)

Part 1: Foundations

Bibliography: Bajons, 'Schadensersatz für gesundheitliche Beeinträchtigungen nach italienischem Recht' *ZVglRWiss* 92 (1993) pp. 76–114; v. Bar, 'Neues Haftungsrecht durch Europäisches Gemeinschaftsrecht' in *FS für Hermann Lange* (Stuttgart 1992) pp. 373–395; Behrends, 'Das Vindikationsmodell als "grundrechtliches" System der ältesten römischen Siedlungsorganisation. Zugleich ein Beitrag zu den ältesten Grundlagen des römischen Personen-, Sachen- und Obligationenrechts' in: Behrends/Diesselhorst (edd.), *Libertas. Grundrechtliche und rechtsstaatliche Gewährungen in Antike und Gegenwart* (Ebelsbach 1991) pp. 1–59; Brasiello, *I limiti della responsabilità per danni* (Milan 1959); Coing, *Europäisches Privatrecht* vol. i (Munich 1985); Denning, 'Review of the 3rd edition of Winfield: A textbook of the law of tort', 63 (1947) *LQRev* pp. 516–518; Deutsch, 'Unfallversorgung statt Haftung in Neuseeland', *RabelsZ* 44 (1980) pp. 478–509; Feenstra, *Romeinsrechtelijke grondslagen van het Nederlandse Privaatrecht*, (5th edn. Leiden 1990); Gaertner, *Verschuldensprinzip und objektive Haftung bei nachbarlichen Störungen (troubles de voisinage) nach französischem Recht verglichen mit dem deutschen Recht*, (diss. Freiburg 1972); Gammeltoft-Hansen/Gomard/Philip, *Danish Law*, (Copenhagen 1982); García Laraña, 'La responsabilidad civil ex delicto en el anteproyecto de Código penal de 1992', *La Ley* 1992 (3) pp. 1048–1053; Giffard/Villers, *Droit romain et ancien droit français (obligations)*, (4th edn. Paris 1976); Hausmaninger, *Das Schadensersatzrecht der Lex Aquilia* (5th edn. Vienna 1996); Hausmaninger/Selb, *Römisches Privatrecht* (Vienna 1987); Heldrich, *Die allgemeinen Rechtsgrundsätze der außervertraglichen Schadenshaftung im Bereich der Europäischen Wirtschaftsgemeinschaft* (Frankfurt/Main and Berlin 1961); Hochstein, *Obligationes quasi ex delicto* (Stuttgart *et al.* 1971); Hohloch, *Die negatorischen Ansprüche und ihre Beziehungen zum Schadensersatzrecht* (Frankfurt/Main 1976); Jørgensen, 'Ersatz und Versicherung', *VersR* 1970 pp. 193–208; id., 'Træk af privatrettens udvikling og systematik' (Copenhagen 1966) *Acta Jutlandica* 38:1; id., *Vertrag und Recht* (Copenhagen 1968); Karakostas, 'Neue Entwicklungen des Umweltschutzes im griechischen Zivilrecht', *ZfU* 1990 pp. 295–305; Kaser, *Das Römische Privatrecht.* 'Part One: Das altrömische, das vorklassische und das klassische Recht' (2nd edn. Munich 1971); Monier, *Manuel élémentaire de droit romain.* 'Vol. ii: Les obligations', (5th edn. Paris 1954); Newark, 'The Boundaries of Nuisance', *LQRev* 65 (1949) pp. 480–490; Parisi, *Liability for Negligence and Judicial Discretion* (2nd edn. Berkeley 1992); Rudden, 'Torticles', *Tulane Civil Law Forum* 6/7 (1991–92) pp. 105–129; Stoll, 'Consequences of Liability: Remedies', *IntEncCompL* XI 8 (1971); Tucci, *Il danno ingiusto*

1

(Naples 1970); Tunc, 'Torts, Introduction', *IntEncCompL* XI 1 (1983, compl. 1973); Visintini, 'Responsabilità contrattuale ed extracontrattuale (Una distinzione in crisi?)', *Rass.dir.civ.* 1983 pp. 1077–1091; Winfield, *The Province of the Law of Tort* (Cambridge 1931); Zimmermann, *The Law of Obligations: Roman Foundations of the Civilian Tradition* (Cape Town *et al.* 1990).

I. THE TERM 'LAW OF DELICT'

1 'Law of delict'[1] describes the field of private law[2] which determines whether a person who has sustained damage has a right to compensation (or where such damage is impending, to injunctive relief)[3] even if the infliction of the damage forms the only legal bond between the two parties.[4] This definition may not include all the characteristics relevant in the various national laws of the European Union to the decision as to whether or not a legal rule is part of the law of delict. However, any additional characteristics, such as fault, or considerations of protected interests, are merely auxiliary criteria designed for the classification of only minor issues. Each of these additional characteristics would be questioned on the European level. Therefore the law of delict, both as a jurisprudential discipline and as positive law, can only be developed from the two elements constituting its very heart, for they find general acceptance everywhere: first, its function as a system to compensate damage and secondly, the fact that its operation requires no prior legal

---

[1] European legal terminology is far from uniform. The word 'delict' is often eschewed in order to avoid any associations with the criminal law; e.g. in Spain and Italy the term 'non-contractual responsibility' (*responsabilidad extracontractual, responsabilità civile extracontrattuale*) is used to refer to the civil law of delict. On the English law of tort see no. 6; on the Portuguese terminology and system no. 9 and fn. 41; and on the *délits* of French law fn. 23.

[2] On the relationship between the law of delict and constitutional, as well as criminal law, see Part 6 below.

[3] The simple explanation for the inclusion of preventive legal protection is that prevention of damage is better than its compensation (on comparative law thereto see Stoll, *IntEncCompL* XI 8–175 ff.) Therefore, the opinion is correct (*contra* e.g. Hohloch, *Negatorische Ansprüche*, pp. 152–153) that preventive legal protection is a necessary component of the law of delict. Only recently has injunctive relief again become a part of the Dutch law of delict (Art. 6: 168). Both the Greek Cc (Arts. 57, 58, 60) and the Portuguese Cc (Art. 70) mention injunctive relief in connection with invasion of privacy. The legislation of the French *Code Civil* is similar (Art. 9, see Cass. civ. 20 Oct. 1993, D. 1994 *Jur.* p. 594, note Picod). In England the equitable remedy of an injunction is particularly important if the tort is actionable *per se*.

[4] Depending on the different doctrines on concurrent claims, the law of delict can even be ousted by a claim for damages in contract: see nos. 431–435 below.

relationship between victim and tortfeasor. A liability law of such residual nature is part of every European legal system; none could exist without a set of rules to regulate the compensation of loss between persons who were in no way connected with each other prior to the infliction of the damage.[5]

Notwithstanding the fact that the very definition of 'damage' depends **2** on the legal system employing it,[6] its use as a systematic criterion has one main advantage:[7] it allows us to separate the law of delict from *negotiorum gestio* as well as from the law of unjustified enrichment. The main concern[8] of *negotiorum gestio*, is the compensation of 'voluntary pecuniary transfers' (*Aufwendungen*), and that the law of unjust enrichment is the annulment of unjustified net transfers of wealth. First and

---

[5] Industrial injuries insurance schemes replace the law of delict only in a limited number of cases. This is also true of the state which has gone furthest in abolishing the law of delict, namely New Zealand; see Deutsch, *RabelsZ* 44 (1980) pp. 487–509.

[6] As most legal systems do not restrict damages to pecuniary compensation, I think Denning was wrong in saying: 'in these days the form of remedy is hardly an appropriate way to define substantive rights and liabilities. The province of delict is to allocate responsibility for injurious conduct' (63 [1947] *LQRev* p. 517). In a substantial number of cases liability law requires no conduct to establish liability for damages.

[7] In some (but by no means in all) European legal systems reliance on the notion of damage also serves to keep certain special compensatory claims out of the law of delict, e.g. in cases of 'necessity' (*aggressiver Notstand*) (compare e.g. § 904 s. 2 BGB with Art. 2045 Ital. Cc), or in cases of 'liability on grounds of equity' (*Billigkeitshaftung*) (compare e.g. Art. 2074, II Ital. Cc, § 829 BGB with Art. 1386*bis* Belg. Cc, Art. 6:101 BW and Art. 20 Span. CP = Art. 118 NCP). Another example are certain disputes among neighbours, see e.g. for Germany § 906 II s. 2 BGB (*angemessener Ausgleich in Geld*), see BGH 2 Mar. 1984, BGHZ 90 pp. 256, 263, BGH 20 Jan. 1993, *VersR* 1993 p. 609, each containing further references, and for Austria Schwimann (-Pimmer), ABGB II, § 364 no. 53, p. 57. The Greek Cc, however, contains no regulation corresponding with § 906 II s. 2 BGB (see Art. 1003 ZGB), so for liability amongst neighbours the general rules of the law of delict have to be applied: see Georgiades/ Stathopoulos (-Georgiades), *Greek Cc* vol. v, Art. 1003 no. 22; Karakostas, *ZfU* 1990 pp. 295, 300 f. The *troubles de voisinage* (see Carbonnier, *Droit Civil* vol. iii, 14th edn. no. 57; Marty/Raynaud, *Droit Civil* vol. ii [1], 2nd edn., nos. 528 ff.; Starck [-Roland/Boyer], *Obligations* vol. i, 4th edn., no. 363; and Gaertner, *Verschuldensprinzip und objektive Haftung* [op. cit. bibliography before no. 1], pp. 161 ff.) form part of the French law of delict (although not of the Belgian: Cass. 6 Apr. 1960, *Pas. belge* 1960, I, p. 915 [combined application of Art. 544 Cc and the 'principle of equity']). In England the rule in *Rylands* v. *Fletcher* (1866) LR 1 Ex. 265, (1868) LR 3 HL p. 330, which in its interpretation in *Read* v. *Lyons* [1947] AC 146 (HL) bears many features of what in Germany is called 'liability for suffering a legally inflicted harm' (*Aufopferungshaftung*) (cf., although with no comparative remarks, Newark, *LQRev* 65 1949 pp. 480, 487–489) is also believed to be law of delict. In the Netherlands, on the other hand, the regulation concerning the respective interests of neighbours in Art. 5:37 BW is understood to be *lex specialis* to the basic rule of the law of delict in Art. 6:162 BW (T&C [-Stolker] 2nd edn., Art. 5:37 BW note 2). For Italy see also the diverging positions of Brasiello, *I limiti della responsabilità*, pp. 51 ff. on one hand and of Tucci, *Il danno ingiusto*, pp. 31 ff. on the other; for Portugal see no. 9 and fn. 41 below.

[8] More about indistinct contours in Part 5 II. The Italian law, which also operates with the term *danno* in its basic regulations concerning unjustified enrichment (Art. 2041 Ital. Cc) solves the problem of concurring claims by imposing general subsidiarity of actions for unjustified enrichment (Art. 2042 Cc).

foremost, however, the law of delict must be contrasted with the law of contract. Since the former requires no legal connection between the parties, a claim for compensation cannot be based on a delict if the loss was sustained solely as a result of a breach of contract. Although regulations for compensation of damages which oust the law of delict can also be found in other areas of law (e.g. in family law[9]), the law of delict has always and universally been seen as the sum of rules governing *non-contractual liability*. § 1295 I ABGB and §§ 1 of both the Finnish and the Swedish Damages Act explicitly mention this point, and every published Danish judgement on the law of delict is given the title *'Erstatning uden for kontraktsforhold'*.

3   To differentiate between contractual obligations and those *quae ex delicto nascuntur* western private law was taught by the Institutions of Justinian[10] and the Institutions of Gaius.[11] In the intervening one and a half thousand years, this differentiation has never been in any real danger of being abandoned, although it is recognized as having only limited effectiveness in some cases.[12] It is not difficult to show that the

---

[9] Here, too, some shifting of the borderline is encountered in Austria (§ 46 AGBG), Spain (Art. 44 Cc), The Netherlands (Art. 1:49 BW; see Rb. 's-Hertogenbosch 30 Sep. 1983, *NedJur* 1984 no. 646 p. 2220), Italy (Art. 81 Cc), Germany (§§ 1298 ff. BGB), and Greece (Art. 1347 ZGB). A claim based on the breach of an engagement to marry, for example, systematically belongs to family law, whereas in France such problems are solved with the help of Arts. 1382, 1383 Cc, which form part of the law of delict. However, French law (see e.g. Art. 450 II Cc: liability of the guardian towards the ward) and Belgian law (e.g. Arts. 379: liability of parents and 450 Cc: guardian; see also § 264 of the Austrian ABGB) both recognize claims for damages based on family law, and one also meets such claims in areas outside child custody (e.g. in marriage law; see only Art. 129*bis* Ital. Cc, in divorce law, e.g. Art 301 Lux. Cc, or in the matrimonial property regime [see only Arts. 1:91, 1:111, and 1:164 BW]). Claims for damages based on the law of succession are also possible, e.g. in the relationship of limited heir/reversionary heir, between the members of a community of heirs or against the executor (see Art. 709 II Ital. Cc.), and even the liability of a notary for faults during the making of a will is occasionally mentioned in the law of succession, see Art. 705 Span. Cc.

[10] Inst. 4.1.

[11] Inst. Gai. III. 88: 'Nunc transeamus ad obligationes. Quarum summa divisio in duas species diducitur: omnis enim obligatio vel ex contractu nascitur vel ex delicto.' For more detailed information see Feenstra, *Romeinsrechtelijke grondslagen* 5th edn., no. 247; Monier, *Manuel élémentaire de droit romain*, vol. ii, 5th edn., no. 23; Giffard/Villers, *Droit romain et ancien droit français* 4th edn., no. 11 (remarking that further subdivisions in delict and quasi-delict were first developed in the Institutions of Justinian).

[12] One sign pointing in this direction is the concept of 'obligation founded in reliance' (*Schuldverhältnis aus Vertrauen*) currently enjoying its heyday, esp. in Germany. This means that the obligation, although governed by contractual rights, is actually implied in law. On the borderline of damage to property and pure financial loss (if this difference is recognized) the traditional dichotomy between contract and delict also poses a problem for other legal orders: see Visintini, *Rass.dir.civ.* 1983 pp. 1077–1091 as well as the displeased remark by Lord Roskill in *Junior Books Ltd.* v. *Veitchi* [1983] 1 AC p. 520, p. 545 (HL): 'I think today the proper control lies not in asking whether the proper remedy should lie in contract or instead in delict or tort, not in somewhat capricious judicial determination whether a particular case falls on one side of the line or on the other, not in somewhat artificial distinctions.'

laws of different European nations reveal diverging opinions about where to draw the line between the law of contract and the law of delict;[13] the same can be said for the latter's relationship with other disciplines. However, everywhere in Europe—even in the English common law[14] which evolved mainly from its own roots—the identity of the law of delict is still strongly influenced by its relationship[15] to the law of contract.[16]

The law of delict is and always has been part of the *law of obligations.*   **4** The origin of the idea of *obligatio* is not yet known in all its details. However, it is probable that, at least in that part of the law of obligations with which we are dealing here, the term *ligare* (= Lat. bind; cf. the Dutch *verbintenissenrecht*) was meant literally.[17] In classical times it was still possible for the injured party to gain the right of access to the body of the tortfeasor; at the conclusion of the judicial proceedings he could be cuffed and deprived of his liberty.[18] It was only later in the development of law that the offender who had to 'answer' to the court (therefore: *respondere, responsabilidad civil, responsabilité civile délictuelle, delictuele aansprakelijkheid, ansvar*) was allowed to free himself by making a payment. Finally, the idea that the delict created an obligation to compensate in cash,[19] not primarily as a forfeiture but to compensate damage incurred, gained precedence. Separation between the law of delict and criminal law had taken place,[20] non-contractual

---

[13] See Part 5 I nos. 13 ff. below.

[14] The most famous, although frequently challenged definition of the term 'tort law' (see no. 6 below) is found in Winfield, *The Province of the Law of Tort* (1931); at p. 32 he says: 'Tortious liability arises from the breach of a duty primarily fixed by the law; the duty is towards persons generally and its breach is redressible by an action for unliquidated damages.' See also Winfield/Jolowicz (-Rogers) *Tort* 14th edn., p. 3.

[15] Indeed, the law of delict and the law of contract partly even depend on each other. For just as a law on the acquisition of pecuniary interests cannot be drafted without the existence of a law protecting pre-existing interests, neither can a law protecting pre-existing interests be conceived without the presence of a law securing the acquisition of such interests.   [16] Tunc, *IntEncCompL* XI pp. 1–5 ff.

[17] For more detailed information see Zimmermann, *Law of Obligations*, nos. 1 and 2. For an independent historic view of the meaning of *obligatio* in the law of contract see Behrends (op. cit. bibliography before no. 1) p. 44.

[18] The Old High German term *haften*, too, derives most likely from the common Germanic adjective for caught, bound: Duden (vol. vii), 2nd edn., *Das Herkunftswörterbuch, Etymologie der deutschen Sprache* (Mannheim/Vienna/Zurich 1989), and Pfeifer, *Etymologisches Wörterbuch des Deutschen* (Munich 1995), headword 'Haft'.

[19] For more detailed information see Giffard/Villers, *Droit romain et ancien droit français*, 4th edn., nos. 316–319; Kaser, *Römisches Privatrecht* vol. i, 2nd edn., §§ 39 and 40; Zimmermann loc. cit. (fn. 17). See also Hausmaninger/Selb, *Römisches Privatrecht*, pp. 241 f and Feenstra, *Romeinsrechtelijke grondslagen* 5th edn., no. 247; Parisi, *Liability for Negligence*, pp. 37–48.

[20] For more detailed information see nos. 600 ff. below. The separation of punishment and compensation was a difficult and often interrupted process which took several centuries to achieve. In Denmark, for example, until modern times forfeitures resulting from

liability law and the non-contractual law of damages had become synonymous.[21]

The development of legal terminology in England points to a very similar historic background. Its modern word *liability* derives from the French *liable* which in turn stems from the Latin *ligabilis* (what can be bound) or *ligare* (bind). A similar symbolic meaning of the term 'to bind' is also to be found in the old Germanic (Saxon) language. Before *law-French* brought Franco-Latin words to England in cases of liability, the expressions 'to bind' and 'being bound by law' were employed up to the 16th and 17th C.[22]

II. LIABILITY FOR PERSONAL MISCONDUCT

5 In every legal system of the EU cases in which a party is found to have non-contractual responsibility for damage caused to another party can be divided into liability with and liability without personal misconduct on the part of the person sued. The title 'law of delict' historically refers

delicts were imposed to punish as well as to compensate (see Gammeltoft-Hansen/ Gomard/Philip (-Kruse), *Danish Law*, p. 161). Differentiating between criminal law, procedural law, and the law of compensation demanded a strict separation of public and private law which was fairly unknown to the *Danske Lov* (1683), and only had its breakthrough during the time of the German Romance. The term 'compensation' first appears in the Danish literature of the 18th C. Even in the 20th C. the idea of combining the criminal law and the law of compensation in one single 'law governing the consequences of delict' (*Reaktionenrecht*) had its supporters (see in more detail Jørgensen, *Træk af privatrettens udvikling og systematik*, pp. 4, 37–41, *id.*, *Vertrag und Recht*, pp. 96–101). Even nowadays the mutual root of the criminal law and the civil law of delict is still visible especially in the adhesion procedure common to the Roman countries (see e.g. Art. 3 French C.proc.pén., and Art. 4 Belg. *Wetboek van Strafvordering*); and in regulations determining that 'each person liable under criminal law for a delict or misconduct is also liable under civil law' as provided in Art. 185 Ital. and Art. 19 Span. CP (= Art. 116 NCP). Consequently the law of delict of the Spanish Cc *only* deals with those obligations 'which are a result of such acts or failures to act where fault or neglect encroach and which are not penalized by law' (Art. 1093 in conjunction with Art. 1092 Cc). During the revision of the Spanish CP (see the recent report in *Actualidad Juridíca Aranzadi* no. 163 dated 8 August 1994) an exclusion of the rules on liability enclosed in the *Código Penal* was considered (see v. Bar [-Santidiu-menge], *DeliktsR in Europa*, Spain, p. 25) but now the civil liability of part V will remain (albeit rewritten) in the *Nuevo Código Penal* (NCP, in force since 24 May 1996). For more detailed information on the long-lasting struggle to separate procedures from criminal procedures in Italian law see Bajons, *ZVglRWiss* 92 (1993) pp. 76, 80–83.

[21] Whether liability law and the law of delict can now be seen as one, or whether the latter is to be regarded as part of (non-contractual) liability law, depends on whether the term 'law of delict' is used in its original sense only (liability for personal misconduct) or whether it is understood as including also so-called strict liability; see no. 9.

[22] According to *The Oxford English Dictionary*, 2nd edn. (Oxford 1989), in 1462 the word 'bind' meant 'to make a person liable for the payment of a debt'.

to the former; in Roman times the term 'quasi law of delict' was applied for the latter (see no. 7 below).

The Latin noun *delictum* derives from the verb *delinquere* (to stray from **6** the right way) to mean an offence, a lapse, or a mistake. Thus, the existence of a law of delict tells us that rules have been developed which entitle a person (and generally only that person) who has sustained damage or loss caused by the misconduct of another person to demand compensation for this damage: a party will be liable if he does not show the necessary respect for the rights and interests of his contemporaries in the given circumstances, whether intentionally or negligently.[23] Therefore, the law of delict demands rigorous case analysis. A legislator who wishes to avoid commenting on the mechanics of such an analysis can simply speak of *'délits'* or obligations *'que nacen de culpa o negligencia'*. This is still the practice in France, Belgium, Luxembourg, and Spain. However, a legislature wishing to remind 'its' lawyers to pursue a specific order in examining a claim will require them first to find out what everybody would have had to take into consideration under normal circumstances (the level of unlawfulness). Only then would the question arise, what could have been expected of this particular tortfeasor in this specific situation (level of fault). The initial question will always be: what went wrong from an objective (standardized) point of view? Hence codes speak of *'unerlaubte Handlungen'*, *'fatti illeciti'*, *'factos ilícitos'*, or *'onrechtmatige daden'*.

There is no practical reason why current[24] English legal terminology calls this field the *law of torts* or tort law, and not the 'law of delict'.[25] The word 'tort' derives from the Latin *tortus* (tortuous, twisted; it was also used for 'to tear out' somebody's arm or leg, so must also have meant to

---

[23] Liability for negligent conduct was already known to the Lex Aquilia (possibly 286 BC: Hausmaninger, *Das Schadensersatzrecht der Lex Aquilia* 5th edn., p. 8), see e.g. Inst. 4.3.3: *'nam alioquin non minus ex dolo quam ex culpa quisque hac lege tenetur'*. The terminology of the French *Code Civil*, however, uses the term *délits* only for damage caused intentionally; 'negligence' is covered by the *quasi-délits*, see the Rapport de Greuille in Locré vol. vi p. 280 no. 9 (*'C'est dans ce défaut de vigilance sur lui-même qu'existe la faute, et c'est cette faute qu'on appelle en droit quasi-délit, dont il doit réparation'*). See also e.g. Marty/Raynaud, *Droit Civil* vol. ii (1) 2nd edn. no. 15; Starck (-Roland/Boyer), *Obligations* vol. i, 4th edn., no. 5; Heldrich, *Allgemeine Rechtsgrundsätze*, p. 29 fn. 1; Ferid/Sonnenberger, *Frz. Zivilrecht* vol. ii, 2nd edn., 2 0 3. This opinion is shared in Belgium: Cornelis, *Buitencontractueel aansprakelijkheidsrecht*, p. 19 and Van Gerven, *Verbintenissenrecht* vol. ii, p. 2. The quasi-delicts of Roman law and the *quasi-délits* of French law are, however, *faux amis*; surprisingly, the latter uses this term for a completely different category of rules.

[24] The use of the term 'law of torts' finally succeeded in the 19th C. Until then the dichotomy of law of contract/law of delict was often expressed with the word-pair contract/duty: Williams/Hepple, *Foundations* 2nd edn., p. 1 fn. 1.

[25] On the famous dispute as to whether it is better to speak of the law of tort (singular) or of the law of torts (plural) see Rudden, *Tul.Civ.Law Forum* 6/7 (1991/92) pp. 105–129.

torture, to torment[26]) and can still be found in the German language (*jemanden einen Tort antun; Tortur*) as well as in French (*avoir du tort; faire du tort*). In medieval French legal terminology 'tort' already meant breach of law, as in 'tortuous act'.[27] With this meaning it finally found its way—via law-French, the language of the old common law courts—into English terminology. There it replaced the word 'wrong' which in turn derives from 'wrung' (German: *gewrungen*), and is none other than the English word for *tortus*.[28] An almost exact equivalent of the term '*Delikt*' is the word 'trespass', the earlier tort of the common law. For trespass derives from the Latin *transpassare* which means both literally and figuratively 'to cross a line'.

III. LIABILITY WITHOUT PERSONAL MISCONDUCT

7 As well as liability for personal misconduct, the law also recognizes liability without personal misconduct. For a first approach to this issue it is advisable to further subdivide it into the categories: liability for misconduct of a third party and liability for dangerous things. Although this distinction is far less strict now than it used to be (too often not only the two main groups but also both sub-categories blend into each other almost unnoticed)[29] it must be stressed that they, too, are included in the law of delict. Again it was the Roman law of obligations that paved the way for the laws of continental Europe, at least in this respect. As mentioned above, the Institutions of Justinian united the respective rules under the heading of *quasi law of delict*.

Part of this was, for example, that 'liability was imposed on the

---

[26] Georgis, *Ausführliches lateinisch-deutsches Handwörterbuch* (unchanged reprint of 8th edn. Darmstadt 1988), '*torqueo*'.

[27] Tunc, *IntEncCompL* XI pp. 1–5 (fn. 19). During the discussions concerning the French *Code Civil* 'torts' were often spoken of, see the Rapport Bertrand Greuille in Locré vol. vi pp. 277–282. [28] Williams/Hepple loc. cit. (fn. 24).

[29] A fine example is the case of *Malaco v. Littlewoods Organisation Ltd.* (HL), *SLT Rep.* 1987, 425/*Smith v. Littlewoods Organisation Ltd* (1987) AC 241. The defendants had purchased an empty, derelict cinema which they wanted to replace with a supermarket. Thieves forced their way into the building where they started a fire which spread to an adjacent building. The plaintiff's complaint against the owner of the building was jointly dismissed by their Lordships, who found that the acts of a third party, and not the state of the buildings, were responsible. HR 1 Apr. 1993, *NedJur* 1994, no. 502, p. 2353, held the defendant liable in a very similar case for his personal misconduct. He had parked 8 trailers packed with straw in an underpass where they were set alight during the night by a third party. Of course, the facts of any one case can involve the liability of a third party as well as liability for things, see e.g. Danish HD 8 Feb. 1991, *UfR* 1991 A p. 274, an accident in a boy scout camp; questions of liability of the group leader and the owner of the land.

occupant of a flat, out of which something was thrown or poured, so that someone was injured—regardless whether he was the owner of the flat, or whether he rented it, or lived in it free of rent . . .[30] [And that he was] not liable on grounds of a delict [was assumed] as, in many cases, he was liable for the misconduct of a third person, whether a slave or a free man. The same can be said for somebody who erects a structure which can injure a passer-by if it falls on land commonly used as a path',[31] and of the ship-owner or the publican who causes damage in or through their business: 'because they employed unreliable persons'.[32] The *actio damni infecti*[33] of the Roman law (although even more complicated in its outline) also belonged under the heading quasi-delicts. It is the root of all European codified law concerning the liability of a house-owner. Further quasi-delicts were held to give rise to noxal liability[34] of an

---

[30] More detailed about this *actio de effusis vel eiectis* (D.9.3.) is Hochstein, *Obligationes quasi ex delicto*, pp. 16–19. It no longer features in the present European codes, except in § 1318 ABGB (which sees it as a liability for the acts of others) and Art. 1910 Spanish Cc (which understands it mainly as liability for effects produced by immovable property. But see also TS 12 Apr. 1984, *RAJ* 1984 no. 1958, p. 1490: a workman failed to turn off taps; liability of tenant for damage caused to the flat below according to Art. 1910 Cc). The authors of the French Cc were satisfied with *L'énonciation du principe* (in Art. 1384 Cc), the *actio de effusis* incorporated in the draft of Art. 16 was therefore seen as only one of its examples, which '*doivent être retranchés*' (Rapport Bigot-Préameneu in Locré vol. vi p. 270 no. 12). During the discussions of the BGB it was decided against incorporating a rule similar to Art. 1910 Span. Cc (although it was well known: Prot. II p. 644) because of considerations regarding its contents. As 'living in buildings is a necessary part of life, which does not hold any extraordinary dangers as such, hence does not provide enough reason to deviate from the basic idea that the only person liable for compensation is he who caused the damage. It is only fair that the injured party who cannot detect the originator of the injury carries the damage, instead of burdening a third party, who is probably innocent, with it', Prot. II p. 645. In Scotland, *Gray* v. *Dunlop*, 1954 SLT 75 (Sh. Ct.) infers that the *actio de effusis* is not part of Scottish law (see Stewart, *Introduction*, p. 16): a pupil sued the owner of a house because an unidentified person poured the contents of a chamber pot out of the house onto his head. The claim was dismissed because the owner was not at fault. [31] Inst. 4.5.1.

[32] Inst. 4.5.3: see § 1316 ABGB (though almost made redundant by the provisions in § 970 ABGB for contractual liability: Schwimann [-Harrer], § 1316 no. 3) and § 431 HGB. The idea that the employer of 'unreliable persons' is liable is clearly expressed in § 1315 ABGB ('he is liable who employs an unfit . . . person to take care of his business'), a rule giving rise to strict liability (OGH 25 Mar. 1987, *SZ* 60/49 pp. 252, 258; Rummel [-Reischauer], ABGB vol. ii, 2nd edn., § 1315 no. 3). [33] D. 39.2.

[34] Noxal liability permitted the defendant to avoid further liability by handing over the animal, slave, and originally also the child causing the damage (Inst. 4.8. pr.). The handing over of children was later 'completely put out of use' (Inst. 4.8.7). Noxal liability as a basic model for liability is still alive, as can be seen in Art. 4 of Greek Act Γ N' dated 4/5 Dec. 1911, concerning criminal and civil liability for motor vehicles, and in Art. 185 III WVW (*Stb.* 1994, 475) and its predecessor Art. 31 IV Dutch Road Traffic Act in the 1935 version. Both limit the strict liability of the owner of a motor vehicle (in The Netherlands they also limit the strict liability of the keeper of the vehicle, where appropriate) in cases of property damage, to the value of the vehicle at the time of the accident: see Rb. The Hague 8 Dec. 1993, *VR* 1994 no. 83 p. 119. In Austria a similar provision is made in § 4 I no. 3 of its Inland Waterways Act (personal liability is limited to the value of ship and freight); see OGH 25 Aug. 1992, *ÖJZ* 1993 p. 59 (EvBl. 10).

animal-keeper[35] and the liability of the *paterfamilias* for delicts by children of the house.[36]

8   The term 'quasi-delicts' may be unfamiliar nowadays; it is found in the *Codes Civils* of France, Belgium, and Luxembourg, where it has from the outset been a synonym for liability for negligence.[37] Yet strict liability has never been of more topicality. Not only does all codified European law devote special rules[38] to this matter of potential social conflict, already distinguished from 'normal' cases by the *Corpus Juris Civilis*, but also a great number of these ancient rules have been modified by modern legal provisions to meet the specific dangers of modern times. Every European legal order contains rules which impose liability for damages on persons who have acted lawfully and therefore cannot be accused of any fault. Even if in most areas of life it can still be said, as in Art. 1306 Austrian ABGB, that 'the damage caused by someone . . . without fault . . . as a rule, need not be compensated by him', and although many European laws still agree with Art. 483 II Portuguese Cc that 'no-fault liability . . . should be limited to cases expressly provided for by statute', the fault principle, which saw its heyday in the nineteenth century, lost its monopoly position long ago. Strict liability is again a feature common to all European countries.[39] Even the basic ideas on which the quasi-law of delict was founded in classical times are (or remain) European public property: if a legal order permits a person—either in the interest of the economy or in his own interest—to use things, to employ staff, or to pursue a profession so as to cause potential danger, then he should not only enjoy the advantages but also assume responsibility to compensate any damage caused to others because of such danger: *cuius commoda, eius et incommoda*. Depending on what the particular legal orders have wanted to emphasize, expressions such as strict liability, *Gefährdungshaftung*,

---

[35] XII table 8.6. and Inst. 4.9.pr., which states: 'Injuries caused by animals are injuries caused without any wrong on the part of the acting party. As an animal cannot reason, it cannot be said that it did wrong.'

[36] Very clearly Ulp. D.9.4.35 (41 Sab.) where in sentencing the (generally responsible) son, the father was liable for his peculium (i.e. the assets given by the father to the son to run his estate).

[37] Fn. 23 above. The *délits ou quasi-délits* are mentioned in Art. 1370 IV, as well as in the heading for Art. 1382 Cc (Dutch: *misdrijven en oneigenlijke misdrijven*). Yet in The Netherlands Art. 1383 Cc, identical to Art. 1402 BW (old), was mainly seen as a regulation tailored to liability for omissions: see no. 24 below and fn. 103.

[38] See Part 2 III and IV, nos. 130 ff. below.

[39] European Community law also plays a major role in this development: see currently only v. Bar, *FS Lange* (1992), pp. 373 ff. Thus esp. the Scandinavian laws and partly also the English common law have come full circle historically. In medieval times Scandinavian liability laws were based entirely on an objective concept: the pain of the injured person, it was thought, would not become any the less if the person causing the injury had done so without fault (detailed on this matter: Jørgensen, *Erstatningsret* 2nd edn., pp. 5–6; see also id. *VersR* 1970 pp. 193, 195).

responsabilidade pelo risco, responsabilité du gardien, responsabilité objective, objektivt ansvar, and *risico-aansprakelijkheid* became common.[40]

Whether the law of strict liability is part of law of delict, or whether **9** the law of delict only concerns that field of modern liability governing illegal acts committed by tortfeasors,[41] is purely a question of terminology with almost no practical effect. We have decided to use 'law of delict' as the generic term for both areas. This is firstly, because most European languages are not really equipped with a better expression, and secondly, because the phrase 'law of delict' (if used at all)[42] now has a wider meaning than previously in European legal terminology as a whole. Finally, and most importantly, one must not be tied down to a specific dogmatic concept just because of a particular word chosen. Even if the demand for order is understandable, one should always be aware of the fact that the obvious differences between liability for one's own delicts, for the wrongdoing of others, and for the realization of dangers resulting from things have blended into each other in the past hundred years. The duties of supervision and control contrived since then through judge-made law have brought so many nuances into the matter that any hasty categorization would be a mistake.[43]

---

[40] Technical advances made since the 19th C. and the escalating manufacture and application of high energy sources were often the cause of such danger; this led to the introduction of new 'objective' bases of liability in the law of delict. Alongside this field, of great importance for road traffic law, emerged the law of industrial injuries (closely linked with the social security law) which gave liability law its second major impetus.

[41] As in the German literature, e.g. in the depiction by Deutsch (*'Haftungsrecht'* vol. i, 1976), whereas Kötz (*Deliktsrecht* 5th edn., 1991) and Brüggemeier (*Deliktsrecht*, 1986) continued to use the traditional name. In Portugal the law itself differentiates: the section headed *'Responsabilidade Civil'*, is subdivided into *'Responsabilidade por factos ilícitos'* (subsec. 1; Arts. 483–498 Cc) and *'Responsabilidade pelo risco'* (subs. 2; Arts. 499–510 Cc). The doctrine usually combines both areas in *responsabilidade extracontratual,* which also includes liability for *factos lícitos* (i.e. permitted acts, see Arts. 339, 1322, 1347–1367 Portuguese Cc): Pires de Lima / Antunes Varela, *Cc anotado* vol. i, 4th edn., p. 471. In The Netherlands, on the other hand, Art. 6:162 III BW states: 'An unlawful act can be imputed to its author if it results from his fault or from a cause for which he is answerable according to law or common opinion.' Therefore the *'aansprakelijkheid buiten schuld'* is also a delict. In Belgium and France there is no demand to make the question an issue because of Art. 1384 I Cc. The *'objektieve (foutloze) aansprakelijkheid'* and the *'responsabilité objective'* naturally form a part thereof.

[42] See fn. 1 above.   [43] Part 2 II, nos. 97 ff. below.

Part 2: Continental Europe's Codified Law of Delict

Every European nation with a codified civil law[1] has devoted a complete **10** section of it[2] to the law of delict.[3]

Of these states, those currently belonging to the EU are: Belgium (Arts. 1382–1386 *bis* Cc),[4] Germany (§§ 823–853 BGB), France (Arts. 1382–1386 Cc), Greece (Arts. 914–938 Cc), Italy (Arts. 2043–2059 Cc), Luxembourg (Arts. 1382–1386 Cc), The Netherlands (Arts. 6: 162–197 BW), Austria (§§ 1293–1341 ABGB), Portugal (Arts. 483–510 Cc), and Spain (Arts. 1902–1910 Cc).[5]

In the following pages we shall examine the subjects regulated by these provisions as well as the methods employed. Once again we shall differentiate between the law of liability for personal misconduct (see I below) and the law of liability for third parties and things (see II–IV below).

---

[1] On the Scandinavian law of delict, and on that of England, Ireland, and Scotland, see Part 3 below.

[2] The location of the provisions concerning the law of delict within the codes varies; 3 basic models are here considered. In the first group, the law of delict is dealt with in the specific part of the law of obligations, where it habitually follows the two other *ex lege* obligations: *negotiorum gestio* and unjust enrichment. Germany, Greece, Italy, and Spain have opted for this model. The Netherlands and Portugal, on the other hand, include the law of delict in the general part of the law of obligations (Boek 6: '*Algemeen Gedeelte van het Verbintenissenrecht*' and Livro II, Titulo 1: '*Das obrigações em geral*' respectively), a solution which the editor v. Kübel also had in mind in his preliminary draft of the German BGB (Schubert [ed.], *Vorentwürfe der Redaktoren*, pp. 653 ff. [§§ 181–195c]). In the third group, consisting of France, Belgium, and Luxembourg, the law of delict (book III, part four) is also part of the general law of obligations (part III). However, it sits uneasily in a book dealing with 'the various means of acquiring property'. In the Austrian ABGB the 'law of compensation and satisfaction' (*Recht des Schadensersatzes und der Genugtuung*) forms part of 'personal property law' (*persönliches Sachenrecht*)(2nd part, 2nd section), and therefore also falls within the third group.

[3] The provisions listed in the previous footnote do not contain all the rules of the law of delict. The *Personenrecht* (legal protection of a person's name and rights of personal privacy, see § 12 BGB and Arts. 57–59 Greek Cc; and liability of mentally disabled persons, see Art. 489–2 French Cc) can also contain elements of the law of delict; the same is true of the law of property. Injunctive relief provided in Art. 5:37 BW, for example, is *lex specialis* relating to the basic regulation found in Art. 6:162 BW. Likewise, the definitions of negligence are usually given in the general part of the law of obligations, see Part 1 fn. 3 above, and fn. 10 below. The following list is therefore not comprehensive.

[4] '*C'est que le principe établi par l'article* (1386 *bis*) *est applicable aux obligations contractuelles comme aux obligations délictuelles ou quasi délictuelles*', that the provision which is not part of the law of delict was placed in a separate part of the code: *Pasin. belge* 1935 pp. 286, 293.

[5] As stated above, the Spanish Criminal Code still governs the major part of the law of delict (formerly Arts. 19–20, 101–108 CP; as from 24 May 1996 part V of the NCP). Further, delictual provisions are found in the compilation of the civil law of Navarra, which is, however, laid out extensively in accordance with the common Spanish law of delict: see e.g. TSJ de Navarra 11 Mar. 1994, *RAJ* 1994 no. 2114 p. 2844.

I. SUBJECTS AND METHODS OF REGULATION WITHIN THE LAW OF LIABILITY FOR PERSONAL MISCONDUCT

Bibliography: Albaladejo, 'Sobre la solidaridad o mancomunidad de los obligados a responder por acto ilícito común', *An.Der.Civ.* 16 (1963) pp. 345–376; Alpa, 'Come fare cose con principi', *NGCC* 1992, II, pp. 383–416; id., 'Il codice e la responsabilità civile: origine di un testo', *Riv.Dir. Com.* 1992, I, pp. 513–524; Asser, *Nederlandsch Burgerlijk Wetboek, vergeleken met het Wetboek Napoleon* (2nd edn. The Hague and Amsterdam 1838); Bajons, 'Schadensersatz für gesundheitliche Beeinträchtigungen nach italienischem Recht', *ZVglRWiss* 92 (1993) pp. 76–114; v. Bar, 'Zur Struktur der Deliktshaftung von juristischen Personen, ihren Organen und ihren Verrichtungsgehilfen', in: *FS Zentaro Kitagawa* (Berlin 1992) pp. 279–295; id., 'Entwicklungen und Entwicklungstendenzen im Recht der Verkehrs(sicherungs)pflichten', *JuS* 1988 pp. 169–174; id., 'Neues Verkehrshaftpflichtrecht in Frankreich', *VersR* 1986 pp. 620–629; id., 'Das "Trennungsprinzip" und die Geschichte des Wandels der Haftpflichtversicherung', *AcP* 181 (1981) pp. 289–327; Berman, *Law and Revolution: The Formation of the Western Legal Tradition* (Cambridge Mass. 1983); Bloembergen, *Schadevergoeding bij onrechtmatige daad* (diss. Deventer 1965); Bocken, *Het aansprakelijkheidsrecht als sanctie tegen de verstoring van het leefmilieu* (Brussels 1979); Boonekamp, *Onrechtmatige daad in groepsverband volgens NBW* (Deventer 1990); Bosdas, 'Astika adikimata kata ton kodika', *EEN* 14 (1947) pp. 430–433; Bucher, 'Der Einfluß des französischen Code Civil auf das Obligationenrecht', in: Caroni (ed.), *Das Obligationenrecht 1883–1983. Berner Ringvorlesung zum Jubiläum des schweizerischen Obligationenrechts* (Berne and Stuttgart 1984) pp. 139–176; Busnelli, 'Capacità ed incapacità di agire del minore', *Dir.fam.pers.* 1982 pp. 54–76; Bydlinski, 'Haftung bei alternativer Kausalität. Zur Frage der ungeklärten Verursachung, besonders nach österreichischem Zivilrecht', *JBl* 1959 pp. 1–13; v. Caemmerer, 'Das Verschuldensprinzip in rechtsvergleichender Sicht', *RabelsZ* 42 (1978) pp. 5–27; id., 'Wandlungen des Deliktsrechts', in: *Gesammelte Schriften*, vol. i: *Rechtsvergleichung und Schuldrecht* (Tübingen 1968) pp. 452–553; Canaris, 'Schutzgesetze, Verkehrspflichten, Schutzpflichten', in: *FS für Karl Larenz* (Munich 1983) pp. 27–110; Carvalho Fernandes, *Teoria Geral do Direito Civil*, ii (Lisbon 1983); Castronovo, *La nuova responsabilità civile. Regola e metafora* (Milan 1991); id., *Problema e sistema nel danno da prodotti* (Milan 1979); id., 'Le frontiere mobili della responsabilità civile', *Riv.crit.dir.priv.* 1989 pp. 539–624; Catala, 'Le droit français de la grève', in: Lovi/Rotondi (edd.), *The Strike* (Milan 1987) pp. 23–39; Cendon, *Infermità di mente e responsabilità civile*

(Padua 1993); Cendon/Gaudino, 'Gli Illeciti di dolo', in: Cendon (ed.), *Responsabilità civile*, pp. 389–472 (Milan 1988); Chianale, 'In tema di responsabilità dei genitori per i danni causati dai figli minori', *Giur.it.* 1986, I, 1, 1527 (note); Cian, 'Fünfzig Jahre italienischer Codice civile', *ZEuP* 1993 pp. 120–131; Conde-Pumpido Ferreiro, 'Los problemas de la responsabilidad civil por los hechos ilícitos de los incapaces', in: *Estudios de Derecho civil en honor del Prof. Castán Tobeñas*, vol. ii (Pamplona 1969) pp. 75–109; Coutinho de Abreu, *Do Abuso do Direito* (Coimbra 1983); Cristóbal Montes, *Mancomunidad o solidaridad en la responsabilidad plural por acto ilícito civil* (Barcelona 1985); van Dam, *Zorgvuldigheidsnorm en aansprakelijkheid* (Deventer 1989); Dejean de la Batie, *Appréciation in abstracto et appréciation in concreto en droit civil français* (diss. Paris 1965); Dekkers, *Précis de droit civil belge. Tome ii: Les obligations, Les preuves, Les contrats, Les sûretés* (Brussels 1955); Deliyannis, 'I paranomia os proipothesi tis adikopraktikis evthinis', *Tim. Tomos G. Michaelides-Nouaros* (Athens 1987) vol. A pp. 303–348; Díaz Alabart, 'La responsabilidad por los actos ilícitos dañosos de los sometidos a patria potestad o tutela', *An.Der.Civ.* 40 (1987) pp. 795–894; Ebenroth, 'Les principes fondamentaux de la responsabilité non-contractuelle en droit français et en droit allemand', *Gaz.Pal.* 1994 *Doctr.* pp. 5–9; Enneccerus/Lehmann, *Recht der Schuldverhältnisse* (15th edn. Tübingen 1958); Fabarius, *Äußere und innere Sorgfalt* (Cologne 1991); Fagnart, 'Les faits générateurs de responsabilité. Aperçu des principales tendences actuelles', in: Dalcq (ed.), *Responsabilité et réparation des dommages* (Brussels 1983) pp. 1–84; de Falco, 'Esercizio del diritto di sciopero, neutralizzazione degli effetti e condotta antisindacale', *Riv.dir.lav.* 1992 pp. 331–368; Ferrari, 'Der neue deliktische Schutz der eheähnlichen Lebensgemeinschaft in Italien. Eine rechtsvergleichende Kritik', *RabelsZ* 56 (1992) pp. 757–765; id., 'Das italienische Recht der außervertraglichen Verschuldenshaftung als Beispiel für einen Ausgangspunkt zur Umdeutung der Rolle des § 823 I BGB', *Jahrbuch für italienisches Recht* 8 (1995) pp. 191–201; id., 'Zwanzig Jahre Generalklausel im italienischen Deliktsrecht', *ZfS* 1992 pp. 2–3; id., *Atipicità dell'illecito civile. Una comparazione* (Milan 1992); Ferrer Correia, 'Da Responsabilidade do Terceiro que coopera com o Devedor na Violação de um Pacto de Preferência', in: *Estudos de Direito Civil, Comercial e Criminal* (2nd edn. Coimbra 1985) pp. 33–51; Forchielli, *Il rapporto di causalità nell'illecito civile* (Padua 1960); Fragistas, 'Der Rechtsmißbrauch nach dem griechischen Zivilgesetzbuch', in: *FS für Martin Wolff* (Tübingen 1952) pp. 49–66; Galgano, 'Le mobili frontiere del danno ingiusto', *Contratto e Impresa* 1985 pp. 1–27; García Cantero, 'Exégesis comparativa del artículo 1.902 del Código Civil', in: Asociación de profesores de Derecho Civil (ed.), *Centenario del Código Civil*, vol. i (Madrid 1990) pp. 875–884; Gasis/Chiotellis, 'Evthini trapesas kat' A.K. 919, *NoB* 40 (1992) pp. 467–484; Georgiades, 'Standpunkt und Entwicklung des griechischen Deliktsrechts', in: *FS für Karl Larenz* (Munich 1983) pp. 175–198; id., *Die Anspruchskonkurrenz im Zivilrecht und Zivilprozeßrecht* (Munich 1968); Ghisalberti, *La Codificazione del Diritto in Italia* (Rome and Bari 1985); Julius v. Gierke, 'Das Zivilgesetzbuch von Griechenland', *ZHR* 115 (1952) pp. 185–294; Gogos, 'Das griechische Bürgerliche Gesetzbuch vom 15. März 1940', *AcP* 149 (1944) pp. 78–101; Gómez Calle, *La responsabilidad civil de los padres* (Madrid 1992); Gorlé/Bourgeois/Bocken, *Rechtsvergelijking* (Ghent 1985); Gutteridge, 'Abuse of Rights', *CLJ* 5 (1933–35) pp. 22–45; Hartig, *Vergleichende Warentests im Recht Deutschlands, Frankreichs, der Niederlande und Großbritanniens* (Frankfurt/Main 1973); Hartkamp, *Judicial Discretion under the New Civil Code of The Netherlands (Centro di studi e ricerche di diritto comparato e straniero)* (Rome 1992); id., 'Das neue niederländische Bürgerliche Gesetzbuch aus europäischer Sicht', *RabelsZ* 57 (1993) pp. 664–684; Haybäch, 'Können wahre Tatsachenbehauptungen Ehrenbeleidigungen im Sinne des § 1330 Abs. 1 ABGB sein?', *JBl* 1994 pp. 732–741; Heck, *Grundriß des Schuldrechts* (Tübingen 1929); Hedemann, *Die Fortschritte des Zivilrechts im XIX. Jahrhundert. Ein Überblick über die Entfaltung des Privatrechts in Deutschland, Österreich, Frankreich und der Schweiz. Part 1: Die Neuordnung des Verkehrslebens* (reprint of the 1910 Berlin edn., Frankfurt/Main. 1968); Heldrich, *Die allgemeinen Rechtsgrundsätze der außervertraglichen Schadenshaftung im Bereich der Europäischen Wirtschaftsgemeinschaft* (Frankfurt/Main and Berlin 1961); Hennings, *Persönliche Haftung und Mitverschulden des Kindes im französischen Deliktsrecht* (Berlin 1992); Herbots, 'Le "duty of care" et le dommage purement financier en droit comparé', *Rev.dr.int.dr.comp.* 62 (1985) pp. 7–33; Hohlbein, *Die neuere Entwicklung des niederländischen außervertraglichen Haftungsrechts* (diss. Münster 1981); Hondius, 'Das neue Niederländische Zivilgesetzbuch', *AcP* 191 (1991) pp. 378–395; Wieland Horn, *Die unberechtigte Verwarnung aus gewerblichen Schutzrechten* (Cologne 1971); Houin/Pédamon, *Droit commercial* (9th edn. Paris 1990); Huc, *Commentaire théorique et pratique du Code civil*, vol. viii (Paris 1895); Jagert, 'Deliktsrechtliche Betrachtungen zur nichtehelichen Lebensgemeinschaft aus der Sicht des deutschen und des italienischen Rechts', *RabelsZ* 53 (1989) pp. 718–728; v. Jhering, 'Das Schuldmoment im römischen Privatrecht' (Gießen 1867), in: Rudolf v. Jhering, *Vermischte Schriften juristischen Inhalts* (reprint of the 1879 Leipzig edition, Aalen 1968) pp. 155–240; Josserand, *Cours de Droit Civil positif Français*, vol. ii: *Théorie générale des Obligations* (2nd edn. Paris 1933); Kapsalis, *Persönlichkeitsrecht und Persönlichkeitsschutz nach griechischem Privatrecht unter Berücksichtigung des deutschen Rechts* (Athens 1983; also diss. Cologne 1983); Karakatsanes, *Wandlungen des griechischen Ehescheidungsrechts* (Athens and Komotini 1985); Karollus, *Funktion und Dogmatik der Haf-*

tung aus Schutzgesetzverletzung (Vienna and New York 1992); Kletecka, 'Solidarhaftung und Haftungsprivileg', *ÖJZ* 1993 pp. 785–792 (part I) and pp. 833–838 (part II); Klinge-van Rooij/Snijder, 'Auf dem Weg zu einem neuen Produkthaftungsrecht. Das DES-Urteil des Hogen Raad', *EuZW* 1993 pp. 569–573; Koch, *Allgemeines Landrecht für die preußischen Staaten*, vol. i (8th edn. Berlin and Leipzig 1884); Koutrakis, *Evthini ek logon epiikias* (2 vols., Athens and Komotini 1982); Koziol, 'Generalnorm und Einzeltatbestände als Systeme der Verschuldenshaftung: Unterschiede und Aufteilungsmöglichkeiten' *ZEuP* 1995 pp. 359–367; Krause, 'Der deutschrechtliche Anteil an der heutigen Privatrechtsordnung', *JuS* 1970 pp. 313–321; Lankhorst, *De relativiteit van de onrechtmatige daad* (Deventer 1992); Lapoyade Deschamps, 'Les petits responsables. Responsabilité civile et responsabilité pénale de l'enfant', *D*. 1988 *Chron*. pp. 299–305; Laurent, *Avant-Projet de Révision du Code Civil*, vol. iv (Brussels 1884); Levi, *Responsabilità civile e responsabilità oggettiva* (Milan 1986); v. Lillienskiold, *Aktuelle Probleme des portugiesischen Delikts- und Schadensersatzrechts* (diss. Bonn 1975); Limpens, 'La théorie de la "relativité aquilienne" en droit comparé', in: *Mélanges Savatiers* (Paris 1965) pp. 559–581; Limpens/Kruithof/Meinertzhagen-Limpens, 'Liability for one's own act', *Int.Enc.Comp.L* XI 2 (1983); Lipovats, 'Note to BGH 10 Apr. 1962', *NoB* 14 (1966) pp. 74–77; Litzeropoulos, 'Tria themeliodi provlimata tis astikis evthinis is ta synchrona dikaia kai ton Ellenikon Astikon Kodika', *AID* 7 (1940) pp. 158–203; Livanis, *I Efarmogi tou arthrou 300 is to pedion tis antikimenikis evthinis* (diss. Athens 1970); López Beltrán de Heredia, *La responsabilidad civil de los padres por los hechos de sus hijos* (Madrid 1988); Macris, 'Die Grundgedanken für die Ausarbeitung des Entwurfs eines griechischen Zivilgesetzbuches', *RabelsZ* 9 (1935) pp. 586–614; di Majo, *La tutela civile dei diritti* 2nd edn. (Milan 1987); Mantzoufas, *Enochikon Dikaion* 3rd edn. (Athens 1959); id., *Das griechische Zivilgesetzbuch und seine theoretischen Grundlagen* (Athens 1954); Markesinis, 'General Theory of unlawful Acts', in: Hartkamp/Hesselink/Hondius/du Perron/Vranken (edd.), *Towards a European Civil Code* (Nijmegen *et al.* 1994) pp. 285–299; Maschio, 'Responsabilità ex art. 2048 Cc e "grandi minori"', *Dir.fam.pers*. 1988, II, pp. 875–886 (annotation); Mastropaolo, 'Morte del minore, provocata da non imputabile, e risarcimento dei danni', *Giur.it*. 1984, I, cols. 149–166; Otto Mayer, 'Gutachten über die Frage: Wie weit hat der Arbeitgeber für das Verschulden seiner Arbeiter zu haften?', Gutachten IV zum 17. Deutschen Juristentag (*Verhandlungen I* 1884) pp. 125–136; Mazeaud, 'La "faute objective" et la responsabilité sans faute', *D*. 1985 *Chron*. pp. 13–14; Meincke, 'Kann § 848 BGB gestrichen werden?', *JZ* 1980 pp. 677–678; Mertz, *Der Schutz primärer Vermögensinteressen im niederländischen Deliktsrecht im Vergleich zur deutschen Rechtsprechung* (Cologne *et al.*

1994); Merz, 'Obligationenrecht (Die privatrechtliche Rechtsprechung des Bundesgerichts im Jahre 1991)', *ZBernJV* 129 (1993) pp. 235–245; Mota Pinto, *Teoria Geral do Direito Civil* 3rd edn. (Coimbra 1985); Nieuwenhuis, 'Welke Belangen worden beschermd door Art. 1401 BW?', *WPNR* 1987 no. 5821, pp. 145–149; Nipperdey, 'Die Generalklausel im künftigen Recht der unerlaubten Handlungen', in: *Grundfragen der Reform des Schadensersatzrechts* (Munich 1940) pp. 36–49; Nobel, *Anstalt und Unternehmen* (Diessenhofen [Switzerland] 1978); Oldenhuis, *Onrechtmatige daad: aansprakelijkheid voor personen* (Deventer 1985; Monografieën Nieuw BW B-46); Pantaleón, 'Causalidad e imputación objetiva: Criterios de imputación', in: Asociación de profesores de Derecho civil (ed.), *Centenario del Código Civil (1889–1989)*, vol. ii (Madrid, date of publication missing [1990?] pp. 1561–1591); Papachristou, 'Chrimatiki ikanopiisi gia ithiki vlavi se periptosi diasigiou', *NoB* 31 (1983) pp. 933–938; Pera, *Diritto del lavoro* 3rd edn. (Padua 1988); Pereira Coelho, *Direito da Família* 2 vols., 2nd edn. (Coimbra 1985); id., *O problema da causa virtual na responsabilidade civil* (Coimbra 1955); Philippe, 'La théorie de la relativité aquilienne', in: *Mélanges Roger Dalcq* (Brussels 1994) pp. 467–486; Pinto Borea, 'I doveri dei genitori verso i figli minori e la responsabilità ex art. 2048 Cc', *Dir.fam.pers.* 1992, I, pp. 364–402; Plagianakos, *Die Entstehung des Griechischen Zivilgesetzbuches* (Hamburg 1963); id., 'To dikaioma epi tis idias prosopikotitas', *EllDik* 7 (1966) pp. 101–176; Potamianos, 'Ai ex adikimaton enochai kai to Schedion tou Ellenikou Ast. Kodikos', *AID* 4 (1937) pp. 244–313; Puill, 'Vers une réforme de la responsabilité des père et mère du fait de leurs enfants?', *D.* 1988 *Chron.* pp. 185–192; Rabel, 'Die Grundzüge des Rechts der unerlaubten Handlungen', in: *Deutsche Landesreferate zum ersten internationalen Kongreß für Rechtsvergleichung* (1932), cited according to Leser (ed.), Ernst Rabel, *Gesammelte Aufsätze* vol. iii (Tübingen 1967) pp. 101–119; Rodière (ed.), *La responsabilité délictuelle dans la jurisprudence* (Paris 1978); Rodotà, *Il problema della responsabilità civile* (Milan 1964); Ronse, *Aanspraak op schadeloosstelling uit onrechtmatige daad* (Brussels 1954); Rosenkranz, *Die Haftung für Schadenszufügung aus unerlaubter Handlung nach italienischem Recht unter besonderer Berücksichtigung der Straßenverkehrshaftung* (diss. Regensburg 1973); Roubier, *Le droit de la propriété industrielle* (Paris 1952); Rummel, 'Zur Verbesserung des schadensrechtlichen Schutzes gegen unlauteren Wettbewerb', *JBl* 1971 pp. 385–390; Sacco, 'L'ingiustizia di cui all'art. 2043', *Foro pad.* 1960 I cols. 1420–1442; Scheffen, 'Vorschläge zur Änderung des § 828 Abs. 1 und 2 BGB', *FuR* 1993 pp. 82–89; id., 'Der Kinderunfall—Eine Herausforderung für Gesetzgebung und Rechtsprechung', *DAR* 1991 pp. 121–126; Schlesinger, 'L'ingiustizia del danno nell'illecito civile', *JUS* 1960 pp. 336–347; Schlüchter, *Haftung für gefährliche Tätigkeit und Haftung ohne Verschulden. Das italienische Recht als*

Vorbild für das schweizerische? (Berne and Stuttgart 1990); K. Schmidt, 'Integritätsschutz von Unternehmen nach § 823 BGB. Zum "Recht am eingerichteten und ausgeübten Gewerbebetrieb"', *JuS* 1993 pp. 985–992; Scholten, 'Burgerlijk onrecht. Aansprakelijkheid van de overheid. Wenschelijke wetswijziging', *WPNR* 1911 nos. 2149–2158; Schrauder, *Wettbewerbsverstöße als Eingriff in das Recht am Gewerbebetrieb* (Bielefeld 1970); Schubert (ed.), *Die Vorentwürfe der Redaktoren zum BGB. Recht der Schuldverhältnisse*. Part 1: *Allgemeiner Teil* (author: Franz Philipp v. Kübel) (Berlin and New York 1980); Soutis, 'Das griechische Zivilgesetzbuch im Rahmen der Privatrechtsgeschichte der Neuzeit', *SavZ Rom. Abt.* 78 (1961) pp. 355–385; Spencer/van Wassenaer, 'Causal links and congenital disabilities', [1993] *CLJ* 206–209; Spier, 'Boekbespreking' (on Boonekamp, *Onrechtmatige daad in groepsverband*, see above), *WPNR* 1991 no. 6029, pp. 857–860; Spier/Sterk, *Rope-Dancing Dutch Tort Law*, Schriftenreihe deutscher Jura-Studenten in Genf, issue 6 (Geneva 1993); Stathopoulos, 'Bemerkungen zum Verhältnis zwischen Fahrlässigkeit und Rechtswidrigkeit im Zivilrecht', in: *FS für Karl Larenz* (Munich 1983) pp. 631–647; Stoll, *Kausalzusammenhang und Normzweck im Deliktsrecht* (Tübingen 1968); Stone, 'Civil Liability for Damages Caused by the Insane: A comparative study', in: *FS für Ernst Rabel* vol. i (Tübingen 1954) pp. 403–419; Tamburrino, 'Der Begriff des Vermögensschadens im italienischen Recht', in: *Hefte der Vereinigung für den Gedankenaustausch zwischen deutschen und italienischen Juristen*, issue 8/9 (Karlsruhe 1973) pp. 11–35; Toullier, *Le droit civil français suivant l'ordre du code* vol. xi (Paris 1824); Traverso, 'L'abuso del diritto', *NGCC* 1992, II, pp. 297–317; Triantaphyllopoulos, 'Der griechische Entwurf eines Obligationenrechts', *RabelsZ* 10 (1936) pp. 53–66; Tucci, 'La risarcibilità del danno da atto lecito nel diritto civile', *Riv.Dir.Civ.* 1967 I 229–268; Vavouskos, 'To astiko adikima eis tas periptosis ithikis simias ypo to kratos tou Astikou Kodikos', *EEN* 22 (1955) 82–87; id., 'I adikos astiki praxis eis tin synchronon epistimin kai nomologian', *Tim. Tomos G. Michaelides-Nouaros* (Athens 1987) vol. A pp. 87–105; id., *I paralipsi os simiogono gegonos eis ta adikimata Astikou Dikaiou* (Athens 1954); Vaz Serra, 'Requisitos da responsabilidade civil', *BolMinJust* 92 (1960) pp. 37–136; id., 'Obrigação de Indemnização (Colocação. Fontes. Conceito e Espécies de Dano. Nexo Causal. Extensão do Dever de Indemnizar. Espécies de Indemnização). Direito de Abstenção e de Remoção', *BolMinJust* 84 (1959) pp. 5–301; id., 'Culpa do devedor ou do agente', *BolMinJust* 68 (1957) pp. 13–149; id., 'Responsabilidade de pessoas obrigadas a vigilância', *BolMinJust* 85 (1959) pp. 381–444; id., 'Abuso do direito (em matéria de responsabilidade civil)', *BolMinJust* 85 (1959) pp. 243–343; Venchiarutti, 'La responsabilità civile dell'incapace', in: Cendon (ed.), *Responsabilità civile* pp. 497–518 (Milan 1988); Vetter, *Geestelijke*

19

stoornis (Deventer 1992; Monografieën Nieuw BW A-9); Viney, 'La réparation des dommages causés sous l'empire d'un état d'inconscience', *Sem.Jur.* 1985, I, 3189; Vranken, 'Einführung in das neue Niederländische Schuldrecht', Part 2: 'Das Recht der unerlaubten Handlung, Schadensersatz- und Bereicherungsrecht', *AcP* 191 (1991) pp. 411–432; Voss, *Fahrlässiges Delikt und reiner Vermögensschaden. Haftungsgrenzen in der deutschen, anglo-amerikanischen und niederländischen Praxis* (diss. Cologne 1987); Warnsink, 'Het DES-arrest in het perspectief van verzekerbare slachtofferbescherming', *A&V* 1993 pp. 6–12; De Wilde, 'Het begrip 'schade'', in: Vandenberghe (ed.), *Onrechtmatige daad—actuele tendenzen* (Antwerp 1979) pp. 181–196; Will, *Quellen erhöhter Gefahr* (Munich 1980); Willems, 'Essai sur la responsabilité édictée par les articles 1382–1386 du Code civil', *Rev.gén.dr.* 1895 pp. 110–150; Yzquierdo Tolsada, 'El pertubador artículo 1092 del Código civil: cien años de errores', in: Asociación de profesores de Derecho Civil (ed.), *Centenario del Código Civil* vol. ii (Madrid 1990) pp. 2109–2135; Zepos, 'Der Schutz der Persönlichkeit nach dem griechischen Zivilgesetzbuch', in: *FS für Ernst v. Caemmerer* (Tübingen 1978) pp. 1129–1139; id., 'Les Solutions du Code Civil Hellénique en Matière de Responsabilité Civile', *Rev.int.dr.comp.* 2 (1950) pp. 297–304; id., 'Der Schadenersatz nach Ermessen des Richters', in: *FS für Martin Wolff* (Tübingen 1952) pp. 167–173.

1. BASIC PROVISIONS GOVERNING LIABILITY FOR FAULT

a. **General**

11   Throughout the codes of continental western Europe tortious acts are governed by a general rule, albeit sometimes made up of several parts. As both main and residual provision, it covers the majority of the doctrinal issues, and most of the case material concerning the law of delict.[6] With one exception,[7] these basic rules are restricted to liability for

---

[6] The exceptions being Spain, where liability law is closely tied to the criminal law, and France. In France, as a set of statistics from 1971 indicates, *gardien* liability under Art. 1384 I, 2nd alt. Cc (on which see nos. 107–114 below) has for some time replaced liability for *faute* under Arts. 1382, 1383 Cc: Rodière, *La responsabilité délictuelle dans la jurisprudence*, p. 2; Hennings, *Persönliche Haftung und Mitverschulden*, p. 33.

[7] Only Art. 6:162 III Dutch BW goes further. Art. 483 II Portuguese Cc acknowledges the existence of no-fault liability. However, such liability is limited to circumstances explicitly prescribed in the law. On the preparatory works to the Italian Cc, which considered all kinds of causes of liability, but finally decided to frame the basic regulation of Art. 2043 Cc in terms of fault only, see Alpa, *Riv.Dir.Com.* 1992, I, pp. 513, 522.

personal misconduct, which in turn depends on fault on the part of the person causing the damage.[8] Thus fault, i.e. intent and negligence, becomes the central notion of the codified law of delict. Other sources of liability are set out either later in the relevant section of the code or in statutes outside the code.

Only § 1294 s. 2 ABGB defines intent: 'with knowledge and **12** design' (*mit Wissen und Wollen*). Even negligence is not universally defined *legaliter*,[9] and where the authors of the codes fought successfully to include such a definition[10] it often no longer meets modern requirements.[11] Furthermore, the provisions have been tailored primarily to the liability of *natural persons*.[12] Legal persons are not usually considered within the basic provisions[13] and there are few specific regulations dealing with this matter. The fact that legal persons committing tortious 'acts' might bring about special problems has not generally been acknowledged. Hence, apart from a few rules based on the organic theory,[14] this area is not regulated by the codes.

b. From the French General Clause to the Restrictive Approach of the BGB

There are two primary problems for the law of delict: first, which interests **13** are to be protected, and second, what type of conduct should give rise to a duty to compensate the victim. These problems must be addressed by the legislature and the judiciary jointly. However, until now it has been neither necessary nor possible to develop a common core of principles

---

[8] Note that this is only true for liability for personal misconduct according to the aforementioned basic regulations. The widespread *Billigkeitshaftung* (special liability on grounds of equity) are discussed below at nos. 75 ff.

[9] Neither the French, Belgian, or Luxembourg Cc, nor the Dutch BW contain a legal definition of negligence.

[10] As in Germany (§ 276 BGB), Greece (Art. 330 s. 2 Cc), Italy (Art. 1176 Cc; for the law of delict, however Art. 43 CP is more important: see no. 625), Portugal (Art. 487 II Cc), and Spain (Art. 1104 Cc).

[11] Even the Portuguese Cc, which only came into force in 1967, still operates in Art. 487 II with the figure of '*diligência de um bom pai de família*'. Clearly a Europe committed to sexual equality should no longer refer to the 'good father of the family' (see also Art. 1176 I Italian Cc; Arts. 1137 I, 1374 I French Cc; and Art. 1104 II Spanish Cc) as the model for a prudent human being; see also Part 6 I no. 565 below.

[12] See Art. 1382 Cc: '*Tout fait quelconque de l'homme, qui cause . . . un dommage.*'

[13] However, García Cantero, *Exégesis comparativa del Art. 1.902 Cc*, pp. 875, 879, quite rightly remarks that the Spanish basic rule on the law of delict deliberately deviated from its French model, to ensure that its wording would not make the imposition of liability on legal persons problematic. See also TS 29 Sep. 1964, *RAJ* 1964 no. 4097 p. 2522.

[14] See e.g. § 31 BGB, Art. 71 Greek Cc, and Art. 571 Port. Cc. In other codes regulations on strict liability of the employer serve a similar purpose. Only the Dutch BW occasionally distinguishes explicitly between legal and natural persons in its law of delict (see Art. 6:170 II).

governing the competence of these authorities in Europe.[15] Only when a European Civil Code of Obligations is seriously contemplated will the subject unavoidably come onto the agenda. It is therefore not surprising that in almost 190 years, between the enforcement of the French Cc and the new Dutch BW,[16] different models of codification have been developed, the extent of whose regulations varies widely. The number of provisions on delict in the various European civil codes has gradually increased.[17] Of the texts still in force the Austrian ABGB is the only exception, adhering firmly to its Roman roots. A contemporary lawyer thus finds it unusually detailed. Furthermore, the authors of the newer codes tended generally to see the older ones as experiments of their time, the results of which were to be examined by means of comparative law.[18]

14   Of all the European codes, the French *Code Civil* gives the courts the least guidance. Its authors were interested solely in laying down the *'vérités éternelles'*.[19] They were interested only in regulating the principle of *neminem laedere*, which can hardly be regarded as an applicable rule of law and which can only be classified to a limited extent. Finding solutions for detailed problems was not the legislature's concern.[20] Thus, the

---

[15] The constitutional question of competence, i.e. what power should be allocated to the courts to extend the law in areas covered by an *already enforced* system of codification, is discussed in Part 6 I, nos. 562 ff. and 597 ff. below.

[16] The French *Code Civil* dates from 20 Mar. 1804. It remains in force in Luxembourg, as well as in Belgium, which separated from The Netherlands in 1830 (see Art. 139 no. 11 of the Belgian Constitution of 1831, abrogated in 1971). The Austrian ABGB came into force on 1 Jan. 1812, the Spanish Cc on 27 July 1889, and the German BGB on 1 Jan. 1900. Italy replaced its *Codice Civile* of 1865 on 21 Apr. 1942 (see Cian, *ZEuP* 1993 pp. 120–123). The Greek Cc of 1940 came into force on 23 Feb. 1946. Portugal substituted its *Código Civil* of 1867 in 1966 (in force since 1 June 1967). The Dutch have had their own Civil Code since 1 Oct. 1838 (on whose history, and on the temporary validity of the French Cc in the Netherlands, see Gorlé/Bougeois/Bocken, *Rechtsverglijking*, no. 233), brought into force books 3, 5, 6, and 7 of the new Dutch BW (the latter only in parts) on 1 Jan. 1992 (Stb. 1991 no. 600). Until then their law of delict was laid down in Arts. 1401–1416c BW (old). Books 1 (family law) and 2 (legal persons) however, came into force in 1970 and 1976 respectively, and book 8 (Transport law) came into force in 1991.

[17] Although the Portuguese Cc of 1867 provided quite extensive regulation in its Arts. 2361–2403.

[18] For general observations on the extent to which western lawyers gained knowledge from these 'experiments' see Berman, *Law and Revolution*, pp. 151–164. The most impressive comparative studies are found in the many articles published prior to the new Portuguese Civil Code by Vaz Serra in *BolMinJust* (Portugal), in the *Dutch Parlementaire Geschiedenis*, in the work of Mantzoufas, *The Greek Civil Code*, pp. 28 ff. On the role played by comparative law in the preparation of the Spanish Cc see e.g. García Cantero, *Exégesis comparativa del Art. 1.902 Cc* (Part 2 Bibliography).

[19] *Exposé de motifs* by Treilhard no. 5 (in Locré vol. vi, p. 275). See also García Goyena, one of those most prominent in the drafting of the Spanish law of obligations: 'El artículo (he means Art. 1900 of his *Proyecto* = Art. 1902 Cc) *encierra una máxima de jurisprudencia universal, fundada en un principio eterno de justicia, sua cuique culpa nocet'* (cited here according to García Cantero, *Exégesis comparativa del Art. 1902 Cc*, pp. 875, 876).

[20] Loc. cit. no. 11. See also Josserand, *Cours de Droit Civil* vol. ii, 2nd edn., no. 422.

legal text contents itself with stating in Art. 1383 Cc that a person is liable not only for intentional acts (Art. 1382 Cc) but also for damage he or she causes *'par sa négligence ou par son imprudence'*. The authors of the code saw no need to include additional provisions governing liability for personal misconduct. The guidelines which the French *Code Civil* provides for the courts have not yet been extended beyond the three constituent elements laid down in Arts. 1382 and 1383 (with the exception of Art 489–2 Cc).[21] They are: *faute*, causation, and damage. The basic rule became a *general clause*, and since then the courts have had to develop French fault-based liability law from this regulation alone.

Whether the criticism of the French legislature,[22] particularly in recent **15** German literature,[23] is fair need not be discussed here. The fact remains that for a long time the law of delict of various countries contented itself with similar broad basic provisions. In this respect the Belgian (1830) and Italian (1865) Ccs are word-perfect copies of the French model.[24] Even the Spanish Cc (1889) met the need for regulation in this area mainly by incorporating Arts. 1382 and 1383 of the French Cc into its Art. 1902.[25] Apart from the Austrian ABGB (which is based on an entirely different legislative concept),[26] in the nineteenth century only The Netherlands, Switzerland,[27] and (more clearly) Portugal had the courage to distance themselves, albeit gingerly, from the French Code

---

[21] See fn. 3 above and no. 66 below.

[22] See e.g. de Page, *Droit Civil Belge* vol. ii, 3rd edn., no. 901 (p. 857), who accused the code's law of delict of *'obscurité d'une part, insuffisance de l'autre'*. The report by Mayer for the 17th German Lawyers' Day in 1884 (see bibliography before no. 11 above) is, in the author's opinion, one of the most balanced comments on this matter, and still worth reading. For a more recent and succinct comparison of the German and the French law of delict (in French) see Ebenroth, *Gaz.Pal.* 1994 *Doctr.*, pp. 5–9.

[23] That 'considerations of legal policy render the German system preferable to a system of tort law based upon a general clause' is an opinion put forward by Canaris, *FS Larenz* 1983 pp. 27, 35. His view was shared by Rabel, *'Unerlaubte Handlungen'* (see bibliography before no. 11 above) pp. 13 f., 27, but not by Enneccerus/Lehmann, *Schuldverhältnisse*, 15th edn., § 229 II, Fikentscher, *Schuldrecht*, 8th edn., § 97 III 2 c, or Nipperdey, *Generalklausel*, pp. 37 ff.

[24] Arts. 1382 and 1383 Belgian (and Lux.) Cc; Arts. 1151 and 1152 Italian Cc (1865). For a more detailed examination of the adoption by unified Italy of the French Cc see Ghisalberti, *La Codificazione del Diritto in Italia 1865–1942* (1985) pp. 42 ff.; Alpa, *Riv.Dir.Com.* 1992, I, pp. 513, 514–517, and Alpa/Bessone, *Atipicità* vol. i, 2nd edn., pp. 369 ff., who concentrate on the law of delict.

[25] *'El que por acción u omisión causa daño a otro, interviniendo culpa o negligencia, está obligado a reparar el daño causado.'* See fn. 13 above.

[26] Although § 1295 ABGB, like Art. 1382 French Cc, only mentions the infliction of damage *'aus Verschulden'*, its co-regulation § 1294 s. 1 ABGB refers expressly to *'widerrechtliche Handlung'*.

[27] Art. 50 Swiss OR (1881) followed to a large extent Art. 1401 BW (old) (more below). Art. 50 OR (1881) reads: 'Whoever unlawfully causes damage to another person, whether intentionally or negligently, is bound to pay compensation to that person.' Here again, only the element of unlawfulness 'separates the mother (French) legal order from its (Swiss) daughter': Bucher, in: Caroni (ed.), *Das Obligationenrecht 1883–1983*, p. 162.

Civil. They divided *faute* into two distinct parts, unlawfulness and fault (to be dealt with in that order), and thus created the first true law of 'unlawful acts' (see no. 6 above). In 1838 the word *'onregtmatig'* had already been incorporated into Art. 1401 of the old Dutch BW, originally also a repetition of Arts. 1382 and 1383 French Cc, and as a result *'onregtmatigheid'* was distinguished from *'schuld'*.[28] With *'faute'* thus structured, the legislature temporarily regained some of its power: it was the legislature—not the courts in *ad hoc* judgments—which decided what kind of behaviour was to be regarded as unlawful.[29]

The Dutch addition to the text of Art. 1382 French Cc had a lasting effect: it resulted in the legal advantage shifting from the plaintiff to the defendant.[30] This development was adopted in Italy in the twentieth century: Art. 2043 Cc (1942) makes unlawful damage (*'danno ingiusto'*) a prerequisite for a claim of compensation. Thus, with only a few exceptions, Art. 2043 Cc was for a long time applied only in cases of infringement of absolute rights.[31]

16   However, Art. 1401 BW (old) did not really bring about other changes to codification policy in Europe. Only the Portuguese Cc of 1867 had pursued the distinction between unlawfulness and fault before it experienced its final breakthrough in the German BGB. Not only did the Portuguese text—again excepting the Austrian ABGB—contain the most elaborate codification of the law of delict of its time (Arts. 2361–2403) but its basic provisions (Arts. 2361 and 2362 Cc)[32] also deliberately concentrated on the protection of absolute rights (*direitos*). Furthermore,

---

[28] For more details, Asser (-Hartkamp), *Verbintenissenrecht* vol. iii, 9th edn., pp. 32 f.; Schut, *Onrechtmatige daad*, 4th edn., p. 40; and Mertz, *Schutz primärer Vermögensinteressen*, pp. 8–12. Also remarkable for their time are Arts. 1382, 1382a, and 1382b of the *Badisches Landrecht*. Although the *'faute'* of Art. 1382 French Cc was only translated with *'unrechte That'* in Art. 1382, it was further shaped by Arts. 1382a and 1382b, which distinguished between unlawfulness and fault (see e.g. Art. 1382b: 'All (victims) of unlawful acts including unintentionally injured persons have a right to compensation'); see also no. 31 and fn. 137 below. Just as interesting is a project by the Belgian François Laurent, whose Art. 1120 was meant to supplement Art. 1382 Cc with the words *'tout fait illicite de l'homme'* and whose Art. 1122 would then further define the *fait illicite* (vol. iv, pp. 103, 107).

[29] C. Asser, a member of the editing commission, confirms in his *Nederlandsch Burgerlijk Wetboek, vergeleken met het Wetboek Napoleon*, 2nd edn., (1838) p. 488 that this was the reason for the introduction of the term *'unlawful'*.

[30] HR 31 Jan. 1919 *NedJur* 1919 p. 161 = W 1919 no. 10365 (with correction no. 10368) = *WPNR* 1919 no. 2564, p. 64 (case *Lindenbaum/Cohen*) marks the reversal of this development; see no. 24 below.

[31] See so far only Alpa/Bessone, *Trattato* vol. xiv, 2nd edn., p. 77 ('Unlawfulness as the key concept for the classification of typical delictual elements') and Alpa, *Riv.Dir.Com.* 1992, I, pp. 513, 523 (the introduction of the term *danno ingiusto* marked a turning point for Italian legislation in this area). Also v. Bar (-Busnelli), *DeliktsR in Europa, Italien*, p. 14; for more details see nos. 20 ff. below.

[32] Art. 2361: *'Todo aquele que viola ou ofende os direitos de outrem constitui-se na obrigação de indemnizar o lesado por todos os prejuízos que lhe causa.'* Art. 2362: *'Os direitos podem ser ofendidos por factos ou por omissão de factos.'*

Art. 2398 recognized 'infringement of a protective statute'[33] (i.e. breach of statutory duty) as a specific tort, although the circumstances in which it applied were strictly limited. Previously only § 1311 s. 2, 2nd alternative ABGB, had specifically considered this matter. On the whole, however, the law of delict of the Portuguese Cc of 1867 still depended largely on criminal law, as did that of the Spanish Cc of 1889. According to Art. 2365 Portuguese Cc (1867), criminal liability was always accompanied by civil liability, although the reverse was not necessarily true, and '*os casos em que esta última é acompanhada da responsabilidade civil estão especificados na lei*'.

When the German BGB entered the European stage on 1 January 1900,   **17** with the express intention of stealing the limelight from the French Cc, it was able to draw from two foreign examples. The authors of the BGB regarded even the starting point of their French counterparts as unacceptable: '*Es entspreche weder der Tendenz des Entwurfes noch der im deutschen Volke herrschenden Auffassung von der Stellung des Richteramtes, die Lösung solcher Aufgaben, die durch das Gesetz erfolgen müsse, auf die Gerichte abzuwälzen.*'[34] Consequently, as in Art. 1401 Dutch BW (old), they divided '*faute*' into unlawfulness and fault. However, the authors of the BGB went a step further by differentiating between the various characteristics of unlawfulness: the 'infringement of a right' (*Rechtsverletzung*) (§ 823 I BGB), the 'infringement of a protective statute' (*Schutzgesetzverletzung*) (§ 823 II BGB), and the 'violation of *bonos mores*' (*Sittenverstoß*) (§ 826 BGB).[35] The BGB thus divides into '*gattungsmäßig ausgestaltete Haftungsgründe*'[36] what the rest of Europe united in one general clause, following the example set by the French Cc. Finally, a ranking order was established by § 823 I, II, and § 826 BGB. The role of basic regulation was attributed to § 823 I BGB, the most detailed rule.[37] If its preconditions are not fulfilled, the facts of the case may still bring it

---

[33] For further details see v. Lillienskiold, *Aktuelle Probleme des portugiesischen Deliktsrechts*, p. 15.

[34] 'To hand over to the courts the function of solving problems which ought to be solved by statute, corresponds neither to the intention of the draft, nor to the view generally accepted by the German people of the judge's function', Prot. II (1898) p. 771.

[35] Mot. II (1888) p. 726.

[36] 'Typecast causes of action.' Deutsch, *Haftungsrecht*, vol. i, p. 107.

[37] According to which any violation of a right or an 'absolute' legal interest is unlawful. Although § 823 II BGB states that the violated rule must be a statutory one (see Art. 2 EGBGB), it remains for the courts to determine which statutes protect the individual. § 826 BGB, built on the Roman *actio de dolo*, itself practically a general clause, does not even give guidance as to what *bonos mores* is to be based on. Besides, § 826 BGB, like the general clauses of other European codes, does not properly differentiate between the reasons for and the consequences of liability (between *Haftungsgrund* and *Haftungsausfüllung*). *MünchKomm* (-Mertens), 2nd edn., on § 826 BGB no. 51 rightly says: 'damage according to § 826 . . . (is) any pecuniary disadvantage, hence impairment of a legal interest', a view shared by *Staudinger* (-Schäfer) BGB, 12th edn., § 826 no. 81.

within one of the few exceptions provided in § 823 II and § 826 BGB, or in further regulations found in supplementary rules. However, the BGB left no room for doubt when it came to the courts' power to develop an independent judge-made law of delict: their powers were as far as possible to be restricted by means of a code. However, the barrier they built to withstand such further developments of the law was soon to be breached. The German BGB had closed the gates too tightly, just as the leniency of the Code Civil had opened them too widely.

18   Within Europe's codified law, only the BGB provides a basic delictual provision containing a *final list of legally protected interests*. It does not include a person's honour or right to privacy. Furthermore, no other nation, apart from Portugal, opted for such a formal concept of unlawfulness as that established in § 823 BGB.[38] Nevertheless, the concept enshrined in § 823 I BGB, that faultless conduct can be unlawful, justifying injunctive relief, is an approach also accepted in other EU Member States.[39] Faultless conduct can be unlawful e.g. if it was caused by a person lacking civil capacity and, under certain circumstances, even where due care was exercised. In addition, the notion that each violation of an *absolute right*, regardless of how the violation came about, is unlawful[40] leads in most cases to a commendable shifting of the burden of proof *vis-à-vis* legal grounds of justification. Thus the surgeon must prove that the patient gave fully informed consent to the treatment given, or that he explicitly waived explanations. However 'relative rights', such as those arising from a contract, are not protected by § 823 I BGB.[41] Yet it soon became obvious that the concept contained in § 823 I BGB needed a number of important adjustments if it was to survive. The legislators' first mistake was to exclude protection of a person's rights to honour, reputation, and privacy; the second was to give the judiciary no scope for independent decisions in the field of pure economic loss.[42] On the

---

[38] Although various attempts have been made by the courts to adopt the concept of § 823 I BGB in the general clauses of the codes of other nations: for Austria see Karollus, *Schutzgesetzverletzung* pp. 37 ff.; Koziol, *ZEuP* 1995 pp. 359–367. For Italy see no. 20 below.

[39] For Greece see Stathopoulos, *FS Larenz* (1983), pp. 631, 644–646.

[40] Mot. II (1888) p. 726.

[41] BGH 24 Feb. 1954, BGHZ 12 pp. 308, 317–318 and BGH 19 Oct. 1993, *NJW* 1994 p. 128. In the later ruling the judges felt compelled to note that this would mean, given the fundamental nature of § 823 I BGB, that § 826 BGB could not be applied as broadly in practice as might seem possible in theory. The courts of the former GDR had given § 823 I BGB (while it remained in force there) a different meaning: according to OG 27 Sep. 1962, OGZ 9 pp. 206, 208–209, contractual rights fell under the 'other rights' of § 823 I BGB (later also the case for § 332 of the later Cc of the GDR). However, this protection was restricted to the 'immediate injured party', see BG Leipzig 2 Feb. 1984, *NJ* 1985 p. 296.

[42] Only recently an Austrian commentator on legal developments in Germany rightly observed that the *modus operandi* (*rechtstechnisches System*) of the BGB 'must long since be regarded as having failed as far as this issue is concerned': Karollus, *Schutzgesetzverletzung* p. 42.

other hand, those authors who supported the idea that *any* violation of an absolute right should give rise to a presumption that the violation was caused unlawfully (the 'indication of unlawfulness') encountered difficulties where there was no direct causation, e.g. in cases of failure to act.[43] In other words, it is incorrect both to assert that a violation of a right is invariably unlawful, and to rely upon the legal system to knit a sufficiently tight net of protective 'statutes' (§ 823 II in conjunction with Art. 2 EGBGB) to cover all eventualities. Even taking into account the need for a conceptually elegant provision, it should still have been obvious that there are cases where the separation of unlawfulness and fault is not possible,[44] or would at the very least make it even more difficult to achieve an appropriate result.[45]

c. The Basic Provisions of the More Recent Codified Laws

The German BGB underwent its first serious test in Europe in the 1930s **19** when *Greece* started to develop its own Civil Code.[46] On the whole, the BGB fared well.[47] Even the section on unlawful acts was largely adopted by the Greek Cc, including verbatim transplants of some provisions.[48] The aforementioned weaknesses of the German BGB were well known and the authors of the Greek Code departed from the German model where necessary.[49]

---

[43] On the failure to include liability for omissions in § 823 I BGB see v. Bar, *Verkehrspflichten*, pp. 15 ff. Yet the first draft of § 704 BGB which, in not providing a conclusive list of protected interests, more closely resembled a general clause, expressly mentioned omissions: 'If a person has acted unlawfully, or failed to act, whether intentionally or negligently, and thus inflicted damage on another person, and if he must or should have foreseen such damage, he is liable to compensate the other person for the damage caused by such act, regardless of whether the extent of the damage could have been anticipated.'

[44] Particularly when considering the German concept of liability for duties of care, recent discussions have shown that the distinction between 'outer' care (unlawfulness) and 'inner' care (fault) is artificial: see Fabarius, *Äußere und innere Sorgfalt* (1991), *passim*. Furthermore, it is hardly possible to attribute provisions such as § 824 II BGB (protection of reputation as worthy of credit) to either unlawfulness or fault, since a person can only legitimately protect this interest if he has made careful investigations beforehand.

[45] For example, liability of the legal person, which can be handled much more easily by applying the undifferentiated term '*faute*', see Mayer, Gutachten IV for the 17th German Lawyers Day 1884, '*Verhandlungen*' pp. 125, 129; and v. Bar, *FS Kitagawa* (1992) pp. 279, 286 ff.

[46] For more details see: Potamianos, *AID* 4 (1937) pp. 244–313; Macris, *RabelsZ* 9 (1935) pp. 586 ff.; and on the law of obligations Triantaphyllopoulos, *RabelsZ* 10 (1936) pp. 53 ff.

[47] For more details see the study by Plagianakos, *Die Entstehung des Griechischen Zivilgesetzbuches* (1963), esp. pp. 68–80; and Mantzoufas, *Das griechische Zivilgesetzbuch*, p. 11.

[48] For more detail see Gogos, *AcP* 149 (1944) pp. 78, 93; J. v. Gierke, *ZHR* 115 (1952) pp. 185, 189. See also nos. 36 ff. and 42 ff. below.

[49] See *Schedion Astikou Kodikos*, vol. ii, p. 10 (extract from the protocols concerning the discussions of the editorial committee, meeting of 30 Nov. 1930): the committee member Triantaphyllopoulos convinced the majority not to follow the German system here, as proposed by Professor Demertzis, on the grounds that 'the German system cannot be called successful since it is impossible to list all delicts in advance'. A general clause would therefore be necessary. See Soutis, *SavZ Rom.Abt.* 78 (1961) pp. 355, 385.

For example, the basic provision of the Greek Cc reads 'a person who through his fault has caused damage to another in a manner contrary to statute shall be liable for compensation'. Thus Art. 914 Greek Cc perpetuates the differentiation between unlawfulness and fault.[50] In contrast to § 823 I BGB, however, but in line with Art. 41 Swiss OR of 30 Mar. 1911,[51] the proposal to limit the scope of Art. 914 Greek Cc explicitly to absolute rights and legally protected interests was abandoned.[52] Moreover, although Art. 914 Greek Cc may appear from its structure and wording to be a *blanket* (or framework) *provision*, depending on *external* regulations for implementation, this did not prevent the Greek judicial system from treating it as a directly applicable *general clause*. It may be considered an established fact that Art. 914 Greek Cc refers not only to abstract standards of conduct, 'special' legal provisions designed for specific situations in life, and provisions defining the scope of absolute rights and legally protected interests. Art. 914 also covers provisions prohibiting the abuse of a legal right (Art. 281 Greek Cc), and the duty to act in good faith (Art. 288 Greek Cc). Thus the courts developed from the legal system as a whole a general 'statutory' prohibition against causing damage to others, and implemented it through Art. 914 Greek Cc; accordingly, any unlawful act is contrary to statute. A person acts unlawfully if his or her conduct violates the spirit of the legal system. Hence, one can base the general 'statutory' duty not negligently to inflict

---

[50] This is the prevailing opinion today. See e.g. Georgiades, *FS Larenz* (1983) p. 181; Mantzoufas, *Das Griechische Zivilgesetzbuch*, p. 22 ('Hence not only contrary to law but also negligently'); Litzeropoulos, *Stoicheia Enochikou Dikaiou* vol. ii, p. 352; Filios, *Enochiko Dikaio* vol. ii (2), 3rd edn., pp. 17 ff.; Stathopoulos, *Geniko Enochiko Dikaio* vol. A1, 2nd edn., pp. 257 ff.; Georgiades/Stathopoulos (-Georgiades), *Greek Cc* vol. iv, p. 699; and Deliyannis, *FS Michaelides-Nouaros*, vol. A, pp. 303, 309. The proposal to strike out the phrase 'contrary to statute' as redundant had already been rejected by the editing committee: *Schedion Astikou Kodikos*, vol. ii, p. 381, no. 91, and only Vavouskos still argues that unlawfulness cannot be treated independently; Vavouskos, *FS Michaelides-Nouaros* vol. i, p. 87; see also id. *EEN* 22 (1955) pp. 82, 83. Bosdas has always been of the opinion that negligent infliction of damage alone indicates unlawfulness, hence will be unlawful unless justifying circumstances exist; Bosdas, *EEN* 14 (1947) pp. 430, 432; and Zepos, *Enochikon Dikaion* vol. ii(2), 2nd edn., pp. 717, 731. However, this rather theoretical dispute is of little practical relevance; see text above.

[51] The text of which has remained practically identical to Art. 50 OR (1881) (see fn. 27 above). It reads: 'A person who unlawfully inflicts damage on another person, whether intentionally or negligently, is obliged to compensate for such damage.' However, it is uncertain that the authors of the Greek Cc knew at the time that they were duplicating Art. 41 OR. It seems more likely that Professor Triantaphyllopoulos was thinking of the 'broad' system of Arts. 1382, 1383 French Cc, as reported in *Schedion Astikou Kodikos*, vol. ii, p. 7; see also Zepos, *Rev.int.dr.comp.* 2 (1950) pp. 297, 301; Triantaphyllopoulos loc. cit. (fn. 46) p. 65; and Gogos loc. cit. (fn. 48) p. 87. However, the wording of Art. 914 Greek Cc more closely resembles the Swiss than the French model; see Potamianos, *AID* 4 (1937) pp. 244, 270.

[52] Georgidades rightly saw this as 'one of the major differences between the Greek Cc and the German BGB'; Georgiades, *Anspruchskonkurrenz*, p 56. See also Kapsalis, *Persönlichkeitsrecht und Persönlichkeitsschutz*, pp. 14 ff.

damage upon a person's legally protected interests (Art. 330 Greek Cc) directly on Art. 914 Greek Cc, and this is precisely what the Areopag did.[53] As a result, liability for failure to act fitted effortlessly into the system,[54] and an adequate basis for the protection of pure economic interests, not specifically dealt with in the Code itself, was established.[55] The same can be said of the protection of specially named rights (i.e. Arts. 58, 60, 920, 921, 932, and, until 1983, Art. 1453 [now rescinded][56] Greek Cc) as well as a general right (Arts. 57, 59 Greek Cc) to personal dignity and autonomy.[57] To a foreign observer things appear to have gone too far, with the Greek courts basing too many claims on the right of personality, far exceeding the lengths to which any other European nation has gone.[58]

The authors of the *Italian* Cc, developed in 1942 and so a contemporary **20** of the Greek Cc, also sought a compromise between the French and German Civil Codes. Arts. 1151 and 1152 of the old Ital. Cc were

---

[53] See Areopag 967/1973 *NoB* 22 (1974) pp. 505 f.; and CA Athens 2510/1975 *NoB* 23 (1975) p. 674. According to these rulings, a damaging act is unlawful 'if it breaches the general duty of Art. 914 Greek Cc not to inflict any damage upon a person through negligent conduct'. Areopag 81/1991 *EllDik* 32 (1991) p. 1215 drew the same conclusion, albeit using another methodological approach: 'Art. 5 § 1 of the constitution in conjunction with Arts. 200, 281, 297, 298, 914 Greek Cc form the basis for the principle that every act or omission which results in negligently inflicted damage compels the tortfeasor to compensate such damage. This obligation arises not only if the act or omission infringes a specific legal provision, but also whenever the general spirit of the legal system, which requires that all conduct must be within the boundaries of *bonos mores*, is violated.' See also CA Salonica 2901/1987, *Arm.* 1988 p. 765; and Potamianos, loc. cit. (fn. 46), according to whom Art. 534 of the draft (= Art. 914 Greek Cc) was intended to categorize an act as unlawful if it violated 'a general or special provision of the code'.

[54] On the arguments for a general duty of care see e.g. Areopag 1891/1984 *EEN* 52 (1985) p. 754 (an omission is unlawful if an act could reasonably have been expected according to the principle of good faith); and CA Salonica 2901/1987 *Arm.* 1988 p. 765 (Art. 914 Greek Cc contains the requirement of *nemimem laedere*).

[55] See CA Athens 3178/1982, *NoB* 31 (1983) p. 519 (causing a power failure was interpreted as a violation of a tenant's contractual right to be supplied with electricity and was considered sufficient cause for liability under Art. 914 Greek Cc). The reasons given in Areopag 1891/1984 loc. cit. (in the same case) were admittedly different.

[56] On the consequences for divorce law of the abolition of this 'claim to satisfaction' see Papachristos, *NoB* 31 (1983) pp. 933 ff.; Karakatsanes, *Wandlungen des griechischen Scheidungsrechtes*, pp. 103–104.

[57] On this issue see esp.: Kapsalis, *Persönlichkeitsrecht und Persönlichkeitsschutz, passim*; Zepos, *FS v. Caemerer*, pp. 1129–1139.

[58] See e.g. Areopag 776/1977 *NoB* 27 (1979) p 561 (the right to use a piece of river bank in public use was based on the basic personal rights); CA Athens 807/1956 *NoB* 4 (1956) p. 624 (preventing a person from entering the premises of a racing club); CFI Athens 5980/1976 *NoB* 24 (1976) p. 1117 (landlady trespassed on tenant's verandah); CA Athens 4248/1992, *EllDik* 34 (1993) p. 224 (unlawful transfer of an employee within the office); CA Crete 65/1963 *NoB* 12 (1964) p. 211 (removal of electricity masts); or CFI Salonica 799/1968 *Arm.* 23 (1969) p. 711 (building deprived its neighbours of fresh air and light). Contrarily, BGH 21 June 1977, *NJW* 1977 pp. 2264, 2265 (it is an established fact that public use is not one of the 'other rights' under § 823 I BGB).

verbatim copies of Arts. 1382 and 1383 French Cc (see no. 15 above), whereas the delictual provisions (Arts 2043–2059) of the new codification are headed *'dei fatti illeciti'*.[59] Thus they moved tentatively closer to the German BGB.[60] Yet Art. 2043 Cc, unlike § 823 I BGB, does not provide a complete list of protected interests, nor is the term unlawfulness applied in the text of Art. 2043 Cc[61] to an *act* resulting in damage, but refers to an element directly related to the *damage* itself: compensatable is *'qualunque fatto doloso o colposo, che cagiona ad altri un danno ingiusto'*. Not only is this construction unique within Europe (as far as this author is aware)[62] but it also proved initially irritating. However, the term 'unlawful damage' is used simply to clarify that not all damage suffered will be compensated, only damage caused *non iure* and *contra ius*. In other words, only that damage will be compensated which results from an unlawful act.[63] In turn, the unlawfulness of an act depends in many cases on the consequences resulting from it. Not only does the unlawfulness of damage in a system opposed to the enumeration of unlawful acts become an *'elemento necessario alla qualificazione dell'atto come illecito'*[64] but it also alters the general understanding of the term

---

[59] Since the Italian law speaks of *'fatti illeciti'* (unlawful events) rather than *'atti illeciti'* (unlawful acts) (see the Italian wording of the heading before Art. 41 Swiss OR), a number of authors believe that it has, from the outset, been chiefly concerned with the interests of the victim. Furthermore, they claim that the Italian wording was intended to pave the way for the introduction of liability without fault. See: Visintini, *La responsabilità civile* (1967) p. 2; Rodotà, *Il problema della responsabilità civile* (1964) pp. 117 ff.; Rescigno, *Manuale* pp. 642–643; Alpa/Bessone, *Responsabilità civile*, vol. i, 2nd edn., p. 214, who share this view. However, the prevailing opinion is that the phrase *'fatti illeciti'* is to be read as *'atti illeciti'*: Cian/Trabucci, *Commentario breve*, Art. 2043 Cc note I 2 (*'osservazione comune e tradizionale'*). See also: Levi, *Responsabilità civile e responsabilità oggettiva*, p. 2; and RR no. 264 (in Pandolfelli, *et al.*, *Codice Civile*, p. 677) (*'Fonte di responsabilità può essere il comportamento della persona [fatto proprio]'*).

[60] See Castronovo, *La nuova responsabilità civile*, p. 113; id., *Problema e sistema nel danno da prodotti*, pp. 118 ff.

[61] Although the article's *heading* speaks again of the *'risarcimento per fatto illecito'*. In addition, the term *'fatto illecito'* is also used in Arts. 2048 (liability for adolescents) and 2049 Cc (liability for employees).

[62] The principle of *'danno ingiusto'* used to figure in Art. 28 Portuguese Act no. 32171 of 29 July 1942, where it regulated the liability of medical doctors and assisting personnel: see Pessoa Jorge, *Pressupostos da Responsabilidade Civil*, p. 295; Antunes Varela, *Obrigações em Geral*, vol. i, 7th edn., no. 137 (pp. 521–523). It was removed when its authors realized that unlawfulness is relevant only to the cause of action, not to the consequences of liability: Antunes Varela loc. cit.

[63] See Corte Cost. 14 July 1986, no. 184, *Foro it.* 1986, I, pp. 2054, 2059 (in conjunction with the note by Ponzanelli): *'Ogni danno è . . . conseguenza dell'atto . . . illecito'*; also the references in Schlüchter, *Haftung für gefährliche Tätigkeit*, pp. 75 ff.

[64] Castronovo, *La nuova responsabilità civile*, p. 115. In agreement, di Majo, *La tutela civile dei diritti* 2nd edn., p. 192; and Tucci, *Riv.dir.com.* 1967 I pp. 229, 252 (an unlawful act is the violation of a duty of care which damages an interest, the protection of which is the objective of that duty).

'*danno*'. In Germany, for example, where the notion of damage *per se* is unknown, one must differentiate between the unlawful act and the loss (*Schaden*),[65] whereas there are Italian cases in which the mere infringement of a legally protected interest is seen as damage.[66]

This method of relating a breach of duty to the damage suffered is **21** reminiscent of the concept of unlawfulness on which § 823 I BGB is based. It may also explain why Art. 2043 Ital. Cc was in the past interpreted as protecting only absolute patrimonial and personal rights.[67] '*Danno ingiusto*' was for some time merely regarded as another form of '*lesione di un diritto assoluto*'. It was a long time before the '*lesione di un interesse giuridicamente rilevante*' was understood to include damage sustained *contra ius*.[68] The starting point in Italy (contemporaneously with a similar development in England)[69] was liability for information issued

---

[65] BGH 8 May 1989, *DB* 1989 pp. 1666, 1667 (dealing with a contractual claim, although the principle also applies here).

[66] A position rightly held by Tamburrino, *Begriff des Vermögensschadens*, p. 13; and elsewhere: de Cupis, *Il danno*, vol. i, 3rd edn., p. 19; Schlesinger, *JUS* 1960 pp. 336 ff.; Rodotà, *Problema della responsabilità civile*, p. 173; Galgano, *Contratto e Impresa* 1985 pp. 1, 7. This understanding of damage had serious consequences when it came to recognition of the '*danno biologico*': see Part 6 I nos. 573–574 below.

[67] See e.g. Cass. 26 Sep. 1970, n. 1717, *Giust.civ.Mass.* 1970 no. 1717 (incorrect entry in telephone directory; no delictual liability). For details see Alpa/Bessone, *Atipicità*, vol. i, 2nd edn., p. 428. See also e.g. Benucci, *Responsabilità civile* p. 17, who, as late as 1955, defined '*l'atto illecito*' as '*come un comportamento dell'uomo (positivo o anche meramente omissivo) da cui deriva una lesione ad un diritto soggettivo assoluto e che, di regola, si qualifica ulteriormente con l'elemento subiettivo della colpa*'. Hardly any information survives on the genesis of Art. 2043 Cc. Although RCR p. 24 (in Pandofelli *et al.*, *Codice civile* p. 677) does point towards a reading of Art. 882 of the draft text (= Art. 2043 Cc) as a general clause, it also states that one would achieve the same results with this general clause as one would, albeit '*con minor chiarezza*', by applying the German BGB. For literature in German see esp. Ferrari, *ZfS* 1992 pp. 2 f.; id., *RabelsZ* 56 (1992) pp. 757, 762; id., *Jahrbuch.f.ital. R.* 8 (1995) pp. 191, 196–198; Schlüchter, *Haftung für gefährliche Tätigkeit*, pp. 73 ff.; Rosenkranz, *Haftung für Schadenszufügung*, pp. 17 ff.; v. Bar (-Busnelli), *DeliktsR in Europa, Italien*, p. 14; Dörner, *WM* 1977 pp. 962, 965; and Heldrich, *Allgemeine Rechtsgrundsätze*, pp. 34–38.

[68] Cass. 4 May 1982, no 2765, *Giur.it.* 1983 I, 1, 786 (789); Cass.sez.un. 6 Dec. 1982, *Giur.it.* 1984, I, 1, 1771 ('The legal basis of civil liability is the term *danno*, which is no longer looked upon from the point of view of its consequences, i.e. as the difference in the financial situation of the victim before and after damage has occurred, as was previously the case; but rather as an independent . . . fact of the case, consisting in the violation of a legally protected interest. *Danno* is defined as a violation of "inter-private" interests . . . The adjective "*ingiusto*" which qualifies the "*danno*" emphasizes the fact that such a violation must be *contra ius*, i.e. it must infringe a protected interest.') Trib. Verona 13 Dec. 1988, no. 1871, *Giur.it.* 1990, I, 2, 135; Trib. Verona 15 Nov. 1990 *Foro.it.* 1991 I, 261; Visintini, *Fatti illeciti*, vol. i p. 80; Schlüchter loc. cit. p. 76. Alpa/Bessone in their *Trattato*, vol. xiv, 2nd edn., p. 80, interpret the term *danno ingiusto* today as a kind of 'general clause within a general clause'. This interpretation leaves enormous scope for the judge's discretion. Franzoni, on the other hand, pursues another line of thought: see Franzoni, *Fatti illeciti*, pp. 189–190.

[69] *Hedley Byrne & Co. Ltd. v. Heller & Partners Ltd.* [1964] AC 465 (HL).

by bank employees[70] and members of other professions concerned with the finances of others.[71] This expanded to cases where an employer suffers damage through the injury of an employee, where compensation was awarded by the application of Art. 2043 Italian Cc.[72] The provision was then applied in cases concerning loss of production due to an interrupted electricity supply.[73] The peak was finally reached in 1982 in the *De Chirico* case, dealing with a false certificate of authenticity for a painting. The judges of the *Corte di Cassazione* stated that they had 'no doubt' that the 'infringement' (*lesione*) of the 'right to integrity of one's assets' (*il diritto all'intregrità del proprio patrimonio*) could be a cause of action.[74] Thus did the Italian judiciary bring Art. 2043 Cc into line with its actual wording. Since Art. 2043 Cc was no longer merely a '*norma secondaria o sanzionatoria*' but had become a '*norma primaria*', there was no further need to rely on other rules to award compensation.[75]

Thus, after a delay of over a hundred years, a development took place

---

[70] See esp.: App. Bari 13 Apr. 1959 and Cass. 10 Apr. 1961, no. 762, *BB* 1961, II, 171 (note Buttaro); and App. Bologna 28 July 1961 and Cass. 30 Oct. 1963, n. 2909, *BB* 1963, II, 500, 501 (note Bile), all concerning banks' liabilities to one another for issuing incorrect information about account balances. However, see also Cass. 1 Aug. 1992, no. 9167, *Giur.it.* 1993, I, 1268, 1269: no liability of the bank to the payee of a cheque, the bank having confirmed the credit-worthiness of the payer's account. The bank was unaware and could not have known of the freezing of the debtor's assets due to bankruptcy, since this had been found only shortly before the information was issued.

[71] App. Palermo 11 June 1959, *Foro.pad.* 1960, I, 1420 in conjunction with an essay by Sacco: false information on the progress of a building site, rendering the guarantor liable to the bank which granted the loan. As a result the person/institution issuing the information was held liable to the guarantor, having violated his '*diritto di credito*'.

[72] Cass. 26 Jan. 1971, no. 174, *Foro.it.* 1971, I, 1285 (note by Busnelli) (the *Meroni* case) departing from Cass. 4 Jul. 1953, no. 2095, *Foro.it.* 1953, I, 1086. See also Cass. (sez. un.) 12 Nov. 1988, no. 6132, *Foro.it.* 1989, I, 742. For similar cases from the French jurisdiction see currently only Colmar 20 Apr. 1955, *D.* 1956 *Jur.* 723 (injury to a footballer; club entitled to compensation); and Cass.civ. 12 June 1987, Bull.civ. 1987, II, no. 128 (p. 73) (damage suffered by a business due to a partner's illness).

[73] Cass. 24 June 1972, n. 2135, *Foro.it.* 1973, I, 99.

[74] Cass. 4 May 1982, n. 2765, *Giur.it.* 1983, I, 786, 788; Cass. 19 Dec. 1985, n. 6506, *Foro.it.* 1986, I, 383, 389; and Cass. 25 July 1986, n. 4755, *NGCC* 1987, I, 386 m. Note by Libertini ('*la norma generale sulla repressione dell'illecito aquiliano [art. 2043 cod.civ.] tutela . . . il diritto di ogni cittadino alla propria integrità patrimoniale, che viene lesa dal . . . comportamento illegìttimo*'). For detailed discussion of this issue see Castronovo, *Riv.crit.dir.priv.* 1989, pp. 539, 551 ff. See also Cass. 13 Jan. 1993, n. 343, *Resp.Civ. e Prev.* 1993 p. 808 (the bank of a payer failed to return bad cheques in good time to the payee's bank: contractual and delictual liability to the payee's bank which had honoured the cheques); Trib. Milan 9 Nov. 1992, *Giur.it.* 1993, I, 2, 576; and 24 Feb. 1994, *NGCC* 1995, I, p. 179 (delictual and contractual liability of a shop assistant, who carelessly examined a cheque and guarantee card, to the account-holder from whom the cheque had been stolen).

[75] An impressive argument in favour of this proposition is found in Schlesinger, *JUS* 1960 pp. 336, 337, 342 (above quotations taken from this article). See also Rodotà, *Problema della responsabilità civile*, pp. 21 ff.

in Italy similar to that in France in the nineteenth century.[76] The *'principio di atipicità'*, according to which neither an infringement of one of a *numerus clausus* of statutory duties, nor one of a *numerus clausus* of absolute rights, is necessary to establish liability, prevailed. This was accompanied and supported by similar developments in the field of protection of right to personal dignity, autonomy, and privacy. Although honour has always been protected by Art. 2043 Cc, it took the *Corte di Cassazione* until 1975 to establish sufficient protection of the right to privacy. The court developed an 'independent right to confidentiality of personal affairs',[77] soon supplemented by the 'right to personal identity'.[78]

In 1966 Portugal also replaced its nineteenth-century codified law.[79] **22** The new law of delict of the Portuguese *Código Civil* was chiefly developed by *Vaz Serra*. Like the more modern codes of other European nations, it is marked by a certain 'legal eclecticism'.[80] European codified law was examined for its strengths and weaknesses, and provisions felt to be suitable for Portuguese law were adopted and combined with national legal traditions. The concept and design of the Portuguese basic delictual provision (Art. 483 I Cc) reveals a strong German influence. At first sight it appears to consist entirely of a combination of the two subsections of § 823 BGB.[81] According to Art. 483 I Cc, a person is only obliged to compensate damage if he negligently and 'unlawfully violates another's rights or a legal provision aimed at the protection of

---

[76] Arts. 1382 and 1383 French Cc were originally also understood as liability norms applying to interference with absolute rights, or to the violation of statutory standards of conduct: Huc, *Commentaire théorique et pratique*, vol. viii (1895) p. 536; Toullier, *Le droit civil français*, vol. xi (1824) no. 121, p. 153 (*'Les actes nuisibles aux droits d'autrui sont naturellement divisés en deux grandes classes; qui les comprennent tous, sans exception: Attentats à la personne ou aux droits personnels d'autrui; Attentats à sa propriété ou à ses droits réels'*); Willems, *Rev.gén.dr.* 1895 pp. 110, 135 ff.; Hennings, *Persönliche Haftung und Mitverschulden des Kindes* (1992) p. 30; and, on Belgium, Van Gerven, *Verbintenissenrecht*, vol. ii, 3rd edn., p. 69. Only in conjunction with delictual protection of extra-marital cohabitation (causing the death of the breadwinner) Cass.crim. 20 Feb. 1863, D. 1864.1.99 (102) clearly stated *'que l'art. 1382 . . . ne limite en rien, ni la nature du fait dommageable, ni la nature du dommage éprouvé'*. In this century Cass.civ. 27 July 1937, *DP* 1938 1.5, said again: 'le demandeur d'une indemnité délictuelle ou quasi-délictuelle doit justifier non d'un dommage quelconque mais de la lésion d'un intérêt légitime, juridiquement protégé', but the discrepancy was corrected by Cass.mixte 27 Feb. 1970, *D.* 1970 Jur. 201, when it said: *'Ainsi le préjudice peut être défini comme la lésion d'un intérêt sous la seule réserve qu'il ne soit ni illicite ni immoral'*. See fn 72 above.

[77] Cass. 27 May 1975, n. 2129, *Foro.it.* 1976, I, 2895 (*'diritto alla riservatezza'*). See also App. Milan 28 Aug. 1960, *Foro.it.* 1961, I, 43; Pret. Rome 25 May 1985, *Dir.inf.* 1985 p. 988; and Pret. Milan 27 May 1986, *Dir.inf.* 1986 p. 924.

[78] Cass. 22 June 1985, n. 3769, *Foro.it.* 1985, I, 2211 (*'diritto all'identità personale'*). See also the ruling in the *Panella* case, Pret. Turin 30 May 1979, printed in Alpa/Bessone, *Atipicità*, vol. ii (1), 2nd edn., pp. 149–155.

[79] For a detailed account of the history of the Portuguese Cc see v. Lillienskiold, *Aktuelle Probleme des portugiesischen Deliktsrechts*, pp. 22–26. See also fn 16 above.

[80] Markesinis, in: Hartkamp *et al.* (edd.), *Towards a European Civil Code*, pp. 285, 290.

[81] Sinde Monteiro, *Responsabilidade por conselhos*, p. 177.

others'.[82] Ergo the Portuguese Cc is based on the principle that a person only commits a delict if either an absolute right[83] is infringed, or a statute defining further private interests and protecting them from unlawful acts is violated (see Art. 1 II Port. Cc). Hence a tortious act is not committed simply because an interest or a standard of conduct is violated, but only if the damage suffered or the interest itself falls within the protection of that standard of conduct.[84] Furthermore, according to the Portuguese basic delictual provision, the standard of conduct must be prescribed by statute; the courts themselves are not a source of law. One must therefore conclude that Art. 483 Cc does *not* serve as a general clause. This in turn means that damage to pure economic interests is generally *not* compensatable unless a protective provision obtains, which will generally but not always be a criminal provision.[85] The authors of the Portuguese law of delict would not accept even a partial general clause in the fashion of § 826 BGB.[86] In addition, the commentators are still divided over whether the 'right to carry on an established trade or business' is covered by the delictual provisions.[87]

---

[82] '*Aquele que, com dolo o mera culpa, violar ilicitamente o direito de outrem ou qualquer disposição legal destinada a proteger interesses alheios fica obrigado a indemnizar o lesado pelos danos resultantes da violação.*'

[83] The history of the legislation itself demonstrates that only an absolute right can be understood as 'a right of another' under Art. 483 Port. Cc, see e.g. Vaz Serra, *BolMinJust* 92 (1960) no. 13 (pp. 37, 112), and this remains the prevailing opinion. See for many Antunes Varela, *Obrigações em Geral*, vol. i, 7th edn., no. 138 (p. 524); Sinde Monteiro, *Responsabilidade por conselhos*, p. 182; Almeida Costa, *Obrigações*, 4th edn., p. 369; Martins de Almeida, *Manual de Acidentes*, 3rd edn., p. 203; and Pires de Lima / Antunes Varela, *Cc anotado*, vol. i, 4th edn., note 5a. Possibly of different opinion: Pessoa Jorge, *Pressupostos da Responsabilidade civil*, p. 301.

[84] Neto/Martins, *Código civil*, 7th edn., Art. 483 note 3 (with a reference to a work by Pereira Coelho, unobtainable for this author); Antunes Varela, *Obrigações em Geral*, vol i, 7th edn., no. 140 (pp. 529 ff.), and Almeida Costa, *Direito das Obrigações*, 4th edn., pp. 369 ff. For a case on this issue: RP 19 May 1981, *BolMinJust* 310 (1981) p. 343.

[85] Sinde Monteiro, *Responsabilidade por conselhos*, pp. 176–177.

[86] Although Sinde Monteiro (loc. cit.) pp. 545–582 has sought to interpret Art. 334 Port. Cc as similar to § 826 BGB, no attempts seem to have been made by the judiciary to make use of it.

[87] On the right to carry on an established trade or business see no. 47 below. There are no Portuguese rulings discussing this issue. Regarding literature on the subject, the author knows only of Vaz Serra, *BolMinJust* 92 (1960) no. 15 (pp. 121–126); and Sinde Monteiro, *BolMinJust* loc. cit. pp. 206–222, who, after an extensive study of the situation in Germany, proposed the recognition of a '*direito sobre uma empresa industrial*' as a right 'similar to the right to property'. Other authors (fns. 83, 84) are silent on the issue. However, one must bear in mind that in Portugal the right to personal dignity, autonomy, and privacy applies in a number of circumstances where in Germany the right to carry on an established trade or business would apply (see nos. 23 and 49 below). Furthermore, the Portuguese judges have hitherto generally been able to find suitable protective laws, see e.g. RC 12 Jan. 1993, *CJ* XVIII (1993–1) p. 17 (the entry of a freelancer in a telephone directory was made two years late; liability was established by reference to an internal administrative regulation), and Procuradoria-Geral da República 31 Aug. 1979 and 8 July 1982, *BolMinJust* 294 (1980) pp. 87, 94 and *BolMinJust* 325 (1983) pp. 247, 255 (the latter includes a general discussion of liability in cases of excessive strike actions). Simple cases of damage to property of course pose no problem: RL 7 May 1987, *CJ* XII (1987–3) p. 80 (rupture of a water pipe, *danos em estabelecimentos comerciais*).

As for liability for incorrect information[88] and failure to act, the Portuguese legislators have adhered to the principle that only a violation of pre-existing rights and obligations can incur liability: according to Art. 486 Cc, simple omissions incur liability only if the tortfeasor was under a duty to act, imposed either by statute or contract.[89] A proposal by Vaz Serra during the drafting process to frame Art. 486 Cc so as to include a general duty of care was rejected.[90] The conclusion that Portugal has ignored developments in this direction in other Member States is justified only to a limited extent, if at all. The liability lacunae left by Art. 486 Cc are in most cases closed by Art. 493 I Cc, imposing general 'liability for risks arising from dangerous property, real and personal' for presumed breaches of a duty to control, which effectively introduces liability for failure to act into this area of Portuguese law.[91] Nevertheless, an examination of the relevant rulings reveals that the courts are still trying to base liability for failure to act when risks arise through dangerous property on independent statutory duties, i.e. statutory duties found outside the delictual part of the code. To give two examples, the duty to illuminate a broken-down trailer at night was found not to arise directly from Art. 493 I Cc, but rather from Art. 483 Cc in conjunction with Art. 20 IV *Código da Estrada*.[92] Further, the liability of local electricity suppliers for badly maintained public cables which caused a shop to burn down was found to be based on a specific statute.[93]

---

[88] In cases of 'simple advice', Art. 485 Port. Cc leaves liability for an intentional misstatement under Art. 483 I Cc unaffected. On the issue of a negligent misstatement Art. 485 establishes that a person is only liable if he has 'accepted liability for information issued, or if a *statutory duty* to show due care when furnishing information has been grossly violated' (italics added).

[89] The text of Art. 486 reads: '*As simples omissões dão lugar à obrigação de reparar os danos, quando, independentemente dos outros requisitos legais, havia, por força da lei ou de negócio jurídico, o dever de praticar o acto omitido.*' 'Simple omissions' are true 'failure to act' delicts. They are complemented by the false 'failure to act delicts', the *comissões por omissão*. If an ordinary citizen does not rescue a drowning person, he is liable only if his failure to act constitutes a crime: whereas if a policeman does not try to prevent violent riots, he can be liable for damage to property even though he has committed no crime, see Martins de Almeida, *Manual de Acidentes*, 3rd edn., p. 210.

[90] Vaz Serra suggested the introduction of an Art. 486 II Cc: '*Aquele que abre uma fonte de perigos tem o dever de adoptar as cautelas indespensáveis para os impedir, mesmo que não sejam impostas pelos regulamentos administrativos*' (wording here according to Martins de Almeida, *Manual de Acidentes*, 3rd edn., p. 213, who rightly states on p. 211 that through Art. 486 Cc, '*estão excluídos os casos de deveres impostos pela moral social ou pela solidariedade humana em geral*').

[91] See esp. Antunes Varela, note in STJ 26 Mar. 1980, *RLJ* 114 (1980) pp. 40–41, 72, 77–79; id., in: Pires de Lima/Antunes Varela, *Cc anotado*, vol. i, 4th edn., Art. 486 note 3; id., *Obrigações em Geral*, vol. i, 7th edn., p. 543; Menezes Cordeiro, *Obrigações*, vol. ii, pp. 835–836; and Sinde Monteiro, *Responsabilidade por conselhos*, pp. 312–314. As for judicial rulings, see e.g. RL 7 May 1987, *CJ* XII (1987-3) pp. 80, 81. On Art. 493 Cc see also no. 121 below.

[92] RL 14 Dec. 1973, *BolMinJust* 232 (1974) p. 166.

[93] STJ 5 June 1985, *BolMinJust* 348 (1985) p. 397. See also RL 13 Oct. 1992, *BolMinJust* 420 (1992) p. 640 (liability of an autonomous province for failing to erect warning signs).

Furthermore, since Art. 493 I Cc was never intended to cover liability for third parties, such liability can be imposed only by statutory or contractual duties. Hence, for example, a psychiatric hospital's duty to prevent its mentally handicapped in-patients from escaping and harming others was based on the *'força do negócio jurídico do internamento no Hospital'* in conjunction with statutory provisions dealing with the running of such hospitals.[94]

23   In conclusion, although the Portuguese law of delict appears rather conservative in some areas, it nevertheless reacted very 'positively' to a number of recent developments concerning the principles of liability law. A development of particular interest to foreign commentators is the incorporation of liability for *culpa in contrahendo*, aimed primarily at the protection of pure economic interests. Although Art. 227 II Cc is regarded as dealing with contractual liability,[95] the connection to the law of delict is obvious. For example, the limitation of actions in Art. 227 II refers to the relevant delictual provision, Art. 498 Cc. However, to understand the true scope of Art. 483 I Cc one must realize that, unlike § 823 I BGB, it does not list a *numerus clausus* of (patrimonial and personal) rights. The authors of Art. 483 I Port. Cc deliberately avoided such an enumeration. Consequently, Art. 483 I Port. Cc can only be fully understood by reference to the provisions of the general part of the code where rights to personal dignity, autonomy, and privacy (*direitos da personalidade*, Arts. 70 ff.) are established.[96] In this respect Art. 483 I Port. Cc and § 823 I BGB are clearly different: the 'rights of personality' of the Portuguese Cc include the right to prevent others from using one's name (Art. 72), the right to prevent others from using one's pseudonym (Art. 74), protection of confidential recordings (Arts. 75–78), rights over one's photographic image (Art. 79), protection of privacy (Art. 80: *direito à reserva sobre a intimidade da vida privada*), and the protection of one's good

---

[94] STJ 25 July 1985, *BolMinJust* 349 (1985) pp. 516, 519. See also RC 12 Jan. 1993 (fn. 87 above) which is similarly structured. For a further instructive ruling see RL 15 Nov. 1988, *CJ* XIII (1988–5) p. 112: a woman left her 14- and 15-year old sons with their grandmother while visiting the USA. The boys broke into a neighbouring house and destroyed the contents. Grandmother not liable as she had concluded no 'contract to supervise' with her daughter. When she agreed to look after her grandchildren, there was no intention to create a legal obligation.

[95] Neto/Martins, *Código civil*, 7th edn., Art. 227 no. 3; see also RL 17 Nov. 1981, *CJ* VI (1981–5) p. 147.

[96] Antunes Varela, *Obrigações em Geral*, vol. i, 7th edn., nos. 138–140 (e.g. p. 532 fn. 2) is of the opinion that only the rights of personality listed in Arts. 72–80 Cc are 'rights of others' in accordance with Art. 483 I, 1st alt. Cc. Since he believes that this does not include the right to privacy or other aspects of private life (freedom, health, life), these interests would only be protected by the criminal law (Art. 483 I, 2nd alt. Cc: protective laws). However, his thesis has not been favourably received. See (in an earlier edn.) v. Lillienskiold, *Aktuelle Probleme des portugiesischen Deliktsrechts*, pp. 34 ff.; see also STJ 28 Apr. 1977, *BolMinJust* 266 (1977) p. 165; STJ 4 July 1978, *BolMinJust* 279 (1978) p. 124.

reputation (*bom nome*). The last has been complemented by the tort of endangering a person's economic reputation, provided by Art. 484 Cc (*ofensa do crédito*). Some of these rights can even, under Art. 71 Cc, be protected *post mortem*. For the *Código Civil*, the right to privacy and other aspects of personal life are all legally protected interests. Art. 70 I Cc states: '*A lei protege os indivíduos contra qualquer ofensa ilícita ou ameaça de ofensa à sua personalidade física ou moral.*' It thus embraces not only the 'right to life' (*direito à vida*)[97] and to physical integrity, health, freedom, and honour, but also allows for progressive updating of the definition of legally protected personal interests. According to the *Supremo Tribunal de Justiça*, the 'right to repose and recovery' (*direito ao repouso essencial à existência*)[98] is just 'one example' of such updating.[99] Thus, Art. 483 I in conjunction with Art. 70 I Cc has considerable potential for development.[100] The legislator evidently attempted to draft Art. 483 I Cc so as to correspond with basic constitutional rights,[101] and from this point of view Art. 483 I Cc seeeks only to protect 'pre-existing' rights.

Although one cannot deny the achievements of the Portuguese codified **24** law of delict, it is nevertheless outdated compared with the new Dutch law, developments in which have led to the recently (1 January 1992) enforced Art. 6:162 BW.[102] This provision replaced Art. 1401 BW (old),[103]

---

[97] See e.g. STJ 16 Jan. 1974, *BolMinJust* 233 (1974) p. 55; STJ 23 Jan. 1974, *BolMinJust* 233 (1974) p. 82.

[98] E.g. STJ 28 Apr. 1977, *BolMinJust* 266 (1977) pp. 165, 167; and RE 21 July 1977, *CJ* II (1977–5) p. 1225 (inhabitants of house entitled to injunctive relief and damages against the owner of café run on the ground floor. The 'right of a citizen to rest and recovery is, as a rule, "legally" (*juristisch*) more important than the right to run a business'. Such opposing interests are assessed by reference to Art. 335 Cc.

[99] STJ 13 Mar. 1986, *BolMinJust* 355 (1986) pp. 356, 358: '*O direito à vida, à integridade física, à honra, à saúde, ao bom nome, à intimidade, à inviolabilidade de domicílio e de correspondência, e ao repouso essencial à existência, são exemplos de direitos de personalidade reconhecidos pela nossa lei, constituindo a sua violação facto ilícito gerador da obrigação de indemnizar o lesado.*'

[100] The question arises whether 'personal family rights' can receive delictual protection through Art. 483 I Cc, and if so under what circumstances liability would be established. Although most Portuguese academics are opposed to such liability (e.g. Pereira Coelho, *Direito da Famiília*, vol. i, p. 37; and Pessoa Jorge, *Pressupostos da Responsabilidade Civil*, p. 301), some remain undecided: see Neto/Martins; *Código civil*, 7th edn., Art. 483 note 2; Pires de Lima/Antunes Varela, *Cc anotado*, vol. i, 4th edn., Art. 483, note 5a.

[101] See Part 6 section I, no. 585 below.

[102] For literature in German on this and Art. 1401 BW (old), see Hartkamp, *RabelsZ* 57 (1993) pp. 664, 671–673; and the dissertations by Hohlbein, *Neuere Entwicklungen des niederländischen Haftungsrechts*, pp. 5 ff., and Mertz, *Schutz primärer Vermögensinteressen*, pp. 23–31. For an instructive and concise discussion in English see Spier/Sterk, *Rope-Dancing Dutch Tort Law* (Geneva 1993).

[103] To be precise one would have to refer to Arts. 1401 and 1402 Dutch BW (old), modelled on Arts. 1382 and 1383 French Cc. First, the term '*onrechtmatige daad*' had to be read into Art. 1402 BW (old) where it was absent. Then the two provisions had to be combined, which was achieved by defining Art. 1402 BW (old) as a provision applicable in cases of failure to act: HR 6 Apr. 1883, *Ned. Rechtspraak* 133 (1883) pp. 358, 365–366 = W 1883 no. 4901 p. 1 ('*notaris*').

a provision adopted from French law, and which, as mentioned above, employed the term *'onrechtmatige daad'* as early as 1838. However, at the time when the German BGB was being developed, the Dutch judiciary had temporarily consolidated their view that (as P. Scholten observed)[104] *onrechtmatigheid* means the same as *'onwettigheid'* (contrary to statute). Hence, an act could only be deemed unlawful if it infringed an absolute right or a statutory duty.[105] It was mainly due to Molengraaff's[106] influence (which met with Meijers'[107] whole-hearted approval) that the *Hoge Raad* soon abandoned this proposal to reduce the law of delict to a mere annex of the criminal law. In the *Lindenbaum/Cohen* case, one of the key rulings of Dutch legal history, the *Hoge Raad* maintained that *'dat immers het woord onrechtmatig niet gelijkwaardig is met strijdig tegen een wetsbepaling'* and declared:

> *'dat onder onrechtmatige daad is te verstaan een handelen of nalaten, dat of inbreuk maakt op eens anders recht, of in strijd is met des daders rechtplicht of indruischt, hetzij tegen de goede zeden, hetzij tegen de zorgvuldigheid, welke in het maatschappelijk verkeer betamt ten aanzien van eens anders persoon of goed.'*[108]

25   Sub-section 2 of Art. 6:162 BW[109] evidently refers to the famous *Lindenbaum/Cohen*, case and to the judgments over some seventy years which have been based on this ruling.[110] Art. 6:162 BW retains much of

---

[104] Scholten, *WPNR* 1911 nos. 2149, 2152.

[105] Although, as far as the author is aware, the *Hoge Raad* never explicitly stated at the time that a *'rechtsplicht'* is only infringed in cases where a statutory duty is violated. However, see Asser (-Hartkamp), *Verbintenissenrecht*, vol. iii, 8th edn., no. 29 (p. 31), who believes that such a ruling was in fact positively given on 20 Feb. 1852. Many rulings from that time—esp. HR 6 Jan. 1905, W 1905 no. 8163 (*'Singer/Ivens'*); HR 24 Nov. 1905, W 1905 no. 8304 (*'Necec'*); and HR 10 June 1910, W 1910 no. 9038 (*'Zutphense waterleiding'*) can only be and always have been interpreted in this way. For further case references see Asser (-Hartkamp) loc. cit.

[106] Who as early as 1887 developed the wording which became law on 1 Jan. 1992, by interpreting Arts. 1401 and 1402 BW (old) as saying: *'Hij die anders handelt dan in het maatschappelijk verkeer den eenen mensch tegenover den ander betaamt, anders dan men met het oog op zijne medeburgers behoort te handelen, is verplicht de schade te vergoeden, die derden daardoor lijden'* (*RM* 1887 pp. 373, 386). For more detail see van Maanen, *Onrechtmatige Daad*, pp. 139 ff.

[107] Meijers, *WPNR* 1919 no. 2564 p. 66 (note). He believes that this decision is as important as an entire new book of the BW.

[108] HR 31 Jan. 1919, *NedJur* 1919 pp. 161, 163 = *WPNR* 1919 no. 2564 (p. 64) = W 1919 no. 10365 (printing error rectified in W 10368). The court here used the text of the draft bill by Heemskerk on the reform of Arts. 1401–1407 BW (old) from 1913 (printed in W 1913 no. 9459).

[109] *'(1.) Hij die jegens een ander een onrechtmatige daad pleegt, welke hem kan worden toegerekend, is verplicht de schade die de ander dientengevolge lijdt, te vergoeden. (2.) Als onrechtmatige daad worden aangemerkt een inbreuk op een recht en een doen of nalaten in strijd met een wettelijke plicht of met hetgeen volgens ongeschreven recht in het maatschappelijk verkeer betaamt, een en ander behoudens de aanwezigheid van een rechtvaardigingsgrond. (3.) Een onrechtmatige daad kan aan de dader worden toegerekend, indien zij te wijten is aan zijn schuld of aan een oorzaak welke krachtens de wet of de in het verkeer geldende opvattingen voor zijn rekening komt.'*

[110] See Vranken, *AcP* 191 (1991) pp. 411, 415 f.

the phraseology, and even expands it. Thus, the new provision states that 'a person who commits an unlawful act towards another which can be attributed to him must repair the damage which the other person suffers as a consequence thereof'. The definition of an unlawful act is found in Art. 6:162 II BW: 'except where there is a ground for justification, the following acts are deemed to be unlawful: the violation of a right or an act or omission violating a statutory duty or an unwritten rule of law pertaining to proper social conduct'.

If a causal connection (Art. 6:98 BW) is established, the unlawful act can be attributed to its author 'if it results from his fault or from a cause for which he is responsible': Art. 6:162 III BW. Thus for the first time in Europe,[111] liability without personal fault was incorporated in a national basic delictual provision. One must conclude that Art. 6:162 BW reflects the lessons learnt from nearly 200 years of developments in the law of delict in Europe. This provision has been crafted so that it is not only far more precise than its French counterpart but also improves on the relevant Italian provision, which is made problematic by its *danno ingiusto*. Art. 6:162 BW has a more open approach towards the protection of interests[112] and the establishment of duties of care[113] and is therefore also an improvement on the German BGB, the Greek Cc, and the Portuguese Cc. Russia considered incorporating this part of the BW into its Cc[114] and would have done better to do so instead of insisting on its own individualistic tort law system, as in the cases of Arts. 1064–1101.

2. INCORPORATING EXTERNAL PROVISIONS INTO DELICTUAL LIABILITY: VIOLATION OF A STATUTE, INFRINGEMENT OF *BONOS MORES*, AND THEIR PURPOSE WITHIN THE LIABILITY SYSTEM OF CODIFIED LAW

To give a complete overview of codified delictual law, it is necessary to **26** examine more closely two causes of action mentioned above: violation of a statute (nos. 27–35) and infringement of *bonos mores* (nos. 36–41). These

---

[111] See no. 11 and fn. 7 above.

[112] It is self-evident that personal rights and, in some cases also pure pecuniary interests, can be covered by Art. 6:162 BW. For an interesting case bringing both matters together, see HR 29 Oct. 1993, *NedJur* 1994 no. 108 pp. 4–9 (unjustified TV criticism of the achievements of a language school). On liability for information issued see HR 10 Dec. 1993, *RvdW* 1993 no. 248 c (incorrect credit information issued negligently by a bank).

[113] The important factor here, as Greek (no. 19) and Portuguese (no. 22) liability law reveal, is that the wording of the Code permits the courts to determine what constitutes an unlawful act.

[114] That the Russians were thinking in this direction emerged as early as summer 1993, see e.g. the report by Lebesque, *de Volkskrant* of 29 July 1993 ('*Burgerlijk Wetboek het voorbeeld voor Russen*'). Meanwhile Byelorussia and Kazakhstan have demonstrated some interest in a partial adoption: editors' note, *NJB* 1994 p. 1023.

causes of action fulfil various purposes, and the significance of many other specific torts can only be discerned by reference to them (nos. 42 ff. below).

a. Determining Causes of Action from Blanket Provisions

27   European codified law provides no auxiliary provisions which precisely define what is meant by (e.g.) infringement of health, or damage to property. On the other hand, there are numerous provisions which instruct the judiciary as to what types of behaviour cannot be regarded as showing proper care for the rights or legally protected interests of others. The codes include blanket rules imposing liability in damages for violations of provisions which are themselves non-delictual. These are mainly criminal, road-traffic, and construction law. Taken on their own these laws have no 'real' links with the law of damages. Yet the law of delict turns some of their norms into auxiliary delictual provisions, whose sole purpose is to define appropriate acts or omissions in legal relationships. If the contents of such provisions change, or if additional provisions are added, the substance of the relevant liability law is also changed. Thus the liability provisions are subject to constant adjustment with no alteration of the delictual legal texts.

28   Although the wording of the codes varies, in practice this makes no difference. Some codes refer expressly to this link between specific non-delictual and delictual provisions (e.g. § 1311 s. 2, 2nd alt. ABGB; § 823 II BGB; Art. 914 Greek Cc; Art. 483 I Port. Cc; Art. 6:162 II BW), while others note only the connections between delict and criminal law (see Art. 1092 Span. Cc in conjunction with Art. 19 Span CP or Art. 116 I NCP[115]), and a third group does not even clearly state that such a link exists (see Arts. 1382, 1383 French, Belg., and Lux. Cc, and Art. 2043 Ital. Cc). The French,[116] the Belgians, and the Italians[117] consider an act

---

[115] See no. 4 and fn. 20 above.

[116] *Rapport* de Greuille no. 9 in Locré vol. vi, p. 280.

[117] See for Belgium the great number of references in the case reviews by Dalcq, *Rev.crit.jur.belge* 1980 pp. 355 ff.; *Rev.crit.jur.belge* 1987 pp. 601 ff.; Vandenberghe/Van Quickenborne/Hamelink, *TPR* 1980 pp. 1139 ff. (nos. 4–8); and Vandenberghe/Van Quickenborne/Geelen/De Coster, *TPR* 1987 pp. 1255 ff. (nos. 3–12). Note Italian civil law regularly relies on the criminal definition of *colpa* (Art. 43 CP); for more details see *inter alia* Alpa, *Responsabilità civile*, p. 229; Cendon (-Gaudino) vol. iv, p. 1985 note 8; Visintini, *Fatti illeciti*, vol. ii, p. 8; ead., *Responsabilità civile*, p. 13; Geria/Breccia/Busnelli/Natoli, *Diritto civile*, vol. iii, pp. 699–700; Giur.sist. Bigiavi (-Figone/Spallarossa) vol. i, p. 53, no. 5; Cass. 28 Apr. 1979, n. 2488, *Giust.civ.Mass.* 1979 no. 2488, pp. 1980, 1081; Cass. 17 Dec. 1973, n. 3420, *Giur.it.Mass.* 1973 col. 1161; and Cass. 21 Mar. 1981, n. 1656, *Giur.it.Mass.* 1981 col. 457. All these state that: 'the term *colpa* in its technical legal meaning is a mode of conduct of the tortfeasor who, without intent, inflicts damage on another person, due to *negligenza, imprudenza, imperizia*, or non-observance of legal provisions and standards of conduct'.

'*fautif*' if it infringes a legal standard of conduct. The importance of such differences in structure and wording should not be overestimated. This holds especially true when one considers that in all the European codes, including the Spanish, the conduct forbidden need not necessarily be criminal. Spanish law says only that if a person commits a criminal offence, questions of liability arising in that context will not be subject to the Cc, *therefore* Art. 1902 Cc will not be applicable. Nevertheless, in cases where liability is based on Art. 1902 Cc the breach of any statutory duty is considered a cause of action, even in Spain.[118]

However, even if a common ground for liability has thus been **29** established for all EU Member States, they do not necessarily agree on how it should operate, although parallels between some laws of delict are apparent. For example, most agree that liability for a statutory violation should generally be stricter than for a breach of a general legal duty not yet established in a written provision (see no. 31 below). Furthermore, most EU Member States agree that diligence on the part of the alleged tortfeasor cannot be presumed simply because he complied with the statutory rules and regulations relevant to the activities he was pursuing: such provisions may be incomplete, outdated, or offer insufficient protection to the plaintiff. Only in Portugal is the situation less clear.[119] At least the laws of delict agree that they are free to require more care regarding damage to health and property than, for example, in construction, road-traffic, or criminal law.[120] However, the question whether the violation of any rule of law indicates delictual misconduct, or whether the protection of the victim from the damage sustained must

They also state that Art. 43 Ital. CP views any violation of a legal provision as a form of negligence: '*Il delitto . . . è colposo, o contro l'intenzione, quando l'evento, anche se preveduto, non è voluto dall'agente e si verifica a causa di negligenza o imprudenza o imperizia, ovvero per inosservanza di leggi, regolamenti, ordini o discipline.*' Thus, the term '*fatto colposo*' in Art. 2043 Cc embraces an infringement of a protective law. Accordingly, Art. 5 CP states that ignorance of a law is no defence. Corte Cost. 24 Mar. 1988, n. 364, *Foro.it.* 1988, I, 1385 restricted this article in respect of criminal liability where the wrongdoer could not have known that the act was unlawful.

[118] For more recent rulings see TS 30 May 1988, *RAJ* 1988 no. 4116, pp. 4052 ff.; TS 25 Feb. 1992, *RAJ* no. 1554, p. 1936. From the relevant literature see *inter alia* Cavanillas Múgica, *Transformación*, pp. 48–50. See also Art. 1089 Span. Cc.

[119] See no. 22 above and, although it is hard to judge whether this ruling has been of general influence, see also STJ 23 Jan. 1970, *BolMinJust* 193 (1970) p. 365: no delictual liability if all safety measures laid down in a building permit were complied with in erecting the building.

[120] However, it is possible that the requirements of the law of delict have been met if different but equally effective protective measures have been taken: STJ 2 June 1977, *BolMinJust* 268 (1977) p. 208. The situation is different when dealing with pure economic interests: here the courts are generally happy to accept the statutory duty of care: e.g. Karollus, *Schutzgesetzverletzung*, pp. 140–141. Also *Deloitte Haskins* v. *National Mutual Life* [1993] 2 All ER 1015.

have been in the mind of the legislator when the provision was drafted, remains heavily disputed in all EU Member States.

30   In a system in which the law of delict is built around a general clause, the principle that everything not explicitly forbidden is permitted certainly does not apply. Indeed, such a general clause by its very nature ousts the notion of *nullum crimen sine lege scripta*.[121] Hence in France,[122] Belgium,[123] Spain, and Italy[124] the opinion prevails that compliance with specific rules of conduct does not 'necessarily' excuse the tortfeasor from liability under Arts. 1382 and 1383 Cc (in the author's opinion quite rightly.) '*Men blijft immers steeds gehouden tot naleving van de behoorlijkheidsnorm welke hogere eisen kan stellen dan wettelijke of reglementaire bepalingen. De goede huisvader gedraagt zich behoorlijk, ook waar de wet hem geen bepaalde gedragswijze voorschrijft.*'[125] The German, Greek, and Portuguese Civil Codes are more ambiguous on this issue, for their links to the principle of *nullum crimen sine lege scripta* are much stronger. The best which can be said of these codes is that their authors have neither discussed the question, nor even recognized it as inherent. However, in general the courts of these three countries find that a person's conduct is not necessarily acceptable[126] simply because the statutory duties were

---

[121] This point is rightly stressed in the French and Spanish literature. For the former see Weill/Terré, *Obligations*, 4th edn., no. 620; and Aubry/Rau (-Dejean de la Bâtie) vol. vi, 7th edn., no. 343. For the latter see e.g. Díez-Picazo/Gullón, *Sistema de Derecho Civil*, vol. ii, 6th edn., p. 599; and de Ángel Yágüez, *Responsabilidad civil*, 3rd edn., p. 49. The Spanish constitutional court expressly stated that the '*principio de tipicidad y legalidad de los delitos*' of Art. 25 no. 1 Spanish Constitution does not apply in civil law: '*El precepto . . . no es directamente aplicable a los simples ilícitos de naturaleza civil, en los que la tipicidad y la legalidad no tienen que actuar de manera tan estricta*', TC 2 Dec. 1982, *BOE* 29 Dec. 1982, no. 34726, pp. 24, 25. This opinion is shared by Austrian jurisprudence: Karollus, *Schutzgesetzverletzung*, pp. 71 ff., 136 ff.

[122] Cass.civ. 14 June 1972, *D* 1973 *Jur.* 423 ('*Mais attendu que le fait que la loi ou le règlement autorisent un acte, en le subordonnant à certaines conditions éditées dans l'intérêt des tiers, n'a pas pour effet de relever ceux qui accomplissent cet acte, de l'obligation générale de prudence et de diligence civilement sanctionnée par la disposition de l'article 1382 C.civ.*') Various older rulings in the same vein in Planiol/Ripert (-Esmein) vol. vi, 1, 2nd edn., no. 521, p. 705.

[123] For extensive case references, see Vandenberghe/Van Quickenborne/Hamelink, *TPR* 1980 pp. 1139, 1154 (no. 8); Vandenberghe/Van Quickenborne/Geelen/De Coster, *TPR* 1987 pp. 1255, 1281 (no. 12).

[124] For Spain see the numerous case references in Cavanillas Múgica, *Transformación*, p. 49 (fn. 2); also TS 27 May 1982, *RAJ* 1982 no. 2603, p. 1795 ('*la diligencia obligada abarque no sólo las prevenciones y cuidados reglementarios, sino también todos los que la prudencia imponga para prevenir el daño*'); TS 12 Dec. 1984, *RAJ* 1984 no. 6039, p. 475; TS 25 Feb. 1992, *RAJ* 1992 no. 1554, p. 1936; and TS 9 June 1992, *RAJ* 1992 no. 5179, p. 6814. For Italy see mainly Cass. 20 July 1993, n. 8069, *Foro.it.* 1994, I, 455 (liability of manufacturers of pharmaceutical products; *in casu* gross negligence was found 'although the established provisions had been complied with'). For references to earlier cases see also Will, *Quellen erhöhter Gefahr*, p. 177; and Schlüchter, *Haftung für gefährliche Tätigkeit*, pp. 156 ff.

[125] Bocken, *Het aansprakelijksrecht als sanctie tegen de verstoring van het leefmilieu*, p. 39.

[126] Vandenberghe *et al.* loc. cit. (fn. 123).

complied with.[127] The law of delict is not just an annex to other parts of codified law, but a compensation system which can and must develop independently. Whether a European law of delict should operate a system in which the notion of unlawfulness is divided into different categories, and thus standardized, or with a general clause, is an issue yet to be resolved. Another, entirely different question is whether the violation of any statute alone should be sufficient to found an action, or whether the law of delict should only apply in cases where standards of conduct intended to protect private interests have been infringed. A further question is whether only damage which the violated norm sought to prevent should be compensatable. In Germany (§ 823 II BGB), Portugal (Art. 483 I Cc), and The Netherlands (Art. 6: 163 BW) the answer to this question can be found in the text of the relevant provisions: liability arises only through violation respectively of a *'den Schutz eines anderen bezweckenden Gesetzes'*, a *'disposição legal destinada a proteger interesses alheios'*, and *'geen verplichting tot schadevergoeding bestaat, wanneer de geschonden norm niet strekt tot bescherming tegen de schade zoals de benadeelde die heeft geleden'*. Hence delictual unlawfulness is seen as a form of relative unlawfulness (so-called *relativité aquilienne*), i.e. a violation of a law or statute which focuses not on the protection of the common good, but on the individual interests of the victim. This view is shared by Greece,[128] Italy,[129]

---

[127] Some inconsistencies, esp. in the German jurisdiction, cannot be denied: e.g. BGH 7 Oct. 1986, *NJW* 1987 p. 372; BGH 22 Apr. 1974, BGHZ 62 pp. 265, 270; BGH 18 Sep. 1984, BGHZ 92 pp. 143, 148; comments by v. Bar, *JuS* 1988 pp. 169, 172–173. However, in all cases a thorough examination was carried out as to whether non-delictual standards of conduct provide sufficient legal protection as regards § 823 I BGB; see OLG Frankfurt 10 Mar. 1993, *VersR* 1994 p. 829. Furthermore, BGH 9 Dec. 1986, *NJW* 1987 pp. 1009, 1011 clearly states that an official permit (*Betriebserlaubnis*) does not exempt the tortfeasor from applying due care. Otherwise the authorities would have to bear undue responsibility for the operational safety of the plant.

[128] See e.g. Areopag 383/1964, *NoB* 12 (1964) 930; and Areopag 1855/1984, *NoB* 33 (1985) 1142 (public building and town planning regulations seek to protect public rather than private interests). In the field of state liability Art. 105 Introductory Statute to the Greek Cc expressly states that violation of a provision 'which has been implemented for the protection of the public interest' is not a sufficient basis for a claim. For literature in German see Karakostas, *ZfU* 1990 pp. 295, 303; and v. Bar (-Vrellis), *DeliktsR in Europa, Griechenland*, p. 13.

[129] Cendon (-Gaudino) vol. iv, p. 1984, note 7.7; Antolisei, *Diritto penale*, 10th edn., p. 317; Visintini, *Fatti illeciti*, vol. ii, pp. 11–12; Marinucci, *La colpa per inosservanza di leggi*, pp. 230 ff.; Cass. 29 Jan. 1982, n. 587, *Giust.civ.Mass.* 1982 no. 587, p. 213; Cass. 2 Feb. 1973, n. 335, *Giust.civ.Mass.* 1973 no. 335, p. 172; Cass. 10 Apr. 1970, n. 1002, *Giust.civ.Mass.* 1970 no. 1002, p. 559 and elsewhere. See also Pret. Palermo 28 Mar. 1992, n. 516, *Lav.prev.oggi* 1992 p. 1161 which deals with an unlawful strike; for a case concerning the duty to control certain stock exchange prospectuses in public law, Cass.sez.un. 14 Jan. 1992, n. 367, *Foro.it.* 1992, I, 1422, 1426 (no liability since the duty arises only *'in una prospettiva di sviluppo del mercato finanziario ed a tutela dell'interesse generale'*).

Spain,[130] and Austria.[131] Yet in France,[132] and more importantly in Belgium,[133] whether the violated statute seeks to protect personal interests, and whether the damage sustained comes within its protection is irrelevant. It is felt that the text of the statutes does not allow for such restrictions, nor are they desirable since they lead to legal uncertainty. The requirement for a protective statute (*relativité aquilienne*), it is (wrongly) said, is not in accordance with Kant's categorical imperative (i.e. the idea of duty-induced activity). Any undue hardship this stance might create is avoided by taking a more lenient position when determining causation and damage.[134] This latter point reveals that even these two legal orders are not as strict as one might think.[135] Likewise,

---

[130] TS 27 May 1982 loc. cit. and TS 12 Dec. 1984 loc. cit. (both in fn. 124 above) make the same statement: '*lo que comporta la indeclinable necesidad de que el acto dañoso tenga que ser antijurídico por vulneración de una norma, aun la más genérica (alterum non laedere), protectora del bien lesionado, y culpable*' (italics supplied). The theory of the protective purpose of a provision seems to have stronger links to criminal than to civil jurisdiction, see e.g. TS 30 May 1988, *RAJ* 1988 no. 4116, p. 4052. The latter discusses this issue mainly in the context of causation; see the analysis by Pantaleón Prieto in: *Centenario del Código Civil*, vol. ii, pp. 1561, 1580–1590.

[131] This is without doubt the prevailing opinion in both case-law and literature: see OGH 15 Apr. 1982, *ZUR* 1983/206 p. 262; Schwimann (-Harrer), *ABGB*, vol. v, § 1311 no. 8; and Rummel (-Reischauer), *ABGB*, vol. ii, 2nd edn., § 1311 no. 4.

[132] Herbots, *Rev.dr.int.dr.comp.* 62 (1985) pp. 7 ff.; Le Tourneau, *Responsabilité civile*, 3rd edn., no. 1884; Limpens, *Mélanges Savatier*, pp. 559, 571 f. Ferid/Sonnenberger, *Frz. Zivilrecht*, vol. ii, 2nd edn., no. 2 0 116. Although Cass.civ. 17 Mar. 1958, *JCP* 1959, II, 10950 (see Stoll, *Kausalzusammenhang und Normzweck im Deliktsrecht*, p. 6) dismissed a complaint giving the remarkable reason that the violated law had not been implemented to protect the '*intérêts particuliers*' of the plaintiff, but rather the '*intérêts généreaux de la Nation*'. However, to this author's knowledge there have been no similar rulings, cf. e.g. Cass.civ. 5 Dec. 1969, Bull.civ. III, no. 804 (p. 610): '*les particuliers peuvent invoquer la violation de règlements administratifs ou de servitudes d'intérêt public . . . à la condition . . . d'un préjudice personnel*'. See also Limpens/Kruithof/Meinertzhagen-Limpens, *IntEncCompL* IX 2–134: 'Despite this isolated case (i.e. Cass.civ. 17 Mar. 1958), it seems that as French law stands at present there is nothing to prevent someone from recovering damages in either the civil or the criminal courts, where he has suffered harm through breach of a law protecting society generally, if he bases his action on the ordinary rules of tortious liability.' Furthermore, see a note by Chambon on Cass.crim. 19 Nov. 1959, *JCP* 1960 II 11444; and De Wilde in Vandenberghe (see bibliography before no. 11 above) p. 191.

[133] Apart from the references in Vandenberghe *et al.* loc. cit. (fn. 123 above) see also e.g. Ronse, *Aanspraak op schadeloosstelling uit onrechtmatige daad*, pp. 70–94 (p. 91: '*Het Belgisch recht kent de relativiteitsleer niet en heeft er niets bij te winnen*'). Belgium and Dutch law differed on this issue even while both were using the same code: Nieuwenhuis, *WPNR* 1987 no. 5821, p. 145.

[134] Vandenberghe/Van Quickenborne/Hamelink, *TPR* 1980 pp. 1139, 1154. See also the work by Philippe, *Mélanges Dalcq*, pp. 467, 484–486, based on extensive comparative analysis.

[135] The Luxembourgeois judiciary, for example, is of the opinion that '*la négligence commise par le propriétaire dans la surveillance de sa voiture automobile, négligence qui rend possible le vol de la voiture, est sans lien causal direct avec le dommage que le voleur cause dans un accident avec la chose volée*' (Trib.Lux. 4 June 1950, *Pas.luxemb.* 15 [1950–1953] p. 89; confirmed by Cour 2 Apr. 1952, *Pas.luxemb.* 15 [1950–1953] p. 352. However, as the *Cour* had already found that there was no fault [loc. cit. p. 354] because it was not possible to lock the vehicle, the question of causation was untouched).

those nations which focus on the victim's individual interests do occasionally operate with ideas closer to French law. Under certain circumstances a plaintiff has a reasonable prospect of success in an action based on a breach of the general duty of care where the protective purpose of the relevant law does not provide a suitable cause of action.[136]

b. Fault and Breach of Statutory Duty

Where a case involves a violation of a statute, the statute serves two **31** functions. First to help define delictual misconduct. Secondly and very importantly, to lower the threshold for proof of fault, i.e. to move towards strict liability. Here again, France and Belgium go the furthest. Both apply the principle that in the absence of a specific *fait justificatif*, a violation of a written legal rule automatically constitutes *faute*.[137] 'Le seul fait de leur inobservation' is sufficient.[138] These legal systems presume that the law is known to everybody[139] and must therefore be obeyed, imposing a strict duty of care. Dutch law achieves the same result by applying Art. 6:162 II 2nd alt. (violation of a statute) in

---

[136] See e.g. HR 17 Jan. 1958 *NedJur* 1961 no. 568 p. 1201, 1206 (the '*Tandartsen*' case). On this case see also Lankhorst, *De relativiteit van de onrechtmatige daad*, pp. 25–27; and Voss, *Fahrlässiges Delikt und reiner Vermögensschaden*, p. 141. The plaintiffs, who were dentists, brought an action against a 'colleague' claiming violation of the duty of care. The latter operated without having completed the necessary training and thus did not satisfy the relevant 'provisions on the establishment of a dental surgery', which clearly serve only to protect the public. They succeeded in an action based on the common law duty of care. See also BGH 8 June 1976, BGHZ 66 pp. 388, 390, 393: an electric cable was damaged due to violation of building regulations. Although these provisions were denied protective quality, possible liability under § 823 I BGB (interference with an established trade or business, see no. 47 below) was considered, but subsequently denied.

[137] France: Marty/Raynaud, *Droit Civil*, vol. ii, 1, 2nd edn., no. 456; Weill/Terré, *Obligations*, 4th edn., no. 620; Planiol/Ripert (-Esmein) vol. vi, 1, 2nd edn., no. 521; Le Tourneau, *Responsabilité civile*, 3rd edn., nos. 1884 ff.; *Encyclopédie Dalloz* (-Rodière), *Rép.Dr.Civ.*, vol. vii, 2nd edn., 'Responsabilité du fait personnel' nos. 24 ff. (all containing references to cases). A particularly rigid ruling was given by Cass.civ. 10 Nov. 1992, Bull.civ. 1993 III no. 292 = *Rev.trim.dr.civ.* 1993 p. 360 (the fact of violation of property can constitute *faute*). Belgium: Vandenberghe *et al.* *TPR* 1980 pp. 1139, 1154 and *TPR* 1987 pp. 1255, 1266 ('*In de mate deze bepalingen een welbepaalde gedraging gebieden of verbieden, leggen ze een resultaatsverplichting op*'); Cass. 3 Oct. 1994 *JT* 1995 p. 26: contrary to statute, the administrator of a bankrupt's affairs innocently failed to pay social security contributions. Also Liège 23 Oct. 1989, *JT* 1990 pp. 23, 24 ('*elle n'a trait qu'à la faute, celle-ci étant constituée précisément par la désobéisance à cette loi*'). Note that the law of the Grand Duchy of Baden of 3 Feb. 1809 (in force from 1 Jan. 1810) translated Art. 1382 French Cc as 'each unlawful act of a person, damaging another person, . . . (obliges) its author to compensate'. In Art. 1382a 'an act' is defined as 'unlawful, if an undertaking is forbidden (*ein an sich verbotenes Unternehmen vollführt*), or if an unlawful undertaking is knowingly carried out by an unauthorized person, or in an unlawful manner') (*Landrecht* of the Grand Duchy of Baden, Official text Gazette, Karlsruhe 1867).   [138] Esmein loc. cit.

[139] v. Bar (-Gotthardt), *DeliktsR in Europa, Frankreich*, p. 18.

conjunction with Art. 6:162 III 3rd alt. (an unlawful act can be imputed to its author if he can reasonably be supposed to have committed).[140] The German BGB seems also to have taken an approach somewhat different to that of the French Cc. § 823 II s. 2 BGB explicitly states that 'if, according to the provisions of a statute, infringement is possible even without fault, the duty to compensate arises only in the event of fault'. However, the French and German positions are not as far apart as may at first glance appear. The German legislator sought from the outset to clarify that fault in § 823 II BGB concerns only the protective law, and neither an infringement of a right or legally protected interest, nor the actual loss sustained.[141] In addition, the German courts (and the Austrian courts in cases concerning §§ 1298 and 1311 Austrian Cc) promptly added a further provision: where the violation of a law has been established, fault is rebuttably presumed whenever a statute prescribes a specific standard of conduct.[142]

32   Germany's approach is shared by Portugal. Although 'a violation of a legal duty . . . does not necessarily result in a finding of fault',[143] the *Supremo Tribunal* has repeatedly said, for example, 'in a traffic accident, where the damage was caused through a violation of provisions of the road traffic code (*Código da Estrada*), carelessness can be presumed *juris tantum* on

---

[140] As far as the author is aware, no direct statements have been made by the HR on this issue since the new BW came into force. However, in support of the statement made in the text above, Art. 6:162 III, 3rd alt. BW not only emphasizes the 'objective test for negligence' (an entrant into the medical profession is subject to the standard of care expected of a specialist) but also seeks to eliminate the 'error in law' defence (see *Parlementaire Geschiedenis*, vol. vi, pp. 621–622; and Hijma/Olthoff, *Compendium*, 4th edn., no. 411). The ruling of HR 23 Oct. 1992, *NedJur* 1992 no. 813 pp. 3495, 3501 = *RvdW* 1992, 236, in the author's view, does not contradict this view. The defendant drove her car off the road. She defended a claim against her by her passenger, stating that he had grabbed the steering wheel and applied the handbrake. The complaint was dismissed due to a *non liquet*: the burden of proof was on the plaintiff and he had failed to discharge it. No violation of Art. 25 WVV, which prohibits the road-user from causing danger to traffic through misconduct, was proved. This provision is only infringed if a driver 'acts carelessly by not paying proper attention and not exercising due care'. Hence, whether a law carries an *'obligation de résultat'* depends on its substance. The burden of proof is not shifted in cases where the law infringed does not explicitly define the correct conduct, but only demands generally that due care be applied. This is also the position in German law: BGH 19 Nov. 1991, BGHZ 116 pp. 104, 115.

[141] Also Jakobs/Schubert, *Beratung des BGB*, pp. 876, 893. See also RG 1 July 1907, RGZ 66 pp. 251, 255; RG 18 Oct. 1917, RGZ 91 pp. 72, 76; OGH 3 Sep. 1992, *JBl* 1993 pp. 396, 397; HR 20 Mar. 1992, *NedJur* 1993 no. 547 p. 1975.

[142] BGH 19 Nov. 1991, BGHZ 116 pp. 104, 115. See also RG 18 Oct. 1917 (see previous fn.); BGH 13 Dec. 1984, BGH *NJW* 1985, pp. 1774, 1775; BGH 17 Jan. 1984, *VersR* 1984 pp. 270, 271. See also HR 23 Oct. 1992, loc. cit. (fn. 140). For Austria, where there is no clear differentiation between abstract standards of conduct and pure rules of care, see OGH 6 July 1987, SZ 51/109 pp. 497, 499–500; OGH 15 Apr. 1982, ZVR 1983/206 p. 262; OGH 31 Aug. 1984, SZ 57/134 pp. 661, 668.

[143] RP 11 Dec. 1981, *CJ* VI (1981–5) p. 274.

the part of the person causing the accident'.[144] In Spain this question plays only a minor role. Its courts have shown themselves willing to shift the burden of proof in tort law, which indeed now lies generally with the defendant. Fault may be presumed (e.g.) if Art. 17 *Código de la Circulación* is violated, which demands only driving behaviour appropriate to the traffic conditions.[145] In Italy the situation is also very clear: the violation of a statutory duty is part of the definition of 'culpable' conduct.[146] In this context Art. 2050 Cc (liability for the pursuit of dangerous activities) is also relevant. The courts have determined that breach of a statutory duty itself deprives the defendant of the defence *'di avere adottato tutte le misure idonee a evitare il danno'* ('to have taken every appropriate measure to avoid the damage').[147]

c. Extension of the Protected Interests

Reliance on the violation of a protective law also serves to increase the **33** number of protected interests, albeit only in some EU countries. Belgium, France, Italy, Luxembourg, and Spain, i.e. those countries with a general clause for delictual liability, do not need such an extension, but rather a restriction of liability. In Greece, which relies on a blanket provision (see no. 19 above), to add 'violation of a protective law' to the causes of action would be meaningless. However, in Germany the opposite is true. § 823 II BGB used to be unique in Europe, being the only provision (except for §§ 824, 826 BGB) to admit the protection of personal honour to the law of delict: personal honour is not covered by § 823 I BGB.[148] Since the German BGB also has no provision similar to § 1330 ABGB, only the introduction of § 823 II BGB opened the way to compensation

---

[144] STJ 5 July 1984, *BolMinJust* 339 (1984) p. 364, RE 16 June 1983, *BolMinJust* 330 (1983) p. 563; STJ 14 Oct. 1982, *BolMinJust* 320 (1982) p. 422. Also RE 6 Jan. 1983, *BolMinJust* 325 (1983) p. 614. See also RC 19 May 1981, *BolMinJust* 310 (1981) p. 343: (*Nas hipóteses de negligência presumida, por violação de uma norma regulamentar que protege interesses alheios, não é necessária a prova da concreta previsibilidade do evento sempre que este se situe no círculo de interesses privados que a norma regulamentar pretendeu acautelar.'*

[145] TS 8 May 1990, *RAJ* 1990, no. 3690, pp. 4895, 4897. Less clear, however, is TS 27 Apr. 1992, *RAJ* 1992 no. 3414, pp. 4519, 4520, where lack of fault and lack of causation in the violation of a statutory duty seem to have been seen as synonymous: *'El hecho de que por ésta* (of the employer's liability) *se apreciara infracción de la reglamentación de las normas de seguridad en el trabajo no comporta por sí sola existencia de culpa civil. Ninguna relación de causa a efecto se ha demostrado entre la falta de barandilla en un andamio en el que trabajaba el oficial primero y su muerte, de la que no consta dato alguno que permita conocer cómo se produjo.'*

[146] See fn. 117 above. Also of interest is Art. 872 II Ital. Cc, concerning land law. It entitles a plaintiff to claim under Art. 2043 Cc for damage sustained through a violation of building provisions (e.g. Art. 878 Cc), see Cass. 30 Jan. 1990 n. 591, *Giust.civ.Mass.* 1990 no. 591 p. 126; and Trabucchi, *Istituzioni*, 33rd edn., pp. 397–398.

[147] For further details see Will, *Quellen erhöhter Gefahr*, pp. 176–177; Schlüchter, *Haftung für gefährliche Tätigkeit*, pp. 158–160.

[148] RG 2 Sep. 1937, RGZ 156 pp. 372, 374, including references to earlier decisions.

for insult and libel.[149] However, in 1954 the German Federal Court of Justice decided that the right to personal dignity, autonomy, and privacy was a 'right' under § 823 I BGB,[150] and soon afterwards ruled that compensation was available for violations thereof resulting in non-material loss.[151] § 823 II BGB then largely ceased to serve this particular purpose. Although §§ 185 and 186 StGB (the Penal Code provisions on defamation) are still 'protective laws', present-day civil judges, unlike those of the Supreme Court of the German Reich,[152] rarely refer to them.[153] Even where an insult is proven, compensation is now generally obtained under § 823 I BGB.[154] Insult seems only to be a sub-category of violations of the right to personal dignity, autonomy, and privacy. Although it is still possible to fall back on § 823 II BGB in particular cases,[155] there is no practical need to do so. Furthermore, it should be noted that rights of personality can be violated negligently,[156] whereas in the criminal offence of defamation intent is required.[157]

34   § 823 II German BGB has therefore more or less lost its meaning in the

---

[149] Prot. II pp. 573–574. However, the first draft of § 704 BGB was different: see Mot. II p. 726. In practice the result was to exclude liability in cases of purely negligent violation of honour.   [150] BGH 25 May 1954, BGHZ 13 pp. 334 ff.

[151] BGH 14 Feb. 1958, BGHZ 26 pp. 349 ff.

[152] See e.g. RG 6 Apr. 1932, RGZ 140 pp. 392, 395; and RG 2 Sep. 1937, RGZ 156 pp. 372, 374.

[153] See the review of cases in *MünchKomm* (-Mertens), 2nd edn., § 823 no. 168.

[154] BGH 5 Mar. 1963, BGHZ 39 p. 124, 129. What is striking in this ruling is that the court subsumed 'the grievous damage to the plaintiff's . . . honour' under § 823 I BGB. Also BGH 22 Dec. 1959, BGHZ 31 pp. 308, 311.

[155] BGH 9 July 1985, BGHZ 95 pp. 212, 214; BGH 8 Mar. 1966, *NJW* 1966 p. 1213.

[156] This is also true of claims for non-material loss: BGH 14 Feb. 1958, BGHZ 26 pp. 349, 357 (violation of the right to one's own photographic image); and BGH 5 Mar. 1963, *NJW* 1966 pp. 904, 905.

[157] The question remains to what extent the introduction of a general right to personality in § 823 I BGB undermines the decision of the legislator that 'the negligent violation . . . of honour' should not 'receive special civil protection' (Prot. II p. 573 f.). Cases of breach of the duty to supervise have always come under either §§ 831 in conjunction with §§ 823 II BGB, §§ 185, 186 StGB or under the general duty of care (see RG 20 June 1935, RGZ 148 pp. 154, 161–162) as long as only the person under supervision acted intentionally. Although cases of mistaken identity are not covered by § 823 II BGB, they are of little practical relevance. Of greater importance, and also not covered by this provision, are cases concerning violation by the press of the 'duty to operate with care' (*Sorgfaltspflicht*) and the 'duty to investigate' (*Nachforschungspflicht*). Here the defendant cannot rely on § 193 StGB (protection of legitimate interests) to justify his conduct. Yet infringement of these duties is only punishable if intent can be proven. Therefore, as far as compensation for the violation of honour is concerned, only in the few cases where intent is negated by the defendant's factual error constituting liability under § 193 StGB (invasion of personal privacy) go further than its sub-sec. II. The general right to personality only 'really' comes into action in cases other than the violation of a personal honour, such as the protection of privacy and the individual's 'right to social recognition' (*Geltungsanspruch*). Remarkably, similar developments can be found in Dutch law, which only abolished liability for intentional insult under Art. 1408 BW (old) (see Art. 1416 BW [old]: different limitations of action) with the introduction of Art. 6: 162 BW. Until then Art. 1408 BW (old) was considered *lex specialis* to Art. 1401 BW (old), as ruled by the *Hoge Raad* (HR 14 Nov. 1958 *NedJur* 1959 no. 15 p. 66). Hence, only on 1 Jan. 1992 did intent cease to be a precondition for liability for insult.

field of protection of personal honour. However, violation of a protective law still constitutes an important instrument incorporating pure economic loss into the list of compensatable interests in Austria, Germany, and Portugal. Pure economic loss, i.e. compensation for damage unrelated physical injury,[158] is covered by neither § 823 I BGB, §§ 1293, 1295 ABGB,[159] nor Art. 483 I 1st alt. Port. Cc.[160] Those codes recognize no general duty of care towards purely economic interests.[161] For them the existence of a protective law is a precondition for the compensation of 'pure economic interests'. In Austria, Portugal, and Germany the criminal principle *nullum crimen sine lege scripta* has to some extent survived in this area of private law. In other words, the opinion in these countries is that such a sensitive matter should not be left in the courts' discretion.

In the modern European legal landscape such rules seem like relics **35** from the past. § 823 II BGB was born of the legislator's mistrust of the judiciary. Its approach was justified by the belief that 'there is no way of predicting the effect on judges of holding such an authoritative position, nor whether German judgments would suffer excesses similar to those found in a great number of French rulings'.[162] Having learnt this, the present-day lawyer should always bear in mind that the identity of a modern constitutional European state is based on its judicial system and its dialogue with its neigbours! It therefore comes as no surprise that in Art. 6:162 BW, the latest European codification, judge-made and statutory standards of conduct enjoy the same level of importance, even in the field of compensation of pure economic loss. The Dutch clearly recognize

---

[158] The term 'pure economic loss', which is often difficult to distinguish from the notion of violation of property, is currently only defined in 2 § Swedish Statute on Damages of 2 June 1972, which reads: 'pure pecuniary loss according to this Act is such economic loss as is not in any way connected to personal injury or damage to property.'

[159] For details see v. Bar (-Schilcher/Kleewein), *DeliktsR in Europa, Österreich*, pp. 60–61. On the compensatability of pure economic loss covered by a protective law, see Schwimann (-Harrer), *ABGB* vol. v, § 1293 no. 2, and § 1311 no. 6. For a very clear ruling see OGH 22 June 1993, *JBl* 1993 p. 788: 'Causation only leads to compensation if there has been a blameworthy violation of a contract, or of a protective law according to § 1311 ABGB, or unethical conduct on the part of the defendant, or if the unlawfulness of the damaging conduct can be deduced directly from a law.'

[160] For details of the protection of primary economic interests in Portuguese law see Sinde Monteiro, *Responsabilidade por conselhos*, pp. 181 ff., 187 ff.; Mota Pinto, *Teoria Geral*, 3rd edn., no. 26; Pessoa Jorge, *Pressupostos da Responsabilidade civil*, pp. 302 ff. See also RL 27 Jan. 1987, *CJ* XII (1987–1) p. 111; and STJ 14 Apr. 1988, *BolMinJust* 376 (1988) p. 593, both referring to the same case: unlawful refusal by a syndicate of dockers to unload a ship. Liability based on Art. 483 Cc: the employees had breached their statutory duty to contract.

[161] On an attempt to place the duties of care on the same level as the protective laws (rejected by the courts: BGH 27 Jan. 1987, *NJW* 1987 p. 2671) and thus to achieve a duty of care towards another's pure economic interest under § 823 II BGB, see v. Bar, *Verkehrspflichten*, pp. 204–238. [162] Prot. II p. 571.

not only the 'classic' facts of criminal offences against assets (fraud, breach of trust, embezzlement) but also other provisions as protective laws, violation of which results in civil liablity.[163] However, the Dutch do not consider this position to be final and absolute. They are quite rightly of the opinion that liability need not depend on the violation of a criminal law,[164] nor indeed of any legislation at all.[165]

d. The Intentional Infliction of Damage *Contra Bonos Mores* and the Abuse of Legal Rights

36 Part of the Roman legacy to continental Europe's[166] law of delict is the *actio de dolo*,[167] which depends on the concept of 'evil intent' (*dolus malus*, as opposed to ordinary intent and *dolus bonus*, employed in cases where the victim outwits his attacker)[168] as an independent cause of action. Of the contemporary codes, only § 826 BGB, and § 1295 II ABGB[169] and Art. 919 Greek Cc which were modelled on the German provision, still clearly display their affinity to the Roman

---

[163] Asser (-Hartkamp), *Verbintenissenrecht*, vol. iii, 9th edn., no. 34 (p. 37). See also e.g. Ktg. Haarlem 4 May 1984, *VR* 1985 p. 117: father's obligation to ensure that his moped-riding son has third-party insurance.

[164] Which was the case under 4 § of the aforementioned Swedish Statute on Damages: (see fn. 158 above) 'a person causing pure economic loss by committing a crime shall compensate for it under the provisions on compensation for personal injury and damage to property of 1–3 §§'. Even some Portuguese and German authors support such a limitation of liability: Canaris, *FS Larenz* (1983) pp. 49 ff.; Sinde Monteiro, *Responsabilidade por conselhos*, pp. 237 ff., 611; also *MünchKomm* (-Mertens), 2nd edn., § 823 no. 138. However, this position was not accepted by the German legislator (Prot. II p. 572) nor has it been adopted by the courts of either country, which have not introduced such a restriction. Although it is correct to say that either penal or administrative sanctions are imposed on most provisions recognized as protective laws, there are exceptions: see for Germany e.g. BGH 25 Feb. 1959, BGHZ 29 p. 344, 351 (§ 27 GWB; non-admission into an 'economic association' (*wirtschaftlicher Interessenverband*); and BAG 19 Aug. 1982, *NJW* 1983 pp. 1391, 1392 (§ 9 II MuSchG; failure to report the resignation of a pregnant employee). For Portugal see e.g. RC 12 Jan. 1993, *CJ* XVIII (1993–1) pp. 17, 18 (entry of a medical practitioner into the telephone directory two years late; violation of the statutory duty to issue annually a complete list of all persons owning a telephone); and Procuradoria-Geral da República 31 Aug. 1979, *BolMinJust* 294 (1980) pp. 87, 94; id., 8 July 1982, *BolMinJust* 325 (1983) pp. 247, 255 (statutes on the right to strike, the striking parties must maintain specific minimum functions of a business).   [165] Nos. 24 f. and fn. 113 above.

[166] On equivalent provisions in English law, which operates with a number of separate torts, see Gutteridge, *CLJ* 5 (1933–35) pp. 22 ff. See also no. 308 below.

[167] *D.* 4.3. ('de dolo malo').   [168] Ulp. *D.* 4.3.1 § 3.

[169] Only in 1916 did the Austrian ABGB incorporate its § 1295 II: 'A person who wilfully causes damage to another in a manner contrary to *bonos mores* is liable for damages. However, should he have been exercising a right, he is not liable unless he acted with purely malicious intent.' This provision effectively combines §§ 226 (prohibition against the exercise of a right if it can only have the purpose of harming another peron) and 826 BGB. On this issue see e.g. Schwimann (-Harrer), *ABGB* vol. v, § 1295 no. 103; and Rummel (-Reischauer), *ABGB* vol. ii, 2nd edn., § 1295 no. 54.

principle. Under Roman law the *actio de dolo* was a subsidiary[170] cause of action, imposed at the discretion of the judge.[171] It only came into effect if other remedies failed. In emphasizing the *dolus malus*, it required especially blameworthy, malicious, and unethical conduct.[172] In Roman times it played an important role in many of the same cases as today, particularly in cases on § 826 BGB and Art. 919 Greek Cc, e.g. malicious litigation,[173] inducement to breach of contract (for instance by tendering a second, higher offer),[174] or where (e.g.) a bank makes a false statement about the solvency of a person.[175] § 826 BGB, § 1295 II ABGB, and Art. 919 Greek Cc constitute both blanket provisions and general clauses. They serve as blanket provisions in differentiating between unethical conduct as a special type of unlawfulness and intent as a form of fault. They are general clauses in that their references to *bonos mores* seem only to refer to non-delictual standards of conduct.[176] Furthermore, it should be noted that one need only have intended to cause injury (in all three provisions *dolus eventualis* is sufficient to establish intent); intention to act unethically is not

---

[170] Ulp. *D.* 4.3.1 §§ 4–7 and *D.* 4.3.7.

[171] Inst. 4.6.31 expressly states that *actio de dolo* is part of the *'actiones arbitrarias'*.

[172] Ulp. *D.* 4.3.1 § 2. Although the term *bonos mores* is not mentioned in the paragraph on *actio de dolo*, links can be found in other areas, e.g. in cases of invalidity of contracts or wills: Papian *D.* 22.1.5; *D.* 28.7.15. How malicious conduct was to be understood, can still be seen in § 276 II BGB: 'ordinary' intent is not *contra bonos mores*; the attempt to exclude in advance liability for a delict committed intentionally is, however, *contra bonos mores*, and the exclusion will be void.

[173] See Inst. 4.16.1; *MünchKomm* (-Mertens), 2nd edn., § 826 no. 169 on one hand, and CFI Athens 11690/1964, *NoB* 12 (1964) p. 812 on the other. See also CA Athens 972/1961, *EllDik* 1961 p. 962 (abuse of a final ruling, obtained for example by deceiving the court); and BG 1 Oct. 1991, BGE 117 II 394 (in conjunction with a report by Merz, *ZBernJV* 129 [1993] pp. 235, 239–240). A denunciation of persons with differing political beliefs is regarded as particularly vicious: OLG Dresden *VersR* 1993 p. 1161: reporting a person intending to leave the country illegally to the GDR authorities.

[174] E.g. BGH 24 Feb. 1954, BGHZ 12 pp. 308, 317 f.; and BGH 19 Oct. 1993, *NJW* 1994 p. 128 in conjunction with Ulp. *D.* 4.3.33; or in conjunction with Mantzoufas, *Enochiokon Dikaion*, p. 527; or in conjunction with Trib. Verona 4 Mar. 1991, *Giur.it.* 1993, I, 2, 286; and *Encyclopédie Dalloz* (-Rodière), *'Rép.Dr.Civ.* vol. vii, 2nd edn., Responsabilité du fait personnel', no. 29 (inducement of breach of contract).

[175] Also remarkable are the similarities between Gai. *D.* 4.3.8 and Areopag 297/1959, *NoB* 7 (1959) p. 1015; HR 10 Dec. 1993, *RvdW* 1993 no. 248c; RG 18 Oct. 1917, RGZ 91 pp. 80, 81 f., and BGH 23 Mar. 1966, *DB* 1966 pp. 2019, 2020. On the relevance of Art. 919 Greek Cc for liability to information issued under Greek law see also Mantzoufas loc. cit. (fn. 174 above).

[176] Mertens (*MünchKomm*, 2nd edn., § 826 no. 2), says: 'the incorporation of *bonos mores* in the modern pluralistic society is not so much a reference to non-statutory standards, as it is an authorization of the judge to make law.' See also Georgiades/Stathopoulos (-Georgiades) *Greek Cc*, vol. iv Art. 919 no. 4, who points to the ability of Art. 919 Greek Cc to adapt to new developments. See also Koziol, *Österr. Haftpflichtrecht*, vol. ii, 2nd edn., p. 95 (*bonos mores* form the 'essence of all law which has not manifested itself in a statute'; the term does not necessarily involve moral standards).

necessary.[177] It therefore comes as no surprise that conduct *contra bonos mores*, and the intention to inflict damage, although they must theoretically always been investigated separately, are in practice two sides of the same coin. The German courts have repeatedly presumed intent when conduct *contra bonos mores* was proved,[178] and vice versa.[179] Hence, intent and conduct *contra bonos mores* remain as closely linked as was the case in the term *dolus malus.*

37   To the question of what the *actio de dolo* tries to achieve in contemporary law, the answer, at least for § 826 BGB, is clear: it has always targeted the same issues as § 823 II BGB: i.e. extension of the interests protected by § 823 I BGB. Originally this included improving the protection of the right to dignity, autonomy, and privacy,[180] as well as establishing a basis for the compensation of pure economic loss. The former aim was made redundant by judicial recognition of the rights of personality. However, in the latter issue of liability for pure economic loss, including liability for misinformation in both German and Greek and Austrian law, it still has a role to play.[181]

38   The difficulties which can arise, particularly in this field, for a legal system which on one hand objects to operating with general clauses, and on the other fails to recognize the intentional infliction of damage *contra bonos mores* as a distinct cause of action, can best be demonstrated by the example of Portugal. Its civil code has always lacked the *actio de dolo*[182] and could therefore only incorporate such an action through the criminal

---

[177] For Austria see OGH 21 Dec. 1929, SZ 11/49 p. 140; OGH 15 Dec. 1993, *WBl* 1994 p. 167. For Germany see RG 8 Feb. 1912, RGZ 79 pp. 17, 23; RG 31 Jan. 1929, RGZ 123 pp. 271, 278; and BGH 8 Mar. 1951, *NJW* 1951 p. 596 (note Coing). For Greece see CA Athens 5025/1990 *NoB* 39 (1991) p. 79. That intent need not refer to the immorality of the conduct is also largely undisputed in Greek literature: see Georgiades/Stathopoulos (-Georgiades), *Greek Cc*, vol. iv, Art. 919 nos. 13 f.; and Stathopoulos, *Geniko Enochiko Dikaio*, vol. ii p. 126. Arguing against this, however, Gasis/Chiotellis, *NoB* 40 (1992) pp. 467, 482. In Austria this fact has never been disputed: Rummel (-Reischauer), *ABGB* vol. ii, 2nd edn., § 1295 no. 56.
[178] E.g. BGH 26 Nov. 1986, *NJW* 1987, pp. 1758, 1759.
[179] E.g. BGH 20 Oct. 1992, *VersR* 1993 p. 330 = *EWiR* § 826 BGB 1/93 p. 33 (v. Bar/Rogge); and OLG Zweibrücken 10 June 1992 *WM* 1992 pp. 1604, 1608.
[180] See RG 2 Sep. 1937, RGZ 156 pp. 372, 374; and RG 6 Apr. 1932, RGZ 140 pp. 392, 395.
[181] OGH 22 June 1993 loc. cit. (fn. 159); Areopag 297/1959 loc. cit. (fn. 175); CA Athens 5025/1990, *NoB* 39 (1991) p. 79 (a bank acted *contra bonos mores* when handling a major loan to a shipyard); also BGH 20 Sep. 1993, *NJW* 1993 pp. 2931, 2934 (judges tend 'generally to improve § 823 I BGB, which they find protects pure economic interests insufficiently, by allowing intent to be more easily established'). Unlike the *actio de dolo*, § 826 BGB is, according to the concept of concurring claims, not simply a subsidiary provision. However, in practice it is treated as such, since such a serious reproach should only be made in cases where other bases for a claim will fail, esp. since under § 152 VVG there is no third-party liability cover in cases of intent. See also BGH loc. cit.; and for Austria Koziol, *Österr. Haftpflichtrecht*, vol. ii, 2nd edn., p. 97. For Greece see fn. 188 below.
[182] In that the Portuguese Cc of 1867 also contained no provisions resembling Art. 919 Greek Cc and § 826 BGB. Vaz Serra, *BolMinJust* 85 (1959) pp. 243, 335–342 was unsuccessful in his proposal to introduce such a norm.

offence of fraud (Art. 483 I, 2nd alt. Port. Cc). Thus non-contractual liability for information issued, i.e. in a case where *culpa in contrahendo* is not applicable, still poses a problem for Portuguese lawyers. Although there seems to be no reason why the prohibition against the violation of a legal right under Art. 334 Port. Cc, which relies (also) on *'bons costumes'*,[183] cannot be regarded as a protective law under Art. 483 I Cc, until now Portuguese law has not followed this line of thought.[184] Sinde Monteiro has proposed to increase the scope of Art. 334 Cc by interpreting it as a general provision on liability for the violation of a legal right; whether this will be successful remains to be seen. His attempt to create a provision similar to § 826 German BGB demands a generous interpretation of the term 'law/right' (*direito*) in Art. 334 Port. Cc, which it does not necessarily permit. The term *direito* would have to be understood as a general freedom of action, and not simply as a subjective absolute right.[185] However, a foreign observer might find it more convincing to interpret the term *direito* in Art. 483 I Cc as including relative rights, an interpretation which the text of the provision would allow.

While Portugal is still struggling to find a new interpretation of the **39** concept of *actio de dolo*, in modern Greek law its incorporation into the Civil Code plays only a minor role. In fact, Greek legislators have from the outset been uncertain whether a version of § 826 BGB was truly necessary to complement Art. 914 Cc.[186] As regards improved protection of personal rights it is unnecessary.[187] However, whether a provision should exist to deal with those types of conduct which do not infringe

---

[183] *'É ilegítimo o exercício de um direito, quando o titular exceda manifestamente os limites impostos pela boa fé, pelos bons costumes ou pelo fim social ou económico desse direito.'*

[184] See e.g. Coutinho de Abreu, *Do abuso de direito*, pp. 76–77; Carvalho Fernandes, *Teoria Geral*, vol. ii, 2nd edn., no. 86; and Almeida Costa, *Obrigações*, 4th edn., p. 370: all say that the abuse of a legal right is unlawful. Yet none of them states that Art. 334 Cc should qualify as a protective law within the meaning of Art. 483 Cc. However, Coutinho de Abreu, loc. cit. p. 77, is of the opinion that abuse of a legal right should be recognized in Art. 483 Cc as a third form of unlawfulness and should therefore also be applicable in tort law *de lege ferenda*. That would bring this field of Portuguese law in line with Germany and Greece, where § 226 BGB (prohibition of chicanery) and Art. 281 Greek Cc (abuse of a legal right) are recognized as protective laws: see no. 39 below. Such a solution would accord with Vaz Serra's intentions to incorporate the abuse of a legal right into a provision similar to § 826 (see fn. 182).

[185] The position held by Sinde Monteiro, *Responsabilidade por conselhos*, pp. 545–582. Coutinho de Abreu (see previous fn.) follows similar lines.

[186] Tryantaphyllopoulos, a member of the drafting committee, thought that Art. 534 of the draft version (= Art. 914 Greek Cc) would suffice: *Schedion Astikou Kodikos*, vol. ii, p. 381, no. 92. In fact, a number of authors considered Art. 919 Greek Cc superfluous: Litzeropoulos, *AID* 7 (1940) pp. 158, 191 (esp. fn. 24); Vavouskos, *I paralipsis os simiogono gegonos eis ta adikimata astikou dikaioñ*, pp. 112 ff.; and Zepos, *Enochikon Dikaion*, vol. i, 2nd edn., p. 403 (esp. fn. 2).   [187] See no. 19 above.

substantive law, i.e. a 'subsidiary remedy,'[188] would depend solely on how Art. 914 Cc was to be interpreted. The Areopag transformed it into a true general clause,[189] so now, against the background of Art. 914 Greek Cc, Art. 919 Cc is almost unnecessary. However, by using Art. 919 Cc in the following cases, the Greek courts have allowed it to retain some of its scope as an independent provision: where a person relies on the invalidity of a legal transaction, despite having himself fraudulently caused the defect of form;[190] where another, for personal reasons, dissuades a debtor from performing a contract;[191] where a person makes use of an incorrect ruling which cannot be challenged; and in other cases of abuse of procedural rights.[192]

40   The situation in The Netherlands largely resembles that in Greece. As stated above, Art. 6:162 II BW has rendered the violation of a *'plicht . . . volgens ongeschreven recht in het maatschappelijk verkeer'* (the general, residual duty of care) secondary to the provision dealing with violation of protective laws, and has made it compensatable.[193] It applies to cases which in Germany and Greece are covered by liability for intentional infliction of damage *contra bonos mores*. For *'deze woorden omvatten hetgeen in het oude recht werd omschreven als de strijd met de goede zeden of de strijd met de zorgvuldigheid die in het maatschappelijke verkeer betaamt. Daar het begrip "goede zeden" in de jurisprudentie nimmer tot wasdom is gekomen is thans gekozen voor een ander redactie.'*[194] In Belgium and France the principle of the *actio de dolo*, which can still be clearly recognized in Art. 1382 Cc (deliberate acts),[195] has been included in the general clause. Yet even here, relying on the violation of *bonos mores* is

---

[188] According to the courts, delictual liability can only be based on Art. 919 Greek Cc in cases where no statutory law has been violated. The Areopag (214/1972, *NoB* 20 [1972] p. 901 and 1969/1990 *EllDik* 32 [1991] p. 1499: refusal to let a person become a member of the 'association of pharmacists' for party-political reasons; abuse of the freedom of contract, Arts. 914 in conjunction with 281 applied instead of Art. 919 Greek Cc) applies this principle of subsidiarity even to Art. 281 Greek Cc (abuse of legal rights), to the general disapproval of academics. See: Georgiades/Stathopoulos (-Georgiades), *Greek Cc*, vol. iv, Art. 919, no. 24; Filios, *Enochiko Dikaio*, vol. ii 2, 3rd edn., p. 51.   [189] See no. 19 and fn. 53 above.
[190] CA Crete 138/1965 *EEN* 33 (1966) p. 366; CA Athens 414/1972 *Arm.* 26 (1972) p. 519.
[191] See fn. 174 above and CA Athens 2169/1958 *NoB* 7 (1959) p. 195.
[192] See fn. 173 above; but see also fn. 181.   [193] See no. 25 above.
[194] 'These words cover what was described under the old law as being contrary to *bonos mores* in breach of the general duty to take reasonable care. As the notion of *bonos mores* had fallen from use in the courts, a new wording was considered appropriate': *T&C* [-Steketee], Art. 6:162, note 2, refering to Parlementaire Geschiedenis, vol. vi, p. 616. See also HR 28 Oct. 1994, *NedJur* 1995 no. 140, p. 595: competitors in the market, the defendant intentionally exploited a breach of a contract between the plaintiff and a third party to force the plaintiff out of the market; Art. 6:162 BW.
[195] See no. 6 and fn. 23 above.

still one way of establishing *faute*.[196] In Italy pure economic loss is 'in any event' recoverable in cases of violation of *bonos mores* and intentional infliction of damage.[197] This also means that, irrespective of the recognition of a 'right to integrity of one's assets',[198] a number of cases come under the scope of the general clause, in which the unlawfulness of the damage (the *danno ingiusto*) depends on whether *animus nocendi* can be determined on the part of the tortfeasor. Alpa, for example, rightly refers to this aspect of Arts. 833 (a proprietor may not use his property to cause damage to others) and 1349 Italian Cc (a third party resolves in bad faith a dispute between the parties to a contract), both of which have come to be regarded, together with *reticenza* (fraudulent concealment) and *induzione in errore*, as intentional torts under Art. 2043 Cc. He also cites in this regard Art. 935 I s. 2 Cc (a proprietor, having used material other than his own in bad faith when erecting a building, and who destroys this material upon its return, is compelled to compensate), and Art. 96 C.proc.civ. (*abuso dei mezzi processuali*).[199] A further example of the requirement of intention for the recovery of *danno meramente patrimoniale*, noted by Busnelli, is the 'classic' situation of inducement of a double sale.[200] It would seem that the *actio de dolo* is also present in the Italian general clause.

Finally, we turn to an outline of the relationship between provisions concerning the prohibition against both the violation of a legal right, mentioned in nearly all European codifications,[201] (and referred to several times above), i.e. the *abus de droit* on one hand and the legal elements of the law of delict on the other.[202] All legal systems make

---

[196] See De Page, *Droit Civil Belge*, vol. ii, 3rd edn., no. 941 (p. 939); Weill/Terré, *Obligations*, 4th edn., nos. 629 and 405; Dekkers, *Précis*, vol. ii no. 220; Mazeaud/Tunc, *Responsabilité civile*, vol. i, 6th edn., no. 409: '*On commet une faute délictuelle, de même qu'on commettait un dolus en droit romain, chaque fois qu'on agit dans l'intention de causer un dommage.*' For literature in German see e.g. Heldrich, *Allgemeine Rechtsgrundsätze*, p. 27.

[197] Cian/Trabucchi, *Commentario breve*, 4th edn., Art. 2043 II 1 Ital. Cc. See also Geri/Breccia/Busnelli/Natoli, *Diritto Civile*, vol. iii, p. 708. See also Cass.sez.un. 2 Nov. 1979, n. 5688, *Foro.it.* 1979, I 2548. Castronovo, *Riv.crit.dir.priv* 1989 pp. 539, 571–573, thinks that the protection of pure economic interests under Art. 2043 Cc should be restricted in a fashion similar to the German solution.   [198] See no. 21 above.

[199] Alpa, *Responsabilità civile*, p. 222. See id., NGCC 1992, II, 383, 394–395; Cendon/Gaudino, in: Cendon (ed.), *Responsabilità civile*, pp. 389–472; Traverso, NGCC 1992, II, 297, 300–302; and Visintini, *Fatti illeciti*, vol. ii, p. 275.

[200] See v. Bar (-Busnelli), *DeliktsR in Europa, Italien*, pp. 13 ff. See also the literature referred to in fn. 174 above.

[201] Art. 7 II Span. Cc; § 226 BGB; Art. 281 Greek Cc; Art. 833 Ital. Cc; Art. 334 Port. Cc; and § 1295 II ABGB.

[202] For further details on comparative law and the history of the law in this area see Limpens/Kruithof/Meinertzhagen-Limpens, *IntEncCompL* XI/1 2–230 ff. See also the still very instructive work by Gutteridge, *CLJ* 5 (1933–35) pp. 22 ff.

the same basic assumption that absolute rights inevitably have inherent limitations, and that a tort is committed where social responsibility, a fundamental component of every right, has been shamelessly ignored. However, the methods by which this initial principle is incorporated into the law of delict vary, as does (occasionally) even the extent of adherence to the principle. Where a special legal provision prohibiting the abuse of a legal right exists, it automatically forms part of the group of protective laws sanctioned by delictual liability,[203] unless a claim to damages is already incorporated into the provision itself.[204] Whether such protective laws have any practical relevance to the law of delict depends, first, on the question of whether they operate with the broad notion of intentional unethical damage,[205] and secondly, on how the concurring claims of abuse of a legal right as *lex specialis,* and the *actio de dolo* as *lex generalis,* are dealt with[206] (although factually there is no difference between them). Legal systems which stress the difference between rights and legally protected interests on one hand, and pure economic interests on the other, operate as follows: if a person, whilst exercising a personal right, violates the right of another, (typical examples are cases of neighbour disputes,[207] family law [abuse, child custody], and violations of personal freedom [malicious report of a political 'crime' in a dictatorial regime]), the notion of the abuse of a legal right is employed to demonstrate that the tortfeasor's rights do not justify his actions. In cases where pure economic interests are violated, the fact that a person has failed to comply with the social responsibilities arising through his (usually absolute) legal right classifies his conduct as *contra bonos mores;* however, it is not unknown for a legislator to ask the court to exercise restraint on this

---

[203] As is the case in Germany and Greece, although suprisingly not in Portugal: see no. 38 and fn. 184 above. Unfortunately RP 11 Oct. 1983, *BolMinJust* 330 (1983) p. 537 (short case report) does not clarify the situation.

[204] As in Art. 7 II Span. Cc; for information on case-law on this issue see de Ángel Yáguez, *Responsabilidad civil,* 2nd edn., pp. 90–102. Remarkably, a combined Franco-Italian project on a common law of obligations of 1928 would have included a very similar provision in its Art. 74 II (text in Alpa/Bessone, *Atipicità,* vol. ii, 2nd edn., p. 412; see also no. 368 below).

[205] As is the case in Germany, where, if the requirements of § 226 BGB (prohibition of chicanery) have been met, the same can also be said for § 826 BGB. See Soergel-Fahse, *BGB,* 12th edn., § 226 n. 11.

[206] For Greece see fn. 188 above (Art. 281 prevails over Art. 919 Greek Cc).

[207] See Traverso, *NGCC* 1992, II, 297, 300–303. The German Federal Court (BGH 18 Sep. 1984, BGHZ 92 pp. 143, 148) is of the opinion that provisions on the respective interests of neighbours (esp. § 906 BGB) provide a definitive list of what can be considered an unlawful violation of property. From the point of view of the abuse of a legal right, this is of special interest, since it means that whether the problem is tackled from the viewpoint of the tortfeasor or the victim is of little relevance.

question.[208] Those countries which have no special provision on the abuse of a legal right, and which operate with a general clause, could in theory operate without the notion of the *abus de droit*. It is sufficient to incorpororate its sense into the concept of *'faute'*.[209] Yet there is a general desire to dissolve the linguistic tension between the concept of an 'absolute' right, which *'confère à son titulaire une certaine impunité'*, and the fact that the exercise of such a right can lead to liablity for damages.[210] Nevertheless, whether one says that a person acts *fautif* when he is guilty of an *abus de droit*,[211] or whether it is argued that no right can sanction (as Arts. 1382, 1383 Cc suggest) a *faute* being committed, makes no difference in practice. This is confirmed by the statement that *'toute faute, même non intentionnelle, commise dans l'exercice d'un droit'* renders a person liable.[212] In practice, this brings the German and Greek provisions into effect.[213] Neither § 826 BGB nor Art. 919 Greek Cc require

[208] As in § 1295 II ABGB (see fn. 169 above), and Art. 281 Greek Cc. According to the latter it must be 'apparent' that, through the exercise of a right, the boundaries set by the principles of *bonos mores* and good faith have been transgressed. On this issue see Fragistas, *FS Wolff*, pp. 49, 51; Koziol, *Österr. Haftpflichtrecht*, vol. ii, 2nd edn., p. 99 (criticizing the wording of § 1295 II ABGB); and Rummel (-Reischauer), *ABGB* vol. ii, 2nd edn., § 1295 no. 59 (the overriding purpose must be to cause damage). This 'classic' position, which strictly adheres to § 1295 II ABGB, has recently been abandoned by the Austrian OGH, which has declared that 'causing purely economic loss is unlawful and thus must be compensated if the interests of the person causing the damage are deemed inferior to those of the person suffering the loss': OGH 8 July 1993, *ÖJZ* 1994 pp. 276, 277 (*EvBl* 58).

[209] Therefore Mazeaud/Tunc, *Responsabilité civile*, vol. i, 6th edn., no. 547 and Cass. 10 Sep. 1971, *Pas. belge* 1972 I 28, 29, in which the Belgian Court of Cassation rightly states: *'L'abus de droit peut résulter non seulement de l'exercice d'un droit avec la seule intention de nuire, mais aussi de l'exercice de ce droit d'une manière qui dépasse les limites de l'exercice normal de celui-ci par une personne prudente et diligente'*, agree with those authors *'qui considèrent que le critère de l'abus de droit est la faute aquilienne commise dans l'exercice d'un droit'*: Fagnart, in: Dalcq (ed.), *Responsabilité et réparation des dommages*, p. 12. In the Spanish literature the view that 'fault practically . . . replaces the concept which previously occupied this area, the abuse of a legal right' (Cavanillas Múgica, *Transformación*, p. 49 and fn. 3) has recently gained strong support. Yet in Italy most courts (however, not Trib. Turin 13 June 1983, *Resp.Civ. e Prev.* 1983 p. 815) have ignored the attempts of a number of legal writers to develop a general theory of *abuso del diritto* through Art. 833 Ital. Cc (Visintini, *Fatti illeciti*, vol. ii, p. 276). For Portugal Vaz Serra defended the (correct) thesis that the abuse of a legal right does not really concern the *'exercício de um direito, mas de falta de direito'*: BolMinJust 85 (1959) pp. 243, 257.

[210] Flour/Aubert, *Obligations*, vol. ii, no. 625. See also Visintini, *Fatti illeciti*, vol. ii, p. 286; Cass. 6 Feb. 1982, n. 688, *Giur.it.* 1983, I, 1, 144.

[211] This is the prevailing opinion. See e.g. Dekkers, *Précis*, no. 220; Josserand, *Cours de Droit Civil*, vol. ii, 2nd edn., nos. 428 ff., and recently Cass.com. 5 July 1994, *Bull.Com.* 1994 no. 258.   [212] Flour/Aubert, *Obligations*, vol. ii, no. 625; Cass. 10 Sep. 1971 (fn. 209).

[213] See Ferrer Correia, *Estudos de Direito Civil*, 2nd edn., pp. 33 and 44, who sums up § 826 BGB *'uma responsabilidade fundada em conduta <contrária aos bons costumes>, uma responsabilidade por abuso de direito.'* See also TS 14 Feb. 1944, *RAJ* 1944 no. 293 p. 160 (prior to the introduction of the latest version of Art. 7 into the *Código Civil* in 1974), where the court defined the abuse of a legal right as unethical damage to the interests of others (note: rights and legally protected interests, which are sufficiently protected elsewhere, were not included); for detail see Díez-Picazo/Gullón, *Sistema*, vol. ii, 6th edn., pp. 455, 457–462.

malicious intent in the infliction of damage.[214] In cases where a person acts negligently, no right can be said to be 'exercised'. In conclusion, it seems that the doctrine of *abus de droit* is concerned more with providing conceptually elegant reasoning than with solving real legal disputes. Its only real relevance appears to be its influence on the transformation of blanket provisions into general clauses in Greece, and to a much more limited extent also in Portugal.[215]

3. FURTHER AREAS OF LIABILITY FOR PERSONAL MISCONDUCT
IN EUROPEAN CODES

a. General Overview

42 There are three main areas of liability for personal misconduct which, if any issues are singled out, are specified in the delictual provisions of the various European codes: protection of economic reputation (see b. below), joint and several liability (see c. below), and liability of persons lacking civil capacity (see d. below). An overview of all the codes would show that many other delictual provisions also exist. However, they are of a purely national character, and their contents and significance vary from code to code. Personal liability of judges and civil servants for breach of duty, for example, is imposed by § 839 BGB.[216] This provision is exceptional not for its content, but for its inclusion in the Code.[217] Provisions are now found only in the two teutonophone nations of Europe (§ 825 BGB and § 1328 ABGB) on damage to a woman's sexual reputation. However, since World War II there have been rulings only on § 1328 ABGB,[218] and that only rarely. The Greek legislator considered its Art. 921 Greek Cc (old version) to be antiquated, and repealed it by Art.

---

[214] Representative of the view of many authors, see Georgiades/Stathopoulos (-Georgiades) *Greek Cc*, vol. iv, Art 919 no. 14; and *MünchKomm* (-Mertens), 2nd edn., § 826 BGB: no. 61. However, under § 1295 II ABGB the legal position is different: Reischauer loc. cit. (fn. 208 above).   [215] See nos. 19 and 38 above.

[216] See also Art. 34 GG, which transfers the personal liability of civil servants onto the state. The most important exception is the liability of those doctors, who are civil servants, for mistreatment of in-patients (BGH 30 Nov. 1982, BGHZ 85 p. 393). Note, however, that mistreatment of out-patients is not excepted (BGH 8 Dec. 1992, BGHZ 120 p. 367 = *VersR* 1993 p. 357).

[217] The most common model in use in Europe is the application of the general provisions of the law of delict to the liability of civil servants (see Part 6, fns. 1–5 below). However, those nations which consider it necessary to apply special provisions on this matter have chosen completely different locations. Furthermore, Art. 501 Port. Cc concerns only the liability of the state regarding those civil servants carrying out public administration under private law. Thus it is compatible with §§ 31 and 89 BGB, and Arts. 71 Greek Cc, 104 Greek Intr. Act to the Cc.

[218] OGH 15 Oct. 1992, *JBl* 1993 p. 595 (abuse of the state of dependency).

7 of Act 1329/1983. Portugal rejected a similar provision in 1967 when its Code was being drafted.[219]

Although the Italian courts have regularly discussed the *seduzione con promessa di matrimonio* ('seduction with the promise of marriage'),[220] they have recently begun to alter their view on this matter. Whereas the *Corte di Cassazione* as recently as 1991 told a court of first instance, which was of the opinion that the claim no longer corresponds with the 'social conscience of a modern society',[221] that although such 'changes of the social conscience' merited careful consideration as regards causes of action, this would not alter the fact that for Art. 2043 Cc *'la mera colpa dell'agente'* is sufficient. For, unlike Art. 526 CP, Art. 2043 Cc does not demand intent.[222] Two years later, however, the Court of Cassation abandoned this position, rendering intent on the part of the man a necessary precondition. The promise of marriage must have been made specifically to overcome her reluctance and modesty, and to influence her will.[223]

Whereas provisions such as §§ 1328 ABGB and 825 BGB are considered **43** antiquated in most European nations, the contents of the regulations of § 848 BGB and Art. 934 Greek Cc are undisputed. It is *jure communi europaeo* that, in cases where a person *steals an object*, or comes into its possession as the result of a delict, he is liable for its later loss even if he was not at fault for that loss. Furthermore, all European nations agree about the reasons for this decision. If a person unlawfully deprives another of an object, that deprivation renders him *ex lege* in default. Art. 934 Greek Cc, for example, states this expressly. Only on the question of whether clarification of this position is needed[224] or, if it is decided to introduce it, whether it should be placed in the general part covering delay,[225] does discord arise. As a result of such conceptual

---

[219] See Vaz Serra, *BolMinJust* 92 (1960) pp. 37, 130–133.

[220] For an overview see Alpa/Bessone, *Trattato*, vol. xiv, 2nd edn., pp. 120–121. For court rulings see esp. Cass. 10 Aug. 1991, n. 8733; *NGCC* 1992, I, 397, but also Cass. 9 Nov. 1973, n. 2947, *Foro.it.Mass.* 42 (1973) col. 826, and Cass. 11 Mar. 1976, n. 846, *Rep.Foro it.* 99 (1976) col. 2595 = *Foro.it.* 1976, I, 961.   [221] Trib. Pisa 3 Feb. 1976, *Giur.it.* 1976, I, 708.

[222] Cass. 10 Aug. 1991 loc. cit. (fn. 220 above).

[223] Cass. 8 July 1993, n. 7493, *Corr.giur.* 1993 p. 1052. So the situation in Italy is similar to that in Greece, where the judiciary can still resort to Art. 919 Greek Cc: Areopag 672/1993, *EllDik* 35 (1994) p. 1271.

[224] The Belgian and French Cc do without it (only in the law of impossibility of performance do they incorporate such a provision: see Arts. 1302 and 1145 Cc). That there is no need for this reminder *'en matière de délits et de quasi-délits'* is one of the *'exceptions unanimement admises'*: de Page, *Droit Civil Belge*, vol. iii, 3rd edn., no. 75. Even some German academic writers consider § 848 BGB to be superfluous: Meincke, *JZ* 1980 pp. 677 ff. Under the old Dutch law, which has no such provision, attempts were made to 'introduce' it by means of analogy: Bloembergen, *Schadevergoeding bij onrechtmatige daad*, pp. 208–209.

[225] As in Italy (Art. 1221 II), Spain (Art. 1185) Cc, and The Netherlands Art. 6:83 (b) in conjunction with Art. 6:74 I BW.

differences, the number of auxillary provisions in the law of delict varies. The provisions on defining negligence,[226] self-defence, and necessity,[227] and those on liability for information issued, clearly demonstrate this point.[228]

b. Endangering the Economic Reputation of a Person or Firm, and Other Delicts Concerning the Protection of a Business

44   Only a few countries in the European Union have special legal provisions dealing with the delict of endangering the credit of a person or firm. Those provisions which do exist are, in historical order: § 1330 II ABGB, § 824 BGB, Art. 920 Greek Cc, and Art. 484 Port. Cc. Under Dutch law, Art. 6:167 BW (claim to a publication rectifying a misrepresentation; see also § 1330 II s. 2 ABGB) requires that such actions be prescribed by Art. 6:162 BW. In Spain the Act on the Protection of Personal Honour of 5 May 1982 extends to economic reputation, i.e. to 'commercial honour' (see no. 49 below). In Italy it was the courts which shaped and reinforced the right to a *reputazione economica*, within the general clause.[229] In France and Belgium, on the other hand, endangering the credit of a person or a firm simply falls under the general clause, and is not separately emphasized.[230]

45   The provisions dealing with endangering the credit of a person or a firm protect, not social, but economic reputations.[231] Hence, they are not

---

[226] See no. 12 and fn. 10 above. Only the Port. Cc integrated its definition of negligence into the law of delict.

[227] Only the Italian law incorporates the relevant provisions into the law of delict: Arts. 2044 and 2045 Cc. It is remarkable that the Dutch legislator deliberately refrained from including these grounds of justification into its code. Their scope was considered so vague that it was felt better to abstain from such a rule: *Parlementaire Geschiedenis*, vol. vi, p. 617. The legislatory consequence of such restraint was that guidance on potential grounds of justification needed to be expressly set out in the basic provision: Art. 6: 162 II BW.

[228] Unlike in Greece (Art. 729 Greek Cc) and Germany (§ 676 BGB), the relevant provisions have been incorporated into the Austrian (§ 1300 ABGB) and Portuguese (Art. 485 Cc) laws of delict. However, they do not form the *basis* for an independent cause of action extending beyond that of the basic provision. See Sinde Monteiro, *Responsabilidade por conselhos*, pp. 451–454.

[229] See the review of cases in Perlingieri (-Maglione), Art. 2043 Cc no. 27, pp. 1787–1789.

[230] For examples of court rulings see Ferid/Sonnenberger, *Frz. Zivilrecht*, vol. ii, 2nd edn., 2 0 120, also Paris 25 Jan. 1988, *D.* 1988 IR 50 and Cass.civ. 12 Feb. 1986, *D.* 1986 *Jur.* 158. For further rulings see the fns. to no. 46 below.

[231] RG 6 Apr. 1932, RGZ 140 pp. 392, 396; OGH 31 Aug. 1983, SZ 56/124, pp. 548, 553; Georgiades/Stathopoulos (-Vosinakis), *Greek Cc*, vol. iv, Art. 920 no. 1; Deliyanis/Kornilakis, *Eidiko Enochiko Dikaio*, vol. iii p. 177, who stresses the main aim of Art. 920: to clarify that credit, occupation, and professional career all come under the general right to privacy (Arts. 914 in conjunction with 57 Greek Cc). Also Vaz Serra, *BolMinJust* 92 (1960) pp. 37, 126–130, and Pires de Lima/Antunes Varela, *Cc anotado*, vol. i, 4th edn., Art. 484 Cc notes 1 and 2, who expressly mentions the similarities between German and Portuguese law. See also TC 14 Dec. 1992, *BJC* 141 (1993) p. 55; CA Salonica 1316/1993, *Arm.* 199 p. 540.

concerned with contractual claims to performance (e.g. repayment of a loan),[232] but rather with economic success in commerce and career, and the value of a favourable business reputation (i.e. of creditworthiness: *il credito di cui gode di fronte ai terzi*). Hence, they concern an issue which poses specific problems, particularly for German law, namely the protection of privacy and purely financial interest. Unlike cases concerning privacy and dignity, the factual elements in a case on endangering a person or firm's credit are not value judgements, but are verifiable (or falsifiable) statements of fact,[233] which are not necessarily disreputable. However, if statements of fact are made which are disreputable, then liability for insult and the general protection of privacy would be appropriate causes of action; the latter may overlap with liability for endangering the credit of a person or firm.[234] Furthermore, the connections between tortfeasor and victim need not arise from competition. If that is the case the principles of fair trading are often also relevant. Thus statements of fact made by journalists, associations operating in the public interest, teachers, and other persons having no immediate economic interests in harming the person criticized are almost always the basis of such claims.[235] Unfavourable statements of fact are regularly made in the media, either written or spoken. According to the BGH 'misrepresentations impairing the relationship between the injured party and persons indispensable for his survival and success in business, i.e. persons who can be called his "business

---

[232] Therefore, endangering the credit of a person or a firm must not be confused with the *tutela aquiliana del diritto di credito* which is currently so hotly disputed in Italy. It concerns the delictual protection of relative rights (to claim); see Castronovo, *La nuova responsabilità civile*, pp. 19 ff., and Perlingieri (-Maglione), Art. 2043 Cc no. 7, pp. 1745 ff. The objective of the provision on endangering the credit of a person or a firm, on the other hand, is to protect 'economic credibility': see Trib. Genoa 24 Nov. 1993, *NGCC* 1995, I, 390 (*credibilità economica*).

[233] On the difference between value judgements and statements of fact: HR 5 June 1992, *NedJur* 1992 no. 542, p. 2180; OGH 28 Jan. 1993, *JBl* 1994 p. 258; OGH 14 Dec. 1993, *ÖBl* 1994 p. 82; BGH 28 June 1994, *WM* 1994 p. 2080; BGH 21 June 1966, BGHZ 45 pp. 296, 302 ff.; and BGH 17 Dec. 1991, *NJW* 1992 pp. 1314, 1315. That distinction is important, first, because an incorrect statement of fact is not covered by the constitutional right to express one's opinion, and secondly, since the remedy of revocation is only available for misstatements of fact. See also Orléans 30 Mar. 1988, *Sem.Jur.* 1988.IV.368.

[234] See e.g. BGH 17 Nov. 1992, *VersR* 1993 p. 193, and OGH 28 Jan. 1993 loc. cit. (fn. 233). For an illustrative case on this distinction see Rb. Utrecht 30 June 1987, *KG* 1987 p. 309: in a review a doctoral thesis was described as a 'breathtaking monument of confusion full of *quasi*-scholarly gibberish, infantile boasting and flagrant blunders'. This statement was not considered to have endangered the credit of the person concerned. Although the review affected the 'good name' and the 'professional career' of the person criticized, the president of the *Rechtbank* considered these value judgments 'just about admissible'. Note also that, unlike cases concerning personal rights, for an infringement of economic protection the accusation must have been published: STJ 29 June 1993, *CJ* (*ST*) I (1993–2) p. 171.

[235] Typical is BGH 23 Oct. 1979, *NJW* 1980 p. 881, where a critique published with the intent to *promote* fell not under § 824 BGB, but under § 823 I BGB (infringing the right to carry on a trade or business, see also no. 47 below).

partners", such as lenders, customers, suppliers, and employers'[236] constitute an actionable violation of interests.

46   European courts provide many examples. *Corte di Cassazione* of 4 February 1992[237] concerned the liability of the RAI (the Italian public television company) for a journalist's assertion, made live on television, that the fish fingers sold by the plaintiff's company were contaminated with antibiotics. He was partly correct, as the fish had been treated with such a substance shortly after being caught. However, the substance was no longer active when the fish were processed. Based on Arts. 2049 (employer's liability) and 2043 Cc, the court allowed the claim: in failing to find out about alternative testing methods, the journalist had not exercised the appropriate professional duty of care.[238] When considering the types of associations mentioned above, the many rulings on the publication of quality tests on goods come to mind. However, these in fact make poor examples because they usually focus on the publication of value judgements.[239] A better example therefore is BGH 17 November 1992[240] which concerns a statement made by an association for the protection of endangered species. They claimed that the plaintiff, a limited company (*GmbH*), had 'illegally' and 'without proper documentation' sold 100,000 furs and skins of protected animal species to Spain. Had the statement only alleged illegality, it would have been a legal assessment (a statement referring to codified law) which would have escaped further investigation: a simple value judgement. However, the allegation of missing papers transformed the criticism into a statement of fact. The same is true in cases where, as in *Cour d'appel* Paris, 25 January 1988,[241] a journalist publishes the news that a company is on the brink of bank-

---

[236] BGH 7 Feb. 1984, BGHZ 90 pp. 113, 119. For a similar ruling see CA Athens 1678/1960 *NoB* 8 (1960) p. 1058; see also TC 14 Dec. 1992, BJC 141 (1993) pp. 55, 58–59.

[237] Cass. 4 Feb. 1992, n. 1147, *Foro.it.* 1992, I, 2127 m., and note by Roppo in *Foro.it.* 1993, I, 3359.

[238] For a similar case decided by a French court see Cass.civ. 18 Feb. 1986, *D.* 1986 *Jur.* p. 158, concerning tests on medicine carried out by a consumer protection association. See also Paris 28 Feb. 1989, *D.* 1989 *Somm.* 337. For German judgments see OLG Stuttgart 21 Mar. 1990, *NJW* 190 p. 2690: an authority was held liable for an unjustified warning about alleged microbiological contamination of pasta. For Belgium see Brussels 14 May 1981, *JT* 1981 p. 415 (information on a cigarette brand), and Brussels 25 June 1969, *JT* 1970 p. 153 (incorrect and poorly researched information on a type of pea). For Dutch rulings see HR 29 Oct. 1993, *NedJur* 1994 no. 108, p. 419 dealing with a television report on a language school implicating the entire establishment, when in fact the criticisms applied only to the French class.

[239] See e.g. HR 9 Oct. 1987, *NedJur* 1988 no. 537 pp. 1959, 1962; Brussels 4 Jan. 1985, *JT* 1985 p. 237; Cass. 18 Oct. 1984, n. 5259, *Foro.it.* 1984, I, 2711 (note Pardolesi); Orléans 30 Mar. 1988, *Sem.Jur.* 1988.IV.368 ; and BGH 9 Dec. 1975, BGHZ 65 p. 325. For even earlier rulings see the national reports in Hartig, *Vergleichende Warentests* (see bibliography before no. 11 above). Schwimann (-Harrer), *ABGB* vol. v, § 1330 no. 14, and Rummel (-Reischauer), *ABGB* vol. ii, 2nd edn., no. 8, correctly emphasize that § 1330 II ABGB only comes into effect in cases where a test comparing goods is based on misrepresentations.

[240] BGH 17 Nov. 1992, *VersR* 1993 p. 193.   [241] Paris 25 Jan. 1988, *D.* 1988 *IR* 50.

ruptcy, has *'du plomb dans l'aile'*. Furthermore, it is not only the credit-worthiness of a firm which is protected. Factual assertions concerning the professional success of an employee are also covered. In a 1953 case in Athens, representatives of the defendant firm alleged that the plaintiff had danced naked during working hours. However, the claim against them was dismissed when the truth of the assertion was proved.[242] The Austrian Supreme Court has even applied the delict of endangering the credit of a person or a firm to a priest[243] and a political party.[244] An inherent weakness in the provisions protecting a person or firm's economic reputation is the insistence on a direct relationship with the person criticized. Thus, cases such as that of the *Cour d'appel* Paris of 29 March 1989,[245] in which the defendant publisher overlooked and thus omitted to mention the plaintiff's company in a *'catalogue de l'ensemble des éditeurs de disques sur le marché français'*, can be handled only by a general clause.

Apart from their immediate objective, the provisions on endangering **47** the credit of a person or a firm serve a second, and equally important, purpose. They demonstrate how many special causes of action in the various codes have lost their precision over the years and given way, at least partly, to general clauses. Liability is no longer necessarily restricted to statements of fact. Nor is making a statement (and so being unable to rely on the *exceptio veritatis*, still to be found in § 1330 II ABGB, § 824 I BGB, and Art. 920 Greek Cc,[246] but given up in Art. 484 Port. Cc[247]) the

---

[242] CA Athens 2252/1953, *Themis* 65 (1954) p. 101. See also Paris 31 May 1988, *D.* 1988 *IR* 219 (incorrect details on the in-house function of a journalist).

[243] OGH 9 July 1987, *ÖJZ* 1988 p. 209 (*EvBl* 32).

[244] OGH 30 Nov. 1987, *JBl* 1988 p. 174.

[245] Paris 29 Mar. 1989, *D.* 1989 *IR* 132. A similar Italian case is Trib. Rome 7 June 1991, *Giur.it.* 1992, I, 2: a restaurant guide truthfully referred to the closure of a restaurant but omitted to mention its reopening in a later edition.

[246] Under all 3 laws the misstatement must be proved by the injured party. Negligent ignorance suffices, although under German and Austrian but not Greek law, the tortfeasor is not liable 'if he or the receiver of the communication has a lawful interest in it'. See § 824 II BGB and § 1330 II s. 3 ABGB, the latter limiting liability to cases concerning 'communications not been made public'.

[247] Art. 484 Port. Cc requires only *'um facto capaz de prejudicar o crédito ou o bom nome de qualquer pessoa'* (a fact likely to damage the credibility or good name of a person). The prevailing opinion among Portuguese commentators is that the *exceptio veritatis* is not necessarily a defence. Even the truth could damage the good name and credit of a person if it is inappropriate in a specific situation: Pires de Lima/Antunes Varela, *Cc anotado*, vol. i, 4th edn., Art. 484 no. 2 (including a case in which a newspaper truthfully but maliciously referred to a doctor's unsuccessful treatment of a patient: c.f. § 826 German BGB). Also Antunes Varela, *Obrigações em geral*, vol. i, 7th edn., no. 143, pp. 539–540; Almeida Costa, *Obrigações*, 4th edn., p. 371. The CA Lisbon (RL 21 May 1987, *CJ* XII [1987–3] p. 88) expressly stated that Art. 484 Cc covers not only untrue statements but also such true statements 'as are intentionally or negligently presented in bad faith, or in defaming circumstances'. The case concerned an accurate press report headed by a photograph of the plaintiff minister and two other persons (to whom the report did not refer) with the insulting caption: 'They queue . . . to sell weapons . . . to Iraq.'

only way to incur liability: in exceptional circumstances liability can arise from making a true statement.[248] Hence, the development by the German courts of the *'right'* to carry on an established trade or business.

Although the *Reichsgericht* had recognized such a 'right' even before the BGB came into force,[249] a judgment of 27 February 1904[250] must be considered the starting point for modern developments. It concerned a person claiming intellectual property rights to which he was not in fact entitled, or at least not to the degree asserted, who commanded another (and the latter's customers)[251] to stop selling (or buying) a particular product, threatening legal proceedings. Such a threat includes no actual statement of fact, but rather a (legal) value judgement,[252] and therefore was not, and is still not, covered by § 824 BGB. The RG nevertheless intended to award injunctive relief or damages. To achieve this, by referring to earlier rulings,[253] it relied on § 823 I BGB, stating that 'an established trade or business constitutes a right which can itself be violated'.[254] 'Since an established and independent business does not mean the business person is simply exercising his free will, but rather that this will has actually been embodied, a right to this business can safely be presumed.'[255]

48   This famous ruling by the Supreme Court of the German Reich constituted the first of the German courts' conceptual innovations with the

---

[248] In France, where competition law is based on the general clause of Arts. 1382 and 1383 Cc, the defence of truth is expressly excluded in cases of *'dénigrement'* (injurious falsehood), whereas Art. 35 of the Act of 29 July 1881 allows it in cases of 'diffamation' (defamation): *'En matière de concurrence déloyale il n'y a pas d'exceptio veritatis comme il y a en matière de diffamation . . . On n'a pas le droit de rélever au public toutes les tares et les fautes de ses concurrents'*: see Roubier, *Le droit de la propriété industrielle*, p. 549., and Houin/Pédamon, *Droit commercial*, 9th edn., no. 553. For court rulings see e.g. Paris 26 June 1986, D. 1986 IR 348: *'En communiquant au nouvel employeur d'une salariée des renseignements défavorables sur des faits qui, de surcroît, étaient totalement étrangers aux aptitudes professionnelles et au comportement au sein de l'entreprise et qui ont eu pour conséquence directe et immédiate la fin de la période d'essai, l'ancien employeur a un comportement fautif et il doit réparation au salarié du préjudice subi.'*
[249] RG 29 Oct. 1888, RGZ 22 pp. 93, 96: unjustified warning based on a non-existent intellectual property right, the claim to injunctive relief was granted; RG 25 June 1890, RGZ 28 pp. 238, 247, and 249: incitement of boycott, right 'of the individual business' to 'a good reputation'. For a detailed overview of the roots of the 'right to one's own enterprise' in German law see Krause, *JuS* 1970 pp. 313, 315; and Nobel, *Anstalt und Unternehmen*, pp. 9, 12–14.   [250] RG 27 Feb. 1904, RGZ 58 p. 24.
[251] That even threats to (potential) customers can establish an infringement of a person's trade or business was confirmed by BGH 7 Feb. 1975, *NJW* 1975 pp. 923, 924, and BGH 19 Jan. 1979, NJW 1979 p. 916 (both refer to further rulings on this issue). See also no. 48 and fn. 261 below.
[252] For further details see Wieland Horn, *Die unberechtigte Verwarnung aus gewerblichen Schutzrechten*, pp. 135–138.
[253] See fn. 249. On 14 Dec. 1902, just after the BGB came into force, the RG—in line with RG 25 June 1890 (loc. cit.)—in a case concerning incitment of a boycott, ruled that 'a running business can be . . . considered a vested right': RGZ 56 pp. 271, 275.
[254] RG 27 Feb. 1904, RGZ 58 pp. 24, 29.   [255] Loc. cit. pp. 29–30.

BGB's law of delict, for the right to carry on an established trade or business is not a right which is protected *erga omnes*. Rather, it is a name for a group of legal duties intended to protect economic reputations and other pure economic interests.[256] In other words, it is a partial general clause within § 823 I BGB.[257] In the relevant cases, the unlawfulness of a specific act does not depend only on the damage caused. Indeed, it is the very purpose of competition to fight over every customer, and anyone who promises not to do so breaches the prohibition against cartels. Thus, when it has been established that certain conduct is an unlawful 'invasion of personal rights', this means that a particular act has been judged as unlawful (antisocial, libellous) in the circumstances of the case. The term 'right to carry on an established trade or business' therefore describes a concept not dissimilar to that of *faute* in French law, albeit restricted to a few conflict-laden areas.[258] Of course, the protection of the right to carry on an established trade or business is in many ways inferior to the protection afforded by a general clause.[259] The former has until now only been applied in relatively few cases and has not developed into a subsidiary cause of action covering all pure economic loss which would otherwise escape liability.[260] On the other hand, the right to carry on an established trade or business has not been developed simply to provide the legal answer to the problem of unlawfully claimed intellectual property rights (an area where it seems no longer to be

[256] As *MünchKomm* (-Mertens), 2nd edn., § 823 BGB no. 484 correctly states. See also K. Schmidt, *JuS* 1993 pp. 985, 986–989; and BGH 22 Dec. 1961, BGHZ 36 pp. 252, 256: 'The right to carry on an established trade or business has been developed by the courts, since the general clause of § 826 BGB, which requires intention to inflict damage, does not fulfil the needs of business, and the law against unfair trading has proved incomplete.' In Austria, however, the existence of such a right is denied, as 'indistinct and conceptually unjustifiable': Koziol, *Österr. Haftpflichtrecht*, vol. ii, 2nd edn., p. 39.

[257] See v. Caemmerer, *Wandlungen des Deliktsrechts* (= *Gesammelte Schriften*, vol. i, pp. 452, 499).

[258] For a comparative study on this matter see Wieland Horn loc. cit. (fn. 252) pp. 53–70.

[259] For example, it fails in cases of liability for information issued and in cases of interrupted power supply (BGH 9 Dec. 1958, BGHZ 29 pp. 65, 75). Neither is it successful in cases where an employer suffers loss as a consequence of injuries to his employees (BGH 19 June 1952, BGHZ 7 pp. 30, 36), nor in a number of other cases which would almost invariably result in delictual liability in other European countries (see no. 46 with fn. 245 above, and e.g. TS 11 Dec. 1990, *RAJ* 1990 no. 9994 p. 12822: professional reputation of a doctor damaged when a pharmacist failed to follow his prescription for obesity medication, resulting in ineffective treatment). Finally, the right to carry on an established trade or business is not protected by environmental liability law.

[260] See BGH 5 Nov. 1962, BGHZ 38 pp. 200, 204: 'due to its position as a subsidiary cause of action, such liability (for infringment of the right to carry on an established trade or business) . . . comes into effect only in cases where other causes of action are lacking, and where, according to the context of the relevant existing provisions, it is obvious that a gap exists which can be closed by means of § 823 I BGB.' Also BGH 23 Oct. 1979, *NJW* 1980 pp. 881, 882: 'Being classified . . . as a "subsidiary cause of action" . . . does not mean that a delict comes under § 823 I BGB in all cases where the relevant provisions would not consider the act as wrong. If the specific law sets standards prohibiting liability under the given circumstances, a claim under § 823 I BGB can usually be excluded.'

needed,[261] and where German law is even more rigid than that of most other European legal systems).[262] In the course of time, the number of acts considered unlawful and resulting in the imposition of damages has increased. Examples are: organization of boycotts,[263] unlawful strikes,[264] actual boycotts or blockades,[265] value judgements damaging to trade and business[266] including goods tests,[267] the latter being of major importance in comprehending the development process overcoming the limits set by § 824 BGB, and finally, the publication of *true* facts intended only to damage another's business.[268]

49   A lawyer trained in the spirit of the French *Code Civil* is likely to criticize the German system for bringing such varied fields as unlawful claims to intellectual property rights, boycott, blockade, strike, stating true facts, and insulting criticism under the same rule of law, i.e. the 'right to carry on a trade or business'. Since he enjoys the benefits of a general clause, the need for such a (makeshift) solution escapes him. In France these causes of action, although they share the objective of protecting the reputation and assets of others, are considered to have nothing in common other than the fact that they are all examples of *fautive* conduct.[269]

---

[261] If victim and tortfeasor are competitors, and the latter threatens either the victim or his customers (BGH 23 Feb. 1995, *DB* 1995 p. 1322), then § 1 UWG (law on unfair trading) would be applicable; see Wieland Horn, *Die unberechtigte Verwarnung aus gewerblichen Schutzrechten*, p. 212. See also Schrauder, *Wettbewerbsverstöße als Eingriff in das Recht am Gewerbebetrieb*, *passim*. One of the reasons why Austria opposes a general delictual right to carry on a trade or business is that pure economic loss cannot be compensated under 1295 ABGB, only under special provisions such as § 1 UWG; see Koziol (-Rummel), *Österr. Haftpflichtrecht*, vol. ii, 2nd edn., p. 258.

[262] Esp. in the field of unlawful claims to rights arising from a patent, the person making this claim is better off in some other countries than in Germany if the threat is aimed at the opponent and not at the opponent's customers. For the situation in The Netherlands see Mertz, *Schutz primärer Vermögensinteressen*, pp. 132–136; for England see Wieland Horn loc. cit. (fn. 261) pp. 9–20; and for France see e.g. Cass.civ. 23 May 1964, *Annal.prop.ind.* 110 (1964) p. 266 (although this case concerned trade marks). Also Cass.civ. 8 Nov. 1967, *Annal.prop.ind.* 1986 p. 73 (claim to hold a patent made to a competitors' customers); and Trib.Com. 9 Mar. 1954, *JCP* 1954 IV 79 (claim to hold a patent made to a competitor).

[263] BGH 10 May 1957, BGHZ 24 pp. 200, 206.

[264] Established practice in the courts since BAG 4 May 1955, BAGE 2 pp. 75, 77.

[265] BGH 30 May 1972, BGHZ 59 pp. 30, 34.

[266] BGH 26 Oct. 1951, BGHZ 3 pp. 270, 279; and BGH 21 June 1966, BGHZ 45 pp. 296, 306.   [267] See fn. 239 above.

[268] BGH 24 Oct. 1961, BGHZ 36 pp. 77, 82. In cases where the communication of a true fact concerns an employee and not an enterprise, liability may be based on an infringement of the general right to privacy: OLG Düsseldorf 22 Jan. 1992, *NJW-RR* 1993 p. 1242.

[269] E.g. Paris 26 June 1986, *D.* 1986 IR 348 (statement about a true fact); Paris 28 Feb. 1989, *D.* 1989 *Somm.* 337, and Cass.civ. 6 May 1987, *D.* 1889 *Somm.* 53 (degrading value judgments); Angers 22 Oct. 1980, *Droit soc.* 1980 p. 547 (illegal strike; see on this case also Catala, in: Levi/Rotondi [ed.], *The strike*, pp. 23, 38; Starck [-Roland/Boyer], *Obligations*, vol. i, 14th edn., p. 174; see also Cass.soc. 7 Apr. 1993, *D.* 1993 IR 115—although this case concerns a legal strike); and Liège 4 Jan. 1983, *JT* 1983 p. 556 (unlawful claim to an intellectual property right).

The Dutch have adopted the French system. In the absence of a special cause of action,[270] the Dutch placed what German lawyers classify as protection of a trade or business in Art. 6:162 II, 3rd alt. BW (*'hetgeen volgens ongeschreven recht in het maatschappelijk verkeer betaamt'*).[271] Examples are: warning issued to a purchaser falsely claiming intellectual property rights,[272] inappropriate publication of true facts about a competitor,[273] an inadequate goods test,[274] a damaging report on goods[275] and services,[276] and an illegal strike.[277] Its weaknesses of construction aside, the German approach of relying on the right to carry on an established trade or business has its advantages. The rulings it has produced are by and large accurate. What is more, without enforcing this right it would have been completely impossible to protect interests in Germany to the extent common to most European countries. Portuguese lawyers learn that in countries without a general clause some gaps can be closed by applying the relevant domestic provisions, such as special protective statutes in the field of strike law,[278] or more onerous liability for endangering the credit of a person or firm, as a result of which the 'protection of reputation' could also make actionable true statements of fact.[279] However, any additional gaps must be closed either by applying the general provisions on the protection of dignity, autonomy, and privacy (Art. 70 Port. Cc) or, as in Austria, by an action based on a violation of *bonos mores*.[280] On the

---

[270] On patents, Art. 43 II Ow (1910) = Art. 70 III Ow (1995).

[271] As Merz correctly argues in *Schutz primärer Vermögensinterressen*, p. 126; see also Asser (-Hartkamp), *Verbintenissenrecht*, vol. iii, 9th edn., no. 47; *Parlementaire Geschiedenis*, vol. vi, p. 615.

[272] For further references to Dutch rulings, although concerning Art. 1401 BW (old), see Wieland Horn loc. cit. (fn. 261) pp. 48–52; and Mertz loc. cit. (fn. 271).

[273] See e.g. Hof Amsterdam 16 Nov. 1951, *NedJur* 1952 no. 33, p. 86: the case concerned an invitation to tender. A builder who failed to win the contract informed the customer that his opponent had collaborated with the Germans during World War II and added that 'a true Dutchman would never sign a building contract' with such a person.

[274] HR 9 Oct. 1987 loc. cit. (fn. 239); and HR 19 Apr. 1968, *NedJur* 1968 no. 263, pp. 863, 872.   [275] Hof The Hague 31 Oct. 1940, *NedJur* 1941 no. 100 (p. 145).

[276] Hof Amsterdam 10 Feb. 1970, *NedJur* 1971 no. 130 p. 366. A post office savings book shown on the dust-cover of a book entitled *The Forgers*.

[277] Hof The Hague 22 May 1987, *NedJur* 1988 no. 646, p. 2281; Hof The Hague 15 Jan. 1988, *NedJur* 1989 no. 672, p. 2518; and Rb. Utrecht 27 Mar. and 13 May 1992, *NedJur* 1993 no. 431 p. 1530 (union liable for collecting and retaining drivers' lorry keys for the duration of strike). However, on boycotts see Rb. Roermond 3 Nov. 1993, *KG* 1993 no. 411: Greenpeace interrupted the plaintiff chlorine manufacturer's railway link for a short time. His complaint was dismissed on the ground that so short an interruption could be justified in the public interest.   [278] See fns. 160, 164 above.

[279] See no. 47 and fn. 247 above.

[280] On both boycott and incitement see OGH 8 July 1980, SZ 53/102 (where § 1 UWG was applied); and Koziol, *Österr. Haftpflichtrecht*, vol. ii, 2nd edn., p. 181 (§ 1295 II ABGB). Where the incitement to boycott is an attempt to damage another's reputation, it is also covered by § 1330 ABGB (Rummel [- Reischauer], *ABGB* vol. ii, 2nd edn., § 1330 no. 33. See also Rummel, *JBl* 1971 p. 385.

face of it, the question of which means are used to protect the right to carry on an established trade or business is academic. Yet in Greece, Filios has recently supported the proposal to establish such a right,[281] whereas both Sourlas and Plagiannakos have declared that strike and boycott in particular must be qualified as violations of the 'economic freedom' of Art. 57 Greek Cc (right to privacy).[282] Derogatory statements of opinion, for instance, which come neither under Art. 920 Greek Cc nor under any criminal provision, can only be dealt with under Art. 57 Greek Cc. The Greek judiciary have so far avoided deciding whether such infringements concern the right to carry on an established trade or business, or the right to privacy; three cases concerning unreasonable obstruction of a shop entrance caused by building work were treated as unlawful acts in contravention of Art. 914 Greek Cc.[283]

A glance at the Italian and the Spanish law is also revealing. *Italy*, for instance, recognizes no delictual protection of enterprises similar to that of the German system. However, some similar elements are covered by the *'diritto alla reputazione economica'*,[284] and others by the 'right to the integrity of one's assets' (see no. 21 above). Yet as far as strike law is concerned, there are parallels to the German law of delict. Not only in contractual, but also in a non-contractual context,[285] the right to strike has certain 'external limitations' (*limiti esterni del diritto di sciopero*).[286] These are, *'l'incolumità fisica e la dignità delle persone'*, and *'l'integrità e funzionalità degli impianti (sotto il profilo della salvaguardia della potenzialità produttiva dell'azuienda')*,[287] the 'protection of the organization of an enterprise',[288] and the freedom *'dell'iniziativa economica privata'*.[289] Taken together, these are no different from the 'right to carry on an established trade or business'—the right protected by the criminal provisions on

---

[281] Filios, *Enochiko Dikaio*, vol. ii (2), 3rd edn., p. 28.

[282] *ErmAK* (-Sourlas), Eis., Arts. 57–60 Greek Cc pp. 68, 68a; Plagiannakos, *EllDik* 7 (1966) pp. 101, 142.

[283] CFI Athens 8861/1956, *EEN* 23 (1956) pp. 638, 639 f.; CFI Athens 6541/1961, *NoB* 10 (1962) p. 920; and CA Athens 217/1967, *NoB* 16 (1968) p. 859. See also Georgiades, *FS Larenz* (1983) pp. 175, 185. In Germany such cases are seen as violations of the right to an enterprise: OLG Düsseldorf 30 June 1961, *NJW* 1961 p. 1925; and BGH 31 May 1974, BGHZ 62 pp. 361, 364.   [284] See fns. 229 and 237 above.

[285] See e.g. Pret. Palermo 28 Mar. 1992, n. 516, *Lav.prev.oggi* 1992 pp. 1161, 1163 ('*risarcimento del danno da responsabilità contrattuale ed extracontrattuale*'). This action failed on the ground that the infringed statute did not seek to prevent this type of conduct (see also no. 30 above). See also Trib. Bolzano 31 July 1989, *Rep.gen.* 1990, no. 139, col. 3546 (liability under Art. 2043 Cc).

[286] See Cass. 28 Oct. 1991, n. 11477, *Foro.it.* 1992, I, 3058, 3059–3060 with references to many further cases. On the '*limiti esterni*' see also Art. 1 of the Act from 12 June 1990, n. 146, Gaz.Uff. 14 June 1990, n. 137. See also Alpa, *NGCC* 1992, II, 383, 395.

[287] Pret. Mestre 30 Jan. 1986, *Lavoro 80* 1986 p. 388; Cass. 7 Feb. 1985, n. 6177, *Arch.civ.* 1986 p. 645.   [288] De Falco, *Riv.dir.lav.* 1992 p. 331, 342.

[289] Cass. 3 May 1984, n. 2696, *Riv.giur.lav.* 1985, II, 530.

boycott, sabotage, and 'taking over the premises of an establishment' (Arts. 507, 508 CP),[290] and Art. 2598 no. 3 Cc (which defines boycotts as an untypical form of unfair competition). In cases where a complaint cannot be based on Art. 2598 no. 3 Cc, e.g. because the boycotting parties are a trade association and thus do not run an independent trading enterprise, the courts apply Art. 2043 Cc by presuming a violation of Art. 41 of the Italian constitution (*iniziativa economica privata*).[291] Finally *Spain* takes us back to the delict of damaging a person's reputation. Its scholars and courts have always reasoned that the reputation and standing enjoyed by business people and freelancers is as important to them as is honour to a private person.[292] Therefore Art. 457 CP (old version) states that '*es injuria toda expresión proferida o acción ejecutada, en deshonra, descrédito o menosprecio de otra persona*'.[293] Furthermore, with a view to Law 1/1982 of 5 May 1982 on the civil protection of honour, personal private life, and photographic images, the *Tribunal Constitucional* has made it absolutely clear that the courts are correct to extend this protection to 'professional reputation and honour'.[294]

c. Liability of Independent Tortfeasors, Accessories and Conspirators, and Group Members

Even more widespread in European codes than the provisions on **50** damaging the reputation of a person or firm are those on the liability of several tortfeasors. They concern two or more tortfeasors, independently responsible for the same damage, accessories, conspiritors, and group members. They are treated as jointly and severally liable in all codes, albeit under different conditions, and in some cases with differing legal consequences. The first group are those who, independently of one another and with no shared intention, inflict the same injury or damage on a third party.[295] Accessories are those who incite or aid others. Group members are also independent tortfeasors. However, the problem here is

---

[290] Pera, *Diritto del lavoro*, 3rd edn., pp. 197 ff.

[291] Cass. 20 June 1973, n. 1829, *Giust.civ.* 1973, I, 1467. See also Cendon (-Gaudino) vol. iv, p. 2014, no. 15.4; (on Art. 2598 no. 3 Cc) Cass. 23 Feb. 1983, n. 1403, *Giust.civ.Mass.* 1983 no. 1403 p. 489; Giur.sist. Bigiavi (-Cendon/Gaudino) vol. i, p. 121.

[292] For more detail, including references to court rulings, see Bajo Fernández/Díaz-Maroto y Villarejo, *Derecho Penal*, 2nd edn., pp. 277–279, 286.

[293] See Art. 208 NCP, according to which '*es injuria la acción o expresión que lesionan la dignidad de otra persona, menoscabando su fama o atentendo contra su propia estimación*'.

[294] TC 14 Dec. 1992, BJC 141 (1993) pp. 55, 58–59.

[295] See e.g. Cass. 13 May 1989, n. 2204, *Rep.gen.* 1989 no. 171, col. 3381 ('*la risultante di una cooperazione di attività nella produzione di un medesimo evento lesivo*'). Factually irrelevant, yet conceptually remarkable, is the fact that Greek law subsumes part of the liability of independent tortfeasors under the term 'an act committed in common by several persons' (Art. 926 s. 1, 1st alt. Greek Cc). However, cases of 'several persons' being 'equally liable for

causation: a person is treated as one of a group if it cannot be determined whether the effects of an act are attributable to that person (e.g. as a combatant in a fight) or to another 'gang member' (Art. 6:166 BW). In order to overcome such problems, accessories and group members are often treated alike. In claims against accessories, too, particularly for aiding and abetting, causation often poses a considerable problem for the continental European laws of delict.[296]

(1) Independent tortfeasors

51   It is now common in Europe for independent tortfeasors to be held individually liable for all damage caused. The plaintiff is not obliged to sue everybody who caused the damage individually. He need only proceed against one perpetrator, who must then ensure that the other tortfeasors pay their share of the damages.[297] Any other solution, especially apportioning shares of damages, is out of the question in a field of law where each link in the causal chain is treated equally, and which generally does not distinguish between the various types of fault (intent, gross negligence, ordinary, and slight negligence). In fact, it would be odd if one person were held liable to a lesser degree simply because another had also done wrong. On the other hand, the victim must only be compensated once for the damage suffered, to avoid unjustified enrichment. Making all tortfeasors jointly and severally liable seems the obvious solution. In Germany (§ 840 I BGB), Greece (Art. 926 s. 1, 1st alt. in conjunction with Art. 927 Cc), Italy (Art. 2055 Cc), The Netherlands (Art. 6:99 BW),[298] and Portugal (Arts. 490 in conjunction with 497 Cc) this solution has been incorporated into the respective code. In

the same damage' (Art. 926 s. 1, 2nd alt. Greek Cc), cases which an independent observer would consider the very core of liability of independant tortfeasors, are usually considered as a combination of vicarious liability and liability for personal misconduct (Art. 922 Greek Cc), or cases of liability of the person in need of, and the person performing, the duty of supervision (Art. 923 Greek Cc). See e.g. Georgiades/Stathopoulos (-Georgiades), *Greek Cc*, vol. iv, Art. 926 nos. 8–10; Deliyannis/Kornilakis, *Eidiko Enochiko Dikaio*, vol. iii, p. 217; Balis, *Enochikon Diakaion, Genikon Meros*, 3rd edn., § 28, pp. 109 ff. Thus the person handling stolen goods is liable under Art. 926 s. 1 Greek Cc ('an act made in common by several persons'): CA Athens 14134/1976, *NoB* 24 (1976) p. 1119. The Austrian ABGB mentions only the participant's liability in § 1301. For independent tortfeasors § 1302 ABGB must be applied. OGH 26 Mar. 1987, SZ 60/55 pp. 282, 284; Koziol, *Österr. Haftungsrecht*, vol. i, 2nd edn., p. 296.

[296] See Deutsch, *Haftungsrecht*, vol. i, p. 347. On common law see also nos. 319–323 below.

[297] See only Cass. 30 Apr. 1984, *Rep.gen.* 1985 no. 167 col. 3468, TS 26 Dec. 1988, *RAJ* 1989 no. 9817, p. 9618; OGH 15 July 1953, *JBl* 1954 p. 44; and Cass. 15 Feb. 1974, *Pas. belge* 1974, I, 632. Cases where independent tortfeasors acting concurrently inflict different injuries distinguishable from one another, however, result in *pro rata* liability. For environmental impairment liability, see Rb. Alkmaar 25 Feb. 1993, *A&V* 1993 p. 19.

[298] On this provision see no. 60 below; also Boonekamp, *Onrechtmatige daad in groepsverband*, p. 28.

Austria, Belgium, France, Luxembourg, and Spain[299] it has been incorporated into the law by the courts.

The legal position in Belgium, France, Luxembourg, and Spain was **52** originally more complicated. First, they were all influenced by the *Code Napoléon*, according to which *'la solidarité ne se présume point; il faut qu'elle soit expressément stipulée'* (Art. 1202 I Belg., French, Lux. Cc; Arts. 1137, 1138 Span. Cc). Secondly, neither the French nor the Spanish Cc explicitly provides for joint and several liability[300] of independent tortfeasors.[301] In Spain Art. 106 CP (now Art. 116 I s. 2 NCP) proved a further obstacle: it stated that 'in cases where two or more persons are civilly liable for a crime or an offence, the courts shall determine the quota of liability for each of them'. Hence, Spanish courts had to ascertain partial (*responsabilidad mancomunada*) and not joint and several (*responsabilidad solidaria*) liability: *'El principio general (art. 106) es un principio de fragmentación.'*[302] However, the contractual context of Art. 1202 French Cc (= Arts. 1137, 1138 Span. Cc)[303] was eventually acknowledged by both systems,[304] and it was decided that liability of *'coauteurs'* is *not 'un cas de solidarité parfaite au sens des articles 1200 et suivants du Code civil'.*

---

[299] See fn 295 above; and OGH 15 July 1953 loc. cit. (fn. 297).

[300] However, in the field of parental liability *responsabilité en solidarité* has been expressly incorporated in Art. 1384 IV French Cc and Art. 1384 II Lux. Cc, whereas liability in Art. 1384 II Belg. Cc is *in solidum*.

[301] The civil codes of these nations do not even refer to joint and several liability of accessories. However, this lacuna is closed by Arts. 50 Belg. CP, 55 French CP, and 107 Span. CP (now Art. 116 II NCP). As a Belgian scholar once wrote, joint and several liability as required by these provisions is to be understood as *'l'application d'un principe de droit commun, de droit civil'*, which, according to Art. 1202 Cc, is itself a 'law'. See de Page, *Droit Civil Belge*, vol. ii, 3rd edn., no. 1032 (p. 1079), who refers to the leading Belgian cases: Cass. 14 Mar. 1907, *Pas. belge* 1907, I, 160; and Cass. 24 Jan. 1924, *Pas. belge* 1924, I, 159. For France see the overview in Capitant (-Terré/Lequette), *Grands arrêts*, 9th edn., no. 161 pp. 679 ff.

[302] Díez-Picazo/Gullón, *Sistema*, vol. ii, 6th edn., p. 615.

[303] Nonetheless, a significant number of scholars still challenges the contractual features of Arts. 1137, 1138 Cc. Although TS 23 Dec. 1903, *Col.Leg.Esp.* 16 (1903–II) no. 160 p. 941 acknowledged the contractual quality of both provisions in a case concerning unjustified enrichment, they maintain that neither the wording nor the position of the provisions support such conclusions. Hence, they argue, non-contractual liability must come under the principle of *mancomunidad*: Cristóbal Montes, *Mancomunidad o solidaridad*, pp. 105–116; Albaladejo, *Derecho civil*, vol. ii (2), 8th edn., pp. 555–557; id., *An.Der.Civ.* 16 (1963) pp. 345–376. However, the fact that the *Tribunal Supremo* itself occasionally reverts to joint and several liabilty in contracual cases (see TS 22 Mar. 1950, *RAJ* 1950 no. 710, p. 420, since then established practice of the courts) weakens their position. I.e. from the point of view of this judge-made law the meaning of Arts. 1137, 1138 is scarcely relevant. For the courts it has at least since TS 20 Feb. 1970, *RAJ* 1970 no. 938 page 662, 663 become established practice to apply the principle of joint and several liability to non-contractual liability law. See fn. 307, and e.g. TS 4 Nov. 1991, *RAJ* 1991 no. 8141 p. 11160 (house-owner and parents jointly and severally liable).

[304] De Ángel Yágüez, *Responsabilidad civil*, 3rd edn., pp. 846–847; v. Bar (-Santdiumenge), *DeliktsR in Europa, Spanien*, p. 34; de Page loc. cit. (fn. 300); Starck (-Roland/Boyer), *Obligations*, vol. i, 4th edn., nos. 1267 ff.

Therefore: *'lorsqu'un fait dommageable résulte des fautes commises par plusieurs personnes et que chaque faute a été directement causale de tout le dommage subi par la victime, sans qu'il soit possible de déterminer la part respective des auteurs du fait dommageable dans la réalisation du dommage, la victime peut demander à chacun des agents en faute la totalité de la réparation.'*[305] Spanish lawyers considered their position strengthened by Art. 107 CP, which divides wrongdoers into the groups of *'los autores, los cómplices y los encubridores'*, amongst which groups the principle of subsidiarity applies. However, the individual members of each group are *'responsables solidariamente'*. Although persons handling stolen goods are not covered by Art. 116 II NCP, the basic principles of Art. 107 CP (old version) have been retained. On the basis of an analogy with Art. 107 CP, Arts. 827 Ccom (joint and several liability in a collision between two ships), and 123 *Ley de Navegación aérea* (aircraft collisions),[306] and 'for reasons of safety and public interest', the *Tribunal Supremo* has accepted the principle of joint and several liability in the majority of cases in which it is not possible to establish the *'influencia personal, por acción u omisión, en la producción del evento dañoso'* with absolute accuracy.[307] The French leading case, Cass. civ. of 11 July 1892,[308] had used almost the same wording ninety years earlier. Two ships had collided. The owner of the damaged cargo successfully sued both captains as jointly and severally liable: *'d'après les principes du droit commun, quand il y a participation de plusieurs à un fait dommageable, la réparation doit être ordonnée pour le tout contre chacun, s'il est impossible de déterminer la proportion dans laquelle*

---

[305] Cour 25 Oct. 1961, *Pas. luxemb.* 18 (1960–62) pp. 386 and 387, representing Luxembourg's view.

[306] De Ángel Yágüez, *Responsabilidad civil*, 3rd edn., p. 862. However, see Cristóbal Montes, *Mancomunidad o solidaridad*, pp. 116–126; Albaladejo, *Derecho civil*, vol. ii, (2), 8th edn., pp. 555–557: arguing these exceptions from the *mancomunidad* does not form a sufficient basis for an analogy.

[307] TS 26 Dec. 1988, *RAJ* 1989 no. 9817, p. 9618; similarly TS 25 Mar. 1991, *RAJ* 1991 no. 2443, p. 3221; TS 31 Oct. 1991, *RAJ* 1991 no. 7248, p. 9804; TS 7 Jan. 1992, *RAJ* 1992 no. 149, p. 174 (also casenote in *VersRAI* 1993 p. 31); and TS 13 Oct. 1994, *RAJ* 1994 no. 7549, p. 9832 (joint and several liability of a community and a business for an accident during a firework display); TS 5 Apr. 1995, *RAJ* 1995 no. 3414, p. 4544 (explosion of a tennis ball which had been 'prepared' with fire crackers: parents and vendor held jointly and severally liable). For a case where, as an exception, partial liability was presumed on the basis that an exact share of the damage could be attributed to each independent tortfeasor, see TS 21 Feb. 1994, *RAJ* 1994 no. 1108, p. 1460 (during the demolition of a building the adjacent building was damaged. Although the demolition was conducted negligently, the owner of the house was only 25% liable, since 75% of the fault was attributed to the property managers who had not properly maintained the water pipes of the house, which led to its demolition).

[308] Cass.civ. 11 July 1892, *DP* 1894.1.513 (note Levillain) = *S.* 1892.1.508; Starck (-Roland/Boyer) *Obligations*, vol. i, 4th edn., nos. 1272 ff. demonstrate however, that some later rulings do follow this decision. Yet in recent cases the courts have again become unequivocal and rejected the restriction cited above. See e.g. Cass.civ. 12 Feb. 1969, Bull.civ. 1969 II no. 46, p. 35: *'le coauteur d'un dommage, ayant concouru à le causer en entier, doit être condamné envers la victime à en assurer l'entière réparation'*; Cass.civ. 29 Apr. 1970, *JCP* 1971 II 16586.

chaque faute a concouru à produire le dommage subi par la partie lésée.' When the Belgian *Cour de Cassation* faced this legal problem nearly half a century later, it ruled accordingly: *'lorsque le dommage a été occasionné par le concours de deux fautes isolées et distinctes et qu'il a fallu ce concours pour causer le dommage, les auteurs des deux fautes sont obligés tous deux à la réparation intégrale du dommage envers la victime, sauf à régler entre eux la question de la contribution à la dette.'*[309] However, in both countries joint and several responsibility of independent tortfeasors leads only to liability *in solidum*, reflecting the fundamental rule of interpretation inherent in § 425 II the German BGB. Unlike the genuine *responsabilité en solidarité* incurred by conspirators (*faute commune*)[310] and in cases of parental liability,[311] reminders, interruptions of limitation periods, notices of assignment, etc. affect only individual tortfeasors.[312]

Road traffic accident law provides abundant material on the joint and   **53**
several liability of independent tortfeasors. In HR 20 February 1981,[313] the driver of a car (K) recklessly attempted to overtake three cars and a bus on a country road: when K overtook the bus, its driver (L) swerved to the left to avoid a cyclist he had noticed late, the cyclist having no lights. K was forced even further left and hit a pedestrian. The court argued that L's conduct was at least slightly negligent. The owner of the bus was therefore found jointly and severally liable, and ordered to compensate the damage in full. In a similar case, BGH 16 June 1959,[314] one defendant suddenly drove out of a petrol station onto the road violating the right of way of the plaintiff, who was forced to swerve to the left. At this moment a driver who was overtaking in a similarly careless fashion collided with the plaintiff. The plaintiff, who was riding a motorbike, had to have his leg amputated. The BGH found joint and several liability for both defendants but the plaintiff was also found negligent. In addition, the defendants were strictly liable under the road traffic legislation (§ 7 StVG). This and the previous HR case of 20

---

[309] Cass. 2 Apr. 1936, *Pas. belge* 1936 I, p. 209.

[310] As for the liability of conspirators, Belgian and French law differ slightly. In France, *responsabilité en solidarité* arises only if a crime has been committed. In other cases liability is *in solidum*. Yet in Belgium Art. 50 CP is regarded as an expression of a general principle. Therefore incitors, joint principals, aiders, and abettors are liable *en solidarité* even where the delict does not constitute a crime. See Mazeaud/Chabas, *Obligations*, 8th edn., nos. 1070–1071; Starck (-Roland/Boyer), *Obligations*, vol. i, 4th edn., nos. 1268; and de Page, *Droit Civil Belge*, vol. ii, 3rd edn., nos. 1032, pp. 1081–1084.

[311] Only Art. 1384 IV French Cc says that *'le père et la mère . . . sont solidairement responsables'*. Art. 1384 II Belgian Cc is silent on the point.

[312] For a concise overview see Capitant (-Terré/Lequette) loc. cit. (fn. 300 above). The legal situation is the same in Belgium: Cass. 15 Feb. 1974, *Pas. belge* 1974, I, 632. Similar results could be achieved under § 425 BGB by arguing that the nature of the obligation is such that *'sich etwas anderes ergibt'*.

[313] HR 20 Feb. 1981, *NedJur* 1981 no. 418, p. 1385. See also HR 25 June 1993, *RvdW* 1993 no. 147.   [314] BGH 16 June 1959, *BGHZ* 30, p. 203.

February 1981 (liability without misconduct by the employer for the employee's negligence), demonstrate that even where the causes of action differ, joint and several liability can still arise. Another case in point is Trib. Milano 13 July 1989:[315] the first defendant inflicted serious injuries on the plaintiff rider of a moped, whose leg was broken and he suffered grave psychological shock. Whilst still in shock he attempted to leave hospital: confused, he jumped out of a window. The car driver and the nursing staff were held jointly and severally liable for the damage sustained as a result of the jump, the latter because they had not properly fulfilled their supervision duty. Two breaches of a *duty to act* have often resulted in the same damage. In such cases both tortfeasors are jointly and severally liable. Product liability law is well accustomed to such cases.[316] Another example of concurrent omissions is BGH of 13 May 1955:[317] sugar-beet was transported in a contaminated railway carriage, its previous cargo having been 'scrap lead'. The beet was fed to dairy cows, which died of lead poisoning. The owner of the cows obtained damages from both the railway and the transport agent: both had breached their duties by failing to examine and clean the carriages.

(2) Problems of Causation by Accessories and Participants

54   Since independent tortfeasors can be held jointly and severally liable for all damage, the same must apply to joint principals, i.e. those who conspire to commit a delict. Incitors and aiders and abettors can also be held liable for all damage to the victim. This finds statutory expression in § 830 I s. 1 in conjunction with § 830 II German BGB, whose authors relied on §§ 1301, 1302 ABGB and Art. 60 OR old version (= Art.

---

[315] Trib. Milano 13 July 1989, *Giur.it.* 1991, I, 2, 54 (note Rubini Tarizzo). See also Trib. Roma 21 Oct. 192, *NGCC* 1993, I, 637 (joint and several liability of editor and publisher); App. Naples 12 June 1992, *Foro.it.* 1993, I, 2347 (joint and several liability of journalist and publisher); and Cass.sez.lav. 4 March 1993, n. 2605, *Giust.civ.Mass.* 1993, no. 2605 p. 424, clarifying that Art. 2055 Cc also applies in cases combining contractual and delictual liability.

[316] For Italy e.g.: Trib. Massa 1 July 1989, *Arch.Giur.circolaz* 1990, p. 600 (puncture of a tyre, subsequent accident, joint and several liability of the *'costruttore, rigeneratore'* and the *'rivenditore professionale di pneumatici'*); and Trib. Roma 27 Apr. 1988, *Resp.Civ. e Prev.* 1989 p. 334. For Spain see: TS 26 Jan. 1990, *RAJ* 1990 no. 69, p. 115 (fatal accident caused by incorrectly installed cable in a bathroom cupboard; joint and several liability of manufacturer and vendor); and TS 26 Dec. 1988, *RAJ* 1988 no. 9817 p. 9618 (fire through faulty gas bottles; joint and several liability of manufacturer and supplier). For The Netherlands: Hof The Hague 7 Dec. 1979, *NedJur* 1981 no. 670, p. 2254 (incorrectly fixed roof insulation, joint and several liability of manufacturer and housing association for attaching faulty instruction leaflets).

[317] BGH 13 May 1955, BGHZ 17 p. 240. For a Belgian example, Cass. 26 Jan. 1922, *Pas. belge* 1922, I, 143.

50 OR new version).[318] In Greece this area is covered by Art. 926 Greek Cc,[319] in Italy by Art. 2055 Cc[320] and Art. 187 II Ital. CP,[321] in Portugal by Art. 490 Cc,[322] and in The Netherlands by Art. 6:166 BW.[323] In France and Belgium these rules form part of the *droit commun*.[324]

---

[318] Mot. II p. 738 on § 714 first draft; on the equal treatment of incitors and aiders and abettors under Austrian law: Schwimann (-Harrer), *ABGB* vol. v, §§ 1301 f. ABGB no. 10; and OGH 4 Dec. 1957, SZ 30/80 pp. 264, 267.

[319] Although Art. 926 s. 1 Greek Cc was evidently modelled on § 830 BGB, it is a broader provision. Art. 926 s. 1 Greek Cc includes independent tortfeasors, which the German BGB mentions only in § 840 BGB. However, regarding accessories the Greek text speaks only of 'an act made in common by several persons'. At first glance this seems to cover independent tortfeasors (see § 830 I s. 1 BGB: 'if several persons through a jointly committed delict have caused damage . . .') Yet it has become generally accepted that Art. 926 s. 1 Greek Cc extends joint and several liabilty to incitors as well as to aiders and abettors. Although Filios, *Enochiko Dikaio*, vol. ii (2), 3rd edn., pp. 90 ff., when considering Art. 926 s. 1 1st alt. Greek Cc, covers only joint principals, he then subsumes incitors, aiders, and abettors, as well as independent tortfeasors under the 2nd alt. Many other authors agree that the term 'an act made in common by several persons' is to be widely interpreted to cover *all* forms of accessories: Georgiades/Stathopoulos (-Georgiades), *Greek Cc*, vol. iv, Art. 926 p. 588; Balis, *Enochikon Dikaion Genikon Meros*, § 28, pp. 109 ff.; Deliyannis/Kornilakis, *Eidiko Enochiko Dikaio*, vol. iii, p. 218; Kavkas/Kavkas, *Enochikon Dikaion*, vol. ii, pp. 876 ff., and Zepos, *Enochikon Dikaion*, vol. ii (2), 2nd edn., pp. 751–752.

[320] Art. 2055 I Cc itself says only that the damaging act can be attributed to several persons (*è imputabile a più persone*). However, this does not mean that Art. 2055 Cc covers only independent tortfeasors. See Cass.sez.lav. 4 Mar. 1993, n. 2605 loc. cit. (fn. 315 above). From the Italian point of view it is unneccessary to distinguish between independent tortfeasors, joint principals, incitors, and aiders and abettors. The relevant question is whether their actions have led to a *fatto dannoso*: Cendon (-Devescovi/Gambi) vol. iv, p. 2160, no. 3; Cian/Trabucchi, *Commentario breve*, 4th edn., Art. 2055 Cc no. 1; Alpa/Bessone, *Trattato*, vol. xiv, 2nd edn., pp. 441–442; and Cass. 15 Jan. 1969, n. 70, *Giust.civ.Mass.* 1969 no. 70.

[321] 'I condannati per uno stesso reato sono obbligati in solido al risarcimento del danno patrimoniale o non patrimoniale.' Art. 110 CP is to be seen in the same context. It regulates sentencing for a crime: '*quando più persone concorrono nel medesimo reato*'.

[322] It covers '*os autores, instigadores ou auxiliares*', including under '*autores*' not only joint principals but also independent tortfeasors: Pires de Lima/Antunes Varela, *Cc anotado*, vol. i, 4th edn., Art. 490 no. 3; Almeida Costa, *Obrigações*, 4th edn., p. 388. Also no. 51 above.

[323] Art. 6:166 BW establishes joint and several liability for 'members of a group' (who belong to a *groepsverband*). For an individual member a '*psychisch causaal-verband*' is sufficient. See *Parlementaire Geschiedenis*, vol. vi, p. 663; Asser (-Hartkamp), *Verbintenissenrecht*, vol. iii, 9th edn., no. 93. If liability can be presumed for all members of a group (e.g. persons participating in a demonstration: Rb. Breda 26 July 1993, *KG* 1993 no. 302) then joint principals and aiders and abettors must therefore also be held jointly and severally liable. See Boonekamp, *Onrechtmatige daad in groepsverband*, p. 94. The only issue is whether they come under Art. 6:166 or remain under Art. 6:162 BW.

[324] For Belgium see Dalcq, *Rev.crit.jur.belge* 1981 p. 87, no. 109; de Page, *Droit Civil Belge*, vol. ii, 3rd edn., nos. 1032 ff. For court rulings see e.g. Cass. 15 Feb. 1974, *Pas. belge* 1974, I, 632; Cass. 2 Apr. 1951, *Pas. belge* 1951, I, 506; and Cass. 26 Jan. 1922, *Pas. belge* 1922, I, 143. For France see e.g. Flour/Aubert, *Obligations*, vol. ii, nos. 675 ff.; Mazeaud/Chabas, *Obligations*, 8th edn., nos. 1058, 1070 ff.; and Starck (-Roland/Boyer), *Obligations*, vol. i, 4th edn., no. 1268. The civil laws of both nations recognise only *coauteurs*. The differentiation between joint principals, incitors, aiders, and abettors is reserved for the criminal law, see Arts. 50 Belg. and 55 French CP.

In Spain the situation is more complicated[325] although the results are broadly similar. As stated above,[326] civil liability for crimes was initially governed by Arts. 106 and 107 CP. According to Art. 106 CP the '*principio de fragmentación*' was the starting point. Art. 107 CP supported this principle insofar as the damaged caused by the three groups mentioned in this provision—*los autores, los cómplices, y los encubridores*—could be shared proportionally between them (otherwise the principle of joint and several liability was also to be applied here).[327] *Los encubridores* were persons handling stolen goods and accessories after the fact, Art. 17 CP. *Autores* were defined in Art. 14 CP, according to which *autores* were joint principals, incitors, and those aiders and abettors 'necessary to carry out the crime' (*los que cooperen a la ejecución del hecho con un acto sin el cual no se hubiere efectuado*), i.e. persons without whom the (principal) offender *ex ante* could not have acted.[328] Liability based on a proportional sharing of responsibility[329] was thus applied only to non-essential accomplices (i.e. 'freelancers' who could be disposed of at any stage). For, according to Art. 16 CP, '*son cómplices*' are only '*los que, no hallándose comprendidos en el artículo 14, cooperan a la ejecución del hecho con actos anteriores o simultáneos*'. The new Spanish Penal Code, in force since May 1996, has retained that system. Unlike the old Art. 107 CP, Art. 116 II NCP makes no mention of persons handling stolen goods, but that is the only change. The area covered by the old Art. 106 CP now falls under Art. 116 I s. 2 NCP, and that covered by the former Art. 14 CP is now governed by Art. 28 NCP. Furthermore, Art. 29 NCP is a verbatim copy of the old Art. 16 CP.

55   The majority of European codes have dealt with the liability of accessories simply for the sake of clarification. Even when the '*Badisches Landrecht*' (Code of the Grand Duchy of Baden, 3 February 1809) was being drafted its authors deemed it necessary to complement its German translation of the *Code Napoléon* with 'supplementary and elucidating provisions'. To Art. 1382 *Code Napoléon* they attached Art. 1382d *Badisches Landrecht*, which stated that of 'those tortfeasors who succeed in their deeds through a joint effort, . . . all those who have acted with intent are jointly and severally liable'.[330] Moreover, particularly regard-

---

[325] For a good summary of the legal situation see TS 17 Feb. 1972, *RAJ* 1972 no. 657 p. 493.   [326] See no. 52 above.

[327] See fn. 307 above. See also TS (crim.) 17 Nov. 1994, *La Ley* 1995 (1) pp. 202, 213 where joint and several liability is imposed on a lawyer employed by ETA members who kidnapped a businessman. Although the laywer was 'only' liable as an accomplice, he was nevertheless held liable for all the damage, since no charges had yet been brought against the terrorists themselves. It was for him to seek recourse against them.

[328] E.g. TS 1 Mar. 1988, *RAJ* 1988 no. 1513, pp. 1451, 1452; TS 11 Mar. 1988, *RAJ* 1988 no. 1627, pp. 1641, 1642.   [329] Morillas Cueva, *Consecuencias del delito*, p. 149.

[330] Law of the Grand Duchy of Baden. 'Authorized edition' (*Amtliche Ausgabe*) Karlsruhe 1867.

ing the liability of incitors, uncertainties had arisen about the common law interpretation of the Roman texts which needed rectifying.[331] Continental European laws of delict have always maintained that conduct which, if viewed on its own is *not* causally linked to a given damage,[332] can nevertheless lead to liability for all damage suffered by third parties if the conduct was intended to support another in the commission of a tort. Whether the other person would have committed the delict (alone or with assistance) even without the support of his accomplice is irrelevant. What must be proven is that the person supporting the tortfeasor participated intentionally. Thus, 'but for' psychological causation need not be proven,[333] which is the second reason why European codes have emphasized the liability of the accessory within the law of delict.

In the words of the Belgian *Cour de Cassation*, it is therefore unnecessary *'de faire une distinction suivant que la participation a été principale ou accessoire, ni suivant la mesure dans laquelle les participants ont contribué aux divers faits qui ont causé le dommage'*.[334] The same would be true if aiders and abettors as well as principal offenders were treated as 'members of a group'. For it is the very intention of (e.g.) Art. 6:166 BW (for more on this provision see no 59 below) to draw the causal link from the damage only to the conduct of the group and not to that of the individual, the group being considered a unit. Thus, if damages are claimed from a member of this group, he cannot escape liability on the ground that he was not the tortfeasor, nor by stating that the damage would have occurred even if he had not participated.[335] Both German leading cases in this field support this line. BGH of 29 October 1974[336] concerned a sit-in organized by students. When the police evacuated the building, stones were thrown. Two police officers were injured and police vehicles were damaged. The plaintiffs, who were found later on the roof of an adjacent building, had not thrown any stones themselves. They had nevertheless participated in the sit-in and vociferously supported the subsequent 'battle'. The BGH ruled: 'whether the riots would have occurred without the defendants is irrelevant. Support given to the principal offender can be considered as aiding and abetting even if it is not the cause of his success.'[337] The situation in BGH of 31 January 1978[338] was similar. It concerned go-slow industrial action by air-traffic controllers. Being civil servants they were prohibited from taking strike action. Thus the BGH judged their

---

[331] Mot. II p. 738.   [332] See Antolisei, *Diritto Penale*, 10th edn., p. 473.

[333] See Bydlinski's fundamental analysis in *JBl* 1959 pp. 1–13; Koziol, *Österr. Haftpflichtrecht*, vol. i, 2nd edn., p. 65. On the exceptional situation under Spanish law, see no. 54 above.   [334] Cass. 2 Apr. 1951, *Pas. belge* 1951, I 506, 508.

[335] Hijma/Olthof, *Compendium*, 4th edn., no. 419; Schut, *Onrechtmatige daad*, 4th edn. § 23; Boonekamp, *Onrechtmatige daad in groepsverband*, p. 17; *Parlementaire Geschiednis*, vol. vi, p. 662.   [336] BGH 29 Oct. 1974, BGHZ 63 p. 124.

[337] Loc. cit. p. 130.   [338] BGH 31 Jan. 1987, BGHZ 70, p. 277.

conduct *contra bonos mores* under § 826 BGB. The defendant air-traffic controllers' federation had supported its members' campaign through its executive organs (*Organe*) by giving interviews and other means. The BGH ruled: 'it is of no relevance whether the "campaign" would have taken place even if the defendant had not supported its members'. So, 'aiding and abetting the air-traffic controllers by giving them psychological support' was sufficient to establish joint and several liability.[339]

56   The situation is more complex when the defendant is neither joint principal, incitor, aider or abettor, nor clearly liable as an independent tortfeasor, i.e. when it is not clear who unlawfully caused the delictually relevant event. This leads to the question: should such participants be jointly and severally liable when the specific tortfeasor cannot be identified, or should they escape liability if the plaintiff cannot prove causation?

A good example of such dilemma, though its solution is outdated,[340] is Cass.civ. 4 January 1957.[341] Mr Richard, Mr Gauthier, and Mr Gaudray went hunting together. Gauthier and Gaudray simultaneously but independently fired in the direction of Mr Richard. The pellets hit his face and hands. His claim against Gauthier and Gaudray was dismissed because it could not be determined whose shot had injured him. The plaintiff failed *'de prouver, d'une part, l'existence d'une relation de cause à effet entre les coups de feu et le dommage dont il demande réparation et, d'autre part, que les projectiles qui l'ont atteint ont été tirés par l'arme placée sous la garde du chasseur auquel il impute la responsabilité dudit dommage'.*[342]

57   Had this accident occurred in Portugal at the same time, the courts would presumably have reached the same result.[343] It seems that this view remains valid,[344] although it must be said that there are no more recent cases on this problem. Art. 490 Port. Cc, which is phrased differ-

---

[339] Loc. cit. p. 285. This view is shared by the Austrian courts: OGH 14 Apr. 1954, SZ 27/103 pp. 241, 244; OGH 2 Sep. 1970, SZ 43/141 pp. 507, 509; OGH 15 Jan. 1986, SZ 59/7 pp. 31, 34.   [340] See no. 58 below.

[341] Cass.civ. 4 Jan. 1957, *D.* 1957 *Jur.* 264. An identical case with an identical ruling is found in 9 Oct. 1957, *D.* 1957 *Jur.* 708 (*'le gardien d'une chose dont il n'est pas démontré qu'elle a occasionné le dommage, ne [peut] être condamné à le réparer'*). However, see Cass.civ. 18 May 1955, *D.* 1955 *Jur.* 520.   [342] Loc. cit. p. 265.

[343] For more detail see Vaz Serra, *BolMinJust* 84 (1959), who not only refers to § 830 BGB, but also mentions such hunting cases. See also Pereira Coelho, *Causa virtual, Introdução N. 5,* who criticizes the German approach and applauds the absence of such a provision in the (old) Portuguese law. Vaz Serra must have been *de lege ferenda* undecided at that time (see fn. 345 below) since his draft on this issue was ambiguous on all major points: loc. cit. pp. 125, 286.

[344] Antunes Varela, *Obrigações em Geral*, vol. i, 7th edn., p. 615 (fn. 2) referring to the works of Vaz Serra and Pereira Coelho mentioned above; Martins de Almeida, *Manual de Acidentes*, 3rd edn., p. 232. Unlike the Spanish Hunting Act (on which more below) its Portuguese counterpart contains no provision specifically governing even this case of liability of participants. Art. 33 Port. Hunting Act (Act No. 30/86 of 27 Aug. 1986) applies to persons carrying hunting weapons liability similar to that of owners and drivers of motor vehicles, according to Art. 503 Cc. Although this is an example of strict liability, it still requires causation.

ently from § 830 I s. 2 BGB, speaks only of independent tortfeasors, joint principals, incitors, and aiders and abettors. Its silence on participants speaks volumes.[345] This placing of the interests of the actors over those of the victim distinguishes Portuguese law from almost every other continental European code. Only in Italy could the same result be achieved by applying the equally unsatisfactory Art. 2055 Ital. Cc.[346] All other continental European legal systems examined here have followed exactly the opposite course. Even in Spain, where the courts formerly decided against the victim,[347] the situation was remedied by the Spanish Hunting Act of 1970,[348] albeit only for the limited area of hunting accidents.[349] Furthermore, by its decision of 8 February 1983[350] the *Tribunal Supremo* extended its application to other cases.

The 1983 case concerned a group of children who, while playing on a public road, threw small metal objects. They injured a person who was unable to say who had thrown the objects. The *Tribunal Supremo* held the parents of all the children jointly and severally liable. The decision was based on an analogous application of Arts. 1910, 1564, 1683, and 1784 Cc and Art. 33 V Spanish Hunting Act. No other solution was considered possible, *'por (ser) inequitativo exonerar de responsabilidad por esos daños, acudiendo a la fuerza mayor, que dejaría sin indemnización a las víctimas, con lo que, además, se orillan las dificultades de prueba atribuyendo la responsabi-*

---

[345] This thesis is confirmed by the history of the legislation. Vaz Serra incorporated in the text of his *Anteprojecto* Art. 741 III, which reads: *'Se o dano foi causado no decurso de uma acção conjunta perigosa, embora não ilícita, não podendo saber-se quem foi o autor efectivo dele, presume-se a culpa no mesmo dano dos que tenham culposamente participado nessa acção'* (*BolMinJust* 101 [1960] pp. 15, 122). Unlike sub-sections I and II of this provision, sub-section III was not reproduced in Art. 490 Cc. Joint and several liability of participants based on presumed causation remains unrecognized in Portuguese law: Martins de Almeida loc. cit. (fn. 344).

[346] See e.g. Cass. 14 June 1978, n. 2962, *Giust.Civ.Mass.* 1978 p. 1215; Cass. 13 May 1989, n. 2204, *Giust.Civ.Mass.* 1989 pp. 556, 557 = *Rep.gen.* 1989 col. 3381, no. 171. In cases of independent tortfeasors doubts about causation were dealt with to the disadvantage of the victim. Art. 2055 Cc does not cover such cases, *'e se non si identifica la precisa imputabilità dell'evento fra due o più persone che, in ipotesi, possono avere prodotto il danno con azioni contestuali ma autonome, la pretesa risarcitoria deve essere respinta non potendosi addossare una responsabilità, per così dire, collettiva, sol perché non si è acquisita la prova dell'imputabilità individuale'*. Hence Forchielli, in *Rapporto di causalità*, pp. 96, 150, 153, is rightly critical and favours the abolition of Art. 2055 Cc, which he indicts based on the principle of *condicio sine qua non*. Trib. Monza 4 Apr. 1991, *Arch.Giur.circolaz.* 1992 p. 21 = *VersRAI* 1993 p. 64, concerned a hunting accident where the person who had fired the round could not be determined. The court considered the Italian legal situation constitutionally questionable. However, since then insurance companies have introduced a guarantee fund, removing any constitutional problems.

[347] This is what was argued by an influential, though unpublished and thus unobtainable, study by Pantaleón, the contents of which are referred to in detail by de Ángel Yáguez, *Responsabilidad civil*, 3rd edn., pp. 874–877.

[348] The (courageous) text of Art. 33 V s. 2 says that if a person is shot when hunting and it cannot be established by whom, then all participants are to be held jointly and severally liable.   [349] E.g. TS 8 June 1988, *RAJ* 1988 no. 5681, pp. 5596, 5597.

[350] TS 8 Feb. 1983, *RAJ* 1983 no. 867, p. 602.

*lidad del grupo a que pertenece el desconocido autor de la infracción dañosa, y a
su vez se fundamenta la solidaridad de los responsables personalizando la
responsabilidad de todos y cado uno de los miembros del grupo'.*[351]

58   That ruling was influenced by the desire to prevent doubts as to
causation, the crucial feature of *alternative tortfeasorship* (*Alternativtä-
terschaft*), from prejudicing the victim, and to disadvantage the possible
tortfeasors. This is also the intention behind the relevant Dutch, German,
and Greek provisions. According to § 830 I s. 2 BGB (the oldest of the
three) 'each is individually responsible for the damage', even in cases 'in
which it cannot be determined which of the several participants actually
caused the damage'. Art. 926 s. 2 Greek Cc is equally clear, stating that 'if
several persons acted concurrently or successively and it is not possible
to ascertain whose act caused the damage', then all persons involved are
to be held jointly and severally liable. Hence, if several hunters fire their
weapons simultaneously, and a beater is hit by one of them,[352] or if
several persons independently strike another,[353] or if, as in the aforementioned case of the *Tribunal Supremo*, several members of a group throw
stones or other objects,[354] and doubts arise as to who caused the damage,
then all potential tortfeasors are liable for all the damage sustained by
third parties.[355] Nowadays this is also the case in Belgium[356] and France,
although, as mentioned above, the latter once took a different view.
However, as early as 1968 the *Cour de Cassation* required a member *'d'une
bande de jeunes gens'* who had attacked a boy scouts' camp to prove he
had not thrown the stone which caused injury.[357] This view soon became
standard, *'selon laquelle les participants à une activité dangereuse peuvent être*

---

[351] Loc. cit. p. 603. See in great detail on this issue de Ángel Yágüez, *Responsabilidad civil*,
3rd edn., pp. 879–882; and Díez-Picazo/Gullón, *Sistema*, vol. ii, 6th edn., p. 616.
[352] RG 19 Jan. 1920, RGZ 98 pp. 58, 60; see also BGH 2 Feb. 1962, *VersR* 1962 p. 430. For
further cases on hunting accidents in Germany see *BGB-RGRK* (-Steffen), 12th edn., § 830
BGB no. 27. For Greece see Georgiades/Stathopoulos (-Georgiades), *Greek Cc*, vol. iv, Art.
926 no. 17; and for The Netherlands see Boonekamp, *Onrechtmatige daad in groepsverband*, p.
13; Spier, *WPNR* 1991 no. 6029, p. 857.
[353] BGH 15 June 1982, *NJW* 1982 p. 1307; Georgiades loc. cit.
[354] RG 11 Jan. 1909, *JW* 1909 p. 136, no. 11; BGH 19 Feb. 1960, *LM BGB* § 830 no. 8; Rb.
Almelo 15 Dec. 1943, *NedJur* 1944 no. 312, p. 463; Rb. Alkmaar 22 Dec. 1949 *NedJur* 1950 no.
447, p. 753; Rb. Turnhout 11 Feb. 1980, *Pas. belge* 1980, III, p. 40; Cass.civ. 6 Mar. 1968,
Bull.civ. 1968, II, no. 76.
[355] See also the illustrative case of BGH 1 Oct. 1957, BGHZ 25 p. 271: 'If a path crossing
several adjacent properties has been intentionally neglected, so that it has become dangerous to use, and if a person while using this path has an accident due to its condition, each of
the land owners is liable to compensate for all the damage if the accident happenend on the
boundary of the properties and it cannot be determined on whose land.'
[356] For a review of cases: Vandenberghe/Van Quickenborne/Gelen/De Coster, *TPR* 1987
pp. 1255, 1536–1537 (no. 175).
[357] Cass.civ. 6 Mar. 1968, Bull.civ. 1968 II no. 76; report by Durry, *Rev.trim.dr.civ.* 66 (1968)
pp. 711, 718–719. In the field of hunting accidents Cass.civ. 5 Feb. 1960, *D.* 1960 *Jur.* 365
already showed signs that the tide was turning.

tous condamnés à réparer le dommage qui a pu en résulter',[358] for cases in which it could not be determined who had actually caused the damage.[359] Placing the burden of proof on the defendant was eventually extended to guardian liability under Art. 1384 I Cc, and also to Art. 1385 Cc on the liability of animal keepers.[360]

The most recent provision in this field is the Dutch BW of 1 January **59** 1992. Not only has it obviously drawn on the French developments, but in some respects it goes even further. Art. 6:166 I refers to the aforementioned liability of members of a group (*groepsverband*): 'if a member of a group unlawfully causes damage, and if the risk of causing this damage should have prevented these persons from their collective conduct, then they are jointly and severally liable if the conduct can be imputed to the group.' This provision is also supplemented by Art. 6:99 BW: 'where the damage may have resulted from two or more events for each of which a different person is liable, and where it has been determined that the damage has arisen from at least one of these events, the obligation to repair the damage rests upon each of these persons, unless he proves that the damage is not a result of the event for which he himself is responsible.' Thus Arts. 6:99 and 6:166 BW approach the subject of liability of participants from a different angle. The latter starts from the notion of *actio libera in causa*: liability results from joining a group, e.g. participating in a demonstration,[361] in situations when the undertaking of the *groepsverband*[362] is evidently dangerous, e.g. the demonstrators intend to exercise violence. Should the damage likely to result from such actions in fact occur, liability will be imputed to all participants, irrespective of whether the person actually causing it is identified. Thus the provision covers not only cases which could also be dealt with by § 830 I s. 2 BGB and Art. 926 s. 2 Greek Cc.

E.g. Rb. Amsterdam 16 March 1962:[363] four boys were playing football.

---

[358] Durry, *Rev.trim.dr.civ.* 71 (1973) pp. 773, 779–780 with further references. Cf. esp. Cass.civ. 12 July 1971, Bull.civ. 1971, II, no. 258 = D. 1972 *Jur.* 227; more recently, Cass.civ. 14 Dec. 1983, *Sem.Jur.* 1984, IV, 65; Cass.civ. 15 Dec. 1980, *D.* 1981 *Jur.* 455.

[359] See Cass.civ. 10 Jan. 1973, Bull.civ. 1973, II, no. 15: joint and several liability of the parents denied, since it was possible to identify the child who had set fire to an aircraft shelter.

[360] See fn. 358. For further references see Weill/Terré, *Obligations*, 4th edn., no. 745; Durry, *Rev.trim.civ.* 82 (1984) pp. 315, 316–318.

[361] See Rb. Breda 26 July 1993, *KG* 1993 no. 302; Asser (-Hartkamp), *Verbintenissenrecht*, vol. iii, 8th edn., no. 94; and *Parlamentaire Geschiedenis*, vol. iv, p. 664, although each explicitly states that as far as the right to demonstrate is concerned, special analysis of each case is required.

[362] For more detail on this term see Boonekamp, *Onrechtmatige daad in groepsverband*, pp. 75–76, 81–96; *Parlamentaire Geschiedenis*, vol. vi, pp. 662–663.

[363] Rb. Amsterdam 16 Mar. 1962, *NedJur* 1962 no. 302, p. 983.

The ball rolled onto the road, collided with a moped, and caused an accident; the question of who had kicked the ball remained unanswered.

Cases where these provisions would not apply are also covered: i.e. where at least one of the tortfeasors, for example the person throwing the stone, is known[364] or, conversely, where it is certain that the group member who is sued is *not* the tortfeasor.[365] According to this convincing[366] provision of Dutch law, he is still liable.

60   Art. 6:99 BW tackles the issue from a completely different angle. It does not focus on the realization of risks arising from joining a group, but bases liability on probable causation. Although some cases covered by Art. 6:99 BW also fall under Art. 6:166 BW, Art. 6:99 BW is an independent provision, and its scope clearly extends beyond that of § 830 I s. 2 BGB and Art. 926 s. 2 Greek Cc. For example, Art. 6:99 BW is relevant to the intense debate[367] generated by BGH of 7 November 1978,[368] where causation was positively established for one tortfeasor but not for his co-accused.

In BGH of 7 November 1978 the car driven by an electrician D collided with a moped-rider R, who had failed to respect D's right of way. R fell and lay motionless on the road. The defendant then approached the scene of the accident and, unable to stop his car in time, ran over R, who died in hospital. It was impossible to determine who caused R's death, since either of the accidents could have been fatal. Unlike earlier similar cases,[369] the BGH rejected joint and several liability of the defendant. According to § 7 StVG (strict liability of the keeper of a motor vehicle) D was liable for all damage, the second accident also being imputed to him. Therefore R's beneficiaries were not in the legal predicament,[370] common under § 830 I s. 2 BGB, of being unable to establish who caused the damage. § 830 I s. 2 BGB does not seek to resolve

[364] See BGH 15 Dec. 1970, BGHZ 55 pp. 86, 94; Filios, *Enochiko Dikaio*, vol. ii (2), 3rd edn., p. 94; Cass.civ. 10 Jan. 1973, Bull.civ. 1973, II, no. 15; Bloembergen, *Onrechtmatige daad*, Art. 166 note 2.1; Boonekamp, *Onrechtmatige daad in groepsverband*, pp. 5–7; Spier, *WPNR* 1991 no. 6029, pp. 857, 858; Hijma/Olthof, *Compendium*, 4th edn., no. 419; and Schut, *Onrechtmatige daad*, 4th edn., § 23.

[365] Neither under Greek nor German law could liability be established in such cases: Filios loc. cit.; BGH 24 Jan. 1984, BGHZ 89 pp. 383, 399.

[366] Ángel Yágüez, *Responsabilidad civil*, 3rd edn., pp. 846 ff., thinks that similar provisions should be developed in the Spanish law: a view shared by this author.

[367] See commentators: e.g. Filios, *Enochiko Dikaio*, vol. ii (2), 3rd edn., p. 94, who considers that Art. 926 s. 2 Greek Cc is inapplicable in such cases. Also Deliyannis/Kornilakis, *Eidiko Enochiko Dikaio*, vol. iii, pp. 225–226, who think that the conduct of the second driver broke the causal chain between the initial accident and the damage suffered. As a result, and this is only too common under Art. 926 s. 2 Greek Cc, the burden of proof lies with the injured person. In German literature: Deutsch, *Haftungsrecht*, vol. i, p. 353.

[368] BGH 7 Nov. 1978, BGHZ 72 pp. 355 ff.   [369] BGH 15 Nov. 1960, BGHZ 33 p. 286.

[370] The hidden problem in this case was that D's third-party insurance cover was insufficient: BGHZ 72 pp. 355, 361.

uncertainty over whether a person other than the tortfeasor can also be held liable.[371] Under Greek law it would have been equally difficult to resolve this issue.[372] In The Netherlands, however, under Art. 6:99 BW the outcome would have been clear: the defendant would have been jointly and severally liable, a more satisfactory solution than that of the BGH.

The immense potential created by Art. 6:99 for establishing liability becomes even more apparent in cases where it is uncertain whether, at the time of the claim, causation can be proved for any of the identifiable probable tortfeasors, and where, in addition, the defendants are neither participants nor members of a group under Art. 6:166 BW. In HR 9 October 1992[373] this led to a view of product liability even wider than that of 'market-share liability' in the US.[374]

Between 1953 and 1967 various manufacturers of pharmaceutical products brought onto the market diethylstiberiol (DES) pills, intended to protect pregnant women from miscarriage and premature birth. Even at that time, research could not totally exclude the risk of foetal abnormalities, and indeed some girls born physically fit did develop urogenital cancer in adolescence. When the disease and its cause were discovered, those affected were unable to identify which of the firms had produced the pills taken by their mothers, nor even whether the drugs taken had been marketed by one of the enterprises being sued (some of whom had ceased to exist). The *Hoge Raad* allowed the claim. Art. 6:99 BW was held to apply to the circumstances in 1953–67, since it reflected a legal opinion already prevalent at that time. Factually it was considered applicable since the very aim of the provision was to prevent a person unable to prove who caused his injury from carrying the burden of such injury himself.[375] Furthermore, the court was of the opinion that *pro rata* liability, after the fashion of market-share liability was unsatisfactory and unacceptable, in that the victim was burdened with the risk of the defendant's insolvency, as well as the risk that the enterprise would cease to exist or become unidentifiable.

d. Liability of Persons Lacking Capacity

Having dealt with interests protected by codified law, with mechanisms **61**
for determining what conduct is tortious, and with the issue of causation,

---

[371] BGH loc. cit. (fn. 370 above); see also BGH 15 Dec. 1970, BGHZ 55 pp. 86, 94.
[372] See fn. 368 above.
[373] HR 9 Oct. 1992, *RvdW* 1992 no. 219 = *TMA* 1993 p. 15, note by van Dunné.
[374] See Spencer/van Wassenaer, [1993] *CLJ* 206–209; Klinge-van Rooij/Snijder, *EuZW* 1993 pp. 569, 570; and Wasink, *A&V* 1993 pp. 6, 10–11.
[375] See *Parlementaire Geschiedenis*, vol. vi, p. 346 (Toelichting Meijers) which supports this view, although it does not expressly refer to product liability.

we now turn to another problem in the field of liability for personal misconduct: liability of persons who, due to age, mental impediment, or any other reason, were at the time when the delict was committed incapable of reason or action, and were thus morally not at fault. These are: children and juveniles (see no. [1] below), disabled persons ([2]), and persons acting under the influence of drugs ([3]). The liability of their carers is a separate issue and is treated later.[376]

(1) Children and Juveniles

62   In European law there are three key questions concerning the misconduct of children and juveniles:[377] first, the age below which children are exempt from liability; second, exceptions which, for reasons of equity, can result in liability for children below that age; and finally, whether the personal liability of children and juveniles should be secondary, not only for practical economic reasons, as is usually the case, but also legally. That is to say, should liability of children and juveniles arise only if there is nobody else (usually the parents) from whom the plaintiff can claim damages?

(a) Exemption from Liability during Early Childhood: Children as Persons Without Capacity to Commit a Delict

63   We begin by considering the lower age limit, which involves four questions. First, should children be allowed to rely on immaturity as a defence? Secondly, if so, should the age limit be fixed or variable, i.e. should it depend on the maturity of the individual child? Thirdly, if the limit is fixed, where should it lie? Finally, should intermediate solutions be found for juveniles beyond the upper age limit of childhood (which varies from country to country) but not yet of full legal age?[378] Europe's answers to these questions are still astonishingly diverse. Continental Europe, with the exception of France (see no. 66 below), unanimously agrees that children, even if they intended to cause injury, must be protected by being deemed to lack civil capacity. However, fixed mini-

---

[376] See nos. 130 ff. below.

[377] On the questions of whether children and juveniles can be liable for their parents, and whether parental negligence should be regarded as contributory negligence on the part of the child, see no. 154 below.

[378] With the exception of Austria (§ 21 II ABGB: 19 years) legal majority in the EU is attained upon completion of the 18th year: Belgium; Art. 488 Cc; Denmark: § 1 I *Myndighe-dsloven* (*Lovbekendtgørelse* No. 443 of 3 Oct. 1985); Finland: 16 § L. *Ang.förmynderskap* No. 34 of 13 Aug. 1898 in the version of Act no. 457 of 3 June 1976; France: Art. 488 Cc; Germany: § 2 BGB; Ireland: sec. 2 Age of Majority Act 1985; Italy: Art. 2 Cc; Luxembourg: Art. 488 Cc; Portugal: Art. 130 Cc; Scotland: sec. 1 Age of Majority (Scotland) Act 1969; Sweden: Chapter 9, 1 § *Lag om ändring i föräldrabalken* of 13 Dec. 1990 (SFS 1990: 1526); Spain: Art. 315 Cc; The Netherlands: Art. 1: 233 BW; United Kingdom: sec. 1 Family Law Reform Act 1969 (chap. 46).

mum ages for liability are found only in the civil codes of Austria (§§ 1308–1310 in conjunction with § 21 II ABGB), Germany (§ 828 I BGB), Greece (Art. 916 Greek Cc), and The Netherlands (Art. 6:164 BW: and each employs a different age. Germany stipulates completion of the seventh year, Greece the tenth, and Austria and The Netherlands protect their children from liability until they have completed their fourteenth year.[379] One could try to explain these differences by assuming that liability law across Europe has become increasingly 'child-friendly'. However, that theory is disproved on closer inspection: for example the modern Danish age limit is four years[380] while the much older Austrian Cc's limit is fourteen. Furthermore, modern French law could hardly be considered child-friendly (see no. 66 below) and the Portuguese legislator only decided in 1965 to follow the German BGB by reintroducing an age limit of seven (Art. 488 II Port. Cc[381]). However, unlike § 828 I BGB, Art. 488 II Port. Cc contains only a rebuttable presumption of absence of civil capacity: the plaintiff can seek to prove that the child who injured him was capable of understanding the wrongful nature of his behaviour and of acting accordingly, even if below the age of seven. Similarly, a child over seven may defend himself by rebutting the presumption of Art. 488 II Cc that he has civil capacity.[382]

Belgian law has followed the same course as its Portuguese counterpart, **64** although its *Code civil* (like those of France, Italy, and Spain) contains no special provisions on liability of children except Art. 1310 (conclusion of contract under the illusion of majority), leaving this issue in the discretion of the courts. *Infantes* must have reached the 'age of reason' (*âge de raison, jaren des onderscheids*) to incur liability for *faute*. Whether that age

---

[379] In earlier rulings of Dutch courts *'kennen en kunnen'* was presumed even for very small children (see e.g. HR 9 Dec. 1966 *NedJur* 1967 no. 69, p. 241 [*Joke Stapper*: concerning a child of $5^1/_2$]; see also HR 26 Oct. 1986, *NedJur* 1987 no. 791, p. 2609 [fault of a child of $5^1/_2$, who freed himself from his mother and caused an accident on a cycle path]). These rulings are now redundant.

[380] See v. Bar (-Nørgaard/Vagner), *DeliktsR in Europa, Dänemark*, p. 13; VLD 24 Nov. 1988, *UfR* 1989 A p. 926 (gross negligence of a 9-year-old); and HD 8 Feb. 1991, *UfR* 1991 A p. 274 (10-year-olds). On § 63 Danish Act no. 443 of 3 Oct. 1985 on minority and guardianship, and on the other Scandinavian laws, see nos. 324–325 below.

[381] *'Presume-se falta de imputabilidade nos menores de sete anos e nos interditos por anomalia psíquica.'*

[382] Pires de Lima/Antunes Varela, *Cc anotado*, vol. i, 4th edn., Art. 488, n. 2; Antunes Varela, *Obrigações em Geral*, vol. i, 7th edn., pp. 555–556; Neto/Martins, *Código civil*, 7th edn., Art. 488 n. 3; Almeida Costa, *Obrigações*, 4th edn., p. 381. Also Vaz Serra, *BolMinJust* 69 (1957) pp. 13, 107–108 (an extensive analysis of comparative law). There seem as yet to be no published court rulings on this issue. RC 14 Oct. 1981, *BolMinJust* 312 (1982) p. 314 says only that if the age of a minor is disputed, the document to be consulted is an ID card and not a medical record. Even in Germany young children would be held responsible if the law had not determined a fixed age limit: OLG Karlsruhe 14 May 1982, *VersR* 1983 p. 252.

has been reached must be determined for each child individually.[383] If the child has attained age seven, civil capacity is usually presumed.[384] In Italy, however, the liability of children is covered by Art. 2046, and indirectly by the provisions governing liability of persons under a duty to supervise: Arts. 2047 and 2048 Cc. According to Art. 2046 Cc: 'liability for damage resulting from an act cannot be imputed to a person who lacked civil capacity at the time he committed it, as long as the deficiency is not his fault.' Art. 2046 Cc further defines a person lacking civil capacity as a *persona incapace d'intendere o di volere*, and Art. 2047 Cc completes this statutory definition by stating that a person 'supervising a handicapped person' will be presumed liable for damage caused by the person lacking civil capacity, whether a minor or an adult.[385] Finally, Art. 2048 Cc, although again mainly concerned with the liability of parents, completes this liability system by dealing with liability for children with civil capacity.[386] So it is necessary to determine the age of capacity, not only to establish a child's liability under Arts. 2043 and 2046 Cc, but also a parent's. Unlike Italian criminal law (Art. 97 CP: age limit of fourteen years), its civil law contains no fixed limit. Not least with regard to parental liability,[387]

---

[383] See e.g. Cornelis, *Responsabilité extra-contractuelle*, pp. 26–28; Fagnart/Denève, *JT* 1986 pp. 297, 301 (no. 52); 1986 pp. 297, 301 (no. 52); de Page, *Droit Civil Belge*, vol. ii, 3rd edn., no. 913, pp. 881 ff.; Vandenberghe/Van Quickenborne/Geelen/De Coster, *TPR* 1987 pp. 1255, 1318–1319 (no. 31). As for court rulings: e.g. Cass. 3 May 1978, *Pas. belge* 1978, I, 1012; Cass. 30 Oct. 1980, *Pas. belge* 1981, I, 262 (no liability for children below the *jaren des onderscheids*); and Antwerp 20 May 1975, *Bull.Ass.* 1975 p. 505 (not accessible to this author, cited here according to Fagnart/Denève loc. cit.): a 9-year-old child was held liable for an accident with an air-gun. However, cf. Antwerp 26 June 1975, *Limb.Rechtl.* 1977 p. 109 (a 5-year-old injured another child with a bottle and ran away: held liable), and Cass. 16 Feb. 1984, *Pas. belge* 1984, I, 684 (a 14-year-old injured herself during a swimming lesson after underestimating the depth of the pool: held not to be contributorily negligent).

[384] At least in the view of Cornelis, loc. cit., p. 27.

[385] See v. Bar (-Busnelli), *DeliktsR in Europa, Italien*, p. 27.

[386] A position held by Benucci, *Responsabilità civile*, p. 167 (with further references to earlier rulings). See also Busnelli loc. cit.; Franzoni, *Fatti illeciti*, Art. 2048 n. 1, p. 347; Perlingieri (-Maglione), *Codice civile*, vol. iv (2), 2nd edn., Art. 2048 n. 2; de Cupis, *Dei fatti illeciti*, pp. 59 ff.; Alpa/Bessone, *Trattato*, vol. xiv, 2nd edn., p. 323; Cass. 10 Apr. 1970, n. 1008, *Giust.civ.* 1970, I, 1379; and Cass. 30 Jan. 1985, n. 565, *Rep.gen.* 1985 col. 3462, no. 112.

[387] First, the cause of action differs in Arts. 2047 and 2048: *culpa in vigilando* and *culpa in vigilando o in educando*. (See Franzoni, *Fatti illeciti*, Art. 2047 n. 2, p. 341; De Martini, *Fatti produttivi di danno*, p. 289; Cendon [-Venchiarutti] vol. iv, p. 2057 no. 1; for more details see no. 136 below). Secondly, according to Art. 2048 Cc, parents can only be held liable if their children 'live with them', a precondition absent from Art. 2047 Cc. Finally, if Trib. di Macerata 20 May 1986, *Foro.it.* 1986, I, 2594 (with a note of approval by Straziota) is upheld, Arts. 2047 and 2048 Cc will also have different legal consequences. In this case only the application of Art. 2048 Cc in conjunction with Art. 2059 would entitle the plaintiff to damages for pain and suffering (this is established practice: see Cass.sez.un. 6 Dec. 1982, n. 6651, *Giur.it.* 1984, I, 150 with an essay by Mastropaolo = *Foro.it.* 1983, I, 1630; and Cass. 18 June 1985 n. 3664, *Giust.Civ.Mass.* 18 June 1985 no. 3664, p. 1127). However, no such compensation is payable for liability under Art. 2047 I (parental liablity) and II (equitable liability of those not in possession of full mental faculties, see nos. 82–83 below).

this is unfortunate.[388] Although civil capacity is usually presumed for children who have attained age fourteen, this does not necessarily mean that it will generally be denied for children below this age, as some authors claim.[389] The basic rule is that the question of a child's civil responsibility must be separated from criminal law, since the civil courts must decide the issue *'in concreto, caso per caso'.*[390] In conclusion, this means not only that parental liability for children over the age of fourteen may in theory be limited to Art. 2047 Cc in individual cases, although this author is unaware of any examples, but also that Art. 2048 Cc can be applied to parents whose children have not completed their fourteenth year.[391] Although such children are not criminally liable, civil ability *d'intendere o di volere* may be presumed, in which case parents and children are jointly and severally liable for damage suffered.[392] Very young children still come under Art. 2046 Cc.[393]

Spain still has in most cases an even higher upper age limit for the   **65** liability of children and minors than The Netherlands or Italy. However, the position is unusually complicated. Although legal scholars have developed a number of solutions, some are so fundamentally contradictory that the situation will remain uncertain until settled by the *Tribunal Supremo*. Since all claims have so far been based on parental liability, its judges have only considered the possibility of the child's contributory negligence, which would limit the claim.[394]

---

[388] Maschio, *Dir.fam.pers.* 1988, II, pp. 874, 884, is in favour of the introduction of a civil law age limit.

[389] Alpa, *Responsabilità civile*, pp. 301 f. (*'ai genitori di minori di età inferiore ai quattordici anni . . . si applica il disposto dell'art. 2047 anziché il disposto dell'art. 2048'*).

[390] Benucci, *Responsabilità civile*, p. 167 (referring to earlier rulings); Busnelli, *Dir.fam.pers.* 1982 pp. 54, 61–62; Franzoni, *Fatti illeciti*, Art. 2046, n. 1, p. 317; Perlingieri (-Magliona), *Codice civile*, vol. iv (2), 2nd edn., Art. 2046, n. 2 (the quotation above originates from this note); Cian/Trabucchi, *Commentario breve*, 4th edn., Art. 2046, n. 3; Alpa/Bessone, *Trattato*, vol. xiv, 2nd edn., p. 93. For court rulings see Cass. 19 Nov. 1990, n. 11163, *Foro.it.Mass.* 1990 no. 11163 (civil law relies on an independent system of legal capacity); Cass. 28 May 1975, n. 1642, *Resp.Civ. e Prev.* 1976 p. 136 (each case must be judged individually). See also Cass. 18 June 1953, n. 1812, *Giust.civ.Mass.* 1953 no. 1812; Cass. 10 Aug. 1964, n. 2291, *Giust.civ. Mass.* 1964 no. 2291; and Cass. 4 Apr. 1959, n. 1006, *Giur.it.* 1959, I, 1, 619 (see fn. 435 below). App. Firenze 27 Feb. 1968, *Giur.tosc.* 1968 p. 611 accepted liability of a 13-year-old minor for the collision of two mopeds (see on this case Bussani, *Colpa soggettiva*, p. 191); App. Firenze 13 Mar. 1964, *Giur.tosc.* 1964 p. 598 (see on this case Venchiarutti, in: Cendon [ed.], *Responsabilità civile*, pp. 497, 499) held a 12-year-old liable.

[391] E.g. Cass. 6 Dec. 1982, n. 6651, *Giur.it.* 1984, I, 150; Cass. 30 Oct. 1984, n. 5564, *Foro.it.* 1985, I, 145; and Cass. 24 Oct. 1988, n. 5751, *Foro.it.* 1989, I, 98. See also Cass. 30 Jan. 1985, n. 565, *Giust.civ.Mass.* 1985, I, no. 565; and Cass. 12 Jan. 1980, n. 269, *Giust.civ.Mass.* 1980 no. 269.

[392] Busnelli, *Dir.fam.pers.* 1982 pp. 54, 62 (no. 8).

[393] Trib. di Macerata loc. cit. (fn. 387) (6-year-old). Also Trib. Piacenza 4 Mar. 1961, *Arch. Giur.circolaz* 1962, II, 290 (for a 6-year-old individual analysis of the case is not necessary: *incapacità* is self-evident. On this issue see Franzoni, *Fatti illeciti*, Art. 2046, n. 1, pp. 318, 330.

[394] See esp. TS 27 June 1983, *RAJ* 1983 no. 3691, p. 2913, concerning a 12-year-old; TS 17 Dec. 1986, *La Ley* 1987 (1) p. 825 (no. 8494R) concerning a 15-year-old.

The confusion has arisen chiefly because the provisions of the *Código civil* and the *Código penal* are incompatible. Whereas the *Código civil*, in line with other European codes, contains only a general clause (Art. 1902) and one provision on parental liability (Art. 1903 II), Art. 20 CP explicitly states that civil liability for criminal acts committed by mentally ill persons, persons with impaired senses, and minors below the age of sixteen (Art. 8 no. 2 CP: *'Están exentos de responsabilidad criminal: . . . 2° El menor de 16 años'*) 'will be imputed to those persons under whose legal power or supervision they are, in cases where fault or negligence on the part of the minors has been proven. In cases where there is no guardian, or where the guardian is insolvent, the (minor) himself is liable to the extent of his assets.' This leaves Spanish law with two incompatible systems. On one hand, parents are liable under Spanish civil law, for presumed fault (Art. 1903 VI Cc) until their children have reached sixteen, and children are liable for proven fault (Art. 1902 Cc) provided they are capable of reason and have acted negligently. On the other hand, under the criminal system, children and juveniles up to age 16 are strictly liable, albeit in default of their parents. That is to say, liability of juveniles who have not completed their sixteenth year (regardless of whether they possess criminal capacity) is only possible in cases where: parents can successfully rebut the presumption that they are at fault (Art. 20 CP); parents are insolvent; or children and juveniles have neither parents nor guardian (Art. 20). However, unlike Art. 1903 Cc, under the Penal Code parents escape tortious liability for the criminal acts of their children who have completed their sixteenth year. In other words, the liability of parents is displaced by that of their children in criminal law, and vice versa in civil law; cases of joint and several liability do not exist.

In order to achieve at least some consistency, the majority of legal authors favour a provision analogous to Art. 20 CP for purely civil delicts.[395] However, little is gained by this 'solution'. The question of which elements should be transferred to the civil system remains. Such an application of Art. 20 CP to sixteen- and seventeen-year-old minors, for instance, would result in them rather than their parents being personally liable: a controversial solution. It contradicts Art. 1903 Cc, and

---

[395] Pro: Conde-Pumpido Ferreiro, *Festschrift Castán Tobeñas*, pp. 75, 91–98; Díaz-Alabart, *An.Der.Civ.* 40 (1987) pp. 795, 876; Díez-Picazo/Gullón, *Sistema*, vol. i, 7th edn., p. 256 and vol. ii, 6th edn., p. 625; Espín Cánovas, *Manual de Derecho civil*, vol. iii, 6th edn., p. 504; Gómez Calle, *Responsabilidad civil de los padres*, p. 210; López Beltrán de Heredia, *Responsabilidad civil de los padres*, p. 170. Contra: Albaladejo, *Derecho civil*, vol. ii, (2), 8th edn., pp. 517, 545; de Ángel Yágüez, *Responsabilidad civil*, 3rd edn., p. 308.

most legal scholars favour the opposite conclusion.[396] Furthermore, the *Tribunal Supremo* firmly resists the removal of parental liability in such cases, albeit not always with the same reasoning. The *Tribunal Supremo*, whose rulings are supported by Art. 22 CP, is of the opinion that parents are in principle at least secondarily liable for crimes committed by their children who are nearing majority.[397] For very young children, lacking the *capacidad de entender y querer*, the legal situation is again controversial. Some authors favour a provision analogous to Art. 20 CP to introduce a secondary but strict liability, while others would prefer to exclude for civil delicts liability for children of this age.[398] The *Tribunal Supremo* has not yet ruled on this moot point. Agreement has not even been reached on whether the (civil) ability to reason must be determined *in concreto* (the opinion of most authors who consider this question important) or whether it should depend on a fixed age limit.[399] So it is no surprise that there is also disagreement about children capable for the purposes of civil law but under the age of criminal responsibility

---

[396] In favour of precedence being given to the liability of minors (for criminal and civil delicts) are e.g. Díaz-Alabart loc. cit. (fn. 395 above) pp. 861–866; Gómez Calle loc. cit. (fn. 395 above) pp. 217–219. Yet López Beltrán loc. cit. (fn. 395 above) pp. 173–183; and Conde-Pumpido loc. cit. (fn. 395 above) pp. 91–94 are generally in favour of giving precedence to parental liability under 1903 Cc, although on some details their opinions differ greatly. Whereas e.g. López Beltrán believes Art. 1903 Cc should be applied (analogously) by criminal courts, Díaz-Alabert thinks that Art. 1903 Cc should be restricted to civil delicts, retaining only for crime the precedence of parental liability over that of children.

[397] This was the position in TS 11 Oct. 1990, *RAJ* 1990 no. 7860 p. 9932 (secondary liability of father for a crime committed by 17-year-old son; *responsabilidad civil subsidiaria*). However, in TS 12 Feb. 1994, *RAJ* 1994 no. 773, p. 1010, the court considered *direct* parental liability under Art. 20 CP and Art. 1903 Cc (homicide caused by negligence; a 17-year-old used his father's service pistol; Art. 20 CP need not necessarily be interpreted so as to exclude civil liability of parents for the crimes of their adolescent children). *Contra*, however, is TS 2 Mar. 1994, *La Ley* 1994 (2) p. 579 (rape committed by a juvenile with criminal responsibility; parental liability denied on the ground that Art. 1903 Cc does not concern liability for crimes): even the *Tribunal Supremo* is not consistent on this issue: see no. 88 below.

[398] In favour of strict (secondary) liability of children of this age group are: Díez-Picazo/Gullón loc. cit.; Díaz-Alabart loc. cit. p. 876; Gómez Calle loc. cit. (all cited in fn. 395 above). Resistant to strict liability for delicts relevant to civil law is López Beltrán loc. cit. (fn. 395 above) p. 178. Conde-Pumpido Ferreiro, *Festschrift Castán Tobeñas*, p. 83, believes that the 'delicts' of very young children are not based on any 'act', which means that liability is excluded *per se*. However, his view that even parents should not be liable in such cases is not shared by TS 22 Jan. 1991, *RAJ* 1991 no. 304, p. 333.

[399] According to Gómez Calle and Díaz-Alabart (loc. cit.) the ability to reason of children who have attained age 16 should only be examined if the circumstances demand it. Below this age liability depends on the *capacidad de entender y querer* of the individual child, as does the question of whether the duty of care specific to children of this age has been violated. Puig Brutau, *Fundamentos*, vol. ii, (3), p. 107 thinks that for persons aged less than 18 capacity can usually be assumed. In the majority of civil cases, the ability to reason is determined individually.

(sixteenth year not yet completed). Here, the question is whether their personal liability (for both criminal acts and civil delicts) and their parents' liability should be treated as joint and several (as is commonly the case in Europe), or whether—based on Art. 20 CP—the child's liability should be only secondary.[400] Both solutions are highly unsatisfactory. In the former, civil law threatens to undermine the protection afforded by criminal law, and the latter could impose strict liability on a fifteen-year-old in cases where an adult would only be liable if at fault. In view of the impending reforms of the Spanish CP, it is of paramount importance that these questions are resolved. The legislator must resolve the uncertainty of the *Código Penal* in this field. How this is to be done has already been established: all questions of liability of minors and their parents should be removed from the Penal Code. However, until the Youth Penal Code is implemented, the old version of Art. 20 CP remains applicable to minors (Art. 1 lit. a *Disposición derogatoria de NCP*); and Art. 19 NCP, which exempts minors from criminal liabilty, has not yet been implemented (Art. 7 *Disposiciones finales* of the NCP).

(b) Counter-Developments in France: *Faute Objective*

66 Although the attitude towards children in continental Europe's laws of delict is by and large protective, French precedents set a striking counter-example. Not least under the influence of Art. 489–2 Cc (*'Celui qui a causé un dommage à autrui alors qu'il était sous l'empire d'un trouble mental, n'en est pas moins obligé à réparation'*) which was incorporated in the 11th title of the First Book in 1968 (*'De la majorité et des majeurs qui sont protégés par la loi'*), a section of the *Code civile* dealing only with adults,[401] the *Cour de Cassation* dramatically tightened the liability of minors in the mid-eighties.[402] Although the implications for liability law have since decreased, the effects of these rulings extend far beyond their original meaning: they have become leading cases on the term *faute*.

It is chiefly due to a more recent legal development, namely Art. 3 II of

---

[400] Gómez Calle and Díaz-Alabart loc. cit. favour joint and several liability; whereas Díez-Picazo/Gullón loc. cit. support the idea of secondary liability although independent of fault; so also, but only for civil delicts, thinks López Beltrán loc. cit., pp. 173–183 (all cited in fn. 395 above).

[401] Cass.civ. 20 July 1976 *Sem.Jur.* 1978, II, 18793 (note, Dejean de la Bâtie) = *Rev.trim.dr. civ.* 1976 p. 783 (Durry) decided that liability under Art. 489–2 Cc could also be extended to minors *'sous l'empire d'un trouble mental'*, irrespective of its position within the Code. However, a more recent case opposed the earlier ruling: Trib.gr.inst. Tours 26 Apr. 1991, *Gaz.Pal.* 1993 Somm. 206.

[402] For a brilliant description and analysis of French law developments see Hennings, *Persönliche Haftung und Mitverschulden von Kindern im französischen Deliktsrecht* (1992), esp. pp. 100–122. See also v. Bar (-Gotthardt), *DeliktsR in Europa, Frankreich*, pp. 19–20.

Act No. 85–677 of 5 July 1985,[403] that the *arrêt Derguini*,[404] the second of five decisions of the *Assemblée plénière* of 9 May 1984,[405] has become outdated, but only regarding its immediate subject-matter and not the general statement made therein. A girl of five ran onto the road without looking and was hit by an approaching vehicle, sustaining fatal injuries. In her parents' claim for damages, based on Art. 1382 Cc,[406] the *Cour de Cassation* considered the question whether the damages should be reduced due to (50%) contributory negligence on the part of the child. It answered in the affirmative: '*Mais attendu qu'après avoir retenu le défaut d'attention de M. Tidu et constaté que le jeune Fatiha, s'élançant sur la chaussée, l'avait soudainement traversée malgré le danger immédiat de l'arrivée de la voiture de M. Tidu et avait fait aussitôt demi-tour pour revenir sur le trottoir, l'arrêt énonce que cette irruption intempestive avait rendu impossible toute manoeuvre de sauvetage de l'automobiliste; qu'en l'état de ces énonciations et constatations, la cour d'appel, qui n'était pas tenue de vérifier si la mineure était capable de discerner les conséquences de tels actes, a pu, sans se contredire, retenir, sur le fondemnet de l'article 1382 c.civ., que la victime avait commis une faute qui avait concouru avec celle de M. Tidu, à la réalisation du dommage dans une proportion souverainement appréciée.*' Contributory negligence was also an issue in the *arrêt Lemaire* of the

---

[403] Translated, the text of the *loi Badinter* reads: 'Art. 3 (I): The injured parties, with the exception of drivers of motorized vehicles, will be compensated for any personal injuries regardless of contributory negligence, except for cases in which their inexcusable fault proves the sole cause of the accident. (II): In cases where the injured parties of sub-section I are below age 16 or above age 70, or have been declared permanently or at least 80% disabled, they are to be compensated for their personal injuries in all cases.'

[404] Cass.Ass.plén. 9 May 1984, *Sem.Jur.* 1984, II, 20256 (no. 1) including note by Jourdain = D. 1984 *Jur.* p. 529 (*4ème espèce*) including note by Chabas. In *Luxembourg* (which lacks a provision similar to the *loi Badinter*) the courts have ruled similarly: Cour 19 Dec. 1984, *Pas. luxemb.* 26 (1984) p. 241: '*Pour attribuer une part de responsabilité à un enfant victime d'un accident, il n'y a pas à rechercher si, en raison de son âge, cet enfant était capable de discerner les conséquences de son acte; il suffit que l'enfant ait commis un acte contribuant au dommage.*' Hence in Luxembourg the law is even stricter than in France.

[405] The remaining 3 decisions concerned (1) the liability of a 9-year-old for intentional arson (*arrêt Dionab*: Cass.Ass.plén. 9 May 1984, *D.* 1984 *Jur.* p. 528 [*1ère espèce*]), (2) parental liability under Art. 1348 IV Cc for a child of 7, who shot an arrow into the eye of another (*arrêt Füllenwarth*: Cass.Ass.plén. 9 May 1984, *D.* 1984 *Jur.* p. 529 [*2ème espèce*] = *Sem.Jur.* 1984, II, 20255 [no. 2], a case in which the *Cour de Cassation* separated parental liability from a child's liability), and (3) the liability of a child under Art. 1384 I Cc (*arrêt Gabillet*: Cass.Ass.plén. 9 May 1984, *D.* 1984 *Jur.* p. 529 [*3ème espèce*] = *Sem.Jur.* 1984, II, 20255 [no. 1]; 3-year-old held liable as *gardien* of a stick).

[406] The article on which the claim was based is relevant since the defence of contributory negligence, which had been denied by the *arrêt Desmares* (Cass. 21 July 1982, *D.* 1982 *Jur.* 449, concl. Charbonnier, note Larroumet = *Sem.Jur.* 1982, II, 19861, note Chabas), which was still good law at the time of the *arrêt Derguini*, was only excluded for gardien liability under Art. 1384 I Cc. Unfortunately the lawsuit was conducted (rather incompetently) before the Criminal Court, in which only liability under Art. 1382 Cc can be examined (Hennings, *Persönliche Haftung und Mitverschulden*, p. 104).

same day.[407] A boy of thirteen was electrocuted while attempting to change the light bulb in an incubator for piglets. A few days earlier an electrician had negligently connected the live wire to the bulb holder. Again the parents' claim was reduced due to contributory negligence on the part of their son, who should have switched off the electricity. The *Cour de Cassation* repeated part of the text of the *arrêt Derguini*, saying: '*la cour d'appel qui n'était pas tenue de vérifier si le mineur était capable de discerner les conséquences de son acte, a pu estimer sur le fondement de l'article 1382 du Code civil que la victime avait commis une faute qui avait concouru avec celle de M. Lemaire, à la réalisation du dommage dans une proportion souverainement appréciée.*' Art. 1382 Cc has thus been used twice to reduce claims on the basis of contributory negligence, and the Second Civil Chamber of the *Cour de Cassation* in the *arrêt Sabatier* of 12 December 1984[408] further extended this position to the liability of minors under Art. 1382 Cc. A boy of seven deliberately bumped into another in the school playground. The latter fell and hit a bench, sustaining a ruptured spleen. Again the court declined to examine the first child's ability to reason. The court accepted liability on his part, and stated once more '*qu'en l'état de ces énonciations, la Cour d'appel, qui n'était pas tenue de vérifier si le mineur Jean-Claude Sabatier était capable de discerner les conséquences de son acte, a caractérisé la faute commise par lui; d'où il suit que le moyen* (i.e. the appeal filed by the father on behalf of the child before the *Cour de Cassation*) *n'est pas fondé*'.

67   Four important aspects of these decision are apparent. First, liability of minors under French law no longer depends on their *discernement*[409] ('ability to distinguish between good and evil')[410] but is now established, judge-made law.[411] The ability to reason is no longer a precondition for civil responsibility, whether liability is based on *garde* or on

---

[407] Cass.Ass.plén. 9 May 1984, D. 1984 *Jur.* p. 529 (*5ème espèce*) = *Sem.Jur.* 1984, II, 20256 (no. 2).

[408] Cass.civ. 12 Dec. 1984, *Sem.Jur.* 1985, IV, p. 71 = *Gaz.Pal.* 1985 *Jur.* p. 235 = Bull.civ. 1985 II no. 193, p. 137.

[409] For more detailed information on the term *discernement* see Carbonnier, *Droit Civil*, vol. iv, 14th edn., no. 94 ('*état de discerner le bien du mal, le discernement supposant à la fois une suffisante raison et une certaine force de volonté*'); and Marty/Raynaud, *Droit Civil*, vol. ii (1), 2nd edn., no. 458 (referring to Savatier) ('*l'agent doit avoir eu la possibilité de connaître le devoir violé et la possiblité de l'observer*').

[410] Hennings, *Persönliche Haftung und Mitverschulden*, p. 76.

[411] The *Assemblée plénière* of the *Cour de Cassation* has thus departed from a long line of decisions which accepted that *discernement* was a precondition for the *imputabilité* of the results of an unlawful act. Most recently: Cass.civ. 7 Dec. 1977, *Sem.Jur.* 1978, Bull.civ. 1978, II, 179 = D. 1979 *IR* p. 64 (Larroumet). The civil and criminal terms *faute* (the latter still requires *discernement*) have been separated for good: see Cass.civ. 7 June 1989, *Gaz.Pal.* 1989 *Jur.* 783 (note Chabas). The provision of Art. 1310 Cc (that the minor '*n'est point restituable contre les obligations résultant de son délit ou quasi-délit*') is only applied to cases in which a minor pretends to be of age in order to conclude a contract.

faute.[412] Although the lower courts sometimes object,[413] this does not seem to have made any significant impression. Secondly, it has been established judge-made law since 1984 that the ability to reason is no longer an issue, and this affects both the cause of action (liability of the child) and the limitation of liability (contributory negligence by the child). The only corrections made by the legislator concern contributory negligence of children in road traffic accidents, where even a *faute inex-cusable* cannot be held against them until they reach age sixteen.[414] According to the strict rules laid down in the decisions of 9 May 1984, the child remains fully liable for damage to third parties: i.e. his damages for his own injuries are not reduced by his contributory negligence; but he is liable for damage sustained by the car which hit him because of his contributory negligence, either in *faute* or in *garde*:[415] a remarkable imbalance between breach of duty and contributory negligence.[416]

The most important aspect of these rulings seems to be the following. **68** In negligence,[417] the simple fact that the ability to reason has ceased to be a precondition for liability does not answer an equally important question: what standard of care should be required of a child or juvenile? Should he be judged by reference to the diligence to be expected of a person of the same age in similar circumstances, or that of the *bon père de famille*? Nearly all scholars who have analysed the more recent French rulings agree that the question was, or at least should have been, answered by

---

[412] This concerns the liability of both child (see fn. 405 and 408 above) and parents (see fn. 405).

[413] Trib.gr.inst. Tours 26 Apr. 1991, *Gaz.Pal.* 1993 *Somm.* 206. See also Jourdain, *Rev.trim.dr.civ.* 90 (1991) pp. 119, 123, whose case reports show the lower courts' tendency to diffuse the results of the decisions of 9 May 1980 wherever possible.

[414] See fn. 403 above.

[415] This view was supported by the very first decisions under the Act of 5 July 1985: Nîmes 9 Oct. 1985, *Gaz.Pal.* 1985 *Jur.* 733 (note Chabas) concerning a 10-year-old. The child was held liable for *faute* and as *gardien* of his bicycle. Chambéry 12 Nov. 1985, *Gaz.Pal.* 1985 *Jur.* 766; and Dijon 11 Dec. 1985, *Gaz.Pal.* 1986 *Jur.* 64 (note Chabas) concerned an 8-year-old cyclist. The *Cour de Cassation* has confirmed similar rulings by the courts of appeal on several occasions: Cass.civ. 4 Mar. 1992, *Gaz.Pal.* 1993 *Jur.* 204; and Cass.civ. 1993, *D.* 1994 *Somm.* 15, concerning a child who, having dishonestly obtained a lighter from his mother, set hay in his grandfather's barn alight. The child was held liable as *gardien* of the lighter. See also Cass.civ. 7 Oct. 1987, *D.* 1987 *IR* 206; and Cass.civ. 18 Nov. 1987, *Sem.Jur.* 1988, IV, 25, although the latter case concerned adults.

[416] In a similar situation, under § 829 BGB in conjunction with § 254 BGB, BGH 10 Apr. 1962, BGHZ 37 pp. 102, 106 expressly described such an outcome as illogical. Even French authors are uneasy about the current position. They consider yet another third-party liability insurance or any other effective insurance to be the *deus ex machina*: e.g. Weill/Terré, *Obligations*, 4th edn., no. 631; Viney, *Sem.Jur.* 1985, I, 3198 nos. 22 ff.; Lapoyade-Deschamps, *D.* 1988 *Chron.* pp. 185, 190.

[417] In the field of liability for 'intent' (whatever that means regarding small children) an (innocent) 'desire to cause damage' is sufficient, *discernement* having become redundant (see fn. 405 above: *arrêt Dionab*). Even small children are capable of this (as Deutsch correctly states, *Haftungsrecht*, vol. i, p. 300).

applying the stringent standard of care demanded of the *bon père de famille*.[418] The current position of French judge-made law[419] is therefore that a civil *faute* is determined solely by the act committed: the age of the tortfeasor, his character, intelligence, and ethical capacity are of no relevance: '*Le type de comparaison doit être placé dans les circonstances "externes", non dans les circonstances "internes" où se trouvait le défendeur.*'[420] '*On ne comparera donc pas la conduite d'un infans à celle d'un infans, . . . mais a celle d'un individu sensé et l'on décidera qu'ils ont commis une faute lorsqu'une personne sensée n'aurait pas agi comme eux.*'[421] If this is correct—and there is no reason to believe otherwise, although the *Cour de Cassation* has not yet made an unambiguous statement on the issue[422]—it means that, following the rulings of 1984, liability for *faute* has been reduced to liability for unlawful conduct.[423] The notion of negligence which takes no intellectual deficiencies into consideration (the *faute objective* or *culpa in abstracto*), recognized by all other members of the EU,[424] has thus been ruthlessly stretched to its limits. This also means that the second line of defence formerly open to a tortfeasor, i.e. the separation of unlawfulness ('the conduct which would be considered objectively appropriate under the circumstances') and fault ('do the

---

[418] See esp. Weill/Terré, *Obligations*, 4th edn., no. 631; Le Tourneau, *Responsabilité civile*, 3rd edn., no. 2087; Hennings, *Persönliche Haftung und Mitverschulden*, pp. 114–117 (although critical) and Marty/Raynaud, *Droit Civil*, vol. ii, (1), 2nd edn., no. 465.

[419] Whether one approves of this situation is a separate matter from an analysis of current judge-made law. Even so, there are authors and courts (see fn. 413 above) who disagree with the position held by the *Cour de Cassation*: see references in Hennings, *Persönliche Haftung und Mitverschulden*, pp. 117–119; Jourdain, *Rev.trim.dr.civ.* 90 (1991) pp. 119, 123; Viney, *Sem.Jur.* 1993, I, 3664 p. 148, nos. 25–28.

[420] Mazeaud/Chabas, *Obligations*, 8th edn., no. 449, p. 447.

[421] Henri Mazeaud, D. 1985 *Chron.* pp. 13, 14. Critical, however: Jourdain loc. cit. (fn. 419 above) p. 124.

[422] According to a 1965 analysis, the French courts, even in earlier times, hardly ever applied a standard of care tailored to the age of the tortfeasor (Dejean de la Bâtie, *Appréciation in abstracto*, no. 27, p. 25). Two Supreme Court decisions of the 1970s, however, did employ an adjusted standard of care: Cass.civ. 6 Feb. 1974, *Sem.Jur.* 1974, IV, 107; and Cass.civ. 29 Apr. 1976, *Sem.Jur.* 1978, II, 18793 (note Dejean de la Bâtie). Yet neither the decisions of 1984 nor the more recent rulings mean that a level of care appropriate to the age of the tortfeasor will be revived. In fact this question is no longer asked: Cass.civ. 27 Feb. 1991, *Sem.Jur.* 1991, IV, 161 concerning the liability of an 8-year-old for a fight in the school playground; Cass.civ. 4 Mar. 1992, *Gaz.Pal.* 1993 *Jur.* 204 concerning the liability of minors—a case in which the age of the juvenile tortfeasor is not even mentioned, and is clearly irrelevant. Although the *Cour de Cassation* takes a different view in Cass.civ. 7 Mar. 1989, *Sem.Jur.* 1990, II, 21403 (note Dejean de la Bâtie), in which a 16-year-old loosened a rock while taking part in a treasure hunt on a mountain range, by admitting liability on the ground '*que son âge lui permettait de comprendre le danger prévisible auquel il exposait ses camérades*') there has been no ruling *denying* liability on ground of the tortfeasor's age.

[423] Starck (-Roland/Boyer), *Obligations*, 4th edn., no. 456 goes so far as to describe this type of liability as a '*responsibilité sans faute*': it is an example of '*l'idée de garantie*'.

[424] Limpens/Kruithof/Meinerzhagen-Limpens, *IntEncCompL* XI 2–31. See also nos. 626–628 below.

circumstances of this case give any reason to believe that this tortfeasor in this specific situation was unable to do what would have been expected of him according to common opinion?) has been abandoned altogether. In other words, liability is based on objective misconduct, and is independent of fault. Although, unlike in cases of true strict liability, the question of whether even the *bon père de famille* could reasonably have been expected to act lawfully, or whether the act of the child could be considered reasonable from the point of view of an adult, is still an issue,[425] nobody seems to remember that fathers too were once children.

The frequently used argument that adults are treated no differently from children, i.e. they too are subject to a strict duty of care, cannot justify the course embarked upon by the *Cour de Cassation*. For to deprive children of the protection of the requirement of *discernement* is to place a heavy responsibility on them before their lives have begun.[426] As for the standard of care, one should always bear in mind that a child cannot act other than as a child. One simply cannot compare[427] a child with a doctor who seeks to excuse mistreatment on the ground that she finds it difficult to learn and forgets easily:[428] the latter can (and must) stop practising. To apply this notion of *actio libera in causa* to children (and mentally handicapped persons) seems absurd.[429]

(c) Juveniles: ability to reason and reduced standard of care

Just as the provisions governing the liability of children are conceptually **69** auxiliary provisions, defining fault within the scope of a specific provision, the provisions on the liability of juveniles also cover privileges. The basic issues are broadly similar: should an inability to reason protect the defendant, in other words, should a minor be subject to a duty of care tailored to persons of his age group, or should his conduct be measured against that of an adult? The second question obviously only arises if (as in France) *discernement* is not a prerequisite, or if it is (which is happily the case in all other European countries[430]) where the circumstances indicate that the tortfeasor's reason must be acknowledged: only then does the

---

[425] Regarding contributory negligence, Viney, *Sem.Jur.* 1993, I, 3664 (no. 27, p. 148) has recently observed a more 'victim-friendly' attitude, which also benefits the *enfant-victime*.
[426] For German rulings on this issue see the dramatic appeal of the OLG Celle 26 May 1989, *VersR* 1989 p. 709 (note Lorenz = *NJW-RR* 1989, p. 791); see also Scheffen, *FuR* 1993 pp. 82–89; and id., *DAR* 1991 pp. 121–126.
[427] Contra: Mazeaud, D. 1985 *Chron.* pp. 13, 14; and Mazeaud/Chabas, *Obligations*, 8th edn., no. 448.   [428] An example given by Heck, *Grundriß des Schuldrechts*, p. 78.
[429] Although, according to a report by Starck (-Roland/Boyer), *Obligations*, vol. i, 4th edn., no. 451 Ripert is supposed once to have pursued such a line. Loc. cit., he is credited with the phrase: *'Le fou ne peut pas commettre de faute, mais c'est une faute d'être fou.'*
[430] The ability to reason is by no means retreating in all areas of liability law, but predominantly in the field of adults' liability: van Dam, *Zorgvuldigheidsnorm en aansprakelijkheid*, p. 272.

question of carelessness arise. Thus, in a system which imposes a strict age limit to mark the end of a liability-free period, questions about minors' liability for negligence concern only juveniles. Below this age limit there is no need to contemplate the term 'ability to reason' or its effects. Even if the absence of this element was the main incentive for the German legislator's choice of seven as the key age (§ 828 I BGB), or its Greek counterpart opting for ten (Art. 916 Greek Cc), and Austria (§ 21 II ABGB) and The Netherlands (Art. 6:164 BW)[431] for the unusually high age of fourteen, the definition of the term 'ability to reason' is only relevant for juveniles who have already passed the respective age limits.

70   Where inability to reason is allowed as a protection against liability, it is merely one example of an unavoidable mistake as to the wrongful nature of an act, and thus does not incur liability. § 828 II BGB and Art. 917 Greek Cc[432] are identical apart from their age limits: seven to eighteen years in Germany, and ten to fourteen in Greece. They are the only two independent provisions in Europe concerning juveniles, and they merely confirm the principle, common to both legal systems, of excusing cases of unavoidable mistake as to the wrongful nature of an act.[433] This of course also applies to all legal systems in which *discernement* remains a precondition for liability.[434] The lowest universal common denominator in the ability to reason has been described variously as the ability: 'to evaluate in a suitable fashion the social value of a specific act',[435] 'to differentiate between good and bad and to recognize that the latter has legal consequences',[436] and 'to recognize the unlawfulness of one's

---

[431] The protocols reveal that a decision was only reached at the very end of the discussions, following an initiative of Ms. Haas-Berger MP (*Parlementaire Geschiedenis*, vol. vi, p. 657). One reason for the swing in this direction was that the exclusion of liability of children under Art. 6:169 BW is compensated by their parents' strict liability (no. 133 below), usually covered by suitable insurance.

[432] Gogos' (see table of translated codes, above) translation of Art. 917 Cc into German reads as follows: '*Wer das zehnte, nicht aber das vierzehnte Lebensjahr vollendet hat, haftet für den von ihm verursachten Schaden, es sei denn, daß er bei der Begehung der schädigenden Handlung die zur Erkenntnis der Verantwortlichkeit erforderliche Einsicht nicht hatte. Das gleiche gilt für Taubstumme.*' The text of § 828 II BGB reads: '*Wer das siebente, aber nicht das achtzehnte Lebensjahr vollendet hat, ist für einen Schaden, den er einem anderen zufügt, nicht verantwortlich, wenn er bei der Begehung der schädigenden Handlung nicht die zur Erkenntnis der Verantwortlichkeit erforderliche Einsicht hat. Das gleiche gilt von einem Taubstummen.*' However, Gogos relies too heavily on § 828 II BGB: Art. 917 Greek Cc in fact only says: 'who . . . shall be liable for the prejudice he has caused unless he lacked the ability to reason'.

[433] On mistake as to the wrongful nature of an act see only BGH 10 July 1984, *NJW* 1985 pp. 134, 135; CA Athens 348/1977, *NoB* 25 (1977) p. 555.

[434] For Belgian law see e.g. Dalcq, *Rev.crit.jur.belge* 1987 pp. 601, 610 who, following the rulings on the *erreur invincible* of admininstrative authorities based on mistake in the law, discusses the problem of the *défaut de discernement des jeunes enfants* (loc. cit. no. 7).

[435] This is how the Ital. Court of Cassation interpreted the *capacità d'intendere o di volere* of Art. 2047 Cc: Cass. 4 Apr. 1959, n. 1006, *Giur.it.* 1959, I, 1, 619; Cass. 19 Nov. 1990, n. 11163, *Giust.civ.Mass.* 1990 p. 1902. Further Franzoni, *Fatti illeciti*, Art. 2046, n. 1 pp. 315–319.

[436] Fns. 383 and 410 above. For Belgium see Cass. 30 Oct. 1980, *Pas. belge* 1981, I, 262.

act'.[437] Unlike German[438] and Greek[439] law, the *capacità d'intendere o di volere* (Art. 2046 in conjunction with Art. 2047 I Ital. Cc)[440] of Italian, and the *capacidade de entender ou querer* of Portuguese law (Art. 488 I Cc)[441] also demand the ability to act voluntarily in accordance with this intellectual understanding.[442] In Germany and Greece[443] the prerequisite of ability to reason and to act accordingly is replaced by a requirement that the juvenile must be able to see 'his responsibility as a result of his dangerous conduct',[444] i.e. 'to recognize the duty somehow to take responsibility for his actions'.[445] Thus both countries still consider an error as to the legal consequences of an act as important. This view, although unambiguous *de lege lata*, is questionable from the point of view of legal policy.[446] Yet a juvenile's awareness of the legal consequences of his action appears to be the only factual difference between the inability to reason and other examples of unavoidable error as to the wrongful nature of an act. In both instances the burden of proof lies on the tortfeasor, and neither a general error as to the wrongful nature of an

---

[437] CA Athens 2494/1977, *NoB* 26 (1978) p. 387; BGH 17 May 1957, *FamRZ* 1957 pp. 254, 255.

[438] In Germany the 'ability to act on one's intellectual understanding' (*Steuerungsfähigkeit*) is relevant only in criminal law (see §§ 3 JGG and 20 StGB): not in civil law only the ability to reason is required: BGH 10 Mar. 1970, *NJW* 1970 p. 1038; BGH 28 Feb. 1984, *NJW* 1984 p. 1958.

[439] In Greek law, the ability to act on one's intellectual understanding is only considered in Art. 33 Greek CP, not in Art. 917 Greek Cc. Georgiades/Stathopoúlos (-Georgiades), *Greek Cc*, vol. iv, Art. 917, no. 5; Stathopoúlos, *Geniko Enochiko Dikaio* vol. i, p. 141; and Deliyannis/Kornilakis, *Eidiko Enochiko Dikaio*, vol. iii, p. 166. *Contra*: Koutrakis, *Evthini ek logon epiikias*, vol. ii, p. 56.

[440] Cass. 19 Nov. 1990 loc. cit. (fn. 435 above); Cass. 28 May 1975, n. 1642, *Resp.Civ. e Prev.* 1976 p. 136; Giur.sist. Bigiavi (Alpa/Bessone) vol. i, p. 207; Visintini, *Fatti illeciti*, vol. i, p. 769.

[441] Vaz Serra, *BolMinJust* 68 (1957) pp. 13, 147; and more recently Martins de Almeida, *Manual de Acidentes*, 3rd edn., p. 223; Antunes Varela, *Obrigações em Geral*, vol. i, 7th edn., p. 555.

[442] The '*kennen und kunnen*' of the old Dutch law also followed these lines: HR 9 Dec. 1966, *NedJur* 1967 no. 69, p. 241 (Joke Stapper); and HR 26 Oct. 1986, *NedJur* 1987 no. 791, p. 2609. In modern Dutch law this term is relevant only in cases concerning a minor's liability for failure to act (see Art. 6:165 I and Art. 6:169 II BW), see *T&C* (-Lankhorst), Art. 6:169, n. 6. A juvenile aged 15 or more lacking the ability to reason should be dealt with under Art. 6:165 I BW, i.e. be judged as a person 'under the influence of a mental or physical handicap'.

[443] This is the prevailing opinion amongst scholars and in the courts: Filios, *Enochiko Dikaio* vol. ii (2), 3rd edn., p. 45; Zepos, *Enochikon Dikaion*, vol. ii (2), 2nd edn., p. 742; Balis, *Genikai Archai tou Astikou Dikaiou*, 8th edn., § 172; Kavkas/Kavkas, *Enochikon Dikaion*, vol. ii, 7th edn., Arts. 915–917, p. 769; CA Athens 2429/1977, *NoB* 26 (1978) p. 387; CA Athens 7550/1979, *NoB* 28 (1980) p. 535. However, compare the authors in fn. 446 below.

[444] BGH 14 Nov. 1978, *NJW* 1979 pp. 864, 865. OLG Cologne 5 May 1993, *NJW-RR* 1993 pp. 1498, 1499 states that it is sufficient 'that (the juvenile has) a general understanding of the fact that (his) conduct is likely to bring about danger'.

[445] BGH 17 May 1957, *FamRZ* 1957 pp. 254, 255, and elsewhere.

[446] Deutsch, *Haftungsrecht*, vol. i, p. 263 and fn. 72; Stathopoulos, *Geniko Enochiko Dikaio*, vol. i, p. 141; Georgiades/Stathopoulos (-Georgiades), *Greek Cc*, vol. iv, Art. 917, no. 4; Deliyannis/Kornilakis, *Eidiko Enochiko Dikaio*, vol. iii, p. 166.

act, nor a general inability to reason are at issue, but only an error specific to the provision infringed.

71   It therefore becomes increasingly likely that provisions such as § 828 II BGB and Art. 917 Greek Cc will become redundant in modern codes. They are of little practical relevance, since there are hardly any decisions in which a court has denied a mentally healthy juvenile's ability to differentiate between right and wrong in matters common in his day-to-day life.[447] Insofar as the ability to reason also covers error as to the legal consequences of one's act, this notion is considered antiquated and has been abandoned even by criminal law. The wide age ranges (seven to eighteen years and, even worse, ten to fourteen years) also provide more cause for irritation than help. For even a mentally handicapped nineteen-year-old (or for that matter a fifteen-year-old) can in certain circumstances lack the ability to reason. All this gives rise to the argument that special provisions such as those mentioned above are vestiges of an antiquated psychiatric thesis: the legislators felt obliged to comment on the ability to reason in cases where there was no indication that it was lacking.

72   The question of which standard of care to apply, which no European code has answered, is much more relevant than a juvenile's (in)ability to reason. Although nearly all codes employ the test of 'negligence based on what would be expected of a reasonable man', the question of whether the applicable standard should be that of a *bonus paterfamilias*, or that of a diligent person of the defendants's age, has been left entirely to the courts. It appears that, with the exception of France,[448] Europe's courts generally determine the liability of juveniles by reference to the standard of care expected from someone of the defendant's age.

73   For example, it is the established practice of the *Areopag* to determine negligence from an objective point of view, but also in light of the care 'expected in the environment of the actor'.[449] Commentators therefore generally conclude that the tortfeasor is to be judged according to the abilities and knowledge expected of those to whom 'he is connected by profession, location, and age'.[450] This corresponds with the opinion of

---

[447] For rulings on similar cases: BGH 27 Jan. 1970, *VersR* 1970 p. 374; HR 9 Dec. 1966, *NedJur* 1967 no. 69 p. 241 (a child of $5^1/_2$), and Cass. 27 May 1982, *Pas. belge* 1982, I, pp. 1128, 1129 (*Cour de Cassation* considered as a question of fact whether a child of 4 who was cycling on the pavement was able to reason when he suddenly rode onto the road in front of a lorry which he should have seen. As the *Cour d'appel* had already answered this question in the affirmative, it was not questioned again by the *Cour de Cassation*).

[448] See no. 68 above.

[449] Areopag 603/1972, *NoB* 20 (1972) p. 1443; Areopag 257/1979 *NoB* 27 (1979) p. 1277; Areopag 1427/1979, *NoB* 28 (1980) p. 1036.

[450] Stathopoulos, *Geniko Enochiko Dikaio*, vol. A i, 2nd edn., p. 95; Deliyannis/Kornilakis, *Eidiko Enochiko Dikaio*, vol. iii, p. 161; Georgiades/Stathopoulos (-Stathopoulos), *Greek Cc*, vol. ii, Art. 330, no. 33. See also Kavkas/Kavkas, *Enochikon Dikaion*, vol. ii, 6th edn., Art. 914, pp. 727–728.

the German Supreme Court, which has frequently employed 'group-specific negligence', declaring 'that an examination of the mental maturity of children must involve a comparison with what can generally be expected of that age group. . . . It also does not contradict the rulings of the Supreme Court, if those courts in which matters of fact can still be raised, on examination of negligence, take into account the special circumstances of a spontaneous and emotional act common to juveniles of a certain age, e.g. the instinctive desire to play,[451] the urge to experiment and explore, lack of discipline, pugnaciousness, impulsiveness, and acts committed under the influence of emotions. . . . If in such circumstances the damaging conduct of the minor would not typically have been avoided, and if his act thus lacks the personal (subjective) aspect of negligence, the "internal" diligence, then his conduct is not negligent'.[452] Portugal has not yet issued such a clear statement, and analysing its literature on the subject, one cannot avoid the conclusion that even scholars favour applying to juveniles the standard of care expected of the *bom pai de família*.[453] In such cases it is doubtful whether the elements—ability to reason and negligence[454]—are always clearly separated.[455] For a practical illustration see STJ 2 March 1978.[456] The defendant (Fernando), aged fourteen, discovered a hunting rifle while visiting a friend. He aimed the rifle at his friends, one after the other. The friend whose home it was shouted when the rifle was aimed at him: 'don't worry, the rifle is certainly not loaded.' Fernando pulled the trigger and his friend died instantly. Fernando suffered enormously for his deed. The STJ upheld the decision of the Court of Appeal which had found no fault on Fernando's part. A breach of the parents' duty to supervise was also refuted. The decision of the STJ not to object to the Court of Appeal's ruling of Fernando's lack of negligence demonstrates (albeit indirectly) that a lower standard of care, adjusted to the relevant

---

[451] Here the court refers to BGH 27 Jan. 1970, *VersR* 1970 pp. 374, 357.

[452] BGH 28 Feb. 1984, *NJW* 1984 pp. 1958, 1959. Further on 'group-specific negligence': BGH 17 Dec. 1963, *VersR* 1964 p. 385; BGH 17 May 1957, *FamRZ* 1957 p. 254; BGH 14 Nov. 1978, *NJW* 1979 p. 864; BGH 10 Mar. 1970, *NJW* 1970 p. 1038; OLG Cologne 5 May 1993, *FamRZ* 1994 p. 831.

[453] Pereira Coelho, *Obrigações*, pp. 151–152 (it is of the utmost importance to differentiate between internal and external circumstances: only the latter are of relevance); Antunes Varela, *Obrigações em Geral*, vol. i, 7th edn., pp. 567–569 (negligence independent of fault within the civil law); Pires de Lima / Antunes Varela, *Cc anotado*, vol. i, 4th edn., Art. 487 nn. 2 and 3; Martins de Almeida, *Manual de Acidentes*, 3rd edn., p. 215.

[454] OLG Schleswig *r+s* 1993 p. 372 (8–year-old wrongly believes he can cross the street in front of a car approaching at excessive speed: although the child's ability to reason was acknowledged, negligence and thus also contributory negligence was not found proven).

[455] Martins de Almeida (loc. cit. fn. 453) p. 222: because the standard of care required is that of the paterfamilias, he says '*interessa sempre averiguar se o menor, pela sua idade, está em condições de entender o valor do seu acto e de se determinar segundo as exigências da conduta que lhe é pedida*'.   [456] STJ 2 Mar. 1978, *BolMinJust* 275 (1978) p. 170.

age group, was applied: an adult would have been expected to examine the gun, and not to point it at anyone.

74   A tension similar to that in Portuguese law is found in its Belgian counterpart. Cornelis writes: *'l'appréciation de la faute ne peut . . ., en principe, être influencée ni par l'âge, ni par le sexe, ni par l'inexpérience du défendeur en responsabilité.'*[457] Vandenberghe summarizes the basic rule as follows: *'Bij het beoordelen van de vraag of de gewraakte handeling onzorg-vuldig is, . . . pleegt de beoordeler te abstraheren van omstandigheden die de persoon van de dader en niet de normale mens betreffen, zoals jeugdige leeftijd, slechte gezondheid.'*[458] Yet, regardless of this 'principle' and of the fact that a number of rulings of the *Cour de Cassation* can be interpreted in line with it,[459] close examination of the rulings shows that, with regard to the predictability of the damage, the age of the child is nevertheless considered by the judges.[460] The *Cour de Cassation* has confirmed an appeal court decision that children playing on the pavement cannot be accused of negligence, although adults should have recognized the danger to cyclists.[461] Moreover, liability was denied in the case of a child who threw pieces of wood at a friend, injuring his eye. The appeal before the *Cour de Cassation* was based on the claim that *'un homme normalement prudent et raisonable ne jette pas des morceaux de bois en visant d'autrui'*;[462] this appeal was dismissed with the comment that the defendant had been engaged in a *'jeu en soi innocent'*.[463] In another case a 14-year-old sustained injuries by diving head first into a shallow pool; she escaped contributory negligence,[464] unlike an adult who had suffered the same mishap just before this incident.[465]

Italian law tackles the problem from an entirely different angle. Instead of operating a construction of rules and exceptions, its authors have come to the conclusion that a duty of care can only be breached where the damage was predictable. Although the predictability of the damage is judged objectively, it is 'subjectivized' in that the experience and ability of the actor are taken into consideration. Age is accordingly

---

[457] Cornelis, *Responsabilité extra-contractuelle*, p. 39.

[458] Vandenberghe *et al., TPR* 1987 pp. 1255, 1295.

[459] Cass. 5 May 1971, *Pas. belge* 1971, I, 802 = *JT* 1971 p. 662. In Cass. 24 Oct. 1974, *Pas. belge* 1975, I, 237 5-, 7-, and 8-year-olds were playing with bows and arrows; the winner was to be the one who shot the highest. A falling arrow injured one of the children. The Court of Appeal ruled that *'ce jeu ne peut être considéré que comme un divertissement normal et innocent pour un groupe de garçons de cet âge'*. The Court of Cassation objected, stating that *'en prenant ainsi en considération le jeune âge de l'auteur de l'accident pour apprécier le caractère illicite ou non de son acte, l'arrêt ne justifie pas légalement sa décision'* (loc. cit. p. 239).

[460] Vandenberghe loc. cit. p. 1309 and elsewhere; see also Fagnart, *JT* 1976 pp. 569, 586–587.   [461] Cass. 16 June 1969, *Pas. belge* 1969, I, 950.

[462] *Pas. belge* 1975, I, 1046.   [463] Cass. 26 June 1975, *Pas. belge* 1975, I, 1046, 1047.

[464] Cass. 16 Feb. 1984, *Pas. belge* 1984, I, 684, 689–690.

[465] Brussels 30 Mar. 1982, *RGAR* 1983 no. 10720.

also relevant when considering the care expected of the *buon padre di famiglia* of that age.[466] According to Bussani, minors fall into three groups. First, those who are nearly adult (sixteen and seventeen years old) to whom the standard of the *buon padre di famiglia* (which is always applied in road traffic accident cases, irrespective of age) can usually be applied.[467] Secondly, the twelve- to fifteen-year-olds, whose conduct will be compared with the duty of care which a person of that age could be expected to demonstrate.[468] Thirdly, the six- to eleven-year-old group, who are rarely found negligent. The courts usually determine causal connection only in order to apply Art. 2048 Cc (parental liability).[469] In appropriate cases, the Dutch also apply a standard of care related to the relevant age group, although there are no recent rulings on this.[470]

(d) Liability in Equity as an Exception

If the standard of care demanded of a minor depends on his age, and if **75** either he met that standard or failed to do so because of restricted ability to reason, there can be no liability based on *fault*. However, this does not necessarily oust other causes of action. Strict liability, for instance, may still apply. As for liability for personal misconduct, *liability in equity* determines who is to compensate for the damage, and to what extent. Let us consider an example. If the victim was particularly vulnerable, and the tortfeasor, though juvenile, was rich, social justice may exceptionally require that the loss be compensated. This principle is applied in most European systems, and where it exists it serves as the functional equivalent to the onerous liability system of French and, to a lesser degree, Spanish law.

This equitable liability, although controversial, has found its way into **76** most European codes. Although of little practical relevance, it has become an object of extraordinary interest for comparative law, chiefly because it is a striking example of a legal concept which, over the course

---

[466] Giur.sist. Bigiavi (-Figone/Spallarossa) vol. i, p. 55; Franzoni, *Fatti illeciti*, pp. 131–133; and Visintini, *Fatti illeciti*, vol. ii, p. 16 (stating that *'l'ossequio alla categoria concettuale dell'uomo di media diligenza'* is *'meramente formale. L'accertamento del requisito della rappresentatività non può essere valutato che in concreto tenendo conto delle circostanze, delle possibilità e della cultura dell'agente'*); all include references to judgments.

[467] On road traffic accidents: App. Roma 31 July 1963, *Resp.Civ. e Prev.* 1964 p. 308; Bussani, *Colpa soggettiva*, pp. 180, 189, 192.

[468] See fn. 466 above together with App. Firenze 27 Feb. 1968, *Giur.tosc.* 1968 p. 611. Bussani loc. cit.; Cass. 31 Mar. 1967, n. 734, *Resp.Civ. e Prev.* 1967 p. 562; Cass. 26 July 1962, n. 2125, *Resp.Civ. e Prev.* 1963 p. 281; Patti, *Famiglia e responsabilità civile*, p. 235; and Chianale, *Giur.it.* 1968, I, 1, 1528.

[469] As did Cass. 10 Feb. 1981, n. 826, *Rass.Avv.Stato* 1981, I, 331; Cass. 16 July 1962, n. 1882, *Resp.Civ. e Prev.* 1962 p. 443; Cass. 4 Mar. 1977, n. 894, *Giur.it.* 1977, I, 1, 1660; Cass. 27 Nov. 1971, n. 3467, *Giur.it.Mass.* 1971 no. 3467; and Cass. 19 Oct. 1965, n. 2132, *Giur.it.* 1966, I, 1, 1281.

[470] Schut, *Onrechtmatige daad*, 4th edn., pp. 102–107; *T&C* (-Lankhorst) Art. 6:169, n. 2.

of 200 years, passed from one nation to the next, altering a little with each move. Although the original principle is always retained, each nation has shaped it slightly differently. This was possible, first because there was no supra-national institution to prevent these changes, and secondly because the codification of this equity-based liability made the provisions less flexible than would have been the case had it been left to courts and scholars.

77   The idea of imposing on children[471] liability based on 'natural equity'[472] stems from the Prussian Civil Code, the *Allgemeines Landrecht* (ALR) of 1 June 1794.

ALR I, 6, §§ 41–44 read as follows: '§ 41: In cases where insane persons, imbeciles, or children below the age of seven injure another, they can be required to compensate only immediate damage[473] with their own assets. § 42: However, the assets of the minor may only be drawn upon in cases where his guardian or his parents are not liable for or cannot compensate the damage. § 43: Moreover, the minor is liable to compensate the victim only to such extent as does not deprive him of his maintenance or an education befitting his standing in society. § 44: In cases where the victim has contributed to the damage, by whatever means, even by the slightest negligence, he is not entitled to damages from the tortfeasor.'

Although E. Koch, the most important commentator on the Prussian *Allgemeines Landrecht*, criticized these provisions a hundred years later for their 'irregularity', and has doubted whether they are truly consistent with the equity argument,[474] one need only picture life in Prussia at that time, and imagine the boisterous children of landowners smashing the windows of farmhands' houses, to set these provisions in context.

78   These four provisions were copied practically wholesale by the Austrian ABGB (§§ 1310 and 1308). Moreover, although the authors of the first draft of the German BGB, who strongly opposed 'such a deviation from the general principles of law' on the ground that 'such outlandish provisions . . . would leave the judge with considerations of equity (*Billigkeitsrücksichten*) rather than giving him fixed provisions to apply',[475] their concerns were ignored in later stages.[476] The second Commission re-introduced equitable liability, remarking that it was 'not possible to exclude a claim for damages demanded by the legal conscience simply because the legislator was unable to phrase it appro-

---

[471] § 41 made no express or analogous reference to those aged between seven and fourteen years: Pr. Obertribunal 14 Mar. 1873, *PrObTrE* 69 pp. 258, 263.

[472] This is the official argument in the draft version of ALR II, 3, § 34 (as cited by E. Koch, *Allg. Landrecht für die preußischen Staaten*, vol. i, 8th edn., p. 299, fn. 37).

[473] 'Immediate damage' is defined in ALR I, 6, § 2; 'consequential damage' in ALR I, 6, § 3.

[474] Loc. cit. (fn. 472 above).   [475] Mot. II p. 734.

[476] For details on the further history of the legislation see RG 13 Dec. 1934, *RGZ* 146 pp. 213, 216–218; and Deutsch, *Haftungsrecht*, vol. i p. 313.

priately'.[477] The result of this argument can be seen in § 829 BGB, a provision which distinguishes itself in a number of ways from both its Prussian and Austrian predecessors. The limitation to 'immediate damage' has been removed, as has the principle that even the slightest degree of negligence on the part of the victim deprives him of his claim, a principle which was recognized in Prussian law, and still is, in § 1308 ABGB, calling to mind the equity maxim that 'he who comes to equity must come with clean hands'. In present-day German law the plaintiff's contributory negligence is only one factor to be considered within an equity-based claim.[478] Furthermore, it has become standard practice for the courts to incorporate a claim for damages for pain and suffering into § 829 BGB.[479] § 829 BGB is now applied even in cases beyond those covered by its wording. It applies not only to 'cases specified in §§ 823 to 826', but also to liability cases under §§ 831 ff. BGB.[480] Further, liability in equity is not only employed where the tortfeasor's liability for damage is excluded by §§ 827, 828: § 829 BGB has also been held to cover cases where liability is excluded by an age limit,[481] or by sudden and unpredictable loss of consciousness,[482] in which it is debatable whether a delictually relevant 'act' has actually been committed.[483] German liability in equity in this field (i.e. in cases of medical crisis or loss of consciousness while driving), which of course applies only to adults, is even more rigid than the tough liability regime of French law.[484] Furthermore, it must be a case where equity *demands* (rather than merely allows) damages. Equity must always take into consideration the degree of causal responsibilty of the juvenile,[485] the effects of his actions on the victim,[486] and the financial situation of both parties. The courts regularly take into consideration any insurance covering either party, whether social insurance for the victim,[487]

---

[477] Prot. II p. 590.

[478] Indeed OLG Cologne 29 Oct. 1980, *VersR* 1981 pp. 266, 267 goes so far as to say that § 829 BGB may be applied where the plaintiff's contributory negligence reaches 50% ('in cases where the responsibility is shared equally'). However, recklessness defeats the claim: BGH 18 Dec. 1979, *VersR* 1980 p. 625.

[479] See e.g. BGH 18 Dec. 1979, *VersR* 1980 pp. 625, 626 (this has never been a moot point); and BGH 11 Oct. 1994, *NJW* 1995 p. 452.

[480] See RG 4 Mar. 1915, *JW* 1915 p. 580 (application of § 836 BGB under § 829 BGB); RG 25 Sep. 1916, *JW* 1917 pp. 38, 39 (§ 833 s. 2 BGB). See also OLG Hamm 14 Dec. 1976, *VersR* 1977 pp. 531, 532 (§ 836 BGB); for more details see *MünchKomm* (-Mertens), 2nd edn., § 829 nos. 3–8.

[481] The foundation-laying decision was BGH 21 May 1963, *BGHZ* 39 pp. 281, 286–287.

[482] BGH 15 Jan. 1957, *BGHZ* 23 p. 90; BGH 11 Oct. 1994 loc. cit. (fn. 479 above).

[483] See *MünchKomm* (-Mertens), 2nd edn., § 829 nos. 10–11, which differentiates even further.

[484] Cass.civ. 4 Feb. 1981, *D.* 1983 *Jur.* 1 = *Sem.Jur.* 1981, II, 19656. See also no. 94 below.

[485] See OLG Hamm 14 Dec. 1976, *VersR* 1977 pp. 531, 532.

[486] OLG Cologne 22 Oct. 1980, *VersR* 1981 pp. 266, 267 (loss of one eye).

[487] OLG Hamm loc. cit. (fn. 485 above); where the victim but not the tortfeasor was insured, equitable liability was refused.

or third-party liability insurance covering the minor.[488] In 1979 the BGH ruled that such considerations could influence only the amount of damages to be paid, and not the determination of the action itself. The BGH also ruled that the simple existence of such cover must not 'result in sums being awarded which would otherwise exceed the financial capacity of the defendant'.[489] However, although it has more recently ceded ground on this position,[490] so far that has been only in the field of compulsory third-party liability insurance in road traffic law. Hence, for minors, the existence of third-party liability insurance still does not found a cause of action. According to § 829 BGB, a person is not 'rich' simply because he is insured: this is known as the 'millionaire's provision'. However, if its preconditions are met, it governs children: the courts then have to determine whether or not the child was contributorily negligent (§ 254 BGB is analogously applied).[491] This approach is shared by the Austrian OGH's rulings on §§ 1304, 1310 ABGB.[492]

79   The *Code Napoléon* did not provide for equitable liability, which the French legislator in 1968 declared incompatible with the liability principles of French law.[493] Belgium is therefore the only Roman-based legal system to adopt (in 1935) the German principle of equity-based liability.

---

[488] BGH 15 Jan. 1957, BGHZ 23 pp. 90, 99–100. See also BGH 26 June 1962, *VersR* 1962 p. 811; BGH 24 June 1969, *VersR* 1969 p. 860; BGH 24 Apr. 1979, *VersR* 1979 p. 645; and BGH 11 Oct. 1994, *NJW* 1995 p. 452. On the similarly problematical issue of determining the quantum of damages for pain and suferring under § 847 BGB, see also BGH 16 Feb. 1993, *NJW* 1993 pp. 1531, 1532. For a general view on the difficult relationship between third-party liability insurance and liability see v. Bar, *AcP* 181 (1981) pp. 289 ff.

[489] BGH 18 Dec. 1979, *VersR* 1980 p. 625 (which describes itself as a 'limitation of BGHZ 23, 90' in its headnote). For rulings following this line, see LG Dortmund 30 Sep. 1992, *VersR* 1994 p. 606. *Contra*, however, OGH 15 June 1972, *SZ* 45 no. 69 p. 298 (a voluntary liability insurance policy is property under § 1310 ABGB); and even more so OGH 3 Apr. 1974, *SZ* 47 no. 43 p. 202: it is of great relevance which of the parties involved could most easily bear the loss. 'Therefore, even a defendant without financial means will be asked to compensate the damage to an amount covered by insurance, notwithstanding that the latter was purchased by a third party.'   [490] BGH 11 Oct. 1994 loc. cit. (fn. 488 above).

[491] BGH 10 Apr. 1962, BGHZ 37 p. 102 (a 3-year-old chased his ball onto the road, hitting the plaintiff's bicycle. The child's claim under § 823 I BGB was reduced by the application of §§ 254, 829 BGB). See also BGH 24 June 1969, *NJW* 1969 p. 1762. *Contra*, however, KG 31 Oct. 1994, *NZV* 1995 p. 109 (§§ 254, 829 BGB are not applicable if the person causing the accident has third-party liability insurance).

[492] OGH 16 Dec. 1992, *JBl* 1993 p. 660. This expressly states that 'although under § 1310 persons below the age of 7 [are] not necessarily unable to take responsibility for a delict, [contributory] fault on their part [is] only exceptionally to be found. It is for the other party to prove such fault.'

[493] The draft of the Act of 3 Jan. 1968, introducing Art. 489–2 Cc, sought to authorize the judge to '*modérer l'indemnité mise à la charge de l'aliéné, eu égard aux situations respectives de la victime et de l'auteur du dommage*' (Weill/Terré, *Obligations*, 4th edn., no. 632, p. 645). v. Bar (-Gotthardt), *DeliktsR in Europa, Frankreich*, p. 20, fn. 85. There are hardly any recent academic works favouring liability in equity: Hennings, *Persönliche Haftung und Mitverschulden*, pp. 119–120. However, strict liability may still be justified under the doctrine of *faute objective*: Mazeaud/Tunc, *Responsibilité civile*, vol. i, 6th edn., no. 467, p. 530.

Art. 1 sub-section II of the Act of 16 April 1935,[494] which introduced Art. 1386*bis* into the Belgian *Code civil*, explicitly authorizes the judge '*selon l'équité* (Dutch: *naar billijkheid*), *tenant compte des circonstances et de la situation des parties*'. However, Art. 1386*bis* Belg.Cc concerns only persons '*se trouvant en état de démence, ou dans un état grave de déséquilibre mental ou de débilité mentale la rendant incapable du contrôle des ses actions*'. This is why it is generally inapplicable to healthy children, even by analogy,[495] for they are neither *déments* nor *anormaux*. Thus, irrespective of Art. 1384 II Cc (parental liability), it applies only to mentally handicapped children.[496]

True liability in equity is recognized in Greek, Italian, and Portuguese   **80** law. The Netherlands appeared for some time to consider joining them.[497] The idea was eventually discarded, partly because the legislator intended to introduce a special provision for the mentally handicapped anyway,[498] and partly to preserve certainty in the law.[499] The *Parlementaire Geschiedenis* mirrors the *Motive*, the published first edition and discussion of the BGB. However, although the Dutch have not totally abandoned the concept inherent in § 829 BGB, they did move it into the law of damages where it influences *all* cases of liability. Art. 6:109 BW reads:

'The judge may reduce a legal obligation to compensate for damage if awarding full reparation would lead to clearly unacceptable results in the circumstances, including the nature of the liability, the legal relationship between the parties, and their financial capacity. The reduction may not exceed the amount for which the tortfeasor has covered, or was obliged to cover, his liability by insurance.'

The Dutch observed and analysed other European developments and drew their own conclusions, which led to a shifting of emphasis: equity is no longer a cause of action, but now limits damages. This means, in turn, that the role of liability insurance must be seen in a new light, as must the victim's insurance cover and the age of the tortfeasor: all are relevant to the reduction of damages payable, and in cases of minor fault (probably also under Art. 6:101 BW, contributory fault),[500] but not to the

---

[494] *Loi sur la réparation de dommages causés par les déments et les anormaux, Pasin. belge* 1935 p. 286 (incl. official commentary); Monit. belge 18 Apr. 1935.

[495] Cass. 18 Oct. 1990, *RGAR* 1992, 12026; de Page, *Droit civil Belge*, vol. ii, 3rd edn., no. 916, p. 887.

[496] Cornelis, *Buitencontractueel aansprakelijkheidsrecht* no. 191. Cass. 18 Oct. 1990 (loc. cit.) states that parental liability under Art. 1384 II Cc is not limited by the fact that the child's liability arises from Art. 1386*bis* Cc; see also no. 86 below.

[497] For details on Art. 6.3.6 (later to be 6.3.1.2a and b = Art. 6:164 and Art. 6:165 BW) (*ontwerp burgerlijk wetboek* = draft by Meijers) which contained liability in equity: *Parlementaire Geschiedenis*, vol. vi, pp. 644–649. For details in German: Hohlbein, *Niederländisches außervertragliches Haftungsrecht*, p. 58.   [498] Art. 6:165 BW; see nos. 91–92 below.

[499] Memorie van Antwoord II, *Parlementaire Geschiedenis*, vol. vi, p. 652.

[500] HR 1 June 1990, *NedJur* 1991 no. 720, p. 3125.

cause of action.[501] Compensation for pain and suffering is covered by Art. 6:106 I BW.

81   Greece was the first European country to introduce equitable liability into its Civil Code. The Greek provision closely resembles § 829 German BGB. However, despite the high age limit, it seems to have led to hardly any decisions. Like its German model, Art. 918 Greek Cc[502] applies not only to cases where liability for fault 'under the provisions of sections 915 to 917' is excluded, but by analogy also to cases in which the rules concerning the group-specific negligence of minors who have attained age ten (Arts. 916 and 917 Greek Cc) exempt them from liability.[503] The same applies where the tortfeasor suddenly becomes unconscious.[504] Yet Art. 918 Greek Cc builds on the notion that the tortfeasor must fulfil all the criteria of Art. 914 Greek Cc,[505] except for the question of delictual responsibility. Utmost restraint is exercised when it comes to equity-based claims where the victim is self-insured.[506] The influence of third-party liability insurance purchased by the tortfeasor has not yet been discussed. All aspects of the individual case, such as the economic situation of the parties involved, the severity of injuries, the mental abilities of the tortfeasor, and the possibility of contributory negligence on the part of the victim, can serve as grounds of equity. In cases where the person lacking civil capacity is the victim, Art. 918 Greek Cc is integrated into Art. 300 Greek Cc, which deals with contributory negligence (just as in Germany § 829 BGB becomes part of § 254 BGB, and in Austria § 1310 ABGB becomes part of § 1304 AGBG).[507] In addition, 'indemnification' under Art. 918 Greek Cc may lead to compensation in full. However, usually only such amount as is considered equitable is ordered.

82   Liability in equity is also a fairly new concept in the Italian and Portuguese codes. The Italian *Codice Civile* of 1865 did not recognize it. It was introduced in its 1942 successor in Art. 2047 II Cc. Under this

---

[501] *Parlementaire Geschiedenis*, loc. cit. (fn. 499 above) pp. 652–653; *T&C* (-Oosterveen), Art. 6:109, nn. 5 and 6; Hartkamp, Judicial Discretion, p. 14.

[502] 'A person who has caused damage may, where he is not liable under sections 915 to 917 inclusive, be ordered by the Court, having considered the parties' respective positions, to pay reasonable damages if the damage cannot be made good in any other way.' For a German overview: Zepos, *FS für Martin Wolff* (1952) pp. 167–173.

[503] Georgiades/Stathopoulos (-Georgiades), *Greek Cc*, vol. iv, Art. 918 nos. 41 f.; Stathopoulos, *Geniko Enochiko Dikaio*, vol. ii, p. 108; Deliyannis/Kornilakis, *Eidiko Enochiko Dikaio*, vol. iii, p. 167.   [504] Stathopoulos loc. cit.

[505] Or of any of the other provisions on no-fault liability of Book 2 Chapter 39 Greek Cc.

[506] Filios, *Enochiko Dikaio*, vol. ii (2), 3rd edn., p. 48; Deliyannis/Kornilakis and Stathopoulos loc. cit. (fn. 503 above).

[507] This is the prevailing opinion amongst legal scholars. See fn. 503 above, and Lipovats, *NoB* 14 (1966) pp. 74, 75 (in a note on BGH 10 Apr. 1962 [see fn. 491 above]); *ErmAK* (-Litzeropoulos), Art. 300 no. 22; and Livanis, *I Efarmogi tou arthrou 300 is to pedion tis antikimenikis evthinis*, pp. 58 ff.

provision, which is much shorter than § 829 BGB and Art. 918 Greek Cc, in cases where the plaintiff cannot get damages from the person responsible for the child, 'in view of the economic situation of both parties [the court may] compel the author of the damage make appropriate compensation'. For the authors of the *Codice Civile* it is a '*responsabilità puramente oggettiva*', which was deliberately taken from German law,[508] to counterbalance liability for fault. The *autore del danno* is responsible for third-party liability. This means in turn that a *condotta cosciente e volontaria* (action knowingly and willingly undertaken) by the tortfeasor is not a necessary precondition.[509] Whether a person is liable, and if so to what amount, are questions for the judge. Moreover, the plaintiff does not have an absolute entitlement, this being only a discretionary remedy.[510] For the authors of Art. 2047 Cc liability arises through the 'solidarity of society' and 'social responsibility'.[511] Thus, although the wealthy may have to accept responsibility to the poor, the latter are not necessarily responsible to the wealthy.[512]

There have so far been few rulings on Art. 2047 II Cc, since parental **83** liability is strict (see no. 135 below) and liability in equity only secondary (see no. 86 below). The leading case in Italy is still a ruling of Trib. Macerata of 20 May 1986.[513] Some children were playing with a sling and paper arrows. The ten-year-old defendant hit the four-year-old plaintiff in the eye with an arrow, permanently blinding it. The damages awarded by the court were determined by an analogous application of the rules of Act no. 39 of 26 February 1977[514] governing compulsory third-party liability insurance for motorists. This prescribes that the loss of an eye causes a permanent invalidity of 25%. The total material damage amounted to one quarter of three times the annual social security pension of 1986.[515] To the material damage, the court added the biological damage, applying the so-called Pisa method.[516] The total amount of damages was reduced by one-third by the application of Art. 2047 II Cc. This figure was chosen after the court had compared the financial situation of both children. Compensation for pain and suffering

---

[508] *Relazione della Commissione Reale al progetto del libro 'Obbligazioni e contratti'* p. 25, cited here according to Pandolfelli *et al.*, *Codice civile*, p. 680. De Martini, *Fatti produttivi di danno*, speaks on p. 286 of a *responsabilità legale oggettiva*.

[509] Geri/Breccia/Busnelli/Natoli, *Diritto civile*, vol. iii, p. 699.

[510] De Cupis, *Il danno*, vol. ii, 3rd edn., p. 24.

[511] Cass. 28 Jan. 1953, n. 216, *Giur.it.* 1953, I, 1, 496; Visintini, *Fatti illeciti*, vol. i, p. 491.

[512] Rodotà, *Problema della responsabilità civile*, p. 143 and fn. 38; Visintini; *Fatti illeciti*, vol. i, pp. 491, 497. [513] Trib. Macerata 20 May 1986, *Foro.it.* 1986, I, 2594.

[514] *Gaz.Uff.* 115 (1977) no. 54 p. 1471, amending Act no. 990 of 24 Dec. 1969 (*Gaz.Uff.* 111 [1970] no. 2, p. 18).

[515] On the 'Genoa evaluation method', originally conceived for biological damage, see Bajons, *ZVglRWiss* 92 (1993) pp. 76, 92–95.   [516] See also Bajon loc. cit. pp. 95–98.

was not awarded. The *Sezione unite* of the Court of Cassation[517] had previously argued that, although Art. 2059 Cc is to be applied in all cases where the requirements of a criminal offence have been objectively fulfilled, the act in this particular case was not reprehensible, and nor did social conscience (*la coscienza sociale*) demand compensation for pain and suffering. Moreover, the economic situations of the parties supported the Tribunales' decision not to compensate the *danno morale*. In conclusion, it seems that the headnote on the decision ('*Il danno non patrimoniale non è risarcibile quando l'autore del fatto, astrattamente previsto dalla legge come reato, è un minore di anni quattordici, incapace di intendere e di volere secondo le leggi civili*') has been worded too broadly. Compensation for pain and suffering is not altogether excluded, but determined according to the principles of equity.[518]

84   Unlike its predecessor, the Portuguese *Código Civil* of 1867, Arts. 2377–2379 of which imposed strict personal liability on children, albeit secondary to parental liability, the authors of the Portuguese Cc of 1965 introduced a separate equity provision (Art. 489) into their codification.[519] Yet it has so far been of little practical relevance, since there are no published precedents. Scholars stress the exceptional status of Art. 489 Port. Cc, whose sub-section II (like § 829 BGB but unlike Art. 2047 II Ital. Cc and Art. 918 Greek Cc) strongly emphasizes that compensation of others is secondary to self-preservation.[520] Yet the only difference between most provisions on liability for fault and Art. 489 I Cc is that the former demand of the tortfeasor the ability to reason, and the latter does not.[521] The application of Art. 489 Port. Cc to juveniles who, according to the doctrine of group-specific negligence, have acted as one could reasonably expect young persons of that age to act, has so far not been considered.[522] Under this provision the courts may award damages for pain and suffering if the economic situation of the tortfeasor and the principles of equity allow (rather than demand). The amount to be awarded depends on the circumstances.[523] A special feature of Portuguese law is that liability in equity extends to keepers of vehicles: Art. 503 II Cc expressly states that 'persons lacking civil capacity . . . are liable under the provisions of Article 489'.

---

[517] Cass.sez.un. 6 Dec. 1982, n. 6651, *Giur.it.* 1984, I, 1, 150, 171. The decision concerned parental liability for a 13-year-old under Art. 2048 Cc.

[518] Supporting the argument: Franzoni, *Fatti illeciti*, Art. 2046, n. 3 (p. 322: '*conseguentemente, che anche il minore di anni quattordici possa essere condannato al risarcimento del danno morale*').

[519] Its introduction can also be attributed to Vaz Serra's studies of comparative law: *BolMinJust* 68 (1957) pp. 13, 89 ff., 110–113.

[520] Martins de Almeida, *Manual de Acidentes*, 3rd edn., p. 225.

[521] Antunes Varela, *Obrigações em Geral*, vol. i, 7th edn., p. 558.

[522] See no. 73 above.   [523] Martins de Almeida loc. cit. (fn. 520 above) p. 227.

(e) The Personal Liability of Children and Juveniles: A Secondary Form of Liability?

The relationship between the liability of children and juveniles on one **85** hand, and the liability of their parents, guardians, and other persons with a duty to supervise (see nos. 131 ff.) on the other, might seem somewhat remote at first glance. Children rarely possess great assets, and family third-party liability insurance usually covers both children and their parents against claims by third parties. Even regarding a right of recourse for damages which parents may claim from their children, a reduction to nil—due to the former being obliged to provide maintenance for the latter—is not uncommon. Nevertheless, it remains an issue for the law of delict. For not only does it set the legal framework for insurance, it must also provide for cases where insurance cover is missing, always bearing in mind that a claim can still be enforced after the youth has become an adult and has his own income.[524]

The following differentiation must therefore be made: liability in **86** equity is always secondary to liability for supervision. This is expressly provided by § 1310 ABGB, § 829 BGB, Art. 489 I Port. Cc, and Art. 2047 II Ital. Cc. Art. 918 Greek Cc says that equity-based liability can only be relied upon if compensation is not otherwise available.[525] Only Belgium has no similar provision, which can be explained by the fact that its equity-based liability concerns only the mentally handicapped.[526] Since this generally involves adults, its authors have simply not contemplated its relationship to liability for supervision under Art. 1384 II.[527] Nevertheless, liability for supervision may influence the scope of a mentally handicapped adult's liability under Art. 1386*bis* Belgian Cc, if he has a carer. However, the carer's liability will not necessarily take precedence. Similarly, parents and their mentally handicapped child are jointly and severally liable for the child's reduced liability, the parents being liable

[524] For instance, under French law (Arts. 2270–1 in conjunction with 2244 Cc) a title to a delictual claim can still be enforced after 10 years; under Greek (Art. 268 Cc), Dutch (Art. 3: 324 I BW), and Portuguese law (Arts. 309 and 311 Cc, see RL 2 Nov. 1979, *BolMinJust* 296 [1980] p. 328) after 20 years; and under Belgian (Arts. 2262 in conjunction with 2244 Cc) and German law (§ 218 I BGB) after 30 years. In a similar fashion, Art. 2953 Ital. Cc extends the 5-year period of Art. 2947 I Cc (from the time the act was committed) to 10 years from the time when the decision became res judicata (Art. 2945 II Cc). Under Spanish law too, *res judicata* starts a new limitation period, albeit, like the basic period of limitation for claims under Art. 1902, only for 1 year (Arts. 1968 no. 2, 1971 Cc).

[525] This wording is intended to stress that liability in equity is secondary, not only to liability for supervision, but also to a claim by the plaintiff against his insurer: Filios, *Enochiko Dikaio*, vol. ii (2), 3rd edn., p. 48; Deliyannis/Kornilakis, *Eidiko Enochiko Dikaio*, vol. iii, p. 166; Georgiades/Stathopoulos (-Georgiades), *Greek Cc*, vol. iv, Art. 918, nos. 11–12; and Stathopoúlos, *Geniko Enochiko Dikaio*, vol. ii, p. 108.　[526] See no. 79 above.

[527] The explanatory notes (*Pasin. belge* 1935 pp. 286, 292) say only: '*Le projet de loi . . . ne modifie en rien les principes suivis par la jurisprudence qui n'applique pas au gardien des déments la règle de l'article 1384.*' Children appear to have been overlooked.

for the rest.[528] Parental claims to recourse are, in turn, subject to Art. 1386*bis* Cc.[529]

Giving priority to liability for supervision over liability in equity does not mean that the latter is *de jure* excluded in all cases where the former exists: liability for supervision must be economically enforceable to oust liability in equity.[530] This does not usually result in both questions, i.e. whether a claim based on liability for supervision exists and whether the supervisors are financially able to pay the damages, being examined in a preceding court action.[531] Only Italy calls for preliminary proceedings,[532] as a result of which liability under 2047 II Cc seems to play a very minor role in practice. Austria only demands that an attempt be made to enforce the claim against the parents where liability for supervision has been established but it is unclear whether they have the means to meet the damages awarded. In cases where both liability for supervision and its enforceability are in question, the plaintiff is usually advised to sue both the guardian and the alleged tortfeasor.[533]

Where both parents and children are liable at civil law for personal fault they are severally liable to third parties.[534] A court may show lenience towards the minor in determining negligence where parental

---

[528] Cass. 18 Oct. 1990, *RGAR* 1992 no. 12026.

[529] *Pasin. belge* loc. cit. (fn. 527 above) p. 293.

[530] Cass. 28 Jan. 1953, n. 216, *Giur.it.* 1953, I, 1, 496; and Giur.sist. Bigiavi (-Venchiarutti) vol. i, p. 224; Martins de Almeida, *Manual de Acidentes*, 3rd edn., p. 224; and Pires de Lima/ Antunes Varela, *Cc anotado*, vol. i, 4th edn., Art. 489, n. 2; Georgiades/Stathopoŭlos (-Georgiades) loc. cit. no. 12; *MünchKomm* (-Mertens), 2nd edn., § 829 BGB no. 17; Rummel (-Reischauer), *ABGB* vol. ii, 2nd edn., § 1310, no. 11. In cases where liability for supervision can only be partially met the guardian and the tortfeasor are jointly and severally liable (Mertens loc. cit.). However, the guardian is exclusively liable to the torfeasor: § 840 II, p. 2 BGB; Art. 927, p. 2 Greek Cc.   [531] Martins de Almeida, Mertens loc. cit.

[532] Thus Cendon (-Venchiarutti) vol. iv, Art. 2047, no. 6, p. 2061.

[533] OGH 22 Nov. 1938, *SZ* 20/241 p. 507, and 14 Oct. 1970, *ÖJZ* 1971 p. 123 (EvBl 74). Yet the plaintiff must 'prove that he was not responsible for the injury, and that the supervisor of the person causing the damage cannot indemnify him': OGH 18 Oct. 1993, *ZVR* 1994 pp. 366, 367.

[534] For Italy: Cass. 22 Oct. 1965, n. 2202, *Arch.resp.civ.* 1967 p. 15; Cass. 31 Mar. 1967, n. 734, *Giust.civ.Mass.* 1967 no. 734; Cass. 21 Dec. 1968, n. 4046, *Giur.it.* 1969, I, 1, 1084 (it is unnecessary to proceed against both parents and child); Cendon (-Venchiarutti) vol. iv, Art. 2048, no. 7, p. 2066; Franzoni, *Fatti illeciti*, Art. 2048, no. 2 pp. 351–352 (also giving his own view on Art. 2048 as *lex specialiter* loc. cit p. 354); Alpa, *Responsabilià civile*, p. 304; De Martini, *Fatti produttivi di danno*, p. 290; and Giur.sist. Bigiavi (-Mantovani) p. 13, no. 6; for Portugal: Antunes Varela, *Obrigações em Geral*, vol. i, 7th edn., p. 585, Martins de Almeida, *Manual de Acidentes*, 3rd edn., p. 237, and Vaz Serra, *BolMinJust* 85 (1959) pp. 381, 431; for Greece: CA Athens 2737/1979 *NoB* 28 (1980) p. 103; CA Athens 1577/1953 *NoB* 1 (1953) p. 196; for Germany: *MünchKomm* (-Mertens), 2nd edn., § 832, no. 30; for Belgium: Vandenberghe/van Quickenborne/Geelen/De Coster, *TPR* 1987 pp. 1255, 1452, no. 118; and Cornelis, *Responsabilité extracontractuelle*, p. 331; for France: Starck (-Roland/Boyer), *Obligations*, vol. i, 4th edn., no. 1268; for The Netherlands: v. Bar (Hondius/van Dam), *DeliktsR in Europa, Niederlande*, p. 11.

liability has been established.[535] The fact that his parents are also liable may, under specific provisions known as reduction clauses, reduce his share of the damages[536] in cases where the courts are of the opinion that neither the child's full liability nor that of his parents is justifiable.[537] Neither fact, however, affects the principle of joint and several liability.[538] Not only could such a reduction clause, in the circumstances of the individual case, also operate to the advantage of the parents, but the courts could even conclude that an older child's responsibility ought to displace his parents' duty to supervise.[539] The Dutch BW took this into account when deciding that, under Art. 6:169 BW, until the child's fourteenth year parents are strictly liable, between the fourteenth and fifteenth year liability for failure to supervise is rebuttably presumed, and afterwards failure to supervise must be established.[540]

As for the rights of recovery between jointly and severally liable parties, the liability of minors regularly prevails over liability for supervision,[541] the latter being often only liability for presumed fault, whereas the former is generally for established fault. Whether and to what extent the parental right of recovery is enforceable depends ultimately on family law. It makes little sense to claim compensation from child, only to lose it in maintenance.

As we saw above, Spanish law makes special provision for the **88** relationship between parental liability for failure to supervise and the liability of their children, and for the time being this situation will not

---

[535] See e.g. Cass. 24 Oct. 1974, *Pas. belge* 1975, I, 237; and observations by Jourdain and Viney (see fn. 419 above).   [536] E.g. Art. 6: 109 BW and Art. 494 Port. Cc.

[537] See *T&C* (-Oosterveen), Art. 6: 109 BW no. 5, p. 534.

[538] The authors of the new Dutch BW have expressly rejected the idea that the liability of minors is only secondary: *Parlementaire Geschiedenis*, vol. vi, p. 646.

[539] BGH 19 Jan. 1993, *FamRZ* 1993 pp. 666, 667 ('therefore in cases under § 832 BGB the child's personal responsiblity for liability, which plays just as important a role as the liability risk on the part of his parents, must increasingly prevail over parental responsiblity'). Also Bloembergen (-Oldenhuis), *Onrechtmatige daad*, Art. 169, no. 57.

[540] Further, see no. 133 below.

[541] For Belgium: de Page, *Droit Civil Belge*, vol. ii, 3rd edn., p. 987; Vandenberghe/van Quickenborne/Geelen/De Coster, *TPR* 1987 pp. 1255, 1452 no. 118; for Germany; § 840 II, 1st alt. BGB; for Portugal: Art. 497 II Cc (the right to recourse depends on the degree of fault of each defendant); for Greece: Art. 927, p. 2 Greek Cc (the same rule); for The Netherlands: Art. 6:102 BW; overview by Oldenhius, *Onrechtmatige daad: aansprakelijkheid voor personen*, pp. 32–36. Whether parents are even entitled to unlimited recourse under Art. 1298 I Ital. Cc (*pro* Franzoni, *Fatti illeciti*, Art. 2048 no. 2, p. 354; and Giur.sist. Bigiavi [-Mantovani] vol. ii [1] p. 13; both in cases where fault cannot be positively established on the part of the parents), or whether Art. 2055 II Cc, which would give parents sole liability for part of the damages, must always be applied (*pro* Cendon [-Venchiarutti] Art. 2048 no. 2, p. 2063) depends on whether parental liability under Art. 2048 Cc is to be interpreted as strict liability or as liability for presumed *culpa in vigilando vel educando*, the latter being true for the majority of schoolchildren (see no. 136 below). Finally, Art. 1904 Span. Cc is an exceptional provision in that employers have rights against their employees and (in cases of gross negligence) schools against their teachers. Not, however, parents against their children.

change.[542] Under Spanish law, parental liability ousts the liability of their children who have not reached age sixteen. It is therefore redundant to differentiate between equity-based and strict liability.[543] Sixteen- and seventeen-year-olds, however, pose a special problem: they have reached the age of criminal responsibility and are therefore liable under both the *Código Penal* and the *Código Civil*. On the other hand, although parental liability ends under Art. 20 CP when their children have reached the age of criminal responsibility, it does not end under Art. 1903 Cc, which creates problems. Should parental liability extend to the criminal delicts of their children aged sixteen and over,[544] and what is its relationship to their children's personal liability?[545] The *Tribunal Supremo* answered the first question in the affirmative, and has for the time being reverted to Art. 22 CP (which speaks of a subsidiary liability), ruling that liability for supervision is secondary only *vis-à-vis* third parties.[546] However, a change of approach is already in sight. Once Spain has revised its criminal law relating to young offenders, parents and their minor children will become jointly and severally liable.[547]

(2) The Handicapped

89 Despite the distinct and disputed rulings of the French *Cour de Cassation*, and differences of detail apart, Europe has managed to achieve remarkable protection from delictual liability for minors. However, in the field of protection against liability for mentally handicapped adults, the approach appears to be changing.[548] In the nineteenth century they were usually exempt from liability (but see § 1310 ABGB) as incapable of committing a fault, although under the BGB they were subject to liability in equity (§§ 827 s. 1, 829). Belgium followed this example in 1935 (Art. 1386*bis* CC), and Greece (Arts. 915 I,[549] 918 Cc), Italy (Art.

---

[542] See no. 65 above.

[543] See again TS 22 Jan. 1991, *RAJ* 1991 no. 304, p. 333: the liability of parents is in no way connected to the child's ability to reason.

[544] Art. 1903 Cc is retained only for civil delicts.

[545] For a summary of academic and court opinions see de Ángel Yágüez, *Responsabilidad civil*, 3rd edn., pp. 307–331. Also Díaz Alabart, *An.Der.Civ.* 40 (1987) pp. 795, 872–811. In German, see v. Bar (-Santdiumenge), *DeliktsR in Europa, Spanien*, pp. 32–33.

[546] TS 11 Oct. 1990, *RAJ* 1990 no. 7860, p. 9932 (secondary liability of the father for a crime committed by his 17-year-old son: *responsabilidad civil subsidiaria*).

[547] See no. 65 above.

[548] For a comparative overview as at 1954 see Stone, *Festschrift Rabel*, pp. 403–419; as at 1964: Heldrich, *Allgemeine Rechtsgrundsätze*, pp. 29–30, 33, 37, and 44; as at 1974: Limpens/Kruithof/Meinertzhagen-Limpens, *IntEncCompL* XI 2–193 ff.

[549] Art. 915 I Greek Cc exempts from liability a person who 'owing to a mental illness was deprived of the use of reason'. The issue here is whether the tortfeasor is able to appreciate the unlawfulness of his act, and not also (as under § 827 BGB: *BGB-RGRK* [-Steffen], 12th edn, § 827 no. 3) whether he can act accordingly (Georgiades/Stathopoulos [-Georgiades], *Greek Cc*, vol. iv, Art. 923 Greek Cc no. 7).

2047 Cc), and Portugal (Arts. 488 I, 489 Cc) also eventually adopted this solution. Although this equity-based liability is secondary to the corresponding liability for failure of supervision,[550] adults lacking the ability to reason are nevertheless, for practical or legal reasons,[551] often not subject to legal supervision. Thus liability in equity has far wider consequences for them than for children. In addition, an adult is usually obliged to prove that he lacked civil capacity[552] at the time of the act.[553] Only Art. 488 Port. Cc still contains the (rebuttable) presumption that persons placed in guardianship after being declared of unsound mind lack civil responsiblity. In all other jurisdiction this question is examined *caso per caso.*[554]

Recent developments have done more than merely tightening the law **90** of equity. For instance, Spanish law takes into account that the mentally handicapped adult can only be secondarily liable (Art. 8 in conjunction with Art. 20 CP). However, in cases where there is no supervisor,[555] or in which the supervisor is not at fault or is impecunious, the mentally handicapped adult must bear responsibility for the full extent of the damage.[556] In 1968 the French legislator, followed in 1982 by its Luxembourg counterpart, introduced the above-mentioned Art. 489–2 Cc, under which *'celui qui a causé un dommage à autrui alors qu'il était sous l'empire d'un trouble mental, n'en est pas moins obligé à réparation'.* According to the French *Cour de Cassation* this provision covers all causes of action under Arts. 1382 ff. Cc.[557] The new Dutch law follows a similar, if slightly less stringent path: with its more moderate approach, it could usefully serve as a model for a common European solution.

The old Dutch BW on delict obliged the *Hoge Raad* to adopt one of two **91**

---

[550] § 1310 ABGB; § 829 BGB; Art. 918 Greek Cc; Art. 2047 Ital. Cc; Art. 489 Port. Cc.

[551] Commonly, guardians alone have a legal duty of care; thus only a formal guardianship would oust liability in equity. Under § 832 BGB the carer (*Betreuer*) is no longer obliged to supervise. See § 1908i BGB, which refers to neither § 1631 nor § 1793 BGB. German law no longer recognizes the guardianship of adults.

[552] BGH 12 Feb. 1963, BGHZ 39 pp. 103, 108; Georgiades/Stathopoulos (-Georgiades), *Greek Cc*, vol. iv, Art. 923, nos. 11–13.

[553] Cornelis, *Responsabilité extra-contractuelle*, p. 18.

[554] For Germany see RG 12 Feb. 1924, RGZ 108 pp. 87, 90; for Italy: Franzoni, *Fatti illeciti*, Art. 2046, n. 2, pp. 319–321; Visintini, *Fatti illeciti*, vol. i, p. 490; and Cendon, *Infermità di mente e responsabilità civile*, pp. 11, 48; for Belgium: de Page, *Droit Civil Belge*, vol. ii, 3rd edn., no. 914; for Greece: Filios, *Enochiko Dikaio*, vol. ii(2), 3rd edn., p. 46; Stathopoulos, *Geniko Enochiko Dikaio*, vol. i, p. 143 (*contra*: Zepos, *Enochikon Dikaion*, vol. ii(2) p. 742, fn. 2).

[555] E.g. TS 8 Mar. 1984, *La Ley* 1984 (2) p. 638.

[556] TS 8 Mar. 1984 loc. cit. (fn. 555 above), in which a 20-year-old sufferer of Down's syndrome stabbed his victim to death after an unsuccessful rape attempt; and e.g. de Ángel Yáguez, *Responsabilidad Civil*, 3rd edn., p. 350.

[557] Cass.civ. 4 May 1977, *D.* 1987 *Jur.* 383 (note Legeais); and 24 June 1987, Bull.civ. 1987, II, no. 137. For Belgium, however, Rb. Charleroi still said on 8 Feb. 1972, *RGAR.* 1974 no. 9338, that an insane person could not be the guardian of an object.

extremes: to impose either liability in full or no liability at all.[558] The *Jaguar I* ruling[559] in 1960 eventually ruled that protection of the tortfeasor should take priority over protection of the victim. By and large this decision was followed by the Dutch courts of first instance.[560] Consider an example. A nineteen-year-old mentally handicapped boy, who was living at home because no other suitable accommodation was available, ran away, stole his neighbour's Jaguar, and wrecked it. The insurer's claim for full compensation was rejected. It was declared '*dat Art. 1401 BW geen toepassing kan vinden, wanneer de dader tengevolge van geestesziekte ieder inzicht miste in het geoorloofde of ongeoorloofde van zijn handeling*' (that Art. 1401 BW does not apply if the tortfeasor lacked comprehension of the illegality of his behaviour due to mental illness).[561] However, Art. 6:165 BW (enforced on 1 January 1992) reads as follows:

(1) The fact that conduct amounting to an act is undertaken by a person aged fourteen or more under the influence of a mental or physical handicap does not prevent it from being attributed to him as an unlawful act.

(2) Where a third party is also liable to the victim for insufficient supervision, that third party is obliged to compensate the wrongdoer for the full amount of the third party's liability to the victim.

When this provision was published, and before it came into force, the Dutch courts were temporarily confused as to whether they should apply the new rule immediately. A number of contradictory decisions resulted.[562] This uncertainly has now been resolved: if the facts resemble the *Jaguar I* case, or that of Rb. Rotterdam 19 July 1985[563] (the defendant co-driver, who suffered from recurring psychosis, jumped out of a moving car while it was driving through a tunnel; the driver braked sharply, causing a collision with the car behind) then under Art. 6:165 BW the mentally handicapped person is fully liable.

92   So Art. 6:165 BW clarifies Art. 6:162 III by determining that the

---

[558] Rb. Rotterdam 19 July 1985, *NedJur* 1986 no. 584, p. 2184: the anticipated application of Art. 6:165 BW was denied with the argument that the provision needs to be complemented by Art. 6:109 BW (the reduction clause of the new law).

[559] HR 9 Dec. 1960, *NedJur* no. 1, p. 5: *Jaguar II*.

[560] Rb. Rotterdam 19 July 1985 loc. cit. (fn. 558 above); and Rb. Dordrecht 14 Mar. 1984, *NedJur* 1985 no. 63: a woman suffered an epileptic fit at the dentist's; no liability for the broken surgery chair. On Art. 1401 BW (old): Rb. The Hague 31 Aug. 1994, *VR* 1995 no. 125: a diabetic unexpectedly lost consciousness while driving his car; no liability as no fault.

[561] Loc. cit. (fn. 559 above) p. 7.

[562] See e.g. Pres. Rb. Haarlem 4 Aug. 1989, *KG* 1989 no. 342, and *Hof* Amsterdam 27 May 1977 *NedJur* 1978 no. 9, p. 28: a mentally disturbed person stole a lorry from a plant, subsequently causing a fatal accident. Based on a strict notion of *culpa*, liability was confirmed, although the tortfeasor had been found by the criminal court to lack criminal capacity.   [563] See fn. 558 above.

unlawful act of a mentally disturbed person can and must be 'attributed to him by application by statute or of generally accepted standards'. However, this stringent delictual liability is moderated by three further provisions. First, Art. 6:109 BW can reduce liability generally.[564] Secondly, under Art. 6:165 BW the relationship between actor and guardian, but not to the plaintiff, to whom they are jointly and severally liable,[565] is different from that under Art. 6:102 BW: under the former the guardian must contribute to the reparation of the damage up to the full extent of his liability to the victim.[566] Finally, to establish liability Art. 6:165 BW demands 'conduct constituting an act' (i.e. not an omission). Thus, for liability for persons and things within the scope of Art. 6:183 I BW, the usual rules governing liability for failure to act apply.

Like Art. 6:183 BW, Art. 6:165 BW also takes account of the physically handicapped.[567] A severely handicapped person's failure to act is the prime example for Art. 6:165 BW (e.g. a deaf person does not notice a drowning person crying for help).[568] This may at first glance seem strange. One would usually assume that such examples lack negligence. If the circumstances were the same but the onlooker was instead wheel-chair-bound, failure to lend assistance would not be considered blame-worthy since it demands a physical ability: although if he had the opportunity to call for help, he would obviously be obliged to do so. If the onlooker were mentally handicapped and saw the person drowning without appreciating the danger, his lack of reason would exempt him from liability, not only due to an error as to the wrongfulness of his act, but also due to an error as to the facts of the case. Exclusion of liability in cases of failure to act occurs on a different level from exclusion liability for positive acts, when only ability to reason plays a major role. However, this does not render Art. 6:165 BW inconsequential. Not only does it usually presume liability on the part of the handicapped person, but it is also directly linked to Art. 6:162 II BW,

---

[564] However, HR 24 Dec. 1993, *RvdW* 1994 no. 11 insists that the rule of road traffic law which exempts children below age 14 from contributory fault (HR 1 June 1990, *NedJur* 1991 no. 720 p. 3125; and HR 31 May 1991, *Ned Jur* 1991 no. 721 p. 3137) does not extend to the mentally handicapped who have reached that age. *In casu* it concerned a girl who had just turned 14: the general 50% rule remained applicable (HR 28 Feb. 1992, *NedJur* 1993 no. 566, p. 2117). This could be reduced by the equitable application of Art. 6: 101 BW. If so, this is more likely to be based on age than on mental disability.

[565] *Parlementaire Geschiedenis*, vol. vi, p. 646: 'De . . . regel van subsidiariteit heeft het ontwerp niet overgenomen.'   [566] *T&C* (-Steketee), 2nd edn., Art. 6: 165 BW n. 2.

[567] Other codes even provide for the deaf and dumb (and those who 'from birth or early childhood, have had a severely distorted awareness of reality due to perception disturbances': Art. 8 sec. 3 Span. CP [old version] = Art. 20 sec. 3 NCP) by placing them alongside juveniles: § 828 II s. 2 BGB and Art. 917 s. 2 Greek Cc. Such provisions seem redundant, esp. as there are hardly any rulings on them.

[568] E.g. Asser (-Hartkamp), *Verbintenissenrecht*, vol. iii, 9th edn, no. 87, p. 79; v. Bar (-Hondius/van Dam), *DelikitsR in Europa, Niederlande*, p. 11.

which in turn demands only a 'violation of a right', not a conscious act. Even reflex actions and actions made by an unconscious person are covered by this provision. Hence Art. 6:165 BW serves to reduce uncertainty.[569]

(3) Unconsciousness and the Influence of Drugs

93 Finally, we come to those persons who act in a state of unconsciousness, or who have lost the ability to reason and to act accordingly under the influence of alcohol or drugs. The first question is whether the defendant caused his delictual incapacity negligently (or even intentionally: *actio libera in causa*) or whether it arose through no fault of his own.[570] However, there are also other aspects to consider.

94 In practice the most important example of the liability of 'unconscious' persons is found in road accident law, where a motorist suffers an epileptic fit,[571] falls asleep due either to fatigue[572] or medicine,[573] or suddenly loses control of the vehicle as a result of a heart attack or stroke.[574] Where the driver knew of the risk, or would have known had he exercised the care expected of a driver, he is liable for fault.[575] A diagnosed epileptic is simply not allowed to drive a car. However, where the heart attack could not have been anticipated, i.e. where the conditions of Art. 489-2 French Cc and Art. 1386*bis* Belgian Cc (*trouble mental*) are not met, the driver escapes liability altogether in *Luxembourg*,[576] in Belgium,[577] and, if the author's interpretation is correct, in France. The driver therefore also escapes *gardien* liability under Art. 1384 I in conjunction with Art. 489-2 French Cc.[578] In such cases the plaintiff's

---

[569] *Parlementaire Geschiedenis*, vol. vi (Inv.) pp. 1349–1354 (1350 gives examples of pure failure to act: failure to warn of a danger, or lend assistance); Vetter, *Geestelijke Gestoornis*, pp. 58–61.

[570] § 1307 ABGB; § 827 s. 2 BGB; Art. 915 II Greek Cc; Art. 2046 Ital. Cc; Art. 488 I Port. Cc; Art. 6:162 III BW; for Belgium: de Page, *Droit Civil Belge*, vol. ii, 3rd edn., pp. 882–883; for France: Starck (-Roland/Boyer), *Obligations*, vol. I, 4th edn., no. 422.

[571] Cass.pen. 16 Jan. 1978, *Resp.Civ. e Prev.* 1978 p. 959; Cass.civ. 18 Dec. 1964, *D.* 1965 *Jur.* 191 (note Esmein); BGH 11 Oct. 1994, *NJW* 1995 p. 452.

[572] STJ 25 July 1987, *BolMinJust* 279 (1978) p. 160; RP 9 Dec. 1977, *BolMinJust* 274 (1978) p. 315; Cass.civ. 8 Nov. 1989, Bull.civ. 1989, II, no. 344.

[573] Rb. Leeuwarden 22 Nov. 1979, *NedJur* 1980 no. 438.

[574] BGH 27 Jan. 1957, BGHZ 23 p. 90; Cour 13 June 1963, *Pas. luxemb.* 19 (1963–1965) p. 109; Cass. 12. Dec. 1977, n. 5411, *Giur.it.* 1978 I, 1, 1481; Cass. 24 Apr. 1980, *Pas. belge* 1980 I 1055; Cass.civ. 4 Feb. 1981, *D.* 1983 *Jur.* 1.

[575] See fns. 571–573 above; App. Brescia 16 Oct. 1974, *Resp.Civ. e Prev.* 1974 p. 162; Cass.pen. 13 Apr. 1979, *Resp.Civ. e Prev.* 1978 p. 809.

[576] Cour 13 June 1963 loc. cit. (fn. 574 above).

[577] Cass. 24 Apr. 1980 loc. cit. (fn. 574 above).

[578] The only possible conclusion, since according to the French rulings Art. 489-2 Cc refers also to Art. 1384 I Cc (fn. 557 above), and because (although the case dealt with Art. 1382 Cc) it has been decided that a heart attack does not constitute a disturbance of mental activity under Art. 489-2 Cc (Cass.civ. 4 Feb. 1981 loc. cit., fn. 574 above); Durry,

only source of compensation is the guarantee fund established for victims of traffic accidents. By contrast, in The Netherlands the actor is liable in full, whether under Art. 6:165 BW—driving a car is 'conduct constituting an act'—or (the better solution, since Art. 6:165 BW should be reserved for long-term handicaps) under Art. 6:162 II and III BW. In Germany,[579] Greece,[580] and Italy[581] a plaintiff may rely on the strict liability of the keeper of a car,[582] as well as equitable liability.

Inability to reason due to alcohol or drugs can only very rarely be used   **95** as a defence, e.g. when an inexperienced youth unknowingly drinks alcohol; when somebody is drugged without his knowledge or consent. This is patently reasonable.[583] Liability in equity may apply in cases where intoxication results from addiction, which has caused mental illness,[584] and then only if the case does not come under a strict liability regime, such as in France, Luxembourg, The Netherlands,[585] and Spain.[586]

Finally, one sole provision amongst the European codes, namely § 827   **96** s. 2 BGB, presumes negligence when delicts are committed under the influence of drugs. Only persons who intoxicate themselves in order to commit a delict ('for Dutch courage') are, under *actio libera in causa*, liable for delicts which can only be committed with intent, such as unethical infliction of damage and insult. If the precondition for the provision is gross negligence, then the actor must have been grossly negligent to make himself temporarily *non compos mentis*.[587] Due to § 276 I s. 3 BGB and § 640 RVO this provision is significant for insurers.[588]

Rev.trim.dr.civ. 80 (1982) pp. 144, 148: '*Un malaise n'est pas un trouble mental au sens de l'article 489–2 du code civil.*' Critical, however, are Flour/Aubert, *Obligations*, vol. ii, p. 108. For a different view: Starck (-Roland/Boyer), *Obligations*, vol. i, 4th edn., no. 612 ('*La garde peut être inconsciente*': a statement true of cases of mental illness and fatigue, but not for sudden and unpredictable mental disturbances).

[579] BGH 15 Jan. 1957; BGH 11 Oct. 1994 loc. cit. (fn. 482 above).   [580] Fn. 504 above.

[581] Cendon (-Venchiarutti) Art. 2046, note 2.2, pp. 2053–2054 for further references.

[582] BGH 15 Jan. 1957, BGHZ 23 pp. 90, 94–97 says an inability to continue driving a car due to sudden unconsciousness is not an unavoidable event excluding liability. Cass.pen. 16 Jan. 1978, *Resp.Civ. e Prev.* 1978 p. 959 refused to deny criminal liability for *caso fortuito* where the driver knew of his ill health.

[583] See e.g. *BGB-RGRK* (-Steffen), 12th edn., § 827 nos. 7, 10.

[584] In favour: Giur.sist. Bigiavi (-Venchiarutti) p. 209, no. 4.

[585] Here liability can anyway probably be attributed to the actor under Art. 6:162 III BW, and need not be based on Art. 6:165 BW.

[586] As there was often no supervision, personal liability under Art. 20 CP (old version) applied: de Ángel Yágüez, *Responsabilidad civil*, 3rd edn., pp. 350 ff, and under Art. 118 II NCP liability is no longer in default of a supervisor.

[587] BGH 6 July 1967, *VersR* 1967 p. 944.

[588] A person driving a car under the influence of alcohol always acts with gross negligence: BGH 6 Mar. 1964, *VersR* 1964 pp. 870, 871; BGH 7 May 1974, *NJW* 1974 pp. 1377, 1378, and elsewhere.

II. VICARIOUS LIABILITY AND LIABILITY FOR DAMAGE
CAUSED BY THINGS: GENERAL QUESTIONS

Bibliography: v. Bar, 'Das "Trennungsprinzip" und die Geschichte des Wandels der Haftpflichtversicherung', *AcP* 181 (1981) pp. 289–327; id., 'Entwicklungen und Entwicklungstendenzen im Recht der Verkehrs(sicherungs)pflichten', *JuS* 1988 pp. 169–174; Barbosa de Melo, 'Responsabilidade civil extra-contratual', *CJ* XI (1986–4) pp. 32–39; Bernardini, 'La responsabilità oggettiva nella piu recente giurisprudenza', *Riv.trim.dir.proc.civ.* 1967 pp. 1184–1188; Blaschczok, *Gefährdungshaftung und Risikozuweisung* (Cologne *et al.* 1993); Buján, 'Die Haftung des Kfz-Fahrers nach dem portugiesischen Bürgerlichen Gesetzbuch', *VersR* 1978 pp. 307; Cian, 'Fünfzig Jahre italienischer Codice civile', *ZEuP* 1993 pp. 120–131; id., 'Il diritto civile come diritto privato comune', *Riv.Dir.Civ.* 1989, I, 1–20; Comporti, *Esposizione al pericolo e responsabilità civile* (Naples 1965); Costanza, 'La responsabilità del produttore di autoveicoli nel caso di incidenti stradali', *Riv.giur.circ.trasp.* 1992 pp. 24–30; Dalcq, 'La notion de garde dans la responsabilité', in: *Liber Amicorum Dumon*, pp. 73–86 (Brussels 1983); Demogue, 'Jurisprudence en matière de droit civil, obligations et contrats spéciaux', *Rev.trim.dr.civ.* 3 (1904) pp. 412–439; Ferrand, 'Deliktische Haftung für Dritte in Frankreich', *ZEuP* 1993 pp. 132–140; Franzoni, 'Responsabilità per colpa presunta e responsabilità oggettiva nel danno aquiliano', in: Galgano (ed.), *Colpa presunta e responsabilità del debitore* (Padua 1988) pp. 77–82; García Cantero, 'Exégesis comparativa del Art. 1902 Cc', in: Asociación de Profesores de Derecho Civil (ed.), *Centenario del Código civil*, vol. ii (Madrid 1990) pp. 875–884; Hartkamp, *Judicial Discretion under the New Civil Code of The Netherlands* (Rome 1992); Hohlbein, *Die neuere Entwicklung des niederländischen außervertraglichen Haftungsrechts* (Diss. Münster 1981); Hübner, 'Zur Problematik der "Verkehrssicherungspflichten" im französischen Recht', *VersR* 1980 pp. 795–797; id., *Die Haftung des Gardien im französischen Zivilrecht* (Karlsruhe 1972); v. Jhering, 'Das Schuldmoment im römischen Privatrecht (Gießen 1867)', in: Rudolf v. Jhering, *Vermischte Schriften juristischen Inhalts* (new impression of the Leipzig 1879 edn. Aalen 1968) pp. 155–240; Jonas, *Die verschuldensunabhängige Haftung für Sachen im Entwurf zum Nieuw Burgerlijk Wetboek der Niederlande. Ein Beitrag zur Reform des deutschen Gefährdungshaftungsrechts* (Diss. Munich 1987); Klaassen, *Risico-aansprakelijkheid. De afdelingen 6.3.2 en 6.3.3 NBW, alsmede art. 31 Wegenverkeerswet* (Zwolle 1991); Koch, *Die Sachhaftung* (Berlin 1992); Legeais, 'Un article à surprises, ou le nouvel essai de généraliser la responsabilité du fait d'autrui', *D.* 1965 *Chron.* pp. 131–

134; Legrand, 'Les nouvelles frontières de la responsabilité civile pour le fait d'autrui', *ERPL* 1 (1993) pp. 225–228; López y López, 'Constitución, código y leyes especiales. Reflexiones sobre la llamada descodificación', in: Asociación de Profesores de Derecho Civil (ed.), *Centenario del Código civil*, vol. ii (Madrid 1990) pp. 1163–1176; Van Oevelen, 'Existe-t-il un principe général de responsabilité extra-contractuelle du fait des personnes dont on doit répondre?', *ERPL* 1 (1993) pp. 229–239; Renner, *Der französische Grundsatz des "non-cumul" vertraglicher und deliktischer Schadensersatzansprüche als Vorbild für eine Reform des deutschen Schuldrechts* (Diss. Mainz 1988); Rosenkranz, *Die Haftung für Schadenszufügung aus unerlaubter Handlung nach italienischem Recht* (Diss. Regensburg 1973); Savatier, 'La responsabilité du fait des choses que l'on a sous sa garde a-t-elle pour pendant une responsabilité générale du fait des personnes dont on doit répondre?', *DH* 1933 *Chron.* pp. 81–84; Schlüchter, *Haftung für gefährliche Tätigkeit und Haftung ohne Verschulden. Das italienische Recht als Vorbild für das schweizerische?* (Berne and Stuttgart 1990); Schreiber, *Die Sachhalterhaftung des Art. 1384 Abs. 1 Code civil, verglichen mit dem deutschen Recht* (Diss. Mainz 1987); Stahlberg, *Gefährdungshaftung für gefährliche Tätigkeiten. Eine rechtsvergleichende Untersuchung französischer Rechtsprechung zu Art. 1384 Abs. 1 Code civil mit deutscher Judikatur* (Diss. Freiburg 1975); Vandenberghe, 'Aansprakelijkheid voor zaken, dieren en gebouwen', in: Vandenberghe (ed.), *Onrechtmatige daad*, pp. 59–83 (Antwerp 1979); Vaz Serra, 'Responsabilidade pelos danos causados por coisas ou actividades', *BolMinJust* 85 (1959) pp. 361–380; Viney, 'Vers un élargissement de la catégorie des personnes dont on doit répondre. La porte ouverte sur une nouvelle interprétation de l'article 1384 alinéa 1 du code civil', *D.* 1991 *Chron.* pp. 157–161; Will, *Quellen erhöhter Gefahr* (1980); Zachert, *Gefährdungshaftung und Haftung aus vermutetem Verschulden im deutschen und französischen Recht* (Frankfurt/M. 1971); Ziviz, 'Le attività pericolose', in: Cendon (ed.), *Responsabilità civile* (Milan 1988) pp. 543–581.

1. THE LAW OF QUASI-DELICT: SCOPE AND OBJECTIVES

The law of liability for personal misconduct, the true law of delict, has **97** always shared the stage with the law of liability for others and for things, known in Roman law as the law of quasi-delict.[589] A right to damages may arise where the plaintiff cannot rely upon the basic grounds of liability. This is the case, first, where damage was caused by someone other than the defendant, i.e. in cases of: parental and *loco parentis*

---

[589] See nos. 7–9 above. See also no. 126 below on liability for dangerous acitivities, which overlaps with the above.

liability (see nos. 131 ff. below), employers' liability for their staff (see nos. 168 ff. below), and the liability of vocational trainers and teachers for trainees and pupils (see nos. 160 ff. below). Secondly, the law of liability for things (including premises) is also relevant here. This wide field has developed dramatically over the past 150 years. It now extends from liability for animals and buildings to liability for products and waste, and even to liability for recovering, storing, and conveying energy for commercial purposes, and modes of transport. Not only its wide scope, but also the increasingly divergent conceptual approaches adopted across Europe mean that it will soon become necessary to divide the law of liability for damage caused by things even further.

98   What may at first glance appear to be a case of quasi-delictual liability 'for damage caused by others' or 'by things' may in some circumstances prove to be a simple case of liability for personal misconduct. A person selling a weapon to a child who then injures another;[590] a person who fits electric cables so close together that in windy weather they are blown together and emit sparks;[591] a motorist who ignores another's right of way: each will be held liable simply because he acted negligently, not as the keeper of a hazardous thing. The true law of quasi-delict only applies where the defendant is liable despite having acted properly. In most legal systems employers' liablity is a good example of liability for acts of other persons. Although encouraged to create new jobs, employers are usually vicariously liable for damage to third parties caused by employees while carrying out their duties, often irrespective of any duty to supervise. A good example of liability for things is that of the keeper or owner of a motor vehicle: almost everywhere in Europe he is liable for accidents involving his car, even if caused by a reliable driver to whom he had lent the vehicle. His liability is only excluded if the car had been stolen.

99   Liability without misconduct may be based on presumed but rebuttable fault. This is a typical feature of: parental liability, liability for buildings, parts of the liability of animal keepers, producers' liability, and liability for persons driving a motor vehicle, as well as a number of other areas. When damage is caused by a child, a loose roof tile, a dog, goods, or a car used in traffic, there is a presumption that responsibility for the damage lies with the parents, owner, or keeper for failure to

---

[590] TS 7 Jan. 1992, *RAJ* 1992 no. 149 p. 174: in this case the *Tribunal Supremo* found not only the weapons dealer liable for personal fault, but also the child's parents for quasi-strict parental liability. See TS 22 Sep. 1992, *La Ley* 1992 (4) p. 765, a case of parental liability (although under 1903 Cc) for damage caused by their son using their car. The parents should have hidden the car keys from the minor.

[591] STJ 5 June 1985, *BolMinJust* 348 (1985) p. 397. But see RC 15 Jan. 1991, *CJ* XVI (1991–5) p. 47: strict liability under Art. 509 Port. Cc for damage arising from *instalações de energia eléctrica ou gás.*

supervise.[592] Such presumptions involve aspects of both liability for fault and liability without personal misconduct. The plaintiff is required neither to demonstrate nor to prove the defendant's failure to supervise. It is for the defendant to disprove the accusation. If he fails to do so, the question of whether he has acted properly or negligently, and in the latter case whether his negligent conduct is causally linked to the damage, is irrelevant. In practical terms this shifting of the burden of proof amounts to strict liability in many cases.

A further reason why vicarious liability and liability for things should **100** be dealt with separately from other non-contractual liability law is that in the former liability is frequently imposed for failure to act. This usually concerns the duty to supervise, especially duties extending beyond those established in the basic delictual provisions. To give but one example, let us consider parental liability. Throughout Europe parents have a duty to supervise their children.[593] However, the provisions establishing that duty stem from family law, and are intended only to protect children; under the doctrine of *relativité aquilienne*[594] they do not extend to third parties. It is only in conjunction with the relevant delictual provisions that this situation is reversed.[595] However, children cannot usually rely on these quasi-delictual provisions to claim against their parents.[596] Although it cannot be denied that the law of quasi-delict extends to some cases of liability for acts (as opposed to omissions), e.g. the erection of a defective building,[597] the law of quasi-delict is nevertheless mainly concerned with liability for failure to act. It is especially relevant where the person held liable was not the last link in the causal chain, and it is precisely for this reason that modern liability law still has such difficulties with its quasi-delictual provisions.

2. THE PROBLEM OF *DECODIFICAZIONE*

The Italian and Spanish terms *decodificazione* and *descodificación* describe **101** a trend in the field of delict concerning the legal sources of liability for

---

[592] In Italy employer's liability under Art. 2049 Cc, but not parental liability under Art. 2048 Cc, qualifies as 'indirect' liability. Theoretically (but see no. 135 below) parental liability remains liability for presumed fault. See, representing the prevailing opinion, Cass. 24 Oct. 1988, n. 5751, *Foro.it.* 1989, I, 98; de Martini, *Fatti produttivi di danno*, pp. 292–293.
[593] See e.g. § 1631 I BGB; Art. 1510 Greek Cc; Art. 316 Ital. Cc; Art. 154 Span. Cc; Art. 1: 247 I BW; Art. 371–2 French Cc.   [594] See no. 30 above.
[595] Cavanillas Múgica, *Transformación*, p. 111; Port. II p. 594; v. Bar, *Verkehrspflichten*, p. 21.
[596] See no. 153 below.
[597] § 1319 ABGB; § 836 I BGB; Art. 2053 Ital. Cc; Art. 925 Greek Cc; and Art. 492 I Port. Cc.

damage caused by things.[598] Liability for the actions of others has also undergone a number of improvements recently, concerning both the threshold of liability (e.g. the introduction of strict parental liability into Dutch law[599]) and its scope. Examples of the latter are: organizer's liability (for violent demonstrations and rampaging spectators), liability for sub-contractors,[600] and liability for delicts committed by escaped residents of a home or institution.[601] Overall, however, the law of vicarious liability has retained its relative stability and clarity: all the changes have been made *within* the codes and through their interpretation by judges (the *'droit commun'*).[602] However, in the law of liability for damage caused by things (and particularly for inanimate objects)[603] the picture is completely different.[604] When the first codes began to be enforced, planes, cars, and in some places even trains had not arrived on the scene, and even after their introduction some years passed before the legal profession became aware of the hazards they posed. The same can be said for the numerous risks inherent in the production of electricity and the like, and for product and environmental liability. Even the third-party liability insurance system, which was the basis for later developments in the field of strict liability, was only established at the end of the nineteenth century.[605] Finally, the fault principle, at that time the basis of

---

[598] Cian, *ZEuP* 1993 pp. 120, 127. See id., *Riv.Dir.Civ.* 1989 pp. 5 ff.: the building of 'legal microcosms' can only be prevented if the numerous special laws are interpreted by reference to the *Codice civile*. For Spain see López y López, in: Asociación de Profesores de Derecho Civil (ed.), *Centenario del Código Civil*, vol. ii, p. 1163.

[599] Art. 6: 169 BW, see also no. 80 above and no. 133 below.   [600] See no. 200 below.

[601] See no. 166 below.

[602] Common law (*gemeines Recht, droit commun, diritto comune*) was not originally codified, but evolved gradually. For, as one can still observe in the title of the Austrian ABGB (das *Allgemeines* Bürgerliches Gesetzbuch), codifications, created *general*, and not *common*, law as a conscious act of legal unification. Today the law created by the codes, in conjunction with the relevant rulings, dictates to lawyers, whose training and work is based on the codified law, to such an extent that what used to be 'general' law is treated as 'common' law.

[603] Liability for animals has been dealt with largely outside the codes, in hunting liability law (damage caused by game). Special liability provisions have also been created for experiments in the field of genetic engineering.

[604] One must bear in mind that vicarious liability and liability for things cannot always be strictly separated (no. 7 and fn. 29 above). For an extreme example see TS 12 Mar. 1975, *RAJ* no. 1798, p. 1355: a manic depressive threw himself out of the window of the defendant hospital, killing one passer-by and injuring another. The *Tribunal Supremo* found against the hospital under Art. 1910 Cc. Yet Spanish scholars regularly and appropriately discuss Art. 1910 Cc in terms of liability for things (de Ángel Yágüez, *Responsabilidad civil*, 3rd edn., pp. 628–632; Díez-Picazo/Gullón, *Sistema*, vol. ii, 6th edn., pp. 629–630). In Austria the corresponding provision, § 1318 ABGB, is part of the law of damage inflicted 'through the actions of third parties' (§§ 1313–1318 ABGB). Another interesting example of the extent to which these areas overlap (and of how unimportant this is) is TS 12 Apr. 1984, *RAJ* 1984 no. 1958, p. 1490: a plumber failed to turn off taps after he had effected repairs. His liability for damage caused to the flat below was based on Art. 1910 Cc. Whether he was held liable for damage caused by 'others' or by 'things' cannot be determined.

[605] See v. Bar, *AcP* 181 (1981) pp. 289, 296–303.

all legal philosophy, prevented the authors of codes from introducing no-fault provisions, even for specific technical hazards, right up until this century. Only after intense discussions did the authors of the German BGB,[606] for instance, manage to introduce a strict liability provision for animal keepers, and even this was restricted just eight years later to certain domestic animals.[607] By and large, however, the codified law of delict was dominated by the famous quotation of Rudolf von Ihering in 1867: 'not damage but fault founds liability. A simple phrase, as simple as the chemist's assertion that it is not light which burns, but the oxygen contained in the air.'[608] That approach also coloured the Greek Civil Code. Although Greece had already created a special law 'on criminal and civil liability for motor vehicles' in 1911, the Greek Code of 1946 went no further than the codes of other countries, i.e. liability for children, employees, animals, and buildings. Only the Italian *Codice Civile* (Arts. 2051, 2054),[609] the Portuguese *Código Civil* (Arts. 503–510), and the new Dutch *Burgerlijk Wetboek* (Arts. 6:173, 185–193) introduced provisions dealing with strict liability for modern hazards. Yet even Arts. 6:182 and 184 Dutch BW, on dangerous materials, were not given substance until 1 February 1995. Moreover, the Dutch law on third-party liability for motorists, the *Wegenverkeerswet* (Road Traffic Act, originally Art. 31 of the Act of 1935,[610] now Art. 185 of the Act of 21 April 1994)[611] still awaits incorporation into Book 8 of the BW, which is dedicated to transport law.

So the term *decodificazione* describes the process by which most modern **102** law on liability for damage caused by things has been established in statutes outside the codes, a phenomenon unfortunately not restricted to the old codes. Even the Italian, Portuguese, and Dutch laws of delict have many special regulations on strict liability for damage caused by things, and EU directives will make the situation even worse, unless incorporated into the civil codes.[612] The number of 'legal microcosms'[613] which exist alongside the respective national *droits communs* is already

---

[606] On the history of law-making in this area: Staudinger (-Schäfer), BGB, 12th edn., § 833 nos. 2–3; also BGH 6 July 1976, BGHZ 67 pp. 129, 132.

[607] § 833 BGB originally omitted sentence 2 (exemption of certain domestic animals), introduced only by the Act of 30 Aug. 1908 (BGBl. 1908 p. 313).

[608] See v. Ihering, 'Schuldmoment im römischen Privatrecht', in: *Vermischte Schriften juristischen Inhalts*, pp. 155, 199.

[609] In addition, Art. 2050 Ital. Cc contains a general clause on liability for dangerous activities (*responsabilità per l'esercizio di attività pericolose)*; see no. 126 below.

[610] Stb. 1935 no. 554; Stb. 1989 no. 491.

[611] Stb. 1994 no. 475; enforced on 1 Jan. 1995, Stb. 1994 no. 918.

[612] The EU Directive on Product Liability (nos. 372–393 below) has so far been incorporated only by the Dutch (Arts. 6:185–193 BW); France has for the time being abandoned its plan to follow suit. All other nations have created their product liability law in special statutes outside the code (no. 393 below).   [613] Cian loc. cit. (see fn. 598 above).

extensive. Whether a specific area of law is incorporated into the code varies from country to country, rendering the situation confusing for anyone seeking an overview of Europe's laws. For instance, road traffic third-party liability law is part of Italy's (Art. 2054 Cc) and Portugal's (Arts. 503–505 Cc) civil codes. Yet all other nations have devoted special laws to it. The only areas so far considered worthy of codification by all European nations are liability for animals and for buildings. (The relevant provisions are dealt with in Part IV below: nos. 206 ff.) Liability for modern hazards (road traffic, production of goods, waste disposal, etc.) will be dealt with in the second volume of this work.

3. SPECIAL PROVISIONS AND JUDGE-MADE AND CODIFIED GENERAL CLAUSES

103 Statutory law outside the codes is not the only field into which the modern quasi-law of delict has entered. Within the codes which impose special forms of strict liability for failure to act, causes of action in quasi-delict have influenced the *droit commun* of most European states, producing a number of further general clauses.[614] In those countries with older codes general clauses were a product of judge-made law. Only with the Italian *Codice Civile* did they start to appear in codified law. As we shall see, knowledge of these general clauses, whether judge-made or codified, is vital for an accurate evaluation of the effectiveness and meaning of the codified law of quasi-delict and its supplementary special laws.

a. The General Duty of Care (*Verkehrspflichten*) in German Law

104 In Germany liability based on duties of care is a product of judge-made law. It has long been established practice for the courts to rule that any

---

[614] In Spain this development finds its equivalent in the established practice of the courts, started by TS 10 July 1943, *RAJ* 1943 no. 856, p. 481, dealing with a car accident, and confirmed by TS 14 Jan. 1974, *RAJ* 1974 no. 166, pp. 123, 124, dealing with an elevator accident, according to which, with only a small number of exceptions (e.g doctors' liablity; TS 6 Nov. 1990, *RAJ* 1990 no. 8528; TS 11 Apr. 1991, *RAJ* 1991 no. 2209; and TS 11 Feb. 1992, *RAJ* 1992 no. 1419) liability under Art. 1902 Cc is *regularly* based on presumed fault, and is thus stricter, although not as strict as liability in France under Art. 1384 Cc. Not only has the Spanish *Tribunal Supremo* upheld the fault principle (e.g. TS 5 Oct. 1994, *RAJ* 1994 no. 7453, p. 9689; TS 14 Nov. 1994, *RAJ* 1994 no. 9321, p. 12215; and TS 5 Dec. 1994, *RAJ* 1994 no. 9406, p. 12353) it has also expressly avoided applying Art. 1903 I Span. Cc to things (see no. 108 and fn. 643 below). This provision is purely *narrative*. As for Greek law, one only has to remember Art. 914 Cc which, as stated in no. 19 above, has been converted from a framework provision into a general clause, separating liability for breach of a duty of care from the law of quasi-delict.

person responsible either for creating a source of danger or for allowing it to persist is required to take all necessary and appropriate steps to protect other people and their absolute rights.[615] Thus the courts have created a partial general clause on liability for indirect infliction of damage. The explanation for this lies in the fact that soon after §§ 823 II and 831–838 BGB came into force, it became evident that they were inadequate. The courts wanted to be able to employ delictual duties founded in other provisions. The very first decision of the Supreme Courts of the German Reich[616] on this issue took that approach to duties of care.

In RG of 30 October 1902[617] a rotten tree belonging to the defendant fell onto the plaintiff's house and damaged it. § 836 did not form a suitable basis for a claim: a tree is neither a 'building' nor 'another structure attached to a piece of land' under that provision. The same would have been true under § 823 II BGB, since there was no law obliging the owner of a tree to check the likelihood of its falling down. § 823 I BGB was the only suitable provision. However, in order for the claim to succeed, another approach had to be found which permitted the imposition of liability for failure to act. The Supreme Court considered that § 836 BGB could by analogy found such liability. Although the *actio legis Aquiliae* did not recognize liability for failures to act, there is 'no doubt that the BGB did not necessarily adhere to this principle; for, with regard to buildings and other structures attached to a piece of land, such a view would be incompatible with § 836 BGB. True, the principles behind § 836 BGB *could* arguably be unique to property of *this* kind, since it requires the possessor of defective premises to prove that he exercised all necessary care to avert the danger . . . nevertheless a cogent argument can be made that this provision should be unique regarding the shifting of the burden of proof but not regarding the duty to act.'[618]

The position of the *Reichsgericht* that liability for failing to prevent **105** damage caused by things need not necessarily be based on codified law has lost none of its validity. The more recent notion of liability based on a

---

[615] To give just a few examples: BGH 28 Apr. 1952, BGHZ 5 pp. 378, 380–381; BGH 15 June 1954, BGHZ 14 pp. 83, 85; BGH 30 Jan. 1961, BGHZ 34 pp. 206, 209. For similar statements of Austrian courts see e.g. OGH 4 Feb. 1993, *ÖJZ* 1994 p. 24 (*EvBl* 1); and OGH 15 Apr. 1993, *ÖJZ* 1994 p. 50 (*EvBl* 8). Yet the legal background of the 2 countries is incompatible: first, because § 1294 ABGB expressly mentions 'failure to act', secondly due to differences in the concept of unlawfulness (unlawful conduct in Austria, unlawful result in Germany), and thirdly because § 836 BGB has a much narrower scope than § 1319, 1319a ABGB. Hence the Austrian courts can continue to treat liability for failure to act in cases of 'conduct initiating potential danger to others' (*Ingerenz*) regarding dangers arising from buildings as among the true duties of care (see fn. 619 below): Koziol, *Österr. Haftpflichtrecht*, vol. ii, 2nd edn., pp. 57–58.
[616] Also RG 23 Feb. 1903, RGZ 54 p. 53 (liability for a bridge not cleared of snow and ice).
[617] RGZ 52 p. 373; BGH 1 July 1993, *NJW* 1993 p. 2612.   [618] RGZ 52 p. 377.

general duty of care[619] soon spread, not only to all kinds of damage caused by things,[620] but also to non-codified liability for damage caused by persons.[621] Eventually, when the duties of care ceased to be restricted to certain specifically named risks,[622] the circumstances covered by §§ 831 ff. BGB became mere examples of such duties. In other words, a general duty to supervise or to act arises from the German law of quasi-delict, which renders the codified provisions redundant. As for the burden of proof in cases of product[623] and environmental liability,[624] however, the judiciary have more recently relied analogously on §§ 831–836 BGB, stressing that the defendant must prove that the conduct was unlawful. In all other areas it is for the plaintiff to prove the violation of a duty of care. Once this has been established, the burden of proof passes to the defendant regarding the question of fault,[625] which aggravates liability under § 823 I BGB.[626] Fault plays a similar role[627] in cases of liability for violation of protective laws.[628] However, since in the context of § 823 I BGB fault is understood as inner carelessness,[629] the general duty of care is generally still less strict than the codified law of quasi-delict.[630] Consequently, it would be wrong to conclude that §§ 831 ff. BGB have become completely redundant. It is true that failure to meet their preconditions does not necessarily preclude liability under § 823 I

---

[619] Initially the term *Verkehrssicherungspflichten* was used, primarily concerning dangers to road traffic arising from structures, under § 836 BGB. However, RG 19 Sep. 1921 RGZ 102 pp. 372, 375 already interpreted this liability as an example of the general duty of care (*Verkehrspflichten*; see § 276 BGB): a butcher had been called to put down a cow suffering from anthrax. He caught the virus, and accused the vet of failing to warn him. The RG allowed the complaint, although there is 'no such thing as a general legal duty to prevent another's health from impairment'. In the case of a vet the situation was found to be different. For 'a profession or business of this type carries with it general legal obligations, or, in other words, duties of care'.

[620] For a general overview see v. Bar, *Verkehrspflichten*, pp. 44–60.

[621] See ibid. pp. 21–25, 59, 60.

[622] On the various duties of care see ibid. pp. 83–100; also id. *JuS* 1988 pp. 169, 170–171.

[623] BGH 26 Nov. 1968, BGHZ 51 pp. 91, 106–107; also BGH 17 Mar. 1981, BGHZ 80 pp. 186, 196–197 clarifying the earlier ruling.

[624] BGH 18 Sep. 1984, BGHZ 92 pp. 143, 150–152.

[625] BGH 11 Mar. 1986, *NJW* 1986 pp. 2757, 2758: '*Die Verletzung der äußeren Sorgfalt indiziert entweder die der inneren Sorgfalt oder es spricht ein Anscheinsbeweis für die Verletzung der inneren Sorgfalt.*' See also BGH 31 May 1994, *NJW* 1994 pp. 2232, 2233.

[626] BGH 27 Jan. 1987, *NJW* 1987 p. 2671 expressly states that liability for breach of a duty of care must come under § 823 I BGB, despite its similarity to liability for violation of a protective law.   [627] See BGH loc. cit. (fn. 625 above); v. Bar, *JuS* 1988 pp. 169, 174.

[628] Nos. 31–32 above.

[629] For 2 cases of objective breach of duty of care, but no liability due to lack of inner carelessness, see BGH 23 Oct. 1984, *NJW* 1985 pp. 620, 621; and BGH 14 Mar. 1995, *NJW* 1995 p. 2631.

[630] That the judiciary have actually created a form of 'concealed' strict liability has frequently been argued, most recently by Blaschczok, *Gefährdungshaftung und Risikozuweisung*, pp. 94–120; and Larenz/Canaris, *Schuldrecht*, vol. ii (2), 13th edn., pp. 427–429.

BGB.[631] However, the outcome of such an examination would influence the apportionment of the burden of proof, and the degree of care demanded. Finally, one must not forget that the concept of a general duty of care, developed in the law of omissions, now has a role in cases of conduct, for example where the careless conduct itself constitutes an unacceptable threat to the rights and legally protected interests of others.[632]

b. *Gardien* Liability in French, Belgian, and Luxembourgeois Law

In Germany liability for breach of a duty of care has always been based **106** on unlawfulness and fault; this is not the case in France. French law's *gardien* liability for others and for things, the equivalent of German law's liability for breach of a duty of care,[633] is unambiguously rooted in objective, fault-free liability. Even a toddler can be liable under French law as a *gardien*,[634] whereas in Germany they have always been protected by §§ 828 and 829 BGB.

(1) *The Development of Liability for Damage Caused By Things Under Art. 1384 I 2nd Alt.* Code Civil

The visible link between the judge-made liability for things of the **107** Romance countries and the text of the *Code Civil* is the latter's Art. 1384 I Cc. The wording has always been identical in Belgium, France, and

---

[631] BGH 16 Dec. 1953, *VersR* 1954 p. 118: step-father failed to take air gun away from step-son: no liability under § 832 BGB, but liability was founded in § 823 I BGB. BGH 8 Dec. 1954, *LM* no. 4 on § 823 (Eb) BGB: liability for snow falling from the roof of a house, not under § 836 BGB, but under § 823 I BGB.

[632] See e.g. v. Bar, *Verkehrspflichten*, pp. 61–65, 157; Larenz/Canaris, *Schuldrecht*, vol. ii (2), 13th edn., pp. 401–403. HR 20 Mar. 1992, *NedJur* 1993 no. 547, p. 1975, concerning a road traffic accident. A taxi driver used a bus lane although it had been constructed so that only buses could safely use it, having a hole in the middle into which other vehicles would fall. The taxi owner's claim for compensation was dismissed on the ground that the lane was well lit and signposted. Had this not been the case its construction would have constituted a violation of the general duty of care.

[633] Hübner, *VersR* 1980 pp. 795–797; id., *Haftung des Gardien*, pp. 150–154; Koch, *Sachhaftung*, pp. 99–104. See also Zachert, *Gefährdungshaftung und Haftung aus vermutetem Verschulden*, pp. 27–29; and fn. 630 above.

[634] Until the 1950s the *Cour de Cassation* usually considered the father to be the 'keeper' and the 'guardian' of objects in the hands of his children. Cass.civ. 18 Oct. 1956, *Gaz.Pal.* 1956, II, 365: a father was held to be the *gardien* of the kitchen appliance with which his 4-year-old son had injured a friend. In later rulings the court found personal liability on the part of the minor under Art. 1384 I Cc, although at first only in cases of *discernement* (see Cass.civ. 14 Mar. 1963, *D.* 1963 *Jur.* 500: '*Un enfant, pourvu qu'il ait un discernement suffisant, peut avoir la garde*'; see also Cass.civ. 10 Feb. 1982, *Sem.Jur.* 1983, II, 20069, obs. Coeuret). In the *arrêt Gabillet*, Cass.Ass.-plén. 9 May 1984, *D.* 1984 *Jur.* 529 (*3ème espèce*) this ceased to be a precondition. A 3-year-old was held liable as the *gardien* of a stick, irrespective of inability to reason. See fn. 405 above. Also Cass.civ. 3 Feb. 1993, *D.* 1994 *Somm.* 15, in which a child, whose age was not mentioned, was held liable as the *gardien* of a fire-lighter. In the 1960s the judiciary made clear that even a person suffering an epileptic fit (Cass.civ. 18 Dec. 1964, *D.* 1965 *Jur.* 191, note Esmein) or other *démence* (Cass. 30 June 1966, Bull.civ. 1966, II, no. 720) can incur *gardien* liability.

Luxembourg: '*On est responsable non seulement du dommage que l'on cause par son propre fait, mais encore de celui qui est causé par le fait des personnes dont on doit répondre, ou des choses que l'on a sous sa garde.*' Art. 1384 I Cc was undoubtedly not intended to be the basis for claims,[635] but rather a provision connecting liability for personal misconduct (Arts. 1382, 1383 Cc) and liability for damage caused by persons and things (Arts. 1384 II-VIII, 1385, 1386 Cc). That is to say, its sole purpose was to inform[636] the uninitiated that tort law '*ne s'arrête pas à la personne qui est l'auteur du dommage, il va plus loin; et pour en assurer de plus en plus la juste indemnité, il autorise le lésé à recourir à ceux de qui cette personne dépend, et contre lesquels il prononce la garantie civile*'.[637]

108   The relevant provisions of both the old Italian *Codice civile* (Art. 1153 I)[638] and the old Dutch BW (Art. 1403 I)[639] were verbatim translations of Art. 1384 I French Cc, and were always treated as merely signposting the following provisions on liability for supervision, animals, and buildings.[640] However, the French courts decided at the close of the nineteenth century to make use of the opportunity offered by the wording of Art. 1384 I Cc. In order to overcome the liability problems arising at the dawn of the industrial age, they decided to construe its second alternative ('*On est responsable . . . du dommage . . . qui est causé par le fait . . . des choses que l'on a sous sa garde*') as an independent provision governing the strict liability for things under a person's *garde*,[641] thus creating

---

[635] Mazeaud/Tunc, *Responsabilité civile*, vol. i, 6th edn., nos. 88 ff.; and Mazeaud/ Mazeaud, *Responsabilité*, vol. ii, 6th edn., nos. 1015, 1138 ff. See also Flour/Aubert, *Obligations*, vol. ii, nos. 736 ff.; Carbonnier, *Droit Civil*, vol. iv, 14th edn., pp. 107 ff.; Bénabent, *Obligations*, 3rd edn., nos. 450 ff.; Le Tourneau, *Responsabilité civile*, 3rd edn., nos. 2218 ff.; Jourdain, *Principes*, pp. 77 ff. For Belgium: Cornelis, *Buitencontractueel aansprakelijkheidsrecht*, nos. 279 ff.; de Page, *Droit Civil Belge*, vol. iii, 3rd edn., nos. 1002 ff. For German commentary: Hübner, *Haftung des Gardien*, pp. 3–10; Koch, *Sachhaftung*, pp. 19–32; Schreiber, *Sachhalterhaftung*, pp. 28–41.

[636] '*Em eerder didactische dan wel imperatieve betekenis*': Vandenberghe, *Aansprakelijkheid voor zaken*, p. 61. See also Flour/Aubert loc. cit. nos. 728, 736 ('*à titre de transition*').

[637] *Rapport* de Greuille no. 10 (in Locré vol. vi, p. 280).

[638] For more detail and a comparison of the old provision with Art. 2051 new Ital. Cc of 1942, incorporating French judgments on 1384 I Cc (see no. 118 below) see Cendon (-Ziviz), Art. 2051 n. 1, p. 2105; Franzoni, *Fatti illeciti*, Art. 2051, n. 1, p. 546; Benucci, *Responsabilità civile*, p. 183. Cass. 20 May 1954, n. 1629, *Giur.it.* 1955, I, 1, 95.

[639] E.g. Asser (-Hartkamp), *Verbintenissenrecht*, vol. iii, 8th edn., nos. 158–160; v. Bar (-Hondius/van Dam), *DeliktsR in Europa, Niederlande* p. 12. Academic attempts to breathe life into Art. 1403 I BW have invariably failed: Hohlbein, *Neuere Entwicklung*, p. 19.

[640] In this context one should also glance at the old *Portuguese* Cc, whose Arts. 2394, 2395 imposed liability for presumed fault only in cases of liability for animals and buildings.

[641] The translation of this expression into other European languages has always been affected by the developments and 'preconceptions' of the respective legal orders. Art. 1384 I as translated for the *Badisches Landrecht* (fn. 330 above), for instance, spoke of '*Sachen, die er in Verwahr bei sich hat*', and the official German translation of Art. 2051 Ital. Cc speaks of '*Sachen . . ., die er zur Verwahrung bei sich hat*'. The Italian wording of the provision is '*cose che ha in custodia*', and the Dutch version of the Belgian Cc has opted for '*zaken, die men*

gardien liability. The Belgian and Luxembourgeois courts soon followed this example.[642] In Italy, Portugal, and The Netherlands this move was later made by the legislator. Thus the Spanish Cc remains the only European legal system related to the *Code civil* with no general provision on liability for things (Art. 1903 I Span. Cc).[643]

Along with the *arrêts Jand'heur*,[644] one of the most famous judgments **109** in the history of European private law is surely Cass.civ. 16 June 1896, the *arrêt Teffaine* (or *arrêt du remorqueur*).[645] The ruling concerned an industrial accident. A ship's boiler exploded, killing an employee, Teffaine. The court of first instance dismissed his widow's claim under Art. 1382 Cc on the ground that fault on the part of the employer had not been proved. However, the Court of Appeal relied upon Art. 1160 Cc (*'On doit suppléer dans le contrat les clauses qui y sont d'usage, quoiqu'elles n'y soient pas exprimées'*) thus excluding fault as a necessary precondition, followed by an analogous application of Art. 1386 Cc (liability for buildings). This only added to the predicament of the *Cour de Cassation*. Now, even if its judges intended to impose no-fault liability, they still had to decide whether to do so in contract by relying on a collateral contractual duty (i.e. an *obligation de sécurité*) in the form of an *obligation de résultat* (a strict duty of care). Under the principle of *non-cumul des responsabilités*, this would have brought the case exclusively within the law of contract.[646] Yet

---

onder zijn bewaring', whereas Art. 1403 I BW (old) decided upon *'zaken, die men onder zijn opzigt heeft'*. However, a modern German translation of Art. 1384 I Cc speaks simply of *'Sachen, deren Halter man ist'*: v. Bar (-Gotthardt), *DeliktsR in Europa, Frankreich*, p. 75.

[642] Although similar moves can be seen in early Belgian rulings (Lawson/Markesinis, *Tortious Liability*, vol. i, pp. 148, 226 and fn. 35); the final breakthrough of *gardien* liability was the result of developments in France.

[643] Although the wording of Art. 1903 I Spanish Cc. at first glance suggests otherwise (it speaks expressly of liability for damage caused by persons) there was no time for the French rulings on Art. 1384 I Cc to influence the Spanish legislator. Even the *Debates parlamentarios* do not disclose how the final version of Art. 1903 was conceived. Prevailing opinion is that it was correct not to adopt a general guardian liability (e.g. García Cantero, in: Asociación de Profesores de Derecho civil, *Centenario del Código civil*, vol. ii, pp. 875, 881)—the Spanish Cc demands a more stable relationship to the object than do the French courts (Cavanillas Múgica, *Transformación*, p. 154). However, the way in which the TS employs the reversal of the burden of proof under Art. 1902 Cc (see fn. 614 above), and the *'agotamiento de la diligencia'* (see TS 29 May 1972, *RAJ* 1972 no. 2590, p. 1950: traffic accident at a level crossing; TS 20 Dec. 1982, *RAJ* 1982 no. 7698 p. 5114: flammable goods caught fire; and TS 10 July 1985, *RAJ* 1985 no. 3965, p. 3338: accident on a building site) could easily produce rulings equivalent to those of its French counterpart. On the latest developments concerning rulings on Art. 1903 Cc see no. 117 below.

[644] See no. 111 and fns. 656, 658 below.

[645] Cass.civ. 16 June 1896, *DP* 1897, 1, 433 (note Saleilles) = 1897, 1, 17 (note Esmein).

[646] See nos. 431–435 below. Cass.civ. 11 Jan. 1922, *DP* 1922, 1,16 = p. 1924, 1, 105 (note Demogue) = Capitant (-Terré/Lequette), *Grands arrêts*, 9th edn., no. 102 explicitly states that *'les art. 1382 et s. c.civ. sont sans application lorsque la faute a été commise dans l'exécution d'une obligation résultant d'un contrat'*, but the principle of *non-cumul des responsabilités* had already interested legal scholars at the time of the *arrêt du remorqueur*: see the illustrative publication by Renner, *Der französische Grundsatz des 'non cumul'*, pp. 238–239.

the Court decided against this and opted for a delictual solution instead, probably due to the fact that the *Cour de Cassation* had ruled only two years earlier that implied *contractual* duties of care did not bind employers.[647] Furthermore, a contractual solution may have been regarded as too restrictive. Finally, the Cour de Cassation abandoned the idea of an analogous application of Art. 1386 Cc, which meant for French law[648] '*qu'il n'est pas nécessaire que la chose ait un vice inhérent à sa nature, susceptible de causer le dommage* [which *is* a precondition for liability for buildings under Art. 1386 Cc: '*par la vice de sa construction*'], *l'article rattachant la responsabilité à la garde de la chose, non à la chose elle-même*'.[649] Instead, the Court applied Art. 1384 I, 2nd alt. Cc directly, declaring that '*art. 1384 c.civ. . . . établit, vis-à-vis de la victime de l'accident, la responsabilité du propriétaire du remorqueur sans qu'il puisse s'y soustraire en prouvant soit la faute du constructeur de la machine, soit le caractère occulte du vice incriminé*'.[650]

110   Notwithstanding the above, *gardien* liability had not yet become established, since this latest judgment of the *Cour de Cassation* could be viewed as applying only to the narrow field of industrial accidents. Moreover, only two years after that ruling the French legislator introduced an independent no-fault right to damages for industrial accidents, which not only clarified the position for insurers but also ousted Arts. 1382–1384 Cc.[651] This caused considerable uncertainty as to whether the new law rendered the principle of the *arrêt du remorqueur* invalid.[652] Even the ruling of 16 November 1920 failed to clarify the situation, again due to legislative action:

---

[647] Cass.civ. 5 Apr. 1894, *DP* 1894, 1, 479.

[648] For differences in Belgian law see nos. 113–114 below.

[649] Cass.civ. 26 Nov. 1920, *DP* 1920, 1, 169 (*Gare de Bordeaux*).

[650] Cass.civ. 16 June 1896, *D.* 1897, 1, 433, 440.

[651] Like the current Art. L 466 *Code de Sécurité Sociale*, Art. 2 of the Act of 9/10 Apr. 1898 (published in *D.* 1898, 4, 49–89 including all legislative material) provided that '*les ouvriers . . . ne peuvent se prévaloir à raison des accidents dont ils sont victimes dans leur travail, d'aucunes dispositions autres que celles de la présente loi*'. Art. 1 contained a contractual claim to damages, excluding an Act of God defence. However, the employer was to escape liability if he took out accident insurance in favour of his employees (Art. 5). The amount of damages awarded depended on the employee's income (Arts. 3–4). As a matter of interest, nearly 90 years later the Act again became important. Its Art. 20 II ('*Le tribunal a le droit, s'il est prouvé que l'accident est dû à une faute inexcusable de l'ouvrier, de diminuer la pension fixée au titre Ier*') served as a model for the equivalent road traffic accident provision of the *loi Badinter* of 1985: fn. 652 below.

[652] For detail see references in fn. 635. The tactic of effecting a ludicrously wide liability rule to coerce Parliament to leglislate was employed by the *Cour de Cassation* in the 1980s in respect of road traffic accident victims. The unsatisfactory contributory fault rules which had been applied since Cass.req. 13 April 1934, *D.* 1934 *Jur.* 41 were replaced by the extremely onerous rules of the *arrêt Desmares* (Cass.civ. 21 July 1982, *D.* 1982 *Jur.* 1982 p. 449), provoking the *loi Badinter* Nr. 85–667 of 5 July 1985, which ensured that such liablity could not arise again in those circumstances.

Wooden barrels stored at Bordeaux railway station caught fire, setting an adjacent building alight. Its owner's claim based on Art. 1384 I Cc was allowed, it being unnecessary for the object (i.e. the barrels) to be defective (*que la chose ait un vice inhérent à sa nature*): the *garde* itself sufficed.[653]

The legislator reacted instantly to this decision by adding two new sections to Art. 1384 French Cc (not included in Art. 1384 Cc of Belgium and Luxembourg): sub-sections II and III, introduced by the Act of 7 November 1922, can be read as a rebuke to the Cour de Cassation:

(II) *Toutefois, celui qui détient, à un titre quelconque, tout ou partie de l'immeuble ou des biens mobiliers dans lesquels un incendie a pris naissance ne sera responsable, vis-à-vis des tiers, des dommages causés par cet incendie que s'il est prouvé qu'il doit être attribué à sa faute ou à la faute des personnes dont il est responsable.*

(III) *Cette disposition ne s'applique pas aux rapports entre propriétaires et locataires, qui demeurent régis par les articles 1733 et 1734 du Code civil.*

So *gardien* liability finally achieved its breakthrough only in connection **111** with the steadily growing problem of liability in road traffic accidents. The *arrêts Jand'heur*, as well as the *arrêts Franck*,[654] and *Desmares*,[655] revolved around it. In the former case, a lorry hit a young girl while she was trying to cross the road, causing severe injuries. The Court of Appeal denied the applicability of Art. 1384 I Cc, and dismissed a claim under Art. 1382 Cc for lack of fault. However, the *Cour de Cassation* dismissed the argument that this was a case of liability for misconduct only and not for damage caused by things: '*La loi, pour l'application de la présomption qu'elle édicte, ne distingue pas suivant que la chose qui a causé le dommage était ou non actionnée par la main de l'homme; il suffit qu'il s'agisse d'une chose soumise à la nécessité d'une garde en raison des dangers qu'elle peut faire courir à autrui*' (*Jand'heur I*).[656] The case was therefore remitted to the Lyon *Cour d'appel*, which again refused to apply Art. 1384 I Cc on the ground that '*l'accident est causé par une automobile en mouvement, sous l'impulsion et la direction de l'homme, cela ne constitue pas un fait de la chose*'.[657] On renewed appeal the case again came before the *Cour de*

---

[653] Cass.civ. 16 Nov. 1920, *DP* 1920, 1, 169. The view that liability under Art. 1384 I Cc does not require an object to be dangerous or faulty is also held by the Luxembourgeois courts: Cour 30 Oct. 1951, *Pas. luxemb.* 15 (1950–1953) p. 229; Cour 2 Dec. 1957, *Pas. luxemb.* 17 (1957–1959) p. 263.

[654] Cass.civ. 3 Mar. 1936, *D.* 1936 *Jur.* 81; and Cass.ch.réunies 2 Dec. 1941, *DC* 1942 p. 25: the owner of a car ceases to be its *gardien* when it is stolen even if it was poorly protected from thieves: for the *garde*, only *l'usage, la direction, et le contrôle* are relevant. This view is shared in Belgium (for more detail see Dalcq, *Liber Amicorum Dumon*, pp. 73,75) and Luxembourg (Trib.Lux. 4 June 1950, *Pas. luxemb.* 15 [1950–53] p. 89; and Cour 2 Apr. 1952, *Pas. luxemb.* 15 [1950–53] p. 352).

[655] Cass.civ. 21 July 1982, *D.* 1982 *Jur.* 449 (fn. 652 above).

[656] Cass.civ. 21 Feb. 1927, *D.* 1927, 1, 97.   [657] Lyon 7 July 1927, *DH* 1927 p. 423.

Cassation, whose *chambre réunie* of 13 February 1930 finally decided in favour of the plaintiff. Its official reasoning has since been treated as law:

La présomption de responsabilité établie par l'article 1384 al. 1 à l'encontre de celui qui a sous sa garde la chose inanimée qui a causé un dommage à autrui ne peut être détruite que par la preuve d'un cas fortuit ou de force majeur ou d'une cause étrangère qui ne lui soit pas imputable; il ne suffit pas de prouver qu'il n'a commis aucune faute ou que la cause du fait dommageable est demeurée inconnue; . . . la loi, pour l'application de la présomption qu'elle édicte, ne distingue pas suivant que la chose qui a causé le dommage était ou non actionnée par la main de l'homme; il n'est pas nécessaire qu'elle ait un vice inhérent à sa nature et susceptible de causer le dommage, l'article 1384 rattachant la responsabilité à la garde de la chose, non à la chose elle-même.[658]

112   The French legislator took no action following this decision. Thus the 'keeper' of an object has for sixty years been liable even where no fault could be proved, or where the true cause of the damage remained unknown, for Art. 1384 I Cc presumes, not fault, but responsibility (*une présomption de responsabilité*). Hence the keeper of an object escapes liability only when an Act of God, a true coincidence, or similar interruption of the chain of causation (a *cause étrangère*) is established. Finally, like a 'keeper', a *gardien* is also *'lié à l'usage et aux pouvoirs de surveillance et de contrôle qui caractérisent la garde'.*[659]

113   Belgium and Luxembourg largely agree with this interpretation of Art. 1384 I, 2nd alt. Cc. Art. 1384 I Lux. Cc is an independent, and by no means secondary, provision[660] which refers to both real property and movable goods.[661] The provision *'établit non pas une présomption de faute, mais une présomption de responsabilité à l'encontre de celui qui a sous sa garde la chose inanimée qui a causé un dommage à autrui. La responsabilité du fait des choses a un charactère purement objectif.'*[662] Even the concept of *garde* is defined in line with the French example. So when a car is stolen, the thief becomes its *gardien*.[663] However, Belgium's interpretation of Art. 1384 I, 2nd alt. Cc does not exactly follow the French provision. Even before the Luxembourg decision it was decided to adopt the approach of the French *Cour de Cassation* in the interpretation of Art. 1384 I, 2nd alt.

---

[658] Cass.ch.réunies 13 Feb. 1930, *D.* 1930, 1, 57.

[659] Cass.civ. 9 June 1993, *Sem.Jur.* 1994, II, 22202 (note Viney). The case concerned barley residues from a malt plant, which were removed from the factory and deposited in an artificial lake, which served as a drinking-water reservoir, together with debris from a warehouse fire. The factory owners neglected to inform the contracted demolition firm that the barley might begin to ferment, so the former retained *contrôle* and remained *gardiens* of the barley.   [660] Cour 25 Oct. 1961, *Pas. luxemb.* 18 (1960–1962) p. 379.

[661] Cour 24 Dec. 1930, *Pas. luxemb.* 12 (1930–32) p. 197 (the leading Luxembourg case).

[662] Cour 25 Oct. 1961 loc. cit. (fn. 660 above).

[663] Trib.Lux. 4 June 1950, *Pas. luxemb.* 15 (1950–53) p. 89; Cour 2 Apr. 1952, *Pas. luxemb.* 15 (1950–53) p. 352.

Cc.[664] However, since this decision was taken, not only before the *arrêt Jand'heur*, but also before the French *Cour de Cassation* judgment on the Bordeaux railway station fire,[665] the laws of the two countries have developed in separate directions.

The leading Belgian case is Cass. 26 May 1904.[666] On 7 August 1904 a fire broke out among goods stored in the warehouse of a commercial company. The fire soon spread to the company's factory and then to an adjacent building belonging to the plaintiff. Her claim for damages under Art. 1384 I Cc, was dismissed. The court held that although damages can be awarded under Art. 1384 I Cc the *modus operandi* of Arts. 1382–1386 Cc must be borne in mind. No-fault liability under Art. 1386 Cc applies only in cases where the object itself is defective: '*La constatation du vice de la chose dont on a la garde est donc, au même titre que celle de la faute de la personne dont on doit répondre, la condition à laquelle l'article 1384 subordonne la responsabilité du dommage; qu'aucune présomption légale ne dispense de la preuve de cet égard; . . . la responsabilité dérive du vice de la chose attribué à une faute.*'[667]

The defect in the inanimate object (*vice de la chose inanimée*) was **114** understood to equate to fault in cases of liability for failure to supervise: where the latter demanded *faute*, the former required a defective object. Thus the Belgian *Cour de Cassation* avoided what it (unlike its French counterpart) saw as stricter responsibility for movable goods than for real property under Art. 1386 Cc.[668] As the goods could not be proven to be defective the case was dismissed, rendering revision of Art. 1384 Belgian Cc unnecessary.[669] It remains the case that the object must *intrinsèquement* bear an 'abnormal' feature; the defect must be 'inherent in its structure'[670] to establish liability under Art. 1384 Belgian Cc.[671] The *gardien*'s only defence is that the damage (and not the defect) was caused by chance: this has considerable drawbacks.[672] Whereas under French law a boy playing 'football' with a bottle could become its *gardien*,[673]

---

[664] For the history of *gardien* liability in Belgium: Dalcq, *Responsabilité civile*, vol. i, 2nd edn., nos. 2028–2039; Cornelis, *Responsabilité extra-contactuelle*, nos. 279–279*bis*; de Page, *Droit civil Belge*, vol. ii, 3rd edn., no. 1002. Also fn. 642 above.

[665] See no. 110 and fn. 653 above.   [666] Cass. 26 May 1904, *Pas. belge* 1904, I, 246.

[667] Ibid. p. 249.   [668] Ibid.   [669] See no. 110 above.

[670] Dalcq loc. cit. no. 2137; Cornelis loc. cit. (both fn. 664 above) nos. 290 ff. Also van Gerven, *Verbintenissenrecht*, vol. ii, 3rd edn., pp. 61 ff. Brussels 8 Feb. 1991, *RGAR* 1994 no. 12288: defective car ignition mechanism—'*comportement anormal de la voiture*'—the precondition of *vice* was thus fulfilled. However, even the French do not *completely* ignore the existence of this problem: their approach is to ask if the object has 'intervened'. See Cass.Civ. 8 June 1994, *Bull.civ.* 1994 II no. 152: accident on a trampoline, liability of the '*installateur*' denied on the ground that the material was free of defects.

[671] It is exclusively for the *juge du fond* to determine the existence of such defects. His conclusions as to the existence of a *vice* may be examined by the Court of Cassation: Cass. 31 Jan. 1952, *Pas. belge* 1952, I, 308.   [672] Cass. 13 May 1993, *JT* 1994 p. 231.

[673] *Arrêt Lindini*: Cass.civ. 10 Feb. 1982, *Sem.Jur.* 1983, II, 20069 (note Coeuret).

under Belgian law the owners of a multi-storey car park are not liable even if a parcel bomb explodes in its elevator:[674] its existence does not render the elevator defective. Similarly, strict liability for things such as spilt cream lying on the otherwise defect-free[675] floor of a supermarket, was for a long time imposed only by French,[676] and not by Belgian,[677] law. For the latter the mere fact that an object is in the wrong place '*ne constitue pas in se vice de celle-ci*':[678] the vegetable leaf does not itself found liability. Not even the fact that a tyre bursts raises a presumption that it was defective.[679] In France, on the other hand, a lemonade manufacturer can remain liable as the *gardien* of the bottles it filled, even after their sale.[680]

The Belgian and French courts differ, not only on the question of whether an object must be defective, but also about who the guardian of an object is. Particularly in the field of product liability, the French courts have[681] differentiated between the *garde de la structure* ('technical custody', incumbent on the producer) and the *garde du comportement* ('actual' or 'material' care incumbent on the current custodian). As a result the manufacturer of an oxygen bottle was held liable as its *gardien* under French law when it exploded during transport[682] (the same was said for a television set which imploded in the customer's house[683]). However, under Belgian law, even where a *vice* has been established, the carrier of the oxygen bottle is still considered its only *gardien*.[684]

(2) Liability Under Art. 1384 I 1st Alt. Cc for Damage Caused by Persons

115 The *gardien* liability of the Romance legal systems was originally devised to govern only damage caused by things, not by persons who were to be

---

[674] Cass. 27 May 1982, *JT* 1983 p. 48.

[675] However, Belgian courts seem subsequently to have altered their position. See Cass. 13 May 1993 loc. cit. (fn. 672 above); Liège 7 Dec. 1993, *RGAR* 1995 no. 12455 (spilt tomato soup on the red terracotta tiles of a self-service restaurant); Cass. 1 Dec. 1994, *JT* 1995 p. 340 (pieces of wood on the floor of a badly lit workshop in the basement of a house).

[676] Cass.civ. 16 May 1984, *Rev.trim.dr.civ.* 1985 p. 585 (obs. Huet); Lyon 5 Oct. 1978, *D.* 1979 *IR* 320; Versailles 5 Oct. 1979 *Gaz.Pal.* 1980 *Somm.* 605; Paris 30 Mar. 1984, *Gaz.Pal.* 1984 *Somm.* 206.

[677] See e.g. Cass. 10 June 1983, *Pas. belge* 1983, I, 1147; Cass. 5 Dec. 1985, *Pas. belge* 1986, I, 431; and Cass. 26 June 1986, *Pas. belge* 1986, I, 1326.

[678] Cornelis, *Responsabilité extra-contractuelle*, no. 293, p. 506.

[679] Ghent 18 Feb. 1986, *Bull.Ass.* 1986 p. 421; 1987 p. 139. However, for a decision pursuing a somewhat different course see Brussels 12 June 1986, cited according to Cornelis loc. cit. p. 509. [680] Cass.civ. 12 Nov. 1975, *Sem.Jur.* 1976, II, 18479 *(1ère espèce)*.

[681] Starck (-Roland / Boyer), *Obligations*, vol. i, 4th edn., no. 590 believes that this position has since been abandoned.

[682] Cass.civ. 5 Jan. 1956, *D.* 1957 *Jur.* 261 (note Rodière) = *Sem.Jur.* 1956, II, 9095 (note Savatier); Cass.civ. 10 June 1960, *D.* 1960 *Jur.* 609 (note Rodière) = *Sem.Jur.* 1960, II, 11824 (note Esmein). Also fn. 680 above.

[683] Cass.civ. 30 Nov. 1988, Bull.civ. 1988, II, no. 240. However, no liability in cases where the customer has tried to mend the set: Cass.civ. 14 Nov. 1979, Bull.civ. 1979, II, no. 262.

[684] Thus Rb. Hasselt 1 June 1981, *Limb.Rechtsl.* 1981 p. 119 (note Vander Graesen).

covered by the later sections of Art. 1384 Cc.[685] Those sections were not even considered appropriate for analogous application when liability for objects had already become established customary law,[686] although the text of Art. 1384 I Cc itself never required such restraint or limitation.[687] On the contrary, if it was to be regarded as a general provision governing liability for damage caused by things, it was merely a question of consistency to do the same for general liability for persons. Indeed, Art. 1384 I Cc in its first alternative refers to *'personnes dont on doit répondre'*.[688] However, in a recent decision, the *arrêt Blieck*, the *Assemblée plénière* of the *Cour de Cassation* did follow the more satisfactory path of treating liability for damage caused by things and by persons alike,[689] and courts examining questions of fact have begun to adopt that approach.[690]

In the *arrêt Blieck*, Weevauters had a mental handicap and lived in, but was not confined to, a mental institution. He set the Bliecks' wood on fire. The couple sued the institution, which denied liability by claiming that its personnel had not failed to perform its supervision duty, and that none of the special circumstances listed under Art. 1384 applied (parents', employer's liability, etc.) The *Cour de Cassation* did not accept these arguments: the institution had *'accepté la charge d'organiser et de contrôler, à titre permanent, le mode de vie de ce handicapé'*, therefore *'la cour d'appel a . . . décidé, à bon droit, qu'elle devait répondre de celui-ci, au sens de l'art. 1384, al. 1ᵉʳ, c.civ., et qu'elle était tenue de réparer les dommages qu'il avait causés.'*[691]

---

[685] Parental liability: Art. 1384 IV, VII French Cc, Art. 1384 II, V Belgian and Luxembourg Cc. Employer's liability: Art. 1384 V French Cc, Art. 1384 III Belgian and Luxembourg Cc. Liability of teachers and and others responsible for training: Art. 1384 VI-VIII French Cc; Art. 1384 IV,V Belgian and Luxembourg Cc.

[686] Cass.civ. 15 Feb. 1956, *D.* 1956 *Jur.* 410; Cass. 24 Nov. 1976, *D.* 1977 *Jur.* 595.

[687] The only reason why Art. 1384 I Cc was for a whole century interpreted differently for objects than for persons was 'social need', the *'nécessités impérieuses de la pratique'*. See Mazeaud/Tunc, *Responsabilité civile*, vol. i, 6th edn., no. 714 discussing those authors who wanted to apply Art. 1384 I Cc to persons from immediately after the *arrêt Jand'heur*, as did e.g. Savatier, *DH* 1933 *Chron.* pp. 81–84.

[688] This position was adopted by: Savatier (loc. cit.); *Procureur général* Matter in his *Conclusions* on the *arrêt Jand'heur*, *Gaz.Pal.* 1930, 1, 393 = *D.* 1930, 1, 57; Legeais, *D.* 1965 *Chron.* pp. 131–134; Trib.enfants Dijon 27 Feb. 1965, *D.* 1965 *Jur.* 439; Trib.enfants Poitiers 22 Mar. 1965, *Rev.dr.sanit.soc.* 1966 p. 262 (unobtainable to this author); and Trib.enfants Chambéry 1 June 1977, *Sem.Jur.* 1977, II, Somm. 340. The same issue had already been discussed in 1904: Trib. de paix de Blois 7 Mar. 1904, *Gaz.Pal.* 1904, I, 587; and Demogue, *Rev.trim.dr.civ.* 3 (1904) pp. 412, 419–420.

[689] Cass.ass.plén. 29 Mar. 1991, *D.* 1991 *Jur.* 324 (note Larroument; see also Viney, *D.* 1991 *Chron.* p. 157) = *Sem.Jur.* 1991, II, 21673 (concl. Dontenwille, note Ghestin). See also the fine overview in Jourdain, *Rev.trim.dr.civ.* 90 (1991) pp. 539, 541–544; Ferrand's analyses, *ZEuP* 1993 pp. 132–140; Legrand, *ERPL* 1 (1993) pp. 229–239. Although the Belgian courts have so far followed suit, they seem at least to be approaching the French position by tightening the duties of care: Brussels 7 Dec. 1993, *RGAR* 1995 no. 12416.

[690] Rouen 25 Sep. 1991, *D.* 1993 *Jur.* 5.

[691] Cass.ass.plén. 29 Mar. 1991 loc. cit. (fn. 689 above).

(3) The Relationship between General Gardien *Liability and Codified Causes of Action*

116 Although it is impossible to predict the way in which general strict liability for damage caused by persons will develop,[692] it will inevitably lead (as in the field of traditional liability for damage caused by things) to legal problems of concurrent causes of action and resultant inconsistency. For example, this area of liability law imposes strict liability on institutions for their residents, while, for instance, holding parents liable for the actions of their children only for presumed but rebuttable failure to supervise. That homes and institutions have a duty to supervise their residents is agreed throughout Europe,[693] so vicarious liability has extended beyond its traditional narrow field. However, France is alone in imposing strict liability regime for damage caused by persons where this falls within the scope of a general clause, whereas damage governed by specific provisions (except for Art. 1384 V French Cc, employer's liability) founds liability only in cases of fault. This arrangement is unfortunate, as well as unique in Europe. In France it has led to a turn-around in the impact of the sections following Art. 1384 I Cc (dealing with certain special circumstances). What was originally intended as a means of lowering the liability threshold has had exactly the opposite effect. For in the field of concurrent claims, these special clauses, when applicable, oust the general liability principle of Art. 1384 I Cc.[694] The

---

[692] Cass.civ. 6 Jan. 1993, *D.* 1994 *Jur.* 95 (see explanation by Viney, *Sem.Jur.* 1993, I, 3727) concerned a claim based solely on Art. 1382 Cc. The authorities of a home for the mentally handicapped transferred a minor resident to a foster home. On his way there the resident raped a girl. The *Cour de Cassation* reversed the judgment of the Court of Appeal on the ground that the presumed *faute* by the authority had been insufficiently examined (*caractérisée*). Since the claim was commenced before the *arrêt Blieck* judgment, the *Cour* referred to it only obliquely (*'que ceux-ci ont demandé à l'association la réparation de ce préjudice sur le seul fondement de l'article 1382 Cc'*).

[693] STJ 25 July 1985, *BolMinJust* 349 (1985) p. 516: liability of a psychiatric hospital for failure to supervise a patient who escaped; *Hof* Leeuwarden 5 June 1991, *NedJur* 1992 no. 78 p. 244; OLG Celle 11 Oct. 1960, *NJW* 1961 p. 223: residents of a geriatric home endangering road users; *Dorset Yacht Co. Ltd.* v. *Home Office* [1970] AC 1004: liability for damage caused by runaway Borstal boys; In Italy the liability of psychiatric institutions was removed from Art. 2047 and given its own special law (n. 180/1978): staff can only be liable under Art. 2043 Cc. However, orphanages and other homes for children and juveniles remain subject to the strict liability regime of Art. 2047 Cc. See Galgano, *Diritto civile e commerciale*, vol. ii (2) pp. 324–325; Franzoni, *Fatti illeciti*, Art. 2047 Cc, p. 334–335; Alpa, *Responsabilità civile*, p. 301; and Visintini, *Fatti illeciti*, vol. i, p. 503.

[694] See e.g. Starck (-Roland/Boyer), *Obligations*, vol. i, 4th edn., no. 652 (notably discussing this issue under the heading *'L'inapplicabilité de l'article 1384, alinia 1ᵉʳ'*); Mazeaud/Chabas, *Obligations,* 8th edn., nos. 513, 551; Dalcq, *Responsabilité civile*, vol. i, 2nd edn., no. 2046; and Cass.civ. 28 Nov. 1949, *D.* 1950 *Chron.* 105 note Lalou (*'l'article 1386 C.civ. . . . exclut l'application de la disposition générale de l'article 1384, § 1ᵉʳ'*). Cass.civ. 16 Mar. 1994, *Sem.Jur.* 1994, IV, 1326 confirms the above position. See also Viney, *Sem.Jur.* 1994, I, 3773, pp. 304, 308: *'Le principe de responsabilité du fait d'autrui fondé sur l'alinéa 1ᵉʳ de l'aricle 1384 laisse, pour l'instant, subsister tels quels les régimes particuliers fondées sur les alinéas 4 et suivants.'*

ensuing contradictions give cause for concern: one need only compare liability under Art. 1384 II French Cc with the liability imposed on juvenile *gardiens*.[695] Likewise, liability for buildings under Art. 1386 Cc has become far less effective than liability for movable goods under Art. 1384 I Cc.[696] Moreover, this development caused a number of difficulties concerning the relationship between vicarious liability and liability for damage caused by things. Three examples are: who should be considered the *gardien*,[697] under what conditions should a *garde en commun*[698] oust the law of liability for others, and finally, should liability for failure to supervise be imposed even where the supervisee is liable only for *garde* and not for *faute*.

c. The General Clauses of Spanish, Italian, Portuguese, and Dutch Law

Although Spain is also attempting to transform its Art. 1903 I Cc into a **117** real basis for a claim,[699] this will not mirror French judge-made law. For even if these efforts bear fruit,[700] the provision would still concern only liability for damage caused by others, damage caused by things having been deliberately excluded from Art. 1903 I Cc. Thus the approach taken by the French *Cour de Cassation* has spread only to those systems described here as Romance systems. Unlike in Belgium and Luxembourg, however, in Italy, Portugal, and The Netherlands it was not the judiciary but the legislature which carried this out. Indeed, Italian and

---

[695] No. 110 and fn. 673 above.

[696] Cass.civ. 28 Nov. 1949 loc. cit. (fn. 694). Thus the abolition of Art. 1386 Cc has become a *desideratum*: Mazeaud/Chabas loc. cit. (fn. 694) no. 551. In short, all the provisions following Art. 1384 I French Cc have become a legal embarrassment.

[697] Mazeaud/Chabas loc. cit. no. 537; Dalcq loc. cit. (n. 694 above) no. 2097.

[698] This question is answered differently in France and Belgium, with France tending to take the 'deep pocket' approach, i.e. to treat the person with the most money as the guardian. A good example is found in Cass.civ. 9 May 1990, Bull.civ. 1990, II, no. 93: a yacht sank with all hands during a regatta. Their families sued the family of the captain. The claim was allowed: only the captain (and not the passengers, whom the *Cour d'appel* had considered *co-gardiens*) is the *gardien* of a boat. See fn. 659.

[699] See: TS 23 Feb. 1976, *RAJ* 1976 no. 880 p. 6779; AP Cuenca 9 Mar. 1985, *La Ley* 1985 (3) no. 6526–R, p. 776: a motorist ignored a stop sign; liability imposed on the car owner; TS 23 Sep. 1988, *La Ley* 1988 (4) p. 395, also concerning a car accident: the parents and the owner of the car were held liable under Art. 1903 I; Arts. 1903 II and IV did not apply. See Santos Briz, *Responsabilidad civil*, vol. i, 6th edn., p. 455. Art. 1903 Cc contains only general examples, although its analogous application is certainly possible.

[700] Opposed to such an expansion of Art. 1903 I Cc is, e.g., de Ángel Yáguez, *Responsabilidad civil*, 3rd edn., p. 323. Moreover, even TS 30 May 1992, *La Ley* 1992 (4) p. 138, in a case concerning a borrowed car did not employ Art. 1903 Cc, but instead applied Art. 22 CP (old version) (secondary liability) analogously. It therefore seems that the Spanish judiciary does not want general liability for damage caused by persons, but rather a separate solution for road traffic accidents.

Dutch judges[701] had refused to transform by judgment alone Arts. 1153 I
Ital. Cc (old version) and Art. 1403 I BW (old), which were identical to
Art. 1384 I French Cc, into independent bases for a claim.[702] This judicial
self-restraint permitted coherent development of the new systems by the
legislator, avoiding internal contradictions. Furthermore, the new role
for those provisions concerns only liability for damage caused by things,
and does not impose general strict liability for damage caused by persons: see (1) below. However Italy and Portugal created new problems
by introducing into their codes liability for both damage caused by
things and dangerous activities (Arts. 2050, 2051 Ital. Cc; Art. 493 I, II
Port. Cc), the latter based on the German concept of strict liability.
Generally, however, the tendency to differentiate between liability for
damage caused by things and liability for dangerous activities seems to
have passed its peak. The Dutch BW of 1992 abandoned this approach,
and in Italy and Portugal the somewhat artificial distinction between the
two areas has become increasingly vague: see (2) below.

(1) Guardian Liability Outside France, Belgium, and Luxembourg

118 The Italian *Codice civile* of 1942 was not only the first European Civil
Code to introduce special provisions on the liability of the driver (Art.
2054 I, II, IV Cc) and owner (Art. 2054 III, IV Cc) of non-rail vehicles
(*veicoli senza guida di rotaie*,[703] usually motor vehicles, but also
bicycles,[704] go-karts,[705] electric wheelchairs,[706] shopping trolleys,[707]
and even roller skates,[708]) it was also the first European Civil Code

---

[701] In Portugal this was not an issue, since the old Portuguese Cc had no provision
corresponding to Art. 1384 I French Cc.
[702] For the first statement on this issue in The Netherlands see HR 31 May 1929, *NedJur*
1929 p. 1441: '*art. 1401 of 1403 BW., welk laatste artikel niet op zichzelf, maar in verband met
eerstgenoemde bepaling moet worden beschouwd.*' This was repeatedly confirmed in later
judgments: e.g. HR 16 Apr. 1942 *NedJur* 1942 no. 394 p. 598; HR 28 June 1946, *NedJur*
1946, no. 723 p. 929; more recently HR 22 June 1979, *NedJur* 1979 no. 535 p. 1741; and HR 20
June 1980, *NedJur* 1980 no. 622 p. 2050. See also fn. 767 below. For Art. 1153 I Italian Cc (old)
see e.g. Cendon (-Ziviz) vol. iv, Art. 2051 Cc p. 2105; Franzoni, *Fatti illeciti*, Art. 2051 p. 546
(who also mentions rulings taking a different position, esp. those of the *Corte d'Appello di
Milano*); Benucci, *Responsabilità civile*, p. 183; and Alpa/Bessone, *Responsabilità civile*, vol. i,
2nd edn., p. 70. See also the commentary in Cass. 20 May 1954, n. 1629, *Giur.it.* 1955, I, 1, 95:
regarding a fire, the court confirmed that under Art. 1153 Cc (old) fault had to be proved,
whereas Art. 2051 Cc (new) shifted the burden of proof.
[703] This term has since been defined in Art. 47 *Codice della strada* (DPR 30 Apr. 1992, n.
285, *Gaz.Uff.* Suppl. n. 114 of 18 May 1992, enforced on 1 Jan. 1993). Yet for railways Italian
law still imposes no strict liability. Railways do not even fall within Art. 2050 Cc (liability
for carrying out dangerous activities). From the Italian point of view railways are apparently not dangerous, so are subject only to Art. 2043 Cc; v. Bar (-Busnelli), *DeliktsR in
Europa, Italien*, p. 32.   [704] Cendon (-Peccenini) vol. iv, Art. 2054, p. 2147.
[705] Cass. 15 Dec. 1972, n. 3671, *Resp.Civ. e Prev.* 1973, p. 94.
[706] Cass.pen. 20 Sep. 1989, *Arch.Giur.circolaz.* 1990 p. 506.
[707] Pret. Pistoia 30 Dec. 1983, *Giust.civ.* 1984, I, 1674.
[708] Franzoni, *Fatti illeciti*, Art. 2054, p. 645, fn. 2.

deliberately to introduce general *custodia* liability in addition to the *leges specialis*[709] covering liability for animals (Art. 2052 Cc) and buildings (Art. 2053 Cc). In 1942 the legislator discarded Art. 1153 Cc (old):

'*ciascuno parimenti è obbligato non solo per il danno che cagiona per fatto proprio, ma anche per quello che viene arrecato col fatto delle persone delle quali deve rispondere, o colle cose che ha in custodia*'

and replaced it with *Art. 2051 Cc*, according to which

'*ciascuno è responsabile del danno cagionato dalle cose che ha in custodia, salvo che provi il caso fortuito*' (liability for damage caused by objects in one's control, unless an act of God can be proven).

Hence, what the authors of the old *Codice civile* conceived as a general **119** introduction became in 1942 an independent basis for a claim, albeit covering only things and not persons. Moreover, Art. 2051 Italian Cc speaks of compensation for damage caused by the object ('*cagionato dalle cose*'), whereas Art. 1153 I Cc (old) spoke of an event connected to the object (the '*fatto colle cose*'). As a result, Italian courts only grant claims under Art. 2051 Cc if the 'capacity to cause damage is inherent in the object' (*un proprio dinamismo*).[710] '*La presunzione di responsabilità per danni da cosa in custodia . . . non può trovare applicazione nella diversa ipotesi di danni che non derivino dalla res in sé, ma da un comportamento, anche omissivo, del detentore della stessa.*'[711] Hence, where damage can be attributed to human misconduct, whether act or omission, Art. 2051 Cc[712] is not applicable. For example, a lawyer who, while conducting his case falls off his platform can claim damages from the authority responsible for the court only under Art. 2043 Cc.[713] Yet where a branch falls off a publicly owned tree, injuring a passer-by, the community is liable under

---

[709] On the issue of concurrent claims under Art. 2052 (animal keeper's liability) and Art. 2051 Cc, see Giur.sist. Bigiavi (-Costanzo) vol. ii(2), p. 546; Cendon (-Ziviz) vol. iv, Art. 2052 Cc n. 2.1, p. 2123; Franzoni, *Fatti illeciti*, Art. 2052 Cc p. 606; and App. Turin 2 May 1958, *Rep.gen.* 1959 no. 258 col. 3010. On concurrent claims under Art. 2053 (buildings) and Art. 2051 Cc see Ziviz loc. cit. Art. 2051 Cc, n. 6.2, p. 2120; Franzoni loc. cit. Art. 2051 Cc, p. 603; Cass. 29 Jan. 1981, n. 693, *Giust.civ.Mass.* 1981 no. 693, p. 258; and Cass. 24 May 1972, n. 1632, *Giust.civ.Mass.* 1972, no. 1632. As a result of liability for buildings (Art. 2053 Cc) being governed by *lex specialis*, the owner and not the *custode* is liable. Furthermore, since one precondition under Art. 2053 Cc is a *rovina* (a partially or wholly derelict building), examples such as snow from a roof (Ziviz loc. cit.), or falling items which are not part of a building (e.g. scaffolding) are not covered by Art. 2053 Cc, but by Art. 2051 Cc: Cass. 31 May 1971, n. 1641, *Giust.civ.Mass.* 1971, no. 1641, p. 895. See also Cass. 18 Oct. 1956, n. 1731, *Resp.Civ. e Prev.* 1957, p. 250.

[710] Cass. 23 Oct. 1990, n. 10277, *Giust.civ.Mass.* 1990, p. 1786; Cass. 15. Dec. 1975, n. 4124, *Giust.civ.* 1976, I, 551; Cass. 22 May 1982, n. 3134, in: Gentile/Guerreri/Guerreri, *La Responsabilità, voce Responsabilità civile: cose in custodia* 69 (111), Cass. 16 Feb. 1976, n. 506, *Arch.civ.* 1976, p. 1209; Cass. 2 Feb. 1983, n. 908, *BB* 1984, II, 459; and App. Genoa 31 Mar. 1989, *Riv.giur.circ.trasp.* 1990 p. 581.

[711] Cass. 23 Mar. 1992, n. 3594, *Foro.it.* 1993, I, 198.

[712] In cases concerning dangerous activities liability may be imposed under Art. 2050 Cc. See no. 126 below. [713] Loc. cit. (fn. 711 above).

Art. 2051 Cc.[714] Where a customer is injured in a bank robbery,[715] or by slipping on rainwater on the floor of a bank,[716] there is no liability under Art. 2051 Cc because both bank and floor lack a *proprio dinamismo*. However, since the 1970s a number of lower courts[717] appear to have departed from this position, deciding in similar circumstances that 'both the capacity to cause damage, inherent in an object, and the danger connected to an object when associated with another object can lead to liability under Art. 2051 Cc',[718] a view subsequently approved expressly by the *Corte di Cassazione*.[719]

120   The Italian judiciary seem therefore to have sought a compromise between the Italian and Belgian approaches. Although *custodia* liability in Belgium demands that the object demonstrate a *'vice inhérent à sa structure'*, in Italy the object need not be objectively dangerous,[720] and Italian judges (more than the French)[721] require the object to have played an active role in causing the damage.[722] Yet in some areas the defectiveness of the object is once again an issue, for example in the field of liability for buildings, where it is the cause of action (Art. 2053 Ital. Cc) and of liability for road vehicles, where it tightens the conditions of liability (Art. 2054 IV Ital. Cc). Whereas French law was forced to accept inconsistency in its liability system following the introduction of Art. 1384 II Cc in 1922,[723] the Italian legislator avoided the same mistake.[724] For example, cases where a fire spreads from one building to another come under Art. 2051 Cc[725] (not Art. 2053 Cc).[726] Cases in which

---

[714] Cass. 21 July 1962, n. 1991, *Resp.Civ. e Prev.* 1963, p. 65.

[715] Cass. 14 Sep. 1983, n. 2619, *Foro.it.Mass.* 1983, no. 2619, p. 544; Cass. 11 Mar. 1991, n. 2555, *Foro.it.* 1991, I, 2802; App. Genoa 21 Dec. 1979, *Giur.it.* 1981, I, 2, 160 (confirmed by Cass. 2 Feb. 1983, n. 908, *BB* 1984, II, 459). Trib. Rome 2 Feb. 1977, *Giur.it.* 1981, I, 2, 159 upheld the applicability of Art. 2051 Cc in such cases: it was overruled by App. Rome 5 Feb. 1980, *Giur.it.* 1982, I, 2, 173, confirmed in Cass. 14 Apr. 1983, n. 2619, *Giust.civ.* 1983, I, 2658.

[716] Cass. 24 Jan. 1975, n. 280, *Giur.it.* 1977, I, 1, 2044. See also Cass. 27 Mar. 1972, n. 987, *Resp.Civ. e Prev.* 1972 p. 547 (defining the term *proprio dinamismo*).

[717] Trib. Milan 3 Feb. 1980, *Resp.Civ.ePrev.* 1980, p. 571; App. Milan 23 June 1978, *Arch.civ.* 1978, p. 1136.   [718] Schlüchter, *Haftung für gefährliche Tätigkeit*, p. 142.

[719] Cass. 23 Oct. 1990, n. 10277, *Giust.civ.Mass.* 1990, p. 1786.

[720] Cass. 24 Feb. 1983, n. 1425, *Rep.Foro.it.* 1983, n. 109, p. 2786. For further case references see Schlüchter loc. cit. (fn. 718 above) p. 140.

[721] See Cass.civ. 12 May 1980, *Sem.Jur.* 1981, II, 19684 (note Dejean de la Batie). Also fn. 722 below.

[722] See no. 111 above. Such differing approaches to the issue do occasionally result in conflicting solutions. To give just one example, compare the Italian ruling noted in fn. 714 with Cass.civ. 29 Mar. 1971, *Sem.Jur.* 1972, II, 17086 (note Boré), both concerning a branch falling from a tree. The French court denied liability under Art. 1384 I Cc.

[723] See no. 110 above.

[724] For further details see RG no. 657; RR no. 264 (in Pandofelli *et al.*, *Codice civile*, pp. 684 f.)

[725] Cass. 20 May 1954, n. 1629, *Giur.it.* 1955, I, 1, 95 (see fn. 702 above). Arguing to the contrary, though not convincingly, Benucci, *Responsabilità civile*, pp. 180 ff. (no. 66).

[726] For more details see Heldrich, *Allgemeine Rechtsgrundsätze*, p. 77.

the custodian (or 'keeper') of an object must be determined also illustrate the operation of Italian *custodia* liability. As for the liability of owners of stolen cars, the relevant Belgian, French, and Luxembourgeois precedents[727] have been directly incorporated into Art. 2054 III Cc.[728] However, in other areas of *custodia* liability separate solutions have been sought.[729] Consider, for example, the case involving the explosion of over-pressurized bottles. The attempt by the French courts to render the producer liable by employing (at least temporarily) the concept of the *garde de la structure*[730] has not been paralleled by the *Corte di Cassazione*. However, it does not follow that such cases can be dealt with only using liability for fault (as under Belgian common law).[731] Instead of applying Art. 2051 Cc, liability is based on Art. 2050 Cc (liability for dangerous activities)[732] which, by resembling both a subsidiary and a general provision, threatens to dominate the entire system of strict liability.[733] Finally, we come to the conceptually difficult task of determining the character of liability under Art. 2051 Cc. To the impartial onlooker, as in the official commentary,[734] it appears to be *responsabilità oggettiva* (strict liability), since liability can only be escaped if a *caso fortuito*[735] is proved. However, the judiciary insists that Art. 2051 Cc concerns liability based on irrebuttably presumed fault,[736] predominantly because of its effects on Art. 2055 II Cc,[737] according to which only joint and several tortfeasors who are liable for *colpa* are liable to each other. The courts therefore aim (as with Art. 2050 Cc)[738] to prevent such joint and several tortfeasors from escaping liability where they are liable only for *custodia* (or for a dangerous activity).[739] *Custodia* liability is

---

[727] See fns. 654, 663 above.

[728] This provision reads: 'The owner of a car, or its keeper, or purchaser not yet in receipt of title, and the driver are liable as joint tortfeasors unless the owner proves that the car was used without his consent.'   [729] See Cass. 18 Apr. 1992, *Foro.it.* 1993, I, 1186.

[730] See no. 114 above.

[731] See fn. 684 above. See no. 393 below on the EC Product Liability Directive.

[732] See Cass. 9 May 1969, n. 1595, *Resp.Civ.ePrev.* 1970, p. 270. See also v. Bar (-Busnelli), *DeliktsR in Europa, Italien*, p. 30.   [733] See nos. 126 ff. below.

[734] RR no. 264 (in Pandolfelli *et al.*, *Codice civile*, p. 685). Cendon (-Ziviz) vol. iv, Art. 2051 nn. 1.1, 1.2, pp. 2105–2106. Heldrich, *Allgemeine Rechtsgrundsätze*, p. 78, goes so far as to refer to 'strict liability'.

[735] Trib. Verona 8 Jan. 1992, *Foro.pad.* 1993, I, 127 (note de Micheli) considered the builder of a pedestrian bridge to be its keeper, thus rendering him liable for an object 'coming from the bridge' which hit a passer-by. The defendant had to prove the course of events which resulted in the damage; furthermore, he should have constructed appropriate safety measures to protect innocent passers-by from falling stones.

[736] Art. 2051 Cc concerns *una presunzione iuris tantum et de iure di colpa a carico del custode*: Cass. 21 July 1962, n. 1991, *Resp.Civ. e Prev.* 1963, p. 65; Cass. 23 Jan. 1976, n. 221, *Rep.Foro.it.* 1976, no. 141, p. 2594, and elsewhere.   [737] See nos. 51, 53 above.

[738] See Ziviz in Cendon (ed.), *Responsabilità civile*, pp. 543, 545.

[739] See Cass. 22 May 1982, n. 3134, *Foro.it.* 1982, I, 2857; and Perlingieri (-Flamini), *Codice civile*, vol. iv (2), 2nd edn., Art. 2055 n. 2, p. 1932. Cass. 23 Apr. 1981, n. 2431, *Foro.it.Mass.* 1981, no. 2431.

not intended to operate 'exclusively in the interest' (Art. 1298 I Cc)[740] of those liable under Art. 2043 Cc.

121   By introducing liability for damage caused by corporal things into subsection I (*responsabilidade por factos ilícitos*) *Secção V* (*responsabilidade civil*, Arts. 483 ff. Port. Cc) of the relevant chapter of the *Código civil*,[741] rather than into subsection II (*responsabilidade pelo risco*, Arts. 499 ff. Cc) the Portuguese legislator from the outset presented Art. 493 I Cc[742] as a special example of liability for fault. Unlike Arts. 2051 Ital. Cc and 1384 I French Cc, which inspired it,[743] Art. 493 I Portuguese Cc permits escape from liability where coincidence or absence of fault has been established. Its aim was not to create strict *gardien* or *custodia* liability, but to provide only for presumed but rebuttable fault.[744] With this judicious provision the Portuguese legislator closed the gap between general liability for failure to supervise under Art. 493 I Cc and special provisions in the field of liability for damage caused by things, also based on breach of the general duty of care. If one compares, for instance, Art. 493 I Cc with liability for defective premises under Art. 492 Cc, it becomes apparent that the defences against liability are the same in both cases. Furthermore, the Portuguese legislator also managed to avoid a mistake, common in older codes, which only judiciary can rectify:[745] that is, the legislator did not differentiate between liability for buildings or other structures on one hand,[746] and liability for (e.g.) trees and unsafe paths on the other. If a dead tree is not removed, its owner is liable under Art. 493 I Cc, and not under Art. 492 Cc (liability for buildings), although the consequences are the same.[747] So the need to draw analogies is removed: anything which slips through the net of the special provisions is caught

---

[740] This provision states that, as between joint tortfeasors, their shares of a joint liability are equal, unless the liability arose in circumstances benefiting one of the tortfeasors exclusively.

[741] On the place of the law of delict in the structure of the Portuguese Cc see also no. 10 and fn. 2 above.

[742] Arts. 493 I, II read as follows: '(1) A person who has a movable or immovable thing under his control (*em seu poder*) and whose duty it is to control it, and equally a person under a duty to control animals, is liable for damage caused by the things or the animals, unless he can prove that he was not at fault or that the damage would have occurred notwithstanding his fault.

(2) A person injuring another while pursuing a dangerous activity, or because he was using dangerous equipment, must compensate the other, unless he can prove that he took necessary precautions to prevent such damage.'

[743] Vaz Serra, *BolMinJust* 85 (1959) p. 361.

[744] See e.g. Pires de Lima/Antunes Varela, *Cc anotado*, vol. i, 4th edn., Art. 493 n. 1.

[745] See no. 104 above. However, for Spanish law see Art. 1908 no. 3 Cc.

[746] §§ 1319 ABGB, 836 BGB, Art. 925 Greek Cc, Art. 2053 Ital. Cc, and Art. 492 Port. Cc all use exactly equivalent wording.

[747] RC 30 May 1989, *CJ* XIV (1989–3) p. 74. See also STA 29 June 1972, *BolMinJust* 220 (1972) p. 197: local authority liable for an unmarked ditch in its town.

by Art. 493 I Cc (liability for things). Even Art 492 Cc is simply an example of the general rule inherent in Art. 493 I Cc.

Art. 493 I Cc thus serves two functions. First, it tightens liability for **122** fault under Art. 483 Cc (which remains applicable in cases where fault has been proven[748]) and secondly, it provides an additional home for liability for failure to act,[749] which has been gravely neglected under Arts. 483, 486 Cc. Liability under Art. 493 I Portuguese Cc does not require the violation of a pre-existing (statutory or contractual) duty to supervise. Such duties are imposed by the provision itself, under which they can be developed. Under Art. 493 I Cc a builder is liable if a plank falls from scaffolding;[750] the owner or occupier of a building with a 'duty of supervision' is liable for accidents involving the lifts;[751] and a gas supplier is liable for damage caused by exploding gas bottles.[752] Finally, under Art. 493 I Cc, if a house is built with the help of a builder, the duty to ensure that the adjacent building sustains no damage rests with the home owner.[753] In conclusion, viewed from the perspective of comparative law, the Portuguese duty to supervise can be seen as bridging two systems. Although influenced by Italian and French law, a close relationship with the German general duties of care is equally apparent. German law shares two features with Portuguese liability for damage caused by things (liability for persons is dealt with in a similarly broad fashion in Art. 491 Cc[754]). Both are 'back-up' provisions, and both establish extracontractual duties to act, which also are not specific delictual duties.[755]

That liability for omissions is therefore often stricter than liability for **123** actions is a curious phenomenon. Be that as it may, Art. 493 I Cc and the German duties of care[756] share a further purpose: both bridge the gap between fault-based and strict liability. Strict liability occupies Arts. 499 ff. Portuguese Cc. Art. 502 Cc deals with damage caused by animals and Art. 503 with damage caused by vehicles. Liability for animals is thus covered by two provisions (the other being Art. 493 Cc, see above): a person keeping or using animals for his own purposes, whether for farming or domestic reasons, is subject to stricter liability than a person whose duty to supervise arises only from contract,[757] for example a farmer paid to provide pasture for another's cattle, which damage a third party.[758] However, motor vehicles and other *veículos de circulação terrestre*

---

[748] STJ 5 June 1985, *BolMinJust* 348 (1985) p. 397.   [749] See no. 22 above.
[750] STJ 10 Jan. 1975, *BolMinJust* 243 (1975) p. 240.
[751] RC 27 June 1989, *CJ* XIV (1989–3) p. 89; STJ 17 Feb. 1977, *BolMinJust* 264 (1977) p. 166.
[752] RL 22 Oct. 1973, *BolMinJust* 230 (1973) p. 155.
[753] RP 30 Apr. 1981, *CJ* VI (1981–2) p. 128.   [754] See no. 136 below.
[755] See nos. 22, 104 above.   [756] v. Bar, *Verkehrspflichten*, pp. 102–111, 128–143.
[757] STJ 9 Mar. 1978, *BolMinJust* 275 (1978) p. 191.
[758] RE 24 Mar. 1983, *BolMinJust* 327 (1983) p. 710.

(which, unlike in Italy, include rail vehicles)[759] do not fall under Art. 493 I Cc. Here the only issue is whether someone who drives a motor vehicle on behalf of another would incur liability under Art. 493 II Cc (for dangerous activities) or under Art. 503 III Cc in conjunction with Art. 504 II Cc.[760] Although earlier judgments opted for the former,[761] the latter has since become the established practice of the courts.[762]

124 It remains to consider briefly Dutch law. Since its enforcement on 1 January 1992, the central provision has been Art. 6:173 I BW, according to which:

'the possessor of a movable thing which is known to constitute a special danger to persons or things if it does not meet the standards which, in the given circumstances, may be set for such a thing, is liable when this danger is realized, unless, pursuant to the preceding section, there would have been no liability even if the possessor knew of the danger at the time it arose.'

As in Belgium, France, Italy, and Luxembourg, Dutch law now also imposes strict[763] liability for damage caused by things. Animals, motor vehicles, ships, and aircraft, which are subject to a special regime, are excluded (Art. 6:173 III BW), thus avoiding problematic concurrent claims. The same can be said of liability for buildings and other structures (Art. 6:174 BW), excluded from Art. 6:173 I BW by its restriction to 'movable things'. The only other link with the traditional provisions of quasi-delict is made by Art. 6:181 BW, which imposes strict liability on the commercial user of property. Finally, Art. 173 II BW was introduced to distinguish liability for commercial property from product liability.

---

[759] STJ 19 June 1979, *BolMinJust* 288 (1979) p. 378.

[760] Art. 503 III Port. Cc: 'A person driving a vehicle for the purposes of another is liable for the damage he causes, unless he can prove that he was not at fault; however, if he is not driving the vehicle in his capacity as an employee he is liable under the provisions of subsection I', i.e. independent of fault.

[761] See esp. STJ 22 July 1975, *BolMinJust* 249 (1975) p. 480 (*acórdão*); STJ 3 Feb. 1976, *BolMinJust* 254 (1976) p. 180; STJ 4 May 1976, *BolMinJust* 257 (1976) p. 121; STJ 25 Jan. 1978, *BolMinJust* 273 (1978) p. 260; and RP 17 May 1978, *BolMinJust* 279 (1978) p. 269 (headnote only).

[762] This approach was first taken in RP 7 June 1978, *BolMinJust* 279 (1978) p. 269 (headnote 1: '*O disposto no artigo 493° do Código Civil não é aplicável à responsabilidade civil por danos causados por veículos automóveis*'). There had already been signs of such a change in RP 4 Apr. 1978, *BolMinJust* 278 (1978) p. 306, which has since become the established practice of the courts: STJ 17 Oct. 1978, *BolMinJust* 280 (1978) p. 266; STJ 21 Nov. 1979, *BolMinJust* 291 (1979) p. 285; STJ 6 Jan. 1987, *BolMinJust* 363 (1987) p. 488. For an overview of the development, see Martins de Almeida, *Manual de Acidentes*, 3rd edn., pp. 244 ff. For German commentary: v. Bar (-Sinde Monteiro/Moura Ramos/Hörster), *DeliktsR in Europa, Portugal*, p. 17. However, due to the similarities between Arts. 493 II and 503 III Cc, the new practice prejudices those transported free of charge: no. 128 and fn. 795 below.

[763] *Parlementaire Geschiedenis*, vol. vi, p. 743.

The provisions on product liability are found in Arts. 6:185 ff. BW, and are based on the relevant EU Directive. They generally take precedence over liability under Art. 6:173 I BW (the wording of which links it to Art. 7:17 II BW).[764] In cases where liability cannot be based on Arts. 6:185 ff. BW, the producer or occupier is also not liable for things.[765] However, in two exceptional cases the possessor is liable under Art. 6:173 I BW. First, if the producer can prove that the goods were free of defects when he brought them onto the market; and secondly, if product liability cannot be relied upon because only minor damage to personal property was caused.[766]

The Dutch BW demonstrates how much easier it is for the legislator **125** than for the courts to avoid internal contradictions in a liability system.[767] Moreover, what we have seen are essentially variations on one position, demonstrating how closely European liability laws are tied to one another. The legal system of any European nation can now only be properly understood in a European context. The *gardien* of French law and the *custode* of Italian law become the Dutch *bezitter* in Art. 6:173 I BW, and Art. 3:107 I BW defines possession (*bezit*) as '*het houden van een goed voor zichzelf*'. However, unlike the *Code civil* and the *Codice civile*, Art. 6:173 I BW only covers movable things (*roerende zaak*, Art. 3:3 II in conjunction with Art. 3:2 BW). So liability for damage caused by trees, which are immovable but not *opstal* under Art. 6:174 BW, can only arise from Art. 6:162 BW.[768] Furthermore, under Dutch law the movable object causing the damage must also possess a *gebrek*: a defect. Unlike Belgian law, which also demands a *vice de la chose*,[769] Dutch law considers an unguarded loaded shotgun or plugged-in razor to be defective.[770] However, the object must display a *bijzonder gevaar* (special danger): a person causing a bicycle accident (for which there are no special strict liability provisions) through brake or light failure is liable under Art. 6:173 I BW; and a cyclist who violates

---

[764] See only *T&C* (-Lankhorst), Art. 173, n. 6.

[765] *Parlementaire Geschiedenis*, vol. vi (Inv.) p. 1376.

[766] Lankhorst loc. cit. fn. 764 n. 7; Klaassen, *Risico-aansprakelijkheid*, p. 100.

[767] Nonetheless, it was the Dutch judiciary which laid the foundations for the Parliament on liability for things by tightening the duties of care: e.g. HR 5 Nov. 1965, *NedJur* 1966 no. 136, p. 225; HR 27 May 1988, *NedJur* 1989, no. 29, p. 83; HR 8 Jan 1982, *NedJur* 1982, no. 614, p. 2130; HR 13 Nov. 1987, *NedJur* 1988, no. 139, p. 583; and HR 14 Apr. 1989, *NedJur* 1990, no. 712, p. 2909; HR 30 June 1989, *NedJur* 1990, no. 652, p. 2596 (*Halcion* case). On the last see Bloembergen (-Oldenhuis), *Onrechtmatige daad*, vol. i, Art. 173 BW, n. 1.

[768] Oldenhuis loc. cit. nn. 26, 54; *Parlementaire Geschiedenis*, vol. vi (Inv.) p. 1373. However, no-fault liability remains a possibility if it is in accordance with 'the generally accepted view' under Art. 6: 162 BW: Klaassen loc. cit. (fn. 766) p. 94.

[769] See nos. 113–114.

[770] *T&C* (-Lankhorst), Art. 173 n. 4; *Parlementaire Geschiedenis*, vol. vi, p. 747.

traffic law is liable under Art. 6:162 BW.[771] Dutch law is also unique in defining the term *bijzonder gevaar* using the terminology of EU product liability law.[772] Similarly, the precondition in Art. 173 I BW that the special danger presented by the movable thing must have been known was also modelled on the Product Liability Directive. However, the danger need not have been known by the possessor himself, only generally recognized in his profession or circumstances.[773]

(2) Liability for Things and for Dangerous Activities

126 According to Art. 6:162 III, 2nd alt. BW, an unlawful act can be attributed to its author even where he was not at fault, if it *in het verkeer geldende opvattingen voor zijn rekening komt* (strict liability if this is in accordance with the generally accepted view). While it is not certain whether this will ever become a 'general clause behind a general clause',[774] this is already the case in Italy and Portugal. Only these two have imposed general liability for things, together with equally broad liability for dangerous activities (Arts. 2050 Ital. Cc, 493 II Port. Cc), Portugal having all the features of a subsidiary and general clause, standing behind the specific provisions covering quasi-delict and *custodia* liability.

127 Although according to the wording of these two nearly identical texts[775] fault is merely rebuttably presumed in both Italy[776] and Portugal,[777] the provisions resemble the German concept of strict liability in many ways.[778] The differences of terminology are of little practical relevance. German strict liability incorporates a number of provisions employing

---

[771] Bloembergen (Oldenhuis), *Onrechtmatige daad*, vol. i, Art. 173, n. 5; *Parlementaire Geschiedenis*, vol. vi (Inv.) p. 1385.

[772] Under Art. 6: 173 I BW a thing poses a special hazard 'if it does not meet the standards which, in the given circumstances, may be set for such a thing'. This largely follows the definition of the term 'fault' under Art. 6 I EU Directive on Product Liability (see no. 393 below).

[773] Bloembergen (-Oldenhuis), *Onrechtmatige daad*, vol. i, Art. 173, n. 36; and *Parlementaire Geschiedenis*, vol. vi, p. 743, which was intended to permit the exclusion of liability in cases of development risks.

[774] Currently this development seems restricted by questions concerning state liability, and liability for damages awarded and received at first instance in judgments subsequently overturned on appeal: Hartkamp, *Judicial Discretion*, p. 11.

[775] Art. 2050 Ital. Cc served Vaz Serra (*BolMinJust* 85 [1959] pp. 361, 375–380) as a model for his first draft of this provision. This derivation from Italian law results in Portuguese courts often relying on the Italian model when interpreting Art. 493 II Cc: see esp. STJ 21 Nov. 1979, *BolMinJust* 291 (1979) pp. 285, 287–289.

[776] See Ziviz in Cendon (ed.), *Responsabilità civile*, pp. 545, 556, 575; and Comporti, *Esposizione al pericolo*, p. 268, who represent the view of the majority of authors.

[777] No. 121 above.

[778] See Schlüchter, *Haftung für gefährliche Tätigkeit*, pp. 116–122; Will, *Quellen erhöhter Gefahr*, pp. 150–195.

similarly worded (and interpreted)[779] exclusions of liability,[780] rendering it no different from liability for 'dangerous activities', albeit covered, not by a single general clause, but by a number of specific
provisions.[781] Yet German law imposes no additional (strict or stricter
form of) liability for things, just as most countries which have developed independent strict liability for movable and immovable goods
have no additional strict liability for dangerous activities at their disposal. By and large European legislators agree, with good reason, that
the presence of both concepts in one code is inadvisable. Apart from
certain martial arts, or where an employer chooses an employee unfit
for the job (neither of which, remarkably, falls within the term 'dangerous activity' of Art. 2050 Ital. Cc)[782] there are very few situations in
which the mere act of a person, involving no physical thing, is considered dangerous. Whether a skier is liable as the *gardien* of his skis[783]
or because he is pursuing a dangerous activity[784] is unimportant: it
depends merely upon which end of the chain of causation one considers. The situation is much the same where one legal system imposes
gardien liability for stored goods which explode or ignite,[785] while

---

[779] In German courts an event causing damage is only 'inevitable' under § 7 II StVG (fn.
780 below) if it could not have been avoided. (BGH 19 Dec. 1967, *VersR* 1968 p. 356). In Italy
a similarly high threshold has to be crossed to meet the preconditions for exclusion of
liability under Art. 2050 Cc ('*adottato tutte le mesure idonee a evitare il danno*'). Although the
Italian wording is not as wide as the German (Perlingieri [-Maglione], *Codice civile*, vol. iv
[2], 2nd edn., Art. 2050, no. 8), time and again only an Act of God has been permitted as a
defence against liability under Art. 2050 Cc (see fn. 798 below). Furthermore, it has always
been maintained that 'the margin for facts constituting an Act of God is very narrow': e.g.
Cass. 13 May 1982, n. 182, *Giust.civ.Mass.* 1982 no. 182, p. 66; Giur.sist. Bigiavi (-Franzoni)
vol. ii, 2, p. 974. In Portugal too the courts demand 'ideal precautions' (STJ 4 Oct. 1984,
BolMinJust 340 [1984] p. 370), with the result that the exclusion of liability is also only
granted in cases where the preconditions of § 7 II German StVG would have been met: RP
28 Jan. 1988 *CJ* XIII (1988–1) p. 202 (building of a dam); RP 21 Apr. 1988 *CJ* XIII (1988–2) p.
217 (storing of flammmable goods in a quarry); and RL 6 Apr. 1989, *CJ* XIV (1989–2) p. 119
(transportation of drinking water in pipes).
[780] Compare the provisions referred to in no. 126 above with, e.g., the wording of § 7 II
German Road Traffic Law (StVG): the keeper is not liable 'if . . . the driver of the vehicle has
taken all possible precautions in the circumstances of the case'.
[781] A case in point is liability for pharmaceutical products. In Germany this is subject to a
special provision, § 84 AMG. In Italy the production of drugs is considered a dangerous
activity: App. Rome 17 Oct. 1990, *Giur.it.* 1993, I, 2, 816; Cass. 27 July 1991, n. 8395, *Giur.it.*
1992, I, 1, 1332.
[782] On boxing see e.g. Cendon (-Gaudino), Art. 2043 n. 33.2 (p. 2030) incl. further
references; if the regulations are complied with, liability under Art. 2043 Cc is also
excluded.
[783] See e.g. Chambéry 19 Oct. 1954, *JCP* 1954, II, 8408 (note Esmein); Toulouse 14 Mar.
1958, *JCP* 1961, II, 11942*bis* (Colombini); and Grenoble 8 June 1966, *JCP* 1967, II, 14928. For
further material on the liability of skiers under Art. 1384 I Cc see Stahlberg, *Gefährdungshaftung für gefährliche Tätigkeiten*, pp. 64–72.
[784] Ap. Bologna 26 Feb. 1972, *Giur.it.* 1973, I, 2, 964.
[785] E.g. Cass.civ. 16 Nov. 1920, *DP* 1920, 1, 169; Cour 4 Feb. 1969, *Pas. luxemb.* 21 (1969–
71) p. 123.

another focuses on the storage itself,[786] or the transport,[787] and deems that to be a dangerous activity. Similarly, 'the taking of X-rays',[788] 'experimenting with electricity in the course of a lesson',[789] and 'driving a coal powered locomotive in a wooded area'[790] could be seen either as dangerous activities or as situations in which the objects causing the damage found *gardien* liability. Whichever of these approaches is chosen the result is the same. Yet despite the practical irrelevance of whether, for example, liability is linked to the *garde* of a hunting gun[791] or to the firing of it,[792] this remains an issue in the courts of many countries. Consider damage caused by the digging of a hole. Should this incur liability by virtue of the dangerous thing (the hole) or the dangerous activity (the digging)?[793]

128   To sum up, scepticism about a single system combining strict *custodia* liability and liability for dangerous activities seems appropriate, not only in view of national legal disputes but also given the gradual assimilation of the various European legal systems in the field of strict liability. On a national level the existence of two general clauses in this area[794] produces difficult problems: first in distinguishing between them, and secondly regarding the special provisions governing liability for animals, buildings, and motor vehicles. For the latter, Portuguese law demonstrates how difficult it is, albeit of what little conse-

---

[786] STJ 24 Mar. 1977, *BolMinJust* 265 (1977) p. 233 (possession of a building in which flammable goods are stored constitutes a dangerous activity); Trib. Firenze 3 Jan. 1952, *Resp.Civ. e Prev.* 1952 p. 365 (explosion of ammunition left on military land).

[787] RL 6 Apr. 1985, *CJ* XIV (1989–2) p. 119 (transport of water in pipelines); RL 7 Mar. 1980, *CJ* V (1980–2) p. 183 (transport of cotton, danger of spontaneous combustion); Cass. 1 June 1968, n. 1647, *Foro.it.* 1968, I, 1760 ('transportation' of electricity); Collegio Arbitrale 10 Aug. 1984, *Rep.gen.* 1986 no. 81, col. 3595 (transportation of flammable goods).

[788] Pires de Lima/Antunes Varela, *Cc anotado*, vol. i, 4th edn., Art. 493 n. 2.

[789] Schlüchter, *Haftung für gefährliche Tätigkeit*, p. 132.

[790] STJ 27 Mar. 1979, *BolMinJust* 285 (1979) p. 304. Cf. Cass.civ. 11 Feb. 1954, Bull.civ. 1954, II, 55.

[791] Cass.civ. 15 Dec. 1980, *D.* 1981 *Jur.* 455 (note Poisson-Drocourt); Cass.civ. 7 Nov. 1988, Bull.civ. 1988, II, 214 (both dealing with the additional problem of *garde collective*).

[792] Cass. 13 Apr. 1963, n. 937, *Giust.civ.Mass.* 1963, no. 937, p. 440; Cass. 23 Dec. 1968, n. 4072, *Giur.it.* 1969, I, 1, 2185.

[793] Liability under 2050 Cc (dangerous activities): Cass. 24 July 1965, n. 1737; *Foro.it.* 1966, I, 557; Cass. 8 Oct. 1970, n. 1895; *Foro.it.* 1970, I, 3058. Further citations at Will, *Quellen erhöhter Gefahr*, pp. 168–169. Liability under Art. 2051 Cc (*custodia* liability): Trib. Genoa 1 July 1971, *Giur.mer.* 1972, I, 122 (unavailable to this author; cited here according to Schlüchter, *Haftung für gefährliche Tätigkeit*, p. 139, fn. 309); and App. Turin 9 Feb. 1985, *Rep.gen.* 1985 no. 88, col. 3459 ('*L'attività di escavazione . . . costituisce esercizio di attività pericolose ai sensi dell'art. 2050 cc*').

[794] Italy suffers the additional problem of having also to distinguish these 2 forms of liability from liability for fault in the form of yet another general clause: Cass. 21 Dec. 1993, n. 13530, *Resp.Civ. e Prev.* 1993 p. 821, concerning a large, slow-moving road-building vehicle. Art. 2043 and not Art. 2050 was applied when a wall, already in poor condition, collapsed due to vibrations caused by the vehicle.

quence,[795] to clarify the position of special provisions in relation to the general clause on liability for dangerous activities (Arts. 503 III, 493 II Port. Cc).[796] If these special provisions are to have any real meaning they must be accorded precedence in their fields.[797] In view of the unproductive conflicts between the general clauses themselves, it should be noted that even the reasons for excluding liability are identical in the two provisions,[798] rendering the disputes redundant even in this respect. It is irrelevant whether an electrically powered garage door which injures a person is an example of a *proprio dinamismo*,[799] or whether the operation of the door is a dangerous activity in line with the Italian Court of Cassation definition, according to which such activities not only come under Art. 2050 Cc as expressly deemed dangerous by the statute,[800] but *'anche tutte quelle altre che, pur non essendo specificate, abbiano una pericolosità intrinseca o relativa ai mezzi di lavoro impiegati'*.[801]

[795] In the late 1970s a major stir was caused by the question of whether, in cases where liability did not arise under Art. 503 III Cc (for presumed fault of the driver), Art. 493 II Cc could be relied upon. (See also no. 123 above). However, this was of practical relevance only for Art. 504 II Cc, according to which, in cases of transport without charge, the driver is only liable 'under the general provisions for fault-based damage', for it had to be decided whether Art. 493 II Cc was such a 'general provision'. There is no other visible difference between Arts. 503 III and 493 II Cc. See also Buján, *VersR* 1978, p. 307.

[796] See fns. 761, 762. As for Italian law, Schlüchter, *Haftung für gefährliche Tätigkeit*, p. 135, even seems to view Art. 2054 as a special case of Art. 2051 Cc, a view not shared by this author.

[797] See fns. 709, 761, 762 above. On the relationship between the above-mentioned special provisions and Art. 509 Port. Cc (liability for electrical cables) see RC 15 Jan. 1991, *CJ* XVI (1991–5) p. 47. Yet in Italy, which has no similar special provision, such damage is covered by Art. 2050 Cc, for *'la produzione di energia elettrica costituisce attività pericolosa ai sensi dell'art. 2050 cc'*: Trib. Messina 27 Sep. 1983, *Riv.Dir.Com.* 1984, II, 215 (note Viale).

[798] Although the Portuguese and Italian Parliaments have not worded them identically, this has no practical effect. Where Art. 2051 Cc demands a *caso fortuito* (coincidence), Art. 2050 Cc requires proof that defendant has adopted *tutte le misure idonee a evitare il danno*. This is nothing other than a definition of the *caso fortuito*. See Giur.sist. Bigiavi (-Franzoni) vol. ii, 2, p. 475; Bernardini, *Riv.trim.dir.proc.civ.* 1967, pp. 1184 ff. For 'all precautions' must have been taken to avoid the damage. Thus each case is looked at with hindsight (Cass. 21 Nov. 1984, n. 5960, Gentile/Guerreri/Guerreri, *La responsabilità, voce Responsabilità civile*, 14, col. 3601) so that the courts habitually conclude that the very occurrence of the damage establishes a presumption that all possible precautions had not been taken (Trib. Savona, 20 Dec. 1965, *Arch.resp.civ.* 1967 p. 144). Furthermore, the defendant must prove compliance with these precautions in a 'concrete' and 'positive' manner, Cass. 29 Apr. 1991, n. 4710, *Rep.gen.* 1991, no. 66, col. 3442. On the term 'Act of God' (literally 'coincidence') see the references in Franzoni loc. cit., p. 480.

[799] As in Cass. 24 Feb. 1983, n. 1425, *Resp.Civ. e Prev.* 1983, p. 774.

[800] This concerns chiefly Arts. 46 and 58 'Public Safety Act' (*Legge di Pubblica Sicurezza*, RD 18 June 1931, n. 773, *Gaz.Uff.* n. 146 [1056 *in suppl.*] of 26 June 1931) and Arts. 81 ff. of the relevant *Regolamento* (RD 6 May 1940 [*in suppl.*]). Cass. 8 July 1955, n. 2136, *Resp.Civ. e Prev.* 1956 p. 47; Cass. 8 Apr. 1978, n. 1629, *Resp.Civ. e Prev.* 1978, p. 856.

[801] Fn. 800 above. Cass. 10 Nov. 1971, n. 3213, *Giust.civ.Mass.* 1971, no. 3213, p. 1726; Cass. 29 May 1989, n. 2584, *Giur.it.* 1990, I, 1, 234; Cass. 27 July 1990, n. 7571, *Arch.civ.* 1991, p. 46. For further references see Giur.sist. Bigiavi (-Franzoni) vol. ii, 2, p. 453.

129   From the European viewpoint the dual systems of Italy and Portugal are particularly interesting: they are best interpreted as an experiment in reconciling and harmonizing German strict liability and French *gardien* liability. Unfortunately, however, that experiment was not completely successful. Distinctly reminiscent of the German system are the attempts of both countries to use the indistinct difference between act and failure to act, in order to differentiate between *custodia* liability and liability for carrying out an activity.[802] Under German law, strict liability is imposed only for positive acts, which is why it is only rarely applicable in the field of liability for hazards arising from premises. Although the situation is theoretically[803]—and sometimes even practically[804]—different in Italy, all analyses of Italian court rulings confirm that Art. 2050 Cc is relied on for the majority of accidents involving movable objects. The conclusions to be drawn are therefore, first, that Portugal and Italy employ liability for dangerous activities more frequently than *custodia* liability,[805] and secondly, that German strict liability needs to be expanded.

III. THE LAW OF LIABILITY FOR THIRD PARTIES UNDER SPECIAL PROVISIONS OF THE CODIFICATIONS

Bibliography: Agallopoulou-Zervogianni, 'Astiki evthini goneon apo praxeis ton anilikon paidion tous', in: *FS für Michaelides-Nouaros*, vol. A (Athens 1987) pp. 31–42; Albilt, *Haften Eltern für ihre Kinder? Zur Haftung von Aufsichtspersonen Minderjähriger* (Pfaffenweiler 1987; also diss. Freiburg/Br. 1985); Archaniotakis, *I astiki evthini tou nomikou prosopou idiotikou dikaiou* (Salonica 1989); Asser (-van der Grinten), *Vertegenwoordiging en rechtspersoon*, vol. i: *De Vertegenwoordiging* (7th edn. Zwolle 1990), vol. ii: *De rechtspersoon* (7th edn. Zwolle 1991); Balomenos, 'Anmerkung zu (frz.) Cass.civ. 12.10.1955', *NoB* 7 (1958) pp. 157–159; v. Bar, 'Zur Struktur der Deliktshaftung von juristischen Personen, ihren Organen und ihren Verrichtungsgehilfen', in: *FS Kitagawa* (Berlin 1992)

---

[802] Ziviz in Cendon (ed.), *Responsabilità civile*, p. 576 (a precondition for Art. 2050 is that a person's activity must manifest itself in the motion of a thing); Perlingieri (-Maglione), Art. 2051, no. 3 (in Art. 2051 the damage occurs '*direttamente da cose*', and in Art. 2050 through a '*momento dinamico dell'attività pericolosa*'); and Schlüchter, *Haftung für gefährliche Tätigkeit*, p. 135 (Art. 2051 sanctions the failure to act). See references in fns. 799, 800 above; App. Milan 18 Oct. 1968, *Resp.Civ. e Prev.* 1969 p. 381. For Portugal see no. 122 above.
[803] By its wording, Art. 2050 Cc is not restricted to immovables.
[804] See fns. 778, 793.
[805] See fns. 801, 802 above; see also e.g. Will, *Quellen erhöhter Gefahr*, pp. 151 ff.

pp. 279–295; id., 'Vertragliche Schadensersatzpflichten ohne Vertrag?', *JuS* 1982 pp. 637–645; id., 'Das "Trennungsprinzip" und die Geschichte des Wandels der Haftpflichtversicherung', *AcP* 181 (1982) pp. 289–327; Baums, 'Haftung für Verrichtungsgehilfen nach deutschem und schweizerischem Recht', in: *FS Lukes* (Cologne *et al.* 1989) pp. 623–638; Becher, *Griechenland: Handels- und Wirtschaftsrecht (Bundesstelle für Außenhandelsinformation)* (Cologne and Berlin 1993); Bonvicini, *La responsabilità civile per fatto altrui* (Milan 1976); Canaris, 'Geschäfts- und Verschuldensfähigkeit bei Haftung aus "culpa in contrahendo", Gefährdung und Aufopferung', *NJW* 1964 pp. 1987–1993; Carrasco Gómez, *Responsabilidad médica y psiquiátrica* (Madrid 1990); Dahlgrün, *Die Aufsichtspflicht der Eltern nach § 832 BGB*, (diss. Munich 1979); Dalcq, 'Les limites de la responsabilité du commettant pour abus de fonction de son préposé', *Rev.crit.jur.belge* 1992 pp. 228–248; Delvaux/Goerens, 'Rapport cadre sur la responsabilité civile de l'employeur privé du fait de son préposé', *Rev.jur.pol.Ind.Coop.* 27 (1973) pp. 549–562; Denck, *Der Schutz des Arbeitnehmers vor der Außenhaftung* (Heidelberg 1980); Desportes, 'Le nouveau régime de la responsabilité pénale des personnes morales', *Sem.Jur.*, Éd. E, 1993, I, 219 pp. 69–77; Dialinas, *Das Mitverschulden des Minderjährigen, seiner gesetzlichen Vertreter und Erfüllungsgehilfen im deutschen, französischen und griechischen Recht* (Munich 1982); Díaz Alabart, 'La responsabilidad por los actos ilícitos dañosos de los sometidos a patria potestad o tutela', *An.Der.Civ.* 40 (1987) pp. 795–894; id., 'Un apunte histórico para la determinación de la responsabilidad de los maestros en el artículo 1903 del Código Civil', in: Asociación de profesores de Derecho civil (ed.), *Centenario del Código civil*, vol. i (Madrid 1990) pp. 691–706; Dontenville, 'L'article 1384 alinéa 1 du Code civil: Source résurgente', in: *Rapport de la Cour de Cassation. Documentation française* (Paris 1991) pp. 65–94; Dreyer, 'Wie weit hat der Arbeitgeber für das Verschulden seiner Arbeiter zu haften?', *Verhandlungen des 17. DJT*, vol. i (Berlin 1884) pp. 46–124; Esser, 'Zur Anrechnungspflicht elterlichen Mitverschuldens bei Verkehrsunfällen deliktsunfähiger Kinder', *JZ* 1953 pp. 691–693; Fagnart, 'Les faits génrateurs de responsabilité. Aperçu des principales tendences actuelles', in: Dalcq (ed.), *Responsabilité et réparation des dommages* (Brussels 1983) pp. 9–84; Ferrand, 'Deliktische Haftung für Dritte in Frankreich', *ZEuP* 1993 pp. 132–140; Fosserau, 'Le principe de responsabilité de l'entrepreneur principal du fait de son sous-traitant', in: *Rapport de la Cour de Cassation 1991. Documentation française* (Paris 1991) pp. 161–175; Franzoni, *Colpa presunta e responsabilità del debitore* (Padua 1987); García Cantero, 'Exégesis comparativa del artículo 1902 del Código civil', in: Asociación de profesores de Derecho civil (ed.), *Centenario del Código civil*, vol. i (Madrid 1990) pp. 875–884; García Laraña, 'La responsabilidad civil ex delicto en el anteproyecto de Código penal de 1992', *La Ley* 1992 (3) pp. 1048–1053; Gasis, 'Peri tin ennian tou voithou ekpliroseos kai tou prostithentos', in: *Eranion pros Maridakin*, vol. ii (Athens 1963) pp. 227–284; id., *Genikai Archai tou Astikou Dikaiou (Allgemeine Grundlagen des bürgerlichen Rechts)*, vol. ii, 2nd book: *Ta Nomika Prosopa* (Legal Persons) (Athens 1974); Gaudino, 'La responsabilità dei padroni e committenti', in: Cendon (ed.), *Responsabilità civile* (Milan 1988) pp. 519–542; Gerlach, 'Die moderne Entwicklung der Privatrechtsordnung in Spanien', *ZVglRWiss* 85 (1986) pp. 247–323; Van Gerven, *Beginselen van Belgisch Privaatrecht I: Algemeen Deel* (Brussels 1987); Gómez Calle, *La responsabilidad civil de los padres* (Madrid 1992); Grillberger, *Österreichisches Sozialrecht* (Vienna and New York 1990); Hager, 'Das Mitverschulden von Hilfspersonen und gesetzlichen Vertretern des Geschädigten', *NJW* 1989 pp. 1640–1647; Hanau/Rolfs, 'Abschied von der gefahrgeneigten Arbeit', *NJW* 1994 pp. 1439–1442; Hofmanns, 'Minderjährigkeit und Halterhaftung', *NJW* 1964 pp. 228–234; Immenga, 'Aufsichtspflichtverletzung und Gleichberechtigung', *FamRZ* 1969 pp. 313–319; Karollus, 'Gleichbehandlung von Schädiger und Geschädigten bei der Zurechnung von Gehilfenverhalten', *ÖJZ* 1994 pp. 257–261; Klaassen, 'Aansprakelijkheid van kinderen voor hun ouders of voogd', *WPNR* 1988 no. 5891 pp. 593–597; id., *Risico-aansprakelijkheid* (Zwolle 1991; also diss. Nijmegen 1990); Kletecka, *Mitverschulden durch Gehilfenverhalten* (Vienna 1991); Koebel, 'Aufsichtspflicht der Eltern und Gleichberechtigung', *NJW* 1960 pp. 2227–2228; Konowalczyk/Sauer, 'Arbeitnehmerhaftung im internationalen Vergleich. Österreich, Schweiz, Bundesrepublik Deutschland', *RIW* 1995 pp. 383–388; Koziol/Frotz, 'Die schadensersatzrechtlichen Folgen der Verletzung von Aufsichtspflichten durch Lehrer', *RdS* 1979 pp. 97–102; Kruithof, 'Aansprakelijkheid voor andermans daad: kritische bedenkingen bij enkele ontwikkelingen', in: Vandenberghe (ed.), *Onrechtmatige daad*, pp. 19–57 (Antwerp 1979); Lepage, 'La responsabilité personelle civile et pénale des dirigeants d'entreprises en raison de dommages', *Dr.prat.com.int.* 1994 pp. 4–40; López Beltrán de Heredia, *La responsabilidad civil de los padres por los hechos de sus hijos* (Madrid 1988); van Maanen, 'Vicarious Liability in a European Civil Code', in: Hartkamp/Hesselink/Hondius/du Perron/Vranken (edd.), *Towards a European Civil Code* (Nijmegen *et al.* 1994) pp. 301–311; Magnus, *Drittmitverschulden im deutschen, englischen und französischen Recht. Zur Auslegung des § 254 Abs. 2 Satz 2 BGB* (Heidelberg 1974); Mammey, 'Zur Anrechnung des Aufsichtsverschuldens des gesetzlichen Vertreters als Mitverschulden des Kindes', *NJW* 1960 pp. 753–756; Maschio, 'Responsabilità ex art. 2048 c.c. e "grandi minori"', *Dir.fam.pers.* 1988, I, pp. 875–886; Mast, *Overzicht van het Belgisch*

Administratief Recht (Ghent 1992); Mastropaolo, 'Morte del minore, provocata da non imputabile, e risarcimento dei danni', *Giur.it.* 1984, I, 1,149–166; Meinertzhagen-Limpens, 'Subordination et conjugaison verticale en matière de responsabilité quasi-délictuelle', *Rev.crit.jur.belge* 1985 pp. 212–232; Michaelides-Nouaros, 'Evthini tou prostisantos gia tis paranomes praxis tou prostithentos (AK 922)', *EllDik* 29 (1988) pp. 1641–1651; Münchener Rückversicherungs-Gesellschaft (ed.), *Die Haftung des Arbeitgebers* (Munich 1993); Van Oevelen, 'De civielrechtelijke aansprakelijkheid van de werknemer in het raam van de uitvoering van de arbeidsovereenkomst', *RW* 1987–1988 pp. 1170–1205; Oldenhuis, *Onrechtmatige daad: aansprakelijkheid voor personen* (Deventer 1985; Monografieën Nieuw BW B-46); Peano, 'L'incompatibilité entre les qualités de gardien et de préposé', *D.* 1991 *Chron.* pp. 51–55; Pinto Borea, 'I doveri dei genitori verso i figli minori e la responsabilità ex art. 2048 Cc', *Dir.fam.pers.* 1992, II, pp. 364–402; Puill, 'Vers une réforme de la responsabilité des père et mère du fait de leurs enfants?', *D.* 1988 *Chron.* pp. 185–192; Rambach, *Die deliktische Haftung Minderjähriger und ihrer Eltern im französischen, belgischen und deutschen Deliktsrecht* (Antwerp and Apeldoorn 1995; Ius Commune, Deel 7); Ravarani, 'La responsabilité civile de l'état et des collectivités publiques', *Pas. luxemb.* 28 (1990–92) pp. 77–426; Rokas, 'Gehilfenhaftung in Griechenland', *KF* 1993 pp. 52–54; Rutten-Roos, *Jeugdigen in burgerrechtelijke relaties* (Deventer 1975); ead., 'Ouders, kinderen en wettelijke aansprakelijkheid', *WPNR* 1970 no. 5069 (pp. 101–106); Schaub, 'Die Haftungsbegrenzung des Arbeitnehmers', *WiB* 1994 pp. 227–230; van Schilfgaarde, *Van de BV en de NV* (9th edn. Arnhem 1992); M. J. Schmid, 'Die Aufsichtspflicht nach § 832 BGB', *VersR* 1982 pp. 822–825; Schmitz, *Die deliktische Haftung für Arbeitnehmer* (Berlin 1994); Schoonenberg, 'De aansprakelijkheid voor onrechtmatige gedragingen, verricht onder invloed van een geestelijke tekortkoming', *NJB* 1985 pp. 1081–1085; Schreiber, '"Kinder haften für ihre Eltern". Zum Mitverschulden des gesetzlichen Vertreters', *Jura* 1994 pp. 164–166; Signes Pascual, 'La responsabilidad de los educadores según el artículo 1903 del Código civil, tras su reforma por Ley de 7 de enero de 1991', *La Ley* 1992 (1) pp. 958–961; Spiliotopoulos, *Encheiridio Dioikitikou Dikaiou*, vol. i (5th edn. Athens and Komotini 1991); Steinbauer, 'Die Handlungsfähigkeit geistig Behinderter nach dem neuen Sachwalterrecht', *ÖJZ* 1985 pp. 385–393 (pt. 1) and pp. 427–432 (pt. 2); Tomandl, *Grundriß des österreichischen Sozialrechts* (3rd edn. Vienna 1985); Vandenberghe, 'De grondslag van contractuele en extra-contractuele aansprakelijkheid voor eigen daad', *TPR* 1984 pp. 127–154; Vaz Serra, 'Responsabilidade de pessoas obrigadas a vigilância', *BolMinJust* 85 (1959) pp. 381–444; Vermeiden, 'Aansprakelijkheid van het ziekenhuis voor beroepsfouten van de aan het ziekenhuis verbonden medici', *WPNR* 1969 nos. 5035 and 5036 (pp. 157–161 and 165–168); Vetter, *Geestelijke stoornis* (Deventer 1992; Monografieën Nieuw BW Bd. A 9); Baron van Wassenaer van Catwijck, *Eigen Schuld* (diss. Leiden 1971).

130 In every European code the law of quasi-delict incorporates, within liability for dangers caused by persons, the law governing parental liability (see nos. 131 ff. below) and the vicarious liability of principals for their servants (see no. 179 below). Some codes exclude pupils, students in secondary education, apprentices, and trainees from this latter category, and liability for any damage which they cause is then allocated to their teachers and instructors (see nos. 160 ff. below). Thus, from a European perspective, some overlap with other fields of law is inevitable. For example, liability for apprentices is often covered by standard employers' liability; and liability for schoolchildren's acts could fall under the law of delict, state liability law, or social security law. However, most problems in these 'fringe' areas chiefly concern delict. On one hand there is the problem of distinguishing between liability for others and for things.[806] On the other there is the need to distinguish between quasi-delict, liability for fault arising from national basic tort law provisions,[807] and that area where there is no duty of supervision and thus no liability. To give just one example: under Art. 6:171 Dutch BW, liability for sub-contractors (see nos. 200 f. below) is seen as a *risico-aansprakelijkheid* of the main contractor. Under other codes, however, he is only held liable for failure to supervise; subcontractors work independently and are thus not covered by employers' liability, the only form of vicarious liability which might have been applicable. The position is similar for handicapped persons, for those confined to institutions, and for prisoners (see nos. 166 f.)

The quasi-delictual causes of action in the field of vicarious liability are equally diverse. They are partly based on a (rebuttably or non-rebuttably) presumed failure of supervision, but liability may also be based on additional duties, and may even arise irrespective of any unlawful conduct, and thus of fault. As for the liability of legal entities for their executive bodies, however (see nos. 168 ff. below) it is unclear whether the law of quasi-delict as conventionally understood is relevant at all. There is a strongly held view that this matter falls under liability for personal fault, since it deals with the misconduct of a legal person, albeit acting through its executive body.

---

[806] See also nos. 7, 101, and fn. 604 above.
[807] For further discussion see nos. 103 ff. above.

1. LIABILITY FOR CHILDREN

a. Liability of Parents and Guardians

Although the family enjoys special constitutional protection throughout **131**
Europe,[808] all codes impose special liability on parents and those *in loco*
parentis, including adoptive parents and often guardians[809] (Art. 1384 IV,
VII French Cc; Arts. 1384 II, V Belgian and Lux. Cc; Art. 1903 II, VI Span.
Cc and Art. 20 Span. Cc; §§ 1309 ABGB, 832 BGB; Art. 923 Greek Cc;
Arts. 2047, 2048 Ital. Cc; Art. 491 Port. Cc; Art. 8:169 Dutch BW). So the
parental right to bring up a child entails a duty to compensate damage
caused to third parties by that child, albeit not an unlimited and general
duty: all European legal systems agree that the scope of parental liability
depends on the age of the child. Although this principle manifests itself
differently in the various countries, the basic concept has been retained.
This is that parental liability for young children should be more stringent
than for older minors.[810] The older children become, the more delictual
responsibility will be imposed on them personally, even before they
reach majority,[811] and their parents' liability decreases accordingly. After
the child reaches puberty, the fact that his parents are responsible for his

---

[808] See part 6 I, no. 591 below.

[809] Guardians have the same legal position as parents if their care of the child incorporates the duty to supervise, or if the ward is a member of the guardian's household. See §§ 832, 1800 BGB; Art. 6:169 BW; Art. 2048 I Ital. Cc; Art. 1903 II, III Span. Cc (for detail on the latter and, on the position under the old CP, see Paz-Ares/Díez-Picazo/Bercovitz/Salvador, *Código civil*, vol. ii, 2nd edn., p. 2011 [sub 5]; v. Bar [-Santdiumenge], *DeliktsR in Europa, Spanien* p. 33); and Art. 923 Greek Cc. However, the French Cc only speaks explicitly of the liability of 'father and mother', and as the *Cour de Cassation* applies this text to the letter (see Cass.civ. 15 Feb. 1956, *D.* 1956 *Jur.* 410 [note Blanc]; and Cass. 9 Nov. 1971, *D.* 1972 *Jur.* 75 [although the cases did not concern guardians, but supervisory staff] liability under Art. 1384 IV Cc does not, according to French law, include guardians. See Cass.crim. 28 July 1949, s. 1950.1.154; *Encyclopédie Dalloz* (-Bénac-Schmidt/Larroumet), *Rép.Dr.Civ.* vol. viii, 'Responsabilité du fait d'autrui', no. 172; and Flour/Aubert, *Obligations*, vol. ii, 5th edn., no. 194. The situation is the same in Belgium: Cornelis, *Buitencontractueel aansprakelijkheidsrecht*, p. 313 (no. 183); and André, *Responsabilités*, p. 152 (no. 102); Brussels 19 May 1983, *JT* 1983, p. 578.

[810] The current situation in Italy is consistent with this. Although for civilly responsible children liability for presumed failure to supervise is supplemented by liability for presumed failure to bring up a child (Art. 2048 Cc, see also no. 135 below) the duty of supervision still decreases as the child becomes older. (See e.g. Cass. 6 May 1986, n. 3031, *Giur.it.* 1986, I, 1, 1527; and App. Venice 8 Oct. 1986, *Dir.fam.pers.* 1988, II, 874). Moreover, when the youth becomes an apprentice or trainee, parental liability is often replaced by employers' liability: see e.g. Cass. 22 Apr. 1977, n. 1501, *Arch.civ.* 1977, p. 772; and Trib. Rome 28 May 1987, *Riv.giur.circ.trasp.* 1988, p. 635. However, from the point of view of current Spanish law, the general validity of the statement in the text above is somewhat problematic. See also nos. 65, 88 above and 134 below.

[811] A view rightly taken by BGH 19 Jan. 1993, *FamRZ* 1993 pp. 666, 667 (see fn. 539 above).

existence no longer suffices to establish their liability for his acts.[812] From then on only failure (albeit presumed) on the part of the parents in addition to the child's misconduct can lead to shared liability for damage to a third party.

(1) Strict Liability and Liability for Presumed and Proven Parental Misconduct

132 No code better demonstrates the different levels of parental liability than the Dutch BW. Its Art. 6:169 BW distinguishes between three age groups, and allocates for each of them a separate cause of action against the parents. Although the classification appears unrefined, it makes the Dutch provision the clearest of its kind. Parents are strictly liable for 'damage done to another by such conduct of a child aged below fourteen years as may be considered an act': this is true *risico-aansprakelijkheid* (strict liability).[813] Parents of 'a child between fourteen and sixteen years of age' are liable only for presumed fault, and are not liable if they can prove that 'one cannot reproach [them] for not preventing the conduct of the child': Art. 6:169 II BW.[814] The situation for sixteen- and seventeen-year olds is therefore clear: parental liability arises from Art. 6:162 BW, which demands proof of fault.[815] When the child reaches fourteen, the law no longer differentiates between acts and omissions.

133 One could perhaps criticize the BW for treating young children in the same way as employees, subcontractors, and agents (Art. 6:172 BW), as well as animals and dangerous objects. However, this outward appearance is misleading, apparently even to the Dutch themselves, who have not fully accepted their new parental liability.[816] One advantage of the

---

[812] TS 2 Mar. 1994, *RAJ* 1994, no. 2097, p. 2830 (parental liability for rape committed by 17-year-old son denied; no *culpa in vigilando*, nor did giving birth to him constitute a source of risk). Furthermore, TS 23 Sep. 1988, *La Ley* 1988 (4) p. 395, no. 9130 clearly states that parental liability under Art. 1903 Cc ends when the child reaches majority. In most countries this has never been in doubt. See e.g. Cass. 9 Nov. 1973, n. 2947, *Dir.fam.pers.* 1974, p. 59: girl became pregnant by her boyfriend after he unlawfully 'kidnapped' her with her consent. The man reached majority while living with the girl. As the child was conceived thereafter, the boy's parents were not liable. However, the position is different if the adult offspring is civilly incapable and lives with his parents: Cass. 1 June 1994, n. 5366, *Foro.it.* 1995, I, 1285, and Art. 120 I Span NCP.

[813] van Dunné, *Verbintenissenrecht*, vol. ii, 2nd edn., pp. 571–574; Bloembergen (-Oldenhuis), *Onrechtmatige daad*, vol. i, Art. 169 BW n. 1; *T&C* (-Lankhorst), 2nd edn., Art. 169 BW n. 1; Oldenhuis, *Onrechtmatige daad: aansprakelijkheid voor personen*, pp. 21–23.

[814] *Parlementaire Geschiedenis*, vol. vi, p. 680 observes that this should not be difficult, since parents cannot possibly prevent all acts by their children which could cause damage.

[815] Bloembergen (-Oldenhuis), *Onrechtmatige daad*, vol. i, Art. 169 BW, n. 57. See also Ktg. Haarlem, *VR* 1985 p. 117: it is a father's duty to ensure that his son, the owner of a moped, has third-party insurance.

[816] HR 22 Sep. 1995, *RvdW* 1995 no. 186: the father of a 13-year-old insisted, up to the Court of Cassation, that he should escape liability as he had not breached his duty of supervision.

Dutch solution is that, where fault is required, parental duties are realistic. At the same time, regarding the age group for which strict parental liability is imposed, its authors have managed to avoid the error, all too common in other codes, of demanding a level of parental care which ignores the reality of life, and which, from an educational point of view, may even be counterproductive. Furthermore, in the case of smaller children it is notable that whether the family wage-earner can exonerate himself by claiming that he was not at home at the relevant time, and was thus unable to exercise parental care, plays no role: both parents have parental custody and are therefore jointly and severally liable (Art. 1:251 III BW). Lastly, the protection afforded to minors by the new BW is extremely effective. Strict parental liability for children under age fifteen was introduced to shield them from equity-based (Art. 6:164 BW)[817] as well as all other forms of liability.[818] Hence they are unaffected if their parents omit to take out third-party liability insurance covering their risks.[819] Parents are expected (but under no obligation)[820] to insure themselves. Although it is true that in cases where uninsured parents are held personally liable the children's maintenance might be affected, that is no counter-argument: children whose parents are answerable with their own property for their own unlawful acts suffer the same fate. Yet the Dutch legislator has managed to prevent children from being burdened at maturity with the debts of their childhood.

Although only the Dutch BW, the most modern civil code, expressly **134** imposes strict liability on the parents of small children, both Spanish and Italian law can also be considered to operate on a no-fault basis.

The complicated situation regarding parental liability under Spanish law was discussed above.[821] Both Art. 20 CP (which remains in force until further notice) and Art. 1903 VI Cc base parental liability on presumed failure of supervision,[822] so parents must prove that they acted

---

[817] See nos. 63, 80 above.

[818] In this context a few remarks should be made concerning Art. 6:183 BW. According to its subsection I, the causes of action of strict liability under Arts. 6:169–181 BW also apply to children under 14. However, Art. 6:183 II BW contains an exception supplementing Art. 169 I BW (parental liability): see nos. 148, 149 below.

[819] On the serious consequences which a lack of third-party liability insurance can have for children see OLG Celle 26 May 1989, *VersR* 1989 p. 709.

[820] That parents must take out a third-party liability insurance against damage caused by their children was denied by HR 14 Feb. 1969, *NedJur* 1969 no. 189 p. 465. This decision is still relevant for parents with children who have completed their 14th year (van Dunné, *Verbintenissenrecht*, vol. ii, 2nd edn., pp. 574–575). Moreover, the Dutch legislator of the new BW had already decided not to connect parental liability with compulsory third-party insurance: *Parlementaire Geschiedenis*, vol. vi, pp. 600, 656; see also Bloembergen (-Oldenhuis), *Onrechtmatige daad*, vol. i, Art. 169 BW, n. 19; v. Bar (-Hondius/van Dam), *DeliktsR in Europa, Niederlande* p. 11.   [821] See nos. 65, 88.

[822] Unlike Art. 1903 VI Cc, a shifting of the burden of proof is not explicitly mentioned in Art. 20 CP, but is nonetheless manifest: Diéz-Picazo/Gullón, *Sistema*, vol. ii, 6th edn., p. 625.

lawfully. According to Art. 1903 VI Cc, they would then have to demonstrate that they showed the level of care expected of a *paterfamilias*. As to children who have not completed their sixteenth year,[823] the standard required is usually so strict that one cannot meaningfully speak of fault-based liability.[824] The *Tribunal Supremo* has meanwhile confirmed the generally accepted view that, irrespective of Art. 1903 VI Cc, liability under Art. 1903 II Cc is *'una responsabilidad por riesgo o cuasi objetiva'*,[825] i.e. effectively strict. Therefore parents must compensate for damage caused if their child uses another's bicycle or moped (even with his permission), ignores a stop sign, and causes an accident.[826] Neither do parents escape liability if they both have to go to work,[827] nor if they had vehemently forbidden their child to act in the fashion which caused the accident.[828] The demands made of guardians are similarly high.[829]

135   With regard to parental liability, Italian law distinguishes between responsibility for children incapable in civil law (Art. 2047 I Cc) and responsibility for children who already have the *capacità d'intendere o di volere* (Art. 2048 I Cc). However, neither provision has a fixed age limit. Which provision is to be applied is decided *caso per caso*: completion of the sixth year is only a rough indicator.[830] For Art. 2048 I Cc to apply, children must live with their parents; Art. 2047 I Cc applies where such parental influence is missing. Either Art. 2048 or Art. 2047 I Cc would probably establish liability for pain and suffering, although not certainly.[831] In either case parents have a good defence if they can prove

---

[823] Díaz Alabart, *An.Der.Civ.* 40 (1987) pp. 872, 849 claims she has found no Spanish decision in the period she has examined (from 1980) in which the parental duty to supervise was applied less strictly to older children so that parents actually escaped liability: however, TS 2 Mar. 1994 loc. cit. (fn. 812) is just such a ruling. TS 12 Feb. 1994, *RAJ* 1994, no. 773, p. 1010 does not contradict this case. The 17-year-old son of a policeman stole his father's gun while he was away, and injured a girl. The TS held the father liable. Although the relationship between Art. 20 CP and Art. 1903 Cc remains uncertain (see fn. 397 above) the result is nonetheless unambiguous: the gun should have been locked out of reach.

[824] Díaz Alabart loc. cit. and Gómez Calle, *Responsabilidad civil de los padres*, pp. 267–275; Cavanillas Múgica, *Transformación*, pp. 103–123; López Beltrán de Heredia, *Responsabilidad de los padres*, pp. 88–91; de Ángel Yágüez, *Responsabilidad civil*, 3rd edn., pp. 327, 335; and v. Bar (-Santdiumenge), *DeliktsR in Europa, Spanien* p. 32.

[825] TS 2 Jan. 1991, *RAJ* 1991 no. 304, pp. 333, 334 = *La Ley* 1991 (2) pp. 241, 242.

[826] TS 22 Jan. 1991 loc. cit.

[827] De Ángel Yágüez, *Responsabilidad civil*, 3rd edn., p. 337.

[828] TS 14 Apr. 1977, *RAJ* 1977, no. 1654, p. 1230.

[829] TS 30 Oct. 1956, *RAJ* 1956, no. 3427, p. 2352.

[830] See no. 64 above. On distinguishing between Arts. 2047 and 2048 Cc see Gentile/ Guerreri/Guerreri, *La responsabilità, voce responsabilità civile—incapaci*, printed in sec. 63 of the case reviews Cass. 17 June 1953, n. 1812 [5] (= *Giur.it.* 1953, I, 1, 837); Cass. 5 Mar. 1955, n. 646 [9]; Cass. 10 July 1958, n. 2485 [15]; and Cass. 10 Aug. 1964, n. 2291 [22]. That the judge when establishing civil capacity must take into account all circumstances of the individual case was confirmed in Cass. 28 Apr. 1975, n. 1642, *Giust.civ.Mass.* 1975 no. 1642 p. 746; and in Cass. 15 Jan. 1980, n. 369, *Giur.it.* 1980, I, 1, 1593.   [831] See fn. 387 above.

'that they could not have prevented the act'. Most legal authors[832] approve the established practice of the *Corte di Cassazione* in construing Arts. 2047 and 2048 Cc as a *'responsabilità diretta per fatto proprio'*, i.e. not as strict liability for others, but liability for personal failure on the part of the parents.[833] Yet the main practical effect of this qualification is peripheral, and concerns the right of recourse under Art. 2055 Cc,[834] and not causes of action. Under Art. 2047 I Cc parents must prove that they took all possible precautions to prevent the damaging act. They must show that they neither instigated a dangerous situation, nor tolerated a situation which made it either possible or easier for the *incapace* to commit a tort.[835] Only very rarely have parents been able to meet this burden of proof.[836] Their task is even harder under Art. 2048 I Cc, where the established practice of the courts is to base liability, not on presumed failure to supervise but on presumed failure to raise the child properly. Hence, parents must not only prove that appropriate supervision would not have prevented their child committing the tort, they must also satisfy the court that they had assiduously taught their child not to harm others.[837] The courts demand positive proof: *'la prova positiva di avere adempiuto gli obblighi educativi ricavabili dall'art. 2048 Cc.'*[838] The

---

[832] See e.g. Visintini, *Fatti illeciti*, vol. i pp. 491–508 (on Art. 2047) and pp. 509–529 (on Art. 2048); Giur.sist. Bigiavi (-Venchiarutti) vol. i, pp. 217–224; Giur.sist. Bigiavi (-Mantovani) vol. ii (1), pp. 3–34; de Martini, *Fatti produttivi di danno*, p. 291; and Galgano, *Diritto civile e commerciale*, vol. ii (2) p. 325. However, Franzoni, *Fatti illeciti*, Art. 2047, pp. 326, 342 and Art. 2048 p. 368 considers them to be cases of strict liability, because it is 'impossible' to prove the opposite. For further references on this dispute see Cendon (-Venchiarutti) vol. iv, Art. 2048, nn. 2, 3.

[833] See e.g. Cass. 14 Sep. 1967, n. 2157, *Giur.it.* 1968, I, 1, 828; Cass. 5 Dec. 1974, n. 4027, *Rep.gen.* 1974, col. 3113, no. 78; Cass. 4 Oct. 1979, n. 5122, *Rep.gen.* 1979, col. 3553, no. 97 (on Art. 2047); Cass. 24 Oct. 1988, n. 5751, *Foro.it.* 1989, I, 98, and Cass. 29 May 1992, n. 6484, *Giur.it.* 1993, I, 1, 588, 590. [834] See fn. 541 above.

[835] See e.g. Cass. 14 Sep. 1967, n. 2157, *Giur.it.* 1968, I, 1, 828; Cass. 4 Mar. 1977, n. 894, *Giur.it.* 1977, I, 1, 1660; and Cass. 15 Dec. 1980, n. 6503, *Giur.it.* 1981, I, 1, 1453. All decisions explicitly state that the duty of supervision must be seen in relation to age, degree of maturity, and personality of the child in question.

[836] See Franzoni (fn. 832 above). Also note by Pinori on Trib. Genua 29 Apr. 1994, n. 1445, *Giur.it.* 1995, I, 2, 555. In an appeal to the Court of Cassation it cannot be argued that the judge, who decides on matters of fact and law, applied too high a standard in the circumstances of the case: it is exclusively within the discretion of the *giudice di merito* to establish which criteria to employ: Cass. 28 June 1976, n. 2460, *Rep.gen.* 1976, col. 3447, no. 56.

[837] For more recent rulings on *culpa in educando*, see Cass. 9 June 1983, n. 3977, *Giust. civ.Mass.* 1983 no. 3977 p. 1417 (child throwing a stone); Cass. 16 May 1984, n. 2995, *Giust.civ.Mass.* 1984 no. 2995 p. 1005 (throwing lime); Cass. 10 Feb. n. 1427, *Giur.it.* 1987, I, 1. 1752 (the *bonus paterfamilias* must prove that he took all possible precautions to prevent the child's dangerous act); Cass. 29 May 1992, n. 6484, *Giur.it.* 1993, I, 1, 588 (a very lively boy, whose upbringing was considered to have been too inadequate); and Trib. Genoa 13 Jan. 1995, n. 199, *Giur.it.* 1995, I, 2, 554 (liability for a fight in schoolyard).

[838] Cass. 29 May 1992 (fn. 837 above) col. 590. Also the cases cited in fn. 837; Cass. 30 Oct. 1984, n. 5564, *Foro.it.* 1985, I, 145; Cass. 18 June 1985, n. 3664, *Giur.it.* 1986, I, 1, 1525; Cass. 24 Oct. 1988, n. 5751, *Foro.it.* 1989, I, 98; Cass. 18 Dec. 1992, n. 13424, *Riv.giur.circ.trasp.* 1993 p. 588.

upbringing of the child (especially in road traffic accident law) must be 'ethically and socially sufficient'.[839] Apart from a few exceptions for *grandi minori*,[840] a child is only considered to have been raised properly if he or she has acted with due care.[841] Moreover, parents are liable for their children's torts even if they cannot fulfil their duty to supervise because they live too far from the children.[842] In conclusion: Art. 2048 I Cc is a quasi-strict liability provision, rendering parents jointly and severally liable for the delicts of their children.[843]

136   Although other European codes neither distinguish between parental liability for children capable of reasoning and those who are not, nor place such heavy emphasis on the duty to raise a child properly as Art. 2048 Ital. Cc, their conclusions are often similar. For instance, Portugal largely followed Vaz Serra's proposal[844] in the official version of Art. 491 Cc, deliberately assigning it to *responsabilidade por factos ilícitos*, and not *responsabilidade pelo risco*, unambiguously demonstrating that the cause of action is a presumed *culpa in vigilando*.[845] Hence in Portugal, as in Italy, it is far from easy for parents to escape liability.[846] Defences have only succeeded where the minor was employed a considerable distance from his parents at the time of the tort,[847] or where there is no causal connection between the parental breach of duty and the infliction of the damage.[848] In the great majority of cases the courts decide against the

---

[839] E.g. Cass. 27 May 1975, n. 2141, Gentile/Guerreri/Guerreri, *La responsabilità, voce responsabilità civile—genitori e tutori* 64 (112); Cass. 21 Oct. 1976, n. 3725, *Giust.civ.Mass.* 1976 no. 3725, p. 1544; and Cass. 27 Nov. 1984, n. 6144, *Giust.civ.Mass.* 1984 no. 6144 p. 2009. See also App. Venice 8 Oct. 1986, *Dir.fam.pers.* 1988, II, 874 (the father of a 16-year-old escapes liability only if he can adduce *'la prova di non avere potuto impedire il danno e di avere impartito al figlio una educazione idonea'*).
[840] E.g. Cass. 6 May 1986, n. 3031, *Giur.it.* 1986, I, 1, 1527: no liability of parents for a tort committed by their 20-year-old son, while still a minor, at a sports club; App. Venice 8 Oct. 1986 (fn. 839 above) with note by Maschio. Also Pinto Borea, *Dir.fam.pers.* 1992, II, pp. 364, 400–401.
[841] Bussani, *Colpa soggettiva*, p. 181; Cass. 6 May 1986, n. 3031, *Giur.it.* 1986, I, 1, 1527.
[842] An objective failure to carry out the duty to supervise is sufficient to found liability: Cass. 18 Dec. 1992, n. 13424, *Riv.giur.circ.trasp.* 1993 p. 588.
[843] Cass. 20 Apr. 1978, n. 1895, Gentile/Guerreri/Guerreri, (fn. 839 above) 64 (120); Cass. 19 Dec. 1978, n. 6104, *Giust.civ.Mass.* 1978 no. 6104 p. 2550; and Franzoni, *Fatti illeciti*, Art. 2048 p. 357.   [844] Printed in *BolMinJust* 101 (1960) p. 124 (Art. 742 of the draft).
[845] See e.g. Pires de Lima/Antunes Varela, *Cc anotado*, vol. i, 4th edn., Art. 491 I, III; Almeida Costa, *Obrigações*, 5th edn., p. 367; Martins de Almeida, *Manual de Acidentes*, 3rd edn., pp. 237–238. Furthermore, since STJ 8 Feb. 1977, *BolMinJust* 264 (1977) p. 154, the courts have repeatedly also applied Art. 491 Cc to minors lacking ability to reason. See also STJ 13 Feb. 1979, *BolMinJust* 284 (1979) p. 187; and STJ 23 Feb. 1988, *BolMinJust* 374 (1988) pp. 466, 469.
[846] For successful defences see STJ 2 Mar. 1978, *BolMinJust* 275 (1978) p. 170; STJ 13 Feb. 1979 (fn. 845 above); STJ 28 Oct. 1992, *BolMinJust* 420 (1992) p. 565.
[847] RP 11 Dec. 1974, *BolMinJust* 242 (1974) p. 362. Similar Italian case and outcome: Cass. 20 May 1958, n. 1662, Gentile/Guerreri/Guerreri (fn. 839 above) 64 (36).
[848] STJ 17 Jan. 1980, *BolMinJust* 293 (1980) p. 308.

parents, especially given that liability also arises from *culpa in edu-cando*.[849] Thus a mother who left her fourteen- and fifteen-year-old sons with their grandmother while she went to the US was held liable because she had failed to leave her children with a reliable person. The grandmother was deemed unreliable because she failed to prevent the delict.[850] In a more recent decision, the *Supremo Tribunal de Justiça* held liable the parents of a sixteen-year-old who, at a disco, broke into premises to obtain cigarettes, was discovered, and fatally injured a guard. The court ruled that the parents, despite having arranged psychological and psychiatric treatment for him, had not raised their son in such a way as to *'promover o seu desenvolvimento físico, intelectual e moral'*.[851]

One country which has not followed the course taken by most of **137** continental Europe is Austria: a country with an old code. At first glance, § 1309 ABGB resembles the corresponding Dutch provision, since it holds liable only those *'denen der Schade wegen Vernachlässigung der ihnen über (Unmündige) anvertrauten Obsorge beigemessen werden kann'*. According to § 21 II ABGB, the *'unmündige'* are those *'die das vierzehnte . . . Lebensjahr noch nicht vollendet haben'* (incompetent by reason of being under fourteen). However, closer inspection reveals that the only thing which § 1309 ABGB and Art. 6:169 I BW have in common is the age limit of fourteen years. § 1309 ABGB is a secondary provision, since by § 1308 ABGB it does not apply if the plaintiff himself caused or contributed to the damage *'durch irgendein Verschulden'*.[852] Secondly, and more importantly, § 1309 ABGB is an example of liability for failure to act (and for the breach of a duty of care).[853] So the burden of proof does not pass to the defendant: in contrast to the rest of continental Europe,[854] the *'Beschädigte'*—as explicitly confirmed in many OGH decisions—must 'prove that the duty to supervise was carried out negligently, whereas the parent has to prove (only) that he was not at fault'.[855] This division of the burden of proof corresponds to the general rule in § 1298 ABGB, as a

---

[849] According to RL 23 Nov. 1979, *BolMinJust* 299 (1980) p. 411, the relevant parental breach of duty may have occurred some time before the accident; RL 17 Mar. 1987, *BolMinJust* 366 (1987) p. 550 establishes that a *culpa in educando* constitutes a breach of the duty of supervision. [850] RL 15 Nov. 1988, *CJ* XIII (1988–5) p. 112.

[851] STJ 20 Mar. 1991, *CJ* XVI (1991–2) pp. 7, 11. See also RL 20 Feb. 1986, *BolMinJust* 361 (1986) p. 597.

[852] See no. 78 above. It is not for the parents to prove the plaintiff's contributory negligence: the plaintiff must prove that no contributory negligence can be attributed to him: Rummel (-Reischauer), *ABGB*, vol. ii, 2nd edn., § 1309 ABGB no. 9. The subsidiarity of § 1309 ABGB is of only minor importance, since it does not prejudice minors. Moreover, the term contributory negligence has in this context been narrowly defined by the OGH. On both issues see OGH 11 May 1960, *SZ* 33/54 pp. 149, 152–153: one person who pushes another to the ground must expect a punch, but not a sharp object being thrown at his face.

[853] OGH 6 Oct. 1961, *JBl* 1962 pp. 263, 264.

[854] On Scandinavian and common law see no. 331.

[855] OGH 6 Oct. 1961, *JBl* 1962 p. 263; OGH 27 Jan. 1971, *SZ* 44/8 pp. 24, 27.

result of which the victim must prove a breach of duty. Hence, the Austrian liability system is more favourable to parents.[856] The interpretation of § 1309 ABGB (its subsidiarity to § 1308 ABGB aside) as a standard provision establishing liability for failure to act automatically entailed the continuation of the duty to supervise beyond completion of the child's fourteenth year. The parental duty to bring up their children 'continues, irrespective of their age, as long as they need supervision'.[857] A culpable breach of this duty could even render a parent (or guardian) liable 'for damage inflicted by a person who, although of age, lacks the capacity to reason'.[858] Since in Austria, too, the 'standard of care' depends on 'what could reasonably be expected of the person, taking into account his age, mental development, and character',[859] the standard demanded decreases as the child grows older. By contrast with The Netherlands, however—the third difference between the codes—the basis of parental liability does not change when the child reaches fourteen.

138   In Belgium (Art. 1384 II, V Cc), France (Art. 1384 IV, VII Cc), Germany (§ 832 BGB), Greece (Art. 923 Cc), and Luxembourg (Art. 1384 II, V Cc), those with parental custody are presumed not to have fulfilled their duty to supervise, unless they rebut that presumption. Originally all these provisions assumed that only the father had parental custody, burdening him alone with the duty to supervise.[860] However, the principle of equality of the sexes has now changed the position.[861] This has created a new problem: liability for breach of the duty to supervise is now likely to fall on the parent without income, who is less likely to be able to meet the claim.[862] To adapt to the new situation, only the actual wording of the relevant *Code civil* provisions had to be altered.[863] In Greece (Art. 923 Greek Cc) and Germany (§ 832 BGB), whose provisions are all but identical, the legislator has always referred to 'a person bound by law

---

[856] E.g. OGH 28 June 1983, *ZVR* 1984/324 (constant supervision of children is not necessary if their social environment does not give any cause for concern, and if incompatible with the parents' occupations); OGH 6 July 1977, *ÖJZ* 1978 p. 154 (*EvBl* 52); OGH 10 Sep. 1981, *ZVR* 1982/109; and OGH 24 June 1981, *EFSlg* 38.569.

[857] OGH 27 Jan. 1971 (fn. 855 above).

[858] OGH 4 Nov. 1963, *ÖJZ* 1964 p. 183 (*EvBl* 124).

[859] Established practice of the courts: see e.g. OGH 27 Jan. 1971 (fn. 855) p. 28 (with further references). However, the courts have always acknowledged that the standard of care required and the occupation and financial situation of the parents are related.

[860] See Art. 373 Cc (version of 1804: '*le père seul excerce cette autorité durant le mariage*'); Arts. 1500–1502 Greek Cc (old version); and §§ 1626, 1627 BGB (old version).

[861] For Belgian developments see Fagnart in Dalcq (ed.), *Responsabilité et réparation des dommages*, § 2 (p. 14–15); for France see *Encyclopédie Dalloz* (-Benac-Schmidt/Larroumet), *Rép.Dr.Civ.*, vol. vii, nos. 136–141; for Greece see Agallopoulou-Zervodianni, *FS Michaelides-Nouaros*, vol. A (1987) pp. 31–42; and for Germany see e.g. Koebel, *NJW* 1960 pp. 2227–2228.   [862] For greater detail see Immenga, *FamRZ* 1969 pp. 313–319.

[863] The original text of Art. 1384 II Cc read: '*Le père, et la mère après le décès du mari, sont responsables du dommage par leurs enfants mineurs habitant avec eux.*'

to exercise supervision over a person needing supervision by reason of minority'. Any adaptations were therefore restricted to family law, and the relevant delictual provisions did not require alteration. On the other hand, Belgium, France, and Luxembourg each for the first time revised its own Art. 1384 Cc, embarking on separate courses. The Belgian *Code civil* now provides in Art. 1384 II Cc that *'le père et la mère sont responsables du dommage causé par leurs enfants mineurs'*. The French and Luxembourgeois version provides that *'le père et la mère, en tant qu'ils exercent le droit de garde, sont solidairement responsables du dommage causé par leurs enfants mineurs habitant avec eux'*. The reader will notice three differences between the Belgian and the French and Luxembourg solutions. First, Belgium retains liability *in solidum*, whereas in France and Luxembourg parents are jointly and severally liable.[864] Secondly, under the French provision minor children must live in their parents' household,[865] a precondition abandoned by the Belgian legislator. Finally, only under Art. 1384 IV French Cc and Art. 1384 II Lux. Cc must the defendant parent be the one exercising the right of custody (*le droit de garde*). Therefore a number of Belgian scholars have argued that, under their Art. 1384 II Cc, action can also be brought against a parent deprived of custody—for example due to divorce—prior to the delict.[866] Those commentators seem to be in the minority,[867] despite the wording of Art. 1384 II Cc, and despite the fact that it is often the other parent who failed properly to perform his duty.[868]

(2) The Preconditions for and Extent of Parental Duties

The requirements for and the extent of parental duties were addressed **139** above. The children are expressly required to live in their parents' household to found parental liability only in French, Italian, and Luxembourgeois law. In practical terms this requirement could cause concern where the parents have separated and the children spend time with each parent in turn.[869] Under French law cohabitation ceases, for example, when the

---

[864] See also no. 52 above.

[865] Hence only Art. 482 II French Cc (and not the relevant Belgian or Luxembourg provision) explicitly states that parents are not liable under Art. 1384 Cc for 'emancipated' minors with limited adult legal capacity. However, this has not prevented the Belgian courts from achieving similar results: see Cass. 11 Feb. 1946, *Pas. belge* 1946, I, 62.

[866] Cornelis, *Buitencontractueel aansprakelijkheidsrecht*, no. 183 (p. 313); and Antwerp 30 Mar. 1984, *Pas. belge* 1984, II, 128.

[867] A view shared by André, *Responsabilités*, no. 102 (p. 152); and Vandenberghe/Van Quickenborne/Geelen/De Coster, *TPR* 1987 p. 1255–1615 (no. 115).

[868] Generally, *culpa in educando* raises the presumption of liability; see no. 140 below.

[869] Antwerp 30 Mar. 1984, *Pas. belge* 1984, II, 128: the other parent's duty to supervise continues throughout the child's absence. In Belgium *cohabitation* with the parents is not a precondition. Yet see also Cass.crim. 13 Dec. 1982, *Rev.trim.dr.civ.* 1983 p. 539 (*observations* Durry): the child was with the father, the mother was released from liability. However, Cass. 8 Jan. 1985, *Pas. belge* 1985, I, 532 states that splitting custody between estranged parents does not in itself constitute a breach of duty.

child starts military service, commences studies in another town,[870] attends a boarding school,[871] or even during a holiday with his grand-parents.[872] However, if the child has ceased to live with his parents other than as a consequence of 'normal circumstances' and *'pour une cause légitime'*, for instance if his parents made him leave, or he left due to an argument, he continues legally to live with them.[873]

The fact that only the three codes mentioned above expressly require the child to live at home should not be over-emphasized. Belgian courts, for example, have on several occasions also decided that parents are relieved of the duty to supervise while their child is under the supervision of another.[874] In such cases, only an unrebutted presumption of fault in the child's upbringing can found liability.[875] On the other hand, both French[876] and Belgian[877] courts seem to be of the opinion that parental liability continues while their children are at school and under the supervision of their teachers if the delict is a direct result of the child's upbringing. In other legal systems too, e.g. in Austria, Germany, and Greece, cohabitation is an element of the duty of supervision. If children are in the care of another person then the extent of parental responsibility is limited, depending on the circumstances of the case. Parents must choose a suitable person to supervise their children, control that person as appropriate, and make appropriate enquiries about him;[878] but this is where their duty to supervise ends. Hence, in cases where guardian and ward live in different places, the guardian is often exempt from liability.[879] Most cases on this issue concern juveniles who entered into a contract of employment or vocational training prior to the delict.[880] If the relevant

---

[870] Starck (-Roland/Boyer), *Obligations*, vol. i, 4th edn., no. 1097.
[871] Cass.civ. 2 July 1991, Bull.civ. 1991 I no. 224.
[872] Cass.civ. 24 Apr. 1989, D. 1990 *Jur.* 519.
[873] Starck (-Roland/Boyer), *Obligations*, vol. i (fn. 870 above); Paris 26 Nov. 1960, D. 1961 *Jur.* 227; Cass.crim. 24 July 1952, S. 1953 *Jur.* 69.
[874] Brussels 19 May 1983, *JT* 1983 p. 578; Trib. Brussels 7 Jan. 1991, *JT* 1991 p. 587; Brussels 7 Dec. 1993, *RGAR* 1995 no. 12416; Liège 19 Feb. 1987, *JT* 1987 p. 648.
[875] Brussels 19 May 1983 (fn. 874 above).
[876] Cass.civ. 16 May 1988, *Gaz.Pal.* 1989, 2, *Somm.* 371.
[877] Cass. 23 Feb. 1989, *JT* 1989 p. 235; and Cass. 28 Sep. 1990, *JT* 1990 p. 22, which abandoned the position of Cass. 22 Sep. 1978, *JT* 1980 p. 508. However, see also Brussels 11 June 1992, *RGAR* 1995 no. 12466: child injured a school-friend on the way home; the parents, and not the teachers, were liable.
[878] See e.g. *MünchKomm* (-Mertens), 2nd edn., § 832 no. 13; Rummel (-Reischauer), *ABGB*, vol. ii, 2nd edn., § 1309 no. 6; and Georgiades/Stathopoulos (-Georgiades), *Greek Cc*, vol. iv, Art. 923 nos. 10–11 (the duty to supervise is always allocated to the person exercising supervision).
[879] CA Athens 442/1972, *Arm.* 1972 p. 322; CA Athens 6779/1987, *EllDik* 29 (1988) p. 1415.
[880] CA Thessalonika 181/1972, *Arm.* 1972 p. 401; STJ 11 Dec. 1974, *BolMinJust* 242 (1974) p. 362; Cass. 20 May 1958, n. 1662, Gentile/Guerreri/Guerreri, *La responsabilità, voce responsabilità civile—genitori e tutori* 64 (36). For Belgium see also the (highly controversial) decision concerning a child of school age Cass. 22 Sep. 1978, *Pas. belge* 1979, I, 508 (*contra*: Brussels 2 Nov. 1977, *JT* 1978 p. 135); also fn. 890 below.

Luxembourgeois decisions of the first half of this century can still be considered 'good law' (there are no recent rulings) then the relationship between parental and employers' liability is still seen in the light of *non-cumul des responsabilités*: '*Si le dommage a été causé par un préposé mineur, la responsabilité du commettant exclut celle du père et les deux actions ne peuvent être cumulées.*'[881] Where the parent is also the employer, the type of liability incurred depends on whether the child's conduct concerns primarily his private life[882] or his occupation.[883]

One of the main objectives of the special delictual provisions govern-   **140** ing parental liability, as stated above, is to apply the duties of supervision rooted in family law for the protection of others.[884] Whether the same can be said of the duty to educate (not mentioned in codified liability law) is controversial. Even those countries generally in favour do not agree on the details. Italian courts have advanced the furthest; they have rendered the notion of *neminem laedere* an objective of parental education, thereby imposing almost strict liability on *culpa in educando*.[885] Likewise, Belgian,[886] French,[887] Luxembourgeois,[888] and Portuguese[889] courts habitually examine *culpa in educando* within the liability question.[890] However, unlike their Italian counterparts, they do examine individual areas of education, such as whether a parent must teach his children about road traffic regulations.[891] *Culpa in educando* is presumed if a delict committed by a minor constitutes an act of considerable mischief. An example is intentional grievous bodily

---

[881] Cour 4 May 1929, *Pas. luxemb.* 12 (1930–32) p. 109.

[882] As in Cour 24 Nov. 1922, *Pas. luxemb.* 12 (1930–1932) p. 420.

[883] As in Cour 29 July 1936, *Pas. luxemb.* 14 (1936–1949) p. 67.

[884] See no. 100 above.   [885] See no. 135 above.

[886] Cass. 30 May 1984, *Pas. belge* 1984, I, 1200; Cass. 8 Jan. 1985, *Pas. belge* 1985, I, 532; Cass. 24 Jan. 1985, *Pas. belge* 1985, I, 603; and Cass. 18 Oct. 1990, *RGAR* 1992, 12026.

[887] Cass.civ. 4 May 1987, Bull.civ. 1987 II no. 63; Cass.civ. 18 Feb. 1987, *D.* 1987 IR 56.

[888] Cour 12 June 1985, *Pas. luxemb.* 27 (1987–89) 182; and Trib. Lux. 6 Feb. 1963, *Pas. luxemb.* 19 (1963–65) 144: the defendant must show that neither a fault in the supervision of the child nor a fault in its education can be attributed to him, '*la preuve de l'absence d'une seule de ces fautes n'étant pas libératoire*').

[889] See fn. 849 above; STJ 20 Mar. 1991, *CJ* XVI (1991–2) pp. 7, 11; STJ 17 Jan. 1980, *BolMinJust* 293 (1980) p. 308 and elsewhere.

[890] That this contradicts the 'classic' and, at least in Luxembourg, still valid (see no. 139 above) principle of *non-cumul* of liability for others (for the relevant Belgian decisions see fn. 880 above) is a seperate issue. Belgium seems to have overcome this problem. Cass. 20 Apr. 1982, *JT* 1983 p. 48 confirmed parental liability for a boy '*alors qu'il se trouvait sous la surveillance de la police*', because his parents '*n'ont pas donné une bonne éducation à leur fils mineur*'. Cass. 23 Feb. 1989, *JT* 1989 p. 235 subsequently confirmed this judgment with regard to teachers. Mons 9 June 1993, *JT* 1993 p. 688, and Vred. Ninove 5 June 1991, *RW* 1993–1994 p. 1336 followed that decision.

[891] For a perceptive and critical overview of Belgian decisions see Fagnart, in Dalcq (ed.), *Responsabilité et réparation des dommages*, no. 20 (p. 20).

harm.[892] However, by and large the prevailing opinion is correct: the mere fact that a child commits an unlawful act does not constitute *culpa in educando*.[893] Neither would his unlawful behaviour incur liability for the father where breach of the duty to supervise is wholly attributable to the mother.[894] Otherwise strict liability would be imposed on parents, and the intellectual connection between the child's upbringing and the delict committed has no real relevance. Parents would then act merely as guarantors for the payment of damages, and would no longer qualify as tortfeasors.

141 For this reason Austria, Germany, and Greece have been more cautious. For example, German courts have stressed that the law does not impose 'a general duty of care on parents and guardians (*Erziehungsberechtigte*) towards third parties, to bring up their children or wards (*Aufsichtsbefohlenen*) so as to limit to an absolute minimum the damage which the minors might cause'.[895] However, closer inspection reveals that in German law (as in Austria and Greece) the child's education and the duty to supervise are closely related. If parents succeed in the former, the latter can be exercised more leniently;[896] conversely, a disobedient child must be supervised more closely.[897] The courts have stressed that the standard of supervision required depends on the degree to which the child's maturity and stability of character entitle him to freedom.[898] If he tends to get involved in fights, likes playing with matches or weapons, or appears more dangerous than other children of his age, then especially intense supervision is required.[899] If a parent cannot prevent a child from behaving in a certain way, these legal systems also hold him responsible for *culpa in educando*. However, it must be remembered that children are not formed from clay. Parents with children who are men-

---

[892] Cass. 20 Apr. 1982, *JT* 1983 p. 48; Liège 20 Dec. 1990, *RGAR* 1994 no. 12249 (liability of the father was based, not on *faute personelle*, but on *culpa in educando*: son shot a passer-by in the eye); Cass.crim. 18 June 1980, *D.* 1981 IR 322 (n. Larroumet); and STJ 20 Mar. 1991, *CJ* XVI (1991–2) p. 7.

[893] Starck (-Roland/Boyer), *Obligations*, vol. i, 4th edn., no. 1122. Contra: Ghent 14 Dec. 1993, *RW* 1994–95 no. 1196.   [894] Cass.civ. 14 Nov. 1984, *Sem.Jur.* 1985, IV, 34.

[895] *MünchKomm* (-Mertens), 2nd edn., § 832 BGB no. 18. OLG Cologne 12 June 1974, *VersR* 1975 p. 162 goes so far as to say: 'A breach of the duties involved in bringing up a child, which must be distinguished from the duties of care, does not incur liability on the part of guardian'.   [896] Mertens (fn. 895 above).

[897] BGH 19 Jan. 1984, *NJW* 1985 pp. 677, 679: 'the duty of supervision is increased for minors who tend to commit mischievous and criminal acts . . . Older children must also be supervised more closely the less successful their education has been.' See also BGH 10 July 1984, *NJW* 1984 pp. 2574, 2575: the standard of supervision depends on the influence that education has had on the child.

[898] See e.g. v. Bar (-Schilcher/Kleewein), *DeliktsR in Europa, Österreich*, p. 83; Georgiades/Stathopoulos (-Georgiades), *Greek Cc*, vol. iv, Art. 923 nos. 5–6; and CFI Thessalonika 976/1989, *Arm.* 43 (1989) p. 967.

[899] The plaintiff must prove that an increased standard of care was required: OGH 24 June 1981, *EFSlg* 38.569; and OGH 10 Sep. 1981, *ZVR* 1982/109.

tally disturbed from early childhood, in particular, should be supported rather than punished.[900]

What constitutes an appropriate degree of supervision depends on the   **142** facts of the case. For instance, children have to be alerted to the danger inherent in certain conduct, and they have to be taught the basic rules of road traffic. Parents must observe whether their bans are heeded. Dangerous toys must be taken away, and dangerous games forbidden. If children are fascinated by fire, all matches and lighters have to be locked away; the circumstances might require certain rooms to be locked, or contact between badly behaved children forbidden. In all legal systems where parental liability is not strict, the type of measures to be taken depend on the danger inherent in the act itself, the age, character, and maturity of the child, the social environment, the number and age of brothers and sisters, and the child's general ability to socialize.[901] In addition, Austrian courts have repeatedly (and rightly) stressed that the duty to supervise must be economically feasible for the parents.[902] One must not forget that, if children are to be raised properly, they have to be allowed to develop the ability to handle danger.[903] It is not for the law to wrap children in cotton wool, nor to encourage parents permanently to reprimand and control their children.

---

[900] Trib. Brussels 7 Jan. 1991, *JT* 1991 p. 587 therefore rightly said: '*Attendu que l'obligation d'éducation doit s'apprécier de façon raisonnable et humaine, sous peine, dans le cas contraire d'obliger tout parent, quel qu'il soit, à l'égard de tout enfant, quel qu'il soit, dans quelque circonstance qu'elle soit, à une obligation de résultat; qu'il ne peut être fait grief aux parents du premier cité d'avoir failli là ou des spécialistes de la problématique de la jeunesse n'ont pu, à ce jour, combler les lacunes affectives initiales dont a eu à souffrir, et souffre encore Frédéric.*'

[901] E.g. OGH 6 Oct. 1961, SZ 34/137; and OGH 15 Apr. 1982, *ZVR* 1983/206; Antwerp 30 Apr. 1984, *Pas. belge* 1984, II, 128; Starck (-Roland/Boyer), *Obligations*, vol. i, 4th edn., no. 1123 (including an extensive case review); Georgiades/Stathopoulos (-Georgiades), *Greek Cc*, vol. iv, Art. 923 no. 6, 12; Deliyannis/Kornilakis, *Eidiko Enochiko Dikaio*, vol. iii pp. 195–196; CA Thessalonika 1809/1990, *Arm.* 44 (190) p. 440; STJ 23 Feb. 1988, *BolMinJust* 374 (1988) p. 466; HR 26 Nov. 1948, *NedJur* 1949 no. 149 p. 281 (on the continuing effect of this decision on children over age 14, see van Dunné, *Verbintenissenrecht*, vol. ii, 2nd edn., pp. 571–572); BGH 27 Nov. 1979, BGHZ 111 pp. 282, 285; and BGH 19 Jan. 1993, *FamRZ* 1993 pp. 666, 667 ('the degree of supervision of minors to be considered appropriate is defined by their age, their personal development, and their character. Which measures are regarded as necessary and appropriate depends on what sensible parents would have to do under reasonable circumstances to avoid damage being inflicted on others by their children').

[902] Established practice of the courts: See OGH 27 Jan. 1971, SZ 44/8 pp. 24, 27; OGH 10 Sep. 1981, *ZVR* 1982/109.

[903] OGH 28 June 1983, *ZVR* 1984/324; CFI Thessalonika 576/1989, *Arm.* 43 (1989) p. 967; Deliyannis/Kornilakis, *Eidiko Enochiko Dikaio*, vol. iii, pp. 196; Georgiades/Stathopoulos (-Georgiades), (fn. 901 above) no. 6; Asser (-Hartkamp), *Verbintenissenrecht*, vol. iii, 9th edn., nos. 137–138; and STJ 2 Mar. 1978, *BolMinJust* 275 (1978) pp. 170, 173 (children need reasonable space to develop). For an interesting decision in this context see BGH 25 Apr. 1978, *NJW* 1978 pp. 1626, 1627, on a local authority's duty to safeguard an adventure playground. The court stated that 'from an educational point of view' it is necessary for children and juveniles 'to learn at an early stage about the dangers of everyday life, i.e. to learn how to face and control them'.

Rather, the task for liability law is to achieve consistency with family law. For example, if § 1626 II s. 1 German BGB requires parents 'to adjust the care and education of their child to his growing need for independent responsible action', liability law is also so bound.

143   The scope and extent of the parental duty of supervision often depend largely on the extent to which parents can rely on others to meet their duty in a reasonable fashion. Parents can be assumed to have breached the duty if an obviously unreliable person is placed in charge of the children, or is insufficiently supervised.[904] Likewise, parents cannot burden others with all their responsibilities. For example, if they allow their son to take a knife to school, they cannot blame his teachers if it is used unlawfully: they have a duty to prevent such a danger.[905] However, in families dependent upon the income of both parents, their duty to provide maintenance might oblige them to place their children in the care of others. Leaving children under the supervision of a third party, who has less liability for the children, or even none, does not in itself constitute a breach of duty. However, the more readily a legal system admits *culpa in educando* as a cause of action, and the more easily it presumes that a failure to educate the child properly was causally linked to his delict, the more readily it will hold parents strictly liable under this alternative to the duty to supervise.[906]

144   As parental care is regularly imposed on both married parents,[907] and as the duties to educate and supervise are merely elements of the child's care, so parents are jointly and severally liable to third parties.[908] However, joint and several liability only arises if the wrongful act can actually be attributed to both parents. In cases of presumed *culpa in educando* that is unlikely to be difficult to prove. However, where liability is based on breach of the duty to supervise, the question arises whether a spouse can avoid responsibility by arguing that his partner ought to have prevented

---

[904] RL 15 Nov. 1988, *CJ* XIII (1988–5) p. 112.   [905] Mons 9 June 1993, *JT* 1993 p. 688.

[906] Cass. 28 Sep. 1989, *JT* 1990 p. 22. Also no. 139 above.

[907] On the dispute about the meaning of the *droit de garde* in Belgian law see no. 138 above; on the meaning of *cohabitation* see no. 139 above. Questions arising in family law cannot be discussed in detail here.

[908] Belgium: Vandenberghe/Van Quickenborne/Geelen/De Coster, *TPR* 1987 pp. 1255, 1449 (*in solidum* liability); France: Art. 1384 II Cc ('*sont solidairement responsables*'); Germany: *MünchKomm* (-Mertens), 2nd edn., § 832 note 14; Greece: CFI Thessalonika 576/1989, *Arm.* 43 (1989) p. 967; CA Thessalonika 1809/1990, *Arm.* 44 (1990) p. 440; Deliyannis/Kornilakis, *Eidiko Enochiko Dikaio*, vol. iii, p. 198; and Georgiades/Stathopoulos (-Georgiades), *Greek Cc*, vol. iv, Art. 923 no. 11; Italy: Cass. 20 Sep. 1978, n. 1895, Gentile/Guerreri/Guerreri, *La responsabilità, voce responsabilità civile—genitori e tutori*, 64 (120); Cass. 19 Dec. 1978, n. 6104, *Giust.civ.Mass.* 1978 no. 6104 p. 2550; Luxembourg: Art. 1384 II Cc; The Netherlands: Bloembergen (-Oldenhuis), *Onrechtmatige daad*, vol. i, Art. 169 BW n. 11; Portugal: Martins de Almeida, *Manual de Acidentes*, 3rd edn., p. 238; Spain: Gómez Calle, *Responsabilidad de los padres*, pp. 398–405; and López Beltrán de Heredia, *Responsabilidad civil de los padres*, pp. 115–126.

the child from inflicting the damage. Liability law traditionally permits this argument[909] if the defendant can disprove any breach of the duty of care on his own part.[910] In a marriage where one partner runs the household while the other provides the income, such a system of liability can easily clash with family law provisions.[911] The partner who stays at home is then usually held liable for accidents which commonly arise from a child playing or dealing with traffic. If third-party family insurance is not compulsory, the plaintiff may be unable to enforce his claim.[912] This author therefore believes that wherever possible under the current liability provisions (i.e. under Art. 491 Port. Cc, Art. 1384 VII French Cc, and Art. 1384 V Belgian Cc[913]) a spouse should only be exempt from liability if no breach of duty can be attributed to either partner, and that this approach should be generally adopted. In countries whioch impose strict liability on parents, they are automatically jointly and severally liable. They should not be treated differently for liability for a presumed breach of duty. The argument that this would render a husband strictly liable for his wife[914] does not convince: they share the care of the child and should therefore also share the duties.

---

[909] See e.g. Cass.civ. 14 Nov. 1984 (fn. 894 above); Immenga, *FamRZ* 1969 pp. 313–319; Vandenberghe/Van Quickenborne/Geelen/De Coster (fn. 908 above); Ghent 18 Sep. 1981, *RW* 1982–83 p. 42; Rummel (-Reischauer), *ABGB*, vol. ii, 2nd edn., § 1309 no. 6; Bloembergen (-Oldenhuis), *Onrechtmatige daad*, vol. i, Art. 169 BW n. 31. *Contra*: Spain *TS* 29 Dec. 1962, *RAJ* 1962 no. 5141 p. 3499, following the path laid by the Spanish legislator, by which parents are quasi-strictly liable. For Portuguese court rulings: fn. 913 below.

[910] BGH 14 Nov. 1961, *VersR* 1962 pp. 157, 158: a 20-year-old 'not overly clever son' (when majority was reached at age 21) handled a weapon carelessly. The co-defendant mother, a 'simple countrywoman', argued that the father was solely responsible for teaching the son to use the weapon and for supervising him. The BGH rejected this argument: 'under the circumstances the mother should have taken the gun from her son.'

[911] Therefore Oldenhuis, *Onrechtmatige daad: aansprakelijkheid voor personen*, no. 20 (p. 27) is right in saying the *individuele disculpatie* is inconsistent with the joint duty of care under Art. 1:251 I BW. See also HR 26 Nov. 1948 *NedJur* 1949 no. 149 p. 281 which demonstrates how little even Dutch courts of that time favoured the possibility of one parent escaping liability. For Spain see TS 29 Dec. 1962 (fn. 909 above).

[912] Damages arising from one spouse's delict are not usually enforceable against the other spouse (§ 1360a BGB), and under marital property laws debts arising from delict are usually personal debts: e.g. Art. 1407 IV (with Art. 1412) Belgian Cc (although the system under Arts. 1409, 1417 French Cc is slightly different).

[913] The French and Belgian provisions render both parents liable as long as *'le père et la mère . . . ne prouvent qu'ils n'ont pu empêcher le fait'*. The use of the plural here is significant. Art. 491 Port. Cc makes the guardian liable if the 'duty of supervision' is violated. It is completely irrelevant who violated it. Hence liability is always imposed on *both* parents: STJ 13 Feb. 1979, *BolMinJust* 284 (1979) p. 187; and RL 21 May 1987, *BolMinJust* 367 (1987) p. 561.

[914] An argument only recently raised in Denmark (in Pagter Kristensen and Bryde Andersen's review of the 2nd edn. of the handbook on liability law by Nørgaard/Vagner in *J* 1992 pp. 320, 325), although Danish courts in particular have long held the view expressed in the text above. See ØLD 30 Dec. 1943, *UfR* 1944 A p. 392; VLD 8 Feb. 1963, *UfR* 1963 A p. 627: a mother let her child play near parked cars; the defendant father was liable, although not at home at the time.

(3) The Unlawful Act of the Child

145 Parental liability is either for, or brought about by, damage caused by the child. Therefore the basis of parental liability is linked to the question of which legal preconditions the child must satisfy to initiate such liability. The answer must be that parents are (only) liable for damages if an adult in the same position as the child would have been answerable. Regarding omissions, if a child could not protect others from a dangerous situation, the parents are only accountable for such damage as a child of that age could be expected to have prevented. For a statutory expression of this principle see Art. 6:169 BW.

146 Parental liability therefore requires, first, a damaging act on the part of the child. If an adult tries to walk past a toddler playing on some stairs and falls as a result, its parents are not liable.[915] Secondly, the conduct of the child which leads to the damage must be unlawful, albeit not necessarily culpable: a position stated by both courts and legislation.[916] The intention has been to establish parental responsibility particularly for children who, at the time of the act, lacked the ability to

---

[915] Cass. 11 Apr. 1991, *RW* 1993–94 p. 1064.

[916] Although European codes do not expressly state that the child's conduct need not be culpable, this is the effect of provisions requiring only unlawful conduct by the child. These are § 832 BGB (see e.g. BGH 19 Jan. 1984, *NJW* 1985 pp. 677, 678), Art. 2048 Ital. Cc (Art. 2047 Cc only concerns children lacking delictual capacity), and Art. 923 Greek Cc (on the dispute concerning fault as a requirement of Art. 923 Cc see fn. 920 below). In Austria the legal situation is the same given that § 1294 and § 1309 ABGB are regarded as one. In Spain Art. 20 CP requires a child below the age of criminal responsibility to have objectively fulfilled the preconditions of a criminal provision, hence also to have acted unlawfully; and Art. 1903 Cc goes so far as to require negligence by the child (see the outstanding comparative examination by Gómez Calle, *Responsabilidad civil de los padres*, pp. 290–297); and Art. 120 NCP (parental liability for crimes of adult children lacking criminal capacity) also requires a *delito o falta*. The well formulated text of Art. 6:169 I BW states the relevance of whether the act 'but for the child's age could be attributed to him as an unlawful act', and Art. 6:169 II BW even employs the term *fout*, which it does not generally employ (see Oldenhuis, *Onrechtmatige daad: aansprakelijkheid voor personen*, p. 26 [no. 18]). As to those codes which are less precise, courts and commentators have 'made up for' deficiences. See for Portugal: Almeida Costa, *Obrigações*, 5th edn., p. 367, who demands a *facto antijurídico* (*ilícito*); STJ 23 Feb.1988, *BolMinJust* 374 (1988) pp. 466, 469; and STJ 20 Mar. 1991, *CJ* XVI (1991–2) pp. 7, 11 ('*o acto do menor deve ser objectivamente ilícito*'); for Belgium: Fagnart, in Dalcq (ed.), *Responsabilité et réparation des dommages*, pp. 15–17 (no. 12–15); from the many decisions Cass. 28 Oct. 1971, *Pas. belge* 1972, I, 200, 202 ('*il faut, mais il suffit . . ., que le mineur ait accompli l'acte lui-même et que cet acte ait été illicite*'); Cass. 26 June 1975, *Pas. belge* 1957, I, 806 (ability to reason is not a prerequisite); Cass. 24 Oct. 1974, *Pas. belge* 1975, I, 237. In France the situation is less clear. Although it used to be usual for the courts to declare only the '*caractère illicite de l'acte commis par le mineur*' to be relevant (Cass.civ. 13 June 1974, Bull.civ. 1974 II no. 1974 II no. 198), the *arrêt Fullenwarth* (Cass.ass.plén. 9 May 1984 *D.* 1984 *Jur.* 529 [see no. 66 and fn. 405 above]) remarked in 1984 that '*il suffit que (le mineur) ait commis un acte qui soit la cause directe du dommage invoqué par la victime*', and thus abandoned the notion of the *fait objectivement illicite* (Starck [-Roland/Boyer], *Obligations*, vol. i, 4th edn., no. 1107). Cass.civ. 13 Apr. 1992, Bull.civ. 1992 II no. 122 is a product of this decision. The Luxembourg courts took the first opportunity to embark on the same course: Cour 12 June 1985, *Pas. luxemb.* 27 (1987–89) p. 182.

reason,[917] or could only exercise such care as could be expected from children of their age (although *in casu* not sufficient to avoid the damage).[918] That a parental obligation to supervise, and with it a delictual responsibility, albeit with different preconditions, exists even for older children who have not yet completed their eighteenth year is undisputed.[919] Liability on the part of the child is not a precondition for parental liability. On the contrary, it is for the parent to compensate for the differences between the standards of care which distinguish a child from an adult.

The notion that parental liability for the child requires merely unlawful **147** but not necessarily culpable conduct could be misconstrued, particularly where a code provides that a duty of care may be breached by mere unlawfulness, rather than fault. Such provisions create the risk that parents could be punished whenever their child injures a person or damages property. This cannot be right: if parents are liable for conduct which would not constitute negligence even if the standards of care required of adults were applied, they would be penalized simply for having brought a child into the world, and no credible legal system counts childbirth as a delict. This leads to the conclusion that parents everywhere are liable only if the child's conduct would have incurred liability if committed by an adult, even where that proposition is not expressly stated.[920]

---

[917] See references in fn. 916 above. Also OLG Oldenburg 19 Oct. 1993, *FamRZ* 1994 p. 833 8 (the headnote of which reads: 'on the requirements of the parental duty to supervise in cases of setting a playmate on fire'); OGH 10 Sep. 1981, *ZVR* 1982/109. In Belgian courts, parents must compensate damage if the minor is *'privé de raison'* not by his age but by ill health (Cass. 18 Oct. 1990, *RGAR* 1992 no. 12026). Although this is at the limit of the scope of parental liability, it does not contradict *lex lata*.

[918] Cass. 26 June 1975, *Pas. belge.* 1975, I, 1046 (1048–49); and Cass. 24 Oct. 1974, *Pas. belge* 1975, I, 237 (8238–239). For a further example see BGH 29 May 1990, BGHZ 111 p. 282.

[919] Even in Austrian (see no. 137 above) and Portuguese law. Although in Portugal Art. 491 Cc employs the term *incapacidade natural*, this includes all minors: see e.g. STJ 20 Mar. 1991, *CJ* XVI (1991–2) p. 7.

[920] In favour of this proposition see for Spain: Gómez Calle (fn. 916). In Greece the courts (e.g. CA Athens 217/1959, *NoB* 7 [1959] p. 741; CFI Thessalonika 2847/1962, *NoB* 11 [1963] p. 957; and CFI Patras 2737/1979, *NoB* 28 [1980] p. 103) and some (earlier) scholars, e.g. Kavkas/ Kavkas, *Enochikon Dikaion*, vol. ii, 6th edn., Art. 923 p. 839; and Zepos, *Enochikon Dikaion*, vol. ii (2), 2nd edn., p. 77) have for the same reason even required fault by the minor, unless he lacks civil capacity. This issue, although controversial, is of little relevance, since those of the opposing view achieve the same result by establishing a breach of duty on the part of the parents; Georgiades/Stathopoulos (-Georgiades), *Greek Cc*, vol. iv, Art. 923 no. 13; Deliyannis/Kornilakis, *Eidiko Enochiko Dikaio*, vol. iii, p. 199; and Filios, *Enochiko Dikaio*, vol. ii (2), 3rd edn., p. 65. The Italian solution is a combination of the two: the impossibility of preventing the act is proved if the conduct of the minor was reasonable from the point of view of the *uomo medio*: Bussani, *Colpa soggettiva*, p. 181; Cass. 6 May 1986, n. 3031, *Giur.it.* 1986, I, 1, 1527. The Belgian Court of Cassation (11 Apr. 1991, *RW* 1993–94 p. 1064) also unambiguously stated: *'Overwegende dat het hof van beroep, nu het de echtgenoten R.-N. op grond van . . . artikel 1384, tweede lid, aansprakelijk verklaart, na te hebben vastgesteld dat hun minderjarige zoon "geen objectieve onrechtmatige daad had vericht", zijn beslissing niet naar recht verantwoordt.'* By contrast, the German course of employing the notion of *'sozialadäquates Verhalten'* as justification (see e.g. OLG Cologne 5 May 1993, *r+s* 1994 pp. 297, 298) is less than convincing: see also no. 199 below.

Consider some examples. At a hotel swimming pool a group of children is playing water-polo. A mother approaches the pool to take photographs. The ball hits the camera, which falls into the water. The child was not negligent, so the question of contributory negligence does not arise: an adult in the same situation would also not have acted negligently, because playing ball in the pool was permitted. The child's parents would therefore not be liable for damages.[921] However, the situation would be altogether different had the boys been playing catch, and if one of them had jumped into the pool, injuring someone. Even if his conduct could not be considered culpable because it was instinctive, his parents would not escape liability. An adult behaving in this fashion would be liable for personal injury caused by negligence. Another relevant case is Rb. Brugge 10 September 1990:[922] two children aged nine and ten entered unsecured private premises. They found a jeep which they thought was damaged beyond repair. They smashed its windows and 'redesigned' its interior. Whether or not their misconception was justified was relevant only regarding the children's liability (which was established). It would not affect their parents' liability, because adults should definitely not make such a mistake.

However, on closer inspection it becomes evident that the position whereby a child whose act complies with the standard of conduct for an adult does not incur liability for his parents is relevant only in legal systems which impose strict liability. For the aim of parental supervision and education is precisely to induce and foster such a sense of care in children.[923]

148   The next question is whether strict liability on the part of the child can incur parental liability. First, one must bear in mind that parental liability (if enforceable) ousts liability in equity, for the latter is always secondary to the former.[924] Secondly, where the keeper is a child, keepers' liability and the special provisions on parental liability are also

---

[921] *VR* 1994 p. 251 (no. 174), decided on 7 Feb. 1994 by the *Raad van toezicht op het schadeverzekeringsbedrijf* (an arbitration body established by Dutch insurers), appears at first glance only to be similar: the plaintiff wanted to film his brother's $1^1/_2$ -year-old daughter while she was playing in the sandpit. The video camera was damaged when the girl threw sand at the plaintiff. Here the *Raad* rightly awarded damages, as the child's act was objectively tortious. However, under Art. 6:101 BW damages were reduced to 75%.

[922] *RW* 1993–1994 p. 651.

[923] In line with this principle, Dutch legislation makes parents liable only if the damaging act would, but for his age, incur liability on the part of the child (see fn. 916). There seems no reason why other countries with strict parental liability should not adopt this idea. In Spain the absence of such a provision causes a number of problems in the field of keepers' liability (see fn. 926). For the same reason Norwegian courts have trouble in arguing convincingly why strict liability can only be imposed on parents if their children have at least acted negligently: see Nygaard, *Skade og ansvar*, 4th edn., p. 428.

[924] See no. 86 above.

mutually exclusive.[925] Under the provisions governing keepers' liability, damages can be claimed even if the dangerous situation was not unlawful and the damage could not have been prevented despite appropriate precautions being taken. In other words, the incident was simply bad luck, with neither breach of a duty of supervision, nor *culpa in educando*. Furthermore, keepers' liability even ousts strict parental liability.[926] In The Netherlands, for instance, house owner's liability under Art. 6:174 BW can—under Art. 6:169 I BW in conjunction with Art. 6:183 I, II BW— be imposed solely on the under-age occupier (*bezitter*, see Arts. 3:107–109 BW), and not on his parents under Art. 6:169 BW.[927]

However, it is very clear that keepers' liability and parental liability   **149** nonetheless share certain objectives. The former also draws on provisions intended to protect minors when establishing the conditions under which a minor may be the legal keeper of a thing which he possesses or owns.[928] The more efforts his parents make to educate and supervise him, the more they (and not the child) are considered the keepers, and the more the strict liability provisions apply to them. Moreover, some codes make the child the keeper, but redirect his strict liability to his parents. This has occurred regarding animal keepers' liability in England and Scotland,[929] and in continental Europe in The Netherlands. Under

[925] In favour: RP 5 July 1979, *CJ* IV (1979–4) p. 1251. For Greece see fn. 920 above. This view is shared in Italy (which always demands an objectively unlawful act, under Art. 2043 Cc, on the part of the minor), Germany (OLG Oldenburg 5 Mar. 1974, *Nds.Rpflege* 1974 p. 135: precondition of an objectively unlawful act under §§ 823 ff. BGB), and Austria (where the issue has apparently never been raised). On the remaining European nations see fns. and no. 150 below.

[926] Spanish commentators also wisely pursue this course. See esp. Gómez Calle, *Responsabilidad civil de los padres*, p. 194 and fn. 151; and Díez-Picazo/Gullón, *Sistema*, vol. i, 7th edn., p. 256: no parental liability if the child is the keeper of the animal; but family law gives the child the opportunity to recover his losses through indemnity. The courts do not seem to oppose their view; see the decision often cited in this context TS 10 May 1985, *RAJ* 1985 no. 2265 p. 1925: two 16-year-olds were riding mules side-by-side on a road at night. The TS decided that they acted negligently. Art. 1905 Span. Cc (animal keepers' liability) therefore did not apply. The mutual exclusivity of keepers' and parental liability was finally acknowledged by AP Lugo of 22 Oct. 1975 (cited by Gómez Calle loc. cit. p. 194): the plaintiff was bitten by a child's dog. The *Audiencia Provincial de Lugo* declared the incident to be within Art. 1905 Cc. As the keeper was under-age, Art. 1903 Cc was employed to transfer liability directly to his father. Although the outcome is justifiable (see also no. 149 below), the court should openly have declared it to be a case of *praeter legem*, judge-made law.

[927] For more detail see *Parlementaire Geschiedenis*, vol. vi, p. 768; *Parlementaire Geschiedenis*, vol. vi, (Inv.) p. 1398. Hence, Art. 6:183 BW ousts Art. 6:164 BW).

[928] For references see fn. 929 below. Also Canaris, *NJW* 1964 pp. 1987, 1989–1992; Hofmann, *NJW* 1964 pp. 228–234.

[929] Sec. 6(3)(b) Animals Act 1971 (c. 22): 'a person is a keeper of an animal if . . . he is the head of a household of which a member under the age of 16 owns the animal or has it in his possession.' Also sec. 5(1)(b) Animals (Scotland) Act 1987 (c.9): 'for the purposes of this Act a person is a keeper of an animal if . . . he has actual care and control of a child under the age of 16 who owns the animal or has possession of it.'

Art. 6:183 II BW parents are liable for children under age fourteen who are *bezitters* of dangerous things or animals, 'unless used to carry out a trade or business'. This concept, which is currently causing problems in Spanish courts,[930] is a move in the right direction. For it is parents who, in exercising their duty of care, decide whether or not their children may keep a pet or a moped.

150   In France and Luxembourg the notion that parental and keepers' liability are mutually exclusive has not taken hold, and it seems to have been ignored in Belgium.[931] Under Art. 1384 II French Cc and Art. 1384 IV Lux. Cc parents are liable if the child is *gardien* (Art. 1384 I Cc) of the thing causing the damage.[932] On studying the relevant cases more closely, it becomes clear that all recent decisions are on cases in which, had the tortfeasors been adults, they would have been presumed negligent. This is precisely where parental liability should end: as stated above, if a child's conduct would not constitute a breach of duty, both breach of duty and *culpa in educando* on the part of his parents should also be denied. France and Luxembourg demonstrate that a liability system which refuses to examine *discernement* regarding the personal liability of a child, and which does not adjust the standard of care to the age of the tortfeasor, is likely to produce controversial results.[933] Were they to apply the more recently developed and stricter form of *faute objective* more rigorously, Art. 1384 I Cc would be rendered redundant regarding parental liability. In other words, not only do *gardien* liability and liability for *faute objective* seem to have been co-ordinated insufficiently, the latter also appears to cause unease amongst the judiciary.

An example of the dilemma caused by *gardien* liability being incorporated in parental liability is Trib.gr.inst. Bernay of 1 June 1988.[934] A group of children of about fifteen years of age stole substances from the house of a boy, B, who later became a co-defendant, to make a

---

[930] See fn. 926 above.

[931] It was discussed (and rightly rejected) by Cornelis, *Buitencontractueel aansprakelijkheidsrecht*, no. 195, pp. 330–331; and Meinertzhagen-Limpens, *Rev.crit.jur.belge* 1985 pp. 212, 223–225. However, Cass. 5 Nov. 1981, *Rev.crit.jur.belge* 1985 p. 207, a decision on the same issue albeit in the field of liability for employees, seems to follow the opposite path. The Court of Cassation found the employee, a riding instructor, to be the *gardien* of his employer's horse. He was therefore held liable under Art. 1385 Cc (animal keepers' liability), and Art. 1384 III Cc (employers' liability) applied to the employer.

[932] For a guideline ruling on this issue see Cass.civ. 10 Feb. 1966, *D.* 1966 *Jur.* 332 (concl. Schmelk): 'si une même personne ne peut être poursuivie à la fois en qualité de gardien de la chose et en qualité de père de l'enfant qui a occasionné le dommage, rien n'empêche que la responsabilité de l'enfant gardien de la chose, et celle du père sur le fondement de l'article 1384, alinéa 4, soient retenues. Si la responsabilité du père suppose que celle de l'enfant ait été établie, la loi ne distingue pas entre les causes qui ont pu donner naissance à la responsabilité de l'enfant.' The decision prompted Luxembourg to set similar new precedents: cf. Lux. 22 June 1982, *Pas. luxemb.* 26 (1984–86) p. 26 and Cour 7 Feb. 1962, *Pas. luxemb.* 18 (1960–62) p. 494.

[933] See nos. 66–68 above.   [934] *Gaz.Pal.* 1991, Somm. 233.

'bomb'. The device exploded causing serious injuries to one of the youths. No liability of the parents of B under Art. 1384 I Cc. They had only been *gardiens* of the original substances, not of the 'bomb', which constituted a new thing. *Gardien* liability on the part of B was not upheld, since under Art. 1384 I Cc *co-gardiens* are not responsible for each other. Even liability under Art. 1382 Cc was not proven. The damage was not an 'immediate result' of B's conduct, but rather *'la conséquence de l'imprudence de la victime'*. Thus Art. 1384 IV in conjunction with Art. 1382 Cc did not apply, and liability under Art. 1384 IV Cc in conjunction with Art. 1384 I Cc was also not established, because the boys had been *co-gardiens*. The question arises of why the court relied upon *gardien* liability at all, which was not only unnecessary, but confused the situation. As where children cause damage by playing with darts or matches, here too parental liability could have been founded on Art. 1382 Cc because the parents of B had exercised less care than should have been expected from a *bonus paterfamilias*. In such cases *faute objective* ought to be employed. To rely on the notion of *garde* is to ignore the purpose for which parental liability is imposed.

What is true of keepers' liability is also true of conduct-related strict **151** liability, predominantly found in product and environmental liability, and which can almost never be imposed on minors. However, the liability of a juvenile for a presumed breach of duty (e.g. as the driver of a vehicle) can actively affect parental liability: his presumed misconduct will lead to a presumption of breach of duty on their part.

A further problem for parental liability is the question of how far they **152** can be held liable if their child fails to take appropriate precautions to protect others. To find a solution one must consider parental duties in relation to the duties of a child. Parents can indeed induce in their children a sense of care for others, but this is hardly achieved by supervision. Moreover, in cases involving failure to supervise, it is nearly always irrelevant whether the child's delict was caused by an act or a failure to act.[935] Where a parent tells his child, who is nearer to the source of danger, to act, the parent is usually concerned, not with the duty to supervise, but with the duty of care towards third parties. It is therefore advisable to exercise restraint in the field of omissions. Regarding parental liability, it would certainly be wrong to apply the same duty of care to children as to adults. Parents are only required to prevent their children from causing danger to others, not to ensure that the children act as guardians. If a seventeen-year-

---

[935] The existence of a grey area between act and omission does not justify van Dunné's harsh criticism of the Dutch legislator for the wording of Art. 6:169 I BW (*Verbintenissenrecht*, vol. ii, 2nd edn., pp. 576–577). It remains for the court to determine whether the circumstances of the case point to an act or an omission, thus limiting the problem by exempting only 'true omissions' from Art. 6:169 I BW, i.e.—unlike in the example above—cases lacking an act which created a danger.

old who lives in his own flat repeatedly fails to comply with his duty to clean the staircase, or regularly neglects to lock his car so that it may be stolen and become involved in an accident, his parents can still be held liable. However, liability for younger children covers only conduct which could have been expected from children of their age. The Dutch legislator has expressed this view by making parents of children under fourteen years of age 'liable [only] for damage done to another by such conduct of that child which must be considered an act' (Art. 6:169 I BW). This provision was prompted by the fact that parental liability in The Netherlands is strict.[936] Nonetheless the provision would also be beneficial for the other European systems, subject only to a little flexibility on the age requirement.

(4) The Objective of Parental Liability

153   The objective of parental liability is to compensate others for damage caused by children.[937] Children falling victim to a breach of parental duty, for example by self-inflicted injury, or owing to the conduct of another, can therefore only rely on the rules of general liability.[938] In such circumstances—depending on the relevant legal system—the special provisions on parental liability are replaced by basic regulations governing liability,[939] provisions on liability for failure to act,[940] or rules on strict and *gardien*

---

[936] The famous *struikelende bakker* case (HR 22 Nov. 1974, *NedJur* 1975 no. 149, p. 452) prompted that provision. Children had been playing outside a bakery, and omitted to warn a baker about a rope streched over the path. Whether the rope had been placed there by the children was unknown. The claim against their parents was dismissed. The children could not have been expected to know that they should warn the baker.

[937] Some codes already specify that special provisions on parental liability only apply in claims for damages made by 'others', and not by their own children: § 832 BGB, Art. 491 Port. Cc, Art. 923 Greek Cc, and Art. 6:169 BW.

[938] This common European principle is also shared by Austria. OLG Innsbruck 11 Mar. 1985, *ZVR* 1986/114 also applied § 1309 ABGB in a case of self-inflicted injury of a ward, but § 1309 ABGB is really only another general provision on liability for established breach of duty of care; see also no. 137 above. Moreover, most codes offer causes of action under family law: for Germany see *MünchKomm* (-Hinz), 3rd edn., § 1664 n. 1, contributing to the discussion as to whether § 1664 BGB constitutes an independent cause of action. For Greece, where the situation is similar, see Agallopoulou/Zervogianni, *FS Michaelides-Nouaros*, vol. a, (1987) pp. 31, 40; and Georgiades/Stathopoulos (-Georgiades), *Greek Cc*, vol. iv, Art. 923 no. 4.

[939] This is common procedure. For Italy see App. Firenze 17 Apr. 164, Gentile/Guerreri/ Guerreri, *La responsabilità, voce responsabilità civile—genitori e tutori* 64 (62); Giur.sist. Bigiavi (-Mantovani) vol. ii, (1) p. 32; Franzoni, *Fatti illeciti*, Art. 2048 Cc p. 351; for Portugal STJ 17 Jan. 1980, *BolMinJust* 293 (1980) p. 308 (child injured in road traffic accident; no presumption of parents' fault); for Greece *Georgiades* (fn. 938 above); for Spain Goméz Calle, *Responsabilidad civil de los padres*, pp. 428–431 (liability under Art. 154 Cc); for Germany OLG Karlsruhe 8 Oct. 1976, OLGZ 1977 pp. 326, 328 (liability only under § 823, not under § 832 BGB, since a person needing supervision cannot himself claim damages under § 832 BGB); for Belgium see Vandenberghe/Van Quickenborne/Geelen/ De Coster, *TPR* 1987 pp. 1255, 1463 (no. 123), and e.g. Brussels 5 Apr. 1979, *Pas. belge* 1979, II, 90, 91 ('tout en ne perdant pas de vue le souci de protéger les tiers victimes').

[940] Pires de Lima/Antunes Varela, *Cc anotado*, vol. i, 4th edn., Art. 491 p. 492 (referring to Art. 486 Cc: *omissões*); BGH 16 Jan. 1979, *NJW* 1979 p. 973.

liability. Moreover, in both Germany (§ 1664 BGB) and Greece (Art. 1531 Greek Cc) liability for parents' fault *vis-à-vis* their children has been defused in that they are only liable for *diligentia quam in suis*, as a result of which they may even be responsible only for gross negligence.[941] Not only in countries employing such provisions, but in general, it seems advantageous to exempt from the special provisions on parental liability both liability for self-inflicted injuries and for injuries caused by persons not related to the child, as well as damage caused by the other parent and the child's minor brothers or sisters.[942] Those persons are also not 'others' within the terms of the provisions: brothers and sisters are excluded because damage which they cause arises from a breach of parental duties both to supervise them and to protect the injured child. The other parent cannot be 'another' because the provisions only envisage him as a defendant. He has no claim as *co-gardien* against the other supervisor.

The next question is whether a child's claim may be countered on the   **154** basis of his parents' failure to supervise him as a form of contributory negligence. Although it is agreed that children cannot be held liable for their parents,[943] no consensus exists as to whether a child's claim against

[941] In Germany the question of whether, and if so to what extent, § 1664 BGB applies to delictual duties is still moot. In RG 22 Dec. 1910, RGZ 75 pp. 251, 254 the question remained unanswered. (Some authors argue that it does not, e.g. *MünchKomm* [-Hinz], 3rd edn., § 1664 n. 6). BGH 16 Jan. 1979, *NJW* 1979 pp. 973, 974 did not discuss it, since *diligentia quam in suis* on the part of the mother had been established. Only shortly before, OLG Karlsruhe 8 Oct. 1976, *OLGZ* 1977 pp. 327, 329 had even held that 'the liability limitation under § 1664 BGB does not cover damage arising from a breach of duty of supervision'. On the other hand, LG Freiburg 3 Aug. 1965, *VersR* 1966 p. 476 declared that § 1664 was applicable 'unless the unlawful act bears no connection to parental authority being exercised'. BGH 1 Mar. 1988, *VersR* 1988 p. 632 then decided that § 1664 BGB is 'in any event' applicable in cases where parental duties *'ganz in der Sorge für die Person aufgehen'*. OLG Hamm 20 Jan. 1992, *VersR* 1993 p. 483 and OLG Hamm 17 Aug. 1993, *r+s* 1994 pp. 15, 16 both followed this decision.

[942] In agreement: Cornelis, *Buitencontractueel aansprakelijkheidsrecht*, p. 308 (no. 179); presumably also HR 6 May 1983, *NedJur* 1983 no. 584 p. 1824. Insofar as the duty to supervise children is also a duty arising from marriage (see Art. 1396 Greek Cc and § 1369 BGB) both marital duties and duties of care oust liability under § 832 BGB and Art. 923 Greek Cc respectively. Suffice it to say that the special provisions on parental liability do not affect a child's liability to his parents: Ghent 19 Sep. 1981, *RW* 1982–83, p. 43; Vandenberghe/Van Quickenborne/Geelen/De Coster, *TPR* 1987 pp. 1255, 1463 (no. 123); and HR 11 Apr. 1975, *NedJur* 1975 no. 373, p. 1131.

[943] However, this view is not necessarily shared by Dutch law, which reads: 'if the conduct of a representative (*vertegenwoordiger*) in the exercise of the powers resulting from the representation commits a fault towards another, the person who is represented is also liable towards that other person.' Hence, Art. 6:172 BW also applies to statutory representatives (Klaassen, *WPNR* 1988 no. 5891 [pp. 593–597]; id., *Risico-aansprakelijkheid*, pp. 72–77) and parents, who have this statutory power. Yet it is suggested that it should be restricted to cases of parental care for property of the child, such as his business (see also no. 200 below), and not for *culpa in educando*. See also *Parlementaire Geschiedenis*, vol. vi, pp. 731–732 (the extent of Art. 6:172 BW should be kept narrow); and Asser (-van der Grinten) vol. i: *De Vertegenwoordiging*, 7th edn., p. 157. Finally, as López Beltran de Heredia, *Responsabilidad civil de los padres*, p. 86 rightly observed, even criminally incapable Spanish children may be held liable for their (insolvent) parents if they committed the crime with the parents.

another can be reduced on the ground of the child's parents' failure to supervise. Hence, the question is not whether the parents' claim for injury to their child is to be reduced. If contributory fault is established, it always entails a reduction of the damages due to the parents.[944] The question is rather whether contributory fault can be attributed to the child where his parents (individually or together) fail in their duty to protect him. According to some European laws the child can be held accountable,[945] but the majority (correctly in this author's opinion) do not place responsibility on the child.[946] There is no good reason to identify the parents with the child.[947] In the law of delict the victim is not usually prejudiced simply because the delict was committed by more than one tortfeasor. For damage caused to children, it follows that the other party and the parents are joint and several tortfeasors, and the former can only bring against the latter a claim for indemnity. Otherwise, if he were liable, for instance, for only 50% of the damage, he could then

---

[944] Cass. 11 Apr. 1986, n. 2549, *Giust.civ.Mass.* 1986 no. 2549 p. 708; Georgiades/Stathopoulos (-Georgiades), *Greek Cc*, vol. iv, Art. 923 no. 19; Versailles 27 Mar. 1980, *BolMinJust* 295 (1980) p. 408; OLG Karlsruhe 7 Dec. 1977, *VersR* 1978 p. 575 (nervous shock; the court correctly applied § 832 BGB within the scope of § 254 BGB). The parents' claim for their own damage can also be diminished if contributory fault is attributed to the injured child. See for Germany: § 846 BGB; BGH 11 May 1971, BGHZ 56 pp. 163, 168–171; for Greece: Dialinas, *Das Mitverschulden des Minderjährigen*, pp. 174–176; and for France: Aix-en-Provence 13 June 1963, *Gaz.Pal.* 1963 Somm. 11; Amiens 23 Nov. 1962, D. 1963 *Jur.* 194; Trib.gr.inst. Caen 10 June 1963, *Sem.Jur.* 1963, II, 13414.

[945] E.g. in Spain, usually by applying Art. 1103 Cc (reduction of damages): TS 27 Nov. 1993, *La Ley* 1993 (4) pp. 547, 549; TS 25 May 1985, *RAJ* 1985 no. 2812 p. 2353; TS 21 Nov. 1985, *RAJ* 1985 no. 5624 p. 4783; TS 4 Nov. 1991, *RAJ* 1991 no. 8141 p. 11160; TS 5 Apr. 1995, RAJ 1995 no. 2882 p. 3846. In Portugal (where Art. 571 Cc supplies a solution) STJ 26 Mar. 1980, *BolMinJust* 295 (1980) p. 408 (a traffic accident in which even risk liability was denied because the child's injuries were primarily caused by his parents' failure to supervise). For Italy: Cass. 7 Apr. 1988, n. 2738, *Giust.civ.Mass.* 1988 no. 2738 p. 671 (child injured by a playmate of the same age; the award was reduced due to contributory fault by the mother, who should have prevented such dangerous games). In a case concerning a contract with protective effect for others (see § 5, nos. 478 ff.) even the BGH 30 Apr. 1968, *VersR* 1968 pp. 673, 674 ordered a reduction in damages for failure to supervise. Agallopoulou-Zervogianni, *FS Michaelides-Nouaros*, vol. A (1987) pp. 31, 40 argues for a distinction between delictually capable and incapable children.

[946] E.g. BGH 8 Mar. 1951, BGHZ 1 pp. 248, 250–252 (although the reference to the supposedly different legal situation in France is misleading); OLG Hamm 14 Dec. 1976, *VersR* 1977 p. 531. Also Cass.crim. 10 Oct. 1963, D. 1964 *Jur.* 20 (note Esmein); Cass.civ. 12 June 1975, *Sem.Jur.* 1975, IV, 252; Dijon 24 June 1994, *Sem.Jur.* 1995, IV, 36; HR 31 May 1985, *NedJur* 1986 no. 690 p. 2569 (note Brunner); Hof 's-Hertogenbosch 27 Apr. 1961, *NedJur* 1962 no. 274 p. 895; Hof 's-Gravenhage 6 Mar. 1957, *NedJur* 1957 no. 429 p. 776; OGH 16 June 1954, *JBl* 1954 p. 593; OGH 28 Sep. 1961, *JBl* 1962 p. 155; OGH 19 Oct. 1955, *ZVR* 1956/29 (pp. 40, 41); OGH 23 Oct. 1975, *ZVR* 1976/318. In Belgium: Vandenberghe/Van Quickenborne/Geelen/De Coster, *TPR* 1987 pp. 1255, 1477 (no. 128); Cornelis, *Responsabilité extra-contractuelle*, no. 181. For Greece: Georgiades/Stathopoulos (-Georgiades), *Greek Cc*, vol. iv, Art. 923 no. 18; Dialinas, *Das Mitverschulden des Minderjährigen*, pp. 163–164; CFI Athens 17485/1956; *NoB* 5 (1958) p. 390; CA Athens 5014/1978, *NoB* 27 (1979) p. 790.

[947] Even in Denmark and under the common law this principle is applied less and less strictly: see no. 326 below.

sue the parents (again under the indemnity/contribution rules) for 50% of the damages for which he was liable. Furthermore, in cases of injury to a child, a breach of the duty of parental care is often presumed, and one should therefore be wary of holding the breach against the child by rendering him liable for contributory negligence. For, as stated above, a child suing his parents (or rather their third-party liability insurer) for a contribution could not base his claim on a presumed breach of duty.

(5) The Problems of Joint and Several Liability

The rules on liability of collateral tortfeasors have been established.[948] **155** If damage to a child results from both the action of another and a failure of parental care, both parties are jointly and severally liable. This rule also applies if parents and child are answerable to a third party,[949] and if the child and the third party are responsible for damage to the parents. However, common liability of and claims between joint and several tortfeasors must be distinguished from cases involving collateral tortfeasorship of parents and a third party, first, because parents are in a better position than the third party. The German *Bundesgerichtshof* considered that the solution which it developed for standard cases of '*gestörte Gesamtschuldverhältnisse*' (according to which the privileged liability position of one tortfeasor automatically releases the other defendant from liability to the plaintiff, thus reducing the latter's damages) does not apply to cases under § 1664 BGB (liability based on *negligencia quam in suis*: the other tortfeasor is liable in full to the child, while his parents, who are protected by this provision, are liable neither to the child, nor (even partially) to the other tortfeasor.[950] Using the same argument, that '*le recours en garantie, exercé par le coauteur d'un accident de la circulation [aurait] pour effet direct ou indirect de priver la victime de l'entière réparation de son dommage*',[951] France has gone yet further and, in cases of *gardien* liability in road traffic accidents, denied the other of the right to contribution from parents who are themselves liable for breaching their duty of supervision;[952] a

---

[948] On the liability of collateral tortfeasors generally: nos. 51–53 above.

[949] On the position in Spanish law see no. 65 above. TS 19 Apr. 1988, *RAJ* 1988 no. 2817 p. 2706 clarifies that, in cases where both child and parents can claim damages, and the latter waive their claim, the child's claim remains, because Art. 166 Span. Cc prohibits the waiving of a child's claim.

[950] BGH 1 Mar. 1988, *VersR* 1988 pp. 632, 633–634, abandoning the position held by BGH 27 June 1961, BGHZ 35 p. 317 (although this decision concerned § 1359 BGB).

[951] Cass.civ. 20 Apr. 1988, Bull.civ. 1988, II, no. 87 (*arrêt no. 1*).

[952] Loc. cit. (fn. 951 above). See also Court of Cassation ruling of the same day (loc. cit., fn. 951 above no. 87, *arrêt no. 2*). This rule does not apply where the other tortfeasor beings his own claim for damages: Cass.civ. 6 July 1994, Bull.civ. 1994, II, no. 184 (p. 106).

privilege which cannot be claimed by their third-party liability insurers.[953]

156 A provision which seems to have ignored these developments is § 840 II German BGB. On a literal reading, parents who must indemnify a second tortfeasor under § 832 BGB can claim full indemnity from their children if these are also liable to the other tortfeasor. This provision, based on an antiquated and pedantic construction of the fault principle, has no equivalent in present-day Europe.[954] All other nations take into account at least the share of fault of the collateral tortfeasor.[955] Some go even further and (usually for the benefit of the child) include the financial situation of the parties in their considerations.[956] One might conclude that indemnity between children and parents would be better placed in family law than in the law of delict.[957]

b. Liability of other Supervisors

157 As explained above, parents may employ others to perform the duty to supervise. If a child commits an unlawful act while under their care, these persons may be liable under all European codes, although subject to different conditions. Although no code imposes strict liability on employees or persons temporarily entrusted with the care of a child,[958] the issues surrounding such person's liability still divide Europe. In the first group, consisting of Germany (§ 832 II BGB), Greece (Art. 923 II Cc), and Portugal, it is suggested that additional carers be treated as parents, so they incur liability for presumed failure to supervise if that duty is contractual. (Although Austria takes the same approach,[959] it belongs to the second group, because its § 1309 ABGB alters the burden of proof).[960] In the second group, Belgium, France, Italy, Luxembourg,

---

[953] This is how Jourdain, *Rev.trim.dr.civ.* 87 (1988) p. 791 (no. 15) interprets both rulings. If the parents are covered by insurance, even an indirect impairment of the child's interests is highly unlikely.

[954] On the discussion about the scope of Art. 2055 Ital. Cc in such cases see fn. 541 above. The criticism of *MünchKomm* (-Mertens), 2nd edn., § 832 BGB no. 25 on § 840 II BGB is justified.

[955] E.g. Art. 2055 II Ital. Cc; Art. 497 II Port. Cc; Art. 927 Greek Cc.

[956] On Arts. 6:101, 6:102 BW see e.g. Asser (-Hartkamp), *Verbintenissenrecht*, vol. iii, 9th edn., nos. 135, 137–138. Although the draft of the new BW included provisions on the equitable liability of children to their parents, the concept never became law.

[957] Rutten-Roos, *Jeugdigen in burgerrechtelijke relaties*, p. 106; and Oldenhuis, *Onrechtmatige daad: aansprakelijkheid voor personen*, no. 26, who argues that it is a principle of family law to deny parents a right of recourse against their children.

[958] Art. 6:169 I BW is expressly limited to persons exercising 'parental authority or guardianship over a child'.

[959] E.g. Schwimann (-Harrer), *ABGB*, vol. v, § 1309 no. 3.   [960] See no. 137 above.

The Netherlands, and Spain,[961] persons employed to supervise the children are only liable for failure to act. Here only teachers and training employers are subject to increased liability.[962]

The latter approach has more to commend it. The system used in **158** Germany, Greece, and Portugal has two unfortunate features. First, all contracts to supervise will protect third parties, which is inconsistent with the principle of privity of contract; and secondly, the contractual burden of presumed fault is shifted to tort law. Such a step is only appropriate for some cases of liability for supervision, and discourages neighbours and relations from stepping in when needed, and it utterly contradicts modern trends towards granting employees protection against liability to others. This may be of little concern to nannies whose employers are ultimately liable for them and who have only a limited right to contribution.[963] However, what of the child-minder looking after the children of a debt-burdened family in which both parents are working?

For relatives, friends, and neighbours who baby-sit only occasionally, **159** the practical effect of the 'German' solution depends on the conditions under which a legal system presumes the existence of a contract.[964] Unfortunately, German law especially is too ready to declare that the conduct of the parties implies intention to create a legal relationship.[965] However, the preparatory works to § 832 BGB, and Arts. 923 II Greek Cc and 491 Port. Cc which were evidently fashioned after the German model, highlight another aspect. The legislator had in mind, not persons supervising children, but rather 'guardians of the mentally handicapped'.[966]

---

[961] E.g. Cass.civ. 9 Nov. 1971, *D.* 1972 *Jur.* 75 (child spending his holidays with his grandparents; *garde* remained with the parents; no *gardien* liability of the grandparents in respect of matches; no liability under Art. 1382 Cc because no fault could be established); and Cass.civ. 25 Jan. 1995, *D.* 1995 *Somm.* 232 (even if a child lives with his grandfather, liability under Art. 1384 IV Cc remains with the parents); and Asser (-Hartkamp), *Verbintenissenrecht*, vol. iii, 9th edn., p. 126 (other supervisors are liable under 6:162 BW); Cornelis, *Buitencontractueel aansprakelijkheidsrecht*, no. 183; André, *Responsabilités*, pp. 152, 735–737 (liability of other persons—step-parents, grandparents, and other relations—only under Arts. 1382 and 1384 I Cc [substantive liability]; Cass. 15 Dec. 1972, n. 3617, *Giur.it.* 1973, I, 1, 1534 someone renting out play-cars is under no duty to supervise the children renting the vehicles); López Beltran de Heredia, *Responsabilidad civil de los padres*, pp. 140–142; and TS 30 Apr. 1969, *RAJ* 1969 no. 2411 p. 1690 (one child injured another with a stone while under his grandfather's supervision; no liability of the latter under Art. 1903 Cc [not applicable *in casu*], nor under Art. 1902 Cc [no fault on the part of the grandfather]). In cases of self-inflicted injury also, liability can only arise from 'normal' liability for fault: OLG Cologne 22 Dec. 1993, *NJW-RR* 1994 p. 862.   [962] See no. 160 below.

[963] See no. 205 below.

[964] E.g. RL 15 Nov. 1988, *CJ* XIII (1988–5) p. 112. Also *MünchKomm* (-Mertens), § 832 BGB no. 13 and Georgiades/Stathopoulos (-Georgiades), *Greek Cc*, vol. iv, Art. 923 no. 10: (a child stayed with relatives for an extended period, rendering it virtually impossible for his parents to exercise their duty of supervision. Intent was implied on the part of the relatives to assume parental duties).   [965] See nos. 464 ff., 500.

[966] Mot. II pp. 735, 736. Also Vaz Serra, *BolMinJust* 85 (1959) pp. 381, 393; and Pires de Lima/Antunes Varela, *Cc anotado*, vol. I, 4th edn., Art. 491 no. 1.

These provisions have always[967] dealt with the liability of natural and legal persons contractually bound to care for mentally handicapped adults. In this light, § 832 II BGB seems a rather 'modern' provision, for French courts have only recently decided to impose strict liability on the *gardien* in such cases, under Art. 1384 I Cc.[968] Hence, it is the supervision of the mentally handicapped, and not the care of children, which should be subject to a stricter form of liability. The mistake of the German model is to equate the two.

2. LIABILITY FOR PUPILS AND APPRENTICES

a. Liability of Teachers and School Governing Bodies

160   Liability for delicts committed by pupils[969] during lessons[970] also comes under liability for unlawful conduct by minors.[971] Although the codes apparently provide clear special provisions governing responsibility for

---

[967] No recent decisions seem to hold domestic staff or even relatives liable for presumed failure of supervision. So far these provisions have only been relevant in cases of psychiatric institutions' liability for run-away patients; see e.g. BGH 19 Jan. 1994, *NJW* 1985 p. 677; and STJ 25 July 1985, *BolMinJust* 349 (1985) p. 516. Furthermore, § 832 II BGB is considered to apply to the staff supervising a children's home: OLG Oldenburg 6 Jan. 1994, *FamRZ* 1995 pp. 600, 601 (although *in casu* breach of duty of care was not proven).

[968] Cass.civ. 29 Mar. 1991, *D.* 1991 *Jur.* 324; Rouen 25 Sep. 1991, *D.* 1993 *Jur.* 5. Also the reference in Cass.civ. 6 Jan. 1993, *D.* 1994 *Jur.* 95; and no. 115 above.

[969] No code provides extra provisions governing liability for students; however, 'pupils' as in the text above, usually includes kindergarten children: e.g. TS 21 Nov. 1990, *RAJ* 1990 no. 9014 p. 11476; and fn. 988 below.

[970] This covers not only lessons but also breaks (e.g. Mons 9 June 1993, *JT* 1993 p. 688; and Cass. 15 Dec. 1972, n. 3617, *Giur.it.* 1973, I, 1, 1534), games (e.g. Cass. 27 Mar. 1984, n. 2027, *Rep.gen.* 1984 col. 3443 no. 119), excursions (e.g. Cass. 5 Sep. 1986, n. 5424, *Rep.gen.* 1986 col. 3602 no. 133; and Vred. Ronse 5 Feb. 1991, *RW* 1993–94 p. 652), and other events for which the school is ultimately responsible. Cass. 19 Feb. 1994, n. 1623, *Giust.civ.Mass.* 1994 no. 1623 p. 182 extends state liability under Art. 28 Italian Constitution in conjunction with Arts. 2043, 2048 Cc to injuries inflicted by school staff after school. Hof 's-Hertogenbosch 15 Apr. 1992, *NedJur* 1994 no. 760 p. 3631 held a school 80% liable for an accident which occurred because a student managed to steal chemicals and experiment with them at home. However, liability for supervision on the way to or from school lies with the parents and not the school: Brussels 11 June 1992, *RGAR* 1995 no. 12466.

[971] According to App. Turin 8 June 1968, *Giur.it.* 1969, I, 2, 492, Art. 2048 II Ital. Cc, for instance, is only applicable to under-age pupils; and Arts. 1903 V Span. Cc and 22 II Span. CP (Art. 120 IV NPC do not mention pupils, but Art. 22 II CP nonetheless remains in force—Art. 1 lit. a *Disposición derogatoria* on the NCP) are expressly limited to liability for damage caused by the 'under-age pupils [of] education centres which do not provide higher education', i.e. schools and not universities. As for 18- and 19-year-olds, Koziol/ Frotz, *RdS* 1979 pp. 97, 99 rightly say that 'they have by and large achieved such a high degree of independence that they no longer need to be supervised'.

pupils (Arts. 1384 IV Belg. Cc, 1384 VI French Cc; 2048 II Ital. Cc; 1903 V Span. Cc; and 22 II Span. CP; and—for provisions which not only affect teachers and pupils—Arts. 923 II Greek Cc and 491 Port. Cc, and § 832 II BGB)[972] this issue has developed into a complicated area of liability law, since it encompasses questions of state liability and social security law.

A law governing industrial injuries insurance generally ousts the other **161** two compensation systems only in cases concerning legal relationships between members of the same school, such as injury inflicted on one pupil by another, or by teachers. It does not affect injuries inflicted upon third parties, e.g. by pupils throwing stones from the school playground at the windows of adjacent buildings.[973] Liability in such cases depends on whether the miscreants are pupils of a state school[974] or a private school. Throughout Europe, only private schools remain subject to private law, and only in so far as they do not provide compulsory education. Here liability is usually based on presumed[975] failure to supervise, but in some cases breach of duty must be positively established[976] *casu per casu*.[977] In either case teachers often escape liability,[978] either because the legislation channels liability directly to

---

[972] In the latter provisions the duty to supervise can only be assumed by means of contract and thus concerns only private schools. Whether liability for presumed breach of duty is incurred by the teacher or the school governing body is determined *casu per casu*; however, in most cases it is suggested that the teacher is merely an employee of the school in performance of its obligation to educate, and therefore its servant.

[973] E.g. Vred. Ronse 5 Feb. 1991, *RW* 1993–94 p. 652: during an excursion to Austria a pupil intentionally damaged the tyres of a coach. The court found the school liable under Art 1384 IV Belg. Cc.

[974] It is not possible here to list all relevant provisions on schools. Thus Art. 10 French *Décret* 60–389 of 22 Apr. 1960 *relatif au contrat d'association à l'enseignement public passé par les établissements d'enseignement privé* (JO 24 Apr. 1960) is just one example in which state liability under the Act of 5 Apr. 1937 (see also fn. 984 below) has been extended to private schools which have been awarded state recognition.

[975] E.g. in Belgium (under Art. 1384 V Cc); in Germany (§ 832 II BGB); in Italy (Art. 2048 III Cc); and in Portugal (Art. 491 Cc). However, Art. 1384 V Belg. Cc has been rendered virtually redundant by Art. 18 of the *Loi* of 3 July 1978 *relative aux contrats de travail*, BS 22 Aug. 1978, a provision dealing with the (personal) external liability of employees which usually also covers employed teachers, thus limiting their liability to cases of *faute grave*.

[976] E.g. in France (Art. 1384 VII Cc); in Luxembourg (Art. 1382 Cc: teachers are no longer mentioned in Art. 1384 Cc); in The Netherlands (Art. 6:162 BW: Art. 6:169 BW is not applicable); and in Spain, where Art. 1903 V Cc is applied, for liability under Art. 22 Span. CP (as well as under Art. 1903 V and Art. 1904 II Cc in the version of Act 1/1991 [BOE no. 7 of 8 Jan. 1991]) liability is strict, although only secondary.

[977] See e.g. Mons 24 Oct. 1984, *Pas. belge* 1984, II, 151, by which the age and number of children to be supervised plays an important role; and Hof 's-Hertogenbosch 24 Feb. 1981, *NedJur* 1982 no. 313 p. 1149 (teacher negligently allowed his pupils to use a delivery bicycle). However, note that both cases concern state, not private, schools.

[978] For Belgium see fn. 975 above.

the school governing body[979] because that body is deemed to be the 'teacher',[980] or because (only) the governing body as the wealthier party is sued in its capacity as employer.[981] In other cases the teacher's share of fault is considered negligible compared to both the parents' failure to supervise and *culpa in educando*.[982]

162   In Belgium and The Netherlands, where the stricter form of liability under Art. 1403 IV BW (old) has been ousted by liability for fault under Art. 6:162 BW,[983] teachers of state schools are also covered only by the general protective mechanisms of liability law; no special rules exist. However, most other nations consider teachers' duty to supervise to be an obligation arising from public law; thus violation renders only the school governing body accountable for claims by third parties.[984] The

---

[979] As in Spain under Art. 1903 V Cc and Art. 22 CP (see fns. 970, 976 above). Responsibility for damage caused by pupils outside school lies with 'persons and institutions responsible for primary and secondary education centres'. Under Art. 1904 II Cc, contribution can only be claimed if the teacher acted intentionally or with gross negligence. The reason for extending this liability regime in 1991 to include state schools was that, despite the moderate judgments of the *Tribunal Supremo* (e.g. TS 21 Nov. 1990, *RAJ* 1990 no. 9014 p. 11476 [lunch in a kindergarten; one child put a fork into the eye of another; no liability of the staff or kindergarten]), the legislator still felt it necessary to reduce the instances of personal liability of teachers. Liability for failure to supervise has been replaced by a 'duty to organize' on the part of the governing body: for more detail see Signes Pascual, *La Ley* 1992 (2) pp. 958–961. The Act of 1 Sep. 1988 (*Mémorial* A 1988 p. 1000) brought Luxembourg a similar solution.

[980] As argued by Kruithof, in: Vandenberghe (ed.), *Onrechtmatige daad*, p. 41. This line is not followed by the Belgian courts: Brussels 2 Nov. 1977, *JT* 1978 p. 135; and Cass. 3 Dec. 1986, *Pas. belge* 1987, I, 410.

[981] That such employers' liability exists (in most cases) has repeatedly been stressed, e.g. by Oldenhuis, see Bloembergen (-Oldenhuis), *Onrechtmatige daad*, vol. i, Art. 6:170 no. 17; and id., *Aansprakelijkheid voor personen*, no. 34.

[982] E.g. Mons 9 June 1993, *JT* 1993 p. 688. See also Cass. 28 Sep. 1989, *JT* 1990 p. 22 (father and teacher jointly and severally liable); Rb. Alkmaar 9 June 1983, *NedJur* 1984 no. 215 p. 808 (accident during a swimming lesson because the water was too shallow; only the owner of the pool was held liable, no liability on the part of the teacher); and Cass. 22 Apr. 1977, n. 1501, *Rep.gen.* 1977 no. 118 col. 3484 (*in casu* parental *culpa in educando* outweighed the teacher's failure to supervise).

[983] For a comparison of old and new law see esp. Asser (-Hartkamp), *Verbintenissenrecht*, vol. iii, no. 138 a, pp. 134–135. However, Dutch precedents under the old BW referring only to Art. 1401 BW (old) and not to Art. 1403 IV BW (old) have lost none of their significance. See e.g. HR 14 June 1985, *NedJur* 1985 no. 736 p. 2410: fatal trampolining accident involving a 17-year-old pupil; teacher held liable for allowing the dangerous jumping and for not having sufficient knowledge of first aid.

[984] Austria: § 1 I *Amtshaftungsgesetz* (Federal Act of 18 Dec. 1948, governing liability of Federal and *Länder* governments, of districts and local authorities, and of other corporative and statutory bodies for damage caused in the execution of the law; Germany: § 839 BGB in conjunction with Art. 34 GG; France: Art. 2 Act of 5 Apr. 1937 (*Loi modifiant les règles de la preuve en ce qui concerne la responsabilité civile des instituteurs et le dernier alinéa de l'article 1384 du Code civil relatif à la substitution de la responsabilité de l'État à celle des membres de l'enseignement public*) JO of 6 Apr. 1937. For German discussion of the issue see v. Bar (-Gotthardt), *DeliktsR in Europa, Frankreich*, p. 35; Greece: Arts. 105, 106 Introductory Law of the Cc in conjunction with Art. 57 Act no. 1811/1951 on the position of civil servants, and in

teachers are only answerable to their governing body, and then usually only in cases of gross negligence or intent.[985] Such liability is of course subject to the requirement that the duty of supervision is for the protection of others.[986]

In Austria and Germany injury to school members is treated differ-   **163** ently again.[987] For instance, if one pupil injures another, or falls victim to a teacher's failure to supervise, these laws not only distinguish between private and state schools, but in state schools also between damage to property and personal injury. Only in cases of damage to property do the rules outlined above apply, i.e. liability for breach of duty, under either civil or state liability law. In cases of personal injury in state schools,[988] however, both countries employ an industrial injuries insurance scheme.[989] Thus, except in cases of intentionally inflicted bodily harm,[990]

conjunction with Art. 85 Presidential Decree 611/1977 on the code of provisions concerning the status of civil servants and of legal persons in public law, also called 'Code for Officials' (for details see e.g. Spiliotopoulos, *Encheiridio Dioikitikou Dikaiou*, vol. i, p. 224); Italy: Art. 61 Act no. 312 of 11 July 1980 (Gaz.Uff., *Supplemento Ordinario* of 12 July 1980, no. 190) (also Corte cost. 24 Feb. 1992, n. 64, *Riv.giur.circ.trasp.* 1992 pp. 650, 654: the purpose of the regulation, which is not contrary to the constitution, is to limit the third-party liability of school staff for *culpa in vigilando*); Luxembourg: Art. 5 Act of 1 Sep. 1988 (*Mémorial* A 1988 p. 100) (for details see Parvani, *Pas. luxemb.* 28 [1990–92] pp. 77–426); Spain: Arts. 1903 V Cc and Art. 22 CP, both holding the school governing body responsible. These provisions also determine whether or not a breach of the duty of supervision is presumed.

[985] This is the case in Austria (§ 3 I *Amtshaftungsgesetz*); in Germany (Art. 34 s. 2 GG); in France (however, regarding claims for contribution Art. 2 IV Act of 6 Apr. 1937 refers to the rules of the *droit commun*); in Greece (Art. 85 I s. 1 of the relevant Presidential Decree [fn. 984]); in Italy (Art. 61 Act no. 312 of 11 July 1980); and in Spain (Art. 1904 II Cc).

[986] See e.g. BGH 15 Mar. 1954, BGHZ 13 p. 25 (civil servant teachers are obliged to supervise pupils during breaks 'in view of possible damage to others'; as the relevant case concerned injury to a fellow pupil, tort law would not apply today).

[987] If Austria and Germany are seen as one extreme of the range of European solutions, then those laws which do not employ privileging (public law) provisions, but which instead rely on the general rules of private law, would be located at the other end. They are (apart from Belgium and The Netherlands, see no. 162) Italy (e.g. Cass. 23 June 1993, n. 6937, *Giust.civ.Mass.* 1993 no. 6937 p. 1065; Cass. 20 Apr. 1991, n. 4290 *Giur.it.* 1992, I, 1, 1350 = VersRAI 1993 p. 26; and Trib. Naples 5 Dec. 1989, *Rep.gen.* 1990 col. 3544 no. 119); and Spain (e.g. TS 10 Nov. 1990, *RAJ* 1990 no. 8538, p. 10940). Yet not even these two systems are identical. In Italy Art. 2048 II Cc applies (exposing pupils of primary schools in particular to an extremely high liability risk), whereas in Spain cases of self-inflicted injury due to failure to supervise come under Art. 1902 Cc, the basic liability provision. Factually, however, employers' liability under both systems should exonerate the teacher, and in view of Art. 1902 Cc one has to bear in mind the established practice of the *Tribunal Supremo* concerning burden of proof in questions of fault; for detail: de Ángel Yágüez, *Responsabilidad civil*, 3rd edn., p. 537.

[988] The same applies to institutes of higher education and universities in both countries, but to kindergartens only in Germany: see fn. 989 below. However, institutions of further education and training for employers and civil servants (see LG Wiesbaden 23 July 1992 VersR 1993 p. 1489) each have their own special regimes.

[989] Austria: § 175 IV ASVG; Germany: § 539 I no. 14 RVO.

[990] Although the courts appear disinclined to admit intent, see e.g. OLG Koblenz 6 Feb. 1992, *NJW-RR* 1993 p. 97.

teachers and school governing bodies, as well as pupils, escape personal liability.[991] Such social security systems share (apart from the exception mentioned above) many of the features of state liability. The one significant difference is that social security systems also impose liability for self-inflicted injuries where nobody was at fault. Here private law would not award damages. The disadvantage of this system is that even a pupil treated unjustly has no claim for damages for pain and suffering.

b. Liability of Training Employers

164   Whether the liability of training employers for injury inflicted upon others during that training by their apprentices should also be covered by a special quasi-delictual provision[992] depends chiefly on the contents and scope of the other two provisions which could also come into effect in such cases: liability for minors and liability for employees. Training employers' liability for under-age apprentices, for instance, might arise from liability for minors. This is the case if the burden of proof (or the strict liability) lies not only with the parents, but also with those persons whose (implied) duty of supervision arises from contract,[993] for example if the apprentice is a member of the training employer's household, a situation not uncommon for craft and farming apprentices. In some respects they attain the status of a child of the house.[994] As employees, they are also subject to the strict rules of employers' liability, regardless of their age. The distinction between under-age and other apprentices is therefore only relevant where an apprentice commits a delict outside working hours but within the sphere of influence of his training employer.[995] Whether adult apprentices and 'normal' employees must be distinguished depends largely on the

---

[991] Austria: § 333 I, IV ASVG in conjunction with § 335 III ASVG; see also OGH 25 Jan. 1984, *JBl* 1985 p. 111; Grillberger, *Österr. Sozialrecht*, pp. 59–60; and Tomandl, *Grundriß des Österr. Sozialrechts*, 3rd edn., pp. 153–158; Germany: § 637 IV s. 1 RVO.

[992] As in the *Code Napoléon* (see Art. 1384 VI, VII French Cc; Art. 1384 IV, V Luxemb. Cc; and Art. 1384 IV, V Belg. Cc) which also served as model for Art. 2048 II Ital. Cc (liability of those who 'train people in a trade or craft'). Spain has a similar provision in Art. 120 IV NCP (secondary liability of training employers in cases of criminal incapacity of tortfeasors); also López Garrido/Garcia Arán, *Código Penal* of 1995, p. 80 of which largely resembles the old Art. 22 CP. The new Dutch BW, however, abandoned the 'training employers' liability' of the old code (Art. 1403 IV BW [old]) (see Asser [-Hartkamp], *Verbintenissenrecht*, vol. iii, 9th edn., no. 138a) and introduced a general employers' liability under Art. 6:170 BW (Oldenhuis, *Onrechtmatige daad: aansprakelijkheid voor personen*, p. 45). They have thus also got rid of the old problem of under-age apprentices: Rb. Amsterdam 9 Dec. 1958, *NedJur* 1959 no. 385, p. 919. The other European nations have no special provisions for training employers' liability.   [993] See nos. 157–159 above.

[994] So the relevant provisions always refer to 'father, mother, and master craftsman'.

[995] See e.g. Cass.civ. 15 Feb. 1956 (no. 165 and fn. 999 below); and Cass. 20 Feb. 1962, n. 341, *Rep.gen.* 1962 col. 3258 no. 220: liability of a master for damage caused by an apprentice outside working hours, because the training employer had permitted him to enter the workshop without adequate supervision.

contents of employers' liability law. Where liability is based only on pre-sumed failure to supervise, the distinction is redundant.[996] Where employ-ers' liability is strict, training employers' liability, if applicable,[997] can only benefit the employer. Finally, the altruistic element inherent in training, as well as the parallels with the traditional rules of law governing the liability of teachers, relieve training employers of all liability in some cases.[998]

A decision of the French *Cour de Cassation* of 15 February 1956[999] is **165** a clear example of how closely the various possible solutions are linked. Noirault was hit at night by an unlit bicycle ridden by Morin, '*âgé de 16 ans, domestique agricole au service de* Parent, *après le temps de son travail'*. The training employer Parent, with whom Morin lived, was held not liable under Art. 1384 Cc; and the conditions of Art. 1382 Cc., which could have applied, were not established. Art. 1384 IV Cc did not 'fit' because it deals only with parents, and Art. 1384 VI Cc was unsuitable as the accident occurred at a time when Morin was not '*sous la surveillance'* of his training employer. The outcome would have been the same in those legal systems which only use employers' liability in this case, for Morin committed the delict in his free time. Under German, Greek, and Portuguese law (yet, to the apparent regret of the *Cour de Cassation*, not in France) the burden of proof could have been shifted, and the courts could have presumed that Parent was under a contractual obligation to ensure the roadworthiness of the bicycle as if it were his son's.

3. LIABILITY FOR OTHER PERSONS UNDER SUPERVISION

A further group demanding special attention are mentally handicapped **166** people resident in homes and psychiatric hospitals.[1000] European legis-lators have developed a number of provisions on damage caused by mentally handicapped persons to others.[1001] What they have in common

[996] This is why it is missing in Germany and Spain, where the codes (§ 831 BGB, Art. 1903 VI Cc) allow the employer to escape liability. However, Art. 120 IV Spanish NCP imposes strict (secondary) liability: López Garrido/García Arán (fn. 992 above).

[997] See fn. 992.

[998] Art. 1384 VII French Cc; Art. 1384 V Belg. Cc; Art. 1384 V Luxemb. Cc; Art. 2048 III Ital. Cc.   [999] Cass.civ. 15 Feb. 1956, *D.* 1956 *Jur.* 410 (note Blanc).

[1000] For the mentally sound inmates of homes (e.g. the old or blind: see Rb. Utrecht 12 Apr. 1950, *NedJur* 1951 no. 278 p. 543) liability is only incurred by fault, e.g. failure properly to organize a business. For escaped prisoners, a special public law regime should generally apply (e.g. TS 15 July 1988, *RAJ* 1988 no. 5896, p. 5824). However, England imposes liability in negligence for omission: *Home Office* v. *Dorset Yacht Co. Ltd.* [1970] AC 1004.

[1001] For self-inflicted injuries of mentally ill persons, liability of such institutions arises for fault. See OLG Koblenz 12 Apr. 1990, *OLGZ* 1991 no. 98 p. 326; OLG Hamm 7 Oct. 1993 *NJW-RR* 1994 p. 863; and RC 20 Nov. 1984, *CJ* IX (1984–5) p. 68. The same rules apply to anaesthetized patients injuring themselves in the recovery room: HR 13 Jan. 1995, *RvdW* 1995 no. 31.

is that the liability imposed on those running such establishments is not limited to failure to act, but is more onerous. What separates them is their wide range of solutions to the question of the extent of such liability. One end of the scale is marked by *gardien* liability under Art. 1384 I French Cc, as developed in the *arrêt Blieck*.[1002] The German and Portuguese equivalents are to be found in judgments intended to increase liability in cases of contractual supervision duties.[1003] In The Netherlands, both the old[1004] and the new[1005] Dutch BW impose liability on institutions for the mentally handicapped 'only' under the basic delictual provision; the new Code has extended liablity under Art. 6:165 II BW to cover the relationship between institution and mentally handicapped patient; only the institution can incur such liability. In addition, the general rules on liability for violation of a protective law[1006] oblige psychiatric institutions to supervise patients, an obligation which entails the protection of others.[1007] The prevailing view in Italy is that under Act No. 180 of 13 May 1978 *sull'assistenza psichiatrica*[1008] the personnel of psychiatric institutions are no longer subject to increased liability; they can only be liable under Art. 2043 Cc, not under Art. 2047 I Cc.[1009] The imposition of strict liability on *centri di igiene mentale* follows the current European trend.[1010]

167   Spanish law[1011] also emphasizes (secondary) liability under the criminal law (Art. 20 CP [old] and Art. 118 I NCP: liability for presumed failure to supervise).[1012] The more stringent liability of the Cc only applies if the institution has been appointed guardian (Arts. 1903 and

---

[1002] On the *arrêt Blieck* see no. 115 above. On the situation in Belgium see André, *Responsabilités*, p. 732, and Cornelis, *Buitencontractueel aansprakelijkheidsrecht*, p. 236.
[1003] See no. 159 and fn. 967 above.
[1004] E.g. Hof Amsterdam 3 June 1959, *NedJur* 1960 no. 188 p. 524; Rb. Roiermond 1 Mar. 1973, *NedJur* 1973 no. 309 p. 888; Art. 1403 BW [old] not applicable); and Hof Leeuwarden 5 June 1991, *NedJur* 1992 no. 78 p. 244 (a pyromaniac was released from a Borstal on probation to live in a boarding house. The Borstal was held liable because the governors allowed him to stay in the boarding house despite renewed arson attacks). For an interpretation of Art. 1403 I BW (old) in accordance with the French decisions on Art. 1384 I Cc: Rb. Amsterdam 16 Mar. 1965, *NedJur* 1966 no. 131 p. 220.
[1005] *Contra*, however: Schoonenberg, *NJB* 1985 pp. 1081, 1082; also Vetter, *Geestelijke stoornis*, pp. 72–73; and HR 12 May 1995, *RvdW* 1995 no. 110 (liability of the institution for a fire set by a 13-year-old mentally handicapped patient; no difference between Art. 1401 BW [old] and Art. 6:162 BW).   [1006] See nos. 31–32 above.
[1007] E.g. OGH 11 Dec. 1969, *SZ* 42/188 pp. 610, 614.
[1008] Gaz.Uff. of 16 May 1978, no. 133.
[1009] For detail see Franzoni, *Fatti illeciti*, Art. 2047 Cc, pp. 334–335; Galgano, *Diritto civile e commerciale*, vol. ii (2), 2nd edn., pp. 324–325; and Perlingieri (-Maglione), *Codice civile*, vol. iv (2), 2nd edn., Art. 2047 no. 3, p. 1828.
[1010] Alpa, *Responsabilità civile*, p. 301; and Visintini, *Fatti illeciti*, vol. i, p. 503. See also references in fn. 1009 above.
[1011] Carrasco Gómez, *Responsabilidad médica y psiquiátrica*, pp. 149–161.
[1012] On Art. 20 CP see no. 65 above; and on Art. 118 I NCP, López Garrido, García Arán, *Código Penal de 1995*, p. 79.

242 Span. Cc).[1013] Note, however, the extraordinary case of the patient who threw himself out of a window onto a passer-by: applying Art. 1910 Cc, the TS found against the institution.[1014] Less unusual, but nonetheless interesting, are TS 6 October 1989[1015] and TS 16 March 1992.[1016] In the former, a mentally ill patient started a fire whilst on day release; in the latter, one psychiatric patient killed another on the premises of the institution. In both cases the *Tribunal Supremo* found against the institution under Art. 20 CP; the fact that Art. 1903 Cc had not been breached was considered irrelevant. Finally, TS 8 March 1984 illustrates the course embarked upon by the *Tribunal Supremo*: a twenty-year-old Down's syndrome sufferer stabbed his victim to death after trying to rape her. As he was not a patient of any institution, his parents were unknown, and he was not a ward, he was held personally liable.[1017] The same result would have been obtained under the NCP.

Finally, in the context of liability for others, excluding liability for the mentally handicapped in homes and other institutions, note that Spanish courts were ready to apply Art. 22 CP analogously if appropriate. On 30 May 1992, in the most prominent decision on this issue, the TS ruled that one person lending a motor vehicle to another was liable for crimes committed with the car by the borrower.[1018] Such an analogous application of Art. 22 CP should still be possible under Art. 120 NCP.

4. LIABILITY FOR EXECUTIVES AND MANAGERS, EMPLOYEES, SUBCONTRACTORS, AND AGENTS

a. Liability of Legal Persons for their Executives and Managers

(1) Liability for Others and for Personal Misconduct

The final aspect of liability for others concerns liability for executives and **168** managers, employees, sub-contractors, and agents (Art. 6:172 BW). Within this group liability for executive bodies occupies a special position, although they also operate in the interests of a principal when executing a contract, and although the conditions for the liability of legal

---

[1013] De Ángel Yáguez, *Responsabilidad civil*, 3rd edn., p. 350.
[1014] TS 12 Mar. 1975, *RAJ* 1975 no. 1798 p. 1355.
[1015] TS 6 Oct. 1989, *RAJ* 1989 no. 8450 p. 9893.
[1016] TS 16 Mar. 1992, *RAJ* 1992 no. 2268 p. 3052.
[1017] TS 8 Mar. 1984, *La Ley* 1984 (2) p. 638.
[1018] TS 30 May 1992, *La Ley* 1992 (4) p. 137. For a similar French ruling see *Cour de Cassation* of 9 May 1990, Bull.civ. 1990, II, no. 93: a sailing boat sank during a regatta. Whereas the Court of Appeal had classed all on board as *co-gardiens* (thus excluding liability under Art. 1384 I Cc), the Court of Cassation reversed the judgment: only the captain was *gardien*.

persons for their duly appointed directors and managers need not necessarily differ from those applicable to a 'normal' employer for damage to third parties caused by his staff. As most differences are peripheral,[1019] most Civil Codes do not differentiate between this special case and 'common' employers' liability,[1020] although there is a good reason for doing so. Only the liability of legal persons must necessarily be absolutely strict,[1021] a principle followed in all European nations.[1022] For legal persons (and companies with partial legal personality under commercial law, which are equal in law to legal persons on the issue of the liability of legal persons for their executives[1023]) are effectively not capable of 'conduct'. They therefore cannot be held responsible for failing properly to select and supervise their board members. This leads to the conclusion that a legal person cannot be at fault, it can only be liable.[1024]

169 The question remains of how liability law should deal with these facts. The liability of legal persons 'for' their executives can be expressed not

---

[1019] Asser (-Hartkamp), *Verbintenissenrecht*, vol. iii, 9th edn., p. 241, refers to HR 10 June 1955, *NedJur* 1955 no. 552 p. 977 and reminds us that under Dutch law a claim can only be based on Art. 6:162 BW (see also no. 169 below) not on Art. 6:170 BW (strict liability for subordinates).

[1020] There is no provision dealing exclusively with the liability of executive bodies (but on a number of company law rules see no. 175 below) in the civil codes of Austria, Belgium, France, Italy, Luxembourg, The Netherlands, or Spain. Only Germany (§§ 31, 89 BGB, liability of private companies and public bodies), Greece (Art. 71 Greek Cc, all legal persons); and Portugal (Arts. 165, 501 Cc and Art. 22 Portuguese Constitution, *pessoas colectivas* and *pessoas colectivas públicas*) have such provisions. Their function is merely clarificatory. Art. 501 Port. Cc also puts executive bodies, personnel, and agents of legal persons on the same level and imposes vicarious liability on the corporate body where it pursues an activity under private law (*comissários*): STJ 15 June 1982, *BolMinJust* 318 (1982) p. 430.

[1021] Therefore Walker, *Delict*, 2nd edn., p. 127 is right to say 'the liability of a corporation is inevitably only and always vicarious'.

[1022] For Germany, Greece, and Portugal see fn. 1020 above; for Austria see e.g. OGH 25 Mar. 1987, *JBl* 1987 p. 254 = SZ 60/49 pp. 252, 257 (the prevailing opinion is that legal persons are liable for their executive bodies' misconduct). For The Netherlands: HR 6. Apr. 1979, *NedJur* 1980 no. 34 p. 79 (*Knabbel en Babbel*). For Belgium: Cornelis, *Buitencontractueel aansprakelijkheidsrecht*, no. 262. For France Starck (-Roland/Boyer), *Obligations*, vol. i, 4th edn., no. 400 ff. For Spain: García Cantero, in: *Centenario del Código civil*, vol. i, pp. 875–884.

[1023] From the German point of view these are in particular the OHG and the KG (§ 124 HGB). Yet § 31 BGB does not apply to 'private law partnerships' (*Gesellschaften bürgerlichen Rechts*) since they do not possess 'legal personality' (*Rechtspersönlichkeit*): BGH 30 June 1966, BGHZ 45 pp. 311, 312. However, in Spain the *Tribunal Supremo* on 29 Apr. 1988, *RAJ* 1988 no. 3326 p. 3299, ruled *obiter dictum* that even communities which are not legal persons can be personally liable.

[1024] A legal person can be held liable e.g. as keeper of an object. See e.g. Cass.civ. 22 Feb. 1984, *D*. 1985 *Jur*. 19 (legal person as *gardienne* of a dog); and the (Austrian) VwGH 20 Nov. 1984, *ZfVB* 1985 p. 331: '§ 138 WRG (Act on the law relating to water, 1959) applies not only where a person negligently violates the rules of the WR, but also if the state of affairs contradicts the provisions of the WRG. Legal persons can also breach its provisions by act or omission'.

only by means of *ex lege* joint liability:[1025] it is also possible to argue that the legal person acts 'via' its executive, i.e. that the natural person appointed as its manager and agent is effectively its head and body. In other words, a legal person is identified with the natural person representing it. Whenever that natural person acts, the company acts. This is the principle concept of the *Organtheorie*, based on the doctrine developed by the German lawyer Otto van Gierke, according to which companies are (albeit only in law) real persons.[1026] Those putting this doctrine into practice, i.e. most European nations,[1027] have to conclude that the liability of legal persons for their executives is not liability for others, but liability for personal misconduct.[1028]

It cannot and need not be decided at this stage which of these views is **170** correct.[1029] It is not necessary to decide, because the principle notion that the liability of a legal person for its executives is strict is undisputed. It cannot be decided because the *Organtheorie* touches a more general problem: the integration of legal persons into non-contractual liability law. The debatable point of the *Organtheorie* is whether, and under what conditions, a legal entity is liable for damages for which its duly appointed representative is not liable. If he has not acted unlawfully

---

[1025] Portuguese law on the liability of legal persons for their executives, at least, has embarked on this course (Arts. 165, 501 in conjunction with Art. 500 I Cc). Under Art. 500 I Cc a corporate body is only liable if 'the obligation to pay damages also affects' the executive. Correct (albeit not universally accepted) are those authors who say that § 31 German BGB was not founded upon the *Organtheorie* (see v. Bar, FS Kitagawa, pp. 279, 281–285). The text of Art. 71 Greek Cc is ambiguous, although the prevailing opinion is that it was shaped in accordance with the *Organtheorie*. (see Archaniotakis, *I astiki evthini tou nomikou prosopou idiotikou dikaiou*, pp. 98 ff., 115 ff.; Balis, *Genikai Archai tou Astikou Dikaiou*, 8th edn., pp. 52, 65; Papantoniou, *Genikes Arches*, 3rd edn., p. 151; and Gasis, *Genikai Archai tou Astikou Dikaiou*, vol. ii (2), p. 58, 65, who is critical.

[1026] O. v. Gierke, *Die Genossenschaftstheorie und die deutsche Rechtsprechung* (Berlin 1887), esp. pp. 607 f.

[1027] For Greece see fn. 1025 above; for Germany, e.g. RG 18 Oct. 1917, RGZ 91 pp. 72, 75 ('from the point of view of civil law the action of a natural person representing a legal person . . . is considered to be the action of the legal person'); and RG 14 Mar. 1939, RGZ 162 pp. 129, 169 (when a representative acts it is as though the legal entity itself acted); for Italy Cass.civ. 5 Dec. 1992, n. 12951, *Giust.civ.Mass.* 1992 no. 12951 p. 1832; for Belgium Vandenberghe *et al. TPR* 1984 pp. 127–154; and Van Gerven, *Beginselen van Belgisch Privaatrecht*, vol. i, no. 56; for The Netherlands van Schilfgaarde, *Van de BV en de NV*, 9th edn., pp. 157–159; and Asser (-van der Grinten), *Vertegenwoordiging en rechtspersoon*, vol. ii, 7th edn., pp. 90–98. See also fns. 1022 above and 1028 below.

[1028] As recognized by all nations with no special provision. For references see fns. 1022, 1027 above; see also Cass.civ. 24 Sep. 1977, n. 4069, *Rep.gen.* 1977, col. 3485 no. 126 (direct liability; Art. 2049 Ital. Cc not applicable); Díez-Picazo/Gullón, *Sistema*, vol. ii, 6th edn., p. 615; Starck (-Roland/Boyer), *Obligations*, vol. i, 4th edn., nos. 403 ff.; Le Tourneau, *Responsabilité civile*, 3rd edn., nos. 496 ff.; and Vandenberghe/Van Quickenborne/Geelen/De Coster, *TPR* 1987 pp. 1255, 1488 ff. The Netherlands rely on Art. 6:162 III BW (Schilfgaarde [fn. 1027] p. 157). Spanish Art. 1902 Cc deliberately omits any mention of 'persons', unlike its French counterpart, Art. 1382 Cc. See García Cantero, *Centenario del Código civil*, pp. 875, 879.

[1029] On Scandinavia and the common law see nos. 335 ff. below.

(since the duty violated was not his personal duty but that of the corporation) then the purpose of a liability system must be examined, an issue which certainly does not belong to the field of 'liability for others': nobody, not even a legal person, is answerable in delict for lawful conduct. Liability in cases where a board member of a legal person commits a tort, for example, does not fall within the *Organtheorie*. It would be somewhat surprising to argue that not only the chief executive but also the company jumped a red light.

(2) The Executive: Issues of Delict

171   Natural persons for whom a company can be made liable are identified principally by company law provisions, and by the company's articles of incorporation. Therefore representatives appointed by law clearly belong to this group,[1030] as do persons allocated a specific area of responsibility by the articles. Under German law they are termed 'duly appointed representatives' (§ 31 and § 30 BGB). Moreover, in order to close gaps in liability law, most European nations now consider that not only duly appointed representatives are included in the provisions on the liability of legal persons for their executives. They rank persons who under company law are merely servants (for which a legal person under special circumstances may not be held liable) together in delict with executives, or else they hold corporate bodies (usually the state or other public bodies) liable for natural persons who, for lack of control, are not even 'servants' (see Art. 6:170 BW). As a result of these developments, European law of delict has created its own definition of the term 'executive', according to which 'executives are all independently working persons responsible for carrying out characteristic duties for the legal person, even if they are not referred to in the articles of association'.[1031]

172   European courts define the term 'executive' generously in delict, as numerous examples show. Hof 's-Hertogenbosch, for instance, recently

---

[1030] According to BGH 8 July 1986, BGHZ 98 p. 148, this is the case even if they are only joint representatives. As to knowledge, even that of a former executive can be attributed to the legal person: BGH 8 Dec. 1989, *NJW* 1990 p. 975.

[1031] Filios, *Enochiko Dikaio*, vol. ii (2) 3rd edn., p. 73 (who uses nearly the same wording as BGH 30 Oct. 1967, BGHZ 49 pp. 19, 21); OGH 15 Apr. 1971, *JBl* 1972 p. 312; OGH 21 Oct. 1975, SZ 48/107; and OGH 7 June 1978, SZ 51/80 (pp. 373, 377: superior, or similarly powerful, sphere of influence; executive position which gives decision-making power and authority); BGH 27 Apr. 1962, *VersR* 1962 p. 664; Cass. 24 Sep. 1977, n. 4069, *Rep.gen.* 1977, 3485 no. 126 (effective conduct for the business suffices); Cass.com. 8 Dec. 1981, *Rev.soc.* 1981 p. 351 (note Bouloc); and Cass.crim. 23 July 1985, *Rev.soc.* 1986 p. 106 (note Jeandidier) (not only the *'dirigeants proprement dits'*, but also the *'personnes qui . . . ont exercé en fait l'administration au lieu . . . des représentants légaux'*). However, Van Oevelen, RW 1987–1988 pp. 1170, 1196 (no. 52) says of Belgium that it is in public rather than in private law that the term 'executive' has a broader meaning.

decided that a local authority is liable for a civil servant although 'from a legal point of view' he is not an executive.[1032] The leading case in The Netherlands is the *Hoge Raad* decision of 6 April 1979, known by the name of the cartoon characters *Chip 'n' Dale*.[1033] A departmental head of a town council made critical remarks about a building contractor, declaring the latter was jointly responsible for the collapse of a school building. The *Hoge Raad* overruled the Court of Appeal, which had based its decision on the head's role as an executive. According to the HR, the important question was whether his conduct was to be seen as the private act of a natural person, or as the act of an authority, thus effectively anticipating Art. 6:162 III BW.[1034] Another remarkable case almost overlapping with public law, and thus close to state liability law, is that of the *Tribunal Supremo* of 28 May 1984,[1035] combining the techniques of piercing the corporate veil and extending the notion of the liability of legal persons for their executives. The plaintiff sustained flood damage, for which the water supplier of Palma de Mallorca, a public limited company, was responsible. The limitation period was only unexpired if the proceedings pending against the town council had interrupted the limitation period for the claim against the water supplier. The TS decided that this was the case, since the town dominated the water company, rendering the latter its 'executive'.

Where liability for employees ('servants') is considered insufficient, **173** the accent is placed on making it impossible for their employers, the relevant legal persons, to escape liability. In the light of §§ 1315 ABGB, 831 BGB, it is understandable that in Austria and Germany editors-in-chief,[1036] senior hospital consultants,[1037] and branch managers,[1038] for instance, are treated as duly appointed representatives. The results in a system imposing liability for failure properly to organize a business would be similar. In its first variation, its aim is to impose on legal persons the provisions governing liability for failure to act, even if none of its employees was personally responsible for the danger, i.e. none had committed a delict.

[1032] Hof 's-Hertogenbosch 9 Nov. 1992, *NedJur* 1993 no. 311 p. 1142.

[1033] HR 6 Apr. 1979, *NedJur* 1980 no. 34 p. 79. Yet in HR 20 June 1980, *NedJur* 1980 no. 622 p. 2050 the *Hoge Raad* found a political party not liable for posters put up by its members, damaging the property of others.

[1034] See Asser (-van der Grinten) vol. ii, 7th edn., p. 90.

[1035] TS 28 May 1984, *RAJ* 1984 no. 2800 pp. 2131, 2132.

[1036] OGH 25 Mar. 1987, SZ 60/49 pp. 252, 258.

[1037] BGH 21 Sep. 1971, *NJW* 1972 p. 334; BGH 27 June 1995, *NJW* 1995 p. 2407.

[1038] BGH 30 Oct. 1967, BGHZ 49 p. 19 (with the remark on p. 21: 'In the circumstances it would be inappropriate to apply § 831 to allow a legal person to escape liability'). For Greece see Papantoniou, *Genikes Arches*, 3rd edn., p. 151; Spyridakis, *Genikes Arches*, vol. A p. 245; and Gasis, *Genikai Archai tou Astikou Dikaiou*, vol. ii (2), p. 66; for The Netherlands see van Schilfgaarde, *Van de BV en de NV*, 9th edn., p. 159.

TS 29 September 1964[1039] exemplifies this. Personal injury was caused by gas escaping from defective pipes, because of a failure to service them by the supplier responsible. The *Tribunal Supremo* considered this to be a case of liability for failure properly to organize a business, and held the company's board of directors directly liable.

Liability for failure properly to organize one's business is also presumed if a usually reliable and efficient member of staff is given so much work that he cannot possibly handle it adequately, or if responsibilities are delegated to persons without sufficient authority in the company hierarchy.

An example of the latter is found in OGH 19 April 1984.[1040] The car mechanic Richard F. negligently caused an accident while test-driving an HGV, for which he did not possess a *Lenkerberechtigung* (driving licence). The OGH presumed liability for failure to properly organize one's business on the part of the plaintiff's managing director, since not one, but two of the company's foremen had failed to notice the missing driving licence. 'If a board of directors leaves it to its foremen to examine whether a member of staff possessed a *Lenkerberechtigung*' it should at least ensure that appropriate forms are issued to and filled in by the staff, and returned to the management.

174 This example shows that the doctrine of liability for failure to organize one's business properly, and the generous definition of the term 'executive', have similar effects. If the foremen had been deemed to be executives, the result would have been the same.[1041] The example also suggests that in some circumstances liability for failure properly to organize one's business may even go beyond what would be considered necessary to protect the rights and legal interests of others. *In casu*, it is far from clear that the managing director of the plaintiff company was better placed than his foremen to supervise the mechanics. Moreover, if the German *Bundesgerichtshof* decides that 'a legal person is usually liable for failure to organize, and cannot escape § 31 BGB, for any business activities, whether private or professional, merely because the task in question had not been explicitly delegated to a duly appointed representative,[1042]

[1039] TS 29 Sep. 1964, *RAJ* no. 4097 p. 2522.

[1040] OGH 19 Apr. 1984, SZ 57/77 pp. 351, 353.

[1041] The OGH presumably could not follow this path, having already ruled in a decision of 24 Nov. 1976 (*JBl* 1977 p. 199) that the foreman of a limited company is not an executive for the purposes of 'representative liability' (*echte Repräsentantenhaftung*).

[1042] BGH 10 May 1957, BGHZ 24 pp. 200, 213. A similar statement had already been made in RG 14 Mar. 1939, RGZ 162 pp. 130, 166 (breach of duty by appointing a person as a servant; the court condemned 'the intolerable possibility of exoneration under § 831 BGB'). RG 9 Mar. 1938, RGZ 157 pp. 228, 235 had previously remarked that a legal person (i.e. its representative) can under certain circumstances violate its duty to organize by appointing 'suitable persons' as servants rather than as executives.

the situation acquires a new perspective. The sole objective seems to be to furnish the plaintiff with a financially viable defendant. But a 'deep pocket' should not be a cause of action. To find a way back to a more coherent system, it might be appropriate to exclude all issues of fault from cases involving the liability of legal persons.

(3) Liable legal persons

The rules on liability of legal persons for acts of their executives govern **175** legal persons under private law, as well as the state and its emanations under public law.[1043] However, for the latter, it is necesary to differentiate between the execution and breach of public duties, and cases where a representative enters into a legal relationship under civil law,[1044] because state liability in its narrower sense is often governed by special provisions.[1045] As for legal persons under private law, it must be noted that, except for Arts. 71 Greek, and 998, 500, 165 Port. Cc, which are truly exemplary, all other codes only impose liability for their executives upon specific types of companies, although the basic concept is regularly applied to all legal persons. For example, if taken literally, § 31 BGB would only apply to clubs. The Italian legislator seems also, by mistake, to have omitted to introduce Art. 18 of the draft (the complementary provision to § 31 BGB) into the *Codice civile*,[1046] which explains why the Italian Cc contains special delictual provisions covering only internal relationships under company law (Arts. 2281 with 2293 and 2315 Cc: damage to property owned by a partnership). Belgium (Arts. 63*bis* and 130 *in fine* of the *Loi sur les sociétés commerciales)* and France (Art. 1849 and Arts. 49, IV, 98 II *Code de sociétés*) also have provisions governing liability for external relationships, although in Belgium only for private companies with limited liability (*BWBA*) and public limited companies (*NV*). In Germany § 31 BGB, originally aimed only at clubs, is also employed for the liability of companies to third parties. The practical relevance of the Belgian and the French provisions (but see also Art. 2384*bis* Ital. Cc) derives from the fact that they all state that *'la société est engagée même par les actes du . . .* [then naming the relevant representative] *qui ne relèvent*

[1043] § 89 BGB, Art. 501 Port. Cc; and Art. 104 Greek Introductory Law of the Cc. *Contra* for France, Le Tourneau, *Responsabilité civile*, 3rd edn., no. 496.

[1044] Difficult to place are cases of breach of duty by consultants working as civil servants in state-run hospitals, e.g. RC 18 Oct. 1988, *BolMinJust* 380 (1988) p. 553 (public law); and BGH . Dec. 1992, BGHZ 120 pp. 376, 380–381 (differentiation between senior and junior consultants, as well as between in- and out-patient treatment). For a case in which public authorities and a private person are jointly and severally liable under the principle of the liability of a legal person for its representative, see Cass.sez.unit. 14 Mar. 1991, no. 2726, *Giur.it.* 1993, I, 1, 1118 (insufficient protection at a firework display).

[1045] See nos. 161–162 above and Part 6 fns. 1–4 below.

[1046] Franzoni, *Fatti illeciti*, pp. 453 f.

pas de l'object social, à moins qu'elle ne prouve que le tiers savait que l'acte dépassait cet objet ou qu'il ne pouvait l'ignorer compte tenu des circonstances'.

(4) Unlawful Conduct by Executives

176   Strict liability of a company in delict requires, first, that its executive or manager has acted unlawfully,[1047] and secondly, that the act cannot be said to be of a private nature. A legal person can be held liable for both acts and failures to act,[1048] as well as for presumed fault.[1049] However, cases of true strict liability similar to § 7 German StVG are insufficient: here a legal person is liable only as keeper of a motor vehicle. Hence, if the managing director of a limited company uses his private car on official business, and an accident occurs through no fault of the MD, the legal person is not liable. As far as responsibility for its executives in delict is concerned,[1050] the executive must have acted unlawfully.[1051] This is also true of all cases of liability for others,[1052] an unsatisfactory but, *de lege lata*, unavoidable consequence, especially in cases of insufficient insurance cover. True strict liability applies only to the keeper of the source of danger, and he alone benefits from its insurance. Even if one

---

[1047] In cases of necessity, damages might even be awarded if the representative acted lawfully, but this is not an issue of delict.

[1048] E.g. TS 5 Jan. 1977, *RAJ* 1977 no. 5 p. 12 (failure to service electrical installations); OGH 15 Apr. 1971, SZ 44/45 (failure of supervision by the duly appointed representative); and BGH 5 Dec. 1989, BGHZ 109 p. 297 (sale of goods under extended reservation of title; failure to examine sales contracts).

[1049] For an example of liability of the driver (not the keeper) of a motor vehicle, see § 18 German StVG. However, this is to be distinguished from cases where the legal entity is directly liable for presumed fault, as the question of whether the representative's fault can be attributed to the company becomes redundant: e.g. TS 13 June 1989, *RAJ* 1989 no. 4629 p. 5334: poisonous gases escaped from a fire extinguisher. It was impossible to establish whether this resulted from misconduct by a member of the company, or if a third party had opened the valves. The court upheld the claim against the company due to a reversal of the burden of proof.

[1050] See fns. 1047, 1049 above. Hence a legal person may be liable even if its representative has not acted unlawfully. However, such cases are no longer based on the notion of *ex lege* joint liability. Examples are employees whose principal is not a representative, but rather the legal person. Cass. 24 Sep. 1977, n. 4069, *Rep.gen.* 1977, col. 3485 no. 126: employers' liability under Art. 2049 Ital. Cc does not demand that the managing director be personally liable.

[1051] The liability of a legal person is thus also excluded in cases lacking delictual conduct (MD has heart-attack whilst driving). However, in cases where liability for positive acts does not demand fault, but only unlawfulness (e.g. in certain cases of water pollution) the relevant legal person can generally be held responsible.

[1052] Which can usually be clearly deduced from the text of the relevant provisions (esp. clear: Art. 6:170 BW). On parental liability see also nos. 145 ff. above; on employers' liability see no. 197 below. For court rulings see e.g. TS 25 Oct. 1980, *La Ley* 1981 (1) p. 72; TS 30 July 1991, *La Ley* 1991 (4) p. 560; and (for France) Cass.civ. 8 Oct. 1969, Bull.civ. 1969 II no. 269 = *Sem.Jur.* 1969, IV, 269. This decision expressly requires *faute* on the part of the *préposé*; no employers' liability if the employee is liable only as *gardien*. Not only is this decision correct, it also demonstrates that decisions on parental liability (see no. 150 above) based on an opposing viewpoint have been poorly reasoned.

deems it necessary temporarily to classify the principal as keeper, rather than the representative or servant, the problem remains.

Where the liability of legal persons for their executives is at issue, the **177** legal and natural persons become jointly and severally liable.[1053] However, the executive is not always personally answerable.[1054] It is often not even necessary to identify the relevant natural person, at least not where the liability of legal persons for their executives and employers' liability are both strict. The only condition is that the damage can be attributed to a group of natural persons. Whether liability arises from *rapporto organico* or from *dipendenza* (Art. 2049 Ital. Cc) the result is always the same.[1055]

Finally, legal persons can also be held liable if their executives **178** intentionally inflict damage on third parties.[1056] Whether an executive is personally responsible depends, not on the type of fault, but on how closely his conduct and the functions to which he is appointed are connected.[1057] The decisive test for employers' liability is the viewpoint of an objective bystander. Even in cases where the director or manager operates outside the *objet social*, the legal person remains answerable if the injured party could not be expected to know that he was exceeding his competence.[1058] The causal connection is only broken if the damage occurred, not in the performance of the duty of service, but merely upon the occasion of such performance.[1059]

[1053] However, regarding the legal person an additional cause of action may be considered, e.g. breach of contract: HR 31 Jan. 1958, *NedJur* 1958 no. 251 p. 513.

[1054] E.g. Cass.civ. 17 July 1967, obs. Durry, *Rev.trim.dr.civ.* 1968 p. 149. Conversely, the representative may be sued alone: Asser (-Hartkamp), *Verbintenissenrecht*, vol. iii, 9th edn., p. 244, no. 262. In such cases the contract for services and the articles of partnership determine whether the representative can claim for indemnity against the legal person.

[1055] Cass. 5 Dec. 1992, n. 12951, *Giust.civ.Mass.* 1992 no. 12951 p. 1832. Also Cass. 3 Nov. 1983, n. 6469, *Rep.gen.* 1983, col. 3842, no. 389; and Cass. 21 Jan. 1985, n. 222, *Rep.gen.* 1985, col. 1335, no. 23.

[1056] Cass. 5 Dec. 1992 (fn. 1005 above); BGH 8 July 1986, BGHZ 98 p. 148; BGH 20 Feb. 1979, *NJW* 1980 p. 115; Luik 26 Apr. 1955, *Rev.crit.jur.belge.* 1956 p. 5 incl. note Renard/Goossens.

[1057] E.g. Cass. 7 Oct. 1993, n. 9935, *Giust.civ.Mass.* 1993 no. 9935 p. 1449 (state liability; it must be possible to connect the act directly with the state); BGH 8 July 1986, BGHZ 98 p. 148 (it depends on the overall framework of the duties appointed to him); Papantoniou, *Genikes Arches*, 3rd edn., p. 154; and Spyridakis, *Genikes Arches*, vol. i, pp. 246–247 (causal connection between the representative's duties and conduct).

[1058] See no. 175 above. This is a consequence of the doctrine of *mandat apparent*, which has a dual function in that it can also lead to an extension of the delictual definition of representative (see nos. 171–174 above).

[1059] Cornelis, *Buitencontractueel aansprakelijkheidsrecht*, no. 265; Mast/Dujardin, *Overzicht*, 12th edn., p. 631, no. 594; Pires de Lima/Antunes Varela, *Cc anotado*, vol. i, 4th edn., Art. 500 n. 4; BGH 8 July 1986 (fn. 1057 above); Filios, *Enochiko Dikaio*, vol. ii (2), 3rd edn., p. 74. Cass. 31 Mar. 1943, *Pas. belge* 1943, I, 117 is a good example. Also STJ 17 Nov. 1977, *BolMinJust* 271 (1977) p. 201.

b. Liability for Employees, Subcontractors, and Agents

(1) Employers' Liability: Strict Liability and Presumed Breach of Duty

179 If a third party[1060] has a claim against a principal who is a natural person, or if the defendant is a legal person and the tortfeasor is an employee below the rank of representative,[1061] liability to the third party could 'technically' be based on (presumed) fault on the part of the principal or the natural person representing him. However, because of the wording of the relevant provisions, this happens only rarely; even where exculpation is possible by law, in fact it exists only on paper. A self-confident judiciary does not indefinitely embrace the obvious misjudgments of its legislature.

180 Under the *Code Napoléon* employers' liability has always been strict: no breach of duty by the principal is needed (Arts. 1384 V French Cc; 1384 III Belg. and Lux. Cc; 1403 III BW [old]). Greece (Art. 922 Cc), Italy (Art. 2049 Cc), and Portugal (Art. 500 Cc) follow the same course; even the authors of the new Dutch BW (Art. 6:170) saw no reason to change this position. They justify their strict (or 'indirect') liability by arguing that the risk inherent in the delegation of work must remain with whoever induces another, in his own interest, to carry out the work.[1062] Moreover, this principle holds even for a master who does not pursue his interests alone, nor does it seem to be altered by the many situations in which a principal is virtually obliged to appoint a specialist to take appropriate measures to protect the rights and legal interests of others. It is argued that the basic conditions (delictually speaking: the sources of danger) are created by the master who finally benefits from them. This general approach is unaltered by exceptions. Furthermore, the concept of *culpa in eligendo*, the key notion of those systems tying employers' liability to the question of fault in staff selection, is becoming redundant. A modern social economy attempts to employ even the weakest members of society.

[1060] The following account concerns the law on liability to third parties. True industrial injury law (compensation of damage sustained by an employee at work due to the negligence of his employer, a colleague, or a third party) is so eclipsed by insurance law that it is appropriate to discuss the relevant provisions together with insurance law's ousting of private liability. For a perceptive overview see Münchener Rückversicherungs-Gesellschaft (ed.), *Die Haftung des Arbeitgebers* (Munich 1993).

[1061] The terms 'employer' and 'employee' are used here in a rather indistinct fashion. Liability for *Verrichtungsgehilfen* (§ 831 BGB; Art. 922 Greek Cc), *Besorgungsgehilfen* (§ 1315 ABGB), *preposés* (Art. 1384 V and Arts. 1384 III Belg. and Lux. Cc) *ondergeschikte* (Art. 6:170 BW), *comissários* (Art. 500 Port. Cc), *dependientes* (Art. 1903 IV Span. Cc), and *domestici e commessi* (Art. 2049 Ital. Cc) often does not require an employer–employee relationship in the technical sense (see also no. 191 below). That is to say, the terms employer/employee only cover the most important cases.

[1062] See e.g. Pires de Lima / Antunes Varela, *Cc anotado*, vol. i, 4th edn., Art. 500, no. 5.

The basic concept of *culpa in eligendo vel in vigilando* emerges in some **181** legal systems even today; but it is no longer the crucial factor for liability. The cases in which such *culpa* was irrebuttably presumed[1063] are historic remnants. Liability has in effect become 'indirect': the master is responsible for the servant's fault. Even where the presumption of fault *in eligendo* and *in vigilando* is still rebuttable, e.g. in Spain under Art. 1903 IV, VI Cc, thus rendering liability 'direct',[1064] this is now a hollow phrase. The reality of Spanish liability law proves that such rebuttal is actually impossible.[1065] An employer only escapes liability if he can prove that his employee was not at fault:[1066] only then can he exonerate himself.[1067] This also applies if liability is still based, not on Art. 1903 IV Cc, but on Arts. 21 I and 22 I CP.[1068] Although it is secondary here, it 'has developed into a predominantly strict form' of liability, for it concerns not so much 'fault in selection or supervision, as the effects of insufficient organization and structuring of a service'.[1069] That discussion became superfluous with the implementation of Art. 120 IV NCP, by which secondary employers' liability is strict.[1070]

An entirely different system is adopted for liability for 'employees' **182** (*Besorgungsgehilfen*) under the Austrian ABGB. Its basic approach is defined in § 1313 s. 1: 'One is generally not responsible for unlawful acts committed by others in which one had no part.' Moreover, according to § 1313 s. 2 ABGB exceptions must be statutory. Examples of exceptions are § 1313a ABGB, which applies only to existing obligations,

---

[1063] Art. 2049 Cc, for instance, is still interpreted in this way (see e.g. Cass.pen. 16 Oct. 1984, *Rep.gen.* 1985, 3462, no. 115; and Trib. Monza 13 Sep. 1988, *Rep.gen.* 1990, 3545, no. 125). In France this view, once popular, has been abandoned: Starck (-Roland/Boyer), *Obligations*, vol. i, 4th edn., no. 989; Viney, *La responsabilité: conditions*, no. 790; and Malaurie/Aynès, *Droit civil*, 3rd edn., no. 158.

[1064] E.g. TS 28 Jan. 1983, *La Ley* 1983 (2) p. 789; TS 22 Feb. 1991, *La Ley* 1991 (2) p. 900; TS 30 July 1991, *La Ley* 1991 (4) p. 560; and TS 21 Apr. 1992, *La Ley* 1992 (3) p. 685.

[1065] E.g. Cavanillas Múgica, *Transformación*, pp.90–95 who justifies this development by reference to Art. 1904 Cc. (It concerns a right to contribution which would be more appropriate in vicarious than in direct liability); Díez-Picazo/Gullón, *Sistema*, vol. ii, 6th edn., p. 626; Gerlach, *ZVglRWiss* 85 (1986) pp. 247, 309–310; v. Bar (-Santdiumenge), *DeliktsR in Europa, Spanien* pp. 33–34; and Albaladejo, *Derecho civil*, vol. ii (2), 8th edn., §§ 152–154.

[1066] It is established practice of the courts on Art. 1902 Cc to presume fault also on the part of the *dependiente*: TS 7 Nov. 1985, *La Ley* 1986 (1) p. 846.

[1067] However, this does not rule out other avenues through which the employer can be made immediately and strictly liable under Art. 1902 Cc for his employee's misconduct (e.g. for insufficient maintenance of a thing): TS 25 Oct. 1980, *La Ley* 1981 (1) pp. 72, 75.

[1068] Art. 21 I CP concerned the secondary liability of persons running an *établissement* for violation of police by-laws; Art. 22 CP dealt with the subsidiary liability of persons and enterprises 'carrying out any kind of industrial business'.

[1069] TS 7 Apr. 1994, *RAJ* no. 2900 pp. 3908, 3911.

[1070] López Garrido/García Arán, *Código Penal de 1995*, p. 80.

and §§ 1314 and 1315 ABGB. Of these, § 1314 ABGB (dealing with damage caused by persons permitted to live in the same household as the injured party, despite his knowledge that their 'physical and mental state' suggested that they were dangerous) is virtually obsolete, and there have been no rulings on it for nearly twenty years. The last concerned a lodger's liability to his landlady whose jewellery was stolen by the lodger's guest. The case was dismissed, as § 1314 ABGB only applied 'if the defendant had positively known that *D* had a tendency to commit thefts'.[1071]

183   § 1315 ABGB forms the core of liability for others. Under this provision a person 'entrusting an incompetent person or someone known to be dangerous with the performance of a task' assumes responsibility 'for the damage inflicted on another by that person in that function'. In the second alternative, the conduct constituting fault occurs earlier: someone who knowingly employs a kleptomaniac or ruffian to carry out business is liable even if he is not at fault regarding the actual unlawful act.[1072] As such cases are rare, the focus is on the first alternative of § 1315 ABGB, a provision which 'does not require that the principal himself be at fault (whether for poor selection, training, or supervision)'.[1073] It is thus totally irrelevant whether the principal knew of the incompetence of his employees, or even whether he negligently lacked this knowledge. When, though, is an employee 'incompetent'? Is it sufficient that he fails in a specific task, or must he be generally unreliable? The answer is always the latter: 'It is the established practice of the courts ... that liability for incompetent employees requires their habitual incompetence'.[1074]

184   In conclusion: Austrian law imposes strict liability on servants, although only within a narrow scope. Moreover, habitual incompetence is not presumed, but must be proved by the plaintiff.[1075] The gaps thus opened could have proved problematic had the courts not developed a number of devices to escape the chains of § 1315 ABGB.

[1071] OGH 14 Apr. 1977, *JBl* 1978 p. 378.

[1072] See v. Bar (-Schilcher/Kleewein), *DeliktsR in Europa, Österreich*, pp. 75–76.

[1073] Established practice of the OGH: e.g. 25 Mar. 1987, *JBl* 1987 pp. 524, 526 (source of quotation); and OGH 8 Feb. 1968, *JBl* 1968 pp. 473, 474 ('liability for incompetent persons is strict').

[1074] OGH 8 Feb. 1968 loc. cit., which refers to OGH 19 Mar. 1952, SZ 25/68; OGH 5 May 1954, SZ 27/118; and OGH 3 Dec. 1954, SZ 27/311.

[1075] OGH 12 Apr. 1967, *ZVR* 1968/126 (p. 238); OGH 21 Nov. 1974, *JBL* 1975 p. 544; however, commentators are increasingly demanding that the harmful result of an act be accepted as *prima facie* evidence of the incompetence of the *Besorgungsgehilfe*: e.g. Schwimann (-Harrer), *ABGB*, vol. v, § 1315 no. 14. Moreover, in cases of failure to act, the burden of proof (in this case of somebody's competence) is shifted to the principal. For the latest case see OGH 24 Nov. 1976, *JBl* 1977 p. 199.

Although it seemed at first that that provision was the sole cause of action, the OGH decided in 1968 that principals could also be sued for *culpa in eligendo vel vigilando* under § 1295 ABGB.[1076] Furthermore, in some circumstances a single instance of incompetence by an employee can indicate that he is generally incompetent. Examples are: an editor who publishes allegations of bribery without conducting his own thorough enquiries and in reliance on third-party information;[1077] or workmen who use inadequate bolts to fit a blind in a hotel.[1078] Such grave mistakes do not arise from a momentary lapse. A solution is to extend the term representative (*Organ*). To qualify as a representative, a 'relatively independent sphere of activity suffices';[1079] by that definition not only legal persons (such as companies) but also sole traders have representatives in their employ.[1080] The fourth way around § 1315 ABGB is to render § 1313a ABGB applicable by referring to implied protective duties arising from contract (if necessary with protective effects for third parties) or from a confidential relationship based on a binding agreement.[1081] However, the Austrian courts have only recently 'discovered' the instrument of *culpa in contrahendo*.[1082] The fifth escape route from § 1315 ABGB was established earlier. It involves the analogous application of special vicarous liability provisions within statutes imposing strict risk liability,[1083] although the OGH has stressed several times that these specific laws[1084] cannot found a *general* vicarious liability.[1085] Extension by analogy is only possible in cases of increased and exceptional danger.[1086] Therefore, it has long been established practice to subject the hazards created by the business of large companies to tougher liability

---

[1076] OGH 19 Nov. 1968, *ZVR* 1969/204, overturning OGH 28 Sep. 1950, SZ 23/273.

[1077] OGH 25 Mar. 1987, *JBl* 1987 p. 524.

[1078] OGH 28 Oct. 1975, *JBl* 1978 p. 91; for further precedents see Harrer (fn. 1075 above).

[1079] OGH 10 Apr. 1991, *JBl* 1991 p. 796. See nos. 173–174 above.

[1080] This is the view of Harrer (fn. 1075 above) no. 22.

[1081] E.g. OGH 25 June 1992, *JBl* 1992 p. 788 (producer's duty to issue a warning; contract with protective effect for third parties); OGH 7 July 1978, SZ 51/111 (p. 505: 'The proprietor of a business is obliged by binding agreement with a person entering his premises intending to buy to ensure the safety of those premises; under § 1313a ABGB, liability for misconduct by his servant is attributed to him'); or OLG Innsbruck 25 Jan. 1994, *ZVR* 1995 p. 109 (liability of a cable railway business which organized nocturnal sledging parties under § 1313a ABGB for fault on the part of the club whose services had been employed).

[1082] OGH 8 Oct. 1975, SZ 48/102 is the leading case.

[1083] For key decisions see OGH 10 Sep. 1947, SZ 21/46; OGH 16 Aug. 1949, SZ 22/110; and OGH 19 Mar. 1952, SZ 25/68.

[1084] See e.g. § 19 II EKHG; §§ 6, 7 MedienG; § 2 RHG; § 29c I LuftVG; and § 35 III AtomG.

[1085] See e.g. OGH 24 Nov. 1976, SZ 49/144; and OGH 19. June 1985, *EvBl* 1986/75.

[1086] OGH 30 Nov. 1977, *JBl* 1978 p. 543.

than is imposed under § 1315 ABGB.[1087] In the light of all these alternatives, § 1315 ABGB no longer causes concern.

185   All these escape devices, apart from the application of strict liability of analogy,[1088] are also found in German law, some aspects of which (failure to organize, contractual duty to protect) actually served as models for the Austrian developments. However, the German problem of liability for servants is essentially of a different nature. Like the Spanish Cc, the German BGB recognizes only 'direct' liability for masters (§ 831 BGB). 'A person who employs another to do any work [is] bound to compensate for any damage which the latter unlawfully causes to a third party in the performance of his work', but that 'duty to compensate does not apply if the employer exercised proper care in selecting the employee and, where he is obliged to supply apparatus or equipment or to supervise the work, he also exercised ordinary care as regards such supply or supervision' (§ 831 I s. 2 BGB). This also applies where a breach of duty by the principal is proved (or presumed and not rebutted), but where there is no causal link between the breach of duty and the unlawful act by the servant.

186   Thus § 831 I BGB—from the outset a highly controversial provision—introduced liability for (presumed) failure in staff selection, and for culpable failure to act, but only in a small number of cases. Adults, unlike children and mentally handicapped persons, do not need constant supervision. *Culpa in vigilando* should only be raised in cases where the principal is in charge of the execution of the work assigned.[1089] 'It is reasonable to hold a master responsible only if it can be proved that he was at fault in the way in which his order was given or executed.'[1090] The final wording of the provision also specified 'the extent of duties of

---

[1087] OGH 10 Sep. 1947; 16 Aug. 1949; and 19 Mar. 1952 (fn. 1083 above); OGH 5 Mar. 1958, *JBl* 1958 p. 550; OGH 9 Apr. 1968, SZ 41/43; OGH 28 Mar. 1973, *JBl* 1974 p. 199.

[1088] Strict liability provisions, due to their exceptional character, cannot be applied by analogy: in German law this was made clear as early as RG 11 Jan. 1912, RGZ 78 pp. 171, 172, and confirmed on several occasions: e.g BGH 25 Jan. 1971, BGHZ 55 pp. 229, 233; and Kötz, *Deliktsrecht*, 7th edn., nos. 371–373. RG 11 Jan. 1912 concerned the emergency landing of one of Count Zeppelin's airships, but was long ago rendered redundant by the strict liability provisions of the LuftVG; and a special provision ousting § 831 BGB (apart from the *adjektizische* liability under § 485 HBG and §§ 3, 4, 114 BinnSchG, see BGH 27 Feb. 1964, BGHZ 41 pp. 203, 204) is found in § 3 HPflG ('a person operating a mine, quarry, excavation site (*Gräberei*), or business is liable for damages if an agent, a representative, or a person appointed to supervise the operation or the personnel negligently causes the death or physical injury of another whilst carrying out his duty'). Liability under § 3 HPflG only concerns accidents arising from installations (not cases of product liability, e.g. failure of those responsible for final quality control.)

[1089] Prot. II p. 598. See also v. Bar, *Verkehrspflichten*, p. 23. This explains why liability for servants (§ 831 BGB) is dealt with before that of persons exercising the duty of supervision (§ 832 BGB), i.e. liability for children and the mentally handicapped.

[1090] Prot. II p. 603. Here the protocols give an incorrect picture of the distribution of the burden of proof.

supervision of principals'.[1091] That other European countries took a different view was irrelevant. It was contemptuously declared that 'the German legal conscience (*Rechtsbewußtsein*), which alone is relevant, has no room for the notions of the *code civil*'.[1092] Moreover, it was felt that the insurance system was insufficiently developed and that it was 'doubtful whether some areas of industry, those which still need to be treated with care, and small farms, can bear such a heavy burden'.[1093]

The history of decisions on § 831 BGB, which lagged behind even **187** § 1315 ABGB and Art. 1903 Span. Cc, soon turned into a race to make up ground in a desperate attempt to raise the level of the German *Rechtsbewußtsein* (or so it now appears). Although the *Reichsgericht* initially imposed liability on the principal for presumed failure to supervise only if he had directed the execution of the task,[1094] it soon took the view that a general duty of supervision arises from § 823 BGB.[1095] Just four years later the court went even further, stating that 'the employee must have been capable of properly performing the assigned function which led to the injury of a third party at the time of its execution, and the principal must prove that he properly exercised his duty of care in his choice of employee at that time'.[1096] It soon became established that 'only properly supervised employees may be deemed properly selected'.[1097] This was clearly an important move. From then on, the employer had to prove that he had not failed properly to instruct and supervise his servants; it was only a question of time before those duties became so stringent as to make principals' liability quasi-strict.[1098] In many areas the defendant/principal was unable to produce such proof so as to escape liability under the BGB.[1099] When the BGH resumed the work of the RG after the Second World War, it considered § 831 BGB to

---

[1091] Id. p. 604.
[1092] Id. p. 603. Just how blatantly anti-French the mood of the 2nd Commission was is clear from the polemic report issued by *Reichsgerichtsrat* Dreyer for the 17th German Lawyers' Conference 1888 (pp. 46, 81–83, 106–107; see Baums, *FS Lukes*, pp. 623, 624), with analysis of some French decisions he thought eminently misguided. His analysis was superficial because in several places he criticized questions either already classed as purely contractual by the French (Trib.civ. de la Seine 28 May 1872, *DP* 1873.3.7) or which could easily have been so classed (Trib.civ. de la Seine 22 July 1857, *DP* 1857.3.51).
[1093] Prot. II p. 603.   [1094] RG 4 Dec. 1902, RGZ 53 pp. 123, 125.
[1095] RG 19 Sep. 1907, *JW* 1907 p. 674 no. 9: example of the extension of quasi-delict by imposing liability for breach of general duties of care (nos. 104–105 above).
[1096] RG 14 Dec. 1911, RGZ 78 p. 107, 109; confirmed by RG 18 Mar. 1912, RGZ 79 pp. 101, 106.   [1097] RG 25 Feb. 1915, RGZ 87 pp. 1, 4.
[1098] Kötz, *Deliktsrecht*, 7th edn., nos. 282–283; *MünchKomm* (-Mertens), 2nd edn., § 831 BGB nos. 9–20; and *BGB-RGRK* (-Steffen), 12th edn., § 831 BGB no. 3. Examples of effectively insurmountable degrees of supervision can be found in e.g. BGH 30 Oct. 1959, *NJW* 1960 p. 335 (building works); BGH 14 Oct. 1964, *VersR* 1965 p. 38 (firework display); and KG 4 July 1966, *VersR* 1966 p. 1036.
[1099] For details see v. Bar, *Verkehrspflichten*, p. 247.

be an 'exception' to the 'principle . . . which dominates German law governing unlawful acts, and contrasts sharply with other laws, that one is generally . . . not liable for the damaging conduct of others . . . but only for one's own misconduct'.[1100]

188   The attempt to evade the 'unacceptable possibility of exoneration under § 831 BGB'[1101] suffered a setback when the BGH introduced a system of decentralized exoneration in 1951.[1102] Furnishing evidence for one's exoneration was 'simplified' for 'large organizations', in that the master only had to exonerate himself regarding his leading employees, a move which can only be described as unfortunate, especially for larger businesses,[1103] and which was doomed to fail, especially as the doctrine of failure to organize soon closed the gap.[1104] Furthermore, another important instrument was soon developed: the employee's indemnity against liability from his employer. This development was sparked off by the fact that under German law an employee is personally and fully liable for injuries which he negligently inflicts upon others during working hours.[1105] Such personal liability, in the context of delegated assignments and the risk involved, is often out of all proportion to an employee's income, and the courts therefore granted employees (particularly those in potentially dangerous work)[1106] a claim in contract against the employer for indemnity against liability to third

---

[1100] BGH 8 Mar. 1951, BGHZ 1 pp. 248, 251–252.

[1101] Stressed by RG 14 Mar 1939, RGZ 162 pp. 129, 166.

[1102] BGH 25 Oct. 1951, BGHZ 4 pp. 1, 2. Yet the two RG decisions to which the judges refer have no relevance to the case: RGZ 87, 61 is misquoted, and RG 27 Nov. 1916, RGZ 89 p. 136 concerned failure to organize.

[1103] Large organizations in particular already had 100% coverage for third-party liability (see v. Bar, *AcP* 181 [1982] pp. 289, 293). That liability for servants was still based on fault was due to the fact that the insurance systems had not yet matured (no. 186 above).

[1104] See no. 173 above. Closer inspection reveals that the German judiciary recogizes two types of failure to organize. One is limited to the liability of legal persons and concerns tasks which, instead of being assigned to a representative, were transferred to an employee (see RG 14 Mar. 1939 [fn. 1101 above]; RG 9 Mar. 1938, RGZ 157 pp. 228, 235, BGH 10 May 1957, BGHZ 24 pp. 200, 212–213; and BGH 8 July 1980, *NJW* 1980 p. 2810 [concerning a case of 'fictitious liability'; the judges treated the servant as a representative]). The other type of failure to organize can also be applied to natural persons (BGH 25 Oct. 1951, BGHZ 4 p. 1, 2–3) and concerns the general duty arising from § 823 I BGB to organize one's business in such fashion that 'the rights of others are not unnecessarily prejudiced', a duty which cannot be delegated to employees (BGH 10 May 1957 loc. cit.)

[1105] This is established practice, and was confirmed by BGH 21 Dec. 1993, *NJW* 1994 p. 852. See also BGH 19 Sep. 1989, BGHZ 108 pp. 305, 307. For a comparison of the positions in Germany and Austria see Konowalczyk/Sauer, *RIW* 1995 pp. 383–388.

[1106] The leading case is BAG 25 Sep. 1957, BAGE 5 p. 1. However, whether the assigned task is potentially dangerous is no longer so important. It is now merely one of the factors to be taken into consideration when weighing the employee's fault against his employer's risk (BAG 12 June 1992, *ZIP* 1993 p. 699; BAG 27 Sep. 1994, *ZIP* 1994 p. 1712; and BGH 21 Sep. 1993, *NJW* 1994 p. 856).

parties.[1107] Even in the rare instances where an employer can exonerate himself on the basis of § 831 BGB, it does not help him much: he will still have to indemnify his employee.[1108] If the employee has already paid the damages, his right to indemnity entitles him to claim against his employer for payment. Since this is also the case where the claim is assigned to the injured third party (whether voluntarily or by the court),[1109] and since neither assignment nor attachment of earnings depend on whether the employee was financially able to satisfy the claim against him,[1110] a creditor will only seek compensation from him if his employer is insolvent. Thus, although a residual risk remains, from the employer's point of view the scope of § 831 I s. 2 BGB has again been greatly reduced.

However, the most important mechanism in the German law of **189** obligations for bypassing § 831 BGB involved contract law: by applying liability for servants under § 278 BGB (instead of § 831 BGB) to existing obligations. This method is no longer favoured,[1111] even in matters which concern, not the cause of action, but the limitation of liability for contributory fault on the part of the servant.[1112] Nonetheless, the contractual part of modern German liability law has been strongly influenced by the requirement for exculpatory proof under § 831 BGB.[1113] Without it the

---

[1107] The scope of such indemnity, repeatedly linked with § 254 BGB, depends largely on the degree to which the employee was at fault. Earlier rulings distinguished between 3 possibilities (slight negligence: indemnification in full; medium negligence: split damages; gross negligence and intent: no indemnity; see BAG 19 Mar. 1959, BAGE 7 pp. 290, 297), whereas today (despite relapses) the degree of indemnity seems to depend on the circumstances. BAG 23 Mar. 1983 (7th Senate) *NJW* 1983 p. 1693 granted full indemnity although a medium degree of negligence had been established. However, BAG 24 Nov. 1987 (8th Senate), *NJW* 1988, p. 2816 reintroduced the old system, albeit subject to considerations of equity and reasonableness. BAG 12 Oct. 1989 (8th Senate), *NJW* 1990 p. 468 concluded that 'concessions of liability in favour of the employee . . . may even be granted in cases of gross negligence'. For detail see Hanau/Rolfs, *NJW* 1994 pp. 1439–1442; and Schaub, *WiB* 1994 pp. 227–230.

[1108] See e.g. OLG Hamburg 29 Oct. 1992, *NJW-RR* 1993 p. 914.

[1109] See e.g. BAG 11 Feb. 1969, *DB* 1969 pp. 841, 843. *Contra*, however: BGH 27 Feb. 1964, BGHZ 41 pp. 203, 205. But BGH 24 Nov. 1975, BGHZ 66 pp. 1, 4 is generally considered the leading case, overturning the latter view.

[1110] BGH 24 Nov. 1975 (fn. 1109 above).

[1111] Cases involving this idiosyncratic reliance on *culpa in contrahendo* were known as the *'department store cases'* (see no. 190 below). Whether the parties entered a contractual relationship is no longer even examined (e.g. BGH 5 July 1994, *VersR* 1994 p. 1128), because § 847 BGB (damages for pain and suffering) does not apply to contractual claims.

[1112] BGH 10 July 1980, *NJW* 1980 pp. 2573, 2575, on contributory fault: § 831 BGB applied to limit the claim against the servant, even if no contractual obligation existed prior to the unlawful act. On the same issue under Austrian law see mainly Karollus, *ÖJZ* 1994 pp. 257–261.

[1113] As early as 1916 Pollock predicted a similar development in English law in response to a commentator's suggestion that it should abandon vicarious liability (Pollock, 32 [1916] LQR 226–227; see also Lawson/Markesinis, *Tortious Liability*, vol. i, p. 167: 'denial of the superior's responsibility in tort would surely have led to a luxuriant and perplexed growth of contracts implied in law, for which the substance of justice would have been no better from any point of view, and the science of law much the worse.'

notions of *culpa in contrahendo*, contractual duty of care, and contracts with protective effect for third parties (all of which are now employed primarily to protect pure economic interests)[1114] would not have been developed as they have been.[1115]

190   There are four famous decisions in this field: the *linoleum case*, the *gas heater case*, the *banana skin case* and the *vegetable leaf case*. In RG of 7 December 1911 the plaintiff entered the defendant's department store intending to purchase linoleum. While examining linoleum two rolls fell on and injured the plaintiff due to an employee's fault. The RG took the view that evidence given in exoneration under § 831 BGB was irrelevant, as the defendant employer was liable under § 278 BGB. The parties had already entered 'a legal relationship preliminary to the purchase which was similar to a contract'. Furthermore, the RG had always stressed 'that a contractual relationship or a relationship based on obligation may entail duties of care for the life and property of another which are unconnected with the immediate legal nature of the relationship, but which are a necessary result of the circumstances of the case'.[1116] In RG 10 February 1930[1117] the 'leading gas fitter' of the defendant firm helped M's plaintiff maid to move furniture whilst fitting a new gas meter in M's bathroom. When the maid smelt gas in the bathroom she tried to locate the leak by inspecting the pipes with a naked light. The gas ignited, injuring the maid. Basing its decision on the law of contract, the RG found against the defendant, although no true contract with protective effect for third parties in accordance with § 328 BGB had been entered into (the maid had no claim against the defendant for defective installation of the gas meter).[1118] The fitter could have forseen that M had entered into the contract intending that her maid should also benefit. Therefore § 278 and not § 831 BGB had to be applied. Moreover, the fitter was grossly negligent. When the BGH resumed the work of its predecessor, it not only recognized but refined the view taken by the RG. BGH 26 September 1961 primarily concerned the the burden of proof. A customer entered the plaintiff department store and slipped on a banana skin. The BGH stressed that it was part of the quasi-contractual duties arising from *culpa in contrahendo* 'that even during business hours the staff are obliged to examine the floor for objects which should not be there'. If it is unclear whether the personnel fulfilled that duty, it is for the defendant to prove that they did.[1119] Finally, in BGH 28 Jan. 1976 a child accompanying her mother to the shops slipped on a vegetable leaf

---

[1114] See Part 5, nos. 492 ff. below.
[1115] As often described, e.g. v. Bar, *JuS* 1982 pp. 637–645.
[1116] RG 7 Dec. 1911, RGZ 78 pp. 239, 240.   [1117] RG 10 Feb. 1930, RGZ 127 p. 218.
[1118] An earlier case concerning a contract with protective effect for third parties is RG 7 June 1915, RGZ 87 p. 64.   [1119] BGH 26 Sep. 1961, *NJW* 1962 pp. 31, 32.

while they were queuing. Here the BGH combined the notion of *culpa in contrahendo* with that of contracts with protective effect for third parties, and also removed the three-year limitation period under § 852 BGB by applying § 195 BGB (limitation period of thirty years). When the Court of Appeal objected that 'the long limitation period, in conjunction with the reversal of the burden of proof, would make it unreasonably difficult for the defendant to exonerate himself', the BGH merely responded that 'the obvious choice of corrective would be the forfeiture of a right, for which no legal grounds exist'.[1120] Thus, in the field of liability for personal injuries, 'the furthest outpost of contractual liability, which had been expanding since 1900, had been reached'.[1121]

(2) Principal and Servant

So far, the person liable has mostly been termed 'employer', and the **191** person acting 'employee' for reasons of simplification and clarity, as stated above.[1122] Employers' liability clearly occupies the largest part of this area of liability for others. However, liability for others also includes cases in which the person liable and person acting are not parties to a contract of employment. The liability principle of *respondeat superior* is connected, not with internal contractual relationships, but with conditions in which the actor is bound to follow instructions.[1123] It is almost unanimously agreed that such a state of dependency exists if the superior usually has the authority to give instructions.[1124] Thus

---

[1120] BGH 28 Jan. 1976, *JZ* 1976 pp. 776, 778 (note Kreuzer).   [1121] Id. Kreuzer p. 778.
[1122] See fn. 1061 above.
[1123] For European precedents see OGH 8 Feb. 1968, *JBl* 1968 pp. 473, 474 (no employer/employee relationship is necessary: it suffices that the servant is bound by instructions); also OGH 28 Oct. 1975, *JBl* 1978 p. 91, note Koziol; RG 25 Mar. 1918, RGZ 92 pp. 345, 346 ('a person has been assigned to perform a function if he more or less depends upon the instructions of the assignor'); and BGH 29 June 1956, *NJW* 1956 pp. 1715, 1716 ('general representative' (*Generalvertreter*) seen as employee, because his performance of the function assigned to him 'depended entirely upon the defendant's will'); STJ 17 Nov. 1977, *BolMinJust* 271 (1977) p. 201 ('*se caracterize por uma relação de subordinação ou dependência do comissário para com o comitente, que autorize este a dar ordens ou instruções àquele*'); Areopag 1345/1980, *NoB* 29 (1981) p. 672; Areopag 102/1983, *NoB* 31 (1983) p. 1537; and Areopag 1095/1983, *NoB* 32 (1984) p. 1009 (each requiring dependency as a result of being bound by instructions); Cass. 24 May 1988, n. 3616, *Giur.it.* 1989, I, 1, 99; Trib. Milan 14 Sep. 1989, *Foro.it.* 1990, I, 1038 (relationship of *preposizione*; both declaration of intention by the *dominus* and state of dependency are conditions); and Cass.civ. 7 Dec. 1983, *Sem.Jur.* 1984, IV, 55 ('*est préposé celui qui remplit une fonction pour le compte d'une autre personne, laquelle possède à son égard un pouvoir de surveillance, de direction et de contrôle*'). On the meaning of these criteria for dependant conditions for liability for sub-contractors see nos. 192, 200 below.
[1124] Areopag 1270/1989 (fn. 1124 above); Cass.civ. 12 Jan. 1977, *D.* 1977 IR 330 (note Larroumet); Cass.civ. 11 Oct. 1989, *Sem.Jur.* 1989, IV, 397; Cass. 4 Apr. 1963, *Pas. belge* 1963, I, 847; and Cass. 13 June 1986, n. 3937, *Rep.gen.* 1986, col. 3602, no. 137.

where specialists (e.g. surgeons[1125] and pharmacists)[1126] are employees, their employers are not exempt from liability for them merely because they lack the expertise to give them detailed orders. The crucial factor is whether the specialist determines his own working hours. Conversely, a person may have acted as a servant if he was bound by strict orders in a specific case. For instance, a lawyer who is given strict instructions as to how he must conduct a case acts as an employee.[1127] The key factor is that *'une personne peut, en fait, exercer son autorité ou sa surveillance sur les actes d'une autre personne'.*[1128] It matters neither whether the other person is permanently employed or merely helping out,[1129] nor whether he is paid for executing the task.[1130] The principal/servant relationship need not even be contractual; it also arises where the damage occurs while the servant is performing a task assigned to him by the principal, from

---

[1125] See e.g. Areopag 1270/1989, *EllDik* 32 (1991) p. 765; CA Athens 197/1988, *EllDik* 29 (1988) p. 1239; Brussels 14 Jan. 1982, *RGAR* 1983 no. 10688; BGH 16 Oct. 1956, *VersR* 1956 p. 714 (temporary replacement employee of the regular surgeon); and BGH 11 Apr. 1951, BGHZ 1 p. 383. Not an employee of the hospital, however, is the surgeon flown in to carry out surgery in a specific case (HR 31 May 1968, *NedJur* 1968 no. 323 p. 1121), and a senior consultant is commonly regarded as a hospital's executive (see fn. 1037 above). For a decision demonstrating great reticence in classing surgeons employed by a hospital as *préposés*, see Cass.ch.req. 21 July 1947, D. 1947 *Jur.* 486.
[1126] Cass. 16 Oct. 1972, *Pas. belge* 1973, I, 165, 170.
[1127] This is the view shared by RG 21 June 1919, RGZ 96 pp. 177, 179 (by extending the applicability to 'representatives/agents' (*Vertreter*) in general), BGH 11 Feb. 1957, *BB* 1957 p. 306 (concerning the power of attorney; far-reaching decision); and, at least *incidenter*, BGH 8 July 1980, *NJW* 1980 p. 2810 (a lawyer experienced in press law who had to determine the admissibility of a certain publication on behalf of the publishers). Both decisions touch upon the perimeters of liability for servants, since (lawyers employed as permanent legal advisers aside) lawyers are generally independent administrators of justice. France therefore exercises much greater restraint in this respect, to the extent that not even an *avocat salarié* qualifies as a *préposé* (Starck (-Roland/Boyer), *Obligations*, vol. i, 4th edn., no. 1005). Architects occupy a similar position. Those in employ are employees, but not those who are self-employed: TS 10 May 1986, *La Ley* 1986 (3) p. 292. Finally, ordinary editors are *employees*, but editors-in-chief are usually executives: OGH 25 Mar. 1987, *JBl* 1987 pp. 524, 526.
[1128] Cass. 2 Oct. 1984, *Pas. belge* 1985, I, 156, Cass. 4 Apr. 1963 (fn. 1126 above), and Cass. 16 Oct. 1972 (fn. 1125 above) reached the same conclusion.
[1129] Pires de Lima/Antunes Varela, *Cc anotado*, vol. i, 4th edn., Art. 500 no. 3; STJ 17 Nov. 1977, *BolMinJust* 271 (1977) p. 201; Asser (-Hartkamp), *Verbintenissenrecht*, vol. iii, 9th edn., p. 137; v. Bar (-Schilcher/Kleewein), *DeliktsR in Europa, Österreich*, p. 76.
[1130] E.g. TS 10 Dec. 1976, *RAJ* 1976 no. 5294 p. 3742 (subsidiary liability for an overseer working free of charge who, while undertaking his work on a melon plantation, shot dead a thief); Hof Amsterdam 30 Dec. 1964, *NedJur* 1966 no. 250 p. 601, Cass.civ. 27 Nov. 1991, *Resp.civ.assur.* 1992 no. 143 (a hunter gutting game acts as employee of the owner of the hunting ground); and RG 25 Mar. 1918, RGZ 92 pp. 345, 346 (the task with which a person has been entrusted 'can be of a factual or a legal nature, paid or unpaid, permanent or casual, higher- or lower-ranking, and it can have been assigned for a range of duties or for a specific task'). According to BGH 14 June 1966, *VersR* 1966 pp. 877, 878 and Rb. Haarlem 15 May 1956, *NedJur* 1956 no. 658 p. 1290, someone who borrows another's car does not automatically become the latter's employee. TS 30 May 1992, *La Ley* 1992 (4) p. 137, on the other hand, applied Art. 22 CP in the same situation.

which the principal would benefit. The possibility of instructing another person is sufficient to prove that the person instructed acted as servant.[1131] Thus a French court held a football club to be the principal of one player who injured another,[1132] a candidate in an election campaign was declared to be the principal of one of his supporters who assaulted an opponent,[1133] and the seller of a car was the principal of the putative buyer who caused an accident on his way to the *centre de contrôle technique*: it was the responsibility of the seller to take the car for a check-up, '*l'acheteur était donc le préposé occasionnel du vendeur au moment de l'accident*'.[1134] Finally, even a legal person may in some circumstances qualify as an employee.[1135]

Just as persons bound to follow orders are considered as servants,[1136] **192** they are classed as principals if they have the authority to instruct. Thus, the nurse's principal is normally the hospital, but during surgery it may be the operating surgeon.[1137] The *Cour de Cassation* went so far as to rule that all twenty owners of a flock of sheep were the *commettants* of the shepherd tending them.[1138] The question of who has *pouvoir effectif* becomes important in practice in cases concerning casual workers.

[1131] Greek courts soon reversed the position taken by Areopag 114/1956, *NoB* 4 (1956) p. 564, according to which the relationship between principal and servant needed to be based on contract. See Areopag 194/1976, *NoB* 24 [1976] p. 718; Areopag 380/1979, *NoB* 27 [1979] p. 1437; CFI Thessalonika 5691/1987, *Arm.* 42 (1988) p. 37; and Filios, *Enochiko Dikaio*, vol. ii (2), 3rd edn., p. 84; Deliyannis/Kornilakis, *Eidiko Enochiko Dikaio*, vol. iii, p. 183; and Rokas, *KF* 1993 pp. 52, 53.

[1132] Trib.gr.inst. Marseille 6 Oct. 1983, *D.* 1985 *IR* 143 (note Karaquillo); a view shared by Limoges 17 Sep. 1992, *D.* 1993 *Somm.* 333 (rugby match; it is irrelevant whether the players are professionals).   [1133] Cass.crim. 20 May 1976, *Gaz.Pal.* 1976 *Jur.*, 545.

[1134] Metz 8 Mar. 1994, *Sem.Jur.* 1994, IV, 1916 (p. 251).

[1135] Filios (fn. 1131 above) p. 85.

[1136] Of course liability for a principal arises not only from misconduct by his servant, but also from unlawful acts directly attributable to him (see no. 7 and fns. 29 and 98 above). For a perceptive example see RL 14 Nov. 1984, *CJ* IX (1984–5) p. 183: *Maria* acted grossly negligently by instructing her worker *Antonio* to set fire to some dry grass although the weather conditions suggested that this would be dangerous. A principal can also be held liable for personal fault if he fails to supervise employees of other companies, when their tasks are his responsibility, see AP Madrid 20 Oct. 1993, *La Ley* 1994 (1) 752: bunjee-jumping accident. Both the organizer of the event and the city of Madrid, which permitted the event but exercised no control over it, were found liable under Art. 1902 Span. Cc. Finally, for cases in which only duties attributed to the employer are violated, see Cass.com. 12 Oct. 1993, *D.* 1994 *Jur.* 124 incl. note Viney = *Sem.Jur.* 1995, II, 22493 incl. note Chabas (competition; *faute personnelle* of the employee was not proved, liability of the employer upheld).

[1137] This is the view of Cass.civ. 15 Mar. 1976, *Bull.civ.* 1976 II no. 100; for a different view see HR 31 May 1968, *NedJur* 1968 no. 323 p. 1121 *Nuboer* arrest; see Vermeyden, *WPNR* 1969 nos. 5035, 5036. BGH 11 Apr. 1951, *BGHZ* 1 p. 383 ignores this question, presuming personal liability on the part of the senior consultant; BGH 30 June 1959, *NJW* 1959 pp. 2302, 2303 regards the hospital, rather than the operating surgeon, as principal of the theatre nurse. The principal of a self-employed midwife is the senior consultant of the gynaecology ward: BGH 14 Feb. 1995, *VersR* 1995 pp. 706, 708.

[1138] Cass.civ. 20 July 1955, *Sem.Jur.* 1956, II, 9052.

Here the courts must determine who is the principal of the employees of a subcontractor who are integrated into the business operations of the main contractor at the time of the damage, and who were following the main contractor's instructions. The courts increasingly tend to view the main contractor as either the sole principal or at least a co-principal.[1139] However, the decision depends on the circumstances of the individual case.

TS 1 February 1994 is a good example.[1140] The plaintiff lent his car to an acquaintance who, while on a business trip, left it in a hotel car park. Due to the negligence of the car park security officer, the car was stolen. The security officer was not an employee of the hotel but of a third party acting on the hotel's instructions. Whereas the *Audiencia Provincial* dismissed the case on the basis that the hotel guest only had a contract with the security firm, the *Tribunal Supremo* upheld the claim of liability in delict: the hotel was held liable for the security man's misconduct under Art. 1903 Cc (employer's liability).

193   A servant who is personally liable to third parties is jointly and severally liable with his principal.[1141] However, this does not mean that a principal is only answerable if his employee is also liable. Detailed analysis is required to decide whether a servant's personal liability is a prerequisite of his principal's liability. All legal systems have in common, first, that the injured plaintiff who sues the principal is not required also to sue the servant. Where it is a necessary precondition for liability, it suffices to establish his fault *incidenter*. Secondly, all agree that the

---

[1139] As well as in TS 1 Feb. 1994 (fn. 1140 below), this was the outcome in: Cass.civ. 18 Jan. 1989, *Sem.Jur.* 1989, IV, 104 (employee of a security firm integrated into the work routine of the plant he was guarding); BGH 14 July 1970, *VersR* 1970 p. 934 (a firm allowed its staff members to work for another firm to operate a complicated machine); OLG Düsseldorf 29 Oct. 1993, *NJW-RR* 1995 p. 160; OGH 28 Oct. 1975, *JBl* 1978 pp. 91, 93 (fitter of a subcontractor also employee of the main contractor); HR 16 Apr. 1943, *NedJur* 1943 no. 352 p. 483; and HR 7 Jan. 1983, *NedJur* 1984 no. 607 p. 2112 (the important factor is the terms on which a person has been integrated; in some circumstances both employers may be principals); Cass. 24 Oct. 1978, n. 4821, *Rep.gen.* 1979, col. 3553, no. 103; Cass. 11 June 1983, n. 4031, *Rep.gen.* 1983, col. 3634, no. 125; and Cass. 6 July 1983, n. 4561, *Rep.gen.* 1983, col. 3634, no. 126 (the key factor for liability under Art. 2049 Ital. Cc is the factual connection between the parties, and not whether their relationship was based on contract). See also the *Nuboer* case HR 31 May 1968 (fn. 1137 above) (a theatre nurse working for a non-employee surgeon remains the *ondergeschikte* of the hospital which employed her. It could not be ascertained whether she had worked on the instructions of the surgeon); HR 14 Oct. 1994, *RvdW* 1994 no. 204 p. 1133 (an authority remained the *ondergeschikte* of the state with liability for its chief officer who, within the scope of his responsibilities whilst working for a private enterprise which produced forgery-proof passports, unlawfully dismissed another employee). [1140] TS 1 Feb. 1994, *RAJ* no. 854 p. 1112.

[1141] These are cases of liability *in solidum*. Liability under Art. 22 Span. CP and Art. 120 IV NCP is secondary in nature. Furthermore, BGH 13 Dec. 1994, *VersR* 1995 pp. 427, 428 holds that the rules on joint and several liability must not result in employees being liable for their employers' fault.

individual who caused the injury need not be identifiable. The conditions for liability are met if it is established that any of the servants committed the delict.[1142] Finally, all European systems share the principle that protection against liability aimed solely at the employee must not be transformed into provisions which also protect his employer from liability. However, limitations of liability on the part of the employee (at least to third parties) have not yet become universal in Europe,[1143] with the result that this principle only operates in some systems.

The best example is currently found in Belgium. Art. 18 of its labour law says in its first two sections: '*En cas de dommages causés par le travailleur à l'employeur ou à des tiers dans l'exécution de son contrat, le travailleur ne répond de sa faute légère que si celle-ci présente dans son chef un caractère habituel plutôt qu'accidentel.*'[1144] That is, the employee is not personally responsible for a momentary lapse. In such cases liability rests solely with employer. For '*de vrijstelling van aansprakelijkheid voor*

[1142] OGH 28 Oct. 1975, *JBl* 1978 p. 91 (it was not established which 'fitter had carried out the work'); STJ 10 Jan. 1975, *BolMinJust* 243 (1975) p. 240; AP Madrid 30 Mar. 1994, *La Ley* 1994 (1) p. 752 (unlawful act of one of the persons in charge, identity unknown); Cass. 15 Oct. 1992, n. 11336, *Giust.civ.Mass.* 1992 no. 11336 p. 1476; Cass. 12 Apr. 1990, n. 3104, *Rep.gen.* 1990, col. 2153, no. 337; and App. Rome 24 Feb. 1976, *Giur.it.* 1978, I, 2, 430 (traffic accident due to a car part's becoming detached; identity of responsible employee could not be established); and RG 27 Nov. 1916, RGZ 89 pp. 136, 137 (the plaintiff need not name the individual responsible).

[1143] Unlimited liability of employees to third parties is still the basic rule in: Germany (no. 188 and fn. 1105 above), Greece, France, Luxembourg (most recently in Cour 13 June 1990, *Pas. luxemb.* 28 [1990–92] pp. 45, 48–49, incl. comparisons with French law), Austria (see § 3 *Dienstnehmerhaftpflichtgesetz*, by which the employee only has a right to indemnity against his employer), The Netherlands (with the exception provided by Art. 6:168 II BW: employee not liable if instructed to act in socially tolerated but unlawful manner), Italy, and Spain. It is irrelevant for the employee's personal liability that such liability was founded on conduct incurring liability on the employer (BGH 5 Nov. 1989, *ZIP* 1990 pp. 35, 37; and TS 1 Dec. 1987, *RAJ* 1987 no. 9170 p. 8499, both of which stress that a patient is not required to sue the hospital. There is no reason why she cannot simply sue the consultant/employee). As for continental Europe, only in Belgium does the degree of fault determine the 'scope of liability' (see below), a solution also found in Scandinavian law (see §§ 19 III, 23 II Danish law on damages; 4th Chapter, 1 § Finnish law on damages; § 2–3 II Norwegian law on damages, and 4th Chapter, 1 § Swedish law on damages). However, despite the basic continental European rule of unlimited liability for employees to third parties, they can indemnify themselves against liability on the basis of non-delict law. A good example is German labour law, which enables an employee to absolve himself (see no. 188 above). A second example is French law, under which the victim usually sues the employer, but rarely the employee. The employer is usually insured against third-party liability and the insurer's right of recourse against the employee requires *faute lourde* under Art. L 121.12 *alinéa 3 Code des assurances* (to be applied in cases of '*malfaisance commise par . . . les préposés, employés, ouvriers ou domestiques*'); for established practice of the courts, e.g. Cass.soc. 27 Nov. 1958, *D.* 1959 *Jur.* 20 (n. Lindon).

[1144] *Wet betreffende de arbeidsovereenkomsten/Loi relative aux contrats de travail* of 3 July 1978, BS/Monit. belge of 27 Aug. 1978.

lichte schuld, die niet gewoonlijk voorkomt, geldt enkel voor de aangestelden en sluit de civielrechtelijke aansprakelijkheid van de werkgever niet uit'.[1145]

194   A more problematic issue is the question of whether the principal should only be liable if the servant is at fault, even in a minor degree. It soon becomes apparent that the answer to this question, like Gaul, has three parts. First, there is the issue of the relationship between principals' vicarious and employees' strict liability; secondly, it must be decided whether principals are liable for employees who are incapable of being at fault, such as mentally handicapped persons. Finally, one must consider whether a principal can be burdened with damages for injuries suffered by a third party even where the servant acted with due care.

195   The first of those questions was discussed above in connection with the liability of legal persons for their executives.[1146] It concerns the issue of whether a principal is also responsible for risks arising from the servant who is the keeper of a dangerous object. Unfortunately, the courts have found against the principal[1147] in far too many cases: those who argue that keepers' and principals' liability are mutually exclusive are correct. First, in those systems which hold principals strictly liable for failure to supervise, this follows from the fact that supervision can never ensure more than careful conduct.[1148] Moreover, strict liability's objective, i.e. ensuring that it is the insured keeper who pays, militates against a merger with principals' liability. Therefore a principal can only be the

---

[1145] Cass. 18 Nov. 1981, *RW* 1982–83 p. 859. Also Vred. Oostende 25 Jan. 1991, *RW* 1994–1995 p. 201.   [1146] See no. 176 above.

[1147] See Art. 500 I Port. Cc, according to which a principal is always liable if the *comissário* 'is under an equal obligation to compensate'. This is considered to indicate that it is sufficient for employer's vicarious liability if the employee is strictly liable as keeper of the object. (Pires de Lima/Antunes Varela, *Cc anotado*, vol. i, 4th edn., Art. 500 no. 2).; See also STJ 5 Nov. 1981, *BolMinJust* 311 (1981) p. 340: *in casu* the court found in favour of the defendant, but only because his employee had misused the car, thus acting outside his function); J. de Paix Lux. 8 Mar. 1979, *Pas. luxemb.* 24 (1978–1980) p. 240; Cass. 5 Nov. 1981, *Pas. belge* 1982, I, 316 (also fn. 1264 below); and Georgiades/Stathopoulos (-Georgiades), *Greek Cc*, vol. iv, Art. 922 no. 24 (a principal is also liable where his servant is strictly liable as animal keeper). Even Bloembergen (-Boumann), *Onrechtmatige daad*, vol. iii, *Verkeersrecht*, n. 193 considers it theoretically possible that an employer can be held responsible in such a case (keepers' liability if an employee uses his employer's car for private purposes). Yet his view appears incompatible with the unequivocal wording of 6:170 BW ('*fout*'). However, such decisions as Rb. 's-Gravenhage 15 May 1978, *VR* 1980 no. 56, are less significant than is frequently claimed. An employee was asked by his employer to help a member of the board to move house. He was expressly permitted to use his employer's private minivan to carry out the task. Only when he had an accident did it emerge that the vehicle was not insured. A *fout* was clearly committed by driving a vehicle without insurance. The only question was who should be considered the principal: the firm (the view of the court) or the board member (view of the Greek, Rokas, *KF* 1993 pp. 52, 53).

[1148] See nos. 148–150 above.

temporary keeper of an object (e.g. a car) belonging to his employee which the latter uses for business purposes.[1149]

The second question, concerning incapable servants, poses no problem **196** if the provision violated demands only an unlawful act, without fault being necessary. Such are the prerequisites of § 831 German BGB, Art. 2049 Ital. Cc, and Art. 922 Greek Cc,[1150] as well as § 1315 ABGB (a mentally handicapped employee is apparently habitually incompetent) and Art. 6:170 I BW, for the term *fout* used therein describes an unlawful act[1151] which can be attributed to the *ondergeschikten*. Moreover, Art. 6:165 I BW provides that 'a mental or physical disability does not prevent . . . conduct, which must be considered an act . . . from being imputed to him as an unlawful act' (see no. 91 above). The French *Cour de Cassation* achieves the same result by integrating Art. 489–2 Cc into employers' liability.[1152] Spain's secondary liability under the NCP has a similar effect, and Portugal can employ liability for failure to supervise based on contract in accordance with Art. 491 Cc. Courts may even rely on Art. 500 I directly.[1153] However, there are no decisions on this issue. Only in Belgium is liability for servants without delictual capacity still an issue.[1154] The problem is that the official commentary to Art. 1386*bis* expressly states that such cases are not covered by employers' liability.[1155]

[1149] The leading case in France, whose recent developments are recorded in detail by Peano, D. 1991 *Chron.* pp. 51–55, is Cass.civ. 24 Jan. 1973, Bull.civ. 1973, III, no. 72: '*Les qualités de préposé et de gardien étant incompatibles, le premier cesse de garder sa propre chose lorsqu'il l'utilise pour accomplir la mission qui lui est confiée, par le commettant dans l'intérêt de ce dernier, qui devient gardien.*' For a more recent case directly concerning the use of private cars see Trib.gr.inst. Saint-Brieuc 5 June 1990 (not reported, cited here according to Peano loc. cit. p. 52 fn. 9), and Cass.civ. 11 Oct. 1989, Bull.civ. 1989, II, no. 175 (accident during the felling of a tree; the court found the owner of the tree to be both *gardien* and *commettant*). This case demonstrates how closely *garde* and *préposition* have approached each other, which development has been codified in Portugal. Under Art. 503 I Port. Cc, a person is liable if he 'has actual power over a farming vehicle and uses it for his own purposes, whether or not through an employee'.

[1150] Although the prevailing view is that liability for incapable servants arises, not from Art. 922, but from Art. 914 Greek Cc, see e.g. Filios, *Enochiko Dikaio*, vol. ii (2), 3rd edn., p. 85.

[1151] Asser (-Hartkamp), *Verbintenissenrecht*, vol. iii, 9th edn., nos. 125, 145; v. Bar (-Hondius/van Dam), *DeliktsR in Europa, Niederlande*, p. 12; van Dunné, *Verbintenissenrecht*, vol. ii, 2nd edn., p. 580.

[1152] Cass.civ. 3 Mar. 1977, D. 1977 *Jur.* 501 (note Larroumet); for more detail see Jourdain, *Rev.trim.dr.civ.* 89 (1990) pp. 667–668.

[1153] The Portuguese legislator co-ordinated liability of principals for their servants, and personal liability in equity of the mentally handicapped clumsily. The former renders the principal responsible for any personal liability of his servant, whereas the latter is merely secondary to liability for failure to supervise.

[1154] See e.g. Cornelis, *Responsabilité extra-contractuelle* no. 225; and Van Oevelen, RW 1987–88 pp. 1170, 1200–1201 (no. 60).

[1155] *Pasin. belge* 1935, pp. 286, 287–288. See also no. 79 above.

197   The third question, whether liability can be imposed if the servant acted with due care, has also been tackled similarly by all European courts, although the texts of the codes themselves differ substantially. The issue is whether the servant must have satisfied all the requirements of the relevant tort (with the exception of *discernement*) in order to incur liability for his employer. In other words, is it necessary that an employee acted culpably, i.e. at least carelessly? To an impartial observer the answer is simple: since employing a servant is not unlawful, and since an employee who works carefully cannot have affected his principal's liability for risks arising from delegating tasks, the latter cannot be held responsible. Therefore the general rule is that a principal is not liable unless he would have been liable had he taken the action himself. Furthermore, if his fault would have had to be positively proved, the same must apply to his servant. However, if the burden of proof is on him, he can only exonerate himself if he can demonstrate that his servant was not at fault.[1156]

198   In some legal systems the relevant text expresses this quite clearly. For example Art. 6:170 BW demands a *fout* by the servant, and Art. 500 I Port. Cc demands that the employee 'would be under an equal obligation to compensate'.[1157] However, in most codes this point is unclear.[1158] Some even explicitly state that an unlawful act on the part of the servant is sufficient.[1159] Is such a provision intended to render an employer liable for any damage related to the conduct of his servant, even if the latter did not act negligently? Is a transport agent to be held liable for his driver if the latter drove onto a damaged quay, not knowing that it would collapse under the weight of the HGV?[1160] Is he to be held responsible if his driver was suddenly blinded by the sun,[1161] or failed to take a preventative measure which even the employer would not have been required to take in the cir-

---

[1156] E.g. TS 7 Nov. 1985, *La Ley* 1986 (1) p. 846: employer was liable because his *dependiente* was presumed to be at fault; and BGH 4 Nov. 1953, BGHZ 11 p. 151: incorporation of § 831 II (personal liability of an employee in charge of supervision for presumed failure to supervise other employees) into § 831 I BGB. The level of care required depends on the circumstances of the case. For instance, if the servant is employed because he has expertise in a certain area, he has to use that expertise.

[1157] Portuguese judges have therefore repeatedly maintained that the liability of principals is based on three pillars: '*Vínculo entre comitente e comissário, prática do acto ilícito no exercício da função e responsabilidade do comissário*': see RP 23 Oct. 1984, *CJ* IX (1984–4) p. 227 (source of quotation); and STJ 17 Nov. 1977, *BolMinJust* 271 (1977) p. 201.

[1158] The *Code civil* refers only to liability for '*dommage causé par leurs domestiques et préposés dans les fonctions auxquelles ils* [= *les maîtres et les commettants*] *les ont employés*'. Art. 1903 IV Span. Cc and § 1315 ABGB are similarly worded.

[1159] See § 831 BGB, Art. 2049 Ital. Cc, and Art. 922 Greek Cc.

[1160] As in Danish HD 9 Aug. 1993, *UfR* 1993 A p. 809 = *NDS* 1994 p. 500.

[1161] As in STJ 29 Nov. 1974, *BolMinJust* 242 (1975) p. 366 (negligence not found: but the case did not directly concern employers' liability).

cumstances?[1162] These questions must be answered in the negative, as agreed by commentators and courts throughout Europe.[1163] This is even true of Italy[1164] and Greece,[1165] although the texts of their codes seem to favour a different solution. Only in Germany has § 831 I BGB given, at least temporarily,[1166] some cause for concern.[1167]

The case concerned was BGH 4 Mar. 1957.[1168] As the plaintiff was **199** about to enter a tram, it started moving. He fell and was so severely injured that his leg had to be amputated. It was impossible to establish the exact circumstances which led to the accident: in particular, it was unclear whether the driver or the conductor was at fault. Under § 831 BGB it was unnecessary to clarify this point in order to establish liability on the part of the tram company; an 'unlawful' act was sufficient. If, in accordance with prevailing opinion at the time, unlawfulness were established by the mere fact that injury was caused by starting the tram, the claim would be upheld, a result which the BGH considered untenable. Hence an entirely new concept of unlawfulness was developed. It had to be 'established that an unlawful act has not been committed if the relevant road traffic regulations (and the duty of care) have been observed'.[1169] Thus the BGH had created the notion of orderly road traffic conduct as a ground for justification, which also solved the problem of how to apportion the burden of proof: 'the principal must . . .

[1162] See *Topp* v. *London Country Buses (South West) Ltd.* [1993] 3 All ER 448.

[1163] For Portugal see fn. 1157 above; for The Netherlands see Asser (-Hartkamp), *Verbintenissenrecht*, vol. iii, 9th edn., no. 145; for Belgium Cornelis, *Responsabilité extra-contractuelle*, no. 225; Cass. 26 Jan. 1988, *Pas. belge* 1988, I, 615; and Antwerp 7 Dec. 1987, *RW* 1989–90 p. 780; for France Flour/Albert, *Obligations*, vol. ii, 5th edn., no. 212; and e.g. Cass.civ. 8 Oct. 1969, Bull.civ. 1969 II no. 269, and Cass.civ. 25 June 1981, *Gaz.Pal.* 1982, 1, pan. 22 (note Chabas); and for Luxembourg Diekirch 17 May 1961, *Pas. luxemb.* 18 (1960–1962) p. 513. A principal is clearly not liable, even where his servant acted negligently, if there is no causal connection with the damage: TS 3 Mar. 1995, *RAJ* 1995 no. 3890 p. 5177.

[1164] Cass. 29 May 1972, n. 1712, *Giur.it.* 1973, I, 1, 917; and Cass. 6 May 1986, n. 3025, *Rep.gen.* 1986, 3602 no. 135.

[1165] Areopag 390/1988, *EllDik* 29 (1988) p. 1672; Areopag 156/1953, *NoB* 1 (1953) p. 192; Areopag 1322/1976, *NoB* 25 (1977) p. 925; Areopag 1125/1977, *NoB* 26 (1978) p. 934; Areopag 194/1976, *NoB* 24 (1976) p. 718; and elsewhere. Yet some commentators disagree with the established practice: Michaelides-Nouaros, *EllDik* 29 (1988) pp. 1641–1651.

[1166] Commentaries now reflect the text of § 831 BGB and maintain that the conduct of the servant need only be unlawful: he need not have been at fault, see e.g. *MünchKomm* (-Mertens), 2nd edn., § 831 no. 52; and Staudinger (-Schäfer), *BGB*, 12th edn., § 831 no. 126.

[1167] Unnecessarily, because RG 31 Mar. 1936, *JW* 1936 pp. 2394, 2396 had already stressed it was common practice that 'an act which, if performed by the principal, would not have rendered her liable . . . (does) not require her to compensate if an employee acted in her place'. The court laid down the rule: 'If staff act without fault when preparing and serving food, the landlord is also free of liability': id. p. 2394. Initially the BGH shared this view (BGH 14 Jan. 1954, BGHZ 12 p. 94: 'no special exculpatory proof is needed to exclude liability under § 831 BGB if the employee acted in a fashion which any carefully selected person would have demonstrated'). It is therefore difficult to see why the BGH strayed from this course, albeit only for a limited period of time.

[1168] BGH (Great Senate) 4 Mar. 1957, BGHZ 24 p. 21.   [1169] Id. p. 26.

prove that his servant's conduct was lawful (in accordance with road traffic regulations). . . . In cases of doubt as to this point, the burden of proof lies with the defendant company' (i.e. the principal).[1170] Both approaches were wrong. To use correct conduct under road traffic regulations as a justification (*Rechtfertigung*) proved damaging to the general liability system, was also completely unnecessary,[1171] and resulted in a bad decision. The burden of proof may only be shifted to the principal's disadvantage if the burden would have been his had he acted instead of his servant. Hence, the BGH could have based its decision on a general reversal of the burden of proof. However, the case was really unrelated to problems of the liability of principals. In conclusion, irrespective of the wording of § 831 BGB, even under German law a principal can only be held liable if negligence on the part of his servant is established.

(3) Liability for Independent Contractors and Agents

200 It is unequivocally established that a principal is liable for unlawful but faultless acts by his *ondergeschikten*, irrespective of his own fault, as also is the rule that *ondergeschikten* are not answerable for faults by their employer.[1172] The question which must be answered is whether, and in what circumstances, someone can (or should) be liable for the conduct of another who is his equal,[1173] but who was working in his interest and on his instructions when the damage occurred. In other words, should no-fault liability be imposed on independent contractors and agents? Only Dutch legislation has so far developed separate provisions: Arts. 6:171, 172 BW permit liability in both cases. The first provision reads: 'if a non-servant (*een niet ondergeschikte*) who performs activities in order to carry on the business of another on the latter's instruction is liable to a third party for a fault committed in the course of those activities, that other

---

[1170] Id. p. 29.

[1171] See fn. 1167. The BGH never again took correct road traffic conduct into consideration as 'grounds for justification', for that would effectively shift the burden of proof of negligence. BGH 28 Feb. 1969, VersR 1969 p. 542, for instance, restates: 'as the caterpillar driver acted correctly, in the manner to be expected of any carefully selected person digging the hole, liability under § 831 BGB would have to be denied without further exculpatory proof.' The BGH thus returned to the position in BGHZ 12 p. 94 (see fn. 1167 above) rather than referring to BGHZ 24 p. 21, a course already adopted by BGH 14 June 1966, VersR 1966 pp. 877, 878.

[1172] This issue was discussed and rejected by OGH 7 Apr. 1992, JBl 1992 pp. 786, 787 regarding contracts with protective effect for third parties: the contract between a ski school and a skiing instructor had no contractual effect upon the students. Therefore the instructor was only held liable for his own delictual duty of care, not for his employer's breach of contractual duty of care (as the instructor's servant). See also BGH 13 Dec. 1994 (fn. 1141 above).

[1173] See Delvaux, Rev.jur.pol.Ind.Coop. 27 (1973) pp. 549, 554: '*ils ne peuvent être considérés comme préposés alors qu'ils traitent d'égal à égal.*'

person is also liable to the third party'. Furthermore, under Art. 6:172 BW the *fout* of the representative (*vertegenwoordiger*) is attributed to the person represented (*vertegenwoordigde*). The Dutch legislator thus adapted the law of delict in line with the law of contract. However, if the term 'agent' under Art. 6:172 BW were construed to include not only 'statutory representatives' (including parents)[1174] but also representatives who were not contractually bound, the scope of the provision would be too wide.[1175]

However, the fact that only the Dutch BW contains such a provision   **201** does not mean that no other system has embarked on a similar course. Although it is the only European nation which categorically imposes liability for one independent contractor upon another, others have taken similar and remarkable steps in the same direction.[1176] Austrian courts, for instance, have sometimes classed independent contractors as employees (*Besorgungsgehilfen*),[1177] and Germany has developed contracts with protective effects for third parties.[1178] There are also countless rulings, cited above, in which a subcontractor's employees were found to be (temporary) employees of the main contractor if they were bound

---

[1174] This is the inevitable conclusion, in view of the term *vertegenwoordiging*, and is also the prevailing opinion. E.g. *Parlementaire Geschiedenis*, vol. vi, pp. 731–732; and Klaassen, *Risico-aansprakelijkheid*, pp. 74–75, who remarks that in accordance with this view children may be held liable for their parents as their statutory representatives.

[1175] See no. 154 and fn. 943 above. That the legislator sought only to incorporate delicts committed during and in connection with the conclusion of contracts (or the issuing of a declaration of intention) can be deduced from the examples given in *Parlementaire Geschiedenis* (fn. 1174 above) on Art. 6:172 BW (deceit and anti-competitive conduct upon conclusion of contract). This view is corroborated by the fact that the provision was to pave the way for an easier solution in cases such as HR 10 June 1955, *NedJur* 1955 no. 552 p. 977 (anti-competitive conduct of an insurance agent) (*T&C* [-Lankhorst], 2nd edn., Art. 6:172 n. 6).

[1176] Cass.ass.plén. 12 July 1991, D. 1991 *Jur.* 549; and Cass.civ. 23 June 1992, Bull.civ. 1992, I, no. 195 aside, one should also point out French rulings on *chaînes de contrats*, although they concern only sales contracts. Where the performance of a service is ordered, however, sub-contractors are liable in delict to the person to whom the service is rendered.

[1177] This can be deduced from OGH 28 Oct. 1975, *JBl* 1978 pp. 91, 93 (note by Koziol); and OGH 8 Feb. 1968, *JBl* 1968 p. 473. Another interesting ruling is Cass.civ. 18 Oct. 1960, JCP 1960, II, 11846, although it only affected an *obligation de sécurité de moyens*. The case concerned the liability of a surgeon for the fault of an equally independent anaesthetist. Whereas the *Cour d'appel* wanted to apply Art. 1384 V Cc, the *Cour de Cassation* held that liability arose in contract.

[1178] E.g. BGH 21 June 1994, VersR 1994 pp. 1202, 1203: independent craftsmen and (sub-contractors) are often not employees (but see also BGH 24 June 1953, VersR 1953 p. 358 ; and BGH 23 Oct. 1973, VersR 1974 p. 243). Craftsmen omitted properly to secure the building site; held not to be employees of the main contractor, as they they did not simply follow his instructions. The BGH reversed the decision of, and remitted the case to, the OLG. The BGH suggested that the OLG should examine whether the plaintiff, an injured construction worker, could sue the main contractor directly, since the protective effect of the contract for work and services concluded between main and subcontractor might also cover the plaintiff.

by the latter's instructions to a sufficient degree.[1179] Moreover, the main contractor can also be liable if the injury is directly attributable to his failure to supervise.[1180] On the other hand, Dutch courts are increasingly reluctant as to the interpretation of Art. 6:171 BW.[1181] This by no means indicates that the gap between the Dutch and other European systems has closed entirely: the basic rule that others are not liable for damage by independent contractors remains.[1182] It merely indicates that the new Dutch system is not as revolutionary as it first appears. In fact, closer consideration reveals that similar attempts have been made in the field of liability for delicts committed by agents.[1183] For example, it used to be the established practice of the *Reichsgericht* to class 'duly appointed representatives' (*rechtsgeschäftlich bestellter Vertreter*) as employees on the basis that their employers had general authority to instruct them, a position adopted by the BGH.[1184]

(4) Responsibility of Employers for Others and of Employees for Themselves

202 A principal is clearly not liable for delicts committed by his employee as a private person against a third party, i.e. for incidents not linked to the function(s) assigned to the employee. On the other hand, principals' liability would be meaningless if it did not cover unlawful conduct simply because the servant was not instructed to commit a delict. For this reason European legal systems often find it problematic to determine whether a specific case comes under principals' liability, or whether responsibility lies solely with the employee.

[1179] See no. 192 above.

[1180] See e.g. BGH 13 Dec. 1960, *LM* § 823 (Db) BGB no. 10 (independent trader, with a stall located at the entrance to a department store, worked with methylated spirits; the department store was liable for breach of duty of supervision).

[1181] Esp. in cases of state liability in delict: Rb. 's-Gravenhage 16 June 1993, *NedJur Kort* 1993 no. 32 p. 32.

[1182] E.g. TS 12 Nov. 1986, *RAJ* 1986 no. 6386 p. 6231 (in contracts for work and services, the person requiring the work is only liable for the contractor and his staff if the person requiring the work has expressly reserved the right to supervise the staff, and if he carried out some of the work himself); Cass. 11 Feb. 1980, n. 970, *Rep.gen.* 1980, col. 141, no. 52; Cass. 16 May 1987, n. 4518, *Giust.civ.Mass.* 1987 no. 4518 p. 1285; and Trib. Latina 23 Apr. 1992, *Foro.it.* 1992, I, 2522 (the court declared that the work of the contractor is autonomous, so the mandator is not liable for him under Art. 2049 Cc); and RL 25 Mar. 1993, *CJ* XVIII (1993–2) p. 124.

[1183] These are, first, liability based on the extension of the term executive (*Organ*) (see nos. 171 ff. above); secondly, Italian decisions that a *mandato* suffices for Art. 2049 Cc if it entails duties of supervision; and thirdly, the generous application of secondary liability under the old Art. 22 Span. Cc, according to which even a chief of police or deputy mayor can be a servant, see TS 26 Mar. 1994, *RAJ* 1994 no. 2599 p. 3534. This position has been largely adopted in Art. 120 IV NCP, under which 'persons carrying out a trade or business' are also strictly and secondarily liable for their '*representantes*'.

[1184] RG 25 Mar. 1918, RGZ 92 pp. 345, 347; RG 21 June 1919, RGZ 96 pp. 177, 179; BGH 29 June 1956, *NJW* 1956 p. 1715; and BGH 15 Feb. 1957, *BB* 1957 p. 306.

The situation is unambiguous if the servant merely acted negligently. **203**
Here a sufficiently strong link between delict and work is commonly
presumed if the incident occurred during working hours,[1185] if the
employee was acting under the instructions of the principal, and if,
but for the injury, the activity would have served the purposes of the
principal. If a nurse negligently gives the wrong medication, liability lies
with the hospital.[1186] If she gives wrong advice, or knocks over a supermarket shelf, in her private capacity, the hospital escapes liability.[1187]

The situation is less clear where the servant acts with intent or **204**
commits a crime. Here the courts must analyse the options. If the way in
which the work was distributed hypothetically increased the danger or
the possibility of committing a crime, and if this danger eventually
materialized, the unlawful act can be attributed to the principal. However, if the task assigned to the employee did not help him to commit the
crime, and did not make it more likely that a crime would be committed,
the crime is not a direct consequence of the task.[1188] Thus an employer is
liable for the overseer of his melon plantation who shoots a thief.[1189]

[1185] The time factor is an important indicator for intentional delicts: see Brussels 8
May 1985, *JT* 1986 p. 252. From the point of view of liability law, delicts occurring on
the way to and from work are committed outside working hours (e.g. Trib. Firenze 12
July 1975, *Rep.gen.* 1976, col. 3449, no. 71; and BGH 24 June 1958, *NJW* 1958 p. 1774).
This is not the case if the servant works while commuting (e.g. Cass. 24 Dec. 1980, *Pas.
belge* 1981, I, 467: sales agent continued negotiations while returning from a trade fair;
employer was liable for an accident occurring). A case on the border between personal
and principals' liability is Cass.crim. 21 Mar. 1989, *Resp.civ.assur.* 1989 no. 217 (employer
exceptionally allowed employee to take a company car home on a Friday evening to
enable him to return to work the next morning; employer liable for subsequent car
accident).

[1186] An interesting variation is found in ØLD 9 June 1942, *UfR* 1942 A 984: a guest in a
restaurant complaining of stomach pains asked for a remedy. By accident the waitress gave
him cockroach poison instead of sodium bicarbonate. The court upheld the claim against
the proprietor for both employers' liability under DL 3–19–2 and personal fault. It was her
responsibility to store the poison in a secure place.

[1187] E.g. Cass. 11 July 1975, n. 2766, *Giur.it.* 1976, I, 1, 1173: a travel agency hired out a car
with a chauffeur. During a break the chauffeur injured a third party with his fishing rod.
The court dismissed the claim against the travel agency.

[1188] Apart from 6:170 I BW, in which the issue of increased risk has been incorporated
into law, see also BGH 24 June 1958, *NJW* 1958 p. 1774 (no liability if it is impossible 'that
the assignment of the performance effected or increased a hazard which was causally
related to the accident'); Cass.pen. 27 Apr. 1992, *Giur.it.* 1993, II, 608 (an employer has to
bear the burden of the risks connected with the assigned work even in case of crime); and
RP 23 Oct. 1984, *CJ* IX (1984–4) p. 227 (*uma conexão adequada* must exist between the
assignment and the delict). Even Greek judges, who have repeatedly stressed that a delict
committed 'on the occasion' of work assigned can be attributed to the employer (CA
Athens 3828/1973, *NoB* 21 [1973] p. 1476; Areopag 1324/1976, *NoB* 25 [1977] p. 926; and
Areopag 380/1979, *NoB* 27 [1979] p. 1437) are increasingly asking whether the servant's
conduct constituted a risk typical of the task: see Georgiades/Stathopoulos (-Georgiades),
Greek Cc, vol. iv, Art. 922 nos. 32–38).

[1189] TS 10 Dec. 1976, *RAJ* 1976 no. 5294 p. 3742.

Fights[1190] and acts of revenge[1191] do not usually incur principals' liability,[1192] nor do cases of sexual harassment of female employees by male colleagues.[1193] On the other hand, injuries caused by an employee in his employer's, or a customer's, stolen or embezzled car should be covered by principals' liability,[1194] at least where the tortfeasor's job is connected with cars. In other cases, for instance if the car was stolen by a clerk, liability can only be imposed on an employer if the car was in a car park to which only members of the firm and customers had access. Liability always arises in theft if the staff were employed to safeguard the property of the victim;[1195] the same applies where employees must be allowed into houses if liability is not already based upon contract. These criteria also apply to all other offences against property, such as fraud, breach of trust, and falsification of documents. Therefore the *Tribunal Supremo* rightly compelled a pharmacist, whose assistant (her husband) helped out in the sales room and deceived a customer, to pay compensation.[1196] Similarly, Italian courts have imposed liability on banks whose employees intentionally issued incorrect information to other financial institutions.[1197] The legal situation is the same if they fabricate false

---

[1190] On whether an employer is liable if the fight occurred for reasons connected with the work, see Cass. 30 Oct. 1981, n. 5724, *Rep.gen.* 1981, col. 3197, no. 143; and Cass. 4 Jan. 1980, n. 20, *Rep.gen.* 1980, col. 1978, no. 297, which take different views. Also excluding liability: Versailles 19 May 1994, *Gaz.Pal.* 1994 *Somm.* 789.

[1191] Rb. Arnhem 3 Dec. 1992, *A&V* 1993 p. 18: no liability of employer where an employee during lunch-break intentionally started a fire in the employer's warehouse, which spread to the adjacent premises of the plaintiff.

[1192] The situation is different if the task principally involves the use of physical strength: Cass.crim. 20 May 1976, Gaz.Pal. 1976 *Jur.* 545: liability of club when a footballer injured opponent; and Cass.crim. 14 June 1990, *Resp.civ.assur.* 1990 no. 316.

[1193] Thus ØLD 6 Dec. 1993, *UfR* 1994 A p. 215: a businesswoman was held not liable for her employee husband, who had committed such a delict for the first time. However, a different view was quite rightly taken in Brussels 8 May 1985, *JT* 1986 p. 252: a male nurse raped a patient; *'il suffit que l'acte ait été effectué pendant la durée du service et qu'il soit en relation avec celui-ci même indirectement et occasionnellement'*.

[1194] A view shared by Cass.civ. 7 Oct. 1968, n. 3137, *Rep.gen.* 1969, 3909, no. 150; *contra*, however: STJ 5 Nov. 1981, *BolMinJust* 311 (1981) p. 340; and Trib. Lux. 15 Nov. 1967, *Pas. luxemb.* 21 (1969–71) p. 42. See also Rb. Amsterdam 4 Dec. 1985, *VR* 1987 no. 96: a car mechanic during working hours copied the key of and stole a customer's car; customer's claim against employer upheld; and Paris 9 July 1991, *Resp.civ.assur.* 1991 no. 367: the security guard of a discotheque pursued a thief, who had stolen a customer's car, in the car of another customer; again the claim was upheld. Cass. 27 Mar. 1987, n. 2994, *Giur.it.* 1988, I, 1, 1833; BGH 3 Nov. 1964, *NJW* 1965 p. 391.

[1195] E.g. BGH 9 May 1957, BGHZ 24 pp. 188, 196–197; and App. Milan 28 Dec. 1984, *Rep.gen.* 1986, col. 3595 no. 78; *contra*: Cass.crim. 29 Oct. 1991, *Resp.civ.assur.* 1992 no. 42.

[1196] TS 23 June 1981, *RAJ* 1981 no. 2789 p. 2309. On fraud committed by employees on principal's instructions, see BGH 14 Oct. 1971, BGHZ 57 pp. 137, 142.

[1197] App. Milan 28 Dec. 1984, *Rep.gen.* 1986, 3595, no. 78. A remarkable French decision is Cass.civ. 13 Dec. 1991, Bull.civ. 1991, II, no. 304. Comex, a company with financial problems bribed M. Monnier, *'directeur'* of an agency of the Banque Nationale de Paris, with a car so that he would recommend Comex to his superiors. He did so and Comex was granted further credit. The plaintiff M. Adoul had ordered a car from Comex and paid a deposit.

documents.[1198] Equally, a bank is liable if its clerks use clients' money for their own purposes.[1199] This was the sort of case which sparked the development of the general rule that employers would escape liability under the *Code civil* only under three cumulative preconditions: the employee must have acted: *hors des fonctions auxquelles il était employé*, and *sans autorisation*, and *à des fins étrangères à ses attributions*.[1200] The burden of proof lies with the employer. In accordance with more recent decisions, an employers' liability can only be reduced by contributory negligence if the victim knew or should have known that the servant was acting in breach of his position.[1201] French courts thus seem to have abandoned their earlier position that Art. 1384 III Cc is positively inapplicable in such cases.[1202]

Another criterion for the balancing of interests is found in the new Dutch BW. Whereas Art. 6:170 I BW refers to general employers' liability, Art. 6:170 II BW says that in cases where 'the servant did not work in the framework of the master's profession or business, he . . . is only liable if the servant, in committing the fault, acted in the performance of the duty which he had been ordered to carry out'. Although this wording also leaves ample scope for interpretation, its aim is clear: the connection between the task assigned and the injurious conduct has to be more direct if the delict occurred in the employer's private sphere.[1203] Probably they should simply have connected liability to negligence by the principal in such cases.

As for claims to indemnity of a principal, who has paid damages to a **205** third party, against his servant, damages are usually split according to the share of fault. If the employer was at fault, the burden of compensation

---

When Comex became insolvent, it was unable to satisfy his claim. He successfully sued both Monnier and the bank: Monnier had not acted '*en dehors de ses fonctions*'. However, according to the decision of Cass. 7 Oct. 1993, n. 9935, *Giust.civ.Mass.* 1993 no. 9935 p. 1449, the state is not liable for customs officers taking bribes, these not being in the principal's interest.

[1198] E.g. RG 14 Mar. 1939, RGZ 162 pp. 129, 169.

[1199] Cass. 26 Oct. 1989, *Pas. belge* 1990, I, 241; Cass.civ. 11 June 1992, Bull.civ. 1992, II, no. 164; and Paris 10 Oct. 1989, *Resp.civ.assur.* 1990 no. 52. See also Cass. 3 Apr. 1991, n. 3442, *Giust.civ.Mass.* 1991 no. 3442 p. 446; and BGH 27 Apr. 1995, *NJW-RR* 1995 p. 936: bank clerk carried out an order although he knew it to have been overtaken by the bankruptcy of the customer.

[1200] Cass.ass.plén. 19 May 1988, *D.* 1988 *Jur.* 513 (note Larroumet); adopted by Belgium in Cass. 26 Oct. 1989 (fn. 1199 above).

[1201] Cass. 11 Mar. 1994, *JT* 1994 p. 611 with note Christine Dalcq; and Cass.civ. 19 Jan. 1994, Bull.civ. 1994 II no. 34.

[1202] For Belgium this can be seen in Cass. 4 Nov. 1993, *JT* 1994 p. 231: but cf. Cass. 11 Mar. 1994 (fn. 1201 above). For details see Dalcq (fn. 1201). French judges now seem to distinguish between positive knowledge and negligent ignorance of the facts: Starck (-Roland/ Boyer), *Obligations*, vol. i, 4th edn., no. 1017. There are no recent Italian rulings on this issue. In earlier rulings Art. 2049 Cc was considered inapplicable in cases of both knowledge and grossly negligent ignorance: Cass. 11 June 1971, n. 1760, *Rep.gen.* 1971, col. 3657, no. 119.

[1203] *Parlementaire Geschiedenis*, vol. vi, p. 718. Also Art. 120 IV NCP (fn. 1183 above).

will also rest on him in the internal distribution.[1204] On the other hand, if his responsibility arises purely from strict liability he can claim full indemnity from his servant.[1205] Tort law sees employers' liability as a secondary (supplementary) liability, intended to protect the victim, not the employee.[1206] In continental Europe only Art. 6:170 III BW impedes that right of indemnity by means of the law of delict: indemnity is usually limited to cases of intent or 'deliberate' negligence (*bewußte Fahrlässigkeit*).[1207] All other nations which have deemed it right to counteract such extreme employee–employer liability have done so by means of contracts of employment and insurance contracts, the most important examples of which are referred to above.[1208] The aim is to protect employees, at least in cases of slight and medium negligence, by exempting them to some extent from liability to their employers.

[1204] RC 21 Jan. 1986, *CJ* XI (1986–1) p. 33.

[1205] This has been expressly stated in a number of rules, such as Art. 1904 Span. Cc; Art. 503 III, 1st alternative Port. Cc; § 1313 ABGB; and § 840 II BGB. In accordance with the prevailing opinion: CA Larisa 147/1987, *EllDik* 29 (1988) p. 929; Areopag 188/1977, *NoB* 25 (1977) p. 1162; Georgiades, *Sitimata asthikis evthinis*, p. 38, (giving references to opposing commentators); and Filios, *Enochiko Dikaio*, vol. ii (2), 3rd edn., p. 99. Greece arrived at the same result by applying Art. 926, 2nd alternative with Art. 927 s. 2 Cc: if the principal is strictly liable, and his servant for established fault, the servant is responsible to indemnify the employer.

[1206] Cass.civ. 6 Feb. 1974, *D*. 1974 *Jur*. 409 (note by Le Tourneau) was particularly unambiguous: '*L'art. 1384 a, dans son alinéa 5, spécialement pour but de protéger les tiers contre l'insolvabilité de l'auteur du préjudice en leur permettant de recourir contre son employeur.*' As a result, Art. 1251 III Cc remains applicable (for only the third party and not the employee benefits from the payment), which in turn leads to a right to full indemnity if the employer was not at fault (Cass.civ. 25 Nov. 1992, *Sem.Jur*. 1993, IV, 336). The right of recourse may not be exercised in the majority of cases, but if it is then its effects are '*extrêmement sévère*' (Viney, *Sem.Jur*. 1993 *Doctr*. 3664 [p. 147]). For exercising this right is positively not '*subordonné à la condition que le préposé ait agi en dehors de ses fonctions, sans autorisation et à des fins étrangères à ses attributions*': Cass.civ. 28 Oct. 1991, *Resp.civ.assur*. 1992 no. 2. In Italy Arts. 2055 II, III, and 1298 I Ital. Cc are seen in a similar light and also create a right to full indemnity for the employer: Franzoni, *Fatti illeciti*, Art. 2049 p. 419 (unconditionally supported); and e.g. Cass. 12 Feb. 1968, n. 471, *Foro.it.Mass*. 1968 no. 471; Trib. Monza 13 Sep. 1988, *Rep.gen*. 1990, col. 3545, no. 125.

[1207] The Dutch legislation thus codified what had been established practice since HR 26 June 1959, *NedJur* 1959 no. 551 p. 1153. See esp. HR 27 Mar. 1992, *NedJur* 1992 no. 496 p. 203. In Scandinavia similar provisions had already been implemented. See § 23 I Danish law on damages; 4th Chap., 1 § in conjunction with 3 § Finnish law on damages; and 4th Chap. 1 § in conjunction with 6. Chap. 2–4 §§ Swedish law on damages.

[1208] See no. 188 (indemnity against liability under German labour law). See no. 193 and fn. 1143 (indemnity against liability under Austrian law; extended by a prohibition of recourse under § 4 *Dienstnehmerhaftplichtgesetz*; limitation of indemnity claims of third-party liability insurers to cases of *faute lourde*). See also no. 193 above (Art. 18 Belgian *Loi relative aux contrats de travail* for all cases indemnifying employees against liability to third parties and in which the employer has no right of indemnity against the employee). Attempts to exempt employees from indemnity, at least in cases of *culpa levissima*, by means of employment law have also been made by Italian courts. See esp. Trib. Milan 16 June 1958, *Rep.gen*. 1960, col. 2972, nos. 188, 189; and App. Brescia 15 Jan. 1971, *Rep.gen*. 1971, col. 3666, no. 189. However, they have not become established practice.

IV. THE LAW OF LIABILITY FOR DANGERS ARISING FROM ANIMALS AND BUILDINGS AND LAND

Bibliography: Antonides, 'Verkehrssicher ungspflichten für Busschleusen', *VersRAI* 1995 pp. 31–32; v. Bar, 'Vorbeugender Rechtsschutz vor Verkehrspflichtverletzungen', in: *25 Jahre Karlsruher Forum* (Karlsruhe 1983) pp. 80–85; id., 'Entwicklung und rechtsstaatliche Bedeutung der Verkehrs(sicherungs)pflichten', *JZ* 1979 pp. 332–337; Branca, 'Rovina di edificio e responsabilità civile', *Foro.pad.* 1966, vol. i, 119–124; Bussani, 'La rovina dell'edificio', in: Cendon (ed.), *Responsabilità civile* (Milan 1988) pp. 583–613; Chapus, *Droit administratif général*, vol. ii, (6th edn. Paris 1992); Cornelis, *De buitencontractuele aansprakelijkheid voor schade veroorzaakt door zaken* (Antwerp 1982); Deutsch, 'Die Infektion als Zurechnungsgrund', *NJW* 1986 pp. 757–759; id., 'Gefährdungshaftung für laborgezüchtete Mikroorganismen', *NJW* 1976 pp. 1137–1138; id., 'Der Reiter auf dem Pferd und der Fußgänger unter dem Pferd. Irrwege der Rechtsprechung zur Haftung für die Tiergefahr', *NJW* 1978 pp. 1998–2002; Edlbacher, 'Die Haftung für den Zustand eines Weges', in: *25 Jahre Karlsruher Forum* (Karlsruhe 1983) pp. 18–23; Fagnart, 'La responsabilité du fait des microbes', *RGAR* 1969 No. 8302; Franzoni, *Colpa presunta e responsabilità del debitore* (Padova 1988); García Cantero, 'La responsabilidad por ruina de los edificios ex artículo 1.591 del Código civil', *An.Der.Civ.* 16 (1963) pp. 1053–1113; Hausheer, 'Haft- pflicht- und Privatversicherungsrecht', *ZBernJV* 130 (1994) pp. 283–299; Holmes, *The Common Law* (Boston 1881); Jabornegg, 'Die Dachlawine als Haftungsproblem', *ZVR* 1974 pp. 321–328; *JClCiv* (-Giraudel), arts. 1382 to 1386, 'Responsabilité du fait des bâtiments', *Fasc.* 152; *JClCiv* (-Carbajo) arts. 1382 to 1386, 'Etat et collectivités publiques, Travaux et ouvrages publics, Le patrimoine responsable', *Fasc.* 370–3; Jonas, *Die verschuldensunabhängige außervertragliche Haftung für Sachen im Entwurf zum Nieuw Burgerlijk Wetboek der Niederlande. Ein Beitrag zur Reform des deutschen Gefährdungshaftungsrechts* (Munich 1987); Klaassen, *Risico-aansprakelijkheid. De afdelingen 6.3.2 en 6.3.3 NBW, alsmede art. 31 Wegenverkeerswet* (Zwolle 1991; also diss. Nijmegen 1991); Kötz, 'Gefährdungshaftung. Empfiehlt sich eine Vereinheitlichung und Zusammenfassung der gesetzlichen Vorschriften über die Gefährdungshaftung im BGB und erscheint es erforderlich, das Recht der Gefährdungshaftung weiterzuentwickeln?', in: Bundesminister der Justiz (ed.), *Gutachten und Vorschläge zur Überarbeitung des Schuldrechts*, vol. ii (Cologne 1981) pp. 1779–1834; Martyn, 'Wordt er gelachen in het oude recht? Een rechtshistorische bloemlezing', *RW* 1993–94 pp. 1041–1050; Van Quickenborne, 'Réflexions d'un point

223

de vue belge sur l'arrêt du BGH du 2 juillet 1991', *ERPL* 1 (1993) pp. 245–255; Ravarani, 'La responsabilité civile de l'état et des collectivités publiques', *Pas. luxemb.* 28 (1990–92) pp. 77–426; Rottler, *Die Tierhalterhaftung und ihre Begrenzung im deutschen, französischen und englischen Recht* (diss. Freiburg/Br. 1994); Scheffen, 'Zivilrechtliche Haftung im Sport', *NJW* 1990 pp. 2658–2665; Seiler, 'Tierhalterhaftung, Tiergefahr und Rechtswidrigkeit', in: *FS für Albrecht Zeuner* (Tübingen 1994) pp. 279–293; Spencer, 'Motor Cars and the Rule in *Rylands* v. *Fletcher*: A Chapter of Accidents in the History of Law and Motoring', [1983] *CLJ* 65–84; Sterk, *Verhoogd gevaar in het aansprakelijkheidsrecht* (Deventer 1994, also diss. Tilburg 1994); Stone, 'Liability for damage caused by things', *IntEncCompL* XI 5 (1971); Terbille, 'Der Schutzbereich der Tierhalterhaftung nach § 833 S. 1 BGB', *VersR* 1994 pp. 1151–1155; id., 'Die Beweislastverteilung bei der Tierhalterhaftung nach § 833 S. 1 BGB', *VersR* 1995 pp. 129–134; Trimarchi, *Rischio e responsabilità oggettiva* (Milan 1961); Vandenberghe, 'Aansprakelijkheid voor zaken, dieren en gebouwen', in: Vandenberghe (ed.), *Onrechtmatige daad*, pp. 59–83 (Antwerp 1979); Vaz Serra, 'Responsabilidade pelos danos causados por edifícios ou outras obras', *BolMinJust* 88 (1959) pp. 13–62; id., 'Responsabilidade pelos danos causados por animais', *BolMinJust* 86 (1959) pp. 21–101; Westerhoff, 'Ist die Entscheidung gerecht? Methodische Wertung am Beispiel eines Reitunfalls', *JR* 1993 pp. 497–501; Zimmermann, 'Der Hund im Clapham Omnibus', *ZEuP* 1994 pp. 733–735; Ziviz, 'Il danno cagionato da animali', *NGCC* 1990, II, pp. 71–80.

206   Together with liability to others there has always been liability for things, as it has unfortunately been called.[1209] Liability 'due to' things would be more suitable, because it is undisputed that things, including live animals,[1210] cannot 'act' in a legal sense. The time when animals

---

[1209] See no. 7.

[1210] See § 285a ABGB which served as the model for § 90a BGB. 'Animals are not things. They are protected by special laws. The provisions dealing with things apply to animals if no special provisions exist.' Therefore in both German and Austrian law damage to (rather than arising from) an animal results in complete restitution, even above the market value of the animal (§§ 1332a ABGB, 251 II s. 2 BGB).

[1211] On noxal liability see also no. 7 and fn. 34 above; Holmes, *Common Law*, pp. 8–12, 25–27; and Stone, *EncCompL* XI 5-1. Clear traces of noxal liability in respect of liability for (and of) animals can still be found in §§ 1321, 1322 ABGB. Furthermore, the view that an animal can be liable with its own body was accepted in all cases where the animal became a party to an action (Martyn, *RW* 1993–94 pp. 1041, 1048). The belief that a thing can be a party to liability proceedings has survived in some modern maritime law; e.g. in England: (see Halsbury's Laws of England [-Ivamy], 4th edn., vol. 43 [Shipping and Navigation] no. 1003); and Greece: (see Arts. 236, 237, 239 of Act no. 3816/1958 on private maritime law which always speaks of the liability 'of the ship'. Ships are considered the most 'agile' of all inanimate things, which is why they are subject of noxal liability: Holmes loc. cit. p. 24; see also Mazeaud/Mazeaud/Chabas, *Responsabilité civile*, vol. iii (1), 6th edn., no. 2346. Its

stood as independent parties in legal actions is definitly past.[1211] This development has had little effect on the legal terminology, however, and liability is still described as being 'for' things. Moreover, although liability is now unanimously believed to be for the realization of a risk embodied by a thing, the original concept that it was this thing which formed the last 'visible' cause is still apparent in the modern legal mind.[1212] A particularly good demonstration is Art. 925 Greek Cc, according to which 'the owner or possessor of a building . . . shall be liable for damage caused to a third party by reason of its collapse'. Since the relationship between owner and possessor is irrelevant in this case, the 'second party' must be the collapsing building.[1213]

The thing most frequently responsible for accidents is the car. Yet the **207** risk arising from motor vehicles has been ignored by most codes, partly because they could simply not have anticipated it, and partly because they did not consider it worth mentioning. Thus, with the exception of Arts. 2051 Ital. and 503 Port. Cc, the law of liability for motor vehicles is a good example of the process of *decodificazione*.[1214] Only two types of perennial risk were regarded as worthy of inclusion in the codes: risks arising from animals and from buildings. Moreover, they (and only they) have been made subject to special provisions in all European civil codes, with the sole purpose of introducing a stricter form of liability than the basic provision on liability for personal misconduct (which remains applicable alongside the special provisions).[1215] Thus, the analysis of these provisions raises similar questions: for which cases has the stricter notion of liability been developed, what does it consist of, at whom is it aimed, and who benefits from it?

1. Liability for Damage Caused by Animals

a. Animals

The special provisions on liability for damage caused by animals (i.e. **208** Arts. 1385 Belg., French, and Lux. Cc; §§ 1320 ABGB, 833, 834 BGB; Arts.

---

equivalent is the old *law of deodand*, under which a person had the right to have the thing causing the damage surrendered or destroyed. It even influenced English railway liability law in its early stages (*R v. Eastern Counties Railway* [1842] 10 M&W 58 = 152 ER 380), and played a role in the development of motor accident liability law (Spencer, [1983] *CLJ* 65–84).

[1212] This is why virtually all codes still speak of damage 'caused' by an animal or by a collapsing building which, strictly speaking, is not correct.

[1213] The authors of the Greek Cc in Art. 924 I had the same predicament, according to which 'the keeper of an animal shall be liable for the damage caused by such animal to *a third party*' (italics supplied), which means that the animal is the second party.

[1214] See no. 101 above.

[1215] For more detail on the relationship between special and basic provisions see part 2 II 3 (nos. 103 ff.)

924 Greek Cc, 2052 Ital. Cc, 493 I, 502 Port. Cc, 1905 Span. Cc; and Arts. 6:179–181 BW) hold responsible the 'proprietor', the 'possessor', the 'keeper', and occasionally also the person contractually bound 'to supervise' the animal on behalf of the keeper. Hence, these provisions only deal with animals belonging to someone or in someone's possession, or which can at least be kept under control.[1216] Liability for injury and loss caused by any animals not within those groups, i.e. animals living wild, cannot therefore arise.[1217] This is also true of 'wild' animals legally belonging to the state or to a regional or local authority: although such animals have owners, they are still not 'kept' in the legal sense.[1218] The only situation in which damage caused by animals living wild must be compensated is *Wildschäden*: damage caused by game animals eating seeds and forest plants which are private property. Unless the person responsible, e.g. a professional hunter, was at fault for failing to limit the game population to a reasonable number,[1219] the question of who must compensate the injured party depends on the hunting laws,[1220] commonly laid down in statutes.[1221]

209   An issue first considered during the development of the 1966 Portugese

---

[1216] See e.g. *MünchKomm* (-Mertens), 2nd edn., § 833 BGB no. 9; Flour/Aubert, *Obligations*, vol. ii, 5th edn., p. 279; and *Encyclopédie Dalloz* (-Bénac-Schmidt/Larroumet), *Rép.Dr.Civ.* vol. viii, 'Responsabilité du fait des animaux' (1993), nos. 12, 13 (animals belonging to no one [*res nullius*] do not come under Art. 1385 Cc; they are not *animaux appropriés*); and Deliyannis/Kornilakis, *Eidiko Enochiko Dikaio*, vol. iii, p. 203.

[1217] Animals in zoos or game parks are deemed to be 'kept' by somebody, even if they are called 'wild' animals, see App. Firenze 17 Sep. 1955, *Foro.it.* 1956, I, 90; and OGH 15 Jan. 1986, *ÖJZ* 1986 p. 402 (*EvBl* 111).

[1218] Thus Cass. 12 Aug. 1991, n. 8788, *Giur.it.* 1992, I, 1, 1795 with a note by Centrofanti (liability of the Italian Regions, as owners of animals living wild, only under Art. 2043, and not under Art. 2052 Cc which only governs domestic and farm animals) was right and not Pret.Cosenza 5 July 1988, *Foro.it.* 1988, I, 3629, nor Trib. Perugia 11. Dec. 1995, *Foro.it.* 1997, I, p. 315. For similar cases in France see Bénac-Schmidt/Larroumet (fn. 1216 above) nos. 14, 15. Even if the public authorities have no title to the animals, they can still take legal action; see TS 1 Apr. 1993, *La Ley* 1993 (2) p. 661: an authority claimed damages from a hunter for killing a protected bear.

[1219] See e.g. BGH 22 Apr. 1974, BGHZ 62 p. 265: not enough pigeons were killed; however, liability under § 823 II BGB for violation of a decree was rejected as the hunting regulations concerning *Wildschäden* were held to be final; Cass.civ. 29 Apr. 1964, *D.* 1964 *Jur.* 642 (liability only under Art. 1382, not under Art. 1385 Cc); and TS 14 July 1982, *RAJ* 1982 no. 4235 p. 2766 (primary liability of a party of hunters for not shooting enough rabbits; subsidiary liability of the owner of the hunting ground).

[1220] Under Art. 45 Dutch *Jachtwet* of 3 Nov. 1954 (Stb. 1954, 523) in the version of the Act of 8 June 1977 (Stb. 1977, 387) liability arises only for fault. The statute obliges every '*jachthouder . . ., datgene te doen, wat een goed jager betaamt*', referring to the general provisions on liability for fault. See also Rb. Assen 8 Feb. 1969, *NedJur* 1969 no. 343 p. 1007; Ktg. 's-Gravenhage 6 Feb. 1961, *NedJur* 1961 no 348 p. 719; Art. 1906 Span. Cc imposes liability in such cases for presumed fault.

[1221] Except for Art. 45 Dutch *Jachtwet* (see fn. 1220 above) which must be read in conjunction with Art. 6: 162 BW. See also the Belgian Act of 28 Feb. 1961 *relative à la réparation des dégâts causés par le gros gibier* (Monit. belge of 28 July 1961); and Liège 14 June 1982, *JT* 1982 p. 742 (damage caused by wild boars; contributory fault on the part of the

Cc,[1222] namely whether micro-organisms are animals within the terms of the statutory provisions, has recently become highly controversial.[1223] In earlier European codes legislators only contemplated animals which could be seen with the naked eye. Bees were commonly considered the smallest potentially dangerous living things. Viruses and bacteria again became an issue during the discussions preceding the new Dutch BW, only to be excluded from Art. 6:169 BW.[1224] It was decided that provisions on strict liability for viruses and bacteria would have to be made subject to the law on liability for dangerous substances.[1225] In particular, in view of an assimilation of European laws this appears the correct approach. The question of whether one should further distinguish between bacteria and viruses, the latter being strictly incapable of reproduction, remains untouched.[1226] Moreover, as a person cannot own or supervise a microbe, the liability of animal keepers and owners would not apply. Bacterial cultures may be used to produce yoghurt, or in a cesspit to clean industrial effluent: although cultivated in laboratories, the bacteria are not 'kept' within the terms of the law, as it would be impossible to single out individual bacteria without a microscope.[1227]

---

proprietor); §§ 29–35 German *BJagdG*; Arts. 33, 52–53 Span. Hunting Act (*Ley de Caza* 1/ 1970 of 4 Apr. 1970, BOE of 6 Apr. 1970 no. 82) and Arts. 35, 52 *Reglamento de Caza* (*Decreto* 506/1971 of 25 Mar. 1971 BOE 30 Mar. 1971, no. 76). For France see Arts. 200 ff. *Code rural* implemented by the *Loi* of 24 July 1937 *pour la réparation des dommages causés aux récoltes par le gibier*, and Act no. 68–1172 of 27 Dec. 1968 (text in *D.* 1969 *Légis* 18) with Cass.civ. 28 Oct. 1991, *D.* 1991 *IR* 263, and the *Décret* of 30 June 1975 *relatif aux dommages dus aux sangliers et gibiers inscrits au plan de chasse* (text in *D.* 1975 *Légis* 219) with Cass.civ. 26 Apr. 1990, Bull.civ. 1990, II, no. 73. The relevant sources of Portugese law are cited in v. Bar (- Monteiro/Ramos/Hörster), *DeliktsR in Europa, Portugal*, vol. IV, V. In Austria legislation on *Wildschäden* is subject to the jurisdiction of the *Bundesländer* (v. Bar [-Schilcher/Kleewein], *DeliktsR in Europa, Österreich*, p. 100). For an overview of the Acts see Koziol, *Österr. Haftpflichtrecht*, vol. ii p, 2nd edn., 412.

[1222] Vaz Serra, *BolMinJust* 86 (1959) pp. 21, 39–40. Vaz Serra wanted the provision to extend to bacilli cultivated in laboratories.

[1223] As the legal world had failed to notice the developments in Portugal (see fn. 1223 below), discussion on this issue was sparked by Fagnart, *RGAR* 1969 no. 8302. He soon found a hesitant supporter in Stone, *IntEncCompL* XI 5–79, who himself reverted to Mazeaud/Mazeaud, *Responsabilité civile*, vol. ii, 6th edn., no. 1115, fn. 3 (a text taken from a previous edition by Tunc). His view was adopted by Deutsch, *NJW* 1976 p. 1137 and *NJW* 1986 p. 757. Subsequently, a more generous interpretation of the provision on liability for animals has been favoured by: Cornelis, *Responsabilité extra-contractuelle*, no. 362; van Dunné, *Verbintenissenrecht*, vol. ii, 2nd edn., p. 489; *MünchKomm* (-Mertens), 2nd edn., § 833 no. 10; and Deliyannis/Kornilakis, *Eidiko Enochiko Dikaio*, vol. iii, p. 203.

[1224] *Parlementaire Geschiedenis*, vol. vi, p. 763.

[1225] Sterk, *Verhoogd gevaar*, pp. 230–231. Arts. 6: 175–178 BW (Stb. 1994, p. 846) were only implemented on 1 Feb. 1995.

[1226] A position taken by Rottler, *Die Tierhalterhaftung und ihre Begrenzung*, p. 6.

[1227] Bénac-Schmidt/Larroumet (fn. 1216 above), no. 20. In Italy microbes have also been excluded from liability for animals. However, there is current discussion about whether liability could arise from Arts. 2050 and 2051 Cc: see Giur.sist. Bigiavi (-Franzoni) vol. ii (2), pp. 499–501; Cass. 15 July 1987, n. 6241, *Foro.it.* 1988, I, 144.

This has been undisputed in rulings on diseases communicated by 'large' animals: the courts have simply asked whether the risk which the diseased host animal carried has been realized.[1228] It would in fact be absurd if a court had to establish when a person had been the keeper of a virus. However, strict liability for micro-organisms demands an independent definition of the risk which they pose. This is why the German legislator considered it necessary to impose strict liability for genetically engineered organisms (§ 32 GenTG), arguing that their effects are unpredictable. However, 'damage due to insufficient safety measures against known sources of potential danger can largely be dealt with by means of liability for fault (duty to safeguard the public in general)'.[1229] Hence, the application of § 833 BGB has quite rightly not been considered.[1230] It does not apply even when living viruses are deliberately transferred to people, as is the case with poliomyelitis innoculations.

b. Farm and 'Luxury' Animals: Liability for Animals and its Causes of Action

(1) Strict Liability and Liability for Presumed Breach of the Duty of Supervision

210 From a legal point of view, except for uncontrolled animals and micro-organisms as mentioned above, it is only necessary to differentiate between different types of animals if an additional cause of action depends on that distinction. This is generally not the case. Art. 1385 Cc in Belg., French, and Lux. Cc, and Arts. 1905 Span. Cc, 502 Port. Cc,[1231]

[1228] Except for injuries sustained though animal bites, the courts have on several occasions denied such a connection, e.g. in HR 24 Feb. 1984, *NedJur* 1984 no. 415 p. 1519 (an infected pig escaped from a farm and spread disease to those on a neighbouring farm, so that piglets on the second farm are stillborn. Damage through infection is only compensated if caused by bites or scratches, not if caused by licking or nuzzling); and Cass. 10 Apr. 1970, n. 1004, *Resp.Civ. e Prev.* 1970 p. 588 (Art. 2052 Cc not applicable to the communication of disease). Rb. Rotterdam 8 June 1990, *NedJur* 1991 no. 210 p. 857 dismissed a claim where infection resulted from the bite of a diseased dog, a decision seemingly incompatible with HR 24 Feb. 1984 (loc. cit.); it does seem unreasonable not to compensate if the sick beast has sniffed other animals (a position shared by RG 19 Oct. 1912, RGZ 80 pp. 237, 239–240: the communication of 'germs' from one horse to another). Whether liability is incurred by transmitting disease-causing agents is irrelevant in this context. Even in cases where liability was established it has always been linked to the host animal and never to the microbes themselves: e.g. RG 19 Oct. 1912 loc. cit.; Cass.civ. 21 July 1992, Bull.civ. 1992, II, no. 220 p. 109 (infection caused by a flock of sheep); and TS 10 Feb. 1959, *RAJ* 1959 no. 1483 p. 898 (an escaped cow was found dead on the land of a neighbour. An employee helping to dispose of the carcass required an anti-rabies innoculation, inducing an allergic reaction; liability under Art. 1905 Cc).

[1229] BRats-Drucks. 387/89, official commentary on § 28 of the draft (= § 32 GenTG).

[1230] E.g. BGH 4 July 1989, *NJW* 1989 pp. 2947, 2948.

[1231] Moreover, under Art. 493 I Port. Cc persons assigned by contract to look after an animal are also liable for presumed breach of the duty to supervise. See no. 216 below.

2052 Ital. Cc, and 6:179 BW[1232] refer simply to 'animals', and in each code the person responsible is strictly liable.[1233] Austrian law also makes no distinction between farm and other animals and holds the keeper strictly liable. Under § 1320 s. 2 ABGB 'the person keeping the animal is responsible if he cannot prove that he had taken the necessary measures for (its) safekeeping and supervision'. Although for a long time the text was interpreted as imposing liability for presumed but rebuttable fault,[1234] the OGH has more recently started to allow claims 'if objectively necessary measures had not been carried out, without anybody being at fault'. No-fault keeper's liability, which had not then been supported by the Supreme Court judges, has since been deemed reasonably justifiable.[1235] Simultaneously, but independently of the developments in Austria, the same position was adopted in Dutch legislation.[1236] However, Austrian keepers' liability retains one distinguishing feature: an objective breach of the duty of care is still required.[1237] Hence no-fault

---

[1232] By Art. 6:181 BW, liability under Art. 6:179 BW for animals used to carry out a business lies with the person carrying out the business (see no. 216 below). Under Art. 6:183 II BW parents are answerable for animals not kept for business purposes and owned by a child under age 14 (see no. 148 above).

[1233] E.g. Pires de Lima/Antunes Varela, *Cc anotado*, vol. i, 4th edn., Art. 502, n. 1, and STJ 9 Mar. 1978, *BolMinJust* 275 (1978) p. 191; *T&C* (-Lankhorst), 2nd edn., Art. 6:179 BW no. 1; *Parlementaire Geschiedenis*, vol. vi, p. 761; and Asser (-Hartkamp), *Verbintenissenrecht*, vol. iii, 9th edn., nos. 193; Cour 14 Dec. 1964, *Pas. luxemb.* 19 (1963–65) p. 490 (the defendant only escapes liability if he can submit proof *'d'un cas fortuit, de force majeure ou d'une cause étrangère'*); and Cour 3 May 1972, *Pas. luxemb.* 22 (1972–1974) p. 132 (cause of action is *garde*); Albaladejo, *Derecho civil*, vol. ii (2), 8th edn., pp. 550–551; de Ángel Yágüez, *Responsabilidad civil*, 3rd edn., pp. 562–567; TS 18 July 1991, *RAJ* 1991 no. 5398 p. 7312; Flour/Aubert, *Obligations*, vol. ii, 5th edn., pp. 279–281; Cass.civ. 24 May 1991, Bull.civ. 1991 II no. 155; Cass.civ. 21 July 1992, Bull.civ. 1992 II no.220; Cass. 20 May 1983, *Pas. belge* 1983, I, pp. 1060, 1061; and Cass. 23 June 1932, *Pas. belge* 1932, I, 200 (however, Belgian courts have consistently spoken of a *présomption de faute*, and French courts of a *présomption de responsabilité*). In Italy, liability under Art. 2052 Cc also for irrebuttably presumed fault (Cass. 9 Dec. 1970, n. 2615, *Resp.Civ. e Prev.* 1971 p. 322; and Cass. 16 Nov. 1955, n. 3745, *Resp.Civ. e Prev.* 1956 p. 229); this is why Pret. Forli 19 Feb. 1986, *Resp.Civ.ePrev.* 1986 p. 176 speaks simply of 'strict liability'.

[1234] For the last ruling along these lines see OGH 23 Nov. 1972, SZ 45/126 (pp. 522, 523: 'no absolute liability but rather liability for fault in conjunction with a reversed onus of proof'); see also the earlier decision of OGH 18 Jan. 1954, SZ 27/8 (pp. 25, 26): a dog being chased by another ran into a bicycle, causing an accident; no liability.

[1235] OGH 20 Oct. 1981, *JBL* 1982 pp. 150, 151.

[1236] Art. 1404 BW (old) used to be interpreted as a no-fault liability provision (for more detail see Bloembergen [-Oldenhuis], *Onrechtmatige daad*, vol. i, Art. 179 n. 1). HR 15 Oct. 1915, *NedJur* 1915 no. 1971 = W 9937 broke with this tradition and allowed the defendant to show that he was not at fault. In anticipation of the NBW, however, HR 7 Mar. 1980, *NedJur* 1980 no. 353 p. 1165 (*Stierkalvern* ruling) reinterpreted Art. 1404 BW (old) as a strict liability provision.

[1237] OGH 20 Oct. 1981 (fn. 1235 above); OGH 15 Jan. 1986, *OJZ* 1986 p. 402 (*EvBl* 111): 'the appropriate level of supervision and safekeeping is flexible and has to be determined in accordance with the circumstances of the case'. Also OGH 11 Oct. 1994, *ÖJZ* 1995 p. 306 (*EvBl* 57): the alleged good nature of a large dog does not justify leaving it entirely unsupervised.

liability is based on the unlawfulness of the act, a situation of considerable practical relevance.[1238]

211   The view of most continental European countries that the keeper of an animal is answerable for any damage 'caused' by his animal, independent of the keeper's fault, is shared by Germany (§ 833 s. 1 BGB) and Greece (Art. 924 I Greek Cc). Yet as early as 1908 a supplementary provision was added to the BGB,[1239] and later to the Greek Cc, to the effect that in these two codes persons keeping a domestic animal 'which aids the business, the earnings, or the prosperity of the keeper of the animal' (§ 833 s. 2 BGB) or which is 'utilized in connection with the exercise of a profession or for guarding the house or for the nourishment of the possessor' (Art. 924 II Greek Cc) are privileged. A keeper of such animals is not strictly liable. Hence, in Germany and Greece strict liability is only imposed on 'luxury' animals. This is an unsatisfactory solution:[1240] first, because these provisions exempt what are effectively the most prominent cases from strict keepers' liability; secondly, because it creates a variety of unnecessary problems in defining the term domestic animal;[1241] thirdly, because equal treatment woud be desirable;[1242] and finally, because they run counter to the general tendency to treat business activities more strictly than private undertakings.[1243] Moreover, it is illogical that the definition of the term 'domestic animal' should depend on what is commonly regarded as a domestic animal in the relevant country. It appears unreasonable that the keeper of a bull which runs onto the motorway can exonerate himself,[1244] whereas the keeper of a camel, born in a zoo or circus, cannot.[1245] Finally, as these Regulations

---

[1238] E.g. OGH 4 June 1985, *JBl* 1986 p. 481: a Rottweiler bit a 13-year-old girl during a scrap; no objective breach of the duty of care on the part of the keeper, no gross negligence on the part of his servant: no liability.   [1239] See no. 101 and fn. 607 above.

[1240] Kötz, *Gefährdungshaftung*, pp. 1802–1803; Deliyannis/Kornilakis, *Eidiko Enochiko Dikaio*, vol. iii, p. 202; Georgiades/Stathopoulos (-Vosinakis), *Greek Cc*, vol. iv, Art. 924 nos. 2–3.

[1241] Typical is the question of whether bees are domestic animals (in favour: CFI Salonica 613/1957, *NoB* 5 [1957] p. 819; and Georgiades/Stathopoulos [-Vosinakis], *Greek Cc*, vol. iv, Art. 924, no. 4; against: RG 19 Nov. 1938, RGZ 158 pp. 388, 391; and e.g. Deliyannis/ Kornilakis, *Eidiko Enochiko Dikaio*, vol. iii, p. 203).

[1242] E.g. if, in professionally run stables, a person is injured by a horse belonging to another, then the latter is strictly liable (OLG Stuttgart 7 Sep. 1993, *NJW-RR* 1994 p. 93); yet if the horse belonged to the stables and was rented out, § 833 s. 2 BGB would apply, so the stable owner could exonerate himself (OLG Schleswig 24 Mar. 1982, *VersR* 1983 p. 1084; OLG Karlsruhe 10 Feb. 1982, *VersR* 1983 p. 928; OLG Düsseldorf 8 Apr. 1975, *NJW* 1975 p. 1892). Ideally the solution should be the opposite way round.   [1243] See fn. 1240 above.

[1244] OLG Celle 3 Mar. 1975, *NJW* 1975 p. 1891. The OLG sets the threshold for *exculpatio* very high, thus at least preventing § 833 s. 2 BGB from coming into effect. When § 1320 ABGB was still thought to impose liability for fault (see no. 210 above), OGH 23 Nov. 1972, SZ 45/126 dismissed the victim's claim altogether in a very similar case (cattle secured only by an electric fence ran onto a busy road).

[1245] See *MünchKomm* (-Mertens), 2nd edn., § 833 no. 29.

(§ 833 s. 2 BGB, Art. 924 II Greek Cc) do not even truly coincide,[1246] they are clear candidates for deletion in a common European Civil Code.

The distinctions between groups of farm animals are unclear and of **212** little relevance. The wording of the German BGB suggests that 'working animals' are those needing special training, such as sheepdogs, hunting dogs, sniffer dogs,[1247] and police horses. Animals kept mainly for financial gain, i.e. for breeding or for slaughter, should come under the term 'animals aiding business and prosperity'. In Greece the latter group would also be defined as 'working animals'. It is therefore of little practical relevance that animals aiding business and prosperity are not mentioned in Art. 924 II Greek Cc.[1248] Horses belonging to stables run for profit are therefore also rented out to aid a business.[1249] That may be true, but are such animals really 'domestic'?[1250] Animals whose products are consumed by the keeper himself, such as dairy cows and hens, also have a maintenance function. Whether a guide dog helps to 'maintain' its owner, whether the owner can only exonerate himself from an injury inflicted by the dog while the owner was carrying out his business, or whether he cannot exonerate himself at all, is still a highly controversial issue.[1251] The mere fact that these questions are raised, whereas the keeper of a bull need only prove that he took all necessary precautions, demonstrates the problems created by the provisions.

(2) The Persons Liable

It is not always easy to decide who should be answerable if a danger **213** arising from an animal becomes a reality. The most convincing, as well as the most appropriate solution, in view of the system of strict liability, seems to be to place liability for animals exclusively on their keeper (see § 833 BGB, Art. 924 Greek Cc, Art. 502 Port. Cc, and § 1320 s. 2 ABGB). However, current European liability law is more complex. Under Art. 1385 Belg., French, and Lux. Cc, for instance, the keeper is

---

[1246] The most prominent difference concerns guard dogs. Under Greek law they are exempt from strict liability (Art. 924 II, 2nd alt. Greek Cc: 'guarding the house'), and under German law their keepers only escape strict liability if they are not used to guard a private house (OLG Stuttgart 27 Sep. 1929, *HRR* 1930 no. 110), but buildings used for business purposes (OLG Munich 29 Sep. 1983, *VersR* 1984 pp. 1095, 1096).

[1247] A group of animals for which OGH 20 Oct. 1981, *JBl* 1982 pp. 150, 151 also considers a 'reduction of the duties of care' appropriate.

[1248] Deliyannis/Kornilakis, *Eidiko Enochiko Dikaio*, vol. iii, p. 208 (pigs, hens, rabbits, and other animals raised purely to be sold on the market also aided the business).

[1249] See fn. 1242 above.   [1250] Mertens (fn. 1245 above) no. 32.

[1251] Without giving further details, LG Wiesbaden 23 July 1992, *VersR* 1993 p. 1489 rightly held that guide dogs were covered by § 833 s. 1 BGB.

only alternatively[1252] liable 'alongside' the owner ('*le propriétaire d'un animal, ou celui qui s'en sert, pendant qu'il est à son usage, est responsable*'). This wording is also adopted by Art. 2052 Ital. Cc. In the otherwise identical Art. 1905 Span. Cc, the possessor (*el poseedor*) and the keeper are alternatively liable.

214   However, closer consideration reveals that the Romance countries also tend to favour the idea that the keeper of an animal should be liable. For '*la présomption de responsabilité édictée par l'art. 1385 à l'encontre du proprié- taire de l'animal ou de celui qui s'en sert est fondée sur l'obligation de garde, corrélative aux pouvoirs de direction, de contrôle et d'usage qui caractérisent le gardien*'.[1253] Hence, modern lawyers conclude that liability for animals is nothing other than a special case of *gardien* liability within the terms of Art. 1384 I Cc.[1254] This means that the owners of animals need not, and therefore should not, be mentioned in Art. 1385 Cc. Yet to take them out of the provision would shift the burden of proof: at present the defendant owner must prove that not he but another was the animal's *gardien* at the time of the injury. In that case he is also exempt from liability under Art. 1385 Cc,[1255] a view shared by the Italian courts.[1256] Spain also comes to the same conclusion concerning the alternative liability between *poseedor* (see Art. 430 Cc) and keeper. The *Tribunal Supremo* went so far as to extend the provision to the owner, stressing that although he is not mentioned in Art. 1905 Cc, he was clearly liable '*salvo que exista algún estado de posesión o servicio del animal . . ., en cuyo caso cesará su responsabilidad, para pasar a quien, de hecho, esté encargado de la custodia del animal*'.[1257]

[1252] Under Art. 1385 Cc there is no liability *in solidum* of owner and keeper; the owner could only be sued alongside the keeper (whose liability arises from Art. 1385 Cc) under Arts. 1382, 1383 Cc. See e.g. Cass. 30 Apr. 1975, *Pas. belge* 1975, I, 857; Cass. 18 Nov. 1993, *JT* 1994 p. 231; and Cornelis, *Responsabilité extra-contractuelle*, nos. 369 ff. This view is shared by HR 8 Oct. 1982, *NedJur* 1984 no. 2 p. 2 on Art. 1404 BW (old).

[1253] Cass.civ. 5 Mar. 1953, *D.* 1953 *Jur.* 473. Since then it has been the established practice not only of the French, but also of the Luxembourg courts (e.g. Cour 3 May 1972, *Pas. luxemb.* 22 [1972–74] p. 132). Belgian decisions are not materially different: e.g. Cass. 18 Nov. 1993, *JT* 1994 p. 231: '*L'art. 1385 du Code civil implique seulement qu'au moment du fait dommageable le gardien ait la maîtrise de l'animal, comportant un pouvoir de direction et de surveillance non subordonné, sans intervention du propriétaire, et un pouvoir de direction et de surveillance non subordonné, sans intervention du propriétaire, et un pouvoir d'usage égal à celui de ce dernier.*'

[1254] For detail on *gardien* liability see nos. 106 ff. above.

[1255] For Belgian rulings see Cass. 18 Nov. 1983, *Pas. belge* 1984, I, 307; Cass. 20 May 1983, *Pas. belge* 1983, I, 1061; and Cass. 5 Nov. 1981, *Pas. belge* 1982, I, 316; for France e.g. Cass.civ. 11 Apr. 1986, *D.* 1986 *IR* 264; Cass.civ. 2 and 8 July 1970, *D.* 1970 *Jur.* 704; Cass.civ. 21 Oct. 1981, *Gaz.Pal.* 1982 *pan.* 147; and for Luxembourg, Cour 15 Feb. 1978, *Pas. luxemb.* 24 (1978–80) p. 125.

[1256] E.g. Pret. Avellino 25 Jan. 1972, *Giur.it.* 1973, I, 2, 388; and Cass. 7 May 1958, n. 1485, *Resp.Civ. e Prev.* 1959 p. 119 (the injured party can choose whether to sue the owner or the keeper; the owner must prove that the animal was beyond his supervision and that the duties of care and supervision had passed to another).

[1257] TS 26 Jan. 1972, *RAJ* 1972 no. 120 p. 119 (a cow escaped from a farm at night, ran onto a road, and collided with a motorcycle; liability of the owner).

Furthermore, where an animal has both an actual possessor who is not the owner, and an original possessor who is the owner (e.g. a borrowed hunting dog), the former is usually held responsible.[1258] The decision of the Dutch legislator to hold, not the keeper, but the *bezitter* liable under Art. 6:179 BW is unfortunate.[1259] Yet the situation is not as serious as first meets the eye: first, *bezit* in accordance with Art. 3:107 BW means '*het houden van een goed voor zichzelf*' (to keep goods for oneself), so that Art. 6:179 BW finds the approval of some non-Dutch lawyers who also see the actual possessor as keeper;[1260] and secondly, liability of the actual possessor under Art. 6:181 BW, in cases of professional keepers, is always channelled to the latter. In other words the *bezitter* nearly always is the keeper.

All European laws now apply the same three criteria to identify the   **215** keeper of an animal: he must have actual control over the animal which he is using with the intention of obtaining usufruct (benefit) from it.[1261] In cases where an animal is 'foisted' upon someone, or where a stray animal adopts somebody as its guardian, such a person is not a keeper as long as he does not look after the animal for his own purposes. Vermin infesting a person or a building are not kept in the legal sense, because no one intends to exercise any but the most final control over the animals.[1262] Children[1263] and persons in positions of dependency, such as service and nursing staff, commonly have no intention to control the animal; or else they objectively lack such control because they are bound by the instructions of a principal regarding

---

[1258] E.g. Albaladejo, *Derecho civil*, vol. ii (2), 8th edn., p. 550, Díez-Picazo/Gullón, *Sistema*, vol. ii, 6th edn., p. 630; Paz-Ares/Díez-Picazo/Bercovitz/Salvador (-De Ángel Yágüez), *Código civil*, vol. i, 2nd edn., Art. 1905 p. 2042.

[1259] The Dutch legislator made the controversial decision to burden the possessor with the responsibility (very much against the views of e.g. van Dunné, *Verbintenissenrecht*, vol. ii, 2nd edn., p. 492), as it was thought that the *bezitter* was the person whom the victim could most easily identify (*Parlementaire Geschiedenis*, vol. vi, p. 745; trans. into German in Jonas, *Verschuldensunabhängige außervertragliche Haftung im Entwurf zum NBW*, pp. 125–128).

[1260] As do e.g. Larenz/Canaris, *Schuldrecht BT*, vol. ii (2), 13th edn., p. 614.

[1261] For an overview see e.g. Larenz/Canaris, *Schuldrecht*, vol. ii (2), 13th edn., pp. 614–615; *Encyclopédie Dalloz* (-Bénac-Schmidt/Larroumet), *Rép.Dr.Civ.* vol. viii, 'Responsabilité du fait des animaux' (1993), nos. 61–85; de Page, *Droit Civil Belge*, vol. ii, 3rd edn., no. 1012; Deliyannis/Kornilakis, *Eidiko Enochiko Dikaio*, vol. iii, p. 206; Georgiades/Stathopoulos (-Vosinakis), *Greek Cc*, vol. iv, Art. 924, no. 7; Koziol, *Österr. Haftpflichtrecht*, vol. ii, 2nd edn., pp. 403–405; Ziviz, *NGCC* 1990, II, p. 71, 73–75. For Portugal e.g. Pires de Lima/Antunes Varela, *Cc anotado*, vol. i, 4th edn., Art. 502 pp. 511–512; Neto Martins, *Código civil*, 7th edn., pp. 392–393.

[1262] Jonas, *Verschuldensunabhängige außervertragliche Haftung im NBW*, p. 126; see also *Parlementaire Geschiedenis*, vol. vi, p. 763; *Tremain v. Pike* [1969] 1 WLR 1556.

[1263] See nos. 148–149 above; also BGH 6 Mar. 1990, *NJW-RR* 190 pp. 789–790 (parents are the keepers of the horse belonging to their 13-year-old daughter).

the animal's care.[1264] The only exception arises on theft: a thief is always a keeper.[1265] On the sale of an animal it is the actual hand-over which effects the change of keeper, rather than the passing of title.[1266] Persons who have another's animals in their safekeeping, or who let them use their grazing areas for payment, are also not keepers of those animals, because they do not use them for their own purposes.[1267] In accordance with the prevailing—and correct—opinion, this is also true for carriers.[1268] If somebody lets or lends his animal to someone, then the duration and purpose of the loan and the agreements on the distribution of costs have to be weighed against each other.[1269] A person leaving his horse with professional instructors to have it taught how to pull a carriage remains the keeper of the horse.[1270] On the other hand, if somebody rents out his horse for an entire competition season, and is freed of any duties with regard to the horse, he cannot be held liable for it during

---

[1264] From the great number of rulings see e.g. HR 29 Nov. 1985, *NedJur* 1987 no. 291 p. 1057 (a moped collided with a pony which had escaped from its 17-year-old groom whilst being led from training ground to arena. Overturning the lower courts, the *Hoge Raad* held the owner of the horse liable); TS 18 July 1991, *RAJ* 1991 no. 5398 p. 7312 (a youth was killed by a horse which had escaped from a groom; the owner and not the groom was deemed responsible under Art. 1905 Cc); Cass.civ. 15 Dec. 1976, *Sem.Jur.* 1977, IV, 34 (an employee is not the *gardien*); Cass. 18 Nov. 1993, *JT* 1994 pp. 231, 232: although Michel Léger was the only person to have known the animal well enough to control it effectively, and although he was '*ainsi chargé comme d'habitude de le maîtriser et de le préparer*', this was not sufficient unless he also had '*le pouvoir non subordonné de direction et de surveillance sans intervention du propriétaire*'); Brussels 15 Feb. 1980, *RW* 1980–81 p. 734 (apprentice); and Cass. 28 Oct. 1969 no. 3558, *Resp.Civ. e Prev.* 1970 p. 588. However, if an employee uses his own animal for business purposes, he is accountable as a keeper, whereas his employer will be answerable under the general rules on employers' liability (Cass. 6 Jan. 1983, n. 75, *Giur.it.* 1983, I, 1, 1481). Yet an accumulation of keepers' and employers' liability, as allowed in Cass. 5 Nov. 1981, *Pas. belge* 1982, I, 316, should not be repeated (see no. 195 and fn. 1147 above). It remains controversial whether the relevant case actually gave rise to a *cumul* at all, since recognizing an employed riding instructor as *gardien* of the animals is a questionable decision.

[1265] E.g. Trib. Parma 29 May 1954, *Giust.civ.* 1954, I, 1386; Larenz/Canaris, *Schuldrecht BT*, vol. ii (2), 13th edn., p. 615; Georgiades/Stathopoulos (-Vosinakis), *Greek Cc*, vol. iv, Art. 924 no. 7. Versailles 26 Feb. 1987, *D.* 1987 *IR* 94 decided wrongly that a visitor who rides a pony without permission is its *gardien*.

[1266] See Almeida Costa, *Obrigações*, 5th edn., p. 504; Cass.civ. 8 July 1970, *D.* 1970 *Jur.* 704; and Cass.civ. 21 Oct. 1981, *Gaz.Pal.* 1982 *pan.* 147. However, someone who is merely trying an animal without having decided to buy it is not its keeper: Vaz Serra, *BolMinJust* 86 (1959) pp. 21, 55.

[1267] HR 31 May 1963, *NedJur* 1966 no. 338 p. 885; Bloembergen (-Oldenhuis), *Onrechtmatige daad*, vol. i, Art. 179 n. 15.

[1268] *Contra*: Vandenberghe/Van Quickenborne/Geelen/De Coster, *TPR* 1987 pp. 1255, 1423 (no. 90B) by reverting to Cass. 20 Apr. 1979, *Pas. belge* 1979, I, 989; and Cass. 26 June 1981, *Pas. belge* 1981, I, 1248.

[1269] Larenz/Canaris (fn. 1265 above); Cass. 30 Apr. 1975, *Pas. belge* 1975, I, 857, 858.

[1270] BGH 19 Jan. 1988, *NJW-RR* 1988 p. 655, 656; *contra*, however: Cass.civ. 15 Jan. 1954, *D.* 1954 *Jur.* 169.

that period. However, if the horse is let to various riding students the owner remains its keeper even while horse and rider are out hacking.[1271] Those authors are right who say that the same is true if the animal is at the vet's,[1272] or the blacksmith's,[1273] or in the case of a dog, it is taken for a walk by a friend.[1274] A person who voluntarily lets his animals out of his immediate control for a limited time remains responsible,[1275] as does e.g. a bee keeper who allows his bees to swarm,[1276] the owner of racing pigeons sending his birds on a journey,[1277] a hunter who sends his dog to retrieve game,[1278] and the owner of bulls who lets them take part in an *abrivado* (*'bandido'*), during which people are chased by bulls through the streets with the consent of the authorities.[1279] A typical case of keepers' liability is where animals escape (Art. 1385 French Cc) and cause an accident. Here the courts should consider when the animal escaped and then establish whether there is a sufficiently close connection with the damage caused.[1280] Where the animals of several keepers cause the same

---

[1271] E.g. Cass. 18 Nov. 1983, *Pas. belge* 1984, I, 307, 308 (it is irrelevant whether the riding student is good or bad. What is relevant is whether or not he possesses a *'pouvoir de direction et de surveillance non subordonné'*); Hof Leeuwarden 13 Jan. 1982, *NedJur* 1982 no. 482 pp. 1679, 1680; BGH 22 Dec. 1992, *NJW* 1993 p. 2611 (a rider to whom the animal is lent as a favour also benefits from the limits on keepers' liability); and OLG Düsseldorf 19 Nov. 1993, *NJW-RR* 1994 pp. 352, 353 (riding student). Although OGH 22 June 1972, *ZVR* 1973/157 (pp. 216, 217) takes an opposing view, that decision was based on § 1320 s. 1 ABGB, according to which someone who goads, irritates, or neglects his duty to supervise an animal is liable. Hence, the provision applies equally to persons who borrow animals.
[1272] Vandenberghe *et al.* (fn. 1268 above) no. 94 A with Belgian citations. Yet this view is not shared by French courts: e.g. Cass.civ. 4 Oct. 1972, *Sem.Jur.* 1973, II, 17450 (note by Starck); and references in *Encyclopédie Dalloz* (-Bénac-Schmidt/Larroumet), *Rép.Dr.Civ.* vol. viii, 'Responsabilité du fait des animaux', nos. 74–75.
[1273] BGH 28 May 1968, *VersR* 1968 pp. 797, 798 (a blacksmith does not 'treat' animals entirely at his own risk as far as damage to his person is concerned); *contra*: Cass.civ. 13 June 1985, Bull.civ. 1985, II, no. 118; and several French judgments: see Bénac-Schmidt/Larroumet (fn. 1272 above).   [1274] Dijon 16 Feb. 1989, *D.* 1989 IR 140.
[1275] Not, however, somebody compelled by the state to relinquish possession: Cass.civ. 5 Mar. 1953, *D.* 1953 *Jur.* 473 (note Savatier).
[1276] Pret. Turin 4 Dec. 1956, *Giur.it.* 1957, I, 2, 1001.
[1277] Cass.civ. 24 May 1991, Bull.civ. 1991, II, no. 155 p. 83.
[1278] Cass. 14 May 1963, n. 1188, *Resp.civ. e Prev.* 1963 p. 391.
[1279] Nîmes 10 Mar. 1980; and Trib.gr.inst. de Tarascon 2 Oct. 1980, *D.* 1981 Somm. 482. If the event was badly organized its organizers are also liable for fault. See TS 30 Apr. 1984, *RAJ* 1984 no. 1974 p. 1510: an old man who relied on the published timetable was trampled by the leading bull at a time when the *encierro* should already have been over; liability on the part of the local authority. The court stressed that in this case the owner of the animal was not liable under Art. 1905 Cc.
[1280] E.g. Cass.civ. 12 Nov. 1986, *Sem.Jur.* 1987, II, 20731; BGH 6 Mar. 1990, *NJW-RR* 1990 p. 789; TS 30 Apr. 1984, *RAJ* 1984 no. 1976 p. 1512; and Brussels 29 Oct. 1992, *RGAR* 1994 no. 12331. In The Netherlands, the question of when a person loses actual possession of a runaway animal and is thus released from liability is governed by Art. 5:19 BW.

damage,[1281] where an animal has more then one keeper,[1282] and where several animals cause damage and the one 'causing' the specific injury cannot be determined[1283] the rules on joint and several liability offer a suitable solution.

216   Joint and several liability always applies to someone obliged to look after an animal without being its *gardien*.[1284] However, such persons are only personally liable if they failed to do what was necessary in the circumstances. This is true even if the obligation to look after the animals is contractual: even persons contractually bound to look after another's animals are not strictly liable unless they are also keepers. Moreover employees are also protected by employment law.[1285] Furthermore, fault on the part of the employee can result in employers' liability: first, if the employer is not the keeper of the animal, secondly, if the keeper can exonerate himself in respect of his farm animals (see no. 211 above), and thirdly, if the event leading to the injury is not solely the fault of the keeper. In otherwise almost identical provisions (§ 834 BGB, Art. 493 I Cc) Germany and Portugal have narrowed the scope of liability for persons actually in control of the animal by shifting the onus of proof of carelessness. This solution can only be considered wise if the provision covers only those who are not employed by the keeper of the animals.[1286] In cases of an independent carrier, for instance, whom some laws even classify as *gardien*,[1287] it might be appropriate to reduce the conditions of liability. Employees fulfilling their employers' duties of care, however, must not have an equal (in the case of farm animals) or similar (in the case of luxury animals) burden of liability to that of their employers.

217   In Austria the position of employees entrusted to supervise animals is peculiar. At first glance no actual problem is apparent, for, as stated

---

[1281] Georgiades/Stathopoulos (-Vosinakis), *Greek Cc*, vol. iv, Art. 924 no. 8; Filios, *Enochiko Dikaio*, vol. ii (2), 3rd edn., p. 145; and Rb. Assen 16 Jan. 1962, *NedJur* 1963 no. 301 p. 742; *contra*, but incorrectly: CFI Lasithion 348/1958, *NoB* 8 (1960) p. 330 (Art. 926 Greek Cc does not apply as liability under Art. 924 I Greek Cc is strict); and Rb. Amsterdam 31 May 1995, *NedJur* (Kort) 1995 no. 30 p. 55: dogs belonging to several keepers were chasing each other in a park. The leader of the pack collided with a cyclist. No joint or several liability of the other keepers.   [1282] STJ 15 Mar. 1983, *BolMinJust* 325 (1983) p. 553.
[1283] App. Cagliari 1 Mar. 1957, *Rep.Giust.civ.* 1957, *voce Resp.civ.*, no. 416.
[1284] Georgiades/Stathopoulos (-Vosinakis), *Greek Cc*, vol. iv, Art. 924 no. 8; Pires de Lima/Antunes Varela, *Cc anotado*, vol. i, 4th edn., Art. 502, n. 1; STJ 17 July 1986, *BolMinJust* 359 (1986) p. 693; TS 17 May 1988, *RAJ* 1988 no. 3674 p. 3595.
[1285] See nos. 188, 193 above. Note also the limitations on industrial injury law; see BGH 19 Oct. 1993, *NJW-RR* 1994 p. 90; and LG Wiesbaden 23 July 1992, *VersR* 1993 p. 1489.
[1286] As in OLG Düsseldorf 15 Jan. 1980, *VersR* 1981 p. 82; OLG Munich 29 July 1983, *VersR* 1984 pp. 1095, 1096; and supposedly BGH 19 Oct. 1993 (fn. 1285 above). *Contra*: RG 9 Dec. 1941, *RGZ* 168 p. 331; and RE 14 July 1992 (*secção criminal*), *CJ* XVII (1992–4) p. 313 (liability of a shepherd who did not use lights at night to warn other road users of the sheep's presence; fault was established).   [1287] See fn. 1268 above.

above, Austrian keepers' liability is based on liability for objectively insufficient supervision of the animal.[1288] As it is the very purpose of a strict liability regime to channel the responsibility to the keeper, it ought to be of little relevance whether he or his servant had failed to exercise due care. Yet the OGH merely asks whether the keeper 'has taken all necessary precautions in view of the known or visible characteristics of the animal which could sensibly have been expected in accordance with the generally accepted standards'.[1289] If one considers, not the actual time of the accident, but an earlier time, it is possible to say that the keeper has fulfilled his duty of 'safekeeping' under § 1320 s. 2 ABGB if he has employed a capable servant to ward off any dangers. This view was taken by the OGH on numerous occasions,[1290] effectively enabling the keeper of the animal to escape liability by delegating the duty of supervision.[1291] Only in the early 1980s did the OGH appear less certain of the course it had adopted and contemplated a path 'to reduce the conditions of vicarious liability by applying the provisions on strict liability' (in particular § 19 II EKHG) to avoid 'such unreasonable results as are regularly achieved under § 1315 ABGB'.[1292] However, no final decision was ever made. When the issue next arose, the OGH had changed its mind again. Although the analogous application of § 19 II EKHG would have imposed strict liability on the keeper only if his servant had been at fault, this was too daring a move for the OGH. It therefore declared that the servant must, in addition, have acted at least grossly negligently.[1293] From an Austrian point of view this may be justified; in a European context it is totally out of line.

c. The Realization of a Danger Arising from an Animal

(1) The Animal's Behaviour

All European codes provide that the keeper of an animal must indemnify   **218** a victim for damage 'caused' by the animal. What exactly is meant by 'caused' in this context is not usually specified. Only the two most recent civil codes, the Portugese Cc and the Dutch BW, give guidance on its

---

[1288] See no. 210 above.

[1289] OGH 15 Jan. 1986, *ÖJZ* 1986 pp. 402, 403 (*EvBl* 111) incl. references to earlier rulings.

[1290] E.g. OGH 30 Mar. 1955, SZ 28/89; OGH 11 Apr. 1962, SZ 35/45; and OGH 6 July 1971, *ZVR* 1973/33. The courts have always applied § 1315 ABGB (see no. 183 above), except OGH 9 Apr. 1924, SZ 6/147. The use of § 1313a ABGB was categorically denied (see no. 182 above). For further rulings see OGH 30 Mar. 1955 (esp. p. 216); OGH 11 Apr. 1962; OGH 18 Mar. 1965, *ZVR* 1965/286 (p. 339); OGH 10 May 1979, *ZVR* 1980/278.

[1291] For similar earlier rulings, see OGH 8 June 1937, SZ 19/188; OGH 12 Mar. 1970, *EFSlg* 13.690; OGH 10 Oct. 1974, *ZVR* 1975/62 ; OGH 27 June 1979, *ÖJZ* 1980 p. 179 (*EvBl* 49).   [1292] OGH 20 Oct. 1981, *JBl* 1982 pp. 150, 151.

[1293] OGH 4 June 1985, *JBl* 1986 pp. 181, 182, by reverting to Koziol, *Österr. Haftpflichtrecht*, vol. ii, 2nd edn., pp. 409, 363.

meaning. Art. 502 Port. Cc holds the keeper liable only for damage 'arising from danger specifically connected to this animal (*do perigo especial*)', and Art. 6:179 imposes on the keeper liability 'for the damage done by the animal unless, pursuant to the preceding section,[1294] there would have been no liability if the actual possessor had had control over the animal'.

219   The authors of Arts. 502 Port. Cc and 6:179 BW clearly intended to close the discussion on the definition of the term 'specific risk arising from an animal' under keepers' strict liability. That discussion produced some strange results[1295] and has repeatedly puzzled lawyers all over Europe.[1296] The keeper of a dog should be held responsible if it bites a passer-by, as should the keeper of a horse that kicks an innocent bystander.[1297] Has the animal truly caused someone injury if the space it takes up and its weight alone caused the injury (a horse falls on its rider;[1298] a visitor trips over a dog lying on the floor;[1299] somebody suffers shock due to the sight of a dangerous looking but harmless animal)?[1300] Has the 'risk specifically posed by the animal' been realized if the animal passes on a contagious disease?[1301] Is the owner to be held liable for the instinctive actions of an animal, such as the anaesthetized or terminally ill dog which bites the vet?[1302] Finally, has an animal damaged someone if it did exactly what its keeper or supervisor wanted it to do: to bite an attacker, to run onto a street,[1303] to ruin a neighbour's garden,[1304] etc.?

[1294] The authors are here referring to section 1 ('General provisions') title 3 ('Unlawful Conduct') book 6; i.e. to Arts. 6:162–168 BW.

[1295] E.g. RG 19 Nov. 1938, RGZ pp. 388, 392. Horses were attacked by bees. The court considered whether the keeper of the bees was liable. The RG followed the Court of Appeal' decision 'that the scent of horse sweat is not an extraordinary event irresistible to the bees, but merely an incentive to attack, and that the conduct is just an *active* and *voluntary* reaction'.

[1296] On comparative preparatory work see esp. Vaz Serra, *BolMinJust* 86 (1959) pp. 21, 41–49; and *Parlementaire Geschiedenis*, vol. vi, p. 763 (*Toelichting* Meijers).

[1297] Although not always: in Austria, Germany, and Greece the keeper escapes liability if he can prove he did not breach his duty of supervision.

[1298] See OLG Düsseldorf 15 Jan. 1980, *VersR* 1981 pp. 82, 83 (if a horse slips on asphalt 'its conduct is not voluntary if it turned at its rider's command').

[1299] LG Wiesbaden 23 July 1992, *VersR* 1993 p. 1489 (keepers' liability was considered); and van Dunné, *Verbintenissenrecht*, vol. ii, 2nd edn., p. 493, reminding us of 'the purely passive role of things' under *gardien* liability in all cases of this kind.

[1300] E.g. JP Verviers 24 Mar. 1978, *JT* 1978 p. 512 (also Van Quickenborne, *ERPL* 1 [1993] pp. 245, 249): a dog barked at a bull, which was so startled it ran off panicking and died of a heart attack soon after; dog owner found liable for 50% damages as the bull had already been ill.   [1301] See fn. 1228 above.

[1302] As in OLG Munich 26 Oct. 1976, *VersR* 1978 p. 334: no liability.

[1303] Against liability in such a case: HR 23 Feb. 1990, *NedJur* 1990 no. 365 p. 1401 (2 men drove a herd of cows across a road; a car collided with a cow. Art. 1404 BW [old] was not applicable as the cow had merely 'functioned' as an instrument of its owner). Rightly in favour of liability: STJ 9 Mar. 1978, *BolMinJust* 275 (1978) p. 191 (a great number of animals on the road in itself poses a special risk); and RP 3 May 1984, *BolMinJust* 337 (1984) p. 413.

[1304] *Parlementaire Geschiedenis*, vol. vi, p. 763 is adamantly against liability: the danger

Before we can answer these questions we need to take a closer look at   **220**
when damage is caused 'by' an animal. The real problem in answering
that question is to recognize that the term 'caused' is used in the physical
rather than a legal sense. The injury inflicted by a dog's bite is clearly
'caused' by the animal, but it cannot legally be attributed to the dog, just
as injury caused by a defective machine cannot legally be attributed to
the machine. An animal can neither be held liable, nor 'act' in the legal
sense of the word; it cannot explain the reasons for its act or omission.
For the actions of a human being, issues of causation create or limit
responsibility. However, this function of the legal concept of causation
does not apply to things, which at law includes animals, or at least how
they are treated.[1305] The risk is attributed, not to the animal but to its
keeper, who is not identified by reference to causation.[1306] Hence, only
one who can 'act' can inflict damage upon another, and acting in the
legal sense is limited to human beings. Therefore, as with all provisions
on strict liability 'for' (better: due to) things, injurious conduct is not
defined from the point of view of the relevant animal (if necessary by
reverting to features specific to the species),[1307] but from the point of
view of the endangered general public. Thus, the question usually asked,
whether the causal connection between the act causing the damage and
the 'independent energy'[1308] of the animal is 'adequate',[1309] does not
help: considerations of adequacy are nothing other than diluted considerations of negligence, and animals cannot be negligent. Furthermore,
for injurious conduct under keepers' liability it is irrelevant whether the

constituted by an animal is not realized where the animal was controlled by its owner. This
view is shared by many commentators: e.g. Deliyannis/Kornilakis, *Eidiko Enochiko Dikaio*,
vol. iii, p. 205; Filios, *Enochiko Dikaio*, vol. ii (2), 3rd edn., p. 145; and Cass. 19 Jan. 1977, n.
261, *Giur.it.* 1978, I, 1, 1791.

[1305] Rb. Amsterdam 31 May 1995 (fn. 1281 above) is therefore correct in this respect.

[1306] See no. 215 above.

[1307] It clearly does not help to think in terms of the categories of due care, nor to try
to distinguish between the risk arising from an average cow and the risk arising from
the cow causing the injury. Indeed, for most domestic animals there are no risks
reserved to specific groups of beasts. Art. 502 Port. Cc, for instance, therefore deliberately speaks only of 'certain hazards of keeping animals', and not of the specific
dangers of an animal or a class of animals. How dangerous an animal is depends
less on its species than on the way it is used. See STJ 9 Mar. 1978, *BolMinJust* 275
(1978) pp. 191, 194.

[1308] It was this criterion which sparked the implementation of the *tenzij* clause (see no.
218 above) in The Netherlands: *Parlementaire Geschiedenis*, vol. vi, pp. 761–766. At the
same time the Dutch legislator attempted, unnecessarily, to regulate the question of self-
defence. The search for 'independent energy' is an impossible task; the notion was
therefore rightly harshly criticized (esp. by van Dunné, *Verbintenissenrecht*, vol. ii, 2nd
edn., pp. 500–501).

[1309] The attempt to define the 'liability risk constituted by animal keepers' by means of
adequacy can be found in e.g. Neto/Martins, *Código civil*, 2nd edn., Art. 502 no. 7; *contra*: TS
10 Feb. 1959, *RAJ* 1959 no. 1483 p. 898.

conduct of the animal is 'normal' or 'abnormal'.[1310] It is inappropriate to limit keepers' liability to 'unpredictable' animal conduct[1311] and to define unpredictable conduct as 'a display of animal energy which is not brought about by reason'.[1312] The 'reasonable dog' does not exist,[1313] therefore it is wholly irrelevant whether it 'acted' or whether the damage was caused because it was simply lying on the ground. There are no criteria suitable to distinguish between conscious and unconscious conduct (e.g. in the case of a bee). Neither is it possible to differentiate between 'reflex actions', reactions to external stimuli, such as pain,[1314] the presence of other animals,[1315] or orders given by people[1316] on one

---

[1310] In Belgium the question whether Art. 1385 Cc only applies if the animal behaved abnormally or unpredictably is controversial: for an overview see Cornelis, *Responsabilité extra-contractuelle*, nos. 366–367; and Vandenberghe/Van Quickenborne/Geelen/De Coster, *TPR* 1987 pp. 1225, 1431 (no. 97). The situation has been further complicated by Cass. 12 Oct. 1984, *Pas. belge* 1985, I, 220. The plaintiff complained that the Court of Appeal had violated Art. 1385 Cc by demanding that the animal's conduct be abnormal and unpredictable (*un comportement anormal ou imprévisible*), which condition is not mentioned in the provision. The Court of Cassation ambiguously found that: '*L'article 1385 du Code civil n'exclut pas une exonération de cette responsablité à défaut de lien de causalité, notamment lorsque le comportement de l'animal n'était ni anormal ni imprévisible et que le dommage a été causé par une faute de la victime, excluant toute faute éventuelle . . . du gardien'.* Hence, the complaint was discussed only in terms of contributory negligence. However, it is clear that the Court of Appeal saw similarities between this case and the *vice de la chose* under Art. 1384 I Cc.

[1311] Notwithstanding BGH 6 July 1976, BGHZ 67 pp. 129, 132.

[1312] Although this has repeatedly been said by the German *Bundesgerichtshof*, e.g. BGH 23 June 1959, *VersR* 1959 pp. 853, 854; BGH 12 July 1966, *VersR* 1966 pp. 1073, 1074. BGH 6 July 1976 (see fn. 1311 above) remarked that 'this does not mean that there are contrasting cases where the conduct of an animal could have been guided by reason'. But what else could it mean?

[1313] Although the idea has been used: Zimmermann, *ZEuP* 1994 pp. 733–735 on *Da Silva v. Otto* [1986] 3 SA 538 (T).

[1314] BGH 9 June 1992, *VersR* 1992 pp. 1145, 1146 therefore rightly says that the danger presented by the animal is also realized if a horse throws the rider who hits it with a crop.

[1315] There is an abundance of cases in which damage was caused by the presence of animals: in all these instances the danger constituted by the animal is realized regardless of whether the external stimulus was classified as overwhelming or as controllable by the animal, e.g. a horse which kicked out when another horse was led past it in a narrow passage (OLG Stuttgart 7 Sep. 1993, *NJW-RR* 1994 p. 93; and Cass. 20 May 1983, *Pas. belge* 1983, I, 1061). Other examples are: the male animal which gets excited if a female on heat walks past (OLG Düsseldorf 28 May 1993, *NJW-RR* 1994 p. 92; OLG Saarbrücken 17 Feb. 1988, *VersR* 1988 p. 752; and BGH 6 July 1976, BGHZ 67 p. 129); the natural herd instinct (Trib.gr.inst. de Tarascon 2 Oct. 1980, *D.* 1981 Somm. 482); the natural play instinct of puppies (OGH 25 June 1992, *JBl* 1993 p. 315); the feeding instinct of cows (BGH 6 July 1976 loc. cit., p. 131); and the hunting instinct of dogs initiated by the presence of a flock of sheep (OLG Munich 29 July 1983, *VersR* 1984 p. 1095).

[1316] See fns. 1303, 1304 above. Consider the *arrêts Jand'heur* of the French *Cour de Cassation* (no. 111 above), which stated that '*la loi ne distingue pas, suivant que la chose qui a causé le dommage était ou non actionée par la main de l'homme; qu'il n'est pas nécessaire qu'elle ait un vice inhérent à sa nature . . . ; l'article 1384 rattachant la responsabilité à la garde de la chose, non à la chose elle-même'.* This is equally true of keepers' liability.

hand, and the 'independent conduct' of an animal on the other.[1317] Such methods not only catapult the law back into those times when it was thought that the demon controlling the animal had to be destroyed,[1318] they also raise questions which are incompatible with the very legal purposes which they are supposed to serve. It is not a specific animal's 'conduct' which is important, but the need to establish the risk which animals pose, and which distinguishes animals from both inanimate things and human beings. This risk arises mainly from the fact that an animal is a living thing which can move but which cannot reason. It instinctively eats and reproduces; it can fall ill or carry germs and viruses. If damage arises from any of these features, the danger arising from the animal has been realized. In this author's view the same is true if the animal's excrement is the source of danger.[1319] However, the biggest threat to the public lies in the mobility of animals, which is why the keeper is held responsible if, for instance, somebody falls over the keeper's dog. It is different if somebody trips over a dustbin bag. Although one could argue that the dustbin bag should also come under *gardien* liability, only the dog can move without external help. The danger presented by an animal is also realized if an animal falls, or if a herd of animals poses an obstacle: cattle usually pose a hazard to traffic as their movements and reactions are unpredictable. Liability also arises where a horse is ridden fast around a bend on a forest path and knocks over a pedestrian,[1320] if it kicks somebody while under anaesthetic, while suffering a colic attack, after being stung by an insect, or hit with a crop. However, the keeper is not liable if he sets his animal on an attacker in self-defence, as long as he has not misjudged the situation

---

[1317] Therefore Italian judges were right to say repeatedly that the sudden, unpredictable reactions of animals, whether caused by internal or external stimuli, come under keepers' liability: e.g. Cass. 7 Sep. 1966, n. 2333, *Giur.it.* 1967, I, 1, 1425; Cass. 9 Dec. 1970, n. 2615, *Resp.Civ. e Prev.* 1971 p. 322.

[1318] As correctly suggested by Deutsch, *NJW* 1978 pp. 1998, 2000.

[1319] *Contra*: RG 20 Sep. 1933, RGZ 141 pp. 406, 407 (bees excreting wax; this is not 'irrational and uncontrolled conduct'). Furthermore, it is this author's view that the rider of a bicycle who skids on cow excrement on the road also has a claim against the cow's keeper.

[1320] How such a case would be solved under Art. 6:179 BW is unclear despite the explanations of *Parlementaire Geschiedenis*, vol. vi, p. 763. If the *bezitter* is not the rider, the former is liable under 6:179 BW only if the latter is also answerable. Under Art. 6:173 III BW Art. 6:173 I BW is not applicable in such cases, therefore everything depends on Art. 6:162 BW. Under Art. 6:162 III BW liability requires either fault or that, according to common opinion, the fast riding constitutes a risk taken by the rider. As it can hardly be denied that the rider is responsible for the pace of his horse, the *tenzij* clause of Art. 6:179 BW has lost its purpose. Conversely, it seems inappropriate to hold the keeper liable even if the rider caused the damage, particularly in view of the fact that other legal systems are considering exempting keepers from liability where fault can be attributed entirely to a third party: see App. Turin 24 Mar. 1950, *Resp.Civ. e Prev.* 1950 p. 467; Cass.civ. 2 Dec. 1982, *Sem.Jur.* 1984, II, 20136.

(and is not at fault). If he has misjudged, the danger presented by the animal has been realized.[1321] The same applies if a person panics on seeing a dangerous-looking and unsecured animal.[1322] For it is the ability of living things to move which generates fear and hasty reactions in human beings and other animals alike. Liability for animals also arises where a person witnesses one animal tearing another to pieces and suffers shock.[1323] Finally, commentators have rightly argued that the provision also applies to dead animals:[1324] it is not logical to make a legal distinction between an animal carcass and a living creature: an animal is a thing both before and after death.

221   This does not mean that the keeper of an animal cannot raise the same defences, even so as to escape liability, as are commonly found in the law of strict liability. Hence, he can show that he or the supervisor of the animal was exercising 'justifiable' self-defence. The keeper can also claim that the damage was due to an Act of God,[1325] or was the 'realization of the general risks of living' (*allgemeines Lebensrisiko*),[1326] or state that the injured party acted at his own risk, i.e. *acceptation du risque*,[1327] and finally, he can claim that the victim negligently contributed to the

---

[1321] The argument that liability for damage caused by things is not incurred if the thing was merely used as a 'weapon' has not found support in the Dutch courts. See Rb. Almelo 18 Mar. 1993, *VR* 1993 no. 20 p. 61: drunken driver was chasing rabbits in his car; no exemption from strict liability to the injured passenger; no contributory fault by the passenger.

[1322] *Pro*: Cass.civ. 24 Feb. 1982, *Gaz.Pal.* 1982 *pan.* 250; Deutsch (fn. 1318 above) p. 2001.

[1323] See the facts of the case KreisG Cottbus 12 May 1993, *NJW-RR* 1994 p. 804. The liability question has thus not been finally decided: it depends for example on the severity of the shock. It has at least been established that the damage need not have been done 'by' the animal. Furthermore, European courts have repeatedly confirmed that no direct contact between person and animal is needed: courts have found against keepers/defendants where a motorbike rider collided with an oncoming car while trying to avoid an animal on the road (Deliyannis/Kornilakis, *Eidiko Enochiko Dikaio*, vol. iii, p. 204; also TS 26 Jan. 1972, *RAJ* 1972 no. 120 p. 119.

[1324] *Pro*: TS 10 Feb. 1959, *RAJ* 1959 no. 1483 p. 898 (fn. 1228 above); van Dunné, *Verbintenissenrecht*, vol. ii, 2nd edn., p. 499.

[1325] Whether an Act of God (*overmacht*) releases from liability is controversial in The Netherlands: for an overview see Bloembergen [-Oldenhuis], *Onrechtmatige daad*, vol. i, Art. 179 n. 38; and van Dunné, *Verbintenissenrecht* vol. ii, 2nd edn., p. 492. It seems undisputed in all other European nations: e.g. Deutsch, *NJW* 1978 pp. 1998, 1999; Cass.civ. 8 Nov. 1984, *Gaz.Pal.* 1985 *pan.* 109; Cornelis, *Responsabilité extra-contractuelle*, no. 382; Rottler, *Die Tierhalterhaftung und ihre Begrenzung*, pp. 79–80; Cour 14 Dec. 1964, *Pas. luxemb.* 19 (1963–65) p. 490; and Trib. Verona 26 Apr. 1979, *Dir.fam. e pers.* 1981, p. 509.

[1326] KreisG Cottbus 12 May 1993 (fn. 1323 above).

[1327] BGH 9 June 1992, *VersR* 1992 pp. 1145, 1146, if a person voluntarily accepts the special danger, e.g. for 'breaking in a horse, dressage, show-jumping'; Deliyannis/Kornilakis, *Eidiko Enochiko Dikaio*, vol. iii, pp. 205–206; HR 24 Jan. 1992, *NedJur* 1992 no. 302 p. 1187 (fighting dogs; at the request of the owner of one dog, the artist owner of the other interferes, is bitten, and loses a finger. The court dismissed the plea of *acceptation du risque*); Nîmes 25 Feb. 1969, *D.* 1969 *Jur.* 375 ('test of courage' during a bull-fighting event; no liability under 1385 Cc); Cass.civ. 16 June 1976, *Sem.Jur.* 1977, II, 18585; and Cass.civ. 5 June 1985, *Sem.Jur.* 1987, II, 20744.

damage in a fashion which reduces his share (possibly even to nil).[1328] The claim can also be reduced if the danger presented by the animal or other thing belonging to the victim added to the damage,[1329] for instance if the damage was caused in a traffic accident involving an animal and a road vehicle under a regime of strict liability. However, for an animal pulling a cart, the question of which liability rules apply depends on whether the animal is treated as a creature or merely as part of a vehicle. The latter is typically presumed in countries such as Italy, where the law does not distinguish between various types of non-railway vehicles, so that motor vehicles and horse-drawn carriages have the same legal status.[1330]

(2) Persons Protected by the Provisions Governing Liability for Animals

In principle, all victims of damage caused by animals are protected by   **222** liability in tort. Problems arising in this context can be solved with the ordinary defences of the law of delict. However, when applying their rules on concurring claims on the relationship of contractual and non-contractual

---

[1328] See e.g. BGH 22 Dec. 1992, *NJW* 1993 p. 2611 (15-year-old mounts a horse without sufficient instruction and against her parents' express wish); Cour 3 Mar. 1992, *Pas. luxemb.* 21 (1969–71) p. 62 (liability was split); Cass. 20 May 1983, *Pas. belge* 1983, I, 1061 (a horseman goes too close to the rider in front; liability reduced to nil); Cass. 12 Oct. 1984, *Pas. belge* 1985, I, 220 (2 horses walking side by side; contributory fault on the part of the victim 100%); BGH 9 June 1992, *VersR* 1992 p. 1145 (riding accident; the owner let the rider use the horse free of charge; § 834 BGB incorporated in the examination of contributory fault); Trib. Pordenone 10 Apr. 1989, *Foro.it.* 1989, I, 2950 (no liability if the faultless supervision of the animal is severely impaired by the victim's conduct); App. Trento 27 May 1959, *Rep.Giust.civ.* 1959, *voce Resp.civ.*, no. 366 (damages split); Bloembergen (-Old-enhuis), *Onrechtmatige daad*, vol. i, Art. 6: 179 BW not 90; HR 7 Mar. 1980, *NedJur* 1980 no. 353 p. 1165 (*Stierkalveren-arrest*; see fn. 1236 above); Hof Leeuwarden 13 Jan. 1982, *VR* 1983 no. 20; Rb. Amsterdam 1 Feb. 1984, *VR* 1985 no. 21; and Rb. Almelo 26 July 1985, *NedJur* (Kort) 1995 no. 42 p. 70 (which all state that the rider's claim against the *bezitter* of the horse is often dismissed if his contributory fault is 100%); Rb. Bruges 8 Oct. 1992, *Pas. belge* 1992, III, 110 (the rider had to warn the pedestrian, therefore *in casu* no contributory fault); Filios, *Enochiko Dikaio*, vol. ii (2), 3rd edn., p. 145. Furthermore, even in France, after abandoning the *Desmares* ruling (see no. 110 and fn. 652 above; also Part 6 I, no. 598 below), limitation of damages in cases of contributory negligence on the part of the victim no longer poses a legal problem: Cass.civ. 1 July 1987, Bull.civ. 1987, II, no. 143.

[1329] OLG Stuttgart 7 Sep. 1993, *NJW-RR* 1994 p. 93; OLG Düsseldorf 28 May 1993, *NJW-RR* 1994 p. 92; Cass. 16 June 1976, *Sem.Jur.* 1977, II, 18585; JP Verniers 24 Mar. 1978, *JT* 1978 p. 512.

[1330] Cass. 9 Dec. 1992, n. 13016, *Giust.civ.Mass.* 1992 no. 13016 p. 1845; Cass. 19 Apr. 1983, n. 2717, *Giust.civ.* 1983, I, 2987; Cass. 5 Feb. 1979, n. 778, *Giust.civ.Mass.* 1979 no. 778; Cass. 12 Sep. 1968, n. 2933, *Foro.it.* 1968, I, 2706; Cass. 16 Aug. 1960, n. 2383, *Resp.Civ. e Prev.* 1961 p. 72. If a car and a horse-drawn carriage collide Art. 2054 II Cc applies, so the drivers are presumed to be equally responsible. If an animal and a car collide, however, conflicting claims arise because Arts. 2052 and 2054 I Cc both apply. Here it has to be established how far each party contributed to the damage; see also Trib. Perugia 14 Mar. 1983, *Rep.Giur.it.* 1985, *voce Circ.strad.*, no. 143; and Trib. Forli 24 Apr. 1985, *Arch.Giur.circolaz.* 1985 p. 816. It was decided in RE 10 Nov. 1983, *BolMinJust* 333 (1984) p. 543 that where an insufficiently supervised animal runs into a motor vehicle whose keeper and driver was not entirely at fault, there is no traffic accident under Art. 508 Port. Cc.

liability, some legal systems may conclude that 'their' keepers' liability—as with everything else in the law of delict—does not apply to parties to a contract.[1331] However, despite such external limitations on liability for animals, such liability also applies to persons supervising animals, using them for private purposes (e.g. for hacking), or who are lent them free of charge for any other reason. Doubts about this view, occasionally found in academic texts,[1332] have always been dismissed by the courts.[1333] Only the keeper of the animal (and sometimes also his *co-gardien*) is exempt from its protective scope.[1334] Consequently, as soon as one labels the rider[1335] or someone working professionally with a horse[1336] as its temporary keeper, the difference between the two positions becomes much less relevant. To classify them as temporary keepers not only makes them liable to third parties, but also deprives them of their claims against the owner.[1337]

2. Liability for Dangerous Buildings and Land

a. The Starting Point: Article 1386 *Code Napoléon*

223 Like liability for risks presented by animals, liability for damage caused by the dangerous condition of real property has also always been part of the law of delict, and is found in all western European codes.[1338]

[1331] See Cass.civ. 16 Jan. 1951, *JCP* 1951, II, 6163; and Cass.civ. 8 Feb. 1961, *D.* 1961 *Jur.* 218: liability of stables for a horse throwing its riders under a contractual *obligation de sécurité de moyens* only, i.e. only in cases of fault. *Contra*: Trib. Brussels 2 June 1994, *RGAR* 1995 no. 12467. See nos. 431 ff on the doctrine of *non-cumul des responsabilités*.

[1332] E.g. Deutsch, *NJW* 1978 p. 1998; a view largely shared by Westerhoff, *JR* 1993 p. 497; to some extent also by Kavkas/Kavkas, *Enochikon Dikaion*, vol. ii, 6th edn., p. 856; *contra*, however: e.g. Terbille, *VersR* 1994 p. 1151.

[1333] E.g. Cass. 11 Feb. 1994, n. 1380, *NGCC* 1995, I, 398: operating stables is a dangerous activity; Art. 2052 Ital. Cc accordingly protects the student riding under supervision; Hof Leeuwarden 13 Jan. 1982, *NedJur* 1982 no. 482 p. 1679; Hof Leeuwarden 16 Nov. 1985, *VR* 1986 no. 113 p. 248; Trib. Brussels 2 June 1994 (fn. 1331 above), RG 6 Mar. 1902, RGZ 50 pp. 244, 248–250; BGH 9 June 1992, *VersR* 1992 p. 1145; BGH 22 Dec. 1992, *NJW* 1993 p. 2611.

[1334] See Cass.civ. 2 Dec. 1982, *Sem Jur* 1984, II, 20136 (n. Chabas): '*La responsabilité de l'article 1385 à l'encontre du gardien d'un animal a été établie en faveur des tiers, . . . et non pas pour le gardien lui-même.*'

[1335] Versailles 26 Feb. 1987, *D.* 1987 IR 94 (a visitor mounted a pony without permission; the court found the visitor to have been the *gardien*).

[1336] Cass.civ. 2 May 1911, *DP* 1991.1.367 was of the opinion that the *gardien* of an animal is '*celui qui, par lui-même ou par ses préposés, en fait l'usage que comporte l'exercice de sa profession*'. The judgments on vets and blacksmiths follow this (see fns. 1272, 1273 above). The judgment led to a series of other rulings, e.g. those declaring a freelance jockey to be *gardien* (see Bénac-Schmidt/Larroumet, fn. 1272 above).   [1337] See fn. 1334 above.

[1338] See no. 207 above. As no special provision on the liability for buildings has been introduced into the compilation of the civil law of Navarra, a reversed onus of proof under *Ley* 488.2. *Fuero Nuevo de Navarra*, which corresponds with Art. 1902 Span. Cc, is employed instead: TSJ de Navarra 11 Mar. 1994, *RAJ* 1994 no. 2114 p. 2844.

Liability for defective premises is distinguished in several ways from liability for animals: first, on the question of who is protected, and secondly, in its legal structure. The most prominent feature is the narrower definition of the risks which result in stricter forms of liability. It is this definition which causes the great majority of problems related to the question of who should be held responsible for damage caused by real property. These problems can best be unfolded from Art. 1386 French (= Belgian, Luxembourgeoise) Cc, which is both the earliest and clearest of the relevant provisions in Europe. '*Le propriétaire d'un bâtiment*', says Art. 1386 Cc, '*est responsable du dommage causé par sa ruine, lorsqu'elle est arrivée par une suite du défaut d'entretien ou par le vice de sa construction.*' Hence, the law operates three restrictions: first, Art. 1386 does not burden all owners of real property, but only the owners of buildings. Secondly, the provision does not cover all dangers constituted by a building, only the risk of its collapse (*sa ruine*). Finally, even where damage is caused by collapse, liability only arises if the collapse is due to insufficient maintenance or a structural defect.

b. Buildings and Other Structures

The first of these conditions, that the structure is a 'building', was **224** obviously intended to exempt paths and plants (trees) from the provision (an issue pursued below).[1339] However, it also excludes many other constructions. According to the definition by Professor Mertens, a building is a space surrounded by walls which are firmly connected to the ground, which can be used to house people or animals, or to store things.[1340] Yet this limitation of liability for premises is inadequate. There are a great number of structures which can be as dangerous to people as buildings under Art. 1386 Cc. All later codes, except Art. 1907 Span. Cc,[1341] have altered the narrow wording of Art. 1386 Cc. § 1319 ABGB[1342] first introduced the phrase 'building or similar construction',

---

[1339] See no. 232 below, letter e.

[1340] *MünchKomm* (-Mertens), 2nd edn., § 836 BGB no. 5.

[1341] 'The owner of a building is liable for the damage resulting from the collapse of the entire building or parts thereof if the collapse occurred because measures necessary to conserve it were not carried out'. The Span. Cc distinguishes itself even further from other codes by implementing additional provisions dealing with risks arising from specific types of property, such as Art. 1908 no. 1 (explosion of machines and material), no. 3 (trees beside highways), no. 4 (leakage from cesspits and storage rooms). Also Arts. 1909 (architects' and builders' liability), and 1910 (things thrown from buildings).

[1342] Even Austria has retained the *actio de effusis* as well as the *actio de posito vel suspenso*: § 1318 ABGB.

which phrase was adopted by § 836 BGB, Art. 2053 Ital. Cc, Art. 925 Greek Cc, Art. 492 Port. Cc, and Art. 6:174 I BW. Art. 6:174 III BW even defines the generic term 'construction' (*opstal*): 'construction means buildings and works, durably united with land, either directly or through incorporation with other buildings or works.'

225 Comparing the provisions and their interpretation by the courts is merely a first step (for more see no. 226 below), which shows only that the gap between the different approaches is in fact much smaller than first appears. In all European countries whose codes impose such liability only for buildings (i.e. France, Belgium, Luxembourg, Spain, and until the end of 1991 The Netherlands, see Art. 1405 BW [old]) it is established practice to interpret the term 'building' to mean construction in general.[1343] According to the French courts, there are only two defining characteristics for a *bâtiment*: it must be a construction, and it must be durably united with the land on which it stands (*son incorporation durable au sol*).[1344] Therefore a dam can qualify as a 'building',[1345] as can a sewer,[1346] a supporting pillar,[1347] and a retaining wall.[1348] Even ground-level and underground constructions have been held to be buildings.[1349] The term *bâtiment* under French law thus not only covers the same objects as the term 'construction' in other codes,[1350] but also

---

[1343] For Belgium see Cornelis, *De buitencontractuele aansprakelijkheid voor schade veroorzaakt door zaken*, pp. 250–251; and Vandenberghe/Van Quickenborne/Geelen/De Coster, *TPR* 1987 pp. 1255, 1442 (no. 107; adaptation of French rulings); for Spain, where Art. 389 Cc ('building, wall, column, or any other construction') expressly suggests a generous interpretation of Art. 1907 Cc, see e.g. Díez-Picazo/Gullón, *Sistema*, vol. ii, 6th edn., pp. 632–634; Puig Brutau, *Compendio*, vol. ii, 2nd edn., pp. 639–642; and de Ángel Yágüez, *Responsabilidad civil*, 3rd edn., pp. 571–574. Art. 1405 BW (old), interpreted the term *gebouw* widely to mean *bouwsel* (Jonas, *Verschuldensunabhängige außervertragliche Haftung für Sachen*, pp. 34, 111) which interpretation was adopted by the NBW. For more recent decisions confirming this position see Rb. Breda 31 Aug. 1993, *NedJur* 1995 no. 335 p. 1526 (gravestone as building); Rb. Arnhem 13 Jan. 1994f, *A&Vá* 1994 p. 78 (no. 23) (water pipe as *gebouw* in accordance with Art. 1405 BW [old]); and Rb. Assen 16 Feb. 1993, *A&Vá* 1993 p. 51 (wall as building).
[1344] *Encyclopédie Dalloz* (-Bénac-Schmidt/Larroumet), *Rép.Dr.Civ.* vol. viii, 'Responsabilité du fait d'autrui', nos. 54–59.
[1345] Cass.civ. 28 Nov. 1949, *D.* 1950 *Jur.* 105 (n. Lalou).
[1346] Cass.civ. 25 June 1952, *D.* 1952 *Jur.* 614.
[1347] Bordeaux 30 Jan. 1953, *D.* 1954 *Somm.* 15.
[1348] Cass.civ. 14 Feb. 1979, Bull.civ. 1979 II no. 48; see also Mons 13 Nov. 1992, *RGAR* 1994 no. 12391.
[1349] Bénac-Schmidt/Larroumet (fn. 1344 above) no. 55; Starck (-Roland/Boyer), *Obligations*, vol. i, 4th edn., no. 740; all refer to earlier rulings. In cases of 'depressions', however, Art. 1386 does not apply: Cass.civ. 2 Nov. 1967, Bull.civ. 1967, II, no. 311; here the relevant provision is Art. 1384 I Cc.
[1350] For Portugal see Vaz Serra: *BolMinJust* 88 (1959) pp. 13, 28–35; and Pires de Lima/Antunes Varela, *Cc anotado*, vol. i, 4th edn., Art. 492 n. 3 (border walls, canals, bridges, aquaducts, pillars, antennae). For Greece: Deliyannis/Kornilakis, *Eidiko Enochiko Dikaio*, vol. iii, pp. 211–212 ('other work' includes all man-made technical constructions or installations indirectly or directly, durably or temporarily connected with the ground, as well as

regularly extends to constructions which are highly controversial elsewhere.[1351] Hence the French system is in practice different from the other European systems in that it does not require constructions to be durably connected with the land. Cases in point are huts, sheds, and mobile homes,[1352] as well as scaffolding and escalators. These have been held not to fall within Art. 1386 in several cases.[1353]

Staying with these examples,[1354] the question of whether scaffolding **226** should come under liability for buildings (as in Germany and Greece,[1355] but not in The Netherlands[1356]) or elevators (as in The Netherlands[1357] but not in France and Portugal[1358]) has some relevance, but this should not be overrated. Nor should one overlook the fact that the circumstances under which this issue arises are sometimes unpredictable. Bringing the facts of a case under a particular rule of law is generally only relevant in cases where the level of liability and the causes of action, as well as the person liable, depend on which special provision on liability for structures is applicable. In all countries whose courts (or legislators[1359]) have followed recent trends and developed general clauses for liability for things[1360] which achieve the same results as those for structures, it is of little importance under which of the possible

walls, fences, scaffolding, and power lines). For Italy: Cendon (-Bussani) vol. iv, Art. 2053 n. 2 (*edificio* includes every man-made construction standing on the ground, even if only for limited time). For Germany: *MünchKomm* (-Mertens), 2nd edn., § 836 BGB no. 7 ('structures' include scaffolding, building workers' huts and kiosks, bridges, dams, telegraph poles, underground oil tanks). For Austria: OGH 22 Sep. 1982, *MietSlg*. 34.290 (§ 1319 ABGB applies where the natural condition of the ground or of a site has been artificially altered, and the state of the alteration is obviously below the required standard).

[1351] Underground constructions are not considered by some to be structures, as they cannot 'collapse': Bussani [fn. 1350 above]; cautiously Koziol, *Österr. Haftpflichtrecht*, vol. ii, 2nd edn., p. 394. The thesis is not very convincing, however, (Franzoni, *Fatti illeciti*, Art. 2053, p. 630), and is not generally accepted: OGH 10 Dec. 1969, *JBl* 1970 p. 623 (excavation); OGH 12 Apr. 1961, *ÖJZ* 1961 p. 662 (*EvBl* 526) (manure pit); BGH 25 Jan. 1971, BGHZ 55 p. 229 (underground water pipeline).

[1352] Cass.civ. 18 Apr. 1993, *D.* 1993 IR 135. For earlier Dutch judgments see: Hof Amsterdam 31 Dec. 1953, *NedJur* 1954 no. 319 (circus tent); HR 28 June 1951, *NedJur* 1952 no. 537 (loose fire escape); and HR 13 June 1974, *NedJur* 1975 no. 17 (pedestrian bridge). Each of those structures was held not to be a building.

[1353] Aix-en-Provence 14 Apr. 1977, *D.* 1978 IR 404; Paris 20 Feb. 1980, *Gaz.Pal.* 1980, 1, Somm. 284.

[1354] Further examples are easy to find: are objects falling from buildings under construction covered by liability for buildings? Yes in most European countries, but not in France, where Art. 1384 I Cc applies: Bénac-Schmidt/Larroumet loc. cit. (fn. 1344 above) no. 71.

[1355] See fn. 1350 above.

[1356] Scaffolding is not a building under Art. 6:174 III BW, as it is not durably united with the land; however, if it collapses liability may arise under Art. 6:173 I BW (strict liability for moveable things).　　　　[1357] *Parlementaire Geschiedenis*, vol. vi, p. 754.

[1358] See fn. 1353 above, and RL 18 Apr. 1991, *CJ* XVI (1991-2) p. 176: liability of the owner for presumed fault under Art. 493 Port. Cc, fault-based liability of the business providing the service, Art. 487 Port. Cc.　　　　[1359] Loc. cit. (Part 2 II, esp. 117–129).

[1360] For detail see part 2 II, nos. 103–129 above.

provisions a case concerning liability for real property is discussed. If, as is often the case, liability for both buildings and other things is based on presumed fault,[1361] or if all the relevant provisions are strict,[1362] then where the line is drawn is often primarily a question of legal aesthetics, a phenomenon found in all marginal areas of liability for constructions. It is not limited to the changing perimeters of the term 'building'.[1363] Today the dividing line has become faint and indistinct in most countries. Not so in Greece, however, which explicitly distinguishes between fault-based liability under Art. 914 Cc and strict liability under Art. 925 Cc. As for the French system, Art. 1386 Cc is always backed up by Art. 1384 I Cc:[1364] if the conditions of the former are *not* met (i.e. either the construction is not a 'building' or it has not 'collapsed'), the owner is only liable for fault. Yet if he is also the *gardien* of the thing, Art. 1384 I Cc renders him strictly liable and here, at least from the point of view of the French courts,[1365] it is no longer relevant whether the construction was faulty or inadequately maintained.[1366] Hence in France, unlike other

---

[1361] The most important German decisions are those regarding the distribution of the onus of proof in cases of violation of the general duty of care (see nos. 105 and fn. 625 above). For Spain: the rulings on Art. 1902 Cc (see no. 103 and fn. 614 above); Tribunal Superior de Justicia de Navarra 11 Mar. 1994, *RAJ* 1994 no. 2114 p. 2844: minors threw stones at a pillar of an empty house, as a result of which a wall collapsed injuring them. The TSJ applied *Ley* 488.2 *Fuero Nuevo de Navarra* (i.e. Art. 488 II of the compilation of the civil law of Navarra): 'A person negligently causing damage to the property of another could compensate the other, as can be expected in the circumstances'. The court applied to this the presumption of fault developed by the Tribunal Supremo on Art. 1902 Span. Cc thereby reaching the same result as would have been reached by applying Art. 1907 Cc.

[1362] See the French and Dutch examples in fns. 1354 and 1356 above. In Italy, ruins and rotten trees lead to similar results: Art. 2053 Cc (liability for buildings) does not apply, but Art. 2051 Cc (*custodia* liability) closes the gap. See Cass. 31 Mar. 1971, n. 1641, *Rep.gen.* 1971 col. 3663 no. 167; and Trib. Verona 26 Jan. 1994, *Foro.it.* 1995, I, 692 (however, liability denied because damage was held to have been due to an Act of God). Art. 2053 Cc is simply a special form of the provision in Art. 2051 Cc: Cass. 17 Nov. 1984, n. 5868, *Foro.it.* 1985, I, 123; and Cass. 29 Jan. 1981, n. 693, *Riv.Dir.Comm.* 1982, II, 47.

[1363] Also often the case if there is no 'collapse'. The liability regime achieved by applying the general rules in such cases often leads to very similar results, see fn. 709 above. A typical example is glazing which is dangerous to the public in general, e.g. the glass entrance of a hotel (TS 4 Nov. 1991, *RAJ* 1991 no. 814 p. 11160), and the glazed outer wall of the staircase of a block of flats (BGH 31 May 1994, *NJW* 1994 p. 2232). See Cass.civ. 11 Jan. 1995, *Sem.Jur.* 1995, IV, 625: building expert climbed onto the roof of a house where a glass brick broke under his weight. Liability under Art. 1384 I was dismissed).

[1364] See no. 116 above.

[1365] Not so in Belgium, due to the precondition of *vice de la chose*: see nos. 113–114 above.

[1366] Conversely, however, Art. 1384 I Cc also applies if part of a structure which alone does not qualify as a building has objectively been inadequately maintained; see fn. 1353 above.

legal systems, it is better for the plaintiff if he is 'only' liable under Art. 1386 Cc, which is why some commentators would like to reinstate its original limitation to genuine buildings.[1367] The current wide interpretation of the term *bâtiment* holds the French system back, rather than aiding it,[1368] for it blocks the way to Art. 1384 I Cc.[1369]

c. Collapse and Falling Parts of Buildings

Art. 1386 Cc would have little practical relevance if it were taken **227** literally, since on the face of it an entire building must collapse to establish a claim. This is why the courts soon declared that *'la ruine d'un bâtiment au sens de l'article 1386 du Code civil s'entend de sa destruction totale ou de la dégradation partielle de toute partie de sa construction, de tout élément mobilier ou immobilier qui y est incorporé de façon indissoluble'*.[1370] Hence a building 'collapses' if individual stones, a projecting beam, a window frame, or a roof tile fall off,[1371] if a gravestone falls over,[1372] or if the floor of a salon gives in.[1373] Thus it usually makes no difference whether the relevant provisions speak of 'collapse' (as in Art. 1386 Cc in Belgium, France and Luxembourg), or whether they also mention the 'detachment of parts' of the structure (as in §§ 1319 ABGB, 836 BGB, and Arts. 925 Greek Cc,

---

[1367] A position taken by Rodière, in a note on Pau, 5 July 1946, *JCP* 1946, II, 3324, and taken up by Cass.civ. 4 July 1974, *D.* 1974 *IR* 223.

[1368] In order to prevent the new Dutch system from similar infelicities, its authors warned the courts against interpreting 6:174 III BW too extensively: Bloembergen (-Oldenhuis), Art. 174 n. 38.

[1369] That Art. 1386 ousts Art. 1384 I Cc, i.e. that there is no *cumul* of owners' and *gardien* liability, is the established practice of French (Cass.civ. 12 July 1966, *D.* 1966 *Jur.* 632) and Belgian courts (Cass. 22 Oct. 1954, *Pas. belge* 1955, I, 149; Rb. Antwerp 19 Mar. 1981; and Antwerp 13 Sep. 1983, *De Verzekering* 1984 p. 465). The *gardien* cannot be held liable under Art. 1384 I Cc even if he is not the owner: Cass.civ. 30 Nov. 1988, *Sem.Jur.* 1989 II 21319.

[1370] This is the standard definition employed by French courts: e.g. Cass.civ. 12 July 1966, *D.* 1966 *Jur.* 632; Cass.civ. 30 Nov. 1977, *D.* 1978 *IR* 201; and Paris 1 July 1992, *Sem.Jur.* 1992, IV, 2593. This wording has by and large been adopted in Belgium, see Cass. 18 Apr. 1975, *Pas. belge* 1975, I, 828; and Cass. 8 May 1924, *Pas. belge* 1924, I, 328 (*'ruine totale ou partielle, chute ou effondrement de tout ou partie de la construction'*).

[1371] See Cass. 17 Nov. 1984, n. 5868, *Foro.it.* 1985, I, 123; TS 7 Oct. 1991, *RAJ* 1991 no. 6891 p. 9363; Hof Amsterdam 14 Dec. 1967, *NedJur* 1968 no. 337; Ghent 16 Nov. 1993, *RW* 1994–95 no. 1094; and Aix-en-Provence 8 Jan. 1951, *D.* 1951 *Jur.* 223. However, Belgian courts unjustly distinguish between one tile coming from a roof (not considered a collapse: Vred. St-Gilles 22 Jan. 1979, *JT* 1979 p. 343) and several tiles or a chimney falling (a collapse: Moucron 7 Dec. 1979, *RGAR* 1982 no. 10464). In Spain there is often also the possibility of strict liability arising under Art. 1910 Cc: TS 5 July 1989, *RAJ* 1989 no. 5297 p. 6092.

[1372] Paris 8 Dec. 1938, *DH* 1939, 72; BGH 5 Oct. 1971, *NJW* 1971 p. 2308; and Rb. Breda 31 Aug. 1993 (fn. 1343 above). However, Ghent 8 Dec. 1993, *RW* 1994–1995 p. 716 did apply Art. 1384 I Cc.   [1373] Cass.civ. 3 Mar. 1964, *D.* 1964 *Jur.* 245.

492 Port. Cc).[1374] Finally, where differences have been retained, this was usually intended to achieve consistency of results rather than to preserve inconsistency. A good example is the widespread desire to impose strict liability on those responsible for water pipes.[1375] A building has not collapsed, however, if a thick layer of snow rather than a tile falls off the roof,[1376] nor if stairs, entrances, or paths are uneven,[1377] nor if overhead powerlines are placed too close together so that they touch and emit sparks in stormy weather.[1378] Furthermore, the prevailing view is that walls which collapse due to inadequate building, repair, or demolition should also not incur liability for build-

---

[1374] Differences in the applicability of the relevant provisions are commonly based on the fact that the first group demands a durable connection with the land. Thus if a board falls from scaffolding this is easily within § 836 BGB (BGH 21 Apr. 1959, *VersR* 1959 pp. 694, 695), but definitely not within Art. 1386 Cc. However, objects intentionally or negligently thrown from a bridge or out of a building do not come within liability for buildings (see STJ 10 Jan. 1975, *BolMinJust* 243 [1975] p. 240: building workers dropped a plank; employers' liability; and Trib. Verona 8 Jan. 1992, *Foro.pad.* 1993, I, 127: an object was thrown from a bridge onto a car. The offender could not be identified. Liability of the keeper of the structure under Art. 2051 Cc, as the burden of proof lay with him). In such cases liability can only be based on general provisions or, where it is provided, strict liability. TS 12 Mar. 1975, *RAJ* 1975 no. 1798 p. 1355 even applied Art. 1910 Span. Cc when a mentally ill, suicidal patient jumped out of a hospital window killing a passer-by.

[1375] CA Athens 4268/1956, *NoB* 5 (1957) p. 325 allowed a tenant to sue the owner under Art. 925 Greek Cc when a house water pipe burst; BGH 25 Jan. 1971, BGHZ 55 pp. 229, 232–233 defended the call for strict liability for water pipes (laid outside a house), subsequently implemented by § 2 HPflG. Furthermore, the Spanish *Tribunal Supremo* has repeatedly applied Art. 1910 Span. Cc (*actio de effusis*) where a water pipe in an upstairs flat was left open or burst and caused damage to a lower flat (TS 20 Apr. 1993, *La Ley* 1993 [3] p. 360; TS 12 Apr. 1984, *RAJ* 1984 no. 1958 p. 1490 [a repairman omitted to turn off the taps]; and TS 26 June 1993, *RAJ* 1993 no. 5383 p. 6869). Finally, RL 7 May 1987, *CJ* XII (1987–3) p. 80 applied Art. 493 II Port. Cc in a case of a burst water pipe belonging to a licensed water supplier. See also OGH 10 Dec. 1969, *JBl* 1970 p. 623 (fn. 1379 below). However, it is unclear whether liability for burst pipes in buildings lies with the tenant (as in Spain under Art. 1910 Cc) or the owner (as in Pret. Trento 11 May 1993, *Foro.it.* 1994, I, 294; Cass.sez.un. 11 Nov. 1991, n. 12019, *Foro.it.* 1993, I, 922; Cass. 17 Nov. 1984, n. 5868, *Foro.it.* 1985, I, 123).

[1376] *Encyclopédie Dalloz* (-Bénac-Schmidt/Larroumet), *Rép.Dr.Civ.* vol. viii, 'Responsabilité du fait des bâtiments', no. 54; and *MünchKomm* (-Mertens), 2nd edn., § 836 BGB no. 12; also fn. 709 above. In favour of the application of § 1319 ABGB: Jabornegg, *ZVR* 1974 p. 321. Yet Austrian courts usually opt for liability for breach of a protective statute (§ 1311, 2nd alt. ABGB in conjunction with § 93 Austrian StVO): OGH 15 Mar. 1972, SZ 45/32; OGH 7 Nov. 1972, *ZVR* 1974/53; OGH 16 Jan. 1975, *ZVR* 1975/269.

[1377] Hence the numerous supermarket and slippery path cases. E.g. BGH 22 Sep. 1992, *NJW-RR* 1993 p. 27; Mons 6 Dec. 1991, *RGAR* 1994 no. 12342 dismissed liability under Art. 1384 I Cc: snow-covered and thus slippery stairs are not defective; BGH 20 Sep. 1994, *NJW* 1994 p. 3348: insufficiently secured garden ponds do not come within liability for buildings. However, OGH 18 Feb. 1986, *JBl* 1986 p. 523 found liability for buildings where a path had become generally unsafe for the public.

[1378] STJ 5 June 1985, *BolMinJust* 348 (1985) p. 397. See also Cass.civ. 3 Mar. 1993, Bull.civ. 1993, II, no. 86: fissures in a chimney caused lethal poisoning; no 'collapse'.

ings.[1379] These situations have nothing to do with the prerequisite of 'collapse', because the damage was not caused by insufficient maintenance. The owner fullfilled his duty to maintain the building: the sole cause of the damage was bad workmanship.

The real problem of the law of liability for buildings is not so much **228** where the wide interpretation of the term 'collapse' should stop, but whether it is a suitable description of the risk which leads to liability. Only recently the Dutch decided not to use this term in the new BW.[1380] Under Art. 6:174 I BW the only issue is whether the construction 'fails to meet the standards which, in the circumstances, may be set for it, and thereby constitutes a danger for persons or things'. The Dutch BW again breaks new ground, and provides a model deserving consideration at European level. It seems much more appropriate to extend this part of liability for real property to all dangers resulting from the unsafe condition of a structure, instead of bringing one case under the general clause and another very similar one under the special provision. There is no good reason why a malfunctioning gate lock should be treated differently.[1381] This is also true for a collapsing, as opposed to a missing, cellar shaft cover,[1382] for shutters with defective locking devices which malfunction.[1383] Why barriers at a level crossing which suddenly dropped should be treated differently from those which suddenly rose[1384] is also unfathomable.[1385] Liability for buildings, which repeatedly acted as a catalyst during the development of liability for damage caused by things,[1386] must now be brought back into line with the latter: yet another problem which the Dutch legislation has tackled with great success by orientating both

---

[1379] E.g. Rummel (-Reischauer), *ABGB*, vol. ii, 2nd edn., § 1319 no. 9 (*contra*: OGH 10 Dec. 1969, *JBl* 1970 p. 623: a water pipe was damaged during excavation work; escaping water damaged an adjacent shop); Bénac-Schmidt/Larroumet (fn. 1376 above) nos. 70–72 with references to French decisions; TS 21 Feb. 1994, *RAJ* 1994 no. 1108 p. 1460: the plaintiff's house was severely damaged by demolition work on the adjacent property which had become uninhabitable due to leaking municiple water pipes; both the neighbour and the town were liable under Art. 1902 Span. Cc); and *MünchKomm* (-Mertens), 2nd edn., § 836 BGB no. 14. Ambiguously, however: BGH 18 June 1968, *VersR* 1968 p. 972 (see also BGH 8 Nov. 1978, *NJW* 1979 pp. 309, 310).

[1380] *Parlementaire Geschiedenis*, vol. vi, p. 753: '*Aansprakelijkheid krachtens dit artikel kan ook bestaan als er niet een gehele of gedeeltelijke instorting van het werk heeft plaatsgevonden.*'

[1381] See Jonas, *Verschuldensunabhängige außervertragliche Haftung für Sachen* p. 115.

[1382] See HR 5 Nov. 1965, *NedJur* 1966 no. 136 p. 225.

[1383] If shutters come out of the guide rail this amounts to a collapse (Cass.civ. 8 June 1994, *D.* 1994 IR 181), but if defective shutters remain inside their rails this is not a collapse (RG 9 Nov. 1908, *WarnR* 1909 no. 101 p. 97).

[1384] OGH 5 Nov. 1980, SZ 53/143 (pp. 642, 646) deemed it necessary to distinguish the two cases.

[1385] Even harder to understand are those French cases where a house collapses having caught fire. Under Art. 1384 II French Cc fault has to be established; it is not sufficient to prove that there was e.g. a defect in the wiring. [1386] See no. 104 above.

Art. 6:173 (movable things) and Art. 6:174 (immovable things) along the same lines.

d. Insufficient Maintenance and Faulty Construction: Liability for Disrepair of a Thing or Liability for Misconduct?

229   When a building collapses, whether totally or partially, this is usually due either to defective construction or to inadequate maintenance,[1387] and often to a combination of the two, because good maintenance reveals and remedies defects of construction.[1388] Although most codes impose liability for 'defective construction' and 'inadequate maintenance' (Art. 1386 French, Belg., and Luxemb. Cc; § 836 BGB; Arts. 925 Greek Cc; 2053 Ital. Cc; 492 Port. Cc; and 1907 and 1909 Span. Cc[1389]), in both cases an 'inadequate condition in the construction' (§ 1319 ABGB), in other words a 'construction which does not meet the standards which, in the given circumstances, may be set for it and thereby constitutes a danger for persons or things' (Art. 6:174 I BW) is required. If the structure has collapsed[1390] it becomes less relevant who bears the onus of proof of either defective construction or inadequate maintenance. If the victim proves a 'collapse' he has often also demonstrated the poor quality of the repair work to the structure.[1391] Thus, in more advanced codes it is for the owner (or the immediate possessor) to prove that the structure is free of defect or that the defect did not cause the collapse and subsequent damage.[1392]

230   Typical cases of collapse with no defect in construction are those where the damage to the building was caused by external forces which are neither controllable nor predictable; for example, damage as a result

---

[1387] E.g. BGH 8 Feb. 1972, BGHZ 58 pp. 149, 155. Under § 836 BGB a structure is only properly constructed and maintained if it does not collapse and no parts of it become detached. See also OGH 15 Apr. 1993, *ÖJZ* 1994 pp. 50, 51 (*EvBl* 8): a retaining wall unsecured against collapse is defective.

[1388] BGH 20 Sep. 1962, *VersR* 1962 pp. 1105, 1106. It is irrelevant which of the two causes of action has been realized.

[1389] Under Art. 1909 Cc both the architect and the person for whom the structure is built are liable for defects in the construction. The provision supplements contractual liability under Art. 1591 Cc with non-contractual protection *vis-à-vis* third parties, and Art. 1591 Cc extends the limitation periods to 10 and 15 years respectively.

[1390] Under Art. 6:174 I BW a structure need not collapse (see no. 228 above): the victim merely has to prove its unsafe condition. Moreover, his position is even stronger as *'die bewijslast niet al te streng dient te worden gehanteerd'* (Bloembergen [-Oldenhuis], *Onrechtmatige daad*, vol. i, Art. 174 no. 5). Moreover, in cases of collapse the *res ipsa loquitur* rule also applies (loc. cit. no. 128).

[1391] Even in French courts the dilapidated condition of a structure (*vétusté*) is often sufficient proof of inadequate maintenance and/or defective construction. For more detail see Bénac-Schmidt/Larroumet (fn. 1376 above) no. 78.

[1392] The more advanced codes are Italy (Art. 2053 Cc) and Greece (Art. 925 Cc; see also CFI Athens 30/1980, *Arm.* 35 [1981] p. 471; CFI Salonica 456/1973, *NoB* 21 [1973] p. 392;

of war, natural disaster,[1393] (but not weather in general), or entirely unreasonable pressure being put on an installation.[1394] There is also no insufficient maintenance when a building collapses, not instantly, but so soon that its owner could not reasonably have prevented the realization of the danger, e.g. after a lorry was driven into it. For this very situation the Dutch legislator introduced the *tenzij* clause in Art. 6:174 I BW ('unless, pursuant to the preceding section, there would have been no liability if the possessor had known of the danger at the time it arose'.) Furthermore, as the BW does not limit liability for buildings to cases of 'collapse', an examination of all the circumstances of each case is needed. The courts have not yet determined which course to pursue.[1395]

It is not as straightforward as one might think to determine whether **231** the structual defects which caused the damage are purely a characteristic of the building, or whether they are also to be regarded as a result of the misconduct of its owner (or *gardien*). If the former is presumed, there must be strict liability for structural disrepair. By contrast, on the latter view a breach of duty is hardly a sufficient cause of action in accordance with the general rules and regulations: fault (albeit presumed) would also have to be shown. Amongst European legislators both views find supporters. Under the civil codes of Greece, The

and CFI Pátrai 603/1973, *NoB* 21 [1973] p. 1509). Less advanced are Portugal (STJ 28 Apr. 1977, *BolMinJust* 266 [1977] pp. 161, 163); Belgium (e.g. Cass. 17 Dec. 1992, *RW* 1993–1994 p. 434); France (e.g. Cass.civ. 4 Aug. 1942, *D.* 1943 *Jur.* 1, note Ripert; and Cass.civ. 11 Oct. 1957, *D.* 1968 *Jur.* 106); Austria (e.g. OGH 8 July 1986, *SZ* 59/121, pp. 616, 620); and Germany (BGH 16 June 1952, *LM* no. 4 on § 836 BGB), where the victim still has to prove the existence of a defect. However, in all countries *prima facie* evidence (*res ipsa loquitur*) is sufficient. For Spain see e.g. Puig Brutau, *Compendio*, vol. ii, 2nd edn., pp. 639–642.

[1393] However, a structure erected in the open air must usually be able to withstand a storm: e.g. Mons 13 Nov. 1994 *RGAR* 1995 no. 12391; Trib. Liège 3 May 1993, *RGAR* 1995 no. 12468; and Rb. Assen 16 Feb. 1993, *A&V* 1993 p. 51.

[1394] If the necessary safety standards for that type of structure have been observed, and if the damage can be wholly attributed to the victim's conduct, it is he who is at fault. E.g. Hof 's-Hertogenbosch 29 Nov. 1993, NedJur 1994 no. 456 p. 2162: the victim leant against a single-wire fence which collapsed beneath his weight; no liability under Art. 6: 174 BW as the structure was not defective.

[1395] For a case in which liability was denied under the old BW, but would probably be admitted under the new Dutch law, see Hof Amsterdam 5 Dec. 1991, *NedJur* 1992 no. 824 p. 3547: a swimmer was caught on a plug at the bottom of a swimming-pool which had caused no trouble since 1917. No liability, although the court described the plug as defective. However, in the case of a 20-year-old elevator which caused severe injuries to a child, Hof 's-Hertogenbosch 28 Dec. 1993, *A&V* 1994 p. 79 (no. 24) rejected the victim's claim. It was argued that the lift was not defective merely because lifts with higher safety standards existed. Moreover, in Rb. Amsterdam 20 Jan. 1993, VR 1994 no. 158 the issue of structural defects was not even considered: to deter drug addicts the defendant had barred his window using iron bars with spiked tips. The plaintiff slipped on snow and fell against the barred window. Liability of the defendant was denied as he had not breached his duty to keep the path gritted.

Netherlands, and Italy (where the character of liability under Art. 2053 Cc is highly controversial) liability is strict.[1396] In Austria, Spain, Germany, and Portugal, on the other hand, the defendant has a good defence if he can prove either that he should not have known of the defect, or that he could not have corrected it even if he had known.[1397] However, the standard of care required for that defence is usually quite high. Additionally, most of the latter group of countries have provisions enabling one neighbour to sue the other for specific performance (e.g. to repair the roof), a cause of action which is independent of fault.[1398]

e. Paths and Trees

232 Streets, roads, and paths used by the public are often subject to a special state liability regime which, despite its closeness to civil provisions, is not an issue for this book.[1399] The remaining cases also do not come under the general provisions on liability for buildings, but under the rules and regulations on negligent breach of the general duties of

---

[1396] For Greece: see fn. 1392 above and Deliyannis/Kornilakis, *Eidiko Enochiko Dikaio*, vol. iii, pp. 209–211; Filios, *Enochiko Dikaio*, vol. ii (2), 3rd edn., pp. 146–147; Balis, *Genikai Archai tou Astikou Dikaiou*, 8th edn., p. 453. For Belgium: Cass. 17 Dec. 1992, *RW* 1993–1994 p. 434. For France: Cass.civ. 19 Apr. 1887, *DP* 1888.1.27; Cass.civ. 4 June 1973, *D.* 1973 *IR* 185. Courts and scholars in Italy disagree on whether Art. 2053 Cc should be regarded as a strict liability provision, or as presumed fault (a position taken by the Court of Cassation, e.g. Cass.civ. 6 June 1973, n. 1632, *Resp.Civ. e Prev.* 1974 p. 202; Cass. 11 Nov. 1977, n. 4898, *Giur.it.* 1978, I, 1, 1508). As in liability for animals (see no. 210 and fn. 1233 above), this is of no legal consequence.

[1397] Austria: OGH 20 Mar. 1951, SZ 24/78; OGH 8 July 1986, SZ 59/121; and OGH 15 Apr. 1993, *ÖJZ* 1994 p. 50 (*EvBl* 8); Spain: de Ángel Yágüez, *Responsabilidad civil*, 3rd edn., pp. 571–574; Díez-Picazo/Gullón, *Sistema*, vol. ii, 6th edn., pp. 632–634; Portugal: STJ 28 Apr. 1977, *BolMinJust* 266 (1977) p. 161; Germany: BGH 7 Oct. 1975, *VersR* 1976 p. 66.

[1398] The *actio cautio damni infecti* of Roman law (Vaz Serra, *BolMinJust* 88 [1959] pp. 13, 55) is probably the origin of provisions enabling a neighbour to force the owner of a building to carry out maintenance work (§ 908 BGB [v. Bar, in: *25 Jahre Karlsruher Forum*, pp. 80–85]; Art. 389 Span. Cc; Art. 1006 Greek Cc; Art. 1172 Ital. Cc; and Art. 1350 Port. Cc).

[1399] See also Part 6 I, no. 553 and fns. 1–5 below. For Austria and The Netherlands see following references; for the liability system created by French administrative courts, esp. for *travaux publics*, see Chapus, *Droit administratif général*, vol. ii, 6th edn., p. 530; and *JClCiv* (-Carbajo), Arts. 1382 to 1386, 'État et collectivités publiques, Travaux et ouvrages publics. Le patrimoine responsable, Fasc. 370–3'. For Luxembourg: see the summary of the new state liability law by Ravarani, *Pas. luxemb.* 28 (1990–1992) pp. 77–426; and Trib. Lux. 27 Jan. 1988, confirmed by Cour 8 May 1989, *Pas. luxemb.* 27 (1987–1989) p. 332. For Belgium see Cass. 7 Mar. 1963, *Pas. belge* 1963, I, 744; Brussels 21 Apr. 1992, *RGAR* 1994 no. 12344; JP Seraing 14 Feb. 1991, *RGAR* 1994 no. 12345; and Cornelis, *De buitencontractuele aansprakelijkheid voor schade veroorzaakt door zaken*, pp. 288–331. For German rulings on § 839 BGB with Art. 34 GG (violation of public duty to safeguard road traffic) see BGH 12 July 1979, BGHZ 75 p. 134; BGH 11 June 1992, BGHZ 118 p. 368; BGH 1 July 1993, *NJW* 1993 p. 2612. Such duties to safeguard the public in general paved the way for the state liability law in Germany. See v. Bar, *JZ* 1979 pp. 323–337.

care,[1400] and on the general principles of *gardien* and *custodia* liability respectively.[1401] Only in The Netherlands are roads expressly treated like any other construction. Liability for public roads (definition in Art. 6:174 V BW) 'rests upon the public authority in charge of the proper maintenance of the roads', Art. 6:174 II s. 2 BW. This new provision, implemented on 1st January 1992, introduced strict liability where the old BW imposed liability only for fault (Art. 1401 BW).[1402]

The Austrian legislator took a step in exactly the opposite direction by **233** implementing § 1319a ABGB on 1st January 1976. Instead of burdening the keeper of roads, whether a private person or a public authority, with strict liability, the provision protects him: under § 1319a ABGB the keeper of a road is only liable for intent or gross negligence.[1403] In view of the general European trend, this provision (which also applies to ski- and sledging-runs,[1404] but not to toll roads[1405]) is retrogressive, particularly considering that the only other provision applicable alongside § 1319a ABGB is § 1319 ABGB, and the former does not oust the latter.[1406] Furthermore, § 1319a ABGB also puzzles impartial observers of the Austrian system, as it has been the 'general practice of the courts, a practice sanctioned by Austrian scholars', to apply § 1319 ABGB 'by analogy even to trees'.[1407] To tighten the conditions of liability for trees, which are clearly not structures because they have not been manufactured but have grown naturally,[1408] was a legitimate step for the Austrian legislator. Strict liability for trees growing alongside highways is found in several European systems.[1409] If strict

---

[1400] E.g. OLG Cologne 19 Aug. 1992, *VersR* 1993 p. 1165.

[1401] E.g. Cass. 31 Oct. 1961, n. 2530, *Rep.gen.* 1961 col. 3137, no. 27.

[1402] The first to be effected by this were the bus-lane cases. See Antonides, *VersRAI* 1995 p. 31. These cases used to be subject to fault-based liability under the general clause (see HR 20 Mar. 1992, *NedJur* 1993 no. 547 p. 1975), whereas now they are dealt with under Art. 6: 174 BW: Hof Amsterdam 30 Dec. 1993, *VR* 1994 no. 151; Rb. 's-Gravenhage 11 Mar. 1994, *VR* 1994 no. 152.

[1403] See Edlbacher, in: *25 Jahre Karlsruher Forum*, pp. 18–23. Under § 1319a ABGB even the breach of an authority's duty to grit roads depends on whether 'the mayor or his officers acted intentionally or grossly negligently': OGH 11 Mar. 1993, SZ 66/30.

[1404] OGH 7 June 1978, *ÖJZ* 1979 p. 16 (*EvBl* 1); OGH 23 Mar. 1983, *ZVR* 1984/176; OGH 7 Nov. 1990, *JBl* 1991 p. 652; and OGH 4 Feb. 1993, *ÖJZ* 1994 p. 24 (*EvBl* 1). However, § 1319a ABGB does not apply to contractual duties to safeguard the public in general, e.g. the duty of care of the organizer to the participants of a skiing race: OGH 22 June 1993, *ZfRV* 1994 pp. 249, 253.

[1405] Toll roads are subject to a contractual liability regime (see e.g. OGH 9 Nov. 1978, *ÖJZ* 1979 p. 185 [EvBl 61]; and OGH 26 Mar. 1981, *ZVR* 1982/193) to which § 1319a ABGB does not apply (OGH 22 June 1993 [fn. 1404 above]; OGH 7 June 1978, *JBl* 1979 p. 433; OGH 5 Nov. 1980, SZ 53/143). [1406] OGH 15 Apr. 1993, *ÖJZ* 1994 p. 50 (*EvBl* 8).

[1407] OGH 8 July 1986, SZ 59/121, pp. 616, 620. Also OGH 31 Mar. 1970, *ÖJZ* 1970 p. 517 (*EvBl* 294). [1408] OGH 10 Apr. 1957, SZ 30/22, pp. 82, 84.

[1409] Yet only Spanish legislation has a specific provision on liability for collapsing trees near thoroughfares (Art. 1908 no. 3 Span. Cc). Under Art. 1908 no. 3 Span. Cc, liability is

liability is imposed for trees, it is consistent to impose it also for roads.[1410]

f. Persons Who Are Liable and Those Who Are Protected

234 The French *Code civil* is unambiguous about who is responsible for damage caused by a collapsing building: only the owner. Not even the *gardien* is liable unless he is the owner. Although this principle no longer fits seamlessly into the French law of delict, it still finds unconditional support from the French courts.[1411] If there are several owners they are jointly and severally liable.[1412] The liability of an owner ends when ownership is passed. Only the owner at the time of the accident is liable.[1413] The same position applies in Belgium,[1414] Italy,[1415] and Spain,[1416] albeit not uncontroversially: some commentators would also like the usufructuary to be strictly liable.[1417]

strict, and also applies if a branch breaks off a tree (TS 28 Mar. 1994, *RAJ* 1994 no. 2526 p. 3423). Many other laws achieve the same result using either their *custodia* liability (Cass. 26 Feb. 1994, n. 1947, *Giust.Civ.Mass.* 1994 no. 1947 p. 217; Cass. 31 Mar. 1971, n. 1641, *Rep.gen.* 1971 col. 3663 no. 167 [application of Art. 2051 Ital. Cc]; RC 30 May 1989, *CJ* XIV [1989–3] p. 74), or *gardien* liability (Cass.civ. 5 May 1993, *Gaz.Pal.* 1993 *pan.* 255; Cass. 27 Nov. 1969, *Pas. belge* 1970, I, 277. For further Belgian judgments, also on the prerequisite of *vice inhérent à la nature de la chose,* see Vandenberghe/Van Quickenborne/Geelen/De Coster, *TPR* 1987 pp. 1255, 1400–1402). In The Netherlands (*Parlementaire Geschiedenis,* vol. vi, p. 753 and ibid. [Inv.], p. 1373). In Greece: e.g. Deliyannis/Kornilakis, *Eidiko Enochiko Dikaio,* vol. iii, pp. 211–215). In Germany liability for trees comes under general liability for fault (e.g. LG Frankfurt 12 Nov. 1986, *NJW-RR* 1987 p. 795). It was such tree cases which paved the way for liability for breach of general duties of care: see no. 104 above.

[1410] Despite such discrepancies, § 1319a ABGB is not unconstitutional: VfGH 1 Mar. 1978, *JBl* 1979 p. 142.

[1411] Cass.civ. 30 Nov. 1988, *Sem.Jur.* 1989, II, 21319. Furthermore, Arts. 1384 I and 1386 are mutually exclusive in cases where the owner is the *gardien:* Cass.civ. 12 July 1966, *D.* 1966 *Jur.* 632. Likewise, tenant and usufructuary are not liable under Arts. 1386, 1384 I Cc for collapsed buildings: Versailles 18 Apr. 1984, *Gaz.Pal.* 1985 *Somm.* 318. Also Mons 13 Nov. 1992, *RGAR* 1994 no. 12391 on *succession vacante.*

[1412] Paris 28 Sep. 1990, *Gaz.Pal.* 1991 *Somm.* 232.

[1413] E.g. Cass.civ. 3 Mar. 1964, *D.* 1964 *Jur.* 245: the defendant buyer bought the house at an auction which had taken place at the house. When people moved into the sitting room, where furniture was to be auctioned, the floor collapsed. The defendant was found liable.

[1414] Ghent 16 Nov. 1993, *RW* 1994–95 no. 1084; Cornelis, *Responsabilité extra-contractuelle,* no. 410; Vandenberghe *et al.* (fn. 1409 above) no. 106.

[1415] For more detail see Cendon (-Bussani), *Responsabilità civile,* pp. 597–599; and de Cupis, *Il danno,* vol. ii, 3rd edn., p. 205. However, the tenant may sometimes (see fn. 1375 above) be liable under Art. 2051 Cc (Cass. 10 Feb. 1994, n. 1364, *Giust.civ.Mass.* 1994 no. 1364 p. 138). He may also be liable under Art. 2043 Cc if he knew, but failed to inform the owner, of the defect: Cass. 29 Jan. 1981, n. 693, *Riv.Dir.Com.* 1982, II, p. 47; Franzoni, *Fatti illeciti,* Art. 2053 Cc p. 627. [1416] Díez-Picazo/Gullón, *Sistema,* vol. ii, 6th edn., p. 633.

[1417] In favour in Spain: Santos Briz, *Responsabilidad civil,* vol. ii, 6th edn., pp. 734–735; against: Díez-Picazo/Gullón loc. cit. For Italy: Bussani (fn. 1415 above). However, in accordance with Art. 1523 Ital. Cc it should be apparent that in cases of conditional sale with reservation of ownership in favour of the seller until payment of the purchase price, which in Italy is possible for premises, liability under Art. 2053 Cc passes to the buyer at completion.

The other legal systems, unlike those mentioned above, often focus on the *Eigenbesitzer*: the person who 'possesses a thing as if it belonged to him' (§ 872 BGB) even if he is not the owner. Only § 1919 ABGB still speaks of the 'possessor': anyone 'who is able to take the measures necessary to prevent the danger, and who, due to his proximity to the structure, has a duty to do so'.[1418] Thus, despite § 309 s. 2 ABGB, in Austria even a tenant can be a possessor in accordance with § 1319 ABGB.[1419] This is not so in Germany, because the BGB (§§ 836 III, 837)[1420] limits liability for buildings to the *Eigenbesitzer*. Tenants and other possessors are only liable for defective premises if they are *Eigenbesitzer* of a construction attached to the soil solely for a temporary purpose (§ 95 BGB).[1421] Greek and Portuguese law declare both the *Eigenbesitzer*[1422] and the owner liable. As for the owner, this is effectively irrelevant because he is only liable if he is in possession of the house. If the *Eigenbesitzer* and the owner are not the same person, only the former is responsible.[1423] In Portugal (Art. 492 II Cc) and Germany (§ 838 BGB) anyone contractually bound to maintain the construction is liable for presumed fault in addition to the *Eigenbesitzer*.[1424] Finally, under the new Dutch BW the burden of liability has also shifted from the owner to the *bezitter* (Art. 6:174 in conjunction with Art. 3:107 BW). However, in order to enable the victim to identify the person responsible, Art. 6:174 IV BW contains the (rebuttable) presumption that 'the person entered in the public registers as owner of the construction or the land, is . . . the possessor of the construction'.[1425] Furthermore, in accordance with Art.

[1418] Koziol, *Österr. Haftpflichtrecht*, vol. ii, 2nd edn., p. 399 with Austrian citations. The 'possessor' in § 1319 ABGB corresponds with the 'keeper': OGH 8 July 1986, SZ 59/121, pp. 616, 621.

[1419] OGH 7 Feb. 1968, *ÖJZ* 1968 p. 322 (*EvBl* 192): the tenant of a flat is the 'possessor' in accordance with § 1319 ABGB; therefore he must compensate for damage caused by a window pane falling to the ground.

[1420] Even liability under § 837 BGB (possession of buildings or structures on the premises of another in the exercise of a right) requires *Eigenbesitz*: RG 28 Oct. 1915, *JW* 1916 pp. 39, 40.

[1421] E.g. BGH 5 Oct. 1971, *NJW* 1971 p. 2308. Austrian courts go even further: OGH 10 Apr. 1957, SZ 30/22.

[1422] The 'possessor' under Arts. 925 Greek Cc, 492 Port. Cc is always the *Eigenbesitzer*: Arts. 974 Greek Cc, 1251 Port. Cc.

[1423] For the prevailing opinion see Deliyannis/Kornilakis, *Eidiko Enochiko Dikaio*, vol. iii, p. 213; Georgiades/Stathopoulos (-Vosinakis), *Greek Cc*, vol. iv, Art. 925 no. 9; Balis, *Genikai Archai tou Astikou Dikaiou*, 8th edn., p. 453; Kavkas/Kavkas, *Enochikon Dikaion*, vol. ii, 6th edn., p. 864. *Contra*: Filios, *Enochiko Dikaio*, vol. ii (2), 3rd edn., pp. 147–148. Whether liability under Art. 925 Greek Cc ought to be applied to the usufructuary instead of the owner is unclear.

[1424] Art. 492 II Port. Cc ('*em lugar do proprietário ou possuidor*') is understood to impose liability exclusively on the person obliged to maintain the structure, but only if the owner/possessor is not at fault. If the latter cannot exonerate himself, they are jointly and severally liable: Neto/Martins, *Código civil*, 7th edn., Art. 492 n. 1.

[1425] See Bloembergen (-Oldenhuis), *Onrechtmatige daad*, vol. ii, Art. 174 n. 8; *Parlementaire Geschiedenis*, vol. vi, p. 753. The *Amercentrale* judgment of HR 13 June 1975, *NedJur* 1975 no. 509 p. 1619 clearly influenced this rule, which still bears resemblances to the French system.

6:181 BW, a building used to carry out a trade or business is the responsibility of the proprietor of the business: he replaces the *bezitter* for both keeper's liability[1426] and liability for structures.[1427]

236 Finally, as for the extent of protection of liability for buildings, all European systems agree on what has been proven to be the most relevant issue in practice. If not barred by the system of *non-cumul des responsabilités*, a tenant can also sue the owner.[1428] Moreover, liability for structures also protects the employees of owner and possessor alike.[1429] However, the German *Bundesgerichtshof* rightly exempts both the principals and the servants of demolition firms from the scope of § 836 BGB. When such firms carry out their work and an employee is injured, this is not the responsibility of the owner of the premises.[1430]

[1426] See no. 214 above.

[1427] E.g. Hof Amsterdam 5 Dec. 1991 (fn. 1395 above): under the NBW the *exploitant* of the swimming pool would be liable.

[1428] For Italy: Cass 7 Oct. 1967, n. 2335, *Resp.Civ. e Prev.* 1968 p. 452 (however, in a case concerning a burst water pipe, Cass. 6 Feb. 1987, n. 1202, *Giur.it.* 1989, I, 1, 206 employed only contract law). For Greece: CFI Athens 30/1980, Arm 35 (1981) p. 471; CA Athens 4268/1956, *NoB* 5 (1957) p. 323. For Germany see BGH 23 Jan. 1951, *NJW* 1951 p. 229. However, for a special case concerning a burst pipe see Rb. Maastricht 1 Dec. 1994, *NedJur* (Kort) no. 26 p. 41: a water pipe was rusted through at a point outside the water meter, and was therefore the responsibility of the supplier. The owner of the flat was refused damages under Art. 6:174 II BW, because as against the owner, the 'administrator of the pipe' (*de leidingsbeheerder*) was liable only for fault.

[1429] OGH 30 July 1963, SZ 36/103: during a break a cook's apprentice fell from a balcony from which he was throwing snowballs when its railing collapsed: not an injury at work).

[1430] BGH 29 Sep. 1978, *NJW* 1979 pp. 309, 310.

Part 3: Scandinavian Liability Laws and the Common Law of Torts

I. THE BASES OF LIABILITY FOR INDIVIDUAL WRONGFUL CONDUCT

Bibliography: Allen, 'Liability for References: The House of Lords and *Spring* v. *Guardian Assurance*', 58 (1995) *MLR* 553–560; Andresen, 'Haftung ohne Verschulden im nordischen, insbesondere norwegischen Recht', *RabelsZ* 27 (1962) pp. 245–262; v. Bar, 'Negligence, Eigentumsverletzung und reiner Vermögensschaden. Zu den Grenzen der Fahrlässigkeitshaftung für reine Vermögensschäden in der neueren Entwicklung des Common Law', *RabelsZ* 56 (1992) pp. 410–442; id., 'Unentgeltliche Investitionsempfehlungen im Wandel der Wirtschaftsverfassungen Deutschlands und Englands', *RabelsZ* 44 (1980) pp. 455–486; id., 'Das "Trennungsprinzip" und die Geschichte des Wandels der Haftpflichtversicherung', *AcP* 181 (1981) pp. 289–327; id., 'Besprechung von Karollus, Funktion und Dogmatik der Haftung aus Schutzgesetzverletzung', *AcP* 192 (1992) pp. 441–445; id., 'Der Einfluß des Verfassungsrechts auf die westeuropäischen Deliktsrechte', *RabelsZ* 59 (1995) pp. 203–229; Bates, 'The Contemporary Use of Legislative History in the United Kingdom', 54 (1995) *CLJ* 127–152; Beaton, *Scots Law Terms and Expressions* (Edinburgh 1982); Bengtsson, 'Torts and Insurance', in: Strömholm (ed.), *An Introduction to Swedish Law* (Stockholm 1988) pp. 297–318; id., 'Svensk rättspraxis: Skadestånd utom kontraktsförhållanden 1976–1979', *SJT* 1981 pp. 519–537; Bird, 'Liability for Defective Products Act 1991', *ILT* 1992 pp. 185–187; Birks, *An Introduction to the Law of Restitution* (Oxford 1990); Björne, *Nordische Rechtssysteme* (Ebelsbach 1987); Blackie, 'Liability as Occupier to User of a Right of Way', *SLT* 1994 pp. 349–352; Bloth, 'Ausdehnung und Verschärfung der Produkthaftung in Schweden', *PHI* 1987 pp. 209–216; Cooke, 'A Development in the Tort of Private Nuisance', 57 (1994) *MLR* 289–296; Cornelius, *Der Schutz des Forderungsinhabers gegenüber Dritten im nordischen und deutschen Recht* (Pfaffenweiler 1985); Cross, 'Does Only the Careless Polluter Pay? A Fresh Examination of the Nature of Private Nuisance', 111 (1995) *LQR* 445–474; Cullen, 'The Liability of the Good Samaritan', *Jur. Rev.* 1995 pp. 20–27; Dahl, *Geschichte der dänischen Rechtswissenschaft in ihren Grundzügen* (Leipzig 1940; trans. K. Haft and H. Henningsen); von Eyben, 'Standardized or Individual Assessment of Damages for Personal Injury and for Loss of Supporter. Some Reflections

259

on the Danish Tort Liability Act', *Scan.Stud.L.* 29 (1985) pp. 49–78; Ferguson, 'Liability in Negligence for Trespassing Criminals', *SLT* 1987 pp. 233–236; Ferrari, 'Produkthaftung und Negligence—Sechzig Jahre *Donoghue v. Stevenson*', *ZEuP* 1993 pp. 354–359; Ford, 'Squaring Analogy with Principle or Vice Versa', 53 (1994) *CLJ* 14–16; Gearty, 'The Place of Private Nuisance in a Modern Law of Torts', 48 (1989) *CLJ* 214–242; Gordley, 'Common law and civil law: eine überholte Unterscheidung', *ZEuP* 1993 pp. 498–518; Hedman, *Ansvar och ersättning vid medicinsk verksamhet* (Stockholm 1984); Hellner, 'Entwicklungslinien im schwedischen Haftpflichtrecht', in: *FS Sieg* (Karlsruhe 1976) pp. 155–169; id., *Haftungsersetzung durch Versicherungsschutz* (Frankfurt/Main 1980) pp. 24–39; id., 'Staatshaftung und Schutznorm im schwedischen Recht', in: *25 Jahre Karlsruher Forum* (1983) pp. 38–40; id., 'The New Swedish Tort Liability Act', *AmJCompL* 22 (1974) pp. 1–16; id., *Speciell avtalsrätt II, 2 häftet: Särskilda avtal* (2nd edn. Stockholm 1993); id., '"Geborgenheitsversicherung"—eine neue Stufe in der Entwicklung des Arbeitsunfallschutzes in Schweden', in: *FS Klingmüller* (Karlsruhe 1974) pp. 159–171; id., 'Sweden', in: Deutsch/Schreiber (ed.), *Medical Responsibility in Western Europe* (Berlin 1985) pp. 683–728; Henrÿ/Pohl, 'Das neue finnische Produkthaftungsgesetz', *PHI* 1991 pp. 42–45; Hertzberg, *Gewährleistung, Produzentenhaftung und Prozeßrecht in Finnland* (Freiburg 1990); Heuston/Buckley, 'The Return of *Rylands v. Fletcher*', 110 (1994) *LQR* 506–509; Hoffmann, '*Rookes v. Barnard*', 81 (1965) *LQR* 116–141; Hopkins, 'Liability for Indolence', 53 (1994) *CLJ* 428–430; Hudson, 'Crime, Tort and Reparation: A common solution', *SLT* 1992 pp. 203–210; Inger, *Svensk rättshistoria* (3rd edn. Lund/Uppsala 1986); Jackman, 'Restitution for Wrongs', 48 (1989) *CLJ* 302–321; Jokela, 'Finland', *IntEncCompL* I, F-33 (1972); Jørgensen, 'Tort Law and Development', *Scan.-Stud.L.* 32 (1988) pp. 69–81; id., 'Die skandinavische Lehre der Vertragsverletzung', in: *FS Larenz* (Munich 1973) pp. 549–573; id., 'Dänische Beiträge zum Karlsruher Forum 1970–1989' (collection of unpublished essays; available at the Law Library of the University of Aarhus); id., 'Ersatz und Versicherung', *VersR* 1970 pp. 193–208; Karollus, *Funktion und Dogmatik der Haftung aus Schutzgesetzverletzung. Zugleich ein Beitrag zum Deliktssystem des AGBG und zur Haftung für casus mixtus* (Vienna 1992); Kelly/Hogan/White, *The Irish Constitution* (Dublin 1994); Kleineman, *Ren förmögenhetsskada* (Stockholm 1987); Korkisch, *Einführung in das Privatrecht der nordischen Länder*, vol. i (Darmstadt 1977); Kruse, *A Nordic Draft Code. A Draft Code for Denmark, Finland, Iceland, Norway and Sweden* (Copenhagen 1963; trans. E. Giersing); Lauridsen, '*Nunc redeam ad meum*—Die Entwicklung der Pressefreiheit und des Persönlichkeitsrechts im dänischen Recht', in: *FS Werner Lorenz* (Tübingen 1991) pp. 677–688; Logie, 'Special Relationships, Reasonable Foreseeability and Distinct Probabilities: The duty to prevent damage to the property of others', *Jur. Rev.* 1988 pp. 77–90; Maguire, 'The Damages (Scotland) Act 1993', *SLT* 1993 pp. 245–249; Markesinis, 'Caparo & Murphy: How two recent decisions of the House of Lords look from the other side of the Channel', *ERPL* 1 (1993) pp. 201–214; id., 'A Matter of Style', 110 [1994] *LQR* 607–628; Markesinis/v. Bar, *Richterliche Rechtspolitik im Haftungsrecht* (Tübingen 1981); Markesinis/ Deakin, 'The Random Element of their Lordships' Infallible Judgment: An Economic and Comparative Analysis of the Tort of Negligence from *Anns* to *Murphy'*, 55 (1992) *MLR* 619–646; McGregor, *Contract Code drawn up on behalf of the English Law Commission* (Milan 1993); Medeen, 'Ersättning i stöd av patientskadelagen och annan lagstiftning tillämplig på hälso-och sjukvården', *JFT* 1994 pp. 38–49; Meierhans, 'Der immer noch nicht bewältigte Reflexschaden. Rechtsvergleichende Anregungen zu mehr Pragmatismus aus dem französischen und dem norwegischen Recht', *recht* 1994 pp. 202–216; Miranda, *'The Negligence Saga*: Irragionevolezza ed ingiustizia del danno nel risarcimento delle *pure economic losses'*, *Riv.Dir.Civ.* 1992 pp. 387–442; Morell, 'Der *Cambridge Water*-Fall: Konsequenzen für Betreiber und Versicherer', *PHI* 1994 pp. 92–94; Mullender, 'Privacy in New Zealand: Are there lessons to be learned?', 53 (1994) *CLJ* 11–14; Newark, 'The Boundaries of Nuisance', 65 (1949) *LQR* 480–490; Nordenson, 'Lagrådsremiss av förslag till skadeståndslag. Riktlinjer för skadeståndsrätten', *SJT* 1971 pp. 363–371; O'Higgins, 'Strict Liability for Supermarket Slippage Cases?', *ILT* 1991 pp. 134–138; O'Sullivan, 'Auditor's Negligence: Getting the balance right', 54 (1995) *CLJ* 25–27; Paanila, 'Das finnische Produkthaftungsgesetz', *PHI* 1991 pp. 560–565; Pedersen/Pontoppidan/Hermann, 'Kommentarer til højesteretsdomme afsagt i tiden oktober-november 1989', *UfR* 1990 B pp. 241–252; Poll, *Die Haftung der freien Berufe zwischen standesrechtlicher Privilegierung und europäischer Orientierung* (Paderborn 1994); Pöxhönen, *An Introduction to Finnish Law* (Paris 1993); Prescott, *'Kaye v. Robertson:* A reply', 54 (1991) *MLR* 451–456; Quill, 'Defective Buildings and the Limitation of Actions', *ILT* 1992 pp. 202–204; Rogers, 'Liability for Environmental Pollution in the Common Law: The *Cambridge Water* case', *A&V* 1994 pp. 64–69; Radau, 'Gefährdungshaftung und Haftungsersetzung durch Versicherungsschutz—das deutsche Arzneimittelgesetz und die schwedische Arzneimittelversicherung', *VersR* 1991 pp. 387–393; id., *Ersetzung der Arzthaftung durch Versicherungsschutz. Eine Untersuchung am Beispiel der Patientenunfallversicherung in Schweden* (Karlsruhe 1993); Rudden, 'Torticles', *Tul.Civ.Law Forum* 6/7 (1991–1992) pp. 105–129; Samuelsson/Søgaard, *Rådgiveransvaret* (Rungsted Kyst 1993 with amendments 1994); Saxén, 'Finlands skadeståndslag jämförd med Sveriges', *SJT* 1977 pp. 148–153; Simpson, 'The Employment Act 1990 in Context', 54 (1991) *MLR* 418–438; Sinding, 'Grundzüge der Produkthaftung in Dänemark', *PHI* 1990 pp. 112–116; Schmidt, 'Integritätsschutz von Unternehmen nach § 823 BGB. Zum "Recht am eingerichteten und ausgeübten Gewerbebetrieb"', *JuS* 1993, pp. 985–992; Schnopfhagen, 'Produkthaftung in England', *ZfRV* 1993 pp. 62–80; Spaude, *Das dänische Rechtswesen* (Cologne *et al.* 1976); Spencer, 'Freedom to denounce your Fellow Citizens to the Police', 53 (1994) *CLJ* 433–435; id., 'Public Nuisance: A critical examination', 48 (1989) *CLJ* 55–84; Steele, 'Scepticism and the Law of Negligence', 52 (1993) *CLJ* 437–469; Stein, 'The *Actio de Effusis vel Dejectis* and the Concept of Quasi-Delict in Scots Law', *IntCompLQ* 4 (1955) pp. 356–372; Stein-Poulsen, 'Das dänische Patientenversicherungsgesetz', *VersRAI* 1995 pp. 19–25; Steininger, *Einführung in das dänische Rechtssystem* (2nd edn. Kiel 1984); Strömbäck, 'Lagrådsremiss av förslag till skadeståndslag. Lagförslagets innehåll', *SJT* 1971 pp. 371–376; Sundberg, 'Civil Law, Common Law and the Scandinavians', *Scan.Stud.L.* 13 (1969) pp. 179–205; Tettenborn, 'Damages in Conversion: the exception or the anomaly?', 52 (1993) *CLJ* 128–147; id., 'Burdens on Personal Property and the Economic Torts', 52 (1993) *CLJ* 382–384; Thomson, 'Delictual Liability for Pure Economic Loss: Recent developments', *SLT* 1995 pp. 135–145; Trindade, 'Some Curiosities of Negligent Trespass to the Person—A Comparative Study', 20 (1971) *IntCompLQ* 706–731; Trolle, 'Außervertraglicher Schadensersatz nach dänischer Lehre', *RabelsZ* 7 (1993) pp. 772–790; Uniken Venema, *Van Common Law en Civil Law, Inleiding tot het Anglo-Amerikaanse recht, in vergelijking met het Nederlande* (Zwolle 1971); Ussing, 'The Scandinavian Law of Torts: Impact of Insurance on Tort Law', *AmJCompL* 1 (1952) pp. 359–372; Weir, 'Chaos or Cosmos? Rookes, Stratford and the Economic Torts', 23 (1964) *CLJ* 225–233; id., 'The Case of the Careless Referee', 52 (1993) *CLJ* 376–379; id., 'Deliktische Haftung für Schäden an benachbarten Gründstücken', *ZEuP* 1995 pp. 840–845; White/Willock, *The Scottish Legal System* (Edinburgh 1993); Wilkinson, '*Cambridge Water Company* v. *Eastern Counties Leather PLC*: Diluting liability for continuing escapes', 57 (1994) *MLR* 799–811; Zimmermann, 'Der europäische Charakter des englischen Rechts. Historische Verbindungen zwischen civil law und common law', *ZEuP* 1993 pp. 4–51.

1. TORT AND THE LAW OF DAMAGES IN STATUTE AND JUDICIAL DECISIONS

237 Efforts to create a unified Nordic Civil Code faltered after the end of the Second World War. Had this code been realized along the lines of the 1962 second edition of Kruse's 1948 work, it would have been the only code whose first book began with the law of delict.[1] After the draft code was abandoned, a number of special *statutes on the law of damages* were rapidly adopted in the Scandinavian countries. Norway (which recently voted against entry to the EU and will therefore be treated in lesser detail) began this process with its Act no. 26 of 13 June 1969.[2] Sweden and Finland followed with their Acts on the law of damages of 2 June 1972[3] and 31 May 1974[4] respectively. Denmark followed suit some ten years later with Act no. 228 of 23 May 1984 'on the duty to pay damages'.[5] The concept of incorporating issues of liability within a statute on the law of damages is found not only in the Scandinavian countries but also in the British Isles.[6] In its original form the Irish Civil Liability Act dates from 1961[7] and the Damages (Scotland) Act from 1976.[8] The

---

[1] Fr. Vinding Kruse, *A Nordic Draft Code* (trans. Copenhagen 1963). Kruse wanted to bring the law of obligations into the first two chapters ('The Rights and their Protection' and 'Special Rules for Liability and General Rules governing Burden of Proof') of the first book ('General Part'). He had in mind 21 comprehensive paragraphs, which in many ways could have been shortened. The same applies to the basic norm of § 2 I, which Kruse introduced on p. 1 as follows: 'Any person who by an act or other conduct causes damage to some other person shall be liable for damages on the following conditions: *if* such act or conduct by a conscientious person solicitous about the welfare of his neighbour might be expected to cause damage so that he would either have omitted it or taken special measures; *if* the damage is inflicted on a right . . .; *if* the act or conduct must be regarded as harmful to the community either in pursuance of law or according to the requirements in the sphere of life concerned; and *if* it is expedient to prevent and remedy such act through damages' (emphasis in the original). On the early Nordic codes see Jokela, *IntEncCompL* I, F-38—F-39, and on the post-war efforts towards a code: Anders Vinding Kruse, *Erstatnings-retten*, 5th edn., p. 14.

[2] *Lov om skadeserstatning* (*Skadeerstatningsloven* = Skl.) (*Norsk Lovtidend* II 1969 p. 419), amended by statute on 25 May 1973, no. 26 (*Norsk Lovtidend* I 1973 p. 579), and again on 10 June 1977, no. 73 (*Norsk Lovtidend* I 1977 p. 572), and yet again on 22 May 1992, no. 49 (*Norsk Lovtidend* I 1992 p. 368).

[3] *Skadeståndslag* (SKL), SFS 1972: 207 as amended by SFS 1975: 404, 1975: 1411, 1977: 272, 1980: 1023, 1986: 445, 1986: 650, 1989: 926, 1990: 153 and 1991: 1555. On the preparatory work see Nordenson, *SJT* 1971 pp. 363–371; Strömbäck, *SJT* 1971 pp. 371–376.

[4] *Skadeståndslag* (SKL), FFS 1974 no. 412 pp. 765; amended by statutes of *inter alia* 17 Nov. 1978, FFS 1978 no. 857 pp. 1876 and of 23 Mar. 1979, FFS 1979 no. 373 p. 790. A detailed comparison of the Finnish and Swedish Acts on damages is to be found in Saxén, *SJT* 1977, pp. 148–153.

[5] *Lov no. 228 om erstatningsansvar* (*Erstatningsansvarsloven* = EAL) (*Lovtidende* A 1984 p. 742), proclamation no. 599 of 8 Sep. 1986 (*Lovtidende* A 1986 p. 2188), amended by statute no. 196 of 29 March 1989 (*Lovtidende* A 1989 p. 676) and statute no. 389 of 7 June 1989 (*Lovtidende* A 1989 p. 1304).

[6] No serious consideration not been given in the British Isles to codifying civil law, including the law of obligations. In recent times the English Law Commission began a project to codify contract law, and the Scottish Law Commission showed interest in this. The project has been halted (cf. Tunc, *Rev.int.dr.comp.* 1984 p. 302); its spiritual father, McGregor, even had to publish his proposal in Italy! (Above bibliography before no. 237).

[7] Civil Liability Act 1961 (c. 41), amended by the Civil Liability (Amendment) Act 1964 (c. 17).

[8] Damages (Scotland) Act 1976 (c. 13) and Damages (Scotland) Act 1993 (c. 5); on the more recent of the two see Maguire, *SLT* 1993 pp. 245–249.

latter has since been ammended. The English Act which comes closest in terms of its content is the Fatal Accidents Act 1976 which draws heavily from sec. 1 of the Law Reform (Miscellaneous Provisions) Act 1934.[9]

238 It would be a mistake to think that all the essentials of a codified system are found in each of these statutes simply because their names are lengthy and somewhat similar. In fact this can only be said (and then with qualifications[10]) of the Swedish and Finnish statutes on the law of damages. Only these two countries develop their law of tort according to the pattern of continental codes, giving pride of place to the basic principle of liability for tort. By contrast, all other statutes are primarily (or exclusively) concerned with the *law of damages*, i.e. the legal consequences of liability. The first paragraph of the 1984 Danish EAL is essentially concerned with the quantum of damages in personal injury cases, supplemented in § 12 with a claim for the loss of a 'provider', similar to Art. 45 Swiss OR. The rules setting out the conditions for liability in cases involving damage to tangible property and economic loss (§ 19 EAL) are found in the second section. § 19 I is of considerable importance. This provides that 'where (either) damage to property or a factory being put out of production is covered by insurance . . . there is no duty to pay damages'.[11] The reponsibility here is to insure oneself and one's property rather than relying on a third party to compensate. As well as issues of joint and several liability (§§ 23, 25) the third section covers the general principle of the reduction of liability for minor fault (§ 24), which appears throughout Scandinavia,[12] and the rule on damage to reputation (§ 26). All questions of the *basis* of liability are specifically excluded. They are subject to the '*culpa* rule' of customary law and the further exceptions provided by Danish judicial decisions.

239 The same concept, with some exceptions, is found in Scotland and Ireland. The *Irish* Civil Liability Act adopts and refines the rule in accordance with sec. 1 of the English Law Reform (Miscellaneous Provisions) Act 1934, that 'on the death of a person . . . all causes of action . . . vested in him shall survive for the benefit of his estate' (sec. 7[1]). The concluding Part Three of the Act governs joint and several liability (sec. 12) of intervening third parties and participants (sec. 11), which, far from being restricted to

---

[9] Law Reform (Miscellaneous Provisions) Act 1934 (c. 41); Fatal Accidents Act 1976 (c. 30).

[10] Neither liability for animals nor liability for buildings was covered by either statute.

[11] § 19 II EAL excludes intentional and gross negligent damage, and § 19 II 2nd alt. EAL excludes all negligently inflicted damage caused in the exercise of public or trade activities.

[12] See further Chapter 6, 2 § Swed. SKL; Chapter 2, 1 §, 2 s. Finn. SKL and § 5–2 Norweg. SKL.

personal injury,[13] concern issues of liability arising from doubts regarding causation.[14] These include rules on contributory negligence by the victim and its effect on liability (sec. 34). The Act ends with provisions on the rights of a deceased person's dependents to claim damages (sec. 48).

Whereas the Danish and the Irish statutes on the law of damages deal **240** partially with issues concerning damage to tangible objects, the Damages (Scotland) Act 1976 restricts itself to damages arising from death and bodily injury. Where an individual is responsible for the death of another he is liable to that person's relatives; their claim is dealt with by the deceased's executors (sec. 1[1]). The old claim for *assythment* by the relatives themselves could therefore be abolished (sec. 8).[15] The executor acquires 'the like rights to damages in respect of personal injuries . . . sustained by the deceased as were vested in him immediately before his death' (sec. 2). The financial (sec. 9) and non-financial (sec. 9A) losses brought about by reduced life expectancy are part of the obligations owed to an injured person. Some basis of liability is a prerequisite (sec. 1[1]), though this is not defined. As stated, the Act concerns not the law of delict but the law of damages.

Even this law of delict[16] is not to be seen as pure common law (as **241** opposed to statutory law). Not only in Denmark is such law subject to a variety of further statutory rules; the same can also be said of England, Ireland, and Scotland.[17] Such rules concern not only areas of modern

---

[13] Cf. *Riordan's Travel Ltd. and Riordan's Shipping Ltd.* v. *Acres and Co. Ltd., G. & T. Crampton Ltd. and Matthew O'Dowd Ltd.* [1979] ILRM 3, 7 (McWilliam, J) (HC): a travel agency was for 18 months unable to conduct its business in its office because mistakes were made whilst taking down the adjacent building; according to sec. 11 Civil Liability Act 1961, the lessor, building contractor, and architect were all jointly liable.

[14] See nos. 54–60 above.   [15] See Walker, *Delict*, 2nd edn., p. 23.

[16] The expression *law of delict* is found in Scotland but not in England. In Scotland it is used above all in support of the interpretation that 'common law nomenclature has been to some extent adopted in Scotland, but without the procedural connotations of the common law, and these names (i.e. of the individual *torts*) are in Scotland no more than convenient titles for sets of circumstances giving rise to liability under one or other of the general principles of delictual liability accepted in Scots law' (Walker loc. cit. p. 31).

[17] The question whether a statute of the London Parliament applies in Scotland is, as a matter of principle, answered in the affirmative (cf. on this point Walker, *Principles*, vol. i, 4th edn., p. 11 and Gloag/Henderson [-Wilkinson/Wilson], *Introduction*, 9th edn., pp. 2–3). The express reference to the fact that the same cannot be said of the Act applying to *Ireland* is pointed to as concrete affirmation of this rule. Where an Act is applicable only in Scotland then its title points to this: e.g. Damages (Scotland) Act. The basic rule that statutes apply to Scotland can be departed from either expressly or by implication. The latter is the case where the matter concerns an Act to amend an Act intended to apply to England alone, or where the Act uses terminology used in England and not in Scotland (e.g. libel and/or slander instead of defamation). Where in such a case it does apply to Scotland (i.e. contrary to the rule) then it has to be arranged in its own particular way. An example is found in sec. 14 Defamation Act 1952 (following fn.) where it expressly states that in Scotland the words libel and/or slander are to be replaced by the word defamation. According to this section a range of provisions of the Defamation Act 1952 are not applicable in Scotland.

liability law which are regarded on the continent as not being worthy of codification, e.g. traffic, product, and environmental law. Large areas of law are governed by statute, including traditional areas of law such as defamation[18] (*injuria verbis* in contrast to *injuria realis*[19]), liability for damage caused by animals,[20] and liability for premises,[21] as well as laws of limitation.[22] So on one hand it is right to say that both codified and uncodified Europe liability systems are moving away from their origins.[23] English common law (the term 'common law' being used here as the opposite of continental 'civil law') acquires ever stronger characteristics of statute-based law, whilst European liability law increasingly resembles a system of jurisprudence based on judges' decisions.[24] It is, however, still impossible for English, Irish, and Scottish tort law to develop from its statutory sources. In the minds of lawyers, statutes remain of secondary importance, despite their number. It is not the statute but the theory of precedent and the deeply ingrained conviction that each case is decided on its own facts, instead of being subordinate to a general theory, which forms the basis of the law of torts.[25] It is this which gives rise to the importance of careful analysis of

---

[18] In this area there is a multitude of statutes. For England see: Libel Act 1843 (c. 96); Libel Act 1845 (c. 75); Law of Libel Amendment Act 1888 (c. 64); Slander of Women Act 1891 (c. 51); Defamation Act 1952 (c. 66); Theatres Act (c. 54); Cable and Broadcasting Act 1984 (c. 46). For Ireland see: Defamation Act 1961 (Number 40 of 1961). For Scotland see the references in fn. 17.

[19] For more on the origin of this distinction, which goes back to Hugo Grotius, see Walker, *Delict*, 2nd edn., p. 21.

[20] *England*: Riding Establishment Act 1964 (c. 70); Animals Act 1971 (c. 22); Guard Dogs Act 1975 (c. 50); Dangerous Wild Animals Act 1976 (c. 38); and Dangerous Dogs Act 1991 (c. 65) (the last, however, is only concerned with criminal responsibility). *Ireland*: Animals Act 1985 (Number 11 of 1985) (sec. 3 loc. cit. introduced a new version of sec. 1 Dogs Act 1906 [c. 32]) and Control of Dogs Act 1986 (Number 32 of 1986) which abolished sec. 3 Animals Act 1985 as well as the entire Dogs Act 1906. *Scotland*: Animals (Scotland) Act 1987 (c. 9).

[21] *England*: Occupiers' Liability Act 1957 (c. 31); Defective Premises Act 1972 (c. 35); Occupiers' Liability Act 1984 (c. 3); and Building Act 1984 (c. 55). *Scotland*: Occupiers' Liability (Scotland) Act 1960 (c. 30).

[22] *England*: Limitation Act 1980 (c. 58). *Ireland*: Statute of Limitations 1957 (Number 6 of 1957); Statute of Limitations (Amendment) Act 1991 (Number 18 of 1991). *Scotland*: Prescription and Limitation (Scotland) Act 1973 (c. 52).

[23] The same applies also to the sources of the law. For example, English courts are obliged, when doubt is raised as to the literal meaning of statutory provision, to give effect to the intention of the legislature, which is often ascertained by reference to *Hansard*: (*Pepper* v. *Hart* [1993] 1 All ER 42. On this area generally see Bates (1995) 54 *CLJ* 127–152; cf. *Pickstone* v. *Freemans PLC* [1988] 2 All ER 803). The House of Lords has also, in tort law, made use of the Practice Statement [1966] 1 WLR 1234 to depart from one of its previous decisions without the interference of the legislature: *Murphy* v. *Brentwood District Council* [1991] 1 AC 398 overruling *Anns* v. *Merton London Borough Council* [1978] AC 728 = [1977] 2 WLR 1024.

[24] Zimmermann, *ZEuP* 1993 pp. 4, 7. Cf. also Gordley, *ZEuP* 1993 pp. 498–518.

[25] The tension between these two principles is found at the heart of the decision in *Murphy* (fn. 23), a decision which criticized the two-stage test in *Anns* (loc. cit. p. 1032 *per* Lord Wilberforce). Cf. v. Bar's German view in *RabelsZ* 56 (1992) p. 410, pp. 415–417. Lord

the factual content of cases and to the art[26] of determining the *ratio decidendi* of cases. In principle, Parliament intervenes only where the common law is incapable of providing a cure. Parliament does not wish to intervene systematically[27] but only where it is deemed necessary to correct erroneous developments. No other European country has as many statutes[28] imposing liability as England, yet, as in Ireland and Scotland, its non-contractual liability law remains essentially judge-made. For this reason the European Court of Human Rights once said with regard to Art. 10 II ECHR[29] that the creations of the common law are covered by the term 'statute' in the sense of the provision. Any other interpretation would not only deprive a common law country, party to the Convention, of the protection of Art. 10, but would also 'affect the roots of the legal system of such a country'.[30]

In the hierarchy of legal sources statute stands above the decisions of **242** judges, but nevertheless often restricts itself to a type of 'surgical' intervention. Section 5 of the Defamation Act 1952[31] is an example of this. Prior to this Act, all the factual assertions made by the defendant in the

---

Reid in *Dorset Yacht Co. Ltd.* v. *Home Office* [1970] AC 1004, 1026–1027 had already observed 'a steady trend towards regarding the law of negligence as depending on principle', by which he meant 'that, when a new point emerges, one should ask not whether it is covered by authority but whether recognized principles apply to it'.

[26] Markesinis, 110 [1994] *LQR* 607, 617, 628.

[27] See *Racz* v. *Home Office* [1994] 2 AC 45: the plaintiff claimed to have been beaten by prison warders. Besides his claims in assault, battery, and negligence, he also brought an action in the tort of misfeasance in a public office. This is one of a group of torts with intentional damage as one of its constituent elements where exemplary damages are being claimed. Cf. *Bennet* v. *Commissioner of Police of the Metropolis and Others* [1995] 1 WLR 488 and *Dunlop* v. *Woollahra Municipal Council* [1982] AC 158, 172 F (*per* Lord Diplock). See also *Bourgoin SA* v. *Ministry of Agriculture* [1986] 1 QB 716 CA). The plaintiff in *Racz* wished his case to be tried before a jury. Under sec. 69(1) Supreme Court Act 1981 (c. 54) 'trial by jury' can only be granted in civil cases for actions in fraud, libel, slander, malicious prosecution, or false imprisonment. Having been isolated in a strip cell he argued that his case was akin to false imprisonment. That this was accepted was, however, insufficient for him to succeed. Lord Jauncey emphasized that there was no common factor linking the causes of action where trial by jury is granted. Legal history, and not logic, was the decisive factor here.

[28] An assertion such as this is naturally difficult to prove; it is based upon the country-by-country series in the v. Bar (ed.) collection, *DeliktsR in Europa*. The report which covers England and Wales (Shaw) lists 62 specific statutes having implications for the law of tort in its jurisdiction. The report does not claim to be exhaustive!

[29] The provision concerns restrictions on freedom of expression 'intended by statute'.

[30] ECHR 26 Apr. 1979 (*Times Newspapers Ltd.* v. *United Kingdom*), EuGRZ 1979 pp. 386–387. The case concerned an injunction based upon contempt of court against a newspaper article covering the background of the Thalidomide scandal.

[31] See fn. 18 above. The text provides: 'In an action for libel and slander in respect of words containing two or more distinct charges against the plaintiff, a defence of justification shall not fail by reason only that the truth of every charge is not proved if the words not proved to be true do not materially injure the plaintiff's reputation having regard to the truth of the remaining charges.'

context of an action for *libel* or *slander* had to be proved as genuine, but since the passage of this Act it is sufficient to prove the truth of those assertions which actually injure reputation. Four years earlier the Law Reform (Personal Injuries) Act 1948[32] had abolished an antiquated rule of common law, namely the defence of common employment in the context of employers' liability (sec. 1[1] loc. cit).[33] A third example is the Occupiers' Liability (Scotland) Act 1960,[34] whose main purpose was to remove the common law classification of persons into three categories (*invitee*, *licensee*, and *trespasser*[35]) to whom the occupier of the premises could be liable according to different circumstances, and to replace this with a general duty of care which would depend upon all the circumstances of the case.[36] The English Occupiers' Liability Act 1984[37] had a similar purpose: its provisions were to replace the common law rules only insofar as the victim is not a 'visitor' (i.e. an invitee or a licensee) but a trespasser. The visitor was already protected in England by the Occupiers' Liability Act 1957,[38] so two Acts were necessary to revise the common law.[39] However, that is not the single most noteworthy aspect of these Acts. Of greater importance is the fact that the Occupiers' Liability Act 1957——although it typically restricts itself to the protection of visitors—used a statutory definition of the general duty of care derived from the tort of negligence, which for its part has for some time been harnessed to provide the defining element of English liability law.[40] Sec. 2(2) Occupiers' Liability Act 1957 reads as follows: 'The common duty of care is a duty to take such care as in all the circumstances of the case is reasonable to see that the visitor will be reasonably safe in using the premises for the purposes for which he is invited or permitted by the occcupier to be there.'

2. The Primary Elements of the Scandinavian Law of Delict

243 The law of non-contractual liability[41] in the three Scandinavian members of the EU has as its basis liability founded on individual wrongful

---

[32] C. 41.

[33] This went back to the decision in *Priestley* v. *Fowler* (1837) 3 M&W 1; 150 ER 1030 (*per* Lord Abinger) that an employer was not responsible for wrongful conduct of his employee resulting in loss and damage to fellow employees.   [34] See fn. 21.

[35] This threefold classification for England and Scotland came from *Dumbreck* v. *Addie & Sons (Collieries)* 1929 SC 51.

[36] Sec. 15(1)(1) loc. cit. See also *McGlone (Appellant)* v. *British Railways Board*, 1966 SLT 2.
[37] See fn. 21.   [38] Loc. cit.   [39] Stewart, *Casebook* p. 268.
[40] See nos. 274 ff. below.

[41] According to its wording (Chapter 1, 1 §) the Swedish statute on damages is not restricted to the field of liability outside contract; in principle the SKL applies to contract law, subject to agreement by the parties and to statutory provisions to the contrary (Hellner, *Skadeståndsrätt* 4th edn., p. 21; Bengtsson/Nordenson/Strömbäck, *Skadestånd* 3rd edn., p. 29).

behaviour. In this respect it is like the codified systems of continental Europe. Reference is made to the *culpa* rule. In Finland and Sweden this rule is primarily anchored in extensive statutory rules; in Denmark it is based on a combination of judge-made and customary law.[42]

Chapter 2, 1 §, 1 s. of the Finnish SKL provides as follows: 'Whoever causes damage to another person, whether intentionally or negligently, has to make good the damage so caused, insofar as there is nothing to the contrary in this Act.' Chapter 2, 1 § of the Swedish SKL is in the following terms: 'Whoever causes personal injury or damage to property, whether intentionally or negligently, shall make good the damage, insofar as nothing to the contrary is laid down in this Act.'

Although one may wish to see in these rules real general principles,[43] **244** such classifications should be treated with genuine caution. According to their actual wording, the distinction between unlawfulness and fault is an alien one.[44] Closer inspection reveals that the structure of Scandinavian laws of delict tends less towards the open system of the *Code civil*, and more toward the multi-layered system of the German BGB.[45] What the BGB achieves in § 823 I is achieved in *Sweden* and *Finland* by the arrangement of specific elements based upon damage to the person and damage to property. To Chapter 2, 1 § Swed. SKL, which in this

---

The matter is treated similarly in Denmark, where the EAL applies 'independently of the basis of liability' (according to the bill at the time of its introduction to Parliament: *Folketingstidende* 1984, *Tillæg* A Sp. 47–126 [120]; also Karnov [-von Eyben] vol. iii, 3rd edn., p. 3280 n. 1 and p. 3291 n. 104; Kruse/Møller, *Erstatningsansvarsloven*, 3rd edn., p. 348). This approach has the result that personal injuries based upon breaches of the duty to provide protection can be founded in tort throughout, cf. SH 14 Sep. 1987, *UfR* 1987 A p. 947 (liability of employer to employee); HD 20 Sep. 1989, *UfR* 1989 A p. 1007 (sterilization of a woman during a caesarian section) or HD 10 Sep. 1993, *UfR* 1993 A p. 908 [treatment of penicillin administered negligently]). In Finland Chapter 1, 1 §, 2 s. of its SKL ('This Act does not apply, subject to any contrary provision in this or any other act, as long as liability for damages is based in contract or is prescribed by another Act') appears to adopt exactly the opposite position. This provision, based upon the Swedish prototype, was not well drafted. It intended to declare the SKL inapplicable only insofar as the law of contract provides differing solutions, for example in the protection afforded to economic loss (Saxén, *Skadeståndsrätt* p. 3). In practice the particular provision leads to complications, cf. HD 23 June 1992, *NDS* 1993 p. 451 (an insurer's agent, acting independently, negligently underwrote a stable which later burned down. The defendant insurer defended itself with the argument that Chapter 3, 1 §, 2 s. SKL [liability for independent contractor where his activity is similar to that of an employee] is not applicable. The HD held that the defendant insurer was liable according to the principles of contract for the fault of its assistants during contractual negotiations).

[42] For a view (in German) on the development of the *culpa* rule in Danish law, see Trolle, *RabelsZ* 7 (1933) p. 772.

[43] v. Bar (-Witte), *DeliktsR in Europa, Schweden* p. 22.

[44] In Denmark this distinction is part of the normal methodology. Unlawfulness is explained on the footing of an objective balancing of interests, whereas negligence is conveyed with the help of the traditional model of the *paterfamilias* (v. Bar [-Nørgaard/Vagner], *DeliktsR in Europa, Dänemark*, pp. 6–7).   [45] See nos. 17–18 above.

context already says what is required, Chapter 2, 4 § SKL adds the clarification that *pure economic loss* is only recoverable according to the rules which govern the recovery of loss for personal injury and damage to property caused by crime. A definition of pure economic loss is found in Chapter 1, 2 § SKL: 'For the purposes of this Act, pure economic loss is to be understood as economic loss which stands separate from and unconnected with personal injury or damage to property.'

245   The equivalent provision in Finnish law is found in Chapter 5, 1 § SKL: 'The damages include compensation for personal injury and damage to property. Where the damage was caused by a criminal act or by action of the authorities or in other cases where substantial reason exists, then the damages include compensation for economic loss.' The similarities with the German method of arranging the basis of liability are obvious. In Finland there is a strong parallel with the threefold (German) division into injury to a legal interest, statutory breach, and breach of custom ('other substantial reason').[46] No such general all-embracing clause was adopted in Sweden; a position similar to that found in Portugal was taken instead (see no. 22 above). It is not simply the case that lacunae in liability law are closed by statutes.[47] It is important to realize that the Finnish Parliament did not intend the rules of Chapter 2, 4 § SKL to be conclusive in all cases: the official commentary to the SKL states that the wording of the Act is not meant to deprive the court of the possibility of establishing liability for pure economic loss should it be appropriate in a context outside criminal law.[48] Thus, for instance, the courts retain the possibility of dealing with the issue of *culpa in contrahendo*,[49] i.e. in those situations which possess all the characteristics of liability in a non-contractual context but do not lead to the formation of a contract.[50] This has become particularly clear in the context of third-party liability in *culpa in contrahendo*.

---

[46] Saxén, *SJT* 1977 pp. 148, 152, gives as a typical example of this a malicious yet legal act resulting in economic loss to the victim.

[47] For an example see HD 13 Dec. 1991, *NDS* 1992 p. 635 = *NJA* 1991: 124 p. 725, and with a German annotation in *VersRAI* 1994 p. 5 (an estate agent gave the purchaser of a property incorrect information as to its size: liable under 14 § of the Act on Estate Agents [*Lag om fastighetsmäklare* of 2 Feb. 1984, SFS 1984: 81]). 'Pure economic loss not caused by a criminal act' is also recoverable under 1 § *Miljöskadelag* (Environment Liability Act, SFS 1986: 225), according to its sec. II, only 'if it is significant'.

[48] *NJA* 1972 II pp. 552, 609 and Hellner, *AmJCompL* 22 (1974) pp. 1, 5–6 under the reference of Kungl. Maj: ts proposition 1972: 5 (*Skadeståndslag* m.m.) p. 628.

[49] See HD 7 Dec. 1990, *NJA* 1990: 122 (p. 745).

[50] See Hellner, *Speciell avtalsrätt* vol. ii (2) no. 28.7.1. (p. 210). In the decisions of the courts there is no clear distinction between contractual and non-contractual claims based on *culpa in contrahendo*. Cf. Kleineman, *Ren förmögenhetsskada*, esp. pp. 428–432.

HD 14 October 1987[51] offers a good example of this: the plaintiff had granted an estate agent a loan of one million Krona, partially secured up to 800,000 Krona by way of a mortgage bond. The basis of the loan was a property valuation given by a valuer appointed by the estate agent. The valuation was grotesquely inaccurate, primarily because planning permission was unresolved. The property was valued at 4,3 million Krona; the true value was only 80,000 Krona. The plaintiff's claim against the estate agent was not satisfied due to the estate agent's bankruptcy. However, the action against the valuer was upheld. From the wording of the official commentary to the SKL it was clear that the Act was not intended to prevent appropriate development of liability law in the context of pure economic loss.

Besides cases of liability for information provided by non-contracting **246** third parties, further exceptions to the basic principle are referred to in the legal literature. Interference to business caused by unlawful strike action, where the strike action is not punishable by the criminal law, is another example.[52] However, the courts have not yet confirmed this view. The same is true of the assertion that damage caused to an employer by injury to one of his employees is not pure economic loss because it is linked to the personal injury of the employee.[53] It appears extremely doubtful whether Swedish case-law will follow the path advocated by Hellner. The position in both Sweden[54] and Finland[55] contrasts with that in Norway.[56] In the former two countries the recovery of such damages from third parties has remained strictly limited. Generally, recovery for *pure economic loss* is governed by the statutory provision that the plaintiff must have been the victim of a criminal offence.[57] A breeding bitch was paired with a mongrel so that

---

[51] HD 14 Oct. 1987, *NJA* 1987: 117 (p. 692).

[52] Hellner, *Skadeståndsrätt* 4th edn., p. 51. Cf. Karlgen, *Skadeståndsrätt* 5th edn., p. 110 (improper use of a right creates liability).   [53] Hellner, *AmJCompL* 22 (1974) pp. 1, 5.

[54] E.g. HD 27 June 1988, *NJA* 1988: 70 (p. 396): loss of a no-claims bonus is treated as a transferred loss (*tredjemansskada*) and as such is not recoverable. Further examples are provided by Roos, *Ersättningsrätt*, p. 142. The emotional value of an object is generally non-recoverable: Roos loc. cit. p. 272.

[55] E.g. HD 21 Oct. 1991, *NDS* 1992 p. 537 (a German version is found in *VersRAI* 1994 p. 6): two 8-year-old children were murdered by their kidnapper. The mother's claim for damages for pain and suffering failed because the provisions of the Finnish SKL allow such a claim only to those directly injured, thus excluding the mother. For comment on these 'tredjemansskada' see Saxén, *Skadeståndsrätt*, p. 69.

[56] See Meierhans, *recht* 1994 pp. 202, 213–215. Norwegian law is traditionally more generous than the Swedish in allowing recovery of pure economic loss. Cf. HD 22 Nov. 1955, *Rt.* 1955 p. 1132 (liability for the late presentation of a gaming licence) and HD 27 May 1967, *Rt.* 1967 p. 697 (disruption to the working of a poultry and trout farm caused by contamination of the water supply).

[57] E.8. Swedish HD 18 Dec. 1989, *NJA* 1989: 131 p. 796: intentional falsification of a certificate for the receipt of a non-existent boat, in order to receive payment for the same;

her entire litter was practically worthless: due to the pregnancy the bitch underwent a physical alteration; the loss of income from the litter was held not to be pure economic loss but damage to property.[58] The result here is identical to that which would have been obtained in Germany.[59]

It need only be added that the liability of the state[60] in both Sweden (Chapter 3, 2 § SKL) and Finland (Chapter 5, 1 §, 2 s. SKL) is more extensive than that of the citizen. It includes responsibility for negligently caused pure economic loss,[61] an illustration of the close relationship between the Scandinavian laws and the principles of German non-contractual state liability (§ 839 BGB with Art. 34 *Grundgesetz*).[62]

247   The starting point of Danish tort law is similar to that of its Scandinavian neighbours. The basic Danish principle is that: 'damage caused by an attributable unlawful act gives rise to liability, whether the damage is caused intentionally or negligently'.[63] It is a fundamental tenet in Denmark that non-contractual liability law protects only absolute legal interests and rights; pure economic interests are protected in contract law.[64] No statutory provisions in Denmark limit the exceptions

liability in deceit. Cf. Swedish HD 19 Dec. 1994, *NJA* 1994: 28 p. 709: attempted insurance fraud; liability for the costs of investigation and administration. Finnish HD 27 May 1994, *NDS* 1995 p. 264: successful claim by a municipality for compensation for salary paid to a civil servant while recovering from an assault. Swedish HD 8 Feb. 1993, *NDS* 1994 p. 149 disregarded the requirement of a crime (liability in a case involving the unauthorized use of a property not amounting to an offence).

[58] Swedish HD 28 Feb. 1990, *NJA* 1990: 16 (p. 80) = *NDS* 1991 p. 106. The case also shows that the rules of the SKL extend to statutory bases of claim. It concerned liability arising from the 1943 version of 4 § Law on Dogs and Cats (*Lagen om tillsyn över hundar och katter*) (SFS 1943: 459). Today's corresponding basis of claim is 6 § *Lag om ändring i lagen om tillsyn över hundar* (SFS 1987: 260) of the amended Statute on Liability for Dogs (SFS 1943: 459).

[59] See no. 220 and fn. 1315 above.

[60] Its introduction was one of the principal material changes which the particular Acts on Damages brought to Finnish and Swedish law (Hellner, *AmJCompL* 22 [1974] pp. 1–3; id., *FS Sieg*, pp. 155–156). No equivalent reform was required in Denmark and Norway, where the notion of state immunity was unknown. This partly explains why the statutes on damages in both the latter countries could be limited to the law of remedies.

[61] HD 18 Apr. 1989, *NDS* 1990 p. 205 gives a good example in Finnish case-law: incorrect information was provided by an immigration officer to a Canadian citizen of Finnish origin as to the procedure for obtaining a work permit. The citizen was thus obliged to return to Canada after four months. The Finnish state was liable for his removal costs and loss of income. A more recent example from Sweden is HD 8 Mar. 1995, *NJA* 1995: 17 p. 112.

[62] It is often asked whether the laws of Scandinavian countries have more in common with the common law or with the civil law of the continental countries. Sundberg, *Scan.-Stud.L.* 13 (1969) pp. 179, 205, answers the question: 'It appears that in our Nordic hearts we are against the King of England.'

[63] V. Bar (-Nørgaard/Vagner), *DeliktsR in Europa, Dänemark*, p. 6.

[64] Gomard, *Obligationsret*, vol. ii pp. 143–144 (recovery of economic loss is allowed in tort only when the loss is consequential or indirect); Jørgensen, *FS Larenz* (1973) pp. 549, 559; v. Bar (-Nørgaard/Vagner), *DeliktsR in Europa, Dänemark*, pp. 16–17 (recovery of transferred

to this rule to actions which contravene the criminal law,[65] and therefore difficult cases can be treated with greater flexibility than in Sweden and Finland. A typical example is, once again, liability to non-contracting third parties for incorrect information given.[66] This gives rise to *erstatningspligt uden for kontraktsforhold* (extra-contractual liability) embedded in tort law.[67] Protection against liability for pure economic loss in the non-contractual context has been sanctioned where a factory was temporarily put out of action following the negligent severing of a cable.[68] Apart from the special cases on liability for the loss of the 'provider',[69]

loss is generally not allowed, the main exception being personal injury to a 'provider'). See also Cornelius, *Schutz des Forderungsinhabers gegenüber Dritten*, pp. 48–49 and HD 13 Dec. 1994, *UfR* 1995 A. p. 185: (the defendant bit the thumb of the plaintiff policeman and claimed, falsely, to be suffering from AIDS. Liability based upon this assertion was rejected. The mere fear of catching a disease was insufficient to establish liability).

[65] Where the elements of a criminal offence are satisfied there is, of course, liability for pure economic loss: this is true also of Denmark. Cf. ØLD 5 Dec. 1977, *UfR* 1978 A p. 406 (fraud by a bank employee against one of the bank's customers).

[66] See Samuelsson/Søgaard, *Rådgiveransvaret*, esp. pp. 21–23 (on the *culpa* rule) and pp. 135 ff. (on the liability of estate agents, an area of law which was formerly the province of judge-made law but has now been placed on a statutory footing: cf. the following footnote).

[67] This liability was originally developed primarily to cover estate agents who gave false information (e.g. ØLD 5 Apr. 1945, *UfR* 1945 A p. 863) or failed to disclose important points (e.g. VLD 4 Sep. 1948, *UfR* 1948 A p. 1297: an estate agent was liable for the cost of new foundations and for the reduction in value because he did not disclose that the house stood on a peat-like foundation and had already begun to tilt). Liability has also been extended to other professional groups and other types of case (cf. again ØLD 10 Oct. 1994, *UfR* 1995 A p. 84: liability of insurers of unemployed people for incorrect information regarding pension entitlement) and VLD 14 Dec. 1994, *UfR* 1995 A p. 247 (incorrect information given by a council regarding drainage costs which disadvantaged the prospective purchaser of the land). That some of the more recent cases have not resulted in liability does not undermine the principle: the failure of each of those claims was due to some other reason. Cf. VLD 17 Dec. 1993, *UfR* 1994 A p. 205: the error of a liquidator in calculating the value of property; liability rejected on account of the contributory negligence of the buyer, which was greater than that of the liquidator; HD 21 Jan. 1994, *UfR* 1994 A p. 280: incorrect valuation by a property valuer; liability only denied because the valuation had been prepared for a purpose other than facilitating the sale of the property; and HD 19 Aug. 1994, *UfR* 1994 A p. 818: incorrect advice by a bank as to the creditworthiness of one of its customers; liability denied on the basis that the information had not been prepared either for the plaintiff sub-contractor or for its bank; that the sub-contractor would rely upon the information is not something of which the defendant bank could have been aware.

[68] HD 9 Dec. 1975, *UfR* 1976 A p. 82. Time and again decisions appear in which it is very difficult to see whether the distinction between property damage and pure economic loss has been made, and what *exactly* was the basis of the action. Cf. VLD 13 Jan. 1995, *UfR* 1995 A p. 314: the unlawful grant of planning permission caused the value of a neighbouring house to drop as the new buildings interfered with the light to the house; the judgment did not elaborate on the type of damage or whether the basis of liability was the general *culpa* rule, breach of protective statute, or liability of a public body.

[69] No. 238 above; cf. on this v. Bar (-Nørgaard/Vagner), *DeliktsR in Europa, Dänemark*, p. 19.

there is also the general rule in Denmark that knock-on damage to third parties need not be compensated.[70]

248 The modern Danish law of delict can use its greater flexibility to advantage in the field of injury to reputation and privacy. At first glance, 26 § of the EAL[71] is scarcely distinguishable from its sister rules in Chapter 5, 6 § Finn. and Chapter 1, 3 § Swed. SKL respectively.[72] All three rules are concerned, amongst other things, with the protection of freedom and reputation. Furthermore, all three rules provide for the compensation of non-material damage. In both the Swedish and the Finnish statutes liability for defamation is dependent upon the commission of a criminal offence; this is not so in Denmark. The reason is historical: the rules have their origins in the criminal statute books.[73] The adoption of this rule in the new SKL leads necessarily to the identical problem which besets Swedish law concerning pure economic loss: whether and how far judge-made law can exceed the text of the statute. The answer remains unclear.[74] The position is clear

---

[70] A good example is HD 8 Aug. 1994, *UfR* 1994 A p. 785: 2 trawlers, the *Libas* and the *Koralhav*, collided in Hanstholm harbour, because of the negligence of the helmsman of the *Libas*. The *Koralhav* always worked in tandem with a third trawler, the *Nesbúgvin*, when fishing at sea. Because the *Koralhav* was damaged the *Nesbúgvin* was unable to work: the latter's dragnets could not be operated from the *Nesbúgvin* alone. The claim of the *Nesbúgvin*'s owner was rejected. The damage was 'reflex damage' and therefore not recoverable. A less clear example is the case reported at VLD 10 May 1994, *UfR* 1994 A p. 659: between 1963 and 1974 the defendant used a former gravel pit as a dump for its chemical waste. Following new statutory rules introduced in the 1980s the ground was analysed and contamination detected. The environment ministry carried out a clean-up and brought an action for the costs of this exercise. The case was viewed as one involving the principles of both tort law and the law of unjust enrichment. The action failed. The reasoning was that the defendant had not acted negligently; between 1963 and 1974 it could not have known that its method of dumping chemical waste endangered the water supply.

[71] 'Whoever commits an offence against the freedom, honour, or person of another is obliged to recompense the other in respect of the insult. § 18 I and II [on transmissability and inheritability] apply to compensation for insult.'

[72] Chapter 5, 6 § Finn. SKL: 'The provisions of this statute for personal injury apply also to suffering caused by crimes (*brott* = indictable and non-indictable offences) against freedom, honour, the sanctity of the home, or other similar acts.' Chapter 1, 3 § Swed. SKL: 'The rules in this Act on compensation for personal injury apply also to harm which one person causes to another: by means of a crime against individual freedom, by means of other unpeaceful conduct which amounts to a crime, by means of an infringement of the privacy of mail and telephone communication, by means of unauthorized interference in a privileged relationship, or by means of unlawful bugging, discrimination, or defamation, or some other similar crime.'

[73] Hellner, *Skadeståndsrätt* 4th edn., pp. 299–300. These criminal norms are considered in Chapter 6, 3 § Swed. Criminal Code and Chapter 9, 2 § Finn. Criminal Code respectively.

[74] See Hellner loc. cit. and Roos, *Ersättningsrätt*, p. 161. The official commentary (*NJA* 1972 avd. II p. 552, p. 731 [on Chapter 5, 1 § SKL in its original version] is not very productive. Cf. also HD 24 Feb. 1977, *NJA* 1977: 9 p. 43 (where one of the parties which found the actual proceedings offensive was sent outside by the judge 'to think about the matter once more'. The claim was rejected, not because there was no crime, but because the conduct could not be categorized as an infringement of the right of personality. The Finnish

for deprivation of liberty, attempted murder, sexual crimes,[75] and criminal insult;[76] it remains unclear for racial discrimination by associations.[77] Unlike in Denmark,[78] non-criminal damage to reputation can be problematic for Swedish law. So it was not until 1978 when the Act on names and pictures in advertizing introduced effective protection for the unlawful, though in the circumstances non-criminal, use of photographs of a person for advertizing.[79]

Liability for omissions causes fewer difficulties.[80] The obligation to act **249** is not (as in the German BGB)[81] based on the trinity of statute, contract,

---

judgment HD 8 Oct. 1991, *NDS* 1992 p. 504 = *VersRAI* 1994 p. 6 points to the same approach: a part-owner of a petrol station was locked out when a fellow owner changed the locks. This was a unilateral criminal act, but was not sufficient to establish liability for damages. The criminal act had given rise only to 'discomfort and irritation', and was not genuine insult in the sense of the statute.

[75] Cf. Swed. HD 7 Apr. 1993, *NDS* 1994 p. 175: attempted murder of a 17-month-old child; liability was affirmed despite the fact that the child could not sense what had happened; and Roos loc. cit. (fn. 74).

[76] E.g. Swed. HD 28 June 1989, *NJA* 1989: 62 (p. 374): a car driver verbally abused a political refugee by calling her a 'damned nigger'; he also threw a bottle at her and kicked her. Besides damages for personal injury, an additional 2,000 Krona were granted in damages for the disparagement: Chapter 1, 3 § SKL, it was said, takes account of basic societal values and the principle of equality.

[77] Swed. HD 31 Oct. 1979, *NJA* 1979: 118 (p. 657).

[78] Cf. VLD 8 Dec. 1993, *UfR* 1994 A p. 199: a photograph of the plaintiff taken at the time of his arrest was incorrectly added to the catalogue of sexual offences and shown to others on several occasions. The plaintiff had never committed a sexual offence. His claim for damages and return of the photograph was upheld. Cf. also HD 11 Jan. 1994, *UfR* 1994 A p. 247: a father was incorrectly accused of sexually abusing his daughter, who as a result was taken away from the family; the liability of the social services was denied only on the ground that since they have responsibility for children they must respond quickly to allegations of abuse.

[79] Expressly reserved in the light of the reforms then being undertaken, esp. the Swedish decision HD 21 May 1976, *NJA* 1976: 50 (p. 282) (on which see Bengtsson, *SJT* 1981 pp. 519, 529 and id., in: Strömholm (ed.), *Introduction to Swedish Law*, p. 305): the defendant used a photograph belonging to the plaintiff actress for advertizing purposes without her consent. Astonishingly, the court based its decision not on Chapter 1, 3 § (injury to personal rights) but on Chapter 2, 4 § (pure economic loss) and decided in favour of the defendant. It did this despite the fact that there are good grounds for stating that no one need allow another to use his or her photograph for advertizing purposes. In Denmark a case based upon very similar facts was without hesitation decided in favour of the plaintiff some 10 years earlier: HD 25 Jan. 1965, *UfR* 1965 A p. 126. For further comment on the protection of the right to personality in Denmark see Lauridsen, *FS Werner Lorenz*, pp. 677–688. According to the provisions of the Act on Names and Pictures in Advertizing, in force since 1978 (SFS 1978: 800) (esp. 1 §, 1 s., and 3 §, I), cases such as those in Sweden (e.g. HD 21 May 1976 above) would now result in the payment of damages in Sweden.

[80] V. Bar (-Nørgaard/Vagner), *DeliktsR in Europa, Dänemark*, p. 6; Hellner, *Skadeståndsrätt*, 4th edn., pp. 74–77; Roos, *Ersättningsrätt*, pp. 103–105; Saxén, *Skadeståndsrätt*, pp. 41–45, 57–58, p. 329. For Norway see also HD 14 Nov. 1947, *Rt.* 1947 p. 723 (smithy poorly secured against unauthorized access by children likely to endanger themselves); and for Denmark a decision reminiscent of *Home Office* v. *Dorset Yacht Co. Ltd.* [1970] AC 1004 (escaped borstal boys) ØLD 13 Dec. 1954, *UfR* 1955 A p. 336 and HD 11 Jan. 1956, *UfR* 1956 A p. 215 (liability for the temporary escape of children from a home for difficult children).

[81] See nos. 104–105 above.

and *Ingerenz* (conduct creating danger); more simply, it is a consequence of the general duty to act with care. As with negligence, there is no statutory definition of fault. The standard of care is objective.[82] In Sweden this is expressed as '*vållande*'. It characterizes action to be avoided; it is independent of subjective blameworthiness.[83] Thus even children and the mentally handicapped can act in a blameworthy way (*vålla*);[84] the necessary adjustment is made by liability reduction clauses. Strict liability is not dealt with in the SKL. The fact that the most important applications of this form of liability are already contained in statutes has not prevented the courts from developing, where appropriate, classes of cases in which compensation is obligatory and independent of fault. In this field statute gives only one answer for the facts it actually considers. It neither forbids analogy nor will it countenance the *argumentum e contrario*. The decisions of the courts are sovereign over both.

250 Judge-led developments in the field of strict liability have a long tradition in Scandinavia, although at varying rates. The jurisprudence of Norway recognized business liability on an objective basis as early as the 1930s,[85] albeit not in statutory form. This advantageous devel-

---

[82] Bengtsson, in: Strömholm (ed.), *Introduction to Swedish Law*, p. 304; Kruse, *Erstatningsretten*, 5th edn., pp. 117–118; HD 10 Sept. 1993, *UfR* 1993 A p. 908 (premature termination of penicillin treatment, the hospital was liable despite the fact that the hospital had followed the advice of a drugs institute); v. Bar [-Nørgaard/Vagner], *DeliktsR in Europa, Dänemark*, p. 7; Roos, *Ersättningsrätt*, pp. 102–110. Cf. the following footnotes.

[83] Hellner, *Skadeståndsrätt*, 4th edn., 8.1, p. 89. In Finnish legal practice objectivization does not go so far; the term *vårdslöshet* is often used instead of the word *vållande* meaning failure to reach the appropriate standard of care: Saxén, *Skadeståndsrätt*, p. 8.

[84] Cf. for Denmark ØLD 14 Sep. 1951, *UfR* 1951 A p. 1096 (a child aged 3 years and 11 months ran in front of a car; the child should have recognized the danger and was therefore liable); HD 8 Feb. 1991, *UfR* 1991 A p. 274 = *NDS* 1992 p. 171 = *VersRAI* 1993 p. 32; VLD 24 Nov. 1988, *UfR* 1989 A p. 278 and HD 25 Oct. 1990, *UfR* 1990 A p. 926 (2 brothers, aged 9 and 10, set fire to a school cupboard; they were held liable under 19 § II no. 1 EAL, because children under 14 are capable of acting with gross negligence as understood by these provisions). In HD 15 Feb. 1963, *UfR* 1963 A p. 303 a girl aged 3 years and $8^1/_2$ months was not liable when her unlawful conduct caused a motorcyclist to fall from his motorbike. The legal position in *Finland* and *Sweden* is unfortunately not clear. From the similarly worded provisions of Chapter 2, 2 and 3 §§ of the Finnish and Swedish SKL it appears that only very young children (cf. Swed. HD 3 Feb. 1977, *NJA* 1977: 36, p. 186: a child aged 3 years and 2 months injured a 5–year-old: no liability) are exempted from liability, and apart from this the basic rule is that liability arises (cf. Swed. HD 18 May 1948, *NJA* 1948: 74 II, p. 342: 5-year-old) but is to be reduced according to the circumstances (Hellner, *Skadeståndsrätt*, 4th edn., pp. 220–223), even to nil in appropriate circumstances. Also, accidents caused by children are judged according to the standard of care specific to children of that age: cf. Swed. HD 7 Oct. 1976, *NJA* 1976: 90 p. 458.

[85] One of the leading cases of this era is HD 25 Apr. 1933, *Rt.* 1933 p. 475: father and son were digging a ditch on their meadow using a metal cable. Part of the cable broke loose and caught in high-tension electricity cables. The *Høyesterett* accepted in principle that the power station had an objective business liability, but on the facts liability was rejected on account of the unusual circumstances. On the general development of strict liability in Norway see Andresen, *RabelsZ* 27 (1962) pp. 245–262.

opment can be seen in a range of cases where other Scandinavian countries still rely on a very strict concept of care.[86] Danish jurisprudence may be a little less developed, but has nevertheless adopted the Norwegian example for at least some types of case. The most important is the strict liability of property developers for excavations of land,[87] subject of the leading case of the *Aalborg Monastery*.[88] Further examples include breaches in water and gas pipelines as a result of the decay of material,[89] and recently employers have been held strictly liable for damage caused by asbestos to employees of a factory.[90] However, the Western High Court refused to grant damages on the basis of strict liability to the victim of an unlawful (but innocent) decision to commit him to a psychiatric hospital.[91] In 1986 such a ground of liability was proposed by the government but was rejected.

With express reference to Danish and Norwegian jurisprudence, the Swedish *Högsta domstol* affirmed the no-fault liability of the operator of a regional heating plant.[92] Relied on as precedents were decisions which submitted especially dangerous activities (e.g. working with explosives) to strict liability, along with construction works with harmful consequences for adjoining land.[93] Finally, in Finland accidents at work involving machines with inherent defects led to the imposition of strict

---

[86] For the Danish position see von Eyben/Nørgaard/Vagner, *Erstatningsret*, 2nd edn., p. 58 and for Norway see Lødrup, *Erstattningsrett*, 2nd edn., pp. 152 and 163 ff. Plenty of voices in Denmark advocate an extension of strict liability to other areas of law (Kruse, *Erstatningsretten*, 5th edn., p. 258). An example is liability for premises, on which reference is all too willingly made to the differently based (although with the same result) Norweg. HD 9 Nov. 1939, *Rt.* 1939 p. 766 (strict liability) and to Dan. HD 10 Mar. 1938, *UfR* 1938 A p. 453 (an enhanced form of fault-based liability; the case concerned falling parts of a building).

[87] E.g. ØLD 18 Apr. 1941, *UfR* 1941 A p. 871; VLD 31 Oct. 1950, *UfR* 1951 A p. 178; VLD 25 July 1961, *UfR* 1961 A p. 939; and HD 24 June 1983, *UfR* 1983 A p. 714. Strict liability does *not* apply to a contractor who damages telephone cables whilst carrying out drainage works: VLD 28 Nov. 1994, *UfR* 1995 A p. 149.

[88] HD 10 Jan. 1968, *UfR* 1968 A p. 84.

[89] HD 18 Aug. 1993, *UfR* 1983 A p. 866; HD 2 Sep. 1983, *UfR* 1983 A p. 895. Cf. HD 11 Dec. 1956, *UfR* 1957 A p. 109; and HD 11 May 1960, *UfR* 1960 A p. 576.

[90] HD 27 Oct. 1989, *UfR* 1989 A p. 1108, with commentary by Judge Pedersen in *UfR* 1990 B pp. 241–246. The decision in the silicosis case had already been given: HD 13 Feb. 1984, *UfR* 1984 A p. 284. [91] VLD 11 Oct. 1994, *UfR* 1995 A pp. 70–71.

[92] HD 11 Dec. 1991, *NJA* 1991: 123 (p. 720) = *NDS* 1992 p. 590 = *VersRAI* 1994 p. 23. However, the decision in HD 8 Apr. 1993, *NDS* 1994 p. 179 reversed the first-instance decision to impose a form of strict liability on a golfer whose ball struck a parked car. It was replaced by a more onerous form of fault liability.

[93] A case involving both aspects is HD 14 Apr. 1966, *NJA* 1966: 46 (p. 248): use of explosives in building an underground station near Östermalmstorg. Objective liability was imposed on the blasting contractor as well as the land-owning council. The principles of this decision have since been fixed by statute in 4 § *Miljöskadelag* (Environment Act) (SFS 1986: 225).

liability in a non-contractual context.[94] Until the EC Directive was adopted by Finnish law, product liability remained subject only to the regime of the SKL, fault being a prerequisite.[95] Even the operation of a ski-lift was not regarded as an especially dangerous activity warranting strict liability.[96]

251   Such judge-made law, which allows the imposition of strict liability in cases other than those governed by statute, is not peculiar to Scandinavian legal systems. Nor is the relatively close *proximity to criminal law*, which characterizes many of their rules,[97] unique to these systems. For on one hand, similar rules are found in the codes of continental Europes (such as Spain[98] and Italy) and on the other, Swedish law has on many important questions developed its jurisprudence beyond its statutory base. Contemporary Swedish law is the culmination of a development in which, over centuries, private liability and criminal law have become parts of a unified system. Both belonged originally to the overarching category of criminal law. It is two hundred years since criminal law began to be regarded as public law, and thus separate from the law of delict.[99]

252   More intensive consideration has been given to the legal consequences of insurance and to techniques for the reduction of damages in Scandinavia than anywhere else in Europe. Nowhere else have such considerations been integrated within private liability law to anywhere near the same extent. If anything comes close to defining the Nordic systems of delict, it is the extensive correlation of liability law and insurance.[100] This is not simply the usual masking of liability law by social security.[101] A range of statutes has achieved the position whereby the victim of a tort is granted, as an *alternative* to his claim, a more favourable claim against an

---

[94] HD 7 May 1990, *NDS* 1991 p. 194 and HD 6 Nov. 1991, *NDS* 1992 p. 547.

[95] Hertzberg, *Gewährleistung, Produzentenhaftung und Prozeßrecht in Finnland*, p. 9.

[96] HD 20 Oct. 1992, *NDS* 1993 p. 615.

[97] A further example is Chapter 2, 5 § Swed. SKL, according to which 'damage caused by an omission to avert a crime' only results in liability where the omission is itself a crime.   [98] See no. 4 and fn. 20 above.

[99] See Björne, *Nordische Rechtssysteme*, pp. 227–228.

[100] Bengtsson, in: Strömholm (ed.), *Introduction to Swedish Law*, says with some justification at p. 229: 'because of the coverage afforded by . . . insurance, the practical importance of the law of torts is today considerably smaller in Sweden that in most comparable countries.' The development which led to the present position began in earnest during the 1960s. A useful analysis in German is provided by Jørgensen, *VersR* 1970 pp. 193–208.

[101] For Sweden, particular mention should be made of Chapter 20, 7 § of the Act on General Insurance (*Lag om allmän försäkring*, SFS 1962: 382), by which the injured party is entitled to demand damages from the tortfeasor according to the general principles of liability law only to the extent that his illness and personal injury are not covered by this insurance. A recourse action by the social security fund was generally abolished by 7 § II of this Act. Cf. Hellner, in: Fleming/Hellner/von Hippel (edd.), *Haftungsersetzung durch Versicherungsschutz*, pp. 24–25.

insurer.[102] Although the quantum is approximately the same, fault need not be proved, and there is less risk of the insurer being unable to meet the claim. In cases involving significant fault the insurer can look to the tortfeasor for redress. The intended consequence was (and remains) that although it continues in theory, the private claim against the tortfeasor effectively falls into abeyance. In these fields there is hardly any case-law; the function of the courts has to all intents and purposes been handed to commissions of inquiry and similar bodies of insurers. By way of medical and so-called safety insurance,[103] bases of claim wholly independent of fault have been established in Sweden[104] on a (collective) contractual basis. The employer-financed 'safety insurance' has a special feature: in order to claim it the plaintiff must abandon any claim in private law.[105] Swedish motor insurance law even contains a 'third-party liability insurance', which really covers all aspects of accident insurance: it also compensates for self-inflicted damage.[106]

---

[102] This path has been trodden several times in Sweden. The first example is found in the law on accidents at work: according to the *Lag om arbetsskadeförsäkring* (SFS 1976: 380), which adds to the achievements of the *allmän försäkring* (previous footnote), insurance for industrial injury leaves employer's liability under the SKL undisturbed (v. Bar [-Witte], *DeliktsR in Europa, Schweden*, p. 56). Loss of income exceeding a basic fixed sum was the prime loss intended to be covered. (With regard to this basic amount the insurance company did not have a right of redress; this has led to a socialization of the risks associated with dangerous activities: Roos, *Ersättningsrätt*, p. 68). This particular provision has become completely obsolete due to additional saftey insurance. A second example is found in the sphere of medical insurance, regarding insurance for patients given treatment (*Patientförsäkring*) or drugs (*Läkemedelsförsäkring*). Both concern optional insurance but if the insurance companies had not provided these services, they would have been introduced by statute. See: Roos, *Ersättningsrätt*, p. 27. Cf. Witte loc. cit. pp. 65–66; Hedman, *Ansvar och ersättning vid medicinsk verksamhet*, pp. 74–78; Hellner, in: Deutsch/Schreiber [edd.], *Medical Responsibility*, p. 700, Radau, *Ersetzung der Arzthaftung durch Versicherungsschutz, passim* and id., *VersR* 1991 pp. 397–393. (The Finnish *Patientskadelag* [Act no. 585 of 25 July 1986, FFS 1986, p. 1236] in so far as it concerns grounds of liability, displaces the Finnish SKL [see Medeen, *JFT* 1994 pp. 38–49]). The same applies in principle for the Danish Act on Insurance for Patients [Act No. 367/91, new version in publication no. 849 of 14 Oct. 1992, *Lovtidende* 1992 A p. 3822; on this see Stein-Poulsen, *VersRAI* 1995 pp. 19–25]: according to its § 7 the more onerous liability of the hospital is passed onto the body responsible. Personal liability of the staff only comes into play when there is no claim under the Act on insurance protection for patients, as where the damage is minor). The third example stems from the law on traffic accidents: 18 § I of the Act on Road Damage (*Trafikskadelag*, SFS 1975: 1410) expressly states that 'independent of the fact that statutory damages for road accidents can be paid . . . the injured party may claim damages under the general law instead'.

[103] *Trygghetsförsäkring för arbetsskador* (TFA). This safety insurance derives from a collective agreement and has the aim of closing lacunae which are covered neither by general insurance nor by insurance for accidents at work (previous footnote). Cf. Hellner, *FS Klingmüller*, pp. 159–171; and Witte, loc. cit. p. 56.

[104] See Hellner, *Skadeståndsrätt*, 4th edn., p. 245 (on TFA), p. 248 (on insurance for patients), and p. 264 (on insurance against the harmful effects of medicines).

[105] Hellner loc. cit. p. 246. It is no longer necessary to proceed under the SKL as the insurance companies barely make use of their right to withold payment in cases involving gross negligence: Hellner, loc. cit. p. 245.   [106] 10 § *Trafikskadelag*.

253   The interplay of liability and insurance is not restricted to such (legal or factual) ousting mechanisms. The presence (or absence) of insurance protection often directly affects the rules of liability and is seized on as a characteristic element of such rules. Mention has already been made of the rule in § 19 of the Danish EAL.[107] When asking which measure of care should be employed to assess negligence, the courts are often swayed by whether the defendant was insured. This phenomenon, which often passes without comment in the literature, has not remained concealed in other parts of Europe. The openness with which the courts in Scandinavia discuss this issue is striking.[108] Furthermore, not only issues of more onerous or enhanced liability are concerned (as in the case of § 19 EAL); in cases involving contributory negligence it is often asked whether the victim, having regard to the value of the damaged article, should have obtained insurance.[109] Such considerations are dealt with in the numerous rules of equity, which everywhere complement and moderate the strict rules of liability law. The liability-limiting clause with its reference to 'the financial and other circumstances of the tortfeasor and of the injured party' was of such importance to the Finnish SKL that it was inserted immediately after the basic liability rule (Chapter 2, 1 §, 2 s. SKL).[110] Such rule adjustments[111] are also found in strict liability statutes.[112] The danger of legal uncertainty arising from the use of equitable principles is recognized and accepted. This is the price which must be

---

[107] See no. 238 above.

[108] Cf. e.g. Danish HD 8 Feb. 1991, *UfR* 1991 A p. 274 (young tortfeasors insured against third-party risks) and HD 2 Oct. 1990, *UfR* 1990 A p. 926 (same). According to Hellner, *Skadeståndsrätt*, 4th edn., pp. 219–220, the situation is very similar in Sweden: the liability of young persons is relaxed in cases where there is no third-party insurance. In Swedish case-law, however, the warning has recently been repeated to allocate an 'essential role' to insurance when attributing fault: HD 29 Oct. 1991 (following footnote).

[109] A striking Danish case is HD 22 Jan. 1959, *UfR* 1959 A p. 160: a tanker driver negligently damaged an aircraft. The Supreme Court reduced to one-third the claim of the Defence Ministry, agreeing with the defence that the plaintiff Ministry, as the owner of such an expensive item, should have made better insurance provision. This decision gave effect to the reasonable proposition that the owner of particularly expensive objects should himself insure them against damage by negligent third parties (v. Bar, *AcP* 181 [1981] p. 289, p. 327). In Sweden this appears to be a common point of view; cf. HD 29 Oct. 1991, *NJA* 1991: 94 p. 567 = *NDS* 1992 p. 540 = *VersRAI* 1994 p. 24: during a shooting party a bullet passed through an elk and killed one of the hounds. The action of the hound's owner was opposed with the argument that the dog's owner should have insured the dog. This reasoning was not accepted by the Supreme Court: in view of the dog's value and age it had not been negligent to leave it uninsured. However, the decision in HD 14 June 1979, *UfR* 1979 A p. 908 possibly points in another direction for Denmark.

[110] See fn. 12 above for similar clauses pertaining to other Acts on damages.

[111] Chapter 2, 2 § (children and young persons) and 3 § (adults) of the Finnish and Swedish SKL respectively. For Denmark §§ 63 and 64 of the Statute on Minority and Guardianship (*Lovbekendtgørelse* No. 443 of 3.10.1985, *Myndighedsloven*).

[112] E.g. 18 § II of the Swedish Road Traffic Damages Act.

paid if the constitutional protection against excess liability is to be applied in a meaningful way in private law.[113]

3. THE COMMON LAW OF TORTS

a. English Liability Law: Nominate Torts and Negligence

(1) An Overview of the Most Important Nominate Torts

A continental lawyer looking for the first time at the English law of torts **254** would, in the way the latter is presented, be reminded of his own criminal law.[114] Continentals are used to the idea of seeing liability law in their own countries develop (albeit with different nuances in different countries) from the general principle that someone who injures the legal interest or right of another, whether intentionally or negligently, is liable in damages to that other. However, Continentals are trained to analyse criminal law on the basis of the numerous elements of the 'Special Part'. Nowhere in the realm of criminal law is there a wide basic principle comparable to that which applies to civil law. Nowhere has the criminal law developed a general rule for the protection of human life (which would be along the following lines: 'whoever kills another, whether intentionally or negligently, will be sentenced to a minimum term of . . . years' imprisonment'). Criminal law distinguishes between murder and manslaughter, personal injury resulting in death, robbery resulting in death, arson resulting in death, death resulting from inadvertence, and much more. So there are, whether necessarily or not, a large number of different specific crimes which may have been committed when one person kills another. In England this is true not only of criminal offences but also of torts, with the so-called *nominate* torts.[115] When Rudden undertook to list them all he counted upwards of seventy-two, and even then he was not sure that his list was comprehensive.[116]

---

[113] More on this in Part 6, nos. 595 f. below. An example from Danish law is VLD 19 Feb. 1993, *UfR* 1993 A p. 430: 2 friends, A and B, met. A had brought with him a pistol which he believed to be defective. B, who had been told by A that the pistol was unloaded, took hold of the pistol and fired a shot which hit A. The court took the view that B had been minimally negligent. Because B was unable to pay the whole amount of the damages ordered his liability was reduced to one-eighth under § 24 EAL.

[114] Cf. Uniken Venema, *Van Common Law en Civil Law*, p. 98.

[115] Strictly speaking the matter is even more complicated, because there are torts 'which are well known to exist but which have no compendious name' (Winfield/Jolowicz [-Rogers], *Tort*, 14th edn., p. 54), and because the tort of most practical significance—negligence—is *not* a nominate tort (see no. 274 below). That private law orders 'its' torts differently from criminal law is clearly illustrated by the example of battery (no. 256 below). This tort covers a range of conduct including murder, manslaughter, rape, assault, and robbery.

[116] Rudden, *Tul.Civ.Law Forum* 6/7 (1991–92) pp. 105, 111–120.

281

When placed alphabetically the list begins with the tort of abduction of a child and ends with a special form of misuse of procedural law, the tort of wrongful civil proceedings which, as has been remarked, is strictly to be distinguished from the tort of abuse of process.[117]

255 Many of these torts—Rudden referred to them somewhat mockingly as 'torticles'—are of such minor significance that we need here only consider them in specific factual contexts. Other torts overlap various legal boundaries. Thus conversion of goods, committed when someone disposes of goods to which he has no legal title, straddles the boundary between tort and unjust enrichment.[118] This tort operates independently of fault[119] and therefore can be counted amongst the so-called stricter forms of liability, analysed in greater detail below. It is important to understand from the outset the bases of the system of liability for tortious actions; at this juncture the following points will suffice.

(a) Trespass

256 Trespass, derived from the latin verb *transpassare*, to overstep, is probably the oldest of all the torts: it is still asserted to be the 'flagship of the fleet'.[120] Trespass is essentially a direct and unlawful interference with: a person (trespass to the person), goods (trespass to goods), or land (trespass to land). Actions brought under trespass to land are based upon infringement of occupation, rather than ownership. Negligence suffices.[121] The most frequent instance of trespass to goods is damage to goods.[122] Torts involving violence to the person are divided into two categories: assault (the threat of violence) and battery (the use of violence).[123] Both may also be crimes. 'An assault is an act which causes another person to apprehend the infliction of immediate, unlawful force on his person; a battery is the actual infliction of unlawful force on another person.'[124] Trespass to the person requires intention; personal injury occasioned unintentionally has been subsumed by the

---

[117] Ibid. p. 120 with reference to *Metall & Rohstoff AG* v. *Donaldson Lufkin & Jenrette* [1989] 3 All ER 14, 50 (*per* Slade LJ).   [118] See nos. 520 ff. and 549 below.
[119] Markesinis/Deakin, *Tort Law*, 3rd edn., p. 407.
[120] Weir, *Casebook*, 7th edn., p. 14.
[121] Cf. *League Against Cruel Sports* v. *Scott* [1985] 2 All ER 489. Also *Burton* v. *Winters* [1993] 1 WLR 1077: one neighbour negligently allowed his earthworks to encroach on his neighbour's property; the other responded by carrying out similar works intentionally.
[122] Trespass to goods can be committed by theft, and by mere secret use (*furtum usus*). It is not easy to comprehend what purpose is served by accepting in private law that trespass is not committed simply because direct causation of damage is absent (but rather some other nameless tort) where someone sets a poison trap in order to kill animals. Yet this appears to be the law (Winfield/Jolowicz [-Rogers], *Tort*, 14th edn., p. 487).
[123] Battery can be committed by words alone: *Wilkinson* v. *Downton* [1897] 2 QB 57. Cf. *Janvier* v. *Sweeney* [1919] 2 KB 316.
[124] *Collins* v. *Wilcock* [1984] 3 All ER 374, 377 (*per* Goff LJ).

tort of negligence.[125] Corporal punishment of a pupil by a teacher is battery.[126]

The third and last form[127] of trespass to the person is false imprison-   **257** ment. This is defined as 'the unlawful imposition of constraint on another's freedom of movement from a particular place'.[128] This tort can also be committed negligently. The victim need not be conscious of the fact that his movement has been restricted.[129] Both these points are significant because false imprisonment (like assault and trespass to land) is actionable *per se*. Torts belonging to this category do not require actual damage to have occurred before they are actionable. That damage is present is to a certain extent inherent in the nature of the thing; after all, one is talking of damage *per se*. However, this clearly does not mean that where such torts have been committed damages cannot be claimed.[130] The remedies which can be claimed are essentially the same, and this is also true of the equitable or discretionary remedies which the courts can impose. If loss is actually suffered it must be compensated. Other options for the court include awards of nominal, aggravated, or exemplary damages,[131] the removal of a continuing interference (mandatory injunction), and the granting of a prohibitory injunction.

(b) Malicious Prosecution

The tort of malicious prosecution lies close to the tort of false imprison-   **258** ment.[132] Malicious prosecution as a tort is concerned more with protecting the individual's good reputation than with guaranteeing his freedom of movement. Apart from this it is essential for the tort of malicious prosecution that the prime mover or instigator intended to act 'indir-

---

[125] *Letang* v. *Cooper* [1965] 1 QB 232, 239–240 (*per* Denning MR) and 244–245 (*per* Diplock LJ), confirmed in *Miller* v. *Jackson* [1977] 1 QB 966, 979 (*per* Denning MR). For an argument critical of the above and in favour of the retention of an action in negligent trespass see Trindade, *IntCompLQ* 20 (1971) 706–731.

[126] Sec. 47 Education (No. 2) Act 1986 (c. 60) made corporal punishment unlawful.

[127] The issue has recently been raised (esp. in cases involving harassment by telephone) of whether there is a further tort of 'personal injury by molestation'. Provided such unwanted telephone calls do not lead to personal injury they do not constitute trespass to the person. In *Khorasandjian* v. *Bush* [1993] 3 All ER 669 (on which see Cooke, *MLR* 57 (1994) 289–296 and Ford, 53 (1994) *CLJ* 14–16) the Court of Appeal gave its majority decision to grant an injunction on the tort of private nuisance. It did this without regard to the traditional requirement of this particular tort, that only a person having 'an interest in land' is able to bring an action in private nuisance. The plaintiff had been harassed while 'only' living at her mother's address.

[128] Loc. cit. (fn. 104) p. 378.

[129] *Murray* v. *Ministry of Defence* [1988] 1 WLR 692, 703 (*per* Lord Griffiths).

[130] See Markesinis/Deakin, *Tort Law*, 3rd edn., pp. 683–685.

[131] *Holden* v. *Chief Constable of Lancashire* [1986] 3 All ER 836; [1987] QB 380.

[132] A recent decision on the borderline between these torts is *Davidson* v. *Chief Constable of North Wales and Another* [1994] 2 All ER 597. See Spencer, (1994) 53 *CLJ* 433–435.

ectly' (i.e. by the organs of the state, most commonly the police) against the victim. The ingredients of the tort are as follows: there must be, first, a criminal prosecution instigated by the defendant which, secondly, is decided in favour of the plaintiff. Thirdly, the defendant must have been motivated by malice, and finally, there must have been no reasonable grounds to bring the prosecution in the first place. Had the decision of the Court of Appeal in *Martin* v. *Watson*[133] been upheld by the House of Lords, then the tort of malicious prosecution would have been reduced to little more than a paper tiger. In evidence at court a woman asserted in what the trial judge described as a 'chain of lies' that her neighbour had exposed himself to her. She told this story to the police, who laid a summons before the magistrates' court for the man's arrest. Although this appeared to represent the 'classic' case of malicious prosecution, the plaintiff's claim was rejected by the Court of Appeal. Contacting the police was not the cause of the criminal action because the police officers concerned had exercised their own discretion in laying the summons before the magistrates. In an era of increasing criminality there are compelling policy considerations in the interests of the community as a whole why the individual citizen who passes on information to the police should not in consequence be exposed to potential liability in civil law. The House of Lords, however, did not follow this line of argument: 'Where the circumstances are such that the facts relating to the alleged offence can be within the knowledge of only the complainant . . . then it becomes virtually impossible for the police officer to exercise any independent discretion or judgment, and if a prosecution is instituted by the police officer the proper view is that the prosecution has been procured by the complainant.'[134]

(c) Deceit, Injurious Falsehood, and Passing Off

259 Since the decision in *Derry* v. *Peek*,[135] involving liability for the content of a company prospectus, the tort of deceit has exhibited the peculiarity that recklessness is sufficient to found fraud, while gross negligence is insufficient as a basis for such an action.[136] Malicious or injurious falsehood lies between deceit and defamation. This 'three-person tort' is not unlike the principle concerning damage to another's credit worthiness[137]

---

[133] *Martin* v. *Watson* [1994] 2 WLR 500.
[134] *Martin* v. *Watson* [1995] 3 WLR 318, 327 (*per* Lord Keith of Kinkel).
[135] (1889) 14 App. Cas. 337.
[136] *Angus* v. *Clifford* [1891] 2 Ch. 449; *Le Lievre* v. *Gould* [1893] 1 QB 491; *Heilbut Symons* v. *Buckleton* [1913] AC 30. See v. Bar, *RabelsZ* 44 (1980) pp. 455, 457–459.
[137] More recent examples are *Joyce* v. *Sengupta and Another* [1993] 1 All ER 897 (CA) (a newspaper reported that the plaintiff, one of The Princess Royal's employees, had stolen some of the Princess's letters, for which she had been dismissed. The plaintiff did not base her action in defamation, because legal aid was not available for such a cause of action. A

found in a number of continental legal systems.[138] At its heart is a false assertion made to a third person which causes loss to the plaintiff. Thus injurious falsehood is not actionable *per se*: malice has to be shown. This tort is added to in the tort of passing off:[139] 'While it is injurious falsehood for a defendant to claim that your goods are his, it is passing off for him to claim that his goods are yours.'[140]

(d) Further Economic Torts

Passing off and malicious (or injurious) falsehood (the latter especially in   **260** the so-called slander of goods) also share characteristics with a rather ill-defined group of torts characterized as economic torts, which from the perspective of continental liability law mostly represent instances involving the intentional infliction of damage *contra bonos mores*.[141] The principle to which Weir has endeavoured to return is: 'that it is tortious intentionally to damage another by means of an act which the actor was not at liberty to commit.'[142] It is also true of English tort law that a mere damage-causing act is insufficient; for liability to ensue there must also be an element of unlawfulness which is 'contrary to good custom'.[143] These torts are called 'economic torts' for two reasons: first, they protect purely economic interests, and secondly, they typically appear in the economic sphere. On closer inspection these torts centre upon interference with contractual relationships (interference with contract), whether to induce a breach of contract (procuring or inducing breach of contract),[144] or to compel, by the direct use of pressure, a

---

further recent example is *Spring* v. *Guardian Assurance PLC* [1994] 3 WLR 354 (an employer was liable for a devastatingly bad incorrect reference; in the absence of the subjective requirement of malice the action succeeded, not in malicious (injurious) falsehood, but in negligence: see Allen, 57 (1994) *MLR* 111–116; Weir, (1993) 52 *CLJ* 376–379; and no. 284 below).

[138] See nos. 44–49 above.

[139] The elements of passing off were stated in *Consorzio del Prosciutto di Parma* v. *Marks & Spencer PLC* [1991] RPC 351, 368–369 (*per* Nourse LJ) and in *Reckitt & Colman Products Ltd.* v. *Borden Inc.* [1990] 1 All ER 873, 880 = [1990] 1 WLR 491, 499 (*per* Lord Oliver). Accordingly: (1) the plaintiff must enjoy a good reputation on account of his goods, his name, or his trademark, and (2) the defendant must have given false information, either intentionally or negligently, which led to confusion, and (3) the plaintiff must have suffered damage. For a case involving the risk of confusion in a limited market in which the professional purchasers know both the vendors and their goods, see *Hodgkinson & Corby Ltd.* v. *Wards Mobility Services Ltd.* [1994] 1 WLR 1564.   [140] Fleming, *Torts*, 8th edn., p. 714.

[141] See nos. 36–41 above.   [142] Weir, [1964] *CLJ* 225, 226.

[143] That malice alone is not enough (*Allen* v. *Flood* [1898] AC 1) reflects the fact that the term 'malice' is not clearly defined (Markesinis/Deakin, *Tort Law*, 3rd edn., p. 378).

[144] The leading case is *Lumley* v. *Gye* [1853] 2 El. & Bl. 216 = 118 ER 749 = Weir, *Casebook*, 7th edn., p. 561 (the defendant, owner of the Royal Italian Opera, Covent Garden, induced the niece of Richard Wagner to terminate her contract with the plaintiff Royal Theatre. Decisions since World War II involving either the use of the principle in *Lumley* v. *Gye* or its limited extension are *BMTA* v. *Salvadori* [1949] Ch. 566 and *Law Debenture Trust Corp. PLC.* v. *Ural Caspian Oil Co. Ltd.* [1993] 2 All ER 355, also Tettenborn (1993) 52 *CLJ* 382–384. The

breach of contract.[145] Where an employer is threatened with strike action to persuade him to dismiss an employee who does not belong to a trade union, then the employee, provided his dismissal was lawful, has an action, not in procuring breach of contract, but in the tort of intimidation.[146] Where two or more persons together cause damage to a third for an unlawful purpose they commit the tort of conspiracy, an action which in practice rarely succeeds because the pursuit of one's own economic interest in a noticeably forceful manner has been accepted as justifiable.[147] In so far as these economic torts extend into employment law[148] there exists an extensive corpus of legislation which has over the years been subject to wide-ranging revision.[149] Interference with the running of an established business[150] is covered by the tort of wrongful interference with trade or business,[151] a tort first developed after the Second World War.

party induced to breach its contract has no cause of action; 'he must resist A's efforts by strength of will' (*Boulting and Another* v. *Association of Cinematograph, Television and Allied Technicians* [1963] 2 QB 606 [*per* Upjohn LJ]). See also no. 310 below.

[145] *J. T. Stratford & Son Ltd.* v. *Lindley* [1965] AC 269.

[146] *Rookes* v. *Barnard* [1964] 1 AC 1129 = [1964] All ER 367; cf. Hoffmann 81 (1965) *LQR* 116–141.

[147] See *Crofter Hand Woven Harris Tweed Co. Ltd.* v. *Veitch* [1942] AC 435.

[148] Besides the references in fns. 144 and 145, see *Universe Tankships Inc. of Monrovia* v. *International Transport Workers' Federation* [1983] 1 AC 366. (This was a claim in unjust enrichment for the return of money paid to a fund as a result of duress by a trade union. Whether the exercise of duress is a tort depends very much upon the circumstances of the individual case. 'Where the particular form taken by the economic duress used is itself a tort, the restitutional remedy for money had and received . . . is one which the plaintiff is entitled to pursue as an alternative remedy to an action for damages in tort') and *Brekkes Ltd. and Another* v. *Cattel and Others* [1972] 1 Ch. 105.

[149] An overview of statutory developments since the beginning of the 1980s is provided by Simpson, 54 [1991] *MLR* 418. Sec. 13(1) of the Trade Union and Labour Relations Act 1974 (c. 52) was the starting point ('An act done by a person in contemplation or furtherance of a trade dispute shall not be actionable in tort on the ground only (a) that it induces another person to break a contract or interferes or induces any other person to interfere with its performance; or (b) that it consists in his threatening that a contract . . . will be broken . . .'). Sec. 14 of the same Act added a far-reaching immunity for trade unions and employer groups and almost completely excluded liability in tort. The Employment Act 1982 (c. 46) broke decisively with this position. Sec. 15(2) of the 1982 Act abolished the immunity of trade unions and rendered them liable provided the conduct giving rise to liability 'was authorized or endorsed by a responsible person'. Sec. 15 of the Employment Act 1982 was further amended by sec. 6 of the Employment Act 1990 (c. 38). Today the relevant provisions are found in the Trade Union and Labour Relations (Consolidation) Act 1992 (c. 52). According to this a trade union is liable for the authorized acts of its members (the statute includes a range of conduct being 'authorized'). A variety of options is available to those on strike which serve as defences at law. They are found in sec. 219(1) and (2) of the 1992 Act and they dovetail with pre-existing defences in sec. 13 of the Trade Union and Labour Relations Act 1974.   [150] See nos. 47–49 above.

[151] See esp. *Merkur Island Shipping Corp.* v. *Laughton* [1983] 2 AC 570, 609–610 (*per* Lord Diplock); *J. T. Stratford & Son Ltd.* v. *Lindley* [1965] AC 269, 324 (*per* Lord Reid); and *Hadmor Productions Ltd.* v. *Hamilton* [1981] 2 All ER 724, [1983] 1 AC 191. See no. 312 below.

A more recent example is the case of *Lonrho PLC* v. *Fayed and Others*.[152]   **261**
Lonrho and Fayed fought for control of a company (House of Fraser)
which counted the renowned department store Harrods amongst its
possessions. Lonrho was temporarily hindered in its bid to control
House of Fraser because, in having to answer to the Monopolies and
Mergers Commission, it was unable by 1985 to acquire more than 30 per
cent of the shares. Lonrho asserted that during the period in which
Lonrho had been blocked, Fayed had intentionally deceived the Monopolies Commission on several occasions in order to acquire for itself the
decisive share interest in House of Fraser and had thereby 'cut out'
Lonrho. The claim was struck out[153] at first instance, but the Court of
Appeal decided that the matter should continue. The claim was based on
the tort of wrongful interference with trade or business. It did not matter
for the purposes of damage that no deceit had in fact been practised
against the Monopolies Commission. Neither must it have been the
predominant purpose of Fayed to damage Lonrho. It was sufficient:
'that the unlawful act was in some sense directed against the plaintiff
or intended to harm the plaintiff.'[154]

(e) Private Nuisance and the Rule in *Rylands* v. *Fletcher*

The tort of nuisance (from the french *nuire*, to damage) is anything but   **262**
new. This tort has some traits of property law, in that it applies especially
to neighbours in the strict sense. The essence of nuisance is to protect the
use and undisturbed enjoyment of land.[155] It also protects against interference by noise, smells, smoke, soot, etc.,[156] and thus resembles § 906
German BGB. It also protects against cross-boundary interference,
whether by flooding[157] or the removal of support provided by the
neighbour's land.[158] Non-physical interference (e.g. the running of a
brothel[159] or a sex-shop on adjacent premises[160]) has been held to constitute nuisance. The traditional limits to this tort were exploded in the
case of *Khorasandjian* v. *Bush*.[161] In its decision the Court of Appeal not
only classified unwanted telephone calls as a nuisance but also did away

---

[152] [1989] 2 All ER 65.
[153] The procedural device of a defence application to strike out a claim as disclosing no
reasonable cause of action tests whether the assertions of the plaintiff disclose any proper
basis for a legal claim.   [154] Loc. cit. (fn. 152) p. 65 (*per* Dillon LJ).
[155] Stanton, *Tort*, pp. 386–405; Rogers, *Tort*, 2nd edn., pp. 130–142; and Markesinis/
Deakin, *Tort Law*, 3rd edn., pp. 418–460. Walker, *Delikt*, 2nd edn., p. 643 is clearly of the
opinion that nuisance liability can arise in personal injury cases.
[156] Cf. *Halsey* v. *Esso Petroleum Co. Ltd.* [1961] 2 All ER 145; and *Bone* v. *Seal* [1975] 1 All
ER 787.   [157] *Sedleigh Denfield* v. *O'Callaghan* [1940] AC 880.
[158] *Leakey* v. *National Trust* [1980] QB 485.
[159] *Thompson-Schwab* v. *Costaki* [1956] 1 WLR 335.
[160] *Laws* v. *Florinplace Ltd.* [1981] 1 All ER 659.
[161] [1993] 3 WLR 476; cf. fn. 127 above.

with the requirement that the plaintiff (who had received the calls whilst living in her mother's house) have an interest in the land. The court found that it would be 'ridiculous if in this present age the law is that the making of deliberately harassing and pestering telephone calls to a person is only actionable in the civil courts if the recipient of the calls happens to have the freehold or a leasehold proprietary interest in the premises in which he or she has received the calls'.[162] The decision in this case reinforces the importance of formulating a clear law for the protection of privacy.[163] This has little to do with nuisance: the mischief here is not the noise of the telephone ringing but the psychological pressure exercised by the ex-boyfriend against his former girlfriend.[164]

263   Serious problems of an altogether different nature are raised by the issue of whether fault has a part to play in the law of nuisance and if so what its role is. The traditional answer is that the law of nuisance does not deal with breaches of duty, but rather with unacceptable conditions: accordingly it compensates for loss irrespective of fault.[165] However, this form of quasi-strict liability has been kept in check by the application of the principle of 'reasonable user'.[166] For example, the principle protected against liability the owner of a tree from which a branch suddenly fell onto the plaintiff's car,[167] as well as a house-owner whose blocked drains caused the adjacent property to be flooded.[168] In each case the defendants neither knew nor could have known of the danger. The effect of the principle of reasonable user is that 'if the user is reasonable, the defendant will not be liable for consequent harm to his neighbour's enjoyment of his land; but if the user is not reasonable, the defendant will be liable, even though he may have exercised reasonable care and skill to avoid it.'[169] In addition, an action based in nuisance requires a continuous condition. (The tort of negligence covers instances where the act or activity complained of is a 'one-off' event).[170] Furthermore, the

---

[162] Ibid. p. 481 (*per* Dillon LJ).   [163] See no. 272 below.

[164] One of the problems in *Khorasandjian* v. *Bush* lay in the fact that the ex-boyfriend was neither married to nor lived with his former girlfriend. For this reason the Domestic Violence and Matrimonial Proceedings Act 1976 (c. 50) was not applicable; a common law solution was necessary.

[165] *St Helens Smelting Co.* v. *Tipping* (1865) 11 HL Cas. 642.

[166] *Bramford* v. *Turnley* (1862) 3 B&S 62, 83 (*per* Bramwell B), according to which the principle is intended to ensure that 'those acts necessary for the common and ordinary use and occupation of land and houses may be done, without subjecting those who do them to an action'.   [167] *Noble* v. *Harrison* [1926] 2 KB 332.

[168] *Hawkins* v. *Dhawan and Mishiku* [1987] 19 HLR 232.

[169] *Cambridge Water Co. Ltd.* v. *Eastern Counties Leather PLC.* [1994] 2 AC 264, 299 (*per* Lord Goff); for comment see Cross, 111 (1995) *LQR* 445, 447–458.

[170] *Cunard* v. *Antifyre Ltd.* [1933] 1 KB 551 (guttering fell through the glass roof of a neighour's kitchen and injured the plaintiff's wife). On the other hand it is possible for nuisance and negligence to be pleaded in the same case: *Miller and Another* v. *Jackson and Others* [1977] 1 QB 966.

successful plaintiff in an action for nuisance can recover compensation only for foreseeable damage.[171]

It is an open question whether this is really a form of 'strict' liability, or **264** whether it is simply negligence with the fault element restricted to instances of unreasonable user. Unreasonable user can of itself constitute unreasonable exposure to danger. What in the context of nuisance appears in the guise of 'quasi-negligence liability'[172] brings to mind the equivalent concept in Austria of *casus mixtus*.[173] A similar notion obtains in Germany[174] in the context of liability for negligent infringement of 'abstract' duties of care (*Verkehrspflichten*).

In the absence of fault, 'as a rule . . . there is no liability' according to § 1306 ABGB. By virtue of § 1311 ABGB s. 1 the same applies to the 'chance accident' (*Zufall*) which damages a person's property or physical integrity. However, according to § 1311 ABGB s. 2: 'If somebody caused the accident (*Zufall*) through negligence . . . he is liable for all the consequences which would not otherwise have occurred'. The point of this rule is obvious: when somebody sets something in motion which, given its tendency to cause damage (perhaps also because it is just the sort of activity which leads to 'chance accidents') it would have been better not to have been done at all, then the person who unreasonably set it in motion cannot rely on the defence that even with the utmost vigilance he could not have controlled the following chain of events. The modern view of liability in nuisance is so close to this position that it is very difficult, if not impossible, to distinguish between the two. Also, because in the example just given the damage must still be foreseeable, it is possible to say from our point of view that today, as long as the act was not committed intentionally,[175] nuisance too is no more than the general duty of care applied in a specific context. It would be different if the test of reasonableness were separated from the same test applied to acts or omissions for other intrinsic sources of danger, but this is not the case. What we have here is the fundamental problem of distinguishing between liability for danger and liability for fault. The issue is whether or not liability for each potential danger can, with the help of the principle of *actio libera in causa*, be placed in the category of fault-based liability.

The definitional uncertainties which stem from the twin characteristics **265**

---

[171] Loc. cit. (fn. 169) p. 300.
[172] Cf. *Wilkinson*, 57 (1994) *MLR* 799, 805. Also *Gillick* v. *O'Reilly* [1984] ILRM 402 (McWilliam J).
[173] See Karollus, *Funktion und Dogmatik der Haftung aus Schutzgesetzesverletzung* (Function and Structure of Liability arising from Breach of a Protective Law), pp. 11–15.
[174] Cf. v. Bar, *AcP* 192 (1992) pp. 441, 442–444.
[175] As in *Hollywood Silver Fox Farm* v. *Emmett* [1936] 2 KB 468.

of nuisance (i.e. being capable of giving rise to both liability based on fault and liability based on the existence of a potential danger) are also evident in another configuration of liability in tort, namely the rule in *Rylands* v. *Fletcher*.[176] This case concerned an occupier of land who had a reservoir built on it. The contractor who carried out the work overlooked the fact that there were underground passageways linking the defendant's land with coal mines belonging to the plaintiff; the plaintiff's mines were flooded by water from the reservoir which ran through the underground passageways. Liability in trespass could not be shown because the cause of damage was not direct, and nuisance failed because there was no continuous interference by the defendant. Therefore Blackburn J. formulated a new principle of liability:

'[a] person who, for his own purposes, brings on his land and collects and keeps there anything likely to do mischief if it escapes must keep it in at his peril, and if he does not do so he is *prima facie* answerable for all the damage which is the natural consequence of its escape. He can excuse himself by showing that the escape was owing to the plaintiff's default; or perhaps that the escape was the consequence of *vis major*, or the Act of God.'[177]

266   *Rylands* v. *Fletcher* could have been developed into a general principle of 'liability for risks', particularly dangerous activities, but it has remained narrowly limited. It has not been extended along the lines of French *gardien* liability, but has repeatedly been restricted. *Rylands* v. *Fletcher* has been held not to apply in cases involving the escape of water, gas, or electricity which had been collected for ordinary daily consumption.[178] In those and similar cases, consent was often readily implied.[179] The rule in *Rylands* v. *Fletcher* was severely limited by the decision in *Read* v. *Lyons*,[180] and later by the decision in *Cambridge Water*.[181] *Read* v. *Lyons* restricted the application of the priciple to those cases involving the non-natural use of land, 'non-natural' meaning extraordinary or unusual, rather than artificial.[182]

A German case involving similar facts[183] illustrates clearly the proximity of *Rylands* v. *Fletcher* to recent developments in the German law of *Aufopferungshaftung* (essentially liability for legally inflicted harm) concerning neighbour disputes. The plaintiff ran a garden producing

---

[176] (1866) LR 1 Ex. 265; (1868) LR 3 HL 330.   [177] (1866) LR 1 Ex. 265, 279.
[178] *Collingwood* v. *Home & Colonial Stores* [1936] 3 All ER 200.
[179] E.g. *Peters* v. *Prince of Wales Theatre (Birmingham) Ltd.* [1943] KB 73: the plaintiff used a room in the defendant's theatre as a store-room. During cold weather the sprinkler system burst. The defendant was held not liable: the plaintiff should have known of the sprinkler system, and having accepted its advantages must also accept its disadvantages.
[180] [1947] AC 156; [1946] 2 All ER 471.   [181] Above, fn. 169.
[182] See citations at Markesinis/Deakin, *Tort Law*, 3rd edn., p. 465.
[183] BGH 2 Mar. 1984, BGHZ 90, p. 255.

organic crops. The defendant, whose land lay above that of the plaintiff, operated a conventional farm, using herbicides. After particularly heavy rain water ran off the defendant's land carrying herbicides onto the plaintiff's land; the latter's products could no longer be classified as organic. The BGH granted the plaintiff's claim by analogy with § 906 II s. 2 BGB.[184] Such a claim was said to exist even 'where the effect emanating from one piece of land and affecting adjacent land is unlawful and for this reason does not have to be tolerated, and the affected owner or occupier is obstructed by special reasons from preventing the effect'.[185] If the facts of this case were decided in England there would be no claim in *nuisance* (no unreasonable user of the higher ground, in that no such interferences had happened before) and neither would *Rylands* v. *Fletcher* be of assistance: whilst herbicide is a non-natural (artificial) substance, its use in agriculture is far from unusual.

Cambridge Water[186] confirmed the decision in *Read* v. *Lyons*. The rule in **267** *Rylands* v. *Fletcher* was further weakened because foreseeability of the type of damage which actually occurred was made a requirement of liability. Since this decision, the rule in *Rylands* v. *Fletcher* appears to have been restricted to cases of nuisance.[187] 'Unreasonable user' in nuisance translates in *Rylands* v. *Fletcher* as 'non-natural' (the two being essentially similar[188]) and thus the priciple contribution of *Rylands* v. *Fletcher* is 'that there should be liability for an isolated escape'.[189] *Rylands* v. *Fletcher* is still regarded in England as a case establishing a form of strict liability not derived from statute. The Australian High Court sees it differently. In a recent decision it held that practically no circumstances remain in which liability under *Rylands* v. *Fletcher* can be distinguished in any meaningful way from liability in negligence. There might be instances in which a claim in nuisance would succeed more easily than one in negligence; but there is no reason why the rule in *Rylands* v. *Fletcher* should be retained as an independent form of tortious liability. 'The rule in *Rylands* v. *Fletcher* with all its difficulties, uncertainties, qualifications

---

[184] The judgment stated: 'Where the owner suffers nuisance, he is entitled to demand equivalent monetary compensation from the user of the other property. This entitlement exists where the nuisance interferes with the owner's use of his property in a way that is typical for its location or where the extent of the nuisance is greater than that which would ordinarily have to be accepted.' [185] Above, fn. 183, p. 262.

[186] Above, fn. 169, p. 306.

[187] This is the point of view of Newark, 65 (1949) *LQR* 480–490, relied upon extensively in *Cambridge Water*, pp. 297–298.

[188] Cf. *Rickards* v. *Lothian* [1913] AC 263, 280 (*per* Lord Moulton): 'not every use to which land is put . . . brings into play that principle [i.e. from *Rylands* v. *Fletcher*]. It must be some special use bringing with it increased danger to others, and must not merely be the ordinary use of the land or such use as is proper for the general benefit of the community', a passage which Lord Goff cited approvingly, loc. cit. p. 299.

[189] Lord Goff loc. cit; also Newark loc. cit. (fn. 187) p. 488.

and exceptions, should now be seen, for the purposes of the common law of this country, as absorbed by the principles of ordinary negligence.'[190] Only a small step would be needed to say the same of the relationship between nuisance and negligence.

(f) Public Nuisance

268 The tortious acts described above are examples of the tort of private nuisance. The word 'private' reflects the tort's concern with damage to one individual or to a limited number of persons. By contrast, nuisance which affects 'the public', 'Her Majesty's subjects generally',[191] or 'a whole section of society'[192] is public nuisance. Private and public nuisance can be regarded as two overlapping circles. Within the portion common to both are instances in which a large number of citizens suffer infringement to their rights by noise, smells, or in other ways relevant to the environment.[193] The most important application of the tort of public nuisance involves obstructions to the public highway caused by physical obstacles.[194] Such cases are no longer regarded as private nuisance, having little or nothing to do with the enjoyment of private land, the interest typically protected by private nuisance. The same is true of cases of injury to a person on a public highway by something originating from land occupied by the defendant. So a customer who, outside a butcher's shop, slipped on a piece of fat which came from the shop succeeded in an action in public nuisance;[195] so too did a pedestrian injured by snow falling from a roof,[196] and another injured when a house collapsed.[197]

269   The tort of public nuisance is still evolving and, given the jettisoning of its historical baggage, it is very much the poor relation. In instances such as those cited above, the decisive factor should be how the person

---

[190] *Burnie Port Authority* v. *General Jones Pty Ltd.*, 120 (1994) ALR 42, 67 (See Heuston/Buckley, 110 (1994) *LQR* 506–509).

[191] *Attorney-General* v. *PYA Quarries Ltd.* [1957] 2 QB 169, 190–192 (*per* Denning LJ).

[192] Stanton, *Tort*, p. 402.

[193] See Spencer, 48 [1989] *CLJ* 55, 76–83. See also *Gillingham Borough Council* v. *Medway (Chatham) Dock Co. Ltd. and Others* [1993] QB 343: noise brought about by heavy goods vehicles being driven through a residential area at all hours of the day and night to and from the docks; no public nuisance because, following changes to planning regulations, the interference actually caused was not atypical of such a designated area. Pleading the case in negligence would have been to no avail as the company running the docks could not be said to have been negligent.

[194] A definition of 'public nuisance on the highway' is found in *Jacobs* v. *London County Council* [1950] AC 361, 375 (*per* Lord Simonds): at its heart is 'any wrongful act or omission upon or near a highway, whereby the public are prevented from freely, safely, and conveniently passing along the highway'. Picketing on the street has also been classified as a public nuisance insofar as it does not serve legitimate employment purposes: *Hubbard* v. *Pitt* [1976] QB 142.   [195] *Dollman* v. *Hillman* [1941] 1 All ER 355.

[196] *Slate* v. *Worthingtons Cash Stores Ltd.* [1941] 1 K.B. 488 (CA).

[197] *Mint* v. *Good* [1951] 1 KB 517.

was injured or the property damaged, not where the damage occured. Now that liability in negligent trespass to the person has been subsumed under liability arising out of the general duty of care,[198] there is no real reason why the related cases of public nuisance should not go the same way.[199] This tort also has fault as a prerequisite.[200] Finally, liability in public nuisance for the collapse of buildings is virtually strict,[201] so meeting exactly the corresponding position in continental Europe,[202] although in the latter strict liability is based on the special danger which the law attributes to buildings, and not on the fact that the damage happened to occur on the public highway. Less convincing is the alternative view of the environmental torts (noise, smells, etc.), according to which it is necessary to consider whether there is a single victim (private nuisance)[203] or a group of victims (public nuisance). That distinction may be relevant for criminal law: public nuisance is both a crime and a tort. However, liability in private law is not dependent on the number of those affected, but on the severity of the injury to each. It is also recognized that not every person can claim damages or an injunction from those who cause interference to the public good. A collective action brought on behalf of the public interest should not be based on public nuisance. Only those who have suffered 'special', 'direct', and 'substantial' damage may bring such an action.[204] The plaintiff must also have suffered more than the general public. Once again the question arises: why should it not be possible simply to replace these diffuse and ill-defined categories with interests protected by the general duty of care in negligence?

This leads to two additional facets of public nuisance. Public nuisance **270** bears an uncanny resemblance to certain rules of Roman law, which, as described in the *Motive* of the German BGB: '(protect) the common use of public things not only according to criminal law but also in accordance with civil law, because (they) grant(ed) the remedy of restitution and

---

[198] Above, no. 256 and fn. 125.

[199] See also Spencer (above, fn. 193) pp. 81–83, an article cited with approval by Buckley J. in *Gillingham Council* v. *Medway Dock* (above, fn. 193) at p. 357. In the decisions cited at fns. 195–197 above the plaintiff's success was based primarily in negligence, and in *Noble* v. *Harrison* [1926] 2 KB 332 the action in public nuisance failed simply because of the absence of negligence. A branch hanging 10m above a road fell during good weather and damaged the plaintiff's car. The defendant could neither have created the danger nor known of its existence.

[200] As in the previous footnote. See also Markesinis/Deakin, *Tort Law*, 3rd edn., p. 449, who are of the view that in public nuisance there is a rebuttable presumption of fault. Whether this is generally so remains doubtful.

[201] Spencer (above, fn. 193) p. 82, with reference to *Mint* v. *Good* (above, fn. 197) and *Wringe* v. *Cohen* [1940] 1 KB 229.   [202] Nos. 223–236 above.

[203] There is no doubt that private and public nuisance can arise in the same case: *Halsey* v. *Esso Petroleum Co. Ltd.* [1961] 1 WLR 683.

[204] See *Benjamin* v. *Storr* (1874), reproduced in Weir, *Casebook*, 7th edn., pp. 196–197.

damages, and in certain circumstances an injunction, against the person who breached the rules regarding the use of public things, other than the *actio injuriarum*.'[205] The authors of the BGB declined to incorporate such rules into the BGB. The rule regarding the common use of public things is 'according to the modern organization of state life' a matter of administrative law. In this way it is not 'incompatible to grant the right to claim damages to the individual whose private interests have been adversely affected by a breach of the rules governing the use of public things. In this context, however, the general rules concerning damages for tortious acts are sufficient. Whoever breaches the statutory rules or police regulations concerning the use of public things acts unlawfully . . . and . . . whoever, whether intentionally or negligently, causes damage to another by unlawful action, is bound to pay damages in like amount to the other.'[206] Where there is on one hand a developed administrative law and on the other a general duty not to act negligently, then, according to the observations made here, torts such as public nuisance can be abolished. English law, once it has addressed this whole issue by extensive legislation[207] and affirmed a general liability for negligent conduct,[208] could then consider whether it really needs the tort of public nuisance, which currently has little application in practice. Whether pure economic loss is recoverable remains to be decided. Such loss is not recoverable in negligence in 'highway cases';[209] yet in public nuisance it was recoverable from an early stage.[210] Whether this circumstance is sufficient to justify maintaining the dual bases of claim is doubtful. Whether pure economic loss is recoverable should no longer be dependant upon 'how the plaintiff chooses to frame his claim—(English law) did bury the forms of action 140 years ago'.[211] Furthermore, it is a moot point whether *Rose* v. *Miles*,[212] the leading case on the recoverability of pure economic loss in public nuisance, in fact centred on damage to property: the case concerned the owner of a lighter prevented from sailing along a stretch

---

[205] Mot. II p. 764.   [206] Ibid. p. 765.

[207] Spencer is correct to say: 'Over the last hundred years . . . virtually the entire area traditionally the province of public nuisance prosecutions has been comprehensively covered by statute. (above, fn. 193).   [208] See nos. 274 ff. below.

[209] Due to the absence of sufficient proximity between the parties. This was confirmed recently in *Wentworth* v. *Wiltshire County Council* [1993] 2 WLR 175, which makes it abundantly clear that a local authority charged with the maintenance of public roads is responsible only to road-users, and then only for personal injury and damage to property where the roads are not properly maintained. This liability derives from sec. 1(2) and (3) of the Highway (Miscellaneous Provisions) Act 1961 (c. 63). So a farmer, who had to stop milk production for more than a year because milk tankers were unable to reach his farm, received no compensation.

[210] *Rose* v. *Miles* (1815) 4 M&W 101; 105 ER 773. Cf. Weir, *Casebook*, 7th edn., p. 197.

[211] Rogers (1994) in a paper to be published for the Centre of Liability Law in Tilburg, a body made up of European experts on the law of obligations.   [212] Above, fn. 210.

of canal blocked by the defendant's barge so that the plaintiff had to transport his cargo overland. In a very similar case the German Federal Court found the defendant liable for damage to the plaintiff's boat.[213]

(g) The Protection of Honour and Rights in Personality

Defamation is a complicated area of English tort law governed by a   **271** variety of statutory provisions.[214] It includes both libel and slander. Libel concerns insults in permanent form, typically written defamatory statements. Slander covers transient, non-permanent forms of defamation, such as the spoken word.[215] Certain forms of statements are defined as libel by statute.[216] Libel is actionable *per se*,[217] as are some forms of slander,[218] where statute so ordains.[219] It is of considerable practical importance that actions in defamation must be financed privately by the plaintiff, legal aid being unavailable, which often causes the plaintiff to plead a different cause of action,[220] most commonly malicious falsehood.[221] It has been accepted that a plaintiff can bypass the constitutional right of someone 'who is charged with libel . . . to have his guilt or innocence determined by a jury':[222] a plaintiff with more than one cause of action is entitled to rely on any one of them.[223] In clear-cut cases the plaintiff has a real interest in bringing his case before a jury:[224] juries generally award higher damages than judges. In order to minimize this trend, sec. 8(2) of the Courts and Legal Services Act 1990[225] empowered the judiciary to substitute its own award of damages for that of the jury. Of special significance here is the threat posed by excessive sums in damages awarded against newspapers to the freedom of the press.[226]

---

[213] BGH 21 Dec. 1970, BGHZ 55 p. 153.   [214] See above, no. 241 and fn. 18.

[215] E.g. Winfield/Jolowicz (-Rogers), *Tort*, 14th edn., pp. 314–321.

[216] E.g. sec. 4 Theatres Act 1968 (c. 54) (defamatory comments from the stage); sec. 1 Defamation Act 1952 (c. 66) (news on the radio); secs. 160 and 201 Broadcasting Act 1990 (c. 42) (programmes on terrestrial and cable television). See also *Youssoupoff* v. *Metro-Goldwyn-Mayer Pictures* (1934) 50 TLR 581.   [217] See no. 257 above.

[218] E.g. an assertion that someone had committed a criminal offence punishable with imprisonment (Rogers [fn. 215]).

[219] A very old example appears in sec. 1 Slander of Women Act 1891 (c. 51): 'Words spoken and published . . . which impute unchastity or adultery to any woman or girl shall not require special damage to render them actionable.' Of far more practical importance is sec. 2 Defamation Act 1952 on assertions against a person's professional or business competence.   [220] Made clear in *Joyce* v. *Sengupta* [1993] 1 All ER 897.

[221] See no. 259 above.

[222] *Rothermere* v. *Times* [1973] 1 All ER 1013, 1017 (*per* Denning MR).

[223] *Joyce* v. *Sengupta* (above, fn. 220) p. 902 (*per* Nicholls V-C).

[224] As in *Racz* v. *Home Office* [1994] 2 AC 45; however, that was not a defamation case, cf. fn. 27 above.   [225] C. 41.

[226] *Rantzen* v. *Mirror Group Newspapers (1986) Ltd.* [1994] QB 670; see *Hopkins*, (1994) 53 *CLJ* 9–11 and below, Part 6 no. 592.

272   A detailed description of libel and slander is beyond the remit of this book.[227] English law in this field displays many 'technical' peculiarities. Above all, the rules on *innocent defamation* created shortly after the Second World War have removed the problems created by the common law's overzealous protection of freedom of expression and freedom of the press.[228] However, when it comes to the protection of rights of personality in general, English tort law[229] is out of step with the common European standard. No tort of 'breach of privacy' has, by any name, ever been recognized in English law.[230] It should be noted that the modern English law of torts recognizes a variety of mechanisms by which loopholes in the protection of the individual's right of personality may be closed;[231] such mechanisms are next considered.

An early case involved the unlawful use of the image of an amateur golfer to advertise chocolates.[232] This was regarded as defamatory. An action in nuisance was also available to the plaintiff. *Khorasandjian* v. *Bush*[233] and *Bernstein of Leigh* v. *Skyviews & General Ltd.* are further examples.[234] In *Kaye* v. *Robertson*[235] the plaintiff was harassed by reporters whilst in a helpless state; the Court of Appeal found an escape route in the tort of malicious falsehood. 'Breach of marital confidence' was another means used to grant a divorcee an injunction against her former husband who intended to publish specific sexual details from their marriage.[236] Even actions in trespass to land are employed to protect the right to be left alone.[237] Anyone who has copyright in a published photograph may use this to claim exemplary damages for 'scandalous behaviour' of the defendant 'in total disregard not only of the legal

---

[227] For an overview in German see v. Bar (-Shaw), *DeliktsR in Europa, England und Wales*, pp. 55–60.   [228] The relevant provisions are in sec. 4 Defamation Act 1952.
[229] In New Zealand there has been some movement in this regard. In *Bradley* v. *Wingnut Films Ltd.* [1993] 1 NZLR 415 it was said at first instance by Gallen J. that the common law of New Zealand recognizes a tort of 'breach of privacy'. A film company filmed a tasteless scene by land which the plaintiff had acquired to use as a grave: the claim was rejected.
[230] This has been repeated on numerous occasions and is still the current position in English law: *Kaye* v. *Robertson* [1991] FSR 62 (*per* Glidewell LJ): 'It is well known that in English law there is no right to privacy'; this despite the fact that Winfield/Jolowicz (-Rogers), *Tort*, 14th edn., describe 'infringement of privacy' as a 'doubtful tort' (p. 586).
[231] The Calcutt Report provides an excellent overview of the present position: Report of the Committee on Privacy and Related Matters, Chairman David Calcutt; HMSO, Cm. 1102 (June 1990).   [232] *Tolley* v. *J. S. Fry & Sons Ltd.* [1931] AC 333.
[233] See no. 260 and fn. 161 above.
[234] [1978] 1 QB 479, 489 (*per* Griffiths J): 'If . . . a plaintiff was subjected to the harassment of constant surveillance of his house from the air, accompanied by the photographing of his every activity, I am far from saying that the Court would not regard such a monstrous invasion of his privacy as an actionable nuisance.'   [235] See fn. 230 above.
[236] *Argyll (Duchess)* v. *Argyll (Duke)* [1967] Ch. 302.
[237] *Ghani* v. *Jones* [1970] 1 QB 693, 708 (*per* Lord Denning).

rights of the plaintiff regarding copyright but of his feelings and his sense of family dignity and pride'.[238]

The fact that help has been offered by these different torts does not **273** alter the basic fact that the protection of the right of personality has remained a stepchild of English law. Apart from defamation, none of the torts referred to above are intended primarily to protect the rights of personality and human dignity. Each claimant in such actions must depend on the willingness of the judge to extend the scope of a tort which was intended to meet some other kind of social conflict. In general, English law today is in the same position as that of Germany before the German Federal Court shed its historical baggage during the 1950s.[239] The English judiciary has undertaken no exercise to rid itself of outdated provisions: it regards itself as hindered (unlike the German Federal Court, which was in a similar position) by a few truncated parliamentary attempts at reform.[240] The objections have always been (and still are[241]) based on the same arguments: a right of privacy would be too uncertain and would threaten press freedom.[242] This is a weak objection given that the British judiciary ranks amongst the most able in the world. The insistence upon legal certainty has overridden the protection of human dignity and fails to protect the individual against excesses of the press.

(2) Liability Based on Negligence

(a) Negligence as an Innominate Tort

If nominate torts are understood to be specified individual causes of **274** action united in one system of nominate torts (as in criminal law) so that it is relatively clear what kind of tort has actually been committed, then

---

[238] *Williams* v. *Settle* [1960] 2 All ER 806, 812 (*per* Sellers LJ).   [239] See no. 33 above.

[240] The Calcutt Report (see fn. 231) recommended in 1990 *against* the introduction of a statutory tort of infringement of privacy, concluding (p. 46) that 'an overwhelming case for introducing a statutory tort of infringement of privacy has not so far been made out . . . We therefore recommend that such a tort should not presently be introduced'). So also found the Younger Committee (*Committee on Privacy*, Cmnd. 5012, July 1972), the McGregor Commission (*Third Royal Commission in the Press*, Cmnd. 6810, July 1977), the Faulks Committee on Defamation (Cmnd. 5909, Jan. 1975), and the Law Commission and Scottish Law Commission on *Breach of Confidence* (Cmnd. 8388, Oct. 1981 and Cmnd. 9385, Dec. 1984); *Review of Press Self-Regulation* (Cmnd. 2135, Jan. 1993, *Calcutt II*); *Privacy and Media Intrusion, National Select Committee* (Fourth Report, 294–1, Mar. 1993); *Infringement of Privacy, Consultation Paper* (Lord Chancellor's Department, July 1993), and *Privacy and Media Intrusion: The Government's Response to the House of Commons National Select Committee* (Cmnd. 2918, July 1995).

[241] See the sharp but unconvincing criticism of the decision in *Bradley* v. *Wingnut Films* (above, fn. 229) by Mullender, 53 (1994) *CLJ* 11–14.

[242] It was precisely on this point that all the committees and commissions listed at fn. 240 recommended against the introduction of a general right to privacy.

the most significant of all the common law torts, negligence, does not qualify as a nominate tort. Trespass, deceit, nuisance, defamation, and the other torts at the very least give a general idea of the protection which the law intends to provide. In the context of general liability in negligence, negligence is not simply one type of fault (as in negligent trespass) but is elevated to an independent tort, so the essential descriptive function of its name is lost. A negligence case can involve product liability, or liability for the actions of children over whom insufficient care was exercised; it may concern the liability of doctors, or of a property owner who has taken insufficient care of his property; it covers the liability of a careless driver and the rights of an investor who has been given incorrect financial advice. If we know only that somebody was found liable in negligence then we know practically nothing of the behaviour or act which was found to be negligent. A basis of liability which covers such a wide range of cases does, however, have the characteristics of a general, albeit restricted, theory of liability, and thereby distances itself from the traditional nominate torts. The latter are far-reaching yet distinct torts which protect certain interests against certain types of behaviour. By contrast, negligence attaches liability to the breach of a general duty of care, in which decisions on both the breach and the interests protected are fundamentally open. Negligence can therefore be moulded with little difficulty into an instrument which, like its continental counterparts, offers a 'catch-all' form of protection[243] against negligent injury to individual interests, rights, and property. In a sense, English substantive law has completed in the twentieth century the development which began with procedural law in the nineteenth. Since 1860 a plaintiff has no longer needed to bring his complaint within one of the prescribed forms of action; he need now only show that he has a cause of action. The defendant is no longer considered by the court as a 'deceiver' (from the tort of deceit), or a 'trespasser', or someone who has committed a nuisance, but merely as someone who is required to pay a certain sum of money in damages.[244] This is precisely the case in continental Europe. In England the court's judgment no longer indicates the nature of the matter from which the complaint arose; in this respect it is very similar to the substantive law of negligence.

---

[243] Cf. on one hand *Hawkins v. Clayton* 78 (1988) ALR 69, 109 (*per* Gaudron J): 'If the statement of duty is transposed in a statement of right, it constitutes an acknowledgement of a right not to be injured by or in consequence of the acts or omissions of one's neighbour in circumstances where the injury is reasonably foreseeable by that neighbour' and on the other hand the statement of K. Schmidt, *JuS* 1993 pp. 985, 987: 'the legal terms property and freedom are defined exclusively in terms of the protective zone which surrounds them and this protective zone is nothing more than the reflection of the duties owed by third parties.'

[244] A more detailed account of the abolition of the medieval forms of action is provided by *Halsbury's Laws of England* (-Jacob), 4th edn., vol. 37, para. 107.

(b) The Development and Requirements of Negligence

Despite its overwhelming importance in English law, negligence is a   **275**
relatively recent tort. *Heaven* v. *Pender*,[245] a Court of Appeal case from
1883, was the first decision to put forward a general theory of liability in
negligence.

The plaintiff, a ship's painter employed by the defendant, fell from the
scaffold which the defendant, the owner of the dock in which the ship
was being repaired, had erected in accordance with his contract with the
ship's owner. The latter had put the execution of the contract at the
disposal of the plaintiff's employer. The scaffolding collapsed because
the ropes attaching it to the hull of the ship had been weakened in a fire.
The defendant could easily have known this. The plaintiff was seriously
injured. His claim was rejected at first instance for want of a cause of
action. The Court of Appeal overturned this decision. Brett MR (later
Lord Esher) said: 'the action is in form and substance an action for
negligence.'[246] Negligence was the cause of action where 'the person
charged with such want of ordinary care had a duty to the person
complaining to use ordinary care in respect of the matter called in
question. Actionable negligence consists in the neglect of the use of
ordinary care or skill towards a person to whom the defendant owes
the duty of observing ordinary care and skill, by which neglect the
plaintiff . . . has suffered injury to his person or property. It is undoubted
. . . that there may be the obligation of such a duty from one person to
another although there is no contract between them with regard to such
duty.'[247]

Almost all of contemporary negligence law can be seen in these few   **276**
sentences. However, it took half a century for his words finally to prevail.[248] In *Heaven* v. *Pender* itself the contrary argument was already
raised: the other two Court of Appeal judges were 'unwilling to concur
with the Master of the Rolls in laying down unnecessarily the larger
principle which he entertains, inasmuch as there are many cases in
which the principle was impliedly negatived.'[249] This was a valid argument. There were already many decisions which primarily provided that
the liability in negligence of the manufacturer of a product was restricted
to his contractual partners;[250] the only exception was if the product was

---

[245] *Heaven* v. *Pender, trading as West India Graving Dock Company* (1883) 11 QBD. 503.
[246] Ibid. p. 506.   [247] Ibid. p. 507.
[248] An interesting summary of the development at this time is found in the dissenting
judgment of Lord Buckmaster in *M'Alister (or Donoghue) (Pauper)* v. *Stevenson* [1932] AC
562, 566–578; cf. no. 277 below.   [249] *Heaven* v. *Pender*, p. 516.
[250] Of note here are *Winterbottom* v. *Wright* 10 M&W 109: collapse of a defectively built
boat; the injured passenger was left without a claim. At p. 115 Alderson B. said: 'The only
safe rule is to confine the right to recover to those who enter into the contract; if we go one
step beyond that, there is no reason why we should not go fifty') and *Longmeid* v. *Holliday* 6

299

inherently dangerous.[251] As late as 1929 it was said of Scottish law (which resembled English law, as was later emphasized in *Donoghue* v. *Stevenson*[252]) that 'where the goods of the defendants are widely distributed throughout Scotland, it would seem little short of outrageous to make them responsible to members of the public for the condition of the contents of every bottle which issues from their works'.[253]

277   Only in the light of this phase of stagnation and retreat can the significance of Lord Atkin's speech in *Donoghue* v. *Stevenson* be recognized. That speech, supported by a bare majority in the House of Lords, was ground-breaking.[254] The decision was truly momentous in English tort law, and it was no coincidence that it occurred at about the same time as *gardien* liability was born in France and the general duty of care (*Verkehrspflicht*) in Germany.[255] The significance of the decision is equivalent to that of the *arrêt Jand'heur*[256] in France and that of the German Federal Court recognizing the general right to personality.[257]

The facts of *Donoghue* v. *Stevenson* were straightforward. The defendant, a manufacturer of ginger beer, stored his bottles prior to filling them so that they were accessible to vermin. A snail got into one of the bottles. The plaintiff, whose friend had bought the bottle of ginger beer, was drinking from it when the remains of the snail appeared. The friend suffered shock and a severe stomach upset.

Wholly at odds with Lord Buckmaster, who wanted to apply the traditional rules and in consequence deny liability, Lord Atkin referred directly back to the speech of Brett MR and restated 'the doctrine of *Heaven* v. *Pender*' in new words:

'In English law there must be, and is, some general conception of relations giving rise to a duty of care, of which the particular cases found in the books are but instances. The liability for negligence, whether you style it such or treat it as in other systems as a species of *culpa*, is no doubt based upon a general public sentiment of moral wrongdoing for

---

Ex. 761, 768: explosion of a defective lamp. The wife had no claim as the lamp had been bought by her husband. A number of decisions were founded on the principle in *Heaven* v. *Pender*, including *Earl* v. *Lubbock* [1905] 1 KB 253 (injury caused by the tyre of a lorry becoming loose) and *Bates* v. *Batey & Co. Ltd.* [1913] 3 KB 351 (exploding soda bottle). The decision in *Le Lievre* v. *Gould* [1893] 1 QB 491 (CA) made clear that the principle in *Heaven* v. *Pender* did not apply to pure economic loss; this had to await the decision in *Hedley Byrne* v. *Heller* [1964] AC 465 (HL) (below, no. 285). Schnopfhagen provides a clear overview in German of the early English decisions on product liability in *ZfRV* 1993 pp. 62, 70–71.

[251] *Dominion Natural Gas Co. Ltd.* v. *Collins and Perkins* [1909] AC 640, 646 (*per* Lord Dunedin).
[252] At p. 566 (Lord Buckmaster), p. 579 (Lord Atkin), and p. 602 (Lord Thankerton).
[253] *Mullen* v. *Barr & Co.* 1929 SC 461, 479 (*per* Lord Anderson).
[254] *Donoghue* v. *Stevenson* (see fn. 248) 578–599.   [255] See nos. 104–116 above.
[256] See no. 111 above.   [257] See no. 33 above.

which the offender must pay . . . The rule that you are to love your neighbour becomes in law, you must not injure your neighbour; and the lawyer's question, who is my neighbour? receives a restricted reply. You must take reasonable care to avoid acts or omissions which you can reasonably foresee would be likely to injure your neighbour. Who, then, in law is my neighbour? The answer seems to be: persons who are so closely and directly affected by my act that I ought reasonably to have them in contemplation as being so affected when I am directing my mind to the acts or omissions which are called into question.'[258]

278 The principle in *Donoghue* v. *Stevenson* has been applied in countless decisions and has never been questioned. The present debate concerns, first and foremost, the problem of which interests are protected by the principle, and the connected issue of the relationship between negligence and the other torts in English law. However important these issues might be for the entire system, from the perspective of negligence alone they raise a range of peripheral problems. A claim based in negligence is then only successful when a fourfold test is satisfied: the plaintiff must show (1) that the defendant owed the plaintiff a duty of care, (2) that the defendant breached that duty, and (3) that as a result of this breach of duty (causation) (4) the plaintiff has suffered damage.[259] If the causation element is considered less worthy of consideration (as being axiomatic), one is left with the trinity of duty, breach, and damage. 'It is now elementary that the tort of negligence involves three factors: a duty of care, a breach of that duty and consequent damage.'[260]

279 At the heart of the tort of negligence is unquestionably the notion of the duty of care, or duty. Whilst also maintaining policy considerations[261] (which serve to highlight further the sovereign position of the English judge) as a control mechanism in determining the issue of the existence or otherwise of a duty of care, the primary test for the existence

---

[258] At 580.

[259] This was made clear at much the same time as *Donoghue* v. *Stevenson*. Cf. Lord Wright in *Lochgelly Iron and Coal Co.* v. *M'Mullen* [1934] 1 AC 1, 25: negligence 'connotes the complex of duty, breach and damage thereby suffered by the person to whom the duty is owing'. See also *Woods* v. *Duncan* [1946] AC 401, 419.

[260] *Burton* v. *Islington HA* [1992] 3 WLR 639, 655 (*per* Dillon LJ). For a clear and wideranging analysis of this topic see Markesinis/Deakin, *Tort Law*, 3rd edn., pp. 65–76.

[261] See also no. 291 below. The decisive factor behind such policy considerations, which allow of no logical classification, was formulated by Lord Goff in *Smith* v. *Littlewoods Organisation* [1987] AC 241, 280: 'It is very tempting to try to solve all problems of negligence by reference to an all-embracing criterion of foreseeability, thereby effectively reducing all decisions in this field to questions of fact. But this comfortable solution is, alas, not open to us. The law has to accommodate all the untidy complexity of life; and there are circumstances where considerations of practical justice impel us to reject a general imposition of liability for foreseeable damage.'

of such a duty is that of foreseeability.[262] The duty concept thus unifies problems of *Rechtswidrigkeit*, objective carelessness, and the *Schutzzweck der Norm*. The starting point of each case is always the question of whether a duty of care was owed to this particular plaintiff; the answer depends essentially (if not entirely) upon whether the damage was foreseeable as a consequence of the defendant's act or omission. A relationship or degree of proximity is required; this is no more than a reformulation of Lord Atkin's neighbour principle. That principle operates as a multi-functional instrument. In cases of physical injury and damage to property, which happen 'directly' and without other causes, the biblical image of the 'neighbour' adds very little, if anything. It is patently obvious that you should not harm your neighbour. This was traditionally the territory of trespass, and is an element of all legal systems. Where the neighbour principle was first applied, namely when damage was caused by more distant 'indirect' factors, the biblical image was, strictly speaking, incorrect from the very beginning: what lay person would come up with the idea that the end consumer of a product was the neighbour of the manufacturer? The neighbour principle sounds good, but in truth it is little more than a pleasing turn of phrase. In reality it concerns what in German law is called the 'positive' statement of *Rechtswidrigkeit*[263] (also no more than fancy waffle): i.e. a value judgement based upon all the circumstances of the case when the end result alone is insufficient to determine the *Rechtswidrigkeit* of the act. As for liability for omissions, the neighbour principle provides that a mere omission will generally not lead to liability unless there was a pre-existing but not necessarily contractual relationship between the parties.[264] 'Proximity' also has an important and independent function in cases involving the recoverability of pure economic loss. In this field other elements (reliance, professional expertise, voluntary acceptance of responsibility) can limit the extent of liability.[265]

280   Two further aspects are crucial to the tort of negligence. The first concerns the test for negligence itself, i.e. that element of the tort from which its name derives: whether someone has acted in a morally wrong way is determined, not by whether there exists a duty, but by whether there has been a breach of duty.[266] Not only in the nominate torts (e.g. trespass) is negligence encountered as a form of fault, but also in the tort of negligence

---

[262] The issue of foreseeability is not restricted to the existence of a duty of care. It is also relevant to causation, because both the extent of damage (*Overseas Tankship [UK] Ltd.* v. *Morts Dock & Engineering Co., The Wagon Mound (No. 1)* [1961] AC 388) and the kind of damage (*Hughes* v. *Lord Advocate* [1963] AC 837) sustained must have been foreseeable. Cf. *Cambridge Water* (above, no. 263 and fn. 171).   [263] See nos. 18 and 105 above.

[264] See no. 288 below. That a duty of care may exist between non-contracting parties was one of the innovations of *Donoghue* v. *Stevenson*.   [265] Below, nos. 285 and 500 ff.

[266] E.g. *Barnett* v. *Chelsea and Kensington Hospital Management Committee* [1969] 1 QB 428.

itself.[267] The fact that foreseeability of damage is the test, not only in the context of duty, but also for an actionable breach of duty gives rise to the question: what is the difference between these two elements? The answer is more difficult than first appears. In *Donoghue* v. *Stevenson* the issue was whether the manufacturer owed any duty of care to the consumer. As far as breach of duty was concerned, the principal question was what exactly had been done wrongly in the storage of the bottles. However, it is not simply a matter of distinguishing between whether on one hand, and how or what on the other. There are a multitude of cases in which it makes little or no sense to distinguish the two issues of whether someone was bound to act carefully 'at all', and what that person 'actually' should have done (or not done, as the case may be); the one is often inseparable from the other.[268] So there is a second aspect which it is easiest to explain by reference to *Donoghue* v. *Stevenson*. To the extent that duty considerations are based upon the foreseeability of damage, a balancing or corrective mechanism is required. The manufacturer of any product (whether cars, knives, or light-bulbs) knows that people can be injured by his product, but he should only be liable if the product has an imperfection for which he is responsible. This principle secured a separate test for breach. That observation in turn leads to a third aspect: it should also be clear that the element of duty dictates the scope of the tort of negligence and the field of protected interests. It is simply not the case, and this point was not made sufficiently clear in the dictum of Lord Atkin, that mere foreseeability of damage is enough to demand that care be exercised by the *reasonable* man. This is capable of the alternative interpretation: the absence of duty is now increasingly relied upon by defendants who, although negligent, deny responsibility for the foreseeable damage sustained.[269] Seen in this light the original role of the duty concept is reversed.[270] Once used as the basis of liability for damage

---

[267] A breach of duty exists if the defendant fails to act with reasonable care. This test is considerably older than the test for negligence, cf. *Blyth* v. *Birmingham Waterworks Co.* (1856) 11 Ex. 781, 784: 'Negligence is the omission to do something which a reasonable man, guided upon those considerations which ordinarily regulate the conduct of human affairs would do, or something which a prudent and reasonable man would not do.' It was put more bluntly by Lord Radcliffe in *Bolton* v. *Stone* [1951] AC 850, 868: 'a breach of duty has taken place if (the plaintiffs) show the appellants guilty of a failure to take reasonable care to prevent the accident.'   [268] E.g *Smith* v. *Littlewoods.* [1987] 1 AC 241.

[269] Of recent cases on pure economic loss see: *Galoo Ltd.* v. *Bright Grahame Murray* [1994] 1 WLR 1360 with commentary by O'Sullivan (1995) 54 *CLJ*, 25, 27: 'Foreseeability alone does not create a duty of care.' Comments such as those of Colman J in *Walker* v. *Northumberland County Council* [1995] 1 All ER 737, 751 can be confusing: 'in the present case it is not necessary to consider foreseeability with respect to the existence of a duty of care, because the relationship of employer and employee itself gives rise to that duty of care.'

[270] Cf. the comment of Lord Goff in *Smith* v. *Littlewoods* [1987] 1 AC 241, 280: 'we have nowadays to appreciate that the broad general principle of liability for foreseeable damage is so widely applicable that the function of the duty of care is not so much to identify cases where liability is imposed as to identify those where it is not.'

caused directly to another, today the requirement of duty operates to block the floodgates and thus to restrict what would otherwise be liability without limit. A person who incorrectly advises on the financial state of a company is not liable to every person who actually relies upon the statement, but only to those whom the adviser must have known would rely upon the statement as the basis of their investment decisions.[271] An individual who fails to maintain his home is liable to a guest but not to a burglar. A barrister owes a duty of care to the court rather than to the litigant.[272] An education authority owes a duty of care to a pupil but this does not necessarily extend to giving professional guidance to the pupil's mother.[273] The prosecuting authorities[274] and the Home Secretary[275] are responsible to Parliament and not to defendants. A duty of care is increasingly required to be fair, just, and reasonable for the good of society as a whole.[276]

281   A final issue of fundamental importance is the relationship between principle and authority. According to the traditional method of case interpretation, a duty of care could only be affirmed when a previously decided case provided an authority for such a duty. The 1970s witnessed a departure from this careful case-by-case approach. In 1970 Lord Reid in *Dorset Yacht* observed 'a steady trend towards regarding the law of negligence as depending on principle', so that 'when a new point emerges, one should not ask whether it is covered by authority but whether recognized principles apply to it'.[277] Lord Denning spoke in similar vein shortly thereafter.[278] Both judgments preceded the expansive 1977 decision in *Anns* v. *Merton*, in which Lord Wilberforce drew up his now famous two-stage test:

'The position has now been reached that, in order to establish that a duty of care arises in a particular situation, it is not necessary to bring the facts of that situation within those of previous situations in which a duty of care has been held to exist. Rather the question has to be approached in two stages. First one has to ask whether, as between the alleged wrongdoer and the person who has suffered damage, there

---

[271] Cf. *Caparo Industries PLC* v. *Dickman and Others* [1990] 2 AC 605: and *Smith* v. *Eric S. Bush, Harris and Another* [1989] 2 WLR 790.

[272] *Rondel* v. *Worsley* [1969] 1 AC 191. On this see Part 6, no. 560 and fn. 34.

[273] E.g. *E (a Minor)* v. *Dorset County Council and Other Appeals* [1994] 4 All ER 640; [1994] 3 WLR 853 (CA); [1995] 3 All ER 353 (HL).

[274] *Elguzouli-Daf* v. *Commissioner of Police of the Metropolis and Another / McBrearty* v. *Ministry of Defence and Others* [1995] 1 All ER 833.

[275] *Bennett* v. *Commissioner of Police of the Metropolis and Others* [1995] 1 WLR 488.

[276] Cf. *Caparo Industries PLC* v. *Dickman* (fn. 271 above) 617–618 (*per* Lord Bridge); and *Marc Rich and Co. AG* v. *Bishop Rock Marine Co. Ltd. and Others, The Nicholas H.* [1995] 3 All ER 307, 326 (Lord Lloyd).

[277] *Dorset Yacht Co. Ltd.* v. *Home Office* [1970] AC 1004, 1026–1027.

[278] *Dutton* v. *Bognor Regis Urban District Council* [1972] 1 QB 373.

is a sufficient relationship of proximity or neighbourhood such that, in the reasonable contemplation of the former, carelessness on his part may be likely to cause damage to the latter, in which case a *prima facie* duty of care arises. Secondly, if the first question is answered affirmatively, it is necessary to consider whether there are any considerations which ought to negative, or to reduce or limit the scope of the duty or the class of persons to whom it is owed or the damages to which a breach of it may give rise.'[279]

Although the two-stage test in *Anns* was applied in over a hundred **282** decisions in the years after it was decided, it has not prevailed. *Anns*, a case covering the twin issues of damage to property and pure economic loss, would have brought to English law a general theory of liability very much akin to that found in the French *Code civil*. In the face of increasing opposition from the House of Lords, this proved ultimately to be a development too far. The structure established by *Anns* was dismantled step by step as regards both subject-matter and principle.[280] As far as subject-matter was concerned, the restriction of liability for extra-contractual pure economic loss[281] was the key. From the point of view of legal principle, the importance in case-law of the basic rule of precedent[282] proved decisive. The decision in *Murphy* v. *Brentwood District Council*[283] stands at the end of this line of cases and is one of the most spectacular decisions in English tort law of recent times.[284] The House of Lords departed from *Anns* and 'all decisions subsequent to *Anns* which purported to follow it'.[285] Also overruled was the decision in *Dutton* v. *Bognor Regis*,[286] one of the decisions which had made *Anns* possible. A duty of care must be derived from the *rationes decidendi* of earlier cases, and not from an all-embracing general theory of tortious liability.

(c) The Protected Interests

The task which confronted the tort of negligence in the first half of its short **283** history was to improve the protection of life, health, and property;[287] all

---

[279] *Anns* v. *Merton London Borough Council* [1978] AC 728, 751–752; [1977] 2 WLR 1024, 1032.

[280] For a more detailed account in German, see v. Bar, *RabelsZ* 56 (1992) pp. 410, 422–430.

[281] Cf. *Yuen Kun Yeu and Others* v. *A-G of Hong Kong* [1988] AC 175; *Caparo Industries PLC* v. *Dickman and Others* [1990] 2 AC 605; and *Clarke* v. *Bruce Lane & Co. (a Firm) and Others* [1988] 1 All ER 364.

[282] *Governors of the Peabody Donation Fund* v. *Sir Lindsay Parkinson & Co. Ltd. and Others* [1985] AC 210; *Hill* v. *Chief Constable of West Yorkshire* [1989] 1 AC 53, 60 (*per* Lord Keith).

[283] [1991] 1 AC 398; [1990] 3 WLR 414; [1990] 2 All ER 908.

[284] *Murphy* is not only a case in which the House of Lords departed from its own earlier decision, but is also an example of the House sitting as a seven-man tribunal.

[285] Lord Mackay LC, in *Murphy*.   [286] See fn. 278 above.

[287] For what amounts to personal injury (above all in nervous shock cases) and where the boundary lies between damage to property and pure economic loss (cf. *Junior Books Ltd.* v. *Veitchi Co. Ltd.* [1983] 1 AC 520; *Tate & Lyle Food & Distribution* v. *Greater London Council and Another* [1983] 2 AC 509, 530 *per* Lord Templeman) see Vol. ii, Part 1 of this book.

other interests originally lay outside the protection of this tort.[288] More recent legal developments have moved away from this position and have thus led to greater convergence between English tort and continental liability law. Meanwhile, negligence has brought the law of torts to a position which, apart from the problems concerning the protection of rights of personality, corresponds substantially to the legal position under Art. 6:162 BW. Already conspicuous in the field of what in continental Europe are called 'absolute rights' are the several extensions to the sphere of application of negligence as a tort. There is nothing to prevent a claim of false imprisonment caused negligently from being brought in negligence, although it may be more usual and beneficial to the plaintiff to bring an action for false imprisonment.[289] Should he sue in false imprisonment which was negligently caused, he is likely to be confronted with policy considerations and other mechanisms to restrict liability which were developed in the context of the tort of negligence.[290] The same applies to actions brought in malicious prosecution[291] and defamation.[292] Touching upon the issue of legal protection for the right of personality and for the subjective rights of the family are a number of recent decisions on whether education authorities and psychiatrists in their employ are liable in negligence for damage to the educational potential and future chances of pupils by their incorrect appraisal and failure to take corrective measures.[293] It is extremely doubtful whether disruption of personality development can be properly described as personal injury.[294] On the other hand, it would be unjust to allow plaintiffs in such cases only to claim either personal injury or pure economic loss, and thereby make their resolution dependent on their fitting into one of those two categories.[295] The most important recent case here is *Spring* v. *Guardian Assurance PLC*.[296] Apart from its relevance for the protection of personality, this decision shows above all how the tort of negligence is becoming increasingly amenable in cases where the prerequisites of more specific torts are absent.

---

[288] Lord Templeman, (fn. 287): 'My Lords, in the cited relevant cases from *Donoghue* v. *Stevenson* to *Junior Books* the plaintiff suffered personal injury or damage to his property.'
[289] See no. 257 above.   [290] *Davidson* v. *Chief Constable of North Wales*, fn. 132.
[291] *Martin* v. *Watson*, fn. 133.
[292] *Derbyshire County Council* v. *Times Newspapers Ltd. and Others* [1993] AC 534.
[293] *E (a Minor)* v. *Dorset County Council and Other Appeals* [1994] 4 All ER 640 and *M* v. *Newham Council/X* v. *Bedfordshire County Council* [1994] 2 WLR 554 (CA); [1995] 3 All ER 353 (HL).
[294] 'Physical harm' was held by the Court of Appeal in *E (a Minor)* to have been caused 'if the plaintiffs . . . have suffered from a pathological condition which accounts for the learning difficulties' (p. 660, *per* Evans LJ). However, the loss to badly taught pupils is irrecoverable pure economic loss (Evans LJ, ibid. p. 670; *Van Oppen* v. *Clerk to the Bedford Charity Trustees* [1989] 3 All ER 389).   [295] Thus Evans LJ in *E (a Minor)*.
[296] [1994] 3 WLR 354 (HL).

In *Spring* v. *Guardian Assurance PLC* the plaintiff sold insurance **284** policies while in the service of the defendant company. The plaintiff began to work for a new employer in insurance who required a reference from the defendant. This reference was so negative as to constitute 'the kiss of death'; the plaintiff became unemployed with no chance of resuming work in the same kind of employment. The plaintiff based his claim in breach of contract, malicious falsehood, and negligence. At first instance he was successful in the negligence action only. The Court of Appeal rejected the plaintiff's claim in its entirety.[297] It could not be shown that the defendant was motivated by the necessary malice since the defendant honestly believed the plaintiff to be dishonest. The Court of Appeal made it clear that negligence should not be introduced to a field 'for which it was not designed and is not appropriate'. In a case of this kind malicious falsehood and defamation were the proper causes of action. The House of Lords overturned the decision of the Court of Appeal and affirmed by a majority the finding of negligence. This was a case of pure economic loss, for which damage is recoverable under the principles in *Hedley Byrne* v. *Heller*.[298] There was no reason to transfer the requirements of liability in defamation to negligence. Lord Woolf, whose speech was the longest, added: 'I can see no justification for creating a fence around the whole of the field to which defamation can apply and treating any other tort, which can beneficially from the point of view of justice enter into part of that field, as a trespasser if it does so.'[299]

Negligence has thus conquered some of the terrain occupied by the protection of reputation. At the same time it has become a residual cause of action, as breach of statutory duty actions can demonstrate: a failure to fulfil the requirements for liability under the statutory breach does not preclude a successful action. Lacunae in the protection of the plaintiff may often be filled by a common law-based duty of care.[300]

Notwithstanding the numerous voices calling for restraint[301] the **285** development of negligence into a theory of general tortious liability on

---

[297] *Idem* [1993] 3 All ER 273 (CA); cf. Weir (1993) 52 *CLJ* 376 and Allen, (1994) 57 *MLR* 111. The Court of Appeal departed from the decision in *Lawton* v. *BOC Transhield Ltd.* [1987] 2 All ER 608, a decision which the court of first instance had regarded as binding upon it. [298] See no. 285 below. [299] Loc. cit. (fn. 296) at p. 399.

[300] Support for this proposition is found not only in *E (a Minor)* (fn. 233) and *Spring* v. *Guardian*, but also in *Stovin* v. *Wise* [1994] 3 All ER 467. The opposite view is reflected in decisions such as *Deloitte Hoskins* v. *National Mutual Life* [1993] 2 All ER 1015 and *West Wiltshire District Council* v. *Garland* [1993] Ch. 409.

[301] The danger 'of extending the ambit of negligence so as to supplant or supplement other torts, contractual obligations, statutory duties or equitable rules in relation to every kind of damage including economic loss' was made clear by Lord Templeman in *Downview Nominees Ltd.* v. *First City Corp. Ltd.* [1993] AC 295, 316. Morritt LJ went on to say in *Elguzouli-Daf* (fn. 274) p. 845: 'I do not understand that warning to have lost its relevance by virtue of the decision of the House of Lords in *Spring* v. *Guardian Assurance.*'

continental lines appears to continue apace. This becomes clearer if one accepts that wherever a general theory of liability covers negligent conduct, the extent of liability for intentional conduct must, at the very least, equal that for negligent conduct. Otherwise a claim of intentional conduct would become a defence against claims of negligence.[302] Also, whether the damage is held to be the consequence of the infringement of a right or as recoverable pure economic loss is a cosmetic matter of legal form. The second decisive point about negligence is that, ever since the decision in *Hedley Byrne* v. *Heller,*[303] pure economic loss is recoverable in prescribed circumstances.

Hedley Byrne involved liability for information. The plaintiff advertising agency was contracted by a firm called Easipower to arrange advertising. The plaintiff initially financed the campaign itself. Accordingly it wished to be sure that Easipower could pay fees. The plaintiff asked the defendant, Easipower's bank, whether Easipower was good for £100,000. The defendant, expressly excluding liability for information given, answered in the affirmative. Within a week Heller withdrew all Easipower's credit and refused to honour cheques draw on Easipower's account. The House of Lords rejected the plaintiff's negligence-based damages claim against Heller on account of the exclusion clause, not because the loss concerned was purely economic.

286   Of course *Hedley Byrne* did not mean that negligence had in one single leap become a comprehensive, all-embracing cause of action of the sort found in Arts. 1382 and 1383 of the French *Code civil. Hedley Byrne* simply established that in certain circumstances there could be a claim for pure economic loss arising out of the 'mere statements' given by professionals whilst conveying information. The *sine qua non* of such liability was (and is) proximity of relationship akin to contract between the provider and the recipient of the information,[304] in which it is fair, just, and reasonable to assume that the giver of the information has voluntarily undertaken responsibility for the accuracy of the information provided.[305] It was not intended that *Hedley Byrne* should disturb the principle that negligently caused pure economic loss is not

---

[302] Gearty, (1989) 48 *CLJ* 214, 223; Williams/Hepple, *Foundations*, 2nd edn., p. 124 fn. 12.
[303] *Hedley Byrne and Co.* v. *Heller and Partners* [1964] AC 465 (HL).
[304] Cf. Part 5 I, nos. 429 and 500 ff. below.
[305] Loc. cit. (fn. 303) p. 487 (*per* Lord Reid) and p. 529 (*per* Lord Devlin: 'a responsibility that is voluntarily accepted or undertaken'). For the test of 'voluntary assumption of responsibility' see *Ministry of Housing and Local Government* v. *Sharp* [1970] 2 QB 223; *Caparo Industries PLC* v. *Dickman* [1989] 2 WLR 316, 326 (*per* Bingham LJ); *Smith* v. *Eric S. Bush, Harris and Another* and *Wyre Forest District Council and Another* [1990] 2 WLR 790, 822 (*per* Lord Jauncey) and *Kuwait Asia Bank EC* v. *National Mutual Life Nominees Ltd.* [1991] 1 AC 187, 219 (*per* Lord Lowry).

recoverable;[306] the House of Lords wanted to restrict this exception to instances involving the provision of services.

Whether it can be said that the above principle is still valid, or whether **287** it is accepted that the common law[307] has developed substantially beyond the territory marked out by *Hedley Byrne*, is an open question. It is clear that the application of *Hedley Byrne* has extended beyond the giving of credit references by banks. The principle has been applied to a range of persons and professional groups whose job involves looking after the financial interests of others.[308] On the other hand, even in these instances the requirement for a close degree of proximity, founded as it is upon reasonable reliance between the professional and the person who has suffered loss, has been strictly maintained.[309] *Caparo* v. *Dickman* is the most significant of the recent decisions in this field.[310] It is also correct to say that *Murphy* v. *Brentwood* demolished what had been a strong and growing tendency to classify a particular type of damage as damage to property[311] instead of pure economic loss (which is what it was).[312] The same applies to the question of whether a manufacturer is

---

[306] Liability for pure economic loss has been repeatedly rejected in a long line of cases in which analogy with *Hedley Byrne* was not possible. In addition to the cases listed at no. 287, see also *Spartan Steel & Alloys Ltd.* v. *Martin & Co. (Contractors) Ltd.* [1973] 1 QB 27 (loss of income caused by interruption of the electricity supply to a factory); *Governors of the Peabody Donation Fund* v. *Sir Lindsay Parkinson & Co. Ltd. and Others* [1985] AC 210 (failure of an authority with responsibility for construction properly to oversee the laying of drainage pipes; no liability); *Leigh and Sillivan Ltd.* v. *Aliakmon Shipping Co. Ltd.* ('*The Aliakmon*') [1986] 1 AC 785 (no liability for damage to goods at a time when they were not the property of the buyer; see also no. 488 below); *Muirhead* v. *Industrial Tanks Specialities Ltd. and Others* [1985] 3 WLR 993 (expenditure on overseeing defective pumping gear) and *D & F Estates Ltd.* v. *Church Commissioners for England* [1989] 1 AC 177 (costs of repairing defectively built housing and damages for loss of use; no liability).

[307] As part of the statutory development in this field, pride of place belongs to sec. 2(1) Misrepresentation Act 1967 (c. 7) which only protects a contractual partner against the *culpa in contrahendo* of the other party.

[308] E.g. *Smith* v. *Bush* loc. cit. (fn. 305); *Ross* v. *Caunters* [1979] 3 WLR 605; *W.B. Anderson & Son* v. *Rhodes (Liverpool)* [1967] 2 All ER 850; *Morgan Crucible* v. *Hill Samuel* [1991] Ch. 295; *Kuwait Bank* loc. cit. (fn. 305). Cf. *Spring* v. *Guardian Assurance* (fn. 296 above).

[309] See *Mutual Life and Citizen's Assurance Co.* v. *Evatt* [1971] AC 793 (recommendation by an insurance company as to the financial stability of an associate company; no liability because advice of this sort did not form part of the kind of advice typically given by an insurance company); in *Yuen Kun Yeu & Others* v. *A-G of Hong Kong* [1988] AC 175; in *Clarke* v. *Bruce Lane & Co. (a Firm) and Others* [1988] 1 All ER 364 or in *Galoo Ltd.* v. *Bright Grahame Murray* [1994] 1 WLR 1360 with commentary, O'Sullivan (1995) 54 *CLJ* 25–27.

[310] [1990] 2 AC 605: auditors not liable to a share purchaser who, having relied upon a defective audit, acquired 90% of the shares in the audited company at too high a price.

[311] E.g. *Anns* v. *Merton* (see fn. 279) and *Junior Books* (fn. 313).

[312] *Murphy* v. *Brentwood District Council* [1991] AC 398: negligence of district council: insufficient foundation; no liability for fracture to the house. Moreover, it was made clear (p. 466, *per* Lord Keith) that the damage in *Anns* was pure economic loss.

liable in tort for damage caused by and to a partially defective product which, although when acquired by the consumer was in a visibly unimpaired condition, contains an inherent imperfection which will later cause damage to the product itself.[313] By contrast, it is unclear whether the decision in *Junior Books* v. *Veitchi*[314] is still valid, despite all that has been said to the contrary. In that decision, a party who had to renew a deficiently laid factory floor in order to prevent further losses was said to have suffered damage to property (and not pure economic loss).[315] To understand what amounts to an extension—and not mere confirmation—of *Hedley Byrne* one must read, not *Spring* v. *Guardian*,[316] but *White* v. *Jones*,[317] one of the most important tort decisions in recent years.

In *White* v. *Jones* the defendant lawyer negligently failed to keep appointments with a client intending to alter his will. The client died without the changes having been made. The disappointed children, whom he had intended to benefit, claimed damages for their loss. The claim was upheld by a majority in the House of Lords. In the leading dissenting judgment Lord Mustill made clear his opinion that the decision of the Court of Appeal[318] could not be upheld either on the footing of existing authority, or on the basis of a new principle of liability.[319] Nevertheless the majority, including Lord Goff, relied upon the decision in *Hedley Byrne*: he said the House of Lords 'should, in cases such as these, extend to the intended beneficiary a remedy under the *Hedley Byrne* principle by holding that the assumption of responsibility . . . should be held in law to extend to the intended beneficiary'.[320]

(d) Liability for Omissions

288 Like the *Verkehrspflichten* in German law,[321] the law of negligence has helped English law to make a significant stride forwards in the field of liability for omissions.[322] It is not widely recognized that the distinction drawn between a positive act and an omission is unsatisfactory.[323] The

---

[313] *Murphy* loc. cit. p. 497 (*per* Lord Jauncey); cf. *Junior Books Ltd.* v. *Veitchi Co. Ltd.* [1983] 1 AC 520, 547.   [314] See previous fn.

[315] For a similar interpretation see Lord Templeman in *Tate & Lyle Industries* loc. cit. (fn. 287 above) and *Simaan General Contracting Co.* v. *Pilkington Glass Ltd. (No. 2)* [1988] 1 All ER 791, 803 (*per* Bingham LJ).   [316] See fn. 296 above.

[317] *White and Another* v. *Jones and Another* [1995] 2 WLR 187 (HL).

[318] *White* v. *Jones* [1993] 3 All ER 481 (CA).   [319] Loc. cit. (fn. 317) pp. 226–227.

[320] Ibid. pp. 206–207.   [321] See nos. 104–105 above.

[322] The development of this area of law began, not with *Donoghue* v. *Stevenson*, but later: cf. Hepple & Matthews, *Tort*, 4th edn., p. 66.

[323] A comment by Steyn J in his first-instance judgment in *Banque Keyser Ullman SA* v. *Skandia (UK) Insurance Co. Ltd. and Others* [1990] 1 QB 665, 712 is a rare exception. He said: 'Leaving aside simple "no duty to rescue" cases, it is today difficult to draw a conceptual line between misfeasance and nonfeasance.'

distinction is often regarded as fundamental[324] and it is pointed out that there is no general duty to rescue another person from danger.[325] It is of note that, in respect of liability omissions, most contemporary judgments favour the defendant.[326] A comparison of the modern law of negligence in England with the position on the continent nevertheless shows that the differences regarding liability for omissions are becoming fewer. The principles are the same; only their application to concrete cases still differs in some respects. Just as there can be no liability without a duty, so there can be no liability for an omission in the absence of an obligation to act.[327] Where there is a duty, a mere omission can result in liability; whether a duty *exists* will depend upon the application of the general rules of negligence. This depends upon reasonableness and foreseeability, upon proximity and assumption of responsibility. In short, it depends upon whether it is fair, just, and reasonable to establish a duty to act in the face of danger. Cases in which such a duty has been imposed in England are legion. The caselaw tends to concentrate on areas where the codified systems have set up special rules, e.g. liability of parents and teachers for children,[328] and liability for premises.[329] Since the decision in *Dorset Yacht*,[330] parallels can be drawn with the *arrêt Blieck* of the French Cour de Cassation[331] regarding liability for the occupants of various homes and

---

[324] According to Slade LJ in *Banque Keyser* (see previous footnote) in the Court of Appeal. At p. 797 he said: 'For better or worse, our law of tort draws a fundamental distinction between the legal effects of acts on the one hand and omissions on the other.' In *Curran v. Northern Ireland Co-ownership Housing Association Ltd.* [1987] AC 718, 724 Lord Bridge had earlier expressly criticized the recent tendency 'to obscure the important distinction between misfeasance and nonfeasance'.

[325] E.g. Lord Keith in *Yuen Kun Yeu v. A-G of Hong Kong* [1988] AC 175, 192.

[326] Cf. *Topp v. London Country Buses (South West) Ltd.* [1993] 3 All ER 448 (CA): passenger bus was left unlocked with its key in the ignition, in order to save time when changing drivers. The bus was usually left like this for 'only' five or ten minutes, but on this occasion it was left for over nine hours because the replacement driver was sick. An unauthorized person took control of the wheel and caused an accident which led to the death of a woman. The plaintiff was the dead woman's husband. His action in negligence was unsuccessful; the Court of Appeal said that there was no general duty to prevent a third party from causing damage. Further conspicuous examples of reluctance to find defendants liable for omissions are cases involving the police: *Hill v. Chief Constable of West Yorkshire* [1988] 2 All ER 238 (CA) and *Osman v. Ferguson* [1993] 4 All ER 344 (CA). Underlying such decisions is the belief expressed in cases such as *Perl v. Camden BC* [1984] QB 342 and *Lamb v. Camden BC* [1981] QB 625, that there should be no liability for the torts of independent third parties.

[327] *Smith v. Littlewoods Organisation Ltd.* [1987] AC 241, 271 (*per* Lord Goff): 'Common law does not impose liability for what are called pure omissions.'

[328] E.g. *Carmarthenshire County Council v. Lewis* [1955] AC 549: child ran in front of a car on leaving her primary school; cf. nos. 330 ff. below.

[329] See nos. 361 ff. below. Unlike the position in France, there is no special liability covering the collapse of buildings.

[330] *Dorset Yacht Co. Ltd. v. Home Office* [1970] AC 1004.   [331] See no. 115 above.

institutions for young offenders. In England liability for omissions is also relevant in a wide range of other situations.[332] This is because the rule in *Hedley Byrne* leads from consideration of the voluntary assumption of responsibility in this direction, not least to the liability of professionals for pure economic loss stemming from their responsibility to protect the financial interests of their clients. *White* v. *Jones* was such a case of negligent omission.[333]

(3) Other Peculiarities of English Tort Law

(a) Rules of Procedure, Limitation, and Damages for Specific Torts

289 The continuing process of convergence between the common law of torts and the continental systems of delict offers a chance which should be seized with both hands. England also has a comprehensive model of liability for blameworthy conduct. Whether viewed from the perspective of methodology or from that of content, it would scarcely make any difference at all if England adopted a codified law of obligations which, like the Dutch BW in the field of non-contractual liability took a position midway between the law of France and that of Germany. If this were achieved, the principle of adherence to precedents could still be retained. Only the occasionally irrational aversion to abstractions would need to yield a little.

290 One should not overlook the fact that the system of nominate torts is responsible for a number of peculiarities in tort law. Nevertheless, they have a function which, strictly speaking, no longer belongs to the law of tort. Procedural law is a point in question. Legal aid is not available for all torts[334] and a jury is available only for some torts.[335] Even the standard of proof changes according to the tort.[336] Limitation law, with its varying limitation periods,[337] can barely be regarded

---

[332] See *Kirkham* v. *Chief Constable of the Greater Manchester Police* [1990] 2 WLR 987; *Stovin* v. *Wise* (*Norfolk County Council, third party*) [1994] 1 WLR 1124; *Hughes* v. *Lord Advocate* [1963] AC 837; *Haynes* v. *Harwood* [1935] 1 KB 146; *Goldman* v. *Hargrave* [1967] AC 645; and *Smith* v. *Littlewoods* (fn. 327).

[333] *White* v. *Jones* [1995] 2 WLR 187, 207 (*per* Lord Goff)

[334] E.g. defamation: see no. 271 above.

[335] See no. 241 and fn. 27 above. 'Trial by jury' can also be demanded by somebody accused of deceit: Supreme Court Act 1981, sec. 69 (c. 54).

[336] Clerk & Lindsell (-Carty), *Torts*, 17th edn., paragraphs 18–20. This rule has its root in the preponderance of probability (cf. *Hornal* v. *Neuberger Products Ltd.* [1957] 1 QB 247, 258, Denning LJ: 'The more serious the allegation the higher the degree of probability that is required').

[337] Under the Limitation Act 1980 (c. 58) the usual limitation period is 6 years (sec. 2); for libel and slander the limitation period is 3 years (sec. 4A). There is a range of special rules for liability in negligence, nuisance, and breach of duty involving personal injury and death: here too the basic limitation period is 3 years (sec. 11[4] loc. cit.)

as procedural law.[338] The third area in which the cause of action pleaded plays an important part is that of remedies.[339] Here one finds a range of subtle distinctions according to the type of conduct on which the claim is based. However, the same can be said of continental systems. This is evident regarding liability for non-pecuniary damages: the fact that exemplary damages, insofar as it can be accepted that damages should have a punitive function at all, are restricted to cases of grave injustice lies at the heart of the matter.[340] That some torts are actionable *per se* does not distinguish English law from that of the continent. The same is true of the fact that mesne profits are a specific remedy for *trespass to land*.[341] Furthermore, by no means all torts entitle the plaintiff to restitutionary damages (as opposed to compensatory damages); this has more to do with the underdeveloped state of the law of restitution in England than with specific problems of tort law.[342] This is evident from the strict character of the tort of conversion of goods. Conversion is an 'antienrichment wrong'.[343] Claims brought in negligence, nuisance, and defamation are for compensation, not restitution, and the remedy of mesne profits embodies both. By contrast, it is more difficult to understand why in respect of contributory negligence distinctions are drawn between different torts. There can be no contributory negligence in the torts of deceit,[344] assault,[345] conversion, or intentional trespass to goods,[346]

---

[338] Sec. 2 Limitation Act 1980 provides that 'an action founded on tort shall not be brought after the expiration of . . . ', but this does not mean that such an action must be disallowed. It merely provides a defence. An action will not be held time-barred by the court acting of its own volition.

[339] Moreover, there is a range of defences which are specific to particular torts, cf. no. 272 above.

[340] Lord Devlin in *Rookes* v. *Barnard* [1964] AC 1129, 1221 set out the general requirements for exemplary damages, see no. 612 below. Exemplary damages are most commonly encountered in severe cases of trespass (e.g. *Louden* v. *Ryder* [1953] 2 QB 202), of libel (*Broome* v. *Cassell & Co. Ltd.* [1971] 2 QB 354), and breach of copyright (*Williams* v. *Settle* [1960] 1 WLR 1072 and sec. 229[3] Copyright Designs and Patents Act 1988 [c. 48]). Exemplary damages are not granted for negligence or nuisance: *AB* v. *South West Water Services Ltd.* [1993] 1 All ER 609. According to that decision exemplary damages are still only recognized where the cause of action is based on a tort which was recognized before 1964 (before *Rookes* v. *Barnard*) as one for which such exemplary damages had been granted. For this reason breach of statutory duty could not give rise to such damages. The position of private nuisance is doubtful: cf. the opposing views of Stuart-Smith LJ (p. 621) and Bingham MR (p. 627). [341] *Inverugie Investments Ltd.* v. *Hackett* [1995] 1 WLR 713.

[342] See Tettenborn, (1993) 52 CLJ 128–147; Jackman, (1989) 48 CLJ 302–321; and Birks, *An Introduction to the Law of Restitution*, pp. 313–357. Also nos. 520 ff. below.

[343] Birks loc. cit. p. 329.

[344] *Central Railway Co. of Venezuela* v. *Kisch* (1867) LR 2 HL 99, 120.

[345] Cf. Lord Denning MR in *Gray and Another* v. *Barr, Prudential Assurance Co. Ltd. (Third Party)* [1971] 2 QB 554, 569: 'Whenever two men have a fight and one is injured, the action is for assault, not for negligence. If both are injured, there are cross-actions for assault. The idea of negligence—and contributory negligence—is quite foreign to men grappling in a struggle.' [346] Sec. 11(1) Torts (Interference with Goods) Act 1977 (c. 32).

whereas it is recognized in respect of negligence, breach of statutory duty,[347] and nuisance.[348] In cases involving strict liability, provided there is no express statutory provision,[349] the position of contributory negligence remains in many respects unclear.[350] It would make greater sense to extend the application of contributory negligence to all forms of tortious behaviour according to the apportionment principle of sec. 1 Law Reform (Contributory Negligence) Act 1945,[351] instead of allowing the misleading expression of contributory negligence[352] to cause confusion.

(b) Policy Considerations

291 The express pleading of policy considerations is a further unique aspect of English law. Policy considerations of a legal nature are used to test whether the final result is consistent with the entire system, i.e. whether the result is just, fair, and reasonable. Policy considerations are most frequently encountered in negligence but their application is by no means restricted to that tort.[353] The main point is to find arguments which allow a claim founded upon general principles to be dismissed; the time when the existence of an insurance policy or other economic advantages of the defendant were used as policy considerations against him[354] seems to be passed.

292 Of course, judges on the continent, as in England, have to deal with policy considerations, and they operate in many fields of liability. So the immunity of those involved in trials (judges, lawyers, and expert witnesses) and the reluctance to grant damages to those who have suffered shock on hearing of an accident, can both be explained as the efforts of a legal system to prevent an avalanche of legal actions arising out of a single event.[355] The way in which policy considerations enter judgments expressly has become a feature of English law. This is a consequence of

[347] *Caswell v. Powell Duffryn Collieries Ltd./Lewis v. Deyne* [1940] AC 921.
[348] *Trevett v. Lee* [1955] 1 WLR 122.
[349] As e.g. in sec. 10(1) Animals Act 1971 (c. 22) and sec. 6(4) Consumer Protection Act 1987 (c. 43). [350] Markesinis/Deakin, *Tort Law*, 3rd edn., pp. 650–651.
[351] Chap. 28.
[352] Contributory negligence involves 'fault against oneself' and therefore cannot be dependent upon the same requirements as negligence. This is why contributory negligence does not require pre-existing duty: *Jones v. Livox Quarries Ltd.* [1952] 2 QB 608, 615, (*per* Denning LJ).
[353] Cf. nos. 283 and 258 above. Policy considerations can also be relevant to questions of vicarious liability (Lord Browne-Wilkinson in *X and Others v. Bedfordshire County Council and Other Appeals* [1995] 3 All ER 353, 368 ff.) and of causation: *Meah v. McCreamer (No. 2)* [1986] 1 All ER 943.
[354] See Denning MR in *Dutton v. Bognor Regis Urban District Council* [1972] 1 QB 373, 397 for radical views on this point, which accepted argument from the plaintiff based upon the 'width of the [defendant's] shoulders' (i.e. financial strength). Like *Anns v. Merton* (no. 281 above), *Dutton* was overruled by *Murphy* (no. 282 above).
[355] See Markesinis/v. Bar, *Richterrechtliche Rechtspolitik im Haftungsrecht*, pp. 9–19.

the fact that a judgment is still regarded as a source of law: the judge therefore has a greater capacity to 'create' law. The dangers arising from this should not be underestimated. The greatest danger stems from the fact that there is no fixed method for the application of policy considerations, so that they are unpredictable. This results in legal uncertainty: a plaintiff risks falling foul of policy considerations which he could not have anticipated when deciding to pursue the action.

The following examples should convey an impression of the capri- **293** ciousness of policy considerations. In *Herrington* v. *British Railways Board*[356] the central, and then uncertain issue was whether the BRB, due to a failure to secure its property, was liable to children who unlawfully exposed themselves to danger. A recent statutory provision was silent[357] on the problem raised by child trespassers. Lord Reid said: 'legal principles cannot solve the problem. How far occupiers are to be required by law to take steps to safeguard such children must be a matter of public policy.'[358] There followed an extensive debate on the competence of the judiciary to make law, and its relationship with Parliament. In *Marc Rich & Co.* v. *Bishop Rock Marine*[359] an employee of a firm of specialists was called out from England to the Caribbean by a ship's owner to resolve a ship's technical problems. Having advised on some relatively straightforward safety measures, the specialist approved the ship's onward voyage. Soon afterwards the ship sank. The owner of the cargo brought an action against the specialist's employer for damages which, according to the Hague-Visby Rules, were not recoverable from the ship's owner. Both the Court of Appeal and the House of Lords refused the claim, despite the fact that all the prerequisites of negligence were satisfied. The Court of Appeal held that it would be unreasonable to transfer to the defendant the obligations of a ship's owner without extending to the defendant the protection afforded by the Hague-Visby Rules. Furthermore, this was not a case 'where an obvious social wrong requires a legal remedy'.[360] This is a pathetic argument: the case was simply a matter of negligently caused damage to property.

Even more dramatic are those cases where policy considerations have operated to the detriment of victims of the police or other public bodies,[361] most recently in *M v. Newham BC*.[362] A child was separated

---

[356] [1972] AC 877.   [357] The Occupiers' Liability Act 1957 was in force at the time.
[358] Loc. cit. (fn. 356) p. 897.
[359] Also known as '*The Nicholas H*' [1994] 1 WLR 1071 (CA); [1995] 3 All ER 307 (HL).
[360] Loc. cit. p. 1089 (*per* Balcombe LJ).
[361] See *Hill* v. *Chief Constable of West Yorkshire* [1989] AC 53; *Elguzouli-Daf* v. *Commissioner of Police of the Metropolis* [1995] 1 All ER 833; *Alcock* v. *Chief Constable of South Yorkshire Police* [1992] 1 AC 310 and *Osman* v. *Ferguson* [1993] 4 All ER 344.
[362] *M v. Newham Borough Council/X* v. *Bedfordshire County Council* [1994] 2 WLR 554.

from its mother because a psychiatrist employee of the defendant local authority incorrectly believed the child had suffered sexual abuse by the mother's boyfriend. The claim was refused by a majority of the Court of Appeal (Bingham MR dissenting). It would be undesirable in this case to go beyond statutory duty by imposing a common law duty. Furthermore, it would be a waste of public funds for the Legal Aid Board to finance such claims and for the defendant to use precious resources to defend itself against such actions. The House of Lords dismissed the appeal: Sir Thomas Bingham's dissenting opinion was 'sound in logic', but the time had come to recognize that it was 'unsound in practice'.[363]

b. The Irish Law of Torts and the Scottish Law of Delict

(1) Ireland: A Law of Torts Influenced by Constitutional Law

294 Ireland is a common law country. As early as the fifteenth century the court of first instance in Dublin was modelled on the courts in Westminster Hall, and for centuries thereafter appeals went to the Court of King's Bench in London. By the end of the seventeenth century hardly any Irish private law remained.[364] With one or two exceptions, it would only really start to develop with the creation of the Irish Free State in 1921.[365] Insofar as there are any specifically Irish peculiarities in the law of extra-contractual obligations, these result from either the 1937 Constitution or more recent Acts of Parliament.

295   Ireland has a number of important statutes concerning tort.[366] The common law of torts in Ireland is nevertheless substantially influenced by its English counterpart. Although Irish cases are cited as authorities, practically all the important cases depend on English decisions. In the course of this reception the most important developments in the tort of negligence have also spread to Ireland,[367] from the basic rule in *Donoghue* v. *Stevenson*[368] to the principle of liability in *Hedley Byrne*.[369] Differences do of course arise, but these mostly concern matters of detail which are discussed here as and when they occur: examples are the differing findings of whether a particular form of conduct was negligent

---

[363] [1995] 3 All ER 353.   [364] O'Higgins, 'Ireland', *Int.Enc.Comp.L* I-67.
[365] Now called either Eire or Ireland: Art. 4, 1937 Constitution.
[366] See nos. 237–240 above.
[367] That the Irish courts have adopted English decisions uncritically, thereby frustrating the development of an independent tort law, is noted with regret by the commentators: McMahon/Binchy, *Irish Law of Torts*, 2nd edn., p. 90.   [368] Ibid. pp. 95–96.
[369] See *Securities Trust Ltd* v. *Hugh Moore & Alexander Ltd.* [1964] IR 417; *Bank of Ireland* v. *Smith* [1966] IR 646; *Wall* v. *Hegarty* [1980] ILRM 124; and *McAnarney* v. *Hanrahan* [1993] 3 IR 492.

or defamatory;[370] the beginnings of a more extensive application of the rule in *Rylands* v. *Fletcher*;[371] and the fact that *Anns* v. *Merton*[372] still enjoys considerable sympathy in Ireland. Occasionally, common law rules are found in Ireland which no longer apply in England: for example the tort of detinue,[373] which was abolished in England by statute;[374] in addition, in Ireland trespass to the person can be committed negligently.[375] Contributory negligence applies to all torts, and not just those to which it applies in England.[376] Finally, the practical effect of the tort of breach of statutory duty naturally depends upon the relevant Irish statute.

As stated above, these are mere details. The significant difference **296** between the modern Irish and English laws of obligations stems, not from isolated adjustments to the common law brought about by Ireland's independence, but rather from the fact that the Republic of Ireland has a constitution which is continental in form. It contains an independent catalogue of basic rights (Arts. 40–44), with provisions of great moment for the law of obligations outside contract.[377]

Sub-sections 3(1) and 3(2) of Art. 40 of the Constitution are of special significance. They read as follows: '(1) The State guarantees in its laws to respect and, as far as practicable, by its laws to defend and vindicate the personal rights of the citizen. (2) The State shall, in particular, by its laws protect as best it may from unjust attack and, in the case of injustice done, vindicate the life, person, good name, and property rights of every citizen.'

Art. 40, sec. 3 is now construed not only to prevent infringements of **297**

---

[370] A nice example is *Berry* v. *Irish Times* [1973] IR 368 (Sup. Ct.), on whether it is defamatory to say that an Irishman contributed to the prosecution in England of a fellow countryman for an act which was criminal in England but not Ireland.

[371] See the *obiter* comments of McCarthy J in *Mullen* v. *Quinnsworth Ltd. T/A Crazy Prices (No. 1)* [1990] 1 IR 59, 69 (Sup. Ct.) for cases involving supermarket customers slipping on icy floors.

[372] Besides the criticism by McMahon/Binchy, *Casebook*, 2nd edn., pp. 62–63 of the decision in *Murphy* v. *Brentwood* (no. 282 above), see the case of *John C. Doherty Timber Ltd.* v. *Drogheda Harbour Commissioners* [1993] ILRM 401; [1993] 1 IR 315, where Flood J years after *Murphy* applied Lord Wilberforce's 'two-stage test' and where, as Byrne & Binchy, *Annual Review of Irish Law 1992* (1994) 553 rightly stated, 'the court was being asked to impose a duty of care well beyond what the case-law in either Ireland or Britain had previously upheld, even in decisions most favourable to recovery for pure economic loss'.   [373] McMahon/Binchy, *Irish Law of Torts*, 2nd edn., pp. 528–533.

[374] Sec. 2(1) Torts (Interference with Goods) Act 1977.

[375] McMahon/Binchy, loc. cit. p. 399.

[376] See no. 290 above and more specifically sec. 34(1) Civil Liability Act 1961: 'Where, in *any action* brought by one person in respect of a wrong committed by any other person, it is proved that the damage suffered by the plaintiff was caused partly by the negligence or want of care of the plaintiff or of one for whose acts he is responsible . . . and partly by the wrong of the defendant, the damages recoverable . . . shall be reduced' (emphasis added).

[377] See also Part 6, no. 558 below.

basic rights by the State, but also to oblige the State to protect the basic rights of the citizen. When an individual's basic rights are infringed by another, the State must provide legal protection. The unlawful interference of one of the rights specified in Art. 40, sec. 3 constitutes a 'civil wrong'.[378] This also applies when the common law provides no appropriate or adequate remedy; in such cases the plaintiff can either await a constitutional extension of the common law,[379] or claim on the basis of a constitutional tort: the plaintiff can claim damages for the tort of wrongful interference with a constitutional right.[380] It is generally said that the normal common law nominate torts provide the protection afforded by the constitution and may thus continue to be used.[381] However, there are exceptions, and these operate in a different way from the common law. Unlike the common law of England, the Irish law of 'constitutional' torts emphasizes legal rights and interests, not obligations, and thus calls to mind Scandinavian and continental European systems of obligations.

298   In *Walsh* v. *Family Planning Services*,[382] the 44-year-old plaintiff, married with five children, underwent a vasectomy, as a result of which he suffered continuous pain. He also became impotent. The plaintiff had spoken with his own doctor about the operation, but at the last moment was operated upon by another doctor. The doctor had carried out the operation without negligence. Nevertheless, McKenzie J found for the plaintiff: 'In my view his constitutional right, that is an unspecified constitutional right to bodily integrity, has been violated . . . All the plaintiff's troubles stem from the operation.' He was awarded £30,000 damages for the infringement of his constitutional rights. This might be to give the judgment too much weight, but it appears that no-fault liability for the consequences of medical operations may have been

---

[378] *Byrne* v. *Ireland* [1972] IR 241 (Sup. Ct.); *Meskell* v. *Coras Iompair Éirann* [1973] IR 121 (Sup. Ct.); *Hanrahan* v. *Merck Sharp and Dohme (Ireland) Ltd.* [1988] ILRM 629 (Sup. Ct.); *Hynes-O'Sullivan* v. *O'Driscoll* [1988] IR 436 (Sup. Ct.).

[379] Such cases are uncommon. An example is *McKinley* v. *Minister of Defence* [1992] 2 IR 333 (Sup. Ct.): an accident caused the husband of the plaintiff to become impotent. The wife's action against the husband's employer for *loss of consortium* was allowed despite the fact that the common law in comparable cases (i.e. husband's claim following injury to the wife) was intended to give the husband alone a right of action, infringing the principle of equality of the sexes.

[380] Kelly/Hogan/Whyte, *The Irish Constitution*, pp. 707–708; and McMahon/Binchy, *Irish Law of Torts*, 2nd edn., pp. 6–16.

[381] An example is *Hanrahan* v. *Merck Sharp* (fn. 378), concerning factory emissions. A shift in the burden of proof for liability in *nuisance* was not regarded as necessary. Henchy J added at pp. 635–636: 'I agree that the tort of nuisance relied on in this case may be said to be an implementation of the State's duties under (Article 40.3.1–2) as to the personal rights and property rights of the plaintiffs as citizens.' See also *Sweeney* v. *Duggan* [1991] 2 IR 274 (HC): Art 40 sec. 3 of the Constitution 'did no more than give the plaintiff a guarantee of a just law of negligence'.   [382] [1992] 1 IR 496 (Sup. Ct.)

founded in *Walsh*.[383] Another group of cases in which the 'constitutional law' aspect of tort plays a significant role comes from employment law.[384] *Meskell* v. *CIE*[385] is particularly instructive: the defendant company and four trade unions agreed that the defendant should cancel its work contracts with the defendant's personnel. The employees were presented with new contracts of employment which obliged them to join a trade union. The plaintiff refused and was therefore sacked. Her claim against the company and the trade unions was upheld on the basis that what had occurred amounted to an infringement of her right to choose not to join an organization. By contrast, no general right in private law of protection of personality, including a tort of infringement of privacy, has yet been finally established. It remains open whether the common law, with its traditional means,[386] is sufficient to provide the protection afforded by the Constitution.[387] It is also unclear whether the general right of privacy belongs to 'personal rights' in the sense intended by Art. 40, sec. 3, sub-sec. 1 of the Constitution.[388] In more recent High Court decisions such a right has been recognized on a number of occasions.[389] All those decisions involved actions between citizens and the state, and therefore the effectiveness in private law of such a basic right, insofar as it has been confirmed by the Supreme Court, cannot yet be determined.

(2) *Scotland: A Law of Delict Under the Influence of the Common Law*

Scotland prides itself on the fact that its law of delict has Roman roots **299** and was developed by the *usus modernus pandectarum*: the expression law of torts is carefully avoided by Scottish lawyers. However, exactly where today's law of delict differs from the common law of torts is unclear.[390] The two have converged in this century to the extent that differences, other than those from statute,[391] are of secondary importance. This process of convergence is partly dependent upon the fact that

---

[383] See Byrne & Binchy, *Annual Review of Irish Law 1992* (1994) pp. 558–560. Also *Hegarty* v. *Loughran* [1990] 1 IR 148 (Sup. Ct.), where McCarthy J said that 'the case for a no-fault system of compensation for those who suffer injury as a result of medical treatment seems so strong as to be virtually unanswerable'.

[384] Cf. *Murtagh Properties Ltd.* v. *Cleary* [1972] IR 330 (HC) and *Educational Co. of Ireland* v. *Fitzpatrick (No. 2)* [1961] IR (Sup. Ct.) 345.   [385] See fn. 378 above.

[386] Cf. no. 272 above.

[387] See McMahon/Binchy, *Irish Law of Torts*, 2nd edn., pp. 684–698.

[388] See Kelly/Hogan/Whyte, *The Irish Constitution*, pp. 767–770.

[389] *Kennedy* v. *Ireland* [1987] IR 587 (HC; *Kane* v. *The Governor of Mountjoy Prison* [1988] IR 757 (Sup. Ct.); *Desmond and Dedair* v. *Glackin, Minister for Industry and Commerce and Others (No. 2)* [1993] 3 IR 67 (Sup. Ct.)

[390] It was stated at no. 7 and in fn. 30 above that the *actio de effusis vel eiectis* of Roman law is no longer part of Scottish law.

[391] See no. 241 above for the most important statutes on obligations.

Scottish liability law is built on case-law. Where a case originating in Scotland comes before the House of Lords, its judgment is binding in Scotland.[392] Cases originating in England are also binding in Scotland when it is said that the legal position in each country is the same.[393] However, in other instances, in the absence of specific characteristics of Scottish law (for example: the less exalted role of trespass;[394] the missing distinction between private and public nuisance;[395] the absence of torts actionable *per se*;[396] the absence of distinction between libel and slander;[397] the rejection of punitive damages;[398] and the non-adoption of the rule in *Rylands* v. *Fletcher*[399]) English decisions are accorded greater, or more persuasive authority.[400] Many significant differences between the English and Scottish laws of obligations only tangentially approach the field of tort law. The law of unjust enrichment is one example, another is that in Scotland the distinction between common law and equity is far less sharp than in England.

300 Scottish terminology includes some terms not used in England. The difference is not, for example, between special and general damages; instead, reference is made to patrimonial loss, *lucrum cessans*, loss of *solatium*, etc. Above all, Scottish law bases its law of delict on a general principle of liability for wrongful conduct, not on a system of nominate torts. Notwithstanding certain peculiarities and shifts in meaning, the nomenclature of English law, based on the nominate torts, is generally used in Scotland, 'but without the procedural connotations of the common law, and these names are in Scotland no more than convenient titles

---

[392] Such complaints are frequent in Scottish legal literature. A recent example appears in the commentaries on *Smith (or Maloco)* v. *Littlewoods Organisation Ltd*. [1987] AC 241 (fn. 327 above); cf. Ferguson, SLT 1987 pp. 233, 235 and Logie, *Jur. Rev.* 1988 pp. 77, 86 (in *Maloco*, a Scottish case, Lord Goff applied English law). *Bourhill* v. *Young* [1943] AC 92 = 1941 SC 395, a leading case on liability for nervous shock, stands alongside *Donoghue* v. *Stevenson* as one of the most important cases from Scotland for the law of England.

[393] Cf. *McGeown* v. *Northern Ireland Housing Executive* [1994] 3 All ER 53 and the analysis by Blackie, SLT 1994 pp. 349–352.

[394] Scottish law recognizes only trespass to land. See Stewart, *Delict*, pp. 18–20.

[395] Ibid. p. 7.

[396] Walker, *Principles*, vol. ii, 4th edn., p. 528. Without damage there can be no cause of action. In a case involving *verbal injuries*, i.e. where the claim is in the tradition of the *actio injuriarum* of Roman law, the loss can be purely non-economic.

[397] Cf. fn. 17 above, and Walker, *Delict*, 2nd edn., p. 741.

[398] *Black* v. *NBR*, 1908 SC 444, 453.

[399] *McQueen* v. *The Glasgow Garden Festival (1988) Ltd*. SLT 1995 pp. 211, 213 (Outer House) (Lord Cullen: 'it has to be recognized that *Rylands* v. *Fletcher* is not authoritative in Scotland') and *RHM Bakeries (Scotland) Ltd*. v. *Strathcylde Regional Council*, 1985 SC 41, 45 (*per* Lord Jauncey: the opposite point of view is 'a heresy which ought to be extirpated').

[400] On the sources and the significance of English decisions for Scottish law see Walker, *Principles*, vol. i, 4th edn., pp. 21–22.

for sets of circumstances giving rise to liability under one or other of the general principles of delictual liability accepted in Scots law'.[401] What this comes down to is often little more than another form of construction, a presentation of the law of delict essentially arranged around the protected interests. When one looks more closely at the general principle of customary law, comparison can readily be made with the decision which, in extending far beyond its content, has presented the United Kingdom torts law with a successful unifying principle: *Donoghue* v. *Stevenson*.[402]

Donoghue v. *Stevenson*, the root of the modern law of negligence, was   **301** after all a Scottish case. All its judges emphasized that Scottish law was no different from English law and that they had based their decisions on considerations arising exclusively from English law. The principle of liability which first took form in *Donoghue* already bore the traits of a basic rule of a type known to continental systems, and consequently contained the characteristics of a general principle, albeit one with only partial application. Therefore it could be integrated into the Scottish law of delict without great difficulty and its modern formulation became the founding principle of delictual liability: 'the fundamental concept', it can be read almost everywhere in the literature of Scottish law of delict in this or similar wording, 'is breach of duty imposed by law not to cause, by act or omission, harm of a legally recognized kind'.[403] The English law of torts can also be reduced to this formula. As far as the law of negligence is concerned, there is no difference between the two systems.[404] *Hedley Byrne*, along with all the decisions in its wake, is applicable law in Scotland;[405] earlier differences in the field of liability for omissions began to disappear a long time ago.[406] The distinctions discussed above in the law of nuisance, trespass, defamation, and the rule in *Rylands* v. *Fletcher* do not have much weight in practice. The same applies to the question of whether nuisance in Scottish law requires

---

[401] Walker, *Delict*, 2nd edn., p. 31.   [402] See no. 277 above.

[403] In this context see Walker (fn. 401); id., *Principles*, vol. ii, 4th edn., p. 527; Stewart, *Delict*, p. 7.

[404] Exceptions to the rule are encountered in the doctrine of causation: Lord Jamieson in *Bourhill* v. *Young* [1941] SC 395, 427 (long before *The Wagon Mound*) said that the rule in *Re Polemis* 'is not part of the law of Scotland'. Further exceptions are found in distinguishing between damage to property and pure economic loss (see Logie, *Jur. Rev.* 1988 pp. 77–90; *Parkhead Housing Association Ltd.* v. *Phoenix Preservation Ltd.* SLT 1990 p. 812 (Outer House).

[405] Recent cases include *Weir* v. *National Westminster Bank PLC* SLT 1994 p. 1251 (First Division) and *Nordic Oil Services Ltd.* v. *Berman* SLT 1993 p. 1164 (Outer House), commented on by Thomson, SLT 1995 pp. 139–145.

[406] Especially on account of *Smith (Maloco)* v. *Littlewoods* (fn. 392). A comparison of Scottish and English law is offered by Logie, *Jur. Rev.* 1988 pp. 77, 79–83. Possibly going beyond *Smith* v. *Littlewoods* is the decision in *Squires* v. *Perth and Kinross DC* 1986 SLT 30 (Outer House): construction workers left a platform unattended, enabling thieves to enter a neighbouring jeweller's shop; liability affirmed. See Cullen, *Jur. Rev.* 1995 pp. 20–27 on liability for failure to offer help.

fault.[407] Although the English point of view is that it must be easier for Scotland, 'where there is a more general concept of *culpa* (wrongful behaviour)', to develop a common law right of privacy,[408] these two UK jurisdictions now differ from each other only slightly. In Scotland one can probably fall back upon *convicium*;[409] nevertheless, there is no judicial confirmation of the existence in Scottish law of a general right to privacy.[410]

II. THE LAW OF SCANDINAVIA AND THE BRITISH ISLES FROM THE PERSPECTIVE OF THE REMAINING LAW OF OBLIGATIONS OF THE CODIFICATIONS

Bibliography: Andresen, 'Haftung ohne Verschulden im nordischen, insbesondere im norwegishen Recht', *RabelsZ* 27 (1962/63) pp. 245–262; Atiyah, *Vicarious Liability in the Law of Torts* (London 1967); v. Bar, 'Liability for Information and Opinions causing Pure Economic Loss to Third Parties: A comparison of English and German case law', in: Markesinis (ed.), *The Gradual Convergence: Foreign ideas, foreign influences, and English law on the eve of the 21st century* (Oxford 1994) pp. 98–127; Beaton, *Scots Law Terms and Expressions* (Edinburgh 1982); Bengtsson, 'Torts and Insurance', in: Strömholm (ed.), *An Introduction to Swedish Law* (2nd edn. Stockholm 1988) pp. 297–317; id., 'Skadestånd utom kontraktsförhållanden 1976–1979', *SJT* 1981 pp. 519–537; Binchy/Byrne, 'Tort Law: The extension of the scope of breach of statutory duty for accidents at work', *ILT* 1995 pp. 4–8 (Part I) and pp. 28–32 (part II); Buckley, 'Liability in Tort for Breach of Statutory Duty', 100 (1984) *LQR* 204–233; Dotevall, 'Die Schadensersatzhaftung von Leitungsorganen der schwedischen Aktiengesellschaft aus rechtsvergleichender Sicht', in: *FS Egon Lorenz* (Karlsruhe 1994) pp. 161–173; Fleming, 'Contributory Negligence and Multiple Tortfeasors', 104 (1988) *LQR* 6–9; Forsberg, *Om ersättning för skada av hund; Uppsatser i försäkringsrätt och Stadeståndsrätt*, vol. i (Stockholm

---

[407] See no. 263 above. On one hand is the view offered by Stewart, *Delict*, p. 23 with reference to *RHM Bakeries* v. *Strathclyde Regional Council* (fn. 399), and on the other is Walker, *Delict*, 2nd edn., p. 643.

[408] Thus *Calcutt Report of the Committee on Privacy and Related Matters* (fn. 231 above), 12.2.

[409] *Convicium* is an ancient form of action (D.47.10.15), believed still to apply in Scotland. (Thus Walker, *Delict*, 2nd edn., pp. 736–740: Stewart, *Delict* p. 173, is doubtful.) *Convicium* exists to protect an individual against exposure to ridicule and contempt.

[410] A wide-ranging survey of the case-law is offered by Walker (previous fn.) pp. 704–708.

1959); Fricke, 'The Juridical Nature of the Action upon the Statute', 76 (1960) *LQR* 240–266; Gutteridge, 'Abuse of Rights', *CLJ* 5 (1933–35) pp. 22–45; Hart/Honoré, *Causation in the Law*, 2nd edn. (Oxford 1985); Hartig, *Vergleichende Warentests im Recht Deutschlands, Frankreichs, der Niederlande und Großbritanniens* (Frankfurt/Main 1973); Hellner, 'Ersättning till tredje man vid sak- och personskada', *SJT* 1969 pp. 332–361; id., 'Développement et rôle de la responsabilité civile délictuelle dans les pays Scandinaves', *Rev.int.dr.comp.* 19 (1967) pp. 779–805; id., 'The New Swedish Tort Liability Act', 22 (1974) *AJCompL* 1–16; Hogan, '*Cook* v. *Lewis* Re-examined', 24 (1961) *MLR* 331–344; Iversen, 'Haftung im Unternehmensbereich, Dänemark', in: *KF* 1993 pp. 50–52; Jackson, 'Liability for Animals in Scottish Legal Literature: From Stair to the modern law', *Jur. Rev.* 1977 pp. 139–163; Jørgensen, 'Solidarität und Regreß im dänischen Recht', in: *FS Karl Neumayer* (Baden-Baden 1985) pp. 337–354; Kleineman, *Ren förmögenhetsskada. Särskilt vid vilseledande av annan än kontraktspart* (Stockholm 1987); Kruse, 'Danske Lovs ansvarsregler om dyr, set i et fremdtidsperspektiv', in: Tamm (ed.), *Danske og Norske Lov i 300 år* (Copenhagen 1983) pp. 677–695; Mannion, 'The Player, Not the Play: The relationship between performers' protection legislation and statutory duties', *ILT* 1992 pp. 276–279; Mathiassen, 'Identifikation', *Jur.* 1961 pp. 327–331; McKendrick, 'Vicarious Liability and Independent Contractors: A re-examination', 53 (1990) *MLR* 770–784; McMahon, 'Conclusions on Judicial Behaviour from a Comparative Study of Occupiers' Liability', 38 (1975) *MLR* 39–51; Miller, 'Liability for Animals', *SLT* 1987 pp. 229–233; Napier, 'Breach of Statutory Duty and Unlawful Means in Strike Law', [1987] *CLJ* 222–225; Newark, 'The Occupiers' Liability Act (Northern Ireland) 1957', 12 (1958) *NILQ* 203–222; North, *The Modern Law of Animals* (London 1972); id., *Occupiers' Liability* (London 1971); O'Higgins, 'Strict Liability for Supermarket Slippage Cases?', *ILT* 1991 pp. 134–138; Pagter Kristensen/Bryde Andersen, 'Anmeldelse af Lærebog i erstatningsret', *Jur.* 1992 pp. 320–328; Peczenik, *Causes and Damages* (Lund 1979); Quill, 'Defective Buildings and the Limitation of Actions', *ILT* 1992 pp. 185–187; Rose, 'Liability for an Employee's Assaults', 40 (1977) *MLR* 420–439; Saxén, 'Finlands skadeståndslag jämförd med Sveriges', *SJT* 1977 pp. 148–153; Simblet, 'Abuse of Power and Vicarious Liability', (1994) 53 *CLJ* 430–433; Spencer, 'The Defective Premises Act 1972: Defective law and defective law reform', (1974) 33 *CLJ* 307–323 (part I) and (1975) 35 *CLJ* 48–78 (part II); Stanton, *Breach of Statutory Duty in Tort* (London 1986); Steele, 'Statutory Strict Liability and the Common Law Judge', (1993) 52 *CLJ* 202–204; Stewart, 'A Degree of Independence: Vicarious liability for an independent contractor', *Jur. Rev.* 1991 pp. 253–256; id., 'Liability of Pupils in Delict', *SLT* 1989 pp. 404–405; Stone, 'Civil Liability for Damage caused by the Insane: A comparative study', *FS Rabel* vol. i (Tübingen

1954) pp. 403–419; Wells, 'Corporate Liability and Consumer Protection: *Tesco* v. *Nattrass* revisited', 57 (1994) *MLR* 817–823; id., *Corporations and Criminal Responsibility* (Oxford 1993); Werlauff, 'Ansvar for hunde', *UfR* 1978 B pp. 266–270. Williams, *Joint Torts and Contributory Negligence: A study of concurrent fault in Great Britain, Ireland and the common-law dominions* (3rd reprint London 1977); id., *Liability for Animals* (Cambridge 1939); id., 'The Effect of Penal Legislation in the Law of Tort', 23 (1960) *MLR* 233–259; Woellert, *Die außervertragliche Haftung für schädigendes Verhalten von Hilfspersonen im nordischen Recht* (diss. Kiel 1972).

1. PARTICULAR ASPECTS OF THE LAW OF LIABILITY FOR WRONGFUL CONDUCT

a. Breach of Statutory Duty

302 The above analysis of the laws of continental Europe clearly shows that the liability of the tortfeasor generally becomes more disadvantageous when his conduct infringes a statutory provision as well as the basic principle to exercise care. On the continent the factors which determine liability not only serve to enable other areas of law to assist in determining blameworthiness, but also bring about higher liability in the field of fault, and wider liability in the field of protected interests. It is also noticeable that specific types of statute were required, those whose purpose was at the very least to protect the interests of private citizens. The infringement of a statute intended only to maintain law and order was generally insufficient to establish liability. On the other hand, it was observed that nowhere was liability law silenced simply because the requirements of a protective statute had been met. In each jurisdiction, having considered all the circumstances of the case, the question was whether the potential tortfeasor could and should in the circumstances have done more than was demanded by the statute.[411]

303   Apart perhaps from the last point, on which there still appears to be no clearly developed line,[412] all aspects of continental theory on breach of statutory duty are found in the laws of the Scandinavian EU mem-

---

[411] See nos. 26–35 above.

[412] Cf. on one hand, VLD 7 Dec. 1993, *UfR* 1994 A p. 194: an employee at a bakery brought an action against his employer for back pain. The employer had provided a fork-lift as required by law, but had failed to insist on its use. The liability of the employer was affirmed with no contributory negligence by the employee. On the other hand, VLD 21 Dec. 1994, *UfR* 1995 A p. 225: unidentified tortfeasors opened an oil tank at a building site run by the local authority. Although there was always a risk of vandalism the subcontractor was not held responsible. The latter had erected the tank according to the applicable rules; also Swed. HD 1 Mar. 1990, *NJA* 1990: 14 (p. 71) = *NDS* 1991 p. 108: observance of the law governing the legal relationships between neighbours is sufficient in such relationships.

bers.[413] Of course there are variations in emphasis and detail. Particularly: in both Finland and Sweden the protection against pure economic loss is dependent on breach of statute and, unlike in Denmark,[414] breach of the criminal law.[415] A breach of administrative provisions is insufficient.[416] The influence of 'protective laws' on the general test of negligence is altogether different. The mere infringement of such a law need not give rise either to a finding of fault or to a reversal of the burden of proof. Infringement of a law intended to protect a particular interest[417] reduces the court's discretion to decide whether the act complained of was in fact negligent. Exceptionally, notwithstanding a breach of such a law, a court may find a defendant not liable.[418] Given the large number of rules in the Scandinavian countries, the standard of the *bonus paterfamilias* has in recent years increasingly yielded to the issue of whether statutory safety standards apply in the circumstances.[419] The more concrete the safety standards, the less discretion the courts have. They may consider other factors to determine fault when a norm is infringed, but generally they rely on the infringement alone;[420] the same effect is then

---

[413] On the Swedish view see Hellner, *Skadeståndsrätt*, 4th edn., pp. 91–94, who states that Swedish law does not recognize protective statutes as understood in Germany.

[414] As stated at no. 247 above, Danish law has a greater tendency to compensate pure economic loss than either Swedish or Finnish law. Even so, a claim for such damage in Denmark is more likely to succeed when a statute intended to prevent such loss is breached. Cf. VLD 16 Jan. 1995, *UfR* 1995 A p. 317.

[415] See nos. 244–246 above. Karlgren, *Skadeståndsrätt*, 5th edn., p. 109 says that such statutes which create a 'special relationship' between the tortfeasor and the victim could give rise to a claim for pure economic loss in accordance with general *culpa* liability (i.e. liability for fault). However, in my opinion there is no explicit confirmation of this in recent case-law.   [416] Hellner (fn. 413) p. 57.

[417] That a statute must be intended to protect the interests of individuals was affirmed by Hellner loc. cit. pp. 93–94. This issue is barely mentioned in the *ratio* of individual judgments. In VLD 19 June 1973, *UfR* 1973 A p. 844 a lorry driver, in contravention of road traffic rules, drove his vehicle into an electricity pylon, resulting in a power cut to a local poultry farm. Animals suffocated. The plaintiff's claim was rejected, not on the basis of the protective traffic rule which had been breached, but because of his contributory negligence: he had had sufficient time to ventilate the poultry farm by other means. In the Swedish case HD 21 Dec. 1993, *NDS* 1994 p. 699 it was accepted that a public body stands squarely within the protection provided by a statutory provision regulating conduct, and can therefore claim damages in the same way as a private individual.

[418] E.g. Swed. HD 12 Dec. 1964, *NJA* 1964: 98 p. 491.

[419] Hellner. (fn. 413) p. 90; Bengtsson/Nordenson/Strömbäck, *Skadestånd*, 3rd edn., p. 37; v. Bar (-Witte), *DeliktsR in Europa, Schweden*, p. 40; and v. Bar (-Nørgaard/Vagner), *DeliktsR in Europa, Dänemark*, p. 8.

[420] Scandinavian case-law on this topic offers a range of examples. From Denmark: HD 17 June 1942, *UfR* 1942 A p. 749 (failure to switch off electricity whilst conducting repairs; breach of the relevant statute was sufficient to establish negligence); VLD 7 May 1965, *UfR* 1965 A p. 702 (explosion of a bottle of gas stored improperly on board ship, causing injury to an employee who was smoking at the time; the ship's owner was held liable). See also VLD 6 Dec. 1968, *UfR* 1969 A p. 441 (breach of road traffic laws). From Sweden: HD 11 June 1976, *NJA* 1076: 72 p. 379 (a pedestrian overlooked a traffic sign forbidding pedestrians to step onto cycle paths; liability of pedestrian affirmed) and HD 20 Dec. 1977, *NJA* 1977: 139 p. 788.

achieved as when the statutory breach must be ascribed to the tortfeasor as a completely objective *faute* or *culpa*.[421] From the viewpoint of a substantive heightening of liability, it is not insignificant that the continuous infringement of a statutory safety provision can sometimes lead to a presumption of cause.

Danish HD 24 October 1989[422] is an example: a garden door leading to a swimming pool had no automatic closing mechanism as required by statute. A child aged three years and eight months was found badly injured in the pool. How the child had entered the garden was unclear. It was possible that the child had used the door, although the owner claimed to have shut it. It was presumed that the accident was caused by the absence of the automatic closing mechanism.

304　The corresponding common law rules are found in the tort of breach of statutory duty. Peculiarities occasionally arise, but the major themes in all European systems are easily recognizable.

305　Breach of statutory duty is an independent tort, distinct from negligence.[423] Where conduct contravenes a statute, the first question is whether Parliament intended that such conduct should give rise to civil liability.[424] If the statute expressly provides either that the breach is actionable,[425] or that action is excluded or restricted,[426] the matter is straightforward. However, if the statute remains silent on the legal consequences of a breach, it is assumed that an actionable right arises in civil law. Courts have intimated that it is unlikely that statutes are intended to communicate only a pious aspiration.[427] The practical application of this rule is somewhat narrow. Generally a statute imposing obligations on citizens intends that sanctions, usually penal, should follow breaches. When a statute is silent as to civil liability, in principle the remedy will be

---

[421] Cf. above no. 31 (Belgium and France), no. 32 (Italy), and no. 249 for discussion of the Swedish and Finnish term for fault (*vållande*), with whose objectivity-oriented tendency the freedom of decision-making referred to substantially accords.

[422] HD 24 Oct. 1989, *UfR* 1989 A p. 1098.

[423] *London Passenger Transport Board* v. *Upson* [1949] AC 155, 168 (*per* Lord Wright). For the relationship between breach of statutory duty and negligence see Stanton, *Breach of Statutory Duty in Tort*, pp. 25–30; for the Scottish view, Walker, *Delict*, 2nd edn., pp. 298–300.

[424] *Lonrho PLC* v. *Fayed and Others* [1989] 2 All ER 65, 69 (Dillon LJ); Weir, *Casebook*, 7th edn., p. 167; Buckley, (1984) 100 *LQR* 204, 205.

[425] Cf. sec 25(3) Resale Prices Act 1976 (c. 53); sec. 35(2) Restrictive Trade Practices Act 1976 (c. 34) and sec. 47(1)(a) Health and Safety at Work Act 1974 (c. 37) (a rule based not on the general duty of care according to sec. 2 loc. cit., but on 'health and safety regulations', cf. Markesinis/Deakin, *Tort Law*, 3rd edn., p. 314).

[426] Sec. 12(1)(b) Nuclear Installations Act 1965 (c. 6) grants damages on the basis of its own rules and not under the auspices of the common law. Examples of statutes which expressly exclude private claims for damages are sec. 13 Safety of Sports Grounds Act 1975 (c. 52) and sec. 5(2) Guard Dogs Act 1975 (c. 50).

[427] *Cutler* v. *Wandsworth Stadium LD* [1949] AC 398, 407; also *West Wiltshire District Council* v. *Garland* [1995] 2 WLR 439, 446. Further comment on similar cases in Stanton, *Breach of Statutory Duty in Tort*, pp. 36–38.

in criminal law: 'Where an Act creates an obligation, and enforces the performance in a specific manner, we take it to be a general rule that performance cannot be achieved in any other manner.'[428]
The above concerns a 'general' rule; it now always depends upon whether either or both of the common law exceptions actually apply.[429] The first exception provides that in every statute creating a 'public right'[430] a cause of action arises for any person who suffers 'particular, direct and substantial damage' by the infringement of his public law right.[431] Cases of this kind are extremely rare. The second exception provides that a cause of action arises on the breach of a protective statute, as recognized in German law, i.e. 'where on the true construction of the Act it is apparent that the obligation or prohibition was imposed for the benefit or protection of a particular class of individuals'.[432] Thus is the doctrine of the protective purpose of laws effectively also applied in the common law. Factory workers thus benefit directly from industrial safety legislation.[433] Such statutes are intended only to protect the health of the employee, not the enforceability of financial claims for breach.[434] In the same way, an act governing betting premises at racecourses is intended to maintain public order, not the financial interests of book-makers.[435] No protective purpose relevant to private law is served by an export embargo[436] created by a statute imposing sanctions for breaches, or by the Education Acts' provisions for the organization of schools.[437] Rules concerned with the transport of cattle by sea must be interpreted as intending only to prevent the outbreak of disease.[438] The Local Government Finance Act 1982 creates a duty of care for the auditors of a local

---

[428] This is the rule in *Doe d. Bishop of Rochester* v. *Bridges* (1831) 1 [1824–1834] B&Ad. 847, 859; 109 ER 1001; cf. Walker, *Delict*, 2nd edn., pp. 307–308.

[429] *Lonrho Ltd. and Others* v. *Shell Petroleum Co. Ltd. and Others* [1981] 2 All ER 456, 461 gives a clear exposition of the current position in England. Irish law goes even further: see *Parsons* v. *Kavanagh* [1990] ILRM 560, 565 (HC); *Attorney General* v. *Paperlink Ltd.* [1984] ILRM 373. See also Mannion, *ILT* 1992 pp. 276–279.

[430] E.g. *Boyce* v. *Paddington Borough Council* [1903] 1 Ch. 109.

[431] This formula was adopted by Brett J in *Benjamin* v. *Storr* (fn. 204 above) and cited with approval by Lord Diplock (fn. 429).

[432] *Lonrho* v. *Shell* (fn. 429); *Cutler* v. *Wandsworth* (fn. 427); *Lonrho* v. *Fayed* (fn. 424); *RCA Corp.* v. *Pollard* [1982] 3 All ER 771, 781 (*per* Oliver LJ); *Re G* v. *Deputy Governor of Parkhurst Prison*, ex parte *Hague* [1992] 1 AC 58, 158 (*per* Lord Bridge).

[433] According to the decision in *Dunne* v. *Honeywell Control Systems Ltd. & Virginia Milk Products Ltd.* [1991] ILRM 595 this applies to works carried out on construction sites. For further on the term 'working operation', often important in this context, see *Dunleavy* v. *Abbey Ltd.* [1992] ILRM 1 (HC) and *Nurse* v. *Morganite Crucible Ltd.* [1989] AC 692, 704.

[434] *Sweeney* v. *Duggan* [1991] 2 IR 274 (HC).   [435] *Cutler* v. *Wandsworth* (fn. 427).

[436] *Lonrho* v. *Shell* (fn. 429).

[437] *E (a Minor)* v. *Dorset County Council and Other Appeals* [1994] 4 All ER 640 (CA); [1995] 3 All ER 353.

[438] *Gorris* v. *Scott* (1874) LR 9 Ex. 125; cf. *Grant* v. *National Coal Board* [1956] AC 649.

authority; it does not protect employees of the authority against their own negligence.[439]

307   Since the differences between common and continental laws amount to little more than varying emphases, it is worth noting their parallels. For example, the task of the tort of breach of statutory duty is to extend the range of interests protected by the law of obligations. This applies in Ireland to some aspects of the right of privacy,[440] and in England, Ireland, and Scotland to the recovery of pure economic loss outside the rule in *Hedley Byrne*.[441] Where a plaintiff belongs to a group of persons protected by statute, and where pure economic loss is within the protective scope[442] of the act infringed, pure economic loss is recoverable.[443] Secondly, entirely independently of the interests protected, note that a sort of competition arises between breach of statutory duty and negligence as possible causes of action.[444] If a statute says nothing to the contrary, or expressly denies a statutory cause of action,[445] liability based in negligence comes into question, whether because the common law

---

[439] *West Wiltshire District Council* v. *Garland* [1993] Ch. 409 (Morritt J); [1995] 2 WLR 439, 446 (Balcombe LJ).

[440] McMahon/Binchy, *Irish Law of Torts*, 2nd edn., p. 687, with reference to sec. 7 Data Protection Act 1988. For England the position is very different. See *Pickering* v. *Liverpool Daily Post & Echo Newspapers PLC* [1991] 1 All ER 622, 632 (*per* Lord Bridge): personal injury, damage to property, and pure economic loss are all recoverable under *breach of statutory duty*. 'But publication of unauthorized information about proceedings on a patient's application for discharge to a mental health review tribunal, though it may in one sense be adverse to the patient's interest, is incapable of causing him loss or injury of a kind for which the law awards damages.' On this see Markesinis/Deakin, *Tort Law*, 3rd edn., p. 311, who rightly say that this was a damages claim 'for breach of privacy'.

[441] See Markesinis/Deakin loc. cit. pp. 311–318; Stanton, *Breach of Statutory Duty in Tort*, pp. 63–73; Walker, *Delict*, 2nd edn., pp. 314–316. McMahon/Binchy loc. cit. (previous footnote) point to the Irish case of *Reilly* v. *Moore* [1935] NJ 196.

[442] Denied in: *Lonrho Ltd.* v. *Shell Petroleum Co. Ltd.* [1982] AC 173; *Watt* v. *Kesteven CC* [1955] 1 QB 408; *RCA Corp.* v. *Pollard* [1983] Ch. 135 (Oliver LJ); and *Sweeney* v. *Duggan* (fn. 434).

[443] Compare the Irish case of *Parsons* v. *Kavanagh* (fn. 429): no licence for carrying people by vehicle; claim brought by a competitor; the Court also relied on the rights granted by the constitution in the English case of *Read* v. *Croydon Corporation* [1938] 4 All ER 631: child suffered damage due to dirty water; the monies which the child's father had to expend were recovered. *Thornton* v. *Kirklees MBC* [1979] 3 WLR 2: local authority held liable for breach of the Housing (Homeless Persons) Act 1977; *Monk* v. *Warbey* [1935] 1 KB 75: lorry driver drove without insurance; the owner of the vehicle was held liable); *An bord Bainne Co-Operative Ltd.* v. *Milk Marketing Board* [1984] 2 CML 584 (breach of Art. 86, EEC Treaty); *In re South of England Natural Gas and Petroleum Co. Ltd.* [1929] AC 158.

[444] See *Bux* v. *Slough Metals* [1974] 1 All ER 262, 273 (*per* Stephenson LJ); *Reffell* v. *Surrey County Council* [1964] 1 WLR 358; and *West Wiltshire District Council* v. *Garland* [1995] 2 WLR 439, 447–448.

[445] E.g. *Deloitte Haskins & Sells* v. *National Mutual Life Nominees Ltd.* [1993] 2 All ER 1015: auditors are obliged to monitor trustees according to the relevant statute only where they are aware of irregularities; There is no wider common law duty to conduct investigations of their own accord.

duty is more extensive[446] than the duties created by the act itself, because the plaintiff does not fall within the protective scope of the statute infringed,[447] or because the act was intended only to serve public interests, not those of private individuals.[448] Finally, and of particular significance, is the third function of this tort, encountered almost everywhere, namely the heightening of the basis of liability. The tort of breach of statutory duty, as already noted, operates independently of negligence, and the applicable standard of care is not that of negligence but the standard which the statute demands. Where the act requires no more than reasonable care, the standard is the same as in negligence. By contrast, where the act contains no such restriction, it again becomes a question of statutory interpretation to determine whether it creates an obligation independent of fault, i.e. a form of strict liability. This latter approach has been affirmed in many cases, the most important concerning legislation regarding safety at work.[449] In this area the employer need only do what is reasonably practical; in practice this can shift the burden of proof of fault.[450]

b. Liability for Damage Caused Contrary to Public Policy, and Interference in the Freedom of Others to Pursue Economic Interests

(1) General

Do the six North European Countries all recognize as contrary to **308** public policy the intentional causing of damage to another?[451] The answer to this question depends in essence upon the measures used to compare them. The criterion of being contrary to public policy (*bonos mores*) is neither expressly stated in any Scandinavian statute on damages, nor part of any tort known to the common law. Leaving aside the old-fashioned expression of §§ 826 BGB, 1295 II ABGB and of Art. 919 Greek Cc (*gute Sitten*), and using a definition of 'contrary to public policy' akin to that found in Art. 6:162 II BW ('an infringement of an unwritten law in social dealings') a parallel becomes clear in Finnish law.

---

[446] Weir, *Casebook*, 7th edn., p. 169. See also *Stovin* v. *Wise* [1994] 3 All ER 467; and *Skelly (a Minor)* v. *Dublin Corporation*, *ILT* 1994 p. 131: ladder of a children's slide was insufficiently secured. Liability in *negligence* was affirmed despite the fact that at the material time the statutory safety provisions concerning the ladder were not in force.

[447] E.g. *Hartley* v. *Mayoh & Co.* [1954] 1 QB 383: injury to a fireman; liability affirmed in negligence but not in breach of statutory duty, as the fireman did not belong to the category of person whom the Act intended to protect. Cf. Jones, *Torts*, 4th edn., p. 299.

[448] E.g. *E* v. *Dorset County Council* [1994] 4 All ER 640 (CA); [1995] 3 All ER 353.

[449] See Stanton, *Breach of Statutory Duty in Tort*, pp. 56–57, 92–107; Binchy/Byrne, *ILT* 1995 pp. 4–8, 28–32; Williams, 23 [1960] *MLR* 233–259; Fricke, 76 [1960] *LQR* 240–266. The defence of *volenti non fit injuria* may be excluded by some statutes, cf. *Wheeler* v. *New Merton Board Mills* [1933] 2 KB 669.   [450] *Nimmo* v. *Alexander Cowan & Sons* [1968] AC 107.

[451] See nos. 36–40 above.

According to Chapter 5, 1 §, 2 s. of Finland's Act on Damages, the term 'damage' is said to include, if damage is 'caused by a criminal act or by an act of the authorities or in another case where there is compelling reason' compensation for further economic loss. According to this wording and its function, the rule comports nothing more than an *actio de dolo*, expressed in terms of modern conditions.[452] Where the act complained of is not criminal, a 'compelling reason' is needed to render pure economic loss recoverable, otherwise the criterion of being contrary to public policy is not satisfied. On the other hand, whether it actually has any effect upon the results achieved by so diverse a law of obligations is questionable. Consider that Germany has the concept of infringement of *bonos mores*; France uses the concept of *faute* (as in Art. 1382 Cc), which is not further defined even in respect of intention; The Netherlands has its unwritten laws in social dealings (Art. 6:162 BW); Finland refers to 'compelling reason'; a number of common law torts require malicious behaviour;[453] Sweden has a general prohibition against chicanery;[454] and in Scotland[455] the basic rule is that *damnum absque injuria* does not lead to liability.[456] What is clear, however, is that all these different wordings have the same purpose, namely to express that nowhere is it sufficient for the purpose of establishing liability simply to want to cause harm to another. Were it otherwise, the free-market system, in which each participant competes for a market share, simply could not operate.

309　In order to analyse more closely how liability is dealt with both in Britain and in Scandinavia for damage caused intentionally in a manner contrary to public policy, more detailed consideration is needed of the solutions and techniques of resolution used in the UK and in Scandinavia for groups of cases which in continental Europe are customarily handled by reference to the criteria listed above. If, in those countries which recognize the *actio de dolo*, a varying degree of use is already made of it,[457] then it is still possible to characterize as contrary to public policy a range of wrongful acts which, wherever there was a cause of action,

---

[452] See no. 245 above. Saxén, *Skadeståndsrätt*, pp. 73–75, repeatedly uses the term 'behaviour contrary to custom'.　　　　　　　　　　　　　　　　[453] See no. 260 above.

[454] See no. 245 above. Note also that under 19 § with 2 § of the Swedish Competition Act (*Marknadsföringslag*, SFS 1975: 1418) breach of good business customs (*god affärssed*) may give rise to liability in damages.　　　　[455] Walker, *Delict*, 2nd edn., pp. 37–40.

[456] Cf. Viscount Simon LC in *Crofter Co.* v. *Veitch* 1942 SC 1, 7: '"Injury" is limited to actionable wrong, while "damage", in contrast with injury, means loss or harm occuring in fact, whether actionable as an injury or not.'

[457] In Germany mainly in the context of § 826 BGB. As far as liability for information is concerned, this has led to the position that because pure economic loss could not be compensated for in any other way, certain types of conduct, which in other legal systems constitute mere negligence, were classified as acts of intention. See v. Bar, in: Markesinis (ed.), *The Gradual Convergence*, pp. 98, 102–106.

one was always wont to associate with the *actio de dolo*: i.e. bringing unjustified legal proceedings, giving bad professional advice to third parties, and inducing breach of contract.[458] In order, on one hand, to avoid the danger that our inventory proceeds too strongly from the viewpoint of only one part of European law and, on the other hand, to avoid repetition (liability for professional advice is considered later),[459] there follows a discussion of liability for inducing breach of contract.

(2) *Inducing Breach of Contract*

Inducing a third party to breach a contract not only constitutes a tort **310** everywhere in Europe, it is also the classic situation in which the *actio de dolo* falls to be considered. This is as true of the Scandinavian countries[460] as of the common law, where procuring breach of contract belongs to the group of economic torts which, as noted above, are very similar in content to the 'causing of damage in a manner contrary to public policy'.[461] The earliest cases on procuring breach concerned instigation to breach contracts of service and employment,[462] a theme which has lost little of its significance,[463] and is still developing. Nowhere is the type of contract[464] any longer relevant; ordinary trade contracts are covered.[465] In principle anybody

---

[458] See no. 36 above.   [459] See no. 497 below.

[460] Inducing breach of contract is one of the rare instances when the Danish literature emphasizes the *actio de dolo*: see Gomard, *Erstatningsregler*, p. 58. In Finland Chapter 5, 1 §, 2 s. SKL is available, cf. Saxén, *Skadeståndsrätt*, pp. 74–75. The position in Sweden is not clear, primarily because of the shortage of decisions on this subject. Perhaps it is not inappropriate to use, for purposes of comparison, the Swedish case-law concerning the shut-down of factories caused by disruption to their electricity supply (HD 4 Apr. 1966, *NJA* 1966: 42 p. 210 [cf. Hellner, *SJT* 1969 p. 332, 357–359] and HD 7 Mar. 1988, *NJA* 1988: 11 p. 62), in which the issue has always been whether the affected party had 'a concrete and direct interest' in the supply of electricity. The protection of such concrete interests also covers claims arising from intentional third-party frustration of contractual expectations.

[461] See no. 260 above. For an English perspective see Gutteridge, (1933–35) *CLJ* 5 22–24: and Lawson/Markesinis, *Tortious Liability*, vol. i, pp. 17–18 and 52–55.

[462] For Denmark see HD 2 Feb. 1932, *UfR* 1932 A p. 308; and ØLD 28 June 1940, *UfR* 1940 A p. 975; in common law see *Lumley* v. *Gye* (fn. 144 above). For Ireland see McMahon/Binchy, *Irish Law of Torts*, 2nd edn., p. 249.

[463] For England see no. 260 above; for Ireland see *British and Irish Steampacket Co. Ltd.* v. *Branigan* [1958] IR 128 (HC); and *Bradbury Ltd.* v. *Duffy & Whelan* [1979] ILRM 51 (HC).

[464] Cf. for Denmark, Ussing (-Kruse), *Obligationsretten*, vol. i, 4th edn., pp. 448–450. For the common law see *Quinn* v. *Leathem* [1901] AC 495, 510, *per* Lord Macnaghton: 'A violation of a legal right committed knowingly is a cause of action, and . . . it is a violation of a legal right to interfere with contractual relations recognized by law, if there be no sufficient justification for the interference'. Inducement not to take part in future dealings is not enough: *Bula Ltd.* v. *Tara Mines Ltd.* [1988] ILRM 157 (HC).

[465] McMahon/Binchy, *Irish Law of Torts*, 2nd edn., p. 560; Walker, *Delict*, 2nd edn., p. 920; Winfield/Jolowicz (-Rogers), *Tort*, 14th edn., p. 520. In *Finlay* v. *Playcock* 1937 SC 21 the tort was extended to cover inducement to breach a contract to marry.

can commit the tort of procuring breach of contract, but in practice most actions are directed against trade unions and their representatives intending to exert pressure by strikes on an unpopular employer. In this context, the scope of the tort (traditionally rather narrow) has been increased in two ways. First, it is no longer necessary that the wrongful act directly caused the breach of contract: 'The principle of *Lumley* v. *Gye* extends not only to inducing breach of contract but also to preventing the performance of it.'[466] A supplier's contract which excludes liability caused by strikes and boycotts does not operate for the benefit of those on strike. Secondly, it is not necessary for the tortfeasor either to have had knowledge of the exact content of the contract[467] or to have been certain that a contract had been signed. He cannot turn a blind eye; it suffices that by exercising only a modest degree of care the tortfeasor could have discovered the contract with the third party.[468]

(3) The Protection of the Individual's Freedom to Pursue Economic Interests

311 To the extent that the tort of procuring breach of contract reaches into employment law, where it joins an extensive range of legislation,[469] the case material with which it is concerned, certainly from the perspective of the majority of continental legal systems, departs from the *actio de dolo*. Unlawful strikes are now everywhere covered by the basic tort principles found in the codes.[470] It will be remembered that the codes place special value on the right to develop one's own economic interest, occasionally expressed as the 'right to set up an enterprise' or 'to operate a business', which in many ways represents an enlargement of the special rule on endangering another's creditworthiness.[471] Although from this starting position it is self-evident that continental countries have not been able to tailor their own economic torts according to like

---

[466] Lord Denning MR, in *Torquay Hotel Co. Ltd.* v. *Cousins and Others* [1969] 2 Ch. 106, 137. Cf. *Bula Ltd.* v. *Mines Ltd.* [1988] ILRM 157, 161.

[467] Lord Pearce in *J. T. Stratford* v. *Lindley* [1965] AC 269, 332.

[468] In purely 'technical' terms, the plaintiff must prove both the defendant's intention to interfere in a contract and the defendant's knowledge of the contract (*British International Plastics Ltd.* v. *Ferguson* [1940] 1 All ER 479, 483, Lord Russell). However, imputed knowledge is now sufficient in the case of gross negligence. Cf. from England *Merkur Island Shipping Corp.* v. *Laughton* [1983] 2 AC 570, 608 (Lord Diplock); *Associated Newspapers Group* v. *Wade* [1979] 1 WLR 697; *Dimbleby & Son Ltd.* v. *NUJ* [1984] 1 WLR 427; *Emerald Construction Co. Ltd.* v. *Louthian* [1966] 1 WLR 691, 700–701 (Lord Denning MR). For Ireland the report by McMahon/Binchy, *Irish Tort Law*, 2nd edn., p. 564 on *Cotter* v. *Ahern* (HC; unreported). The defendant cannot be liable where he could not have known of existing contractual links: *Flogas Ltd.* v. *Ergas Ltd. & Irish National Gas Ltd.* [1985] ILRM 221 (HC).

[469] See no. 260 and fn. 149 above.

[470] Until the right to an established business (*Recht am Unternehmen*) was fully developed, it was necessary to invoke the *actio de dolo* together with § 826 BGB: *BGB-RGRK* (- Steffen), 12th edn., § 823 BGB at no. 61. [471] See nos. 44–49 above.

criteria (i.e. in the form of a number of separate torts),[472] a variety of recent noteworthy developments have nevertheless occurred in this field in English and especially Irish tort law.

Those developments have in part been concerned with the tort of **312** wrongful interference with trade or business.[473] This developed from the tort of procuring breach of contract, and was originally intended to cover disputes about working conditions between employer and employee. In *J. T. Stratford & Sons Ltd.* v. *Lindley*, a trade union prevented the plaintiff's barges from being manned or loaded. No distinction was made between barges operated by the plaintiff company and those it let out to be run by other operators. It became impossible for the plaintiff to continue the business of letting out barges during the 'hot phase'. Lord Reid said: 'it was not disputed that such interference with business is tortious if any unlawful means are employed.'[474] The employees had induced the hirers of the barges to breach their contracts: this was unlawful. A very similar situation occurred in *Merkur Island Corp.* v. *Laughton*: tug crews were incited, in breach of their employment contracts, not to tow the plaintiff's tanker out of port whilst the tanker sailed under a flag of convenience. Lord Diplock used this opportunity to make clear that such conduct not only constituted 'interfering with the trade or business of another person by doing unlawful acts', but also that 'to fall within the genus of torts the unlawful act need not involve procuring another person to break a subsisting contract or to interfere with the performance of a subsisting contract.'[475] Finally, in *Lonrho* v. *Fayed* a new tort was applied to the relationship between two firms, one of which had, to the detriment of the other, deceived the Monopoly Commission.[476]

The tort of wrongful interference with trade or business clearly has **313** tremendous potential for expansion; how far its scope will spread cannot be easily predicted. It is primarily directed at damage caused to the plaintiff intentionally and directly (mere reflex damage as in boycotts are not enough[477]) by unlawful means.[478] The position in Germany is similar: there too, wrongfulness must be proved in instances involving

---

[472] A further issue is whether the different styles of particular torts affect the actual decision when applied to similar factual circumstances. An example is found in the law applicable to tests on comparable products. In Germany recourse is usually had to the law covering the right to an established business, whereas in the common law world only the tort of slander of goods (a sub-category of injurious falsehood) is available. See Hartig, *Vergleichende Warentests*, pp. 34–42, 108–110.   [473] See nos. 260–261 above.
[474] [1965] AC 269, 324.
[475] *Merkur Island Shipping Corp.* v. *Laughton* [1983] 2 AC 570, 606–607.
[476] See no. 261 above.
[477] The same is true in Danish law: see Kruse, *Erstatningsretten*, 5th edn., p. 291; HD 16 June 1928, *UfR* 1928 A p. 700; and ØLD 26 Oct. 1928, *UfR* 1929 A p. 165.
[478] *Barrets & Bairds (Wholesale) Ltd.* v. *Institution of Professional Civil Servants* [1987] IRLR 3, 10 (Henry J). Cf. Napier, (1987) 46 *CLJ* 222–225.

interference with business. However, greater value is given in the common law to bringing the 'unlawful means' under precise control, often by actions in other traditional torts. The arc extends from deception, through breach of statutory duty, inducing breach of contract, and misfeasance in a public office,[479] to breach of fiduciary duty.[480]

314   Influenced by its Constitution,[481] a further step has recently been taken in Ireland. There, even if the requirements of the common law tort of interference with trade or business are absent, a further cause of action comes into play: wrongful infringement of the right to earn a livelihood. This is one of the 'personal rights' referred to in Art. 40(3)(1) of the Irish Constitution[482] and, like all such rights, guards against infringements not only by the state, but also by private citizens.[483] In practice this has created a recognized right to injunctive relief for employees who intended but were unable to reach their workplace on account of measures taken by a trade union.[484] The right to earn a livelihood includes the right to work.[485] That fundamental right is actionable even if there is no wrongful interference with trade or business because the breach did not concern a statute intended to grant a right of compensation for pure economic loss. In *Parsons* v. *Kavanagh*[486] one bus operator won damages against another operating buses on the same route but without a licence. *Parsons* v. *Kavanagh* also illustrates that it makes no difference whether the plaintiff earns his livelihood as employer or employee: notice of this point should be taken throughout Europe.[487]

c. Liability of Joint Tortfeasors

(1) An Overview of Statutory Principles

315   The liability of joint tortfeasors is now governed extensively by statute. In England and Scotland the only relevant provisions are those of the Civil Liability (Contribution) Act 1978[488] concerning the apportionment

---

[479] Cf. *Bourgoin SA* v. *Minister of Agriculture* [1986] QB 716.
[480] *Prudential Assurance* v. *Lorenz* (1971) 1 KIR 78.   [481] See nos. 296–298 above.
[482] See *Ryan* v. *A-G* [1965] IR 294 (Kenny J); *Yeates* v. *Minister for Post and Telegraphs* [1978] ILRM 22 (Kenny J).
[483] *Parsons* v. *Kavanagh* [1990] ILRM 560, 566 (O'Hanlon J). Also *Moyne* v. *Londonderry Port & Harbour Commissioners* [1986] IR 299, 316–317 (Costello J).
[484] *Murtagh Properties Ltd.* v. *Cleary* [1972] IR 330.
[485] *Murphy* v. *Stewart* [1973] IR 97, 117 (Sup. Ct.)
[486] See fn. 483. Cf. *RCA Corp.* v. *Pollard* [1983] Ch. 135.
[487] For a commentary from the German perspective on the problem of balancing the right to run a business against the right to work see *BGB-RGRK* (-Steffen), 12th edn., § 823 BGB at no. 38.
[488] Chap. 47. The most important provisions are found in secs. 1 and 2. It is also noteworthy that for Scotland sec. 3 of the Law Reform (Miscellaneous Provisions) (Scotland) Act 1940 (c. 42) obliges the court which finds joint liability to quantify the extent of liability of each joint tortfeasor; Walker, *Delict*, 2nd edn., p. 115.

of liability between joint tortfeasors.[489] By contrast, the Irish Civil Liability Act 1961[490] addresses all the main issues of outward liability (secs. 11 ff.). Likewise, much of the law on joint liability in Denmark (§ 25 EAL) and Finland (Chapter 6, 2 § and 3 § SKL) is governed by statute. Chapter 6, 3 § of the Swedish SKL contains at the very least the basic rule that 'where two or more people are responsible to meet the same damages [they should] be jointly liable for the damage, provided that the extent of the duty of any of them to pay damages is not restricted'. As for apportionment amongst joint tortfeasors, 8 §, II of the Environmental Liability Law[491] provides that apportionment should proceed 'according to rules of equity having regard to the basis of liability, possible precautionary measures, and other circumstances'. This guideline presumably also applies outside environmental law.[492]

(2) Joint Tortfeasors, Concurrent Tortfeasors, and Concurrent Wrongdoers

Legal systems which apply to the issue of joint liability concepts drawn   **316**
from the criminal law distinguish between joint tortfeasors, participants, 'subsidiary tortfeasors', and parties involved (i.e. subsidiary tortfeasors whose responsibility for causing damage is doubtful).[493] The common law has a different system of classification. There the term joint tortfeasors denotes persons who are all responsible for the same wrong. In other words, the wrong which one of the tortfeasors has committed is sufficient at law, without proof of any further breach of duty, to render the other person liable.[494] Joint tortfeasors are not only those who have agreed to undertake a wrongful act together,[495] but also employers who are vicariously liable for the acts of their employees, principals responsible for agents, persons who breach a duty owed jointly, main and subcontractors who owe non-delegable duties, and finally all those

---

[489] Such statutory rules were necessary because the common law did not contain the wherewithal to resolve the issue of apportionment between joint tortfeasors: Markesinis/ Deakin, *Tort Law*, 3rd edn., p. 740. Until 1937 Sweden did not recognize a civil right of action between co-defendants to criminal charges: Dufwa, *Flera Skadeståndsskyldiga*, vol. ii, no. 4322.   [490] See no. 237 and fn. 7, and no. 239 above.

[491] *Miljöskadelag*, SFS 1986: 225.

[492] Bengtsson, in: Strömholm (ed.), *Introduction to Swedish Law*, pp. 297, 313. See Dufwa, *Flera Skadeståndsskyldiga*, vol. ii, nos. 4308–4314 for an overview of additional statutory rules on rights of recourse.

[493] See nos. 50–60 above; Dufwa, loc. cit., vol. iii, nos. 5403–5416 provides an extensive comparative analysis of the relationship between criminal and civil law in this field.

[494] Charlesworth & Percy (-Percy), *Negligence*, 8th edn., p. 123; Clerk & Lindsell (-Carty), *Torts*, 16th edn., 2–55, p. 181.

[495] This group also includes those who incite the commission of a tort or an offence. The incitement is an independent tort (*CBS Songs Ltd.* v. *Amstrad Consumer Electronics PLC* [1988] 1 AC 1013, 1057 [Lord Templeman). Incitors and 'doers' are joint tortfeasors because 'whoever gives a mandate or order for doing a wrong is held as the doer': Walker, *Delict*, 2nd edn., p. 110.

who have acted 'in furtherance of a common design'.[496] All other cases concern several tortfeasors.[497] Where they cause the same damage they are several concurrent tortfeasors. The textbook example is that of two car drivers who negligently collide as a result of which a pedestrian is injured.[498] Parents and children also belong to this category: fault is a prerequisite of the liability of parents.[499] It is suggested that all several concurrent tortfeasors are equivalent to the *Nebentäter* of German law, but some *Nebentäter* are joint tortfeasors.

317   Concerning the traditional distinction between joint and several concurrent tortfeasors, it must be noted that very little turns on the distinction in practice, because both groups incur joint and several liability. Throughout Europe,[500] every joint or several tortfeasor can be held solely (or severally) liable for all the damage caused. Even the joint tortfeasor is, however confusing it sounds, severally liable. He is also jointly liable. The addition of several to joint liability was of real procedural significance. Previously, joint tortfeasors, against whom there was only one cause of action, could not be proceeded against successively (one after the other); if they were to be held jointly responsible then they had to be proceeded against in the same action. This rule was abolished before the Second World War,[501] and the cause of action no longer distinguishes between the two groups of tortfeasors.[502] However, another historic common law rule in respect of joint tortfeasors remains in force: a discharge from liability[503] of one joint tortfeasor works to the benefit of all joint tortfeasors.[504] A mere commitment not to pursue an action is not sufficient; joint and several tortfeasors are, in this respect at least, on the same footing.[505] In general, therefore, the traditional classification system of the common law has survived. This is a state of affairs

---

[496] Also *CBS Songs* v. *Amstrad*, previous fn.

[497] Markesinis/Deakin, *Tort Law*, 3rd edn., p. 738; Jones, *Torts*, 4th edn., p. 416.

[498] *Drinkwater* v. *Kimber* [1952] 2 QB 281.   [499] See nos. 330 ff. below.

[500] See nos. 51–53 above for the position in continental Europe. For Scandinavia see Dufwa, *Flera Skadeståndsskyldiga*, vol. i, nos. 1798–1809 (Denmark), nos. 1810–1834 (Finland), and vol. iii, nos. 4998, 5056 ff., and 5427 ff. (Sweden, a summary from a comparative perspective). For additional material on Denmark see von Eyben/Nørgaard/Vagner, *Erstatningsret*, 2nd edn., pp. 290–292, and for Sweden see Hellner, *Skadeståndsrätt*, 4th edn., pp. 203–205. The corresponding statutory rules appear at no. 315 above.

[501] By the Law Reform (Married Women and Joint Tortfeasors) Act 1935 (c. 30).

[502] Sec. 1(1) Civil Liability (Contribution) Act 1978: 'Subject to the following provisions of this section, any person liable in respect of any damage suffered by another person may recover contribution from any other person liable in respect of the same damage *whether jointly with him or otherwise*' (italics added).

[503] According to general contract rules, such discharge requires either consideration or a contract executed under seal.

[504] *Cutler and Another* v. *McPhail* [1962] 2 QB 292 (Salmon J) and for New Zealand, *New Zealand Guardian Trust Co. Ltd.* v. *Kenneth Stewart Brooks* [1995] 1 WLR 96, 99 (*per* Lord Keith).   [505] As in the previous footnote.

from which Ireland escaped in 1961, when it pursued the sensible option: in the Civil Liability Act 1961 all such tortfeasors are classified as concurrent wrongdoers.[506] The Act simplified the consequences of the discharge of liability for both joint and several tortfeasors.[507]

In theory, the law of tort intends that the victim should not suffer by **318** virtue of the fact that more than one person was responsible for the damage.[508] Irish tort law has achieved that effect with the unambiguous statement that 'concurrent wrongdoers', as provided by sec. 12(1) of the 1961 Act, 'are each liable for the whole of the damage in respect of which they are concurrent wrongdoers'. This basic rule is common throughout continental Europe.[509] (The notion of partial responsibility only arises where individuals acting independently of each other each cause damage to the same third person by different means.[510]) For example, if two demonstrators jointly throw stones at a policeman, and one stone hits his head and the other his stomach, both demonstrators are liable for the entire damage.[511] In general, joint and several liability can arise irrespective of the ground of liability,[512] the age of the tortfeasor,[513] and the measure of fault of each of them.[514] In addition, joint and several liability can arise even if one of them commits a positive act while the other is 'only' responsible for a wrongful omission.[515] Account must also be taken of any contributory negligence by the victim.[516] By contrast,

---

[506] Sec. 11(2)(a): 'Persons may become concurrent wrongdoers as a result of vicarious liability of one for another, breach of joint duty, conspiracy, concerted action to a common end or independent acts causing the same damage.'   [507] Sec. 17.

[508] See Dufwa, *Flera Skadeståndsskyldiga*, vol. iii, nos. 5417–5426.   [509] See fn. 500.

[510] *Byrne* v. *Triumph Engineering Ltd.* [1982] ILRM 317 (Sup. Ct.) is an example from Ireland. An employee suffered 2 similar injuries, one before and one after a change of job; both employers were held liable. For Sweden, Hellner, *Skadeståndsrätt*, 4th edn., p. 177, takes the view that joint liability accrues, according to Chapter 6, 3 § SKL, where a person suffers 2 or more injuries, each of which was sufficient to render the person unfit for work.

[511] See Walker, *Delict*, 2nd edn., p. 112 with reference to *Hook* v. *McCallum* (1905) 7 F. 528, 532; 12 SLT 770 (*per* Macdonald LJC); and Hellner, *Skadeståndsrätt*, 4th edn., p. 178.

[512] See sec. 11(2)(b) Civil Liability Act 1961 ('the wrong on the part of one or both may be a tort, a breach of contract or breach of trust, or any combination of them') and the similarly worded sec. 6(1) Civil Liability (Contribution) Act 1978 (see Jones, *Torts*, 4th edn., p. 416). See also von Eyben/Nørgaard/Vagner, *Erstatningsret*, 2nd edn., p. 291 (confluence of *culpa* based and no-fault liability). For consideration of the interplay between liability based in contract and liability founded in tort from the perspective of the Irish Civil Liability Act see *O'Sullivan* v. *Noonan and Transit Ltd.* [1969] IR 253 (Sup. Ct.) and *Cole (An Infant)* v. *Webb Caravans Ltd.* [1983] ILRM 595 (HC).

[513] Dan. HD 8 Feb. 1991, *UfR* 1991 A p. 274: joint liability of boy scouts aged between 10 and 13; Dan. HD 25 Oct. 1990, *UfR* 1990 A p. 926: joint tortfeasors aged 9 and 10.

[514] von Eyben/Nørgaard/Vagner and Jones (fn. 512).

[515] Hellner, *Skadeståndsrätt*, 4th edn., p. 179; *Conole* v. *Redbank Oyster Co.* [1976] IR 191 (Sup. Ct.); *Ward* v. *McMaster* [1986] ILRM 43 (HC); *Riordan's Travel* v. *Acres* [1979] ILRM 3 (HC); *Cowan* v. *Freaghaile* [1991] 1 IR 389 (HC).

[516] E.g. *Fitzgerald* v. *Lane* [1989] AC 328. For Ireland, see *Lynch* v. *Lynch & Alliance & Dublin Consumers Gas Co.* (High Court 24 Nov. 1976).

factors which are of universal importance in apportioning liability between tortfeasors and the procedure of apportionment have, as previously stated, very little to do with the law of torts. As far as the relationship between tortfeasors is concerned, several factors come to mind which are of little or no importance in establishing liability to the plaintiff. Factors governing the extent of the damage caused by each tortfeasor, or the degree of fault[517] (simple negligence usually suffices[518]) attributable to each tortfeasor, and especially the effects of contractual agreements and special features relating to the financial position[519] of those involved, or from the issue of insurance cover,[520] can all be decisive. Also, where an employer and an employee are jointly and severally liable, the employee must have been pursuing the employer's interests when the negligence occurred.[521] Finally, in the internal relationship between co-tortfeasors there are often provisions on limitation allowing one to recover, by way of contribution from the other, that portion of the damages which equates to the other's liability, where the other was not proceeded against because he was able to rely upon the defence of limitation.[522]

---

[517] Whether it depends upon causation alone or whether negligence and causation are factors of equal weight, the matter is treated differently as between England and Scotland (Walker, *Delict*, 2nd edn., pp. 119–120); however, it is far from clear that this difference has any practical effect.

[518] In cases where negligence is only slight, the difference between the internal relationship (between the tortfeasors themselves) and the external one (between tortfeasors and victim) becomes particularly clear. It is possible for the victim to claim his total loss from, and for the *concurrent wrongdoer* to be completely free of any responsibility to, the other tortfeasor: *O'Shea* v. *Hegarty & Sons Ltd.* ILT 1995 p. 2.

[519] Cf. Chapter 6, 3 §, II, 2 s. of the Finnish SKL: 'Where one of the persons bound to pay damages is obviously in financial difficulties or their place of abode is unknown, then each of the others who are bound to pay damages must pay the deficit according to his share.'

[520] It has been repeatedly expressed in a range of cases in § 25 I from the Danish EAL that 'regard can be made to the present insurance position when apportioning responsibility to pay damages amongst the defendants'.

[521] See § 23 I of the Danish EAL: 'damages which an employer has to pay as a result of the negligent conduct of one his employees can only be demanded (by the employer) from the employee to the extent that this appears reasonable having regard to the fault of the employee, the position of the employee and to all the circumstances of the case.' In this way the ability of the employer to recover the damages from the employee is all but excluded (v. Bar [-Nørgaard/Vagner], *DeliktsR in Europa, Dänemark*, p. 9; for early history see Jørgensen, *FS Neumayer*, pp. 337, 341). In Sweden the necessary protection is afforded by limiting the liability associated with the external relationship (Chapter 4, 1 § SKL). The Finnish SKL has enlarged the protection afforded in respect of the external relationship (i.e. Chapter 4, 1 § SKL: no liability for simple negligence, with the possibility of liability where equitable) by supplementing the protection in the internal relationship (i.e. between the tortfeasors: Chapter 6, 2 § Finn. SKL). In English law the cases of *Lister* v. *Romford Ice and Storage Co. Ltd.* [1957] AC 555 and *Morris* v. *Ford Motor Co. Ltd.* [1973] QB 792 followed precisely the opposite course, but in practice such recourse actions are rare (Markesinis/Deakin, *Tort Law*, 3rd edn., pp. 743–744). For the position in Ireland see McMahon/Binchy, *Irish Law of Torts*, 2nd edn., p. 81.

[522] See sec. 1(3) Civil Liability (Contribution) Act 1978; sec. 31 Civil Liability Act 1961 and esp. *Neville* v. *Morgan Ltd.* [1988] IR 734, and 4 § of the Swedish Limitation Act.

(3) Causation

The law of delict is again put to the test when it has to decide **319** whether a defendant is liable (either singly or jointly and severally) when it is not clear whether that person caused or contributed to the causation in the victim's injury. If, as a result of two simultaneous acts or omissions, two or more people injure a third, the matter is straightforward. In the case of two hunters who both shot a beater, each has 'done something' to the beater; neither of them can say with certainty that the victim would have died, or been hospitalized, if the other person alone had fired. In the case of a group of surgeons overseeing treatment for a foreign object left in a patient, it is arguably worse that not only one of them, but other colleagues also failed to exercise proper care.

A more complicated group of cases concerns the liability of joint **320** tortfeasors, instigators, and abettors. As in continental theory,[523] the new Swedish theory of 'psychic causation' is relevant here. However, as on the continent, it need not be decisive for liability to be established.[524] This is because the intention to promote the act of another, and the objective promotion itself, are sufficient to result in the liability of the person who does not actually carry out the deed, and ultimately even when the deed would have come about without that person's intervention.[525] Given this starting point, there is a lot to be said for the advice of Hart and Honoré and for not talking at all of causality in this context, and consequently, insofar as it concerns the contribution of the man in the background (i.e. the instigator), not to make causality a prerequisite of liability. According to Hart and Honoré this is a matter of 'interpersonal transactions', and nothing to do with causation.[526] From such transactions we learn very little about causation, and a great deal less than we do from the tangible world. Thus all that can be said is that the 'doer' of the damage was probably given a further reason to act by the man behind him; whether the person in the background initiated the idea or only strengthened the existing resolve of the doer is only relevant to apportionment between co-tortfeasors, which is of no significance for the victim. For the victim's claim, any degree of influence must suffice, depending on three conditions: the person carrying out the deed must have understood what the other intended; the intervention must have preceded the act; and the intended damage must have occurred.[527] In the

---

[523] See nos. 54–55 above.

[524] Dufwa, *Flera Skadeståndsskyldiga*, vol. ii, no. 3835–3841; Kleinemann, *Ren förmögenhetsskada*, pp. 163 and 417.   [525] See fns. 523 and 524.

[526] Hart/Honoré, *Causation in the Law*, 2nd edn., pp. 51–57, 125–127, and 457–458.

[527] Ibid. p. 53. Cf. Atiyah (-Cane), *Accidents*, 4th edn., p. 87 on no-fault liability, 'because the defendant is held liable for damage which he or she may not even have caused, in the sense that the damage may well have occurred even without that person's assistance'.

English decisions on conspiracy and inducing breach of contract, the question of whether one tortfeasor caused the act of the other which in fact caused damage is not rigorously addressed: the two acts tend to be treated separately. However, the result is similar to that reached elsewhere in Europe. In judging the first act, account is taken of the quality of the extra-reason which the person in the background gave to the actual doer. A demand suffices; advice does not.[528] As yet there appear to be no decisions in which this distinction was used to determine the liability of demonstrators or squatters.

321   All European legal systems discuss the problem of how the victim is to be compensated when it is unclear which of a number of participants harmed the victim. The textbook example is again the beater unintentionally shot by one of several hunters firing simultaneously. A statutory solution is provided by sec. 11(3) Irish Civil Liability Act: 'Where two or more persons are at fault and one or more of them is or are responsible for damage while the other or others is or are free from causal responsibility, but if it is not possible to establish which is the case, such two or more persons shall be deemed to be concurrent wrongdoers in respect of the damage.' On one hand this provision operates very narrowly as it only applies where fault attaches to each of the participants; on the other hand it is excessively 'victim-friendly', because it completely removes the requirement of showing causation. Decisions of the kind found in the DES judgment of the Dutch *Hoge Raad*[529] are covered by such wording.[530]

322   As for the remaining jurisdictions, the problem of liability of participants who may have been causally responsible has been left to the judges, and as this issue appears to have been considered only rarely, it is not easy to make definitive statements on it. A Danish 1944 decision of the Western High Court touches on the issue:

Two people were shooting sparrows in a garden; two horses grazing nearby were injured. It remained unclear which of the defendants had hit the horses and whether the injuries were caused by one or two shots. The VLD held both defendants responsible for the entire damage.[531]

Sweden has a similar decision on this point:

In 1947 the plaintiff was beaten about the head. In 1952 he was struck again on the head in a road accident. It could not be determined to what extent each of the

---

[528] This is clear from *Camden Nominees* v. *Forcey* [1940] Ch. 352, 360 (Simonds J). A similar case is *Crofter Hand Woven Harris Tweed Co.* v. *Veitch* [1942] AC 435, 440 (Viscount Simon LC). The elegant formulation of dependence on 'extra-reason' is derived from Hart and Honoré, loc. cit. p. 54.   [529] See no. 60 above.
[530] Cf. McMahon/Binchy, *Irish Law of Tort*, 2nd edn., p. 58, and from the same authors, *Casebook*, 2nd edn., p. 39.   [531] VLD 10 Jan. 1944, *UfR* 1944 A p. 358.

injuries was responsible for the pain endured by the plaintiff. In order to protect the victim, the Supreme Court held each party responsible liable to the victim for the entire damage.[532]

This Swedish case does not go exactly to the heart of the problem, because it was clear that each defendant had wrongfully injured the victim. The only issue was to attribute the consequences to the various wrongful acts, and one can only surmise that the Swedish Supreme Court, given the facts of the Danish case, would probably have reached the same decision as the Danish court.

That is not so certain of the common law. There is as yet no decision on **323** whether the victim or the possible tortfeasors should bear the risk in cases where causation is not clear-cut, when any of the possible tortfeasors may have been causally responsible.[533] This subject is hotly debated by commentators.[534] Two North American cases (one Canadian, the other from the USA) were decided in favour of the victims of hunting accidents.[535] It is extremely doubtful how much weight can be accorded to these decisions, given that in England and Scotland strong words have been used to stress the requirement of showing causation.[536] There is an *obiter dictum* of the Court of Appeal dating from 1958 which appears to doubt that possible tortfeasors should be liable.[537] However,

---

[532] HD 31 July 1961, *NJA* 1961: 57 p. 425. See Dufwa, *Flera Skadeståndsskyldiga*, vol. ii, nos. 2969–2972 and Hellner, *Skadeståndsrätt*, p. 179.

[533] None of the English decisions discussed in this context can be cited as authority for either solution. In *Wilsher v. Essex Area Health Authority* [1988] AC 1074, that a premature baby was born blind could have resulted as much from natural causes as from doctors confusing arteries with veins; liability was not affirmed. In *McGhee v. National Coal Board* [1973] 1 WLR 1 the defendant firm failed to provide coal miners with showering facilities. The defendants were held liable, as the danger of dermatitis was known. In *Bonnington Castings Ltd. v. Wardlaw* [1956] AC 613 the plaintiff contracted a lung disease whose cause could be traced to a machine which, for the most part, was run in accordance with the statutory rules, but which was not wholly in conformity with them. The action succeeded. However, all these cases are irrelevant to the specific problems of causation by concurrent wrongdoers.

[534] For joint liability see Hart/Honoré, *Causation in the Law*, 2nd edn., p. 424; and Markesinis/Deakin, *Tort Law*, 3rd edn., p. 175. For a contrary view see Winfield/Jolowicz (-Rogers), *Tort*, 14th edn., p. 139; and Hogan 24 (1961) *MLR* 331, 344.

[535] *Cook v. Lewis* [1951] SCR 830 (cf. Hogan loc. cit.) and *Summers v. Tice* (1948) 119 P.2d 1.

[536] Extensive analysis is found in Walker, *Delict*, 2nd edn., pp. 207–212.

[537] *Baker v. Market Harborough Industrial Co-Operative Society Ltd.* [1958] 1 WLR 1472, 1475 (Somervell LJ): 'It is, of course, possible that a plaintiff injured by negligence may fail because he is unable to establish whether the negligence was A's or B's. If his difficulties are due to any failure of A or B or both to call available evidence, adverse inferences may be drawn . . . If the natural inference was that the accident was due to negligence on the part of one or other of the drivers but not to both I would have thought that the plaintiff would fail.' A contrary *obiter dictum* was provided by Denning LJ in *Roe v. Minister of Health* [1954] 2 QB 66, 82: 'If an injured person shows that one or other or both of two persons injured him, but cannot say which of them it was, then he is not defeated altogether. He can call on each of them for an explanation.'

the balance of probabilities test can work against the plaintiff. The rule is that the plaintiff must prove that it was more than 50 per cent probable that the defendant caused the injury.[538] However, where stones are thrown from a crowd of demonstrators, or it is unclear whether the defendant manufactured the product which caused damage, the balance of probabilities test does not help the victim.

d. Liability of Children and Mentally Handicapped Adults

(1) Children and Young Persons

324 There are strong parallels in the six North European countries on the liability of children and young persons. Most conspicuously: nowhere does statute fix a minimum age below which a child cannot incur liability. In Scandinavia statutes provide that children who have not yet reached age fifteen (§ 63 of the Danish Act on minority and guardianship) or the age of majority (Chapter 2, 2 § Swed. SKL and Chapter 2, 2 § Finn. SKL) are subject to the usual rules on liability, but the judge may reduce the amount of damages awarded according to equitable principles. In principle then, children are subject to the same rules on liability as adults.[539] An exceptional form of liability based on equity, developed on the continent,[540] is alien to the legal systems of both Scandinavia and the British Isles. Equitable principles are applied, not to exclude liability for fault, but merely to reduce the extent of liability for that fault.[541]

325 The liability-reducing procedure is based in all Scandinavian countries on the age and development of the child, but in practice it now applies only to children below age four.[542] Above this age, lack of discernment

---

[538] See *McGhee* (fn. 533) p. 8 (Lord Simon), p. 10 (Lord Kilbrandon), and pp. 11–12 (Lord Salmon); also *Wilsher* v. *Essex AHA* (fn. 533) pp. 1089–1091 (Lord Bridge).

[539] v. Bar (-Nørgaard/Vagner), *DeliktsR in Europa, Dänemark*, pp. 12–13; Saxén, *SJT* 1977 pp. 148, 149; Hellner, *Skadeståndsrätt*, p. 220. [540] See nos. 75–84 above.

[541] The special rules on reducing liability apply only to liability for actual negligence; they are not applicable to strict liability: Hellner, *Skadeståndsrätt*, 4th edn., p. 219, and Swed. HD 3 Feb. 1978, *NJA* 1978: 6 p. 14. The general rules on reducing liability (e.g. Chapter 6, 2 § Swed. SKL) however, also apply to strict liability.

[542] There is no statutory basis for this particular age-limit but in Denmark it is a rule of thumb: Nørgaard/Vagner (fn. 539) p. 13 ØLD 14 Sep. 1951, *UfR* 1951 A p. 1096, held a 3-year-old child liable for causing an accident by running onto the street. The driver was held 50% contributorily negligent. VLD 24 Nov. 1988, *UfR* 1989 A p. 278 found 2 brothers aged 4 and 6 jointly liable for the damage caused after they had opened almost 2,000 cages at a pelt farm. In the Danish case HD 15 Feb. 1963, *UfR* 1963 A p. 303 a child aged 3 years and 8 months ran out onto the street. A driver managed to avoid hitting the child but turned the car over in doing so: no liability because of the child's age. The Swedish case HD 3 Feb. 1977, *NJA* 1977: 36 p. 186 concerned a child aged 3 years and 2 months who threw a metal object at a friend. The child was not liable. However, a different result was achieved in Swedish case HD 18 May 1948, *NJA* 1948: 74 II p. 342: a 5-year-old rode his bicycle the wrong way along a road, and was held responsible for two-thirds of the damage resulting from the consequent accident.

does not preclude liability. When judging negligence of defendants under age fifteen, the courts employ an age-related lower standard of care.[543] The position adopted by the Scandinavian countries is thus largely the same as that in the British Isles. Age-limits have never been successfully relied upon as a defence; also, at common law there is no fundamental difference between the liability of minors and that of adults. Relevant case reports are conspicuously sparse—most cases deal with contributory negligence rather than the liability of a child to a third party—but the main issue is apparently whether the child has satisfied the requirements of a tort. If the child is not old enough to have the intent required by law, he cannot be liable in respect of an intentional tort, but can be, and often is, liable in trespass.[544] In negligence cases involving children, the care demanded of them is that expected of the average child of the same age.[545] This is an effective form of legal protection. In practice it has the same effect as an express provision that very young children will not be held liable in negligence,[546] since the 'averagely careful' two- or three-year-old does not exist.[547] It can be different where the child has reached the age of six.[548] When a sixteen- or seventeen-year-old minor takes to the road there is no reason why he should not be measured according to the standard applicable to adults.[549]

The fundamentals of the Scandinavian and British approaches are **326** broadly similar; however, the contrast with the continental systems[550] should not be overlooked. A widespread degree of unity is achieved across Europe on one point: that the conduct of a child or young person should only be viewed as negligent if it was not of a standard to be expected from a person of that age. There is now also widespread

---

[543] Nørgaard/Vagner (fn. 539) p. 13; ØLD 18 Apr. 1963, *UfR* 1963 A p. 862; VLD 22 Nov. 1965, *UfR* 1966 A p. 179; Dan. HD 29 May 1967, *UfR* 1967 A p. 524; Hellner, *Skadeståndsrätt*, p. 222; Swed. HD 7 Oct. 1976, *NJA* 1976: 90 p. 458: a 9-year-old fired a cork from a bicycle pump; negligence was not established.

[544] *O'Brien* v. *McNamee* [1953] IR 86, 87–88 (HC). The position in Scotland is unclear, esp. concerning schoolchildren (girls under 12 and boys under 14: see Beaton, *Scots Law Terms*, pp. 82–83). Citing very old authorities, Walker, *Delict*, 2nd edn., p. 87 is of the view that they are capable of being found liable; Stewart, SLT 1989 pp. 404–405 contradicts this ('a pupil is not liable at all in delict').

[545] McMahon/Binchy, *Irish Law of Torts*, 2nd edn., pp. 714–715; Markesinis/Deakin, *Tort Law*, 3rd edn., pp. 148–149; *Gough* v. *Thorne* [1966] 3 All ER 398, 399 (*per* Lord Denning MR).

[546] *Gough* v. *Thorne* (fn. 545) and *Flemming* v. *Kerry County Council* (Sup. Ct.)

[547] Contributory negligence of a child was considered neither in *Ducharme* v. *Davies* (1984) 1 WWR 699 nor in *Oliver* v. *Birmingham and Midland Omnibus Co.* [1933] 1 KB 35.

[548] *Harvey* v. *Cairns* 1989 SLT 107. In *Barnes* v. *Flucker* 1985 SLT 142 it was expressly stated that 5-year-old boys can be held contributorily negligent for traffic accidents. Cf. Walker, *Delict*, 2nd edn., p. 88. For Ireland see *Brennan* v. *Savage Smyth* [1982] ILRM 223 (Sup. Ct.) (25% contributory negligence of a 7-year-old involved in a traffic accident).

[549] Markesinis/Deakin, *Tort Law*, 3rd edn., p. 150.   [550] See nos. 62–68 above.

consistency on another point: where a child in need of supervision is not the tortfeasor but the victim of blameworthy conduct, then a failure by that child's parents to supervise does not operate to the child's disadvantage.[551] Children cannot be held liable in place of those whose duty it is to take care of them. The old doctrine of identification was abandoned long ago. Parental failure to supervise cannot now be charged on children as contributory negligence.[552]

327   Such theoretical bases by no means guarantee that the law of obligations works in a similar way in the real world. From the published decisions, it occur that actions against children are very common in Scandinavia, whereas in common law legal systems they appear only very occasionally. This paucity of English cases has been explained by the fact that children usually have very little property and that actions against them therefore make very little economic sense.[553] However, Scandinavian children are no wealthier than their English or Irish counterparts. In Scandinavia, especially in Denmark and Sweden,[554] third-party liability insurance is far more extensive than in the British Isles, so the reason given may in fact be correct, even though in England the customary householder's insurance has for some time covered all household members. In the Scandinavian legal systems the most important issue today is whether the child or young person responsible for the damage was insured against liability to a third party. If at the time of the damage insurance existed against liability, there is in principle no reason why liability should be reduced.[555] Such reduction operates only in

---

[551] However, the position is not the same where a child suffers disadvantage from the death of a parent. Where the child's provider was negligent then the child's claim is reduced correspondingly: cf. sec. 5 Fatal Accidents Act 1976 (c. 30). The same applies where parents of a dead child bring an action and it is shown that the child was partly to blame for the accident: see *Durlin* v. *Strathclyde Regional Council* SLT 1993 p. 699. Sec. 1(7) of the Congenital Disabilities (Civil Liability) Act 1976 (c. 28) provides that where a child is injured whilst in the mother's womb and one or both of the parents is partly to blame, 'the damages are to be reduced to such extent as the court thinks just and equitable having regard to the extent of the parent's responsibility'.

[552] For Denmark see Mathiassen, *J* 1961 pp. 327, 330; from case-law see: VLD 3 Apr. 1916, *UfR* 1916 A p. 802; ØLD 28 Nov. 1922, *UfR* 1923 A p. 210 (reduction to 50%), cf. VLD 18 Nov. 1969, *UfR* 1970 A p. 223. For England: *Waite* v. *North Eastern Railway Co.* (1858) EB&E 719; 120 *ER* 679, cf. *Mills* v. *Armstrong*, *'The Bernina'* (1888) 13 App. Cas. 1; *Oliver* v. *Birmingham & Midland Omnibus Co.* [1933] 1 KB 35. In Ireland the issue has been resolved to the advantage of the child by secs. 34 and 35 Civil Liability Act 1961. For Scotland see *Taylor* v. *Dumbarton Tramways Co.* 1918 SC 96.

[553] McMahon/Binchy, *Irish Law of Torts*, 2nd edn., p. 715.

[554] Cf. Saxén, *SJT* 1977 pp. 148–153: it is pointed out at p. 149 that the liability of children is greater in Sweden than in Finland, despite an almost identical statutory background because 'quite simply, in Sweden insurance is more widespread than in Finland'.

[555] Saxén loc. cit; Hellner, *Skadeståndsrätt*, 4th edn., pp. 219–223. It is emphasized in Danish decisions which find children liable to pay damages that, as a matter of practice, the damages are to be met by insurance companies and not by the children themselves, HD 25 Oct. 1990, *UfR* 1990 A p. 926; HD 8 Feb. 1991, *UfR* 1991 A p. 274.

exceptional instances when there is no such insurance. In Denmark private insurance in respect of damage to property applies principally to damage caused by third parties.[556] This protects minors provided that they have acted neither intentionally nor with gross negligence.[557] Where the wrongful conduct was intentional, or even a crime, then of course there is neither insurance cover against nor reduction of liability to third party. Young people must answer personally for the consequences of intentional tortious conduct.[558]

(2) Handicapped Adults

The rules on the liability of mentally handicapped adults and those on **328** the liability of children are essentially alike.[559] A mental illness making it impossible for the sufferer to recognize the wrongfulness of his act provides relief at law only if the particular tort requires that the tortfeasor recognizes what he is doing.[560] As for trespass and negligence, insanity neither spares a person from responsibility, nor justifies a lowering of the standard of care, as one is concerned with adults.[561] The Scandinavian laws are similar in effect. In principle no distinction is drawn between mentally healthy and mentally handicapped adults. The latter are protected by proscriptive rules very similar to those protecting minors.[562]

2. Liability for Others

Besides the liability of children and mentally handicapped adults, there **329** are further provisions concerning liability for others and liability arising

---

[556] See no. 238 above.

[557] HD 25 Oct. 1990 (fn. 555): 2 boys aged 9 and 10 dug a 'cave' in a school cupboard and lit a fire so that they could see. The Supreme Court allowed the action of the school's insurers against the children (themselves insured). Even children this young are capable of gross negligence under § 19 II no. 1 EAL.

[558] Cf. Swed. HD 23 Mar. 1976, *NJA* 1976: 23 p. 121; and Swed. HD 15 Dec. 1980, *NJA* 1980: 127 p. 670.

[559] A comparative analysis is provided by Stone, *FS Rabel*, vol. i, pp. 403–419.

[560] *Emmens* v. *Pottle* (1885) 16 QBD 354, 356 (*per* Lord Esher).

[561] See McMahon/Binchy, *Casebook*, 2nd edn., p. 627. In the tort of trespass the question was decided in *Morris* v. *Marsden* [1952] 1 All ER 925, whilst for negligence the issue remains open. Cf. *Kingston* v. *Kingston* 102 (1965) *ILTR* 65, 67 (Sup. Ct., *per* Walsh J). In *Kelly* v. *Board of Governors of St Laurence's Hospital* [1988] IR 402 (Sup. Ct.) a patient jumped from a window during an epileptic fit; his action against the hospital was upheld; no consideration was given to the possible contributory negligence of the patient. Conversely, Dan. HD 20 Jan. 1928, *UfR* 1928 A p. 269 denied the benefit of insurance against fire to a mental patient who, not knowing what he was doing, set fire to his own home.

[562] See § 64 of the Danish Statute on Minority and Guardianship; Chapter 2, 3 § Swed. SKL and Chapter 2, 3 § Finn. SKL. Swed. HD 24 Sep. 1979, *NJA* 1979: 103 p. 581: the liability of a mentally abnormal bank robber who did not understand what he was doing was not reduced.

from the realization of danger, which, in their content and construction, disclose the historical influence of Roman law. What was called quasi-delict[563] by Roman lawyers, and still forms part of the fixed rules of the European codes, is also found under other names in the Scandinavian and British Isles legal systems. Alternative methods of classification of legal material are an outward expression of differing evaluations of the content of that material.

a. Liability for those in Need of Supervision

330   An example of this phenomenon is found in the law governing liability for those in need of supervision, i.e. damage caused by children, pupils, and residents of institutions, hospitals, and homes. Only in continental legal systems is this described as liability 'for others'. Scandinavian and British laws concentrate solely on the negligence of those responsible for exercising supervision. Strict liability does not apply. Neither is the burden of proof shifted to the detriment of supervisors. There is no legal reason to bring together different categories of persons in need of supervision. It is also unnecessary to distinguish between one person in need of supervision who injures himself, and another who injures somebody else, because in both cases the liability of the supervisor is determined according to the principles of negligence.[564]

331   Parents are not liable for their children: parental liability is nothing other than a special form of liability in negligence.[565] Each parent[566]

---

[563] See no. 7 above.

[564] On the liability of parents who fail to prevent their children from damaging themselves, see von Eyben/Nørgaard/Vagner, *Erstatningsret*, 2nd edn., p. 32; and *Surtees* v. *Kingston-upon-Thames BC* [1992] 2 FLR 559. A case on liability of a psychiatric clinic for the attempted suicide of a female patient is *G's Curator Bonis* v. *Grampian Health Board* SLT 1995 p. 652 (Outer House); for liability of a hospital to an epileptic see *Kelly* v. *Board of Governors of St Laurence's Hospital* [1988] IR 402 (Sup. Ct.); for the liability of a grandfather who failed to look after his grandson, *Oliver* v. *Birmingham and Midland Omnibus Co.* [1933] 1 KB 35; for the liability of a leader of a group of 13-year-old scouts, Dan. HD 8 Feb. 1991, *UfR* 1991 A p. 274; and liability of a school and its teachers, *Dolan* v. *Keohane and Cunningham* (Sup. Ct.) 8 Feb. 1994, reproduced in Byrne & Bynchy, *Annual Review of Irish Law 1992* (1994) pp. 579–581 (children injured themselves in dangerous horseplay whilst waiting for the schoolbus; the school was not held liable) and *Barnes* v. *Hampshire County Council* [1969] 1 WLR 1563 (a 5-year-old let out of school five minutes early on the last day of term was hit by a car; liability upheld).

[565] Hellner, *Skadeståndsrätt*, 4th edn., p. 225; von Eyben/Nørgaard/Vagner, *Erstatnings-ret*, 2nd edn., p. 84; Saxén, *Skadeståndsrätt*, p. 91; *Donaldson* v. *McNiven* [1952] 2 All ER 691, 692 (*per* Lord Goddard LJ: 'Some people have thought that parents ought to be responsible for the torts of their children, but they are not'); Walker, *Delict*, 2nd edn., p. 86; and McMahon/Binchy, *Irish Law of Torts*, 2nd edn., p. 294.

[566] In a system of fault-based liability each parent is only liable for his/her own share of the failure to exercise proper supervision, and is not responsible for the shortcomings of the other parent (this is the correct view, expressed by Pagter Kristensen/Bryde Andersen, *J*

owes a duty of care appropriate to the circumstances of the particular case to prevent his or her children from causing damage to others,[567] but there is certainly no tendency to make these obligations as onerous as strict liability for parents. Indeed the opposite can often be observed;[568] furthermore, breach of the general duty to educate the child is not an independent basis of liability.[569] Parents must of course take action if they know that their children have become involved in dangerous activities,[570] and small children must not be given dangerous toys or weapons.[571] Particular duties arise if one parent takes a direct part in a child's activity.[572] Apart from this, the rules are rather generous. For children over the age of fifteen or so, the duty to supervise decreases greatly;[573] case-law indicates that flagrant negligence is then required of parents before they will be found liable in negligence.[574] As soon as a young person enters employment, the nature of claims arising from wrongful

1992 pp. 320–328). To leave the financially weaker housewife liable and not the husband would clearly be unfair. This problem can only be resolved fairly in a system of no-fault liability where the parents are jointly liable (no. 144 above). In the case-law the issue of whether the action should be directed against the mother or the father is seldom raised; most actions are directed against the father (McMahon/Binchy, *Irish Law of Torts*, 2nd edn., p. 297) even in cases where only the mother was present at the material time (e.g. VLD 8 Feb. 1963, *UfR* 1963 A p. 627). A father has also been held responsible for leaving the children without sufficient supervision when the mother was doing housework (ØLD 30 Dec. 1943, *UfR* 1944 A p. 392).

[567] It is of no relevance whatsoever whether specific duties of supervision are set down in statutory form. An example is Chapter 23, 6 § of the Swedish Criminal Code (*Brotts-balken*), according to which parents, teachers, and guardians are obliged to prevent those in their care from committing crimes. Chapter 6, 3 § of the Swedish Act on Parents (*Föräldrabalken*) imposes a statutory duty to provide supervision which protects only the children.

[568] From Denmark see HD 15 Feb. 1963, *UfR* 1963 A p. 303; ØLD 7 June 1973, *UfR* 1973 A p. 872; HD 4 Jan. 1945, *UfR* 1945 A p. 227; and VLD 22 Nov. 1965, *UfR* 1966 A p. 179. For Sweden see HD 7 Oct. 1976, *NJA* 1976: 90 p. 458. From England: *Prince* v. *Gregory* [1959] 1 All ER 133; *Gorley* v. *Codd* [1966] 3 All ER 891; and *Donaldson* v. *McNiven* [1952] 2 All ER 691.

[569] Hellner, *Skadeståndsrätt*, 4th edn., pp. 225–226.

[570] McMahon/Binchy, *Irish Law of Torts*, 2nd edn., p. 295.

[571] See the Swedish case HD 29 Oct. 1954, *NJA* 1954: 86 p. 450 and *Newton* v. *Edgerley* [1959] 3 All ER 337: a farmer allowed his 12-year-old son to possess an air rifle. *Donaldson* v. *McNiven* [fn. 568] was distinguished. In *Donaldson* the 13-year-old was said to be 'mature', whereas in *Newton* the 12-year-old was immature for his age. Moreover, the weapon in *Newton* was more dangerous than that in *Donaldson*).

[572] *Curley* v. *Mannion* [1965] IR 543 (Sup. Ct.); Swed. HD 18 Oct. 1945, *NJA* 1945: 123 p. 471.

[573] The age of 15 is only a rough guide. There is no fixed age at which liability starts or finishes. Even those who have attained majority may need supervision: 'It would appear that the age of majority has no magic in this context': McMahon/Binchy (fn. 570) p. 297.

[574] E.g. Swed. HD 14 Dec. 1970, *NJA* 1970: 89 p. 463 (a father noticed that his 3 sons between 14 and 18 were playing with a home-made gun. He did not immediately tell them to stop but merely murmured his displeasure. When the gun was fired it exploded injuring a 15-year-old onlooker; the father was held not liable; his prohibition proved sufficient).

acts at work obviously alters. The employer is strictly liable for every employee, including minors.[575]

332   Whether and to what extent, in addition to or in place of parents, duties of supervision are owed by other persons (grandparents, crèches, etc.) depends on the general rules of liability for negligence.[576] Where these other supervisors are dependent employees, then, according to the relevant rules on liability, either the employer will be liable as well as the employee supervisors, or the employer alone will be vicariously liable for the employee who breached the supervision duty. The negligence of an employee is a prerequisite for an employer's vicarious liability; where the employee conducted himself properly the employer can only be personally responsible in negligence, e.g., due to organizational breakdown.[577]

333   English case-law on the liability of teachers provides a rich source of material on liability for breach of duty to exercise supervision over children. In principle, the care demanded of teachers is the same as that expected of parents.[578] Here too the requirement is in reality rather low.[579] Striking the necessary balance between supervision and encouraging the independence of pupils is regarded as important.[580] Where a school event takes place outside the class-room, the general duty to supervise continues. According to the Irish Supreme Court this general duty does not extend to children waiting for a bus.[581] Adult pupils are in

---

[575] See e.g. VLD 10 July 1963, *UfR* 1963 A p. 912 (strict liability of the owner of a farm for the damage which a child caused in fetching goods for the wife of the farm-owner. The child was staying on the farm during his holidays). The limit of such liability is illustrated by Swed. HD 15 Oct. 1981, *NJA* 1981: 116 p. 929: a girl was riding a horse which bolted and damaged a car. The horse-owner was not held responsible because the girl was not acting on behalf of the owner; it was simply a pleasure ride.

[576] Dan. HD 4 Nov. 1975, *UfR* 1976 A p. 10; and 8 Feb. 1991, *NDS* 1992 p. 171 = *UfR* 1991 A p. 274; Swed. HD 9 Nov. 1984 *NJA* 1984: 143 p. 764. Other people can also be liable on account of their own negligence as a result of the tortious act of a child: *Ricketts* v. *Erith BC* [1943] 2 All ER 629.

[577] *Carmarthenshire County Council* v. *Lewis* [1955] AC 549: a 4-year-old ran out from the nursery school onto the street; trying to avoid hitting the child, a lorry driver was killed. The child's teacher, momentarily absent at the material time, was not held liable. However, the local authority was liable because it had been possible for such a young child to run out onto the street.

[578] E.g. *Ricketts* v. *Erith BC* (fn. 576); *Rawsthorne* v. *Ottley* [1937] 2 All ER 902; *Camkin* v. *Bishop* [1941] 2 All ER 713.

[579] E.g. *Crouch* v. *Essex County Council* 64 (1966) LGR 240 (a 15-year-old squirted sodium chloride into the face of a class-mate during a chemistry lesson at school. Neither the teacher nor the school authorities were held liable); *Butt* v. *Cambridge and Isle of Ely County Council* 119 (1969) *New LJ* 1118 (a schoolboy injured a class-mate's eye with a pair of scissors; the teacher, at the time attending to another pupil, was held not liable); *Camkin* v. *Bishop* (previous fn.): children indulged in horseplay during a school outing; one threw mud which hit another in the eye. The accompanying teacher was not liable.

[580] *Camkin* v. *Bishop* (fn. 578); *Dolan* v. *Keohane* (fn. 564).

[581] *Dolan* v. *Keohane* (fn 564).

principle no longer in need of supervision. According to a decision of the Finnish Supreme Court, liability only arises in specific circumstances, e.g. where a sports teacher fails to stop an unreasonable contest developing in front of him.[582] As regards liability for dangers arising out of buildings, in England and Scotland the owner of an empty building can be obliged to take considerable steps to prevent children from gaining access to the building and, from within it, endangering adjacent property.[583]

A special duty rests on those who exercise supervision of the occu- **334** pants of homes and institutions, whether or not the occupants are minors, and whether their tendency to wrongful behaviour results from their personal disposition, from mental defects, or because they are being punished for crimes. Long before the *arrêt Blieck* of the French Cour de Cassation,[584] strict liability for failure to supervise in such homes was considered in Denmark, following a case of two boys aged nine and eleven absconding from a school for difficult children and setting fire to a farm. The proposed introduction of judge-made strict liability for dangers of this sort has, however, been rejected.[585] Transporting inmates in a normal tourist bus from which they can easily escape is sufficient to give rise to liability.[586] Despite its general reluctance to affirm liability for omissions, the House of Lords finally upheld the negligence claim of yacht owners whose boats were damaged by Borstal boys on the run. The yacht owners' action was against the Home Office, which had ultimate responsibility for the Borstal.[587]

b. Liability of Legal Persons for the Wrongful Acts of their Officers, Liability for Employees and for Independent Contractors

(1) Legal Persons

Legal persons, like natural persons, are strictly liable for their employ- **335** ees,[588] but not for their executive bodies. Vicarious liability does not apply, because a tort committed by an executive body is viewed as the

---

[582] Finn. HD 10 Jan. 1994, *NDS* 1995 p. 38 (PE lessons were conducted in a business school; football was played in a hall which was too small for the purpose. A free kick was taken by an adult pupil and a 'wall' of defenders made only three metres away. Both the kicker and the teacher were held liable for the injury sustained by a girl in the 'wall'.
[583] *Smith (or Maloco)* v. *Littlewoods Organisation Ltd.* [1987] AC 241; 1987 SLT 425.
[584] See no. 115 above.   [585] Dan. HD 11 Jan. 1956, *UfR* 1956 A p. 215.
[586] ØLD 30 Apr. 1974, *UfR* 1974 A p. 830.
[587] *Dorset Yacht Co.* v. *Home Office* [1970] AC 1004. Cf. *Holgate* v. *Lancashire Mental Hospitals Board* [1937] 4 All ER 19.
[588] Cf. Walker, *Delict*, 2nd edn., p. 127 and McMahon/Binchy, *Irish Law of Torts*, 2nd edn., p. 708.

wrongful act of the legal person.[589] Thus it is always possible to bring an action against a legal person in any tort which requires fault;[590] there is no need to distinguish between acts and omissions.[591] As for the executive body, it is always a question of whether the relevant natural person embodied 'the directing mind and will of the corporation'.[592] A branch manager is not an executive body in this sense.[593] As for doctors it has never been a matter of whether they can be regarded as being in overall charge of a given hospital; there the issue has always been whether they are employees.[594] Unlike on the continent,[595] where tort law has developed its own term of 'executive body' which in many respects goes much further than the equivalent notion of company law, in the UK there has never been a definition of such a term which could be applied specifically to tort. Liability 'for' executive bodies is restricted to the 'central governing authority'; clearly it is irrelevant whether the company was acting *ultra vires*.[596]

336   Whether the potential tortfeasor is an executive body or a mere employee, in other words: whether the company itself is believed to have acted wrongfully or whether it is liable on account of the conduct of its employees, is in most cases not important because the principle of vicarious liability usually leads to the same result.[597] Leaving aside the issue of the criminal liability of a company, where the difference can be of the utmost importance,[598] two particular points in the context of private law need to be highlighted. First, the liability of an employer by reason of agency (or vicarious liability) presupposes a tort committed

---

[589] This is made very clear by the judgment in *Lennard's Carrying Co. v. Asiatic Petroleum Co.* [1915] AC 705, 713 ('A corporation is an abstraction. It has no mind of its own any more than it has a body of its own; its active and directing will must consequently be sought in the person of somebody who for some purposes might be called an agent, but who is really the directing mind and will of the corporation, the very ego and centre of the personality of the corporation' per Lord Haldane). Cf. *Beaton v. Glasgow Corp.* 1908 SC 1010, 1013 (*per* Dunedin LP) and *Campbell v. Paddington Corp.* [1911] KB 869 (nuisance committed by a corporation). That the 'board of directors' is not a mere agent of the company but an organic part of it stems from sec. 35A of the Companies Act 1985 (c. 6).   [590] See also *Lennard's Carrying Co.* (previous fn.)
[591] In *Carmarthenshire CC v. Lewis* (fn. 577) a legal person was liable following an omission amounting to wrongful conduct. The decision also shows that little distinction is made between legal persons in private law and in public law. On this see also Dan. HD 26 Jan. 1993, *UfR* 1993 A p. 311; and von Eyben/Nørgaard/Vagner, *Erstatningsret*, 2nd edn., p. 46.   [592] Fn. 589.
[593] *Tesco Supermarkets Ltd. v. Nattrass* [1972] AC 153; also Wells (1994) 57 *MLR* 817–823.
[594] See no. 340 below.   [595] See nos. 171–174 above.
[596] McMahon/Binchy (fn. 588) pp. 708–709.
[597] See nos. 337 ff. Because of these extensive rules the traditional distinction between employees and officers of a company is essentially no longer drawn in Denmark. E.g. HD 4 Nov. 1958, *UfR* 1959 A p. 1: the CEO of a limited company drove a company car into a garage and injured a mechanic. Liability was based on DL 3–19–2, according to the general rules on employer liability. Cf. no. 337 below.
[598] See Wells, *Corporations and Criminal Liability*, esp. pp. 100–101.

by the employee, whereas according to the executive body theory, liability depends solely upon whether the legal person has committed a tort. It is possible but by no means necessary that, in addition to the legal person, the executive head personally acted in a tortious manner.[599] In Sweden and Finland these two types of liability must be distinguished because the special rules which tend to restrict employer liability[600] are concerned with the liability of the executive body alone, and not with the liability of the legal person for its own wrongful act. Hellner pointed to 25 § of Sweden's Act on Insurance Contracts (*Lagen om försäkringsavtal*), and emphasized that the exclusion of a right of action under an insurance contract for those liable for others is not relevant to the relationship between a legal person and its executive body.[601]

(2) Liability for Employees, Agents, and Other Persons Under Some Form of Control

(a) Vicarious Liability

Genuine liability 'for others' depends in all six jurisdictions upon the **337** responsibility of employers to compensate for the wrongful acts of their employees. The common law talks of vicarious liability. This expression, although firmly entrenched, is inappropriate: true vicarious liability is liability by agency. The employer's liability to compensate does not replace, but supplements that of the employee: employers and employees are concurrent wrongdoers (sec. 11[2][a] Irish Civil Liability Act), and are therefore liable as joint tortfeasors. Effective protection of employees against third-party claims (which is properly vicarious liability) exists only in the three Scandinavian countries,[602] not in the British Isles.[603] In the latter, in the absence of a contrary agreement between the parties, the employer is not bound to insure against third-party damage by his employees or even to desist from commencing third-party proceedings against them. Tortious behaviour by an employee which injures a third party and gives rise to the liability of the employer is treated as a breach of the contract between employer and employee, rendering the latter

---

[599] Cf. *C. Evans & Son Ltd.* v. *Spriteband Ltd.* [1985] 2 All ER 415 (joint liability of the director and the company was upheld in respect of breach of copyright) and *Nordic Oil Services Ltd.* v. *Bermon* SLT 1993 p. 1164.

[600] See esp. Chapter 3, 6 § Swed. SKL; cf. Chapter 3, 6 § Finn. SKL.

[601] Hellner, *Skadeståndsrätt*, 4th edn., pp. 116–117.

[602] See § 23 II Dan. EAL; Chapter 4, 1 § Finn. SKL and Chapter 4, 1 § Swed. SKL. A comparison of the solutions offered by Sweden and Finland is given by Saxén, *SJT* 1977 pp. 148, 150–152.

[603] *Lister* v. *Romford Ice and Cold Storage Co. Ltd.* [1957] AC 555; Cf. Walker, *Delict*, 2nd edn., p. 573.

liable to the former.[604] Sec. 1 of the Employer's Liability (Compulsory Insurance) Act 1969[605] only obliges an employer to insure against his (mostly strict) liability for personal injuries and damage sustained by his employees.

338   So what does the expression vicarious liability mean? More important than the label is the effect: the liability of an employer in the UK, as in Scandinavia, is strict. An employer is liable regardless of any fault either in selecting his employees or in their supervision.[606] In the common law this principle,[607] already developed in the seventeenth century, has been strengthened by a chain of authority.[608] In Denmark it developed from a continuation of DL 3–19–2 (1683), originally intended to regulate the liability of public officials and contractual liability.[609] Finland and Sweden adopted it during the 1970s in their Acts on Damages.[610] For both jurisdictions, which until then had only recognized very restricted strict liability of employers in the non-contractual context, and certainly not that of 'simple employees',[611] this represented an important advance. Only in Denmark,[612] and not in Finland or Sweden,[613] did the common law doctrine of common employment[614] play a part. According to this doctrine, an employer is only vicariously liable where an employee injures a third party who is not a fellow employee. In Denmark, as in the UK, the rule which prevented an injured employee from relying as a 'third party' on

---

[604] Atiyah, *Vicarious Liability*, pp. 426–427, states that the decision in *Lister* is only of limited significance because the insurance companies who have to meet the payments in cases of vicarious liability committed themselves only to take recourse action against the negligent employee with the consent of the employer. Cf. Atiyah (-Cane), *Accidents*, 4th edn., p. 211.   [605] 1969 c. 57.

[606] If an employer is negligent in some other way, then he is liable according to the general rules of tort, regardless of whether his employee committed a tort. For this reason case ØLD 9 June 1942, *UfR* 1942 A p. 984 is less convincing. A diner in a restaurant asked for a cure for indigestion. The waiter offered him powder from a box labelled 'bicarbonate of soda'. The powder was actually a poison. The owner of the restaurant was held liable because she was responsible for the storage of the powder. It was, however, incorrect to base the decision on the *principal-ansvar* under DL 3–19–2. It could not be said that the *waiter* had acted negligently.

[607] McMahon/Binchy, *Irish Law of Torts*, 2nd edn., p. 748. Cf. citations in *Riddick* v. *Thames Board Mills* [1977] QB 881, 893 (Lord Denning MR).

[608] From the modern era see *Stavely Iron & Chemical Co. Ltd.* v. *Jones* [1956] AC 627 and *Imperial Chemical Industries* v. *Shatwell* [1965] AC 656, 685 (Lord Pearce).

[609] Von Eyben/Nørgaard/Vagner, *Erstatningsret*, 2nd edn., p. 127; Iversen, *KF* 1993 pp. 50–51.   [610] Chapter 3, 1 § Finn. SKL; Chapter 3, 1 § Swed. SKL.

[611] See Hellner, *Rev.int.dr.comp.* 19 (1967) pp. 779, 782–785 and id., *AmJCompL* 22 (1974) pp. 1, 2–3. Swedish law certainly recognized and still recognizes a number of circumstances which give rise to no-fault liability. These include 233 § *Sjölagen* (Sea Act, liability of the ship owner), Chapter 1, 4 § *Järntrafiklagen* (Railways Act; liability for independent contractors) and special rules on landlords and tenants which impose liability on the tenant to the landlord for the actions of the tenant's guests.

[612] Cf. Kruse, *Erstatningsretten*, 5th edn., p. 193.

[613] Hellner, *Rev.int.dr.comp.* 19 (1967) pp. 779, 784.

[614] This goes back to *Priestley* v. *Fowler* 3 M&W 1; 150 ER 1030 (1837) (*per* Lord Abinger).

the strict liability of his principal has long since been abolished.[615] Contributory negligence by an employee is attributed to the employer, and regarded as contributory negligence by the employer as well.[616]

(b) Employees, Agents, and Other Persons Under Some Form of Control

Which persons can be vicariously liable is decided in these juristictions **339** in essentially the same way as on the continent.[617] In both Scandinavia and Britain it depends less on the presence of a contract of employment in the strict sense, and much more on issues of control, and the state of dependence of the parties involved. The common law tends to throw a wider net around those persons for whom one is responsible regardless of individual fault[618] than is the case in Denmark, Finland, and Sweden.[619] Nevertheless, Denmark's case-law recognizes instances of liability for those working without remuneration,[620] and the Finnish and Swedish Acts on Damages contain rules in which certain persons are expressly placed on the same footing as employees for purposes of employer liability.[621]

---

[615] Sec. 1(1) Law Reform (Personal Injuries) Act 1948 (c. 41) for England; sec. 1 Law Reform (Personal Injuries) Act 1958 (No. 38) for Ireland. From Scotland's recent case-law see *McMillan* v. *Wimpey Offshore Engineers and Constructors Ltd.* SLT 1991 p. 515 (Outer House) and from Denmark Kruse, *Erstatningsretten*, 5th edn., p. 193 and HD 21 Feb. 1963, *UfR* 1963 A p. 329. This decision is far from clear. On one hand it says it holds 'in itself' to the doctrine of common employment, and yet in a case which satisfies the exact criteria thereof, the doctrine was not applied and no reason was given for this. The Supreme Court added that it need only adhere to the previous legal position if there was no possibility of there being some strict form of employer liability. Because this has been introduced by § 23 EAL it can be said that the doctrine of *common employment* has been abolished; cf. ØLD 6 Dec. 1993, *UfR* 1994 A p. 215 (fn. 620 below). According to a dictum of Lord Denning MR in *Riddick* v. *Thames Board Mills* [1977] QB 881, 893, the principle should still apply in libel cases, as the doctrine was abolished in personal injury matters only.

[616] For Ireland see sec. 34(1) Civil Liability Act 1961; for England Winfield/Jolowicz (-Rogers), *Tort*, 14th edn., p. 184; for Sweden Chapter 6, 1 § SKL; for Finland Chapter 6, 1 § SKL and for Denmark Kruse, *Erstatningsretten*, 5th edn., pp. 329–331.

[617] See nos. 191 ff. above.

[618] Exceptionally, statute intervenes. E.g. sec. 1(1) Employer's Liability (Defective Equipment) Act 1969 (c. 37), by which an employer who provides his employees with faulty equipment is liable for the negligence of the manufacturer as if it were his own. See *Knowles* v. *Liverpool City Council* [1994] 1 Lloyd's Rep. 11. The common law would deny a such claim: see *Keenan* v. *Bergin* [1971] IR 192, 199.

[619] A particularly important Irish case is *Moynihan* v. *Moynihan* [1975] IR 192 (Sup. Ct): strict liability of a mother in her capacity as head of the household for her adult daughter who made tea and, momentarily distracted by the telephone, allowed her 2-year-old niece to scald herself.

[620] E.g. ØLD 6 Dec. 1993, *UfR* 1994 A p. 215: a husband working without pay for his wife sexually molested one of his wife's employees. The wife's liability was denied, not on the basis that the husband was not one of her employees, but because the wrongful conduct was 'out of character' and hence unforeseeable.

[621] Under Chapter 6, 4 §, no. 3 Swed. SKL ('For the purposes of this Act a person is treated as an employee . . . (3) if he works for somebody for reward where the work performed equates to that associated with a relationship of employer–employee') and according to Chapter 3, 1 §, III of the Finn. SKL ('by somebody, who performs a particular task under conditions comparable to a relationship of employment, without being an independent contractor').

340   The key problem is how to distinguish dependent employees or servants from independent contractors. The general rule is that vicarious liability does not apply to the latter.[622] An independent contractor has a contract for services; an employee a contract of service. One of the essential distinguishing characteristics is the question of control.[623] Where the manner in which the service to be supplied is determined by the person carrying it out, the contract is deemed to be for services; where the recipient of the service determines how the work is to be done, the relationship is probably that of master and servant.[624] A group of musicians can be regarded as employees and render its employer vicariously liable for its breach of copyright.[625] The criterion of control enables the principle of *respondant superior* to be brought into play in relation to temporary activities,[626] and in some circumstances even to one-off events.[627]

The criterion of control is, however, not the only one on which vicarious liability depends. The control criterion does not apply to specialists, particularly doctors, because their employers lack the specialist knowledge to determine the manner in which their work is done. Employers of doctors are nonethless strictly liable for their work[628] and other factors have been developed to regulate this. Perhaps the most important is the notion of integration.[629] In a contract of service, the work performed represents an integral element of the employer's business, whereas a contract for services is concerned with accessory or marginal functions.[630] Moreover, it is occasionally asked, even when the criterion of

---

[622] *D & F Estates Ltd.* v. *Church Commissioners for England* [1989] AC 177, 208 (*per* Lord Bridge): 'It is trite law that the employer of an independent contractor is, in general, not liable for the negligence or other torts committed by the contractor in the course of the execution of the work.' See no. 351 below for the exceptions to this basic rule.

[623] *Collins* v. *Herts. County Council* [1947] KB 598; *Cassidy* v. *Minister of Health* [1951] 2 KB 343.

[624] *Honeywill and Stein Ltd.* v. *Larkin Brothers Ltd.* [1934] 1 KB 191, 196 (Slesser LJ).

[625] *Performing Rights Society Ltd.* v. *Mitchell and Booker (Palais de Danse) Ltd.* [1924] 1 KB 762; Markesinis/Deakin, *Tort Law*, 3rd edn., p. 499.

[626] ØLD 15 Feb. 1957, *UfR* 1958 A p. 628 is an example from Denmark: an architect engaged 3 workers to cut down some trees. Their payment was that they could keep the trees. The architect was held liable for the workers' negligence under the principle in DL 3–19–2.   [627] An Irish example is *Moynihan* v. *Moynihan* (fn. 619).

[628] Cf. for England the references provided by Markesinis/Deakin, *Tort Law*, 3rd edn., p. 500; for Sweden Hellner, *Skadeståndsrätt*, 4th edn., p. 115; and for the liability of hospital authorities for their doctors under DL 3–19–2 see Dan. HD 10 Sep. 1993, *UfR* 1993 A p. 908.

[629] *Stevenson Jordon & Harrison* v. *Macdonald & Evans* [1952] 1 *TLR* 101; *Argent* v. *Minister of Social Security and Another* [1968] 1 WLR 1749.

[630] Cf. from the Danish perspective von Eyben/Nørgaard/Vagner, *Erstatningsret*, 2nd edn., pp. 127–129; and HD 17 Dec. 1948, *UfR* 1949 A p. 112: a council delegated its responsibility for pest control to a rat-catcher who had developed a special extermination device; the council was not liable for the rat-catcher or his employees because he had not been integrated into the council's organization.

control is satisfied, whether any contractual terms point in the other direction. For example where, although the manner of doing the work lies outside the would-be employee's control, the worker himself bears some economic risk associated with the job.[631] In a complicated judgment it was accepted that lorry drivers who had been compelled by a finance company with which their employer was associated to buy their own vehicles under a system of payment by instalments no longer stood in a contract of service.[632] Finally, it is also significant whether the person engaged is able to determine his own working hours and the extent of his responsibilities.[633]

Although the criterion of control is only one of many, it is of supreme **341** importance where employees are 'on loan', i.e. where they work under the control of a party which does not pay them; then it must be determined whether the hirer is to be regarded for legal purposes as a temporary employer.

An elegant example is the recent Swedish decision HD 8 January 1992.[634] A quarrying business hired an experienced welder for two weeks from the firm Svetsmekano to carry out repairs to their quarrying plant. The welder acted generally under the instructions of the quarrying company but was himself responsible for the precise manner in which the work was performed. His negligence brought about a large fire. The Supreme Court decided that the key issue was whether the worker had been integrated into the quarrying company's business such that, viewed from outside, he appeared to be on a footing equivalent to that of the latter's employees. This could not be said to be the case due to the short duration of the contract, and also to the degree of autonomy enjoyed by the welder over the manner in which his work was to be performed. In this instance the liability of Svetsmekano as employer was based on a more important factor: the party who suffered the fire damage was Svetsmekano's contractual partner; Svetsmekano was obliged to provide the contractual partner with a reliable welder, it was Svetsmekano and not the quarrying company which should have controlled him.

The basic rule that the requirement for integration into the business of **342** the temporary employer should be applied strictly is expressed concisely by Lord Denning: 'Just as with employers who let out a man with a machine, so also with an employer who sends out a skilled man to do

---

[631] *Market Investigations Ltd.* v. *Minister of Social Security* [1969] 2 QB 173.

[632] *Ready Mixed Concrete (South East) Ltd.* v. *Minister of Pensions and National Insurance* [1968] 2 QB 497.

[633] *WHPT Housing Association Ltd.* v. *Secretary of State for Social Services* [1981] ICR 737; Markesinis/Deakin (fn. 628) p. 501.

[634] HD 8 Jan. 1992, *NDS* 1993 p. 17 = *NJA* 1992: 4 p. 21 = *VersRAI* 1994 p. 57.

work for another, the general rule is that he remains the servant of the general employer throughout.'[635] So, when an employee is lent out together with a machine, and the operation of the machine causes a loss of service, this is almost always attributable to the providing employer.[636] It is necessary to consider all the circumstances of the case: the duration of the hiring, the extent of the recipient firm's ability to direct how the work is done, whether the arrangement is gratuitous[637] or supported by consideration, the negligence exhibited by the employee, the demands of the work expected of him,[638] and whether the recipient firm is active in the same kind of operations as the firm providing the worker.[639] Contractual arrangements between the two employers[640] may also be relevant, as well as the issue of whether the employee, on account of any clothing requirements of the job, is recognizable as an employee of either firm.[641]

343   Vicarious liability is not restricted to employers' liability for the misconduct of employees. It also describes the relationship between principal and agent. The term 'agent' cannot simply be understood as 'representative', as in the Dutch Civil Code.[642] An agent (or mandatary,[643] where he acts without reward) is somebody who undertakes a particular task for and with the consent of the principal, or at least partly on the principal's behalf. An example of such a task is the concluding of a contract, and in that context the use of the term agency is correct. The partners in a firm in relation to each other are both principals and agents.[644] However, the task undertaken by an agent can be of a purely *de facto* nature, and therefore has absolutely nothing in common with representation as understood in contract law. Transporting a friend's vehicle to a place intended by both parties to be the meeting place at

---

[635] *Savory v. Holland & Hannen & Cubitts* [1964] 3 All ER 18, 20.

[636] *Mersey Docks & Harbour Board v. Coggins and Griffiths* [1947] AC 1; *Lynch v. Palgrave Murphy Ltd.* [1964] IR 150 (Sup. Ct.); Swed. HD 20 Dec. 1979, *NJA* 1979: 136 p. 773; Dan. HD 8 Apr. 1959, *UfR* 1959 A p. 444; and Dan. HD 31 Aug. 1961, *UfR* 1961 A p. 895. See also Iversen, *KF* 1993 pp. 50, 51.

[637] The Danish view is that where the worker is provided without reward, then in cases of doubt the recipient firm should be held responsible for any negligence of the worker: see HD 29 Mar. 1955, *UfR* 1955 A p. 472; and HD 22 Dec. 1959, *UfR* 1960 A p. 145.

[638] In the Danish case HD 9 Feb. 1971, *UfR* 1971 A p. 262 the recipient firm was regarded as the employer because the operation of the machine in question 'did not call for any special expertise', cf. Iversen (fn. 636). A similar result was achieved in *Lynch v. Palgrave* (fn. 636), pp. 150, 163.   [639] Cf. Dan. HD 12 May 1970, *UfR* 1970 A p. 483.

[640] In *Mersey Docks* (fn. 636) it was accepted that the firm providing the worker remained that person's employer despite an express provision that the worker was to be regarded at the critical time as the employee of the recipient firm.   [641] Cf. Iversen (fn. 636).

[642] See no. 200 above.

[643] This is a Scottish term: Walker, *Principles*, vol. ii, 4th edn., p. 540 and Beaton, *Scots Law Terms and Expressions*, p. 6.

[644] Walker loc. cit. provides extensive references from Scotland.

the start of a shared holiday suffices as such a task.[645] It is the authorization by a principal with an interest in the task undertaken which is important, not the nature of the task. Mere permission to use an article does not establish a principal–agent relationship. A husband who uses his wife's car to drive to work is no more her agent than the man who drives the now-drunken husband home again in the latter's wife's car.[646] On the other hand, someone who spontaneously helps a housewife to serve her guests, taking her instructions in her kitchen, can thereby become her agent; the housewife is then vicariously liable for him.[647] Similarly, the master of a hunt can be liable for hunt members hunting beyond the marked boundary of the hunt area.[648]

(c) Other Prerequisites of Vicarious Liability

The remaining prerequisites for vicarious liability are practically the **344** same as those found elsewhere in the European Union.[649] The employee must have committed a tort, which must be closely linked to the work which the employee had to perform.

Vicarious liability is strict, and it is therefore irrelevant whether the **345** employer acted negligently; it depends solely upon whether the worker 'has made a mistake or omission in the course of his employment'.[650] Where this is not the case, employer liability is excluded.[651] The employer can still be liable for some other reason: negligence in his choice of employee, negligence in some other regard, or liability for a risk over which his employee without fault lost control.

Scandinavian jurisprudence has a number of examples. In Swedish HD 20 December 1979[652] the driver of a mechanical excavator damaged a house because he did not allow a sufficient gap between the excavator

---

[645] *Ormrod* v. *Crossville Motor Services Ltd.* [1953] 1 WLR 1120 and *Smith* v. *Moss* [1940] 1 KB 424. [646] *Launchbury* v. *Morgans* [1973] AC 127.
[647] *Moynihan* v. *Moynihan* (fn. 619).
[648] *League Against Cruel Sports Ltd.* v. *Scott* [1986] QB 240.
[649] See nos. 202–205 above.
[650] As expressed in Chapter 3, 1 §, 1 s. Finn. SKL and Chapter 3, 1 § Swed. SKL.
[651] *Imperial Chemical Industries Ltd.* v. *Shatwell* [1965] AC 656, 686 (*per* Lord Pearce): 'Unless the servant is liable, the master is not liable for his acts; subject only to this: that the master cannot take advantage of an immunity from suit conferred on the servant.' Cf. *Stavely Iron & Chemical Co. Ltd.* v. *Jones* [1956] AC 627: the basis of the liability of the employer in tort is the wrongful conduct of the employee. Also Dan. HD 25 June 1985, *UfR* 1985 A p. 755: no liability of a hospital authority where it could not be proved that the doctor had been negligent. A particularly difficult case is Dan. HD 10 Sep. 1993, *UfR* 1993 A p. 908: on the advice of a specialist serum institute, hospital doctors stopped the treatment by penicillin of a heart disease patient. This decision was shown to have been wrong. By majority vote (3:2) the Supreme Court found the hospital authority (and not the serum institute) liable.
[652] HD 20 Dec. 1979, *NJA* 1979: 136 p. 773, with critical comment by Bengtsson, *SJT* 1981 pp. 519–520.

and the house. The court said (which was quite astonishing in the light of the objective standard used for negligence in Swedish law) that the driver had not personally been negligent, because he was inexperienced. There was therefore no question of the employer being held liable vicariously. Nevertheless he was held liable in that he had negligently allowed the work to be carried out by an inexperienced person. An example of the second type of negligence is case ØLD 9 June 1942,[653] in which a waiter gave a diner poisonous flakes from a box labeled 'bicarbonate of soda' and which had not been guarded with appropriate care by the restaurant's owner. Also illustrative is case VLD of 19 April 1994:[654] a young girl was injured when a horse, which the defendant's stable lad was collecting from its box, reacted angrily. Because the lad had in no way acted negligently there was no question of the employer being liable under DL 3–19–2. Nevertheless he was found liable under DL 6–10–2 for his failure to control the animal.[655]

346 Where a firm allows a large number of its lorries to travel continuously through a residential area it will be directly liable;[656] this is not vicarious liability. The totality of journeys undertaken by the lorries amounts to a nuisance. The tort is committed not by the individual drivers but by the firm itself. Neither is this an example of the *anonym culpa*, to adopt the term used in Sweden. *Anonym culpa* operates when it is uncertain which of several employees have acted negligently, where all are in the service of the same employer.[657] The requirement that the employee must have committed a tort usually leads to the employer also being freed from liability where the employee raises a successful defence, for example, the consent of the victim, the victim's acceptance of the risk or contributory negligence, or some other general rule of private law excluding liability.[658] This does not mean that the employer can only be liable where the employee can be successfully sued. There are independent bases for excluding the liability of the agent and not of the principal. Perhaps the best known examples are the excluding provisions in Scandinavian legal systems which protect employees against third-party claims.[659] A corresponding example from England, in as much as there were such rules in England,[660] would be the privileges

---

[653] See fn. 606 above.

[654] VLD 19 Apr. 1994, *UfR* 1994 A p. 573. Cf. *Knott* v. *London County Council* [1934] 1 KB 126: a dog owned by a school caretaker bit a cleaning lady. The caretaker personally, and not the school, was held liable because the dog served the caretaker's purposes and not those of the school. [655] See no. 355 below.

[656] Cf. the facts of *Gillingham BC* v. *Medway* (fn. 193 above).

[657] Hellner, *Skadeståndsrätt*, 4th edn., p. 120.

[658] *Imperial Chemical Industries* (fn. 651). [659] Cf. no. 337 above.

[660] Abolished by sec. 1 Law Reform (Husband & Wife) Act 1962 (c. 48).

enjoyed by spouses, which were said not to produce any third-party effects for the benefit of employers or principals.[661]

Much case-law is devoted to the issue of when an employee is acting **347** 'in the course of his employment'. The starting point is straightforward: the employer is not liable for tortious conduct which has nothing to do with the labour which he requires of the employee. Torts committed in the employee's free time are his own responsibility. The only exception is if the employee is at the disposal of his employer after the end of the working day. In Sweden a tram-driver on a tram outside his working hours prevented a drunk from boarding but failed to warn the driver against making a premature departure.[662] As for negligent acts during working hours, even where the employee is involved in a job other than that normally expected of him, tortious conduct will in cases of doubt be regarded as having occurred 'in the course of employment'. That the conduct which leads to damage is either unreasonable (juvenile thieves beaten by an employee negligently overstepping the bounds of necessity[663]) or grossly negligent (a burning match tossed away whilst a petrol tank was being filled[664]) is not the issue; the conduct in question (protecting the employer's property, supplying oil) clearly occurred in the course of the employment. Even an express prohibition by the employer against the particular conduct (the striking of matches whilst filling oil-tanks, smoking in the vicinity of saltpetre,[665] or accepting the help of children when delivering milk[666]) does not alter the fact that the conduct was linked with the work; indeed the prohibition is evidence that the particular risk was inherent in the work required of the employee. It therefore appears to be incorrect that a bus company should not be liable for damage caused by one of its conductors in trying to move another bus which had been incorrectly parked.[667] That he had been expressly forbidden from driving buses does not sever the link between his actions and his employment. The same principle would apply where a driver, who should only have driven his fellow employees to work,

---

[661] *Broom* v. *Morgan* [1953] 1 QB 597; *Smith* v. *Moss* [1940] 1 KB 424.

[662] HD 29 Apr. 1948, *NJA* 1948: 55 p. 262. Another elegant borderline example is Dan. HD 30 May 1958, *UfR* 1958 A p. 821: a boy working for a shopkeeper as a messenger caused an accident on his way home. At the time of the accident he was carrying goods which the shopkeeper had given him for his mother and was therefore active on the shopkeeper's behalf. For this reason the shopkeeper was held liable under DL 3–19–2; cf. Iversen, *KF* 1993 pp. 50, 51.

[663] *Poland* v. *Parr & Sons* [1927] 1 KB 236; cf. Markesinis/Deakin, *Tort Law*, 3rd edn., p. 508.

[664] *Century Insurance Co.* v. *Northern Ireland Road Transport Board* [1942] AC 509.

[665] SHD Copenhagen 5 Aug. 1965, *UfR* 1967 A p. 664.

[666] *Rose* v. *Plenty* [1976] 1 WLR 141.

[667] Cf *Iqbal* v. *London Transport Executive* [1973] 16 KIR 39.

gave someone else a lift.[668] It is precisely his job description which brings the driver into conflicts of this sort.

348   Even intentional and criminal acts can have a sufficiently close connection with employment. For example, a person required by his firm to retrieve from customers furniture which has not been paid for and, in so doing, injures a resisting customer, is acting not only during but also in the course of his employment.[669] In *Racz* v. *Home Office*[670] it was recently said that the tort of misfeasance in public office can render the state vicariously liable. The plaintiff was placed in a 'strip cell' and beaten by prison warders. Whether it is consistent with *Racz* that a bus company should not be held liable when one of its conductors attacked a passenger who laughed at the conductor's accent appears doubtful.[671] It is worth considering whether the employer was at fault in employing as a conductor somebody so quick-tempered: employees of public transport authorities are likely to be faced with such passengers. Since the abolition of the doctrine of common employment an employer can be liable for violence between his employees, for example where a foreman attacks a charge-hand for no apparent reason.[672] Deceit on the part of employees entrusted with financial matters,[673] and theft and embezzlement by those employed to look after the goods of others,[674] are all capable of occurring in the course of employment. Danish HD 15 October 1964[675] clearly illustrates the differences in this field between liability in contract and in tort.

A hotel guest gave his car keys to the concierge who was to drive his car to the hotel garage. The concierge, however, drove the car around the city, causing an accident damaging the guest's and a third party's car. The guest's insurance paid for the damage to both vehicles, the damage to the other car being paid because of the strict liability of the insured under the Danish Road Traffic Act. The insurance company's claim against the hotel was upheld in respect of damage to the guest's car, but excluded the damage to the third party's car. The hotel was not liable to the third party according to DL 3–19–2, because the concierge had not acted in the course of his employment. The hotel was, however, liable to the guest by virtue of their contractual relationship.

349   Although the reasoning is far from obvious, it is assumed that acts of

---

[668] A case decided differently is *Conway* v. *George Wimpey & Co. Ltd. (No. 2)* [1951] 2 KB 266.
[669] *Dyer* v. *Munday* [1895] 1 QB 742.
[670] [1994] 2 AC 45; cf. Simblet, (1994) 53 CLJ 430–433.
[671] *Keppel Bus Co. Ltd.* v. *Sa'ad bin Ahmad* [1974] 1 WLR 1082.
[672] *Macmillan* v. *Wimpey Offshore Construction PLC* SLT 1991 p. 515.
[673] *Lloyd* v. *Grace, Smith & Co.* [1912] AC 716.
[674] *Johnson & Johnson* v. *CP Security* [1986] ILRM 559 (HC); *Morris* v. *Martin* [1966] 1 QB 716.
[675] HD 15 Oct. 1964, *UfR* 1964 A p. 806.

revenge[676] in reaction to insults,[677] and 'emergency' measures[678] exceeding all notions of proportionality, entitle the employer to escape liability. Fault-based liability only arises if fault in selecting or supervising employees can be proved against the employer. Danish case-law has adopted similar measures in regard to sexual harassment in the workplace.[679]

(3) Liability for Independent Contractors

By contrast with his employees, the basic rule is that an employer is not **350** liable for independent contractors.[680] Contractors are 'independent' precisely because they are not under the control of the main contractor. As a rule, the latter is exempt from liability for any damage caused to third parties by independent contractors. The only exception is where the injured third party is a contractual partner of the main contractor: in that case the main contractor is liable in contract for the fault of those who carried out the work (in this instance the subcontractor and its employees).[681] Outside contract law there is in principle no strict liability for independent contractors. The hirer of independent contractors is not answerable for them, and can only incur personal liability, for example, if damage results from a risk for which he is strictly liable,[682] or if he fails to select a suitable contractor for the task, or to give sufficient instruction to a contractor otherwise capable of carrying out the task without causing damage.

The exceptions to the principle that employers are not vicariously **351** liable for independent contractors are found in statutory provisions and in non-delegable contractual duties which bind the main contractor. The

---

[676] *Warren v. Henly's Ltd.* [1948] 2 All ER 935.

[677] *Irving & Irving v. The Post Office* [1987] IRLR 289.

[678] *Poland v. Parr & Sons* [1927] 1 KB 236, 245 (Atkin LJ); Iversen, *KF* 1993 pp 50, 51.

[679] ØLD 6 Dec. 1993, *UfR* 1994 A p. 215: a wife who employed her husband was not liable for sexual harassment committed by him against another employee; the employer had no knowledge of her husband's behaviour and could not have taken any preventative measures.

[680] For England see *D & F Estates Ltd. v. Church Commissioners for England* [1989] AC 177 (see fn. 622); for Scotland *Parkhead Housing Association Ltd. v. Phoenix Preservations Ltd. SLT* 1990 p. 812 (Outer House); for Ireland *McGowan v. Masterson* [1953] IR 101, 106 (*per* Murnaghan J, Sup. Ct.); for Denmark von Eyben/Nørgaard/Vagner, *Erstatningsret*, 2nd edn., pp. 96–99; v. Bar (-Nørgaard/Vagner), *DeliktsR in Europa, Dänemark*, pp. 11–12; HD 10 Dec. 1973, *UfR* 1974 A p. 91; and ØLD 16 Oct. 1975, *UfR* 1976 A p. 229; and for Sweden Hellner, *Skadeståndsrätt*, 4th edn., p. 124; and HD 27 Jan. 1942, *NJA* 1947: 7 p. 23.

[681] Cf. Swed. HD 14 Apr. 1965, *NJA* 1965: 23 p. 124. To fulfil its contracts a transport company used another company whose employees injured the CEO of the transport company when unloading goods; the liability of the transport company was affirmed.

[682] McMahon/Binchy, *Irish Law of Torts*, 2nd edn., p. 761 (with reference to the strict liability of *Rylands v. Fletcher*). Liability for animals is another example. Where liability is strict it must be to prevent the person responsible for the animal from escaping liability by claiming that he had entrusted the animal to an independent contractor.

Finnish SKL primarily adopts the former approach. Chapter 3, 1 §, 2 s. provides that 'the party which commissions an independent contractor who, having regard to the continuing type of relationship (that of receiving orders), to the character of the work, and to the remaining aspects of the relationship, is placed on the same footing as an employee . . . is an employer'.[683] This provision is wider than that contained in Chapter 6, 4 §, 3 no. of the Swedish SKL, according to which 'whoever carries out works on the account of another which are similar to those found in an employee context' is placed on the same footing as an employee. This is an elegant way of avoiding the unfortunate results of *Ready Mixed Concrete (South East) Ltd.* v. *Minister of Pensions and National Insurance*.[684] The Scottish equivalent to this Finnish rule is found in *Marshall* v. *Williams Sharp & Sons*, a 1991 decision of the Inner House.[685]

A quarry manager climbed into the burner of a large drying plant to examine its ignition. Dean, an independent electrician, was permanently entrusted with supervising the mine's electrical apparatus, this being his speciality. He was the only electrician working at the mine, was on permanent stand-by, and was paid on an hourly basis. When the manager was in the burner Dean, instead of pressing only the ignition button, also pressed the fuel-injector button. The manager died. In the action brought by the deceased's widow against the employer the issue was whether the employer was vicariously liable for Dean. This was affirmed: Dean had become a part 'of the defenders' workforce' and had been 'under their supervision and control'.[686] According to Lord Dunpark he was independent but not totally so,[687] whilst Lord Justice-Clerk Ross described Dean as 'an independent contractor or a contractor with a degree of independence', for whom in the circumstances the employer should be vicariously liable.[688]

352   The concept of the non-delegable duty allows the main contractor to be liable for independent contractors, as an exception to the general principle. A person under a duty which he cannot avoid by delegation is personally liable for any breach. He is entitled to transfer to others the carrying out of the obligation, but the risk remains his. Where the person to whom the task is delegated acts negligently, it is no defence for the main contractor to prove that he was not personally at fault: the duty imposed upon him has been breached, and that suffices. That the main

---

[683] A comparison of Finnish and Swedish law on this point is provided by Saxén, *SJT*, pp. 148–149.   [684] See fn. 632 above.

[685] *SLT* 1991 p. 114; cf. Stewart, *Jur. Rev.* 1991 pp. 253–256.

[686] *Marshall* v. *Williams Sharp*, p. 125 F (Lord Dunpark).

[687] Ibid. p. 125 L ('a contractor of his own labour, [not] . . . an independent contractor').

[688] Ibid. p. 121 J.

contractor is able to pursue a remedy against the subcontractor[689] does not erase the former's personal liability. The practical result is the same as vicarious liability.

Notwithstanding various national peculiarities in result, reasoning,[690] **353** and legal construction, the most important conditions in which a main contractor may be liable for an independent contractor are the following:

- liability to ensure a safe place of work;[691]
- liability for the possession of hazardous, and especially explosive and highly combustible, materials and substances;[692]
- liability for making works on public streets safe;[693]
- liability for protecting shafts and manholes in places to which the public has access;[694]
- liability for damage to the foundations of buildings on adjacent land;[695]
- liability for extra-hazardous activities;[696] and
- liability for works occasioned by the employer which risk amounting to a private nuisance.[697]

---

[689] Cf. for Denmark ØLD 28 Nov. 1940, *UfR* 1941 A p. 204.

[690] Note the Danish provision by which main contractors can be held liable where, had they acted themselves, they would have been subject to a particularly extensive liability, approaching strict liability; see von Eyben/Nørgaard/Vagner (fn. 680).

[691] *Wilsons & Clyde Coal Co. Ltd. v. English* [1938] AC 57; *Wilson v. Tyneside Window Cleaning* [1958] 2 QB 110; *Paine v. Colne Valley Electricity Co.* [1938] 4 All ER 803, 807 (Goddard LJ); *Connolly v. Dundalk Urban District Council* [1990] 2 IR 1 (HC). *Marshall v. Williams Sharp & Sons* (fn. 685) indicates some tension with this group of cases.

[692] Cf. Swed. HD 7 Mar. 1941, *NJA* 1941: 26 p. 89; VLD 10 Mar. 1981, *UfR* 1981 A p. 564; *Salsbury v. Woodland* [1969] 3 All ER 863, 869 (*per* Widgery LJ, general statement); *Honeywill & Stein Ltd. v. Larkin Bros. Ltd.* [1934] 1 KB 191.

[693] *Penny v. Wimbledon Urban District Council* [1899] 2 QB 212; *Clements v. Tyrone County Council* [1905] 1 IR 415; *Weir v. Dun Laoghaire Corporation* [1984] ILRM 113 (Sup. Ct.); *Holliday v. National Telephone* Co. [1899] 2 QB 392; VLD 18 July 1928, *UfR* 1928 A p. 953; ØLD 19 Nov. 1932, *UfR* 1933 A p. 176; ØLD 28 May 1959, *UfR* 1959 A p. 753.

[694] *Pickard v. Smith* (1861) 10 CB (NS) 470. Danish case-law is particularly rich in references: ØLD 28 Nov. 1940, *UfR* 1941 A p. 204; VLD 10 Oct. 1942, *UfR* 1943 A p. 137; ØLD 30 Mar. 1944, *UfR* 1944 A p. 667; ØLD 30 Dec. 1948, *UfR* 1949 A p. 488; VLD 24 June 1952, *UfR* 1952 A p. 920; VLD 21 Sep. 1954, *UfR* 1954 A p. 1017; and HD 4 Feb. 1958, *UfR* 1958 A p. 300.

[695] Jones, *Torts*, 4th edn., p. 286, with reference to *Bower v. Peate* (1876) 1 QBD 321. The corresponding provision in Sweden stems directly from Chapter 3, 3 § *Grannelag* (Statute on Legal Relationships between Neighbours) in conjunction with 5 § *Miljöskadelag* (Act on Environmental Damage).

[696] *Balfour v. Barty-King* [1957] 1 QB 496; *Hobbs (Farms) Ltd. v. Baxenden Chemical Co. Ltd.* [1992] 1 Lloyd's Rep. 54, 69; *Honeywill & Stein v. Larkin* (fn. 692); *Salsbury v. Woodland* (fn. 692). Perhaps going too far is the decision in VLD 21 Feb. 1991, *UfR* 1991 A p. 347: a gas company was held liable for damage caused to a private road by heavy lorries belonging to a transport company which the gas company had engaged.

[697] *Matanca v. National Provincial Bank and Elevenist Syndicate* [1936] 2 All ER 633. For Sweden see 6 § 2 s. of the *Miljöskadelag* (Act on Environmental Damage), by which the commercial and sovereign users of land who 'carry out or allow to be carried out an activity which causes damage' are liable.

3. LIABILITY FOR ANIMALS AND DANGEROUS PREMISES

a. Liability for Animals

(1) An Overview of the Statutory Sources

354 As in the continental legal systems, Scandinavia and the British Isles also add[698] statutory elements to their customary fault liability,[699] based upon *culpa* (Scandinavia) or trespass,[700] negligence,[701] and nuisance[702] (Britain), which subject the keeper of an animal to strict liability.[703] Unlike most continental systems, the statutes of the North European countries do not recognize strict liability for all animals. The animals which can give rise to strict liability are narrowly prescribed. If an animal which causes damage does not fall within the ambit of the statute,[704] or if responsibility falls on someone other than the person specified in the statute,[705] or if damage arises from a risk other than that envisaged by the statute,[706] then the common law rules determine who is at fault. The somewhat ethereal discussion by many continental authors about whether liability for the transmission of viruses or bacteria falls under this heading[707] is not entered into by their North European colleagues: the abstract question of what constitutes an animal is not debated in Northern Europe. On the other hand, in Scotland there are special provisions governing liability for the transfer of germs by animals.[708]

---

[698] Common law rules remain applicable alongside the statutes, cf. McMahon/Binchy, *Irish Law of Torts*, 2nd edn., p. 505. See also *Henderson* v. *John Stuart (Farms)* 1963 SC 245, 248.

[699] At common law the rule in *Rylands* v. *Fletcher* is also applicable, esp. where animals are kept on land, amounting to non-natural use of the land, and some animals escape, cf. *Manton* v. *Brocklebank* [1923] 2 KB 212; and *Knott* v. *London County Council* [1934] 1 KB 126, 139: application of the rule in *Rylands* v. *Fletcher* to dangerous dogs.

[700] *Manton* v. *Brocklebank* (previous fn.); *League Against Cruel Sports* v. *Scott* [1985] 2 All ER 489; *Cronin* v. *Connor* [1913] 2 IR 119.

[701] *Gomberg* v. *Smith* [1962] 1 All ER 725; *Pitcher* v. *Martin* [1937] 3 All ER 918; *Draper* v. *Hodder* [1972] 2 QB 556.

[702] *Pitcher* v. *Martin* (previous fn.); *Gilleck* v. *O'Reilly* [1984] ILRM 402 (HC); *O'Gorman* v. *O'Gorman* [1903] 2 IR 573.

[703] See fn. 20 above; for Denmark and Sweden see nos. 355 and 356 below.

[704] E.g. domestic cats: cat scratches are not covered by any of the North European statutes on strict liability.

[705] E.g. an inspector of animals, who is neither the keeper nor the owner of the animal, is only liable under the general rules on liability; cf. no. 358 below.

[706] E.g. the Danish rules on the sanctuary of fields and footpaths (Act no. 818 of 11 Dec. 1987), whose provisions apply only when other animals are injured or when agriculture is impaired. For a comparison with the common law these provisions should be set against sec. 4 Animals Act 1971.   [707] See no. 209 above.

[708] Sec. 1(4) Animals (Scotland) Act 1987: no liability under the Act for the spread of diseases 'transmitted by means which are unlikely to cause severe injury other than the disease'. Where a dog licks but does not bite there is no liability under the Act. See also *Tremain* v. *Pike* [1969] 3 WLR 1556: an employee contracted Weill's disease after contact with rat's urine; employer was held not liable.

The oldest surviving statutory provisions on this issue are contained **355** in the *Danske Lov* of 15 April 1683. DL 6–10–2 concerns free-ranging cattle[709] and dogs which injure faultless victims. This provision expressly allows damages for pain and suffering. Of considerable interest is the legal reasoning, expressed in DL 6–10–4,[710] that a person who feeds and cares for wolves and bears should likewise be liable. This particular provision was extended in this century to cover beasts maintained in circus confinement.[711] Also worthy of mention is DL 6–10–5, reminiscent of the technique used in noxal liability,[712] which as early as 1683 introduced a ceiling to liability according to which: 'where the animals or cattle of one man bite, butt, or kick to death the animals or cattle of another, then the person who owns the offending animal or cattle must pay to the other half the value of the dead animal or cattle, provided the animal which was killed was as valuable as or more valuable than the offending animal; but where the animal which was killed was of lesser value than the animal which killed it, then its full value must be paid.'

Modern Danish jurisprudence on liability for animals no longer recog- **356** nizes such 'liability maxima'. Nevertheless, it distinguishes between types of animal and types of damage. So the Act on the Sanctuary of Fields and Footpaths is, on one hand, applicable only to domesticated animals, and on the other, only to agricultural damage and injuries to other animals.[713] Only the Dogs Act, the most recent version of which dates back to 1969,[714] recognizes liability for personal injury and damage to property of whatever kind. Liability is strict (8 § I). This is supplemented by a duty to insure against third-party risk, which in turn has been made into an *action directe* (8 § II). Insurance protection is even granted where a dog (and consequently also its keeper) cannot be identified.[715] By

---

[709] Horses which have bolted also belong in this category: VLD 19 Apr. 1994 (fn. 654).

[710] DL 6–10–3 (no longer valid law) provided that: 'where a horse or some other livestock animal, which may legally be held, kills a human, then the owner must pay three lots of silver and make oath that he did not know that the animal had this propensity. Should this happen a second time whilst he has such an animal in his charge then he has to pay off the heirs according to the extent of his own wealth.'

[711] ØLD 25 June 1936, *UfR* 1937 A p. 158: whilst practising on the circus stage a female singer was so shocked at seeing a free-roaming lion that she became unconscious, fell, and injured her spine. The lion trainer was held liable as owner under DL 6–10–4. The *répétiteur* controlling the rehearsal was held jointly liable, as was his employer, the circus, under DL 3–19–2.   [712] Cf. no. 7 above.

[713] See fn. 706 above.

[714] *Lovbekendtgørelse* No. 380 of 26 June 1969 *om hunde* (*Hundelov*). This was the republication of an Act from 1937, which followed Acts on Dogs dated 1889 and 1925 (von Eyben/Nørgaard/Vagner, *Erstatningsret*, 2nd edn., p. 143). The 1969 Act was twice revised in 1992: Karnov (-Hansen), vol. ii, 13th edn., p. 1507. For an overview of its rules on liability see Werlauff, *UfR* 1978 B pp. 266–270.

[715] The publication (*bekendtgørelse*) no. 485 of 25 Sep. 1984 *om ansvarsforsikring af hunde* (Text by Karnov [-Hansen, previous fn.] p. 1511) secures this.

contrast with DL 6–10–2, contributory negligence by the victim reduces his claim, but the claim is only lost entirely where the contributory negligence is so overwhelming that the liability of the animal's keeper is completely eclipsed.[716] On this point 6 § of the Swedish Act on Dogs and Cats[717] accords with section 21 of Ireland's Control of Dogs Act 1986: both impose strict liability for damage caused by dogs. Sweden has two further provisions which largely correspond with the provisions on liability in DL 6–10–4 and DL 6–10–5 of the Danish Act on the Sanctuary of Fields and Footpaths.[718]

The prime purpose of the Irish Control of Dogs Act 1986 was to remove the anomaly,[719] still present in England,[720] that greater protection against dogs is given to cattle than to humans: when cattle are bitten or killed by a dog, the dog's keeper cannot defend a claim on the ground that the dog did not belong to a dangerous breed and had not previously attacked cattle. Had the dog bitten a human, this defence would have remained under sec. 2(2)(b) and (c) Animals Act 1971.[721]

357   By contrast with Ireland, where liability for damage caused by animals is still governed by the common law,[722] the relevant principles in England and Scotland have been put into statute,[723] albeit in a somewhat altered form. With only a few differences of detail, both jurisdictions specify three categories of animal for which the keeper, under both Animals Acts and by virtue of his supervisory duty, is personally responsible regardless of fault. The categories are as follows.

(1) Animals classified as dangerous because they are not normally found in the British Isles in a domesticated state and which when fully grown, if not properly controlled, pose a substantial risk of causing damage: secs. 2(1) and 6(2) Animals Act 1971 and sec. 1(1)(b) and 1(3)(a) Animals (Scotland) Act 1987.[724]

---

[716] For further detail see VLD 12 Jan. 1979, *UfR* 1979 A p. 421.

[717] *Lag om tillsyn över hundar och katter*, original version in SFS 1943: 459, republication in SFS 1987: 260. Although in principle the Act also applies to cats the rule on liability in 6 § is expressly restricted to dogs.

[718] Chapter 22, 7 § *Byggningabalken* (Building Act) (liability is strict, but limited in extent, for the killing of livestock by animals); Chapter 22, 8 § (liability of the keeper of animals of prey); and 47, 48 §§ *Ägofredslagen* (liability for damage to a harvest by domestic animals).

[719] Sec. 3 Animals Act is based on sec. 1 of the original Dogs Act 1909 (c. 32) which at that time also applied to Ireland.   [720] See also no. 357.

[721] For further detail see McMahon/Binchy, *Irish Law of Torts*, 2nd edn., p. 513.

[722] Cf. fn. 729 below. The precursor to the Control of Dogs Act 1986, the Animals Act 1985, had in sec. 2(1) abolished 'so much of the rules of the common law relating to liability for negligence as excludes or restricts the duty which a person might owe to others to take such care as is reasonable to see that damage is not caused by an animal straying on to a public road.'   [723] See sec. 1(1) Animals Act 1971 and sec. 1(8)(a) Animals (Scotland) Act.

[724] These rules reflect the old common law rule on strict liability for animals *ferae naturae*. This rule is still applicable in Ireland. Animals such as these are contrasted with the animals *mansuetae naturae*: see North, *Modern Law of Animals*, pp. 34–35.

Neither the individual character[725] of a creature nor the fact that animals of a particular kind are kept as pets in other countries is relevant. As for the risk of damage, the English Act gives equal weight to two virtually indistinguishable factors: a high probability that damage will be caused, and a high probability that if any damage does occur (and this need not be probable) it will be extensive. Unlike in England, sec. 1(3)(a) of the Scottish Act expressly puts dogs on the same footing as wild animals, so that under Scots law liability for damage caused by dogs is strict.

(2) Animals which belong to a non-dangerous group, but which can be dangerous as individuals. The principal requirement is that either the damage must be of a type which an unrestrained animal of this species was likely to cause, or that any damage actually caused was likely to be severe. The foregoing is subject to the proviso that the likelihood of damage or of its severity must be attributable to the characteristics of an individual animal, (characteristics) which in this species are mostly exhibited at certain times or under certain conditions,[726] and that these individual characteristics must have been known to the keeper or the person to whom the knowledge of the keeper is imputed: sec. 2(2) Animals Act 1971.

Sec. 2(2) Animals Act, with its imprecise language and numerous unnecessary alternatives, is one of the worst examples of English legislative drafting.[727] The object was to codify the old common law *scienter* principle, according to which an owner (today the keeper) was only strictly liable for a tame animal if he knew that it had the tendency[728] to dangerous behaviour of the type actually exhibited;[729] that he ought to have known this to be the case was not sufficient.[730] Comments on sec. 2(2) are found in *Wallace* v. *Newton*[731] and *Curtis* v. *Belts*.[732] In *Wallace* the plaintiff was injured by a horse which escaped control while being loaded into a horsebox. The keeper was liable because he knew that the horse was unreliable whenever it had to be loaded into a box. In *Curtis* a bull mastiff bit a child which had known and loved the dog for a long

---

[725] *Behrens* v. *Bertram Mills Circus Ltd.* [1957] 2 QB 1.

[726] An Alsatian is usually not dangerous, except when employed as a guard dog. Cf. *Cummings* v. *Grainger* [1977] QB 397.

[727] The wording of the Act has come in for heavy criticism from English courts, e.g. the comment of Ormrod LJ in *Cummings* v. *Grainger* (previous fn. p. 407) ('remarkably opaque language') or the numerous critical comments in *Curtis* v. *Belts* [1990] 1 WLR 459.

[728] See Williams, *Liability for Animals*, p. 273. The *scienter* action has been abolished in England and Scotland but not in Ireland (McMahon/Binchy, *Irish Law of Torts*, 2nd edn., p. 513) where it also applies to dogs; see *Kavanagh* v. *Centreline Ltd.* [1987] ILRM 306 (HC).

[730] Markesinis/Deakin, *Tort Law*, 3rd edn., p. 482.

[729] See *Glanville* v. *Sutton* [1928] 1 QB 571: a man was bitten by a horse. It was of no help to the victim that the defendant was aware of the horse's propensity to bite other horses.

[731] [1982] 2 All ER 106.   [732] See fn. 727.

time. The dog had just been put into a vehicle, the backseat of which the dog regarded as its territory and wanted to defend. The keeper was neither negligent nor liable under sec. 2(1) Animals Act because fighting dogs are still dogs and in consequence do not belong to the dangerous category of sec. 6(2). However, the owner was liable under sec. 2(2) because he knew that dogs of that sort could be aggressive when they regarded their territory as threatened. Whilst the result is acceptable, the route is absurdly complicated: it is time that the law was reconsidered.

(3) Deer, horses, donkeys, mules, pigs, goats, poultry,[733] and animals suitable for being hunted which are maintained in enclosures:[734] secs. 4 and 11 Animals Act 1971; sec. 3(b) Animals (Scotland) Act. Where such animals cause agricultural damage the keeper is strictly liable.

(2) The Persons Liable and the Scope of Strict Liability for Animals

358   In the older provisions of continental legal systems the person held strictly liable for animals is the owner; more recent legislation has placed this liability upon the keeper.[735] In the North European countries a similar change has taken place since the Second World War. In 6 § of the Swedish Act on Dogs and Cats, the 1987 wording still referred to the owner. By contrast, the Danish Act of the same year on the Sanctuary of Fields and Footpaths[736] referred to the *besidder*, defined in § 2 II: 'According to this Act a *besidder* is the person who keeps the animal, regardless of whether the right of ownership over the animal rests in another person.' Almost twenty years earlier the Dogs Act of 26 June 1969[737] had referred to the *besidderen af en hund*. The *Danske Lov* of 1683 naturally still refers to the owner; in Danish legal literature, however, this term is defined to mean keeper.[738] Swedish commentators also argued that not only the owner but also the beneficiary of the dog's use should be strictly liable.[739] Parliament responded in 1992 by adding a provision to 6 § of the Dogs Act imposing liability also on the keeper of an animal.

359   Section 21 of the Irish Control of Dogs Act 1986 has retained the term owner; not only the Dogs Act 1906 but also the Irish Animals Act 1985 made the owner liable. By contrast, both the English and Scottish Animals Acts impose liability on the keeper: sec. 2(1) and (2) Animals Act 1971 and sec. 1(1)(a) Animals (Scotland) Act 1987. The difference from Irish law is not as great as it appears: according to the relevant defini-

---

[733] Only the English Act mentions and defines poultry, on which the Animals (Scotland) Act 1987 is silent.

[734] Here too there are small differences between the Acts, e.g. the Scottish Act mentions only deer, whilst the English also refers to pheasants.   [735] See nos. 213–217 above.

[736] See fn. 706 above.   [737] See fn. 714 above.

[738] Kruse, in Tamm (ed.), *Danske og Norske Lov i 300 år*, pp. 677, 686.

[739] Hellner, *Skadeståndsrätt*, 4th edn., p. 150; cf. Forsberg, *Om ersättning för skada av hund* (1959) p. 21.

tion, the owner of an animal is always its keeper; only a person in actual possession of the animal attains the same status as the keeper.[740] The same animal can have several keepers simultaneously;[741] they are then jointly liable.[742] When an animal belongs to a child under the age of sixteen, the head of the household, and not the child, is the keeper.[743] A similar statutory provision exists in Dutch law:[744] the person who looks after his employer's animals is not the keeper, nor is the person who temporarily takes charge of animals belonging to another to protect them or others from harm.

The most interesting provisions on the scope of liability for damage **360** caused by animals are in the Animals (Scotland) Act 1987. This requires that the damage caused be directly referable to the animal's physical attributes or tendencies. For this reason the transfer of germs, referred to above, falls under the Act only where it results from bodily injury (typically a bite).[745] When the animal plays a purely passive role, liability is expressly denied.[746] As in England, Scotland has specific rules on victims protected by keepers' liability. The keeper's employees benefit from the keeper's strict liability.[747] Excluded from such protection are people who voluntarily risk the danger posed by the animal.[748] Also excluded from protection are trespassers either injured by an animal not being used to guard the premises, or injured by an animal used to guard the premises where the keeper can prove that it was reasonable to keep the animal on his land.[749]

An example is *Cummings* v. *Grainger*,[750] in which a barmaid was 'badly bitten by a big dog'.[751] The defendant allowed his untrained Alsatian to roam freely at night on land in London's East End used as a scrap metal depot. The dog, whose presence was advertised by a placard, was there

---

[740] Sec. 6(3)(b) Animals Act 1971 and sec. 5(1)(a) Animals (Scotland) Act 1987.

[741] Jones, *Torts*, p. 262. If an animal is stolen its owner remains liable with the thief: *Kavanagh* v. *Centreline Ltd.* (fn. 729).

[742] The fact that the 1986 Act specifies both owner and keeper as potentially liable enables the owner to show that some person other than himself was in possession of and used the animal.

[743] Sec. 6(3)(b) Animals Act 1971. It is not always easy to determine who is the 'head of the household'. The Scottish Act avoids this term and renders liable the person who 'has actual care and control of a child under the age of 16'.   [744] See no. 149 above.

[745] See no. 354 with fn. 708 above.

[746] Sec. 1(5) Animals (Scotland) Act 1987: 'Subsection (1) above shall not apply to injury or damage caused by the mere fact that an animal is present on a road or in any other place.' This excludes strict liability where a person trips over a dog, and probably also where someone (as in ØLD 25 June 1936, fn. 711 above) is shocked by the mere presence of an animal.   [747] Sec. 6(5) Animals Act 1971 says so expressly.

[748] Sec. 5(2) Animals Act 1971; sec. 2(1)(b) Animals (Scotland) Act 1987.

[749] Sec. 5(3) Animals Act 1971; sec. 2(1)(c) Animals (Scotland) Act 1987.

[750] [1977] 1 QB 397; [1977] 1 All ER 104.

[751] According to the inimitable introduction to the judgment of Lord Denning MR, p. 106.

to guard the yard, itself surrounded by a high wall. The plaintiff barmaid's boyfriend was allowed to park his car in the yard at night. The plaintiff knew of the dog and was frightened of it. One night as she followed her boyfriend (without the permission of the defendant) to the car she was bitten by the dog. The requirements of sec. 2(2) Animals Act 1971 were satisfied: damage caused by an Alsatian was (1) 'likely to be severe', (2) attributable to the characteristics found in Alsatians used as guard dogs, and (3) it could be assumed that the plaintiff knew the dog would attack people at night. Nevertheless, the defendant was not liable. He could rely not only on sec. 5(2) Animals Act 1971 (voluntary assumption of a known risk by the plaintiff) but also on sec. 5(3). The plaintiff was trespassing and it was not unreasonable to allow a guard dog to run free on the premises at night in an area 'where persons of the roughest type come and go'.[752]

b. Liability for Dangerous Premises

(1) The Common Law

361   Unlike the codified legal systems of the continent,[753] North European countries do not recognize any special provisions for the 'collapse' (*ruine*) of all or part of a building. Roman civil law has failed to leave any recognizable influence in this respect.[754] That failure has both advantages and disadvantages. Liability for dangerous premises (including buildings, streets, paths, and trees) in principle follows the rules of the common law; only in the British Isles, with the exception of Ireland, has a specific statutory occupiers' liability developed:[755] a liability to persons who suffer damage on the premises of the defendant. (This is addressed below.[756])

362   Scandinavian and British laws in this field are similar in that neither distinguishes between the 'collapse' of a building and other dangers associated with premises. Whether a victim is injured by parts of a house,[757] a falling tree,[758] snow falling from a roof,[759] or a poorly con-

---

[752] Ibid. p. 108.   [753] See nos. 227–228 above.

[754] The same applies to Scotland, cf. no. 7 and fn. 30 above.

[755] An overview of the relevant statutory sources is found at fn. 21 above. Northern Ireland has its own Occupiers' Liability Act (Northern Ireland) 1957, printed with a commentary by Newark, 12 (1956–1958) *NILQ* 203–222. The English Occupiers' Liability Act 1957 does not apply to Northern Ireland (sec. 8[2]), and neither does the Occupiers' Liability Act 1984 (sec. 4[3]).   [756] See no. 363 below.

[757] Dan. HD 10 Mar. 1938, *UfR* 1938 A p. 453; *Cunard v. Antifyre Ltd.* [1933] 1 KB 551; *Taylor v. Liverpool Corporation* [1939] 3 All ER.

[758] Dan. HD 15 Apr. 1953, *UfR* 1953 A p. 519; BD 24 Feb. 1983, *UfR* 1983 A p. 762; *Noble v. Harrison* [1926] 2 KB 332.

[759] Dan. HD 4 Sep. 1958, *UfR* 1958 A p. 1103; *Slate v. Worthington* [1941] 1 KB 488.

structed door,[760] whether he falls on a slippery floor,[761] suffers damage to property due to a defective overflow system[762] or a deficiency of construction,[763] or whether he simply falls into a ditch: the starting point is the same. In continental and Northern Europe the standard of care has clearly been raised.[764] Where extra-hazardous activities are carried out there is also a specific statutory regime of strict liability.[765] Nowhere in Northern Europe has the collapse of buildings been reckoned with, or the dangers inherent in all artificial constructions considered. In general, for dangers of whatever kind emanating from buildings the usual rules of *culpa* (fault) liability and the torts of the common law apply.[766] In common law liability may arise in negligence,[767] nuisance,[768] or under the rule in *Rylands* v. *Fletcher*,[769] depending on the circumstances. The principles of non-delegable duties can also be relied upon by the injured party.[770] The suggestion of introducing no-fault liability for accidents caused by unsafe floors in business premises has not yet been taken up.[771]

(2) Occupiers' Liability as Governed by Statute

Whilst the rules on liability for premises in the codified systems of   **363** continental countries are chiefly concerned with the safety of passers-by, and for that reason are as closely linked to nuisance as to negligence, occupiers' liability is concerned with liability to those suffering damage

---

[760] Finn. HD 23 Sep. 1992, *NDS* 1993 p. 576; Swed. HD 3 Apr. 1985, *NJA* 1985: 42 p. 269.

[761] Finn. HD 6 Oct. 1989, *NDS* 1990 p. 533 (slippery floor in an airport entrance hall). Cf. *Dollman* v. *Hillman* [1941] 1 All ER 355.

[762] *Hawkins* v. *Dhawan and Mishiku* (1987) 19 HLR 232: liability not established as it was the first time that there had been any flooding of this sort.

[763] E.g. Dan. HD 5 Jan. 1940, *UfR* 1940 A p. 228 (the question was posed and then rejected of whether the flats of a particular building could have been better protected against the escape of gas from the other flats); *Siney* v. *Corporation of Dublin* [1980] IR 400 (Sup. Ct.) (liability in negligence because water was able to enter the plaintiff's flat).

[764] See no. 250 and fn. 86 above. A more recent example is ØLD 17 Mar. 1995, *UfR* 1995 A p. 550.

[765] An important example are the provisions of the Swedish Act on Environmental Damage, which serve only to codify existing judge-made law (e.g. HD 14 Apr. 1966, *NJA* 1966: 46 p. 248). 4 § *miljöskadelag* imposes strict liability for the consequences of working with explosives, and 3 § 7 of the same law imposes liability for damage caused by vibration.

[766] See Dan. HD 8 Feb. 1991, *UfR* 1991 A p. 274; and *Maloco* v. *Littlewoods Organisation Ltd. SLT* 1987 p. 425.

[767] E.g. *Dollman* v. *Hillman* (fn. 761); *Slate* v. *Worthington* (fn. 759); *Hawkins* v. *Dhawan and Mishuku* (fn. 763). From Ireland see *Carthy (A Minor)* v. *Sligo Corporation* ILT 1994 p. 103.

[768] *Lynch* v. *Hetherton* [1991] 2 IR 405 (HC) (a tree fell on a moving car: negligence and public nuisance); *Noble* v. *Harrison* [1926] 2 KB 332; *Mills* v. *Smith* [1964] 1 QB 30; *Smith* v. *Giddy* [1904] 2 KB 449. See also *Dollman* v. *Hillman* (fn. 761) and *Slate* v. *Worthington* (fn. 759). See no. 269 above.

[769] E.g. *Mulholland* v. *Baker* [1939] 3 All ER 253: negligent use of fire; liability also for damage caused in putting out the fire.

[770] *Balfour* v. *Barty-King* [1957] 1 QB 496; see no. 353 above.

[771] See O'Higgins, *ILT* 1991 pp. 134–138.

on the premises on which the source of danger originated. An occupier is not dissimilar to a *gardien*. An occupier is a person with premises in his possession or under his control,[772] and who must ensure their safety.[773] A tenant, a trustee, an organizer, or a contractor working on premises[774] can assume the same liability as an occupier. A single property can have more than one occupier simultaneously.[775] The expression 'premises' includes all similar alternatives, 'fixed or movable'.[776]

364   All British statutes on this topic affirm that occupiers' liability is negligence-based; strict liability does not apply.[777] Moreover, the burden of proof of negligence has not been altered to the detriment of the occupier.[778] The relevant legislation has in essence achieved only two advantages: it makes clear in whose favour the duty exists, and it sheds light on the content of that duty.

365   To whom is the duty of care owed? The primary intention behind occupiers' liability legislation since the Second World War has been to subject this question to all the circumstances surrounding the case. In other words: it has been the intent of the legislature to free the courts[779] from the strait-jacket of having to decide between invitees, licensees, and trespassers.[780] The general rule that the occupier had no duty of care towards trespassers led to particularly extensive criticism.[781] The problem became particularly acute with regard to children.[782] Today liabi-

---

[772] Cf. sec. 1(2) Occupiers' Liability Act 1957 ('occupation or control of premises'); sec. 1(1) Occupiers' Liability (Scotland) Act 1960 ('a person occupying or having control of land or other premises'); sec. 1(2) Occupiers' Liability Act (Northern Ireland) 1957 ('duty . . . in consequence of a person's occupation or control of premises'). For further details see North, *Occupiers' Liability,* pp. 16–36.

[773] *Feely* v. *Co-operative Wholesale Society Ltd.* 1990 *SLT* 547 (Lord Dervaird); *H & N Emanuel Ltd.* v. *GLC* [1971] 2 All ER 835; *Jackson* v. *Hall* [1980] AC 854.

[774] See Walker, *Delict,* 2nd edn., pp. 581–582 for further information

[775] *Wheat* v. *Lacon & Co. Ltd.* [1966] AC 552.

[776] Sec. 1(3)(a) Occupiers' Liability Act 1957. A ladder can be a movable structure: *Wheeler* v. *Copas* [1981] 3 All ER 405.   [777] Walker, *Delict,* 2nd edn., p. 578.

[778] *Wallace* v. *City of Glasgow DC SLT* 1985 p. 23; Stewart, *Casebook,* p. 268.

[779] Irish courts themselves had to overcome this excessively rigid three-pronged classification, which had made necessary all manner of legal fictions. They have parted company with the rule that the occupier of property need not take care of trespassers. See *McNamara* v. *Electricity Supply Board* [1975] IR 1 (Sup. Ct.) and *Rooney* v. *Connolly* [1987] ILRM 768 (Sup. Ct.).

[780] This division, whose roots lay in nineteenth-century English case-law, was carried over into Scottish law by the decision in *Dumbreck* v. *Addie & Sons (Collieries) Ltd.* [1929] AC 358.

[781] The most important 'trick' to create a duty of care in favour of trespassers was the device of implied licence: e.g. *Lowery* v. *Walker* [1911] AC 10.

[782] For a commentary see *The Laws of Scotland* (-Macdonald/Mullin/Smith/Wallace), vol. 22, para. 651. The position of English law prior to the Occupiers' Liability Act 1984 is best illustrated by the case of *British Railways Board* v. *Herrington* [1972] AC 877 which introduced the idea of the duty of common humanity. It has to be said that this decision also introduced a considerable degree of legal uncertainty: cf. *Halsbury's Laws of England* (-Bowman), 4th edn., vol. 31, p. 214.

lity towards trespassers depends generally upon whether the occupier recognized or could reasonably have recognized the danger, whether he had taken account of the presence of trespassers, and whether it could, in the circumstances of the case, reasonably be expected of him to safeguard trespassers.[783] Children are still not protected against the consequences of all the mischief they cause,[784] but their position has improved immeasurably.[785] Quite properly, rules still apply to trespassers which are not valid for visitors.[786]

The common law general duty of care is intended to guarantee that **366** people, wherever they are entitled to be,[787] can move around in safety.[788] In each individual case the courts, and not the Acts, decide the claims. It is expressly stated in the Acts that the occupier must take account of the fact that children customarily act with less care than adults.[789] The Acts also provide that a prior warning of the source of danger only suffices if it covers the damage actually suffered.[790] There are rules to protect the occupier, whereby the occupier is not answerable either for damage caused by an independent subcontractor, nor for damage which he himself incurs on site due to substandard work.[791] Business people may not disclaim liability to their customers either by contract or by a warning notice.[792]

---

[783] Sec. 1(3) Occupiers' Liability Act 1984.

[784] See *Devlin* v. *Strathclyde Regional Council SLT* 1993 p. 699: a 14-year-old jumped five feet from a school roof onto a dome-shaped roof made of transparent plastic material, which collapsed and the boy fell to his death. No liability.

[785] This is also true of Ireland where the development of the law on occupiers' liability has taken place exclusively within the common law: see the recent decisions *Clancy* v. *Commissioners of Public Works in Ireland* [1992] 2 IR 449; and *Crowley* v. *Allied Irish Banks Ltd.* [1988] ILRM 225.

[786] It is easier to discharge the duty to trespassers by warnings and express prohibitions than it is to discharge the duty to those with a right to be on the property. Compare sec. 1(5) Occupiers' Liability Act 1984 with sec. 2(4)(a) Occupiers' Liability Act 1957. According to sec. 1(8) of the 1984 Act the occupier is liable to trespassers only for personal injury, not for property damage.

[787] A person entitled to be on the property, but not on the particular part of it where the accident happened, will be treated as a trespasser and can thus see his claim collapse: cf. *Daly* v. *Avonmore Creameries Ltd.* [1984] IR 131 (Sup. Ct.).

[788] In English law the landowner is not liable for accidents which occur on a public right of way: *McGeown* v. *Northern Ireland Housing Executive* [1994] 3 All ER 53. It is not the same in Scotland (*Johnstone* v. *Sweeney SLT* 1985 p. 2 [Sh. Ct.]) but the position there is not totally clear (Blackie, *SLT* 1994 pp. 349–352).

[789] E.g. sec. 2(3)(a) Occupiers' Liability Act 1957.   [790] See fn. 786.

[791] Secs. 3(2) and 2(4)(b) Occupiers' Liability Act 1957.

[792] Sec. 2(1) in conjunction with secs. 1(1)(c) and 3 Unfair Contract Terms Act 1977 (c. 50).

Part 4: Unification and Approximation of the Law of Delict within the European Union

Bibliography: Acosta Estévez, 'La acción de la CEE en materia de responsabilidad por productos defectuosos y reparación de los daños sufridos por el consumidor: adaptación del Derecho español a la Directiva del Consejo 85/374/CEE', *La Ley* 1990 (1) pp. 1141–1149; Alpa, 'La responsabilità per il danno derivato dai "servizi" nel progetto di direttiva comunitaria', *Giur.it.* 1990, IV, 177–182; id., 'Il codice e la responsabilità civile: Origine di un testo', *Riv.Dir.Com.* 1992, I, pp. 513–524; Ancel, 'Rapprochement, unification ou harmonisation des droits?', in: *Mélanges Marty* (Toulouse 1978) pp. 1–13; d'Atena, *Zur Problematik der EG-Richtlinien, vornehmlich in Italien* (Saarbrücken 1986); Aubin, 'Die rechtsvergleichende Interpretation autonom-internen Rechts in der deutschen Rechtsprechung', *RabelsZ* 34 (1970) pp. 458–480; Azara, 'Voce "Codice civile"', in: Azara/Eula (edd.), *Novissimo Digesto Italiano*, vol. iii (1964 impression of the 1957 Turin ed.) pp. 386–387; Bangemann, 'Privatrechtsangleichung in der Europäischen Union', *ZEuP* 1994 pp. 377–380; v. Bar, *Internationales Privatrecht*, vol. i: *Allgemeine Lehren* (Munich 1987); id., 'Neues Haftungsrecht durch Europäisches Gemeinschaftsrecht', *FS Lange* (Stuttgart 1992) pp. 373–395; id. (ed.), *Auf dem Wege zu einer Konvention über das Internationale Umwelthaftungsrecht*, 2 vols. (Cologne *et al.* 1995); id., 'Deliktsrecht. Empfiehlt es sich, die Voraussetzungen der Haftung für unerlaubte Handlungen mit Rücksicht auf die gewandelte Rechtswirklichkeit und die Entwicklungen in Rechtsprechung und Lehre neu zu ordnen?', in: Bundesminister der Justiz (ed.), *Gutachten und Vorschläge zur Überarbeitung des Schuldrechts*, vol. ii (1981) pp. 1681–1778; Bercovitz Rodríguez-Cano, 'La responsabilité pour les dommages causés par des produits défectueux dans le Droit Espagnol: l'adaption à la Directive 85/374/CEE', *ERPL* 2 (1994) pp. 225–235; Betlem, 'Europees Onrechtmatig Daadsrecht', *NTBR* 1992 pp. 151–156; id., 'Een vierde type van rechtsvinding', *NJB* 1991 pp. 1363–1371; Bierbooms/Brans, 'Milieuschade en civiele aansprakelijkheid voor olielozingen', *NJB* 1993 pp. 85–91; Bingham, '"There is a World Elsewhere": The changing perspectives of English Law', 41 [1992] *IntCompLQ* 513–529; Blaurock, 'Europäisches Privatrecht', *JZ* 1994 pp. 270–276; id, 'Wege zur Rechtseinheit im Zivilrecht Europas', in: Starck (ed.), *Rechtsvereinheitlichung durch Gesetze. Bedingungen, Ziele, Methoden* (Göttingen 1992) pp. 90–116; Boch/Lane, 'A New Remedy in Scots Law' *SLT* 1992 pp. 145–148; Bocken, 'L'assurance responsabilité civile pour dommages causés par la pollution', in: *Les assurances de l'entreprise (Actes du colloque tenu à l'Université Libre de Bruxelles les 2 et 3 décembre 1993)* vol. ii (Brussels 1993) pp. 239–280; De Boeck, 'Het voorstel van E.G.-richtlijn inzake de aansprakelijkheid voor gebrekkige diensten', *RW* 1993–94 pp. 585–612; de Boer, 'Risicoaansprakelijkheid voor gevaarlijke stoffen en milieuverontreiniging', *NJB* 1993 pp. 225–231; von Bonsdorff, 'Det svenska lagspråket i Finland', *JFT* 1984 pp. 402–423; Borchmann, 'Die Bundesgesetzgebung zu internationalen Abkommen in den Jahren 1994 und 1995', *NJW* 1995 pp. 2956–2965; Braams, *Buitencontractuele aansprakelijkheid voor gevaarlijke stoffen* (Deventer 1989); Broekema-Engelen/Cleyndert/ Maters, 'Met kunst en veel vliegwerk: de reisovereenkomst', *NJB* 1993 pp. 157–162; Brüggemeier, 'Unternehmenshaftung für "Umweltschäden" im deutschen Recht und nach EG-Recht', in: *FS Jahr* (Tübingen 1994) pp. 223–250; Bundesamt für Justiz (ed.), *Bericht der Studienkommission für die Gesamtrevision des Haftpflichtrechts* (typescript, Berne 1991); Capponi, 'Responsabilità oggettiva del prestatore di servizi', *Riv.Dir. Com.* 1989, I, pp. 567–589; Caranta, 'Governmental Liability after Francovich', [1993] *CLJ* 272–297; Castronovo, 'La responsabilità del prestatore di servizi nella proposta di direttiva comunitaria', *Foro.it.* 1994, V, 273–285; Cleton, 'Aansprakelijkheid en schadevergoeding als nasleep van luchtvaartongevallen', *NJB* 1993 pp. 621–629; Coing, *Europäisches Privatrecht*, vol. ii (Munich 1989); Commissione reale per la riforma dei Codici/Commission française d'études de l'Union législative entre les nations alliées et amies, *Progetto di Codice delle obbligazioni e dei contratti. Testo definitivo approvato a Parigi nell'ottobre 1927/Projet de Code des Obligations et des contrats. Texte définitif approuvé à Paris en octobre 1927* (Rome 1928); Council of Europe, Committee on Legal Co-operation (CCJ). *Report drawn up by the sub-Committee on Fundamental Legal Concepts set up by the European Committee on Legal co-operation* (no place or year of publication given, probably Strasbourg 1976); id., *Empfehlung des Ministerkomitees des Europarates of 19 Mar. 1975, Entschließung (75) 7 über den Schadensersatz im Falle von Körperverletzung oder Tötung*, published *inter alia* in a note of 5 Feb. 1976, BGBl. 1976 II 323–332; van Dam, *Politieke Infiltratie in het Privaatrecht* (Deventer 1994); id., 'De EG-richtlijn dienstenaansprakelijkheid: uitstel of afstel?', *A&V* 1994 pp. 113–118; Damm, 'Europäisches Verbrauchervertragsrecht und AGB-Recht', *JZ* 1994 pp. 161–168; van Delden (ed.), *Hoofdstukken handelsrecht*, 2nd edn. (Deventer 1993); Dessertine (ed.), *L'évaluation du préjudice corporel dans les pays de la CEE* (Paris 1990); Deutsch, 'Aspekte für ein europäisches Haftungsrecht. Versuch einer kritischen, dogmatischen Bestandsaufnahme', *KF* 1992 pp. 4–14; id., 'Einheitliche Dienstleistungshaftung in Europa', *ZRP* 1990 pp. 454–455; Deutsch/Taupitz (edd.), *Haftung der Dienstleistungsberufe. Natürliche Vielfalt und europäische Vereinheitlichung* (Heidelberg 1993);

Dorhout Mees, *Nederlands handels- en faillissementsrecht*, 8th edn., vol. ii (Arnhem 1989); Drobnig, 'Ein Vertragsrecht für Europa', in: *FS Steindorff* (Berlin and New York 1990) pp. 1141–1154; id., 'Rechtsvergleichung in der deutschen Rechtsprechung', *RabelsZ* 50 (1986) pp. 610–630; id., *The Use of Comparative Law by Courts, General Report, XIVth International Congress of Comparative Law* (Athens 1994; typescript not yet published); id., 'The Use of Foreign Law by German Courts', in: Jayme (ed.), *German National Reports in Civil Law Matters for the XIVth Congress of Comparative Law in Athens 1994* (Heidelberg 1994) pp. 5–24; Drobnig/Zimmermann (trans.), 'Die Grundregeln des Europäischen Vertragsrecht, Teil I, der Kommission für Europäisches Vertragsrecht', *ZEuP* 1995 pp. 864–875; Eckert, 'Die EG-Richtlinie über mißbräuchliche Klauseln in Verbraucherverträgen und ihre Auswirkungen auf das deutsche Recht', *WM* 1993 pp. 1070–1078; van Erp, 'Van onredelijk bezwarend naar oneerlijk, of: van Nederzwart en Nedergrijs naar Euro-blauw', *WPNR* 1993 Nr. 6079; Evans, 'Convention sur la responsabilité civile pour les dommages causés au cours du transport de marchandises dangereuses par route, rail et bateaux de navigation intérieure (CRTD)', *Rev.dr.uniforme* 1991 pp. 77–183; Fallon, 'La loi du 25 février 1991 relative à la responsabilité du fait des produits défectueux', *JT* 1991 pp. 465–473; Faure, 'Enkele rechtseconomische kanttekeningen bij de dienstenaansprakelijkheid', *A&V* 1994 pp. 33–41; Flessner, 'Rechtsvereinheitlichung durch Rechtswissenschaft und Juristenausbildung', *RabelsZ* 56 (1992) pp. 246–260; Florijn, *Rechtsvergelijking in het wetgevingsproces* (Zwolle 1993); Fraselle, *La responsabilité du prestataire de services et du prestataire de soins de santé—une proposition de Directive européenne* (Louvain-la-Neuve 1992); Frietsch, 'Der europäische Vorschlag einer Haftung für Dienstleistungen', *DB* 1992 pp. 929–936; Fubini, 'Vers le nouveau Code civil italien', *Rev.trim.dr.civ.* 27 (1928) pp. 75–98; Gaidzik, 'Der EG-Richtlinienentwurf über die Haftung bei Dienstleistungen', *JR* 1992 pp. 323–328; Gandolfi, 'L'attualità del quarto libro del codice civile nella prospettiva di una codificazione europea', *Riv.Dir.Civ.* 1993, I, pp. 415–425; id., 'L'unificazione del diritto dei contratti in Europa: mediante o senza la legge?', *Riv.Dir.Civ.* 1993, II, pp. 149–158; Georgiades, 'I enarmonisi tou Idiotikou Dikaiou stin Evropi', *NoB* 42 (1994) pp. 321–346; Van Gerven, 'Noncontractual Liability of Member States, Community Institutions and Individuals for Breaches of Community Law with a View to a Common Law for Europe', *MJ* 1 (1994) pp. 6–40; Ghestin, 'L'influence des Directives communautaires sur le droit français de la responsabilité', in: *FS Werner Lorenz* (Tübingen 1991) pp. 619–634; Giampietro, 'Le proposte della comunità europea e l'iniziativa del Consiglio d'Europa sulla responsabilità per danno all'ambiente', *Riv.dir.eur.* 1992 pp. 813–826; Giemulla/Schmid, *Warschauer Abkommen* (Frankfurt, loose leaf, as at

May 1993); Grabitz (ed.), *Kommentar zum EWG-Vertrag* (Munich, loose leaf, as at 1992); Großfeld/Bilda, 'Europäische Rechtsangleichung', *ZfRV* 1992 pp. 421–433; Haak, *De aansprakelijkheid van de vervoerder ingevolge de CMR* (The Hague 1984); Hanssens, 'Le Code civil en Belgique', in: La Société d'Études Législatives (ed.), *Le Code Civil 1804–1904: Livre du Centenaire* (unaltered reprint of the 1904 Paris edn., Vaduz and Paris 1979) pp. 679–722; Heinemann, 'Auf dem Wege zur europäischen Dienstleistungshaftung', *ZIP* 1991 pp. 1193–1204; Heinrichs, 'Die EG-Richtlinie über mißbräuchliche Klauseln in Verbraucherverträgen', *NJW* 1983 pp. 1817–1822; Hodges, *Product Liability: European laws and practice* (London 1993); Hohloch, 'Produkthaftung in Europa', *ZEuP* 1994 pp. 409–445; Hondius, 'Naar een Europees contractenrecht: de richtlijn oneerlijke bedingen in consumentenovereenkomsten', *NTBR* 1993 pp. 108–112; id., 'EC-Directive on Unfair Terms in Consumer Contracts: Towards a European Law of Contract', 7 (1994) *Journal of Contract Law*, pp. 34–52; Hondius/Braams, *Auf dem Wege zu einem europäischen Haftungsrecht. Beitrag der Niederlande* (Saarbrücken 1989); Horsmans, 'L'utilisation de droit comparé par le législateur', in: Centre interuniversitaire de droit comparé (ed.), *Rapports belges au XIe Congrès de l'Académie internationale de droit comparé* (Cararcas 1982) (vol. ii, Antwerp and Brussels 1985) pp. 1–19; Hoskins, 'Garden Cottage Revisited: The Availability of Damages in the National Courts for Breaches of the EEC Competition Rules', 6 [1992] *ECLR* 257–265; Hulst/Klinge van Rooij, 'Europäisches Haftungsrecht. Das "Umwelt-Grünbuch": Ökologie oder Ökonomie?', *PHI* 1994 pp. 108–120; International Institute for the Unification of Private Law, 'Protocol of 1992 to Amend the International Convention on Civil Liability for Oil Pollution Damage' (London, 27 November 1992), *UniflRev* 1992 II pp. 61–92; International Institute for the Unification of Private Law, 'Protocol of 1992 to Amend the International Convention on the Establishment of an International Fund for Compensation for Oil Pollution Damage' (London, 27 November 1992), *UniflRev* 1992 II pp. 93–135; Irti, *L'età della decodificazione* (Milan 1979); Joerges/Brüggemeier, 'Europäisierung des Vertragsrechts und Haftungsrechts', in: Müller-Graff (ed.), *Gemeinsames Privatrecht in der Europäischen Gemeinschaft* (Baden-Baden 1993) pp. 233–286; Jongbloed, 'Requiem voor de Unificatie van het recht in Beneluxverband', *NJB* 1985 pp. 1227–1232; Jongeneel/Wessels, 'Onredelijke bedingen in consumentenovereenkomsten', *NJB* 1993 pp. 897–899; Karakostas, *I evthini tou paragogou gia elattomatika proionta* (Athens 1995); v. Kempis, 'La proposition de Directive communautaire concernant la responsabilité civile pour les dommages causés par les déchets', *Eur.Transp.L.* 26 (1991) pp. 155–160; Kommission der Europäischen Gemeinschaften, 'Mitteilung der Kommission an den Rat und das Europäische Parlament und den Wirtschafts- und

Sozialausschuß: Grünbuch über die Sanierung von Umweltschäden', *Doc.KOM* (93) 47 final version 14 May 1993 (typescript, cited in OJ C 149/12 29.5.1993); Kornilakis, *Auf dem Wege zu einem europäischen Haftungsrecht: Der Beitrag Griechenlands* (Saarbrücken 1986); id., 'I evthivi tou paragogou elattomatikon proionton', *Arm.* 44 (1990) pp. 201–211; Kötz, 'Rechtsvergleichung und gemeineuropäisches Privatrecht', in: Müller-Graff (ed.), *Gemeinsames Privatrecht in der Europäischen Gemeinschaft* (Baden-Baden 1993) pp. 95–108; id., 'Alternativen zur legislatorischen Rechtsvereinheitlichung', *RabelsZ* 56 (1992) pp. 215–218; id., 'Gemeineuropäisches Zivilrecht', in: *FS Zweigert* (Tübingen 1981) pp. 481–500; id., 'Europäische Juristenausbildung', *ZEuP* 1993 pp. 268–278; id., 'A Common Private Law for Europe: Perspectives for the Reform of European Legal Education', in: de Witte/Forder (edd.), *The common law of Europe and the future of legal education* (Deventer 1992) pp. 31–41; id., 'Die Ungültigkeit von Verträgen wegen Gesetz- und Sittenwidrigkeit', *RabelsZ* 58 (1994) pp. 209–231; Kurer/McIntosh/Schwenninger, 'Produkthaftpflicht, Produktsicherheit und andere EU-Richtlinien zum Konsumentenschutz', *SJZ* 90 (1994) pp. 169–178; Kwiatkowska/Soons (edd.), *Transboundary Movements and Disposal of Hazardous Wastes in International Law: Basic Documents* (Dordrecht *et al.* 1993); Lando, 'Principles of European Contract Law', *RabelsZ* 56 (1992) pp. 261–273 and 40 [1992] *AmJCompL* pp. 573–585; Lando/Beale (edd.), *The Principles of European Contract Law*, Part I (Dordrecht *et al.* 1995); Lambert-Faivre, *Le droit du dommage corporel* (Paris 1990); Laurent, *Avant-Projet de Révision du Code Civil*, vol. iv (Brussels 1884); Larroumet, 'La responsabilité civile en matière d'environnement. Le projet de Convention du Conseil de l'Europe et le livre vert de la Commission des Communautés Européennes', *D.* 1994 *Chron.* pp. 101–107; Lecheler, *Das Subsidiaritätsprinzip: Strukturprinzip einer europäischen Union* (Berlin 1993); Legeais, 'L'utilisation du droit comparé par les tribunaux', *Rev.int.dr.comp.* 46 (1994) pp. 347–358; Linkis/Hjortnæs, 'Ny civilretlig lovgivning om pakkerejser og om ændring af reglerne om fortrydelsesret', *J* 1994 pp. 112–123; Llorente San Segundo, 'Régimen jurídico de la responsabilidad de productos: normativa comunitaria y adaptación del Derecho español', *La Ley, Comunidades Europeas*, Año XIV, núm. 81, 2 Nov. 1993, pp. 1–5 (I was not able to gain access to a paginated sample); López y López, 'Constitución, código y leyes especiales. Reflexiones sobre la llamada descodificación', in: Asociación de profesores de Derecho civil (ed.), *Centenario del Código Civil*, vol. ii (Madrid 1990) pp. 1163–1176; Lukoschek, *Das anwendbare Deliktsrecht bei Flugzeugunglücken* (Karlsruhe 1984); de Ly, *Europese Gemeenschap en privaatrecht* (Zwolle 1993); Magnus, 'Einheitliches Schadensersatzrecht—Reformüberlegungen für das österreichische Haftpflichtrecht', in: *Verhandlungen des zwölften österreichischen Juristentages*

Wien 1994, part ii/1: *Bürgerliches Recht* (Vienna 1994); Malaurie/Aynès, *Cours de Droit Civil*, vol. VIII: *Les contrats spéciaux. Civils et commerciaux*, 7th edn. (Paris 1993–1994); Malinvaud, 'L'application de la Directive communautaire sur la responsabilité du fait des produits défectueux et le droit de la construction', *D*. 1988 *Chron*. pp. 85–95; Mansel, 'Rechtsvergleichung und europäische Rechtseinheit', *JZ* 1991 pp. 529–534; Mário Raposo, 'Sobre a responsabilidade civil do produtor e a garantia do seguro', *BolMinJust* 413 (1992) p. 5–28; Markesinis, 'The Destructive and Constructive Role of the Comparative Lawyer', *RabelsZ* 57 (1993) pp. 438–448; id. (ed.), *The Gradual Convergence: Foreign Ideas, Foreign Influences, and English Law on the Eve of the 21st Century* (Oxford 1994); id., 'General Theory of Unlawful Acts', in: Hartkamp/Hesselink/Hondius/du Perron/Vranken (edd.), *Towards a European Civil Code* (Nijmegen *et al.* 1994) pp. 285–300; id., 'L'enseignement du droit comparé sous l'éclairage de la jurisprudence', *RRJ* 1985 pp. 866–887; Mengoni, *L'Europa dei codici o un codice per l'Europa?* (Rome 1993); Mouly, 'La doctrine, source d'unification internationale du droit', *Rev.int.dr.comp.* 1986 pp. 351–368; de los Mozos, 'Il codice italiano come "modello" per la codificazione europea', *Foro.pad.* 1992 col. 46–51; Mullany, 'Implementation of the EC Directive on Freedom of Access to Information in Ireland and other Member States', *ILT* 1994 pp. 138–144; Mullerat, 'New Product Liability Law in Spain', *Int.Bus.Lawyer* 1994 pp. 418–421; Müller-Graff, 'Europäisches Gemeinschaftsrecht und Privatrecht', *NJW* 1993 pp. 13–23; O'Callaghan Muñoz, 'Hacia un único Derecho Civil Europeo. De los Derechos Forales a un Derecho Europeo', *Poder Judicial* 1982 pp. 37–44; Odersky, 'Harmonisierende Auslegung und europäische Rechtskultur', *ZEuP* 1994 pp. 1–4; Padoa-Schioppa, 'Dal Code Napoléon al Codice Civile del 1942', *Riv.Dir.Civ.* 1993, I, pp. 531–553; Pagh, 'I hvilket omfang er skader på almentilgængelige værdier omfattet af forurenerens erstatningsansvar', *UfR* 1991 B pp. 121–128; id., 'EF-retten og affaldsproblemerne', *J* 1991 pp. 267–280; id., 'EF-retlige og andre juridiske problemer i dansk affaldsregulering', *UfR* 1994 B pp. 27–36; Parker, 'State Liability in Damages for Breach of Community Law', 108 [1992] *LQR* pp. 181–186; Pellet, *Die reisevertragliche Gewährleistung in Deutschland, England und Frankreich und die Auswirkungen der EG-Pauschalreisenrichtlinie* (Frankfurt/Main *et al.* 1993); Piper, 'Zum Vorschlag der Kommission der Europäischen Gemeinschaften für eine Richtlinie des Rates über die Haftung bei Dienstleistungen aus Sicht des innerstaatlichen Transportrechts', *TranspR* 1992 pp. 92–95; Pouliadis, *I anaklisi epikindinon proionton* (Athens and Komotini 1988); Remien, 'Illusion und Realität eines europäischen Privatrechts', *JZ* 1992 pp. 277–284; id., 'Ansätze für ein europäisches Vertragsrecht', *ZVglRWiss* 87 (1988) pp. 105–122; Renger, 'Haftung und Entschädigung für Ölverschmutzungsschäden auf See', *TranspR* 1993 pp.

132–135; id., 'Perspektiven einer Vereinheitlichung von Haftung und Versicherung', *VersR* 1992 pp. 653–657; Roca Guillamón, 'Codificación y crisis del Derecho civil', in: Asociación de profesores de Derecho civil (ed.), *Centenario del Código Civil*, vol. ii (Madrid 1990) pp. 1755–1775; Romeo Casabona, 'Responsabilidad penal y responsabilidad civil de los profesionales. Presente y futuro de los conceptos de negligencia y riesgo. Perspectivas', *La Ley* 1993 (4) pp. 979–994; Ross, 'Beyond *Francovich*', 56 [1993] *ModLRev.* pp. 55–73; Roth, 'Die Freiheiten des EG-Vertrages und das nationale Privatrecht', *ZEuP* 1994 pp. 5–33; de Sadeleer, 'La Convention du Conseil de l'Europe sur la responsabilité civile des dommages résultant de l'exercice d'activités dangereuses pour l'environnment', *RGAR* 1994 Nr. 12367; Salvador Coderch/Santdiumenge, 'La influencia del Avant-projet de révision du Code civil Belga de François Laurent en el Código civil español de 1889', in: Asociación de profesores de Derecho civil (ed.), *Centenario del Código civil (1889–1989)*, vol. ii (Madrid 1990) pp. 1921–1966; Salvestroni, 'Codice Civile e responsabilità del produttore', *Riv.Dir.Com.* 1993, I, pp. 19–39; id., 'Principi o clausole generali, clausole "abusive" o "vessatorie" e diritto Comunitario', *Riv.Dir.Com.* 1995, I, pp. 11–19; Sandrock, 'Die Europäischen Gemeinschaften und die Privatrechte ihrer Mitgliedstaaten. Einheit oder Vielfalt?', *EWS* 1994 pp. 1–8; Schlechtriem, 'Rechtsvereinheitlichung in Europa und Schuldrechtsreform in Deutschland', *ZEuP* 1993 pp. 217–246; Schmidlin (ed.), *Vers un droit privé européen commun?— Skizzen zum gemeineuropäischen Privatrecht* (Basle 1994); Schwartz, 'Perspektiven der Angleichung des Privatrechts in der Europäischen Gemeinschaft', *ZEuP* 1994 pp. 559–584; Lord Slynn of Hadley, 'The European Community and the Environment', *J.Environ.L.* 5 (1993) pp. 225–231; Snijders, 'Aansprakelijkheid voor milieuverontreiniging: het verzekeringsaspect', *A&V* 1993 pp. 2–6; Spier, 'Wederom: de EEG en gebrekkige diensten', *NJB* 1991 pp. 663–665; Spier/Sterk, 'Aansprakelijkheid voor gebrekkige diensten. Een gebrekkig voorontwerp richtlijn', *NJB* 1990 pp. 1517–1523; eid., 'Een nieuwe ster aan het milieubeschermingsfirmament', *NJB* 1992 pp. 232–233; Sterk, *Verhoogd gevaar in het aansprakelijkheidsrecht* (diss. Tilburg; Deventer 1994); id., 'De aansprakelijkheid voor gevaarlijke stoffen en afvalstoffen', *WPNR* 1991 no. 5991; Stilfried/Stochenhuber, 'Schadensersatz bei Verstoß gegen das Kartellverbot des Art. 85 EG-V', *WBl* 1995 pp. 301–308 (part I) and pp. 345–352 (part II); Storm, 'En købelov for tjenesteydelser?—Om implementering af EF-Direktivet om Pakkerejser', *UfR* 1992 B pp. 313–320; Strømholm, 'Rechtsvergleichung und Rechtsangleichung. Theoretische Möglichkeiten und praktische Grenzen in der Gegenwart', *RabelsZ* 56 (1992) pp. 611–623; Tallon, 'Vers un droit européen du contrat?', in: *Mélanges Colomer* (Paris 1993) pp. 485–494; Taupitz, *Europäische Privatrechtsvereinheitlichung heute und morgen* (Tübingen 1993); id., 'Privatrechtsvereinheitlichung durch die EG: Sachrechts- oder Kollisionsrechtsvereinheitlichung?', *JZ* 1993 pp. 533–539; Tonner, 'Die EG-Richtlinie über Pauschalreisen', *EuZW* 1990 pp. 409–413; Toriello, '"Applicabilità" ed "efficacia" delle direttive comunitarie', *NGCC* 1993, II, pp. 497–532; Tuerlinckx, 'Aansprakelijkheid voor produkten en diensten', in: Storme (ed.), *Recht halen uit aansprakelijkheid* (Ghent 1993) pp. 357–394; Tunc, *La Directive européenne sur la responsabilité du fait des produits défectueux: son incorporation en droit français* (Saarbrucken 1988); Ulmer, 'Vom deutschen zum europäischen Privatrecht', *JZ* 1992 pp. 1–8; Vanel, 'Code Civil', *Rép. Droit Civil*, vol. II (Paris 1971) pp. 1–13; Vigneron, 'L'unification du droit privé européen', *JT* 1991 p. 15; Viney, *Vers la construction d'un droit européen de la responsabilité civile. Les apports possibles du droit français* (Saarbrücken 1986); Walker/Lohkemper, 'Die vorgeschlagene EG-Richtlinie über die Haftung bei Dienstleistungen und ihre Bedeutung für Haftungsfragen im Arbeitsrecht', *RdA* 1994 pp. 105–111; Baron van Wassenaer van Catwijck, *Naar een Europees verkeersschaderecht* (Deventer 1993); Widmer, 'Die Vereinheitlichung des schweizerischen Haftpflichtrechts—Brennpunkt eines Projekts', *ZBernJV* 130 (1994) pp. 385–410; de Witte/Ferder (edd.), *The common law of Europe and the future of legal education* (Antwerp and Deventer 1992); Witz/Wolter, 'Frankreich: Die Umsetzung der EG-Richtlinie über mißbräuchliche Klauseln in Verbraucherverträgen', *ZEuP* 1995 pp. 885–892.

I. INSTRUMENTS OF UNIFICATION AND

APPROXIMATION OF LAWS

367   Whereas the English common law instilled legal uniformity throughout its realm, its continental namesake, the *ius commune*, neither achieved nor even pursued this objective. From the very beginning the common law propagated *ratione imperii*, while Roman law influenced continental laws *imperio rationis* only. However, it was thereby able to provide a common framework for all civil law systems until the early nineteenth century, when those systems finally broke apart. From then on Latin ceased to be the *lingua franca* of the academic world, and the first rush towards codification more or less put paid to the perception of a common European legal system, which was buried under a tidal wave of nationalism. The discrepancies between the three main legal systems— English common law, and Scandinavian and continental European laws—grew wider than ever. To make matters worse, the codifications themselves soon became confusing ragbags of laws. The devastating effect of less than ten years of legislation by each nation on this area of private law is readily apparent from a comparison of the law of delict in the *Code Napoléon* and in the Austrian ABGB. The sole aim was for national legal unification. Each legal world at that time was limited by its own national borders. The French *Code Civil*, for instance, devoted only one single article to international private law, consisting of purely unilateral rules as to choice of law. Furthermore, for the first time in European legal history one of these rules was linked to the principle of nationality (Art. 3 III Cc). Bridges between the various nations and their legal orders were burnt. Even today many regulations of one country seem strange to lawyers of another, not because their substance is unfamiliar but simply because they are in foreign code, often presented in a different systematic order, and nearly always written in another language. This is enough to make it seem like 'foreign' law.

Occasionally, however, the reverse is achieved. When English lawyers dress a legal rule in Latin wording their European counterparts often wrongly believe that they are referring to a principle familiar to Europeans: *ex turpi causa non oritur actio* is a fine example of such a *faux ami* in the law of delict.[1]

After the first wave of euphoria had passed it became apparent that it **368** was inappropriate to study and cultivate law, especially private law, on a national level only. Towards the end of the nineteenth century, therefore, the mood gradually changed. From the turn of the century no code was drafted without a profound comparative analysis, although not necessarily with the intention or the result of achieving unification. The authors of the Spanish Cc, for example, were discussing contemporary Belgian drafts in detail at the turn of the century.[2] Their German counterparts, however, were generally willing to be guided only by other German-speaking countries. That is not to deny that they studied French law closely. However, they were so heavily influenced by the *Zeitgeist* that comparative discussions often resulted in provisions flaty contradictory to those of French law. The German law of delict, as well as other parts of the German code, can thus be regarded in some sense as an 'anti-*Code Civil*'. The consequences are numerous and still felt. For this reason

---

[1] Cf. amongst others *Pitts* v. *Hunt* [1991] 1 QB 24 (CA); *Ashton* v. *Turner* [1981] QB 137 and *Saunders* v. *Edwards* [1987] 1 WLR 116. These deal with several persons committing a crime during which one perpetrator injures another (e.g. an accident during the escape after a break-in). The complaints were dismissed on grounds of public policy. It is true, however, that *ex turpi causa* often overlaps with contributory fault.

[2] For further details see Salvador Coderch, in: *Centenario del Código civil*, vol. ii, pp. 1921–1966 (on the revision project by François Laurent).

the reconciliation of French and German law, rather than the integration of common law, poses the greatest problem for the approximation of laws within Europe. Fortunately such marked tensions faded with the nineteenth century. In the late 1920s Italy and France drafted a joint law of obligations, a major part of which was later incorporated into the Italian *Codice Civile* of 1942.[3] Together with the Greek and the Portuguese Cc, and the Dutch BW, the Italian *Codice Civile* represents a bridge of compromise between the German and the French laws of delict. As demands grow for approximation of laws within the European Union, these codes will merit greater attention than they currently receive. It is, however, an amusing sign of their overdeveloped self-confidence when Italian lawyers recommend their *Codice Civile* as a practically complete European Civil Code![4]

369   In the twentieth century the climate of opinion has swung in favour of renewed internationalization of private law, with special emphasis on Europe. This is demonstrated by a steadily increasing readiness to take foreign achievements into consideration when new legal texts are drafted. In addition, *unification* as well as approximation of laws (remarkably: the former before the latter) has also begun in many fields of private law. However, the law of delict first entered the scene some time after the end of the Second World War. Even then its steps were comparatively tentative, as its authors restricted themselves to the relatively moderate aim of approximating laws rather than the far higher goal of unifying them. Only very reluctantly do European nations relinquish their law of delict. For many, the ties to the *ordre public* are still far too strong. Even a joint effort by Scandinavian countries in the 1960s and '70s only achieved an approximation of their laws, not an identical text.[5] The uniform trademark law of the Benelux countries remains the only

---

[3] Cf. Azara/Eula (-Azara), *Novissimo Digesto Italiano* (1957/1964) III p. 387. The Commission, chaired by Scialoja and Larnaude, included famous names: Henri Capitant, Ambroise Colin, Georges Ripert, and Jacques Bouteron for the French, and Alfredo Ascoli, Roberto de Ruggiero, and Antonio Azara for the Italians. Their draft was published in 1928 (cf. bibliography Part 4 I, *Commissione reale*). However, it was received rather coolly in the literature of that time; positive remarks, e.g. Fubini, *Rev.trim.dr.civ.* 27 [1928] pp. 75, 84 remained the exception. For the text of the regulations concerning the law of delict see Alpa/Bessone, *Atipicità*, vol. i, pp. 412–413; the comparative analyses on which he based the provisions can be found in Alpa, *Riv.Dir.Com.* 1992, I, pp. 513–524.

[4] This confident position is taken chiefly by Gandolfi, *Riv.Dir.Civ.* 1993, I, pp. 415–425; cf. id., *Riv.Dir.Civ.* 1993, II, pp. 149–158. The plan initiated by him (cf. reports on meetings by Vigneron, *JT* 1991 p. 15; Tilmann, *IPRax* 1992 p. 62 = *JZ* 1991 p. 1023; Sturm, *JZ* 1991 p. 555; Posch, *NJ* 1991 p. 70) has no chance of success as the work of the Lando group has almost been completed (no. 409 below). Besides, the Gandolfi plan has as yet shown no definite results. The criticisms made by de los Mozos, *Foro.pad.* 1992 cols. 46–51; and Alpa, loc. cit. (fn. 3) p. 524 (with special regard to the law of delict) are valid.

[5] See Kruse, *Erstatningsretten*, 5th edn., p. 14; for more details see Part 3 I above.

truly realized regional unification of laws which is related to the law of delict in western Europe.[6]

The state treaty is undoubtedly the 'classical' instrument of the **370** *unification of law*. Although such treaties have over the course of time also been developed for matters concerning liability law (see section II below) their scope of application is limited and they concern only projects for the unification of law, without specifically aiming at harmonization within the European Union. Member States have so far used treaties only to protect industrial property and in international private and procedural law as an instrument to unify laws specific to the Union itself. They have not yet even managed to agree upon a joint ratification policy for treaties with third (non-EU) parties, although agreement needs to be found soon. In future, at the very least, those unifying treaties which concern the free movement of goods and services should either be signed by the EU *en bloc* or not at all. As long as EU member states continue to ratify unifying treaties with third countries individually, new problems are bound to arise within the EU. Even where the harmoniza-tion of legislation within the Union is being, or about to be, undertaken, the approximation achieved by a directive can be undermined if higher standards of liability apply to some members of the EU than to other signatories of the same Treaty. On the other hand, if the Union entered such treaties unanimously a directive would become superfluous. Within the law of environmental liability this issue has already arisen.[7]

---

[6] *Beneluxverdrag met eenvormige wet inzake de warenmerken* of 19 Mar. 1962, Stb. 1963 p. 221, and Monit. belge 14 Oct. 1969 (BMW), and *Beneluxverdrag inzake tekeningen of modellen met eenvormige Beneluxwet inzake tekeningen of modellen* of 25 Oct. 1966, Trb. 1966 p. 292, and Monit. belge, 29 Dec. 1973 (BTMW) respectively. The treaties differ in that, according to Art. 13 BMW, *'het gemene recht betreffende aansprakelijkheid uit onrechtmatige daad'* can still be applied without restrictions, whereas the provisions for liability in Art. 14 V BTMW are not only final, they also oust the law of delict. More detailed information on these diverse provisions can be found in Dorhout Mees (-van Nieuwenhoven Helbach), *Nederlands handels- en faillissementsrecht*, 8th edn., pp. 530–532; and van Delden (-Holzhauer), *Hoofd-stukken handelsrecht*, 2nd edn., no. 1381. The provisions made in the *Beneluxverdrag betref-fende de verplichte verzekering van autovoertuigen*, 24 May 1966 (Monit. belge, 21 May 1976) 'only' concern a uniform third-party liability insurance law, not liability law itself. A project partially to unify the law of obligations, the *Benelux-overeenkomst inzake nakoming van verbintenissen* of 2 June 1973 was never concluded. The Dutch legislator considered it for the 6th book of the NBW (Jongbloed, *NJB* 1985 pp. 1227, 1230 and fn. 17). However, the many similarities between Belgian and French law must have derailed the Benelux project. Cf., on the slowly progressing unification of laws in the Benelux countries, Horsmans, in: *Rapports belges au XIe Congrès de droit comparé*, vol. ii, pp. 1, 3–5.

[7] Here the European Convention of 21 June 1993 on Civil Liability for Damage Resulting from Activities Dangerous to the Environment (Lugano Convention) which is not yet in force anywhere (cf. no. 383 below) and the proposal of the Council for a directive on civil liability for damage caused by waste (original version in OJ C 251 4.10.1989 p. 3; text of altered proposal in OJ C 192 23.7.1991 p. 6; see no. 387 below) are partly inconsistent with each other. They are distinctly dissimilar as far as the scope of strict liability law is concerned. It was thus necessary to clarify in Art. 25 II of the Lugano Convention that

371   A treaty (in this case a 'mixed' treaty[8]) would also be the most appropriate instrument to embody a *European Civil Code*, should one ever be drafted. Although the European Parliament demanded as early as 1989 that the necessary steps to this end be taken,[9] strictly speaking the Union lacks a Community instrument with which to enforce such a code. A simple directive is not an adequate instrument to effect codification. A regulation (Art. 189 II Treaty of Rome), on the other hand, which might appear appropriate, would be doomed to failure due to the principle of subsidiarity provided in Art. 3b Treaty of Rome (see e.g. Art. 23 GG). It is true that not only directives but also regulations can be based on either Art. 235 or Art. 100a Treaty of Rome,[10] but in a declaration on Art. 100a Treaty of Rome the Commission itself favoured the directive.[11] Furthermore, it is extremely doubtful whether jurisdiction can be based on Art. 235 Treaty of Rome at all. This question must be asked at least in those cases where private law does not affect the free movements of goods and services in the sense of Arts. 3 lit. h, 100, and 100a Treaty of Rome. Although by far the greater part of the law of obligations does have such an effect[12] this cannot be said of land law, family law, or the law of succession. Should a codification of European private law ever be

'Parties which are members of the European Economic Community shall apply Community rules and shall therefore not apply the rules arising from this Convention except in so far as there is no Community rule governing the particular subject concerned'. Such a self-contradictory European liability law is unsatisfactory. Therefore the EU Commission felt compelled to try to rewrite the Directive on Waste to bring it into harmony with the Lugano Convention. However, Germany, for example, will oppose this plan, having so far refused to ratify the Convention. For an interesting overview on the Convention and the *Green Book* of the EU Commission on Environmental Liability see Larroumet, D. 1994 *Chron.* pp. 101–107.

[8] 'Mixed' because it would deal with both matters within the competence of the Council of Ministers of the EU and matters capable of agreement by national governments. The legal nature of such a mixed treaty, which would have to be prepared on the basis of Art. 220 Treaty of Rome, has not yet been convincingly determined.

[9] Resolution of the European Parliament of 26 May 1989 on the approximation of private law of Member States OJ C 158/400; Doc. A 2–157/89; text (in German) also in *RabelsZ* 56 (1992) pp. 320–321; and in *ZEuP* 1993 pp. 613–615. The European Parliament demands in this resolution that the necessary preliminary work for the development of a joint European Civil Code should commence. The European Parliament renewed and confirmed this resolution on 6 May 1994: EP-Doc A3–329/94; cf. *EuZW* 1994 p. 612 and *ZEuP* 1995 p. 669.

[10] Grabitz (-Langeheine), *Kommentar zum EWG-Vertrag* I, Art. 100a no. 45, and Grabitz (-Grabitz) loc. cit. II Art. 235 no. 83.

[11] Single European Act of 28 Feb. 1986, OJ 1987 L 169/1 in the version found in the Treaty of Maastricht (fn. 14 below): 'In its proposals pursuant to Article 100a(1) the Commission shall give precedence to the use of the instrument of a directive if harmonization involves the amendment of legislative provisions in one or more Member States.'

[12] Not only was Council Dir. 93/13/EEC of 5 Apr. 1993, on unfair terms in consumer contracts, (OJ L 95 21.4.1993, p. 29) based on Art. 100a Treaty of Rome, but the opinion that even a directive on road traffic accidents could be based on Art. 100a Treaty of Rome also finds its supporters; see no. 386 and fn. 113 below.

accomplished, it will only be as a result of a step-by-step development. Although that part of the law of contract which deals with general principles would be a suitable starting point, a clear and comprehensive code would soon have to be developed. Such a concept might even be needed from the outset. Furthermore, the resolution of the European Parliament of 12 July 1990 on the principle of subsidiarity supports the use of a treaty rather than a regulation, by stating in paragraph 9 that in accordance with the principle of subsidiarity, ultimate jurisdiction, especially in the field of private law, will remain with the member states.[13] A Civil Code must be agreed and not imposed.[14] This is also the position held by the Commission.[15]

By its very nature, the unification of law can be achieved only by **372** legislative means. Therefore it can only be accomplished by treaty, parallel legislation, or—within the European Union—by regulation.[16] The *approximation of laws*, on the other hand, can be achieved in a number of ways. Naturally, as far as the territory of the European Union is concerned, the *directive* (Art. 189 III Treaty of Rome) is the appropriate legislative medium. A great number of such directives (as well as proposals and draft proposals therefor) already exist. They have entered the law of delict, to which they have regularly added new and complete causes of action, or at least provisions defining unlawful behaviour.[17] Directives are European framework laws, which must be implemented through concrete incorporation by national legislators. Should a state refuse to implement a directive or unduly delay doing

---

[13] Doc. A 3–163/90, printed in OJ 1990 C 231 p. 113. Cf. on this matter Lecheler, *Subsidiaritätsprinzip*, p. 25.

[14] In addition, a treaty would render obsolete the objection of Mengoni, judge of the Italian Constitutional Court: *L'Europa dei codici o un codice per l'Europa?*, p. 3. He is of the opinion that in Art. F of the Treaty of Maastricht (Treaty of 7 Feb. 1992 on the EU, OJ C 224 p. 6, enforced 1 Nov. 1993, cf. BGBl. 1993 II 1947) '*è implicata una riserva a favore della Europa dei codici*'.

[15] See the answer of EC Commissioner Bangemann to the question posed by Pierros MEP, OJ C 32 4.2.1993, pp. 7, 8.

[16] Even Arts. 85 and 86 Treaty of Rome could be seen as setting unifying standards of conduct, the violation of which gives rise to liability under (albeit not standardized) national laws of delict, cf. *Garden Cottage Foods* v. *Milk Marketing Board*, [1984] AC 130 (HL); and Hoskins, 6 [1992] *ECLR* pp. 257–265: Stilfried/Stochenhuber, *WBl* 1995 pp. 301–308 and 345–352. If one emphasizes Art. 119 Treaty of Rome rather than Dir. 76/207/EEC on the implementation of the principle of equal treatment for men and women as regards access to employment, vocational training, and promotion and working conditions (OJ L 39 p. 40), it could be argued that the ECJ *Dekker* ruling of 8 Nov. 1990 (Case no. C-177/88, *NedJur* 1992 no. 224 p. 853; cf. HR 13 Sep. 1991, *NedJur* 1992 no. 225 p. 855) also contains a piece of '*europees onrechtmatig daadsrecht*' (Betlem, *NTBR* 1992 p. 151; cf. id., *NJB* 1991 p. 1363). Furthermore, on 13 Oct. 1993 the ECJ decided that compensation based on *culpa in contrahendo* for failure to make full disclosure at a pre-contractual stage does not violate Art. 30 Treaty of Rome (Case no. C-93/92, *CMC Motorradcenter GmbH* v. *Pelin Baskiciogullari*), *JZ* 1994 p. 623, with note by Fezer.   [17] See fn. 16.

so, non-compliance proceedings (Arts. 169–171 Treaty of Rome)[18] and state liability can result.[19] However, a directive creates neither rights nor obligations between two subjects of private law.[20] Therefore, product liability in Spain, for example, remained exclusively subject to Spanish law for years after the Product Liability Directive had been enforced and the time given to incorporate it into national law (Art. 19 I: three years) had elapsed;[21] there is no way of knowing when the French will comply.[22] As the nature of a directive is to deliver only the framework for national laws, member states are usually left with some discretion as to details. This applies equally to the law of delict; here too directives have been

---

[18] France has already been sentenced in such proceedings for failure to implement the Product Liability Directive (Council Dir. 85/374/EEC of 25 July 1985 on the Approximation of the Laws, Regulations, and Administrative Provisions of the Member States concerning Liability for Defective Products, OJ 1985 L 220 p. 29): ECJ 13 Jan. 1993, Case no. L-293/91m, *Kommission der Europäischen Gemeinschaft* v. *Französische Republik*, EWS 1993 p. 157. On the binding effect of directives from a French point of view see Conseil d'Etat 11 Mar. 1994, *D.* 1995 *Jur.* 49 (note Pastorel). However, it is important also to realize that the Court of Cassation has meanwhile become active and has 'turned around' the directive on product liability *de facto* through a change in its judgments: Cass.civ. 17 Jan. 1995, Bull.civ. 1995, I, no. 43 = *D.* 1995 *Jur.* 350 (note Jourdain); see also esp. Viney, *Sem.Jur.* 1995, I, 3853 no. 9.

[19] ECJ 19 Nov. 1991, Joint Cases C-6/90 and 9/90, *Francovich and Bonifaci* v. *Italy, Reports of cases* 1991, I, p. 5357; *Giur.it.* 1993, I, 1, p 1585 (with note by Luco); [1990] *IRLR* 84; cf. Caranta, [1993] *CLJ* pp. 272–297; Parker 108 [1992] *LQRev* pp. 181–186; and Ross, 56 [1993] *ModLRev* pp. 55–73. A later *Francovich* ruling was given in ECJ 16 Dec. 1993, Case no. C-334/92, *Fondo de Garantía Salarial*, NJW 1994 p. 921.

[20] A citizen can only invoke a directive against his government (in cases where the latter incorporated it insufficiently or too late), and only if the provisions made therein are clear and specific, cf. only ECJ 23 Feb. 1994, Case no. C-236/92, *Comitato di coordinamento per la difesa della Cava* et al. v. *Regione Lombardia* et al., *EuZW* 1994 p. 282; and ECJ 14 July 1994, Case no. C-91/92, *Paola Faccini Dori* v. *Recreb Srl.*, NJW 1994 p. 2473. A general outline of the Italian jurisdiction on this issue can be found in Toriello, *NGCC* 1993, II, pp. 497–532.

[21] In Spring 1993 a draft product liability law was presented to the Spanish Parliament: Boletín Oficial de las Cortes Generales of 26 Mar. 1993. It was passed by the plenary session of the *Congreso de los Diputados* on 28 Apr. 1994 (*Boletín Oficial de las Cortes Generales, Congreso de los Diputados* of 10 May 1994, no. 40–8). After it had been given the consent of the Second Chamber the Act came into effect on 8 July 1994 (*Ley* 6 July 1994, no. 22/1994; *Responsabilidad civil por los daños causados por productos defectuosos*, BOE of 7 July 1994, no. 161). On the difficulties of the implementation the EC Directive in Spain cf. Acosta Estévez, *La Ley* 1990 (1) pp. 1141–1149. Until that time consumer protection law applied (law no. 26/1984 of 19 July 1984, BOE no. 176 of 24 July 1984). For detailed explanations of the new Spanish product liability law see *inter alia* Bercovitz Rodríguez-Cano, *ERPL* 2 (1994) pp. 225–235; Mullerat, *Int.Bus.Lawyer* 1994 pp. 418–421.

[22] On 23 May 1990 the French Minister of Justice submitted a bill to amend the *Code Civil* to the French Cabinet (*Projet Arpaillange* of 23 May 1990, Doc.Ass.nat. 1989–1990, no. 1395; also printed in Hommelhoff/Jayme, *Europäisches Privatrecht, Textausgabe* [Munich 1993] no. 10 b; cf. *PHI* 1993 p. 112). However, according to the Ministry of Justice the project is *'au point mort'*, the bill was withdrawn, and no second introduction is currently envisaged. Since Cass.civ. 17 Jan. 1995 loc. cit. the results of this immobility have however lost their relevance.

much criticized on these grounds:[23] unjustifiably, from my point of view. Directives do help to revive a *jus commune Europaeum*. This is the case even where the additional causes of action which they create play only an insignificant part in day-to-day litigation, for example in product liability. Hardly any judgments relying specifically on statutory provisions of the EC Directive[24] have yet been handed down. European courts still rely as far as possible on the rules of their national *droit commun*, and one must acknowledge that to a surprising extent it has remained a *droit commun européen*. However, without the Product Liability Directive we would never have become so conscious of this fact. That Directive has even encouraged national courts to interpret their domestic law of delict in a pro-European fashion.[25] In fact, courts everywhere are prepared to interpret national product liability legislation in the light of the Directive;[26] even legislators frequently anticipate drafts of directives in their national legislation.[27] It is nonetheless true that directives, which have to be extremely detailed, usually produce special statutes accelerating the process of *decodificazione*. However, the Dutch example in the field of product liability proves that such a result is not inevitable.[28] (It is currently uncertain whether France will follow this example[29]). This process of decodification nevertheless gives grounds to hope for further efforts towards the europeanization of private law.[30]

[23] Greek literature especially has vehemently criticized the directive on product liability. As the individual nations are given much scope to shape their product liability law, proper unification of laws is impaired: Kornikalis, *Arm.* 44 (1990) pp. 201, 204 ff.; Deliyannis/ Kornilakis, *Eidiko Enochiko Dikaio*, vol. iii, p. 328, and Pouliadis, *I anaklisi epikindinon proionton*, p. 69. Cf., however, the very balanced comment by Georgiades, *NoB* 42 (1994) pp. 321, 328–329.

[24] Listed in Kurer/McIntosh/ Schwenninger, *SJZ* 90 (1994) pp. 169, 174. For an excellent analysis based on an extensive evaluation of case-law across EU member states, see Hohloch, *ZEuP* 1994 pp. 409–445.

[25] See e.g. BGH 19 Nov. 1991, BGHZ 116 pp. 104, 111 ('With a view to this uniform EC legislation . . . [it does not seem] . . . appropriate to differentiate between large and small enterprises in the field of damages for non-economic loss, which are not covered by the German statute implementing the product liability directive, and are therefore treated according to the principles of § 823 I BGB'). Cf. also BGH 5 May 1992, *VersR* 1992 p. 1010 (concerning disclaimers in product liability).

[26] Boch/Lane, *SLT* 1992 pp. 145, 147 with examples of Scottish and English case law.

[27] Blaurock, in Starck (ed.), *Rechtsvereinheitlichung durch Gesetze*, pp. 89, 112–113. § 92 of the German drug law (*Arzneimittelgesetz*) prohibiting disclaimers is a good example of such a development. For French law Cass.civ. 17 Jan. 1995 (see fn. 18 above) should not be forgotten.

[28] The EC Directive on Product Liability promptly became part of the Dutch code: Arts. 6:185–193 BW.

[29] It was planned by the *Projet Arpaillange* (fn. 22 above) to incorporate the new product liability law into the French code, too. Arts. 1386–1 to 1386–19 Cc should have been implemented accordingly. Amendment of the respective provisions of the law of contract would also have become necessary.

[30] Markesinis is therefore right when he speaks of the 'destructive and constructive role of the comparative lawyer', *RabelsZ* 57 (1993) p. 438.

373   *The recommendations of the Council of Europe* have always allowed for the fact that the approximation of law can also be pursued by non-legislative means (see section IV below). Unfortunately, these recommendations have so far received scant recognition, although they are of remarkable quality. Those concerning non-contractual liability law met the same fate.[31] Furthermore, approximation of laws can also be undertaken by the courts, if only to a limited extent. Due to lack of time it is obviously difficult for them to follow the latest developments abroad, and to incorporate them into their work. However, it would be a positive step if they would use foreign material when preparing key decisions. Databases[32] and case-books[33] designed to meet European needs could help here. Such resources together with new text and reference books on *Ius Commune Europaeum* would be a valuable contribution by legal scholarship to the furtherance of European lawyers' mutual understanding. The legal training of future generations would also be improved, as their studies could be undertaken from the outset in a common European context.[34] The national Ministries of Justice could support this development, for example by making a period of work abroad a prerequisite for judicial promotion.

II. UNIFIED LAW THROUGH STATE TREATIES

1. UNIFIED LAW IN PERIPHERAL AREAS OF LIABILITY LAW

374   No true unified law text designed specifically for the territory of the European Union has yet been composed, and none even drafted for the civil law of delict. The European Union has left this field to other organizations, chiefly the Council of Europe.[35] On the whole, existing

---

[31] Recommendation 75(7) of 14 Mar. 1975 on compensation in case of bodily harm or fatal accidents, as well as the 'Report on Fundamental Legal Concepts' (probably from 1976). Both are cited above in the Part IV bibliography under *Council of Europe*.

[32] They should not only include material on uniform law (Schneider, *WM* 1993 p. 1839), but *idealiter* also give access to decisions of the national supreme courts on their domestic law. On the improvement of the supply of information on European law see the Council decision of 20 June 1994 on the electronic dissemination of Community law and national implementing laws and on improved access conditions, OJ C 179 of 1.7.1994, p. 3.

[33] Professor van Gerven, who was Advocate-General at the ECJ, has initiated a major project dealing with this issue. It involves academics from all over the European Union who want to develop, *inter alia*, case-books on contract and on delict.

[34] Cf. Mouly, *Rev.int.dr.comp.* 1986 pp. 351–368.

[35] For an overall picture of developments to 1987 see v. Bar, *IPR* vol. i, nos. 56–60 and 69–72.

unified law consists of multilateral state treaties; bilateral treaties in this field usually deal only with the law relating to aliens.[36] At present the focus of multilateral unification is increasingly on environmental liability law (no. 379 below). Since the attempts of the Council of Europe to introduce a convention on product liability[37] were forced to give way[38] to the regime of the relevant EC Directive,[39] multilateral treaties still touch only peripheral areas of liability law, namely the relationship between delict and contract, and issues of third-party insurance cover.[40]

A convention typical of those concerning peripheral areas of liability law is the *Convention on the Liability of Hotel-keepers Concerning the Property of their Guests*.[41] Its liability system, which imposes strict liability on innkeepers, and which is limited in amount but irrespective of fault, depends only on the admittance of the guest, and is therefore non-contractual in nature. In its time it doubtless proved an important advance in the field of international consumer protection. However, from the perspective of the present European Union the Convention has already become problematic. It forced the authors of the EC Directive on Unfair Terms in Consumer Contracts[42] to give the Convention precedence (Art. 1 II of the Directive)[43] in all EU countries which have ratified the treaty.[44] This is unsatisfactory. At present the hostelries of some countries of the Union only are subject to the provisions of the

375

---

[36] In this respect treaties generating reciprocity in state liability have been of particular practical importance. The European Union, however, has always regarded reciprocity as an unlawful requirement: cf. no. 567 below. The only bilateral state treaty known to me containing separate (strict) liability provisions ousting the domestic law of delict concerns a pipeline between Pernis and Antwerp (*Wet Buisleidingenstraat Pernis-Antwerp* of 11 Mar. 1972, Stb. 1972 p. 145); cf. Braams, *Buiten-contractuele aansprakelijkheid voor gevaarlijke stoffen*, no. 7.13, pp. 522–523.

[37] European Convention of 27 Jan. 1977 on Product Liability in Regard to Personal Injury and Death, European Treaty Series no. 91 (never enforced).

[38] The Convention of the Council of Europe became obsolete as a consequence of the Directive because as part of the EEA treaty the Directive bound EFTA countries (Convention of 2 May 1992 on the European Economic Area, Art. 7 in conjunction with Annex II thereof [BGBl. 1993 II 267, 1294]). [39] Fn. 18 above.

[40] The so called 'London Green Card Agreement' is not a state treaty but a contract between insurance companies, or their parent organizations. It remains an important instrument for settling claims arising from accidents outside the European Union. The Vienna Convention of 8 Nov. 1968 on Road Traffic (BGBl. 1977 II 811) is a state treaty but concerns liability law only to the extent that it sets certain uniform standards of behaviour. [41] UNTS 590 p. 81; BGBl. 1966 II 269.

[42] Council Dir. 93/13/EEC of 5 Apr. 1993 on Unfair Terms in Consumer Contracts, OJ L 95 21.4.1993 p. 29. Cf. no. 390 below.

[43] 'The contractual terms which reflect mandatory statutes or international conventions to which the Member States or the Community are party, particularly in the transport area, shall not be subject to the provisions of this Directive.'

[44] They are: Belgium, France, Germany, Ireland, Italy, Luxembourg, and the UK, as well as Croatia, Cyprus, Macedonia, Malta, Slovenia, and Yugoslavia (BGBl. II, reference directory B, concluded on 31 Dec. 1994, 401).

Directive,[45] whereas licensed premises and restaurants throughout the entire EU have been subject to its provisions since 1 January 1995.

376   Of course, innkeepers' liability only marginally concerns the international unification of laws. More important, along with some conventions on traffic law mainly the *Brussels International Convention of 23 September 1910 on a Standardized Determination of Rules on the Collision of Ships*,[46] the *Geneva Convention of 15 March 1960 Relating to the Unification of Certain Rules Concerning Collisions in Inland Navigation*,[47] and the *Rome Convention of 7 October 1952 on Damage Caused by Foreign Aircraft to Third Parties on the Surface*,[48] are the major state treaties dealing with *transport law*, which to some extent also involve non-contractual liability. They do not upset EU legal uniformity as virtually all its members have signed them. The oldest treaty of this kind is the *Warsaw Convention*[49] which regulates the liability, deliberately characterized as being neither fully contractual nor fully tortious, of the carrier towards its passengers. Its Hague derivative, dating from 1955,[50] has been ratified by all EU member states, and only Portugal and Spain[51] have not yet signed[52] the *Supplementary Convention of Guadalajara*.[53]

However, the provisions of the Warsaw Convention are somewhat antiquated. Its Arts. 17 ff. deal with liability for presumed but rebuttable

---

[45] More precisely: only disclaimers relating to non-contractual liability come under the Council of Europe Convention. True contractual liability of lodging businesses is therefore subject to the directive.   [46] RGBl. 1913 p. 49, p. 89.

[47] UNTS 572 p. 133; BGBl. 1972 II 1005.

[48] UNTS 310 p. 181. The Convention followed the model of the Warsaw Convention (see fn. 49), imposing liability up to a financial maximum on the basis of Poincaré Gold Francs, and was for that reason not ratified by many European nations, in particular the UK, France, Germany, The Netherlands, and the Scandinavian countries. In The Netherlands, following the crash of an El Al aircraft in de Bijlmer near Amsterdam, non-ratification of the Rome Convention resulted in the disaster being treated under common liability for fault rules, since at that time Dutch law did impose strict liability for accidents of that type. See Cleton, *NJB* 1993 pp. 621, 624–625.

[49] Convention of 12 Oct. 1929 for the Unification of Certain Rules Relating to International Carriage by Air (Convention pour l'unification de certains règles relatives au transport aerien international), LNTS 137 p. 11, RGBl. 1933 II 1039.

[50] *Protocol to amend the Convention for the Unification of Certain Rules Relating to International Carriage by Air signed at Warsaw on 12 Oct. 1929. Done at The Hague, on 28 Sep. 1955,* UNTS 478 p. 371; BGBl. 1958 II 291.

[51] Data according to reference directory B (see fn. 44) pp. 223–225.

[52] However, this is of some significance to the law of delict because Art. II of the Convention of Guadalajara expressly states that the executing carrier as well as the contractual carrier are liable under the Warsaw Convention. For further details see Lukoschek, *Anwendbares Deliktsrecht bei Flugzeugunglücken*, p. 12. On the legal nature of liability under the Warsaw Convention see id. pp. 13–15.

[53] *Convention, Supplementary to the Warsaw Convention, for the Unification of Certain Rules Relating to International Carriage by Air Performed by a Person Other than the Contracting Carrier. Signed at Guadalajara, on 18 Sep. 1961,* UNTS 500, p. 31; BGBl. 1963 II 1159.

(Art. 20) fault for bodily harm in accidents (including hijackings),[54] for demolition and loss[55] of goods, and for damage through delay (Art. 19). To the disadvantage of the carrier such liability carries a mandatory minimum (Art. 23). Contributory negligence on the part of the passenger, on the other hand, reduces the sum awarded (Art. 21). Liability is limited in its amount[56] if the carrier acted neither intentionally nor recklessly (Art. 25). The Convention is only applicable in cases of international carriage (defined in Art. 1 II).

As its name suggests, the *Geneva Convention of 19 May 1956 on the* **377** *Contract for the International Carriage of Goods by Road (CMR)*[57] mainly regulates questions of contract law. However, it is also of relevance to the law of delict. According to Art. 28 of the CMR,[58] grounds for excluding or limiting liability are common to contract and tort.[59] The authors of the Convention skirted round the problem of concurrent claims in contract and delict, and simply admitted the same defences for contractual and delictual liability.[60] The original Convention and Supplementary Protocol of 5 July 1978[61] have been ratified by all members of the European Union.[62]

A verbatim copy of Art. 28 CMR can be found in Arts. 46 s. 1 CIV[63]

---

[54] Correctly decided in Cass.civ. 16 Feb. 1982, *RFDA* 1982 p. 392; *Hussert* v. *Swissair* 351 F.Supp. p. 702; 485 F.2d p. 1240 (2nd Cir. 1973); and *Day* v. *TWA* 528 F.2d p. 31; 429 US p. 890. According to the Warsaw Convention 'an accident' includes the shooting down of a civil aviation aircraft by military aircraft: Cass.civ. 15 Dec. 1981, *RFDA* 1982 p. 215. The term 'accident' also includes a passenger falling on an uneven runway surface on his way to an aircraft: TS 17 Dec. 1990, *RAJ* 1990 no. 10282 p. 13170.

[55] For more details on the term 'loss' under the Warsaw Convention see BGH 22 Apr. 1982, BGHZ 84 p. 101.

[56] Among the member states which are signatories to the Treaty, the relevant sums vary drastically. In addition, some of them still operate with Poincaré Francs, whereas others use the SDRs (Special Drawing Rights) of the International Monetary Fund. For a general outlook see Giemulla/Schmid, *Warschauer Abkommen*, nos. 14–20.

[57] *Convention relative au contrat de transport international de marchandises par route*, UNTS 399 p. 189; BGBl. 1961 II 1119.

[58] '(1) In cases where, under the law applicable, loss, damage, or delay arising out of carriage under this Convention gives rise to an extra-contractual claim, the carrier may avail himself of the provisions of this Convention which exclude his liability or which fix or limit the compensation due. (2) In cases where the extra-contractual liability for loss, damage, or delay of one of the persons for whom the carrier is responsible under the terms of Article 3 is in issue, such person may also avail himself of the provisions of this Convention which exclude the liability of the carrier or which fix or limit the compensation due.'

[59] Art. 28 concerns only damage to the transported goods, not damage to other property, e.g. to the place of unloading through contaminating a tank with chemicals: HR 15 Apr. 1994, *RvdW* 1994 no. 90.　　　　[60] Haak, *Aansprakelijkheid van de vervoerder*, p. 269.

[61] BGBl. 1980 II 721, 723.　　　[62] Reference directory B p. 325 (fn. 44 above).

[63] *Convention internationale concernant le transport des voyageurs et des bagages par chemins de fer*; International Convention of 7 Feb. 1970 on Railway Transport of Passengers and Luggage, BGBl. 1974 II 359.

and 51 s. 1 CIM,[64] now Annexes A and B of the *Convention of 9 May 1980 on International Railway Traffic (COTIF).*[65] The maritime *Convention of 19 November 1976 on Limitation of Liability for Maritime Claims,*[66] and the *Strasbourg Convention of 4 November 1988 on Limitation of Liability for Inland Navigation (CLNI),*[67] conceived especially for the Rhine and the Mosel, point in a similar direction. The latter, not yet in force, provides in Arts. 11 ff. for the establishment of a compensation fund. Although the *Brussels International Convention on Tourist Travel Contracts*, of which Art. 15 provides for presumed but rebuttable fault where a duty of care has not been complied with, is in force. However, within Europe it is binding only on Belgium and Italy, and only as regards Argentina, Benin, Cameroon, Taiwan, and Togo.[68] The value of such conventions is questionable.

378   The situation is altogether different with the *European Convention of 20 April 1959 on Compulsory Insurance against Civil Liability in Respect of Motor Vehicles.*[69] Since this does not touch on substantive third-party liability law[70] it is of limited significance for the law of delict. Furthermore, it was only ratified by Austria, Denmark, Germany, Greece, Norway, and Sweden.[71] It was nevertheless the first international instrument to introduce compulsory third-party liability insurance together with an *action directe*[72] for road traffic accident victims (Art. 1 I). In addition it paved the way for the introduction of compensation funds, so that in

---

[64] *Convention internationale concernant le transport des marchandises par chemins de fer* of 7 Feb. 1970; BGBl. 1974 II 381. The text reads in each case (this author's translation): 'In all cases to which the standard provisions apply, a claim for damages against the railway, regardless of the cause of action, can only be made with respect to the preconditions and limitations made therein.'

[65] *Convention relative aux transports internationaux ferroviaires*, BGBl. 1985 II 130.

[66] BGBl. 1986 II 786; BT-Drucks. 10/3553.

[67] Text (in Dutch/French) in Trb. 1989 p. 43, and (in German) in *TranspR* 1989 p. 36.

[68] Text (in French) in BT-Drucks. 8/786 p. 10; details in Pellet, *Reisevertragliche Gewährleistung*, pp. 141–145.   [69] UNTS 720 p. 119; BGBl. 1965 II 281.

[70] The *European Convention of 14 May 1973 on Civil Liability for Damages caused by Motor Vehicles* (European Treaty Series no. 79), however, did focus on road traffic liability. In May 1973 it was submitted for signature. It was signed, but not ratified, by Germany, Norway, and Switzerland (BT-Drucks. 8/108 pp. 5, 8). As ratification by a minimum of 3 parties was necessary, it was never enforced. The Convention would have excluded 'Acts of God' as a defence against liability, and extended the scope of strict liability of the keeper of the vehicle (Arts. 8 and 10 s. 1: strict liability was to have extended to the driver and passengers transported free of charge. However, as far as the driver was concerned, reservations could have been made, Arts. 8 and 10 s. 2). Contributory negligence (Art. 5) was admitted as a defence. However, the maximum limit of liability for financial loss would have remained subject to national legislation, as would the question of whether or not to award damages for non-pecuniary loss (Art. 12 I lit. a). For an insight into the causes of the failure of this convention see Renger, *VersR* 1992 p. 653.

[71] Reference directory B (fn. 44 above) p. 371.

[72] Annex I, Art. 6 I provides that an injured person has a personal claim against the insurer. Cf. the reservation clause in Art. 3 I of the Convention in conjunction with its Annex II, para. 12.

cases of personal injury in which the liability of another person is established, the injured person can gain compensation even where the duty to insure has not been complied with or the person liable could not be identified (Art. 9 I). Mirroring developments in the field of product liability, the Convention was, however, only a first step towards the subsequent *Second Council Directive*[73] *84/5/EEC of 30 December 1983 on the Approximation of the Laws of the Member States Relating to Insurance against Civil Liability in Respect of the Use of Motor Vehicles.*[74] This forced *all* states of the European Union to introduce compulsory third-party liability insurance for damage to property (Art. 1 I),[75] to provide a minimum level of cover (Art. 1 II),[76] and to establish a body to compensate for personal injury or damage to property caused by an unidentified or uninsured vehicle, within the limits of the duty to insure, see Art. 1 IV.[77] In contrast to the Convention of the Council of Europe,[78] under the Directive insurance against liability for personal injury may no longer exclude family members (Art. 3). The Directive, which became binding on 1 January 1989 (Art. 5 II), was less comprehensive than the Convention as it did not require national legislations to introduce an *action directe*.[79] Particularly in Spain, the Second Directive on third-party liability insurance caused lasting changes on a national level.[80]

2. UNIFICATION OF THE LAW ON LIABILITY FOR DAMAGE TO THE ENVIRONMENT

a. Conventions in Force

The protection of the environment, rather than protection for travellers   **379** and traffic, has now moved into the limelight of internationally co-ordinated legislation on the law of delict.[81] Its beginning was marked

---

[73] *(First) Dir. 72/166/EEC of 24 Apr. 1972 on the Approximation of the Laws of Member States Relating to Insurance against Civil Liability in Respect of the Use of Motor Vehicles, and to the Enforcement of the Obligation to Insure Against Such Liability* (OJ L 103 2.5.1972, p. 1 with amendment by Dir. 72/430/EEC of 19 Dec. 1972, OJ L 291 of 28.12.1972, p. 162) predominantly concerned the introduction of compulsory third-party liability insurance for personal injury, as well as ending checks by member states as to whether vehicles of one EU member state entering another carry the 'green card' (definition in Art. 1 para 5, see fn. 40 above). On the latest developments see also no. 385 below.   [74] OJ L 8 11.1.1984, p. 17.

[75] Even the UK, which had no previous duty to insure for damage to property, introduced such a duty in 1988: sec. 143 Road Traffic Act 1988 (1988 c. 52).

[76] Transition periods are provided for in Art. 5 III, according to which, e.g. the latest date for Greece to lift its minimum level of cover to the EU standard was not until 31 Dec. 1995.

[77] Such compensation funds have been established by all EU member states; see the national reports in v. Bar (ed.), *DeliktsR in Europa.*   [78] Annex I, Art. 4 I.

[79] In England even today under the Third Parties (Rights Against Insurers) Act 1930 (c. 25) an *action directe* can only be pursued in England if the tortfeasor has gone into bankruptcy (sec. 1).   [80] v. Bar (-Santdiumenge), *DeliktsR in Europa, Spanien*, p. 37.

[81] Extensive documentation on this issue in Kwiatkowska/Sooms, *Transboundary Movements and Disposal of Hazardous Wastes in International Law* (1993).

by three related conventions on liability in the field of nuclear energy, namely:

- the *Paris Convention of 29 July 1960 on Third Party Liability in the Field of Nuclear Energy and Additional Protocol of 28 January 1964,*[82] a *Brussels Supplementary Convention of 31 January 1963,*[83] and two further *Protocols of 16 November 1982;*[84]
- the *Convention of 25 May 1962 on the Liability of Operators of Nuclear Ships and Additional Protocols;*[85] and
- the *Convention of 17 December 1971 on Civil Liability During the Transport of Nuclear Material at Sea.*[86]

The Paris and Brussels Conventions have been ratified by all EU member states except Austria, Ireland, and Luxembourg, and since Turkey is the only non-EU signatory[87] these Treaties can be seen as common Community law. The Paris and Brussels Conventions deal mainly with the strict liability of the nuclear plant operator, which, as in other areas, is limited in its level of cover.

380   However, the biggest success of environmental liability law so far is not in the field of atomic energy law but in that of liability and compensation for *oil pollution at sea.* The basis of such liability was set out in the *International Convention of 29 November 1969 on Civil Liability for Oil Pollution Damage*[88] after the accident involving the *Torrey Canyon* in the English Channel. The Convention has been ratified by more than seventy-five states. Since 1969 it has been updated by a number of Protocols,[89] and is now simply titled 'Liability Convention of 1984'. Under the Convention the owner of a ship carrying a bulk cargo of oil is liable irrespective of fault (Art. III subs. 1) and to the exclusion of all others (Art. III subs. 4). Maximum levels of liability are calculated according to the tonnage of the ship, and expressed in Gold Francs (as defined in Art. V s. 9).[90] The owner can rely on these if he personally is not at fault (Art. V subs. 2) and if he has demonstrated his financial

---

[82] UNTS 956 p. 251; BGBl. 1975 II, 959, 1007 (Convention of 1960 and Additional Protocol).

[83] BGBl. 1975 II 992, 1021. The latest version of both Conventions is published in BGBl. 1985 II 963.   [84] BGBl. 1985 II 690.

[85] BGBl. 1975 II 977.   [86] BGBl. 1975 II 957, 1026.

[87] Reference directory B (fn. 44 above) p. 381.

[88] UNTS 973; BGBl. 1975 II, 301, 305; Trb. 1970 p. 196.

[89] Of 19 Nov. 1976 (BGBl. 1980 II 724); of 25 May 1984 (BGBl. 1988 II 705; not yet enforced) and of 27 Nov. 1992 (not yet enforced; text in *UnifLRev* 1992 II pp. 61–92 and in BT-Drucks. 12/6364 *et al.*) Cf. on the Protocol of 27 Nov. 1992 esp. Bierbooms/Brans, *NJB* 1993 pp. 85–91; and Renger, *TranspR* 1993 pp. 132–135. Germany ratified it with the Act of 25 July 1994 (BGBl. 1994 II 1150): for more details see Borchmann, *NJW* 1995 pp. 2956, 2961.

[90] Meanwhile they have been replaced by the Special Drawing Rights (SDRs) of the International Monetary Fund.

means to meet the liability (Art. V subs. 3 and Art. VII subs. 1). Those who have suffered loss have the right of *action directe* against the insurer (Art. VII subs. 8). Should the liability ceiling be exceeded, or the owner not have adequate financial capacity, or a ground for exclusion of liability under the Convention apply (e.g. intent of a third party to cause damage; as a result of war), the fund established by the *International Convention of 18 December 1971 on the Establishment of an International Fund for Compensation for Oil Pollution Damage*[91] will provide cover to a limited maximum amount. This Treaty, now simply called the Fund Convention of 1984, has also been subject to numerous supplementary protocols.[92] Due to the financial burdens it imposes, the number of signatories to the Fund Convention has remained small. In the EU, for example, Austria, Belgium, and Ireland have not yet signed it. Nonetheless, the overall system has recently been rightly celebrated as the 'the only functioning international liability regime for damage to the environment'.[93]

In addition, the liability provisions of Art. 10 of the *London Convention of 29 December 1972 on the Prevention of Marine Pollution by Dumping of Wastes and other Matter*[94] as well as Art. 12 of the *Barcelona Convention of 1976 for the Protection of the Mediterranean Sea against Pollution*[95] also serve to protect the marine environment. Like the latter, the *Convention of 20 March 1974 on the Protection of the Marine Environment of the Baltic Sea Area*[96] (amended on 22 April 1991)[97] also focuses on a specific sea region.

b. Conventions not yet in Force

Two Conventions, although not yet in force, are casting their shadows **381** before them. They are the *Convention of 1 February 1990 on Civil Liability for Damage Caused During Carriage of Dangerous Goods by Road, Rail, and Inland Navigation*,[98] developed within the framework of the Inland

---

[91] BGBl. 1975 II 301, 320.

[92] Of 19 Nov. 1976 (BGBl. 1980 II 721, 729), of 25 May 1984 (BGBl. 1988 II 705, 724) and of 27 Nov. 1992 (*UniflRev* 1992 II pp. 93–135; BT-Drucks. 12/6364; the latter two Protocols have not yet been enforced).　　　　　　　　　　　[93] Renger, *TranspR* 1993 pp. 132, 135.

[94] BGBl. 1977 II 180. The Convention has been enforced in all Union member states with direct access to the sea.

[95] The (English) text is published in BT-Drucks. 7/5223 pp. 4–9. The Convention merely required that 'the Contracting Parties undertake to co-operate as soon as possible in the formulation and adoption of appropriate procedures for the determination of liability and compensation for damage resulting from the pollution of the marine environment' (Art. 12).

[96] OJ L 73 16.3.1994, p. 2; BGBl. 1992 II 502. The German ratifying Act of 23 Aug. 1994 is in BGBl. 1994 II 1355; see also Borchmann, *NJW* 1995 pp. 2956, 2963.

[97] BGBl. 1979 II 1229.

[98] Text (in English) in *TranspR* 1990 pp. 83–88; details (and French text) in, *inter alia*, Evans, *Rev.dr.uniforme* 1991 pp. 77–183.

Waterways Committee of the UN Economic Commission for Europe (ECE), and the *European (Lugano) Convention of 21 June 1993 on Civil Liability for Damage Resulting from Activities Dangerous to the Environment.*[99]

Further Conventions not yet enforced are: the *Basle Convention of 22 March 1989 on the Control of Transboundary Movements of Hazardous Wastes and their Disposal*[100] which promotes a special liability rule in Art. 12; two Conventions of the UN ECE: the *Convention of 17 March 1992 on the Protection and Use of Transboundary Watercourses and International Lakes* (Art. 7),[101] and the *Convention on Transboundary Effects of Industrial Wastes* (Art. 13).[102] The Hague Conference on Private International Law may also produce a convention which, in addition to conflict of laws, touches on problems of substantive liability law.[103]

382   The main focus of the ECE Convention of 1 February 1990, which deals only with non-contractual liability law (Art. 3), is once again the introduction of strict liability (Art. 5 I), limited in its amount (Art. 9), and falling on the carrier (Art. 5 VII). Liability is unlimited if the carrier or one of his staff acted intentionally or recklessly (Art. 10). Compulsory third-party insurance (Art. 13) and the right of *action directe* (Art. 15 I) have been planned. Liability is excluded if damage occurred as a result of war or similar events, or if 'the damage was wholly caused by an act or omission with the intent to cause damage by a third party' (Art. 5 IV lit. a and b). Hence the Convention has been designed using the same well established patterns as are found in environmental liability provisions of international uniform law.

383   While the ECE Convention of 1 February 1990 needs ratification by five states (Art. 23 I), the *Lugano Convention of the Council of Europe* requires only three (Art. 32 III). It is not clear whether this will ever be achieved.[104]

---

[99] Fn. 7 above. For a detailed discussion see de Sadeleer, *RGAR* 1994 no. 12367.
[100] BGBl. 1994 II 2704 (text in English, French, and German)
[101] Text in, *inter alia*, BT-Drucks. 12/7190 p. 7.
[102] No source can be given. However, according to the German Ministry of Justice, Art. 13 of the draft contains a provision corresponding to Art. 12 of the Basle Convention, and the Convention for the Protection of Transboundary Waterways respectively, according to which the contracting states support suitable international attempts to determine provisions, criteria, and procedures in the field of liability. No 'ready-to-use' basis for a claim yet exists.
[103] The delegates of those governments represented at the 17th Conference at The Hague decided in May 1993 'to include in the Agenda for the work programme of the Conference the question of the determination of the law applicable, and possibly questions arising from the conflicts of jurisdictions, in respect of civil liability for environmental damage' (Final Act of the 17th Session, The Hague, 29th May 1993, p. 17). Yet, should such a convention emerge, it is possible that it will include a statement concerning substantive liability law: see v. Bar (ed.), *Auf dem Wege zu einer Konvention über das Internationale Umwelthaftungsrecht*, 2 vols. (1995).
[104] Germany will probably not sign the Convention (information from the German Ministry of Justice), whereas in The Netherlands, whose preliminary national work influenced the Convention (de Boer, *NJB* 1993 pp. 225–231; Spier/Sterk, *NJB* 1992 pp. 232–233) ratification is underway (see the note in *NJB* 1993 p. 976).

The European Community can itself become a contracting party (Art. 32 I); indeed its Council granted the Commission a mandate for negotiations on this Convention on 26 March 1992.[105] The Council of Europe Convention breaks new ground in that provisions governing practically the entire field of environmental liability law (not limited to transboundary issues) have been constituted for the first time.[106] It covers personal injury, damage to property, and expenses for measures of reinstatement (Art. 2 VII), introduces duties to furnish members of the public with information (Arts. 13–16), and provides for compulsory third-party insurance, or similar financial safeguards, against the liability introduced by the Convention. This liability is extensive: Art. 6 I of the Convention imposes a strict liability on the 'operator in respect of a dangerous activity. . . for the damage caused by the activity'. Although it is nowadays common practice to dispense with the fault principle, the liability imposed by Art. 6 threatens to become too powerful a weapon, since it relies to a large extent on undefined legal terms. According to the Convention 'dangerous activities' (complete definition in Art. 2 I lit. a–d) are *inter alia* 'the production, handling, storage, use or discharge of one or more dangerous substances or any operation of a similar nature with such substances' (lit. a). 'Dangerous substances' are 'substances or preparations which have properties which constitute a significant risk for man, the environment, or property' (Art. 2 II lit. a). Finally, it defines 'environment' as: 'natural resources, both abiotic and biotic, such as air, water, soil, fauna and flora and the interaction between the same factors; property which forms part of the cultural heritage; and characteristic aspects of the landscape' (Art. 2 X).

Even leaving aside the question of whether a balanced legal policy can support such a regulation (for industrial policy it looks like an unconditional surrender!) it will 'technically' become difficult to achieve uniformity between the judicial decisions in the contracting countries without the existence of a supranational court. Although many conventions on the environment impose liability on plant operators such that national law may not make any other person liable for negligence, no such provisions have been made here. The Lugano Convention deals *exclusively* with the plant operator. However, the strict liability of the plant operator ceases after proper delivery to a waste disposal site, at which point the site operator becomes exclusively liable (Art. 7 II). The provisions on contributory negligence by the plaintiff 'or a person for whom

---

[105] Mandate of the Commission for negotiations on an International Convention on Civil Liability Resulting from Activities Dangerous to the Environment (Council of Europe), SEK (91) 750 final.
[106] Its relationship to other treaties concerning environmental law is dealt with in Art. 25 I Lugano Convention; Art. 25 II tackles its relationship with Community law (see. fn. 7 above).

he is responsible under internal law' (Art. 9) are new, as is the provision headed 'Causality' (Art. 10). Causation is measured in terms of probability, the court having to 'take due account of the increased danger of causing such damage inherent in the dangerous activity'. Should the causal link not be known, a number of plant operators will share joint and several liability (Art. 6 II and III). Only an operator who can prove that only a specific part of the total damage was caused by him escapes this joint and several liability. It is still unclear whether the European insurance market can handle such a rigid liability system.[107]

III. THE EUROPEAN UNION AND ITS DIRECTIVES: ESTABLISHED LAW, PROPOSALS, AND PROJECTS

1. GENERAL OUTLOOK ON THE CURRENT STATE OF THE LEGISLATIVE APPROXIMATION OF LAWS IN THE EUROPEAN UNION

384 The legislative approximation of laws within the EU comprises all topics dealt with in the international unification of laws except transport law. Although the EU is primarily concerned with consumer protection, it also deals with the other two 'big' issues of international legal policy: road traffic accidents and environmental liability.

a. Road Traffic Accidents

385 As for the law of *motor vehicle liability insurance*, the key dates of relevant Community provisions are listed above, in connection with the Second Liability Insurance Directive.[108] The *Third Council Directive of 14 May 1990 on the Approximation of the Laws of the Member States Relating to Insurance against Civil Liability in Respect of the Use of Motor Vehicles*[109] achieved three clarifications: first, compulsory liability insurance must cover personal injuries of all passengers, excluding the driver (Art. 1); secondly, such insurance must cover the entire area of the Community

---

[107] The *Green Book* of the Commission of the European Communities (Doc. Com [93] 47 final) admits on pp. 14–16 that many insurance companies are still inexperienced as far as environmental liability is concerned, nor do they have the staff and technology at their disposal to design adequate policies. Bocken, in *Les assurances de l'entreprise* II pp. 239–280, discusses this question in great detail; see also Snijder, *A&V* 1993 pp. 1, 5, who discusses similar issues within Dutch national law. He feels that the Dutch provisions would make adequate insurance possible.   [108] No. 378 above.
[109] 90/232/EEC; OJ L 129 19.5.1990, p. 33.

with a single premium (Art. 2 I); and thirdly, the guarantee fund must operate whether or not the injured party can demonstrate that the person liable is unable or refuses to make payment (Art. 3). A Directive of 8 November 1990[110] decided that companies offering motor vehicle liability insurance 'through an establishment situated in a Member State' must contribute to the guarantee fund of that member state (Art. 6).

Little has been heard of the harmonization of *substantive liability for* **386** *road traffic accidents* since the aforementioned 1973 initiative of the CE[111] failed. An international working party (led by the presiding judge at the Paris *Cour d'appel*, Dessertine) considered this issue[112] again some years ago, and even produced a draft text[113] (which was chiefly rejected by the German members); but for the time being it does not look as if the Commission is at all interested in adopting it. The proposal deals with accident victims who are nationals of, or habitually reside in, other EU member states. National legislation would provide that each vehicle is to be covered by a single insurance policy protecting the car and its passengers. Consequently, passengers would claim damages only under the policy of the car in which they were travelling. Victims other than passengers (i.e. cyclists and pedestrians) would also have a claim against the insurer of the car involved. It is clear that these provisions do not reflect conventional liability law; instead the authors of the draft have attempted to establish a no-fault insurance scheme, independent of liability law.[114] In this author's opinion these proposals stand no chance of success in the foreseeable future.

b. Environmental Liability Law

At present it is impossible to say if (and when) the European Union will **387** start legislating in the field of *environmental liability law*. The Council explicitly instructed itself over a decade ago to determine by 30 September 1988 the conditions under which civil liability should attach to a waste producer in cases of damage, and to list all persons who could be

---

[110] *Council Dir. of 8 Nov. 1990 amending, particularly as regards motor vehicle liability insurance, Dir. 73/239/EEC and Dir. 88/357/EEC which concern the co-ordination of laws, regulations and administrative provisions relating to direct insurance other than life assurance (90/618/EEC), OJ L 330 29.11.1990 p. 44.* [111] Fn. 70 above.
[112] Cf. Dessertine, *L'évaluation du préjudice corporel dans les pays de la CEE* (Paris 1990); and the *Farewell Lecture* of Baron van Wassenaer (fn. 113).
[113] Published (in English) in: Baron van Wassenaer van Catwijck, *Naar een Europees verkeersschaderecht*, pp. 20–22. The working party assumes that Art. 100a EEC provides a sufficient basis for such a directive.
[114] It is the author's considered opinion that this system could only work satisfactorily if the personal liability of the keeper and/or driver of the car were abolished. However, the draft makes no mention of this point.

made liable for particular damage.[115] Furthermore, in a 1986 Resolution the Council instructed the Commission for Water Pollution to examine this problem,[116] and the European Parliament ordered the Commission to propose a strict liability regime for all high-risk chemical operations.[117] In the same year Art. 130r II s. 2 Treaty of Rome became law. Thus the 'polluter pays' principle which had already been incorporated in the Directives on Waste,[118] Waste Oils,[119] and Toxic and Dangerous Waste,[120] attained constitutional status within the Community. The 1987 EC action programme for the protection of the environment reasserted the need for approximation of civil environmental liability.[121] The legal policy of the Community regarding this issue has been established for some time, as have proposals for its execution. The starting point was the *proposal for a Council Directive on Civil Liability for Damage Caused by Waste*[122] submitted by the Commission on 1 September 1989. Roughly two years later, on 28 June 1991, the Commission proposed an amendment[123] and attached a *Proposal for a Council Directive on the Landfill of Waste.*[124] Art. 14 of the latter document states that the operator of a site shall be strictly liable for all damage to and impairment of the environment arising from waste storage.

388   The (amended) Waste Directive proposal is similarly based on the no-fault liability of the waste producer.[125] Under this proposal, based on terms which are already international standards, the producer escapes liability only in cases of interference by a third party with intent to cause damage, or 'if the damage or injury to the environment results from *force majeure* as defined in Community law' (Art. 6). In cases of contributory negligence liability can be reduced (to nil if appropriate) (Art. 7 II). Not only are personal injury and damage to property covered (Art. 2 I lit. c),

---

[115] See Art. 11 III of the *Council Dir. of 6 Dec. 1984 on Monitoring and Inspection within the Community of Transboundary Transportation of Hazardous Materials,* 84/631/EEC, OJ L 326 13.12.1984 p. 31.   [116] Bull.EC 11–1986, no. 2.1.146.

[117] OJ C 7 12.1.1987, p. 116.

[118] Council Dir. on Waste 75/442/EEC of 25 July 1975, OJ L 194 25.7.1975, p. 39.

[119] Council Dir. on the Disposal of Waste Oils 75/439/EEC of 16 June 1975, OJ L 194 25.7.1975, p. 23.

[120] Council Dir. on Toxic and Dangerous Waste 78/319/EEC of 20 Mar. 1978, OJ L 326 13.12.1984, p. 31.

[121] OJ C 328 7.12.1987, p. 6. Cf. in this context Council Resolution of 17 May 1977, OJ no. C 139 of 13 June 1977, p. 1.   [122] OJ C 251 4.10.1989, p. 3.

[123] OJ C 192 23.7.1991, p. 6. Cf. on this issue the Parliament declaration, OJ C 324 24.12.1990, p. 257.

[124] OJ C 190 22.7.1991, p. 1. *Council Dir. 89/428/EEC of 21 June 1989 on Procedures for Harmonizing the Programmes for the Reduction and Eventual Elimination of Pollution Caused by Waste of the Titanium Dioxide Industry* (OJ L 201 14.7.1989, p. 56) was declared null and void in the *Titanium Dioxide* ECJ ruling of 11 June 1991, Case no. C-300/89, JZ 1992 p. 578. A new Dir. 92/112/EEC of 15 Dec. 1992 with the same name is found in OJ L 409 31.12.1992, p. 11.

[125] The relationship between the liability of the producer and persons subsequently in control of the waste is governed by Art. 7 Waste Directive.

but liablity extends to environmental damage, defined in Art. 2 I lit. d as every 'significant and persistent interference in the environment caused by a modification of the physical, chemical, or biological conditions of water, soil, and/or air'. This is especially relevant to the provisions on measures of reinstatement, the costs of which can be considerable. The Directive would allow such measures to be carried out by the relevant authority on behalf of the tortfeasor without first obtaining authority, the tortfeasor remaining liable for the cost. Furthermore, environmental organizations would be given standing to insist upon such action (Art. 4 III in conjunction with Art. 4 I lit. b [3]). The cornerstone of this liability regime is the definition of the term 'waste'. It is unusually broad. Hence the amended version of the proposal attempts, as did the original,[126] comprehensive regulation of emissions of all kinds. Council Directive 75/442/EEC[127] already operated with a General Clause (Art. 1) defines waste as: 'any substance or object which the holder disposes of or is required to dispose of pursuant to the provisions of national law in force'. Art. 2 I lit. b of the amended Waste Directive adopts this definition.

The combination of the proposed Waste Directive and the Lugano **389**
Convention of the CE[128] would impose enormously extended liability and could create serious problems for industry.[129] Furthermore, such an extensive liability regime is clearly only feasible if covered by insurance, hence Art. 11 I calls for insurance or equivalent financial guarantee. Whether the European insurance industry could afford to offer such cover is by no means certain. For this reason, despite pressure to advance, the European Commission has been forced to delay for a time. The proposed Council Directive was not withdrawn, but was *de facto* replaced by a *Green Book*[130] listing questions still to be addressed, and proposing and promising further investigations. Thus the approximation of environmental liability law within the European Union has been put back on ice for the foreseeable future.

---

[126] The original draft Waste Directive (see fn. 122 above) referred only to 'Art. 1' of Dir. 75/442/EEC (see fn. 118 above) to define waste; the amended draft, however, identifies as waste for its purposes (in Art. 2 I lit. b) all materials or objects 'defined as waste in Council Directive 75/442/EEC'.   [127] See fn. 118.

[128] Before nos. 381 and 383 above.

[129] Cf. the in-depth analysis by Pagh, *J* 1991 pp. 267–280; *UfR* 1991 B pp. 121, 124–127; and *UfR* 1994 B pp. 27–36; Sterk, *WPNR* 1991 no. 5991; Bierbooms/Brans, *NJB* 1993 pp. 85, 88–91; Lord Slynn of Hadley, *J.Environ.L.* 5 (1993) pp. 225–231; v. Kempis, *Eur.Transp.L.* 26 (1991) pp. 155–160; Giampietro, *Riv.dir.eur.* 1992 pp. 813–826; and Brüggemeier, *FS Jahr* pp. 23, 242–250.

[130] Com. (93) 47 final; OJ C 149 29.5.1993, p 12. Cf. the note in *A&V* 1993 p. 13; Hulst/Klinge van Rooij, *PHI* 1994 pp. 108–120; and Larroumet, *D.* 1994 *Chron.* pp. 101–107.

c. Consumer Protection Law

390 Consumer protection directives have been established as Community law for some time. Two of these also affect non-contractual liability law: *Council Directive 90/314/EEC of 13 June 1990 on Package Travel, Package Holidays, and Package Tours*[131] and *Council Directive 93/13/EEC of 5 April 1993 on Unfair Terms in Consumer Contracts.*[132] According to Art. 10 I s. 2 of the latter, its provisions apply to all contracts entered into after 31 December 1994.[133] The Package Tours Directive should have been implemented on 1 January 1993 (Art. 9 I s. 1), but Germany only fulfilled this obligation in April 1994.[134] Both Directives are significant for the law of delict in that they prohibit disclaimers of liability for personal injury. Although they show differences of detail, these appear to be coincidental rather than deliberate. For example, the Package Tours Directive does not differentiate between specific individual agreements and general terms and conditions, whereas the Directive on Unfair Terms regulates only contract clauses which have not been negotiated individually (Art. 3 I). In another example, the Directive on Unfair Terms states that a contractual term which excludes or limits 'the legal liability of a seller or supplier' may be declared unfair, and therefore void 'in the event of the death of a consumer or personal injury to the latter resulting from an act or omission of that seller or supplier' (Annex no. 1 lit. a in conjunction with Art. 3 III). Yet the Package Tours Directive permits only 'damage other than personal injury' to be excluded from liability (Art. 5 II, subs.

[131] OJ L 158 23.6.1990, p. 59; German text also in *EuZW* 1990 p. 413. See on this Directive *inter alia* Broekema-Engelen/Cleyndert/Maters, *NJB* 1993 pp. 157–162; Tonner, *EuZW* 1990 pp. 409–413.

[132] OJ L 95 21.4.1993, p. 29; German text also in *EuZW* 1993 p. 352, *NJW* 1993 p. 1838 and *EWS* 1993 p. 178. Of those discussing this Directive, see esp. Damm, *JZ* 1994 pp. 161–168; Eckert, *WM* 1993 pp. 1070–1078; van Erp, *WPNR* 1993 no. 6079; Heinrichs, *NJW* 1993 pp. 1817–1822; Jongeneel/Wessels, *NJB* 1993 pp. 897–899; Hondius, *NTBR* 1993 pp. 108–112 and id., 7 (1994) *Journal of Contract Law* pp. 34–52.

[133] In Belgium the Directive was implemented by statute dated 12 June 1991 (Monit. belge, 6 Aug. 1991 p. 17209), i.e. before the Directive was enforced. The EU has (as of Jan. 1996) been informed of 5 further implementations: *Celex* Doc. no. 793 L 0013.

[134] BGBl 1994 I 1322. *Denmark* incorporated it with the *Lov om pakkerejser* (statute No. 472 of 30 June 1993, *Lovtidende* A 1993 p. 2499). For details see Storm, *UfR* 1992 B pp. 313–320; and Linkis/Hjortnæs *J* 1994 pp. 112–123. The *Dutch* implementing statute of 24 Dec. 1992 (Stb. 1992 no. 689), enforced on 27 Jan. 1993 (Stb. 1993 no. 43, cf. the note in *NJB* 1993 p. 217), incorporated the text of the Dir. in Arts. 7: 500 ff. BW; the terms prohibiting liability disclaimers can be found in Art. 7: 508 I BW (for details see Broekema-Engelen/Cleyndert/Maters [fn. 131] p. 162). In *England*, according to sec. 2(1) of the Unfair Contract Terms Act (c. 50) it has for many years been impossible to exclude liability for personal injury caused by negligence. The Directive was implemented through The Package Travel, Package Holidays, and Package Tours Reg. 1992 (Statutory Instruments 1992). *France* implemented it with statute No. 92/645 of 13 July 1992 (JO of 14 July 1992, p. 9457), *Portugal* with *Decreto Lei* ('decree statute') No. 198/93 of 27 May 1993 (Diário Rep., 27 May 1993 p. 2904), and *Belgium* with a statute dated 16 Feb. 1994 (Monit. belge, 1 Apr. 1994).

4). The overlooking of loss of life in these provisions is a blunder unfortunately typical of European legislators.[135]

391 Although these two prohibitions against disclaimers have already become established law, the approximation of all law governing professional services, probably the most ambitious EU project to date, shares the fate of environmental liability law. Like the proposed Waste Directive, the *proposal of the Commission for a Council Directive on the Liability of Suppliers of Services*[136] has been dropped. After criticism in legal publications,[137] a massive veto on the part of all concerned parties, and protests from the respective Committees in the European Parliament[138] the Commission withdrew the proposal.[139] Even before this it had been decided that medical practice and the construction industry[140] would be exempt from this directive.[141]

392 The Commission originally planned simply to apply the basic provisions of the Product Liability Directive to the entire service sector.[142] However, due to strong resistance they were forced at an early stage[143] to replace the planned strict liability with liability for presumed but rebuttable, fault (Art. 1 II of the proposal for the Services Directive). Protected interests were to be health, bodily integrity, and moveable property 'including the persons or property which were the object of the service' (Art. 1 I). Thus it incorporated claims based on contract as well as delict. Service was defined in Art. 2 I as 'any transaction carried out on a commercial basis or by way of public service and in an independent manner, whether or not in return for payment, which does not have as its direct and exclusive object the manufacture of moveable property or the transfer of rights or intellectual property rights'. Damage

---

[135] See also nos. 396 ff. below.

[136] Com. (90) 482 final of Dec. 20 1990; OJ C 12 18.1.1991, p. 8.

[137] Authors from across the EU united in a publication edited by Deutsch/Taupitz, *Haftung der Dienstleistungsberufe*. See from the predominantly critical literature also, *inter alia*: Alpa, *Giur.it.* 1990, IV, cols. 177–182; De Boeck, *RW* 1993–94 pp. 585–612; Castronovo, *Foro.it.* 1994, V, cols. 273–285; Deutsch, *KF* 1992 pp. 4–14; Faure, *A&V* 1994 pp. 33–41; Frietsch, *DB* 1992 pp. 929–936; Gaidzik, *JR* 1992 pp. 323–328; Heinemann, *ZIP* 1991 pp. 1193–1204; Piper, *TranspR* 1992 pp. 92–95; Romeo Casabona, *La Ley* 1993 (4) pp. 979–994; Spier, *NJB* 1991 pp. 663–665; Tuerlinckx, in: Storme (ed.), *Recht halen uit aansprakelijkheid*, pp. 357–394 and Walker/Lohkemper, *RdA* 1994 pp. 105–111; Fraselle, *La responsabilité du prestataire de service* (Louvain-la-Neuve 1992) has devoted an entire monograph to the proposed directive.

[138] See Braun-Moser MEP in a query put to the Commission: OJ 1992 C 317 p. 35 = *ZEuP* 1993 p. 383.   [139] For details see van Dam, *A&V* 1994 pp. 113–118.

[140] Cf. the query of the MEP Banotti, OJ C 309 p. 22 = *ZEuP* 1993 p. 381.

[141] Answer of the Commission to the query of Braun-Moser MEP (fn. 138).

[142] See on this early preliminary draft Capponi, *Riv.Dir.Com.* 1989, I, p. 567, pp. 587–589; Deutsch, *ZRP* 1990 pp. 454–455; Spier/Sterk, *NJB* 1990 pp. 1517–1523 (with the text of the latest *Avant-projet* on pp. 1522–1523).

[143] Cf. COM/90/482 final; SYN 308 of 20 Dec. 1990 pp. 14–15 ; and Joerges/Brüggemeier in Müller-Graff (ed.), *Gemeinsames Privatrecht in der EG*, pp. 233, 268.

(defined in Art. 4) and causation were to be proved by the injured party (Art. 5); contributory negligence on his part or on the part of a person for whom he is liable could be taken into account in reducing or excluding a claim (Art 6). However, the authors were never able to produce a convincing argument for a general reversal of the burden of proof for fault in non-contractual matters. Largely as a consequence of this, the proposal was abandoned.

393   Notwithstanding some unfortunate inadequacies regarding both implementation[144] and scope for national variations, permitted under Arts. 15 and 16,[145] *Council Directive 85/374/EEC of 25 July 1985 on the Approximation of the Laws, Regulations, and Administrative Provisions of the Member States Concerning Liability for Defective Products*[146] is still the European Union's most successful attempt at the approximation of liability law within its boundaries. Some years later it was rounded off by *Council Directive 92/59/EEC of 29 June 1992 on General Product Safety.*[147] The most significant provisions of the *Product Liability Directive* have become a routine part of European legal training. It imposes strict liability[148] on the 'producer' (defined in Art. 3) of a 'product' (defined in Art. 2) whose defect (defined in Art. 6) caused the damage. The term 'damage' includes only death, personal injury, and damage to property, other types of damage being excluded. Furthermore, liability for damage

---

[144] No. 372 above (France and, until mid-1994, Spain).

[145] They concern:—

1. the inclusion of primary agricultural products and game within the term 'product' (cf. Art. 15 lit. a Product Liability Dir.), of which Finland (1 § II Product Liability Act; Act no. 694 of 17 Aug. 1990, FFS 1990: 694); Greece (Art. 6 II Consumer Protection Act; Act no. 2251/1994, FEK A 191 of 16 Nov. 1994); Luxembourg (Art. 2 of the Act of 21 Apr. 1989, *Mémorial* no. A 25 of 28 Apr. 1989); Norway (§ 1–2 of Act no. l. 104 of 23 Dec. 1988, *Norsk Lovitidende* 1988 p. 1025); and Sweden (2 § Product Liability Act, SFS 1992: 18) are in favour. The French draft pointed in the same direction in Art. 1386–3 Cc (fn. 22 above);

2. the application of the strict liability regime to development risks (cf. Art. 15 lit. b Product Liability Dir.) which Finland favoured (7 § loc. cit.), Luxembourg (Art. 7 loc. cit.), and Norway (§ 2–2 loc. cit.; cf. also § 2–7 lit. b loc. cit.: shortened time limits), and which was also included in the French draft (Art. 1386–9 I loc. cit.);

3. the introduction of a liability ceiling in cases of death or personal injury (Art. 16 I, Product Liability Dir.) approved by Germany (§ 10 ProdHG), Portugal (*Decreto Lei* No. 383/89 of 6 Nov. 1989, Diário Rep. 1989 no. 255, Art. 9), and Spain (Art. 11 *Ley de responsabilidad por productos defectuosos* of 6 July 1994, BOE No. 161 of 7 July 1994; cf. Llorente San Segundo, *La Ley*, Comunidades Europeas, Año XIV, núm. 81 of 2 Nov. 1993 pp. 1 ff.) The Greek Consumer Protection Act of 1994 did not reaffirm Art. 14 of the former Act no. 1967/1991 (Consumer Protection Act) of 3 Sep. 1991, FEK no. 132/1991, p. 1879. Hence, a liability ceiling is no longer provided for.   [146] OJ L 210 7.9.1985, p. 29.

[147] OJ L 228 11.9.1992, p. 24. The German text can also be found in *EWS* 1992 pp. 262–267.

[148] The legal classification of this so-called strict liability is unclear (see no. 398 below). Based on the wording of Art. 3 I Product Safety Dir. ('producers shall be obliged to place only safe products on the market') it is clear that the Product Liability Dir. deals with liability for unlawful behaviour.

to property arises only from consumer contracts, and extends only to the damage or destruction of property other than the defective product itself (Art. 9). Damage arising from a defective part of a purchased item which affects a defect-free part *(Weiterfresserschäden)* is not included.[149] In addition, the Directive makes provision for an 'excess' (which it terms a 'threshold') of 500 ECU (Art. 9 lit. b); thus minor damage to property can only be compensated under non-approximated national law. 'The injured person shall be required to prove the damage, the defect, and the causal relationship between defect and damage' (Art 4). The producer, on the other hand, can largely avoid liability by proving that: he did not put the product into circulation; the defect did not exist when the product was placed on the market; or according to the scientific and technical knowledge available at that time the defect could not have been recognized: the 'state of the art defence' (Art. 7 lit. a, b, and e). The Directive provides for an *additional* cause of action; existing contractual and non-contractual domestic remedies are left intact (Art. 13). At the risk of sounding cynical: of all the provisions of the Directive, Art. 13 is probably the most significant in practice. This, and the fact that compensation for non-material damage is determined by national law (Art. 9 s. 2 Product Liability Directive) mean that most domestic courts in European member states continue to apply their own pre-existing product liability law. However, non-material damage can be recovered where national legislation combines the regime of the Directive with pre-existing domestic law, for example on pain and suffering. Whether the Italian concept of *danno biologico*, recently granted[150] under Presidential Decree No. 224/88,[151] is to be regarded as non-material damage (as most European lawywers would see it) or whether it is nearer to the concept of material damage (as most Italian lawyers would say) is open to discussion.

2. DIRECTIVE LAW FROM THE PERSPECTIVE OF THE COMMON LAW OF DELICT

a. General

With the European Waste and Services Directives currently on ice, it may **394** seem unnecessary to compare their provisions with Community law already in force. However, such a *Differentialdiagnose*,[152] when applied to the more general provisions, is worthwhile, since on one hand it reveals European tendencies, and on the other it highlights missed

---

[149] More on this subject in Part 5, nos. 442 f. below.
[150] Trib. Monza 21 July 1993, *Resp.Civ. e Prev.* 1994 pp. 141, 143.
[151] Supplemento ordinario alla Gaz.Uff. n. 146 of 23 June 1988. For more see Salvestroni, *Riv.Dir.Com* 1993, I, pp. 19–39.   [152] This expression is from Deutsch, *KF* 1992 pp. 4, 6.

opportunites to pave the way for a common European law of torts. The real problem, as van Dam said, is that 'each proposal for a directive of the European Commission is the beginning of a new adventure in the search for a political compromise'. There is no standard terminology for directives and thus they are often not completely compatible.[153] Van Dam has a point here. The authors of exisiting and proposed directives probably assumed that, like the law of contract, the law of delict has both a 'special part' dealing with legally differentiated categories, which could be successfully tackled one after the other, and a core of generally applicable terms and rules. Only if such a separation existed in the law of torts could one properly proceed with the approximation of distinct fields within the special part. However, no such distinction exists. Although 'special' types of contract with distinct legal features are found (e.g. property and possession in return for money = purchase, possession in return for money = rent etc.) non-contractual liability law, at least in continental Europe (and arguably since the development of negligence in Britain as well) has made distinctions, not so much according to *legal categories*, but rather according to *factual situations* (road traffic accidents, products, environmental pollution etc.) One could distinguish between provisions which always have been and always will be needed in a civilized society (e.g. liability towards victims of violence) and rules specifically tailored to modern aspects of life (e.g. accidents caused by modern energy production or modes of transport). However, although this is interesting it is not helpful to a lawyer. The law of delict must almost always be approached from its basic provisions, whose application tends to be enlarged by courts. To operate directives which use the *lex specialis* approach threatens not only the inner balance of national legal systems but also the approximation of law itself. If directives are treated discretely, rather than as an interconnected body which not only regulates specific matters but also takes reponsibility for the creation of an internally consistent system of Community liability law, this can contribute to the disintegration of Community law. What, seen in isolation, looks like a success for the approximation of laws can, if seen as a part of a whole, prove to be the source of retrogressive disunion.

b. Common Provisions

395 Let us begin with the positive aspects. All five texts prohibit disclaimers of liability for personal injury;[154] in the case of damage to property,

---

[153] van Dam, *Politieke infiltratie in het privaatrecht*, p. 11. Similar observations in Georgiades, *NoB* 42 (1994) pp. 321, 328–329.
[154] Art. 12 Product Liability Dir.; Art. 8 Waste Dir.; Art. 7 Services Dir.; Art. 5 II, sub-sec. 4 Package Tours Dir., and Art. 3 I and Annex no. 1 lit. a Contract Terms Dir.

however, they differ.[155] In the field of consumer protection the degree of protection of the injured seems justified. One could even argue that private persons should never be allowed to alter obligations arising *ex lege* rather than from contracts. However, once a delictual obligation to make good the damage has been established there is no reason why it should not be allowed to waive the right to compensation.[156] The Product Liability Directive is also the source of rules imposing joint and several liability on groups of tortfeasors;[157] it seems therefore that the Romanistic system of partial liability[158] has no relevance for future legal development in Europe. Furthermore, both directive law and uniform international law further the possibility of a reduction of liability (even, where appropriate, to nil) in cases of contributory negligence.[159] My impression is that a uniform limitation period is also within sight: all three texts establish a three-year limitation period for claims based on delict, commencing from the date on which the 'damage'[160] and its originator were or should reasonably have been discovered.[161] Whereas these limitation periods will only be considered by the court if pleaded as a defence by the tortfeasor, they exist against a background of other limitation periods (varying in length) which apply *ipso iure*.[162] This seems a reasonable compromise. It has been unanimously agreed that the whole field of non-pecuniary losses ('non-material damage') should be exempt from the directives' regime.[163] This is probably due to Germany's unfortunate negative influence on the issue. Art. 6 I lit. b of the proposed Waste Directive, on the other hand, swings to the other extreme in assuming that the expression *force majeure* is already a term of art of Community law. The European legislator has simply presupposed a legal definition. One can only guess at the reasons for this. In all

---

[155] Only under Art. 12 Product Liability Dir., Art. 8 Waste Dir., and Art. 7 Services Dir. is liability mandatory.

[156] This is not mentioned explicitly in any of the texts, but can be taken for granted: see e.g. § 14 German ProdHG ('. . . *darf im voraus weder ausgeschlossen noch beschränkt werden*') and Art. 12 of the Italian presidential decree (. . . *che escluda o limiti preventivamente . . . la responsabilità*). Cf. the more ambiguous Art. 6: 192 I BW and sec. 7 English Consumer Protection Act 1987.

[157] Art. 5 Product Liability Dir., Art. 5 Waste Dir., Art. 8 Services Dir.

[158] See Part 2, no. 52 above.

[159] Art. 8 II Product Liability Dir.; Art. 7 II Waste Dir.; Art 6 II Services Dir. Cf. also Art. 21 Warsaw Convention and Art. 9 of the CE Lugano Convention (no. 383 above).

[160] Although this term is problematic throughout: see no. 397 below.

[161] Art. 10 I Product Liability Dir. (knowledge, real or constructive, 'of the damage, the defect, and the identity of the producer'); Art. 10 I s. 1 Services Dir. (with special provisions for buildings [10 years] in s. 2) and Art. 9 I Waste Dir.

[162] Art. 11 Product Liability Dir. (10 years), Art. 10 Waste Dir. (30 years), Art. 9 Services Dir. (5 years).

[163] Art. 9 s. 2 Product Liability Dir. ('non-material damage'); Art. 4 V Waste Dir. ('non-material damage'); Art. 4 Services Directive (only 'direct' and 'financial' damage can be recovered).

probability the term stems from Art. 7 of the preliminary draft (!) of the Services Directive.[164] Finally, of particular significance to the law of torts is the fact that not only do all these directives bring stricter forms of liability, but that this stricter liability also attaches to commercial rather than to private activities.[165] The explanation cannot simply be that western Europe has merged into one economic Community, which does not interfere with the liability law of the individual. One could more plausibly argue the reverse: that the law of individual liability must retain the principle of fault, which always has and always will underpin the personal freedom of the individual.

c. Missed Opportunities

396   The authors of the directives so far published have missed a number of significant opportunities. First, they have made mistakes in drafting legislation which experienced national legislators would never have allowed. A prime example is the definition of damage to property, of which—as also of non-economic damage[166]—various versions exist.[167] Similarly, it is clumsy to refer in the context of contributory negligence to persons 'for whom the injured person is responsible',[168] since the issue is reduction rather than establishment of liability. Furthermore, it is unclear to whom the definition refers: for example, are parents 'responsible' for their children (or even vice versa, e.g. in negligently failing to recognize a defective product which caused injury to their child?) In other areas a terminology common to Community law is incorrectly assumed. We have seen this in the use of the term *force majeure*; the expression 'in the course of a business' (especially in the case of 'freelance professions') poses similar difficulties.[169]

397   The problems become even greater with the use in these directives of

---

[164] This at least contained a standard 'Community law' definition of the expression *force majeure*: '*un événement extérieur, imprévisible et irréversible*' (Spier/Sterk, *NJB* 1990 pp. 1517, 1523).

[165] Art. 3 Product Liability Dir.; Art. 3 I Services Dir.; Art. 1 lit. a Waste Dir. A parallel can be seen between these provisions and liability for *gevaarlijke stoffen* under Art. 6:175 I BW ('*Degene die in de uitoefening van zijn beroep of bedrijf een stof gebruikt . . ., is aansprakelijk*') see Sterk, *Verhoogd gevaar*, p. 213.   [166] See fn. 163 above.

[167] Art. 1 I Services Dir., for example, speaks of the 'physical integrity of movable or immovable property', Art. 2 I lit. c (ii) Waste Dir. of 'damage to property', and Art. 9 lit. b Product Liability Dir. of 'damage to, or destruction of, any item of property'. No adequate reason for this inconsistency is discernible.

[168] As in Art. 8 II Product Liability Dir., Art. 6 II Services Dir., and Art. 7 II Waste Dir. Reduction of liability due to contributory negligence of persons 'for whom one is responsible' is, however, also found in uniform law: see Art. 9 Lugano Convention of the CE.

[169] Many laws do not recognize the occupations of lawyers, physicians, architects etc. as businesses; they would nevertheless have been subject to liability under the Services Dir. For more detail see v. Bar, *FS Lange*, pp. 373, 381–382.

certain basic terms of the law of delict. Consider the word 'damage'.[170] Although all three directives cover only personal injury and damage to property (although it is often doubtful whether simple possession alone or full title is required to found a claim for damages),[171] no clear differentiation is made between the establishment of and the consequences of liability. This failure to distinguish between interference with legally protected interests and the remedies available, discernible in all three texts, poses a problem, at the very least wherever liability is based on fault. For here it must be determined to which of the issues fault is relevant. In addition, the Services Directive proposal refers to direct damage recoverable from a direct damage. In Art. 4 lit. 'damage' was defined as 'death or any other direct damage to the health or physical integrity of persons', and lit. c went on to say that such 'financial material damage' is recoverable which is 'resulting directly from the damage referred to at (a) . . .' It is hard to excuse such a blunder, even given that the expressions 'remoteness of damage', '*préjudice*', '*dommage*', '*Rechtsgutsverletzung*' and '*Schaden*' must have given the authors nightmares. The secret of what direct damage arising through a direct damage actually is will remain theirs.

'Fault', another expression of fundamental concern, has been dealt **398** with in a similarly ill-considered manner.[172] The Product Liability Directive says in its second introductory statement that the problem it addresses can only be adequately solved by the imposition of 'liability without fault on the part of the producer'. According to the wording of the proposed Waste Directive, the waste producer is liable 'irrespective of fault on his part' (Art. 3 I), and the (former) proposal for a Services Directive provided that 'the burden of proving the absence of fault shall fall upon the supplier of the service' (Art. 1 II). But what exactly is meant by 'fault'? It has not been defined by directive law, nor do the texts make clear whether fault and unlawfulness are to be considered as one and the same. If the authors of the directives focused on *faute*, rather than on tort law systems for which unlawfulness is the key element, this might explain the lack of clarity. One could also argue that the distinction between unlawfulness and fault is no longer of much relevance. However, a system which treats liability based on fault as more rigid than no-fault liability makes no sense. However, this is exactly what would have resulted had the Services Directive come into force. According to Art. 4 Product Liability Directive the injured person must, *inter alia*, 'prove . . . the defect', and according to the definition in Art. 6 I a product is

---

[170] See Spier, *NJB* 1991 pp. 663, 665.
[171] The Product Liability Directive protects, according to the 6th opening statement, property of the consumer only.
[172] See v. Bar, *FS Lange*, pp. 373, 382–384, for more detailed comment.

'defective when it does not provide the safety which a person is entitled to expect, taking all circumstances into account'. The Services Directive contained no definition of 'defective services' in its Art. 1 III, but it integrated into the notion of 'fault' elements contained in a provision headed *'définition du défaut d'un service'* in the preliminary draft.[173] The final wording of the proposal was: 'in assessing the fault, account shall be taken of the behaviour of the supplier of the service, who, in normal and reasonably foreseeable conditions, shall ensure the safety which may reasonably be expected'. Despite the narrower definition,[174] the wording first used in the Product Liability Directive to define a defect here reappears in the definition of fault. But now, alarmingly, 'the burden of proving the absence of fault shall fall upon the supplier of the service': hence of proving the *absence* of a 'defect' in his service. Had both these texts become Community law, considerable interpreting skill would have been needed to make sense of them! The random use of the terms 'defect' (to denote unlawful act) and 'fault' produced entirely contradictory results.

IV. NON-STATUTORY APPROXIMATION OF LAWS

399 To spend too much time discussing the above problems would be to fail to acknowledge the enormous achievements of the Commission in the field of approximation of law. Nevertheless, such mistakes reveal the limits of what can be achieved by the statutory approximation of law. Even in specialized fields of tort law, such approximation can only succeed if the principles governing the law have been properly analysed. The approximation of law must therefore be supported by other, non-statutory means.[175]

1. THE RECOMMENDATIONS OF THE COUNCIL OF EUROPE

400 The Recommendations of the Council of Europe constitute just such a non-statutory instrument. In so far as the Recommendations concern the

---

[173] Art. 5 I of the *avant-projet* (text in Spier/Sterk, *NJB* 1990 pp. 1517, 1523) provided: *'Un service présente un défaut lorsqu'il n'offre pas la sécurité à laquelle on peut légitimement s'attendre quant à la santé et l'intégrité physique des biens meubles corporels ou immeubles y compris ceux qui en fait l'objet de la prestation.'*

[174] The Product Liability Dir. demands that *'all* circumstances' be taken into account. However, the inclusion of unpredictable circumstances cannot be intended.

[175] Kötz, *RabelsZ* 56 (1992) pp. 215–218 is therefore right when speaking of the necessity to look for *'Alternativen zur legislatorischen Rechtsvereinheitlichung'*.

law of delict, they fall into two groups. One provides an aid for the interpretation of common private law terms found in treaties creating uniform international law. The other contains recommendations for its member states unilaterally to eliminate wherever possible their differences from other legal systems.

The 1976 *Report* of the *Subcommittee on Fundamental Legal Concepts* of   **401** the Committee on Legal Co-operation of the Council of Europe deals with the law of treaties.[176] It defines the terms 'contractual liability', 'fault', and *'force majeure'*[177] and outlines 'different degrees of fault'. Yet a closer look reveals that some of these definitions are superficial. For example, 'non-contractual liability' has been defined as 'the obligation to repair damage resulting from a fact other than the failure to perform, or the defective performance of, a contractual obligation'. On one hand, this definition is banal; on the other, it has not been properly thought through in many respects. It assumes, for example, an agreed definition of 'defective performance of a contractual obligation'. However, it is precisely here that the gulfs between national legal systems emerge.[178] In addition, it is simply wrong to regard the law of delict as always operating independently from that of contract. One glance, for example, at the law concerning failure to perform a contractual obligation to supervise persons or property proves that the opposite is true; many complicated ties link contract law to the law of delict. The expression 'fault' also seems to have been defined carelessly. 'Fault' is said to be 'a failure, by an act or omission, of the behaviour one could reasonably expect from the person responsible for that failure'. The description of fault (did they perhaps mean unlawfulness?) as 'behaviour' and the reference in the the definition to the notion of 'reasonable expectation' are equally questionable.

More interesting is therefore *Resolution (75) 7 of the Committee of*   **402** *Ministers of the Council of Europe of 14 Mar. 1975 on Compensation in Cases of Personal Injury or Death*.[179] It suggests that member state governments should, when legislating, 'consider' a total of nineteen recommendations in the field of damages. Especially valuable are those

---

[176] Council of Europe, Committee on Legal Co-operation (CCJ). Report drawn up by the Sub-Committee on Fundamental Legal Concepts set up by the European Committee on Legal Co-operation (no year and place given, probably on the turn of 1976/1977).

[177] The definition of the CE (*'Force majeure* is an event which is inevitable—in particular because it is unforeseeable—unavoidable and external to the person whose liability is invoked or external to his sphere of control') (probably) corresponds only partially with the term *force majeure* in the sense of Community law (no. 395 and fn. 164 above).

[178] See further nos. 413 ff. and 459 ff. below.

[179] Text (German) in BGBl. 1976 II 323. No English text available to the author. On these recommendations see Lambert-Faivre, *Le droit du dommage corporel*, p. 12 (reproducing the French text); and Stoll, *Haftungsfolgen*, nos. 270, 275, and elsewhere.

suggestions concerning damages for *non-material loss*, part of liability law so far excluded from international legislation. Proposition number three calls for (much needed)[180] rulings from national courts on 'which specific compensation for the various kinds of damage suffered by the injured person shall be awarded to him or her'. Proposal number eleven suggests compensating the injured person for damage to aesthetic appearance as well as to mental health, and explains what should constitute damage to mental health. Compensation is payable whichever cause of action is succesfully relied upon. In cases of personal injury, victims and their parents and spouse only shall be entitled to compensation, and the latter two only if they suffer damage 'of a special quality' to their mental health (no. 13). Equally convincing is the long-term approach taken to the standardizing of damages awarded for pain and suffering following the death of a relative (no. 19). Those legal systems still resisting are urged to approach the compensation of parents, spouses, fiancés, and children more liberally, 'upon the establishment of a close mental relationship to the injured person at the time of his death'. On the other hand, those legal systems in which awards have been most generous are asked to 'extend neither the circle of persons entitled to compensation nor the sums awarded'. In view of such sensible guidance it is disappointing that the German *Schuldrechtskommission* (Committee for the Reform of the Law of Obligations) has not merely ignored these recommendations, despite the general sympathy of its members towards unification and approximation of laws,[181] but has gone so far as to submit contradictory proposals. They suggest that German contractual liability for 'breach of a contractual duty of care' (*Schutzpflichtverletzung*) should continue to deny damages for non-material loss for the foreseeable future.[182]

2. APPROXIMATION THROUGH CASE-LAW

403 The aforementioned Committee recommendation number nineteen demonstrates very clearly that approximation of law need not be the result of externally imposed international measures; the reduction of differences can also come 'from within'. However, such development cannot be achieved by national legislators acting alone: it requires the support of all those responsible for private law. The adjudicating body, the courts, must also play a leading part. They should be encouraged not only to refer to comparative law in their decision-making in domestic

[180] Cf. Part 6, no. 568 below.   [181] Cf. Schlechtriem, *ZEuP* 1993 pp. 217–246.
[182] See Part 5, no. 464 below. The 60th German Lawyers' Day (Münster 1994) vindicated the opinion of the Committee; see resolution II 7, printed *inter alia* in *DB* 1994 p. 2016.

414

cases,[183] but also to give comparative law a specifically European emphasis. How this should be understood has recently been explained by the President of the German Federal Court:

'Not only is the national judge entitled to consider the opinion of other legal systems and courts; within the boundaries of his national law and whilst weighing up all aspects relevant for the interpretation and development of law, he may also emphasize the fact that the solution in question could help to harmonize European law. In conclusion, he could then use this argument to turn towards foreign legal systems for the solution of the problem. Such reasoning ought to be used increasingly as part of the European process of unification'.[184]

In this century tentative steps towards judge-made comparative law **404** have occasionally been seen. Even rulings of the French *Cour de Cassation*, which cite only the *Code Civil*, are not entirely free from the influence of comparative law: the *rapports* of the Advocate-General are evidence for this proposition. The *Jand'heur*[185] case is one excellent example. Here *M le Conseiller Le Marc'hadour* pointed out how outdated French industrial injury law had become, and why the extension of *gardien* liability under Art. 1348 I Cc had therefore become unavoidable.[186] However, even he did not attempt a detailed comparative analysis, nor have any of his successors or the French courts themselves.[187] In both Portugal and Greece, judge-made comparative law has always been of significant practical relevance. Each looks especially towards those legal systems on which their own code was modelled: namely the German,[188] the Swiss,[189] the French,[190] and the Italian.[191] For them

---

[183] For a French perspective see Legeais, *Rev.int.dr.comp.* 46 (1994) pp. 347–358; for the German point of view see Drobnig, *RabelsZ* 50 (1986) pp. 610, 621–624; and id., in: Jayme (ed.), *German National Reports for the XIVth Congress of Comparative Law*, pp. 5–24.

[184] Odersky, *ZEuP* 1994 pp. 1, 2.

[185] For more detailed consideration see Part 2, nos. 106, 111 above.

[186] DP 1930, I, p. 57.

[187] See in more detail Legeais, *Rev.int.dr.comp.* 46 (1994) pp. 347, 354–358.

[188] See e.g. Areopag 12263/1990, *NoB* 39 (1991) pp. 583, 584 (concurrence of claims in contract and delict) or CA Athens 11518/1986, *EllDik* 29 (1988) pp. 916, 917. Greek courts refer so often to German literature and cases (the latter being often translated, see e.g. BGH 28 June 1978, *NoB* 27 [1979] p. 637 or BGH 15 Apr. 1959, *NoB* 11 [1963] p. 287) that it is impossible to produce a complete reference list here.

[189] E.g. CFI Athens 9363/1975, *NoB* 24 (1976) p. 92 (liability of a person not party to the contract for giving misleading information regarding the object purchased); and CA Crete 138/1965, *EEN* 33 (1966) p. 366 (damage *contra bonos mores*; detailed analysis of German literature).

[190] E.g. STJ 18 Feb. 1986, *BolMinJust* 354 (1986) pp. 567, 569 (Art. 266 French Cc as source for Art. 1792 Port. Cc); CFI Salonica 2530/1967 EEN 35 (1968) p. 56 (liability based on Art. 919 Greek Cc); and CFI Athens 17187/1983 *EllDik* 25 (1984) p. 1220 (likewise dealing with Art. 919 Greek Cc; discusses case-law of the *Cours de Cassation*).

[191] E.g. STJ 21 Nov. 1979, *BolMinJust* 291 (1979) pp. 285, 287–289 (interpretation of Art. 493 II Port. Cc with reference to the Italian code on which it was based) and CFI Athens 30/ 1980 *Arm.* 35 (1981) pp. 471, 472 (problems arising through concurrent claims).

historical and comparative interpretation are two sides of the same coin. When delivering rulings of fundamental importance it may even be that their judges look at a wide range of western European legal systems in order to deliver a considered opinion.[192] Some remarkable developments have been taking place in The Netherlands. Not only has the *Hoge Raad*[193] 'legislated'[194] to restrict the scope of the contributory negligence of pedestrians injured by cars, obviously influenced by the French *Loi Badinter* of 5 July 1985,[195] it has also overturned long-standing precedents regarding the level of damages for non-material loss following developments in surrounding countries.

A trainee doctor accidentally used a syringe with which blood had just been taken from an AIDS patient. Forty days later it was found that the plaintiff had contracted the HIV virus and was likely to develop AIDS symptoms within 24 months. The plaintiff received Dfl. 150,000 from the hospital's insurers. Dissatisfied, he sued the hospital for Dfl. 800,000 and in summary proceedings he demanded an advance of Dfl. 300,000. The highest amount awarded (although the facts of that case were not identical) had, until that time, been 250,000 Guilders. Whereas formerly only the Advocat General had consulted foreign material,[196] here it was used by the judges of the *Hoge Raad* themselves. They noted that there was no legal rule forbidding a judge from examining developments in surrounding countries. Although such developments could not be the sole basis for their decision, they were one of the elements which influenced it. They further noted that neighbouring countries awarded far higher levels of damages than The Netherlands and, partly as a result of this observation, the plaintiff was awarded the 300,000 Guilders.[197]

405   As is well known, it has become almost standard procedure in Austria to incorporate German developments and judgments; Sweden and Finland, which share a common language, regularly examine each other's

---

[192] Very impressive are e.g. STJ 13 Mar. 1985, *BolMinJust* 345 (1985) pp. 414, 416–417 (liability for damages for non-material loss arising from adultery or divorce; German, English, Belgian, Swiss, and French law examined and compared). See on this subject also the comparative analysis by Areopag 6581/1979, *NoB* 27 (1979) pp. 1645, 1646 (with reference *inter alia* to BGH 6 Mar. 1962, *NJW* 1962 p. 958).

[193] The reports of the Advocate General have more than once referred to comparative law. A convincing more recent example from the field of prospectus liability can be found in HR 2 Dec. 1994, *NedJur* 1996 no. 246 p. 1201.

[194] See esp. HR 28 Feb. 1992, *RvdW* 1992 no. 72; further details in Part 6 no. 599 below.

[195] Law no. 85–677 of 5 July 1985 *tendant à l'amélioration de la situation des victimes d'accidents de la circulation et à l'accélération des procédures d'indemnisations*, JO of 6 July 1985 p. 7584.

[196] See (in an earlier case dealing with damages for non-material loss) the report of the Advocat General in HR 21 May 1943, *NedJur* 1943 no. 455, p. 609.

[197] HR 8 July 1992, *NedJur* 1992 no. 714 pp. 3088, 3095.

cases.[198] German courts, on the other hand, scarcely acknowledge the work of their Austrian counterparts.[199] In addition, German courts have analysed foreign developments in tort law in domestic cases concerning the protection of privacy through awarding damages for non-material loss only.[200] In its first major ruling in a *wrongful life* case the BGH, unusually, discussed American and English precedents, which were accepted as basically correct.[201] Meanwhile the English courts have begun to 'respond'. Lord Goff in *R* v. *Reid*, to my knowledge, for the first time ever in an English judgment, analysed a term of English law (the expression 'recklessness') in the light of the corresponding German term *Leichtfertigkeit*.[202] Furthermore, in a later case he discussed the state of German law on an aspect of unjust enrichment.[203] Following Sir Thomas Bingham's repeated demands for improvements in the legal protection of privacy under English law[204] (also referring to German law) the case of *White* v. *Jones*, dealing with a solicitor's liability towards third parties, was the first hearing in the House of Lords in which comparative law played a significant role. References to German law can be found in the Court of Appeal report and (in much more detail) in Lord Goff's House of Lords judgment.[205] Lord Goff of Chieveley, who had previously referred to comparative law when considering the problem of concurring claims in contract and delict,[206] promoted it once again in the House of Lords.

Although such decisions are important they must not be overrated, **406** especially since they constitute as yet only a very small body of case-law. However, they may well be the first tentative steps towards, not only the greater use of comparative law techniques, but a pro-Europe interpretation of law, which would at last bring comparative law out of its ivory tower and give it some practical role. It would indeed be real progress if

---

[198] Swedish courts make wider use of comparative law: e.g. HD 11 Dec. 1991, *NJA* 1991: 123 (p. 720): development of judge-made strict liability for district heating mains based on Danish and Norwegian case-law.

[199] Comparative references to Austrian (and Swiss) law are rare and, as far as liability law is concerned, they do not extend beyond the pronouncement of statutory provisions. Cf. e.g. RG 19 Nov. 1917, *RGZ* 91 pp. 269, 270 f. and BGH 8 Jan. 1958, BGHZ 26 pp. 217, 233. Cf. also Aubin, *RabelsZ* 34 (1970) pp. 458, 463, 478.

[200] BGH 19 Sep. 1961, BGHZ 35 pp. 363, 369; BGH 5 Mar. 1963, BGHZ 39 pp. 124, 132; BVerfG 14 Feb. 1973, BVerfGE 34 pp. 269, 289, 291. Cf. Drobnig, *RabelsZ* 50 (1986) pp. 610, 621–622.   [201] BGH 18 Jan. 1983, BGHZ 86 pp. 240, 250–251.

[202] *R* v. *Reid* [1992] 3 All ER pp. 673, 688–689 (HL) (*per* Lord Goff of Chieveley).

[203] *Woolwich Building Soc.* v. *Inland Revenue Commissioners* [1992] 3 WLR pp. 36, 393 (HL) (*per* Lord Goff of Chieveley). See case-note on this matter Hill, *ModLRev* 56 (1993) pp. 856–865.

[204] *Kaye* v. *Robertson* [1991] FSR (62) (CA) (also in Weir, *Casebook*, 7th edn., pp. 20, 24).

[205] *White* v. *Jones* [1993] 3 All ER pp. 481, 501 (*per* Steyn LJ); and [1995] 2 WLR 187 (*per* Lord Goff).

[206] *Henderson and Others* v. *Merrett Syndicates Ltd.* [1994] 3 All ER pp. 506, 523–525 (HL).

the highest courts of the member states of the European Union were to grant one another some sort of persuasive authority: if they took it upon themselves to examine whether the issue before them had already been decided elsewhere within the Union, or even whether any 'prevailing European opinion' existed. It might even become necessary to give reasons why, under current domestic law, the 'European line' could not be followed *in casu*! How much livelier would the reasoning behind judicial rulings become if they were infused with European spirit! How much easier it would be to entice the intellectual elite into the study of law! Such visions are obviously limited by the enormous volume of work required of all higher courts and their lawyers. However, for important rulings additional expense is justifiable and should be made available. After all, in European legal history the domestic judicial systems have repeatedly made it their business to participate in the formulation of joint law.[207] In order to serve justice one must not simply promote 'one's own' law, one must be fully open to foreign ideas.

3. LEGAL TRAINING AND SCHOLARSHIP

407 The still small number of comparative lawyers (as they have unfortunately named themselves) know of course that even the current legal training falls far short of what, in the previous section, we are asking from the courts. Very often the supranational dimension of law is still of little relevance to courses of study and to the boards of examiners of most European universities. Apart from genuine Community law, international law subjects have often been sidelined. Brilliant examination results and rapid career advancement are possible without the slightest knowledge of neighbouring legal systems other than that which can be read in the press. 'Just as the old idea of the *ius commune* has been displaced in the age of codifications . . . so European lawyers are trained primarily in doctrines and conceptual tools specific to the laws of their own countries. The provincialism and narrowness of European legal education is reinforced by . . . its lofty neglect of ideas . . . from the outside world.'[208] The law student needs to be pointed towards integration.[209] Of course, only the elite will follow in the footsteps of those currently trying to rediscover Europe's common legal culture and jurisprudence, which have for so long been buried. If, from the very beginning, basic legal education were to incorporate foreign material, all those

---

[207] Van Gerven, *MJ* 1 (1994) pp. 6, 40.
[208] Kötz, in: *The common law of Europe and the future of legal education*, pp. 31, 35–36.
[209] See Kötz, *ZEuP* 1993 pp. 268–278; Flessner, *RabelsZ* 56 (1992) pp. 246–260.

new to law would at least be encouraged to participate. It is just as important—and fortunately attempts in this direction have already been made—that national examination regulations acknowledge the qualifications which 'their' students have obtained abroad—be they intermediate or final examinations. It should be possible for that part of an exam which does not consist of a written test or an oral examination, but rather of a piece of academic research (written in the language of the host country) to be assessed by an examiner in the host country, and to be recognized in the candidate's home country.

Of a slightly different nature is the role played by legal scholarship in **408** the ongoing process of European unification. First and foremost it must demystify current private law practices in Europe in order to reduce prejudices and to enable contemorary lawyers again to understand law as an international phenomenon. However, examination of individual foreign jurisdictions, no matter how helpful,[210] can only be the first step. The real task of academic lawyers goes much further. They must present from the outset a framework which enables the presentation and analysis of entire fields of law from a European point of view.[211] European case-books and journals on private law in Europe[212] are needed to complement this work. However, it is the role of treatises (and I hope that this work will meet these expectations) to develop a basic system which allows diversity to flourish without details being lost, to emphasize corresponding solutions, to appreciate discrepancies, and to relate different legal systems so that international disputes can be dealt with as if within *one* legal system. It is of the utmost importance to capture living law, and not to remain on the level of mostly colourless statute law. Therefore the emphasis must be on case-law. The judgments produced, as well as methodological and policy explanations, must be fully comprehensible.[213] This would reveal an existing common European standard in many areas; in other areas developments would become

---

[210] Cf. e.g. the reports by Hondius/Braams (The Netherlands), Kornilakis (Greece), and Viney (France) (Part 4 bibliography above) in a series of lectures in the European Institute of the Saarland (*Europainstitut des Saarlandes*) headed '*Auf dem Wege zu einem europäischen Haftungsrecht*', and the collection by v. Bar (ed.), *DeliktsR in Europa* (Cologne et al. 1993–1994).
[211] This idea originates from Kötz, FS *Zweigert*, pp. 481, 498–500; cf. id., in: Müller-Graff (ed.), *Gemeinsames Privatrecht in der Europäischen Gemeinschaft*, pp. 95–108; Georgiades, *NoB* 42 (1994) pp. 321, 344 ff., and Karakostas, *I evthini tou paragogou gia elattomatika proionta*, pp. 35–36. Kötz and Flessner are currently trying to do just this for parts of the law of contract: cf. the pre-print Kötz, *RabelsZ* 58 [1994] pp. 209–231.
[212] See esp. *European Review of Private Law* (ERPL) and the *Zeitschrift für Europäisches Privatrecht* (ZEuP), as well as *Aansprakelijkheid en Verzekering* (A&V) and the *Maastricht Journal of European and Comparative Law* (MJ), 4 recently founded journals (for bibliographical details see list of abbreviations).
[213] An idea originating from Markesinis, *RRJ* 1985 pp. 866–887.

apparent which would encourage national courts to rule in a less insular manner. Finally, the publication of more such treatises will inevitably help to overcome the manifold problems of language and terminology. Only on the basis of such preliminary work will it become possible, with the necessary political will, to crown the European unification project with a uniform code of obligations.

4. APPROXIMATION OF LAW THROUGH STANDARD CLAUSES:
FIRST STEPS TOWARDS A EUROPEAN CODE OF OBLIGATIONS

409 To find a section dealing with the 'approximation of law through standard clauses' in a study of the law of delict might come as a surprise, as we are obviously outside the field of contract law. However, the many existing approaches to the question of where the law of contract ends and the law of delict begins[214] suggest that the international text of standard clauses can be of relevance. On the level of the European Union, the *Principles of European Contract Law* drawn up by the Commission on European Contract Law (the Lando Commission) are the most important example of such influence.[215] The 'principles' in Art. 4.501 II lit. a explicitly state that a breach of contract shall also result in liability for non-material loss, thus touching on delictual questions. The chapter on 'Formation of Contract', still to be published, will contain provisions dealing with parts of the *culpa in contrahendo* issue. Art. 6.106 is intended to establish liability for negligent misrepresentation as to the object of the contract, even in so far as it causes damage to health. The chapter on agency will incorporate a provision on the third-party liability of an agent acting without authority which, e.g. from a French point of view, would come under the law of delict (Art. 1382 French Cc).[216]

---

[214] For more detail see Part 5 I below, esp. nos. 459 ff.

[215] The first 4 chapters drafted by the '1st Commission' of the Lando Commission (General Provisions, Terms and Performance of the Contract, Non-performance and Remedies in General, Particular Remedies for Non-performance) have just been released by Lando and Beale (Part 4 bibliography above); a pre-print (without comments and notes) is found in Hartkamp/ Hesselink/Hondius/du Perron/Vranken (edd.), *Towards a European Civil Code* (Nijmegen and Dordrecht 1994) pp. 405–415. The last 4 chapters (currently under preparation by the 2nd Commission) should be ready for publication by the end of 1996. The final publication of the Principles will contain amendments to the already published first 4 chapters.

[216] See Dijon 19 May 1931, *D*. 1931 *Jur.* 405 (delictual liability of the *falsus procurator*). More recent French rulings do not seem to exist, but there appears to be general agreement on this issue: cf. *JClCiv* (-Alexandre), *Mandat*, Arts. 1991 to 2002, Fasc. 2, no. 120; and Malaurie/Aynès, 'Cours de droit civil', *Tome* VIII: *Les contrats speciaux*, 7th edn., no. 575. A similar liability provision appears in Art. 16 I of the Geneva (*Unidroit*) Convention of 17 Feb. 1983 on the Agency in the International Sale of Goods (Engl. and French text in *Rev.dr.uniforme* 1983 I-II p. 133 with *Rapport explicatif* in *Rev.dr.uniforme* 1984 I p. 72). However, the treaty has not yet been enforced.

However, these provisions will be applied only if both parties have submitted to them by contract (Art. 1.101 II of the Principles).[217]

For the law of delict, the Principles of European Contract Law are far **410** more significant than appears from the consideration of these rather peripheral issues. In the long run they do more than simply offering a set of standard clauses. Their second, and from a long term-point of view probably more important aim is 'to serve as a basis for any future European Code of Contract. They could form the first step in the work'.[218] This controversial,[219] yet to my mind correct and substantive role for these Principles, will finally force the law of delict to examine how and on the basis of which principles it could follow suit.[220] It is evident that the law of delict and the law of contract complement and depend upon each other. One cannot codify one without also codifying the other, for the law of obligations must be considered in its entirety. A commission similar to the Lando Commission should be set up to develop a draft code of delict, which could become the second pillar of the law of obligations. Obviously, the preconditions for such an undertaking are different in a field of law consisting mainly of *jus cogens*, but this does not necessarily mean that the task is harder to accomplish.[221] Today the law of delict should be seen first and foremost as the protection of constitutionally granted fundamental rights through private law,[222] indeed such protection of fundamental rights has always been a driving force behind the unification of laws in Europe. Even if it is not possible to make the European Parliament's wish for codification come true, the work of such a commission would nevertheless have

---

[217] However, according to Art. 1.101 III the Principles can also be applied '(a) when the parties have agreed that their contract is to be governed by "general principles of law", the *"lex mercatoria"* or the like; or (b) when the parties have not chosen any system or rules of law to govern their contract.' For the time being only arbitrators, and not national courts, which are bound by their international private law, will be able to apply these Principles as *lex contractus*. The only possible exception are actions concerning the contractual liability of the EU itself (cf. Art. 215 I Treaty of Rome).

[218] Introduction 2(a) on the Principles of European Contract Law (see fn. 215 above).

[219] It surprised nobody that even Continental European lawyers strongly opposed the demand of the European Parliament for the creation of a European Civil Code. See e.g. Taupitz, *JZ* 1993 pp. 533–539; id., *Europäische Privatrechtsvereinheitlichung heute und morgen*, pp. 55–66; Remien, *JZ* 1992 p. 277–284; and Sandrock, *EWS* 1994 pp. 1, 5–8. Also sceptical but more cautious: Ulmer, *JZ* 1992 pp. 1, 5; Blaurock, *JZ* 1994 pp. 270–276; Großfeld, *ZfRV* 1992, pp. 421, 426; and Müller-Graff, *NJW* 1993, pp. 13, 23. Furthermore, it is a cause for concern that for years the demand of the European Parliament has apparently only been discussed in Germany. Only the book by Hartkamp *et al.* issued in 1994 *'Towards a European Civil Code'* (see fn. 215 above) provoked a noticeable reaction elsewhere.

[220] Some first approaches towards this issue by Markesinis, in: Hartkamp *et al.* (edd.) loc. cit. (previous fn.) pp. 285, 290–297.

[221] O'Callaghan Muñoz, *Poder Judicial* 1982 pp. 37–44 wrote as early as the beginning of the 1980s that *'un Cc único europeo occidental'* is desirable (p. 44). He believes it to be especially easy to realize in the field of delict (p. 42). [222] Part 6 I, nos. 556 ff. below.

value. It could serve as a model statute, in the hope that it would influence most national legislators. Although western Europe has seen many unsuccessful attempts to overhaul its codified law of delict,[223] there is still the possibility that the latest 'rush for recodification' might finally lead to a restoration of the idea of Civil Codes.[224] This entails both risks and opportunities. On one hand there is the risk of a renewed attempt to fortify differences; on the other the chance for a conscious approximation of national texts. Particularly for the latter goal, a model statute would be of great help.

[223] One of these remarkable projects was the *avant-projet de révision du Code civil* by the Belgian Professor François Laurent (Part 4 bibliography above; cf. Hanssens, *Code civil en Belgique*, pp. 679, 682), who wanted to add to Art. 1382 Cc the word 'tout fait *illicite* de l'homme' in 'his' Art. 1120, and to define the expression '*fait illicite*' in Art. 1122 (loc. cit., vol. iv, pp. 103, 107). Immediately after World War II ended, France appointed an unsuccessful revision commission (Carbonnier, *Droit Civil*, vol. i, 16th edn., no. 72; as well as *Encyclopédie Dalloz* [-Vanel], *Rép.Dr.Civ.* vol. iii [1971], 'Code Civil', nos. 161–195). This text did not find its way into the code. A project initiated by Spain in the early 1990s was also predominantly unsuccessful (details in v. Bar [-Santiumenge], *DeliktsR in Europa, Spanien*, p. 25, fn. 33). The various German endeavours towards the reform of the law of delict of the BGB have been listed by v. Bar, *Gutachten Deliktsrecht*, pp. 1681, 1749–1760. More successful from a long-term point of view was the draft by Heemskerk of a revised Dutch law of delict (text in *W* 1913 p. 4) at that time competing with the draft by Regout (text in *WNPR* 1911 nos. 2149 [pp. 106–108], 2150 [pp. 120–122], 2151 [pp. 132–135], and 2152 [pp. 148–149]), whose proposed wording for Art. 1401 BW (old) ('*Onder onregtmatige daad wordt verstaan een handelen of nalaten, dat of in strijd is met des daders regtspligt, òf inbreuk maakt op eens anders regt, òf indruischt tegen de regelen van betamelijkheid, die in het maatschappelijk verkeer gehooren te worden in acht genoomen*') finally prevailed in Art. 6:162 BW. On this and other Dutch reformatory efforts see van Maanen, *Onrechtmatige Daad*, pp. 72–78.

[224] Following The Netherlands' near completion of the revision of their Civil Code, a commission appointed by the Swiss *Bundesamt für Justiz* submitted a draft for revision of the entire law of delict (Part 4 above; see also Widmer, *ZBernJV* 130 [1994] pp. 385–410). Furthermore, the Austrian Lawyers' Day 1994 discussed reforming the law of delict on the basis of a report by Magnus, *Verhandlungen des 12. Österreichischen Juristentages* II 1, and the German Lawyers' Day 1994 considered the proposals of the *Schuldrechtskommission* (Bundesminister der Justiz [ed.], *Abschlußbericht der Kommission zur Überarbeitung des Schuldrechts*, 1992) which dealt only with limitation periods and the general remedies for non-performance of a contractual obligation. Of course, the 4 Nordic Damages Acts (Norway 1969, Sweden 1972, Finland 1974, and Denmark 1984; see Part 3 I above, nos. 237–240) must not be forgotten.

Part 5: The Law of Delict in the Context of Private Law

A legal system is always a compact whole. In a myriad ways each area **411** affects its neighbouring fields of law, and is influenced by them, in terms of its own content and system of design. This is particularly so in the law of delict or torts, the branch of law most often described, albeit rather simplistically, as 'liability outside contract'.[1] It is only by understanding the forces affecting the law of delict at its margins that one can properly appreciate the full range of the field. We therefore consider next the position of delict in private law. The relationship between the law of torts and constitutional and criminal law is then considered (Part 6, nos. 553 ff.)

Within private law delict is most clearly related to contract law; it is at **412** the juncture between them that the most taxing problems of demarcation and co-ordination occur (see below, section I). Even within one national legal system a range of overlaps and intersections arise with both the law of *negotiorum gestio* (conducting the affairs of another without his authority: see below at section II 1, nos. 507 ff.) and the law of unjust enrichment (below at II 2, nos. 516 ff.) These points of overlap become even clearer when the different national solutions are projected onto a common European screen. Particular points of overlap, with corresponding problems of concurrence of actions, can be traced back to the law of property, whose concept of absolute rights can affect the law of obligations in various ways (below at III, nos. 526 ff). However, the connections between the general rules of delict and special economic torts (the law of unfair competition, monopolies, liability for breach of commercial rights, and copyright) are not dealt with here. Although many legal systems overcome the *concurrence déloyale* with the help of the general law of obligations (as in France, Portugal, the UK, and The Netherlands, whose sixth book of the civil code [BW] devotes an entire section to unfair advertising) it would greatly exceed the framework of a comparative analysis of this size to include those areas. Our point of reference is therefore the law of obligations in the context of 'civil law', and not 'private law' as a whole. Indeed, a further limit is necessary. This study is restricted to civil property law, omitting inheritance and family law. This avoids discussion of conflicts with family-law founded obligations to pay damages, which are anyway marginal in nature. Family law and delict are only interwoven in their essentials where each assigns specific

---

[1] Above at nos. 1–3.

423

protection in the face of liability or provides certain privileges by way of excluding liability for family members in specific instances.

I. THE LAW OF DELICT AND CONTRACT LAW

Bibliography: Adams/Brownsword, 'Privity of Contract: That pestilential nuisance', 56 (1993) *ModLRev* 722–732; Albaladejo, 'La representación', *An.Der.Civ.* 11 (1958) pp. 767–803; Altenburger, 'Grundlagen der Dritthaftung von Sachverständigen für fahrlässig falsche Beleihungswertgutachten', *WM* 1994 pp. 1597–1611; Amsberg, *Anspruchskonkurrenz, Cumul und Samenloop. Eine rechtsvergleichende Untersuchung der Konkurrenz von Ersatzansprüchen aus Vertrag und Delikt im belgischen, niederländischen und deutschen Recht und ihrer Funktion in der Rechtsprechung* (diss. Frankfurt/Main 1994); Androulidaki/Dimitriadou, *Ai ypochreosseis synallaktikis pisteos* (Athens 1972); Arens, 'Zur Anspruchskonkurrenz bei mehreren Haftungsgründen', *AcP* 170 (1970) pp. 392–425; Arlie, 'L'obligation de sécurité du vendeur professionnel', *RJDA* 1993 pp. 409–414; Asser (-Abas), *Bijzondere Overeenkomsten II*, 7th edn. (Zwolle 1990); Assmann, *Die Prospekthaftung* (Cologne *et al.* 1985); Banakas, 'Negligence and Property Rights in the Common Law and the Civil Law', *Rev.Hell.* 40/41 (1987–1988) pp. 41–99; v. Bar, *Probleme der Haftpflicht für deliktsrechtliche Eigentumsverletzungen* (Mannheimer Vorträge zur Versicherungswissenschaft, vol. 55; Karlsruhe 1992); id., 'Negligence, Eigentumsverletzung und reiner Vermögensschaden. Zu den Grenzen der Fahrlässigkeitshaftung in der neueren Entwicklung des Common Law', *RabelsZ* 56 (1992) pp. 410–443; id., 'Tagung für hohe deutsche und englische Richter in Braunschweig-Riddagshausen', *RabelsZ* 58 (1994) pp. 421–464; id., 'Vertragliche Schadensersatzpflichten ohne Vertrag?', *JuS* 1982 pp. 637–645; id., 'Liability for Information and Opinions Causing Pure Economic Loss to Third Parties: A comparison of English and German case-law', in: Markesinis (ed.), *The Gradual Convergence* (Oxford 1994) pp. 98–127; Bénabent, 'Conformité et vices cachés dans la vente: l'éclaircie', *D.* 1994 Chron. 115–116; Bernstein, *Economic Loss* (London 1993); Billiet, 'Haftung und Schadensausgleich bei Aidsinfizierung nach Bluttransfusion in der neueren Entwicklung des französischen Rechts', *VersRAI* 1994 pp. 42–45; Bittner, *Schutz des französischen Käufers vor Mangelfolgeschäden* (diss. Regensburg 1987); Blaikie, 'The Dilatory Solicitor and the Disappointed Legatee', *SLT* 1993 pp. 329–333; Blaurock, 'Haftungsfreizeichnung zugunsten Dritter', *ZHR* 146 (1982) pp. 238–258; Bloth, *Produkthaftung in Schweden, Norwegen und Dänemark* (Heidelberg

1993); Bonell, *An International Restatement of Contract Law: The Unidroit principles of international commercial contracts* (New York 1994); Brügge-meier, 'Die vertragsrechtliche Haftung für fehlerhafte Produkte und der deliktsrechtliche Eigentumsschutz nach § 823 Abs. 1 BGB', *VersR* 1983 pp. 501–511; Büdenbender, *Vorteilsausgleichung und Drittscha-densliquidation bei obligatorischer Gefahrentlastung* (Tübingen 1995); id., 'Wechselwirkungen zwischen Vorteilsausgleichung und Drittschadensli-quidation', *JZ* 1995 pp. 920–928; Bundesministerium der Justiz (ed.), *Abschlußbericht der Kommission zur Überarbeitung des Schuldrechts* (Cologne 1992); Bungert, 'Compensating Harm to the Product itself— A comparison of American and German product liability law', *Tul.L.Rev.* 66 [1992] pp. 1179–1266; Busnelli, 'Itinerari europei nella "terra di nes-suno tra contratto e fatto illecito": La responsabilità da informazioni inesatte', *Contratto e Impresa* 1990 pp. 539–577; Bydlinski, 'Zur Haftung für Erfüllungsgehilfen im Vorbereitungsstadium', *JBl* 1995 pp. 477–488 (part 1) and pp. 558–572 (part 2); v. Caemmerer, 'Das Problem des Dritt-schadensersatzes', *ZBernJV* 100 (1964) pp. 341–382; Calvão da Silva, *Responsabilidade civil do produtor* (Coimbra 1990); Canaris, 'Geschäfts- und Verschuldens-fähigkeit bei Haftung aus "culpa in contrahendo", Gefährdung und Aufopferung', *NJW* 1964 pp. 1987–1993; id., 'Schutzwirkungen zugunsten Dritter bei "Gegenläufigkeit" der Interes-sen', *JZ* 1995 pp. 441–446; Cane, 'Negligent Solicitor escapes Liability', 108 (1992) *LQR* 539–545; Castronovo, 'Liability between Contract and Tort', in: Wilhelmsson (ed.), *Perspectives of Critical Contract Law* (Dart-mouth 1993) pp. 273–291; id., 'L'obbligazione senza prestazione. Ai confini tra contratto e torto', in: *Le ragioni del diritto. Scritti in onore di Luigi Mengoni*, vol. i (Rome 1995) pp. 147–240; Cavanillas Múgica/Tapia Fernández, *La concurrencia de responsabilidad contractual y extracontrac-tual. Tratamiento sustantivo y procesal* (Madrid 1992); Choi, *Die vorvertrag-liche Haftung (Culpa in Contrahendo) und der deliktsrechtliche Schutz primärer Vermögensinteressen: rechtsvergleichende Untersuchungen zum deutschen, englischen und französischen Recht* (Frankfurt *et al.* 1990); Clark, *Contract Law in Ireland*, 3rd edn. (London 1992); Collins, 'Interaction between Contract and Tort in the Conflict of Laws', 16 (1967) *IntCompLQ* 103–144; Contractenrecht VI (-de Groot) (Deventer, loose leaf, as of August 1989; von Bloembergen and Kleijn (edd.); Cornelius, *Der Schutz des Forderungsinhabers gegenüber Dritten im nordischen und deutschen Recht* (Pfaffenweiler 1985); Cornu, *Le problème du cumul de la responsabilité con-tractuelle et de la responsabilité délictuelle* (Paris 1962); Cousy, 'Het verbod van samenloop tussen contractuele en extra-contractuele aanspra-kelijkheid en zijn weerslag', *TPR* 1984 pp. 155–196; Dahm, *Die dogma-tischen Grundlagen und tatbestandlichen Voraussetzungen des Vertrages mit Schutzwirkung für Dritte* (Cologne 1988); id., 'Vorvertraglicher

The Law of Delict in the Context of Private Law

Drittschutz', *JZ* 1992 pp. 1167–1172; Dalcq/Glansdorff, 'Responsabilité aquilienne et contrats', *Rev.crit.jur.belge.* 1976 pp. 20–33; eid., 'Prohibition du concours des responsabilités et irresponsabilité des préposés et agents d'exécution', *Rev.crit.jur.belge* 1978 pp. 431–439; Damman, *Die Einbeziehung Dritter in die Schutzwirkung eines Vertrages. Eine Studie des französischen Rechts im Lichte einer rechtsvergleichenden Betrachtung des deutschen Rechts* (Munich 1990); Deliyannis, 'To paranomon os stoicheion tis ennoias tou astikou adikimatos', *AID* 15 (1951/52) pp. 153–195; Denck, *Der Schutz des Arbeitnehmers vor der Außenhaftung* (Heidelberg 1980); Derleder, 'Deliktshaftung für Werkmängel', *AcP* 195 (1995) pp. 137–170; Dietz, *Anspruchskonkurrenz bei Vertragsverletzung und Delikt* (Bonn and Cologne 1934); Dirix, *Het begrip schade* (Antwerp *et al.* 1984); Dupeyroux/Prétot, *Droit de la sécurité sociale*, 6th edn. (Paris 1993); Fallon, 'Le concours en responsabilité?: Tâtonnements et certitudes de la Cour de Cassation', *Dr.europ.transp.* 1974 pp. 541–562; Elvinger, 'La responsabilité des constructeurs dans les législation et jurisprudence luxembourgoises', *Pas. luxemb.* 28 (1990–1992) pp. 427–456; Feldthusen, *Economic Negligence*, 2nd edn. (Toronto 1989); Ferraz de Brito/Luso Soares/Romeira Mesquita, *Código de processo civil anotado*, 8th edn. (Coimbra 1992); Figueiredo Dias/Sinde Monteiro, 'Portugal', in: Deutsch/Schreiber (edd.), *Medical Responsibility in Western Europe* (Berlin *et al.* 1985) pp. 513–554; Fleming, 'The Solicitor and the disappointed Beneficiary', 109 (1993) *LQR* 344–349; Foerste, 'Deliktische Haftung für Schlechterfüllung?'; *NJW* 1992 pp. 27–28; Furnston (ed.), *The Law of Tort: Policies and trends in liability for damage to property and economic loss* (London 1986); García Rubio, *La responsabilidad precontractual en el Derecho español* (Madrid 1991); ead., 'Responsabilidad por ruptura injustificada de negociaciones', *La Ley* 1989 (4) pp. 1112–1119; Gasis, 'Peri tin ennoian tou voithou ekplirosseos kai tou prostithentos', in: *Eranion Maridaki*, vol. ii (Athens 1963) pp. 227–284; Georgiades, 'I syrroi axioseon epi syndromis symvatikis kai adikopraktikis evthinis', *Diki* 6 (1975) pp. 43–63; Giardina, *Responsabilità contrattuale e responsabilità extracontrattuale* (Milan 1993); Grandmoulin, *Nature délictuelle de la responsabilité pour violation des obligations contractuelles* (thesis Rennes 1894); Grunewald, 'Eigentumsverletzungen im Zusammenhang mit fehlerhaften Werkleistungen', *JZ* 1987 pp. 1098–1104; Helm, *Haftung für Schäden an Frachtgütern* (Karlsruhe 1966); Herbots, 'Quasi-delictuele aansprakelijkheid en overeenkomsten', *TPR* 1980 pp. 1055–1099; id., 'De nalatige antiquairs', *RW* 1983–84 pp. 163–169; id., 'Samenloop contractuele en delictuele aansprakelijkheid', in: Vandenberghe (ed.), *Onrechtmatige daad* (Antwerp 1979) pp. 133–158; id., 'Les relations mouvementées entre le droit de la responsabilité civile et le droit des contrats au Royaume-Uni', *Rev.dr.int.dr.comp.* 70 (1993) pp. 205–219; id.,

'L'affinage du principe de la transmission automatique des droits "propter rem" du maître de l'ouvrage à l'acquéreur de l'immeuble', *Rev.crit.-jur.belge* 1992 pp. 512–549; Hondius (ed.), *Precontractual Liability* (Deventer 1991); Hogg, 'Negligence and Economic Loss in England, Australia, Canada and New Zealand', 43 (1994) *IntCompLQ* pp. 116–141; Horn, 'Culpa in Contrahendo', *JuS* 1995 pp. 377–387; Hübner, 'Beweislastverteilung bei der Verletzung von Vertragspflichten im französischen und deutschen Recht', in: *FS Baumgärtel* (Cologne *et al.* 1990) pp. 151–161; Huet, *Responsabilité contractuelle et responsabilité délictuelle. Essai de délimitation entre les deux ordres de responsabilité* (thesis Paris vol. ii 1978); International Chamber of Commerce (ed.), *Formation of contracts and precontractual liability* (Paris 1990) (*et al.* with country reports: Federal Republic of Germany [Ebke], England [Goode], and France [Schmidt-Szalewski]); Jackson, 'Injured Feelings resulting from Breach of Contract', 26 [1977] *IntCompLQ* pp. 502–515; Jansen, *Onrechtmatige daad: algemene bepalingen* (Deventer 1986); Jassagne (sous la direction de), *Traité pratique de droit commercial*, vol. i (Brussels 1990); *JClCiv* (-Jourdain), 'Responsabilité fondée sur la faute. Application de la notion de faute: imprudences et négligences; fautes commises à l'occasion d'un contrat', arts. 1382 to 1386, *Fasc.* 130–1; *JClCiv* (-Espagnon), 'Rapports entre responsabilités délictuelle et contractuelle', arts. 1146 to 1155, *Fasc.* 16–1; *JClCiv* (-de Poulpiquet), 'Notaire. Responsabilité civile. Situations diverses', arts. 1382 to 1386, *Fasc.* 420–5; v. Jhering, 'Culpa in contrahendo oder Schadensersatz bei nichtigen oder nicht zur Perfection gelangten Verträgen', *JhJb* 4 (1861) pp. 1–112; Jørgensen, 'Berufshaftpflicht für Beratung im dänischen Recht', *KF* 1988 pp. 42–43; id., 'Die skandinavische Lehre der Vertragsverletzung', in: *FS Larenz* (Munich 1973) pp. 549–573; Jourdain, 'L'obligation de sécurité. A propos de quelques arrêts récents', *Gaz.Pal.* 1993 Doctr. 1171–1176; id., 'La nature de la responsabilité civile dans les chaînes de contrat après l'arrêt de l'Assemblée plénière du 12 juillet 1991', *D.* 1992 *Chron.* 149–156; Karassis, *Culpa in contrahendo im griechischen Recht* (Thessalonika 1978); Karollus, *Funktion und Dogmatik der Haftung aus Schutzgesetzverletzung* (Vienna and New York 1992); Katzenmeier, *Vertragliche und deliktische Haftung in ihrem Zusammenspiel, dargestellt am Problem der 'weiterfressenden Mängel'* (Berlin 1994); Keitel, *Rechtsgrundlagen und systematische Stellung des Vertrages mit Schutzwirkung für Dritte* (Frankfurt/Main *et al.* 1988); Kennedy, 'England', in: Deutsch/Schreiber (edd.), *Medical Responsibility in Western Europe* (Berlin *et al.* 1985) pp. 113–162; Knöpfle, 'Zur Problematik der Beurteilung einer Norm als Schutzgesetz im Sinne des § 823 Abs. 2 BGB', *NJW* 1967 pp. 697–702; Kocks, 'Grundzüge des belgischen Produkthaftungs- und Gewährleistungsrechts', *PHI* 1990 pp. 180–196; Kötz, 'The Doctrine of Privity of Contract', *Tel Aviv Univ.Stud.L.*

10 (1990) pp. 195–212; Koziol, 'Delikt, Verletzung von Schuldverhältnis-sen und Zwischenbereich', *JBl* 1994 pp. 209–223; Lambert-Faivre, 'Fon-dement et régime de l'obligation de sécurité', *D.* 1994 *Chron.* 81–85; Lando/Beale (ed.), *The Principles of European Contract Law*, vol. i (Dor-drecht *et al.* 1995); Larroumet, 'L'effet relatif des contrats et la négation de l'existence d'une action en responsabilité nécessairement contrac-tuelle dans les ensembles contractuels', *Sem.Jur.* 1991, I,3531; *Law Commission, Consultation Paper No. 121*, 'Privity of Contract: Contracts for the benefit of third parties' (London 1991); Leenen, 'Der "Pferdefutter"-Fall', *Jura* 1993 pp. 534–539; Lefebvre, 'De la responsabilité, délictuelle, contractuelle. Responsabilité des locataires envers le propriétaire en cas d'incendie (art. 1734 C.civ.). Loi du 5 janvier 1883. Responsabilité du patron envers l'ouvrier. Propositions des lois', *Rev.crit.légis. et juris* 1886 pp. 485–523; Litten, *Die Haftung für Drittvermögensschäden nach Art. 1382 Cc verglichen mit dem deutschen Recht* (diss. Göttingen 1970); Stephan Lorenz, 'Die culpa in contrahendo im französischen Recht', *ZEuP* 1994 pp. 218–243; Werner Lorenz, 'Some Thoughts About Contract and Tort', in: Wallington and Merkin (edd.), *Essays in Memory of F. H. Lawson* (London 1986) pp. 86–100; id., 'Dogmatismus, Evolution und Reform im englischen Privatrecht: Privity of Contract', in: *FS für Arthur Kaufmann* (Heidelberg 1993) pp. 709–727; id., 'Contract Beneficiaries in German Law', in: Markesinis (ed.), *The Gradual Convergence* (Oxford 1994) pp. 65–97; Lorenz/Markesinis, 'Solicitor's Liability towards Third Parties: Back into the troubled waters of the contract/tort divide', 56 (1993) *ModLRev* 558–563; Lupoi, 'Il contratto a favore di terzo in diritto inglese', *Riv.Dir.Com.* 1967, I, pp. 171–240; Markesinis, 'Caparo & Murphy: How two recent decisions of the House of Lords look from the other side of the Channel', *ERPL* 1 (1993) pp. 201–214; Markesinis/Munday, *An Outline of the Law of Agency*, 3rd edn. (London 1992); Marty, *La responsabilidad civil en Derecho comparado* (Barcelona 1962); Meller, *Obligation de Sécurité* (Berlin 1974); Menezes Cordeiro, *Da Boa Fé no Direito Civil*, vol. i (Lisboa 1984); Michaelides/Nouaros, 'Evthini ek symvaseos kai evthini ex adikimatos kata to schedion tou Astikou Kodi-kos', *AID* 4 (1937) pp. 674–718; Middleton/Rogge, 'Anwaltshaftung gegenüber Dritten im englischen und deutschen Recht', *VersR* 1994 pp. 1027–1033; Moitinho de Almeida, 'A responsabilidade civil do médico e o seu seguro', in: *Scientia juridica* 1972 pp. 327–355; Monateri, *Cumulo di responsabilità contrattuale ed extracontrattuale (analisi comparata di un pro-blema)* (Padua 1989); Mota Pinto, 'A responsabilidade pré-negocial pela não conclusão dos contratos', *Boletim da Faculdade de Direito*, Suplemento XIV (Coimbra 1966); id., 'Garantia de bom funcionamento e vícios do produto', *CJ* X (1985–3) pp. 17–29; Müller, 'Zur Haftung des Gesellschaf-ter-Geschäftsführers aus culpa in contrahendo und aus § 64 Abs. 1

GmbHG', *ZIP* 1993 pp. 1531–1538; Müller-Boruttau, 'Entwicklung und heutige Funktion der allgemeinen Prospekthaftung', *JA* 1992 pp. 226–334; Muñoz de Dios, 'Artículo 1591 Cc: ruina de construcción. Responsabilidad y legitimación activa para exigirla', *La Ley* 1990 (1) pp. 1081–1089; Namgalies, *Das französische Arbeitsunfallrecht* (Berlin 1981); Nieuwenhuis, *Anders en Eender. Beschouwingen over samenloop van wanprestatie en onrechtmatige daad* (Deventer 1982); Norrie, 'Liability of Solicitors to Third Parties', *SLT* 1988 pp. 309–321; id., '"Binding" precedent and disappointed beneficiaries', *Jurid.Rev.* 1990 pp. 107–110; O'Connor, *Good Faith in English Law* (Aldershot 1989); Papaeleftheriou, 'Tina peri tis theorias tis mi syrrois dikaiopraktikis kai exodikaiopraktikis evthinis', *NoB* 6 (1958) pp. 1101–1106; Pauwels, 'Over metaalslakken en vergiftigde koeien: een geval van samenloop?', *RW* 1986–87 pp. 330–332; Percival, 'After *Caparo*: Liability in business transactions revisited', *ModLRev.* 54 (1991) pp. 739–745; Peretti Griva, 'Concorso di responsabilità contrattuale ed extra-contrattuale', *Foro.pad.* 1960, I, 639–642; Pfeifer, 'Die Haftung der Wirtschaftsprüfergesellschaft in der italienischen Rechtsprechung', *Jahrb. f. ital. Recht* 8 (1995) pp. 203–209; Phillips, 'Lost Chances in Delict: All or nothing?', *Jurid.Rev.* 1995 pp. 401–413; Pinto Monteiro, *Cláusulas limitativas de exclusão de responsabilidade civil* (Coimbra 1985); Posch, 'Österreich: Leitentscheidung zum Ersatz von "Weiterfresserschäden" nach umgesetztem Gemeinschaftsrecht', *PHI* 1994 pp. 149–153; Pouliadis, *Culpa in contrahendo und Schutz Dritter* (Berlin 1982); Prata, *Notas sobre responsabilidade précontratual* (Lisbon 1991); Preuss, *Vertragsbruch als Delikt im anglo-amerikanischen Recht* (Heidelberg 1977); Princigalli, *La Responsabilità del Medico* (Naples 1983); Quick, 'Die zivilrechtliche Haftung des französischen Abschlußprüfers', *RIW* 1993 pp. 305–309; Van Quickenborne, 'Réflexions sur le dommage purement contractuel', *Rev.crit.jur.belge* 1988 pp. 344–370; Quill, 'Subcontractors, Exclusion Clauses and Privity', *ILT* 9 (1991) pp. 211–214; Rasir, 'Cumul de la responsabilité contractuelle et aquilienne', *JT* 1976 pp. 164–165; Reindl, 'Die zivilrechtliche Haftung bei Unfällen mit Pistengeräten', *ZVR* 1994 pp. 193–198; Reinhart, *UN-Kaufrecht* (Heidelberg 1991); Van Rijn, 'Responsabilité aquilienne et contrats', *JT* 1975 pp. 505–506; Rivero Hernández, 'Naturaleza y situación del contrato del "falsus procurator"', *An.Der.Civ.* 29 (1976) pp. 1047–1136; Roller, *Die Prospekthaftung im Englischen und im Deutschen Recht* (Berlin 1991); Sacco, 'Concorso delle azioni contrattuale ed extracontrattuale', in: Visintini (ed.), *Risarcimento del danno contrattuale ed extracontrattuale* (Milan 1984) pp. 155–163; Sánchez Calero, *Instituciones de Derecho mercantil*, 16th edn. (Madrid 1992); van de Sande Bakhuijzen, 'De wisselwerking tussen vertrouwen en zorgvuldigheid', *WPNR* 1981 no. 5559 pp. 220–225, no. 5560 pp. 236–241, no. 5561 pp. 257–262; Santos Briz, 'La responsabilidad civil en supuestos de prestación de servicios', in: Deutsch/Taupitz (edd.), *Haftung der Dienstleistungsberufe* (Heidelberg 1993) pp. 93–125; van Schellen, *Toerekening naar redelijkheid* (Zwolle 1985); Schlechtriem, *Vertragsordnung und außervertragliche Haftung* (Frankfurt/Main 1972); id., 'Vertragliche und außervertragliche Haftung', in: Bundesminister der Justiz (ed.), *Gutachten und Vorschläge zur Überarbeitung des Schuldrechts* (Cologne 1981) pp. 1591–1679; id., 'Abgrenzungsfragen bei der positiven Vertragsverletzung', *VersR* 1973 pp. 581–595; Schmidt-Szalewski, 'La période précontractuelle en droit français', *Rev.int.dr.comp.* 42 (1990) pp. 545–566; Schoordijk, 'De toepasselijkheid van buiten contractuele diligentienormen in contractuele verhoudingen', *WPNR* 1964 no. 4810 pp. 189–192 and no. 4812 pp. 213–216; id., 'Bookreview' (Asser [-Hartkamp]), *WPNR* 1987 no. 5818 pp. 104–106; v. Schroeter, *Die Drittschadensliquidation in europäischen Privatrechten und im deutschen Kollisionsrecht* (Frankfurt/Main 1995); Schwark, 'Kaufvertragliche Mängelhaftung und deliktsrechtliche Ansprüche', *AcP* 179 (1979) pp. 57–84; Sinde Monteiro, 'Haftung des Dienstleistenden. Der EWG-Richtlinienvorschlag und das portugiesische positive Recht', in: Deutsch/Taupitz, *Haftung der Dienstleistungsberufe* (Heidelberg 1993) pp. 127–135; id., 'Responsabilidade médica em Portugal', *BolMinJust* 332 (1984) pp. 21–79; Stalfort, *Der Schutz von Unfallopfern durch die Sozialversicherung in den Niederlanden und in Deutschland* (diss. Osnabrück 1993); Staub, 'Die positiven Vertragsverletzungen und ihre Rechtsfolgen', in: *FS für den 26. Deutschen Juristentag* (Berlin 1902) pp. 29–56; Steele, 'Two Cheers for *Caparo*: *Ravenscroft* v. *Rederiaktiebolaget Transatlantic*', 56 [1993] *ModLRev* 244–247; Steffen, 'Haftung im Wandel', *ZVersWiss* 1993 pp. 13–37; id., 'Die Bedeutung der "Stoffgleichheit" mit dem "Mangelunwert" für die Herstellerhaftung aus Weiterfresserschäden', *VersR* 1988 pp. 977–980; Strauch, 'Rechtsgrundlagen der Haftung für Rat, Auskunft und Gutachten', *JuS* 1992 pp. 897–902; Symmons, 'The Problem of the Applicability of Tort Liability to Negligent Misstatements in Contractual Situations: A Critique on the *Nunes Diamonds* and *Sealand* Cases', 21 (1975) *McGillLJ* 79–112; Tercier, 'Le concours d'actions selon la directive européenne et les projets suisses sur la responsabilité du fait du produit', in: *Aspects du droit européen/Beiträge zum europäischen Recht. Festgabe der rechtswissenschaftlichen Fakultät der Universität Freiburg an den Schweizerischen Juristenverein* (Freiburg/Switzerland 1993) pp. 191–210; Tettenborn, 'Enquiries before Contract: The wrong answer?', (1992) 51 *CLJ* 415–418; Thomson, 'Delictual Liability Between Parties to a Contract', *SLT* 1994 pp. 29–34; Tiedtke, 'Zur Haftung des Herstellers eines fehlerhaften Produktes bei Schäden an der gelieferten Sache', *ZIP* 1992 pp. 1446–1452; Treitel, *The Law of Contract*, 7th edn. (London 1987); id., 'Remedies for Breach of Contract', *IntEncCompL* VII 16 (Tübingen *et al.* 1976); Urban,

"Vertrag" mit Schutzwirkung zugunsten Dritter und Drittschadensliquidation (Bergisch Gladbach and Cologne 1989); Uría, *Derecho mercantil*, 17th edn. (Madrid 1990); Ussing, *Aftaler*, 3rd edn. (Copenhagen 1950); Vagner, 'Die Haftung bei Dienstleistungen aus Sicht des dänischen Rechts', in: Deutsch/Taupitz, *Haftung der Dienstleistungsberufe* (Heidelberg 1993) pp. 221–230; Vaz Serra, 'Responsabilidade contratual e responsabilidade extracontratual', *BolMinJust* 85 (1959) pp. 115–241; id., 'Reparação do dano não patrimonial', *BolMinJust* 83 (1959) pp. 69–111; Visintini, 'Responsabilità contrattuale (Una distinzione in crisi?)', *Rass.dir.civ.* 1983 pp. 1077–1091; Vollkommer, *Anwaltshaftungsrecht* (Munich 1989); Waddams, 'Privity of Contract in the Supreme Court of Canada', 109 (1993) *LQR* 349–352; v. Walter, *Die Konkurrenz vertraglicher und deliktischer Schadensersatznormen im deutschen, ausländischen und internationalen Privatrecht* (diss. Regensburg 1977); Weir, 'Suit by First Contractor for Damage to Second Contractor's Goods', (1977) *CLJ* 24–27; Welser, *Schadenersatz statt Gewährleistung* (Vienna 1994); id., *Die Haftung für Rat, Auskunft und Gutachten* (Vienna 1983); Graf v. Westphalen, '"Weiterfressende" Schäden und kein Ende?', *Jura* 1992 pp. 511–514; Whittacker, *The Relationship between Contract and Tort: A comparative study of French and English law* (diss. Oxford 1987); Wiegand, *Die "Sachwalter-haftung" als richterliche Rechtsfortbildung* (Berlin 1991); Wilts, § 635 BGB und Deliktsansprüche, *VersR* 1967 pp. 817–820; Winfield, *The Province of the Law of Tort* (Cambridge 1931); Witz/Wolter, 'Vertragliche oder deliktische Haftung im Rahmen von "Vertragsgruppen" (groupes de contrats) in Frankreich? Cour de Cassation (Ass.plén.) vom 12.7.1991', *ZEuP* 1993 pp. 592–598; Manfred Wolf, 'BGH-Rechtsprechung aktuell: Prospekthaftung und Verschulden bei Vertragsschluß', *NJW* 1994 pp. 24–26; Wolfer, 'Frankreich: Die Rechtsprechung des Kassationshofes zu Vertragsketten', *PHI* 1991 pp. 220–225 (part 1) and *PHI* 1992 pp. 30–40 (part 2); Zepos, 'Le problème du cumul des responsabilités contractuelle et délictuelle en droit hellénique', *Rev.Hell.* 15 (1962) pp. 256–262; Zoppini, 'Informatizzazione della conoscenza e responsabilità: I sistemi esperti', *Dir.Inf.* 1989 pp. 581–605.

1. AN OVERVIEW OF THE PROBLEMS OF LIABILITY STRADDLING CONTRACT AND TORT

The overlap between the liabilities to pay damages in contract and in tort **413** gives rise to two major questions. The first is how each area of law complements the other, and the second is how to resolve situations in which a single act gives rise to a claim for damages in both areas but with a different result in each. What must then be determined is which claim takes precedence.

414   The second question is clearly the more problematic (see nos. 418 ff.) Often the first is essentially a problem of characterization only, which, from the comparative law perspective, must be analysed so as to allow for European discourse in respect of the substantive points upon which it rests. One may speak of a complementary role for both contract and tort where the level in abstraction of a codified legal system is insufficient, i.e. where the absence of a sufficiently precise General Part necessitates reference to specific rules of either branch: specific rules may be found which according to their systematic position affect only liability in tort, but which in practice also necessarily affect liability in contract.[2] Further, some general concepts, such as that of the *bonus paterfamilias,* are found under only one of contract and tort titles, but are also significant in the other.[3] Phenomena such as these concern us as little as the cases in which liability in tort is considered only because the contract-based obligations are void for, say, breach of a statutory prohibition or some other reason. Of interest here are those mechanisms which a legal system develops to plug specific lacunae within a given legal area, such that recourse is had to another area which is developed instead. Of particular interest[4] are duties implied for the benefit of a contractual partner's health and property, the concept of *culpa in contrahendo,* contracts having protective effects for the benefit of third parties, and cases of transferred loss (*Drittschadensliquidation*). Because of the above shift between contract and tort, a comparative analysis is compelled to present them as part

---

[2] Cf. e.g. Arts. 2044 and 2045 Ital. Cc on self-defence and emergency, on which Cendon (-Venchiarutti) vol. iv, Art. 2044 n. 1 ('l'art. 2044 c.c. . . . esonera da ogni responsabilità'). By Cass. 3.1.1994, n. 6, *Foro.it.* 1994, I, 1783 the rule of *restitutio in integrum* contained in Art. 2058 ital. Cc. has a 'general character'. Although it is located in the law of tort it can also be applied to contracts. Further examples of rules and definitions which, although located by the respective code within tort law, apply equally to contract are: Port. Cc Arts. 485 sec. 2 (liability for information), 487 sec. 2 (definition of negligence), and 489 (liability of persons *non compos mentis*) (cf. Almeida Costa, *Obrigações,* 5th edn., pp. 432–433) and French Cc Art. 1384 sec. 5 (liability of principal for assistants, cf. Viney, *Sem.Jur.* 1994, I, 3773 pp. 304–305). In contrast, German BGB § 276 sec. 1 sub-sec. 3 refers expressly to §§ 827, 828 BGB.

[3] Cass.civ. 11.1.1922, *D.P.* 1922, 1, 16 concluded that in contract law a different standard of care applies from that which applies in tort. However, it is by no means certain whether this differentiation still holds today: see Marty/Raynaud, *Droit Civil II (1),* 2nd edn., no. 448; Terré/Simler/Lequette, *Obligations,* 5th edn., no. 829. This based on the fact that the *Code civil* retains the concept of *bon père de famille* in contract (e.g. Art. 1137 sec. 1) and in the law of the carrying on of a business by an agent without the principal's authority (e.g. Art. 1374 sec. 1), but not in Arts. 1382–1386. See the principle of *non-cumul des responsabilités.*

[4] A further example is the liability of a tenant who does not return property to his landlord on time. That interest on the rent becomes payable as damages is based on contract law in Germany (§ 557 BGB: BGH 27.4.1977, *NJW* 1977 p. 1335), whereas in England it is tort-based (trespass to land: *Inverugie Investments Ltd.* v. *Hackett* [1995] 1 WLR 731).

of the non-contractual law of obligations: the blurring of the borders between contract and tort has been a theme of both areas for some time. Indeed this development may well have reached its zenith in respect of liability for information resulting in pure economic loss (see below, nos. 492 ff).

The second major question concerning the overlap of contract and tort **415** is whether, and if so under what conditions and with what consequences, a breach of contract might (or must) be treated as giving rise to tortious liability. This question leads to the rules on concurrence of actions. In all jurisdictions, when a plaintiff has a right of action in both tort and contract, he is not permitted double recovery but must choose the more favourable of the two causes of action.[5] To turn the question around and consider whether a tortious act may be treated as a contractual breach would be less meaningful: as soon as it is specified which breaches of contract amount to a tort, then the converse is also fixed. In a typical tort case the tortfeasor and the victim are not linked by any pre-existing contract, and it would therefore be ill-conceived to project the law of tort onto contract.

Although the present discussion is limited to the two central ques- **416** tions, the great web of complexities at the border between contract and tort cannot be developed from discussion of these questions alone. Some of the remaining facets of our general theme have been discussed above, some will be discussed at a later point, and some are of no significance whatever for the study of delict. One issue, already discussed in relation to protected interests, is whether third parties should be liable in tort for affecting or frustrating contractual rights.[6] It has also been shown that intentionally inducing a breach of contract[7] (*actio de dolo*[8]) is a tort everywhere. A rich seam of material exists in which tort law takes account of the voluntary (contractual or quasi-contractual[9]) assumption of duties of care, and meets breach with liability whether the assumption was in

[5] See: Gomard, *Obligationsret II*, pp. 143–144; Mazeaud/Chabas, *Obligations*, 8th edn., no. 404; *Archer* v. *Brown* [1984] 2 All ER 267 (Pain J).

[6] Cf. BGH 24.2.1954, BGHZ 12 pp. 308, 317–318 (simple breach of contractual obligation not founding cause of action in tort; contractual claim not a 'right' under § 823 sec. 1 BGB) with Cass. 19.12.1985, n. 6506, *Foro.it.* 1986, I 383; Cass. 12.11.1988, n. 6132, *Foro.it.* 1989, I, 742; Trib. Milano 9.11.1992, *Giur.it.* 1993, I, 2, 576; CA Athens 3178/1982, *NoB* 31 (1983) p. 519 (negligent interference with third party's contractual rights regarded as cause of action in tort).

[7] Based on *Lumley* v. *Gye* 118 ER 749 (1853). See above, nos. 260 and 310.

[8] Above, nos. 36 ff.; also Cass. 20.10.1983, n. 6160, *Giur.it.* 1984, I, 1, 439; Trib. Verona 4.3.1991, *Giur.it.* 1993, I, 2, 286; BGH 9.7.1992, *FamRZ* 1992 p. 1401; and BGH 19.10.1993, *NJW* 1994 p. 128.

[9] Lord Reid in *Hedley Byrne* v. *Heller* [1964] AC 465, 485 ('so as to bring them virtually in the position of parties contracting with each other') and HR 18.11.1994, *NedJur* 1995 No. 170 p. 721 (liability of sole shareholder of bankrupt company for creditor's loss; shareholder had led the creditor to believe that the company was creditworthy).

relation to the subsequent plaintiff[10] or to an unharmed third party.[11] Article 923 sec. 2 Greek Cc, Arts. 486, 491, and 492 sec. 2 Port. Cc, and §§ 831 sec. 2, 832 sec. 2, 834, and 838 BGB are all codified examples of the second constellation of cases, in which the law of tort imposes a duty to act (and sanctions breaches), on someone who, in relation to another person (usually his employer) is already bound by contract to make safe the source of danger from which the damage to the victim later arises.[12] Once such contractual duties of care[13] are regarded as sufficient to establish tortious duties of care towards the contractual partner, then

[10] Cf. *Esso Petroleum Co. Ltd.* v. *Mardon* [1976] 2 All ER 5, 7; *Walker* v. *Northumberland County Council* [1995] 1 All ER 737; Hof 's-Hertogenbosch 5.3.1991, *NedJur* 1993 No. 438 p. 1546; Hof Leeuwarden 29.1.1992, *NedJur* 1992 No. 830 pp. 3552, 3553 (tortious liability for breach of contractual professional duties); OGH 23.3.1993, SZ 66/40 p. 201 (tortious duty of organizer of ski race to ensure safety of participants based on contract); OLG Karlsruhe 7.6.1978, *VersR* 1979 p. 61 (pre-contractual relationship of reliance as basis of an occupier's duty to make premises safe); OLG Düsseldorf 5.11.1992, *NJW-RR* 1993 p. 315 ('tortious liability of a travel organizer on account of the breach of his duty to render premises safe depends on the contractual obligations he had to the travellers'); and RC 20.11.1984, *CJ* IX (1984–5) p. 68 (tortious liability of hospital to a mentally ill patient who absconded and was injured during his outing affirmed on basis of a breach of a contractual duty to supervise the patient). See Dias/Markesinis, *Tort Law*, 2nd edn., p. 76; Hepple & Matthews, *Tort*, 3rd edn., p. 162 ('contract may provide the source of . . . a duty [to act] in tort'), and Thomson, *SLT* 1994 pp. 29, 33.

[11] Cf. HR 1.10.1993, *RvdW* 1993 No. 189 (tortious liability of nurse affirmed for breach of employment contract in placing leaking hot-water bottle in child's bed); BGH 1.2.1994, *NJW* 1994 p. 1594 (tortious liability of consultant for misorganization in respect of hot-water bottles in incubators) and Cass.civ. 16.12.1992, *Sem.Jur.* 1993, IV, 505 (liability of estate agent for the impossibility of construction project to the purchaser in contract and to vendor in tort). French decisions show a general tendency to deduce *faute* from a breach of contract in respect of a third party injured thereby, cf. *JClCiv* (-Jourdain), Application de la notion de faute, Arts. 1382 to 1386, Fasc. 130–1, nos. 70 ff. and id., *Rev.trim.dr.civ.* 1993, pp. 362–364. Position is different where purpose of contractual duty was to protect the contractual parties against the third party. E.g. *Pacific Associates Inc. and Another* v. *Baxter and Others* [1989] 2 All ER 159: plaintiff had a building works contract with the Sheikh of Dubai, under which payments to contractors were to be increased should unforeseen difficulties arise with ground workings. The defendant engineers were employed to supervise the works. The engineers refused to affirm that difficulties encountered were unforeseeable. The Court of Appeal rejected negligence liability of the engineers: no duty of care owed to the plaintiff. Cf. BGH 22.4.1965, BGHZ 43 pp. 374, 376, where in reliance on §§ 317 and 319 BGB it was said that an arbitrator is only liable for his expert opinion if 'it is manifestly incorrect'. *Gran Gelato Ltd.* v. *Richcliff Group Ltd.* [1992] 1 All ER 865 (no liability of a vendor's lawyer for incorrect information to the vendor as that information was provided in the lawyer's capacity as vendor's representative and was hence attributable to vendor); this decision is doubtful in the light of *Smith* v. *Eric Bush* [1990] 1 AC 831 (Tettenborn, (1992) 51 *CLJ* 415–418).

[12] It is unclear whether a contract should be regarded as the dominant source of duties to protect third parties; where a contract is void a tortious claim will usually also fail, and the notion of the contract having protective effects for the benefit of third parties comes to the fore: OGH 7.4.1992, *JBl* 1992 p. 786. See also Scottish law on third-party liability of lawyers failing to meet contractual obligations to clients (explained in *Weir* v. *J. M. Hodge & Sons* 1990 *SLT* 266, 269 D).

[13] The same applies to duties arising from negotiations (*culpa in contrahendo*) and/or from a special relationship of a public law nature: OGH 24.4.1991, *JBl* 1991 p. 586.

one must accept the principle of concurrence of actions. It would be meaningless to expand contractual duties into universal rules, and at the same time to say that tort law was no longer applicable.

Finally, it is worth recalling that the exact opposite situation is often encountered regarding no-fault liability, namely that tortious liability applies only in respect of non-contractual third parties, and *not* to the contractual partner of the keeper of the risk.[14] In respect of animals, there are differing opinions[15] as to whether persons employed to care for animals[16] or those to whom the animal has been lent,[17] can rely on the benefits of strict liability. In respect of road traffic accidents there is a range of rules creating a special regime which softens the normal strict liability of occupants of vehicles to third parties.[18]

Not only does contract affect tort law. The converse situation, in which **417** a tort constitutes a contractual breach, is more common. That someone cannot legally be bound to commit a tort is self-evident everywhere.[19] For example, where a person whose employment requires integrity acts dishonestly outside work, such conduct may justify dismissal. This example is unrelated to the issue of conflict between two alternative causes of action with which we are concerned. It is not important whether a crime has been committed, nor that the crime caused loss to a third party. Whether or not the crime also constitutes a breach of contract is unimportant. The situation is the same where the tenant of a flat becomes involved in a motor accident with his landlord, or where a purchaser defames his contracting vendor (which in some circumstances

[14] It is unclear whether there are any examples of fault liability for this phenomenon. Cases of liability for incorrect information or authentication might fall into this category. When the sale of goods law limitation period is shorter than that of tort (or its equivalent in *culpa in contrahendo*) the question arises whether the conduct of the expert constitutes a tort, and if so whether the shorter limitation period prevails over the longer statutory period. Cf. nos. 429, 449 ff. below and *Henderson* v. *Merrett Syndicates Ltd.* [1994] 3 All ER 506.

[15] See above, nos. 222 and 360.

[16] Affirming Cass.civ. 9.3.1886, *S.* 1886, 1, 244 and RG 6.3.1902, RGZ 50 pp. 244, 248–250. Cass.civ. 9.3.1886 was overruled by Cass.civ. 16.1.1951, *JCP* 1951, II, 6163. The departure from the old case-law was based, not on a new interpretation of Art. 1385 Cc, but on the application of the principle of *non-concours des responsabilités* which had been established in the interim.

[17] See BGH 9.6.1992, *NJW* 1992 p. 2474; BGH 22.12.1992, *NJW* 1993 p. 2611. In contrast see sec. 5(2) Animals Act 1971. French contract law prevails under the principle of *non-cumul* (below, nos. 431 ff). Cf. Cass.civ. 8.2.1961, *D.* 1961 *Jur.* 218 (liability of stables for a bucking horse). Analogous problems may appear elsewhere, such as duties to maintain buildings. Cf. CA Athens 4268/1956, *NoB* 5 (1957) p. 325: the application of Art. 925 Greek Cc to the relationship of landlord/tenant affirmed. BGH 9.7.1959, *VersR* 1959 pp. 948, 949 states that a contract between the parties does not exclude the application of § 836 BGB.

[18] See e.g. §§ 8 and 8a StVG (German equivalent of the English Road Traffic Acts), Art. 12 of the Greek statute of 4./5.12.1911 on criminal and civil liability for vehicles, and Art. 185 Dutch WVW (see HR 19.3.1993, *NedJur* 1993 Nr. 305 p. 1124). On Spain, see Santos Briz, *Responsabilidad civil*, 6th edn., II pp. 604–608. In contrast, see Arts. 1 and 2 of French statute No. 85–677 of 5.7.1985. [19] See Clark, *Contract Law in Ireland*, 3rd edn., pp. 292–293.

can justify withdrawal from the contract[20]). Issues of conflict in the relationship between contract and tort can only arise when a single act gives rise to liability in damages in both areas.[21] This point is absent from both examples: in the first there is no breach of contract (the accident is unrelated to the tenancy[22]) and in the second the breach of contract (if any) does not give rise to an action for damages. Thus the problem is not whether the law of tort applies between contractual partners[23] (which is patently the case in all European legal systems). Rather, it is as follows: if a breach of contract gives rise to a right to damages in both contract and tort, does the two-pronged approach subsist, or does the contractual claim take precedence?[24]

2. DEVELOPMENT OF BASIC PRINCIPLES OF CONCURRENCE OF ACTIONS FROM THE LAW OF OBLIGATIONS RELATING TO PURE ECONOMIC LOSS

418 The first objective is to find an approach to the most important European intersections between liability in contract and in tort. Not surprisingly, these areas of overlap vary in size in different countries. The smaller the set of interests protected by tort law, the fewer the breaches of contract actually covered by it. Not only are the problems of conflict less pressing when the scope of tort law is narrow, but such a system itself suggests the application of the principle of concurrence of actions (see below, nos. 419 ff). Conversely, a broad concept of tort can co-exist with a narrow

---

[20] E.g. BGH 25.5.1951, *LM* No. 1 to § 276 (Hd) BGB and RG 1.10.1921, RGZ 102 pp. 408, 409. Cf. BGH 30.3.1995, *NJW* 1995 p. 1954 (termination of contract with a lawyer on suspicion of his embezzlement of *other* clients' money). Bianca, *Diritto Civile*, vol. iv, p. 94 explains that a person may resile from a contract where he has reason to believe the creditor cannot protect the person and goods of the debtor who is otherwise ready to perform his obligations. For a Danish analysis of this see Gomard, *Erstatningsregler i og uden for Kontraktsforhold*, pp. 122–180, 468. Less convincing is the widespread idea that intentional acts are automatically and exclusively within the remit of tort law. Cf. Herbots, *Samenloop*, p. 141: no breach of contract by jealous hotelier assaulting guest. Had this occurred in the hotel there would be a breach of contract, for if a hotel-keeper must ensure the safety of his guests in the hotel, he may not intentionally harm them.

[21] Correctly emphasized by Asser (-Hartkamp), *Verbintenissenrecht* I, 9th edn., pp. 4–7, and Mazeaud/Chabas, *Obligations* 8th edn., No. 401.

[22] Cf. Jourdain, *Principes*, p. 31; Van Gerven, *Verbintenissenrecht* II, p. 18.

[23] This is how the question is formulated under the influence of the easily misunderstood Cass.civ. 11.1.1922, *D.P.* 1922, 1, 16 = S. 1924, 1, 105 (note Demogue) (*'les art. 1382 et s. c.civ. sont sans application lorsque la faute a été commise dans l'exécution d'une obligation résultant d'un contrat'*) and repeatedly so: e.g. Bénabent, *Obligations* 3rd edn., No. 384 (*'. . . la responsabilité délictuelle ne peut pas être invoquée entre les cocontractants'*) and v. Bar (-Gotthardt), *DeliktsR in Europa, Frankreich* p. 15 (no 'validity of the rules of tortious liability within an existing contractual relationship').

[24] *MünchKomm* (-Mertens), Introduction to §§ 823–853, no. 29, fn. 33, rightly states that 'the controversial question, whether one should speak of concurrence of claims or only of concurrence of bases of claim, does not yield the solution to the issue'. See below, no. 422.

concept of contractual duties of care. Where this occurs the area of overlap is reduced by the smaller scope of contract law (below, nos. 440 ff. and 459 ff.) It would be futile, however, to attempt to determine *a priori* which obligations are by their nature exclusively contractual and which exclusively tortious. Terminology provides no key to determining what lies in the respective provinces of contract and tort, and what is common ground. This can only be ascertained by analysing both regimes. Anything less would be simply to beg the question, producing a result implicit in the initial hypothesis. For this reason an ordered approach to the issue is only possible from the perspective of protected interests. It will soon become apparent that a distinction between pure economic loss on one hand, and loss consequential on injury to absolute rights and legal interests on the other, is the most promising approach.

a. Restricted Tortious Liability and Concurrence of Actions

(1) Germany

In many legal systems the majority of ordinary contractual breaches are **419** not relevant to tort law because they result in pure economic loss, which is rarely recoverable outside contract.[25] The standard instances of breach of contract make this manifestly clear. A contracting party unable to supply goods, not performing its duties on time, or providing goods of a non-merchantable quality or deficient advice is not liable under the terms of § 823 sec. 1 German BGB; such conduct rarely causes damage to property or injury to persons. Conflicts between contract and tort do not usually appear in this way; they are avoided at the factual level. This is also the case with liability under § 823 sec. 2 BGB (breach of statutory duty); what is manifested here is a fact-based solution similar to the prohibitions developed in other legal systems on simultaneous liability in contract and tort. In German law, provisions obliging a contractual party to perform contractual duties are not deemed to be protective statutes within § 823 sec. 2 BGB. Statutes alone are to be treated as laws by the BGB (Art. 2 EGBGB), and neither civil law contracts nor the principle of *pacta sunt servanda* constitute statutes: 'BGB and EGBGB consider them to be separate legal entities.'[26] The notion of a protective law covers 'all the rules specified in a legal order as opposed to the terms established by contractual agreement for certain relationships'.[27]

---

[25] See e.g. for Sweden Hellner, *Skadeståndsrätt*, 4th edn., pp. 62–62; for Austria Koziol, *Jbl* 1994, pp. 209, 210; and for Denmark Jørgensen, *FS Larenz* (1973) pp. 549, 559.

[26] *Staudinger* (-Merten/Kirchhof), BGB Art. 2 EGBGB no. 86. See also Prot. II p. 572 and Dietz, *Anspruchskonkurrrenz*, pp. 84–87.

[27] RG 24.2.1923, RGZ 135 pp. 242, 245; BGH 9.12.1964, *NJW* 1965 p. 2007; BGH 27.4.1971, *NJW* 1971 pp. 1367, 1368.

Regarding § 823 sec. 2 BGB, the matter is one of statutory law,[28] 'directed by politics'[29] rather than by the parties themselves.

420   The plainness of this statement should not disguise the fact that its deduction remains problematic. For it cannot be doubted that statutory provisions which attribute legal liability to independent acts of human will are rules of objective law.[30] Equally irrelevant is the argument that § 823 sec. 2 BGB must not be employed to rebut the principle in § 823 sec. 1 BGB of caution in respect of the recoverability of pure economic loss.[31] For only the beneficiary of a contractual obligation to perform is protected by a law compelling contractual performance. The protective value of the concept of *pacta sunt servanda* within delict can only be rebutted by the argument that the rule is too imprecise to satisfy § 823 sec. 2 BGB.[32] The parties themselves would have to give substance to the principle for it to acquire the form of an order or prohibition. However, the argument remains that other laws also need to be given substance (by administrative authorities, say) and that an administrative act is then classified as a protective law.[33] The effort to distinguish protective laws from contractual rules is motivated by conflict between different areas of law. One must ensure that 'the duty to pay damages, which arises upon the passage of a statute . . . does not contradict the system and inner integrity of the legal system as a whole, of civil law and of the tort law of compensation'.[34] The question remains the same, whether it is claimed that a breach of contract does not constitute a tort, or that there is a tort but that tort rules are inapplicable. Finally there is the 'methodology of the code' from which it can be argued with some conviction 'that the relationships between the contractual creditor and debtor are governed elsewhere'.[35] It is only a slight exaggeration to conclude that the French principle of *non-cumul des responsabilités* (see below, nos. 431 ff.) exists in German law under the definition of a protective law.

421   The potentially ruinous consequences threatening contract law, namely that breaches of contractual duties giving rise to pure economic loss would amount to breaches of protective laws (or, which amounts to the same thing, that contract law in such cases is to be denied the effect of excluding tort law) are certainly exaggerated. It is not uncommon for rules establishing liability in contract to be stricter (e.g. § 463 sec. 1 BGB:

---

[28] BGH 9.12.1964, *NJW* 1965 p. 2007.
[29] Brüggemeier, *Deliktsrecht*, nos. 790 and 794.
[30] Cf. Dietz, *Anspruchskonkurrenz*, p. 14.
[31] This is emphasized generally by, amongst others, *BGB RGRK* (-Steffen), § 823 BGB no. 536, and BGH 8.6.1976, BGHZ 66 pp. 388, 391.
[32] For the requirement of certainty in the field of classification of protective laws, see amongst others BGH 9.12.1964 (fn. 27); BGH 27.11.1963, BGHZ 40 pp. 306, 307.
[33] BGH 22.4.1974, BGHZ 62 pp. 265, 266–267. Likewise OGH 2.7.1979, SZ 52/109 p. 523.
[34] Knöpfle, *NJW* 1967 pp. 697, 700.   [35] See Prot. II p. 572; cf. p. 566.

no-fault liability where a promised characteristic is absent, or § 538 BGB: no-fault liability where leased residential premises are unfit for habitation). Thus any application of tort would be redundant, or would merely lead to the same results regarding damages (e.g. liability for frustration of contracts, of contractors, and for delay[36]). Nevertheless, were § 823 sec. 2 BGB to be applied, several provisions of German contract law would become redundant, such as the shorter limitation periods,[37] and such rules as §§ 463 sec. 2 and 708 BGB, which require that a claim for damages for poor performance must plead some degree of fault. If it is necessary to preserve the scope of such rules of contract law, and if that is to be achieved by a restrictive application of § 823 sec. 2 BGB, then it would surely be otiose to protect from tort law a party so heavily in breach of its contractual obligations as to have committed a criminal offence. This is especially so in cases of fraudulent deception[38] and some other forms of intentional damage.[39]

An elegant example is the case of AG Brilon 14 April 1993:[40] a client, who had argued with his lawyer whom he had not paid, was ordered by the court to pay him DM 1,114. The client paid by means of 1,114 transactions of DM 1. As a result, the lawyer incurred bank charges of DM 536.50. On the basis of § 826 BGB the court ordered the defendant to pay this sum to the lawyer.

The following conclusions may be drawn from the above observations **422** on German law. The free concurrence of actions is the natural starting point for a legal system with a tort law of narrow scope which does not cover most breaches of contract. 'For every claim arising from the breach of a duty, the injured party is free to choose the legal basis (i.e. contract or tort) on which to make his claim.'[41] Were that not the case, it could result in the exclusion of indispensable protection for the creditor. The conflict between competing causes of action does not only cover relationships with §§ 823 sec. 2, 826 BGB. Clearly, claims for damages can arise

---

[36] The thief alone is always in default (§§ 848, 849 BGB; general principle); in other cases a warning is required (§ 284 BGB); a party owing a duty in tort is often permitted a longer period for review than a similarly placed party under a contractual duty; BGH 27.4.1964, *VersR* 1964 p. 749; OLG Cologne 22.1.1982, *VersR* 1983 p. 451. By § 282 BGB, the burden of proof is generally more favourable to the contractual than to the tortious creditor ('creditor' used here in the law of obligations means someone to whom something, including damages, may be owed, i.e. the plaintiff).　　　　　　　　　　　　　[37] See nos. 449 ff.

[38] See OLG Cologne 1994, *VersR* 1994 p. 870. It is noteworthy that deceit, fraudulent deception, and causing intentional damage were excluded from the Hague Convention Relating to Uniform Law on International Sale of Goods (Art. 89). The UN Convention on International Sale of Goods no longer deals with these (Reinhart, *UN-Kaufrecht*, Art. 71 no. 10), and cedes them to tort law. Cf. Schwark, *AcP* 179 (1979) pp. 57, 68–69. The position in France is similar (Cass.com. 18.10.1994, *D.* 1995 *Jur.* 180).

[39] Cautiously exceeding this is OGH 8.7.1993, *WBl* 1993 p. 329.

[40] *NJW-RR* 1993 p. 1015.　　　　[41] BGH 24.11.1976, BGHZ 67 pp. 359, 362–363.

from interference with the right to an established business, or damage caused to a person's creditworthiness[42] (§ 824 BGB) alongside liability for breach of contract. The same is true of the non-contractual regime governing liability of notaries public (see § 19 sec. 1 BNotO [Federal Notaries Act] in conjunction with § 839 BGB).[43] This is perfectly acceptable. However, liability for pure economic loss is particularly problematic where the general rules of contract meet tort rules on liability for negligent misinformation, which are themselves very close to contract rules. This theme is dealt with below.[44] The point to be grasped here is that it is not the duties protecting the property and health of the contractual partner, but rather the normal cases on disappointed performance expectations which provide a country's basic rule on concurrence of actions. Such cases provided the ratios later applied, albeit in modified form, to the relationship between contractual protective duties and tort.

(2) Greece, Denmark, and Portugal

423 The above problem is treated in the same way in the Greek legal order, in which the basic delictual provision (Art. 914 Cc) consists of a blanket norm. Thereunder, were all systematic control mechanisms to be ignored, the law would appear to disapprove of breach of contract, in that non-performance of contractual duties should, or indeed must, be classified as 'contrary to statute'.[45] In the context of Art. 914 Cc, however, the term statute is to be interpreted narrowly, as the rules relating to breaches of contract are more specific than, and thus take preference over, those of Art. 914 Cc. Moreover, damages are not the only possible legal consequence of a contractual breach.[46] It may thus be argued 'from Articles 914, 343 sec. 1, 345 Cc[47] [that] breach of contract is not a tort

---

[42] Cf. BGH 20.6.1978, *NJW* 1978 p. 2151. Typical cases are those in which a bank incorrectly asserts that its customer is insolvent. § 824 BGB always requires that the assertion be made to a third party and *not* solely to the party affected: see RG 17.2.1921, RGZ 101 pp. 335, 338.

[43] BGH 24.6.1993, *WM* 1993 p. 1889: a notary who acts negligently can be sued as a lawyer in contract and, if that claim is time-barred, as a notary in tort.

[44] Below at no. 435.

[45] Stathopoulos, *Geniko Enochiko Dikaio*, A I, 2nd edn., p. 251; Deliyannis/Kornilakis, *Eidiko Enochiko Dikaio*, III, pp. 108–109; Georgiades/Stathopoulos (-Georgiades), *Greek Cc*, IV, intr. to Arts. 914–938, no. 7.

[46] As above no. 45. Also Balis, *Genikai Archai tou Astikon Dikaiou*, 8th edn., pp. 444–445; and Areopag 754/1990, *NoB* 39 (1991) p. 1097 (after contracting to sell a motor car but before transferring possession, the vendor demanded a higher price and threatened to retain possession. The purchaser paid the extra sum and then reclaimed it in tort. The Areopag rejected the claim: the breach of contract did not amount to an unlawful act within Art. 914 Greek Cc because the extra demand could only be classified as an unlawful act in the context of the contractually agreed price.

[47] Arts. 343 and 345 Greek Cc concern delay; Art. 345 distinguishes expressly between rates of interest for delay which have been set 'by statute or by the legal transaction'.

within the meaning of Art. 914'.[48] So the path is cleared for the basic rule of competing causes of action, usually described thus: 'a non-contractual claim can exist in respect of a damaging and contract-breaching act or omission, where that act or omission would be unlawful irrespective of the contractual relationship, for opposing the general duty contained in Art. 914 not to cause damage to another person in a blameworthy manner.'[49] This formulation is not free of difficulty, as will be seen later.[50] However, it shows clearly that the doctrine regarding concurrence of laws vitalized by earlier Greek commentators is now dead.[51] Deception with intent[52] is the typical case of pure economic damage covered both by contractual and non-contractual law; intentional non- or late performance alone is not sufficient to constitute a tort.[53]

The position is essentially similar in Denmark and Portugal. In **424** Denmark non-contractual economic loss may only be claimed as a consequence of damage to property or the person.[54] Damage ensuing from late payment or poorly performed work rarely meets these criteria. However, where a breach of contract meets the delictual criteria, the principle of competing causes of action applies: the creditor may choose the more favourable cause.[55] The prevailing principle

[48] CA Athens 1846/1971, *NoB* 19 (1971) p. 1443 (although the non-payment of wages amounted to a crime, it was regarded only as a breach of contract and not a tort: hence Art. 938 Cc not applicable. Again the aim is to make an exception to the principle of concurrence of actions by interpreting the term 'breach of protective law' narrowly: cf. no. 420 above). See further CA Athens 7712/1985, *EllDik* 27 (1986) p. 125; and CA Athens 10288/1986, *EllDik* 28 (1987) p. 886.

[49] Areopag 967/1973, *NoB* 22/1974 p. 505. Identical formulations in Areopag 1058/1977, *NoB* 26 (1978) p. 929; CA Athens 10288/1986, *EllDik* 28 (1987) p. 886; and CA Athens 14428/1988, *EllDik* 31 (1990) p. 606. Similar: Areopag 18/1993, *EEN* 1994 p. 34.

[50] Below at no. 433.

[51] E.g. Papaeleftheriou, *NoB* 6 (1958) pp. 1101 ff. Contrary view put convincingly by Zepos, *Rev.Hell.* 15 (1962) pp. 256, 262.

[52] Cf. CA Athens 7801/1990, *EllDik* 32 (1991) p. 1676: assurance given by vendor who failed to warn of a fault in goods sold. In addition to the rights in Arts. 534 ff. Greek Cc, an action under Art. 914 Cc was also allowed to cover the 'overreaching' damage, such as a claim for non-pecuniary damages under Art. 932 Cc.

[53] Areopag 422/1958, *NoB* 6 (1958) p. 130; CA Athens 1848/1971, *NoB* 19 (1971) p. 1343; CA Athens 7712/1985, *EllDik* 27 (1986) p. 125.

[54] Exceptionally, liability to third parties for information given: VLD 22.12.1992, *UfR* 1993 A p. 217; and HD 18.11.1992, *UfR* 1993 A p. 52 (vendor's claim upheld against estate agent employed by buyer's bank for negligent valuation of property). Cf. no. 247 above.

[55] Gomard, *Obligationsret*, II, pp. 143–144; id., *Obligationsretten i en nøddeskal II*, pp. 131–132. Cf. Jørgensen, *KF* 1988 p. 42; Bloth, *Product Liability in Sweden, Norway and Denmark*, pp. 296 ff., 306. See also VLD 21.1.1927, *UfR* 1927 A p. 452; ØLD 20.11.1929, *UfR* 1930 A p. 163; and ØLD 8.6.1943, *UfR* 1943 A p. 1037. Gomard criticizes these decisions in *Erstatningsregler i Kontraktsforhold*, pp. 40 ff. and 467–468, and argues for a case-by-case development of rules on a *non-cumul* rule basis to determine whether a claim be based on contract or tort.

in Portugal[56] of free concurrence of actions, reinforced by the principle of *da mihi facta, dabo tibi jus* (see Art. 664 C.proc.civ.)[57] is not entirely without controversy;[58] but here too it is clear that a mere breach of contract does not necessarily constitute a breach of a law within the meaning of Art. 483 sec. 1 Cc.[59] Only exceptionally is the protection of pure economic interests regarded as a function of tort law.[60]

(3) Italy and The Netherlands

425 In Italian thinking, the mere disappointment of contractual performance expectations does not result in *danno ingiusto*.[61] Here also, the principle of competing causes of action controls the relationship between tort and contractual damages claims.[62] It was long felt that *'solo quando il medesimo fatto abbia violato la legge del contratto, e insieme, la legge penale, la responsabilità contrattuale ed extracontrattuale possono concorrere'*.[63] However, the doctrine of concurrence of actions has probably conquered futher territory by developing liability in tort[64]

---

[56] Vaz Serra, *BolMinJust* 85 (1959) pp. 115, 230–231; Figueiredo Dias/Sinde Monteiro, Portugal, in: Deutsch/Schreiber (edd.), *Medical Responsability*, pp. 513, 530–531; Antunes Varela, *Obrigações em Geral*, I, 7th edn., pp. 508–512; Calvão da Silva, *Responsabilidade civil do produtor*, p. 251; Moitinho de Almeida, *Scientia juridica* 1972 pp. 327, 329. For case-law regarding protective duties of care, see STJ 22.10.1987, *BolMinJust* 370 (1987) p. 529; RC 20.11.1984, *CJ* IX (1984–5) p. 68; and RL 14.5.1991, *CJ* XVI (1991–3) p. 139.

[57] The judge is bound by the parties' submissions of fact but not law; he may come to different conclusions: STJ 7.3.1975, *BolMinJust* 245 (1975) p. 465; STJ 2.4.1976, *BolMinJust* 256 (1976) p. 83; RL 14.5.1991, *CJ* XVI (1991–3) p. 139; Ferraz de Brito, *Código de processo civil anotado*, 8th edn., p. 430.

[58] Almeida Costa, *Obrigações*, 5th edn., develops a *princípio da consunção* pp. 436–442, according to which contractual liability subsumes tort liability. RC 26.11.1991, *CJ* XVI (1991–5) p. 69 is unclear: due to an interruption in electricity supply eggs could not be incubated. The court confirmed the plaintiff's contractual claim, and, without further consideration of whether a tortious claim could be raised, stated *'a responsabilidade pelos danos causados pela interrupção no fornecimento de energia eléctrica insere-se no domínio da responsabilidade contratual'*.

[59] On the basis of contract-based duties to act in tort, see no. 22 above. Cf. RL 17.11.1981, *CJ* VI (1981–5) p. 147 (liability for ceasing negotiations only 'in cases of great unfairness').

[60] Above, no. 22. See further Sinde Monteiro, in: Deutsch/Taupitz (edd.) *Haftung der Dienstleistungsberufe*, pp. 127, 130.

[61] Cf. Cendon (-Gaudino) IV, Art. 2043 no. 37 (p. 2032); Cendon (-Santoro) IV, Art. 1218 no. 21 (p. 108); and de Martini, *Fatti produttivi di danno*, p. 67. Some uncertainty in Giur.sist. Bigiavi (-Rossello) I, p. 297 § 2 and Sacco, in: Visintini (ed.), *Risarcimento del danno contrattuale ed extracontrattuale*, pp. 155, 160 insofar as protection of related rights is afforded under Art. 2043 Cc (cf. no. 21 above).

[62] Cases predominantly concerned with breaches of protective duties. See Cass. 26.9.1970, n. 1717, *Giust.civ.Mass.* 1970 No. 1717; Cass. 19.1.1977, n. 261, *Giur.it.* 1978, I, 1, 1791; Cass. 27.2.1980, n. 1376, *Giur.it.* 1980, I, 1459; Cass. 13.3.1980, n. 1696, *Giur.it.* 1980, I, 1, 1460; Cass. 7.8.1982, n. 4437, *Resp.Civ. e Prev.* 1984 p. 78; Cass. 29.3.1983, n. 2278, *Riv.giur.circ.trasp.* 1983 p. 709; Cass. 22.9.1983, n. 5638, *Giur.it.Mass.* 1983 n. 5638; Cass. 14.5.1987, *Giust.civ.* 1987, I, 1628.

[63] Trib. Reggio Emilia 12.1.1959, *Foro.pad.* 1960, I, 640.

[64] At no. 21 above; cf. in German v. Bar (-Busnelli), *DeliktsR in Europa, Italien*, pp. 42–43.

for false information.[65] Emphasis is laid upon the avoidance of the term *cumulo* in favour of *concorso* as there is no question of double recovery. A *concorso proprio* is constituted if an act of the debtor causes the same damage to the creditor as a breach of both contractual and general duties of care (liability of doctors etc.)[66] A *concorso improprio* arises if the damage is caused without reference to the content of a contract, where the same harm is brought about by two people, one contractually and the other tortiously liable,[67] or where one act constitutes a tort against one person and a breach of contract in respect of another (e.g. liability in contract to one party, with tortious liability to that person's dependents).[68] Of practical importance, particularly in respect of liability for pure economic loss, is the rule in Art. 1225 Cc. This rule, derived from Art. 1150 French Cc, is analogous to rules widely used elsewhere[69] and

---

[65] Had the painter in the *De Chirico* case (Cass. 4.5.1982, n. 2765, *Giur.it.* 1983, I, 1, 786; at no. 21 above) also been the vendor, then by the general rules the case would have been one of *concorso proprio*. The question whether liability in tort could subsist alongside contractual liability in such cases is of little practical significance due to the contractual limitation period's being twice as long, at 10 years, under Art. 2946 Cc as that in tort under Art. 2947 Cc). However, the problem of concurrence of actions arises with regard to the extent of liability and there may be concurrence of actions. Cass. 9.2.1980, n. 921, *Giust.civ.Mass.* 1980 No. 921 (Visintini agreeing, *Fatti illeciti* II, pp. 249 ff.) held that the purchaser of a house, intentionally deceived by the vendor with regard to achievable rent, could claim damages under Art. 2043 Cc rather than rescinding the contract.

[66] See Cass. 27.2.1980, n. 1376, *Giur.it.* 1980, I, 1, 1459; or Cass. 30.5.1980, n. 3565, *Giust.civ.Mass.* 1980 No. 3565 (a *concorso proprio* is constituted where an act 'breaches not only the rights based in contract but also rights which a person has independent of the existence of the contractual relationship'). See also Cass. 14.5.1979, n. 2773, *Resp.Civ. e Prev.* 1980 pp. 403, 408 (where the *danno aquiliano* is the 'direct result' of the contractual breach).

[67] E.g. inducing breach of contract and assisting in such breach (Cass. 20.10.1983, n. 6160, *Giur.it.* 1984, I, 1, 439; Pret. Milano 28.6.1973, *Foro.pad.* 1974, I, 310 and App. Torino 2.10.1969, *Giur.it.* 1969, I, 2, 865) or manufacturer's product liability combined with that of the vendor (e.g. Cass. 27.2.1980,n. 1376, *Giur.it.* 1980, I, 1, 1459).

[68] Cf. e.g. Cass. 13.3.1980, n. 1696, *Giur.it.* 1980, I, 1, 1460 (manufacturer's liability). Also Alpa/Bessone, *Trattato XIV*, 2nd edn., pp. 174–175 and Giur.sist. Bigiavi (-Rossello) I pp. 316–321. A vivid *Danish* case is HD 18.8.1988, *UfR* 1988 A p. 858 (employer provides employee with defective electric saw. Employer liable to the injured employee in contract and to his wife, for dependency loss, in tort). For *Dutch* case-law see Hof Amsterdam 27.6.1957, *NedJur* 1958 No. 104 p. 295 (manufacturer of goods may be liable to purchaser in tort and contract without more); HR 2.4.1982, *NedJur* 1983 No. 367 pp. 1145, 1150 (lawyer failed to apply in time for extension of lease. Held liable to tenant in contract and to sub-tenants in tort); and Hof Leeuwarden 29.1.1992, *NedJur* 1992 No. 830 p. 3552 (liability of a private limited company in contract, of its managing director in tort). For *France* see Cass.civ 16.12.1992, *Sem.Jur.* 1993, IV, 505 (liability of broker to vendor in contract, to purchaser in tort. For *England and Scotland* see *Donoghue* v. *Stevenson* [1932] AC 562, 610 (*per* Lord Macmillan: 'There is no reason why the same set of facts should not give one person a right of action in contract and another person a right of action in tort); *Edgar* v. *Lamont* 1914 SC 277.

[69] Axiomatic in English law is *Hadley* v. *Baxendale* (1854) 9 Exch. 341 = 156 ER 145 (contrary to tort law: *Re Polemis & Furness & Withy Ltd.* [1921] 3 KB 560). For Luxembourg see Trib. Lux. 1.11.1960, *Pas. luxemb.* 18 (1960–1962) p. 288 (Arts. 1146–1153 Cc are not applicable in tort). Castronovo, in Wilhelmsson, *Perspectives of Critical Contract Law*, pp. 273, 274, points out that the European Commission on Contract Law has agreed this rule. The position in Austria is probably different: OGH 2.9.1992, *JBl* 1993 pp. 396, 397.

limits recoverability for negligent non- or late contractual performance to losses foreseeable at the time of contracting. This limitation on liability does not apply for the purposes of Art. 2043 Cc. The aim of excluding contractual breaches covered by Art. 1225 Cc from tort rules is to preserve the function of contractual rules.[70]

426   In The Netherlands the initial question is whether the non-performance of a contract constitutes an *onrechtmatige daad* within the meaning of Art. 6:162 BW. In other words, whether it can be either an *inbreuk op een recht* or an *doen of nalaten in strijd met een wettelijke plicht of met hetgeen volgens ongeschreven recht in het maatschappelijk verkeer betaamt*. Literally interpreted, this is by no means unproblematic. The third alternative requires a systematic analysis of the law of obligations in order to separate and juxtapose 'social' and contractual dealings. The second question: whether a person failing either to perform a contractual duty or to perform properly thereby always breaches a 'statutory' duty, may also be negatived only by the same systematic argument and it is notable that several authors write of the 'non-applicability' of tort.[71] The same problem is apparent for the first alternative (breach of right). For *'de schuldenaar die zijn verplichting niet tijdig, niet behoorlijk of in het geheel niet nakomt, maakt inbreuk op het subjectief recht van de schuldeiser en handelt derhalve onrechtmatig'*.[72] The *'schending van een contractuele plicht'* is more or less *'in strijd met het recht'*.[73] Law on contractual breaches is contained elsewhere in the BW; the term 'right' in Art. 6:162 BW must be narrowly interpreted. Leaving aside leases,[74] the term covers only absolute and personal rights.[75] If they are not breached (and the requirements of the alternatives in Art. 6:162 sec. 2 BW are not fulfilled) a breach of contract within the meaning of Art. 6:74 sec. 1 BW cannot constitute a tort. The attempts by earlier commentators to interpret the French system of *non-cumul*[76] against the background of Arts. 1401, 1402 (old) BW have been abandoned regarding Art. 6.162 BW. Thus tort law has been drawn narrowly enough to render the application of the principle of concurrence of actions probable. What had already been accepted by Dutch

---

[70] See Castronovo (fn. 69) and Visintini, *Rass.dir.civ.* 1983 pp. 1077, 1084–1086.
[71] E.g. T&C (-Steketee), Art. 6: 162 BW Annotation 2. Cf. Parlementaire Geschiedenis VI p. 715 and esp. Jansen, *Onrechtmatige daad*, pp. 28–29 (all instances of non-performance of a contract are unlawful acts. They would not be decided according to Art. 6:162 BW because Art. 6:74 BW must be understood as *lex specialis* having a derogating function).
[72] Asser (-Hartkamp), *Verbintenissenrecht III*, 8th edn., no. 307, p. 254. Cf. commentary by Rutten on HR 9.12.1955, *NedJur* 1956 No. 157.
[73] Schut, *Onrechtmatige daad*, p. 16. Cf. Jansen (fn. 71) p. 29.
[74] T&C (-Steketee) (fn. 71).
[75] See Parlementaire Geshiedenis VI p. 614 and Bloembergen (-Jansen), *Onrechtmatige daad* I, Art. 162, lid 2, aant. 7.
[76] Esp. van de Sande Bakhuijzen, *WPNR* 1981 no. 5559, pp. 220 ff. Cf. Schoordijk, *WPNR* 1987 no. 5818, pp. 104, 105 and ibid., *WPNR* 1964 no. 4812, p. 216.

law, namely that a creditor disrupting the creditor–debtor relationship in a manner not amounting to breach of primary or secondary contractual obligations may be subject to a tortious liability independent of the contract,[77] must now be certain.[78] In contrast, there is now a more precise basic tort principle, which is a better instrument for identifying the overlap between tort and general contractual liability, under Art. 6: 74 sec. 1 BW.[79] The principle of concurrence of causes of action means that claims brought in contract but which cannot succeed on that basis must be assessed by the judge regarding their potential in tort.[80]

(4) The Common Law

English law has recognized the problems of concurrent causes of action **427** since the middle of the nineteenth century, when the Common Law Procedure Act 1852 abolished the forms of action.[81] Tindal CJ said as late as 1842: 'the principle in all cases would seem to be that the contract creates a duty, and the neglect to perform that duty, or nonfeasance, is a ground of action upon tort.'[82] Originally there was only one claim for damages and it was seen as a claim in tort. With the independence of contract, liability for pure economic loss became almost its sole domain. Since then the general tort rule was that pure economic losses were recoverable only for intentional torts.[83] Liability for deceit, intimidation, injurious or malicious falsehood, slander of goods, and interference with contracts belong to this category. In consequence, the overlap of contract and tort liability for pure economic loss remained narrow. It became still

[77] Cf. HR 11.6.1926, *NedJur* 1926 p. 1049; and HR 9.12.1955, *NedJur* 1956 No. 157 (p. 323). HR 26.3.1920, *NedJur* 1920 p. 476 follows the same principle, albeit in consideration of a contractual exclusion clause. That intentional acts are covered by tort law is clear from HR 19.5.1967 *NedJur* 1967 no. 261 p. 705; and HR 20.2.1976, *NedJur* 1976 no. 486 p. 1418.

[78] Cf. Asser (-Hartkamp), *Verbintenissenrecht I*, 9th edn., nos. 6–10; ibid., *II*, 8th edn., no. 552; ibid., *III*, 8th edn., no. 307; Schut, *Onrechtmatige daad*, pp. 13–16; and Hijma/Olthof, *Compendium* no. 409. The principle of concurrence of actions is a necessary prerequisite of the case-law considered at no. 416 above (contract as a source of a duty of care in tort).

[79] Art. 6:74 sec. 1 BW which does not differentiate between late performance, poor performance, impossibility, and breach of protective duties or duties of loyalty in respect of harm resulting from contractual breach, provides as follows: '*Iedere tekortkoming in de nakoming van een verbintenis verplicht de schuldenaar de schade die de schuldeiser daardoor lijdt te vergoeden, tenzij de tekortkoming de schuldenaar niet kan worden toegerekend.*'

[80] E.g. Schut, *Onrechtmatige daad*, 4th edn., p. 14.

[81] See Winfield, *Province of the Law of Tort*, pp. 65–67; Whittacker, *Relationship between Contract and Tort*, p. 207; Herbots, *Rev.dr.int.dr.comp.* 1993 pp. 205, 212–213. Cf. Monateri, *Cumulo di repsonsabilità*, p. 187.

[82] *Boorman v. Brown* (1842) Ex. Ch. 3; QB 511, 525. Confirmed by the House of Lords, albeit with the modification that 'wherever there is a contract, and something is to be done in the course of the employment which is the subject of the contract, if there is a breach of duty in the course of that employment, the party injured may recover either in tort or in contract': 8 ER 1003; 1844 concerning damages for breach of contractual duty not to supply third party with oil. See also below, fn. 101.

[83] Above, nos. 259 ff. and 283 ff.; below, nos. 497 ff.

narrower as claims of inducing breach of contract could not compete with contractual liability. Liability in tort in such cases is only incurred by the person encouraging a third party to breach his contractual obligations; the third party[84] incurs only contractual liability.[85]

428 Protection in tort of the victim of an intentional contractual breach thus became otiose. Where conduct constitutes both a breach of contract and a tort the principle of concurrence of actions applies. The principle enables the plaintiff 'to invoke a more favourable tort rule'.[86] An English court cannot apply the principle *ex officio*, but many lawyers would ensure that a claim was pleaded in both tort and contract.

It is easy to imagine a case of intimidation in which an employer attempts to gain an employee's compliance by threatening dismissal. The English[87] case of *Archer* v. *Brown*[88] provides an elegant example in deceit: the defendant purported to sell to the plaintiff company shares which he had already sold several times to other unsuspecting purchasers. The plaintiff had borrowed money to buy the shares, and had himself been engaged by the defendant as joint managing director. It was held that 'the plaintiff was entitled to recover damage under whatever head he chose, provided he did not duplicate his claim'.

429 Until recently, rules applicable to intentional acts could not simply be transferred and applied to negligence claims. Even at a time when the idea was generally accepted by commentators, the common law developed a general principle of concurrence of actions,[89] caution, however, dictating that a distinction be drawn between damage to the person or to goods and pure economic loss. The principle of concurrence of actions

---

[84] The third party has no action against the person who induced the breach. 'If A procures B to break his contract with C, C can complain . . . but B has no right at law . . . He must resist A's efforts by strength of will' (Upjohn LJ in *Boulting* v. *Association of Cinematograph, Television and Allied Technicians* [1963] 2 QB 606, 639–640).

[85] Cf. *inter alia* Dias/Markesinis, *Tort Law*, p. 190. Of judgments, esp. *Said* v. *Butt* [1920] 3 KB 497: theatre manager denied entry to customer with valid ticket. Whether the manager had committed the tort of inducing breach of contract by preventing theatre company from fulfilling its contractual obligation. McCardie J. denied this: 'the servant who causes a breach of his master's contract with a third person . . . is not a stranger. He is the *alter ego* of his master. . . . In such a case it is the master himself, by his agent, breaking the contract he has made, and in my view an action against the agent under the *Lumley* v. *Gye* principle must therefore fail, just as it would fail if brought against the master himself' (pp. 505–506). See also *Brekkes Ltd. and Another* v. *Cattel and Others* [1972] 1 Ch. 105, 114 (*per* Pennycuick VC).

[86] Fleming, *Torts*, 6th edn., p. 169.

[87] For Ireland see *Barnett* v. *Hyndman* (1840) 3 Ir.LR 109.

[88] [1984] 2 All ER 267.

[89] Cf. Charlesworth & Percy, *Negligence*, 8th edn., 9–05 and 9–06 (pp. 512–513); Cane, in Furmston (ed.), *Liability for Damage to Property and Economic Loss*, pp. 113 ff.; Dias/Markesinis, *Tort Law*, 2nd edn., p. 11; and Fleming, *Torts*, 8th edn., p. 187. For the Scottish perspective see Stewart, *Introduction*, p. 61 and Walker, *Delict*, 2nd edn., p. 14 ('the fact that a person does or does not owe any duty *ex contractu* to another does not by any means exclude the possibility of his also owing a duty *ex delicto* to that person'). For the Irish view see McMahon/Binchy, *Irish Law of Torts*, 2nd edn., pp. 159–160.

could only be considered preserved in respect of the former.[90] Progress was slow regarding pure economic loss stemming (additionally) from breaches of contract.[91] It is particularly interesting to observe the development of English law in this respect. As early as the late 1930s judgments regarding negligent breaches of obligations by stockbrokers[92] and lawyers[93] attributed these questions solely to contract law; additional liability in tort was rejected.[94] The problem posed by these cases,[95] given that they were decided after *Donoghue* v. *Stevenson*[96] but long before *Hedley Byrne* v. *Heller*,[97] was whether they were based on a rule on concurrency or whether they simply resulted from the fact that, at the time, no pure economic losses at all could be recovered in negligence, so that the possibility of tort claims was not even considered. In any event, *Groom* v. *Crocker*[98] 'has never been overruled',[99] which has made it difficult to decide whether the pre-eminent rule regarding professional liability in *Hedley Byrne* v. *Heller* applies not only in respect of third

[90] Based on *Donoghue* v. *Stevenson* [1932] AC 562, 610 (*per* Lord Macmillan): 'The fact that there is a contractual relationship between the parties which may give rise to an action for breach of contract does not exclude the co-existence of a right of action founded on negligence as between the same parties, independently of the contract, though arising out of the relationship in fact brought about by the contract.' See further Lord Simmons in *Lister* v. *Romford Ice & Cold Storage Co. Ltd.* [1957] AC 555, 573 ('It is trite law that a single act of negligence may give rise to a claim either in tort or for breach of a term express or implied in a contract'); and *Bell* v. *Travco Hotels Ltd.* [1953] 1 QB 473. Extensive further references in Clerk & Lindsell (-Dias), *Torts*, 16th edn., 1–03. The position in Scotland has been clear since *Edgar* v. *Lamont* 1914 SC 277: Stewart, *Introduction*, p. 61.
[91] Scottish law proceeded on this point. It had long been clear there that 'when a solicitor is negligent in his dealings with his client, then not only will there be a breach of an implied term of his contract with the client, but there will also be a breach of a duty of care which arose from the contractual relationship, this providing a remedy in delict as well as in contract' (Norrie, *SLT* 1988 p. 309; *Robertson* v. *Bannigan* 1964 *SLT*. 318, 319, *per* Lord Hunter). The Irish Supreme Court had already accepted in *Finlay* v. *Murlagh* [1979] IR 249 that a lawyer owed his client concurrent duties in contract and tort. McMahon/Binchy (fn. 89) assert that *Tulsk Co-Operative Livestock Mart Ltd.* v. *Ulster Bank Ltd.* accords with this (13.5.1983 [1981–3555 P]). More cautious in approach is a range of Canadian (see Feldthusen, *Economic Negligence*, pp. 83–89 and Symmons, 21 (1975) *McGill LJ* 79–112) and New Zealand cases (see McMahon/Binchy [fn. 89] p. 158). A summary in German of the position in the USA is offered by v. Walter, *Konkurrenz vertraglicher und deliktischer Schadensersatznormen*, pp. 88 ff.
[92] *Jarvis* v. *Moy, Davies, Smith, Vandervell and Co.* [1936] 1 KB 399, 403 (Greer LJ). Cf. *Bean* v. *Wade* 2 (1885–86) *Times* 157.
[93] *Groom* v. *Crocker* [1939] 1 KB 194, 205 (Greene MR).
[94] The position is different if the breach of contract simultaneously endangers the creditworthiness of a person or firm: *Wilson* v. *United Counties Bank Ltd.* [1920] AC 102, 109.
[95] Similarly *Bagot* v. *Stevenson Scanlan & Co. Ltd.* [1966] 1 QB 197, 204 (*per* Diplock LJ, liability of an architect for damage ensuing from failure properly to oversee construction works); cf. Preuss, *Vertragsbruch als Delikt*, p. 118.
[96] [1932] AC 562 (at no. 277 above).   [97] [1964] AC 465 (at no. 285 above).
[98] See above, fn. 93.
[99] Nicholls V-C in *White and Another* v. *Jones and Another* [1993] 3 WLR 730, 742–743 (CA). Cf. Fleming, 109 [1993] *LQR* 344.

parties[100] but also between contractual partners.[101] Lord Scarman said in *Tai Hing Ltd.* v. *Liu Chong Hing Bank*,[102] regarding the liability of a bank to its customers, that:

'their Lordships do not believe that there is anything to the advantage of the law's development in searching for a liability in tort where the parties are in a contractual relationship [because] their Lordships believe it to be correct in principle and necessary for the avoidance of confusion in the law to adhere to the contractual analysis: on principle because it is a relationship in which the parties have, subject to a few exceptions, the right to dertermine their obligations to each other, and for the avoidance of confusion because different consequences do follow according to whether liability arises from contract or tort, e.g. in the limitation of action'.[103]

Thereafter it became doubtful whether *Midland Bank* v. *Hett, Stubbs & Kemp*[104] was still good law. There, Oliver J had affirmed the converse, namely a comprehensive concurrence of actions between contract and tort, an opinion incompatible with the observation of the Court of Appeal in *White* v. *Jones* that 'the liability must be the same whether the solicitor is liable to his client in contract alone or both in contract and tort'.[105] The House of Lords judgment in *Henderson* v. *Merrett Syndicates Ltd.*[106] clarified the point. That case concerned the liability of Lloyds of London managing agents towards the Names on the syndicates they managed. After an extensive comparative analysis, Lord Goff affirmed the judgment of Oliver J in *Midland Bank* and came to the crux of the matter:

'an assumption of responsibility coupled with the concomitant reliance may give rise to a tortious duty of care irrespective of whether there is a contractual relationship between the parties, and in consequence, unless his contract precludes him from doing so, the plaintiff, who has available to him concurrent remedies in contract and tort, may choose that remedy which appears to him to be the most advantageous.'[107]

---

[100] See esp. *Ross* v. *Caunters* [1980] Ch. 297 (liability to a third party who failed to inherit on account of procedural error by lawyer preparing a will) and *White* v. *Jones* [1995] 2 WLR 187 (HL: liability of lawyer for failure to prepare will before testator's death; cf. no. 405 above). *White* v. *Jones* is applicable only in England: it is not Scottish law: Blaikie, *SLT* 1993 pp. 329–333 under the aegis of *Robertson* v. *Fleming* (1861) 4 Macq 167, 184 (HL) and *Weir* v. *J. M. Hodge & Son* 1990 *SLT* 266, 269 D.

[101] Cf. the opposing view of Collins, *IntCompLQ* 16 (1967) pp. 103, 104; and Charlesworth & Percy (-Percy), *Negligence*, 7th edn., p. 512. The view of Lord Haldane LC in *Nocton* v. *Lord Ashburton* [1914] AC 932, 956 is noteworthy: 'the solicitor contracts with his client to be skilful and careful. For failure to perform his obligation he may be made liable at law in contract or even in tort, for negligence in breach of a duty imposed on him. In the early history of the action of *assumpsit* this liability was indeed treated as a tort.'   [102] [1986] AC 80.

[103] P. 107. Only 3 years later the opposite view was put in *Smith* v. *Bush* [1989] 2 WLR 790, 800 (*per* Lord Templeman: 'The contractual duty of a valuer to value a house did not prevent the valuer coming under a tortious duty to Mrs Smith . . .').

[104] [1979] Ch. 384.   [105] Nicholls V-C in *White* v. *Jones* [1993] 3 WLR 730, 743 (CA).

[106] [1995] AC 145; [1994] 3 All ER 506 (HL).   [107] Id. p. 533.

Even after the decision in *Henderson* it is uncertain how the courts will   **430**
deal with cases concerning incorrect information given by one party to
the other in pre-contractual negotiations. Where one party makes a
misrepresentation and no subsequent contract results, liability will be
based exclusively in tort, since English law lacks an equivalent to *culpa in
contrahendo*. The tort is deceit where the misrepresentation was intentional;[108] where negligent, liability will be based on the principle in
Hedley Byrne.[109] The bases of claim only change if the parties actually
enter into a contract after a misrepresentation, whether made by a party
directly or through an agent.[110] It is thus doubtful whether there is a
practical need for the rule in *Hedley Byrne*.[111] Liability is based more on
contract, as sec. 2(1) Misrepresentation Act 1967 introduced the concept
of implied fault.[112] With this rule the tort of negligence became otiose.[113]
The tort of deceit remains applicable[114] but has been integrated into the
Misrepresentation Act. This has resulted in a peculiar basis of liability:
liability in contract, under rules which mirror those of the tort of deceit,
but which apply even when the absence of negligence cannot be proved!

b. Broad Liability in Tort and *Non-Cumul des Responsabilités*

(1) France: The Primacy of Contract

Unlike all other legal systems in the European Union, France unashamedly   **431**
gives contract law primacy over tort.[115] However, detailed analysis is
required to discover how the different theoretical starting points yield

---

[108] *Derry v. Peek* (1889) 14 App.Cas. 337 (HL).

[109] *Box v. Midland Bank Ltd.* [1979] 2 Lloyd's Rep. 391; [1979] 2 All ER 391.

[110] Whether and when the agent may himself be tortiously liable (not in *culpa in contrahendo*) is unclear. Cf. no. 416 and fn. 11 above.

[111] This point is justifiably made by Dias/Markesinis, *Tort Law*, 2nd edn., p. 69.

[112] The text provides: 'Where a person has entered into a contract after a misrepresentation has been made to him by another party thereto and as a result thereof he has suffered
loss, then, if the person making the misrepresentation would be liable to damages in respect
thereof had the misrepresentation been made fraudulently, that person shall be so liable
notwithstanding that the misrepresentation was not made fraudulently, unless he proves
that he had reasonable ground to believe and did believe up to the time the contract was
made that the facts represented were true.'

[113] Because sec. 2(1) renders a person liable according to the deceit rules. Where intention
is shown, the rule on foreseeability of the extent of damage (at fn. 69 above) does not apply.

[114] At no. 428 above (*Archer v. Brown*).

[115] On this and the following see: Le Tourneau, *Responsabilité civile*, 3rd edn., nos. 262–272;
Encylopédie Dalloz (-Tunc), *Rép.Dr.Civ. VIII, Responsabilité (en général)* nos. 140–198; Starck (-
Roland/Boyer), *Obligations II*, 4th edn., no. 1831; Malaurie/Aynès, *Droit civil*, 3rd edn., nos.
870 ff.; Mazeaud/Chabas, *Obligations*, 8th edn., nos. 390 ff.; JClCiv (-Espagnon), Arts. 1146 to
1155, Fasc. 16–1; and Mazeaud/Tunc, *Responsabilité civile I*, 6th edn., nos. 96 ff. For German
literature see Ferid, *Das Verhältnis des Anspruchs aus unerlaubter Handlung zum Anspruch aus
Vertragsverletzung*, pp. 23 ff. and Penner, *Der französische Grundsatz des 'non-cumul'*, esp. pp. 177 ff.
and 261 ff.

differing results. Construed dogmatically, French liability law has devel-oped in a radically different way[116] since Cass.civ. 11.1. 1922.[117]

In planning the construction of a ditch under a wall separating two properties, the occupiers each employed a non-legal 'expert' (the case reports are not precise) to draft a contract regulating issues arising from the works. The experts had been required to ensure, and had agreed, '*que la formule employée n'impliquait aucune renonciation à un droit de propriété ou de copropriété sur le mur*'. The resulting contract varied the ownership of the wall and the adversely affected neighbour claimed damages against the experts. The claim would have been sufficiently founded had it been made under Arts. 1382, 1383 Cc; simple negligence (*une faute la plus légère*) would have sufficed for delictual liability. Regarding con-tract, the *Cour de Cassation* was clear that liability would depend upon a breach of the standard of care of the *bon père de famille*. The experts were not in breach of that standard in respect of the difficult (and for them unfamiliar) questions of property law concerned. The court rejected the claim with the oft repeated[118] words: '*C'est seulement en matière de délit ou de quasi-délit que toute faute quelconque oblige son auteur à réparer le dom-mage; les arts. 1382 et p. c.civ. sont sans application lorsque la faute a été commise dans l'exécution d'une obligation résultant d'un contrat.*'

432   Although the expression *non-concours des responsabilités* would be more correct, it has been customary since that decision to describe the prohibition of concurrence of actions as *non-cumul des responsabilités*. Of course there has never been any question of double recovery by the plaintiff on both bases of action. The question was whether the same conduct could found a claim in both contract and tort, and '*non-cumul*' thus merely means that is not generally the case: '*En droit français la responsabilité est soit contractuelle, soit délictuelle. Et elle l'est exclusive-ment.*'[119] Thus where a claim is brought in delict, it may be opposed on the ground that liability must be contractual. The judge must then notify the parties under Art. 16 C.proc.civ. and allow the claim to con-tinue only under contract law as *per* Art. 12 C.proc.civ.[120] Should the

---

[116] Cf. earlier law: Cass.req. 21.1.1890, *S*. 1890, 1, 408.

[117] Cass.civ. 11.1.1922, *DP* 1922, 1, 16 = p. 1924, 1, 105 (note Demogue) = *Gaz.Pal.* 1922, 1, 344 = Capitant (-Terré/Lequette), *Grands arrêts*, 9th edn., no. 102.

[118] Cf. Cass.civ. 6.5.1946, *JCP* 1946, II, 3236 (note Rodière); Cass.civ. 9.1.1957, *JCP.* 1957, II, 9915 (note Rodière); *Cass.civ.* 9.10.1962, *D*. 1963 *Jur.* 1 (note Liet-Veaux); Cass.civ. 22.5.1968, *Gaz.Pal.* 1968 *Jur.* 290; Cass.civ. 17.3.1969, *D*. 1969 *Jur.* 532; Cass.civ. 24.2.1981, *D*. 1981 *Jur.* 560; Cass.com. 26.2.1985, *Sem.Jur.* 1985, IV, 172. Further, on case-law, see Cornu, *Le problème du cumul*, esp. pp. 240 ff. and Huet, *Resp. contractuelle et resp. délictuelle*, passim.

[119] *Encyclopédie Dalloz* (-Tunc) (fn. 115) no. 172.

[120] See also Cass.civ. 19.3.1985, *Sem.Jur.* 1985, IV, 197 and Cass.civ. 31.10.1989, *Sem.Jur.* 1990, II, 21568. Further, *JClCiv* (-Espagnon), Arts. 1146 to 1155, Fasc. 16–1, No. 69. The position in Luxembourg was differently decided: see Trib.Lux. 27.5.1981, *Pas. luxemb.* 25 (1981–1983) p. 311.

defendant not assert contractual primacy, the court retains discretion either to reject the action on a delictual basis, or to allow it to continue in contract for reasons of procedural economy.[121]

The success of the *non-cumul* principle cannot be explained solely by **433** situations similar to that in Cass.civ. 11.1.1922. That case concerned damage to property resulting from incorrect advice,[122] in the light of which the case's particular result was unconvincing, being concerned with fault based on an assumption of responsibility, which is itself not based solely on simple negligence (an *erreur excusable*). The 'experts' should not have attempted matters of which they knew nothing. This development of French law is only understandable if one appreciates that the broad scope of Arts. 1382, 1383 Cc provided an emergency brake for the benefit of contract law, the case-law on Art. 1384 para. 1 Cc not yet being settled and the problems of the relationship between contractual and *gardien* liability thus also not yet in issue.[123] At the turn of the century opinion was strong in France that one should distinguish between the basis of contractual obligations, on one hand, and the legal consequences in terms of damage caused by their breach, on the other. The latter were felt to be covered by Arts. 1382 ff. Cc. '*L'obligation de réparer . . . prend sa source dans les articles 1382 et suivants*',[124] and '*la responsabilité est nécessairement délictuelle.*'[125] To conclude that every breach of contract constitutes a delict would be to go too far;[126] after all, it was never doubted in Belgian and Spanish case-law that poor performance of a contract was covered by tort law.[127] Nevertheless one can easily understand the temptation in such an intellectual climate to remove the problems of concurrence of actions at a stroke. From the text of Arts. 1382, 1383 Cc alone it was, and remains, virtually impossible to characterize 'pure' breaches of contract as such, thereby avoiding the

---

[121] At least in Cass.com. 17.2.1987, D. 1987 Jur. 543 (note Jourdain).

[122] Infringement of property rights can prejudice not only the person whose material possessions are damaged but also the person who loses property on account of a transaction of legal character: BGH 5.12.1989, BGHZ p. 397. The fact that in Cass.civ. 11.1.1922, in the absence of 'dominant knowledge', there was no direct involvement by the experts is for the purposes of attributing civil liability as unimportant as the fact that the owner had signed the contract. Unlike say, the case of deceit, the owner did not intend to act. Only a person who intends to relinquish his property suffers legal pure economic loss when he is led to dispose of it by incorrect and blameworthy information. Negligence suffices: HD 18.11.1992, UfR 1993 Å p. 52.

[123] For the 'disapplication' of Art. 1384 sec. 1 Cc by means of contract law see below, nos. 468–470.

[124] Grandmoulin, *Nature délictuelle de la responsabilité pour violation des obligations contractuelles* (thèse Rennes 1894) II p. 4.

[125] Lefebvre, *Rev.crit.légis. et juris.* 1886 p. 485.

[126] As argued by Mazeaud/Tunc, *Responsabilité civile I*, 6th edn., no. 101.

[127] Below, nos. 436 and 437.

application of delict law.[128] Even the differentiation between pure economic loss and damage to property was often unhelpful as, under the principle in Art. 1138 Cc (mere contract of sale is sufficient to transfer title) impossibility of performance in a contract of sale resulting from negligence can itself amount to damage to property. Above all, no mechanism exists which is capable of differentiating *a priori* between duties in contract and in tort in cases (typically involving professional liability) in which a contractor is obliged to exercise care. The paramount question for tort law, whether there is a duty of care, has already been answered here; and as tort law almost everywhere regards contractual relationships of proximity as founding duties,[129] the key question[130] of whether the act would have been unlawful but for the contract is of little assistance. In any event, it is impossible in the legal systems of modern Europe to distinguish, as regards duties protecting legal rights interests, between primary and secondary contractual and tortious obligations: between primary and secondary contractual obligations because the criterion of actionability has no effect on damages,[131] and between secondary contractual and tortious obligations because both are intended to protect the *status quo*.[132] It was initially noted that the border between contract and tort neither has nor is capable of having a generally applicable theoretical definition, as comparative law attests. The limits of delict in any country are set by its national law. A law of delict like that of France, however, which generally incorporates pure economic loss within its reach, lacks any theoretical means to exclude from its compass *dommage purement contractuel*.[133]

---

[128] Cf. Dietz, *Anspruchskonkurrenz*, p. 43; Ferid, *Verhältnis des Anspruchs aus unerlaubter Handlung*, p. 28; and Cass.civ. 9.6.1993, Bull.civ. 1993, II, No. 204: construction company failed to adhere to the architect's plan as a result of which the owner of the building lost a subsidy. The claim was brought in tort. The Court said that *'l'article 1382 du Cc est inapplicable à la réparation d'un dommage se rattachant à l'exécution d'un engagement contractuel'*.

[129] Cf. no. 416 above.

[130] See no. 423 above. Also Herbots, *Samenloop*, p. 153 (with additional references); Cass. 7.12.1973, *Pas. belge* 1974, I, 376 (*'La responsabilité quasi délictuelle ne peut être engagée qu'à la double condition que la faute constitue la violation, non de l'obligation contractuelle, mais d'une obligation qui s'impose à tous, et que cette faute ait causé un autre dommage que celui qui ne résulte que de l'exécution défectueuse du contrat'*); *Jarvis* v. *Moy, Davies, Smith, Vandervell and Co.* [1936] 1 KB 399, 403 (*per* Greer LJ) and references above at fn. 77 (The Netherlands) and below at nos. 436 (Spain) and 437 (Belgium).

[131] This is not only the result of the fact that, for instance, English law recognizes specific performance only as an equitable remedy, but primarily from the fact that, due to the procedural law principle of certainty, an action cannot be brought to enforce a duty of care. Moreover, if actual damage has been suffered the issue of the existence or otherwise of a claim to performance is of only academic importance. It has already been settled.

[132] BGH 5.12.1989, BGHZ 109 p. 297 is a clear example from German case-law: resale in breach of contract by vendor of an item for which he had not paid, and which therefore was not his to sell; treated as a tort.

[133] A similar point is made by Van Quickenborne, *Rev.cit.jur.belge* 1988 pp. 344, 355–370.

In adopting the principle of *non-cumul des responsabilités*, French case-law was merely drawing the inevitable conclusion from the *Code Civil's* general clause regarding liability in tort. For this reason, attempts to appreciate that doctrine of concurrence inevitably become a cornerstone in endeavours to define the advantages and disadvantages of a general tort liability clause. However, the prohibition against accumulation in France should have the same effect as that achieved in other European countries as a side-effect of a more narrowly defined law of delict: the preservation of the scope of special rules (primarily but not solely) on the division of pure economic losses between contractual partners.[134] The parallel goes further. As elsewhere, it is not deemed necessary in France to protect by means of the non-application of tort law those who commit crimes in the course of contractual dealings to the detriment of the contractual partner (deceit, negligent personal injury, etc.) Theoretically, the general rule remains that liability may be based either in contract or in tort, but it is relaxed in that the plaintiff may choose not only the forum but also the applicable law. Liability is *'de nature délictuelle'*[135] before the criminal courts, but contractual before the civil.[136] For an intentional non-criminal act by a contractor, the *Cour de Cassation* allows genuine concurrence in civil actions.[137] It has been said of this solution *'qu'elle est aujourd'hui très fragile et peut-être, n'a plus cours que pour la responsabilité d'un architecte ou entrepeneur'*.[138]

434

Disregarding temporarily the manner in which, against the background of strict *gardien* liabilty under Art. 1384 sec. 1 Cc, the prohibition of accumulation affects both the extent and the basis of liability for contractual breaches of duties of care[139]—the more they are based on fault, i.e. regarded as *obligations de sécurité de moyens*, the less potential for liability—one is struck by the degree of legal certainty which the French courts have achieved in respect of liability for pure economic loss. Typically, only cases involving third parties cause difficulties regarding the *non-cumul* principle.[140] Otherwise, French law has been spared many of the difficulties which continue to afflict other legal systems. Liability for incorrect advice and information is an excellent

435

---

[134] Viney says correctly at *Sem.Jur.* 1993 *Doctr.* 3664 pp. 144, 145: *'la règle dite du non-cumul . . . est destinée à éviter que l'application des règles délictuelles ne vienne détruire l'equilibre du contrat.'* Clearly this observation is generally correct and does not apply solely to compensation for pure economic loss.

[135] For consistent jurisprudence of the Cass.crim., see e.g. Cass.crim. 12.12.1946, *JCP* 1947, II, 3621 (note Rodière); Cass.crim. 26.11.1964, *Gaz.Pal.* 1965, *Jur.* 312; and Cass.crim. 9.6.1975, *D.* 1976 *Jur.* 116.

[136] Cass.com. 17.11.1987, *Sem.Jur.* 1988, II, 20568 (note Viney).

[137] Cass.civ. 18.12.1972, *D.* 1973 *Jur.* 272 (note Mazeaud).

[138] *Encyclopédie Dalloz* (-Tunc), *Rép.Dr.Civ. VIII, Responsabilité (en général)* no. 186. Cf. Cass.civ. 9.5.1979, *D.* 1980 *Jur.* 414 (note Espagnon).   [139] Nos. 468 ff. below.

[140] See no. 438.

example. Non-contractual liability of experts, banks, and professionals has been developed for the benefit of third parties. To subject particular groups to a potentially more extensive form of non-contractual liability additional to those duties already owed to their partners in contract is a problematic step. *Henderson* v. *Merrett Syndicates*[141] would have been decided differently in France.[142] In Germany too, the analagous problem of the relationship between contract-based and *culpa in contrahendo*-based liability (considered below at no. 500) has now been resolved in favour of contractual liability.[143]

(2) Spain and Belgium

436 Some concluding observations on the laws of Spain and Belgium demonstrate the increase in legal certainty which *non-cumul* law provides for a country with a general tort liability clause. Both countries have attempted, with the help of general considerations on the 'nature' of liability in contract and tort, to avoid the strict form of *non-cumul*. In Spain, in cases where economic loss results from pre-contractual dealings, the concept of *culpa in contrahendo* is usually abandoned in favour of exclusively tort-based liability (Art. 1902 Cc),[144] thereby avoiding the problem of dual liability. Lawyers' liability for negligent drafting of wills under Arts. 705, 712 sec. 2, and 715 Cc is set in a contractual context in so far as third-party claims are concerned, but the rules are classified as special rules of non-contractual liability.[145] There is heated discussion among commentators as to whether all breaches of contract may be regarded as torts (thus requiring reference to the principle of primacy of contract) or whether, for the purposes of Art. 1902 Cc, only such acts as would be unlawful even without a contractual duty of care. However, there is no breach of contract (only a tort) where, for example, a bus driver attacks and robs a passenger, a plumber steals from a house where he has been employed, or a landlord and tenant come to blows whilst arguing over rent.[146] The Tribunal Supremo clearly views the matter

---

[141] No. 429 and fn. 106 above.   [142] Cf. Cass.civ. 24.3.1987, Bull.civ. 1987, I, No. 104.
[143] BGH 4.3.1987, BGHZ 100 p. 117; BGH 6.7.1993, *NJW* 1993 p. 2433.
[144] Cf. TS 16.5.1988, *La Ley* 1988 (3) p. 399: bank employee, having spoken to his superior, believed he was to be transferred to Miami. The employee prepared for the transfer, sold his car, and his wife gave notice to her employer. Shortly before the transfer was to take place it was cancelled. Liability neither for *culpa in contrahendo* nor for breach of contract. Damages were granted under Art. 1902 Cc. (Cf. no. 373 and fn. 408 above for Spanish *culpa in contrahendo*.)
[145] Santos Briz, *Responsabilidad civil*, in: Deutsch/Taupitz (edd.), *Haftung der Dienstleistungsberufe*, pp. 93–125; Paz-Ares/Díez-Picazo/Bercovitz/Salvador (-Uberos), *Código civil I*, 2nd edn., pp. 1789–1791 (Art. 705 is an exception to Art. 1902 Cc, being subject not to the tort 1-year limitation period but the 15-year period under Art. 1964 Cc).
[146] Examples and references from the contribution of Cavanillas Múgica and Tapia Fernández to *La concurrencia de responsabilidad contractual y extracontractual* pp. 6–55; most of the literature referred to therein is not accessible to the author.

thus[147] and attempts to limit the overlap (seen as *tertium genus*) of contract and tort both by viewing as the sole domain of contract that which belongs to 'the strict sphere of what has been agreed by the parties' (*la rigurosa órbita de lo pactado*)[148] and reducing the scope of tort by excluding from it pure economic losses resulting from breach of primary contractual duties.[149] Medical liability cases are thus among the most important regarding concurrence of actions.[150] Indeed, the Tribunal Supremo has commented *obiter*, albeit in a different context, that it cannot be said that *'la responsabilidad contractual opere necesariamente con exclusión de la aquiliana'*.[151] It thus appears that the Tribunal Supremo generally employs all means at its disposal to base liability either in contract or in tort, to that extent approaching the bases of French law. There is no general line, and it is felt that there cannot be one in such a context.[152] Indeed, even procedural law is applied to ensure that only one base of liability may be employed in a particular case.

Thus damage caused by a tenant to a landlord's property has been based, dependent on the wording of the writ, on both contract[153] and tort.[154] (That could perhaps be interpreted as an expression of the principle of concurrence of actions[155]). Where a writ is based solely in either contract or tort, the Tribunal Supremo is extremely reluctant to employ *ex officio* another basis. By virtue of Arts. 359 and 548 LEC, *jura novit curia* should not result in the defendant's being surprised at trial by a basis for which he is not prepared.[156]

Belgian law fluctuates between *non-cumul* and concurrence of actions. **437** For the same reasons as in Spain, this results in great legal uncertainty. A clear statement is found in Cass. 13.2.1930, and has been at the centre of the debate ever since.[157] That case concerned the liability of the Belgian

---

[147] Cf. TS 20.7.1992, *La Ley* 1992 (4), p. 405: boiler incorrectly installed by plumber. Plaintiff employed an electrician who discovered the defect but failed to install as promised the necessary replacement part. Plaintiff used the boiler believing it to have been repaired. The boiler exploded, killing the plaintiff's daughter and severely injuring the plaintiff. The Tribunal Supremo held (primarily for reasons of procedural law) that only tort was applicable, but added *obiter* that there would have been no contractual liability in any event.

[148] See fn. 147. Also TS 16.12.1986, *La Ley* 1987 (1) p. 654; TS 10.6.1991, *La Ley* 1992 (3) p. 231 (liability of ski-lift operator to its customers in tort only). TS 10.6.1991 departs from TS 23.3.1988, *RAJ* 1988 No. 2226, p. 2178 (contractual liability of ski-lift owner affirmed).

[149] Cavanillas Múgica/Tapia Fernández (fn. 146) p. 128. (The Tribunal Supremo does not apply the law of tort in cases of breach of primary contractual duties.)

[150] E.g. TS 7.2.1990, *La Ley* 1990 (2) p. 481.

[151] TS 20.7.1992, *La Ley* 1992 (4) pp. 405, 406.   [152] No. 433 above.

[153] TS 22.7.1991, *La Ley* 1991 (4) p. 890.   [154] TS 24.6.1969, *RAJ* 1969 No. 3635, p. 2463.

[155] Cf. Cavanillas Múgica/Tapia Fernández (fn. 146) pp. 129–130.

[156] E.g. TS 10.5.1984, *La Ley* 1984 (3) p. 370. Cf. TS 20.7.1992, *La Ley* 1992 (4) p. 405 and TS 15.3.1993, *La Ley* 1993 (2) p. 477.

[157] Cass. 13.2.1930, *Pas. belge* 1930, I, 115. Less expressive but often cited, Cass. 28.3.1889, *Pas. belge* 1889, I, 161 (165). Liability for accident at work in tort; no contractual breach by employer found.

State Railway for lost freight. The *Cour de Cassation* said '*qu'en prescrivant la réparation par chacun de tout dommage causé à la personne d'autrui ou à ses biens, l'article 1382 du Code civil a édicté une règle dont l'observation s'impose, en principe, à tous et en toutes circonstances*', that the provisions of tort thus remain applicable between contractors, and consequently: '*le fait de s'engager, dans un contrat, à veiller tout spécialement aux biens ou à la personne d'un contractant n'enlève pas, par lui-même, toute action quasi-délictuelle à ce dernier, pour lui réserver seulement, en cas de dommage, l'action née du contrat.*'[158] The principle affirmed here of concurrence of actions for damage to property was later extended to cover personal injury[159] and applied by Cass. 18.5.1961[160] to the third-party action of a house owner against an architect and builder after the completion of works. ('*La réception ne décharge pas l'entrepeneur de sa responsabilité [quasi-délictuelle], même, sauf stipulation contraire, envers le maître de l'ouvrage, quant aux dommages que, dans l'exécution des travaux, il a causés à des propriétés appartenant à des tiers.*'[161]) When the Brussels Court of Appeal wished to go further and treat as a tort the contractual breach of failing to supply electricity, the Cour de Cassation intervened: '*La responsabilité d'une partie est de nature exclusivement contractuelle, lorsque le droit dont la violation constitue le fondement de l'action intentée trouve uniquement son origine et ses conditions d'existence dans le contrat conclu entre parties, et que le dommage n'est dû qu'au seul manquement aux obligations résultant d'un contrat.*'[162] Here the breach was 'purely' contractual. At first glance it is unclear whether this concept favours the *non-cumul* or the concurrence of actions solution. The court's statement apparently construed the term *faute* in Art. 1382 Cc narrowly, suggesting that the principle of concurrence of actions, '*que l'inexécution d'une obligation contractuelle ne constitue pas un acte illicite et ne constitue, dès lors, pas un fondement pour intenter une action en dommages et intérêts sur la base de l'article 1382 du Code civil*', is of no more assistance in answering the

---

[158] Id. fn. 157, p. 116.

[159] E.g. Cass. 7.9.1969, *Pas. belge* 1970, I, 215, 217 ('*de la seule circonstance, qu'une convention existe entre celui qui a causé le dommage et celui qui en est la victime ne résulte pas qu'une responsabilité extra-contractuelle soit exclue*'). Similarly, Brussels 4.2.1992, *RGAR* 1995 No. 14260. Differences between French and Belgian law are clearly illustrated by cases involving liability for animals to third persons with contractual rights to their use (e.g. child at riding stables). In Belgium Art. 1385 Cc (e.g. Trib. Bruxelles 2.6.1994, *RGAR* 1995 No. 12467) is applied, whereas liability in France is exclusively contractual. (E.g. Cass.civ. 16.1.1951, *JCP* 1951, II, 6163.)

[160] Cass. 18.5.1961, *Pas. belge* 1961, I, 1006. Where no damage to third parties, '*la responsabilité décennale de l'architecte* [is] . . . *de nature contractuelle*': Cass. 15.9.1989, *Rev.crit.-jur.belge* 1992 p. 509 (with comment by Herbots).

[161] Id. For the French position see Cass.civ. 9.5.1979, *D.* 1984 *Jur.* 414 (note Espagnon).

[162] Cass. 4.6.1971, *Pas. belge* 1971, I, 940. Cf. Van Ryn, *JT* 1975 p. 505 and Fagnart, *JT* 1976 p. 569.

particular question than the assertion that a contractual party can only be sued in tort by a contract party '*si la faute qui lui est imputée constitue un manquement non pas à une obligation contractuelle mais à l'obligation générale de prudence*'.[163] It is clear that a breach of the criminal law inevitably entails a breach of a general duty.[164] The distinction between *faute* or *dommage purement contractuel* and *faute purement délictuelle*, however, is anything but clear. This particular problem of Belgian legal doctrine has been further confused by Cass. 7.12.1973.[165]

Whilst loading a ship a stevedore damaged a hydraulic crane on the wharf. The Cour de Cassation said that the stevedore could only be held personally liable in tort if the ship's master were liable as his principal. That was not the case: '*la responsabilité quasi délictuelle ne peut être engagée qu'à la double condition que la faute constitue la violation, non de l'obligation contractuelle, mais d'une obligation qui s'impose à tous, et que cette faute ait causé un autre dommage que celui qui ne résulte que de l'exécution défectueuse du contrat.*'[166]

(3) Problems of Demarcation when Integrating Third Parties into a System Prohibiting Concurrence of Actions

As can be seen from the above Belgian cases, much of the legal certainty   **438** gained by *non-cumul des responsabilités* is lost as soon as one tries to integrate third parties into the prohibition against concurrence of actions. A legal system which bases liability principally in only contract or tort will in some cases of *concorso improprio*[167] inevitably face the problem that a negligent act constitutes a breach of contract in respect of one person and a tort in respect of another. If the tort claim is granted, the person to whom the contractual duty is owed must be allowed to '*demander au contractant réparation d'un dommage dû à l'inexécution d'une obligation contractuelle en éludant l'application des règles contractuelles (prescription, clause limitative ou exonération de responsabilité)*'.[168] Whether this leads to different liabilities depends upon two considerations: whether the defendant was party to a chain of contracts transferring ownership of an object, and if not, whether he was responsible for fault which 'by its nature' is non-contractual.

---

[163] Quotations from Cass. 14.10.1985.
[164] Cass. 26.10.1990, *Rev.crit.jur.belge* 1992 p. 497. Children entrusted temporarily to Mrs Niels. Child-minding responsibility passed by her to 2 men who not only drank alcohol but also allowed the children to do so. One of the children fell from a balcony whilst drunk. The Cour d'Appel did not hold the men liable as they could only be liable in tort if Mrs Niels were not liable in contract alone. The court found that liability under Art. 1382 Cc was always possible where a breach of contract also constituted a criminal offence. This was so in the present case (Art. 418 CP: *coups et blessures involontaires*).
[165] Cass. 7.12.1973, *Pas. belge* 1974, I, 376.
[166] Loc. cit. Similarly Cass. 25.10.1990, *Rev.crit.jur.belge* 1992 pp. 493, 495 (note Dalcq).
[167] No. 425 above.   [168] Capitant (-Terré/Lequette), *Grands arrêts*, 9th edn., p. 454.

439   That a contractual partner may only be contractually liable to non-contractual third parties sustaining damage due to his performance is something which has only been affirmed in France and Belgium in respect of (product) liability in multiple contract cases[169] and in cases involving the liability of supplying firms.[170] (However, French law on product liability has been classified by the European Court of Justice for the purposes of the European Convention on Civil Jurisdiction as law of delict.)[171] It is worth repeating that only in France and Belgium in such cases of (product) liability is the liability of the contractual partner in contract alone guaranteed.[172] The same cannot be said of *prestations de services*, matters concerning the personal liability of an agent to the beneficiary of obligations owed by the agent's principal. The starting point is that such an agent is not responsible to the third party in contract.[173] There is also the problem of whether, and if so under what circumstances, the agent may be liable in tort to the third party: a particularly 'uncomfortable' question, as it seems unjust to deny an agent, and especially an employee, the same legal protection as his employer has *vis-à-vis* the injured party. The answer depends upon whether the matter involves both *faute* and *dommage purement contractuelle*. The Belgian Cour de Cassation adopts the following formulation: '*Si l'inexécution d'un contrat résulte d'une faute du préposé ou de l'agent d'exécution de l'un des contractants, l'autre partie ne dispose que d'une action contre son contractant, à savoir une action contractuelle, sans que ce préposé ou cet agent puisse être considéré au regard du contrat comme un tiers dont la responsabilité quasi délictuelle peut être engagée.*'[174] In France it is also crucial whether the vicarious agent was guilty of a '*faute extérieure à l'exécution du contrat*'. So decided the Cassation regarding the heads of legal persons,[175] and it would be unacceptable if a simple employee were exposed to greater liability. The distinguishing criterion here is unfortunate; who can decide whether, say, the painter's apprentice who inad-

---

[169] For France Cass.Ass.plén. 7.2.1986, *D.* 1986 *Jur.* 293 (note Bénabent) = *Sem.Jur.* 1986, II, 20616 (note Malinvaud) = *Rev.trim.dr.civ.* 1986 p. 605 (note Rémy). For Belgium Cass. 9.10.1980, *JT* 1981 p. 70 (contractual liability for latent defect).

[170] Cass.civ. 26.5.1992, *Sem.Jur.* 1992, IV, 2120; Cass.civ. 4.11.1992, *Sem.Jur.* 1993, II, 22058.

[171] ECJ 17.6.1992, *Rev.trim.dr.europ.* 1992 p. 709.

[172] Viney, *Sem.Jur.* 1993, I, 3663 (pp. 144–145) and Jassagne, *Droit commercial I*, nos. 353 ff. and 466 ff.

[173] E.g. Cass. 25.10.1990, *Rev.crit.jur.belge* 1992 p. 493; and Cass.Ass.plén. 12.7.1991, *Sem.-Jur.* 1991, II, 21743 (note Viney. Cf. Witz/Wolter, *ZEuP* 1993 p. 592). Also Cass.civ. 11.4.1995, *D.* 1995 *Somm.* 231 and Cass.civ. 23.6.1992, *Sem.Jur.* 1988, II, 21125 (note Jourdain). As a result, Cass.civ. 8.3.1988, *Sem.Jur.* 1988, II, 21070 may now be meaningless.

[174] Cass. 7.12.1973, *Pas. belge* 1974, I, 375, 377. Cf. Dalcq, *Responsabilité et réparation des dommages*, pp. 67–69. Subsequently confirmed by Cass. 25.10.1990 (fn. above). The special protection afforded to employees may apply in addition to such general protection: cf. above no. 193 above.   [175] Cass.civ. 31.5.1978, *D.* 1978 *IR* 403.

vertently allows a paint pot to fall from a ladder has committed a *faute contractuelle* or a *faute extérieure à l'exécution du contrat*? Perhaps it is more important to note that the French approach tends strongly to attribute contractual liability to the principal. Removing the leading personnel of a company from the firing line of potential liability can lead all too quickly to the overprotection of such persons against company law duties, above all in cases of bankruptcy.[176]

A further instance of *concorso improprio* occurs in the law of carriage of passengers.[177] Until the road traffic law reform, French law allowed the relatives of a deceased passenger to choose whether to base their claim in contract, with reference to a *stipulation tacite pour autrui*, or in tort, with the limitation advantages which that could encompass.[178]

3. ISSUES OF CONCURRENCE OF ACTIONS REGARDING LIABILITY FOR PERSONAL INJURY AND DAMAGE TO THE PROPERTY OF CONTRACT PARTNERS

a. Introduction

(1) Case Types

The second area of wide overlap between the laws of damages in contract   **440** and in tort is that of liability for damage to the legal rights and interests of a contract partner. In continental systems such rights and interests are defined as 'absolute'. In the German-speaking world this area is called *Schutzpflichtverletzung*[179] (lit: breach of protective duty) and covers such cases as the customer injured in a supermarket, the supplied goods which damage other property of the purchaser, the carrier who fails to transport his passenger or goods safely, the hirer who damages the hired goods, the landlord who lets property dangerous to health, and the garage which fails to repair a car handbrake causing the driver to be injured.[180] Generally it concerns issues of liability within a contractual relationship arising not only out of disappointed expectations of performance but also from the harm caused by one contract partner to the essential interests of the other due to, or in the course of, his performance. The primary examples are again damage to property and personal injury. Such cases are the foundation of tort in all jurisdictions. Two

---

[176] BGH 5.12.1989, BGHZ 109 p. 297 is more convincing
[177] Damman, *Einbeziehung Dritter*, pp. 206–208 for German analysis.
[178] Cass.civ. 19.6.1951, D. 1951 *Jur.* 717 (note Ripert).
[179] The terminology is inconsistent in the German-speaking world: OLG Cologne 17.9.1993, *RIW* 1993 pp. 1023, 1024 also refers to *Schutzpflichten* ('protective duties') as including liability for pure economic loss under a contract for the protection of third parties.   [180] BGH 15.12.1992, *NJW* 1993 p. 655.

issues arise. First, does this area affect contract law, and secondly, does the fact that the avoidance of such injury was part of a contractual duty touch at all upon tort.

441 There are three recognizable groups of breach of protective duties cases. In the first, the contractual law of damages is stricter than that of tort. Thus although a right or interest has been damaged, there has been no tort or breach of non-contractual duty. This position may be described as a non-genuine concurrence of actions. Questions of priority are now resolved in Germany in much the same way as in practically all jurisdictions: priority is given to contract law; the absence of liability in tort does not relieve a party from liability in contract (below at b., nos. 446 ff.) The position is more complicated in the other two groups. The situations envisaged are those in which contract and tort claims have identical prerequisites, but where the respective results differ. This is especially clear when limitation periods or measures of recoverable damages vary due to, *inter alia*, foreseeability, contributory negligence, damages for pain and suffering (below at c., nos. 449 ff.) In the third and final group, liability in tort is stronger than in contract. Conspicuous examples are where non-contractual liability is strict while contractual liability is fault-based, or where in tort any form of negligence suffices, whereas in contract a qualified form is required. It is essential here to decide whether, and if so to what extent, the less severe regime established by contract law displaces the tort regime.

(2) Concurrence of Actions and Protection of Property: Liability for Damage Caused by a Product to Itself

442 Before these three groups are considered it is important to highlight two other facets of the general theme. There is no common understanding in Europe of the terms personal injury, damage to health,[181] or damage to property. Divergences can have a direct result upon the law of concurrence of actions of the legal systems under consideration. Nowhere is this more clear than in respect of liability for self-inflicted damage to a product,[182] which is expressly excluded from the EC Directive on Product Liability (Art. 9 b with Art. 13). This concerns items composed of two of more parts, which are unsatisfactory because of an isolated defect

---

[181] In the law on damage to health there are different reactions to disturbance to peace and quiet by noise. BGH 9.11.1993, *NJW* 1994 p. 127 is a remarkable decision: destruction of frozen sperm is a personal injury; non-pecuniary loss compensated.

[182] Cf. Art. 2. lit. b, Hague Convention of 2.10.1973 on product liability law which provides: '. . . the word "damage" shall mean injury to the person or damage to the property as well as economic loss; however, damage to the product itself and consequential economic loss shall be excluded unless associated with other damage.' (*RabelsZ* 37 [1973] pp. 594, 595.)

in one of the constituent parts (a car throttle cable jams,[183] or a car has the wrong type of tyre,[184] or the cork does not fit the wine bottle[185]). If, after ownership of the item has been transferred, that part causes damage to the item as a whole, the question arises whether the seller liable in contract for the 'small' defect is also liable in tort for the 'greater' damage ensuing. Legal German has a colourful word for this phenomenon: *Weiterfresserschäden* (lit: further-corroding damage).

Negligence is not the only prerequisite for tort liability: many jurisdictions also require that the damage to the whole constitutes damage to property rights. Opinions vary in Europe as to whether this should be the case. In England and Ireland such cases are not viewed as involving damage to property: even where property is completely destroyed the matter is one of non-recoverable pure economic loss.[186] This somewhat surprising position derives from the approach to the problem of concurrence of actions: 'when a product injures only itself the reasons for imposing a tort duty are weak and those for leaving the party to its contractual remedies are strong.'[187] Quite the opposite was decided by the German Federal Court (Bundesgerichtshof) in the celebrated *Schwimmerschalter* case of 1976,[188] to the central passage of

---

[183] BGH 18.1.1983, BGHZ 86 p. 256. Cf. *Murphy* v. *Brentwood* [1990] 2 All ER 908, 928 (*per* Lord Bridge).

[184] BGH 5.7.1978, *NJW* 1978 p. 2241. Also, albeit only *obiter*, *M/S Aswan Engineering Establishment Co.* v. *Lupdine Ltd. and Another* [1987] 1 WLR 1, 21 f. (*per* Lloyd LJ).

[185] Lloyd LJ, fn. 184; BGH 21.11.1989, *NJW* 1990 p. 908.

[186] There is no binding English precedent but *Murphy* v. *Brentwood* (fn. 183 and no. 282 above) leaves little doubt. Analysis of judgment by v. Bar, *RabelsZ* 56 (1992) p. 410, esp. pp. 435–441, confirmed by Lord Goff of Chievely at the first Anglo-German Judges' Conference. (Report v. Bar, *RabelsZ* 58 (1994) pp. 421, 439.) If not overruled, *Junior Books Ltd.* v. *Veitchi Co. Ltd.* [1983] 1 AC 520 (HL) remains at best an isolated case decided on its own facts. In that case it was accepted that a subcontractor's imperfect laying of a factory floor caused damage to property, as opposed to pure economic loss only. (Cf. v. Bar, *RabelsZ* 56 [1992] pp. 410, 421). This classification was made possible by finding the plaintiff and subcontractor to be in a relationship 'akin to contract', a peculiar argument in the circumstances. Regarding *Dutton* v. *Bognor Regis* and *Anns* v. *Merton* (no. 218 above) Irish case-law has stated that the vendor of a house may be liable in tort to the purchaser if the condition of the house endangers the health or property of the latter. E.g. *Sunderland* v. *McGreavey* (1987) IR 372 (HC). Cf. *Siney* v. *Corporation of Dublin* (1980) IR 400 (Sup. Ct.) and *Ward* v. *McMaster* (1985) IR 29 (HC). It was clear from the outset that damage to a product sold does not give rise to tort liability in negligence: *Sunderland* v. *McGreavey* loc. cit. p. 383 (Lardner, J) and *Colgan* v. *Connolly Construction Co. (Ireland) Ltd.* [1980] ILRM 33, 36–37 (McMahon, J).

[187] *East River Steamship Corp.* v. *Transamerica Delaval Inc.* 476 US 858, 870 (1986). The leading American decision which, like the Canadian decision *Rivtow Marine Ltd.* v. *Washington Iron Works* (1973) 40 DLR (3rd) 530 has greatly influenced opinion in England, esp. the decision in *Murphy* (fn. 183). Cf. Bungert, *Tul.L.Rev.* 66 [1992] pp. 1179–1266. Similar thoughts have been decisive in Irish jurisprudence. Cf. Lardner J in *Sunderland* (fn. 186): 'The obligation of a builder or manufacturer in regard to the quality of his product is . . . something which ought to rest in contract only.'

[188] BGH 24.11. 1976, BGHZ 67 p. 359.

which German courts have adhered ever since,[189] albeit with changes in detail.[190]

The defendant manufactured industrial cleaning and degreasing plants. A plant which the defendant supplied to the plaintiff's insuree was destroyed by fire only weeks after commencing operations due to a defective floater switch which failed to switch off heating elements at the correct time. The plaintiff's contractual claim was statute-barred when the writ was issued. Moreover, the defendant had effectively excluded contractual liability. Above all it was extremely doubtful whether there was in fact any contractual liability for the destruction of the entire plant. BGH 8.3.1967 had expressly stated some ten years earlier that claims based on breach of contract in the supply of defective goods gave rise only to liability to compensate for damage to the recipient's legal interests,[191] and not damage caused to the goods themselves.[192] Consequently the purchaser would be left without a remedy were he not given a right of action in tort. The BGH recognized this: the matter was treated as involving fault-caused damage to property within the meaning of § 823 sec. 1 BGB.

Since then the BGH, when distinguishing between pure economic loss (contractual) and damage to property (tort), has maintained the view that only when the damage 'coincides with the reduction in value which was inherent in the thing at the time of acquisition on account of its defectiveness'[193] could the plaintiff succeed in a contractual claim. Otherwise, the 'greater' damage is treated as damage to property and founds only tort liability.

443   It is submitted that the correct solution lies somewhere between the English and German approaches, the English being the closer. It may appear artificial not to categorize as damage to property a negligently initiated chain of events resulting in damage to goods, yet the internal balance of the law of obligations requires that precedence in such cases be given to contract law. The problems in cases of self-induced damage to goods cannot be dealt with solely by reference to the definition of 'damage to property'. All European jurisdictions could usefully apply

---

[189] E.g. BGH 5.7.1978 (fn. 184); BGH 18.1.1983 (fn. 189); BGH 14.5.1985, *NJW* 1985 p. 2420; BGH 12.2.1992, *NJW* 1992 p. 1225; and BGH 24.3.1992, *NJW* 1992 p. 1678. Cf. analysis by Steffen, *VersR* 1988 pp. 977–980.

[190] Originally dependent essentially on whether the defect lay in a 'functionally restricted' component; BGH 18.1.1983, BGHZ 86 pp. 256, 259 altered the criterion to one of 'similarity of substance', as in the cases cited in fn. 193.

[191] BGH 8.3.1967, *LM* BGB § 276 [K] No. 3; see BGH 24.11.1976, BGHZ 67 pp. 359, 365.

[192] OLG Celle 18.2.1993, *VersR* p. 1070 for the corresponding law on contracts for services.

[193] BGH 18.1.1983, BGHZ 86 pp. 256, 259. Also BGH 18.3.1986, *VersR* 1986 p. 1125.

the French concept of *non-cumul des responsabilités* to this area.[194] Indeed, several solutions outside Germany are based upon precisely that. Spanish commentators considered whether to adopt the jurisprudence of the German *Schwimmerschalter* case, but generally rejected it.[195] There is so far no Spanish case-law following the German path.[196] The problem, dealt with by the House of Lords in *Murphy*, namely damage to buildings, is governed expressly by Art. 1591 Span. Cc regarding works contracts: 'the contractor of building work which collapses due to errors in its construction is liable for resulting damage and disadvantages where the decay occurs within ten years from the date on which the construction was completed; the architect is subject . . . to the same liability . . .'[197] In Denmark one must refer extensively to product liability law[198] to establish the priority of warranties for goods.[199] This law allocates problems involving self-induced damage to goods ('component damage') to sale of goods law, precisely as in Germany.[200] The problem is rarely discussed in The Netherlands; where it has been discussed the apparently self-evident assumption has been made that such cases belong to sale of goods law (regarding negligently constructed buildings, Art. 7A:1645 BW[201]

---

[194] Treated comprehensively by v. Bar, *Probleme der Haftpflicht für deliktsrechtliche Eigentumsverletzung*, pp. 17–25. Also noteworthy, BGH 16.2.1993, *NJW-RR* 1993 p. 793: if 'in conflicts between sale of goods and tort law, the contractual and tort claims of the injured party are congruent, the tort claim will exceptionally be limited by the shorter § 477 BGB limitation period'.

[195] Cavanillas Múgica/Tapia Fernández, *Concurrencia de responsabilidad*, p. 13, with further references.

[196] With the decision of TS 5.3.1985, *RAJ* 1985 No. 1108 p. 927 Spanish law affords a particularly elegant case of *Weiterfresserschaden* concerning a floor damaged by woodworm, but even here German law would not apply tort. The TS treated the case as contractual, without considering the application of tort.

[197] The Italian equivalent to Art. 1591 Span. Cc, Art. 1669 Ital. Cc. illustrates the uncertainties attendant upon every statement in this field of law. The Cassazione states that the rule '*configura una responsabilità di tipo extracontrattuale*'. Thus, not only can the person who commissioned the building bring an action under Art. 1669 Ital. Cc against the contractor, but every subsequent purchaser can claim against any person 'under whose direct leadership and responsibility it was built'. (Cass. 27.8.1994, n. 7550, *Giur.it.* 1995, I, 1, 375.) If one considers this as an Italian parallel to the *chaînes de contrat* of French law, it is again clear how pointless it is to distinguish *a priori* between liability in contract and in tort.

[198] *Lovforslag* No. L 54, Folketingstidende 1988–89, Tillæg A, col. 1616 (defective car brakes; liability for damage to goods under sale of goods law only).

[199] Kruse, *Erstatningsretten*, 5th edn., p. 234; Bloth, *Produkthaftung in Schweden, Norwegen und Dänemark*, pp. 182–185, 306.

[200] BT-Drucks. 11/2447 p. 13: 'The protection afforded by the Product Liability Act only covers other objects. This is reasonable because damage to the product itself is adequately covered by special rules on guarantees and in particular by sale of goods and works contracts law.' This has clearly made little impression on the German Federal Court.

[201] Cf. HR 14.11.1929, *NedJur* 1929 No. 1776. Collapse of a house built on sand. Also, Hof van Justitie van de Nederlandse Antillen 31.3.1981, *NedJur* 1981 No. 453 p. 1499' roof defects only apparent after heavy rainfall after transfer of title to house. Liability arose from non-performance (*wanprestatie*). Case also concerned the collapse of the works (*vergaan*).

corresponds to Art. 1591 Span. Cc). Sale of goods law also deals adequately with problems arising from increases in value of the acquired
goods.[202] The same applies in Italy. Changes to the value of the damaged
article are covered by sale of goods law under Arts. 1494 sec. 1 and 1223
Cc.[203] This contractual liability is based on implied fault. Tort liability
arises alongside contract liability under Art. 1494 sec. 2 Cc. only where
other goods (or legal interests) belonging to the purchaser are damaged
in consequence of the original defect. Damage to the product itself
cannot found tort liability.[204] This is because the purchaser buys, not
individual components of a car, but a whole car.[205] There appears to be
no Portuguese material on this issue. The French *Code civil* makes it
clear that contractual liability alone is in issue. The only question is thus
whether liability is *responsabilité contractuelle* (Art. 1147 Cc) or founds an
action *en garantie des vices cachés* (Art. 1641 Cc), which must be validated
dans un bref délai. The most recent deliberations of the Cour de Cassation
suggest that the latter must be the case.[206] The Austrian High Court has
recently expressly rejected[207] the *Schwimmerschalter* case-law. The Swedish Statute on Product Liability[208] provides in para. 1 sec. 2 sub-section 2
with finality that 'damage to the product itself . . . is not recoverable'.
Considering that para. 67, sec. 2 of the Swedish Sale of Goods Act treats
cases of damage to goods other than defective goods purchased as tort
cases, one must accept that the product liability provision is tort law.

(3) Differences of Classification of Duties Generally

444 Our second preliminary observation concerns an analogous problem,
located not in the area of protected interests but in the field of conduct
giving rise to liability, and specifically of duties. The starting point here is
that a legal system's contractual concepts of protective duties can only be
fully understood and developed against the background of the complementary tort law. Contractual protective duties are only required insofar as
their functions are not already achieved by tort law. The complementary

---

[202] Art. 7: 24 (on purchases by consumers) and Art. 6:74 sec. 4 BW. *T&C* (-Lankhorst),
Art. 6: 190 BW annot. 1 (for damage to the product itself, so-called *transactieschade*, *'de
benadeelde [is] aangewezen op het bepaalde bij de consumentenkoop'*). Cf. Hof Amsterdam
27.6.1957, *NedJur* 1958 No. 104 p. 295: accident due to a vehicle's defective steering. The
passenger victim's tort claim did not prevent the owner from bringing a contractual action
against the vendor.   [203] Cendon (-Schiavone) IV, Art. 1494 annot. 2.
   [204] E.g. Cass. 13.3.1980, n. 1696, *Giur.it.* 1980, I, 1, 1460. Also Schiavone loc. cit. annot. 4.
   [205] Pret. Torino 7.5.1991, n. 4326, *Riv.giur.circ.trasp.* 1992 p. 141.
   [206] Cass.civ. 5.5.1993, D. 1993 *Jur.* 506 (note Bénabent) concerning the supply of roof tiles
which rapidly began to crack so that *'le phénomène de délitage s'est étendu en 1982 à la quasi-
totalité de la toiture'*. Cf. Cass.civ. 20.3.1989, D. 1989 *Jur.* 381 (note Malaurie): implosion of a
television set; Art. 1641 Cc.
   [207] OGH 3.2.1994, *JBl* 1994 p. 477 = *ÖJZ* 1994 p. 772 (*EvBl* 159); for a comparative law
view, see Posch, *PHI* 1994 pp. 149–153.   [208] *Produktansvarslag*, SFS 1992: 18.

and corrective function of the law of contract can only truly develop on the basis of a co-ordinated concurrence rule. There is no need to develop a wide range of contractual protective duties alongside a sufficiently developed law of tort, nor could one effectively temper strict tort law in particular circumstances by means of milder contractual provisions without reliance on the *non-cumul* principle. Thus differing approaches to questions of concurrence of actions need not lead to differing results. The same is true of the classification of a case or a basis of liability as being in contract or in tort. Differences in dogmatic classifications of protective duties, viewed from a comparative law perspective, often serve only to secure the same or similar outcomes as those of a neighouring legal system. Such interactions of contract, tort, and concurrence rules are considered below (at sections 4, nos. 459 ff., and 5, nos. 492 ff.) It is also necessary to refer to them here. Without understanding these interactions the basic principles of concurrence of actions cannot be properly understood. It need hardly be emphasized that the three types of case considered at no. 441 are variously weighted in different European Union countries. For example, where employers' liability for accidents at work gives way to social insurance, neither contract, tort law, nor consequently private law concurrence of actions rules, have a part to play. Also, in some countries medical practitioners' liability leads the way regarding the application of concurrence convictions, whereas elsewhere such dependence is inconceivable. In England, for example, where doctors were predominantly employed within the National Health Service, it was said that contract law 'has no role to play in the vast majority of contacts between doctors and patients'.[209]

(4) The Significance of the Distinction Between Contract and Tort Liability in Other Areas of Law

Given the risk of overestimating the importance of classifying protective **445** duties as contractual or tort, it pains the comparative lawyer to observe the significance afforded to such classifications in areas other than liability law. International private and procedural law come readily to mind, although most national vagaries have thankfully now been contained by the European Court of Justice's interpretation of the European Civil Jurisdiction and Judgment Convention.[210] Similarly,

---

[209] Kennedy, in Deutsch/Schreiber (edd.), *Medical Responsibility in Western Europe*, pp. 113, 134.

[210] Cf. EuGH 17.6.1992, *Rev.trim.dr.europ.*1992 p. 709 = BullEG no. 18/92 pp. 4 ff. (contractual liability of producers in France is tort in the sense of Art. 5 ECJC). BGH 23.5.1993 WM 1993 p. 1215 has referred to the European Court the question of 'how the claims for breach of precontractual duties/*culpa in contrahendo* in the present case are to be classified according to the categories (contract/tort) of the European Civil Jurisdiction Convention'. *Matthews* v. *Kuwait Bechtel Corp.* [1959] 2 QB 57 is an English example, jurisdiction being dependent on the classification of the duty breached.

national procedural laws often provide for factual and local competencies of contract and tort; costs rules may also diverge.[211] Legal liability immunity law, theoretically only accessory to liability law but of great practical effect, is a further example of the effects of such classification. Even if it is assumed that a party may in principle enjoy immunity from tort liability, it remains questionable whether such immmunity based on the will of the parties should actually pervade the law of tort.[212] Where such immunity is found in standard-form contracts, the interpretation of which is unclear, it is construed as applying only to contract liability leading, in accordance with the principles of concurrence of actions, to full tort liability. The German *Schwimmerschalter* case-law is on that footing.[213] The last area to be considered here is personal liability insurance. Depending upon the wording of the policy, it may be highly significant whether a case is classified as contract or tort. A dramatic example in Cass.civ. 27.1.1993:[214]

A man helping his brother to fell a tree on the latter's property was injured when the tree touched an electric cable. The property owner was insured against liability under Arts. 1382 and 1384 sec. 1 Cc. The court accepted that there existed between the brothers a gratuitous contract (*une convention d'assistance bénévole*), which '*emporte nécessairement pour l'assisté l'obligation de réparer les conséquences des dommages corporels subis par celui auquel il a fait appel*', and held him liable for damages in contract, for which there was no insurance cover.

b. Liability in Contract Without Liability in Tort

446 Throughout Europe, where a contractor by his act prejudices the rights or interests of the other party, liability often arises exclusively in contract, not merely on the principle of *non-cumul*, but from the simple fact that tort-based immunity does not give rise to contractual immunity. In contrast to tortfeasors, who are unidentifiable prior to the event, contract

---

[211] E.g. *Jarvis v. Moy, Davies, Smith, Vandervell, and Co.* [1936] 1 KB 399, 403.

[212] Cf. Brussels 4.2.1992, *RGAR* 1995 No. 12460: release from strict contract and tort liability, but not from liability under Art. 1383 Cc.

[213] Cf. BGH 24.11.1976, BGHZ 67 pp. 359, 360, and 363 (no. 442 above): injured party 'not prevented from resorting to liability for an unlawful act (i.e. in tort) where contractual claims . . . no longer exist on account of an immunity covering such claims only'.

[214] Cass.civ. 27.1.1993, *Gaz.Pal.* 1993 *Jur.* 434 (note Chabas). Similarly, Cour 10.3.1992, *Pas. luxemb.* 29 (1993–1995) p. 5: neighbour assisting in the slaughtering of a sheep; *contrat d'assistance*. Contrast BGH 9.6.1992, *JR* 1993 pp. 507, 508 (with comment by Haase): 'favours lacking a declaration of intent to be legally bound cannot base contractual claims. In contrast, tort claims arising from favours remain undisturbed, according to BGB jurisprudence.' Cass.civ. 26.1.1994, *Rev.trim.dr.civ.* 1994 p. 864 (Jourdain) corresponds: man assisted another to fell trees and was injured in so doing. Court of Cassation denied existence of a contract; tort liability based on *faute* was thus considered.

parties generally receive consideration for liabilities to which they expose themselves, which justifies imposing on them, not merely a duty of care, but a strict obligation to secure a particular outcome and to bear responsibility for any damage to the other's interests.

This consideration has led a minority[215] of European legal systems to **447** objectivize a lessor's liability for personal injury and damage to property sustained by his tenant due to deficiencies in the premises. Although it only provides for 'damages for non-performance', German courts have interpreted § 538 sec. 1, 1st alt. BGB[216] as laying down a strict contractual liability for damage to property and personal injury,[217] whereby the latter may also lead to liability for leased movables.[218] Belgian and French law provide similarly in Art. 1721 Cc, which has been extended by case-law to cover damage to property[219] and '*pertes résultant des dommages corporels*'.[220] In the exceptional case of fire, Art. 1384 sec. 3 Fr. Cc refers expressly to stricter contract law provisions. Art. 1384 sec. 2 Cc, which bases tort liability on fault,[221] therefore does not apply to '*rapports entre propriétaires et locataires, qui demeurent régis par les articles 1733 et 1734 du Code civil*'. Additionally, innkeepers' liability for their

---

[215] Landlord and tenant law in Greece recognizes objective lessor's liability for conseqential damage at best only in respect of absent guaranteed characteristics, although even that is contentious: see Georgiades/Stathopoulos (-*Rapsomanikis*), Cc III, Arts. 577, 578, margin no. 8. If the property is merely defective, however, liability is fault-based, founded on Arts. 576 and 577 Cc even though those provisions, read literally, apply only to damage arising from non-performance. See CA Athens 9000/1988, *EllDik* 31 (1990) p. 139. Claims arising from damage to property and to health caused by buildings may also be based on tort in which, in the absence of strict liability, the burden of proof may be shifted (Art. 925 Cc). See CA Athens 4268/1956, *NoB* 5 (1957) p. 325. The Spanish position is similar. Despite Art. 1553 sec. 1 Cc (reference to strict sale of goods law warranty liability, Arts. 1484 and 1485 Cc) the leasehold liability conditions of Art. 1556 Cc are of little assistance here as Art. 1554 Cc to which it relates gives no protection to the lessee. Liability in tort thus arises only on the basis of presumed fault. Portuguese law provides for strict lessors' liability for neither defects nor damage resulting from defects (Art. 1032 in conjunction with 798 Port. Cc). In Italy the lessor's liability for the lessee's personal injury or damage to health is only contractual when particular maintenance duties have been expressly undertaken. E.g. App. Roma 30.3.1971, *Foro.pad.* 1972, I. 552: flat provided for concierge did not correspond to particulars in employment contract. Liability for breach of contract, which even provided third-party benefits for the plaintiff's wife and children. No liability when no 'specific' contractual breach. E.g. Cass. 20.1.1960, n. 46, *Rep.gen.* 1960 Nos. 38 and 39, col. 2955. Cinema-goers injured due to failure to observe safety regulations: liability in tort only. In The Netherlands there is also no provision corresponding to § 538 BGB: *de facto* strict contractual liability is effected by the courts' over-stringent demands of care. E.g. Rb. Zutphen 8.2.1990, *NedJur* 1991 no. 228 p. 935.

[216] The defect subsequently causing the damage must be inherent when possession is transferred. If not, liability only if fault can be shown: § 538 sec. 1, 2nd. alt. BGB.

[217] See BGH 21.2.1962, *NJW* 1962 p. 908; BGH 9.12.1970, *NJW* 1971 p. 424; and BGH 5.12.1990, *NJW-RR* 1991 p. 970 with references.

[218] E.g. BGH 21.2.1962 (above) and OLG Koblenz 7.12.1992, *VersR* 1993 p. 1494: leasing of a trailer with defective brakes.   [219] Cass.civ. 26.2.1971, Bull.civ. 1971, III, Nr. 146.

[220] Cass.soc. 29.3.1957, *Gaz.Pal.* 1957, II, 59. Brussels 4.2.1992, *RGAR* 1995 No. 12460.

[221] See no. 110 above for the historical context of the provision.

guests' possessions is related to lessors' liability. (In many legal systems the lessee is also subject to strict contractual liability.[222]) In states signatory to the European Convention on the Liability of Hoteliers for Guests' Property,[223] such liability is strict but limited. Although in most codifications hoteliers' liability is in contract, this particular claim is statutory and for that reason is only a conditional example: the claim originates from the mere acceptance of a guest; no contract is required. Carriage of goods is thus a better example of an area in which contractually based duties to keep goods safe may have the character of a duty to achieve a particular outcome. Both international[224] and national carriage of goods law (e.g. Arts. 1602 Cc, 361 Span. Ccom[225]) provide appropriate examples. In France the law on the carriage of persons was the source of the *obligations de sécurité de résultat*[226] which subsequently took root in the contractually based law of producers and product liability.[227] In contrast, medical practitioners' liability is essentially fault-based, except in respect of instruments and other equipment.[228] It is of course questionable whether a stricter form of liability is really behind this, or whether it is merely a case of applying the rationale of Art. 1384 sec. 1 Cc whilst maintaining the appearance of applying *non-cumul*. Astonishingly little recent use has been made in employment law of strict contractual liability for breaches of protective duties. In England there are pointers in this direction,[229] but these are more likely to be qualified as tort than contract. Disregarding the reversal of the burden of proof, German contract law (§ 618 BGB) on liability for breach of implied protective duties

---

[222] See on The Netherlands Asser (-Abas), *Bijzondere Overeenkomsten II*, 7th edn., no. 50 (pp. 58–59).   [223] 17.12.1962, UNTS 590 p. 81 (no. 375 above).

[224] Art. 17 secs. 1 and 3 CMR.

[225] Liability for damaged freight is strict, the quantum of damages being limited to the freight's value (Art. 371 Span. Ccom.). Cf. Uría, *Derecho mercantil*, 17th edn., pp. 610–612; Sánchez Calero, *Instituciones de Derecho mercantil*, 16th edn., pp. 562–563.

[226] Cass.civ. 21.11.1911, 27.1.1913, and 21.4.1913, all printed in D. 1913, 1, 249. Cass.civ. 7.2.1949, D. 1949 *Jur.* 377 limited the extension of that principle. Where the victim is actively involved (here by using a ski-lift) the case involves an *obligation de sécurité de moyens*. Cf. Cass.civ. 4.11.1992, *Sem.Jur.* 1993, II, 22058 (note Sarraz-Bournet). An *obligation de sécurité de résultat* may apply if the contract partner has sole control over, and responsibility for, his safety. On The Netherlands see HR 26.2.1971, *NedJur* 1971 no. 270 p. 779.

[227] Recent survey and analysis of decisions by Arlie, *RJDA* 1993 pp. 409 ff. Cf. nos. 483 ff. below.

[228] E.g. Rouen 7.2.1984, D. 1985 *IR* 405. French courts accept the existence of obligations to blood-donors: Paris 12.5.1959 and 26.1.196, D. 1960 *Jur.* 305 (note Savatier) and Rennes 14.4.1977, D. 1978 *IR* 36 (note Larroumet). Also Cass. 16.11.1965, D. 1966 *Jur.* 61 (fn. 123 above). Obligations beyond those in the narrow medical sense (e.g. ensuring the safety of floors) are not contractual: these cases were dealt with in tort. Cass.civ. 28.4.1981, D. 1981 *IR* 438; Cass.civ. 10.1.1990, Jourdain, *Rev.trim.dr.civ.* 88 (1990) p. 481.

[229] Sec. 1(1) Employer's Liability (Defective Equipment) Act 1969. *Knowles* v. *Liverpool City Council* [1994] 1 Lloyd's Rep. 11.

arising from the employment relationship is primarily in tort,[230] insofar as it has not, as is now usual, been regulated by social security law.[231]

Whilst courts 'will be slow to superimpose an added duty of care **448** beyond that which was in the contemplation of the parties',[232] parties may everywhere agree higher standards of care between themselves than those statutorily imposed.[233] Some circumstances involving fault-based liability in contract but not in tort are based on liability for third parties. Provisions regulating the strict liability of lessees to lessors for the fault of sub-lessees or members of household extend across the legal systems of Europe (cf. Arts. 539 Gr. Cc, 1564 Span. Cc, 1588 sec. 2 Ital. Cc, and § 549 sec. 3 BGB). It is also important to note that there is everywhere contractual liability for the fault of both employees[234] and independent contractors.[235] Indeed, a tort concept of vicarious liability is not universally recognized. In Germany in particular, where the exonerating rule in § 831 sec. 1 BGB threatened a breach between national law and the European standard,[236] the judiciary admits that, *inter alia*, 'the contract with protective effects for third parties . . . has been developed due to the shortcomings of German tort law, which has restricted the scope of vicarious liability and does not grant sufficient protection of property'.[237] This is the primary basis of the contractual aspect of German tort law,[238] which has uniquely developed *culpa in contrahendo* into an

---

[230] E.g. in Denmark: HD 18.8.1988, *UfR* 1988 A p. 858; and SH 14.9.1987, *UfR* 1987 A p. 947. In The Netherlands: HR 25.6.1993, *RvdW* 1993 no. 145; and Rb. Rotterdam 19.11.1993, *A&V* 1994 p. 53 (shifting of burden of proof rejected). Regarding Portugal; RP 11.7.1983, *BolMinJust* 329 (1983) p. 617. Regarding Italy, see next fn. Liability in England is incurred either by breach of statutory duty (no. 307 above) or negligence. One need not search for a special relationship of proximity in tort as it arises from the contract. See *Walker* v. *Northumberland County Council* [1995] 1 All ER 737.

[231] Private liability for accidents at work has gained significance in Italy recently. Art. 2087 Cc (contractual obligation of the employer 'to protect the physical integrity and mental personality of the employee') is employed by integration into Art. 2043 Cc as a protective law and in order to support a self-contained liability for *danno biologico*, although not independent of the social security system. See Cass. 8.7.1992, n. 8325, *Foro.it.* 1992, I, 2965, 2972; Corte Cost. 15.2.1991, n. 87, *Foro.it.* 1991, I, 2967. The positions in France (see Namgalies, *Das französische Arbeitsunfallrecht*, passim and Dupeyroux/Prétot, *Droit de la sécurité sociale*, pp. 3 ff.) and Germany are very different. Regarding The Netherlands, see Stalfort, *Schutz von Unfallopfern durch die Sozialversicherung in den Niederlanden und in Deutschland, passim*.

[232] *Pacific Associates Inc. and Another* v. *Baxter and Others* [1989] 2 All ER 159, 160.

[233] Stewart, *Introduction*, p. 61. For Dutch, e.g. HR 6.11.1987, *NedJur* 1988 no. 192 p. 806: particular standard of care required of lessee regarding property let. In Austria, OGH 5.6.1984, *ÖJZ* 1985 p. 304: heightened duty of care based on contract to accommodate guest.

[234] Further, on France, Viney, *Sem.Jur.* 1994 *Doctr.* 3773, pp. 304–305.

[235] Cf. OLG Innsbruck 25.1.1994, *ZVR* 1995 pp. 109, 110.

[236] Nos. 185–190 above.   [237] OLG Cologne 17.9.1993, *RIW* 1993 pp. 1023, 1024.

[238] E.g. Steffen, *ZVersWiss* 1993 pp. 13, 16: 'when we [6th *Zivilsenat* of the BGH] decide upon a slight extension of the protection of property . . . we believe it less dangerous to base that extension on contract, or at least on related concepts, because the contractual agreement and trust in the given word facilitates appropriate limits.'

all-purpose weapon.[239] Often a contract party, having breached a protective duty, is obliged to exculpate[240] itself to the extent that in cases of *non liquet* liability may be based on contract only and not in tort.[241] The practical effect of this depends upon the extent to which a legal system is prepared to work with breaches of protective duties based in contract. Nevertheless it is not uncommon to meet decisions attempting to transfer contract-developed reversals of the burden of proof to tort law.[242] Such operations only make sense in the light of limitation rules, and not in respect of the division of the burden of proof, if one views[243] a breach of a protective statute as a breach of an implied contractual protective duty; in such cases these are in any event identical.[244]

c. Common Prerequisites of Liability, Differing Limitation Periods, and Variations in the Extent of Liability

(1) Differing Limitation Periods

449 Differences in limitation periods are traditionally held up as the principal field of application for rules of concurrence of actions regarding tort and contract liability. However, there have been recent developments in precisely that field. The rigid fronts are gradually fragmenting; a degree of approximation among European solutions is discernible regarding

---

[239] Nos. 472 ff. below.

[240] The bases of this vary. Opinion varies as to whether the burden of proof should shift in every case of breach of protective duties, or only under certain circumstances. On Portugal see: Art. 799 sec. 1 Cc and, *inter alia*, Almeida Costa, *Obrigações*, 5th edn., p. 433; Pires de Lima/Antunes Varela, *Cc anotado II*, 4th edn., p. 55; RL 14.5.1991, *CJ* XVI (1991–3) p. 139. Further, RC 26.3.1985, *CJ* X (1985–2) p. 50. On Denmark, *inter alia*, Gomard, *Obligationsret I*, 2nd edn., p. 139; ibid., *Civilprocessen*, 2nd edn., p. 327; Kruse, *Erstatningsretten*, 5th edn., p. 26; HD 18.8.1988, *UfR* 1988 A p. 858; and SH 14.9.1987 *UfR* 1987 A p. 947. On Austria: § 1298 ABGB and, *inter alia*, OGH 3.9.1992, *JBl* 1993 p. 396; OGH 10.10.1991, *ÖJZ* 1993 p. 166; OGH 5.6.1984, *ÖJZ* 1985 p. 304, 305. Further, Welser, *Schadensersatz statt Gewährleistung*, pp. 55–62, and Koziol, *JBl* 1994 pp. 209, 210. On Greece: Georgiades/Stathopoulos (-Stathopoulos), *Greek Cc* II, Intr. Arts. 335–348, no. 28; *ErmAK* (-Michaelides-Nouaros) Art. 330 no. 55. Further: Androulidaki/Dimitradou, *Ai ypochreosseis synallaktikis pisteos*, p. 229; *contra: ErmAK* (-Gasis), Intr. Arts. 335–348 no. 77. On Germany, where despite § 282 BGB there is no general statutory shift of the burden of proof, *inter alia*: BGH 27.9.1951, BGHZ 3 pp. 162, 174; BGH 18.12.1952, BGHZ 8 pp. 239, 243; BGH 14.4.1958, BGHZ 27 pp. 79, 84; BGH 26.9.1961, *NJW* 1962 pp. 31, 32; BGH 4.10.1972, BGHZ 59 pp. 304, 309; BGH 28.9.1992, *DNotZ* 1993 pp. 685, 686; BGH 17.1.1995, *NJW-RR* 1995 p. 684. For The Netherlands: Schut, *Onrechtmatige daad*, 4th edn., p. 13; and Rb. Rotterdam 19.11.1993, *A&V* 1994 p. 53. For Italy: Art. 2018 Cc; de Martini, *Fatti produttivi di danno*, p. 67; and Galgano, *Diritto civile e commerciale II* (1), 2nd edn., p. 75. For France: nos. 469–470 below.

[241] OLG 13.1.1993, *r+s* 1994 pp. 215, 216. Cf. BGH 9.6.1994, BGHZ 126 p. 217 (shifting of burden of proof rejected regarding liability of lawyers).

[242] E.g. OGH 22.6.1993, *ZfRV* 1994 pp. 249, 252; and OLG Schleswig 30.1.1992, *NJW-RR* 1992 p. 796 (on *prima facie* evidence).   [243] E.g. OGH 3.9.1992, *JBl* 1993 p. 396.

[244] No. 31 above.

breaches of protective duties, where the co-ordination problems of limitation rules are concentrated.[245]

Matters are relatively straightforward where tort liability alone is   **450** time-barred. Here, whether the matter is decided on concurrence of claims or on *non-cumul*, the tort limitation does not affect the contractual period, which may thus be fully exploited.[246] Regarding limitation rules, it is also true that the stronger contractual liability ousts the weaker tort liability. It was precisely this circumstance, with the deficient vicarious liability provisions (§ 831 BGB) and the insufficient protection of purely economic interests by tort law, which led Germany to develop its unique protective duties based on the initiation of contract negotiations (*culpa in contrahendo*), the existence of a contractual relationship (so-called positive breach of contract), and contracts with protective effects for third parties.[247] Under § 195 BGB liability for breach of such duties is generally time-barred after thirty years: ten times longer than the limitation period in tort (§ 852 BGB).

Such a period is unconscionably long in respect of accidentally caused personal injury,[248] especially where the burden of proof regarding fault is reversed to the detriment of employers.[249] How is an employer to investigate in the 1990s the facts of an accident in the 1960s? That in such cases, as the BGH says, 'the doctrine of forfeiture offers a corrective'[250] is

---

[245] Corresponding issues of liability for pure economic loss are less common as those legal systems in particular employing a system of concurrence of actions are restrained in compensating for such loss. A neat, albeit now obsolete, example is HR 10.9.1993, *RvdW* 1993 No. 171: the defendant employer had not paid the plaintiff former employee's pension contributions for 1977–1981. As the contractual limitation period had expired under Art. 2012 BW (old), the plaintiff brought his action in tort under Art. 1401 BW (old). The Supreme Court rejected the arguments of the bank to apply Art. 2012 BW analagously in tort. Nor, in the opinion of the court, was Art. 3:312 BW applicable. Cf. *Henderson* v. *Merret Syndicates*, no. 429 above.   [246] E.g. Cendon (-Santoro) IV, Art. 1218, n. 21 p. 108.

[247] E.g. BGH 1.12.1964, *VersR* 1965 p. 240. Plaintiff sustained head injuries in the defendant's shop in 1949. The claim was served in 1960. The tort limitation period had long expired. Nevertheless, damages were awarded on the basis of a 'positive breach of contract'. See also BGH 28.1.1976, BGHZ 66 p. 51 = *JZ* 1976 p. 776 with comment by Kreuzer. The 14-year-old plaintiff slipped on vegetables on the defendant's supermarket floor in November 1963. She commenced her action in March 1970. Compensation was awarded by means of *culpa in contrahendo* having protective effects for the benefit of third parties.

[248] The 30-year limitation period must be the longest in the EU on liability for accidents. Belgium, France, and Luxembourg have similar limitation periods for particular cases of *obligations de sécurité* under Art. 2262 Cc, but this is rarely applied. For product liability it covers only breaches of a general duty of care, not *actions directes* against the manufacturer or retailer pour *la garantie de vice caché*, which *'doit être intentée dans le bref délai prévu par la loi'* under Art. 1648 Cc: Cass. civ. 9.10.1979, *Gaz.Pal.* 1980 *Jur.* 249 (note Plancqueel). In most other countries the standard limitation period for contract is shorter: 10 years in Italy (Art. 2946 Cc), 15 in Spain (Art. 1964 Cc), and 20 in Denmark (DL 5–14–4), Greece (Art. 249 Gr.civ.cod.), and Portugal (Art. 309 Cc).

[249] BGH 26.9.1961, *NJW* 1962 pp. 31, 32 (fn. 240 above).

[250] BGH 28.1.1976, *JZ* 1976 pp. 776, 778.

only a palliative: the author is unaware of any German decision[251] which has used this corrective mechanism. Of interest are the efforts of the BGH, employing numerous analogies, to press for shorter limitation periods,[252] especially in respect of the form of tort liability which it developed itself, based on contract, for misinformation of investors in the grey capital markets where no personal reliance is asserted. Such efforts indicate that the BGH is uncomfortable with the thirty-year rule wherever contract law adopts, as it increasingly does, the role of extending the law of tort.

451   Such substantial differences between limitation periods for breaches of contract and tort protective duties stem from the fact that the German Civil Code, subject to a few exceptions, does not recognize those tort duties. Further, the courts, which developed it against the background of § 195 BGB, have barely had the opportunity to reduce the thirty-year limitation period to a more conscionable level.[253] There have also been proposals for statutory reform of this unfortunate legal position, amounting to synchronization of the contractual and the statutory limitation periods in this field.[254] The concurrence problem on limitation periods would then finally lose its bite, and the German position would once more resemble legal developments in other parts of Europe. Where that which has in Germany been treated as contractual law, under the various titles of *'culpa in contrahendo'*, *'positive contractual breach'*, and *'contract with protective effects for the benefit of third parties'*, has been ascribed to, or left as part of, tort law (below, nos. 459 ff.) the legislature has endeavoured to achieve the necessary synchronization. Recognizing the consequences of the German limitation laws, the codifications of Greece (Arts. 197 and 198, especially 198 sec. 2 Cc[255]) and Portugal

---

[251] HR 1.10.1993, *RvdW* 1993 No. 189 (*'Lekkende Kruik II'*) is of interest. Plaintiff suffered continuing damage as a result of a nurse putting a leaking hot-water bottle in her bed 24 years before the action was commenced. The case *'Lekkende Kruik I'* concerned the claim of the health insurance company against the bottle manufacturer: HR 2.2.1973, *NedJur* 1973 no. 315 p. 897; and Hof Amsterdam 1.3.1974, *NedJur* 1974 no. 486. The defendant argued that it was seriously prejudiced in having to put its case so long after the event: *'daarom moest worden aangenomen dat Van Uitert haar vorderingsrecht heeft verspeeld.'* The Hoge Raad rejected the claim without considering that argument.

[252] BGH 26.9.1991, BGHZ 115 pp. 213–227 provides a useful summary of the present position: no. 496 below.

[253] It might have been possible when § 852 sec. 2 BGB was promulgated to use the opportunity to resort to the tort rule (cf. v. Bar, *JuS* 1982 pp. 637, 640) but the courts ignored that opportunity.

[254] Bundesministerium der Justiz (ed.), *Abschlußbericht der Kommission zur Überarbeitung des Schuldrechts*, p. 36, with § 200 of the Commission's Proposal on the BGB (BGB-KE; loc. cit. p. 72: 'Where statutory damages claims coincide with contractual or quasi-contractual claims, the provisions of the Second Part apply to limitation) and §§ 241 sec. 2 and 305 sec. 2 KE (loc. cit., pp. 289 and 291: rules on breach of protective duties caused by positive breach of term or *culpa in contrahendo*).

[255] Which provides: 'The tort limitation provision applies correspondingly to such a claim as this [in *culpa in contrahendo*].'

(Art. 227 secs. 1 and 2[256]) apply the same limitation period to *culpa in contrahendo* as to the corresponding tort law, despite the fact that (like Italy and Spain) neither country accepts the precontractual protective duties which are recognized in Germany. In The Netherlands the matter has been taken even further[257] to resolve the problem of the *Samenloop*: under Art. 3:310 BW, effective from 1.1.1992, all claims for damages based on *'wanprestatie en uit onrechtmatige daad'*[258] are subject to a five-year limitation period. Section 11 of the English Limitation Act 1980 provides a unified three-year limitation period for personal injury claims arising from breach of either contractual or non-contractual duties of care.

Such extensive harmonization is a happy state of affairs. In countries **452** observing a system of concurrence of claims, the limitation period in tort may be fully exploited, even in those exceptional cases in which it is longer than the period for contractual claims. If a video cassette is ruined by the adding of subtitles,[259] or bed linen by the use of overstrong cleaning agents,[260] in Greek law tort liability remains under Arts. 937 and 693 Cc, even when the contractual claim is time-barred. The position in Germany, although not in The Netherlands,[261] is similar: where 'the customer . . . may claim damages from the contractor both for deficiency of the works under § 635 BGB and on account of a tort act . . . the claim in tort is limited according to § 852 BGB and independently of § 638 BGB which applies to contractual breaches.'[262] Sometimes in tort time runs from the date of knowledge of both the damage and the identity of the tortfeasor, rather than from the breach of duty. In such cases the tort period may be fully exploited so long as it commences after the contract period, even if their duration is essentially equal. This is standard at common law.[263]

There are of course exceptions to the rule that the limitation period in **453** tort is unaffected by a shorter contract period. Such exceptions, although

---

[256] *'A responsabilidade* [resulting from *culpa na formação dos contratos*] *prescreve nos termos do artigo 498.'* [257] Cf. Jansen, *Onrechtmatige daad*, p. 26.
[258] *T&C* (-Stolker), Art. 3: 310 n. 1. [259] Areopag 967/1973, *NoB* 22 (1974) p. 505.
[260] Areopag 1058/1978, *NoB* 26 (1978) p. 929. On carriage of goods: Areopag 18/1993, *EEN* 1994 p. 34: carrier liable in tort for damage to goods carried by sea although the 1-year limitation period had expired.
[261] On breach of duty of care under carriage contract: Rb. Arnhem 2.1.1975, *NedJur* 1976 No. 229 p. 638: short contractual limitation period applied in tort action.
[262] BGH 4.3.1971, *NJW* 1971 p. 1131 with commentary by Ganten, *NJW* 1971 p. 1804. Regarding breach of duties under freight contract, BGH 12.12.1991, *BGHZ* 116 p. 297. See BGH 15.12.1992, *NJW* 1993 p. 655 for the general position on works contracts. Where the claim may be based on positive breach of contract (causing of damage by a defect in goods) the limitation period is extended to 30 years in cases of 'indirect' consequential loss caused by a defect. See *inter alia* BGH 27.4.1961, *BGHZ* 35 p. 130; BGH 13.4.1972, *BGHZ* 58 p. 305.
[263] Dias/Markesinis, *Tort Law*, 2nd edn., p. 11; James/Browne, *Principles*, 4th edn., p. 6; Weir, *Casebook*, 6th edn., p. 51; Chitty (-Guest), *Contract I*, 27th edn., no. 1841. Of particular interest is *Pirelli General Cable Works Ltd. v. Oscar Faber* [1983] 2 AC 1, 12.

a move in the right direction, confuse the matter further. The classic example is the lessee's liability to the lessor for damage to the let property. In Greece Art. 602 Cc provides that 'compensation claims' become time-barred six months after the return of the property. The courts have ruled that the plural must be construed to include both contract and tort claims.[264] German courts have applied § 558 BGB[265] with the argument that in such cases the requirements of § 823 sec. 1 must be satisfied. This line has been held even where the lease itself was ineffective,[266] the person causing the damage merely being within the protective scope of the contract but not a party to it,[267] and where the owner was not the lessor but was closely linked to him financially.[268] Where the property is completely destroyed[269] or the conduct satisfies the conditions of § 826 BGB,[270] say the courts, § 852 sec. 1 BGB may be applied. That § 558 BGB also covers tort breaches does not prevent the BGH from using § 852 sec. 2 BGB analogously in the context of § 558 BGB.[271] Regarding 'initially unrecognizable consequential losses', the BGH resorts to § 195 BGB.[272] Regarding sale of goods law limitation periods, the BGH has held that in principle neither § 477 BGB[273] nor § 377 HGB[274] apply to simultaneous tort claims in respect of consequential harm caused by defects. An exception is where 'the contractual liabilities and interests are congruent with those in tort'.[275] The position in Greece is different: questions of such consequential harm tend to be regulated by contract law,[276] but the courts have prevented contract limitation from having any effect on limitation in tort.[277] Even commentators

---

[264] CA Athens 2203/1977, *NoB* 26 (1978) p. 60; and CA Piraeus 1130/1989, *EllDik* 31 (1990) p. 1073.

[265] *Inter alia*: BGH 31.1.1967, BGHZ 47 pp. 53, 55; BGH 18.9.1986, BGHZ 98 pp. 235, 237.

[266] BGH 31.1.1967.

[267] Most recently: OLG Celle 16.9.1992, *VersR* 1993 p. 1493. Consistent jurisprudence of BGH: *inter alia* BGH 7.2.1968, *NJW* 1968 p. 694. Liability of assistants corresponds: BGH 19.9.1973, *NJW* p. 2059.   [268] BGH 11.12.1991, BGHZ 116 p. 293.

[269] BGH 15.6.1981, *NJW* 1981 pp. 2406, 2407; and BGH 21.6.1988, *WM* 1988 p. 1537.

[270] BGH 17.6.1993, *WM* 1993 pp. 1798, 1800 (*obiter*); Schlechtriem, *Vertragsordnung und außervertragliche Haftung*, p. 393. However, § 558 BGB applies to intentionally caused (but not immoral) damage: BGH 17.6.1993 loc. cit. p. 1799.

[271] BGH 28.11.1984, BGHZ 93 p. 64: 'Regardless of their legal basis, lessors' claims resulting from changes to, or deterioration of, the let property, shall not be time-limited so long as the lessor and lessee negotiate and neither party refuses to continue negotiating.'

[272] BGH 24.11.1993, *NJW* 1994 p. 251.

[273] BGH 24.5.1976, BGHZ 66 pp. 315, 320–322. Where the plaintiff pleads damage to his material interests caused by deficient goods as a positive breach of contract, the claim is subject to § 477 BGB: BGH 27.1.1971, *NJW* 1971 pp. 654, 655.

[274] BGH 16.9.1987, BGHZ 101 pp. 337, 341–346.

[275] BGH 16.2.1993, *NJW-RR* 1993 p. 793.

[276] CFI Agrinion 24/57, *ArchN* 8 (1957) p. 512. Comment by Pouliadis (includes further citations), *Culpa in contrahendo und Schutz Dritter*, pp. 174–176; 185.

[277] CA Athens 951/1967, *NoB* 16 (1968) p. 279; CA Athens 3341/1976, *Arm.* 3 (1977) p. 105.

who advocate extending the concept of contractual protective duties to cover the law of consequential harm would apply the standard tort limitation period.[278] However, that begs the question as to the purpose of the proposed extension of contractual liability.

(2) Differences in the extent of liability

The extent of liability is the second major area affected by whether an action is pursued in contract or tort, notwithstanding that the requirements for liability may be effectively equal. It has been seen that liability for negligent non-performance of contractual duties is limited to foreseeable damage.[279] Furthermore, different rules may apply on interest payable on damages.[280] In England exemplary damages can be awarded in tort but not in contract,[281] and rules on remoteness of damage vary according to the basis of liability.[282] The same discrepancy is found in The Netherlands BW, although that Code has generally synchronized contract and tort law on damages. Art. 6:98 BW expressly links the attribution of responsibilty to, *inter alia*, 'the type of responsibility', thereby distinguishing between contract and tort.[283] The differences between contract and tort to be resolved by the doctrine of concurrence of actions extend even to contributory negligence rules. In England and Scotland[284] sec. 1(1) Law Reform (Contributory Negligence) Act 1945[285] provides for an equitable division of responsibility 'where any person suffers damage as the result partly of his own fault and partly of the fault of any other person or persons', but continues: 'that this subsection shall not operate to defeat any defence arising under a contract'.

It remains unclear what this means in cases involving the simultaneous breach of a contract and a duty of care in tort.[286] The Court of Appeal at least made clear in *Forsikringsaktieselskapet Vesta* v. *Butcher*[287] that 'where a defendant's liability in contract was the same as his liability in the tort of negligence independently of the existence of any

---

[278] E.g. Androulidaki/Dimitriadou, Ai *ypochreosseis synallaktikis pisteos*, esp. pp. 231–232; Mangivas, *I evthyni tou kataskeuastou typopoiimenon proionton* (1978 Athens Ph.D.)

[279] No. 425 and fn. 69 above.

[280] Areopag 1654/1984, *NoB* 33 (1985) p. 1391 states that Arts. 345–347 Greek Cc (on delay) do not apply to tort claims.   [281] *Addis* v. *Gramophone Co. Ltd.* [1909] AC 488.

[282] *Hall* v. *Meyrick* [1957] 2 QB 455: incorrect advice by lawyer regarding will classified as breach of contract. The will became invalid after a subsequent marriage. Ensuing damage too remote under the rule in *Hadley* v. *Baxendale* (1854) 9 Exch. 341. Cf. Phillips, *Jurid.Rev.* 1995 pp. 401–403 on similar problems regarding liability of medical practitioners.

[283] Schut, *Onrechtmatige daad*, 4th edn., p. 15. A similarly worded rule is found in § 24 sec. 1 of the Danish Damages Act of 1984 (no. 238 above).

[284] Cf. Stewart, *Introduction*, p. 146.   [285] Ch. 28.

[286] Treitel, *Contract*, 7th edn., pp. 759–761.   [287] [1988] 2 All ER 43, 44.

contract the court had power to apportion blame under the 1945 Act and to reduce the damages recoverable by the plaintiff even though the claim was made in contract.'[288]

455 Whilst important, rules to the effect that damages for pain and suffering are recoverable only in tort and not contract[289] are now rare. Only Germany (§§ 253, 618 sec. 3 and 847 BGB[290]) and Greece (Arts. 299 and 932 Cc) retain such rules.

Damages for non-pecuniary loss have always been granted in contract by the Civil Codes of Belgium, France, and Luxembourg.[291] The position is similar in Spain,[292] The Netherlands,[293] Denmark,[294] Finland and Sweden,[295] Austria,[296] and the common law countries.[297] It is now also the established view in Portugal,[298] despite reservations regarding Art. 496 Cc's position in tort law.[299] In Italy the issue is

---

[288] A different view is found in *AB Marintrans* v. *Comet Shipping Co. Ltd.*, 'The Shinjitsu Maru No. 5' [1985] 3 All ER 442.

[289] Treitel offers a comparative European analysis in *IntEncCompL* VII 16, 110–113.

[290] Contract law recognizes claims for non-pecuniary loss: § 651f sec. 2 BGB.

[291] Mazeaud/Tunc, *Responsabilité civile I*, 6th edn., nos. 329 ff. and Starck (-Roland/Boyer), *Obligations II*, 4th edn., no. 1373. On Belgium Dirix, *Het begrip schade*, p. 63 with additional references. (Kocks, *PHI* 1990 pp. 182, 193 is incorrect.)

[292] Cf. TS 3.6.1991, *RAJ* 1991 no. 4407 p. 6033; and TS 23.3.1988, *RAJ* 1988 no. 2226 p. 2178: For details: Cavanillas Múgica/Tapia Fernández, *Concurrencia de responsabilidad*, p. 39.

[293] Art. 6: 106 BW.

[294] § 3 of the Damages Act of 1984, whose '*regler gælder uanset ansvarsgrundlagets karakter*': Karnov (-von Eyben) III, 20–9 p. 3280 n. 1.

[295] As in Denmark, this arises from the fact that both damages statutes apply to contractual relationships. See Bengtsson/Nordenson/Strömbäck, *Skadeståndslag*, 3rd edn., pp. 29–32; Hellner, *Skadeståndsrätt*, 4th edn., pp. 58–64.

[296] The legal basis of liability is irrelevant in the context of § 1325 ABGB (personal injury). Non-pecuniary loss is only compensated for breach of contractual protective duty: Schwiman (-Harrer) v, § 1325 no. 58; and Rummel (-Reischauer) II, § 1325 no. 9.

[297] Jackson, *IntCompLQ* 26 [1977] pp. 502–515; Walker, *Delict*, 2nd edn., pp. 14–15; White, *Irish Law of Damages I*, pp. 257–259; Burrows, *Remedies*, pp. 163–168. Of interest in the case-law: *Matthews* v. *Kuwait Bechtel Corp.* [1959] 2 QB 57 and *Graham* v. *Ladeside of Kilbirnie Bowling Club SLT* 1994 pp. 1295, 1296 (Outer House). Jackson loc. cit. offers additional references.

[298] For currently unpopular arguments to restrict damages for pain and suffering to contract law: Antunes Varela, *Obrigações em Geral I*, 7th edn., p. 599; Pires de Lima/Antunes Varela, *Cc anotado I*, 4th edn., Art. 496 n. 8.

[299] Art. 496 Cc undoubtedly applies to contract. See RP 4.2.1992, *CJ* XVII (1992–1) p. 232 (lawyers' professional liability). RC 14.4.1993, *CJ* XVIII (1993–2) p. 39 (lessor switched off electricity and water supplies to a family of 5); and STJ 10.11.1993, *CJ (ST)* 1 (1993–3) p. 132 (inadvertent publishing of ex-directory number in telephone directory). Further, STJ 2.12.1976, *BolMinJust* 262 (1977) p. 142 (agency failed to forward plaintiff's Hackney cab licence application. Non-pecuniary loss compensated as plaintiff had not become an independent contractor). Also, although *in casu* the breach was not sufficiently serious to base a claim for non-pecuniary damages: STJ 18.11.1975, *BolMinJust* 251 (1975) p. 148 (distress over condition of holiday home). Accepted opinion of commentators is that Art. 496 Port. Cc provides a general principle applicable to contract: Galvão Telles, *Obrigações*, 6th edn., pp. 383–384; Almeida Costa, *Obrigações*,

controversial[300] but abstract.[301] Art. 2059 Cc founds damages claims for pain and suffering on a breach of criminal law, and a contractual breach satisfying the elements of a criminal offence will almost always amount to a tort.

Although the restriction of damages for non-pecuniary loss to non-contractual liability has become the exception, it nevertheless confirms the connection between concurrence of actions rules and substantive law: a system of *non-cumul* would be pointless and would exclude such damages from contract law; a legal order granting damages for pain and suffering in tort alone must at the very least guarantee this by means of the doctrine of concurrence of actions. However, this does not alter the fact that it is plainly wrong to refuse damages for pain and suffering in contract.[302] That is shown in the recent German case-law. As such damages are not available for personal injuries resulting from a *culpa in contrahendo* or other instrument of contract law, the courts apply tort law in cases for the benefit of which protective duties in contract were originally devised.[303]

d. The Effects on Tort of Relaxing Contractual Liability

In the final group of cases the contract rules prescribe more stringent **456** conditions for liability, and are thus less strict, than tort law. Where the parties agree either to exclude or to limit liability it must be considered whether they intended that this should also cover simultaneous liability in tort. Where (exceptionally) that is not the case, tort liability is undiminished.[304] Where the parties did intend to affect non-contractual

5th edn., pp. 485–486; Pinto Monteiro, *Cláusulas limitativas*, p. 88; Pereira Coelho, *Obriga-ções*, p. 158. Vaz Serra argues for compensation of non-economic loss in contract also: *BolMinJust* 83 (1959) pp. 69, 109.

[300] Cf. Giur.sist. Bigiavi (-Rossello) I pp. 302–303; de Cupis, *Il danno I*, 3rd edn., pp. 127, 134.

[301] Thus Giardina, *Responsabilità contrattuale e responsabilità extracontrattuale*, p. 13.

[302] According to the Commission on the Law of Obligations, whose task it was to submit revision proposals regarding interference with the performance of obligations, the present position in German law should be retained. Nor should § 253 BGB be changed, nor breach of contractual protective duties give rise to claims for damages for pain and suffering. Such proposals appeared to the Commission to be so misconceived that the final report (above at fn. 247) did not mention them.

[303] E.g. OLG Düsseldorf 28.7.1993, *NJW-RR* 1994 p. 24; BGH 5.7.1994, *VersR* 1994 p. 1128; and OLG Schleswig 30.1.1992, *NJW-RR* 1992 p. 796. Similar tendencies are seen in Greece, despite different approaches. See CA Athens 4284/1992, *EllDik* 34 (1993) p. 224: transfer of employee at telephone switchboard in abuse of powers. Breach of contract constituted breach of rights of protection of personality and entitled the plaintiff to damages for pain and suffering under Art. 59 Greek Cc.

[304] See BGH 24.11.1976, BGHZ 67 pp. 359, 363 (fn. 198 above); *Rutter v. Palmer* [1922] 2 KB 87, 92.

liability, which is a matter of interpretation,[305] the extent of the effect is dependent on their intention.[306]

457   Statutory contract law often creates special systems of liability between parties. Where such a system exists it generally overrules tort law, notwithstanding any other rules on concurrence of actions. Whilst the BGH in Germany has rejected the application of § 708 BGB (limiting the mutual liability of company members to 'that level of care which they would apply to their own affairs', § 277 BGB) in respect of road traffic liability,[307] that may have been influenced by unvoiced considerations of compulsory insurance. The statutory limitation on carriers' liability in § 430 of the German Commercial Code does not affect the law of tort.[308] However, the BGH has consistently affirmed its position on gratuitous contracts: that where there is a statutory limitation on contractual liability to particular forms of fault, more extensive liability in tort cannot be allowed to subsist for the same conduct,[309] even where that liability would otherwise be strict.[310] Similar considerations obtain on liability for intentional acts: under § 464 BGB the purchaser of goods has no claim under § 463 sec. 2 BGB for deceitfully concealed defects where the goods were purchased with knowledge of the defect. A claim for damages under § 826 BGB is also barred.[311]

458   The principle upon which the German case-law is based is effectively *iure communi europaeo*. Art. 2236 of the Italian Cc ('where the required performance involves the solution of technical problems of particular

---

[305] E.g. *Smith v. Eric Bush* [1989] 2 WLR 790, 800; *Pacific Associates Inc. and Another v. Baxter and Others* [1989] 2 All ER 159, 192. Insofar as a case concerns protective duties, it should be accepted (where there is doubt) that an extension covering tort is desired. Winfield/Jolowicz (-Rogers), *Tort*, p. 281 fn. 49 justifiably criticize as 'excessively mechanical' the decision in *Coats Patons (Retail) Ltd. v. Birmingham Corp.* 69 (1977) LGR 356: 'exemption clause applicable to contractual duty but not to concurrent duty in tort, even though both duties were of reasonable care.'

[306] Cases involving immunity from contractual suit, or reduction of the measure of fault required, may meet in the question of whether such preferential treatment should also apply for the benefit of assistants in respect of third parties. It is suggested, and increasingly accepted, that should be the case. Cf. Waddams, *LQR* 109 (1993) pp. 349–352; Quill, *ILT* 9 (1991) pp. 211–214; Blaurock, *ZHR* 146 (1982) pp. 238–258; Denck, *Schutz des Arbeitnehmers*, pp. 130–135; BGH 7.12.1961, *NJW* 1962, p. 388; BGH 23.6.1965, *LM* § 328 BGB no. 28; and BGH 12.3.1985, *ZIP* 1985 p. 687. Further, *Marc Rich & Co v. Bishop Rock Marine* [1994] 1 WLR 1071. But see HR 12.1.1979, *NedJur* 1979 no. 362 p. 1138.

[307] BGH 20.12.1966, BGHZ 46 pp. 313, 316–318.

[308] BGH 23.3.1966, BGHZ 46 p. 140.

[309] BGH (previous fn.) p. 145; BGH 20.12.1966 loc. cit. (fn. 286) p. 316; BGH 4.3.1971, BGHZ 55 pp. 392, 396; BGH 20.11.1984, BGHZ 93 pp. 23, 29; and BGH 9.6.1992, *JR* 1993 pp. 506, 508. Cf. Wilts, *VersR* 1967 pp. 817, 820.

[310] BGH 14.7.1977, *VersR* 1977 pp. 864, 865.

[311] RG 26.10.1904, RGZ 59 p. 104. On the relationship between deceitful silence and tort in Greece: CA Athens 7801/1990, *EllDik* 32 (1991) p. 1676 (fn. 52 above). OLG Cologne 19.8.1992, *VersR* 1993 p. 1494 covers the analogous provision § 539 BGB (lessor's knowledge of a defect in the property let).

difficulty, the party undertaking the work is liable only for intentional damage or damage arising out of gross negligence') is an elegant example, in that it is often referred to regarding Art. 2043 Cc.[312] It is unclear, however, whether this applies in cases of *concorso improprio*: that is, where a non-contracting third party sustains damage.[313] Contractual liability for gratuitous arrangements,[314] that is, for agency agreements, gratuitous loans, gifts, and bailments, is in Germany restricted to intent and gross negligence, which limitation generally also covers tort.[315] In contrast, persons receiving simple favours are often treated more strictly.[316] Instead of restricting liability for gratuitous contracts to particular forms of fault, some systems merely reduce the extent of liability. A party may thus be liable in contract for simple negligence but the court may reduce damages along equitable lines.[317] The principle remains, however: restrictions of liability apply equally to simultaneous tort claims in such cases.[318] The lessening of liability refers to the non-contractual field.

---

[312] Cass.sez.un. 6.5.1971, n. 1282, *Giust.civ.* 1971, I, 1417; Cass. 17.3.1981, n. 1544, Gentile/Guerreri/Guerreri, *La responsabilità, voce Responsabilità civile-Professionisti*, 102 (40) concerning architects; and Cass. 7.8.1982, n. 4437, Gentile *et al.* loc. cit. 102 (48) concerning engineers.

[313] See Cass. 8.11.1979, n. 5761, *Giust.civ.* 1980, I, 340 on liquidators and trustees in bankruptcy; Giur.sist. Bigiavi (-Vigotti) IV p. 263; Cass. 17.3.1981 loc. cit.

[314] In the absence of consideration or seal, no contract can exist at common law. Liability for gratuitous bailment is the English analogy to such arrangements. Here too the absence of payment in the transaction results in a lower standard of care: *Houghland v. R. R. Low (Luxury Coaches) Ltd.* [1962] 1 QB 694. Also *Port Swettenham Authority v. T. W. Wu and Co.* [1979] AC 580, 589; *Chaudhry v. Prabhakar* [1988] 3 All ER 719.

[315] On Denmark: HD 15.6.1966, *UfR* 1966 A p. 561: father lent defective car to son who died in resulting accident. Father not liable to daughter-in-law. On Greece: Areopag 384/1973, *NoB* 21 (1973) p. 1205 (*obiter*) for lending and bailment: CA Athens 951/1967, *NoB* 16 (1968) p. 279; Filios, *Enochiko Dikaio II* (2) pp. 9–10, Balis, *Genikai Archai tou Astikou Dikaiou*, 8th edn., p. 372; and Deliyannis/Kornilakis, *Eidiko Enochiko Dikaio III*, p. 112.

[316] BGH 9.6.1992, *JR* 1993 p. 506; Cass.civ. 27.1.1993 (no. 445 above); Rb. s'Hertogenbosch 17.11.1978, *NedJur* no. 15 p. 37; and Cour 10.3.1992, *Pas. luxemb.* 28 (1990–1992) p. 5. (In cases of gratuitous favours, only *faute lourde* constitutes contributory negligence.)

[317] This is the position in Italy: e.g. Art. 1768 sec. 2 (gratuitous bailment) and Art. 1804 Cc (lending) (Cendon [-Memmo] IV, Art. 1768 no. 4). So too in Spain, where the general standard of care demanded in respect of bailment (*depósito*, Art. 1766 Cc) and agency (*mandato*, Art. 1726 Cc) is that of the *bonus paterfamilias*. However, the court can limit the scope of liability by applying the general 'reduction clause' (Art. 1103 Cc) or Art. 1726 Cc. (Cf. Santos Briz, *Responsabilidad civil II*, 6th edn., pp. 604–609 and Pas-Ares/Díez-Picazo/Bercowitz/Salvador [-León Alonso], *Código Civil II*, 6th edn., p. 1565). The position in The Netherlands is essentially similar. The BW deliberately did not adopt Arts. 1743, 1744 (bailment) and 1838 BW (rpld) (agency) which reduced the standard of care (*Parlementaire Geschiedenis* VI, MvA II, p. 450). In their place is the general reduction clause Art. 6:109 BW (loc. cit. p. 449).

[318] In France the same result is achieved via the *non-cumul* route. Indeed, it was the purpose of that principle of concurrence of actions to preserve the leniency of contract law in the area of degree of fault. See no. 431 above.

4. PROTECTIVE DUTIES AND TRANSFERRED LOSS BETWEEN CONTRACT AND TORT

459 Drawing the boundary between contractual and non-contractual liability is, as has been pointed out, the second great theme of liability for damages in the intersection between contract and tort. It concerns, not questions of concurrence of actions rules *per se*, but the phenomenon that the same area of rules may appear in one system to belong to contract, and in another to tort, and the effects of such dogmatic crossovers on the concepts of justice which determine the attribution of damage.[319]

a. Differences of Characterization of Liability for Personal Injury and for Damage to the Property of Contracting Parties

460 Differences in the characterization of liability for damage to the essential interests of contractual partners, whilst perhaps the least pronounced, are usefully considered here. It is self-evident throughout Europe that a person who has contracted, for example as a doctor or bailor, to care for the health or property of his contract partner is contractually liable if he fails to ensure the agreed care and protection. Where in a contractual relationship damage occurs which is beyond the 'strict sphere of what is agreed'[320] (e.g properly treated patient slips and falls on waiting-room floor[321]) the question arises as to the possibility of contractual liability. Such liability would result from a 'legal' extension of contractual obligations, independent of the parties' wishes. That is, liability for implied contractual obligations, without the agreement of the parties, and without even the requirement that they be typical of such contracts.

(1) A Broad Law of Tort, a Narrow Law of Contract

461 The question of whether a legal system creates such obligations relates primarily to contract law. However, it is equally important to tort law because the two exist in equilibrium. The former may be adapted to compensate for the latter's deficiencies (equally, tort law is employed by those legal modernizers[322] whose hands are bound by contract law). Legal systems which employ general liability clauses allowing the judge a wide discretion, in which employers' liability is strict, and having

---

[319] For the importance for liability of such different positions (e.g. in private international, procedural, and insurance law) see no. 445 above. On burden of proof, limitation, and damages for pain and suffering see nos. 448 ff. above.

[320] Cf. no. 436, fn. 148 above.

[321] Thus Cass.civ. 10.1.1990, reported by Jourdain, *Rev.trim.dr.civ.* 89 (1990) p. 481: liability in tort only: *'le contrat médical passé entre le patient et le centre médical se limite à la consultation et aux soins'*.

[322] On the consideration-derived liability of experts in England: no. 287 above. Also nos. 479 and 497 ff. below.

apparently reasonable tort limitation periods, appear particularly reluctant to adopt statutory contractual protective duties. There, the necessary protection of the physical integrity of contractual partners is ensured by non-contractual liability. As previously seen, that is ordinarily the case in Spain.[323] Despite numerous contrary opinions,[324] Greek and Italian courts have so far shown little enthusiasm for employing such protective contractual duties beyond established sale of goods liability for losses consequential upon defective goods. In Greece the liability, for example of lessors to lessees for damage caused by deficient plumbing maintenance,[325] is exclusively in tort. The same is true of employers' liability for employees'[326] personal injuries. (This despite the fact that Art. 662 Greek Cc, modelled on § 618 BGB, expressly provides that the employers' duty to protect the health of employees is contractual.) Only very rarely have Italian courts found a breach of a protective duty outside Art. 1494 sec. 2 Cc to be *colpa contrattuale*,[327] otherwise relying invariably on tort.[328] Those cases concern, *inter alia*,

---

[323] No. 436 above. Also TS 4.11.1991, *RAJ* 1991 No. 8141 p. 11160: insufficiently safe glass door in hotel. TS 23.3.1988, *RAJ* 1988 no. 2226 p. 2178 (fn. 148 above); and TS 26.5.1995, *RAJ* 1995 no. 4129 p. 5504 is an exception to the approach generally taken by Spanish courts. A coach became stranded on a snow-bound road. Whilst the driver fitted chains, the passengers made their way to the next village. The travel guide subsequently sent the plaintiff to the village to inform the passengers that the bus could proceed. The plaintiff slipped and sustained bone fractures. Her claim in contract succeeded, based on the fault of the guide. (Liability in tort was not tested.)

[324] On the recognition of such protective duties in respect of the principle of good faith, see Bianca, *Diritto civile IV*, pp. 93–94. Also Giur.sist.Bigiavi (-Rossello) I, pp. 308–314. Recognition of protective duties in contract is favoured by numerous Greek commentators: Stathopoulos, *Geniko Enochiko Dikaio A I*, 2nd edn., pp. 51, 80; Zepos, *Enochikou Dikaiou I*, p. 36; Androulidaki-Dimitriadou, *Ai ypochreosseis synalladtikis pisteos*, pp. 1, 2, 93 ff.; Michaelides-Nouaos, *Enochiko Dikaio*, p. 168; ErmAK (-Koumantos), Arts. 197–198 Gr.civ.cod. no. 48; and Georgiades/Stathopoulos (-Stathopoulos), *Greek Cc. II*, Art. 288 no. 46 (*contra*: Pouliadis, *Culpa in contrahendo*, pp. 174–188). Giardina, *Responsabilità contrattuale e responsabilità extra-contrattuale*, pp. 88–90, takes the view that whilst there may be good reason not to supercede those cases expressly provided for by law regarding physical injury, tort should protect relative rights.

[325] CA Athens 4268/1956, *NoB* 5 (1957) p. 325; CA Athens 9228/1979, *NoB* 28 (1980) p. 545. Cf. CA Athens 737/1957, *EEN* 25 (1958) p. 143; and Areopag 1274/1977, *EEN* 45 (1977) p. 323.

[326] CA Athens 405/51, *EEN* 19 (1952) p. 321 (breach of Art. 662 constituting tort); CFI Athens 3732/56, *EED* 15 (1956) pp. 771, 772. Georgiades/Stathopoulos (-Spiliopoulos), *Greek Cc III*, Art. 662, nos. 10–11 and ErmAK (-Kapodistrias), Art. 662 Greek Cc, nos. 33–38 take the view that liability for breach of duties in Art. 662 Greek Cc is in contract, resulting in the application of the 20-year limitation period. Pouliades, *Culpa in contrahendo*, pp. 187–188, agrees. That a vendor's liability for loss resulting from defective goods is also contractual was found in CFI Agrinion 24/57, *ArchN* 8 (1957) p. 512. Similarly, CFI Athens 22888/1965, *ArchN* 9 (1958) p. 345.

[327] Cass. 14.4.1981, n. 2242, *Giust.civ.Mass.* 1981 p. 850 (letting of a sports centre, safety of the premises and apparatus).

[328] See e.g. Trib. Roma 10.11.1982, *Resp.Civ. e Prev.* 1983 p. 793; Trib. Roma 2.2.1977, *Giur.it.* 1981, I, 2, 159; and App. Roma 5.3.1980, *Giur.it.* 1982, I, 2, 173.

the obligations of cinema operators,[329] motorway snack vans,[330] shops,[331] and parks[332] to ensure their customers' safety. The same applies to the liability of a bank to customers injured during a robbery,[333] and of a drinks manufacturer to direct customers injured by exloding bottles.[334] In these cases, protection of the physical well-being of the contractual partner has not been elevated to a performance obligation;[335] Arts. 2043, and especially 2050 and 2051 Cc, suffice for this problem.

462   The essentially similar position in Danish law is demonstrated in SH 14.9.1987[336] and HD 20.9.1989.[337] In the former, a sailor was robbed on board his ship in Dar-es-Salaam; the employer was held liable in tort as he had been aware of the danger but had not instructed the sailor to lock the cabin door. In the latter, a doctor sterilized a patient without her consent whilst carrying out a Caesarian section. The court again viewed this merely as *'erstatningsret uden for kontraktsforhold'*. In The Netherlands, employers' obligations to ensure employees' safety under Art. 1638x BW (old) are contractual,[338] as is lessees' liability to lessors for waste.[339] Despite this, the law of protective duties demonstrates many characteristics of tort.[340] Portuguese law has also rejected the derivation from contractual relationships of general protective duties for the benefit of the person or property of contract partners[341] which are neither

---

[329] Cass. 20.1.1960, n. 46, *Resp.Civ. e Prev.* 1960 p. 356.

[330] Trib. Piacenza 15.3.1965, Gentile/Guerreri/Guerreri *I, voce Responsabilità civile—cose in custodia*, 69 (36).

[331] App. Genova 17.2.1977, Gentile/Guerreri/Guerreri loc. cit. 119; cf. no. 119 above, fn. 717 (liability under Art. 2051 Cc).

[332] Gentile/Guerreri/Guerreri, *La responsabilità, voce Responsabilità civile—giuochi*, 98 (9a) (court unspecified).

[333] Cass. 11.3.1991, n. 2555, *Foro.it.* 1991, I, 2802 with comment by Lenoci; cf. Cass. 14.4.1983, n. 2619, *Resp.Civ. e Prev.* 1984 p. 73.

[334] Cass. 27.2.1980, n. 1376, *Giur.it.* 1980, I, 1, 1459.   [335] Lenoci (fn. 333) 2808.

[336] SH 14.9.1987, *UfR* 1987 A p. 947.

[337] HD 20.9.1989, *UfR* 1987 A p. 1007. Cf. Gomard, *Obligationsret II*, pp. 143–144.

[338] HR 21.6.1974, *NedJur* 1974 No. 453, p. 1295; HR 25.6.1993, *RvdW* 1993, 145. Cf. HR 16.10.1992, *NedJur* 1993 No. 264 (plaintiff employee claimed compensation for damage to his car sustained in accident in course of employment. Liability found on basis of contract of employment but in that context it was argued purely in terms of tort law).

[339] HR 6.11.1987, *NedJur* 1988 no. 193 p. 807. Noteworthy because the legal representatives of both parties argued on the basis of tort, and Advocate-General Asser alone contended that contractual liability must 'surely' have been intended because the lease expressly stated that the lessee would be liable for any fault-related fire damage.

[340] Cf. Hof 's-Hertogenbosch 25.6.1968, *NedJur* 1969 no. 218 p. 534; Rb. Arnhem 2.1.1975, *NedJur* 1976 no. 229 p. 638 (ferry doors closed as car was driven on board); HR 1.10.1993, *RvdW* 1993, 189 (baby injured by leaking hot-water bottle); HR 6.11.1981, *NedJur* 1982 no. 567 p. 1969 (circulatory collapse after donating blood); and HR 24.12.1993, *RvdW* 1994, 12 (product liability to contractual partner). Cf. HR 10.9.1993, *RvdW* 1993, 171 (non-payment of national insurance contributions).

[341] Cf. Prata, *Responsabilidade pré-contratual*, p. 83; Menezes Cordeiro, *Boa Fé*, I p. 553; and Mota Pinto, *Responsabilidade pré-negocial*, pp. 155–156.

specifically agreed nor typical of the type of contract.[342] This is due not least to Arts. 493 sec. 1 (liability for dangerous things) and 500 (liability for assistants) Port. Cc. The decision not to impose such general contractual liability (which regarding pre-contract negotiations is indirectly statute-driven[343]) follows inevitably from Arts. 486 and 799 Port. Cc once a contract is complete. In the former, liability in tort for omissions is linked to a contractual obligation to act; in the latter, contractual liability is based upon presumed fault. Breaches of obligations to protect persons and property are almost invariably instances of omission liability, and Art. 486 Cc would be rendered practically ineffective if it were intended to base such liability upon a system of contractual damages. By its wording, contractual obligations to safeguard a victim are enforced by liability in tort,[344] and in that unique case it must follow that sanctions for breach of such secondary obligations remain the preserve of non-contractual liability. This is unlikely to be relied upon, however, given the differences in the burden of proof (Arts. 799 and 487 Port. Cc), the longer contract limitation period (Arts. 209 and 498 Port. Cc), and the fact that breaches of contract may give rise to claims for non-material loss.[345]

(2) The Common Law Duty of Care

Percy Winfield said that 'lawyers were thoroughly familiar with negligence as one mode of bungling a contract or a bailment long before it became an independent tort. Nor has it ever ceased to retain this earlier signification, though it has acquired the later one'.[346] As Winfield demonstrated, nineteenth-century English legal history saw numerous cases of contract law-based protective duties. These were the decisions on which a majority of the House of Lords relied in deciding the case of *Donoghue v. Stevenson* in 1932.[347] The issue was whether a duty of care was owed by a manufacturer to final consumers. The preliminary issue of whether a manufacturer owed a duty of care to immediate contractual partners had been answered long before;[348] this was the starting point

---

[342] On liability of medical practitioners in Portugal see Figueiredo Dias/Sinde Monteiro, *BolMinJust* 332 (1984) pp. 21, 43, 51; RL 4.7.1973, *BolMinJust* 229 (1973) p. 231 (liability in contract and tort; the injured party may choose the more favourable). Regarding the employer's contractual obligation to ensure his employees' safety, see RP 11.7.1983, *BolMinJust* 329 (1983) p. 617 (failure to comply with hygiene regulations; liability of the employers' federation); RP 14.11.1983, *BolMinJust* 31 (1983) p. 599.

[343] Vaz Serra's proposal expressly referred to protective duties in its provision on *culpa in contrahendo*, but the legislature excluded them from Art. 227 Port. Cc, Arts. 483 and 500 Cc being regarded as sufficient. See Prata, *Notas sobre responsabilidade pré-contratual*, p. 82.

[344] Similarly RC 20.11.1984, *CJ* IX (1984–5) p. 68.   [345] No. 455 above.

[346] Winfield, *Province of the Law of Torts*, p. 63.   [347] [1932] AC 562.

[348] Cf. *Winterbottom v. Wright* (1842) 10 M & W 109, 115 (*per* Alderson B): 'The only safe rule is to confine the right to recover to those who enter into the contract.'

for all further consideration.[349] That view remains in the three common law jurisdictions.[350] The common law basis of the relationships between negligence, contract, and tort is very different from that of the continental systems considered above. It depends on whether the requirements for breach of a duty of care are fulfilled. If so, the breach of duty is actionable in either contract or tort. The former makes available the use of implied terms; the latter is self-evident. Attempts have been made to introduce a distinction so that 'the right of a plaintiff who sues in contract, where the facts giving rise to the breach of contract would also constitute a breach of the common law duty apart from contract, to have the judgment entered on both heads is limited to cases where the common law duty is owed by one who conducts a common calling and thus is under a special type of legal liability, and to cases where the duty is owed by a professional man in respect of his professional skill'.[351] They have been successful neither in England nor Scotland.[352] A plaintiff remains 'entitled . . . to have judgment entered in (his) favour on the basis of tortious liability as well as on the basis of breach of contract, assuming that the plaintiff had established a breach by the defendant of [the] common law duty of care owed to the plaintiff'.[353]

Of course, both the nature and the specific terms of a contract affect the content of the duty of care, just as the level of the 'ordinary common law duty of care' determines what the contract may be interpreted to cover. Whether that duty is contractual or non-contractual is merely incidental. Increasingly the view is taken that 'the law of contract and the law of tort are, in a modern context, properly to be seen as but two of a number of imprecise divisions, for the purpose of classification, of a general body of rules constituting one coherent system of law'.[354]

---

[349] Lord Atkin in *Donoghue* loc. cit. pp. 581–583. Cf. Lord Devlin in *Hedley Byrne v. Heller and Partners* [1964] AC 465, 528: 'there is ample authority . . . that the categories of special relationships which may give rise to a duy to take care in word as well as in deed are not limited to contractual relationships'.

[350] Regarding England, Ireland, and Scotland see *Bell v. Travco Hotels Ltd.* [1953] 1 QB 473 (general contractual duty of care of hotelier); *Davey v. Cosmos* [1989] CLY 2561; *Buther v. McAlpin* [1904] 2 IR 445; *Siney v. Dublin Corporation* [1980] IR 400; *Burke and Others v. Corporation of Dublin* [1991] IR 341 (the same). On employment law; *Matthews v. Kuwait Bechtel Corp.* [1959] 2 QB 57 and Thomson, *SLT* 1994 p. 29 (employer's obligation to ensure the safety of employees was 'obviously' an implied term). On Scots law generally see *Middleton v. Douglas* 1991 SLT 726, 728–729 (Lord Marnoch).

[351] As the plaintiff argued in *Batty v. Metropolitan Realisations Ltd.* [1978] QB 554, 566.

[352] *Middleton v. Douglas* loc. cit. Also *Longworth v. Coppas International (UK) Ltd.* 1985 SLT 111 (Outer House): plaintiff's husband killed in Iranian rocket attack whilst working in Iraq. The case turned upon whether the defendant should previously have evacuated the deceased. The defendant argued that the matter was purely one of tort. Lord Davidson was not persuaded.

[353] Megaw LJ in *Batty* loc. cit. Cf. no. 429 above and *Thake and Another v. Maurice* [1986] 1 All ER 497, 506 (Kerr LJ).

[354] *Hawkins v. Clayton and Others* 78 [1988] ALR 69, 101 (*per* Deane J); cited approvingly by Steyn LJ in *White v. Jones* [1993] 3 WLR 730, 753.

(3) A Narrow Law of Tort and a Broad Law of Contract: Germany and Austria

German law provides the textbook example of functions ordinarily ful- **464**
filled by tort law being accomplished by contract. Many of its solutions
and constructions are also found in Austria.[355] The similar positions in
these countries result from essentially the same causes: on one hand, the
absence of the requirement of consideration, and on the other, tort law's
problems regarding burdens of proof, liability for omissions, limitation,
and the protection of purely economic issues.[356] The Commission on the
Law of Obligations (*Schuldrechtskommission*) in putting forward its proposal for a new § 241 sec. 2 BGB summarized the current position in
Germany thus: 'Relationships of obligation may, depending on their
content and nature, impose upon each party a duty to have special
regard to the rights and legal interests of the other party. The relationship of obligation may be thus restricted.'[357] The latter sentence was
intended to resolve cases involving liability for misinformation and
supply of services. The unusual use of the term *Rechtsgüter* also has
this objective. Hitherto it was understood to mean those personal interests listed alongside 'rights' in § 823 sec. 1 BGB: life, body, health, and
freedom. The Commission employs it to mean 'pure economic interests'.
That contractual partners owe a duty of 'particular' care to each others'
rights should 'suggest a distinction from the general tort duties of
care'.[358] Where this distinction *actually* exists is not disclosed; whether
it may be drawn at all is uncertain. What is decisive is the attempt to
codify a jurisprudence which has long recognized all contracts as being
sources of protective duties, thus going beyond the text of the BGB. The
BGB provides for breach of contractual protective duties only in § 618,
section three of which refers directly to tort law regarding remedies,
whilst excluding damages for pain and suffering under § 847 BGB.

That part of German contract law named *positive Vertragsverletzungen* **465**
(positive breaches of contract), after Hermann Staub's[359] similarly
named article, originated in the jurisprudence of imperial Germany. It
developed duties remarkably similar to the English common law duty of

---

[355] Cf. OGH 5.6.1984, *ÖJZ* 1985 p. 304 (contractual protective duties for the benefit of
third parties arising from contract to take in guests); OGH 3.9.1992, *JBl* 1993 p. 396; OGH
24.4.1991, *JBl* 1991 pp. 586, 587 (it is now 'uncontested that comprehensive protective duties
and duties of care come about where a transaction having a legal character . . . occurs').
OGH 7.4.1992, *JBl* 1992 p. 786; OGH 10.10.1991, *ÖJZ* 1993 p. 166 (general statement); and
OGH 22.6.1993, *ZfRV* 1994 p. 249.
[356] For a detailed study of Austrian law see Koziol/Welser, *Grundriß des bürgerlichen
Rechts I*, 9th edn., pp. 185 f., 195 f.; and Koziol, *JBl* 1994 pp. 209–223. Also Reindl, *ZVR* 1994
pp. 193–198. For the position in Germany see no. 190 above.
[357] Bundesminister der Justiz (ed.), *Abschlußbericht der Kommission zur Überarbeitung des
Schuldrechts*, p. 113.　　　　　　　　　　　　　　　[358] Loc. cit. pp. 114–115.
[359] Staub, *Die positiven Vertragsverletzungen und ihre Rechtsfolgen: FS für den 26. DJT* (1902)
pp. 29–56.

care. The originating case was the 'Horse Fodder' case of 1907.[360] The plaintiff bought horse fodder from the defendant and sold it on to farmers. Several horses belonging to the latter died; the fodder contained poisonous seeds of castor oil plants. The plaintiff settled the claims of the farmers and then proceeded against the defendant, his supplier. The claim thus centred around a purely economic loss irrecoverable under § 823 sec. 1 BGB. Coincidentally, the *Reichsgericht* (German Imperial Court) was at that time engaged with the liability of sellers for consequential harm suffered by purchasers. A recourse action was only possible if the plaintiff had been obliged to compensate the farmers. The Imperial Court concluded that a contractual damages claim existed in both supply relationships. Regarding the plaintiff's liability to his purchasers, the Court referred to a decision of 13.6.1902 in which it had been stated that 'on account of the contractual relationship a claim for damages can exist beside rescission and can be asserted if . . . one party has caused damage in a blameworthy manner which [damage] cannot be remedied by rescission and the claim's enforcement is not opposed by any specific statutory provision. This follows from § 276 BGB.'[361] Thus was the the first step taken. Although the BGB contained no provision akin to the subsequent Art. 1494 sec. 2 Ital. Cc, the *Reichsgericht* based analogous liability on § 276 BGB, under which the debtor must without prejudice bear responsibility for 'intention or negligence'. So a rule which 'properly interpreted provides only a standard of liability but is silent as to legal consequences'[362] developed into a cause of action. The second step was to extend the newly created cause of action to cover pure economic loss, enabling the plaintiff in the Horse Fodder case to claim against the supplier.

The Imperial Court (*Reichsgericht*) retained the concept of general contractual liability for breach of duty of care until its demise.[363] It was only in 1953 that the German Federal Court corrected the doctrinal basis. Admittedly, nothing of substance changed with the clarification that German law only recognizes care in respect of the performance of a duty, and not a general duty of care. The BGH has always accepted that the positive breach of contract, 'a concept recognized both in doctrine and case-law, ...[is] to be treated as good law'.[364]

466   The comparative lawyer would consider this unexceptional, if the sole purpose of liability for *positive Vertragsverletzung* were merely to subject cases such as that of the horse fodder to contract law. The sale of

---

[360] RG 9.7.1907, RGZ 66 p. 289. Good analysis of this in Leenen, *Jura* 1993 pp. 534–539.
[361] RG 13.6.1902, RGZ 52 pp. 18, 19 (emphasis in the original); confirmed by RG 9.7.1907 loc. cit. p. 291.   [362] Thus, correctly, BGH 13.11.1953, BGHZ 11 pp. 80, 83.
[363] E.g RG 29.11.1922, RGZ 106 pp. 22, 25–26. Also (on § 278 BGB) RG 9.5.1939, RGZ 160 p. 310.   [364] BGH 13.11.1953 loc. cit.

goods law of many European countries imposes liability for consequential harm. This is true of Portugal,[365] Spain,[366] Italy, Greece, and the common law jurisdictions. A distinctly 'German' liability for positive breach of contract thus developed only when the courts began to extend the concept to cover personal injury and other damage not caused by inadequate performance of primary contractual obligations. As early as 1911 the Imperial Court admitted that it had 'recognized in numerous decisions that a contractual or other relationship of obligation may give rise to duties of care regarding the life and property of the parties, having no basis in the legal nature of the relationship, but being the necessary consequence of that relationship'.[367] That was no exaggeration. By 1903 it had been decided that a railway company was contractually obliged 'to provide passengers with a safe exit from stations'.[368] In 1906 a test drive prior to the sale of a car was regarded as part of a 'preparatory contract' upon which liability for personal injury could be based.[369] A year later the *Reichsgericht* based contractual liability for damage caused by fire on *positive Vertragsverletzung*: carriers had temporarily stored bales of flax at a railway station without protection from flying sparks.[370] Liability was similarly based when, on another occasion, a customer fell into an unsecured and ill-lit loading bay.[371]

It would be futile to extend the list of examples: we would lose ourselves in the case-law of the Imperial and Federal Courts (the latter following the former seamlessly[372]) if we attempted even a semi-comprehensive list. What is important is that analysis shows that the Imperial Court in its earliest decisions was regularly concerned with the problem of liability for assistants. The aim was to circumvent the 'intolerable'[373] § 831 BGB whenever either the case concerned independent contractors, or the exculpatory function of § 831 sec. 1 sub sec. 2 BGB appeared likely to apply. From the outset the creditor of a contractual claim was denied damages for pain and suffering resulting from

[365] Cf. RL 6.12.1988, *CJ* XIII (1988–5) p. 114 (supply of poisonous pig-feed: contractual liability for death of pigs) and RP 31.1.1985, *CJ* X (1985–1) p. 259 (supply of defective photographic developing machine, resulting in destruction of films: contractual liability).
[366] E.g. TS 13.2.1991, *RAJ* 1991 no. 1200 p. 1462 (supply of poisonous cattle-feed: contractual liability for cattle deaths), TS 19.12.1984, *RAJ* no. 6134 p. 4844 (sale of defective textiles: contractual liability for consequential losses).
[367] RG 28.11.1911, RGZ 78 pp. 238, 240 (linoleum roll); cf. no. 190 above.
[368] RG 5.10.1903, RGZ 55 p. 335. [369] RG 13.12.1906, RGZ 65 pp. 17, 19.
[370] RG 24.10.1907, RGZ 66 p. 402. [371] RG 9.3.1910, RGZ 7 p. 148.
[372] BGH 18.12.1952, BGHZ 8 pp. 239, 241; BGH 26.9.1961, *VersR* 1961 pp. 1078, 1079; BGH 25.6.1968, *VersR* 1968 pp. 993, 994. Also OLG Hamburg 21.1.1971, *VersR* 1972 p. 650. For additional material: Schlechtriem, *VersR* 1973 pp. 581, 583; v. Bar, *Verkehrspflichten*, pp. 251–254.
[373] Thus RG 14.3.1939, RGZ 162 pp. 129, 166 with reference to the 'undesirability of exoneration under § 831 BGB'.

breach of a protective duty. The rule in § 253 BGB was, and still is, regarded as insuperable.[374] Since the development of general liability in tort for breach of duties of care[375] has helped[376] to defuse the problem of § 831 sec. 1 sub sec. 2, ever more frequent recourse is made to tort law due to § 847 BGB. Liability for breach of protective duties has nevertheless remained alive. Often the § 282 BGB-based division of the burden of proof regarding the fulfilling of duties of supervision and control is more advantageous to the injured party than that of tort.[377] Perhaps even more important is the thirty-year contract limitation period (§ 195 BGB).[378] Additionally, the positive breach of contract concept plays a significant role in the enlargement of the class of interests protected by tort.[379]

A trend towards tort has become noticeable at the boundary with the law of consequential harm, primarily as a result of the case-law on damage caused to a product by itself, and the consequent effects on the understanding of what is to be regarded as damage to property. The BGH in any event moved in that direction in a decision reminiscent in many respects of the Horse Fodder case of 7.12.1993.[380] The plaintiff fitter used the defendant's wholesale-sold thread-cutting agent on water pipes on a building site. The agent produced a nauseating smell. The plaintiff settled the claim of the site owner and commenced proceedings; the BGH held that the defendant manufacturer had damaged the plaintiff's property. Interference with the substance of property is not a precondition for presuming damage to it. Interference 'may crystallize in the subsequent obligation of the injured party to his customers to repair the thing itself'. Further, 'the defendant's duty in tort to compensate is without prejudice to the principle that it is generally the function of contract law to protect consumers' or users' interests in the quality of products, whereas tort is generally concerned with absolute rights'.

(4) Contractual Obligations de Sécurité, *Non-Contractual Fault Liability, and Non-Contractual* Gardien *Liability*

468 The issue of whether liability for damage to the health or property of another is contract- or tort-based is nowhere more important than in France. Nor is the boundary between the two fields so unclear and so

---

[374] RG 13.12.1906, RGZ 65 pp. 17, 21 is the leading case: 'whoever is solely contractually liable for personal injuries or damage to health need not compensate for resulting immaterial damage, although an internal reason for such distinction between contractual and tortious liability may not be evident.' [375] Nos. 104–105 above.
[376] Nos. 185 ff. above.
[377] Cf. BGH 26.9.1961 and BGH 25.6.1968 loc. cit. Also no. 448 above, fn. 240.
[378] E.g. BGH 8.5.1956, *VersR* 1956 p. 500; BGH 1.12.1964, *VersR* 1965 p. 240; and BGH 28.1.1976, *JZ* 1976 p. 776. [379] Nos. 497 ff. below.
[380] BGH 7.12.1993, *NJW* 1994 p. 517 = *EWiR* § 823 BGB 2/94 p. 135 (Schlechtriem).

cluttered by considerations of equity. Neither of the typically 'German' problems of damages for pain and suffering and liability for assistants play a role in France, nor is the extension of contractual liability linked to liability for pure economic loss. The presence of varying limitation periods (thirty years in contract if no special rules apply [e.g Art. 1648 Cc], ten years in tort [Art. 2270–1 Cc]) is not a French peculiarity. Problems do arise, though, concerning co-existing *non-cumul*[381] and general *gardien* liability[382] on one hand, and the staggered development of contractual protective duties and stricter non-contractual liability on the other. Given the rules on concurrence of actions, every contractual protective duty developed in France results in tort law being disapplied. The development of contractual protective duties may thus in some circumstances fulfil a very different function from those, say, in Germany. In France the function of augmenting the subsisting tort liability between contractors can only be fulfilled where there is a *garde* within the meaning of Art. 1384 sec. 1 Cc and where contractual liability is strict (*obligation de sécurité de résultat*) or operates with a reversed burden of proof for fault. In all other cases the presumption of a contractual duty of care results in either the extension of the relevant limitation period or a privilege for the contract partner.[383] The latter was the case in the original decision on *non-cumul*.[384] Once the jurisprudence on Art. 1384. sec. 1 Cc (which was itself only developed because of the lack of a concept of contractual protective duties at the end of the nineteenth century[385]) had crystallized, the *non-cumul* principle resulted in a new objective regime in which non-contractual liability was displaced by contractual liability. For the area of overlap with Art. 1384 sec. 1 Cc, extension of the latter implies either another exercise in limitation law or, insofar as contractual liability is based on the breach of an *obligation de sécurité de moyens*, a return to liability based on fault and the displacement of *gardien* liability. Liability becomes less strict rather than stricter.[386] Every *obligation de sécurité de moyens* must thus harmonize with tort law and will only conform with the overall system if that effect is desired; the alternative is unjustifiably unequal treatment.

Examples are easily found. A 'classic' field of the *obligations de moyens* **469** is doctors' and lawyers' liability. Doctors do not guarantee successful

---

[381] Nos. 431 ff. above.   [382] Nos. 107 ff. above.
[383] Viney, *Sem.Jur.* 1994, I, 3773 No. 4.   [384] No. 431 above.   [385] No. 109 above.
[386] Jourdain correctly contends at *Gaz.Pal.* 1993 *Doctr.* 1171, 1172: '*Dès lors, à chaque fois que la victime n'est créancière que d'une obligation de sécurité de moyens, elle se trouve privée du bénéfice de l'art. 1384, alinéa 1ᵉʳ du Code civil.*' Cf. Bonnard, comment on Cass. 10.2.1993, D. 1993 *Jur.* 605, 607; Viney loc. cit. (fn. 383); Lambert-Faivre, D. 1994 *Jur.* 81, 83; Dalcq/ Schamps, *Rev.crit.jur.belge* 1995 pp. 525, 553 (No. 4); and Ghestin, *Sem.Jur.* 1992 I 3572 pp. 157, 158.

treatment, nor lawyers successful actions.[387] What, then, is the position when a patient trips on the surgery carpet? According to the *Cour de Cassation* it is not the contractual obligation of the doctor, lawyer, or supermarket[388] to protect clients or customers against such risks. *'Le contrat médical passé entre le patient et le centre médical se limite à la consultation et aux soins.'*[389] Had such a limitation on contractual liability not been established, the patient would probably have been without a remedy. As it is, the patient may claim under Art. 1384 sec. 1 Cc. The opposite is the case regarding use of medical equipment,[390] injections,[391] or blood analyses.[392] There—at least for injections—liability is in contract, based on an *obligation de sécurité de moyens.*[393] A further example is liability for railways. French jurisprudence long held that a carrier owed passengers an *obligation de résultat* during the period of transport by train; but accidents in railway buildings were covered by an *obligation de moyens*, so passengers had to prove fault by the railway company.[394] In 1989 that *'fractionnement'* was abandoned: a contractual *obligation de sécurité* lasts only while the passenger is on a train; all else is subject to tort law. In following the original view, the Cour d'Appel had breached Art. 1384 sec. 1 Cc by non-application.[395]

470   Similar decisions are unexceptional. Except for hospital liability, modern French liability law continues to replace fault-based liability with contractual protective duties.[396] Initially, *obligations de sécurité* were a

---

[387] Hübner, *FS Baumgärtel*, pp. 151, 156.

[388] Case-law in this area increasingly departs from old concepts of fault-based contractual duties. (Overview and criticism in JClCiv [-Veaux], *Entreprise. Responsabilité civile*, Arts. 1382 to 1386, Fasc. 365–2 no. 5). Cf. Cass.civ. 19.11.1964, *Sem.Jur.* 1965 II 14022 (note Rodière); Cass.civ. 5.6.1991, Bull.civ. 1991, II, 176 (*'La responsabilité d'un commerçant à l'égard de ses clients quant à l'organisation et au fonctionnement d'un établissement dont l'entrée est libre est de nature quasi-délictuelle'*: so Art. 1384 Cc applied). Also, Cass.civ. 20.7.1994, *D.* 1995 *Jur.* 315 (comment by Charollois). The plaintiff, who was to carry out control tests in a hospital, injured himself whilst using the lavatory. The *Cour de Cassation* made no reference to contractual liability and decided the case against the hospital as *gardien*). In Belgium such cases are based exclusively in tort: Liège 25.3.1992, *RGAR* 1994 No. 12341. See also further, no. 114 above.

[389] Cass.civ. 10.1.1990, *Resp.civ. assur.* 1990, *comm.* no. 112 = *Rev.trim.dr.civ.* 1990 p. 481 (reported by Jourdain); also Cass.civ. 28.4.1981, *D.* 1981 *IR* 438.

[390] Rouen 7.2.1984, *D.* 1985 *IR* 405. Also Cass.civ. 16.11.1965, *D.* 1966 *Jur.* 61.

[391] Cass.civ. 4.2.1959, *Sem.Jur.* 1959, II, 11046.

[392] Toulouse 14.12.1959, *Sem.Jur.* 1960, II, 11402. Hospitals and blood transfusion centres (the latter under a *stipulation tacite pour autrui*) are subject to an obligation as to outcome in respect of quality of the blood product. Cf. Paris 28.11.1991, *Sem.Jur.* 1992, II, 21797 and comment by Billiet, *VersRAI* 1994 pp. 42–45.

[393] Contrary to the position previously adopted, under which hospitals were subject to an obligation as to outcome, see Cass.civ. 12.4.1995 (*2ème espèce*), *Sem.Jur.* 1995, II, 224 67 = *Gaz.Pal.* 1995 *Jur* p. 344. Jourdain is critical: *Sem.Jur.* 1995, II, 22467.

[394] Cass.civ. 21.7.1970, *Sem.Jur.* 1970, II, 16488 and Cass.civ. 1.7.1969, *D.* 1969 *Jur.* 640.

[395] Cass.civ. 7.3.1989, *Gaz.Pal.* 1989 *Jur.* 632 (comment by Paire).

[396] Veaux, Jourdain, and Bonnard (fns. 388 and 386). Also Viney, *Sem.Jur.* 1992, I, 3572.

form of *obligations de résultat*,[397] particular to law on the carriage of passengers, and functioning as a contractual analogy to *gardien* liability. *Obligations de moyens* developed alongside because of the necessity of reconciling[398] Arts. 1137 and 1147 Cc.[399] Factually, it enabled *gardien* liability, long perceived as being too strict, to be removed from certain areas. Gradually the floodgates opened to wash away *gardien* liability, either by denying the existence of a contractual duty[400] or, expressly[401] or tacitly,[402] by transforming duties to act in a particular manner into obligations to ensure a particular result. There is a parallel regarding liability for consequential harm: here the *responsabilité contractuelle* begins to encroach upon the area of guarantees in sale of goods law (*garantie pour vices cachés*) thus cutting down the application of Art. 1648 Cc (assertion of a claim within a short period of time).[403] The current position in French law is unclear. Whilst it recently appeared that the the death knell[404] had sounded for *obligations de sécurité de moyens*, there have since been several examples of distinctions being drawn between victims remaining passive and placing trust in the other party (e.g. as a guest) and those adopting an active role.[405] Regarding the former, there has been a tendency to accept a duty to ensure a particular result,

---

[397] No. 447, fn. 226.　　　[398] Hübner, *FS Baumgärtel*, pp. 151, 152 for more detail.

[399] In cases involving breach of a duty to supervise, Art. 1137 Cc demands proof that the defendant failed to exercise the standard of care of the *bon père de famille*. Art. 1147 Cc demands merely the presence of *cause étrangère* to exonerate the defendant in cases of *inexécution de l'obligation*.

[400] Fns. 388, 389, and 395 above. Also Cass.civ. 28.4.1981, Bull.civ. 1981, I, 137.

[401] E.g Cass.civ. 28.10.1991, Bull.civ. 1991, I, 289; and Cass.civ. 13.11.1974 *Sem.Jur.* 1976, II, 18344.

[402] Cass.civ. 10.2.1993, *D.* 1993 *Jur.* 605 is an example. Duty to supervise children at holiday camp was described as an *obligation de moyens* but applied so strictly that Bonnard commented that '*dans ce cas, la Cour de Cassation n'est pas hostile à admettre une pseudo-obligation de moyens, transformée de fait en une obligation de résultat par de présomptions jurisprudentielles de faute et de lien de causalité*'. Similarly, Cass.civ. 27.1.1982, *Gaz.Pal.* 1982 *Jur.* 537 (comment by Chabas) and Cass.civ. 19.7.1983, *Rev.trim.dr.civ.* 1984 p. 729 (obs. Huet). Further, Montpellier 20.1.1992, *Sem.Jur.* 1993, II, 22125 (comment by Bories): obligation to ensure the safety of visitors to a holiday park offering '*une série de jeux et d'amuse-ments nautiques*' described as an *obligation de moyens*. However, liability was based on the fact that the operating company could not prove contributory negligence by the victims in a case in which '*les circonstances exactes de l'accident n'ont pas été établies*'.

[403] Cass.civ. 11.6.1991, Bull.civ. 1991, I, 201 = *Sem.Jur.* 1991, IV, 320: sale of a mobile home, in which the buyers were found asphyxiated after 1 night. No liability under warranty, so Art. 1648 inapplicable. Vendor held contractually liable '*pour manquement à son obligation de sécurité . . . laquelle consiste à ne livrer que des produits exempts de tout vice ou de tout défaut de fabrication de nature à créer un danger pour les personnes et pour les biens*'.

[404] So Jourdain was able to opine, *Gaz.Pal.* 1993 *Doctr.* 1171, 1176, '*soit l'obligation de sécurité est de résultat, soit elle n'est pas contractuelle*'. Cf. Lambert-Faivre, *D.* 1994 *Doctr.* 81–85.

[405] Further Viney, *Sem.Jur.* 1994, I, 3773 no. 4. Luxembourgeois case-law differentiates similarly. See Trib. Diekirch 16.1.1990, *Pas. luxemb.* 28 (1990–1992) p. 42 (no. 142). The position in Belgium is more circumspect where the victim only plays a passive role: e.g Brussels 11.6.1992, *RGAR* 1995 No. 12456.

whereas a mere *obligation de sécurité de moyens*[406] appears to have been applied regarding the latter.

b. Contractual Damages in the Absence of a Contract?

471   Where no contract exists between parties at the time of an accident, one would assume that the plaintiff could only claim damages in tort. In fact the position is rather more complicated. First, many legal systems regard the initiation of contractual negotiations as not only creating a relationship of obligation belonging to the law of contract, but also establishing protective duties whose breach constitutes a *culpa in contrahendo* and founds a contract-type duty to compensate for loss. (See [1] below). The second type of exceptional case involving contract-type obligations to compensate is the *contract with protective effects for the benefit of third parties*. (See [2] below). Examples are found only in a few countries and take several forms. Finally, there are concepts similar to the contract with protective effects for the benefit of third parties which enable the consumer of a product to bring an action against its manufacturer. Such claims are based not in tort but contract. (See [3] below).

(1) Culpa in Contrahendo

(a) The Origins and Essence of *Culpa in Contrahendo*

472   The concept of *culpa in contrahendo* was the creation of the German lawyer Rudolf von Jhering.[407] He attempted to establish that, following Roman law sources, liability could be based on blameworthy conduct occurring before the making of a contract (hence *in contrahendo*). Whether or not this was historically accurate quickly became irrelevant. The idea so convinced Jhering's contemporaries that its derivation scarcely mattered. Several German laws soon embodied the concept. The imperial legislature soon followed suit and applied Jhering's idea in §§ 122 (liability for rescission on the basis of mistake) and 307 BGB (fault-based liability for objective impossibility of performance). The Greek Civil Code appied the same principle in Arts. 145, 335, and 336; moreover, its Art. 198 sec. 1 has is a general provision that 'a party to contractual negotiations which causes loss to the other by way of blame-

---

[406] Cass.civ. 24.11.1993, Bull.civ. 1993 I No. 344 = *Sem.Jur.* 1994, IV, 285. A salvage contract contained only *'une obligation accessoire de moyens de veiller à l'intégrité physique du contractant dès lors que celui-ci n'était pas passif, mais participait à l'excution de la convention'.* Further, Cass.civ. 9.2.1994, *Sem.Jur.* 1994, II, 22313: the supervisory duty of a ski-instructor *'est une obligation de moyens.'* Cf. fn. 393 above. Cass.civ. 17.1.1995, *D.* 1995 *Jur.* 350, 351 accepts contractual *gardien* liability in a case involving both product liability and the liability of a private school for safety in its playground. Cf. no. 480 below.
[407] von Jhering, *JhJb* 4 (1861) pp. 1–112.

worthy conduct . . . (is) obliged to compensate for the damage caused even if no contract comes into existence'. The Italian *Codice civile* provides in Art. 1338 that 'a contractual party who knew or ought to have known of the invalidity of the contract and did not make this known to the other party . . . [is] obliged to compensate for damage sustained by the other due to his innocent reliance upon the contract's validity'. Art. 1337 Ital. Cc provides a general obligation 'to act in good faith . . . in conducting negotiations and establishing contracts'. Art. 227 sec. 1 Port. Cc similarly provides that persons 'negotiating with another with a view to creating a contract [must] observe the rules of good faith in both the preparation and completion of the contract; he shall otherwise be liable for damage culpably caused to the other party'.

Clearly, these provisions have no effect on liability for breach of **473** protective duties, i.e. liability for personal injury. *Culpa in contrahendo* expanded into that area as a result of judge-led developments, predominantly in German-language countries (see [b]). Those developments cannot properly be understood without considering the core of *culpa in contrahendo*, namely fault during contractual negotiations. This core area involves pure economic loss and concerns cases in which the injured party brings an action on the basis that no contract was entered into because of the fault of the (other) negotiating party, or that the resulting contract was not what was initially agreed. The general clauses of Greek, Italian, and Portugese law illustrate that the older and more narrowly drawn paragraphs 122 and 307 of the German BGB are mere examples of a general principle. A duty to compensate arises not only from the avoidance of obligations on the basis of mistake or the withholding of information regarding the impossibility of performance. Rather, *culpa in contrahendo* is committed by anyone who in bad faith denies success to contractual negotiations, such as someone who merely pretends to enter into them, or abandons them in bad faith. It is generally the case that a claim arises only on the so-called negative interest (i.e. in respect of reliance loss). So the claimant is entitled merely to be put into the position in which he would have been had he not entered contractual negotiations.[408]

---

[408] That claims in *culpa in contrahendo* provide for recovery only of reliance loss is *iure communi europeo*. Cf. Prata, *Responsabilidade pré-contratual*, pp. 167–180; García Rubio, *Responsabilidad precontractual*, p. 242; Díez-Picazo/Gullón, *Sistema II*, 6th edn., p. 271; Georgiades/Stathopoulos (-Karassis), *Greek Cc*, I Arts. 197–198 no. 9; *ErmAK* (-Koumantos), Arts. 197–198 nos. 77 ff. (both stating that reliance loss must be ascertained using rules of causation); CFI Thessaloniki 831/1977, *NoB* 26 (1978) p. 539; Van Ommeslaghe, *Rev.crit.jur.belge* 1986 pp. 33, 150–152; Cian/Trabucchi, *Commentario breve*, 4th edn., Art. 1337 n. 5; Cendon (-Benatti) IV, Art. 1337 p. 508; Cass. 26.5.1992, n. 6294; *Resp.Civ. e Prev.* 1993 p. 838; Gomard, *Almindelig kontraktsret*, pp. 98–99; Hellner, *Speciell avtalsrätt II (2)*, p. 210; Horn, *JuS* 1995 pp. 377, 382–383. There are of course exceptions to the restriction of

474   Two aspects of *culpa in contrahendo* have remained unchanged from the outset: the content of the concept, and the question of whether statutory provisions relating to it were of tort or contract law. The *Materialien* of the German BGB (official publications of the reasoning and background to the BGB) state that the 'question of construction [as to whether] liability in *culpa in contrahendo* can be reduced to an interference with the legal rights of others and as such constitute a tort, or whether it is to be traced to the breach of a contractual duty . . . may be left to jurisprudence'.[409] Over one hundred years later, the issue has been laboured over in almost every European jurisdiction, but remains unresolved, with arguments continuing not only within national systems but also between academics and courts of different systems. Perhaps the continuing discussion indicates that the question was ill-conceived, and that it should instead be asked whether the continuing distinction between contractual and tortious liability has any virtue. Doubts that the distinction has any virtue have arisen frequently in this analysis. European lawyers have, however, become so accustomed to these categories that they show no sign of relinquishing them.

475   To the *Code Napoléon* jurist, liability under *culpa in contrahendo* lies in tort. The Belgian[410] and French[411] courts refer consistently, and in accord with the commentators, to Arts. 1382, 1383 Cc.[412] Without a contract there can be no contractual liability. Even the generally non-binding nature of contractual offers is balanced by non-contractual law: a party revoking an offer before a *délai raisonnable* has elapsed commits a *faute* in tort.[413] An expressly *culpa in contrahendo*-based tort is also committed by

---

liability to reliance loss: for Italy see: Cass. 12.3.1993, n. 2973; *NGCC* 1994, I, 120; for France: Cass.civ. 8.10.1958; Bull.civ. 1958, I, No. 413 (further St. Lorenz, *ZEuP* 1994 pp. 218, 230); For Germany: Horn loc. cit.; and for Spain: García Rubio loc. cit. (in some cases reliance loss may cover foregone profit) and Díez-Picazo/Gullón loc. cit.

[409]   Mot. I p. 195.

[410]   E.g Brussels 22.1.1985, *JT* 1985 p. 718; Cass. 1.10.1976, *Pas. belge* 1977, I, 133; Trib.-com.Brussels 24.6.1985, *JT* 1986 p. 236; and Trib.com.Brussels 3.2.1988, *JT* 1988 p. 516.

[411]   E.g Cass.civ. 5.10.1994, Bull.civ. 1994, I, no. 276; Cass.com. 22.2.1994, Bull.civ. 1994, IV, no. 79; Cass.civ. 5.6.1991, Bull.civ. 1991, II, no. 176; Cass.com. 20.3.1972, *Sem.Jur.* 1973, II, 17543; and Cass.civ. 29.11.1968, *Gaz.Pal.* 1969 *Jur.* 63 (liability for the withdrawal of a declaration to contract where the latter was made mistakenly). The position is the same for *culpa post pactum finitum*, 'continuing effect contractual duties'. Cf. Paris 26.6.1986, *D.* 1986 *IR* 348 (foreman speaks to current employer perjoratively about employee: *faute* in respect of the employee).

[412]   See Schmidt-Szalewski, *Rev.int.dr.comp.* 42 (1990) pp. 545, 547–554; JClCiv (-Jourdain), Arts. 1382 to 1386, Fasc. 130–1; JClCiv (-Veaux), Arts. 1382 to 1386, Fasc. 365–2; Cornelis, *Buitencontractueel aansprakelijkheidsrecht*, nos. 65–69; de Page, *Droit Civil Belge II*, 3rd edn., nos. 555–560; St. Lorenz, *ZEuP* 1994 pp. 218–243.

[413]   Cass.civ. 22.3.1972, *D.* 1972 *Jur.* 468. Cf. Cass.civ. 28.6.1995, Bull.civ. 1995, II, no. 225: company gave *Mme Langlois* to believe that she had won 60,000 FF; in fact she was entitled to only a fraction of that sum. The *Cour de Cassation* allowed an action under Art. 1382 Cc for the entire sum; the company had committed a *faute*.

a party who dishonestly ceases negotiations and thereby disappoints '*la légitime confiance*' of the other party.[414] The common law has no developed doctrine of 'good faith',[415] so the concept of *culpa in contrahendo* has not developed there: the term is as unknown as the concept. Until a contract is created, each party negotiates at its own risk; the law seldom offers protection, and then only non-contractual protection.[416] Deceit and breach of confidence may be of assistance, occasionally also negligence under the rule in *Hedley Byrne*.[417]

The characterization of *culpa in contrahendo* has been granted little **476** attention by the Scandinavian legal systems, although the concept is significant.[418] In the absence of a contract, the tendency is to view liability as being in tort.[419] The position may be very different from that in France and Germany, both because compensation statutes apply to contract as well as to tort, and because the laws on the formation of contracts are considerably different from those on the continent.[420] In The Netherlands the law of tort is used extensively in this regard.[421] The Italian courts are clear that liability under Arts. 1337 and 1338 Cc is in tort; a party acting in bad faith in pre-contractual negotiations will be liable under Arts. 2043 ff. Cc. This is significant primarily in respect of the five-year limitation period under Art. 2947 Cc.[422] However, some

---

[414] Cf. Brussels 22.1.1985 and Trib.com.Brussels 3.2.1988 (fn. 410).

[415] See O'Connor, *Good Faith in English Law*, esp. pp. 23 ff., 35–36: 'there is no general rule in English law requiring the parties to negotiate in good faith'; also Bonell, *International Restatement of Contract Law*, p. 84.

[416] Liability under sec. 2(1) Misrepresentation Act 1967 (c. 7) is in tort. Cf. v. Bar (-Shaw), *DeliktsR in Europa*, England and Wales, p. 13. The statute introduced liability in negligence for cases 'where a person has entered into a contract after a misrepresentation has been made to him'.

[417] O'Connor (fn. 415) p. 36. Cf. *Esso Petroleum Co. Ltd.* v. *Mardon* [1976] 2 All ER 5 (duty of care in tort applied to 'pre-contract negotiations'); *Box* v. *Midland Bank Ltd.* [1979] 2 Lloyds Rep. 391 (similarly; unlike *Esso Petroleum* no contract was formed) and Hondius (-Allen), *Precontractual Liability England*, pp. 125, 135–136.

[418] Cf. VLD 27.3.1981, *UfR* 1981 A p. 572. Also, in Sweden, HD 7.12.1990, *NJA* 1990: 122 p. 745.   [419] Cf. no. 245 and fn. 50 above.

[420] Gomard, *Almindelig kontraktsret*, pp. 98–99. Also Andersen/Madsen/Nørgaard, *Aftaler og mellemmænd*, pp. 118–120.

[421] HR 18.6.1982, *NedJur* 1983 No. 723 p. 2297 (costs of preparing contractual estimate: '*goede trouw*' and '*onrechtmatige daad*'). Cf. HR 10.6.1994, *RvdW* 1994 No. 130 (personal liability of the MD of a limited company for misinformation as to the company's ability to meet its debts; liability under Art. 6:162 BW rejected; no shift of the burden of proof). The interpretation of HR 18.6.1982 loc. cit. appears ever more uncertain: see Hondius (-van Dunné), *Precontractual Liability, Netherlands*, pp. 225, 227.

[422] Most usefully: Cass. 18.6.1987, n. 5371, *Foro.it.* 1988, I, 182; Cass. 11.5.1990, n. 4051; Gentile/Guerreri/Guerreri, *La responsabilità II voce responsabilità civile—contratto trattative precontrattuali*, 127 [273]; Cass. 18.6.1987, n. 5371, loc. cit. 127 [179]; Cass. 19.4.1983, n. 2705, loc. cit. 127 [130]; Cass. 7.8.1974, n. 2385, loc. cit 127 [70]; and Cass. 1.2.1995, n. 1163, *Giust.civ.Mass.* 1995 no. 1163 p. 254 (liability for rescinding contractual relations, which requires malice, is based upon the 'broadest category of non-contractual liability' (*essendo riconducibile alla picè ampia categoria della responsabilità extracontrattuale*).

Italian commentators are committed proponents of the contractual view.[423] Teaching in Portugal is similarly divided.[424] Its Civil Code has devalued the characterization issue[425] but the problem remains due to differing rules on burden of proof. Portuguese case-law appears to treat liability in *culpa in contrahendo* as being in tort.[426] In Spain the disagreement appears to reach the Tribunal Supremo.[427] Its Senate for Employment and Social Law tends towards the contractual view,[428] whilst the Civil Senate argues for the tort view.[429] In Greece there have also been decisions classifying *culpa in contrahendo* as tortious in order to enable the court to allow compensation for non-material loss.[430] The dominant force in Greece, however, is provided by the contractual or quasi-contractual classifications. At its heart is a 'special relationship of obligation' which, although not a primary performance obligation, adopts contractual rules.[431] This corresponds closely with the position in Austria[432] and

---

[423] Thus Franzoni, *Fatti illeciti*, Arts. 2043–2059 p. 21, but contrary to most Italian writing. Cf. Vigotti, NGCC 1986, II, p. 175; Bianca, *Diritto Civile*, III p. 163 and Giur.sist.Bigiavi (-Vigotti) I p. 266. By contrast, several first-instance courts have viewed *culpa in contrahendo* as contractual: e.g App. Milano 15.1.1988, *Foro.pad.* 1988, I, 411; and 2.2.1990, Giur.Comm. 1990, II, 767.

[424] Summary by Prata, *Responsabilidade pré-contractual*, pp. 198–214; Prata favours the contractual view.

[425] Cf. nos. 451 (limitation) and 455 with fn. 298 (non-pecuniary damage).

[426] Thus at least RL 17.11.1981, *CJ* VI (1981–5) p. 147.

[427] García Rubio, *La responsabilidad precontractual en el Derecho español*, pp. 94 ff., provides a detailed analysis of the Spanish theory on *culpa in contrahendo*.

[428] TS 2.5.1984, *La Ley* 1984 (3) no. 5473–R p. 628.

[429] E.g TS 16.5.1988, *La Ley* 1988 (3) p. 399: bank employee discussed his transfer to Miami with bank managers and made preparations relying thereon. His wife gave notice to her employer. At the last moment the transfer was cancelled. The employee proceeded successfully against the bank in tort (Art. 1902 Cc) because of the absence of a collateral contract. See García Rubio's analysis, *La Ley* 1989 (4) pp. 1112–1119.

[430] CA Athens 11518/1986, *EllDik* 29 (1988) p. 916: seller of real property concealed defective title from buyer; liability under Art. 198 Greek Cc for reliance loss. Plaintiff also recovered non-pecuniary loss under Art. 932 Greek Cc 'due to the tort nature of precontractual liability'. Amongst commentators, esp. *ErmAK* (-Koumantos), Arts. 197–198 no. 9, favours the view that *culpa in contrahendo* is part of the law of tort.

[431] Assuming no concurrent tortious liability, Art. 932 Greek Cc cannot apply. Thus those who assist in negotiations are liable under Art. 334, rather than 922 Greek Cc: Pouliades, *Culpa in contrahendo*, pp. 193–201; *ErmAK* (-Michealides-Nouaros), Art. 334 no. 12; Stathopoulos, *Geniko Enochiko Dikaio I*, pp. 61, 234; CA Athens 2403/1962, *NoB* 12 (1964) p. 101.

[432] For a summary of dominant opinions in judgments and commentaries: OGH 22.2.1995, *JBl* 1995 pp. 522, 524; Koziol, *JBl* 1994 pp. 209, 211–212; and Koziol/Welser, *Grundriß des bürgerlichen Rechts I*, 9th edn., p. 205. A legal relationship without performance obligations is presumed, with equal practical importance for vicarious liability and for protection against pure economic loss. There is considerable opposition to this view. The tort general clause could be employed to compensate for pure economic loss, but 'continuous squinting at the German BGB has obscured the view' and led to *culpa in contrahendo*'s being developed into an independent cause of action: Rummel (-Reischauer), *ABGB II*, 2nd edn., § 1294 no. 16.

Germany, where *culpa in contrahendo* is said to constitute a concept of statutory liability law, without that resulting in the application of non-contractual liability laws. Rather, *culpa in contrahendo* remains subject to contract law even in the absence of any contract.[433] It remains unclear how the relevant parts of the Unidroit Principles of International Commercial Contracts[434] and the Principles of European Contract Law[435] are to be classified. Both are, after all, devoted to contract rather than tort law.

(b) Liability for Breaches of Protective Duties

Notwithstanding the above, in respect of the present *lex lata* the core area **477** of *culpa in contrahendo* (liability for failure to create a contract) is undoubtedly viewed predominantly as being tort. It is thus hardly surprising that matters which in German law are similarly treated as involving fault during contractual negotiations, namely breaches of protective duties, should be viewed similarly. Only in Germany, Greece, and Austria has this area been affected by *culpa in contrahendo.* Only in these countries can mere contractual negotiations give rise to legal obligations to protect the person and property of each party.[436] The cause of this development, based on vicarious liability for assistants, has been discussed above,[437] as have the grotesque consequences of the shift of tort law issues into contract in Germany.[438] From a common European perspective it must be accepted that the route taken in the 'Linoleum Roll' decision of the *Reichsgericht*[439] was misguided. Elsewhere this area of law is regarded as exclusively[440] belonging to

---

[433] Horn provides an excellent restatement of the current position: *JuS* 1995 pp. 377–387. Also St. Lorenz, *ZEuP* 1994 pp. 218–243; and v. Bar, *JuS* 1982 pp. 637–645.

[434] Bonnell, *International Restatement of Contract Law*, pp. 82–83, 115, and 161 (Art. 2.15 of the Unidroit Principles).

[435] Art. 5301 ('Liability for Negotiations', as yet unpublished) is for the most part co-extensive with Art. 2.15 of the Unidroit Principles. Both provide that a party having no intention to form a contract will be liable for reliance loss resulting from its (continued) negotiations.

[436] Cf. for Germany: no. 190 above; for Austria: nos. 184 and fn. 1082, 464 and fn. 355, and references in OGH 24.4.1991, *JBl* 1991 pp. 586, 587. For Greece: Androulidaki-Dimitriadou, *Ai ypochreosseis synallaktikis pisteos*, pp. 98–99; Barbalias, *NoB* 22 (1974) pp. 733–738; *ErmAK* (-Koumantos), Arts. 187–198, no. 48; Georgiades/Stathopoulos (-Karassis), *Greek Cc*, I Arts. 197–198, no. 4. Also CA Athens 2403/1962, *NoB* 12 (1964) p. 102.

[437] Nos. 184 and 190 above.

[438] No. 450 above. No. 596 for a constitutional law perspective on the German 30–year limitation period. There are no such limitation problems in Greece, as Art. 198 sec. 2 Greek Cc refers expressly to tort limitation law.

[439] RG 7.12.1911 (no. 190 above with fn. 1116).

[440] In Germany, Greece, and Austria fault-related personal injuries occurring in precontractual dealings are clearly the subject of tort law; under concurrence of actions rules, contractual liability may also be possible.

tort,[441] a view which is gaining increasing support in Germany, Greece, and Austria.[442] In Germany, the fact that under §§ 253 and 847 BGB non-pecuniary loss due to personal injuries may only be compensated when resulting from a tort clearly suggests that such protective duties should be treated as law.[443] No recent decisions have based liability for negligently caused personal injury exclusively on *culpa in contrahendo*. Nonetheless, the old cases remain engrained in the psyche of the German lawyer.

(2) Contractual Duties for the Benefit of Third Parties

478   The contract with secondary protective effects for the benefit of third parties is also the creation of German jurists. The doctrine is related to *culpa in contrahendo* in that it was intended to entitle a person with no contractual rights against the defendant to damages on contractual principles. Strictly speaking, liability to a third party under such a contract with secondary protective effects constitutes contractual liability without a contract. The function of such liability is to fill lacunae in the tort system using contractual means.[444] There are, however, numerous significant differences between contracts protecting third parties and *culpa in contra-hendo*. It is immediately apparent that the former has not been provided for in any European code, although many recognize the genuine contract for the benefit of third parties. The concept that a third party may rely upon a contract entered into by other persons for protection of his person and property is a principle developed entirely by the courts; it deos not appear in the statute books. The second difference is that, whereas *culpa in contrahendo* does not require the existence of a contract, there must by definition be a contract for liability to arise regarding the protection of third parties. It remains for the court to assess *in casu* whether the plaintiff is a third party entitled to rely on the contract.[445] Viewed thus,

---

[441] Regarding France, see nos. 475–476 above, from which this necessarily follows, and nos. 361–366 and 468–470 above. Also Cass.civ. 5.6.1991, Bull.civ. 1991, II, no. 176; Cass.civ. 12.2.1964, *D.* 1964 *Jur.* 358; Cass.civ. 18.1.1978, Bull.civ. 1978, I, no. 27; Cass.civ. 7.11.1961, *D.* 1962 *Jur.* 146; Cass.civ. 24.5.1978, Bull.civ. 1978, II, no. 139; Cass.civ. 14.2.1979, Bull.civ. 1979, II, no. 51; and Cass.civ. 28.11.1979, Bull.civ. 1979, II, no. 276. For England, see *Ward* v. *Tesco Stores Ltd.* [1976] 1 WLR 810. For Belgium: Liège 25.3.1992, *RGAR* 1994 no. 12341. For The Netherlands: 's-Hertogenbosch 25.6.1968, *NedJur* 1969 no. 218 p. 534. For Spain: TS 4.11.1991, *RAJ* 1991 no. 8141 p. 11160.

[442] v. Bar, *Verkehrspflichten*, pp. 312 ff.; Pouliades, *Culpa in contrahendo*, pp. 174 ff.; Rummel (-Reischauer) (fn. 432).

[443] Cf. OLG Schleswig 30.1.1992, *NJW-RR* p. 796; OLG Cologne 19.10.1994, *NJW-RR* 1995 p. 861; and BGH 5.7.1994, *NJW* 1994 p, 2617.   [444] v. Bar, *JuS* 1982 pp. 637, 641–642.

[445] German law allows the concept of '*culpa in contrahendo* with protective effects for the benefit of third parties'. Cf. BGH 28.1.1976, *BGHZ* 66 p. 51 = *JZ* 1976 p. 776 with comment by Kreuzer: 14–year-old accompanying mother shopping slipped on vegetables; the child's contract action was successful although brought more than six years later. It is perhaps better to view such cases as examples of *culpa in contrahendo* than as contracts with protective effects for third parties.

contracts with secondary protective effects for third parties are much more like contract law than is *culpa in contrahendo*. It may be for this reason that such contracts are more readily accepted in Europe—as instruments of contract law—than *culpa in contrahendo*. A further difference between the two is that the contract secondarily protecting third parties developed from liability for personal injury and damage to property, rather than for purely economic loss.[446] Only after a lengthy period did such contracts begin, at least in Germany and Austria, to affect the latter area.[447]

The concept of a contract protecting third parties is only realizable **479** under three conditions. First, there must be a law of contract allowing exceptions to the principle of correlative rights and duties (e.g Art. 406 sec. 2 Port Cc). This is absent from the common law, the requirement of consideration preventing any extension of contractual liability beyond the parties.[448] The second prerequisite is a legal order which at least regards the protection of the person and property of the immediate contractual partner as being the object of contract law. A legal system which regards that protection as the exclusive territory of tort, in the absence of a corresponding primary contractual duty, cannot entitle a third party to that contractual protection. For this reason the contract with protective effects for the benefit of third parties is not found in The Netherlands,[449] Spain,[450] or Denmark.[451] It also explains why Greek case-law has not employed the device[452] and why in Portugal it is

---

[446] The view shared by BGH 28.4.1994, *WM* 1994 p. 1724.   [447] Nos. 501 ff. below.

[448] Cf. Steyn LJ, *White* v. *Jones* [1993] 3 WLR 730, 752: 'as the law stands, binding precedent prevents us from adopting a contractual solution. There is either a remedy in tort or there is no remedy.' Also Lord Goff [1995] 1 All ER 691, 708 (HL): the doctrine of consideration prevents the solution of the case by means of a contract with protective effect for third parties.

[449] The NBW (Dutch Cc) has not adopted Art. 1376 sec. 1 BW (old) ('agreements only take effect between the negotiating parties') but it is clear that such a principle is central to the Code (*Parlementaire Geschiedenis* VI p. 916). Thus where in Austria, Germany, or France an action is based on a contract with protective effects for third parties, tort law would be applied in The Netherlands. Cf. HR 7.5. 1976, *NedJur* 1977 no. 63 p. 225; also HR 3.5.1946, *NedJur* 1946 no. 323 p. 420: where third-party interests are affected by a contract, the contractors must take these into account in performance. Failure to do so may give rise to liability for negligence in tort.

[450] The closest Spanish equivalent is found (as in France, cf. nos. 483 ff. below,) in the case-law on tacit assignment of claims. E.g TS 5.5.1961, *RAJ* 1961 no. 2310 p. 1473. The contract with protective effects for third parties is unknown: cf. Cavanillas Múgica/Tapia Fernández, *Concurrrencia de responsabilidad*, pp. 15–17, TS 4.11.1991, *RAJ* 1991 no. 8141 p. 11160; TS (crim.) 5.4.1995, *RAJ* 1995 no. 2882 p. 3846.

[451] Danish law recognizes contracts for the benefit of third parties, but not contracts with protective effects for the benefit of third parties: these are not discussed at all. Cf. Andersen/Madsen/Nørgaard, *Aftaler og mellemmænd*, p. 156–157.

[452] Despite the commentators (e.g Stathopoulos, *Geniko Enochiko Dikaio I*, pp. 89–92 and Lipovats, *NoB* 11 [1963] p. 288) Greek case-law adheres to the view that harm causing reliance loss is to be regarded as tortious rather than contractual. Cf. Areopag 951/1967, *NoB* 16 (1968) p. 279; CA Athens 2688/1969, *Arm*, 24 (1970) p. 313. Also Pouliades, *Culpa in contrahendo*, p. 182 ff.

employed solely to establish lessors' liability to the families of lessees on the basis of presumed fault (Art. 1132 lit. a Port. Cc).[453] Lastly, legal systems which deem it necessary to keep contractual protective duties between contractual partners within restraints may allow recourse to the concept of such contracts, but usually only in cases involving breaches of context-typical obligations. Recent Italian medical negligence developments provide good examples.[454] There are also Belgian judgments in which breach of context-typical obligations is clearly seen to constitute *ipso iure* a *faute* in tort against third parties.[455] Moreover, it is noticeable that French jurisprudence is resiling from *stipulations tacites pour autrui*[456] as readily as it is from contractual *obligations de sécurité*.[457]

480   The third prerequisite for contractual liability in the absence of a contract is that the law of tort be deemed to be deficient. This applies equally to contracts with protective effects for third parties. The tort law must suffer deficiencies which, although not remediable in tort, may be countered in contract. The contract with protective effects for the benefit of third parties is none other than a safety valve for tort; the greater the pressure, the more legal competence is transferred to contract law. Hence the differences between the legal systems which recognize contracts with protective effects for third parties. Thus, in Austria, due to § 1489 ABGB, limitation periods are of no importance; contrarily, in Germany, France, and Italy limitation periods are of considerable importance. In France and Italy questions of liability for assistants are practically never encountered, whereas they have for many years been central to academic debate in Germany and Austria. The same is true of compensation for purely economic loss.[458] Austrian academics emphasize both burden-of-proof issues and the fact that 'enhanced duties of care' flow from certain contracts, such as those between a hotelier and his guests, to the effect that the guest's relatives and visitors should be included within the

---

[453] Thus Mota Pinto, *CJ* X (1985–3) pp. 17, 21–22. No supporting case-law is to be found. However, the concept is not without difficulties, due to Art. 406 sec. 2 Port. Cc.

[454] Cass. 22.11.1993, n. 11503, *NGCC* 1994, I, 690 (comment Zeno-Zencovich): plaintiff injured at birth due to interrupted oxygen supply. The accident occurred in 1971 but the action was commenced in 1978 and so time-barred in tort. In order to benefit from the 10-year contractual limitation period the *Cassazione* based its judgment on a contract with protective effect for the benefit of the plaintiff. These had been introduced to Italian law in App. Roma 30.3.1971, *Foro.pad.*, 1972, I, 552 but had been referred to for some time by first-instance courts.

[455] Cf. Brussels 4.2.1992, *RGAR* 1995 no. 12460 (liability of lift company to users of the lift; *faute*, as it had not fulfilled its duty to the building owner). Similar decisions are found in France (cf. no. 416 above, fn. 11) and Germany. BGH 27.6.1995, *NJW* 1995 pp. 2407, 2408 describes the failure to inform a vasectomy patient of the risks of the operation as a breach of a 'duty arising from the contract of treatment'. In respect of an unintentionally pregnant wife, it was held that where there is a negligent breach of a doctor's duty, there can be 'no reservations about allowing claims for pain and suffering'.   [456] Nos. 468–470 above.

[457] C.f. Cass.civ. 6.7.1994, Bull.civ. 1994, II, no. 182.   [458] Nos. 492 ff. below.

protection afforded.[459] In Germany tenancy agreements protecting third parties lead to no-fault liability of the landlord if the property let was deficient when it became available to the lessee; in Portugal the same circumstances give rise to a rebuttable presumption of fault.[460] The desire to employ contract law to extend the ambit of strict liability claims was the root cause of the development of the French concept of tacitly accepted duties to protect third parties.[461] Today, *gardien* liability being long established, things have moved on. Often, the aim of litigation is to establish the liability of a person without proof of fault in relation to something over which he is not *garde*. The liability of blood-collection centres for Aids-infected blood products is an example.[462] Meanwhile, French law has its hands full ensuring that it does not, by combining contractual third-party protection with *non-cumul*, deny to a deserving third party the benefits of Art. 1384 sec. 1 Cc. In carriage of goods law, for instance, where the *stipulation tacite pour autrui* persists, the unhappy result is that the third party, whose rights originate from the contract between the first and second parties, may, contrary to principle, be better protected than they are.[463] Regarding the law on the carriage of persons, the concept of *stipulation tacite pour autrui* became redundant when Art. 6 of statute Nr. 85–677 of 5.7.1985 came into force.

Cass.civ. 17.1.1995,[464] a peculiar decision whose significance for the entire system cannot yet be properly assessed, broke new ground for two reasons. A four-year-old was injured by improperly constructed play equipment at a private school. The child was successful in its action against the manufacturer, the supplier, and the school. According to the court the school was *'contractuellement tenu d'assurer la sécurité des élèves qui lui sont confiés'*, and was for that reason *'responsable des dommages qui leur sont causés non seulement par sa faute mais encore par le fait des choses qu'il met en oeuvre pour l'exécution de son obligation contractuelle'*. This is no less than contractual *gardien* liability. In addition to the manufacturer, who was liable only as between the defendants, the

---

[459] OGH 5.6.1984, *ÖJZ* 1985 p. 304 (*EvBl* 63).

[460] Mota Pinto (fn. 453). Also OLG Hamburg 17.8.1988, *NJW* 1988 p. 1481 (protection of plaintiff's cohabitee); BGH 7.7.1976, *NJW* 1976 p. 1843; and BGH 22.1.1968, *BGHZ* 49 p. 350.

[461] Cass.civ. 6.12.1932 and 24.5.1933, *DP* 1933, I, 137 (comment Josserand).

[462] Cf. Billiet, *VersRAI* 1994 pp. 42–45. Also Aix-en-Provence 12.7.1993, *D.* 1994 *Jur.* 13.

[463] German case-law has always emphasized that the third party must not be placed in a more advantageous position than the contracting party from whom he derives his rights (BGH 15.6.1971, *BGHZ* 56 pp. 269, 272; BGH 23.6.1965, *LM* § 328 BGB No. 28). French law only applies liability-limiting clauses (Viney, *Sem.Jur.* 1995, I, 3853 no. 1) and forum agreements (Cass.com. 18.10.1994, *Bull.civ.* 1994, II, No. 308) to third parties which have agreed to them. As long as the issue was relevant to passenger transport law, the third party was allowed the choice of proceeding either in contract or under Art. 1384 sec. 1 Cc. Cf. Cass.com. 19.6.1951, *D.* 1951 *Jur.* 717 (comment Ripert).

[464] Cass.civ. 17.1.1995, *D.* 1995 *Jur.* 350 (comment Jourdain); Bull.civ. 1995, I, no. 43.

professional salesman or *vendeur professionnel* was also liable to the child. The seller owes an *obligation de securité* not only to the purchaser but also to the child. That obligation is *extra-contractuelle* but the *Cour de Cassation* did not even attempt an analysis of fault under Art. 1382 Cc. Thus one reaches a second point of overlap with the approaches employed above to solve such problems: the *Cour de Cassation* created an *obligation de sécurité de résultat* in tort.

481   A comprehensive account of the legal systems which recognize contracts protecting third parties (essentially Germany, France, Italy, and Austria) is not possible here.[465] Suffice it to say that the concept varies in importance in those systems. In Italy, the author understands, only contracts between parents and hospitals for medical treatment of children have given rise to third-party protection, in that case for the benefit of the child.[466] In contrast, contracts with protective effects for third parties occupy a remarkably wide area in the case-law of the Austrian OGH;[467] indeed, in personal injury claims it is perhaps used even more frequently than in Germany. In France medical treatment contracts are rarely encountered in this context;[468] instead, the development originated in carriage contracts and cases of *victimes par ricochet*.[469] In Germany it originated in leasehold law, but has gradually been extended to cover sale of goods and services contracts.[470] However, the French functional equivalent of sale of goods contracts having protective effects for third parties, namely assignment in the context of contractual chains,[471] is not recognized in Germany. There are further differences between these four legal systems on the question of who is regarded as a third party within a contract's protection.[472] Clearly, that demarcation is significant in all systems, as it determines the degree to which the boundaries between contract and tort have been blurred.

482   Contracts with protective effects for the benefit of third parties may be

---

[465] Dammann, *Die Einbeziehung Dritter in die Schutzwirkungen eines Vertrages* (1990), provides a detailed comparison of German and French law. Similarly for German and Austrian law: Koziol, *JBl* 1994 pp. 209–223.

[466] Fn. 454 above. In Germany BGH 6.12.1988, *BGHZ* 106 pp. 153, 162 and OLG Oldenburg 27.10.1992, *VersR* 1993 p. 1235 correspond to the rudiments of the Italian position. In contrast, BGH 27.6.1995, *NJW* 1995 pp. 2407, 2408 comes very close to a tort view of contracts with protective effects for third parties. French law assumes a contract between the child and the doctor or hospital in such cases, avoiding problems of third-party protection (Dammann loc. cit. no. 258). Astonishing parallels of legal construction are to be seen in BGH 27.6.1995 and Cass.civ. 17.1.1995 (fn. 464).

[467] Cf. OGH 15.12.1992, *ÖJZ* 1993 p. 422 (*EvBl* 97); OGH 21.12.1992, *ÖJZ* 1993, p. 384 (*EvBl* 91); OGH 5.6.1984, *ÖJZ* 1985 p. 304 (*EvBl* 63); OGH 17.3.1986, *JBl* 1986 p. 381; OGH 23.10.1986, *JBl* 1987 p. 40; and OGH 9.11.1989, *SZ* 62/173 p. 225.   [468] As in fn. 466.

[469] Nos. 447 and 469 above.

[470] E.g BGH 28.4.1991, *WM* 1994 p. 1724; BGH 13.2.1990, *WM* 1990 p. 1208; and BGH 15.5.1959, *NJW* 1959 p. 1676.   [471] See no. 483.

[472] Austrian law is particularly liberal in this respect: OGH 15.12.1992 (fn. 467).

distinguished on four fronts. They differ from genuine contracts for the benefit of third parties in that the third party has no right to enforce primary obligations against the contractor. Outwardly at least, liability under such contracts is distinguishable from French contractual chain-based product liability in that it operates without recourse to the assignment of contractual claims (no. 483 above). By contrast with the case of transferred loss (*Drittschadensliquidation*) it is not the intention here to avoid sale of goods provisions intended to protect the seller from protecting tortfeasors. Thus, again unlike the case of transferred loss, the aim has not been merely to shift the direction of development of an area of liability law which is unproblematic *per se*. Rather, judges have extended liability law beyond the parameters of statutory tort law. The question of whether and under what conditions a person employed by a contractor to perform the latter's contractual obligation may benefit from the protection against liability enjoyed by his employer against the other contractor is not to be confused with the contract with protective effects for third parties.[473] In such cases it may be said that the contract protects the third party: however, the intention is not to provide the third party with an additional cause of action but merely to protect him against liability. Whether, and if so under what circumstances, such protection exists depends on policy considerations and has nothing to do with the issue of whether the third party's liability is in contract or tort.

(3) Protective Duties in Contract Chains

The concept of protective duties in a chain of contracts is also, particularly as regards results, dealt with variously in different European countries in terms of either contract or tort law. At the heart of the matter are rules governing whether the last person to acquire goods (whether movable or immovable) can bring an action not only against the person from whom they were bought but also against the person at the head of the contract chain. This claim can follow contractual principles either where the first sale (or the first contract for work and services) is qualified as a contract intended to benefit all persons in the chain, or where

483

---

[473] On France see no. 439. On Austria: OGH 8.7.1993, *JBl* 1994 p. 44. On The Netherlands: HR 12.1.1979, *NedJur* 1979 no. 362 p. 1138: On Germany, Blaurock, *ZHR* 146 (1982) pp. 238–258. For an English view: *Marc Rich & Co. v. Bishop Rock Marine* [1994] 1 WLR 1971 (CA); [1995] 3 All ER 307 (HL): mechanical problems caused a ship sailing from South America to Europe to interrupt its voyage. After a provisional inspection, an expert surveyor negligently advised that the voyage could safely be continued. The ship was lost soon afterwards. The cargo owner proceeded against the surveyor's employer. The claim was rejected for lack of a duty of care, on policy grounds. The cargo owner had to be content with his (more limited) claims against the ship's owner. To allow otherwise would be to allow circumvention of the Hague-Visby Rules; see no. 293 and fn. 359 above.

it is assumed by implication that each subsequent vendor passes to his purchaser any right of action which the subsequent vendor had against the initial vendor. The actual difference between these two routes is very small. As a rule, the private consumer, i.e. the last person acquiring something, should be better protected than a wholesaler or middleman. In practice the most frequent solution is the assignment option. Eliminated from consideration as third parties, as understood in the term contract with protective effects for the benefit of third parties, are those persons who, when the first contract in the chain was made, could not be determined. Only Austria differs (see no. 485 below).

484   The most important area of application of assignment (if it is used at all) would be in the field of product liability. However, the issue is not restricted to this field. An equivalent concept is found in construction law. Spanish case-law on Art. 1591 of its Cc (liability of the contractor and the architect for buildings with structural defects) accepts that in the sale of a house the corresponding rights of action would be assigned by implication to the subsequent purchaser.[474] He is thus entitled to a claim in contract, and the sole purpose of this operation is to extend to him the ten-year limitation period of Art. 1591 Span. Cc.[475] The Italian equivalent of this rule is found in Art. 1669 Cc, also with a ten-year limitation period. Just as in Spain, the Italian rule extends this benefit to the subsequent purchaser. Italian law states that this is only possible if the rule is regarded as an extra-contractual rule of liability, and that is precisely how it is treated. The notion of assignment is rejected and instead it is said that Art. 1669 Ital. Cc protects not only the purchaser but also the public. The building contractor (and even the head of the building project[476]) has a duty of care towards third parties for ten years according to the statutory duty in tort.[477]

485   As stated above, the 'classic' contract chain is met, not in the transfer of title to real property, but in goods sold on the market, where the chain extends from the manufacturer to the final consumer via wholesaler and retailer. The latter's claims against the manufacturer are viewed almost

---

[474] TS 5.5.1961, *RAJ* 1961 no. 2310 p. 1473; TS 11.10.1974, *RAJ* 1974 no. 3798 p. 2903; TS 17.10.1974, *RAJ* 1074 no. 3896 p. 2976. Cf. Muñoz de Dios, *La Ley* 1990 (1) pp. 1081–1089. It is interesting to compare these cases with BGH 28.4.1994, *WM* 1994 p. 1724. In the latter, the existence of a contract with protective effects for the benefit of third parties was argued but rejected in the light of the special circumstances of the case.

[475] Cavanillas Múgica/Tapia Fernández, *Concurrencia de responsabilidad*, pp. 15–17.

[476] Cass. 27.8.1994, n. 7550, *Giur.it.* 1995, I, 1, 375.

[477] Cass. 27.8.1994 loc. cit. and Cass. 3.2.1969, n. 323, *Resp.Civ. e Prev.* 1969 p. 524; Cass. 11.7.1977, n. 3102, *Rep.Giust.civ.* 1977, *voce* Appalto, 34, 52; and Cass. 11.11.1986, n. 6585, *Foro.it.Mass.* 1986 no. 6585.

everywhere as being in tort.[478] Several European legal systems considered contractual solutions (or solutions very similar to contract) but ultimately rejected them.[479] Only Austria relied on the notion of the contract with protective effects for the benefit of third parties together with the general law of tort.[480] This was because the law on employees' liability was perceived as being too narrow;[481] however, this problem has now been resolved by new legislation on product liability. It is therefore no longer advisable for the injured party to rely on the contract with protective effects for the benefit of third parties because the injured party cannot then prevent the manufacturer from successfully raising as a defence against him the contract with the manufacturer's purchaser.[482] Despite the superficial similarities, one should be wary of equating the traditional position in Austria with that met most often in France—and, under its influence, also in Belgium and Luxembourg, albeit with considerable differences in detail.[483] Only in the 1990s did French product liability law acquire its present form, after much vacillation in a legal system which for a long time seemed only to agree on one point: that a solution had to be found outside the *Code Civil*.[484] The French law is based on three assumptions. The first is that each person who resells[485] an item assigns to the subsequent purchaser the contractual guarantees which he himself had against the person from whom he purchased the

[478] *Donoghue* v. *Stevenson* was also concerned with who was liable in a 'contract chain'; in essence the same question arose: whether the manufacturer owed a duty of care only to his contract partner or also to the purchaser further down the chain. In this context the rules of 46 § of the Swedish Statute on Consumer Protection (*konsumentköplagen*) are of real interest. They allocate to the final consumer under certain restricted circumstances (insolvency, inability to locate the direct contractual partner, or cessation of the latter's trading) a direct right of action against one of the businesses 'higher up' the sales chain. Where damage is caused to the final consumer in respect of goods other than the goods sold, the latter's claim is in the nature of a tort and, to the extent that the rules of the product liability law (in force since 1.1.1993) do not apply, via the SKL to be determined according to the *culpa* rule (Lagrådet, in: *NJA* 1990 *avd.* II pp. 354–361, 356).

[479] Cf. for Portugal Mota Pinto, *CJ* X (1985–3) pp. 17, 21–22; and for Germany the substantial discussion in BGH 26.11.1968, *BGHZ* 51, pp. 91, 93–100.

[480] OGH 4.2.1976, *SZ* 49/14 p. 60.

[481] Koziol, *Österr. Haftpflichtrecht II*, 2nd edn., pp. 90–94.

[482] See also OGH 28.11.1978, *SZ* 51/169 p. 748.

[483] Belgian law recognizes liability for hidden defects (*vices cachés*): Cass. 9.10.1980, *JT* 1981 p. 70, and it is said that the direct contractual claim against the manufacturer is *un accessoire de la chose vendue* (Cass. 5.12.1980, *Pas. belge* 1981, I, 398), and any presumption of *mala fides* against the manufacturer (cf. Art. 1645 Cc) is rebuttable. (Cass. 13.11.1959, *Pas. belge* 1960, I, 313). See Elvinger, *Pas. luxemb.* 28 (1990–1992) pp. 417–486 for the position in Luxembourg.

[484] See esp. Jourdain, *D.* 1992 *Chron.* 149–156; id. *Gaz.Pal.* 1993 *Doctr.* 1171–1176; Arlie, *RJDA* 1993 pp. 409–414; and Wolfer (in German) *PHI* 1991 pp. 220–225.

[485] The fact of the transfer of property is decisive. Where the chain involves contracts for services, the final consumer is left only with a claim in tort. There was a variety of divergent decisions from different senates before the matter was finally resolved by Cass.ass.plén. 12.7.1991, *Sem.Jur.* 1991, II, 21743; cf. Cass.civ. (1ère) 4.11.1992, *Sem.Jur.* 1993, II, 22058.

item: the right to bring an action passes by operation of law with the property in the item.[486] This is how the final consumer acquires rights against the initial manufacturer. The second assumption arises from the principle of *non-cumul des responsabilités*: because the final consumer has a contractual claim, he can only bring that contractual claim; the final consumer's rights are necessarily in contract only.[487] The third assumption is that the manufacturer is strictly liable for product defects. This liability is no longer based on the legal fiction developed from Art. 1645 Cc that a professional purchaser always has knowledge of latent defects in his products;[488] it is now based on the *obligation de securité de résultat* of the manufacturer.[489] This is important because claims need no longer be brought within the *bref délai* prescribed in Art. 1648 Cc, and can now be brought at any time within the usual contract limitation period. The manufacturer is also increasingly prevented from raising defences against the final consumer which arise only from the contract between the manufacturer and the initial (usually professional) purchaser.[490] Despite the assignment, a subsequent vendor who has already assigned the item retains his right to damages for breach of the contract of sale as long as the subsequent vendor has *un intérêt direct et certain*.[491] It is clear that the French *Cour de Cassation* is trying to ensure that French product liability law is consistent with the EU Directive on Product Liability. Given the traditionally contractual approach of French law, it is easy to see why the French government is reluctant to implement the Directive.[492] It is equally clear that the implementation of the Directive would be exceedingly difficult in France, for which reason the European Court of Justice treats the contractual product liability law as a part of tort law for the purposes of the Brussels Convention.[493]

---

[486] Cass.civ. 19.1.1988, Bull.civ. 1988, I, no. 20: '*l'action en garantie des vices cachés se transmet, en principe, avec la chose vendue au sous-acquéreur*'.

[487] Cass.civ. 9.10.1979, Bull.civ. 1979, I, no. 241; Cass.com. 17.5.1982, Bull.civ. 1982, IV, no. 182; Cass.civ. 4.3.1986, Bull.civ. 1986, I, no. 57; Cass.com. 24.11.1987, Bull.civ. 1987, IV, no. 250. If a party suffers injury (e.g a pedestrian hit by a vehicle with a causative manufacturing defect), the claims of the third party arise in tort: Cass.civ. 20.3.1989, *D.* 1989 *Jur.* 381 (note Malaurie); Cass.civ. 17.1.1995 (fn. 464).

[488] Fundamental here is Cass.civ. 19.1.1965, *D.* 1965 *Jur.* 389.

[489] Cass.civ. 27.1.1993, *Sem.Jur.* 1993, IV, 388 = Bull.civ. 1993, I, no. 44. It is not clear whether liability for breach of contract which is still based on the acceptance of an assignment of contractual rights (Arlie, *RJDA* 1993 pp. 409, 412) displaces liability based on a guarantee that against latent defects (*action en garantie pour vices cachés*), neither is it clear whether the latter continues alongside the former. Pointing in the first direction is Cass.civ. 27.1.1993 loc. cit. (the action *obéissait, non aux règles de la garantie, mais à celles de la responsabilité contractuelle'*).

[490] See Jourdain, *Rev.trim.dr.civ.* 1993 pp. 131, 132–134. Cf. fn. 463 above.

[491] This is certainly the case for the *action en garantie des vices cachés*; Cass.civ. 19.1.1988 (fn. 486).   [492] Above, no. 372.

[493] Above, no. 445 and fn. 210.

c. Transferred Loss Between Contract and Tort

It may not be immediately apparent why 'transferred loss' is best under- **486**
stood as a means (for those European legal systems which recognize it)
of expanding tort law by way of contract. Transferred loss cases
involve three parties: a debtor (the 'first party'), a creditor (the 'second
party'), and a loss-suffering 'third party' who is not a party to the
contract between the other two. From the perspective of the second
party, the issue is whether the second party can be the creditor of a
claim for damages for a loss suffered not by himself but by the third
party as a consequence of the first party's breach of duty. Put this way
the issue is general. It is immaterial whether the second party's claim
against the first is in contract or tort, or indeed on some altogether
different basis. The problem is not linked to the source of the injustice
to the second party, but arises from the fact that injustice and damage
burden another party. In such cases the rule is that neither the second
nor the third party has a cause of action against the first party. The
second party has no cause of action because for him the matter is one
of *injuria sine damno* (a legal right has been infringed but there is no
material loss). The third party also has no cause of action because he
has suffered a *damnum sine injuria* (a loss without infringement of his
rights).

The law of transferred loss involves exceptions to the basic principles **487**
of contract and tort set out above. The question is whether the combination of the two principles could unjustly exonerate a debtor who has
clearly caused damage in a blameworthy manner. Where this question is
answered in the affirmative, the construction must meet the following
requirements: the third party's losses are added to the claims of the
second party, and the third party must be able to claim from the second
party his entitlement to sue the first party (or his share of damages
already paid). The result is strikingly similar to the concept applied by
French courts to contract chains.[494]

Few statutory provisions allow loss to be transferred in the way **488**
described above, but such rules are found in both contract and tort.
Examples of the first type are contracts for professional services

---

[494] In the German discussion on product liability the question long remained open
whether the problem could be solved by providing the last vendor in the sales chain
with a right to realize the consumer's loss (see BGH 7.8.1959, *DB* 1959 p. 1083; this line
of reasoning was given up in BGH 10.7.1963, *BGHZ* 40. pp. 91, 99 ff.) The arguments
against the transfer of third-party losses are: first, the loss does not fall on the final
consumer by chance (below at no. 491) and secondly, its impracticality. The final purchaser
would need to sue the vendor for the assignment of the latter's rights of action: i.e. the final
purchaser could not withhold payment until the vendor had transferred to him the vendor's right of action.

(*Geschäftsbesorgungsvertrag*).[495] Examples of the second are statutes enabling the victim of personal injury to sue the tortfeasor for losses incurred by relatives who have visited and cared for the injured person.[496] Where a statute provides the recipient of damaged goods with a direct contractual claim against the carrier,[497] or where relatives of a tort victim can claim damages directly against the tortfeasor in respect of the

---

[495] Cf. esp. Art. 7:419 BW, which goes back to the '*Kribbebijter*' decision HR 11.3.1977, *NedJur* 1977 no. 521 p. 1722 (the debtor is 'obliged in respect of the business purchaser to compensate the damage which his principal suffered on account of the debtor's breach of duty'). Appealing to the German doctrine of transferred loss, Santos Briz, *Responsabilidad civil I*, 6th edn., pp. 327–328, is of the view that Art. 1717 Span. Cc must be construed as entitling a party accepting a commission, and who deals with a third party in its own name, to realize the loss suffered by the commissioning party. Whether this is the view of the Spanish legal system is unclear. Rules like Art. 1183 Port. Cc, Art. 1705 sec. 2 sub-sec. 2, and Art. 1259 Ital. Cc have a provision similar to the German *Drittschadensliquidation* (transferred loss) which enables a third party to enforce the rights of the second party under the contract which the second party entered. A statutory form of transferred loss is found in §§ 701 and 703 BGB.

[496] See the English Administration of Justice Act 1982 sec. 8(1), which expressly obliges the tortfeasor to compensate the injured person in respect of the costs which the latter's relatives incur in respect of 'necessary services . . . rendered to the injured person'. Sec. 8(2) states that the relatives have 'no direct right of action in delict against the responsible person . . . but the injured person shall be under an obligation to account to the relative for any damages recovered from the responsible person under this section'. Sec. 8 applies only in Scotland. The Scottish statutory provision mirrors the permanent practice of many European systems, some of which (e.g. Austria) are based expressly on the notion of transferred loss (v. Bar [-Schilcher/Kleewein], *DeliktsR in Europa, Austria*, p. 44). Moreover, the far-reaching Dutch notion of damage (Art. 6:96 BW) covers some cases of transferred loss. The case of *Hunt* v. *Severs* [1994] 2 All ER 385 (HL) describes the boundaries of transferred loss in English law. The tortfeasor fell in love with his victim, cared for, and later married her. Some time later his wife brought an action against him (in reality his insurers) and claimed the expenses he had incurred in caring for her. This part of the claim was rejected. In Italy Cass. 3.12.1993, n. 11999, *Giust.civ.Mass.* 1993 p. 1715 rejected the claim of an injured party for loss of earnings incurred by his relatives.

[497] The function of such rules in sec. 2(1) Carriage of Goods by Sea Act 1992 (c. 50) is particularly clear. This Act resulted directly from the decision in *Leigh & Sillavan Ltd.* v. *Aliakmon Shipping Co. Ltd.*, '*The Aliakmon*' [1985] QB 350, 359 (Goff LJ); [1986] AC 785, 820 (Lord Brandon). This statute and its history are referred to by Lord Goff in *White* v. *Jones* [1995] 1 All ER 691, 707. Comparable rules are found in Arts. 1689, 1693 Ital. Cc, governing the rights of the recipient against the carrier in respect of loss or damage to the articles carried. These rules are particularly important where someone outside the tripartite contractual relationship damages the goods being carried. Even where the purchaser has not yet acquired property in the goods in accordance with Art. 1523 Ital. Cc, a tort is committed against him: the person causing the accident has frustrated the right of the purchaser against the carrier, which suffices to found liability in tort, here including the purchaser's pure economic loss. According to Art. 1693 Ital. Cc, ownership is irrelevant to the existence of a right of action (Cass. 23.3.1985, n. 2079, *Giust.civ.Mass.* 1985 p. 651, no. 2079). However, neither Italy nor England really recognizes transferred loss; see esp. *Concord Petroleum Corp.* v. *Gosford Marine Panama SA, 'The Albazero'* [1977] AC 774, 846–847. Exceptions to the rule that 'a plaintiff can only recover for his own loss' were highlighted by Lord Browne-Wilkinson in *Linden Gardens Trust Ltd.* v. *Lenesta Sludge Disposals Ltd.* [1994] AC 85, and Steyn LJ in *Darlington Borough Council* v. *Wiltshier Northern Ltd.* [1995] 1 WLR 68, 69.

complete or temporary removal of their 'provider',[498] these rights are only the equivalents of transferred loss, and not transferred loss proper. The characteristic of these last two examples is that a direct action can be brought to achieve what could only otherwise be managed by employing the concept of transferred loss: that is, enabling someone to claim for pure economic loss within a tort system which in principle regards such loss as unrecoverable. A second special feature is also immediately apparent: these are not typical cases of pure economic loss. The carrier's case involves damage to property[499] as well as breach of contract, whilst the case of the provider rendered unable (albeit only temporarily) to provide for his family involves the tort of personal injury or even death. Therefore, only for the third party is the damage always purely economic.

Only in this last scenario does the possibility of transferred loss arise. **489** There is no room for the application of transferred loss where either the third party suffers damage to property (i.e. not pure economic loss) or where the ordinary tort rules allow him to claim for pure economic loss. If the third party is the owner of something damaged by the first party or one of his employees,[500] then the third party is not dependent on the participation of the second party. The same is also true where the third party can for some other reason appeal to tort either directly or, as in the case of assignment, indirectly[501] or where the third party finds himself

---

[498] Such claims were previously (incorrectly) classified as applications of the doctrine of transferred loss: cf. v. Caemmerer, *ZBernJV* 100 (1964) pp. 341, 344.

[499] Who is the owner of goods being carried depends on the law applicable to the transfer of ownership, and above all on the validity and extent of the principle of transfer of possession. Where this does not apply, the purchaser is the owner of the goods from the moment of conclusion of the contract. Consequently, the question of transferred loss does not arise. The buyer can sue and the vendor has no loss. This is the position in e.g. France and Belgium.

[500] See TS 1.2.1994, *RAJ* 1994 no. 854 p. 1112: the plaintiff lent his car to a friend. The friend left the car in the car-park of a hotel from where it was stolen. The hotel had engaged an independent company to watch over the cars in its car-park. The second-instance decision of the *Audiencia Provincial* rejected the plaintiff's claim. The car owner should either have enforced borrowed rights of action in his own name, or assigned them. The *Tribunal Supremo* said that this complicated construction was inappropriate in such a case: the hotel was liable under Art. 1903 Cc (employers' liability) because the personnel employed to watch over the car park were integrated in the hotel staff.

[501] In England there would have been no need for the Carriage of Goods by Sea Act 1992 if Lord Goff's tort-based theory of transferred loss in 'The Aliakmon' had been followed (fn. 497). The study of the relationship between transferred loss and the extent of tort liability in Austrian case-law on claims by those who lease out cars against those who destroy them requires careful attention. Cf. on one hand OGH 27.5.1992, *SZ* 65/83 p. 416, and on the other OGH 17.6.1993, *JBl* 1994 p. 121. Under the heading of transferred loss, OGH 24.3.1994, *ZVR* 1994 p. 224 = *SZ* 67/52 restored to the employer, obliged to continue paying wages to his injured employees, the right to enforce in his own name the employee's action in tort. This was achieved by a judge-made transfer of legal entitlement (cf. OLG Wien 17.5.1993, *ZVR* 1994 p. 146). The Dutch rule in Art. 6.107a BW is unnecessarily complicated: the tortfeasor can escape liability to the injured employee if the latter receives his wages (sec. 1); the employer who continues to pay the employee's wages obtains an independent right of action in tort (sec. 2).

within the protective scope of a contract between the first and second parties.[502] In these instances the third party does not depend on the participation of the second party,[503] but can bring an action directly against the first party. Where the third party has an action 'only' in tort, he cannot revert to a claim in transferred loss simply because his claim is time-barred in tort. If the third party were allowed to claim against the second party by transfer of the latter's extant claim against the first party, this would blur the boundary with contracts having protective effects for the benefit of third parties, as would the use of the claim against the second party to provide the third party with the benefit of no-fault liability or with a more favourable rule on liability for assistants.

490   When is it just, fair, and reasonable to enable a third party to claim compensation for damage which, as far as he is concerned, is pure economic loss? The answer must start from the debtor's point of view, i.e. the point of view of the 'first party'. The sole purpose of transferred loss is to neutralize the legal consequences of shifting risks which have nothing to do with the 'first party'. The concept of transferred loss is intended to prevent someone appealing to rules whose purpose is not to protect that person, but to protect others. On the other hand, transferred loss does not extend liability beyond the level with which the first party would have had to reckon. Where the first party is responsible for a traffic accident as a result of which goods in a transporter are damaged, the tortfeasor is clearly obliged to compensate the damage. If the first party benefits from the fact that the vendor ('second party') still owns the goods, and under the sale of goods law receives payment from the purchaser ('third party') because the goods were carried at the purchaser's risk, that is irrelevant: the rules governing the burden of risk as between vendor and purchaser would unjustly favour the tortfeasor ('first party'); he should not be allowed to say that the vendor had suffered no loss and the purchaser no infringement of his legal rights.[504] It is fairer to grant the purchaser a claim against the

---

[502] As in cases of safe-keeping (*Obhutsfälle*). In such cases (e.g TS 1.2.1994, fn. 500) someone gives goods not belonging to him to another person for safe-keeping. If the latter fails to meet his obligations in respect of the custody his liability to the owner is either in tort or in contract with protective effects for the benefit of third parties (BGH 22.1.1968, *BGHZ* 49 p. 350) and not by way of transferred loss, as was said to be the case according to traditional German doctrine (cf. v. Caemmerer, *ZBernJV* 100 [1964] pp. 341, 365–368). Paras. 701, 703 BGB are also based on this misunderstanding.

[503] The same applies where a purchaser, not yet the owner of the goods, with no express statutory claim (cf. fn. 495) is granted a direct right of action against a carrier. This is said to be the position in Denmark: Cornelius, *Schutz des Forderungsinhabers gegenüber Dritten*, pp. 70–72; Ussing (-Kruse), *Obligationsretten I* 4th edn., p. 446.

[504] It is widely accepted, but by no means certain, that a vendor who receives the sale price from his purchaser suffers no loss if he still owns the goods when they are damaged. Cf. on one hand: BGH 14.7.1972, *VersR* 1972 pp. 1138, 1139; OGH 27.5.1992, *SZ* 65/83 pp.

tortfeasor, namely the owner's claim, by which means the purchaser's loss can be recovered.[505] The purchaser need not pursue the vendor on the assignment of the latter's claim; he can withhold the purchaser's price until the vendor passes to him the vendor's claim against the party who caused the accident.

The decisive factor in cases of transferred loss is that the tortfeasor **491** (first party) who is clearly liable must not benefit from rules which could by pure chance exclude him from liability. The circumstances in which such coincidental shifts of damage occur naturally vary between legal systems and fields of law. Moreover, it often depends on the specific consideration in a given case.[506] Rules on the burden of risk in contracts of sale and in contracts for work and services play as great a part as the rules on the transfer of property in movable objects, whether *inter vivos* or *mortis causa*.[507] Where the liability of the 'first party' is based in contract, and where the case concerns breach of duty, the 'first party' must expect to compensate for pure economic loss, the applicability of transferred loss depends on the rules governing the law of agency. If, despite the fact that the 'second party' acted in his own name, the third party became a direct contract partner then he will be able to bring an action directly against the 'first party'. The 'third party' is only dependent on the 'second party' where the latter is the only carrier of the contractual rights. The classic case (from the perspective of the 'first party' in breach of his own contract) of accidental shifting of loss concerns a person who contracts with another in his own name but on account of a third party (the principal). The rules of transferred loss only come into play when the principal cannot be regarded as a party to the contract between the first and second parties. Finally, the criterion of accidental shifting of loss, which is at the heart of transferred loss,

---

416, 417; Stathopoulos, *Geniko Enochiko Dikaio I*, pp. 85–89; *ErmAK* (-Litzeropoulos) Art. 298 Greek Cc nos. 65–71 (who opines in no. 68 that it is possible to protect third parties directly by Art. 914 in conjunction with Art. 281 Greek Civil Code) and on the other hand: *Obestain Inc. v. National Mineral Development Corp. Ltd., 'The Sanix Ace'* [1987] 1 Lloyd's Rep. 465; *'The Charlotte'* [1908] P. 206, 217; and *Gatewhite Ltd. v. Iberia Líneas Aéreas de España SA* [1990] 1 QB 326, 328. The problem has been analysed more closely by Büdenbender, *Vorteilsausgleichung und Drittschadensliquidation bei obligatorischer Gefahrentlastung* (1995); cf. by the same author *JZ* 1995 pp. 920–928. Observations from the perspective of comparative law are found in v. Schroeter, *Drittschadensliquidation in europäischen Privatrechten* (1995).

[505] Consequently, in calculating loss, reference is had to the third and not to the second party: BGH 14.7.1972, *VersR* 1972 pp. 1138, 1140; cf. OLG München 27.1.1994, *NJW-RR* 1994 pp. 673, 674; and BGH 9.2.1995, *NJW* 1995 pp. 1282, 1283.

[506] See OGH 27.5.1992, *SZ* 65/83 p. 416 (compensation for the cost of car-hire because of damage to a leased vehicle).

[507] In German law the issue of transferred loss arises where a third party destroys an article forming part of an inheritance not yet given to a beneficiary. There have been no decisions directly on this.

distinguishes it from its neighbouring concepts of law. The liability of producers under a chain of sales from producer to consumer is not transferred loss because the producer knows from the outset that his goods will be sold and resold. A complicated area of law which cannot be solved by means of the concept of transferred loss is that involving liability to third parties for defective services: the giving of false information to a person who suffers no loss as a result of that misinformation. Typical examples are probate cases in which a lawyer incorrectly advises, or fails to advise, depriving the person to whom the testator intended to give property. The same problem applies here as so often occurs in transferred loss cases: the person with the right of action suffers no loss, and the person who suffers the loss has no right of action.[508] However, this is not the decisive point. The lawyer knows from the outset that his deficient performance will not affect the testator (or his assets). Depending on the standpoint adopted by a legal system in such cases, they must be dealt with either in tort or by using the special form of contract with protective effects for the benefit of third parties. From the perspective of such contracts with protective effects for the benefit of third parties these cases display atypical features only insofar as they concern, not so much an increase in liability, as a shifting of risk (which was evident from the beginning).[509]

5. OVERLAP BETWEEN CONTRACT AND TORT: LIABILITY FOR PURE ECONOMIC LOSS
SUFFERED BY THIRD PARTIES

492 Other than in the cases of transferred loss considered above, concerned essentially to allow the party who has actually suffered loss a position equal to that of the of the party whose legal right has been breached, all the remaining cases of overlap between liability in contract and in tort concern the situation in which nobody has suffered damage to property or personal injury. The perspective from which the event is observed is irrelevant; the loss will be classified as purely economic. Liability arises from a false declaration ('words') and not dangerous physical activities ('deeds'). Three groups of cases must be distinguished. The first concerns the liability of individuals who have concluded a contract, either with or without the power to act as agent. The second group concerns someone

---

[508] Cf. Sir Donald Nicholls VC in the Court of Appeal in *White v. Jones* [1993] 3 WLR 730, 737: ' . . . if there is no liability the result . . . is striking: the only person who has a valid claim against the solicitor has suffered no loss, and the only person who has suffered a loss has no valid claim.' See also the views of Lord Goff in the same case in the House of Lords [1995] 1 All ER 691, 706. Also BGH 11.1.1977, *NJW* 1977 pp. 2073, 2974.
[509] This is the view of Middleton/Rogge, *VersR* 1994 pp. 1027, 1031–1033.

who, without the involvement of others, seeks or receives commercially important information from another person who is not contractually bound. The final group confronts the problem caused when one party's economic interests are adversely affected by information or another service commissioned, not by that person but by a third party. Negligence is required in all three groups.[510] Where intention is present, an avenue of extra-contractual redress is also available,[511] and where liability is independent of fault, the relevant rules can no longer be understood as rules of tort proper.[512]

a. Liability of Agents and Assistants to the Principal's Contractual Partners

Such strict rules are met only in the liability of the *falsus procurator*. **493** Several European legal systems share the viewpoint adopted in Art. 3.205 of the revised version of the Principles of European Contract Law, that one who concludes a contract in the name of another guarantees his authority to act as agent. Where this authority is lacking then he is liable according to the rules of contract law, whether or not there is fault on his part.[513] Some legal systems have not developed such special provisions within the law of agency. In those systems either *culpa in contrahendo*[514] or the general principles of tortious liability[515] must suffice, so that in practice the agent who operates without authority from the principal is only liable for damages where fault can be shown. These systems do not recognize a specific remedy of performance against an agent without authority.

The liability of the *falsus procurator* is a special case, one of the rare **494**

---

[510] On the other hand, esp. in Greece (Areopag 295/1959, *NoB* 7 [1959] p. 1015) and Germany (see esp. BGH 20.9.1993, *NJW* 1993 pp. 2931, 2934, where this trend is openly admitted) there is a tendency to classify as intentional conduct what in other countries is deemed to be gross negligence. The intention is to enable the application of the *actio de dolo*. For a thorough comparison of German and English law see v. Bar, in: Markesinis (ed.) *The Gradual Convergence*, pp. 98, 102–106.

[511] Cass. 29.3.1952, n. 862, *Foro.it.* 1952, I, 1529; Cass. 20.2.1962, n. 343, *Giust.civ.Mass.* 1962 No. 343: if a contract partner is deceived intentionally by a third party this can lead not only to the contract being held null and void by virtue of Art. 1439 sec. 2 Ital. Cc but also to liability of the third party in tort.

[512] Markesinis/Munday, *Law of Agency*, 3rd edn., pp. 88–89.

[513] This is the position in Germany (§ 179 BGB), England (*Yonge* v. *Toynbee* [1910] 1 KB 215), Greece (Art. 231 Cc), Italy (Art. 1398 Cc), and The Netherlands (Art. 3:70 BW).

[514] This is the position in Portugal: cf. Prata, *Responsabilidade pré-contratual*, pp. 130–138.

[515] As in Belgium (Cornelis, *Responsabilité extra-contractuelle*, p. 439), France (above at no. 409 with fn. 216), and Spain, where it is assumed from Art. 1725 Cc that liability is based upon Art. 1902 Cc (García Rubio, *Responsabilidad precontractual*, pp. 199–204; Albaladejo, *An.Der.Civ.* 11 [1958] pp. 767, 793; and Rivero Hernández, *An.Der.Civ.* 29 [1976] pp. 1047, 1124).

examples where classification affects the basis of liability. Everywhere else, where third parties conclude a contract their personal liability depends on fault. For example, brokers,[516] or people involved in negotiations[517] who in their position of special trust provide incorrect information on the subject matter of the contract or on the element of economic risk inherent in it. Whether use is made of *culpa in contrahendo* or of the law of tort is a matter which affects only the marginal issues of liability, such as the limitation period.

495   Most importantly: persons authorized to contract in the name of their principal can be personally liable[518] where they are responsible for a mistake in the course of contractual negotiations. At the very least, they will always be liable to their principal in contract. Liability to the contract partner can be in either contract or tort. An elegant example is the independent businessman, who sells goods to one private customer, not in his own name but in the name and at the commission of another private customer. Should false information be proferred as to the condition of the item for sale, the purchaser who relies on the expertise of the dealer will attempt to bring an action against him, rather than the unknown vendor. In Germany the plaintiff can sue on the basis of *culpa in contrahendo*,[519] in France on the basis of Art. 1382 Cc,[520] and in England under the rule in *Hedley Byrne*.[521] Despite the different approaches, the results are very similar. So also when the negotiator in the above example is a legal person on whose behalf a managing director is engaged.[522] That the legal person is liable for the negotiator does not exclude the possibility that in some circumstances the director is also personally liable to third parties whilst negotiating

---

[516] See Cass.civ. 16.12.1992, Bull.civ. 1992, I, no. 316 (estate agent liable to the party who commissioned him in contract and to the other side in tort); Dan. HD 21.1.1994, *UfR* 1994 A p. 280; or Swed. HD 27.12.1991, *NDS* 1992 p. 645 (estate agents; incorrect details as to the size of an apartment; liability to the purchaser in tort).

[517] BGH 12.5.1986, *NJW-RR* 1986 pp. 1478, 1479: 'on the quasi-contractual liability extending beyond the protection of property in tort' of a commercial assistant who, in explaining the contents of a company prospectus, gave investors incorrect information, on which they relied, as to the reserves of a coalpit. Cf. BGH 19.12.1977, *BGHZ* 70 p. 337. In contrast, in VLD 17.12.1993, *UfR* 1994 A p. 205 the question of the liability of a lawyer to purchasers of residential properties who relied upon documents prepared by him when acquiring the properties from a liquidator was based in contract.

[518] For the opposite issue, whether the party with whom the agent is contracting on behalf of the principle can be liable to the agent, see the Scottish case of *Weir v. National Westminster Bank PLC SLT* 1994 p. 1251 (1st Div.): a lawyer opened an account on a client's behalf from which a bank employee withdrew money using falsified cheques. The lawyer, the only person entitled to draw on the account in the name of the client, had to compensate for the client's loss. The lawyer brought a successful action in negligence against the bank.   [519] BGH 28.1.1981, *BGHZ* 79 p. 281.

[520] Cass.civ. 5.10.1994, Bull.civ. 1994, I, no. 276.

[521] Cf. *Box v. Midland Bank Ltd.* [1979] 2 Lloyd's Rep. 391; and Chitty (-Reynolds), *Contracts II*, 26th edn., no. 2594.   [522] These were the facts in Cass.civ. (fn. 520).

with the principal's authority. Exactly when the director is liable is analysed in detail below. However, the answer is certainly not dependent on whether the obligation is classified as arising in tort or in contract.[523]

The German courts have long favoured the contractual approach. **496** They turned to a new and radical form of non-tort liability when they set about protecting private investors against incorrect information on tax-favourable capital investments contained in a company prospectus.[524] At the beginning it concerned freelancers who, in order to enjoy tax benefits, bought into limited companies and partnerships which made losses, so that the acquired shares were worthless. The partnership itself was liable in contract for incorrect information, but this was commercially worthless. The same applied to the liability in *culpa in contrahendo* of its agent, a second limited company. If the investor was to have a meaningful cause of action then the managing director of the limited company had to be made personally liable on the ground that he had a personal interest in the outcome of the contract. This is what happened.[525] However, matters did not stop there. What had started as liability of an agent's agent turned into liability of every person responsible for the drafting of a company prospectus.[526] It was no longer necessary that the party liable was either known to the investor or specifically named in the prospectus.[527] When, as a result of a change in tax law, the conditions changed, these principles were applied also to other (and partly new) forms of capital investment outside the stock exchange, namely to company prospectuses offering tax-favourable investment in real property (*Bauherrenmodell*)[528] or advertising shares

---

[523] In most cases liability in this field is based in tort; for the common law countries see *New Zealand Guardian Trust Co. Ltd.* v. *Brooks* [1995] 1 WLR 96. For the Netherlands: HR 10.6.1994, *RvdW* 1994 no. 130; and HR 18.11.1994, *RvdW* 1994 no. 251 = *NedJur* 1995 no. 170 p. 721 (the sole shareholder and managing director of the company commissioned in the name of the company a security firm to undertake work on the former's behalf. The company proved unable to meet its financial responsibilities; managing director held liable under Art. 6:162 BW, because the security firm had been given to believe that its fee would be paid). The position in Germany on the liability of the managing director of a limited liability company, very clearly summed up in BGH 6.6.1994, *DNotZ* 1995 p. 455, is based in *culpa in contrahendo* in cases of pure economic loss (cf. BGH 1.3.1993, *WM* 1993 p. 1882; and Müller, *ZIP* 1993 pp. 1531–1538). Significantly, where the case involves damage to property, the personal liability of the managing director is in tort: BGH 5.12.1989, *BGHZ* 107 p. 297.

[524] E.g. Assman, *Die Prospekthaftung* (1985); v. Bar, *ZGR* 4 (1983) pp. 476–512; Müller-Boruttau, *JA* 1992 pp. 225–234; and Reithmann/Meichssner/v. Heyman (-Thode), *Kauf vom Bauträger* (1992) pp. 435–486. [525] BGH 24.4.1978, *BGHZ* 71 p. 284.

[526] BGH 16.11.1978, *BGHZ* 72 p. 382. [527] BGH 6.10.1980, *BGHZ* 79 p. 337.

[528] BGH 31.5.1990, *BGHZ* 111 p. 314; BGH 26.9.1991, *BGHZ* 115 p. 213; BGH 1.6.1994, *WM* 1994 p. 1371; BGH 1.12.1994, *NJW* 1995 p. 1025. Cf. OLG Kön 23.1.1991, *NJW-RR* 1992 p. 278.

outside the regulated share markets.[529] So a general liability for negligence[530] arose with all the properties of non-contractual liability,[531] but which must not be characterized as such because German tort law does not recognize pure economic loss. It is noteworthy that in Austria liability for incorrect information in a company prospectus has—with recourse to the German position—for many years been based on 'fault in concluding a contract'.[532]

b. Liability for Misinformation Given by One Party Directly to Another

497 Another link in the long chain of examples which illustrate how difficult it has become to distinguish between contractual and non-contractual liability is the law on liability for misinformation. Here too the results govern the classification, in contrast to what pure theory demands. The latter can be seen only in marginal areas,[533] and even then it works more by chance than by intention. Whether the European legal systems are right to continue to organize themselves according to a distinction between contract and tort is an issue to be discussed at some length. The alternative is to organize the material according to the remedies for the claims. How successful such a change of perspective would be is a subject beyond the scope of this book. We must confine ourselves to considering the current position.

498 In the field of liability for misinformation, wherever the laws of contract and tort lie particularly close together, cases are usually characterized by three factors. First, inaccurate information is imparted by a specialist in the course of his profession or business. Because of his specialist knowledge he is regarded as trustworthy in respect of the information.[534]

---

[529] BGH 5.7.1993, *BGHZ* 123 p. 106.
[530] Even the separation of unlawfulness and fault has to all intents and purposes been abandoned, because from the incorrect details of a company prospectus arises 'in the usual case not only a breach of the obligation to provide information correctly but also the fault of the person who is acting' (BGH 24.5.1982, *BGHZ* 84 pp. 141, 148; BGH 28.9.1992, *WM* 1992 p. 1892).
[531] That cases of this kind 'belong' to tort is blindingly obvious outside Germany and Austria (see following fn.) For The Netherlands see HR 2.12.1994, *RvdW* 1994 no. 263; Hof Amsterdam 27.5.1993, *NedJur* 1993 no. 682 p. 2831 (the same case at a lower level).
[532] OGH 12.7.1990, *ÖJZ* 1990 p. 810 (*EvBl* 169).
[533] The consequences for the law governing the limitation of actions resulting from the classification of the particular case (as either tort or contract) are unavoidable. In most cases involving pure economic loss the differences have little effect: cf. *Banque Bruxelles Lambert* v. *Eagle Star* [1995] 2 All ER 769, 838.
[534] When information is provided privately or informally the position is clearly different. The codes then often require intention to harm (cf. § 1300 p. 2 ABGB; §§ 676 and 826 BGB; Art. 729 Greek Cc; and Art. 485 sec. 1 Port. Cc). The relationship 'alters fundamentally where the advice is imparted in a professional capacity' (Kruse, *Erstatningsretten*, 5th edn., p. 104).

Secondly, the person providing the information recognizes or should reasonably have recognized that the recipient would rely on it to make important commercial decisions. Finally, there is direct contact between the parties, even where the provider of the information is under no obligation to provide it.[535] Where all these criteria are met, any information he gives must be correct. This is *iure communi europaeo*, irrespective of how the problem is approached.

The most important example of direct provision of information of the **499** type described is information on creditworthiness provided by banks. X plans to contract with Y but is unsure whether Y can pay for the services X is to render. X approaches Y's bank and asks whether Y is 'good for' such services. If the bank incorrectly answers affirmatively, it is liable for any loss caused to X, namely the unpaid cost of X's sevices.[536] The same applies where a bank pays out on a cheque having been misinformed as to the account limit by the bank drawn upon.[537] Liability for misinformation as to creditworthiness can also be incurred by, for example, lawyers,[538] tax advisers, and business partners of Y, if Y has a particular interest in X and the third party doing business together.[539] Information on creditworthiness is only one example of many. Where a nurse is misinformed as to her pension rights by an insurance company,[540] where misinformation is provided by a pensions insurer ignorant of the legal position,[541] where a party assigns a debt with inaccurate information as to its nature,[542] where an estate agent assures the would-be purchaser that a property is free of encumbrances,[543] where someone wishing to

---

[535] Where the information is the subject matter of a contract, the matter is clearly contractual. Cf. Dan. HD 18.11.1992, *UfR* 1993 A p. 52.

[536] *Hedley Byrne* v. *Heller* (above, no. 285) is the principal common law decision in this field. For Denmark see above no. 247 and fn. 67, and VLD 22.12.1992, *UfR* 1993 A p. 217. For the Netherlands see Rb. Utrecht 21.12.1938, *NedJur* 1939 no. 876 p. 1354; HR 10.12.1993, *RvdW* 1993 No. 248c. For Italy: App. Milano 14.3.1986, Gentile/Guerreri/Guerreri, *La responsabilità, voce Responsabilità civile—Banca*, 136 [113]. For Greece: Areopag 295/1959, *NoB* 7 (1959) p. 1015. For Austria: OGH 29.11.1984, *SZ* 57/184 p. 887. For Germany: BGH 12.2.1979, *NJW* 1979 p. 1595; BGH 28.1.1985, *WM* 1985 p. 381. For an overview of the French case-law see JClCiv (-Grua), Arts. 1382 to 1386, Banquier, Fasc. 335–4 nos. 3–9.

[537] Such cases have been very important in Italy. The leading case is Cass. 10.4.1961, n. 762, *BB* 1961 p. 171 (note Buttaro). A later decision of importance is Cass. 30.10.1963, n. 2909, *BB* 1963 p. 500 (note Bile). Both decisions based liability on Art. 2043 Cc. Cass. 13.1.1993, n. 343, *Resp.Civ. e Prev.* 193 p. 808 confirms this view but also envisages scope for concurrent liability in contract.

[538] E.g. *Dutton* v. *Bognor Regis UDC* [1972] 1 QB 373, 394–395 (*obiter, per* Lord Denning MR); *Midland Bank PLC* v. *Cameron, Thone, Peterkin & Duncans*, SLT 1988 p. 611; Cass.civ. 26.4.1978, Bull.civ. 1978, I, no. 156; liability based on Art. 1382 Fr. Cc).

[539] E.g. BGH 4.3.1987, *BGHZ* 100 p. 117   [540] ØLD 10.10.1994, *UfR* 1995 A p. 84.

[541] Cass.civ. 19.10.1994, Bull.civ. 1994, II, no. 200.

[542] Cf. BGH 25.9.1985, *KTS* 1986 p. 176, on one hand, and BGH 17.10.1989, *WM* 1989 p. 1836 on the other.

[543] HR 4.2.1977, *NedJur* 1977 no. 278 p. 961. Cf. Cass.civ. 16.12.1992, Bull.civ. 1992, I, no. 316.

buy a painting from its present owner is told by an artist that the artist painted it,[544] or where the purchaser of goods or a share interest asks the person previously commissioned by the vendor to value the article or share interest whether he still stands by the valuation[545]—in all these cases the basic structure outlined above applies.

500   In all these cases, information is provided, not as a favour but in connection with the business or profession of the person who imparted it. It is this which gives the information its binding characteristic. Furthermore, it is decisive that the person giving information had special expertise, that he knew or should have known that the party requesting the information would rely on it,[546] and that he could either have refrained from giving the information if the risk of liability attached to the information appeared too great,[547] or expressly denied liability from the outset for reliance on the information provided.[548] Otherwise he voluntarily assumes responsibility and with it liability; he can be held to his word. This leads back to the question of whether such voluntary assumption of liability can amount to a contractual bond, a contract for information, or whether the obligation to furnish accurate information is rooted in a general duty of care in tort. Where there is a long established business relationship between provider and recipient, the relationship itself is more likely to be seen as the source of the duty of care, even if the information is given outside the terms of the contract.[549] Where there was only one transaction between recipient and giver this is usually regarded as insufficient to give rise to contractual

[544] Cass. 4.5.1982, n. 2765, *Giur.it.* 1983, I, 1, 786 (the *'de Chirico'* case, cf. no. 21 above).
[545] *Galoo Ltd.* v. *Bright Grahame Murray* [1995] 1 All ER 16, 36 (Glidewell LJ); BGH 23.1.1985, *JZ* 1985 p. 951.
[546] In the context of this concept of reliance, an important issue much discussed in both Germany (by Canaris, *JZ* 1995 pp. 441–446) and England (e.g. *Gran Gelato Ltd.* v. *Richcliff Group Ltd.* [1992] 1 All ER 865) is whether a person owes a duty of care to a third party because he is contractually bound to safeguard the interests of his client.
[547] HR 10.12.1993, *RvdW* 1993 no. 248c rightly emphasizes that a bank must not embellish the financial position of one of its customers even where it might be in the latter's interest to do so; the bank must remain silent. Cf. *Hedley Byrne* v. *Heller* [1964] AC 465, 486 (*per* Lord Reid).
[548] The relationship between exclusion clauses and liability for misinformation remains cloudy. Although it is clear that where liability is expressly excluded ('without any obligation on our behalf' or similar term) there is no reliance meriting protection (cf. *Hedley Byrne* v. *Heller* p. 504), then two aspects are often separated. See OGH 22.11.1984, *SZ* 57/184; OGH 11.6.1992, *JBl* 1993 p. 397.
[549] This is the position in Austrian case-law with respect to § 1300 sentence 1 ABGB: cf. fn. 548 and OGH 11.7.1990, *JBl* 1991 p. 249. BGH 4.3.1987 (fn. 539) even accepts that where a customer asks a bank to recommend investments, this suffices to create a contract for the provision of advice. The contract arises when the talks occur. Cf. *Banque Bruxelles Lambert* v. *Eagle Star* (fn. 533) where it remained undecided whether liability was in contract or tort. Art. 485 sec. 2 Port. Cc recognizes liability in tort where the provider of information was legally obliged (cf. RL 22.5.1992, *CJ* XVII [1992–3] p. 188) to provide information.

duties of care;[550] almost everywhere in Europe, such liability is based in tort. Again, Germany is the exception. The *Reichsgericht* decided very early that if someone with a recognizable desire for reliable information contacted a person with the expertise to provide that information, then the imparting of the requested information gave rise to a contract. This 'contract' suffices to render the specialist liable if the information provided is inaccurate. Liability does not depend upon consideration for the information, but is based on the qualifications of the expert, on the non-expert's reliance, and on the fact that the expert should have recognized that the information would be used for a commercial transaction.[551] The BGH followed this and stated expressly that it was irrelevant whether the parties actually intended to enter into a contract.[552] This construction is rather daring; it is scarcely encountered in other countries.[553] The weighty criticism in German literature[554] on this subject should not disguise the fact that only the classification of the basis of this liability, not the subject matter itself, is problematic. Elsewhere in Europe the idea of voluntary assumption of responsibility based upon professional expertise and reliance is commonplace, and where the courts clothe this idea in a mantle of tort,[555] or apply *culpa in contrahendo*,[556]

---

[550] Interesting non-German analyses of the German position are from Italy: Busnelli, *Saggi* 1990 pp. 539–541; Castronovo, *FS Mengoni I*, pp. 147–240 (calling at pp. 179 and 209 for pure economic loss to be treated as the preserve of contract law), from Portugal: Sinde Monteiro, *Responsabilidade por conselhos*, pp. 59–71, from Austria: Welser, *Haftung für Rat, Auskunft und Gutachten*, pp. 63–67, and from England: Markesinis, *German Law of Torts*, 3rd edn., pp. 285–293. Apart from the decisions cited in fn. 553 no other European courts accept the German course.

[551] RG 27.10.1902, *RGZ* 52 pp. 365, 366–367.

[552] Fundamental here is the case BGH 29.10.1952, *BGHZ* 7 pp. 371, 375. An overview of the entire BGH case-law on contracts for information is found in BGH 13.2.1992, *VersR* 1992 pp. 964–965 and BGH 19.3.1992, *VersR* 1992 p. 966.

[553] OGH 17.11.1970, *SZ* 43/209 p. 727 creates an exception for Austria; in Sweden HD 14.7.1980 *NJA* 1980: 76 p. 383 appears very close to the German solution.

[554] For recent literature see Strauch, *JuS* 1992 pp. 897–202; Altenberger, *WM* 1994 pp. 1597–1611.

[555] Cf. the references in fns. 536 ff. and for Italy: Giur.sist. Bigiavi IV (-Maganza) pp. 89–91 and Cendon (-Gaudino) IV, Art. 2043, no. 27, p. 2022. For the Netherlands: HR 28.11.1947, *NedJur* 1948 no. 135 p. 241. Art. 485 sec. 2 Port. Cc states expressly in a rule of tort that an obligation to pay damages arises 'if liability for the damage was undertaken': cf. esp. RL 22.5.1992, *CJ* XVII (1992–3) p. 188. Just as it is irrelevant whether such assumption of responsibility is given effect by tort or by contract, so also in all legal systems, where the party providing information neither knew nor should have known that the eventual recipient would rely upon his information, then he is not liable. See Dan. HD 19.8.1994, *UfR* 1994 A p. 818; *Morgan Crucible Co. PLC* v. *Hill Samuel Bank Ltd.* [1991] 1 All ER 148, 158.

[556] In cases involving liability for misinformation it is immaterial whether priority is given to *culpa in contrahendo* or to contracts for the provision of correct information; this is shown by comments in OGH 22.2.1995, *JBl* 1995 pp. 522, 524 according to which 'the legal concept of *culpa in contrahendo* and positive breach of contract, liability for prospectuses, contracts with protective effects for the benefit of third parties, and liability for the mere initiation of business contacts (are located) in the border zone between tort and the breach of a pre-existing obligation (i.e. contract)'; all these result in liability for pure economic loss.

the opposite criticism is made: that the limits of contract law have been overridden by the law of tort.[557] This argument will probably continue until someone accepts that it is not the parties who create law by concluding a contract, but the law which allows the parties to form a binding relationship. In other words, what we call a contractual relationship is no more than a type of relationship of proximity, which will always give rise to duties of care. A contract is only one of many important relationships of proximity, so there is no fundamental difference between the concepts of contract and of tort. It is already clear that each person who asks whether the classic *Hedley Byrne* situation[558] suffices to create a contract as understood by the principles of contract law must accept that the question may be answered both positively and negatively.[559]

c. Liability of Professionals To Third Parties to a Contract

501   The last group of cases also concerns liability for sub-standard services which cause pure economic loss. These cases involve: inaccurate balance sheets and valuations prepared by experts; mistakes in cheque payments or money transfers; sub-standard performance by lawyers drafting contracts and wills; and employment references which portray an employee in an unduly favourable light, to the detriment of the new employer. In contrast to the situations described above at nos. 497 ff., in those listed here there is no direct contact between the provider and the victim. The vendor commissions and pays for the expert opinion or balance sheet. The victim neither commissioned the opinion nor asked the expert whether he still stands by his opinion. The bank customer suffers loss, not because of a mistake by his own bank, but because of the oversight of the transfer or debit department of the intervening bank. The new employer may know the former employer only by name. Until the inheritance comes to light the disappointed beneficiary may not even have known that the testator sought legal advice. However few scruples one might have in confirming a contract which ousts the law of tort, even German law can do little other than admit that the injured party is a 'third party' to the contract.

502   The mere fact that some of these cases have been dealt with in specific

---

[557] For discussion in England see v. Bar in: Markesinis (ed.), *The Gradual Convergence*, pp. 98, 111–113; Lorenz/Markesinis, 56 (1993) *Mod.L.Rev.* 558, 561–563. For Italy: references above in fn. 550, and Franzoni, *Fatti illeciti*, pp. 241–247.   [558] Above, no. 285.
[559] The Principles say in Art. 2.101 (1): 'a contract is concluded if (a) the parties intend to be legally bound and (b) they agree on terms which are sufficiently definite—without any further requirement.' Art. 2.108 states that 'a promise which is intended to be legally binding without acceptance is binding'. The 'voluntary assumption of responsibility' under the rule in *Hedley Byrne* is barely distinguishable from this 'intention to be legally bound'.

statutes[560] does not, of course, justify placing them in a group of their own. It makes no practical difference whether the basis of liability is deemed to be a 'contract' for information, or a contract with protective effects for the benefit of third parties (the BGH even recognizes the contract for correct information with protective effects for the benefit of third parties[561]) and it is equally evident that in cases with a tripartite relationship, contract law is only relied upon when tort law cannot avail.[562] It is also true that in most cases the criteria for liability are the same on both sides of the contract–tort divide: professional expertise, reliance, and voluntary assumption of responsibility. These factors have nothing to do with whether liability is regarded as non-contractual[563]

---

[560] Art. 705 Span. Cc (considered above at no. 2 and fn. 9) governs the liability of a notary if a will is declared void due to mistakes in its preparation. Liability to the would-be beneficiaries requires fault. In Germany liability of the *Notar* for improperly drafted wills is subject to special rules. Cf. BGH 19.5.1958, *BGHZ* 27 p. 274; BGH 28.9.1959, *BGHZ* 31 p. 5; and BGH 2.5.1972, *BGHZ* 58 p. 343. Because a provision of non-contractual liability law in § 839 BGB applies to notaries, there is no need to rely on the contractual constructions of liability developed in respect of lawyers. A statutory rule governing the liability to a new employer for incorrect references is found in Art. 7A: 1638aa sec. 3 BW. Liability depends on the old employer recommending the employee 'against his better knowledge'. Intention is assumed by Rb Utrecht 11.2.1920, *NedJur* 1920 pp. 861, 862 where the reference is objectively incorrect. France has special rules on the liability of auctioneers and experts for incorrect catalogue details; see the decree of 21.11.1956 (text in *D.* 1956 *Légis.* 487). See also Cass.civ. 23.4.1969, *D.* 1969 *Jur.* 493; Cass.civ. 23.2.1970, *D.* 1970 *Jur.* 604. Finally, there are statutory rules on the liability of accountants. § 323 German HGB is interpreted to exclude third-party liability for those carrying out statutory audits. In contrast, Art. 1 of the Decree of the President of the Italian Republic No. 136 of 31.3.1975 (Gaz.Uff. 7.5.1975 no. 119) envisages liability in tort to third parties (Trib. Turin 5.3.1993, *Le società* 1994 p. 87 with comment by di Majo loc. cit.; Pfeifer, *Jahrbuch für italienisches Recht* 8 [1995] pp. 203–209; and Trib. Mailand 18.6.1992, *Giur.it.* 1993, I, 2, 1). The position is similar in France under Art. 234 of Statute No. 66–537 of 24.7.1966 on trading companies; the text is in *Gaz.Pal.* 1966 *Légis.* 72. According to the statute, the *commissaires aux comptes* (auditors) are liable in negligence to third parties; cf. Cass.com. 2.7.1973, *D.* 1973 *Jur.* 674.

[561] BGH 23.1.1985, *JZ* 1985 p. 951; cf. BGH 28.4.1982, *NJW* 1982 p. 2431.

[562] Exceptions to this rule are readily encountered in France. See Paris 18.6.1957, *JCP* 1957, II, 10134: liability in contract of expert to purchaser, based on a *stipulation tacite pour autrui*, where the expert commissioned by the vendor gave an opinion on a stamp. This approach has since given way to a solution based in tort (Viney, *Sem.Jur.* 1992, I, 3625 no. 11).

[563] This is the predominant view. See no. 287 above for the common law; for Scotland see *Leeds Permanent Building Society* v. *Walker Fraser & Steele*, SLT 1995 p. 72; for France *JClCiv* (-Poulpiquet), Arts. 1382 to 1386, *Notaire, Responsabilité civile*. Fasc. 420–5 no. 40–47 (concerning the liability of notaries to third parties). For The Netherlands: HR 18.12.1993, *NedJur* 1994 no. 91 p. 312 (liability of notaries to third parties). For Italy: Cass. 16.2.1957, n. 553; Cass. 24.5.1960, n. 1327; and Cass. 25.10.1972, n. 3255, all in Gentile/Guerreri/Guerreri, *La responsabilità, voce Responsabilità civile—Notaio* 107 [1], 107 [6] and 107 [37] respectively. For Denmark: HD 13.12.1989, *UfR* 1990 A p. 164.

or arises under a contract[564] with protective effects for the benefit of third parties.[565]

503   The real difficulty with cases of professional liability[566] for pure economic loss lies in identifying the criteria which determine, not only who has a cause of action arising from an intentional act, but more problematically: who can claim where the defendant acted only negligently. Where the information is conveyed directly there will always be sufficient proximity between the parties. But when is a person entitled to rely upon services which he did not ensure were correctly rendered? Although this question has not yet been fully answered in Europe, it now seems possible to generalize as follows: for expert opinions which over-value an object, the expert will only be liable if he knew or should have known that his opinion would be communicated to a purchaser whose decision to buy would be affected by that valuation. There is no liability in negligence where an expert could not have known that the party commissioning his opinion was also acting in the interest of a third party.[567] Otherwise, whether the expert knows the third party by name is irrelevant. Normally, an expert must bear in mind that whoever commissioned his opinion is interested, not only in his conclusion, but also whether it will induce a third party to enter into a commercial transaction.[568] That the vendor deliberately fails to inform the expert of factors which reduce the value of the object does not exonerate the expert.[569] The only exception is if the expert states expressly that his report was made in reliance on the vendor's statements or where it is otherwise

[564] Whether Swed. HD 14.10.1987, *NJA* 1987: 117 p. 692 (liability of property valuer to finance company) is to be classed as a tort or a contract case is not readily apparent; the issue appears to be meaningless: cf. Hellner, *Speciell avtalsrätt II (2)* 2nd edn., p. 193. This is one of the cases where the highest court in the land has expressly exceeded Chap. 2 § 4 SKL (above, no. 245).

[565] Courts in both Germany (see fns. 567 ff.) and Austria (OGH 19.2.1992, *JBl* 1992 p. 713; OGH 11.7.1990, *JBl* 1991 p. 249) tend in this direction.

[566] The closely related law on liability of supervisory authorities has its own rules: e.g. Cass.sez.unite 14.1.1992, n. 367, *Foro.it.* 1992, I, 1421: no liability of the stock-exchange supervisory authority for incorrect details in a company prospectus. For Art. 2043 Ital. Cc the infringement of a legitimate interest is sufficient but the supervisory function is not intended to protect individual investors.

[567] OGH 23.4.1992, *VersR* 1993 p. 863; Dan. HD 21.1.1994, *UfR* 1994 A p. 280: incorrect valuation by an estate agent; liability rejected because in the circumstances of the case he correctly assumed that his estimate would not form the basis of a sale. Cf. OLG Saarbrücken 12.7.1978, *BB* 1978 p. 1435: no liability where the expert stipulated that the information should not be passed to third parties without his express prior consent.

[568] *Smith* v. *Carter SLT* 1995 p. 295 (Outer House, Lord McCluskey); Swed. HD 14.10.1987 (fn. 565); BGH 26.11.1986, *NJW* 1987 p. 1758, 1760. Perhaps more narrow is *Galoo Ltd.* v. *Bright Grahame Murray* [1995] 1 All ER 16, 44 (Evans LJ): it depends whether 'the statement is made to an identifiable person and the maker not only knows that it will or is likely to be acted upon but also intended that it should be acted upon for a particular purpose.'

[569] BGH 10.11.1994, *JZ* 1995 p. 306.

clear that the commission was limited in extent.[570] A person who professionally undertakes to evaluate a property must also consider that his opinion may be used as a basis for granting credit. He is therefore liable for his mistakes to the provider of credit,[571] and often also to those who offer their guarantee or property to secure the credit.[572]

Where the owner of a business commissions an expert opinion on the **504** fiscal consequences of the transfer of company shares to his son, then the tax adviser is also liable to the son for mistakes in the opinion.[573] The advisor's risk in such cases is clear. For those who prepare company accounts it is suggested that a distinction must be made between a statutory and a non-statutory audit. Whether the accounts produced for a statutory audit protect third parties (usually those acquiring company shares) is much debated.[574] In statutory audits the official certificate often states explicitly that the accountant has restricted himself to an evaluation of the papers made available to him. He is not responsible for the accuracy of the papers. As for non-statutory audits commissioned by the owner of the company in order to obtain credit or sell the company, there is sufficient proximity to the third party where the person who commissioned is informed of the purposes to which they will be put. For that reason an employer is also liable to a subsequent employer where the first employer recommends an employee who embezzles money from the new employer as he had done from the first. According to the BGH the original employer has a duty to inform the new employer as soon as he is aware of the employee's dishonesty.[575]

A dealer who, by exercising care, would have recognized that a **505** cheque card presented by a customer was stolen is liable to the card owner both in contract and tort under Italian law.[576] It is accepted in Austria[577] and Germany[578] that in money transfers the intervening banks are liable to bank customers for breaches of their duties of care. In this way professional liability to third parties has been opened up as a new field of application, because in this field—very similar to liability for company prospectuses—the protection of genuine reliance interests no

---

[570] OLG Hamm 2.7.1992, *NJW-RR* 1993 p. 1497.

[571] Swed. HD 14.10.1987 (fn. 565); BGH 26.11.1986 (fn. 568); BGH 23.1.1985, *JZ* 1985 p. 951; BGH 18.10.1988, *WM* 1989 p. 375.   [572] BGH 21.1.1993, *WM* 1993 p. 897.

[573] Thus the decision in OLG Munich 1.6.1990, *NJW-RR* p. 1127.

[574] This point of view is rejected by German (§ 323 HGB, above at fn. 560) and English law (*Caparo Industries PLC* v. *Dickman* [1990] 2 AC 605; more generous are the Italian (Art. 12 of the presidential decree referred to at fn. 560 and in respect of this Trib. Milano 18.6.1992, *Giur.it.* 1993, I, 2, 1 with observation by Montalenti) and French positions (*JClCiv* [-Lemaignan/Moreau], Arts. 1382 to 1386, *Responsabilité civile, Expert-comptable*, Fasc. 376, no. 51–53).   [575] BGH 15.5.1979, *BGHZ* 74 p. 281.

[576] Trib. Milano 24.2.1994, *NGCC* 1995, I, 179.   [577] OGH 19.2.1992, *JBl* 1992 p. 713.

[578] OLG Frankfurt 31.1.1995, *WM* 1995 p. 1179; OLG Düsseldorf 11.2.1982, *WM* 1982 p. 575.

longer depends on the personal integrity of an individual.[579] Neither is professional liability solely a matter of liability for incorrect information or other positive act: it can arise from a mere omission. A dramatic 1977 BGH decision illustrates just how empty the concept of the contract with protective effects for the benefit of third parties can be.

The case concerned a direct-debit procedure (*Lastschriftverfahren*). A vendor received from the purchaser the right to deduct sums directly from the purchaser's bank account. Several deliveries were not paid for because the purchaser's bank failed to inform the vendor's bank that no funds remained in the purchaser's account. The obligation to pass on such information arose from a contract between the banks which expressly provided that third parties could not derive any rights from the contract. The BGH nevertheless found that the vendor was protected by the particular contract. Moreover, the *Senat* added that the protective duty of the purchaser's bank was not based on the internal contract between the banks: the duty 'would have existed even if there were no contract between the banks'.[580]

506   There is a group of cases concerning lawyers and notaries[581] sued by third parties for breach of a duty of care towards them. A lawyer who attends during contractual negotiations between his client and a third party is under a duty not to provide the third party with inaccurate information.[582] Liability to third parties may also be incurred where a lawyer advises a testator incorrrectly,[583] omits to take the necessary formal steps in probate,[584] or fails to keep an appointment to prepare a will.[585] In such cases the law has gone so far as to grant a right of action to persons who have thereby lost an inheritance, the quantum of the claim being the value which they would have inherited had the lawyer correctly fulfilled his obligations.[586] The criterion of reliance has been

---

[579] BGH 28.2.1977, BGHZ 69 pp. 82, 88.   [580] Ibid. 89.

[581] In most countries little turns on the distinction; it is important in Germany only because of § 839 BGB (fn. 560 above).

[582] See references in fn. 563; also HR 2.4.1982, *NedJur* 1983 no. 367 p. 1145: liability of a lawyer in tort to a sub-lessee because the contract between the head landlord and tenant, drafted by the tenant's lawyer, was invalid. A different decision was reached in *Hemmens* v. *Wilson Browne* [1993] 4 All ER 826, with the reasoning that the invalid promises of an *inter vivos* donor could be repeated because he was still alive; this decision is doubtful.

[583] BGH 13.6.1995, *VersR* 1995 p. 1096; BGH 11.1.1977, *NJW* 1977 p. 2073 (failure to draw up a separation agreement which was relevant to the inheritance; liability to the son); Cass.civ. 14.1.1981, *Sem.Jur.* 1982, II, 9782; Cass.civ. 23.11.1977, *Sem.Jur.* 1977, II, 21943; *Ross* v. *Caunters* [1979] 3 All ER 580 (Ch. D.)   [584] Dan. HD 13.12.1989, *UfR* 1990 A p. 164.

[585] Hof Amsterdam 19.1.1984, *NedJur* 1985 no. 740 p. 2432; *White* v. *Jones* [1995] 2 WLR 187 (cf. above, no. 287); BGH 6.7.1976, *NJW* 1965 p. 1955. Decided differently is *Weir* v. *J. M. Hodge & Son* 1990 SLT 266 (Outer House, Lord Weir); cf. critical comment by Norrie, *Jurid.Rev.* 1990 pp. 107–110. For a critical analysis of *White* v. *Jones* from a Scottish perspective see Blaikie, *SLT* 1993 pp. 329–333.

[586] Rb. Leuven 5.10.1994, *RW* 1994–95 p. 1061 (commentary by Hens).

done away with in cases of this sort. Whether the third party knew that a lawyer had been consulted is immaterial to the lawyer's liability. It suffices that the lawyer knew he was instructed to protect the interests of intended beneficiaries.

II. TORT: UNAUTHORIZED CONDUCT OF ANOTHER'S AFFAIRS AND UNJUST ENRICHMENT

Bibliography: Álvarez-Caperochipi, *El enriquecimiento sin causa*, 3rd edn. (Granada 1993); Bengtsson, 'Svensk rättspraxis: Skadestånd utom kontraktsförhållanden 1976–1979', *SJT* 1981 pp. 519–537; Bianchini, 'Die Generalklausel der ungerechtfertigten Bereicherung im italienischen Recht', *Jahrb. f. ital.R.* 7 (1994) pp. 197–211; Birks, 'Restitution for Wrongs', in: Schrage (ed.), *Unjust Enrichment: The Comparative Legal History of the Law of Restitution* (Berlin 1995) pp. 171–195; id., *An Introduction to the Law of Restitution* (Oxford 1990); Blackie, 'Enrichment and Wrongs in Scots Law', *Acta Juridica* 1992 pp. 23–47; Clark, *Contract Law in Ireland*, 3rd edn. (London 1992); Cooke, 'Trespass, Mesne Profits and Restitution', 110 (1994) *LQR* 420–430; Cullen, 'The Liability of the Good Samaritan', *Jurid.Rev.* 1995 pp. 20–27; Dornwald, 'Ersatzansprüche des Helfers bei Verkehrsunfällen und Pannen', *DAR* 1992 pp. 54–56; Gallo, 'Remedies for Unjust Enrichment in the History of Italian Law and in the Codice Civile', in: Schrage (ed.), *Unjust Enrichment: The Comparative Legal History of the Law of Restitution* (Berlin 1995) pp. 275–288; id., 'Unjust Enrichment: A Comparative Analysis', *AmJCompL* 40 (1992) pp. 431–465; Gething, 'The Action in Unjust Enrichment to Recover the Proceeds of a Tort', 3 (1995) *Tort Law Review* 123–142; Goff/Jones, *The Law of Restitution*, 3rd edn. (London 1986); Gomard, 'Erstatningsansvar for miljøskader forårsaget af nedgravet kemikalieaffald', *UfR* 1978 B pp. 53–71; Habermeier, 'Schadensersatzanspruch und Eingriffskondition bei Berechtigung mehrerer am Gegenstand des Eingriffs', *AcP* 193 (1993) pp. 364–389; Hakulinen, 'Zur ungerechtfertigten Bereicherung im finnischen Recht', in: *FS Dölle*, vol. i (Tübingen 1963) pp. 401–413; Hellmann, *Die Anwendbarkeit der zivilrechtlichen Rechtfertigungsgründe im Strafrecht* (Cologne et al. 1986); Jackman, 'Restitution for Wrongs', (1989) 48 *CLJ* 302–321; *JClCiv* (-Bonet), id. 'Quasi-contrats. Enrichissement sans cause', *App.* arts. 1370 to 1381; Jones, 'Remoteness and Rescues', 45 (1982) *Mod.L.Rev.* 342–345; Kallimopoulos, *I mi gisia dioikisi allotrion* (Athens 1978); Kupisch, *Ungerechtfertigte Bereicherung.*

Geschichtliche Entwicklungen (Heidelberg 1987); Lejman, *Obehörig vinst och värdeersättning* (Stockholm 1982); Werner Lorenz, 'A Civil Lawyer looks at some recent Developments of the English Law of Restitution', in: *Studi in memoria di Gino Gorla*, vol. ii (Milan 1994) pp. 1051–1064; MacQueen/Sellar, 'Unjust Enrichment in Scots Law', in: Schrage (ed.), *Unjust Enrichment: The Comparative Legal History of the Law of Restitution* (Berlin 1995) pp. 289–321; Minoggio, 'Die Anwendung der Rettungs-klausel gemäß § 63 VVG in der Fahrzeugteil- und Voll(kasko)versicher-ung', *DAR* 1989 pp. 288–291; Oberhofer, 'Die Risikohaftung wegen Tätigkeit in fremdem Interesse als allgemeines Haftungsprinzip', *JBl* 1995 pp. 217–227; Oppermann, 'Konstruktion und Rechtspraxis der Geschäftsführung ohne Auftrag', *AcP* 193 (1993) pp. 497–528; Pagh, 'Selvhjælpshandlinger og erstatningsansvar for miljøskader', *UfR* 1990 B pp. 393–400; Reichard, 'Negotium alienum und ungerechtfertigte Bereicherung', *AcP* 193 (1993) pp. 567–602; Roos, 'För mycket obehörig vinst', *JFT* 1992 pp. 75–97; Schildt, 'Konkurrenzprobleme im Bereicher-ungsrecht', *JuS* 1995 pp. 953–959; Schluep, 'Über Eingriffskonditionen', in: *Mélanges Piotet* (Berne 1990) pp. 173–213; Stathopoulos, *Axiosis adi-kaiologitou ploutismou* (Athens 1972); Steffen, 'Persönlichkeitsschutz und Pressefreiheit sind keine Gegensätze', Interview, *ZRP* 1994 pp. 196–198; Stoljar, 'Restitution: Unjust enrichment and *negotiorum gestio*', *IntEnc-CompL* X 17 (Tübingen *et al.* 1984); Tettenborn, 'Damages in Conversion: The exception or the anomaly?', (1993) 52 *CLJ* 128–147; Vaz Serra, 'Enri-quecimento sem causa', *BolMinJust* 81 (1958) pp. 5–245, 82 (1959) pp. 5–287; Wacke, 'Vorzüge und Nachteile des deutschen Bereicherungsrechts', in: Beiträge zum deutschen und israelischen Privatrecht (ed.) *der Gesellschaft zur Förderung der wissenschaftlichen Zusammenarbeit mit der Universität Tel Aviv* (Cologne 1977) pp. 131–153; Whitty, 'Die Reform des schottischen Bereicherungsrechts', *ZEuP* 1995 pp. 216–241; Wilburg, 'Die "Subsidiarität" des Verwendungsanspruches', *JBl* 1992 pp. 545–557.

507   German tort law is particularly narrow. The English common law of tort is very much the opposite. Other legal systems are situated at various points between the two extremes. This description applies not only to the relationship between tort and contract: the same can be said of the boundaries between tort and neighbouring disciplines, particu-larly *negotiorum gestio* (the unauthorized conduct of another's affairs) and unjust enrichment. According to English common law, 'no special institution called *negotiorum gestio* officially exists',[587] and much of the material which in Germany and elsewhere falls under the law of unjust enrichment is covered by tort.[588] Three issues call for discussion: what type of cases are covered by these overlapping areas; how do they affect

---

[587] Stoljar, *IntEncCompL* vol. x pp. 17–54.   [588] See nos. 516 ff. below.

the content of the relevant tort law; and what significance do they have for the results achieved?

1. TORT AND UNAUTHORIZED CONDUCT OF ANOTHER'S AFFAIRS

a. Overview

Like tort law, unauthorized conduct of another's affairs belongs to those **508** relationships of obligation which arise *ex lege*. We shall consider two groups of cases. In the first, one person (*gérant* or *gestore*) acts on behalf of another (*maître, interessato*, or *Prinzipal*) without being commissioned by the principal in respect of the services rendered, or without being authorized.[589] The action undertaken is altruistic and, according to the information available to the person at the time of carrying out the action, it corresponds with the probable will of the principal.[590] In the tradition of continental civil law[591] this situation has been understood as quasi-contractual, despite its legal character as an obligation;[592] for these reasons, there is a relationship akin to contract between the actor and the principal.[593] In contrast, the second group of cases concerns first the person who becomes involved in the affairs of a principal regardless of the fact that the principal is actually or presumably opposed to the course of action adopted, and secondly the person who uses the reputation or assets of the principal for his own purposes.

It is possible to distinguish a benign (authorized) agent from a malign **509** (unauthorized) agent, and overlaps between the law of tort and *negotiorum gestio* are strongly suggested for unauthorized persons. It is a matter of making the agent more liable than under the usual tort rules (below, no. 515). However, the rules governing the actions of benign agents can also affect tort law. Such rules are intended to improve the

---

[589] The conduct of another's affairs without authority also occurs where one person does another a favour, e.g. *Cutler v. United Dairies (London) Ltd.* [1933] 2 KB 297: rescuer injured.

[590] The notion of 'initial utility' (*utilità iniziale*) is decisive, rather than the 'utility of the final result' (*utilità finale*). Cf. Cendon (-Breccia) vol. iv, Art. 2031 no. 1.

[591] Here lies the intersection with the common law. The common law takes as its starting point the opposite point of view: 'The general principle is, beyond all question, that work and labour done or money expended by one man to preserve or benefit the property of another do not according to English law create any lien upon the property saved or benefited, nor, even if standing alone, create any obligation to repay the expenditure' (Bowen LJ) *Falcke v. Scottish Imperial Insurance Co.* (1887) 34 Ch. D. 234, 248).

[592] Even today Art. 1371 French Cc and Art. 1887 Spanish Cc define such 'quasi-contracts'.

[593] Particularly clear on this point is Art. 2030 I Ital. Cc ('The principal is subject to the same obligations which would arise from contract'). Art. 1372 II French Cc is equally clear: '*Il se soumet à toutes les obligations qui résulteraient d'un mandat exprès que lui aurait donné le propriétaire*'.

legal position of the agent, either by exempting him from liabilty or by granting him a right of action against the principal. Rights of action such as these only have points in common with the law of tort to the extent that they concern compensation for damage to property, personal injury, or other loss resulting from an accidental act. However, a rescuer who does not expose himself or his goods to risk and who demands payment for his services[594] may have a right of action in quasi-contract or *negotiorum gestio*, but has none in tort. For the law of *negotiorum gestio* grants the agent rights to claim damages against the principal,[595] but the law of tort does not restore pure expenditure or grant payment for services rendered in the absence of a contract.

Payment demanded by a genealogist for research undertaken without prior commission is an example of a claim merely for expenditure.[596] Another example is a swimmer who assists another and demands compensation for the time expended, or even a reward. This is also mere expenditure. Where in consequence of the action undertaken he is injured, or suffers commercial loss on account of the time he has spent, this constitutes damage and is nearer to the law of tort. Expenditure and damage are both suffered where a motorway franchise holder demands compensation not only for repairing material damage to the crash barriers and markings but also for the cost of temporarily fencing the accident spot;[597] where a waterways authority removes a crane which has fallen into a canal;[598] and where a local authority cleans a gravel pit used for many years as a chemical waste disposal site.[599]

b. The Legal Status of the Authorized Agent acting on Another's Behalf

(1) Favourable Changes to Liability

510 An authorized act on another's behalf is in principle recognized and welcomed, but not usually demanded, by law.[600] The act has to be well

---

[594] Such claims are often granted to professional helpers (e.g. doctors). See Art. 6:200 II BW; OGH 21 Apr. 1982, *JBl* 1984 p. 256; § 1835 III BGB (applied similarly within the scope of §683 BGB) and Goff/Jones, *Restitution*, 3rd edn., p. 343.

[595] As expressed in 6:200 I BW and Art. 1893 Span. Cc; for Germany see no. 513 below.

[596] Cass.civ. 31 Jan. 1995, Bull.civ. 1995, I, no. 59.

[597] Cass.civ. 8 June 1994, Bull.civ. 1994, II, no. 154.

[598] HR 14 Oct. 1994, *RvdW* 1994 no. 202 p. 1118.

[599] VLD 10 May 1994, *UfR* 1994 A p. 659. An interesting borderline case is VLD 29 Nov.1976, *UfR* 1977 A p. 183: following a factory accident an electric pump restarted and began pumping oil from a tank. The factory floor and surrounding area became polluted, as did a nearby brook. The local authority cleaned up both and obtained compensation according to the rules on the conduct of another's affairs without authority. The costs of cleaning up *other* plots of land were recovered by the local authority according to the *culpa* rule, in negligence. For further detail see Gomard, *UfR* 1978 B pp. 53, 69–70; Pagh, *UfR* 1990 B pp. 393, 394.

[600] Only a contractual duty to intervene would render rules on *negotiorum gestio*

intentioned:[601] no tort is committed by the person who sees a fire in his neighbour's empty house and breaks one of its windows to extinguish the fire.[602] Were he to take the same measures because his own house or that of a third party were endangered, there would be a justifying emergency.[603] Where he acts to protect the property of the owner of the burning house, then either the prerequisites of the tort of trespass to land are satisfied but negated, or his authorized action on another's behalf is regarded as a justification. The same applies where someone has possession of another's perishable goods and, unable to obtain instructions from the owner, decides to sell the goods before they perish.[604] Neither does a doctor act unlawfully who without consent operates on or transfuses blood to an unconscious patient to save his life. The result for the actor is the same[605] whether he is treated as acting with deemed consent,[606] in necessity,[607] or according to the concept of *negotiorum gestio*.

A minimum degree of care is expected from a person acting in the **511** interests of another. He is liable not only for intentional acts which cause damage but also for negligence, and it is no defence that the defendant actor misread the situation or acted clumsily. It must not be forgotten that in all these cases the intervening party acts out of altruism. The statute books of mainland Europe which contain rules on the *negotiorum gestio* all state either that one who acts on behalf of another is liable only for gross negligence,[608] or that the usual rules on negligence apply, in

---

inapplicable, and not criminal law provisions which establish a duty to assist. The same can be said of the general duty of care in tort. Only in exceptional circumstances is there a duty to protect strangers from imminent danger; a duty to intervene on behalf of another which involves a risk to the actor is generally rejected in the absence of a special relationship. OLG Hamm 22 Oct. 1993, *NJW-RR* 1994 p. 153.

[601] The person who provides help in an emergency enjoys the special protection of statutory accident insurance. For Germany see Dornwald, *DAR* 1992 pp. 54–56.

[602] Goff/Jones, *Restitution*, 3rd edn., p. 339; Georgiades/Stathopoulos (-Georgiades), *Greek Cc*, vol. iv, Art. 914 no. 62; Filios, *Enochiko Dikaio*, vol. ii (2) 3rd edn., p. 37 (both state that lawful protection of the property of strangers, in the sense of Arts. 730 ff. Gr. Cc, is a justification); Stoljar, *IntEncCompL*, vol. x 17–57.

[603] See *Cope v. Sharpe* [1912] 1 KB 496: no liability in trespass; although it later became clear that the fire would not in fact have reached the property of the defendant, the defendant acted reasonably in the circumstances.

[604] Goff/Jones, *Restitution*, 3rd edn., p. 339. From Austria: OGH 4 Nov. 1981, *ÖJZ* 1982 p. 297 (EvBl 83).

[605] Rightly pointed out by Walker, *Principles*, vol. ii (4) 4th edn., p. 514.

[606] The notion of deemed consent is used in Germany where the issue arises in criminal law: Hellmann, *Zivilrechtliche Rechtfertigungsgründe im Strafrecht*, pp. 174–175.

[607] In the view of Winfield/Jolowicz (-Rogers), *Tort*, 14th edn., p. 725, in the context of private law necessity should take priority over 'the alternative basis of implied consent'.

[608] As in § 680 BGB (applied in BGH 16 Mar. 1965, BGHZ 43 p. 188 on the misreading of a situation) and Art. 732 Greek Cc.

which case equitable principles reduce damages.[609] In Scotland, where *negotiorum gestio* is recognized, and in England and Ireland, where it is not, there has been little effort to distinguish between different degrees of negligence. Nevertheless, that the matter was one of real emergency is not simply passed over; even in those countries, this is taken into account to determine whether a breach of duty has been committed.[610]

(2) Rescue Cases

512   The next question is under what circumstances a rescuer who endangered himself and suffered injury[611] can claim compensation from the other. A number of issues immediately arise. First, it is clear that the rescuer is not entitled to claim damages if he knowingly acts against the express lawful will of the rescuee: it is clearly different where someone tries to prevent an unlawful suicide or attempts to disarm a bank robber. Should the hero in the second example be shot, the bank would meet his claim with the argument that banks have given their personnel instructions not to endanger themselves to defend cash tills.[612] Even if no such instructions had been given, the bank would not be liable because of

---

[609] The usual solution: see Art. 2030 II Ital. Cc; Art. 1889 II Span. Cc; Arts. 1374 II French, Belg., and Luxemb. Cc; Art. 6:199 I in conjunction with Art. 6:109 BW (see *Parlementaire Geschiedenis*, vol. vi, pp. 449–450) and Art. 466 I with Art. 494 Port. Cc.

[610] For Scotland see Cullen, *Jurid.Rev.* 1995 pp. 20–27 and esp. *Kolbin & Sons* v. *United Shipping Co.*, 'SS Eduard Woermann' 1931 SC 128, 139: 'What measure of care is required from a *negotiorum gestor* . . . has been the subject of much discussion. *Culpa lata, levis, levissima* have been assigned their own boundaries, although to define them in particular cases has proved no easy task. In my humble opinion the more scientific treatment of the problem is not to predicate different degrees of negligence, but to concentrate on the duty, breach of which constitutes negligence'. Very similar with regard to the common law is McMahon/Binchy, *Irish Law of Torts* p. 372. See also *Rigby* v. *Chief Constable of Northampton* [1985] 1 WLR 124.

[611] The position is different where somebody interferes with the rights of another when trying to save himself or his own property. Such interferences are lawful where the protected interest clearly outweighs the damaged interest. The property owner in such a case has no claim against the driver in *negotiorum gestio* (as suggested by Malaurie/Aynès, *Droit civil*, 3rd edn., no. 121) but under the law of necessity (e.g. § 904 II BGB; Art. 2045 Ital. Cc; Art. 286 Greek Cc; and Art. 339 II Port. Cc). *Negotiorum gestio* only plays a part when it provides the car driver (and in some circumstances also the owner of the damaged article, see Art. 339 II Port. Cc) with a claim for compensation against the person originally responsible for bringing about the emergency: Art. 286 Greek Cc. Where a threatened party injures a legal interest of equal value, his actions are not legal but may be excused. Contrary to Cass. 21 Mar. 1979, *Rev.crit.jur.belge* 1982 p. 139 (note by Verhaegen) a claim for damages should be granted to the injured party: see STJ 3 Mar. 1990, *BolMinJust* 395 (1990) p. 534; Cass. 21 June 1972, n. 2025, *Giust.civ.Mass.* 1972 p. 1136; App. Firenze 26 Mar.1960, *Resp.Civ. e Prev.* 1961 p. 453: injury to the occupants of a bus when the driver avoided another road user. The driver and the third party were jointly liable to the injured; as between the two drivers, the third party alone was liable.

[612] The correct view, reached by OLG Karlsruhe 23 Mar. 1977, *VersR* 1977 p. 936; an almost identical case with a different result is Cass.civ. 26 Jan. 1988, *D.* 1989 *Jur.* 405 (note Martin).

overwhelming contributory negligence by the intervening party[613] who risked far more than he could have expected to achieve.[614] Furthermore, an intervening party clearly only has a case where he intended to avoid imminent damage to the principal: the intention of a driver who takes evasive action to avoid a head-on collision is to save his own skin and not to protect the interests of his windscreen insurer. It would be absurd if the windscreen insurer had to pay for the entire damage to the vehicle.[615] There must also be a sufficiently causative relationship between the emergency and the event which causes loss. Where a fireman is injured in the course of duty it should make no difference whether he fell victim to a usual risk or an extraordinary one.[616] However, if after the fire is extinguished the fireman sprains his ankle while boarding the tender, that is a risk inherent in everyday life, and nothing to do with the person who negligently caused the fire.[617]

Whether or not the rescuer has a right of action based on *negotiorum*   **513** *gestio* is of course unimportant where a claim in tort is available. There will be a claim in tort where the defendant caused the emergency, whether he endangered himself[618] or a third party, and thereby brought about the intervention of the rescuer.[619] However, it does seem to be significant in tort whether a judge can refer to a complementary claim in *negotiorum gestio*. English law, for example, responds to rescue and self-sacrifice cases by imposing a heightened form of liability in negligence.

[613] BGH 16 Mar. 1965, BGHZ 43 p. 188 states that restrictions on liability for gross negligence also come into play in the context of contributory negligence.

[614] See Oppermann, *AcP* 193 (1993) pp. 497, 501. In contrast: someone who uses his own car to pursue the thief of another's car should be granted a right of action: see Cass. 23 Oct. 1956, n. 3843, *Rep.gen.* 1956 col. 1229 no. 11.

[615] BGH 13 July 1994, *NJW-RR* 1994 p. 1366. For a more detailed analysis of the background to such cases from the insurance point of view see Minoggio, *DAR* 1989 pp. 288–291.

[616] *Ogwo* v. *Taylor* [1987] 3 All ER 961.

[617] BGH 4 May 1993, *r+s* 1994 p. 134 (claim rejected in tort and *negotiorum gestio*). See also *Crossley* v. *Rawlinson* [1981] 3 All ER 674: rescuer running with a fire extinguisher to an accident fell into a hole hidden by grass; liability rejected because the damage was too remote; see Jones, 45 (1982) *MLR* 342–345.

[618] See *Ogwo* v. *Taylor* (fn. 616 above); McMahon/Binchy, *Irish Law of Torts*, 2nd edn., p. 372, and Kruse, *Erstatningsretten*, 5th edn., pp. 48–49.

[619] As in Areopag 23/1988, *EllDik* 30 (1989) p. 1150: a pedestrian was injured in an accident. While attending to him the plaintiff, another pedestrian, was hit by a vehicle; liability of the person who caused the initial accident was affirmed; no break in the chain of causation; because the person who caused the first accident could not be identified the fund for damages for road accidents victims was liable. In *Haynes* v. *Harwood* [1935] 1 KB 146 a horse running loose endangered children; a police officer running to the scene was injured; action in negligence was affirmed. In Trib.Brussels 20 Feb. 1970, *Rev.crit.jur.belge* 1974 p. 55 (note by Glansdorff/Legros) a 17-year old pushed the family car from the garage on to the sloping yard with her parents' permission. The concierge tried to stop the car and was injured. The court divided responsibility between the parents and the concierge, finding that the latter had contributed to the accident).

Carmarthenshire County Council v. *Lewis*[620] is an example. A four-year-old ran out of a nursery school onto the street. Taking evasive action, a lorry driver hit a telegraph post and was killed. Although negligence could not be proved against the school staff, the local authority responsible for the school was held liable 'since the unexplained fact that . . . it was possible for so young a child to wander from the school premises onto the highway . . . disclosed negligence on their part'.

514   The next question is whether the rescued party should be liable to the party who sacrificed himself for his benefit even where the rescuee was not at fault. What would have been the outcome in *Carmarthenshire* if, instead of the local authority, the young child had been proceeded against? In a Danish case a motorcyclist who flung himself to the ground to avoid hitting a four-year-old was denied a right of action; the girl was not old enough to be capable of fault.[621] No fault could be proved against the parents. The fully incapacitated motor bike rider was therefore left to suffer his losses alone: an intolerable result unless the State at the very least provides statutory insurance cover for such cases. How an English court would decide the case is unclear; the motocyclist's chances would not be high. In The Netherlands Art. 6:200 sec. 1 BW (as in Art. 1893 sec. 2 Span. Cc[622]) expressly recognizes[623] a right of action, independent of fault, in authorized *negotiorum gestio*. Hartkamp takes the view that the rule should not be applied to traffic cases involving self-sacrifice: that would enable the circumvention[624] of Dutch tort law[625] designed to protect minors. Whether this argument will triumph remains to be seen. The position in The Netherlands is in principle very different from that in Denmark or England:[626] parents are strictly liable in the Netherlands.[627] A different voice is heard in Austria: Oberhofer argues for a general 'liability for risk independent of fault when acting in another's interest'.[628] The case-law of the German Federal Court points in more or less the same direction; the BGH has on several occasions decided that 'personal injury and death arising out of action taken to protect another from imminent danger are to be counted amongst the heads of compensation for expenditure as understood by

---

[620] [1955] AC 549. See also Lord Denning MR in *Videan* v. *British Transport Commission* [1963] 2 All ER 860, 868: 'Whoever comes to the rescue, the law should see that he does not suffer for it'. The contrary tendency expressed in *Cutler* v. *United Dairies (London) Ltd.* [1933] 2 KB 297 should no longer be followed.

[621] HD 15 Feb. 1963, *UfR* 1963 A p. 303.

[622] This rule also imposes liability of the *dominus*, independent of fault on his behalf: see Paz-Ares/Díez-Picazo/Bercovitz/Salvador (-Lasarte), *Código Civil*, vol. ii, pp. 1951–1953.

[623] See fn. 595 above.

[624] Asser (-Hartkamp), *Verbintenissenrecht*, vol. iii, 9th edn., p. 293. See *Parlementaire Geschiedenis*, vol. vi, pp. 795–797.   [625] See no. 63 above.

[626] See nos. 330 ff. above.   [627] See no. 132 above.   [628] *JBl* 1995 pp. 217, 218.

§§ 670, 683 BGB'.[629] The most important effect of this enlargement of the term 'expenditure' is that damages can be claimed irrespective of fault by the rescued party.

The BGH decision of 27.11.1962[630] used particularly baffling reasoning, which shows the strength of the influence of equitable considerations in this sensitive area of liability. A car driver was preparing to overtake three young cyclists (aged 10–11 years) travelling in single file when suddenly one of them, for a reason which remains unclear, moved towards the centre of the road. The driver took immediate evasive action, drove into a field, and suffered serious injury. The BGH accepted that as far as the driver was concerned the incident was an unavoidable event as understood by § 7 sec. 2 StVG (road traffic statute), affirmed in principle an action in damages based in *negotiorum gestio* against the blameless schoolboy,[631] reduced the damages payable by 50%, and gave the reason that the position of the parties' interests corresponded to the general average. Maritime law governing this situation states expressly that the damage is to be borne by the parties together.[632]

c. Liability for Unauthorized Conduct Against the Will of Another, and Liability for Unauthorized Conduct for Personal Gain

Where the obligation stemming from *negotiorum gestio* is viewed as a **515** quasi-contractual obligation, it can no longer be relied on for claims based on unauthorized conduct against the will of another, nor even for claims based on unauthorized conduct for personal gain.[633] One who acts against the will of the principal does not thereby create a contract-type relationship with the principal,[634] but commits a wrongful act for whose consequences he alone is responsible.[635] None the less, there are scattered rules which address this obvious truth less in the context of tort,[636] and more of *negotiorum gestio*.[637] *Negotiorum gestio* is then expanded along quasi-tort lines, and so is not especially convincing.

---

[629] BGH 4 May 1993, *r+s* 1994 pp. 134, 136; BGH 10 Oct. 1984, BGHZ 92 pp. 270, 271; BGH 27 Nov. 1962, BGHZ 38 pp. 270, 277 and BGH 7 Nov. 1960, BGHZ 33 pp. 251, 257; see BGH 16 Mar. 1965, BGHZ 43 p. 188.   [630] Fn. 529 above.

[631] Loc. cit. p. 277.   [632] Loc. cit. p. 278.

[633] This is the position under the *Code Napoléon*, the Italian and Spanish Cc, and the Dutch BW.

[634] Except where the principal authorizes the conduct after the event: see e.g. Arts. 2032 Ital. Cc, 1892 Span. Cc, 469 Port. Cc, and 6:202 BW.

[635] See Díez-Picazo/Gullón, *Sistema*, vol. ii, 6th edn., pp. 567–569; *BGB-RGRK* (-Steffen) 12th edn., § 678 no. 3; Bianca, *Diritto civile*, vol. iii, p. 157.

[636] This is the view in § 1311 s. 2, 3rd alternative ABGB.

[637] As in § 678 BGB and Art. 466 II Port. Cc. In contrast, Art. 2031 II Italian Cc has no independent basis of claim, but merely refers to Art. 2043 Cc. Art. 2031 is often compared with § 678 BGB: Geri/Breccia/Busnelli/Natoli, *Diritto civile*, vol. iii, p. 806.

However, that expansion is always justified on the ground that the unauthorized agent in *negotiorum gestio* should be liable for pure economic losses[638] and that liability is always incurred when the action involved fault. When an unauthorized person in *negotiorum gestio* makes a mistake in carrying out the act, it is no defence that this mistake was unavoidable even for someone acting with the utmost care (§§ 678 BGB, 1311 ABGB).

An elegant example of the interweaving of the rules on authorized and unauthorized *negotiorum gestio* is provided by a BGH decision of 30.11.1971.[639] The defendant had been celebrating with the husband of the plaintiff widow. The defendant took the place of his inebriated colleague at the wheel of the car against the latter's protests and drove the car although he too was drunk. He drove the car into the back of a lorry, killing the plaintiff's husband. The BGH rejected the claim of the widow for damages. The deceased had not been competent to consent at law; his protest at the defendant taking the wheel taken was irrelevant. The case therefore turned on the deceased's probable will, determined from an objective assessment of the circumstances. No reasonable person would allow himself to be driven by a person as drunk as the defendant. It was accordingly found that this was an unauthorized act, carried out against the will of another. Because *in casu* the defendant had acted to prevent his insensible colleague from driving, the benefit of § 680 BGB (which limits liability in rescue cases to gross negligence) applied as much to the fault in so acting (driving at all) as to the fault in performance (crashing). No gross negligence was proved on either count, and the defendant was therefore not liable to the widow. (The limitation of the defendant's liability did not of course apply to the claim by the lorry owner.)

516   Where a person exploits the good name or property of another for his own purposes, knowing that he is not entitled to do so, he commits a tort: Art. 472 II Port. Cc, Art. 739 Greek Cc, § 687 II BGB, and § 1040 ABGB. *Negotiorum gestio* is only useful in such cases if there is no cause of action in the complementary law of tort. The person who takes over another's transaction as his own is not only liable under the strict rules of unauthorized *negotiorum gestio*, but also obliged to return to the principal any profit obtained by exploiting the latter's legal rights. The clarification of this point is the primary purpose of § 687 II s. 1, with §§ 681 s. 2, 667 BGB, and Arts. 739 ss. 1 and 734 Greek Cc.[640] These

---

[638] BGH 5 Dec. 1983, *NJW* 1984 pp. 1461, 1462.
[639] BGH 30 Nov. 1971, *NJW* 1972 p. 475 with note by Batsch, p. 818.
[640] Closer analysis in *ErmAK* (-Saketas) Art. 739 Greek Cc no. 6 (where the view is expressed that claims in Arts. 914 and 739 Greek Cc could have a cumulative effect) and Kallimopoulos, *I mi gnisia dioikisi allotrion*, pp. 81 ff., 140 ff., and 206 ff.; and Georgiades/Stathopoulos (-Georgiades), *Introduction to Arts. 914–938 Greek Cc*, no. 51.

provisions are not necessary in The Netherlands whose tort law allows for the recovery of profits as damages (Art. 6:104 BW). To achieve comparable results in the common law world, English tort must be prepared, at least in areas such as trespass to land, to grant not only mesne profits[641] but also restitutionary damages.[642] It remains an open question whether this can in fact happen.[643]

2. COMPARISON OF LIABILITY FOR UNJUST ENRICHMENT AND LIABILITY IN TORT

a. *Condictio indebiti, condictio sine causa,* and Tort Law

As with *negotiorum gestio,* so also the law of unjust enrichment[644] has   **517** several areas of overlap with the law of tort. They occur where someone without authority (but not necessarily in a blameworthy manner[645]) interferes in the rights of another and thereby acquires advantages,

---

[641] See no. 290 above.

[642] Markesinis/Deakin, *Tort Law,* 3rd edn., pp. 38–40 are in favour of this. See also *Edwards* v. *Lee's Administrator* 96 SW 2nd 1028 (Court of Appeals of Kentucky 1936: the defendant had for reward led visitors through underground passageways below his property and shown them sights below the property of his neighbour. The defendant was proceeded against in trespass and had to pay over to the plaintiff a portion of his earnings). For an analysis of this decision from an English perspective see Birks, in: Schrage (ed.), *Unjust Enrichment,* pp. 171, 172–173.

[643] See *Stoke-on-Trent City Council* v. *W & J Wass Ltd.* [1988] 1 WLR 1406, 1415. See no. 521 below for cases in which restitutionary damages were awarded in trespass to land.

[644] This term is used in its widest sense, as in § 812 BGB, Art. 904 Greek Cc, and Art. 473 Port. Cc. In the remaining continental legal systems the term 'unjust enrichment' is used in a narrower sense. For example, some commentators in Austria want to bring only *condictio indebiti* (explained above) under the heading of unjust enrichment (Gschnitzer/Faistenberger/Barta/Eccher, *Schuldrecht BT,* 2nd edn., p. 392), whereas this *condictio indebiti* appears in the *Code civil* as *répétition de l'indu* (Arts. 1376–1381 Fr. Cc. Arts. 1895–1901 Span. Cc are very similar), which only by later judicial developments (Cass.req. 15 June 1892, DP 1892, 1, 596) was widened to a general law of *enrichissement sans cause.* This development was based on a broadening of the old version of the *actio de in rem verso.* This narrow/broad division is still visible in Italian law (Arts. 2033–2040: *'del pagamento dell'indebito'*; Arts. 2041–2042: *'dell'arricchimento senza causa'*) and in The Netherlands (Arts. 6:203–211 BW: *'onverschuldigde betaling'*; Art. 6:212 BW: *'ongerechtvaardigde verrijking'*). The common law countries do not recognize any general principle of unjust enrichment. For a thorough analysis see Goff/Jones, *Restitution,* 3rd edn., pp. 12–30; Clark, *Contract Law in Ireland,* 3rd edn., pp. 475–476); Scotland divides its material between repetition, restitution, and recompense (see Whitty, *ZEuP* 1995 pp. 216–241). The Scandinavian legal systems, which are by no means homogenous (see Roos, *JFT* 1992 pp. 75–79) do not recognize a statutory definition of the term unjust enrichment. The extent of the principle of liability linked with it is unclear. From the standpoint of terminology, issues of the *condictio indebiti* as well as those of all other forms of unjust enrichment (e.g. conversion) are discussed under the heading *obehörig vinst* and *berigelsesret* respectively. See also Lejman, *Obehörig vinst och värdeersättning,* pp. 100–108; Kruse, *Erstatningsretten,* 5th edn., pp. 264–275.

[645] If he acts in the knowledge that he is not entitled to exploit the right, this is unauthorized action undertaken for personal gain (no. 516 above).

but not where a party mistakenly believes that he is performing a contractual obligation and has to be returned to his original position. From the point of view of tort, the core area of *conditio indebiti*[646] has very little relevance. This term concerns the return of property or the payment of compensation for valuable services[647] obtained without legal entitlement. Examples are a person mistakenly paid too much money, or who was not the person to whom performance was owed, or where for some other reason there was no right to claim an increase of assets. Where the obligation which formed the basis of the performance is not a duty in tort (e.g. when parents pay in the mistaken belief that they are obliged, even in the absence of negligence on their part, to compensate for damage caused by their children),[648] then non-contractual liability is incurred only where the recipient conveys an acquired item to a third party, or uses it for his own purposes, or fails to return it to its rightful owner on demand.[649] Moreover, it is obviously also an offence to blackmail someone or to cause someone to pay a third party where no obligation is owed.[650] A very general connection between unjust enrichment and tort is revealed by the provision that a tort victim may not claim twice for the same damage because he must not enrich himself.[651]

[646] The ideas expressed in the various legal expressions vary greatly. Even in those legal systems whose law of unjust enrichment distinguishes between payment of a non-existent obligation and conversion, the term *conditio sine causa* is used almost without distinction. The *conditio sine causa* (no. 518 below) is often encompassed within the *conditio indebiti*, and under the heading of '*enrichissement sans cause*' the French legal system deals with cases in which someone acts without reference to a contract: see Cass.civ. 12 July 1994, *Sem.Jur.* 1995, II, 22425.

[647] That services can be allocated to a category other than money and benefits in kind (see Whitty, *ZEuP* 1995, pp. 216, 218 for Scotland and for France as well as Cass.civ. 12 July 1994 loc. cit. [fn. 546 above] e.g. also Cass.civ. 6 Mar. 1979, *Gaz.Pal.* 1979 *Somm.* 327) is of no real significance for the border between tort and unjust enrichment.

[648] Whether in such a mistake a person has a claim based on unjust enrichment is a question which can be answered in different ways. For the English perspective see *Woolwich Equitable Building Society* v. *Inland Revenue Commissioners* [1992] 3 WLR 366, 402–404; for Ireland: *Rogers* v. *Louth County Council* ILRM 1981 p. 144. Germany (§ 814 BGB) and Greece (Art. 905 Greek Cc) do not employ the common law distinction between mistakes of law and mistakes of fact, but both require the actor to have had positive knowledge of the non-existence of an obligation for the claim for repayment to be denied.

[649] All these acts satisfy the requirements of the tort of conversion: Tettenborn, (1993) 52 *CLJ* 1993 pp. 128, 129–130; McMahon/Binchy, *Irish Law of Torts*, 2nd edn,. pp. 534–543. In other legal systems the unjustified but blameless disposal of another's goods is one of the most important cases in which unjust enrichment complements tort: see Art. 1380 French Cc and § 816 BGB.

[650] See OGH 18 Mar. 1992, JBl 1992 p. 720; BGH 31 May 1994, *ZIP* 1994 pp. 1098, 1101; and no. 260 and fn. 148 above.

[651] It is here that, amongst others, the rules on the liability of joint tortfeasors are based; see no. 51 above. Particularly difficult questions, which can only be referred to here, appear where used articles (e.g. vehicles) are damaged and either the cost of repair is greater than the value of the vehicle or the value of the vehicle is increased by the addition of new parts, something which e.g. RP 12 June 1990, *CJ* XV (1990–3) p. 221 does not envisage as an *enriquecimento sem causa*.

The few exceptions to this principle, all in cases of liability for personal injury, are justified on the ground that the efforts of third parties should not exonerate the tortfeasor from liability.[652] In contrast, there is no rule which limits the liability of the tortfeasor to the extent of his own enrichment.[653]

The law of tort can also largely ignore those cases which one tries to **518** classify as *condictio sine causa*. These involve compensation for performance rendered under legally void contracts. Examples are: transactions lacking the necessary formal requirements; contracts void for breach of either law or custom; and contracts which fail due to the incapacity of one of the parties, and under which property accordingly cannot pass. Areas of overlap with tort are found mostly where the nullity of the contract which brings the law of unjust enrichment into play itself reflects a tortious act, e.g. deceit.[654] In such cases the only problem is that of duplicity of actions: does the other party have an action in tort as well as in unjust enrichment?[655] It should also be noted that certain

---

[652] Whilst e.g. § 843 IV BGB states only that the injured will not be denied damages 'by reason [of the fact] that another has to provide for the injured person', Art. 930 III Greek Cc states that the claim will not be denied 'by reason [of the fact] that another has to pay damages or provide compensation for the injured person'. In both systems these rules can mean, for example, that a tortfeasor is not exempt from liability where an injured employee continues to draw wages from his employer (see BGH 22 June 1956, BGHZ 21 p. 112; CA Athens 6064/1981, *NoB* 30 [1982] p. 1079). Whether this means that the injured employee actually receives double compensation (as in CA Athens loc. cit. and many other cases in Greek law, e.g. Areopag 147/1953, *NoB* 1 [1953] p. 189; Areopag 317/1971, *NoB* 19 [1971] p. 893; and Areopag 89/1983, *NoB* 32 [1984] p. 1341) depends upon the extent to which the claims of the injured person can be passed on *legaliter* to his employer or insurer. In contrast Cass. 3 Dec. 1993, n. 11999, *Giust.civ.Mass.* 1993 p. 1715 does not grant damages 'if the injured person was supported throughout the period of his incapacity by a family member who has satisfied the obligation to provide as understood by Art. 147 Cc'. The same position has been accepted in Portuguese law: a civil servant cannot demand compensation from both the state and the tortfeasor. If both have paid damages the state is entitled to demand repayment of its share on the basis of unjust enrichment: Procuradoria-Geral da República 8 May 1969, *BolMinJust* 192 (1970) p. 126. See no. 489 and fn. 501 above.

[653] For Spain TS (crim.) 21 Nov. 1994, *La Ley* 1995–1 p. 104; and from Denmark HD 25 Jan. 1965, *UfR* 1965 A p. 126: unauthorized publication of the picture of an actor for advertising; compensation was calculated not by reference to price which the defendant agency usually paid for such pictures, but according to the greater loss to the plaintiff. See also no. 522 above.

[654] There is normally no deceit or deception without unjust enrichment. Cf. for Portugal RC 19 Feb. 1986, *CJ* XI (1986–1) p. 63.

[655] Cass.com. 18 Oct. 1994, Bull.civ. 1994, IV, no. 293 says that even where the nullity of a contract (Arts. 1116 and 1117 French Cc) is appealed to, damages for an intentional wrongful act (i.e. tort) are not excluded; see also Cass.com. 7 Mar. 1995, *D.* 1995 IR 88 (void business sale contract, deception, damages for particular expenses incurred based on Art. 1382 Cc). STJ, 13 Jan 1977, *BolMinJust* 263 (1977) pp. 236, 241 allows a claim in unjust enrichment where the corresponding claim based upon nullity can no longer be used. Above all, Art. 498 IV Port. Cc expressly allows a claim for unjust enrichment to be brought where the corresponding tort action is time-barred. The subsidiarity of the unjust enrichment claim as against the claim in tort is a subject of controversy in Greece; see

defences which in one legal system appear alongside *condictio sine causa* are employed in another as a typical instrument of tort. *Ex turpi causa non oritur actio* is a good example.[656]

b. Liability Independent of both Fault and Loss for Interference with the Rights of Others

(1) General

519   We shall now look more closely at cases in which a person receives goods or services which are not bestowed on him 'by way of performance' but which he has annexed to his own property. The unauthorized disposal or use of another's property comes readily to mind, as does the unlawful use of the image, name, or other intangible asset of another for one's own benefit. Anyone who takes such action in a blameworthy manner generally commits a tort. The law on unjust enrichment is not entirely excluded because the loss to the party whose rights have been infringed is often smaller than the profit obtained by the tortfeasor. In contrast, where the party in breach acts without fault it must be determined whether the absence of fault is sufficient reason to allow him to keep all or part of the fruits of his actions. The answers which the various European legal systems give to this question are once more notably similar. He who interferes with the rights of another must return the commercial advantage thereby acquired even if the injured party suffered no corresponding loss which would form the basis of an action. Further, the obligation to make restitution should be independent of fault by the interfering party. These similar results, however, stem from two different origins. Either concepts taken from the law of unjust enrichment are integrated within the law of tort, as described in (2)

Georgiades/Stathopoulos (-Stathopoulos), *Greek Cc*, vol. iv, Intr. Arts. 904–913, nos. 28 ff., 36. In the older case-law the principle of subsidiarity was rarely employed: Areopag 72/1966, *NoB* 14 (1966) p. 801; CA Athens 7401/1976, *NoB* 25 (1977) p. 752; CFI Patras, *NoB* 16 (1968) p. 1083. More recent decisions tend towards it: Areopag 1567/1983, *NoB* 32 (1984) p. 1354; CA Athens 9612/1989, *NoB* 38 (1990) p. 107; CA Athens 1712/1989, *NoB* 37 (1989) p. 1445; and CA Athens 14073/1988, Arm. 43 (1989) p. 438. This can be significant on account of liability according to equitable principles in Art. 132, and above all due to the reference to tort by way of Art. 149 Greek Cc and for cases of *condictio sine causa*. Where a doctor's assistant continued working for nothing because the doctor had promised deceitfully that he would marry her, Areopag 672/1993, *EllDik* 35 (1994) p. 1271 applied tort exclusively (Art. 919 Greek Cc) to grant the plaintiff her lost wages as well as damages for non-pecuniary loss. Schildt, *JuS* 1995 pp. 953, 958–959 provides an account of the interplay of unjust enrichment and tort in German law.

[656] In German law § 817 II BGB applies only to actions of unjust enrichment, not to actions in tort (RG 1 Oct. 1914, RGZ 85 pp. 293, 295), whilst in English law the defence applies only in tort; see *Pitts v. Hunt* [1991] 1 QB 24; *Ashton v. Turner* [1981] QB 137; *Saunders v. Edwards* [1987] 2 All ER 651.

below, or the opposite occurs and the law of unjust enrichment is expanded to incorporate principles of a quasi-tort nature, as described in (3) below.[657]

(2) Elements of Unjust Enrichment in the Law of Tort

Features from the law of unjust enrichment are typically taken up by the **520** law of tort in two sorts of cases. In the first, the law of tort recovers from the defendant profits gained by his use of the plaintiff's property. In the second, tort law grants to the plaintiff payment for use by the defendant of the plaintiff's property, even where the plaintiff has suffered no loss of assets. (If such losses are suffered the plaintiff can claim compensatory but not restitutionary damages). The alternative nature of such claims was mentioned above in the context of usurpation of another's business for one's own ends,[658] which in essence is nothing other than a wrongful interference with the rights of another.[659] The tendency to extend the notion of damage to unjust enrichments is particularly pronounced in jurisdictions where the general unjust enrichment action is met with scepticism, whether because the *condictio indebiti* is not accepted[660] in its entirety, or because of its equitable and therefore subsidiary character[661] originally developed from the *actio de in rem verso* by French courts.[662] Such legal systems strive to apply principles of delict. In the law of unjust enrichment it can be more beneficial to the injured party if,

---

[657] See *Barclays Bank PLC* v. *Glasgow City Council* [1994] 2 WLR 466.

[658] No. 516 above.

[659] In Austria both actions, usurpation of the rights of another for personal gain and general liability for enrichment (the latter developed from the *actio de in rem verso*) based upon interference with the rights of others (Kupisch, *Ungerechtfertigte Bereicherung*, p. 41) are covered by § 1041 ABGB (Schluep, *FS Dutoit*, pp. 173, 176). It is important that the word '*Sache*' ('thing') in § 1041 has the same sense as in § 285 ABGB. For this reason the rule covers the use of customer lists belonging to somebody else (OGH 17 Mar. 1982, SZ 55/37 p. 183), the claims of somebody else (OGH 11 July 1985, *JBl* 1986 pp. 235, 236), and the use of somebody else's image (OGH 16 Feb. 1982, SZ 55/12 p. 54). It is the function of § 687 II BGB, outside § 816 BGB and beyond § 812 BGB, to facilitate claims for the return of profit.

[660] For England see *Woolwich Building Society* v. *Inland Revenue Commissioners* [1992] 3 WLR 366, 391 (*per* Lord Goff: 'That law might have developed so as to recognize a *condictio indebiti*—an action for the recovery of money on the ground that it was not due. But it did not do so'). See also Wacke, *Vorzüge und Nachteile des deutschen Bereicherungsrechts* pp. 131, 134–137.

[661] The principle of subsidiarity of an action in unjust enrichment as against an action in tort is also found outside French law (see fn. 662), esp. in Italy (Art. 2042 Cc, on which see Bianchini, *Jb. f. ital. Recht* 7 [1994] pp. 197, 203 with references to numerous cases), Portugal (Art. 474 Cc), and Greece (fn. 655 above), but no longer in Spain (fundamental here is TS 12 Apr. 1955, *RAJ* 1955 no. 1126 p. 602; see also TS 24 Jan. 1975, *RAJ* 1975 no. 95 p. 99, and on the entire subject Álvarez-Caperochipi, *Enriquecimiento sin causa*, 3rd edn., pp. 116–120). For The Netherlands generally, see *Parlementaire Geschiedenis*, vol. vi, pp. 789, 830; Asser (-Hartkamp), *Verbintenissenrecht*, vol. iii, 9th edn., p. 327. For a more thorough analysis of the Austrian position see Wilburg, *JBl* 1992 pp. 545–557.

[662] Cass.req. 15 June 1892, *DP* 1892, 1, 596; Cass.civ. 2 Mar. 1915, *DP* 1920, 1, 102.

along with the enrichment of the wrongdoer, a corresponding impover-
ishment of the person whose right was infringed is also required.[663]

521   During the preparation of the Dutch civil code it was said that Art.
6:212 BW would play a subsidiary role to the law of tort.[664] This is most
significant. In Dutch tort law the word 'damages' includes more than just
recovery of losses.[665] Where someone disposes of an object belonging to
another and obtains a high sale price reflecting the skilful negotiations of
the wrongdoer, or where somebody exploits for profit the intangible
assets of another where that other would never have marketed those
assets himself, the law of tort only faces a problem if the judge is not
free to determine the quantum of damages independently, as a question
of fact.[666] Spanish courts apply tortious liability for enrichment imposed
in the criminal code under Art. 108 CP[667] to persons subsidiary to the
tortfeasor who knew nothing of the offence from which they benefited.[668]
Mesne profits in the tort of trespass to land[669] possess in part the character of restitutionary damages, trespass to land being a tort for which
restitutionary damages have often also been granted in other contexts.[670]

---

[663] For a discussion from the Spanish perspective see Álvarez-Caperochipi, *Enriquecimiento sin causa*, 3rd edn., pp. 87–88; Díez-Picazo/Gullón, *Sistema*, vol. ii, 6th edn., pp.
575–576. For The Netherlands: *Parlementaire Geschiedenis*, vol. vi (Inv.) p. 1266 and Asser
(-Hartkamp), *Verbintenissenrecht*, 9th edn., vol. iii, p. 325.

[664] *Parlementaire Geschiedenis*, vol. vi, p. 826. As yet that prediction has been confirmed;
there are scarcely any decisions on Art. 6:212 BW. An exception is HR 29 Jan. 1993, *NedJur*
1994 no. 172 p. 728.

[665] Art. 6:104 BW gives the judge the option of measuring 'the damages in terms . . . of
the profit or a part thereof'; see no. 516 above.

[666] Numerous techniques are used in such cases to allow for recovery of damages. For
example, the loss has been said to lie in not allowing the plaintiff to be involved in the
realization of the profit (Trib.gr.inst. Paris 12 Dec. 1984, *D.* 1985 *IR* 323), and in not being
allowed the chance to exploit the thing himself (e.g. Cass. 17 Apr. 1961, *Pas. belge* 1961 I 882;
Cass. 31 Mar. 1969, *Pas. belge* 1969, I, 676). It has been pointed out in connection with the
damage caused that, where the tortfeasor has been exceptionally successful (Paris 19 Apr.
1985, *D.* 1986 *IR* 189), damages have been calculated according to the use and price which
would have been demanded for the exploitation of somebody else's image (Trib.Rome 20
July 1991, *Dir.inf.* 1992 p. 88) or for the use of somebody else's property (Douai 19 May
1952, *D.* 1952 *Jur.* 644). It has also been said that the quantum of damages should reflect the
profit which the injured party could have realized (Trib.Milan 8 Feb. 1990, *Dir.inf.* 1993 p.
126), and it has been asserted that the tort occasioned the plaintiff loss even where he did
not intend to commercialize his image (Cass. 16 Apr. 1991, n. 4031, *NGCC* 1992, I, 45; see
also Rb. Rotterdam 4 Feb. 1994, *NedJur* 1995 no. 39 p. 149, although there it was asserted by
the plaintiff that he was already in negotiations with another firm).

[667] 'Someone who has profited from participation in a crime or assault must pay damages
to the extent of his participation.'   [668] TS 31 Oct. 1994, *RAJ* 1994 no. 8007 p. 10409.

[669] *Inverugie Investments Ltd.* v. *Hacket* [1995] 1 WLR 713; see Cooke, 110 (1994) *LQR*
420–430.

[670] E.g. in *Whitwham* v. *Westminster Byrmbo Coal and Coke Co.* [1896] 2 Ch. 538; in
Swordheath Properties Ltd. v. *Tabet* [1979] 1 WLR 285; and in *Penarth Dock Engineering Co.
Ltd.* v. *Pounds* [1963] 1 Lloyd's Rep. 359 (where Lord Denning MR said: 'the test of the
measure of damages is not what the plaintiffs have lost, but what benefit the defendant has
obtained by having the use of the berth').

Almost everywhere, when assessing the quantum of damages for non-physical losses arising from infringement of privacy, means are found to recover profits made.[671] In cases of *comportement parasitaire* French courts appear to grant damages wholly independent of any loss to the person whose branded goods or reputation the wrongdoer has appropriated.[672] Italian courts estimate financial damages for cases of breach of intellectual property rights by referring to, amongst other things, the number of copies sold.[673] In many legal systems the level of damages is increased where the wrongdoer had calculated that he would make a profit if the court ordered a simple equalization of losses.[674] Finally, it can generally be said that all forms of punitive damages make it possible to return to the person whose rights were infringed any unjustified profit arising from the breach.[675]

That tort laws contain elements of the law of unjust enrichment is **522** apparent, not only from the legal remedies available, but also in many cases from the basis of liability itself. Because the whole point of the law of unjust enrichment is to cancel out unjustified transfers of wealth, it usually provides causes of action independent not only of damage[676] but

---

[671] An express statutory basis for that process is found in Art. 9 III of the Spanish Statute 1/1982 of 5 May 1982 concerning the civil law protection of reputation and the private life of the individual and the family, and the control of the use of a person's image. In most cases it is not greatly important whether or not there is a statutory basis for this. German judges very often concede that this is precisely their objective when deciding cases based on the law of privacy. See BGH 15 Nov. 1994, *NJW* 1995 p. 861: 'Where interference in the rights of privacy of the affected person is intended to increase circulation and hence profits, then the notion of prevention commands that the profit realized be included as a factor when calculating the quantum of damages.' See also the interview with the former Chairman of the 6th Senate, Steffen, *ZRP* 1994 pp. 196, 197.

[672] Paris 21 Nov. 1991, *D.* 1992 IR 37: a toy manufacturer called a product the 'Orient Express', infringing the trademark of the SNCF; liability of the toy manufacturer in tort; no discussion of quantum. See also Trib.gr.inst. Paris 1 Apr. 1992, *Gaz.Pal.* 1995, Somm. 217: unauthorized use of a picture of a castle with only minor changes for advertising purposes; *utilisation commerciale et parasitaire*; FF 30,000 damages for non-pecuniary loss.

[673] E.g. Trib. Rome 3 Nov. 1993, *Giur.it.* 1995, I, 2, 66.

[674] According to Clark, *Contract Law in Ireland*, 3rd edn., p. 446, this was the position adopted in the unpublished decision in *Hickey & Co. Ltd.* v. *Roches Stores (Dublin) Ltd. (No. 1)*.

[675] For a consideration of *violent profits* in Scottish law: Blackie, (1992) *Acta Juridica* pp. 23, 31–35; see also Walker, *Delict*, 2nd edn., pp. 937–938 and Stewart, *Introduction*, 2nd edn., pp. 24–28. They are granted in cases of *spuilzie* (removal of a thing against the will of its owner), ejection, and intrusion (forms of unlawful occupation of land). For exemplary damages in English law see *Rookes* v. *Barnard* [1964] AC 1129, 1227 (Lord Devlin); *Broome* v. *Cassell* [1972] AC 1027; *Riches* v. *News Group Newspapers* [1986] QB 256. From the literature see Markesinis/Deakin, *Tort Law*, 3rd edn., pp. 688–689. In French law, on the issue of whether he has suffered damage, the plaintiff is often assisted by the *concurrence déloyale* which enables the tortfeasor to be disciplined: see Houin/Pédamon, *Droit commercial*, 9th edn., no. 557.

[676] Despite the possibility of restitutionary damages in individual torts, it is still important to distinguish between the law of unjust enrichment and the general law of tort. This point is emphasized by Gething, *Tort Law Review*, 1995 pp. 124, 126.

also of fault.[677] The law of tort also often operates independently of fault, and where it waives the fault of the wrongdoer for the purpose of alloting to the entitled party by way of damages the increase in wealth obtained by the wrongdoer in contravention of the principles governing the allocation of property, one can justifiably talk of an area of tort law which is akin to that of unjust enrichment. In such legal systems, tort law equalizes deficiencies in the development of unjust enrichment in exactly the same way as other legal systems complement their narrow laws of tort by applying the law of unjust enrichment. Consequently, lacunae in the available protection exist only where either one or other is inadequate.[678]

523   Adoption by the law of tort of elements of unjust enrichment takes a wide variety of forms. In Danish law a number of provisions impose liability for damages on a party who breaches another's copyright or commercial interests, and for *bona fides* activities 'as long as it is reasonable' to declare them liable, the compensation 'not to exceed the level of profit yielded by the breach'.[679] A Danish Supreme Court decision in 1965 broke with the *culpa* rule. The unauthorized use of another person's image for advertising was unlawful 'according to general principles of law', so the wrongdoer was ordered to pay damages irrespective of fault.[680] Another piece of enrichment law is applied in French case-law: any infringement of property rights of another is *ipso facto* deemed to be a *faute*.[681] The clearest example of an 'anti-enrichment wrong'[682] is the English tort of conversion,[683] whose very name brings to mind the *actio de in rem verso*. 'Conversion consists of any act relating to the goods of another that constitutes an unjustifiable denial of his title to them.'[684] A person who sells another's goods commits the tort of conversion. Contributory negli-

---

[677] See Schluep, *Mélages Piotet*, pp. 173, 193–196; Deliyannis/Kornilakis, *Eidiko Enochiko Dikaio*, vol. iii, p. 14; and BGH 14 Apr. 1992, *ZIP* 1992 p. 857.

[678] A recent example is Swed. HD 21 May 1976, *NJA* 1976: 50 p. 282: unauthorized use of a photograph for advertising. Damages were refused on the ground that the matter was one of 'pure economic loss'; the law of unjust enrichment was not tested. On this see Bengtsson, *SJT* 1981 pp. 519, 529. The Swedish legislature immediately recognized the gap in protection which this case brought to light and closed it: 3 § *Lag om namm och bild i reklam* (SFS 1978: 800) provides that a suitable fee (*vederlag*) is payable to the injured party whose name or image are used with no fault. Where fault is shown, damages (*ersättning*) are payable over and above pure economic loss.

[679] A compilation of such Danish statutory formulations (e.g. in § 56 II Danish Copyright Act) is offered by Kruse, *Erstatningsretten*, 5th edn., p. 227.

[680] HD 25 Jan. 1965, *UfR* 1965 A p. 126, 134.

[681] Cass.civ. 10 Nov. 1992, Bull.civ. 1992, III, no. 292: '*L'empiètement sur la propriété de l'association était suffisant à caractériser la faute de la société.*'

[682] Birks, *Introduction to the Law of Restitution*, p. 329.   [683] See no. 290 above.

[684] McMahon/Binchy, *Irish Law of Torts*, 2nd edn., p. 534.

gence by the owner is as irrelevant[685] as fault by the defendant.[686] The no-fault character of conversion imposes liability not only on the *bona fide* vendor but also on the *bona fide* purchaser who acquires the goods and treats them as his own (save that if property in the goods was acquired in good faith in market overt,[687] the purchaser was not liable.

(3) Elements of Tort in the Law of Unjust Enrichment

It is often more advantageous for the person whose rights have been **524** infringed to base his claim in unjust enrichment than in tort.[688] Leaving aside issues of limitation[689] and the notorious difficulties of obtaining compensation for pure economic loss in tort,[690] it is usually preferable to claim in unjust enrichment where there is no damage[691] (and no possibility of an action for restitutionary damages) and the 'wrongdoer' was not at fault.[692] The person who without fault disposes of another's

---

[685] See no. 290 above. For Ireland see sec. 34(2)(d) Civil Liability Act 1961: 'The plaintiff's failure to exercise reasonable care in the protection of his own property shall, except to the extent that the defendant has been unjustly enriched, be deemed to be contributory negligence in an action for conversion of the property'.

[686] Tettenborn, (1993) 52 *CLJ* 128, 130; *Hollins* v. *Fowler* (1875) LR 7 HL 757.

[687] Sec. 22(1) Sale of Goods Act 1979 (c. 54): 'Where goods are sold in market overt, according to the usage of the market, the buyer acquires good title to the goods, provided he buys them in good faith and without notice of any defect or want of title on the part of the seller.' This was abolished on 3 Jan. 1995 by Sale of Goods (Amendment) Act 1994 (c. 32). The rule on acquisition in good faith from market overt also applied to stolen goods: *Reid* v. *Metropolitan Police Commissioner* [1973] QB 551.

[688] Continental commentators often assert (e.g. Schluep, *Mélanges Piotet*, pp. 173, 178) that in English law the plaintiff must renounce his right of action in tort in order to achieve this purpose. This is not the true legal position in England; see *United Australia Ltd.* v. *Barclays Bank Ltd.* [1941] AC 1, 13 (Viscount Simon), 28 (Lord Atkin), and 48 (Lord Porter); Goff/Jones, *Restitution*, 3rd edn., p. 605.

[689] Limitation periods for claims in unjust enrichment are mostly, but not always (see Arts. 482, 498 Port. Cc) longer than in tort. See for Austria §§ 1478 and 1489 ABGB and OGH 24 Sep. 1981, SZ 54/131 pp. 653, 656; for England Goff/Jones *Restitution*, 3rd edn., p. 606; for Spain TS 12 Apr. 1955, *RAJ* 1955 no. 1126 p. 602; and for Germany e.g. BGH 2 July 1971, BGHZ 56 pp. 317, 319. Whether a legal system accords equal importance to actions based in unjust enrichment and in tort, or whether it accords priority to the latter, becomes important at precisely this point: see above, nos. 518 and 520.

[690] Someone who collects on another's claim or in some other way disposes of it commits no tort under German, Austrian, Swedish, or Portugese law. He is not entitled to retain the equivalent value of the claim but must return it according to the general principles of unjust enrichment. See only OGH 11 July 1985, *JBl* 1986 p. 235 (claim as a 'thing' in the sense of § 1041 ABGB) and § 816 BGB (disposal of an 'object', i.e. of something more than a 'thing' as in the sense of § 90 BGB).

[691] 'The enriched party must repay the value of the use which he acquired. It is not necessary that the owner has suffered damage': OGH 17 Mar. 1982, SZ 55/37 pp. 183, 186.

[692] Where there is a requirement that enrichment give rise to a corresponding loss ('*danno*' in the sense of Art. 2041 I Ital. Cc) the decisive point is naturally that there is no requirement to show fault. This does not mean that there is no requirement to show damage; see e.g. for Spain TS 15 Nov. 1990, *RAJ* 1990 no. 8712 p. 11114: a purchaser acquired land at an auction ordered by the court. The land register did not show that a bungalow had been built on the plot, so the purchaser paid the value of an empty plot. The

property so that the other is deprived of his rights to that property commits an objective infringement of property rights, but in many legal systems no tort is committed. There, this form of conversion incurs a liability based on the law of unjust enrichment. This typically imposes an obligation to return the price achieved at sale,[693] and especially sums in excess of the objective value of the object.[694] The law of unjust enrichment has for some time extended beyond infringements of property rights. It has acquired real practical significance in connection with infringement of personality rights, especially in Germany[695] and Austria.[696] Many situations which other legal systems deal with under tort law[697] are in these two countries treated as unjust enrichment. The general practice in both countries has been to keep the application of tort within as narrow an area as possible. However, on a European scale this attitude has practical effects only at the margins of liability, for example on limitation.[698]

525   An elegant example is the BGH decision of 26.6.1981.[699] The plaintiff, an advertising agency, owned several racing cars on whose windscreens

---

mistake only became apparent some time later. The purchaser sold the plot for a higher price. He was ordered by the court to repay the difference on the basis of a claim brought in unjust enrichment. On the other hand, see TS 5 Oct. 1985, *RAJ* 1985 no. 4085: unlawful use of land; damages for the accrued loss but not for other benefits obtained by the defendant.

[693] Where an object is sold by an unauthorized person for less than the market price, according to an elderly Danish decision, reference should be made to the objective value of the thing: ØLD 4 Oct. 1921, *UfR* 1922 A p. 1. However, the (correct) tendency today is the opposite, because the price actually realized on the market usually represents the objective value of the article. See VLD 10 Feb. 1919, *UfR* 1919 A p. 483.

[694] See for France Art. 1380 Cc ('*prix de la vente*'); for Portugal Pires de Lima/Antunes Varela, *Cc anotado*, vol. i, 4th edn., pp. 460–461; for Austria OGH 10 Nov. 1954, SZ 27/286 p. 700; for Italy Geri/Breccia/Busnelli/Natoli, *Diritto civile*, vol. iii, pp. 829–832; for Germany BGH 8 Jan. 1959, BGHZ 29 p. 157. For Greece, Georgiades/Stathopoulos (-Stathopoulos), *Greek Cc*, vol. iv, Art. 904 nos. 21, 22 are of the opinion that the part which is exclusively referable to the personal contribution of the person enriched should not be deducted. The author does not share that view. Equally suspect is CA Athens 2073/1987, *EllDik* 29 (1988) p. 550: the defendant used the plaintiff's land without permission and rented parts of it as parking lots to third parties. The CA said that the term 'damage' in Art. 904 Greek Cc went beyond that in Art. 914 Greek Cc, but the defendant only had to repay the amount which he should have paid for renting the property. He was allowed to keep any profit as that was referable to his entrepreneurial skill. This decision amounts to an open invitation to use the property of others.

[695] BGH 8 May 1956, BGHZ 20 pp. 345, 354; BGH 26 June 1981 (no. 525); BGH 26 June 1979, *NJW* 1979 p. 2205; BGH 14 Oct. 1986, *GRUR* 1987 p. 128; BGH 14 Apr. 1992, *VersR* 1993 p. 66.

[696] See esp. OGH 16 Feb. 1982, SZ 55/12 p. 54: use of a picture of a sportsman for advertising.

[697] See no. 521 above; cf. the *Carrera* case (no. 525 below); Paris 21 Nov. 1991 (fn. 672 above).

[698] It is only with very great difficulty that infringements of privacy rights can lead to abolition of enrichment which exempts the infringer from liability (§ 818 III BGB).   [699] BGHZ 81 p. 75.

the name of the firm was clearly legible. The defendant firm, Carrera, manufactured toy racing cars. On its packaging Carrera used a photograph of the plaintiff's cars without authority. The name of the plaintiff company on the windscreen had been retouched so as to read 'Carrera'. The BGH found a breach of the plaintiff's general right of personality. For this infringement 'the defendant had to grant (the plaintiff) compensation by way of enrichment according to § 812 sec. 1 sub-sec. 1, independent of the defendant's fault or of any damage suffered by the plaintiff'.[700] The sum due was that which the plaintiff could reasonably have demanded for its consent. Whether the plaintiff would have given consent and whether the defendant should have advertised as it did, had it known that it would have had to pay for the plaintiff's consent, were irrelevant. This is because an enrichment claim is not intended to compensate the loss to the party whose rights have been infringed, but to neutralize the additional wealth (where there is no legal basis for this increase) which the enriched party has acquired.[701]

III. TORT AND PROPERTY LAW

Bibliography: Alonso Pérez, 'Las relaciones de vecindad', *An.Der.Civ.* 36 vol. i (1983) pp. 357–396; v. Bar, 'Zur Dogmatik des zivilrechtlichen Ausgleichs von Umweltschäden', *KF* 1987 (published 1989) pp. 4–18; Boukema, *Samenloop* (Deventer 1992; Monografieën Nieuw BW A-21); Chartier, *La réparation du préjudice* (Paris 1983); Cornelis/Van Ommeslaghe, 'Les "faits justificatifs" dans le droit belge de la responsabilité aquilienne', in: *In memoriam Jean Limpens* (Antwerp 1987) pp. 265–287; Derine, 'Hinder uit nabuurschap en rechtsmisbruik', *TPR* 1983 pp. 261–291; Drion, 'De betekenis van het bezit voor ons huidige recht', *WPNR* 1967 no. 4941 pp. 109–113, 4942 pp. 121–127, and 4943 pp. 133–137; *Encyclopédie Dalloz* (-Cadiet) vol. i, *Abus de droit* (Paris 1992); *Encyclopédie Dalloz* (-Gaillot-Mercier) vol. ix, *Troubles de voisinage* (Paris 1994); Georgiades, *Empragmato Dikaio*, vol. i (Athens 1991); Gursky, 'Zur neueren Diskussion um § 1004 BGB', *JR* 1989 pp. 397–402; Hecht/Muzak, 'Umwelthaftung im Nachbarrecht', *JBl* 1994 pp. 159–165; *JClCiv* (-Agostini), arts. 1382 to 1386. 'Régimes divers. Troubles de voisinage', *Fasc.* 265 (Paris 1987); *JClCiv* (-Jourdain), arts. 1382 to 1386, 'Droit à réparation. Responsabilité fondée sur la faute. Imputabilité et faits justificatifs', *Fasc.* 121 (Paris 1986); *JClCiv* (-Panouil), arts. 711 to 717, 1er App., *Action en*

---

[700] Ibid. p. 81.   [701] Ibid. p. 82.

revendication (Paris 1991); Karakostas, 'Rechtsmittel zum Schutz der Umweltgüter im griechischen Recht', *NuR* 1993 pp. 467–473; Kerschner, 'Umwelthaftung im Nachbarrecht', *JBl* 1993 pp. 216–222; Köbl, *Das Eigentümer-Besitzer-Verhältnis im Anspruchssystem des BGB* (Berlin 1971); Kremhelmer, *Die Regelung des Herausgabeanspruchs und der Nebenansprüche nach dem französischen und deutschen Zivilrecht* (diss. Munich 1965); Lawson, 'Common law', in: *Structural Variations in Property Law, IntEncCompL* VI 2 (Tübingen *et al.* 1975); López-Nieto y Mallo, *Manual de actividades molestas, insalubres, nocivas y peligrosas* 2nd edn. (Madrid 1986); Malaurie/Aynès, *Les biens. La publicité foncière*, 2nd edn. (Paris 1992); Marshall, *General Principles of Scots Law*, 5th edn. (Edinburgh 1991); Moreno Trujillo, *La protección jurídico-privada del medio ambiente y la responsabilidad por su deterioro* (Barcelona 1991); Van Neste, *Beginselen van Belgisch Privaatrecht*, vol. v: Zakenrecht. Book 1 (Brussels 1990); Pagh, *Erstatningsansvar for miljøskader* (Copenhagen 1990); Roca Juan, 'Sobre el deber general de respeto a la persona (Derecho civil y medio ambiente)', *An.Der.Civ.* 39 vol. ii (1986) pp. 763–786; Rodenburg, *Misbruik van bevoegdheid* (Deventer 1985; Monografieën Nieuw BW A-4); Roussos, 'I arnitiki agogi: Metaxi rei vindicatio kai aposimioseos', *NoB* 35 (1987) pp. 1122–1131; Rummel, 'Erfolgshaftung im Nachbarrecht?', *JBl* 1967 pp. 120–126; Spyridakis, 'Gedanken über einen allgemeinen privatrechtlichen Aufopferungsanspruch', in: *FS Sontis* (Munich 1977) pp. 241–251; Terré/Simler, *Droit civil. Les biens*, 4th edn. (Paris 1992); Tucci, 'La risarcibilità del danno da atto lecito nel diritto civile', *Riv.Dir.Civ.* 13 (1967) pp. 229–268; Visonà, 'Tutela della persona a fronte dell'intollerabilità delle immissioni di rumore', *NGCC* 1992, I, pp. 853–857.

1. GENERAL

526 There is a fundamental difference between the legal systems of the common law countries and those of mainland Europe concerning the relationship between tort and property law. The English law of property (perhaps with the exception of real property or land law) cannot be described as a closed, independent, and systematic body of law. It is much more a cross-section of law containing elements of contract, trust, and tort. It would therefore be erroneous to regard property law and tort law as neighbouring areas of law. Rather, each is a necessary element of the other. This is perhaps seen most clearly from the perspective of the civil law systems when it is said that 'common law . . . has never known a vindication of movables'.[702] Conversion, and therefore the law of

---

[702] Lawson, *IntEncCompL* VI 2–31.

torts,[703] takes over the function of *rei vindicatio* (the owner's right to the return of an object from the person in possession). Thus a tort is committed where someone retains an item which the owner has rightfully claimed. Until the return is demanded, however, there is no need for a common law rule.[704] If the owner does not claim the return, even where he does not know who is in possession of the goods (and the person in possession does not know who the owner is) then quite simply there is no case.

The common law adopts the bilateral perspective of an action between **527** the individual plaintiff and defendant and thereby emphasizes the position of the defendant rather than that of the plaintiff. The notion of absolute right is not recognized: a notion which for continental property lawyers is at the very heart of their understanding of property law. Quite alien to English law is the pomp, reflecting as it does a combination of natural law and ideology, with which sole control over an item is bestowed upon its owner in all mainland European civil codes.[705] On sober analysis there is much to be said for the view that the difference, of such importance to the civil codes of Europe, between absolute and relative rights reflects a notion which is lacking in content. Be that as it may, the concept of absolute rights and the *rei vindicatio* belong inseparably together.[706] *'L'action en revendication est l'action réelle par excellence puisque'elle tend à la reconnaissance de la propriété'.*[707] Where the *rei vindicatio* exists there also exists an independent law of ownership or, as it is more commonly expressed in Europe,[708] an independent law of

---

[703] Until 1977 there were 2 co-existing torts: namely conversion and detinue. Detinue was abolished in English law by sec. 2(1) Torts (Interference with Goods) Act 1977 but it remains part of Irish law, in which a plaintiff can resort to either form of action, see *British Wagon Co. Ltd.* v. *Short* [1961] IR 164.

[704] It is difficult for an English-trained lawyer to comprehend how the position can be any different in continental legal systems. One answer (and there may well be others) is that a legal system can return to such a 'silent' claim for the return of an item in other contexts. For example, according to § 931 German BGB it is possible, by assigning a particular claim, to convey the property in a goods in the possession of somebody who remains unknown to a new owner.

[705] See Art. 544 French, Belgian, and Luxemb. Cc; § 362 ABGB Art. 348 I Span. Cc; § 903 BGB; Art. 832 Ital. Cc; Art. 1000 Greek Cc; Art. 1305 Port. Cc; Art. 5:1 BW.

[706] Among the more noteworthy points of legal history is the fact that the *Code civil* allocates the *rei vindicatio* a subsidiary importance (Art. 2279 II Cc), a fact which is linked to the great value attributed to possession as far as ownership is concerned (Art. 2279 I Cc). Apart from this the *rei vindicatio* is found in all European civil codes (§ 366 ABGB; § 985 BGB; Art. 948 Ital. Cc; Art. 1094 Greek Cc; Art. 1311 Port. Cc). In Spain (Art. 348 II Cc) and The Netherlands (Art. 5:2 BW) it is given expression immediately following the definition of property.

[707] *JClCiv* (-Ranouil), Arts. 711 to 717. 1er App., no. 3.

[708] The Scottish literature also refers to the 'law of things': Marshall, *General Principles of Scots Law*, 5th edn., p. 155.

things,[709] whose core is the protection and realization of the exclusive powers of ownership. By contrast, where there is no such thing as an absolute right the expression 'property law' has only a descriptive function.

528 Other factors determine both the content of the rules and the scope of property law within the legal systems of mainland Europe. However, they do not define this particular area of law. Which of these other factors is most important clearly depends on how property and other rights in things are passed. Where the change in ownership is completed by a contract of sale (as in France) the law of property is not at all wide. Essentially it need only proscribe the extent of an owner's powers and the means, e.g. lien or licence, by which ownership of the property may be altered. In practice, however, the law of property becomes ever more detailed because changes to ownership depend on transfer of possession; an independent contract for the procurement of the property may even be demanded, as in Germany. Lastly, in all systems where transfer of title depends upon transfer of possession, many more rules are needed to define the law of possession.

529 From the point of view of tort all questions concerning changes in the legal relationships of things are referable to the law of tort. Although the laws of property and tort do not see eye to eye here, they do share a common approach to the issues surrounding the preservation of absolute rights. Two aspects are particularly important. The first concerns the fact that legal systems based on a developed doctrine of absolute rights tend to organize their tort law around the protection of such absolute rights. § 823 I of the German BGB ('Whoever either intentionally or negligently . . . damages the property or other right . . . is liable . . .') is by no means the only example.[710] Its wording reveals a clear link with concepts from the law of property, although rights in things other than property are also important. Irrespective of the extent to which each

---

[709] One possible reason why the civil codes of Germany, Greece, The Netherlands, Portugal, and Austria speak, not of the law of ownership, but of law of things is that the law of things recognizes other 'absolute rights' besides ownership, such as the right of lien and legal possession. In fact the different terms used are not decisive. The official bilingual edition of the Italian *Codice civile* translates the heading of the third book *'Della proprietà'* quite easily into the 'law of things' (*Sachenrecht*). It is worth mentioning that the term 'thing' (*Sache*) encompasses a variety of concepts. For most legal systems things are physical objects (§ 90 BGB; Art. 810 Ital. Cc; Art. 947 Greek Cc; and Art. 3:2 BW). In contrast, French law recognizes *meubles par la détermination de la loi* (Art. 529 Cc) comparable to the *choses in action* of English law. Similarly, Austrian law differentiates between things *in rem* and *in personam* (§ 367 ABGB) and counts tort with contract law as part of 'law of things *in personam*' (see the heading to §§ 859–1341 ABGB). Finally, the term *bienes* (goods) in Art. 333 Span. Cc covers more than physical goods: see TS 26 Feb. 1979, *RAJ* 1979 no. 525 p. 439.
[710] See above at nos. 11–25 on the structural principles of the fundamental tortious norms of the codified systems.

country's tort law protects interests other than absolute rights, those rights also have to be included in tort's protection. This is now the case everywhere in mainland Europe. In contrast, the common law has at its disposal only the category of damage, which is not further developed. Damage in the context of negligence covers only physical injury, whether to person or thing. This is important because, whilst every physical injury to a thing also constitutes damage to a proprietary interest, a proprietary interest can be breached without physical damage to property. In the common law such damage-free breaches are dealt with by various other torts. For example, trespass to land is said to be actionable without proof of actual damage:[711] there is a right of action even in the absence of physical damage. In the civil law systems of mainland Europe such a statement is self-evident: it is the breach of a right which gives rise to liability and, because the right is property, property is damaged even without physical damage. The right to undisturbed possession is part of the right of ownership, and can therefore even be protected by the law of tort as one of the 'other rights' under § 823 I BGB.

The law of property is important for the law of tort not only in laying **530** down rules whose breach must be compensated by tort. It is equally important to note that in many countries property law has developed techniques for creating compensatory rules to complement those dealing solely with the content and scope of absolute rights.[712] Thus has arisen a suction effect of the law of property on the law of tort. This development is discernible, to a greater or lesser degree,[713] in all the legal systems of

---

[711] See no. 257 above. The same problem is encountered in *trespass to goods*. If it is true that someone who uses my toothbrush does not 'damage' it, then I can only claim damages if trespass to goods is 'actionable *per se*', see McMahon/Binchy, *Irish Law of Torts*, 2nd edn., p. 524.

[712] The difference between common law and civil law should not be overemphasized. However, it is clear in many special statutes that on the continent the starting point is the legal principles concerning the law of ownership (e.g. § 905 BGB: 'the right of the owner of land extends over the space above the ground . . . The owner may not prevent interferences undertaken at such an altitude . . . that he has no interest in their being prevented'). By contrast, English law goes straight to the issue of liability, e.g. sec. 40(1) Civil Aviation Act 1949 (c. 67): 'No action shall lie in respect of trespass or in respect of nuisance, by reason only of the flight of an aircraft over any property at a height above the ground which . . . is reasonable.'

[713] The Italian *Codice civile* has the strong tendency to adopt rules on liability directly into its law of property. See Arts. 843 II Cc (damage caused by stepping onto somebody's property); 913 III Cc (damage resulting from interference with the natural flow of watercourses); 917 Cc (costs for the upkeep of dams); 924 (damage caused in pursuing a swarm of bees); 936 III s. 2 Cc (damage caused by building on someone else's land); 938 Cc (building works extending onto neighbouring land); 939 III Cc (different things becoming mixed together; damage caused by gross negligence); and 949 II Cc (*actio negatoria*). For further examples see Arts. 1079, 1148, and 1171 Cc. The new Dutch Civil Code (BW) has deliberately kept its 5th Book ('*Zakelijke rechten*') slim, and many issues concerning liability are covered in Book 6 (see *Parlementaire Geschiedenis*, vol. v, p. 2; Arts. 5: 37, 5: 39, and 40 BW). Exceptions such as those in Art. 5:23 II BW (damage caused by stray animals) are rare.

Europe[714] for example, in cases of (aggressive) necessity,[715] referred to above.[716] The rule is that the owner must tolerate damage to his belongings by someone in an emergency; this rule has the character of property law. The complementary rule, that the owner is not obliged to accept damage without the right to compensation, derives its characteristics from the law of obligations.

531   Cases of 'aggressive necessity' concern only one aspect of the wide topic of justification, which need not be explored in depth at this point. Three other areas of overlap between property law and tort are more significant here: obligations between neighbours; the relevance of the *actio negatoria* from the perspective of the law of obligations; and the problem of how compensation is addressed in the 'owner–possessor relationship', as it is called in many legal systems. The first area has been chosen because at the heart of disputes between neighbours is a social conflict common to almost every legal system. Most systems have developed mechanisms allowing compensation independent of fault (section 2 below). In the second and third areas, substantial differences of opinion are encountered. In some systems the issue is whether there is a general right of action to rectify wrongful interference (section 3 below); in others the issue is whether a wrongful but *bona fide* possessor requires any form of special protection when he damages something he believes to be his own (section 4 below).

2. LIABILITY FOR LAND USE DAMAGING ADJACENT PROPERTIES

a. Content and Extent of Property Law

532   Liability law subjects the relationships between neighbours to a special legal regime only to the extent that, because of the location of their respective properties, the parties have a particular dependency on each other. This only arises where excessive use by one party of his property interferes with or frustrates the reasonable use of the other's

---

[714] The sharpest division is offered by the modern Swedish legislation. E.g. chap. 3 § 3 Land Act (*jordabalk*) lays down a number of protective duties for owners carrying out earthworks, and refers to the Environmental Liability Act (*miljöskadelag*) in respect of liability for paying damages to compensate breach.

[715] Not be confused with 'defensive necessity', where the danger arose from the thing which is subsequently damaged. E.g. TS 24 Jan. 1995, *RAJ* 1995 no. 141 p. 214: a hunter shot a bear which had earlier attacked him, and which was protected by a conservation provision). In such a case the owner naturally has no right to claim damages. See *Gerrard* v. *Crowe and Another* [1921] 1 AC 395 (PC): To prevent flooding a land-owner built a dam which caused another plot of land to be damaged by water; liability rejected.

[716] See no. 512 and fn. 611 above. There is no principle in common law corresponding to § 904 II BGB. Cf. *Southport Corporation* v. *Esso Petroleum Co. Ltd.* [1953] 3 WLR 773; *Cooper* v. *Sharp (No. 2)* [1912] 1 KB 496.

property. Not every tort between neighbours brings into play the law on the respective interests of neighbours: someone who neglects a disused and dilapidated property so that children gain access to and light a fire on it which spreads to adjacent buildings[717] is liable under the usual rules of tort. The same applies to someone who throws a yew tree onto his compost heap which is then eaten by and kills a horse from a neighbouring paddock.[718] The law governing relationships between neighbours does not cover personal injury or rights to personality.[719] Genuine cases of the law governing relationships between neighbours only arise where emissions or other comparable substances affect another's property. In other words, it covers those cases which today are covered essentially by environmental law.[720] The neighbour is the first to be affected when a property owner causes noise or vibrations or fails to prevent substances escaping from his property.

For the majority of European countries with civil codes, the law **533** governing relationships between neighbours has traditionally been a part of property law; this is because property law has been the most concerned to demarcate two equally valid 'absolute' subjective rights so that each is allowed to develop to its fullest potential despite the inherent conflict between them. This is why rules have been drawn up which prescribe what an owner may and may not do with his property relative to his neighbour.[721]

---

[717] *Smith* v. *Littlewoods Organisation Ltd.* [1987] AC 241.

[718] HR 22 Apr. 1994, *RvdW* 1994 no. 101.

[719] As in BGH 15 May 1970, BGHZ 54 pp. 56, 61 (breach of the right to personality), so too in Cass. 19 May 1976, n. 1796, *Giur.it.* 1978, I, 1, 412 and Cass.sez.un. 19 July 1985, n. 4263, *NGCC* 1986 p. 226 (injury to health). Also see BGH 18 Sep. 1984, BGHZ 92 p. 143 with its theory that 'the rules governing the legal relationships between neighbours in the area where they apply are to determine authoritatively whether an unlawful act in the sense of § 823 I BGB is at issue' must not be understood to apply to issues of personal injury (v. Bar, *KF* 1987 pp. 4, 10). Cases on relationships between neighbours always involve 'a claim originating from property ownership' (BGH loc. cit. p. 145). It must not be overlooked that this view of the matter is not universally shared. Art. 1346 Port. Cc also protects rights to health and personality; this is confirmed by RC 25 Oct. 1983, *CJ* VIII (1983–4) p. 60. Similarly, recent Italian decisions indicate that Art. 844 of the *Codice civile*, enabling a claim in property law, also allows a 'personal' action under Art. 2058 (e.g. Trib. Milan 10 Dec. 1992, *NGCC* 1993, I, 786). Cass. 1 Feb. 1995, n. 1156, *Giur.it.* 1995, I, 1, 1836 moves the matter back into position and says that a claim based on Art. 844 Cc requires lasting, or at least periodic emissions; for occasional emissions the plaintiff must rely on the right of action in tort under Art. 2043, with its 5-year limitation period.

[720] The wider the definition of the term 'neighbour', the closer environmental law and the law governing relationships between neighbours approach one another: see Kerschner, *JBl* 1993 pp. 216–222; Hecht/Muzak, *JBl* 1994 pp. 159–165. OGH 11 June 1981, *JBl* 1982 p. 595 says: 'the law, in order to prevent infringements, reaches beyond immediate neighbours [and continues] to the extent that emissions have any effect at all'.

[721] A particularly successful formulation is found in Art. 367 I of the Compilation of regional law of Navarre: 'The owner or other user of property must not injure his neighbour and must desist from causing him any more nuisance than that which arises from the reasonable use of their (owner/other user) rights taking account of the needs of each property, the use to which the locality is put, and equitable factors'.

Norms of conduct are found within the definition of property law, to which the law of tort also refers. Conduct permitted by the law governing relationships between neighbours does not constitute breach of a proprietary interest as understood by the law of obligations.[722] If there is no breach of the rights of an owner of neighbouring property, there can be no wrongful act against a mere occupier (tenant or lessee) of that property. The occupier cannot have a better right than the owner.[723] Regulations of the law governing relationships between neighbours work their way into the legal obligations between occupiers (i.e. non-owners) of adjacent properties. Even a plaintiff land-user who merely leaves his vehicle in a parking place where its paintwork is damaged by emissions from an adjacent copper factory, can find his action successfully defended with the argument that only those acts against him are forbidden which would constitute wrongful conduct between neighbouring land-owners.[724]

b. Substantial Interferences

534 What land-owners may and may not do is determined by whether or not there is any substantial interference.[725] All land-owners must accept minor interference with the use of their property, that constitutes neither a nuisance nor an actionable interference with property. It has never been the purpose of property law to protect such interference.[726] By contrast, substantial interference represents a breach of a proprietary right which, in the absence of a specific justification,[727] amounts to a

---

[722] See only BGH 18 Sep. 1984 (fn. 719 above); CFI Athens 16768/1980, *NoB* 29 (1981) p. 1423 (conduct within the boundaries of Art. 1003 Greek Cc is lawful in the sense of Art. 914 Greek Cc); Swed. HD 1 Mar. 1990, *NJA* 1990: 14 p. 71; Swed. HD 28 Mar. 1994, *NJA* 1994: 34 p. 162.

[723] This applies to the occupier not only as injured party (see Cass. 21 Feb. 1994, n. 1653, *Giust.civ.Mass.* 1994 no. 1653 p. 187) but also in his capacity as the person causing the emission. In The Netherlands *Parlementaire Geschiedenis*, vol. v, p. 4 rightly states that Art. 5: 37 BW, which governs the owner's liability for any disturbances caused to his neighbour, also applies by way of analogy to non-owners (i.e. users and occupiers of the property). The position is very similar in Austria: OGH 11 June 1981 (fn. 720 above), and Germany, where BGH 2 Mar. 1984, BGHZ 90 pp. 255, 262 is just one example of many.

[724] BGH 18 Sep. 1984 (fn. 719 above).

[725] See § 906 BGB (and no. 536 below); Arts. 1346 Port. Cc; 1003 Greek Cc; 844 Ital. Cc; and § 364 II ABGB.

[726] In this context the concept of abuse of legal rights is not relevant. The latter is much more likely to depend upon essential interference, such as where building works, without fault on anybody's part, extend onto the property of the neighbour who has seen and allowed this: Rodenburg, *Misbruik van bevoegdheid*, p. 82. For the limits to the remedy of self-help in English law see *Burton* v. *Winters* [1993] 1 WLR 1077.

[727] Such justification arises in certain circumstances in the granting of operating licences, but this is rarely a good defence (see v. Bar, *KF* 1987 pp. 4, 14; HR 26 Nov. 1993, *RvdW* 1993 no. 238; and OGH 20 Jan. 1981, *JBl* 1981 p. 534): such licences are not

wrongful act. Whether the interference is substantial depends on the facts of each case; the law of nuisance states that interference is largely, if not exclusively, 'a matter of fact'.[728] In some cases the interference is so trivial that no further consideration is warranted.[729] For the most part, however, it depends on what is regarded as normal for the location of the property. Normative criteria play a part in deciding, for example, whether the use complained of is allowed in public law,[730] or is otherwise reasonable.[731]

c. Forms of Liability without Fault

Where negligence results in a substantial interference with the use of   **535** adjacent property the owner of that property has a right of action in tort for damages. There is nothing controversial in this. The topic becomes a little more complicated when one asks whether it is reasonable to stand by this so as to deny the affected property owner the right to claim damages when the party from whose land the interference arose was not at fault.[732] In modern Europe this position has been overwhelmingly

---

generally intended to interfere with the rights of third parties to claim damages. There is no liability for essential emissions where the land-owner is expressly forbidden from removing the source of the emission (as in BGH 20 Nov. 1992, BGHZ 120 p. 239, where the emission was caused by frogs enjoying legal protection).

[728] Walker, *Delict*, 2nd edn., p. 959.

[729] A good example is HR 28 Apr. 1995, *RvdW* 1995 no. 105: a gardener sued an agricultural school which had, for the purposes of instruction, acquired a swarm of bees. The bees flew over the gardener's greenhouses on their way to feed on the waste from a nearby jam factory. In so doing they left excreta on the greenhouse roofs. The *Hoge Raad* rejected a claim in tort for the cost of cleaning. At most the bees were responsible for 1% of the soiling to the greenhouse roofs. A similar decision on liability for weed seed carried by the wind was given in HR 3 May 1991, *NedJur* 1991 no. 476, p. 2063. In Swed. HD 26 July 1988, *NJA* 1988: 68 p. 376 the aesthetic interference and general discomfort brought about by a magnetic field created by an electric cable laid through an industrial estate was held to be insignificant. The significance of noise emissions was an issue in BGH 20 Nov. 1992 (fn. 727 above) and Danish HD 17 Mar. 1995, *UfR* 1995 A p. 466; smells emanating from a pig sty were at the centre of RC 12 Apr. 1988, *CJ* XIII (1988–2) p. 63; and BGH 16 Dec. 1977, BGHZ 70 pp. 102, 108–111 concerned the level of fluorine gas emissions.

[730] E.g. HR 15 May 1992, *NedJur* 1992 no. 510 p. 2057: a neighbour does not have to put up with his neighbour's house being used for a purpose inconsistent with a building scheme; an injunction was granted under Art. 1401 BW (old). The decision was different in Cass.sez.un. 27 Nov. 1974, n. 3873, *Foro.it.* 1975, I, 317, where building work was undertaken without the necessary licence, because the requirement for such a licence was not intended to benefit individual members of the public. In Italy when building law which is intended to protect the interest of individuals is infringed, a claim for damages and/or an injunction will be granted: see Cass. 5 Apr. 1984, n. 2207, *NGCC* 1985, I, 175.

[731] See no. 263 above for the concept of 'reasonable user' in nuisance.

[732] The Portugese Cc recognizes very few circumstances in which one neighbour can be liable to another in the absence of fault (e.g. Arts. 1347 III and 1348 II [see STJ 7 Nov. 1972, *BolMinJust* 221 (1972) p. 195)]; none of these applies to cases involving emissions. Art. 1346 Cc, on this issue, governs only the circumstances under which injunctions can be granted.

repudiated, as explained above. For most countries the issue is to determine the circumstances (by no means everywhere the same) in which strict liability can apply between neighbours. The legal and technical concepts employed to bring this about in the different countries are anything but uniform. Common law operates exclusively within the system of tort. Recall that nuisance and breach of the rule in *Rylands* v. *Fletcher* are torts which can be committed without negligence.[733]

536   Unfortunately, German law starts, not from the law of tort, but from the perspective of property law, which creates a range of difficulties. § 906 sec. 1 BGB refers to the obligation to accept non-substantial interferences such as 'gases, steam, smells, smoke, soot, heat, noise, vibrations, and similar effects originating from another property'. Leaving aside the implication that tangible emissions always represent substantial interference (which may not be the case[734]) it is not controversial. It is § 906 II BGB which contains the potential for error. By virtue of s. 1 a property owner is obliged to accept substantial interference to his property so long as it is typical of the locality, and provided that it cannot be prevented by reasonable expenditure by the owner of the land from which it emanates. § 906 II 2 BGB states that the affected property owner is entitled to claim damages arising from such interference. The law not only recognizes substantial interferences which are typical of the locality in question, but also allows damages to compensate for having to accept the interference. Whilst it is not particularly important whether the substantiality can be defined regardless of the vicinity in which the interference arises, the entitlement to damages is a grave mistake. This is because it creates a relationship between victim and tortfeasor which resembles that between an individual and the state which expropriates his property.[735]

537   The intention was to compel property owners to accept substantial interferences while providing that those interferences did not constitute

---

An action for damages requires fault. The position is identical in Greece. There is no claim to damages akin to that contained in § 906 II BGB (see Art. 1003 Greek Cc); decisions of Greek courts have held firm to the requirement of fault (e.g. CFI Athens 16678/1980, *NoB* 29 [1981] p. 1423). Art. 1003 Greek Cc is exceeded to the extent that substantial interferences (albeit ones which are typical of the locality) are present: a person who in such a case omits to carry out necessary measures acts unlawfully under Art. 914 Greek Cc (CA Athens 1773/1982, *Arm.* 37/1983 p. 215; CA Athens 7800/1982, *EllDik* 24/1983 p. 807). The literature follows this. See Georgiades, *Empragmato Dikaio*, vol. i, p. 295.

[733] See nos. 262–267 above.

[734] No substantial interference occurs when a tile falls from one dilapidated building onto another which is adjacent.

[735] The BGH has stated repeatedly that the quantum of damages is to be determined by the principles applied to compensation for compulsory purchase of property (e.g. BGH 2 Mar. 1984, BGHZ 90 pp. 255, 263.)

unlawful acts. As a result, the injured property owner has a claim against his neighbour akin to that of a land-owner against the state which compulsorily purchases his land. The individual can no longer prevent the activity of his neighbour with an injunction (which could be very damaging for industry). It is not, however, sufficient to say he should be entitled only to compensation for pecuniary loss (*Ausgleich*) (as according to § 906 II 2 BGB) and not to full damages in tort. A substantial interference with property is and remains unlawful in the absence of justification. It is not clear how substantial interference in such cases could be justified. Consequently, it is not unreasonable that German courts are rewarding levels of compensation almost equal to full damages in tort.[736] To define the prerequisites for a claim for compensation under § 906 II 1 BGB is truly problematic. First, it is hard to understand why the rules which apply to intangible emissions should not also apply to tangible emissions. Secondly, it is difficult to understand why the claim for compensation should depend on the property owner having no right to injunctive relief. For it may be argued that not bringing an action for an injunction amounts to contributory negligence; yet it would be absurd for someone who, after a protracted trial, finally obtains an injunction only to be denied compensation for the damage suffered in the interim.[737] In § 906 II 2 BGB German jurisprudence has encountered a difficult problem which has not been resolved. Within the confines of the rule, German courts solved the problem in the most reasonable way possible, permitting a general claim for compensation in the law governing the relationships between neighbours which exceeds the text of that law. This claim ignores the factors listed in § 906 I BGB and requires only that it was impossible to prevent the actual impairment.[738] This claim for compensation within the law of neighbours has become the nearest thing in German law to the rule in *Rylands* v. *Fletcher*.

The *cause célèbre*, decided by the BGH on 2.3.1984[739] comes up again: **538** the parties owned properties on a slope, with that of the defendant above that of the plaintiff. The plaintiff farmed its property organically,

---

[736] Not only reductions in value are to be compensated. Loss of income (BGH 31 May 1974, BGHZ 62 pp. 361, 371) and even benefits from private use which have been lost (BGH 29 Mar. 1984, BGHZ 91 pp. 20, 24–25) are also recoverable. On the other hand, it is no surprise that compensation 'need only be paid where the interference goes beyond what can reasonably be borne' (BGH 31 May 1974, BGHZ 62 p. 361). Yet the same end will be achieved by classifying the action as one in tort: see. Swedish HD 30 June 1977, *NJA* 1977: 76 p. 424.

[737] As was the result in BGH 29 Oct. 1954, BGHZ 15 pp. 146, 150–151.

[738] A compilation of decided cases on the topic of '*de facto* compulsion to tolerate interference' is provided by BGH 20 Apr. 1990, BGHZ 111 p. 158 (concerning lead waste from a shooting gallery). From more recent cases see BGH 18 Nov. 1994, *NJW* 1995 p. 714.

[739] BGHZ 90 p. 255; see no. 266 above.

whereas the defendant farmed conventionally. After particularly heavy rain, the run-off carried chemicals onto the plaintiff's land so that its vegetables could no longer be described as organic. The BGH held that § 906 was applicable because the interference had a natural cause.[740] It added that it was not decisive whether before the event which led to the damage the plaintiff could have demanded of the defendant either to stop using pesticides or to prevent the outflow of the chemicals. 'For according to BGH case-law a claim for compensation analogous to § 906 II 2 BGB exists where the interference from one property affecting the adjacent one is unlawful and for that reason need not be tolerated, the affected property owner or occupier is for some special reason prevented from keeping this interference under control according to §§ 1004 sec. 1, 862 sec. 1 BGB . . .'.[741]

539   Considered more closely, the 'compulsion to accept interference' on which the BGH has, both here and elsewhere, so authoritatively relied, is not merely a prerequisite of, but virtually the reason for, granting a claim between neighbours independently of fault. In cases of this type, as in Austria,[742] there is nothing to prevent absolute no-fault liability from developing. The extent to which such no-fault liability is required between neighbours depends on how far the problem of damage caused by excessive use of property already falls within general no-fault environmental liability. The latter can be drawn so narrowly that it allows wide scope to apply no-fault liability specific to the legal relationships

---

[740] P. 259.   [741] P. 262.

[742] The starting point was property law: §§ 364a (damages independent of fault for emissions from a licensed plant) and 364b ABGB (the rule against carrying out works to a property so as to cause loss of support to the neighbouring property). In a case where works were carried out with the necessary authority (19 Nov. 1929, *SZ* 11/233 p. 672) the OGH transferred the concepts behind § 364a and 364b ABGB by analogy. In consequence, strict liability was introduced to cases covered by § 364b ABGB (OGH 9 Apr. 1968, *SZ* 41/42 p. 133; OGH 23 Apr. 1968, *SZ* 41/51 p. 166). This absolute liability was transferred to cases under § 364 II ABGB ('effluent, smoke, gases, heat, odours, noise, vibrations'); to cases of gross emissions (e.g. OGH 25 Jan. 1972, *SZ* 45/7 p. 36; OGH 15 Oct. 1992, *JBl* 1993 p. 387; and OGH 12 Dec. 1977, *SZ* 50/160 p. 773); and to chemicals (OGH 1 July 1959, *SZ* 32/88 p. 215: herbicides carried by wind onto neighbouring vines). In this way a special form of strict liability between neighbours arose. In support of this it was pointed out that neighbours, by virtue of their physical proximity, are exposed to interferences which cannot be avoided or anticipated (OGH 12 Dec. 1977, p. 775). However, it is said in the context of § 364b ABGB that a building permit lulls a neighbour into a false sense of security and removes from the victim the possibility of obtaining injunctive relief (e.g. OGH 21 May 1975, *SZ* 48/61 p. 297; and BGH 20 Jan. 1981, *JBl* 1981 p. 534). The same argument was raised in respect of noise generated by a licensed moto-cross tournament (OGH 11 June 1981, *JBl* 1982 p. 595). Finally, the position is analogous to § 364a ABGB when 'a plant creates a particularly dangerous situation and all the damage suffered is foreseeable for the plant operator' (OGH 16 Jan. 1991, *JBl* 1991 p. 580). From the literature, see the criticism offered by Kerschner, *JBl* 1993 p. 217 and the rejoinder by Hecht/Muzak, *JBl* 1994 pp. 159–165.

between neighbours.[743] It could, however, also cover the entire law of liability between neighbours, which would make the latter redundant. This is the position in Sweden.[744] In Denmark the case described at no. 538 above would have been determined by applying the original 'legal principles governing relationships between neighbours' (*naboretlige regler*). It would be dealt with as environmental pollution within the terms of § 1, and as material damage within the terms of § 2 no. 2 of the Danish Environmental Liability Law No. 225 of 6.4.1994.[745] The requirement of no-fault liability under § 3 of that Act would not have been satisfied, because the defendant farmer was not involved in 'commercial or public activity' within the terms of that provision and the Annex of the Environmental Liability Law. The 'legal principles governing relationships between neighbours' concern compensation independent of fault, as repeatedly confirmed in Danish case-law.[746] Noise[747] and damage from vibrations[748] are covered, as well as damage caused when water collects on one property as a result of vibrations on another.[749]

Netherlands environmental law imposes no-fault liability (Art. 6:175   **540** sec. 1 BW) only on those who 'in the exercise of their profession or business have used matter or had it under their control'. This allows the law on liability between neighbours to exist outside environmental law. In addressing this issue the Dutch legislature has avoided all the embarrassing mistakes introduced into German law by § 906 II BGB: Dutch Art. 5:37 BW[750] governs only conduct, and is silent as to the legal

---

[743] The rules governing the distinction between specific provisions of tort applicable between neighbours and general environmental law liability vary in the different legal systems studied here. The German Environmental Liability Law concerns environmental damage caused by 'plant' (§ 1); the Danish equivalent concerns environmental pollution stemming from commercial or public activity (§ 3); the Italian Act on the Creation of an Environment Ministry (see fn. 754 below) only provides a cause of action to the state (Art. 18); Greek Statute No. 1650/1986 on the Protection of the Environment requires 'pollution or some other detriment to the environment' (Art. 29, more in Karakostas, *NuR* 1993 pp. 467, 471); and in The Netherlands environmental liability is in essence liability for dangerous 'matter' (Art. 6:175 I, VI BW).

[744] For more detail see 1 § ('Damages are granted under this statute for personal injury, damage to property, and pure economic loss caused in the vicinity of land on which a harmful activity is carried out') and 3 § I Environmental Liability Act (*miljöskadelag*) (SFS 1986: 225), by which damages are payable not only for pollution to water, soil, and air but also for 'noise, vibrations, or any similar interference'; see also HD 29 Dec. 1992, *NJA* 1992: 136 p. 896, concerning damage due to vibrations caused by explosives.

[745] 'Damage to property' in the sense of § 2 no. 2 includes damage to land: Karnov (-Linkis) vol. vii, 13th edn., p. 8858 no 8.

[746] For an overview see Pagh, *Erstatningsansvar for miljøskader*, pp. 62–64; Kruse, *Erstatningsretten*, 5th edn., pp. 252–258.   [747] HD 17 Mar. 1995, *UfR* 1995 A p. 466.

[748] HD 10 Jan. 1968, *UfR* 1968 A p. 84.   [749] HD 23 Nov. 1978, *UfR* 1979 A p. 56.

[750] 'The owner of one property must not encroach upon the owner of another property in any measure or form which is unlawful according to Article 162 of Book 6, such as by spreading noise, vibrations, smells, smoke, or gases, or by impeding access to light or air, or by removing supporting matter.'

consequences of a property owner interfering with his neighbour's property 'by way of noise, vibrations, smells, smoke or gases . . .'. The rules governing claims for injunctive relief and damages are found in the law of tort (Art. 6:168 and Art. 6:162 BW respectively); claims must indicate at what stage the interference became sufficiently damaging to be regarded as unlawful (Art. 5:37 BW). Thus property law and liability law remain clearly separate; the anomaly that countervailing public interest renders a substantial emission 'lawful' so that it must be tolerated by the affected party (Art. 6:168) is avoided.[751]

One issue not covered in detail in Dutch law is when the affected neighbour's claim is independent of fault, and when fault is required. Art. 6:162 sec. 3 BW states only that this depends on whether the unlawful emission is to be attributed to the owner of the property from which the interference originates 'according to generally accepted standards', even in the absence of fault;[752] where this is the case, more precise clarification is left to the courts, as with other matters in the field of obligations.[753]

541   The position in Germany, Sweden, Denmark, and The Netherlands is very different from that in Spain, Italy,[754] France, and Belgium, where there is not only no comprehensive legal basis for private environmental law, but also no general property law rule prescribing compensation for emissions between neighbours. The second book of the Spanish Cc (which is very similar to the Dutch BW) confines itself to rules which define the content and the extent of property. Questions of legal liability have, correctly,[755] been confined to the law of tort, where Art. 1908 Cc in its No. 2 ('excessive smoke') and No. 4 ('discharges of noxious matter from pits or storage areas') have established no-fault liability for specific

---

[751] See *T&C* (-Stolker) 2nd edn., Art. 5:37 no. 2.

[752] This also applies if a property owner is compelled to tolerate interference for 'reasons of important social interests' (Art. 6:168 I s. 1 BW). But by Art. 6:168 I s. 2 BW the 'victim retains his right to reparation of damage according to this present title', i.e. only under the conditions of Art. 6:162 BW.

[753] There is much to support the argument that in such cases liability without fault will be the next step. If a property owner has to pay the costs of removing a tree which, in the absence of any fault on his part, fell onto the land of his neighbour (HR 7 May 1982, NedJur 1983 no. 478 p. 1521: failing to remove the tree amounts to a breach of obligation) then there is no clear reason why the same should not apply to emissions. See also HR 4 Nov. 1988, *NedJur* 1989 no. 854 p. 3382.

[754] Italian statute No. 349 of 8 July 1986 on the Creation of an Environment Ministry and Rules on Damage to the Environment is, strictly speaking, not a true environmental liability act because according to Art. 18 only the state and not individual citizens may bring an action for damages. On the other hand the statute does not prevent individuals from suing each other under the general rules of civil law: see part 6, no. 560 below.

[755] See Paz-Ares/Díez-Picazo/Bercovitz/Salvador (-Coca Payeras), *Código Civil*, vol. i, 2nd edn., Art. 590, p. 1498.

injurious emissions.[756] The problem there is that Art. 1908 Cc is far too narrowly drawn. According to its wording noise,[757] gases, dust, smells, and vibrations are not covered, nor any other tangible emissions, apart from the 'discharges' considered above. The problem is easily resolved. By analogy (above all with Art. 590 Cc), Spanish law has developed a general prohibition against emissions,[758] breach of which entitles a claim for injunctive relief and damages, independent of fault.[759]

For some time now the result has been largely the same in Italy, **542** France, and Belgium, in whose legal systems the starting point was slightly more complicated because the civil code of each contained no rules such as those in Art. 1908 Span. Cc. Relevant Italian law was based on Art. 844 Ital. Cc. Section 1 of this Article corresponds to § 906 I BGB; this refers to the obligation to tolerate 'emissions of smoke or heat, smells, noises, vibrations [and similar effects] where they do not exceed the customary measure of what is tolerable, with due consideration to the conditions prevailing within the locality'. The clear corollary is the principle that substantial interference can be prevented by injunction, independent of fault by the party from whose property the interference arises.[760] Art. 844 II Cc adds that the judge 'in applying this rule . . . must balance the requirements of production with the rights of the property owner', and can 'take account of the priority of a specific use'. The Italian courts have interpreted Art. 844 II to apply also where the measure of what can reasonably be tolerated in the terms of Art. 844 I is exceeded. The judge can also consider opposing interests and make an exception by refusing injunctive relief to stop the emission but granting the victim financial compensation.[761] The consideration here is essentially the same as that which formed the background to § 906 II 2 BGB: compensation should be paid for an act which is exceptionally deemed lawful by virtue of the countervailing common

---

[756] For an account of the nature of liability in the different rules of Art. 1908 Span. Cc, see above at no. 233 with fn. 1409; further, Paz-Ares/Díez-Picazo/Bercovitz/Salvador (-de Ángel Yáguez), *Código Civil*, vol. ii, Art. 1908, pp. 2045–2050 and Albaladejo, *Derecho civil*, vol. ii (2), 8th edn., pp. 549–551 (for whom liability based on no. 2 is absolute, in contrast to that based on no. 4 where rebuttable fault is presumed).

[757] For an analogous application of Art. 1908 Cc to noise: Santos Briz, *Responsabilidad civil*, vol. ii, 6th edn., pp. 797–798.

[758] On the prohibition against *immittere in alienum*, see Santos Briz (fn. 757 above) pp. 781–783; and Alonso Pérez, *An.Der.Civ.* 36 I (1983) pp. 357, 386–396.

[759] See esp. TS 14 May 1963, *RAJ* 1963 no. 2699, p. 1699; TS 12 Dec. 1980 no. 4747, p. 3818; TS 17 Mar. 1981, *RAJ* 1981 no. 1009, p. 808; and TS 14 July 1982 no. 4237, p. 2768.

[760] Fundamental here are Cass. 16 July 1943, *Giur.it.* 1944, I, 1, 19; and Cass. 30 Sep. 1948, n. 1648, *Giur.it.* 1949, I, 1, 442; this has since been the established practice of the courts. An action for an injunction based on Art. 844 I Cc is available to the tenant: Cass. 21 Feb. 1994, n. 1653, *Giust.civ.Mass.* 1994 no. 1653, p. 187.

[761] Cass. 19 May 1976, n. 1796, *Giur.it.* 1978, I, 1, 412.

interest.[762] More recently, however, Italian law has begun to view excessive emissions for what they are: unlawful breaches of property rights and therefore *fatti illeciti* as understood by Art. 2043 Cc.[763] Thus the mere obligation to pay compensation has given rise to a duty to pay damages and, because a person who exceeds the statutory levels[764] acts negligently under Art. 2043 Cc, as a matter of practical analysis there is now strict liability in Italian law.

543   The French law on no-fault liability for interference with the property of a neighbour (*troubles de voisinage*) lacks any statutory basis. It was initially developed by the French courts[765] and has now been adopted, with slight modification,[766] by the Belgian legal system.[767] The only thing to which recourse could be had was the definition of property in Art. 544 Cc,[768] which provides that adjacent property owners have identical rights. A neighbour who disturbs that balance abuses his right;[769] he is liable for damages independent of fault.[770] The issue is sometimes approached by viewing each excessive interference with the use of adjacent property as giving rise *ipso iure* to a *faute* which opens the

---

[762] More detail on the theory of liability for *atti leciti dannosi* in connection with Art. 844 II Cc is found in Visintini, *Fatti illeciti*, vol. i, pp. 332–335; Tucci, *Riv.Dir.Civ.* 13 (1967) pp. 229, 244–247.

[763] See esp. Cass. 30 July 1984, n. 4523, *Giust.civ.Mass.* 1984 no. 4523. From the literature, all of which now states that emissions exceeding the measure of Art. 844 I Cc give rise to damages under Art. 2043 Cc: *Cendon* (-Salvi) vol. iii, Art. 844, n. 6.1 (p. 310); and Visintini, *Fatti illeciti*, vol. i, p. 51.

[764] See Cass. 18 Feb. 1977, n. 740, *Giur.it.* 1977, I, 1, 1672; and Cass. 18 Oct. 1978, n. 4693, Rep.Gen. 1978, 22, 3386 and 35, 3387.   [765] See Cass.civ. 27 Nov. 1844, *DP* 1845.1. 13.

[766] In France the special law on liability for *troubles de voisinage* ousts the application of Art. 1384 I Cc (Cass.civ. 20 June 1990, *Sem.Jur.* 1990, IV, 317); by contrast *gardien* liability in Belgium remains applicable between neighbours (Cornelis, *Responsabilité extra-contractuelle*, no. 448; see also fn. 774 below).

[767] Cass. 6 Apr. 1960, *Pas. belge* 1960, I, 915 was fundamental to the early development of Belgian law. See Dalcq/Schamps, *Rev.crit.jur.belge* 1995 pp. 525, 574–586, for a lively overview of recent Belgian cases.

[768] '*La propriété est le droit de jouir et disposer des choses de la manière la plus absolue, pourvu qu'on ne fasse pas un usage prohibé par les lois ou par les règlements.*'

[769] Even today the theory of abuse of legal rights—used in this context for the first time by the Cour d'appel Colmar 2 May 1855, *DP* 1856.2.9 (the *arrêt Doerr*)—remains for many the central plank of liability in *troubles de voisinage* (e.g. Cornelis, fn. 766 above, no. 441); in French academic writings on this subject the relationship between *abus de droit* and *troubles de voisinage* is said to be represented by two intersecting circles (e.g. Starck [-Roland/ Boyer], *Obligations*, vol. i, 4th edn., nos. 362 ff.; and *Encyclopédie Dalloz* [-Cadiet] vol. i, 'Abus de droit', nos. 18 ff.).

[770] E.g. Cass.civ. 4 Feb. 1971, *Sem.Jur.* 1971, II, 16781; Cass.civ. 27 May 1975, D. 1976 *Jur.* 318; Paris 15 Jan. 1993, D. 1993 IR 117; and Cass. 6 Apr. 1960 (fn. 767 above). Regardless of its theoretical basis, the fact that liability for *troubles de voisinage* does not require fault is not subject to any controversy; see Dalcq/Schamps (fn. 767 above) p. 574 with extensive references to Belgian decisions, and from the *Encyclopédie Dalloz* (-Gaillot-Mercier) vol. ix, '*Troubles de voisinage*', nos. 13 ff., with extensive references to French case-law.

way to Arts. 1382 and 1383 Cc.[771] However, the French *Cour de Cassation* takes the view that the matter is one of an autonomous principle of liability *'suivant lequel nul ne doit causer à autrui un trouble anormal de voisinage'*.[772] The similarities with the *naboretlige regler* of Danish law and the *immittere in alienum* prohibition of Spanish law should no more be overlooked than the proximity to the solution favoured in Italy.

In France the right of action depends on an atypical interference, *'un* **544** *trouble anormal'*. Whether there has been such interference in any given case is a question of fact. The circumstances of the locality and the duration of the interference are decisive.[773] Great weight is given to the issue of priority: the party who was there first enjoys considerable privileges over the subsequently arriving neighbour.[774] Where the interference is noise the basic provision is a decree of 1988.[775] A licence granted by an authority to run a business is not an automatic defence against liability.[776] Liability based on *troubles de voisinage* is not limited to intangible interferences; someone whose property is polluted by oil spreading from underground is entitled to claim damages.[777] 'Negative emissions', as they are bizarrely known to German lawyers with a firm grasp of the language, (e.g. the blocking out of sunlight) are also covered.[778] Belgian law requires that the interference be attributable to a specific legal entity,[779] i.e. there must be

---

[771] E.g. *JClCiv* (-Agostini), Arts. 1382 to 1386, Fasc. 265 no. 56; also Trib.gr.inst. 3 July 1990, *D.* 1991 *Somm.* 310 (Arts. 1382 and 544 were cited as bases of liability).

[772] Cass.civ. 19 Nov. 1986, Bull.civ. 1986, II, no. 172.

[773] See Gaillot-Mercier (fn. 770 above) no. 41; and Agostini (fn. 771 above) no. 15. See also e.g. Reims 2 Mar. 1994, *Sem.Jur.* 1995, IV, 897. Cass.civ. 17 Feb. 1993, Bull.civ. 1993, II, no. 68 states that in each case it must be determined whether the interference exceeded the normal level, which question is not satisfied merely by reference to the breach of administrative provisions.

[774] For Belgian law see e.g. Rb. Antwerp 22 Nov. 1993, RW 1995–96 p. 160: as a result of friction between train wheels and track, shards of metal were released which damaged the paintwork of cars. The action of the car owner in *troubles de voisinage* against the Belgian railway was rejected because the stretch of track had been in operation for twelve years; an action in Art. 1384 I failed in the absence of *vice*. For French law, where the problem is governed partly by special law, Cass.civ. 10 Oct. 1984, Bull.civ. 1984, III, no. 165 provides that an industrial concern can only rely on *antériorité* if it has not itself exceeded the statutory limits for emissions.

[775] *Décret* no. 88–523, dated 5 May 1988, *relatif aux règles propres à préserver la santé de l'homme contre les bruits de voisinage*, JO 6 May 1988, p. 6307.

[776] Gaillot-Mercier (fn. 770 above) no. 25; Agostini (fn. 771 above) no. 24.

[777] Cass.civ. 6 July 1994, Bull.civ. 1994, II, no. 182: a transport company supplied a garage with oil. Some of the oil seeped into an underground passage and thence onto neighbouring land. The garage paid damages by way of *troubles de voisinage* and successfully joined the transport company as third party in the capacity of *gardien*.

[778] E.g. Cass.civ. 18 July 1972, *Sem.Jur.* 1972, II, 17203; Versailles 30 Nov. 1989,*D.* 1990 *IR* 18.

[779] Cf. Brussels 2 June 1982, *RW* 1984–85 p. 1523: contractor and architect caused abnormal interference to neighbouring property; liability of the principal was affirmed as he had authorized both to work on his property. See also Paris 13 May 1990, *D.* 1990 *IR* 86: owner let his flat to his mother who was very ill and regularly suffered psychological crises during which she shouted a lot; liability of the owner for audible interference affirmed).

deliberate behaviour (*'fait, omission, comportement quelconque'*).[780] The plaintiff must also be the occupier of the affected property;[781] but the property from which the interference comes need not be situated immediately adjacent to the affected property.[782] Liability entails an obligation to pay, not only compensation for pecuniary loss, but full damages.[783] Unlike claims for damages, injunctive relief may not be claimed against activities licensed by the authorities.[784]

3. LIABILITY FOR OTHER INTERFERENCE WITH PROPERTY

545 Liability may arise independently of fault in all EU legal systems for emissions which harm the property of a neighbour. There are differences between the individual legal systems, but these only concern marginal issues, such as which types of emissions are covered, how the quantum of compensation is calculated, and whether the corresponding claim is in tort or property law. By contrast, there is very little unity on the issue of whether and to what extent other interferences with property found claims for damages independent of fault. This question is related to property law when viewed from the perspective of those European systems whose civil codes have adopted the *actio negatoria*. This is the case in Germany (§ 1004 BGB), Greece (Art. 1108 Cc), and Italy (Art. 949 Cc).[785] According to the wording of Art. 949. II Ital. Cc the intended claim to damages concerns a very special factual situation, of no concern here: it requires that someone, without justification, claim a right over the property of another. The owner can bring an action to prove that no such right exists (Art. 949 I Cc), and then obtains the additional right under Art. 949 II Cc to demand an injunction and damages 'where there is either interference or intrusion'.[786]

---

[780] Cass. 7 Dec. 1992, *JT* 1993 p. 473.

[781] Mere ownership is not sufficient in Belgian law, whereas occupation is sufficient: Cass. 10 Jan. 1974, *Pas. belge* 1974, I, 488. As for French law, Cass.civ. 28 June 1995, Bull.civ. 1995, II, no. 222 states that an owner who is not living on his property can also require interference caused by a neighbour to cease.

[782] Cass. 28 Apr. 1983, *Pas. Belge* 1983, I, 965; Cass.civ. 8 May 1968, *D.* 1968 *Jur.* 609; Cass.civ. 16 May 1994, *Sem.Jur.* 1994, IV, 1824.   [783] Cass. 27 Sep. 1973, *Pas. belge* 1974, I, 89.

[784] Terré/Simler, *Droit civil. Les biens*, 4th edn., no. 318.

[785] The Austrian ABGB governs only a few facets of the *actio negatoria* (§§ 364 and 523 ABGB); the Portuguese Cc considers only the claim to 'recognition' (*reconhecimento*) of property law and then in connection with the *acção de reinvindicação* (Art. 1311 Port. Cc). The *acção negatória* is generally recognized although it is not found in statute (Prata, *Dicionário Jurídico*, 3rd edn., p. 16). The nearest Scottish equivalent to the *actio negatoria* is the delict of *encroachment* which operates independently of both fault and damage (see Walker, *Delict* 2nd edn., pp. 944–946).

[786] The word 'also' (*anche*) in the statute makes it clear that the claim only arises if the interference or intrusion is connected with the exercise of the asserted right: Cendon (-Gambaro) vol. iii, Art. 949 Cc. n. 2 (p. 257); Geri/Breccia/Busnelli/Natoli, *Diritto civile*, vol. ii, p. 158.

In almost identical terms § 1004 I BGB and Art. 1108 I 1 Greek Cc state **546** that where 'property is interfered with other than by the removal or the withholding of it',[787] the owner is entitled to demand 'the removal of the interference' from the party causing it.[788] Neither legal system makes fault a condition of the claim to have the interference removed. The only issue is the meaning of the provision that the property owner can demand 'removal of the interference'. Is he 'interfered with' in his property rights only to the extent that the interference itself continues, or do other negative consequences of this interference constitute a continuous interference with his property rights?[789] Can someone demand not only that his car not be interfered with, but where it has been damaged, demand that the damage be remedied? Must the owner of a tree which falls during a storm pay for its removal from neighbouring property and other costs (such as roof repairs rendered necessary) incurred by the neighbour?

The answer must be affirmative in the two alternatives of the second **547** example given above. If the cost of repair of damaged movable goods amounts to the 'removal' of a continuous interference with property, then general liability, independent of fault, is created for damage to things; with this the entire law of tort would be converted into a system of no-fault liability. This would not be in keeping with existing law, and would be non-sensical. How could one justify making someone 'strictly' liable for damage to goods, but not for personal injury? Events concerning interference to property must be regarded as closed at the moment when the damage actually occurred. In other words, after this point it is no longer possible to apply § 1004 BGB and Art. 1108 Greek Cc. Neither rule distinguishes between movable and fixed goods, so the same rules apply to both. The consequence for the second of the above examples is that liability to remove the interference based on the *actio negatoria* does not include compensation for the the roof.[790] As for that damage, provided that the owner of the tree was not at fault, only a claim based upon no-fault liability outside contract[791] will suffice,

---

[787] § 1004 BGB refers to the withholding of 'possession', which is connected to the idea that in German law this term includes not only possession as owner but also 'detention'.

[788] Both § 1004 and Art. 1108 Greek Cc deal with claims for injunctions. Only Art. 1108 Greek Cc adds, that 'an additional claim for damages according to the rules on unlawful acts . . . [is] not excluded'.

[789] This issue was clearly disposed of in RG 19 Dec. 1929, RGZ 127 pp. 29, 34–35.

[790] See Roussos, *NoB* 35 (1987) pp. 1122, 1130–1131; and Gursky, *JR* 1989 pp. 397–402, who refer to divergent opinions on Greek and German law. A representative of those opposing views is Georgiades/Stathopoulos (-Georgiades), *Greek Cc*, vol. v, Art. 1108, nos. 10–13.

[791] The corresponding position also applies to liability based on presumed fault, see no. 233 above; see also RC 30 May 1989, *CJ* XIV (1989–3) p. 74 in connection with Art. 493 Port. Cc.

which must be either justified by a general liability for dangerous things,[792] or based on a special responsiblity between neighbours.[793] In Germany, whose strict liability law is underdeveloped, only a general claim to damages based upon the law governing legal relationships between neighbours remains.[794] Even this has recently been denied by the BGH, which reasoned that such a claim requires a dangerous use of property of which the defendant was aware. There is no such requirement where someone merely plants or maintains a healthy tree on his land.[795]

548   Even where a legal system intends to compensate damage of this kind only where such damage is referable to a fault, equity demands at the very least that the owner (using the same example) be obliged to remove the fallen tree.[796] The position is no different where a third party takes my car and parks it in front of somebody else's garage: my property 'interferes' with his property; in consequence I am obliged not to allow it to remain there.[797] The result is the same if the case is one of *actio negatoria* or, if this is missing, a corresponding claim is developed within the law of tort, as in the Netherlands.[798] It is not acceptable[799] that relinquishing ownership should relieve a person from the responsibility of removing a continuing interference;[800] it is not good enough

---

[792] For Belgium see Brussels 18 Nov. 1993, *RW* 1995–96 p. 112: a tree unable to withstand wind of 60 km/h has a deficiency (*vice*) in terms of *gardien* responsibility.

[793] See Art. 1908 no. 3 Span. Cc, which complements Art. 390 Span. Cc. A claim for damages in tort arises if a danger materializes whose removal could have been demanded under Art. 390 Cc: Díez-Picazo/Gullón, *Sistema*, vol. iii, 6th edn., pp. 123–137, 197–206; Díez-Picazo, *Fundamentos*, vol. iii, 4th edn., pp. 867–873.   [794] See no. 537 above.

[795] BGH 23 Apr. 1993, BGHZ 122 p. 283.

[796] Gursky (fn. 790 above) p. 402 is entirely correct in opposing German commentators who, along the lines of BGH 2 Mar. 1984, *NJW* 1984 p. 2207 reject liability because the owner of the tree, in the absence of a tortious omission, is no 'tortfeasor' in the sense of § 1004 I BGB. Likewise, Roussos (fn. 790 above) pp. 1128–1129 argues that liability for the costs of removing such a thing only arises where a duty of care has been breached. Decisions in Austria go the other way: during demolition work, with no fault of the owner, masonry fell onto the roof of the adjacent property: an interference was established which led to liability (OGH 12 Dec. 1977, *SZ* 50/160 p. 773).

[797] See also OLG Dresden 24 Apr. 1995, *VersR* 1995 p. 836: obligation to remove environmentally damaging waste stored unlawfully by a contractor.

[798] HR 7 May 1982, *NedJur* 1983 no. 478 p. 1521 (obligation to remove a tree which had toppled over; no fault was shown, so the obligation to remove the tree arose from the 'generally accepted view'; see now Art. 6:162 III BW) and HR 4 Nov. 1988, *NedJur* 1989 no. 854 p. 3382, with note Brunner (same reasoning in a case where garden waste and soil ended up on the lower-lying property of the plaintiff following a landslide; see fn. 753). HR 14 Oct. 1994, *RvdW* 1994 no. 202 confirms yet again the principle that a person acts unlawfully if he fails to remove an object which, without fault on his part, has fallen onto neighbouring property; but it refused to apply the rule to a case where a ship's crane had fallen into a canal and lain there for some 23 years; moreover, the crane belonged not to the defendant, but to his legal predecessor.

[799] See HR 7 May 1982 (fn. 798 above); and BGH 14 Oct. 1955, BGHZ 18 pp. 253, 258.

[800] Staudinger (-Gursky) *BGB*, 13th edn., § 1004 no 107.

for a person to retrieve the useful parts and leave the useless parts behind.[801] Where the removal of the interference is impossible (e.g. contamination of the ground by oil which dispersed) then the other mechanisms for securing damages apply, i.e. tort and the rules of *troubles de voisinage*.[802]

4. EXEMPTIONS FROM LIABILITY FOR THE *BONA FIDE* POSSESSOR OF ANOTHER'S GOODS

The final issue is under what circumstances a person is liable for a **549** thing which he believes to be his own but which in fact belongs to another, where the thing is either lost or damaged. In English law this is a pure tort problem, resolved primarily by conversion, linked by the Torts (Interference with Goods Act) 1977 with the group of torts referred to as wrongful interference with goods.[803] The law of conversion is unusually severe on the *bona fide* non-owner, wrongfully in possession but believing himself to be the owner. For: 'at common law one's duty to one's neighbour who is the owner, or entitled to possession, of any goods is to refrain from doing any voluntary act in relation to his goods which is a usurpation of his proprietary or possessory rights in them. Subject to some exceptions . . . it matters not that the doer of the act of usurpation did not know, and could not by the exercise of any reasonble care have known of his neighbour's interest in the goods. This duty is absolute; he acts at his peril.'[804] A usurpation in this sense is any act which appears to be an adoption or use of rights which belong to the owner alone;[805] damage to or destruction of something in one's possession are examples.[806] This

---

[801] The result was different in a case where tiles from one house ended up on a neighbouring property due to military action: OGH 13 Apr. 1949, *SZ* 22/48 p. 114.

[802] Most German commentators disagree. References and criticism in Staudinger (-Gursky), *BGB*, § 1004 no. 3. See also RG 19 Dec. 1929, RGZ 127 pp. 29, 35: a fire which started on a neighbouring property spread onto a railway embankment. The fire was extinguished on the property where it started but continued on the embankment; the claim under § 1004 I BGB for the cost of repair to the embankment was granted.

[803] Id. sec. 1: conversion of goods, trespass to goods, negligence and 'any other tort so far as it results in damage to goods'.

[804] *Marfani & Co. Ltd. v. Midland Bank Ltd.* [1968] 1 WLR 956, 970–971 (*per* Diplock LJ); see also Clerk & Lindsell (-Tettenborn), *Torts*, 16th edn., p 1259.

[805] See Winfield/Jolowicz (-Rogers), *Tort*, 14th edn., p. 490; Markesinis/Deakin, *Tort Law*, 3rd edn., p. 406.

[806] Tettenborn (fn. 804 above). A positive act is required: an omission does not suffice at common law; a breach of a duty of care is required (e.g. *Coldman v. Hill* [1919] 1 KB 443). A bailee can be liable in conversion by virtue of express statutory provisions: sec. 2(2) Torts (Interference with Goods) Act 1977.

strict liability in conversion is controversial[807] but nevertheless remains law.

550   At the opposite end of the spectrum are those legal systems which do not hold the *bona fide* possessor of somebody else's property liable in respect of his negligent acquisition of it. By Art. 457 I Span. Cc, 'the *bona fide* possessor . . . (is liable) only in cases involving either the deterioration or the loss of the object in his possession, where it can be proved that he acted intentionally'. It is not altogether clear which facts this rule was intended to cover: probably where the item either detoriates or is destroyed after the owner has sued for its return and before judgment is given for the owner.[808] As long as the possessor has no reason to doubt his own entitlement,[809] he cannot act 'intentionally' if he destroys an item which he assumes to be his own.[810] However, as soon as proceedings have been issued his *bona fides* status comes to an end.[811]

551   A third group of legal systems protects from any liability to pay damages the possessor of an object who, had he acted with the necessary care at the time of acquiring possession, would have questioned his proprietary rights to the object. The possessor's liability requires gross negligence.[812] The motive for this degree of protection is to save the

---

[807] See the observations of Lord Denning in *Willis & Son* v. *British Car Auctions* [1978] 1 WLR 438, 441–442, a case which centred upon the sale of an article rather than its destruction. Tettenborn (fn. 804 above) reports at no. 2219 on p. 1231 of the case *AVX* v. *EGM Solders Ltd.* [1982] *Current Law Yearbook* 175: Staughton J said that a person was not liable for the destruction of goods in his possession which he reasonably believed belonged to him. This statement is not easily reconciled with the basic principles of common law.

[808] This point is made convincingly by Paz-Ares/Díez-Picazo/Bercowitz/Salvador (-Miquel González), *Código Civil*, vol. i, 2nd edn., Art. 457, pp. 1227–1229.

[809] According to Art. 433 I Span. Cc the *bona fide* possessor is the person 'who does not know that there is an error in the title or manner of acquisition which renders it of no effect'.

[810] In civil law, intention requires the person to be aware of the unlawfulness. According to French law, pending an action to have property returned, the *bona fide* possessor of an article is only liable for the proceeds of sale or assignment of the article. He is not liable for damages for deterioration of the article during this time: see Art. 1380 Cc and the references in fn. 811 below.

[811] In all legal systems, from that moment the possessor is liable where the thing deteriorates due to simple negligence. For Spain see Miquel González (fn. 808 above); for France: *JClCiv* (-Ranouil), Arts. 711 to 717, 1. App., no. 50; Terré/Simler, *Droit civil*, 'Les biens' 4th edn., no. 510; and Ferrid/Sonnenberger, *Frz. Zivilrecht*, vol. ii, 2nd edn., 3 C 437. For Germany: § 989 BGB; for Greece: Art. 1097 Greek Cc; and for Austria: § 338 ABGB. There is a good argument for the same applying to Portuguese law, whose Art. 1260 Cc expressly states that the possessor is *bona fide* where he does not know that he is infringing another's right ('*quando o possuidor ignorava . . . . que lesava o direito de outrem*'). The relationship of this provision to Art. 1269 Port. Cc, which states that the *bona fide* possessor is liable for loss or damage only where negligent ('*se tiver procedido com culpa*') is just as unclear as the interpretation of Art. 457 Span. Cc.

[812] A good example of a case in which gross negligence was affirmed is Swedish HD 11 Dec. 1987, *NJA* 1987: 146 I, p. 845: the parties circumvented some of the formalities of selling a property. After obtaining possession the purchaser failed to pay the electricity bill as a result of which the water pipes froze and the house was damaged. The purchaser was grossly negligent not only in respect of title but also in respect of the damage caused.

possessor from requiring extensive investigation of the person from whom he obtains possession.[813] In property law special rules[814] are intended to ensure that the possessor is liable only under the double requirement of gross negligence in acquiring the object and ordinary negligence whilst in possession of it. This is the position in Germany and in Greece.[815] The reason is that one does not wish to render liable somebody who negligently but with *bona fides* acquires an object either stolen from or lost by the owner (to which nobody can claim property, § 935 BGB and Art. 1038 Gr. Cc), because the person who receives a non-stolen item from a non-owner under the same circumstances acquires property in it (§ 932 sec. 2 BGB, Art. 1036 Gr. Cc).[816]

Without harmonizing the different national rules on the *bona fide* **552** acquisition of title, it is impossible to recommend, by way of a European compromise, the route which the law of obligations would suggest: making liability dependent simply on whether the possessor acted negligently in both the acquisition of the property and his conduct towards it. This is the position in Austrian,[817] Dutch, Italian, French, and Belgian law.[818] Together they show that neither extra protection of the owner (as found in the common law) nor extra protection of the possessor (as in several mainland European systems) is needed to achieve a well balanced compromise of interests.

---

[813] See Köbl, *Das Eigentümer-Besitzer-Verhältnis* (The Owner-Possessor-Relationship), pp. 161–163.

[814] That these particular privileges against liability apply in property law and not in tort could be explained by the fact that the claim for damages arising from the destruction of a thing appears to be subsidiary to the claim of an owner for the return of his property: see Kruse, *Erstatningsretten*, 5th edn., pp. 266–267.

[815] §§ 990, 989 in conjunction with § 932 II BGB; Arts. 1098 and 1037 Greek Cc.

[816] Köbl (fn. 813 above).

[817] According to § 329 ABGB a *bona fide* possessor can 'on the basis of his actual possession and as he thinks fit, without any responsibility therefor use, consume or even destroy the thing which he possesses'. The possessor is the person who has the thing under his conscious control 'to keep as if it were his own' (§ 309 II ABGB). The *bona fide* possessor is the person 'who has probable cause to regard the thing which he possesses as his own' (§ 326 I. ABGB). Simple negligence excludes *bona fides* (OGH 13 Nov. 1979, *JBl* 1980 p. 589).

[818] None of these three codified systems has special privileges against liability for someone who acts negligently in respect of title; the usual tort principles apply. For France, where due to Art. 2279 Cc this problem has some very special features, see Art. 1379 Cc and Kremhelmer, *Regelung des Herausgabeanspruchs*, pp. 91–95, with further references.

Part 6: The Law of Delict, Constitutional, and Criminal Law

I. THE LAW OF DELICT AND CONSTITUTIONAL LAW

Bibliography: Albamonte, *Danni all'ambiente e responsabilità civile* (Padova 1989); Androulidaki-Dimitriadi, *I ypochreossi enimerosis tou asthenous* (Athens und Komotini 1993); Bajons, 'Schadensersatz für gesundheitliche Beeinträchtigungen nach italienischem Recht', *ZVglRWiss* 92 (1993) pp. 76–114; v. Bar, 'Entwicklung und rechtsstaatliche Bedeutung der Verkehrs(sicherungs)pflichten', *JZ* 1979 pp. 332–337; id., 'Schmerzensgeld und gesellschaftliche Stellung des Opfers bei Verletzungen des allgemeinen Persönlichkeitsrechtes', *NJW* 1980 pp. 1724–1729; Bargagna/Busnelli, *La valutazione del danno alla salute* (Padua 1988); Battistig, 'Italien: Einsetzung eines Garantiefonds für Opfer von Jagdunfällen', *VersRAI* 1992 pp. 39; Bedoura, 'Les incidences de la loi du 27 décembre 1973 sur les concepts traditionnels relatifs au préjudice', *D.* 1980 *Chr.* pp. 139–144; Bellekom/Heringa/Koopmans/ Winter, *Compendium van het staatsrecht*, 6th edn. (Deventer 1992); Billiet/Nieper, 'Zur Bemessung des immateriellen Schadens bei Verlust der Wahrnehmungs- und Empfindungsfähigkeit des Verletzten', *VersRAI* 1994 pp. 6–9; Boch/Lane, 'A New Remedy in Scots Law', *SLT* 1992 pp. 145–148; Bullinger, 'Verfassungsrechtliche Aspekte der Haftung', in: *FS für von Caemmerer* (Tübingen 1978) pp. 297–312; Bungert, 'Verhältnismäßigkeitsprinzip und US-amerikanische Punitive damages', *VersR* 1994 pp. 15–23; Busnelli/Breccia (edd.), *Tutela della salute e diritto privato* (Milan 1988); Canaris, 'Grundrechtswirkungen und Verhältnismäßigkeitsprinzip in der richterlichen Anwendung und Fortbildung des Privatrechts', *JuS* 1989 pp. 161–172; id., 'Verstöße gegen das verfassungsrechtliche Übermaßverbot im Recht der Geschäftsfähigkeit und im Schadensersatzrecht', *JZ* 1987 pp. 993–1004; id., 'Zur Problematik von Privatrecht und verfassungsrechtlichem Übermaßverbot', *JZ* 1988 pp. 494–499; Chapus, *Droit administratif général*, vol. i, 7th edn. (Paris 1993); Christensen, 'Domstolene og lovgivningsmagten', *UfR* 1990 B pp. 73–83; Dagtoglou, 'I tritenergeia ton atomikon dikaiomaton', *NoB* 30 (1982) pp. 780–789 id., 'O dikastikos elenchos tis sintagmatikotitas ton nomon', *NoB* 36 (1988) pp. 721–731; Dejemeppe, 'Pouvoir judiciaire et responsabilités', *JT* 1987 pp. 278–279; Denning, *What next in the Law* (London 1982); Deutsch, 'Schadensrecht und Verfassungsrecht': Akt II, *NJW* 1994 pp. 776–778; id., 'Neues

Verfassungszivilrecht: Rechtswidriger Abtreibungsvertrag gültig—Unterhaltspflicht aber kein Schaden', *NJW* 1993 pp. 2361–2363; id., 'Das Kind oder sein Unterhalt als Schaden', *VersR* 1995 pp. 609–616; Doris, 'Ermineia ton nomon me anagogi se syntagmatikes diataxeis sti nomologia ton poletikon dikastirion', *EllDik* 32 (1991) pp. 1188–1198; Drion, 'Civielrechtelijke werking van de grondrechten', *NJB* 1969 pp. 585–594; Dürr/Schubert, 'Schmerzensgeld bei Gefährdungshaftung', *ZRP* 1975 pp. 225–229; Eichenhofer, 'Co-ordination of social security and equal treatment of men and women in employment: Recent social security judgments of the Court of Justice', *CMLR* 30 (1993) pp. 1021–1042; *Encyclopédie Dalloz* (-Bach), vol. vi, *Jurisprudence* (Paris 1973); Engel, 'Eigentumsschutz für Unternehmen', *AöR* 118 (1993) pp. 169–236; Engelhardt, 'Kind als Schaden?', *VersR* 1988 pp. 540–544; Fernández Segado, *El sistema constitucional español* (Madrid 1992); Fleming, 'Defamation: Political Speech', 109 [1993] *LQR* 12–16; García Gómez de Mercado, 'El nuevo sistema de responsabilidad patrimonial de la Administración', *La Ley* 1993 (4) pp. 955–965; Giesen, 'Schadensbegriff und Menschenwürde', *JZ* 1994 pp. 286–292; Glazebrook, 'Unseemliness Compounded by Injustice', [1992] *CLJ* pp. 226–228; Gomard, *Civilprocessen*, 2nd edn. (Copenhagen 1984); id., 'En retskildemæssig vurdering af de konklusioner, anbefalinger m.v., der udgår fra kommissionsdomsstole og undersøgelsesretter', *J* 1993 pp. 325–336; Grabitz (ed.), *Grundrechte in Europa und USA*, vol i. (Kehl *et al.* 1986); Gralla, *Der Grundrechtsschutz in Dänemark* (Frankfurt 1987); Gray, 'European Convention on Human Rights: Freedom of Expression and the Thalidomide Case', [1979] *CLJ* 242–245; Gulphe, 'A propos de la présente réforme de la Cour de Cassation', *Sem.Jur.* 1981 Doctr. 3013; Haas, 'Unfallversicherungsschutz und ordre public', *ZZP* 108 (1995) pp. 219–239; Baron van Haersolte, *Inleiding tot het Nederlandse staatsrecht*, 9th edn., (Zwolle 1988); Hecht/Muzak, 'Umwelthaftung im Nachbarrecht', *JBl* 1994 pp. 159–165; Heldrich, *Freiheit der Wissenschaft: Freiheit zum Irrtum?* (Heidelberg 1987); Herbert, *Uncommon Law: Being 66 Misleading Cases* (Methuen Humour Classic 1935, reprint of the 1935 edn., Trowbridge 1984); Hesse/Kauffmann, 'Die Schutzpflicht in der Privatrechtsprechung', *JZ* 1995 pp. 219–223; Hopkins, 'A Terrible (but Transient) Ordeal', [1994] *CLJ* 9–11; Horn/Weber (edd.), *Richterliche Verfassungskontrolle in Lateinamerika, Spanien und Portugal* (Baden-Baden 1989); Iliopoulos-Strangas, *I 'tritenergeia' ton atomikon kai koinonikon dikaiomaton tou Syntagmatos 1975* (Athens 1990); *JClCiv* (-Rieg), 'Application de la loi par le juge', art. 5 (Paris 1982); *JClCiv* (-Blumann), 'Etat et collectivités publiques: Règles générales de la responsabilité de la puissance publique', arts. 1382 to 1386, fasc. 370–1 (Paris 1983); Jensen, 'Højesterets arbejdsform', in: Jensen/von Eyben/Koktvedgaard (edd.), *Højesteret 1661–1986* (Copenhagen 1986) pp. 115–143; Karakostas, 'Rechtsmittel zum Schutz der Umweltgüter im griechischen Recht', *NuR* 1993 pp. 467–474; id., 'Neue Entwicklungen des Umweltschutzes im griechischen Zivilrecht', *ZfU* 1990 pp. 295–305; id., *Perivallon kai Astiko Dikaio* (Athens 1986); Kasimatis, 'To sitima tis tritenergeias ton atomikon kai koinomikon dikaiomaton', *ToΣ* 7 (1981) pp. 1–41; Katranis, 'I theoria tis tritenergeias ton dikaiomaton tou anthropou', *ToΣ* 4 (1978) pp. 237–267; Kerameus/Kozyris (edd.), *Introduction to Greek Law*, 2nd edn. (Deventer and Boston 1993); Kindler, *Einführung in das italienische Recht: Verfassungsrecht, Privatrecht und internationales Privatrecht* (Munich 1993); Kottenhagen-Edzes, *Onrechtmatige daad en milieu* (Arnhem 1992; also diss. Rotterdam 1992); Kötz, 'Schmerzensgeld bei Gefährdungshaftung?', *VersR* 1982 pp. 624–628; Koutsakis, 'Periorismeni i aperioristi i chrimatiki ikanopoiis tis ithikis vlavis me vasi ton Astiko Kodika?', *Arm.* 45 (1991) pp. 841–846; Kremer, 'Omvang schadevergoeding bij ongewenste zwangerschap: in het bijzonder smartegeld en kosten van expertise', *Vrb* 1993 pp. 69–70; Krings, 'Considérations sur l'État de droit, la séparation des pouvoirs et le pouvoir judiciaire', *JT* 1989 pp. 521–532; Lepa, 'Die Einwirkung der Grundrechte auf die Anwendung des Deliktsrechts in der Rechtsprechung des BGH', in: *FS Steffen* (Berlin 1995) pp. 261–272; López Pina (ed.), *Spanisches Verfassungsrecht* (Heidelberg 1993); Luther, *Die italienische Verfassungsgerichtsbarkeit. Geschichte, Prozeßrecht, Rechtsprechung* (Baden-Baden 1990); di Majo, *La tutela civile dei diritti*, vol. iii (Milan 1987); Mann, 'Fusion of the Legal Profession', 93 [1977] *LQR* 367–377; Markesinis, 'Comparative Law: A Subject in Search of an Audience', 53 [1990] *ModLRev.* 1–21; Mencarelli/Mazzeo/Fravolini, 'Questioni di etica e di responsabilità nella diagnostica prenatale', *Dir.fam.pers.* 1994, II, pp. 411–430; De Meuter, 'Wrongful life—Wrongful birth—Wrongful conception or pregnancy claim: inventarisatie van de begrippen—theoretisch raamwerk—proeve van probleemoplossing', in: *Liber Amicorum Krings* (Brussels 1991) pp. 61–74; Norrie, 'Wrongful Life in Scots Law: No Right, no Remedy', *Jurid.Rev.* 1990 pp. 205–224; id., 'Liability for Failed Sterilisation', *SLT* 1986 pp. 145–148; Van Oevelen, 'Schade en schadeloosstelling bij de schending van grondrechten door private personen', in: Rimanque (ed.), *De toepasselijkheid van de grondrechten in private verhoudingen* (Antwerp 1982) pp. 421–461; id., 'De aansprakelijkheid van de staat voor ambtsfouten van magistraten en de orgaantheorie na het ANCA-arrest van het Hof van Cassatie van 19 december 1991', *RW* 1992–1993 pp. 377–396; Palin, *Il principio costituzionale d'eguaglianza* (Milan 1965); Papachristou, 'I prostasia tis prosopikokotikas kai to arthro 299 A.K.', *ToΣ* 7 (1981) pp. 42–57; Papadimitriou, 'Der Einfluß des Grundgesetzes auf die griechische Verfassung', in: Battis/ Mahrenholz/Tsatsos (edd.), *Das Grundgesetz im internationalen Wirkungszusammenhang der Verfassungen: 40 Jahre Grundgesetz* (Berlin 1990) pp. 117–129; Peters, 'Zur Gesetzestechnik des § 823 II BGB', *JZ* 1983 pp. 913–926; de la Quadra-Salcedo, *El recurso de amparo y los derechos fundamentales en las relaciones entre particulares* (Madrid 1981); Ramm, 'Drittwirkung und Übermaßverbot', *JZ* 1988 pp. 489–493; Ravarani, 'La responsabilité civile de l'Etat et des collectivités publiques', *Pas. luxemb.* 28 (1990–92) pp. 77–426; Reinhardt, 'Die Umkehr der Beweislast aus verfassungsrechtlicher Sicht', *NJW* 1994 pp. 93–99; Rigaux, *La protection de la vie privée et des autres biens de la personnalité* (Brussels and Paris 1990); Rimanque, 'Nationale bescherming van grondrechten', *TBP* 1981 pp. 33–42; Robertson, 'Wrongful Life', 45 [1982] *ModLRev* 697–701; Scheffen, 'Vorschläge zur Änderung des § 828 Abs. 1 und 2 BGB', *FuR* 1993 pp. 82–89; ead.,'Der Kinderunfall: Eine Herausforderung für Gesetzgebung und Rechtsprechung', *DAR* 1991 pp. 121–126; Schmid, *Schmerzensgeld und Gefährdungshaftung*, (diss. Bonn 1971); Schockweiler, 'La responsabilité extra-contractuelle de l'autorité publique et la loi du 1er septembre 1988 relative à la responsabilité de l'Etat et des collectivités publiques', *Pas. luxemb.* 27 (1987–1989) pp. 1–29; Schut, 'Wetgevende rechtspraak', *RM-Themis* 1992 pp. 353–355; Skouris/Veniselos, *O dikastikos elenchos tis sintagmatikotitas ton nomon* (Athens and Komotini 1985); Sendler, 'Unmittelbare Drittwirkung der Grundrechte durch die Hintertür?', *NJW* 1994 pp. 709–710; Sommermann, *Der Schutz der Grundrechte in Spanien nach der Verfassung von 1978* (Berlin 1984); Sørensen, *Statsforfatningsret* (2nd edn. Copenhagen 1988); Sprung, 'Das neue System zur Bewertung von Personenschäden in Spanien', *Vw* 1992 pp. 49–54; Starck/Weber (edd.), *Verfassungsgerichtsbarkeit in Westeuropa*, vol. i (Baden-Baden 1986); Stolker, *Aansprakelijkheid van de arts in het bijzonder voor mislukte sterilisaties* (Deventer 1988; also diss. Leiden 1988); id., 'Wrongful Life: The limits of liability and beyond', *IntCompLQ* 1994 pp. 521–536; Vavoukos, 'To astikon adikima is tas periptoseis ithikis simias ypo to kratos tou Astikon Kodikos', *EEN* 22 (1955) pp. 82–87; Vaz Serra, 'Requisitos da Responsabilidade civil', *BolMinJust* 92 (1960) pp. 37–137; Verhey, *Horizontale werking van grondrechten, in het bijzonder van het recht op privacy* (Zwolle 1992; also diss. Utrecht 1992); Villiger, *Handbuch der Europäischen Menschenrechtskonvention (EMRK) unter besonderer Berücksichtigung der schweizerischen Rechtslage* (Zürich 1993); de Vries, *Wettelijke limitering van aansprakelijkheid* (Zwolle 1990; also diss. Leiden 1990); Westermann/Karakatsanes, *Schuldrechtsreform in Deutschland und Griechenland* (Athens and Komotini 1986).

1. THE INFLUENCE OF HUMAN RIGHTS ON RELATIONSHIPS BETWEEN INDIVIDUALS

a. General Overview

Questions about the relationship between constitutional law and the law   **553**
of delict outside the field of state liability have only recently arisen. State
liability and delict law have always been interrelated and mutually
complementary[1] both from within one legal system[2] and from the point
of view of comparative law.[3] Yet many important problems of state

---

[1] Private law has even stepped in occasionally to fill gaps in public law: see v. Bar, *JZ*
1979 pp. 332, 334–337. For a remarkable Portugese decision see STJ 14 Feb. 1991, *BolMinJust*
404 (1991) pp. 403, 408: '*O Estado pode ser responsabilizado civilmente por ter emitido uma lei,
ainda que geral e abstracta, desde que ofenda direitos de terceiros. E, responsabilidade continuará a
existir, mesmo na hipótese de a norma jurídica não estar inquinada de qualquer vício de incons-
titucionalidade ou ilegalidade.*'
[2] Constitutional provisions on state liability are found in Germany, Italy, Spain, and
Portugal. In Germany the state assumes liability for its officers; the erstwhile personal
liability of civil servants in the course of their duty towards fellow citizens has been
abolished. However, the state has retained a right of recourse against its employees for
intent and gross negligence: Art. 34 s. 1 and s. 2 GG. In Italy, on the other hand, the civil
servant is personally liable *vis-à-vis* the citizen; the state is liable only as joint and several
debtor: Art. 28 ss. 1 and 2 Italian Constitution of 27 December 1947. The situation is
basically the same in Spain and Portugal (Arts. 22, 271 Portugese Constitution, as amended
on 2 April 1976). Today, after the repeal of Art. 1903 V Cc (old) (by Act 1/91 of 7 Jan. 1991
on the Modification of the Civil and Criminal Code in the Field of Civil Liability of
Teaching Staff, BOE no. 7 of 8 Jan. 1991), Spanish state liability law is found in Art. 106
II Spanish Constitution of 29 Dec. 1978 (CE), and in Arts. 139–144 of Act 30/92 on the
System of Public Administration and Joint Proceedings in Contentious Administrative
Matters of 26 November 1992 (BOE no. 285 of 27 Nov. 1992).
[3] There are no constitutional provisions on state liability for breach of official duty in
Belgium, Denmark, France, Greece, Ireland, Luxemburg, and The Netherlands. In Belgium
and The Netherlands a breach of official duty is basically an unlawful act which must be
assessed in accordance with the relevant private law provisions (see e.g. Liège 23 Oct. 1989,
JT 1990 p. 23, which also gives an account of Belgian case-law developments; Cass. 19 Dec.
1991, *RW* 1992–1993 p. 396 = *JT* 1992 p. 142: ANCA case concerning the state's liability for
its judges; HR 30 Nov. 1990, *NedJur* 1992 no. 94 p. 310; HR 11 Oct. 1991, *NedJur* 1993 no. 165
p. 516; HR 31 May 1991, *NedJur* 1993 no. 112 p. 317; HR 12 Feb. 1993, *RvdW* 1993 no. 55; and
HR 26 Nov. 1993, *RvdW* 1993 no. 238). The Greek law governing the liability of officials is
found in Arts. 104–106 Introductory Statute to the Greek Cc. In Luxembourg the Act of 1
September 1988 '*relative à la responsabilité civile de l'État et des collectivités publiques*' principally restics liability to cases of fault. *Responsabilité sans faute* still arises in some circumstances: for details see Ravarani, *Pas. luxemb.* 28 (1990–92) pp. 77–426; and Schockweiler,
Pas. luxemb. 27 (1987–89) pp. 1–29. In France state liability is covered by public law: see e.g.
JClCiv (-Blumann), Arts. 1382 to 1386, fasc. 370–1, nos. 9, 15; and Chapus, *Droit administratif*
vol. i, 7th edn., p. 977. Although it has more or less adopted the liability system of the *Code
civil* (e.g. Conseil d'État 9 Apr. 1993, *D.* 1993 *Jur.* 312 confirms that '*la responsabilité de l'État
peut être engagée par toute faute, et non pas seulement par une faute lourde*'), it pursues its very
own course in certain relationships (e.g. in the field of public hospital liability, Conseil
d'État 9 Apr. 1993, *Sem.Jur.* 1993 II 22061, a second decision of the same day, admits no-fault
liability). The (often misinterpreted) proverb 'the king can do no wrong' does not mean that
the state is immune to liability; this has been recognized by Irish law since *Byrne* v. *Ireland*
[1972] IR 241 (Sup. Ct.) Any other interpretation would be unconstitutional: *Ryan* v. *Ireland*
[1989] IR 177, 183 (Sup. Ct.)

liability law are based in private law,[4] and are therefore still often decided by civil courts.[5] In other areas, non-contractual liability law and constitutional law only meet by chance, without the latter having any lasting impact on the rules of the former. Such areas include: the prohibition against decisions based on points not previously raised,[6] the right to be heard by a court, the right to a judge who has been allocated in accordance with special rules set up long before the proceedings start (*gesetzlicher Richter*), and the right to constitutionally guaranteed procedures.[7] For example, it was probably not altogether wise for the Appeal Court judge who, in a case concerning nuisance emanating from a neighbouring cricket ground, began his (dissenting) judgment with the words: 'In summertime, village cricket is the delight of everyone.' Such an introduction predicts the outcome. This was particulary the case given that the High Court had granted injunctive relief, upon which the Appeal Court judge commented: 'he has done it at the instance of a

[4] E.g. personal liability of civil servants, which in turn is often a paramount precondition for state liability (but not e.g. in Belgium since Cass. 19 Dec. 1991 [fn. 2], commented on in an essay by Van Oevelen, *RW* 1992–1993 pp. 295–305). Cases of breach of official duty (e.g. by violating a human right), however, are decided by public law. For the effects of this in private international law see OGH 17 Feb. 1982, *JBl* 1983 p. 260.

[5] E.g. in Germany (Art. 34 s. 3 GG), Luxembourg, The Netherlands, and Denmark (the last 3 have no administrative courts), and in Belgium in cases of liability for *faute* (Cass. 17 Mar. 1963, *Pas. belge* 1963, I, 744); strict liability cases, on the other hand, come under the jurisdiction of the *Conseil d'État*, Art. 11 *Wet Raad van State*. In Greece state liability for breach of official duty is a matter for the administrative courts: Act 1406/1983; for details see e.g. Kerameus/Kozyris (-Dagtoglou), *Introduction to Greek law*, 2nd edn., p. 43. This is also true for France (details in *JCLCiv* [-Blumann] [fn. 21] no. 15) and Spain, where Art. 142 of Act 30/92 (see also fn. 1 above) has introduced administrative procedures, and where the Preamble to *Real Decreto* 429/1993 of 26 Mar. 1993 (BOE No. 106 of 4 May 1993), which complements this Act, confirms the competence of administrative courts in the relevant cases. Yet some details still seem to need clarification (for more see García Gómez de Mercado, *La Ley* 1993, 4, pp. 955, 961). It is also true for Portugal, where the civil courts still decide cases of personal liability of civil servants: Tribunal de Conflitos 5 Nov. 1981, *BolMinJust* 311 (1981) p. 195. In Italy a matter always falls within civil jurisdiction of a civil court (Art. 113 I Ital. Constitution) if a personal right has been violated. Infringements of mere economic interests, on the other hand, are regularly dealt with by administrative courts (Art. 103 I Italian Constitution). On the borderline between public and private state liability law see for Spain TS 14 June 1988, *RAJ* 1988 no. 4908 (policeman negligently uses his gun off duty); and for Portugal STJ 11 Oct. 1983, *BolMinJust* 330 (1983) p. 499; STA 20 Oct. 1983, *BolMinJust* 331 (1983) p. 587.

[6] E.g. BVerfG 25 Mar. 1993, *NJW-RR* 1994 p. 188; and (albeit in a different procedural context) *Hadmor Productions Ltd. and Others* v. *Hamilton and Others* [1982] 2 WLR 322, 337 (HL): 'one of the most fundamental rules of natural justice: the right of each to be informed of any point adverse to him that is going to be relied upon by the judge and to be given an opportunity of stating what his answer to it is' (*per* Lord Diplock).

[7] See e.g. *Rothermere* v. *Times* [1993] 1 All ER 1013 (CA); *Joyce* v. *Sengupta and Another* [1993] 1 All ER 879 (CA): 'He who is charged with libel has a constitutional right to have his guilt or innocence determined by a jury'. To deduce from the fact that someone is the keeper of a motor vehicle that he is also its driver has been deemed to violate the prohibition against arbitrariness: BVerfG 31 Aug. 1993, *NJW* 1994 p. 847 (albeit concerning a case of breach of administrative laws).

newcomer who is no lover of cricket', remarking also that the plaintiff's house had been built on a meadow previously grazed by cattle, and that 'the animals did not mind the cricket'.[8]

Whether the law should tolerate such judicial comments need not be   **554** discussed in detail here. What is relevant is the alignment of the law of delict with that of human rights, and thus with the system of values established by the Constitution(s) governing it. For in contemporary Europe the law of delict is increasingly seen as a manifestation of constitutional rights of personal liberty.[9] Therefore it has to be brought into line with them, and where this does not happen a collision between them is virtually inevitable. The three key areas in which this transformation has occurred are damages, damage, and duty. The concept of 'duty' helps distinguish between right and wrong. 'Damage' determines which interests are protected by tort law. The two often overlap. In tort as well as in constitutional law, protected interests, duty, and damages are all related. The scope of liability for personal injury, for example, can only be increased (as in Italy for the past decade) if the constitutional duty to promote 'social solidarity' (Art. 2 Constitution of 27 December 1947) is also increased.[10] Likewise, to improve the legal protection of personal privacy, the freedom of the press must also be considered. Finally, those who would increase the amount of damages awarded should bear in mind the constititional requirement of reasonableness.

b. The Legislator's Freedom to Choose a System of Compensation

That the law of delict is one avenue to compensation for breach of   **555** human rights is undisputed. Yet the legislator is not obliged to provide delictual compensation for all circumstances. Although the French *Conseil Constitutionnel* promoted Art. 1382 French Cc almost to the rank of a

---

[8] *Miller and Another* v. *Jackson and Others* [1977] 1 QB 966, 976 (*per* Lord Denning, MR).

[9] View shared by the Constitutional courts of: Germany (see BVerfG 11 Oct. 1978, *JZ* 1979 pp. 60, 62 [note Starck]), France (Conseil Constitutionnel 22 Oct. 1982, *Gaz.Pal.* 1983 *Jur.* 60 [note Chabas] = *D.* 1983 *Jur.* 189 [note Marzo]); Portugal (Tribunal Constitucional 3 May 1990, *BolMinJust* 397 [1990] p. 51; and essentially also of Spain (TC 21 Dec. 1992, 240/1992, BJC 141 [1993] p. 124). For further similar decisions see e.g. Areopag 81/1991, *EllDik* 32 (1991) p. 1215, for Greece; for Portugal see STJ 4 July 1978, *BolMinJust* 279 (1978) pp. 124, 128–129; and for Ireland *Byrne* v. *Ireland* [1972] IR 121, 132 (Sup. Ct.); and *Meskell* v. *Coras Iompair Eireanne* [1973] IR 121, 132 (Sup. Ct.). Markesinis, 53 [1990] *Mod.L.Rev.* 1, 10 therefore rightly speaks of the 'constitutionalisation of private law'.

[10] That Art. 2 is not simply a hollow statement has been demonstrated by Corte Cost. 6 May 1985, n. 132, *Riv.dir.int.priv.proc.* 1985 p. 325 (the limitations of liability of the Warsaw Convention pose a breach of the principle of solidarity). In a much earlier ruling the Italian Court of Cassation had already strongly linked equitable liability under Art. 2047 Cc to social solidarity and social responsibility (Cass. 28 Jan. 1953, n. 216, *Giur.it.* 1953, I, 1, 496).

human right some years ago,[11] this was not intended to block other avenues to compensation.[12] In a social state which is based on the rule of law, liability for fault can, and in some circumstances must, be replaced by strict liability, which could in turn be overtaken by an insurance solution. When a German teacher was held personally liable for an accident on a school trip in Italy by an Italian court the BGH refused to recognize the decision, ruling that it 'offends against German public policy if a person covered by mandatory accident insurance (or his surviving dependant) obtains judgment against someone who is indemnified against liability under §§ 636, 637 RVO in the country where the accident happened, granting him compensation for personal injury for an accident (sustained in this country) which is covered by his insurance'.[13] In other words, the German supreme court considered it contrary to German public policy to reintroduce tort law into an area where it had been superseded by compulsory insurance. Even the Danish model, in which someone whose personal property is unlawfully damaged is normally obliged to claim under his own insurance and to renounce his claim against the tortfeasor (§ 19 EAL), would be constitutionally in keeping in most European countries. Where a legislator allows insurance law to prevail over tort law, he must still heed the principle of equal treatment. This was temporarily a very real problem in the field of compensation funds in Italy.[14]

c. The State's Duty to Protect Human Rights as between its Individual Citizens

556 The freedom of a state to choose a suitable system for compensation does not release it either from the duty to provide sufficient delictual protection or from the duty to align that protection with human rights if a sufficiently effective alternative does not already exist. Whether that

---

[11] Conseil Constitutionnel 22 Oct. 1982 (fn. 9 above). The Constitutional Court creates a direct link between Art. 1382 Cc and Art. 4 Declaration of Human and Civil Rights of 26 Aug. 1789 ('freedom means being allowed to do everything which does not cause any harm to others'), which in turn has been adopted by the French Constitution in the Preamble of 4 Oct. 1958. Similarly, BVerfG 11 Oct. 1978, *NJW* 1979 pp. 305, 306, declares the protection of rights under § 823 I BGB to be the 'basis of every legal system and an essential ingredient of the law'.   [12] As rightly noted by Chabas (fn. 9 above) p. 61.
[13] BGH 16 Sep. 1993, *JZ* 1994 p. 254 note Eichenhofer = *IPRax* 1994 p. 118 incl. essay by Basedow, *IPRax* 1994 pp. 85–86. See also Haas, *ZZP* 108 (1995) p. 219–239.
[14] Compare Trib. Monza 4 Apr. 1991, *Arch.Giur.circolaz.* 1992 p. 21 (summary in German in *VersRAI* 1993 p. 64). The court considered it constitutionally problematic that a compensation fund existed for cars but not for hunting accidents in cases where the person causing the accident could not be identified. This situation has since been remedied by Act No. 157 of 11 February 1992 (Gaz.Uff. no. 46 of 25 Feb. 1992) which introduced a similar fund for the victims of hunting accidents: see Battistig, *VersRAI* 1992 p. 39.

obligation arises from the states's duty to protect the human rights of its citizens, or whether it is based on the concept of the direct effect of human rights on the relationships between individuals, is purely academic. The former view may be more appropriate where the state has placed the 'law-abiding' citizen at the mercy of his less honourable neighbour. The latter position has been taken in cases where an existing liability provision is interpreted in the context of human rights, producing what is known as an indirect effect on the relationships between individuals, i.e. where such common delictual terms as 'right', 'damage', 'unlawful', 'contrary to public policy', and *'fautif'* are interpreted in a constitutional light. Yet the two approaches often follow the same course, and in the law of delict, which relies much more on state enforcement, it is therefore not necessary to distinguish sharply between them. Moreover, the law of contract and that of delict differ in another important respect. The German *Bundesverfassungsgericht* once declared that tort law belongs to 'those rules of private law which contain mandatory provisions and thus form a part of the *ordre public,* in the wide sense, i.e. those principles which also apply to private legal relationships, as this is in the public interest, and the applicability of which is therefore not subject to private negotiations. Due to their purpose these provisions are not only closely related to, but also complement public law. They must therefore be especially open to the influence of constitutional law.'[15]

Human rights may well also influence relationships between individuals in other areas of private law; as far as the law of delict is concerned, the doctrine of the state's duty to protect its citizens' human rights is as undisputed as its twin concept. By defining the rules of liability governing the 'horizontal' relationships between individuals, the state also fulfils its 'vertical' protective duty.[16] So the only question remaining today is how far this duty reaches, or should reach. The differentiation between the direct and the indirect influence of human rights on relationships between individuals need be pursued no further. One illustration of the closeness of the links between constitutional and delictual law is found in Belgian law, where the violation of a human right automatically constitutes a *'faute'* under Arts. 1382, 1383 Cc.[17] In **557**

---

[15] BVerfG 15 Jan. 1958, BVerfGE 7 pp. 198, 206. However, *in casu* the BVerfG went too far. As far as the (supposedly) manadatory character of law of delict is concerned, it more closely mirrored the French (see currently only Mazeaud/Chabas, *Obligations,* 8th edn., no. 638) than the German position (see § 276 II BGB). Moreover, even in Belgium Arts. 1382 ff. Cc are not *'d'ordre public'*: see e.g. Cass. 10 Feb. 1981, *Pas. belge* 1981, I, 621.

[16] See e.g. Drion, *NJB* 1969 pp. 585, 589–591; Hesse/Kauffmann, *JZ* 1995 pp. 219–223.

[17] Rimanque, *TBP* 1981 pp. 32, 41; Van Oevelen, in Rimanque (ed.), *Toepasselkijkheid van de grondrechten,* p. 423. For France see also Grabitz (-Savoie), *Grundrechte in Europa, Frankreich,* pp. 203, 233.

Greece the influence of human rights on the relationships between individuals is highly controversial. The question there is whether the constitutional provisions granting human rights can be 'directly' interpreted as a protective statute in accordance with Art. 914 Greek Cc, or whether human rights should be regarded as aids for interpreting Art. 281 Greek Cc (the prevailing opinion). Art. 281 prohibits the abuse of a right; the infringement of such a right would amount to such an abuse, and Art. 281 Greek Cc is a statute in accordance with Art. 914 Greek Cc.[18] Clearly, both approaches lead to the same result.

558   Irish law illustrates more clearly that the protective duty of the state is the main issue, and that this approach almost inevitably makes the distinction between the direct and indirect influence of human rights on the relationships between individuals irrelevant. The starting point is Art. 40 III of the Constitution: 'the State guarantees in its laws to respect and, as far as practicable, by its laws to defend and vindicate the personal rights of the citizen. The State shall, in particular, by its laws protect as best it may from unjust attack and, in the case of injustice done, vindicate the life, person, good name, and property rights of every citizen.' This provision not only sparked off a controversy about the delictual protection of the right to privacy, of which only some features are known to common law,[19] but also about the development of 'constitutional torts', i.e. the delict of 'wrongful interference with a constitutional right'.[20] If the constitution grants to a citizen a human right, it equally obliges his fellow citizens to respect that right.[21] Each violation constitutes a delict resulting in liability.[22] 'Therefore, if a person suffers damage by virtue of a breach of a constitutional right or an infringement of a constitutional right, that person is entitled to seek redress against the

---

[18] The question of whether the effect of human rights through general clauses is 'direct' or 'indirect' is often purely theoratical and does not effect the actual result, as rightly stressed by Kasimatis *ToΣ* 7 (1981) pp. 1, 11–13; see also Karakostas, *NuR* 1993 p. 468 (in German); and Westermann/Karakatsanes (-Karakatsanes), *Schuldrechtsreform in Deutschland und Griechenland*, p. 100 (Art. 281 Greek Cc, prohibition against abuse of a right, covers not only absolute rights, but also the general freedom of action). However, other scholars follow either one of the the doctrines. Those supporting the doctrine of the direct influence of human rights are e.g.: Doris, *EllDik* 32 (1991) pp. 1188, 1198 (but a solution consistent with the Constitution); Iliopoulou-Stanga, *I 'tritenergeia' ton atomikon kai koinonikon dikaiomaton tou Syntagmatos*, p. 71; Kasimatis loc. cit. p. 20; and Katranis, *ToΣ* 4 (1978) pp. 237, 266. Supporters of the other camp are e.g.: Dagtoglou, *NoB* 30 (1982) pp. 780, 788; Stathopoulos, *Geniko Enochiko Dikaio* A1, 2nd edn., p. 10; Karakostas, *Perivallon kai Astiko Dikaio*, p. 39; and Spyridakis, *Genikes Arches*, vol. i p. 73. For court decisions see Areopag 81/1991, *EllDik* 32/1991 p. 1215 (no. 560 below); Areopag 717/1985, *NoB* 34 (1986) p. 560; and CA Patras 326/1982, *NoB* 31 (1983) p. 1020, concerning a private company wholly governed by public authorities: delict based on the notion of unequal treatment, see no. 569 below.

[19] More detail in McMahon/Binchy, *Irish Law of Torts*, 2nd edn., pp. 691–698.

[20] Id. p. 9.   [21] E.g. *Educational Co. of Ireland v. Fitzpatrick (No. 1)* [1961] IR 323.

[22] *Byrne v. Ireland* [1972] IR 241, 279–280 (Sup. Ct., *per* Walsh, J), although in the context of a decision resulting in state liability.

person or persons who infringed that right.'[23] This is especially true if the common law does not cover such a claim.[24]

This may be seen as a bold move by the Irish courts, yet their basic **559** concepts are shared by many of their European counterparts. The French Constitutional Court, for example, rejected a draft bill granting unions and employees immunity from liability in cases of strikes; it undoubtedly based its decision on the notion of the state's protective duty.[25] If England had a constitutional court, it would probably have taken a similar position. At around the same time Lord Denning said (out of court) on this issue: 'I wish . . . that we had had some doctrine authorising judicial review of statutes'.[26] Moreover, in a case in which he sat as Master of the Rolls, he went so far as to stress that 'a trade union has no right to use its industrial strength to invade the freedom of the press. They have no right to interfere with the freedom of commercial firms to advertise their wares. These freedoms are so fundamental in our society that no trade union has any right to interfere with them. Interference with the freedom of the press is so contrary to the public interest that it is to be regarded as the employment of unlawful means.'[27] His attempts to advance yet further[28] were thwarted by the House of Lords,[29] but this is the closest an English judge could ever come to imposing a constitutionally based law of tort!

One of the decisions compelling the German state to impose liability **560** for breach of an individual's constitutionally protected rights is the *Bundesverfassungsgericht* ruling, which quashed the decision of the BGH[30] to grant immunity to experts appointed by the court.[31] The Italian *Corte Costituzionale* ruled that the state of Italy, which had provided for a claim for damages in environmental liability law from which it alone could benefit,[32] could only do this if it did not interfere with the

---

[23] *Meskell v. Coras Iompair Éireann* [1973] IR 121, 133 (Sup. Ct., *per* Walsh, J). Under certain circumstances this basic rule can even affect the law governing the limitation of actions, see *Cahill v. Sutton* [1980] IR 269 (HC), and 275 (Sup. Ct.). However, *in casu* there was no breach of the Constitution.

[24] *Meskell v. Coras Iompair Éireann* pp. 132–133; see also *Hanrahan v. Merck Sharp and Dohme* [1988] ILRM 629, 636 (Sup. Ct., *per* Henchy, J).

[25] Conseil Constitutionnel 22 Oct. 1982 (fn. 9 above).

[26] Denning, *What Next in the Law*, p. 231.

[27] *Associated Newspapers Group v. Wade* [1979] 1 WLR 697, 709 (CA).

[28] In *Hadmor Productions Ltd. v. Hamilton* [1981] 3 WLR 139 (CA).

[29] *Hadmor Productions Ltd. v. Hamilton* [1982] 2 WLR 322 (HL).

[30] BGH 18 Dec. 1973, BGHZ 62 p. 54.

[31] BVerfG 11 Oct. 1978, JZ 1979 p. 60 incl. note by Starck. Liability for violation of personal liberty. BVerfG quashed the rule laid down by the BGH loc. cit. that liability does not arise even in cases of gross negligence. In cases of every-day negligence, the exclusion of liability has been retained, as the vote on this issue ended in a draw (4:4).

[32] Art. 18 of Act no. 349 of 8 July 1986 on the Establishment of a Ministry for the Environment and Rules on Damage to the Environment, sub-section 1: 'each intentional

claims of individuals whose personal rights had been violated by the polluter.[33] Against this background one may well ask whether the English liability provision that a barrister has no duty of care to his client even in a criminal case[34] still meets the continental European constitutional standard. Furthermore, the state may even have a duty to secure the economic enforceability of private liability claims. The Austrian OGH decided that customs officers who allow a motor vehicle without third-party liability insurance to enter Austria commit a breach of official duty, rendering the state of Austria liable for damages.[35] This may be right, but for the present purpose it is sufficient to note that, for the law of delict, the doctrine of the influence of human rights on relationships between individuals, and the notion of the state's protective duty, are not only equally popular but also achieve similar results. This is also true for countries which adhere to the concept of the 'indirect' influence of human rights on private law relationships.[36] In Italy, for instance, the *Corte Costituzionale* has called repeatedly for a '*lettura costituzionale*' (constitutional reading), particularly of Art. 2043 Cc, and has drawn

---

or negligent act violating statutes or regulations made on the basis of a statute and endangering the environment by causing damage to it, changing it, impairing, or partially or totally destroying it, renders those causing such acts liable for damages *vis-à-vis* the state'.

[33] Corte Cost. 30 Dec. 1987, n. 641, *Foro.it.* 1988 I, 694, 707 ('*per il privato cittadino il danno ambientale potrebbe essere ingiusto nei limiti in cui si assume la rilevanza. Rimane, comunque, ferma la tutela del cittadino che ha subíto nocumento dal danno ambientale*'). See also Albamonte, *Danni all'ambiente*, pp. 51–52; v. Bar (-Busnelli), *DeliktsR in Europa*, pp. 39–40. On a similar general tendency of a number of decisions on the *danno biologico*, see no. 574 below.

[34] *Rondel* v. *Worsley* [1969] 1 AC 191 (HL): no duty of care where a barrister's negligent conduct is supposed to have earned his client a prison sentence. Meanwhile this privilege of barristers has been acknowledged in sec. 62 Courts and Legal Services Act 1990 (c. 41). The decision is based on the concept that barristers (like experts appointed by a German civil court) are first and foremost answerable to the court. For more detail see Mann, 93 (1977) *LQR* 367, 369.

[35] OGH 1 Apr. 1992, *ZfRV* 1993 p. 125. See also, albeit in a different context, BGH 16 Feb. 1970, BGHZ 53 p. 226; and Corte Cost. 2 May 1991, n. 188, *Foro.it.* 1991, I, 1981 (Art. 4 Act of 24 Dec. 1969, no. 990, on third-party liability for motor vehicles, is unconstitutional insofar as the provision excludes certain 'third parties' as persons entitled to compensation).

[36] For The Netherlands see e.g. Baron van Haersolte, *Inleiding tot het Nederlandse staatsrecht*, 9th edn., pp. 38–39, arguing that the doctrine of the direct influence of human rights is gaining strong support; Verhey, *Horizontale werking van grondrechten*, pp. 89, 175; Grabitz (-de Blois/Heringa), *Grundrechte in Europa, Niederlande*, pp. 511, 541–543. For court rulings see esp. HR 10 Dec. 1982, *NedJur* 1983 no. 687 p. 2156. For Spain see de la Quadra-Salcedo, *El recurso de amparo y los derechos fundamentales en las relaciones entre particulares*, pp. 47–79; Fernández Segado, *El sistema constitucional español*, pp. 484–486; and Sommermann, *Schutz der Grundrechte in Spanien*, pp. 234–238. For Denmark see Grabitz (-Germer), *Grundrechte in Europa, Der Grundrechtsschutz in Dänemark*, p. 105; Gralla, *Grundrechtsschutz in Dänemark*, pp. 176–181; and HD 29 Oct. 1980, *UfR* 1980 A p. 1038, on the freedom of expression in the context of remarks damaging a person's business reputation. For Italy, which has a reputation for venturing a long way on this issue, see e.g. di Majo, *Tutela civile dei diritti*, vol. iii p. 10; Palin, *Principio costituzionale d'eguaglianza*, p. 238; and Alpa/Bessone, *Atipicità*, vol. ii (2), 2nd edn., p. 132.

far-reaching conclusions from this duty.[37] The Portuguese Constitutional Court considered that it was unconstitutional, albeit in the context of government liability, for the state-governed telephone company to benefit from a special liability regime, which protected it against liability in negligence to its *consumidores*.[38] Finally, it was at least partly due to the impact of the Constitution that Art. 914 Greek Cc was converted from a blanket provision into a true general clause. In a 1991 product liability case, the *Areopag* reverted to Art. 5 § 1 Greek Constitution,[39] and confirmed yet again that: 'the basic principle that each act or omission resulting in culpable infliction of damage obliges the actor to compensate such damage, not only if his act or omission violates a specific provision, but also if it infringes upon the general spirit of our legal system which demands that the conduct of a business must not result in a transgression of public policy.'[40]

d. Further Problematic Areas between Constitutional Law and Delict

The second link between human rights and tort law is the need, increasingly recognized, to bring tort law into line with rights of equal treatment. Both the special features of and the general principle inherent in the latter, i.e. to treat equal situations alike and different ones differently, call for such alignment. Furthermore, human rights and the right to equal treatment both play an important role in deciding how far the Constitution allows tort law to be developed by the courts. The principles governing the separation of powers are strongly influenced by all human rights, which focus ultimately on the '*großen Gleich- und Weichmacher der Verfassungsmaßstäbe*' (the great softener of constitutional standards),[41] the principle of reasonableness. Yet those who believe that the constitutional balance between legislator and judiciary is impaired if judges decide which laws constitute protective statutes under § 823 II

561

---

[37] E.g. Corte Cost. 18 July 1991, n. 356, *Foro.it.* 1991, I, 2967, 2974; and Corte Cost. 14 July 1986, n. 184, *Giust.cost.* 1986, I, 1430, 1442 (= *Foro.it.* 1986, I, 2053). See also no. 573 below.

[38] Tribunal Constitucional 3 May 1990, *BolMinJust* 397 (1990) p. 51.

[39] 'Everybody has the right to free development of his personality, and to participate in the social, economic, and political life of the country, insofar as he does not violate the rights of others, the Constitution, or *bonos mores*'.

[40] Areopag 81/1991, *EllDik* 32 (1991) p. 1215. The decision is even more remarkable in that, for the first time, the court established a duty to act by reverting to the Constitution. Usually, liability for failure to act is based on good faith, abuse of legal rights, and generally accepted standards (Arts. 200, 281, and 288 Greek Cc), provisions dealt with in Art. 914 Greek Cc as protective statutes: see e.g. OLG Athens 1039/1979, *NoB*, 27 (1979) p. 984; CA Salonica 2901/1987, *Arm.* 42 (1988) p. 765; Areopag 343/1968, *NoB* 16 (1968) p. 943; Areopag 854/1974, *NoB* 23 (1975) p. 479; and Areopag 9228/1979, *NoB* 28 (1980) p. 545.

[41] As *per* Ossenbühl, *VVDStRL* 39 (1981) p. 189.

BGB are over-cautious.[42] From a constitutional point of view, there is nothing wrong with allowing judges to decide whether a given statute is protective. On the contrary, most of the deficiencies suffered, especially by German tort law, evolved from the reverse situation. The legislature of the *Reich* knit its law of delict so tightly precisely because it distrusted its judges more than was the case in France.[43]

2. JUDICIAL REVIEW OF STATUTES

562 It might be helpful here to outline some of the most important features of constitutional (procedural) law in various national contexts. England, for instance, has no constitutional court: the principle of the supremacy (or sovereignty) of Parliament itself has constitutional status. So an English court cannot reject an Act of Parliament as unconstitutional:[44] an 'unconstitutional Act' is a contradiction in terms. The furthest a judge can venture is to dismiss a provision which does not amount to an Act because it does not pass the reasonableness test[45] or appears otherwise unconstitutional.[46] The courts may refer to the European Convention on Human Rights to seek an approximation of values.[47] If this proves insufficient, however, they must ask the legislator to intervene, which is quite common practice.[48] However, in one extremely sensitive area, the protection of personal privacy, the judiciary's call for an effective right to privacy[49] has not so far been answered.

---

[42] Position taken by Peters, *JZ* 1983 pp. 913, 926.   [43] See no. 17 above.

[44] See e.g. *Cartledge* v. *E. Jopling & Sons Ltd.* [1963] AC 758; *Burmah Oil Co.* v. *Lord Advocate* [1965] AC 75. In both cases the legislature reacted immediately: the 1963 Limitation Act was passed in response to *Cartledge*, and the War Damages Act 1965 to *Burmah*. However, English courts have always reviewed the compatibility of English law with Community law. For 'it has always been clear that it was the duty of a United Kingdom court, when delivering final judgment, to override any rule of national law found to be in conflict with any directly enforceable rule of Community law': Lord Bridge in *R* v. *Secretary of State for Transport*, ex parte *Factortame* [1991] 1 AC 603, 659. For further references on both English and Scottish law see Boch/Lane, *SLT* 1992 pp. 145–148.

[45] *Associated Provincial Picture Houses* v. *Wednesbury Corporation* [1948] 1 KB 223, 229 (CA, per Greene MR); *Wheeler* v. *Leicester City Council* [1985] 2 All ER 1106.

[46] Irrelevant considerations: *Bromley London Borough Council* v. *Greater London Council* [1983] 1 AC 768; legitimate expectation: *Council of Civil Service Unions* v. *Minister for the Civil Service* [1989] 3 All ER 935; natural justice: *Ridge* v. *Baldwin* [1964] AC 40. But cf. *R* v. *Chief Rabbi of the United Hebrew Congregations of Great Britain and the Commonwealth*, ex parte *Wachmann* [1983] 2 All ER 249; discretion: *Padfield* v. *Minister of Agriculture* [1968] AC 997.

[47] *Ahmad* v. *Inner London Education Authority* [1978] 1 QB 36, 41 (Lord Denning MR); and 48 (Scarman LJ) (CA).

[48] E.g. *Malone* v. *Metropolitan Police Commissioner* [1979] Ch. 344, 380 (Megarry VC) (CA). In response to this decision the Interception of Communications Act was passed in 1985.

[49] Last made in *Kaye* v. *Robertson* [1991] FSR 62 = Weir, *Casebook*, 7th edn., pp. 20–25 (Glidewell LJ: 'The facts of the present case are a graphic illustration of the desirability of

Article 61 II of the French Constitution of 4 October 1958 provides that **563** the *Conseil Constitutionnel* can only declare an Act unconstitutional before it is promulgated. Once enacted a statute binds all courts. France has no procedure for individuals to make a constitutional complaint, so the problem of its *Conseil Constitutionnel* overstepping its jurisdiction does not exist. Not so in Germany, however, where it has become a serious problem,[50] as the Constitutional Court tends to be elevated to the role of supervising the Supreme Court, particularly with respect to the law of delict. Dutch judges also cannot review 'the constitutionality of Acts and Treaties' (Art. 120 GrW); they can only confirm the (un)constitutionality of regulations. Article 6:110 BW, for example, says that 'maximum limits for liability can be prescribed by regulations, so that the liability which may arise from damage does not exceed that which can reasonably be covered by insurance. Separate amounts can be fixed according to, amongst others, the nature of the event and the damage, and the ground for liability'. Although no such regulation has yet been made, Dutch scholars are already firing warning shots about the need to examine it closely in the light of Art. 1 s. 1 GrW ('All persons residing in The Netherlands shall be treated equally in equal cases').[51] However, even more important than the possibility of judicial review of a regulation is Art. 94 GrW, according to which 'legal provisions shall not apply within the Kingdom if their application does not comply with the generally binding provisions of treaties and resolutions of organizations under international law'. For the Dutch, treaties—including the European Convention on Human Rights—rank higher than their Constitution. This explains why Dutch scholars increasingly refer to treaties when defining the 'violation of a right' (*inbreuk op een recht*) under Art. 6:162 BW.[52] However, were the *Hoge Raad* to violate the principle of the separation of powers, which seems not to be a purely academic possibility,[53] the

---

Parliament considering whether and in what circumstances statutory provisions can be made to protect the privacy of individuals'; and Bingham LJ: 'This case nonetheless highlights, yet again, the failure of both the common law of England and statute to protect in an effective way the personal privacy of individual citizens').

[50] Recent decision: BVerfG 19 Oct. 1993, *NJW* 1994 p. 36: terms in contracts for loans which require relatives without personal income and possessions to guarantee the loan are unfair.   [51] See de Vries, *Wettlelijke limitering van aansprakelijkheid*, pp. 216–219.

[52] E.g. Jansen, *Onrechtmatige daad*, p. 34; Asser (-Hartkamp), *Verbintenissenrecht*, vol. iii, 8th edn., p. 36. An illustrative, but since Art. 6:106 I BW outdated, decision is HR 1 Nov. 1991, *NedJur* 1992 no. 58 p. 177: a policeman told the plaintiff's girlfriend that he was suspected of a burglary. As a result she called off their relationship, for which the (innocent) plaintiff demanded general damages. As the officer had not committed an insult, the *Hoge Raad* dismissed the case under Art. 1408 BW (old). Yet a claim under Art. 1401 BW (old) was successful, as this provision applied to violations of Art. 8 European Convention on Human Rights, by which a person has a right to privacy (cf. HR 30 Oct. 1987, *NedJur* 1988 no. 277 p. 1097).   [53] See no. 599 below.

absence of a Constitutional Court would prevent it from being sanctioned. Luxembourgeois[54] judges are in the same position as their Dutch counterparts. Their Belgian colleagues, or to be precise, the Belgian Court of Arbitration, has only recently been authorized to review the constitutionality of Acts, particularly regarding the principle of equality before the law.[55]

564   An entirely different situation obtains in Greece, where the 'courts must not apply a statute whose content is unconstitutional': Art. 93 § 4 in conjunction with Art. 87 § 2 of the Constitution of 11 June 1975. The right to declare statutes void (and to interpret them in a constitutional light *erga omnes*) lies solely with the Special Constitutional Supreme Court. There is no appeal to it from the Courts of First Instance, who can only disapply a statute in a specific case.[56] Danish courts can also judicially review statutes. However, they cannot declare a statute void.[57] Individuals cannot make constitutional complaints in either Greece or Denmark. In Ireland the Supreme Court also functions as the Constitutional Court (see Arts. 26, 34 of the Constitution of 1 July 1937 as amended on 26 Nov. 1992). Moreover, in certain circumstances even the High Court has the power to undertake a judicial review (Art. 34 III *loc. cit.*) Only Italy, Spain, Portugal, and Germany have established fully functioning and wholly independent Constitutional Courts. In Italy, cases touching on delict reach the *Corte Costituzionale* mostly by the *via incidentale*: if the court or one of the parties disputes the constitutionality of a statute (and in the latter case the relevant court decides that there is a basis for the claim), a situation only too common, particularly to the Courts of First Instance, then the argument must come before the *Corte Costituzionale*.[58]

---

[54] Art. 95 Lux. Constitution (regulations) and Cour 8 June 1950, *Pas. luxemb.* 15 (1950–1953) p. 41 (international treaties).

[55] Art. 142 II in conjunction with Arts. 10, 11 Belgian Constitution, as amended on 17 Feb. 1994. The first decision to have an impact on tort law is Cour d'Arbitrage 21 Mar. 1995, *RW* 1994–1995 p. 1324: the principle of equality is impaired if liability in private law becomes statute-barred sooner for a criminal act than for a non-criminal act).

[56] In Greece judges have traditionally been responsible for examining the constitutionality of laws. The *Areopag* is supposed to have done so since 1897, even before the Constitution of 1927 which expressly granted the courts this right for the first time (Dagtoglou, *NoB* 36 [1988] pp. 720, 722). The basic principle is laid down in Art. 93 § 4 Constitution of 1975; Art. 87 § 2 repeats that judges are not compelled to apply unconstitutional law. For more detail see esp. Skouris/Veniselos, *O dikastikos elenchos tis sintagmatikotitas ton nomon*, p. 49; however, cf. (in German) Starck/Weber (-Dagtoglou), *Verfassungsgerichtsbarkeit in Westeuropa*, vol. i, *Griechenland*, pp. 363, 372. On the jurisdiction of the Special Constitutional Supreme Court see also Art. 100 lit. e of the Greek Constitution (contradicting decisions of the Council of State, the *Areopag*, and the Audit Office); on proceedings before the Special Constitutional Supreme Court see the comprehensive detail in Skouris/Veniselos loc. cit. p. 68.

[57] For more detail see Sørensen, *Statsforfatningsret*, 2nd edn., pp. 302–304; Grabitz (Gralla), *Grundrechte in Europa, Dänemark*, pp. 75–77. So far only one statute has been found to be unconstitutional: HD 18 Mar. 1971, *UfR* 1971 A p. 299.

[58] Cf. Art. 1 Constitution Act no. 1/1948 (Gaz. Uff. 20 Feb. 1948, n. 43); and Art. 23 Constitution Act no. 87/1953 (Gaz. Uff. 14 Mar. 1953, n. 62).

The situation in Portugal is similar[59] (Arts. 280–283 Portugese Constitution of 2 April 1976 as amended in 1989). Moreover, under Art. 280 IV even parties to civil proceedings can appeal to the Constitutional Court for review of a specific legal provision. A final point of interest is that Spain, like Germany,[60] distinguishes between law implemented before and after the Constitution. As delictual provisions were mostly made before that date, the civil courts themselves must determine their constitutionality (as *lex posterior*). Post-constitutional statutes must be brought before the Constitutional Court, which alone has the right to declare a legal provision unconstitutional and void.[61] Constitutional complaints may be made by individuals.[62] If the complaint concerns the application of human rights to relationships between individuals, the appellant challenges the constitutionality of a civil decision by arguing that the state has breached its duty to protect one individual against unlawful conduct by another.[63] Thus procedural and tort law are neatly interwoven again.[64]

3. TORT LAW AND EQUAL OPPORTUNITIES

a. Sexual Equality

The issue of sexual equality illustrates how substantive tort law can **565** conflict with higher-ranking constitutional law. One has only to consider those European countries which link negligence to the standards required by the *paterfamilias*,[65] an expression which no post-constitutional legislator could employ. Countries with older codes can overcome the problem simply by interpreting the expression constitutionally. Even if men and women do not always agree on what constitutes reasonable conduct, there is no reason why the 'male standard' only (if such exists) should be legally binding. Therefore, it is best to take the entire 'reasonable man' concept with a pinch of salt, as Herbert did in *Fardell* v. *Potts*, a fictional negligence case involving two women. He had his tormented

---

[59] For more details in German see Horn/Weber (-Miranda), *Richterliche Verfassungskontrolle, Portugal*, pp. 81, 92–96.

[60] For a comprehensive discussion of this issue see BVerfG 24 Feb. 1953, BVerfGE 2, 124, 128 ff.   [61] Arts. 163, 164 CE.

[62] Arts. 161 I lit. b, 162 I lit. b, 53 II CE in conjunction with *Ley Orgánica del Tribunal Constitucional* of 3 Oct. 1979 (BOE no. 239 of 5 Oct. 1979), whose Arts. 35 ff. also deal with the procedural details of a judicial review.

[63] For more detail: Starck/Weber (-Rubio Llorente), *Verfassungsgerichtsbarkeit in Westeuropa, Spanien*, pp. 268–269; López Pina (-Tomás y Valiente), *Spanisches Verfassungsrecht*, pp. 149, 158–160.   [64] See nos. 556 ff. above (influence of human rights).

[65] See no. 12 above.

judge say: 'I find that at common law a reasonable woman does not exist'![66] A relaxed view should be taken where, as in Spain,[67] the Civil Code still links the *actio de effusis vel eiectis* to the 'head of the family'. This, too, is merely an archaic expression which can easily be interpreted in a constitutional light.[68]

566   However, § 1300 BGB (liability in general damages for sexual intercourse with an honourable/faithful fiancée) a quasi-delictual rule of pre-constitutional law, cannot be seen simply as an ill-worded provision,[69] but rather as a breach of Art. 3 II GG (the equality of sexes before the law), as decided by AG Münster,[70] and as correctly, although indirectly, approved by the BVerfG.[71] Similarly, the provisions protecting the 'sexual reputation' of women (§ 1328 ABGB, §§ 825, 847 II BGB),[72] and regulations (such as § 1326 ABGB) by which disfigurements of abused persons 'especially if they are of the female gender' have to be given special consideration, are controversial. However, as § 825 BGB no longer has any practical relevance,[73] its constitutionality need not be discussed in detail here. It suffices to say that it is based on an attitude to women which does not meet modern standards, and its Greek equivalent (Art. 921 Greek Cc)[74] was repealed in 1983, when the concept of equality was finally pushed through.[75] In Spain Art. 479 CP used to cause constitutional concern. It imposed quasi-damages on men knowingly committing bigamy, because men had to provide a dowry for honourable women, but not vice versa. The situation became intolerable in 1983, when the Spanish legislator abolished the duty to pay dowry as compensation for crimes (Art. 444 CP; now Art. 193 NCP).[76] No provi-

---

[66] Herbert, *Uncommon Law*, p. 6.

[67] Art. 1910 Cc. In § 1318 ABGB, which concerns the same cause of action, gender implications have been avoided. Moreover, in Scotland the *actio de effusis vel eiectis* seems no longer to be applicable law: cf. no. 7, fn. 30 above.

[68] Díez-Picazo/Gullón, *Sistema*, vol. ii, 6th edn., p. 635.

[69] BVerfG 26 Jan. 1972, *NJW* 1972 p. 571.

[70] AG Münster 8 Dec. 1992, *NJW* 1993 p. 1720.

[71] BVerfG decision of 5 Feb. 1993, mentioned in *NJW* 1993, p. 1721 in an editorial note.

[72] Compensation for pain and suffering in such cases allowed under German, but not Austrian, law.   [73] As rightly stated in *BGB-RGRK* (-Steffen) 12th edn., § 825 no. 1.

[74] 'If a woman's honour has been insulted by sexual intercourse with her as a result of a punishable act or as a consequence of threats or deceitful promises, or of an abuse of her subordinate position, she shall be entitled to compensation by payment of such sum of money as would enable her to get married.' On the same occasion the Greek legislator also deleted the last sentence of Art. 931 Greek Cc: compensation for physical disability or disfigurement 'if such may affect the victim's future, particularly as regards a woman's prospects of marriage'. Both provisions had long been constitutionally controversial: Machairas, *NoB* 27 (1979) p. 24 on Areopag 28/1978.

[75] By Arts. 4 II, 116 I of the Greek Constitution of 11 June 1975, law infringing the principle of equality became ineffective at the end of 1982.

[76] More detail in Bajo Fernández/Díaz-Maroto y Villarejo, *Derecho Penal*, 2nd edn., p. 327.

sion similar to Art. 479 CP was included in the NCP in May 1996, so the problem simply ceased to exist. In Italy, on the other hand, the number of decisions on *seduzione con promessa di matrimonio*[77] demonstrates that, under certain social circumstances, the 'sexual reputation of women' may still require special protection. None the less, the German legislator should follow the Greek example and delete § 825 BGB.

b. Further Cases of Unequal Treatment

Tort law also discriminates on issues other than gender. In 1972, for **567** instance, the *Corte Costituzionale* had to decide a road traffic accident case.[78] Under Art. 2054 II Ital. Cc, 'in cases of collisions between vehicles, it is presumed, until the contrary is proved, that each driver contributed equally to the damage suffered by either vehicle'. The Italian Constitutional Court decided that it was a breach of Art. 3 of the Italian Constitution (principle of equality) that equal contribution was not presumed in cases where one of the cars involved in the accident sustained no damage. Ten years later the French *Conseil Constitutionnel* regarded a draft bill on employment law relating to strikes as a '*discrimination manifeste*': a clear breach of the right to '*l'égalité devant la loi et devant les charges publiques*'.[79] Yet in 1978 the Austrian Constitutional Court declined the claim that § 1319a ABGB (liability for damage suffered on public paths only in cases of the occupier's intention and gross negligence), implemented only a few years earlier, violated the principle of equality before the law. It was argued that 'liability had to be lessened as the path was free of tolls and did not benefit any particular person'.[80] An Act imposing a limitation period of five years for liability in damages arising from crime and of thirty years for liability in damages arising from unlawful but *not* criminal conduct is unambiguously inappropriate and discriminatory: the Belgian Constitutional Court therefore declared those provisions void.[81] The principle of equality before the law and the concept of sexual equality can also clash in pre-contractual, and thus (as is often the case) also in extra-contractual areas, for instance when a national legal system imposes an upper limit for damages (Art. 6 EEC Directive 76/207) for employment policies which discriminate on the ground of sex (Art. 3 loc. cit.) without taking the circumstances of the

---

[77] See no. 42 above; cf. Cass. 8 July 1993, n. 7493, *Foro.it.* 1994, I, 1878.

[78] Corte Cost. 29 Dec. 1972, n. 205, *Arch.Giur.Circolaz.* 1973 p. 23; see also v. Bar (-Busnelli), *DeliktsR in Europa, Italien*, p. 34. Against the background of this decision, Cass. 17 June 1993, n. 6750, *Riv.giur.circ.trasp.* 1993 p. 975 extends the application of Art. 2054 II Cc even to a moving vehicle hitting one which is stationary.

[79] Conseil Constitutionnel 22 Oct. 1982 (fn. 9 above).

[80] VfGH 1 Mar. 1978, *JBl.* 1979 pp. 142, 143.

[81] Cour d'Arbitrage 21 Mar. 1995 (fn. 55 above).

individual case into consideration.[82] Moreover, the German Bundesverfassungsgericht reviewed §§ 636, 637 RVO insofar as they exclude compensation for pain and suffering under industrial accident law, primarily
with regard to Art. 3 I GG (equality before the law), not under Art. 2 II
GG (protection of personal integrity). It held that even in cases where
third-party motor insurance had to indemnify the employee, the provisions were not unconstitutional.[83] Other cases which are similarly controversial but constitutionally sanctioned by the courts are those of
soldiers[84] and foreigners whose home countries and whose countries
of residence have not entered into any reciprocal agreements,[85] e.g. in
the fields of government liability[86] and compensation schemes for victims of traffic accidents.[87] The Austrian OGH once generously declared
that it was 'for the home country', and not for Austrian constitutional
law, to overcome deficits in reciprocity.[88] So only after the implementation of European Community law did member states begin to realize
that an individual should not be held liable for deficiencies of his country![89] However, should a foreigner ever truly be in a better position than

[82] Directive 76/207/EEC on the implementation of the principle of equal treatment for
men and women as regards access to employment, vocational training, promotion, and
working conditions of 9.2.1976, OJ L 39 p. 40. For an overview of decisions on this issue see
Eichenhofer, *CMLR* 30 (1993) pp. 1021, 1037–1041. See also *Marshall v. Southampton and
South West Hampshire Health Authority (Teaching) (No. 2)* [1994] QB 126, 165–166 (ECJ), albeit
in casu against a background of an unlawful termination of contract. Violation of dignity by
discrimination during selection procedures for a job was the issue in BAG 14 Mar. 1989,
NJW 1990 p. 65. Pret. Ferrara 25 Nov. 1993, *NGCC* 1995, I, 70 regarded the termination of
the contract of a woman, absent from work for three days without notifying her employer
after her child died, as a violation of the constitutional right to human dignity.
[83] BVerfG 7 Nov. 1972, *VersR* 1973 pp. 269, 272; recently confirmed by BVerfG 8 Feb.
1995, *NJW* 1995 p. 1607, which expressly stated that this also applied to 'gravely injured
persons'. [84] See BVerfG 22 June 1971, BVerfGE 31 pp. 212, 218.
[85] OGH 1 July 1976, *SZ* 49 no. 89 pp. 426, 431; decisions cited in fn. 86 below; and BVerfG
17 Jan. 1991, *NVwZ* 1991 p. 661.
[86] For German law see e.g. Palandt (-Thomas), 53rd edn., § 839 BGB no. 5. There are no
reciprocal treaties between Germany and Italy (see BGH 14 July 1988, *VersR* p. 1047),
Germany and Sweden (see ObGerBrZ 17 Nov. 1949, *NJW* 1950 pp. 65, 66), Germany and
Poland (BGH 10 May 1954, BGHZ 13 p. 241), or Germany and Turkey (BGH 17 Dec. 1981,
WM 1982 p. 241).
[87] See e.g. § 2 IV German *Opferentschädigungsgesetz*, and § 11 *VO über den Entschädi-
gungsfonds für Schäden aus Kraftfahrzeugunfällen* in accordance with §§ 12, 14 PflVG (BGBl
1965 I 2093, 2094).
[88] OGH 1 July 1976 (fn. 85 above). Meanwhile a reciprocity treaty has been implemented
between Germany and Austria: Austrian BGBl. 1982, 204.
[89] *Ian William Cowan v. Trésor Public*, Rs. C-186/87, European Court 2 Feb. 1989, *InfAuslR*
1989 p. 147 = *NJW* 1989 p. 2183: French law governing the compensation of victims of
crimes infringes European Community law: an English tourist, the victim of an assault in
Paris, was denied compensation. The court argued that reciprocity between France and the
United Kingdom was not guaranteed. BGH 14 Mar. 1988, *VersR* 1988 p. 1047, however, saw
no reason to appeal to the European Court pursuant to Art. 177 EEC Treaty! On the
collision of reciprocal rules under the Copyright Act and European Community law, see
also *Phil Collins et al.*, Rs. C-92/92 and C-326/92, European Court of Justice 20 Oct. 1993,

a national, some national courts are more prepared to apply the principle of equality. Art. 38 Introductory Statute to the German BGB is one example. The BGH refused to recognize an American decision imposing punitive damages, arguing that it would 'enable foreign creditors to gain access to national debtors to a far greater extent. . . . To place the few creditors from a country which recognizes punitive damages in a better position than everybody else . . . is . . . not justified by reasons deserving protection in accordance with the German legal system';[90] from the viewpoint of conflict of laws this is a truly amazing justification.

Controversial issues also arise in the calculation of damages. When- **568** ever an adjustment of claims is governed by aspects of 'equity', and thus by 'the circumstances of the individual case', particularly in cases where the level of non-material damages has to be determined on the basis of such aspects, it is extremely difficult to determine whether the principle of equality has been violated. This problem is exaggerated where the courts do not explain how they reach the figure upon which they decide, as for example in Denmark and Spain. Nonetheless, the 'System to Assess Damage to Persons Caused by Traffic Accidents'[91] suggested by the Ministry for Economy and Finances to Spanish insurers, as well as the many data banks and volumes recording the quantum of damages awarded in individual cases, demonstrate the great need for equal treatment in this field. The Italian Court of Cassation was therefore right to ask for a detailed explanation when the Court of Appeal simply ordered the defendant's insurance company to pay five million lire for biological damage.[92] Finally, it still seems to be a tremendous problem for judges to resist being influenced by a victim's popularity, wealth, and social standing when deciding 'equitable' compensation for pain and suffering.[93]

c. Discrimination Against Individuals by other Individuals

Rules which, especially under German law, exclude immaterial damages **569** in cases of strict liability and breach of contractual duty of care (and *culpa in contrahendo*) can be constitutionally tested not only against Art. 3 I GG (equality before the law) but also, and most effectively, against Art.

NJW 1994 p. 375, including an essay by Loewenheim, *NJW* 1994, pp. 1046–1048; and BGH 21 Apr. 1994, *ZIP* 1994 p. 1384.

[90] BGH 4 June 1992, BGHZ 118 pp. 312, 345. When the *Kammergericht* took a different view, the BVerfG 3 Aug. 1994, *RIW* 1994 p. 769 passed a provisional order against it. Yet in the main proceedings the BVerfG held that the German courts were obliged to issue a writ against a German national being sued for punitive damages under US law before a US court: BVerfG 7 Dec. 1994, *JZ* 1995 p. 716 and note Stadler.

[91] For details: Sprung, *Vw* 1992 pp. 49–54.

[92] Cass. 18 Feb. 1993, n. 2008, *Giur.it.* 1994, I, 1, 44.

[93] Cf. v. Bar, *NJW* 1980 pp. 1724, 1729.

2 II GG (bodily integrity as a human right). Although the *Reichsgericht* held as early as 1906 that it 'did not see any obvious reason to distinguish between contractual and delictual liability on this issue',[94] the aim of keeping the extent of liability at a reasonable level was reason enough to allow such strange rules to slip through the net of the general prohibition against arbitrariness.[95] Thus, the only remaining question on equal treatment before the law is under what conditions an individual commits a delict by discriminating against his fellow man. This would usually only occur if the relationship between one private person and another resembled that of the state to its citizen. It is against this background that national economic laws and the EC Treaty (Art. 86 s. 2 lit. c) have contrived to create the delict of abuse of a dominant position in the market.[96] This was also the background to the European Court's confirmation of the decisions of the Dutch *Hoge Raad* and the German *Bundesgerichtshof* that invasion of personal privacy occurs (and may result in compensation for pain and suffering) if an employer refuses to employ a woman for reasons related to her sex.[97] The 1983 decision against an electricity supplier in CA Patras was also made against this background.[98] An electricity supplier (organized under private law, but completely controlled by the state) turned a natural lake into a dam after the Greek state had expropriated the relevant land in its favour. The dam rendered other land, not expropriated, virtually inaccessible and thus worthless to its owners, who were awarded damages for violation of property under Art. 914 Greek Cc. The court argued that the owners of the land which had not been expropriated (and who had not been compensated by the state) had been prejudiced contrary to the principle of equality before the law. In an even more impressive ruling by CA Athens 1990 on the conduct of a bank which terminated credit agree-

---

[94] RG 13 Dec. 1906, RGZ 65 pp. 17, 21.

[95] Breach of the prohibition against arbitrariness is only presumed if a specific provision is objectively wholly unjustifiable: see e.g. BVerfG 5 Mar. 1958, BVerfGE 7 pp. 305, 318; STA 5 July 1979, *BolMinJust* 304 (1981) p. 462.

[96] See e.g. for Greece Areopag 1969/1990, *EllDik* 32 (1991) p. 1499; liability for damage caused by refusal to admit into a professional association; breach of public policy deduced from Art. 281 Greek Cc (abuse of a legal right) in conjunction with Arts. 5 § 1, 25 § 3 Greek Constitution. Art. 86 s. 2 lit. c EEC Treaty contains no compensatory sanctions, but infringement incurs liability under national law: see *Garden Cottage Foods* v. *Milk Marketing Board* [1984] AC 130 (HL).

[97] HR 13 Sep. 1991, *NedJur* 1992 no. 225 p. 855 (specific damages), a reaction to European Court of Justice 8 Nov. 1990, C-177/88, *NedJur* 1992 no. 224 p. 853, and BAG 14 Mar. 1989, *NJW* 1990 p. 65 (general damages). The European Court even remarked (loc. cit.) that the employer is strictly liable. Discrimination occurred when the best qualified of a number of female applicants was not employed because she was pregnant. In this context see also ØLD 6 Dec. 1993, *UfR* 1994 A p. 215 (breach of § 4 Danish Equal Treatment Act in a delictual context considered, but *in casu* rejected).

[98] CA Patras 526/1982, *NoB* 31 (1983) p. 1020.

ments, the court decided, in view of Art. 919 Greek Cc (breach of public policy, and thus of *bonos mores*) that in such situations the principles of reasonableness and equality had also to be considered under private law.[99] In HR 10 December 1982[100] a foreign plaintiff, who had lived in The Netherlands since 1973, put his name on a waiting list in 1977 to occupy a flat built by the defendant's construction company. In 1981, when his wife and child followed him to The Netherlands, the defendant had still not considered his application. In the six years since he had registered, the defendant had rented out 543 flats, only one of them to a non-national, while other companies had 7.2% of foreign tenants. The *Hoge Raad* upheld the decision of the Court of Appeal ordering the defendant to restitute in kind by allocating the plaintiff a flat. The defendant had used unlawful discrimination, resulting in liability under Arts. 1401, 1402 BW (old). However, it might have been more appropriate to deal with that case as a breach of the right to personal dignity. Such a breach is committed if e.g. the manager of a 'sophisticated' discotheque refuses a person entry for being the 'wrong' colour.[101] The usual excuse that the maximum number of guests has already been admitted only makes matters worse: a blatant lie adds to the humiliation.

4. TORT LAW AS THE MANIFESTATION OF THE GUARANTEE OF
HUMAN RIGHTS OTHER THAN THOSE TO EQUAL TREATMENT

As stated above, tort law is one of the tools by which a state can protect **570** its citizens from each other. Although human rights can always be relied upon by both defendant and plaintiff, some are more often used by one than the other. Although this distinction is sometimes blurred in practice, the following text assumes this basis.

a. Human Rights Protecting Primarily the Plaintiff

(1) Freedom of Movement

The most obvious right to personal liberty is freedom of movement. In **571** recognition of its status as a constitutionally guaranteed right, the German *Bundesverfassungsgericht* overruled a BGH decision to render

---

[99] CA Athens 5025/1990, *NoB* 39 (1991) p. 79.

[100] HR 10 Dec. 1982, *NedJur* 1983 no. 687 p. 2156.

[101] BayObLG 7 Mar. 1983, *NJW* 1983 p. 2040 (*in casu* it was even considered a criminal insult). See also Swedish HD 28 June 1989, *NJA* 1989: 62 p. 374: black political refugee was hit and called a *jävla svartskalle* (bloody nigger). The court, assessing the amount of damages, held that it was imperative to take into consideration the fact that such discrimination was incompatible with the fundamental values of a legal system.

expert witnesses liable only for intent, even where an unreliable report led to a prison sentence.[102] The status of the right to freedom of movement should prompt English law also to reconsider its position on the liability of barristers as decided in *Rondel* v. *Worsely*.[103] The privileged position of witnesses in tort cases of malicious prosecution seems also to need thorough review. In the 1993 Scottish decision *B* v. *Burns*,[104] the plaintiff accused one of six defendants of having raped her. The accused called the other five defendants to confirm that they had been with him in two pubs in Glasgow at the time of the crime. They confirmed the alibi, and the plaintiff was charged with misleading the police and making false allegations. She was taken into custody, searched, and arrested. When it was eventually proved that the two pubs in question were closed at the relevant time, the plaintiff sued both perpetrator and witnesses. The Court of Appeal dismissed the claim, arguing that witnesses compelled to give evidence enjoy absolute immunity from civil action. The court held that 'if a person makes a statement in circumstances which attract absolute privilege then the fact that the statement may have been made maliciously and may cause harm does not remove the operation of the privilege. Were the position otherwise, then the privilege would not be absolute.'[105] In continental Europe this decision would be seen as a breach of human rights. In The Netherlands, where state liability follows the rules of the civil law of delict,[106] tort law in conjunction with Art. 5 V of the European Convention on Human Rights[107] was even relied on to find the state liable for a prosecutor who wrongly interpreted a legal provision.[108] Similarly, the *Hoge Raad* held the state liable for a judge in a guardianship court who committed the plaintiff to a closed psychiatric hospital, on the demand of his father, without assigning a legal adviser to him.[109] Furthermore, the German BGH, who once regarded a claim under Art. 5 V European Convention on Human Rights as 'a case of strict liability requiring unlawful conduct'(!),[110] now, like the Austrian OGH,[111] grants compensation for

---

[102] See no. 560 and fn. 31 above.   [103] See no. 560 and fn. 34 above.
[104] 1994 *SLT* 250 (2nd Division).   [105] Id. p. 253 (Lord Caplan).
[106] See no. 553 and fn. 3 above.
[107] 'Everybody who has been taken into custody or arrested contrary to the provisions of this Article, has a right to compensation.'
[108] HR 11 Oct. 1991, *NedJur* 1993 no. 165 p. 516.
[109] HR 12 Feb. 1993, *RvdW* 1995 no. 55. For unlawful arrest see also Hof 's-Gravenhage 17 Feb. 1993, *NedJur* 1993 no. 294 p. 1081. However, if an innocent person is lawfully remanded in custody, he has no claim under Art. 6:162 BW: Hof 's-Gravenhage 18 Feb. 1993, *NedJur* 1994 no. 282 p. 1245. On the extension of the state's liability for judges in Belgium see Cass. 19 Dec. 1991, *RW* 1992–1993 p. 396 (although the case concerned, not deprivation of freedom of movement, but unlawful commencement of bankruptcy proceedings).
[110] BGH 31 Jan. 1966, BGHZ 45 p. 58.
[111] Most recent decision: 7 Oct. 1992, *ÖJZ* 1993 p. 276 (*EvBl* 57).

pain and suffering under this provision.[112] In a case concerning a person wrongly imprisoned for seven years, the Danish Western Court of First Instance went so far as to award over 50% of the total damages (about £300,000 of the total of £590,000) for injustice suffered.[113]

(2) Life and Bodily Integrity

Life, bodily integrity, and health are generally protected by tort law, so **572** the consequences of liability (i.e. the law of damages in its narrower sense) rather than the cause of action have lately been influenced by constitutional law, principally to improve the position of the injured party. The Dutch *Hoge Raad* has only recently placed the victim's interest in the integrity of his body ahead of that of the perpetrator. A rapist waives his human right under Art. 11 GrW[114] to the extent that he must undergo an AIDS test as part of the restitution in kind.[115]

The most dramatic changes have occurred in Italy.[116] Its *Codice civile*, **573** like so many others, distinguishes between two kinds of compensation for physical harm. Pure economic loss (*danno patrimoniale*) is compensated under the general clause in Art. 2043 Cc, and its special provisions. Non-material damage (*danno non patrimoniale*) depends primarily on whether the perpetrator has committed a criminal offence (Arts. 2059 CC, 185 II CP). Both this concept and the official commentary[117] clearly suggest that the legislator was thinking of damages for pain and suffering (*pretium doloris*). However, it was not long before the question arose whether Art. 32 I Italian Constitution was already sufficiently complied with,[118] or whether an infringement of bodily integrity and biological conditions, regardless of any loss of property and/or physical pain, had to be regarded as damage. Yet, if a *danno alla salute* and a *danno biologico* were constitutionally called for, would not either Art. 2043 or Art. 2059 Cc have to be considered unconstitutional? When the Italian Constitutional

---

[112] BGH 26 Nov. 1992, *VersR* 1993 pp. 972, 975–976.

[113] VLD 24 June 1994, *UfR* 1994 A p. 751.

[114] 'Everybody has the right to bodily integrity regardless of restrictions based on a law or by virtue of the law.'

[115] HR 18 June 1993, *RvdW* 1993, 136 = *NedJur* 1994 no. 347 p. 1590.

[116] See (in German) Bajons, *ZVglRWiss* 92 (1993) pp. 76, 84–90; Stoll, *Haftungsfolgen*, p. 353. In Italian see e.g. Franzoni, *Fatti illeciti*, p. 993; Giur.sist. Bigiavi (-Barone and Pellegrino) vol. v p. 329; anthology by Busnelli/Breccia (edd.), *Tutela della salute e diritto privato* (1988); and Bargagna/Busnelli (edd.), *La valutazione del danno alla salute* (1988).

[117] Pandolfelli *et al.*, *Codice civile*, p. 691. For details on the history of Art. 2059 Cc see Corte Cost. 14 July 1986, n. 184, *Giur.cost.* 1986, I, 1430 = *NGCC* 1986, I, 534 (Alpa) = *Foro.it.* 1986, I, 2053 (Ponzanelli).

[118] 'The Republic protects health as a fundamental right of the individual and as a public interest, and guarantees free medical treatment for the needy.'

Court first addressed these questions in 1979, it answered in the negative.[119] It nonetheless approved the course taken by the civil courts and defined the *danno biologico* initially as a *danno non patrimoniale* in accordance with Art. 2059 Cc.[120] It was established that biological damage was compensatable, but only if a criminal act was committed. In order to break this chain the non-constitutional courts took advantage of the unique wording of Art. 2043 Cc. This is the only basic delictual provision in Europe which recognizes the concept of 'unlawful damage'.[121] In Italy, therefore, damage can be both the result of an unlawful act and a cause of action. Therefore, one must distinguish between *danno conseguenza* and *danno evento*. The former is subdivided into damage for pure economic loss and *danno non patrimoniale* in accordance with Art. 2059 Cc, the latter being merely a *danno morale*. However, *danno biologico* is a form of *danno evento*. Thus it has become the prevailing view that '*il danno biologico è risarcibile a norma dell'art. 2043 Cc in tutti i casi di illecita menomazione dell'integrità psico-fisica della persona*' ('biological damage is recoverable under Art. 2043 Cc in all cases of wrongful infringement of the psychophysical integrity of the person).[122] This step, too, was carried by the *Corte Costituzionale* as it complied with the concept of the '*lettura costituzionale*' under Art. 2043 Cc.[123]

574   Subsequently the Constitutional Court also advanced the notion of biological damage in the field of industrial injuries law. Although there is *de lege lata* no reason why industrial injuries insurance should cover *danno biologico*, a reform of the law would be desirable. The relevant Presidential Decree of 30 June 1965[124] only covers compensation for physical-psychological inability to work.[125] For this reason the exclusion of employers' liability under Art. 10 I of the Decree[126] (which applies only in cases not involving crime) would have to be limited to cases covered by industrial accident insurance.[127] Hence, in matters relating to the law of damages, where it neither could nor would be effective,

---

[119] Corte Cost. 26 July 1979, n. 87, *Giur.cost.* 1979, I, 652 = *Foro.it.* 1979, I, 2543 (Art. 2059 Cc); and Corte Cost. 26 July 1979, n. 88, *Giur.cost.* 1979, I, 656 (Anzon) = *Giur.it.* 1980, I, 1, 9 (Alpa) = *Foro.it.* 1979, I, 2542 (Art. 2043 Cc).

[120] In ruling no. 88 (fn. 119 above), Corte Cost. 14 July 1986, n. 184 loc. cit. (fn. 117 above) then established that compensation for biological damage 'constitutes a first, important, and predominant form of compensation independent of any other (liability) precondition'. See also v. Bar (-Busnelli), *DeliktsR in Europa, Italien*, p. 22.   [121] See no. 20 above.

[122] Cass. 8 July 192, n. 8325, *Foro.it.* 1992, I, 2965, 2971 (incl. further references to rulings of the Court of Cassation, which has pursued this course since the mid-1980s).

[123] Corte Cost. 14 July 1986, n. 184 (fn. 117 above).

[124] DPR no. 1124 of 30 June 1965, Gaz. Uff. 13 Oct. 1965, no. 257.

[125] Corte Cost. 15 Feb. 1991, n. 87, *Foro.it.* 1991, I, 1664.

[126] 'The insurance in accordance with this Decree exempts the employer from civil liability for industrial injuries.'

[127] Corte Cost. 18 July 1991, n. 356, *Foro.it.* 1991, I, 2967; and Corte Cost. 27 Dec. 1991, n. 485, *Foro.it.* 1993, I, 72.

liability would still come under the *Codice civile*. Consequently, employers could not escape liability for biological damage by reliance on Art. 10 of the aforementioned Presidential Decree.[128] Unlike the German Constitutional Court, its Italian counterpart has considered it unconstitutional to exempt employers from liability for infringements which are non-work related or immaterial in nature.[129] Moreover, the Italian Constitutional Court has recently discussed with remarkable intensity the rights of relatives of a person killed in an industrial accident.[130] The decision of the *Corte di Cassazione* that a breach of Art. 2087 Cc (regulation of working conditions) is sufficient to found a claim under Art. 2043 Cc, i.e. that no criminal conduct is necessary (cf. Art. 10 II, III Presidential Decree)[131] also deserves special attention. The relevant German provision (§ 618 III BGB) has always positively excluded § 847 BGB (damages for pain and suffering) by referring only to §§ 842–846 BGB! So the position unanimously supported in Germany on damages for pain and suffering, and recently adopted in France by means of *préjudice personnel*,[132] still needed to be confirmed by the Italian Constitutional Court: compensation for biological damage under Art. 2043 Cc is not

---

[128] Fn. 124, col. 2975; and again in Cass.sez.lav. 8 July 1992, n. 8325, *Foro.it.* 1992, I, 2965.

[129] The discrepancy between the decision of the BVerfG 7 Nov. 1972 (see fn. 83 above) and the rulings of the *Corte Costituzionale* appears less striking in the light of the fact that the Italian *danno biologico* does not cover immaterial damage. Consequently Corte Cost. 17 Feb. 1994, n. 37, *Foro.it.* 1994, I, 1326 (note Poletti) did not lift the restrictions on compensation of the *danno morale* under Italian industrial injuries law on the basis of Art. 32 Italian Constitution.

[130] The unresolved problem is whether the relatives of a deceased person are entitled to damages for biological injury *iure hereditatis* or *iure proprio*. This is in practice relevant to all cases where death occurs immediately, rather than after a long illness. Only in the latter case has the deceased been entitled to compensation for biological damage passed to his relatives as his legal successors (Cass. 27 Dec. 1994, n. 11169, *Riv.giur.circ.trasp.* 1995 p. 529 = *Resp.Civ. e Prev.* 1995 p. 281 incl. note Giannini). Trib. Milan 2 Sep. 1993, n. 8166, *Corr.giur.* 1994 p. 115 = *Foro.it.* 1994, I, 1954 (Salmè) = *Giur.it.* 1994, I, 2, 886 (Pellechia) = *Riv.dir.civ.* 1995, II, 311 (d'Amico) first awarded compensation to parents for their own biological damage (*iure proprio*) caused to their children's suffering. It was confirmed by App. Milan 11 Oct. 1994, *NGCC* 1995, I, 490. Meanwhile, however, Trib. Firenze 10 Nov. 1993, *Giur.it.* 1994, I, 2, 81 had appealed to the Constitutional Court, as *danno biologico* following a death could only be regarded as *danno conseguenza*, not as *danno evento*, and could not therefore be transferred to the relatives *iure proprio*. Corte Cost. 27 Oct. 1994, *Giur.it.* 1995, I, 406 (Jannarelli) = *Riv.giur.circ.trasp.* 1995 p. 162 considered the appeal unfounded; Arts. 2043, 2059 Cc were constitutionally approved. It is also correct that relatives only succeed to a person's rights *de iure successionis*, i.e. they could only claim for biological damage if it had already manifested in the deceased. As this will not be the case in instant death, relatives of such victims must be granted a claim under Art. 2059 Cc, which incorporates what would otherwise have qualified as biological damage. Trib. Firenze 10 Dec. 1994, *Resp.Civ. e Prev.* 1995 p. 159 conveys this new view.

[131] Cass. 8 July 1992, n. 8325, *Foro.it.* 1992, I, 2965.

[132] E.g. Bordeaux 18 Apr. 1991, D. 1992 Jur. 15 = *VersRAI* 1994 p. 6. For more detail see Bedoura, D. 1980 Chr. 139; Viney, *La responsabilité: effets*, p. 149; and Billiet/Nieper, *VersRAI* 1994 p. 7.

passed onto either the social insurer by statutory assignment under Art. 11 of the aforementioned Presidential Decree,[133] or by *diritto di surrogazione* under Art. 1916 Cc.[134]

575   The closest German parallel to these Italian developments is the change in the *Bundesgerichtshof*'s position on damages for pain and suffering in cases of grievous bodily harm. Due to a midwife's malpractice a child suffered such serious brain damage that his receptive faculty was seriously impaired. The BGH regarded the 'destruction of the child's personality as immaterial damage, which was to be compensated financially'.[135] Furthermore, the Fourth Senate abandoned its earlier and much more restrictive position[136] and held, convincingly, that 'with regard to the system of values under Art. 1 GG . . . impairments on this scale would have to carry a greater weight'.[137] In its first ruling on abortion the BVerfG had already stressed that 'human life was entitled to dignity wherever it existed; it is not relevant whether the bearer of that right was aware of this honour and could defend it himself. The potential abilities present from the very beginning in every human being are sufficient to establish a right to human dignity'.[138]

576   Not least because of this BGH judgment, which has brought German law back into line with the common European position,[139] it is now even more important that Germany should remedy another constitutional shortcoming: its restrictive view on damages for pain and suffering in

---

[133] Corte Cost. 27 Dec. 1991, n. 485, *Foro.it.* 1993, I, 72 = *Giur.it.* 1992, I, 1, 794 incl. note Dogliotti, *Giur.it.* 1994, I, 162. Consequent decision: Cass. 14 Dec. 1993, n. 12333, *Giust. civ.Mass.* 1993 no. 12333 p. 1761: a pension paid by the insurer to the employee has no effect on the latter's claim to biological damage since the pension and the damage are unrelated. This is true even if the pension exceeds the amount which would have been due as *danno patrimoniale* under civil law.

[134] Corte Cost. 18 July 1991, n. 356, *Foro.it.* 1991, I, 2967; Cass. 8 July 1992, n. 8325 (fn. 131 above); Cass. 15 Apr. 1993, n. 4475, *Riv.giur.circ.trasp.* 1993 p. 967; Cass. 11 June 1994, n. 5683, *Riv.giur.circ.trasp.* 1994 p. 893; and Trib. Rome 15 Sep. 1994, *Riv.giur.circ.trasp.* 1995 p. 539. See generally Cass. 15 Sep. 1995, n. 9761, *Foro.it.* 1995, I, 3140, incl. note Poletti).

[135] BGH 13 Oct. 1992, BGHZ 120 p. 1 = *NJW* 1993 p. 781 (German) = *JZ* 1993 p. 516 (Giesen). This was followed by OLG Stuttgart 2 May 1994, *NJW* 1994 p. 3016.

[136] BGH 16 Dec. 1975, *NJW* 1976 p. 1147; BGH 22 June 1982, *NJW* 1982 p. 2123.

[137] *NJW* 1993 pp. 781, 783; confirmed by BGH 16 Feb. 1993, *JZ* 1993 p. 521.

[138] BVerfG 25 Feb. 1975, BVerfGE 39 pp. 1, 41.

[139] For England see e.g. *H. West & Son v. Shephard* [1964] AC 326, 349 (*per* Lord Morris of Borth-y-Gest); and *Lim Poh Choo v. Camden and Islington Area Health Authority* [1980] AC 174, 188 (*per* Lord Scarman). For France see e.g. Bordeaux 18 Apr. 1991 (fn. 132 above); and Cass.civ. 28 June 1995, Bull.civ. 1995, II, no. 224: '*L'état végétatif d'une personne humaine n'excluant aucun chef d'indemnisation, son préjudice doit être réparé dans tous ses éléments*'; but see also Cass.civ. 20 Jan. 1993, Bull.civ. 1993, II, no. 23: for constitutional reasons no objection to a low award of compensation for pain and suffering for an elderly traffic accident victim who died after having been in a coma for 2 months. For Austria see OGH 5 Ob 608/84. The decision was not accessible to this author, and is quoted here from v. Bar (-Schilcher/Kleewein), *DeliktsR in Europa, Österreich*, p. 46. For Belgium see Brussels 16 Feb. 1993, *RGAR* 1995 no. 12505. For Switzerland see BG 6 July 1982, *BGE* 108 II 422, 428–432.

its narrower sense, even where liability for grievous bodily harm arises from contract,[140] and where it is strict.[141] The reasons for this are twofold: first, because the BGH has accepted 'the concept of adjusting the consequences of liability for bodily harm to the values of the Constitution',[142] and secondly, because it has acknowledged that it is constitutionally appropriate to interpret the objective 'loss of privacy, (the) loss of personal quality'[143] as immaterial damage. In the light of the state's duty to protect human dignity (Art. 1 I s. 2 GG), and thus human personality, it is only necessary to distinguish between the various causes of action for damages for pain and suffering if there are substantial objective reasons stemming from these human rights. It is arguable whether any such reasons can exist in the field of strict liability. Regarding contractual and quasi-contractual liability, however, they are, as already rightly concluded by the Reich Court,[144] invisible. This is exactly what comparative law teaches us. Germany is the only remaining legal system in Europe which generally does not impose damages for pain and suffering for breach of a contractual duty resulting in physical injury.[145] Despite the fact that Art. 299 Greek Cc and § 253 German BGB appear almost identical, they cannot be directly compared, because the German 'violation of contractual duty of care' generally comes under the law of delict in Greece.[146] It has none the less been suggested that Art. 299 Cc should be deleted.[147] That it was § 831 BGB which brought about the implementation of contractual duties of care is no consolation. As for the transfer of loss (*Schadensanlastungsfunktion*),[148] the concept of exculpatory proof has become constitutionally controversial in the law of delict. The exclusion of damages for pain and suffering from contractual liability cannot even be justified on the ground that it is tort law, which ranks below constitutional law. On the contrary, the German *Schuldrechtskommission* even argued for contractual duties to be incor-

---

[140] See no. 455 above.   [141] See no. 577 below.

[142] As correctly remarked by Stoll, *Haftungsfolgen*, p. 354.

[143] BGH 16 Feb. 1993, *JZ* 1993 p. 521. That the protection of a person's physical integrity comes under the general protection of the human personality was already the view of Prot. II p. 567. BGH 27 June 1995, *NJW* pp. 2407, 2408 also speaks of the 'right to physical integrity being a part of the right to personality as defined by statute'.

[144] See no. 569 and fn. 94 above.   [145] See no. 455 above.   [146] See no. 461 above.

[147] Westermann/Karakatsanes (-Karakatsanes), *Schuldrechtsreform in Deutschland und Griechenland*, pp. 112–114, 127. Papachristou, *ToΣ* 7 (1981) pp. 43, 51 even argues that breaches of contract impairing the creditor's integrity would, via Art. 59 Greek Cc, unquestionably result in an obligation also to compensate immaterial damage (e.g. damage to the reputation of an architect caused by breach of contract). Similarly generous interpretations of Art. 59 Greek Cc have been suggested by Vavouskos, *EEN* 22 (1955) pp. 82, 86; and Koutsakis, *Arm.* 35 (1991) pp. 841, 844–845. Papachristou (loc. cit. p. 56) also remarks that Art. 299 Greek Cc is in significant contrast to the constitutional protection of the human personality, which contrast has to be dissolved by applying Art. 59 Greek Cc.

[148] Bullinger, *FS für von Caemmerer*, pp. 297, 301.

porated into the BGB, albeit without considering liability for pain and damages; it has recently stressed that one party to a contract must treat other parties 'with great care'.[149] It must therefore be wrong to exempt such a party from liability for pain and suffering in cases of fault, since compensation is already due, even if only a 'lower degree of care' applies. Regarding the question of 'whether § 847 BGB ranks as a consideration in its own right (*Sachgesetzlichkeit*) within the BGB, or whether it is an exemption from the exclusion of monetary compensation for non-economic loss'[150] (a question left unanswered by the BVerfG twenty years ago), a modern lawyer would have to favour the former view. In all cases of infringement of human personality in the broader sense, damages for pain and suffering are a necessary correlative consequence of liability,[151] not a claim with lower status. Non-material damages are the appropriate form of compensation for violations of this object of legal protection, and must therefore be granted at least for grave impairments. Unfortunately, the BGB only mentions contractual duties of care in relation to bodily harm in § 618, a provision long superseded by the law on industrial injuries. Therefore, a constitutional interpretation of § 847 BGB would demand that this provision be taken literally, i.e. to award the 'injured party . . . fair compensation in money . . . in the case of injury to the body or to health'. Against this background the argument that the position of § 847 BGB within the BGB would prohibit such a step is not convincing.[152] As contractual duties of care have developed *praeter legem*, and because they have been necessary to overcome shortcomings in tort law, it was, and still is, wrong not to apply the provisions on unlawful acts, and thus § 847 BGB, to them. Under the regime of the *Grundgesetz* it is imperative that judge-made law is brought (back) into line with human rights law.

577   The exemption of damages for pain and suffering from strict liability law in cases of physical harm in Germany is unique in Europe.[153] The European policy on the harmonization of laws has so far ignored this problem,[154] not because Europe agrees with the German position, but

---

[149] See no. 464 above. Moreover, the overwhelming majority of those attending the 60th German Lawyers' Day rejected the motion to 'award damages for pain and suffering in cases of personal injury based on contract: Resolution no. II 7, printed e.g. in *NJW* 1994 p. 3075.   [150] BVerfG 7 Nov. 1972, *VersR* 1973 pp. 269, 271.

[151] See BG 6 July 1982, BGE 108 II 422, 430; also esp. Stoll, *Haftungsfolgen im bürgerlichen Recht*, nos. 13, 17, 275; and Papachristou (fn. 147 above) p. 56.

[152] A view surprisingly shared by Austria. Its § 1325 ABGB—like § 847 BGB!—says nothing about the conditions for liability. Thus the legal basis of the obligation is wholly irrelevant: Rummel (-Reischauer) *ABGB*, vol. ii, 2nd edn., § 1325 no. 9; and Schwimann (-Harrer) *ABGB*, vol. v, § 1325 no. 58, both with further references. On the relevant recommendations of the Council of Europe see Part 4 no. 402 above.

[153] E.g. Stoll, *Haftungsfolgen im bürgerlichen Recht*, no. 17.

[154] See no. 395 above.

because Europe took another wrong turn, for which it is at least partly responsible. The German commentators who have strongly opposed this situation, and criticized its many inconsistencies, are legion.[155] Moreover, it is amusing that animal keepers' liability has been incorporated into the BGB, so that they may be liable under § 847, purely to pay tribute to Roman law,[156] whereas in (nearly) all other cases special laws have to be applied. Although these special laws have also included provisions from the law of delict, § 253 BGB, and not § 847 which would have been much more appropriate, has attained the status of a basic rule covering the entire ambit of private law. The judiciary did not object to the fact that until 1969 no German legislator deemed it necessary to explain why immaterial damages were excluded.[157] A surprising exception to the rule against granting immaterial damages is found in an area where strict liability has been rigorously construed,[158] the field of liability for military aircraft (§ 53 LuftVG). Oddly enough, this exception stems from the fact that the *Reich Luftwaffe* wanted to outdo other armed forces with its compensation policy (even in 1943)![159]

It is therefore surprising to learn that the discussion on the constitu- **578** tionality of the exclusion of compensation for pain and suffering from strict liability delicts under (here, what used to be) German law emanated, not from Germany, but from Austria. That country is reviewing German laws implemented during the time of Austria's annexation, for example the (*Reich*) LuftVG. Still valid in its original version, it is one of the rare instances in the Austrian strict liability system where liability is not imposed for pain and suffering; it is thus considered by important Austrian commentators to constitute a breach of the principle of equality and of the Constitution.[160] Despite this, the Austrian OGH decided against an appeal to the Constitutional Court as recently as 1991.[161] The decision was based on the fact that the Constitutional Court had

---

[155] See e.g. Kötz, *VersR* 1982 p. 624; Dürr/Schubert, *ZRP* 1975 p. 225.

[156] Originally in RG 6 Mar. 1902, RGZ 50 pp. 244, 253.

[157] For an analysis of all relevant legal texts see Schmid, *Schmerzensgeld und Gefährdungshaftung* (diss. Bonn 1971) pp. 3–14.

[158] See BGH 27 May 1993, BGHZ 122 p. 363 = *VersR* 1993 p. 1012 (yet also stating that due to such liability being of the strictest kind, the term 'accident' would have to be taken literally. Therefore the BGH found against an inhabitant of a military low-flying zone who claimed damages for pain and suffering for the permanent headache caused by the air traffic).

[159] Official reasoning printed in *DJ* 1943 p. 123. On the reasoning see Schmid (fn. 157 above) p. 13. On the predecessor of the current § 53 LuftVG, see § 29k LuftVG of 26 Jan. 1943 (RGBl.- 1943 I p. 69), by which limiting damages to a maximum amount and excluding liability for pain and suffering was inappropriate for the air force, as it would have put persons injured by air force planes in a worse position than those injured in other *Wehrmacht* accidents or by enemy planes.

[160] Gimpel-Hinteregger, *ÖJZ* 1992 pp. 561, 568; v. Bar (-Schilcher/Kleewein), *DeliktsR in Europa, Österreich*, p. 47. [161] OGH 30 Oct. 1991, *ÖJZ* 1992 p. 165 (*EvBl* 35).

not held until 1979 that the principle of equality was not violated by §
1319a ABGB (limitation of liability for gross negligence) because it was
counterbalanced by extended vicarious liability.[162] The OGH therefore
also decided that the particularly strict liability of the LuftVG was sufficient reason to withhold damages for pain and suffering. If the causes of
action differed, the scope of liability would have to differ also.[163]

579 From the point of view of arbitrariness, this concept also appears
acceptable for German law, although it is wholly uncertain whether any
consideration of arbitrariness in fact guided the legislator. However, in
view of the fact that damages for pain and suffering affect not only the
principle of equality but also the concept of bodily integrity and the
protection of the human personality, it becomes increasingly necessary
to justify such fundamentally different solutions on liability. On the
other hand, the chances for the legislator to influence legal relationships
are decreasing as the border between unlawful acts and strict liability is
blurred. As far as the 'classic' provisions on strict liability are concerned,
by which a keeper is liable for damage resulting from the recovery,
maintenance, or transport of high energy sources, excluding damages
for pain and suffering is constitutionally just about justifiable. However,
when considering liability for unlawful, non-culpable conduct in a commercial context, particularly for product liability under the German
Pharmaceutical Products Act, the insignificant differences between strict
liability and the liability regime under civil law do not justify such
significant differences between the legal consequences of the two systems. In a momentous disaster such as that of Thalidomide (for which §§
84, 87 AMG do not provide an adequate remedy) Arts. 2 II, 3 I GG
require the compensation of extreme immaterial damage. In the field of
product liability, particularly under the Pharmaceutical Products Act,
Germany definitely does not protect the human rights of its citizens.
Many desperate fights for damages for pain and suffering have to be
fought today, simply because company executives do everything possible to stop their liability insurers, who are usually willing to pay (!), from
doing so. Companies fear that payment of compensation would be
regarded as an admission of fault which could result in criminal proceedings for negligent bodily injury.

(3) Protection of Privacy

580 Another area in which constitutional law strongly influences the civil
law of delict is the protection of privacy. This covers not only the
protection of personal honour, privacy, and reputation, but also such

---

[162] VfGH 1 Mar. 1978, *JBl* 1979 p. 142 (see fn. 80 above).
[163] (Fn. 161 above) p. 166.

matters as the liability of medical practitioners and damage to the environment. The law on protection of the human personality partly supplements and partly defines those human rights which are closely linked to tort law, the rights to life, bodily integrity, and health.

(a) Wrongful Birth and Wrongful Life

The first problems to be considered are those concerning the fact of a **581** child's birth. Two basic rules outline the common European position. First, it is accepted that nobody has a right to his own non-existence,[164] so the fact that a person was conceived or not aborted cannot found a cause of action for that person. This is true of children born with serious disabilities due to knowingly ignored infection in the womb or genetic defect (wrongful life).[165] The second rule is that the unborn have a right to human dignity.[166] Liability is therefore iresepective of whether damage was inflicted before or after birth.[167] The cynicism inherent in the argument that because the unborn have no legal capacity they cannot sue for antenatal injury when they become legally capable is constitutionally intolerable. Portuguese courts reasonably hold that parents of an unborn child who dies in the womb due to accidental injuries are entitled to compensation for their own pain and suffering but not for that of the unborn child.[168] However, it would be a grave violation of

---

[164] This clearly does not mean that human life must be preserved in all circumstances. In *Airedale NHS Trust* v. *Bland* [1993] 1 All ER 821 the HL rightly held, regarding a victim of the Sheffield football stadium disaster, that there was no duty to prolong the life of a patient who would not regain consciousness. See also the subsequent case of *Frenchay Healthcare National Health Trust* v. *S* [1994] 2 All ER 403 (CA).

[165] For English law: sec. 1(5) Congenital Disabilities (Civil Liability) Act 1976 (c. 28) 'The defendant is not answerable to the child for anything he did or omitted to do when responsible in a professional capacity for treating or advising the parent'. Also *McKay and Another* v. *Essex Area Health Authority and Another* [1982] 1 QB 1166, 1180–1181 (CA, *per* Stephenson LJ). For Scotland: Norrie, *Jurid.Rev.* 1990 pp. 205, 207; for France: Trib.adm. Strasbourg 17 July 1990, *Gaz.Pal.* 1991 *Jur.* 52; Versailles 8 July 1993 and Paris 17 Dec. 1993, both in *D.* 1995 *Somm.* 98; Bordeaux 26 Jan. 1995, *Sem.Jur.* 1995, IV, 1568. For Germany: BGH 18 Jan. 1983, *VersR* 1983 pp. 396, 398–399. However, Deutsch, *NJW* 1993 pp. 2361, 2362 and Neto/Martins, *Código civil*, 7th edn., p. 356 no. 49 argue that in such cases a child should be entitled to compensation for its additional needs.

[166] *Conseil Constitutionnel* 15 Jan. 1975, *Rev.dr.publ.* 91 (1975) p. 205: French constitutional law guarantees '*respect de tout être humain dès le commencement de la vie*'. Also Art. 40 III no. 3 Irish Constitution; BVerfG 25 Feb. 1975, BVerfGE 39 pp. 1, 41 (fn. 138 above).

[167] English Congenital Disabilities (Civil Liability) Act 1976, sec. 2: 'liability of women driving while pregnant' expressly provides thus in respect of the mother's liability to the child. That those injuring a child in the womb are liable to the child after its birth is general policy in Europe. Cf. Karnov (-v. Eyben) vol. iii, 13th edn., 20–9 (*Patientforsikring*) p. 3299 n. 2; HR 9 Oct. 1992, *RvdW* 1992 no. 219; Trib. Verona 15 Oct. 1990, *Foro.it.* 1991, I, 261; BGH 11 Jan. 1972, BGHZ 58 p. 48; BGH 18 Jan. 1983, *VersR* 1983 pp. 396, 398; also BGH 20 Dec. 1952, BGHZ 8 p. 243 (child not even conceived at the time of the injury); Conseil d'État 27 Sep. 1989, *D.* 1991 *Jur.* 80; RP 13 Apr. 1989, *CJ* XIV (1989–2) p. 221.

[168] STJ 23 May 1985, *BolMinJust* 347 (1985) p. 398; also RP 13 Apr. 1989 (fn. 167 above).

human dignity to treat a disabled child as being legally the same as defective goods. This is also true of failed abortions which injure a foetus subsequently carried to full term.[169] If a child is born alive but then dies of injuries negligently inflicted before its birth it is usually not difficult to establish third-party liability. The Scottish Outer House recently expressed what should be common European policy: 'that it is not necessary to rely on the "legal fiction" to give a child who is born alive a title to sue for injuries sustained *in utero* and that if a child dies after being born alive and the death is caused by injuries sustained *in utero* the parents of that child have a title to sue for damages for the death of that child.'[170]

582   It has not yet been conclusively resolved, however, whether and to what extent parents of children who were either unwanted or who would have aborted had their 'defects' been known have a claim for damage. The case of the unwanted healthy child is known by the unfortunate American title of 'wrongful birth'. These cases usually concern children conceived after either the purported sterilization of one parent or the sale of inappropriate contraceptive devices to the parents, or those born after an unsuccessful abortion. Irrespective of whether the defendant's conduct is considered in contract or tort, the course which should generally be adopted is to regard neither the cost of the child's maintenance nor the material or immaterial disadvantages connected with birth as recoverable damage. No more than half the European systems take this view.[171] Exponents are Denmark,[172] some Dutch courts,[173] the

---

[169] Conseil d'État 27 Sep. 1989 (fn. 167 above): liability even if the unsuccessful abortion does not injure the foetus. *Dommage par ricochet* is an issue which has escaped discussion so far: if a woman undergoes an abortion against her husband's wishes, the father may have a claim to material and/or immaterial damages even if the abortion is not a criminal offence, as it is technically unlawful. A Spanish judgment ordered a father culpably responsible for the death of his son to pay the divorced mother damages for her pain and suffering: TS 15 Apr. 1988, *RAJ* 1988 no. 2780 p. 2676.

[170] *McWilliams* v. *Lord Advocate*, Outer House 28 July 1992, *SLT* 1992 pp. 1045, 1048 (Lord Morton of Shuna). Also *Burton* v. *Islington Health Authority* [1992] 3 All ER 833 (CA); Trib. Verona 15 Oct. 1990 (fn. 167 above) grants siblings their own claims.

[171] Neither Greek nor Portuguese relevant rulings are available. Androulidaki-Dimitriadi, *I ypochreossi enimerosis tou asthenous*, pp. 415–417, states that under Art. 690 Greek Cc (on contracts for services) the doctor is liable for the costs of birth, lost earnings, and maintenance of the child if he was aware that the parents could not afford the maintenance costs. In all other cases the 'moral enrichment' which parents gain from their child breaks the causal chain.

[172] VLD 15 Mar. 1954, *UfR* 1954 A p. 540 (vasectomy); VLD 19 Nov. 1960, *UfR* 1961 A p. 239 (damages in respect of unsuccessful sterilization of a woman. Yet the birth of a child is considered such a blessed event that *ordre public* prohibited compensation for maintenance). Also v. Eyben/Nørgaard/Vagner, *Erstatningsret*, 2nd edn., p. 235; v. Eyben, *Patientforsikring*, pp. 211–212.

[173] Rb. Arnhem 28 Nov. 1974 and 26 Feb. 1976, *NedJur* 1977 no. 281 p. 971 (child born after vasectomy. The court accepted that the man had suffered damage but compensation

French *Conseil d'Etat*[174] and *Cour de Cassation*,[175] and the Italian Court of Cassation, which declared that the 'economic damage which parents suffer as a result of an unsuccessful abortion is not compensatable'.[176] Belgian,[177] Spanish,[178] and English courts favour limited compensation for maintenance costs,[179] thereby adopting a position similar to that of

for maintenance would not have accorded with the Dutch legal system); Hof 's-Hertogenbosch 17 May 1983, *NedJur* 1984 no. 240 p. 884 (unsuccessful sterilization; no damages for pain and suffering, compensation only for lost earnings and expenses connected with pregnancy); Rb. Leeuwarden 1 Mar. 1984, *NedJur* 1986 no. 334 p. 1325 (sterilization; no breach of duty on the part of the surgeon). Compare Stolker, *Aansprakelijkheid van de arts*, pp. 99–104. Rb. Leeuwarden 28 Jan. 1993 (author has no access: quoted from Kremer, *Vrb* 1993 pp. 69, 70) compensation for costs related to child's upbringing, but no damages for either lost earnings or pain and suffering. Similarly Rb. Utrecht 27 Apr. 1994, *NedJur* 1995 no. 295 p. 1368: costs of child's upbringing compensated, but not incidental costs of circumcision, books, school uniform, visit to Israel, and supervision. Rb. 's-Gravenhage 21 Sep. 1994, *NedJur* 1995 no. 296 p. 1370 refused to presume incorrect administration of a vasectomy solely because patient's wife became pregnant 8$^{1}/_{2}$ years later.

[174] Conseil d'État 2 July 1982, *D.* 1984 *Jur.* 425 (n. d'Onorio) = *Gaz.Pal.* 1983 *Jur.* 193 (n. Moderne) (unsuccessful abortion: *'la naissance d'un enfant . . . n'est pas génératrice d'un préjudice de nature à ouvrir à la mère un droit à réparation . . . à moins qu'existent . . . des circonstances . . . particulières'*).

[175] Cass.civ. 25 June 1991, *D.* 1991 *Jur.* 566 (n. le Tourneau): confirmation of Riom 6 July 1989, *D.* 1990 *Jur.* 284 (n. le Tourneau) = *JT* 1990 p. 643 (n. Kefer), albeit with amendments. Case concerned an unsuccessful abortion. *Cour de Cassation* held that only *'un dommage particulier'* had to be compensated, whereas *'l'existence de l'enfant qu'elle a conçu ne peut, à elle seule, constituer pour sa mère un préjudice juridiquement réparable'*; view shared by Paris 17 Feb. 1989, *D.* 1989 *Somm.* 316 (handicapped child; no compensation for material damage; immaterial damages for upbringing of the child).

[176] Cass. 8 July 1994, n. 6464, *Giur.it.* 1995, I, 1, 790, thus Trib. Padova 9 Aug. 1985, *Foro.it.* 1986, I, 1995 invalid. The same should be true of App. Bologna 19 Dec. 1991, *Dir.fam.pers.* 1993, I, p. 1081 inc. n. Lei (70 m. lire awarded as maintenance, but not the personal claim of husband).

[177] Corr. Courtrai 3 June 1989, *RW* 1988–1989 p. 1171; also, under different circumstances, Brussels 8 May 1985, *RGAR* 1985 no. 10979 = *JT* 1986 p. 252.

[178] Audiencia Provincial Badajoz 22 Apr. 1991, *La Ley* 1991 (3) p. 485 (ineffective ligature of Fallopian tubes. The couple already had 3 children and were expecting twins. Estimated maintenance costs for the twins until completion of their 18th year and immaterial damages were awarded). TS 25 Apr. 1994, *RAJ* no. 3073 p. 4169 confirms the decision on a contractual basis. At p. 4173 the court remarks, albeit expressly as *obiter dictum*, that it considers it 'unusual' that part of the compensation should contribute to the upbringing of the unwanted children. Also TS 10 Oct. 1995, *RAJ* 1995 no. 7403 p. 9826.

[179] Regarding compensation for maintenance *Emeh* v. *Kensington, Chelsea and Westminster Area Health Authority* [1984] 3 All ER 1044 (CA): compensation for economic maintenance obligations, but immaterial damages only if child disabled; *Thake* v. *Maurice* [1986] 1 All ER 497 (CA) (unsuccessful vasectomy, claim in tort and and contract allowed on basis of insufficient information to parents; maintenance costs, compensation for loss of earnings, and damages for distress, pain, and suffering awarded. Also Norrie, *SLT* 1986 pp. 145–148); *Allen* v. *Bloomsbury Health Authority and Another* [1993] 1 All ER 651 (Brooke, J) (pregnancy overlooked when mother was sterilized. She would have aborted had she known. Court took into account that she was spared abortion. Maintenance incl. private school fees until adulthood awarded). On the effects of such rulings on limitation see *Walkin* v. *South Manchester Health Authority* [1995] 4 All ER 132 (CA). Although concerning wrongful life see *McKay* v. *Essex Area Health Authority* (fn. 165 above), cf. Robertson, 45 [1982] *ModLRev*

the Sixth Civil Division of the BGH.[180] Despite maintaining that the opposite was true,[181] that court contradicted a judgment of the German Federal Constitutional Court. In its second pregnancy termination decision the BVerfG unambiguously declared the decisions of the civil courts to be in need of review. For 'the duty of all public authorities to respect every person's existence prevents the duty to maintain a child from being viewed as damage. . . . the legal pronouncement that the existence of a child is a source of damage . . . is constitutionally unacceptable' (Art. 1 I GG).[182]

583   The BGH's sensitivity to such *obiter*[183] comments is understandable, especially given its superfluity, the constitutional question having been on criminal and not private law. Additionally, the BGH has always seen itself as the guardian of the human dignity of children.[184] Further, a surgeon defending himself by a constitutional appeal against a judgment ordering maintenance payments could rely not only on Arts. 2 I, 12, and 14 GG but also on Art. 1 GG, claiming that to require him to violate the child's dignity would constitute an attack upon his own dignity. Nonetheless, the conclusion drawn by the *Bundesverfassungsgericht* is convincing. Human life cannot be sustained without maintenance, so to judge the former positively and the latter negatively appears impossible.[185] That a child cannot constitute damage might appear to be a meaningless platitude, but the principle has consequences which are not initially apparent. To relax the principle that a child's care and upbringing are both a natural right and a primary duty of its parents (Art. 6 II s. 1 GG) is to provoke an avalanche of problems. Not only would such relaxation

697. That lost earnings are compensatable is confirmed: *Udale* v. *Bloomsbury Area Health Authority* [1983] 1 WLR 1098 (Jupp, J). The latter decision must be considered overruled in so far as it denied compensation for normal maintenance. Glazebrook [1992] *CLJ* 226, 228 is in favour of differentiating between cases where the surgeon culpably fails to prevent conception (liability must be admitted) and improper termination of pregnancy: no duty 'to save the pocket of the fertile people of England and Wales the cost of rearing the children they would rather not have had'.

[180] No European court has discussed the issue as much as the Sixth Senate of the BGH. BGH 18 Mar. 1980, BGHZ 76 p. 249 (unsuccessful sterilization); BGH 18 Mar. 1980, BGHZ 76 p. 259; BGH 30 June 1992, *VersR* 1992 p. 1229; BGH 27 June 1995, *NJW* 1995 p. 2407 (damages for pain and suffering: the unwanted pregnancy constituting bodily injury); BGH 9 July 1985, BGHZ 95 p. 199; BGH 25 Feb. 1992, *VersR* 1992 p. 829. Further references in BGH 16 Nov. 1993, BGHZ 124 p. 128 = *JZ* 1994 pp. 305, 306.

[181] BGH 16 Nov. 1993 (fn. 180 above) appears to attack the BVerfG which, the Senate opined, interfered unnecessarily in the competence of the lower court. Lower courts now face the dilemma of which to follow: OLG Düsseldorf 15 Dec. 1994, *NJW* 1995 p. 788; Deutsch, *VersR* 1995 pp. 609–616.

[182] BVerfG 28 May 1993, *NJW* 1993 pp. 1751, 1764 (= BVerfGE 88 p. 203).

[183] Hence not binding under § 31 I BVerfGG: Giesen, *JZ* 1994 pp. 286, 287–289.

[184] BGH 16 Nov. 1993, *JZ* 1994 pp. 305, 309: 'the exemption of parents from all maintenance costs, even in such wrongful life cases, therefore does not indicate a disregard for the child's dignity but is rather a suitable means for protecting and guaranteeing it.'

[185] Stoll, *Haftungsfolgen*, no. 230; *contra*, BGH loc. cit. (fn. 184 above).

grossly contradict family law,[186] it could also lead to claims by older siblings regarding the reduction of their inheritance. Moreover, compensation of maintenance costs resulting from the birth of a healthy child[187] would necessitate many new regulations, because current liability provisions would cease to apply by virtue of their incompatibility with human rights. Moreover, it would be necessary to adjust the damages for which the doctor was liable to reflect the benefits received by the parents, since a child brings joy to his family and may also be 'useful'.[188] Which aspect of liability law would justify limiting the compensation period to the child's minority, even though parents must often maintain children beyond that point? Would the parent's right to maintenance have to be withdrawn if they had another child after successfully suing the surgeon? Should one not also ask whether the couple were contributorily negligent in not refraining from intercourse, or not studying the contraceptive's instructions more thoroughly, or whether the purportedly sterilized man is to blame for his partner's failure to undergo an early pregnancy test?[189] Should it really be asked whether the decision not to abort,[190] or not to give the child up for adoption, interrupted the chain of causation?[191] Even in this age of contraceptives, a child is not something for which one may cancel the order. The argument that the mother should be compensated so as to prevent her from desiring an abortion on financial grounds[192] is untenable: to hold doctors liable for the birth of children may encourage women to terminate their pregnancies.[193] The loss resulting from temporary interruption to training and employment is entirely separate from liability for maintenance; nearly all countries consider that this should be compensated.[194] Finally, in cases of rape the offender should bear all the financial consequences of his act.

---

[186] Rb. Arnhem 28 Nov. 1974; 26 Feb. 1976 (fn. 173 above).

[187] Compensation for the additional maintenance costs of unhealthy children (wrongful life) is constitutionally unproblematic. Trib. Rome 13 Dec. 1994, *Dir.fam.pers.* 1995, I, 662, comment by Dogliotti loc. cit. p. 1474, awarded compensation for their own biological damage to parents who became aware of their child's deformity only on his birth. However, maintenance was not awarded as, the deformation having been recognized too late for an abortion to be performed legally, there was no causal connection between the failure to inform the parents and the non-performance of the abortion.

[188] Argued and rejected in Hof 's-Hertogenbosch 17 May 1983 (fn. 173 above); discussed in the judgment of *Udale v. Bloomsbury Health Authority* (fn. 179).

[189] Argued in Rb Leeuwarden 1 Mar. 1984 (fn. 173).

[190] Argued in Hof 's-Hertogenbosch 17 Mar. 1983 (fn. 173). Moreover, in *Emeh v. Kensington Chelsea Westminster AHA* (fn. 179 above) the court of first instance considered the decision against a termination of pregnancy unreasonable.

[191] Hence Riom 6 July 1989 dismissed. Cass.civ. 25 June 1991 later confirmed the decision for different reasons (fn. 175 above).

[192] Argued in *Emeh v. Kensington Chelsea Westminster AHA* (fn. 179 above).

[193] BVerfG (see fn. 182 above) was almost certainly, though tacitly, thus influenced.

[194] See fns. 173–180.

(b) The Right to Privacy and Environmental Protection

584 Less spectacular, although more surprising, is the effect of protecting privacy on some areas of environmental protection law, a field in which Greek courts currently lead. Art. 57 Greek Cc has been applied not only where public access (e.g. to the coast) is reduced,[195] but also to grant injunctive relief and removal where the sea is polluted.[196] Claims for damages have so far been dealt with under traditional rules of tort law, especially provisions protecting personal property.[197] It is the author's view that this should not change. It would overstretch the civil law, for instance, to attempt to compensate the loss of amenity caused by damage to flora and fauna by means of either Art. 24 I s. 1 Greek Constitution ('It is the duty of the state to protect the natural and cultural environment') or the law of privacy.[198]

585 By contrast, the application of constitutional principles to the civil law to improve protection against noise pollution is acceptable. Unlike German courts,[199] those in Italy have already embarked on that course, relying occasionally on Art. 32[200] of the Constitution.[201] However, Portuguese law leads the field here. Its starting points are Arts. 64 I (protection of health) and 66 I of the Constitution, according to which 'every person . . . is entitled to a humane, healthy, and ecologically balanced environment' and every person is 'obliged to care for its maintenance'. From the outset Portuguese courts have implied those rights into Art. 70 Cc[202] and regarded the proffered protection as a 'right' under Art. 483 Cc. Consequently, in the 1970s a resident of Lisbon city centre was awarded damages for discomfort caused by the noise of pneumatic drills lasting nineteen hours a day as a result of misplanning the city's underground railway extension. That was considered to be a breach of the plaintiff's constitutionally granted *direito à saúde e ao repouso* (to repose, tranquility, and rest).[203] In the same year and for the same reason the

---

[195] Areopag 743/1963, *NoB* 12 (1964) p. 514; Areopag 623/1956, *NoB* 5 (1957) p. 316; Areopag 470/1963, *NoB* 12 (1964) p. 195. Analysed by Karakostas, *ZfU* 1990 pp. 295, 297–300; id., *NuR* 1993 p. 467; id. *Perivallon kai Astiko Dikaio*, pp. 40–45.

[196] Thus CFI Volos 1097/229/1989, *NoB* 38 (1990) p. 308 and CFI Nauplio 163/1991, *NoB* 39 (1991) p. 786. The judgments are always based on the Civil Code rather than the Constitution.

[197] CA Athens 1773/1982, *Arm.* 1983 p. 215: grazing ground of plaintiff's sheep contaminated by fluorine emissions; claim for damages for violation of personal property.

[198] Similarly, Kottenhagen-Edzes, *Onrechtmatige daad en milieu*, pp. 155–156 (Art. 21 Grw has no immediate effect on third parties).

[199] BGH 26 Nov. 1980, *BGHZ* 79 pp. 45, 51; BGH 27 May 1993, *VersR* 1993 p. 1012; OLG Hamm 20 Dec. 1977, *VersR* 1979 p. 579.   [200] Fn. 118 above.

[201] Trib. Milan 10 Dec. 1992 and App. Milan 17 July 1992, *NGCC* 1993, I, 786. Also Cass. 20 Feb. 1992, n. 2092, *Giust.civ.Mass.* 1992 no. 2092 p. 249 (air pollution).

[202] 'The law protects all persons from the unlawful violation, impending or actual, of their physical and mental personality.'

[203] STJ 28 Apr. 1977, *BolMinJust* 266 (1977) pp. 165, 167.

Relação de Évora granted a tenant damages and compelled the defendant neighbouring restaurateur, who had not properly insulated his ceiling against noise and air pollution, to close his restaurant. The *Relação* held that under Art. 335 II Cc[204] the right of the individual to rest and recuperation was legally more important than the right of another to run a commercial or industrial business which caused noise pollution or other irritation.[205] The duty of the state to protect constitutionally granted rights *ao repouso, à tranquilidade e ao sossego*, which is manifest in tort law, has regularly been taken up by the *Supremo Tribunal* and other Portuguese courts,[206] to protect an individual from nuisance caused by a school playground[207] or from the unbearable noise and odour of a pigsty.[208] Moreover, in all those cases both injunctions and compensation were granted. This illustrates how a state's declared objective of environmental protection, when combined with constitutional rights to health and dignity, may influence the development of tort law.

(c) Self Respect, Reputation, and the Protection of Privacy

For most European lawyers, the protection of dignity includes the **586** protection of self respect, reputation, and privacy. Immediately after the Second World War the Greek Cc reacted to the failure of its model, the German BGB, by introducing Arts. 57–59; by 1965 the draftsmen of the Portuguese *Código civil* (Arts. 70, 71, 79–81) were able to rely on the encouraging German developments since 1954.[209] In that year the BGH initiated the constitutional rights-based development of the private law of tort, and held that 'the Basic Law now recognizes the individual's right to the protection of his dignity [Art. 1 *Grundgesetz*] and the freedom to develop his personality as a private right to be respected by every person'.[210] That decision was subsequently confirmed by the BVerfG, as was the BGH judgement[211]

---

[204] '(1) In the case of conflict between equal or similar rights, the beneficiaries must waive their rights in so far as it is necessary to honour all rights equally without major damage to any of the parties. (2) In cases of unequal or different rights, the higher-ranking right prevails.'   [205] RE 21 July 1977, *CJ* II (1977–5) pp. 1225, 1227.
[206] STJ 6 May 1969, *BolMinJust* 187 (1969) p. 121; RL 29 June 1977, *CJ* II (1977–4) p. 918.
[207] STJ 4 July 1978, *BolMinJust* 279 (1978) pp. 124, 128–130.
[208] STJ 15 Oct. 1985, *BolMinJust* 350 (1985) p. 301.
[209] Vaz Serra, *BolMinJust* 92 (1960) pp, 37, 82–111, whose preparations for the Portuguese Civil Code included studies of German developments. See RL 21 May 1987, *CJ* XII (1987–3) p. 88, concerning a press report on arms sales to Iraq. The text was flawless but the caption beneath the photographs of 3 politicians not involved in the sale read: 'they are lining up . . . in a dirty deal . . . to sell arms to Iraq.' The *Relação de Lisboa* regarded this as an abuse of the freedom of the press, incurring liability for the infringement of the politicians' reputation.   [210] BGH 25 May 1954, BGHZ 13 pp. 334, 338.
[211] BVerfG 14 Feb. 1973, BVerfGE 34 p. 269 (Soraya).

ordering compensation for pain and suffering caused by breach of the general right to dignity. Arts. 1, 2 GG 'directly protect that area of the legally recognized personality which is principally subject only to the free self-determination of the individual, violation of which by definition leads primarily to immaterial damage, being a degradation of the personality. To respect that area . . . is a legal obligation imposed by the Basic Law itself'.[212]

587   Those two decisions join a number of important judgments which not only made German legal history but persuaded other legal systems to improve their protection of the personality. Reference has already been made to the influence of German law on that of Portugal. Even English courts have referred to those BGH decisions when asking for Parliament to take action.[213] Italy also rapidly followed Germany's lead. The *Corte di Cassazione* held in a 1956 case concerning Enrico Caruso that Italian tort law did not protect privacy,[214] but in 1963 it conceded that its citizens had an 'absolute right to free self-determination of the development of the personality'.[215] In 1973 the *Corte Costituzionale* added the right to the protection of private life.[216] The *Corte di Cassazione* awarded Princess Soraya Esfandiari (who also appeared in the German courts)[217] damages for the publication of photographs showing her in compromising positions in her own house in 1975.[218] Reliance on Art. 2 Ital. Constitution (free development of the personality) had by then become common practice in tort law. The right to personal identity (the personal social profile)[219] and improved protection of reputation under Art. 7 Cc soon followed.[220]

588   Nowhere in tort law is the influence of human rights as strong and immediate as in the protection of dignity. Reliance on the constitution has long been common practice in non-constitutional European courts, although under the supervision of their respective constitutional courts. The Spanish *Tribunal Constitucional* only recently decided that the protection of personal honour includes the protection of professional reputation.[221] In that context Italian[222] and Dutch[223] broadcasters have been ordered to exercise more care when criticizing goods and services. In

---

[212] BGH 14 Feb. 1958, BGHZ 26 pp. 349, 354.
[213] *Kaye* v. *Robertson* [1991] FSR 62 (Weir, *Casebook*, 7th edn., pp. 20, 24) (*per* Bingham LJ, quoting Markesinis, *German Law of Torts*).
[214] Cass. 22 Dec. 1956, n. 4487, *Giur.it.Mass.* 1956 no. 4487 p. 941 = *Giur.it.* 1957, I, 1, 366.
[215] Cass. 20 Apr. 1963, n. 990, *Giur.it.* 1964, I, 1, 470.
[216] Corte cost. 12 Apr. 1973, n. 38, *Foro.it.* 1973, I, 1707.   [217] Fn. 211 above.
[218] Cass. 27 May 1975, n. 2129, *Giur.it.* 1976, I; 1, 970 = *Foro.it.* 1976, I, 2895.
[219] Cass. 22 June 1985, n. 3769, *Foro.it.* 1985, I, 2211.
[220] Cass. 7 Mar. 1991, n. 2426, *Dir.fam.pers.* 1992, I, p. 139.
[221] TC 14 Dec. 1992, 223/92, BJC 141 (1993) p. 55.
[222] Cass. 4 Feb. 1992, n. 1147, *Foro.it.* 1992, I, 2127.
[223] HR 29 Oct. 1993, *NedJur* 1994 no. 108 p. 419.

view of the special constitutional status of the right to dignity, Portuguese courts even found a newspaper negligent for failing to check the telephone number given incorrectly in the advertisement of a notorious massage parlour, so that an innocent telephone subscriber was pestered by calls to 'Otilia'.[224] The freedom of the press is in all European systems a serious and powerful competitor with the protection of dignity. This point is elaborated below.[225]

(4) Other Rights and Objects of Legal Protection

A state can violate citizens' rights by enacting strict liability law, but this **589** is rarely the case. An example is Art. 1916 II Ital. Cc, concerning exemptions from an insurer's right to subrogation after paying compensation. Under that provision, except in cases of intent, there is no subrogation by the insurer 'when the damage is caused by children, foster-children, ancestors, or other persons related by blood or affinity to the insured and permanently living in his household, or by his domestic staff'. The *Corte Costituzionale* was clearly obliged to declare the provision unconstitutional in so far as it excluded the insured's wife.[226] In private law the enforcement of other constitutionally granted liberties is usually covered by tort's protection of personal dignity. Defending the subjective rights of the family against violation by others,[227] for instance, would be covered, an area which includes more than just adultery in the familial home and the abduction of children. Both the CA Athens, referring to Art. 9 I s. 2 Greek Constitution ('the private and family life of the individual is inviolable'), and the *Corte di Cassazione*, referring to Art. 29 Italian Constitution, have awarded to plaintiffs whose spouse was rendered incapable of sexual intercourse in a traffic accident compensation for the plaintiff's pain and suffering: it was held, *inter alia*, that the plaintiffs' right to have children by their respective partners had been violated.[228] The *Bundesgerichtshof* should also have relied on the protection of personal dignity, rather than the right to bodily integrity, when it awarded DM 25,000 to a man for pain and suffering when his frozen sperm was destroyed.[229] German courts even recognize links between the freedom of information under Art. 5 I GG and the right to personal development under Art. 5 I GG, as was seen when the Turkish tenants of a block of flats were granted the right to instal satellite dishes to receive

---

[224] RL 18 Apr. 1989, *CJ* XIV (1989–2) p. 139.   [225] See no. 592.

[226] Corte Cost. 21 May 1975, n. 117, *Giur.it.* 1975, I, 1, 1741.

[227] On the constitutional implications of parents' refusal to allow children necessary medical treatment: Procuradoria-Geral da República 16 Jan. 1992, *BolMinJust* 418 (1992) pp. 285–318.

[228] CA Athens 6055/1989, *ArchN* 41 (1990) p. 776; Cass. 11 Nov. 1986, n. 6607, *Foro.it.* 1987, I, 833 (claim by the husband on the ground of wife's inability to have sexual intercourse).   [229] BGH 9 Nov. 1993, *NJW* 1994 p. 127.

Turkish television broadcasts.[230] The protection of dignity can also be relied on when there is deliberate interference with the freedom of religious practice or the memory of dead relatives.[231] In serious cases of the latter kind, e.g. the desecration of a Jewish cemetery with swastikas, the families of the dead should also be entitled to damages.

590   That tort law often protects assets in different and narrower circumstances than constitutional law is particularly obvious in Germany, but that poses no constitutional problems. Whilst there may be examples of a subjective civil right, recognized by tort, which is not 'property' pursuant to Art. 14 GG (for instance the right to carry on a trade or business [nos. 47–48 above] under the *sonstigen Rechte* of § 823 I BGB)[232] it is more usual to find economic interests protected by the constitution but not by the Civil Code: whereas the term 'property' in § 823 I denotes certain property law rights, under Art. 14 GG it may comprise merely relative rights.[233] Such differences demonstrate only that rules governing private individuals may differ from those of public law. By subjecting itself to stricter liability, the state does not violate its duty to protect its citizens' property from others; and the courts clearly do not protect too stringently the right to carry on a trade or business. The series of recent BGH judgments which has pushed the boundary away from (non-compensatable) purely economic loss in favour of (compensatable) damage to property[234] is a step in the right direction regarding Art. 14 GG. Finally, it is generally recognized that the copyright protection established in most European constitutions requires substantive implementation by tort law.[235]

---

[230] OLG Dusseldorf 2 Dec. 1992, *NJW* 1993 p. 1274; OLG Düsseldorf 12 Nov. 1993, *NJW* 1994 p. 1163; OLG Frankfurt 22 July 1992, *NJW* 1992 p. 2490; BVerfG 9 Feb. 1994, *NJW* 1994 p. 1147.

[231] BGH 20 Mar. 1968, BGHZ 50 pp. 133, 143. Remarkably, the headnote refers only to Arts. 2, 5 GG as authoritative sources.

[232] It is questionable whether the right to operate a trade or business is constitutional: Engel, *AöR* 118 [1993] pp. 171–236. BVerfG 13 June 1961, BVerfGE 13 pp. 225, 229 treated it as proprietary, but BVerfG 22 May 1979, BVerfGE 51 pp. 193, 221, and BVerfG 18 Dec. 1985, *NJW* 1986 p. 1601 considered the question to be open.

[233] BVerfG 18 Mar. 1970, BVerfGE 28 pp. 119, 141 (claims based in general law of obligations); BVerfG 8 June 1977, BVerfGE 45 pp. 142, 179 (claim for purchase price); and BVerfG 9 Jan. 1991, BVerfGE 83 pp. 201, 208 (purchase option arising independently of claim *in rem*). BVerfG 26 May 1993, *NJW* 1993 p. 2035: tenant's possessory rights as property. Critical: Sendler, *NJW* 1994 pp. 709–710.

[234] BGH 7 Dec. 1993, *NJW* 1994 p. 517 (product liability: injury to property may 'also manifest itself in the injured party's subsequent obligation to his buyers to repair qualitative defects'); BGH 25 Oct. 1988, BGHZ 105 pp. 346, 350 (fish rendered unsaleable by the possibility that they had been fed contaminated food); BGH 21 Dec. 1970, BGHZ 55 pp. 153, 159 (ship unable to leave canal due to collapsed bank; violation of property in ship); BGH 21 Nov. 1989, *NJW* 1990 p. 908 (wine required rebottling due to defective corks); BGH 16 Feb. 1993, *VersR* 1993 p. 1368; BGH 17 Mar. 1981, BGHZ 80 pp. 186, 189 (unsaleability of apples with imperfections).   [235] RL 11 Jan. 1994, *CJ* XIX (1994–1) p. 83.

b. The Liberties and Protection of the Tortfeasor

We now turn from the victim to the culprit, and consider in which areas **591** tort law may (entirely or partially) exempt someone who causes damage from liability by virtue of his constitutional rights. The first area examined is the general right of freedom of action, closely related to freedom of expression and the prohibition against disproportionality. Remember, however, that there are other areas in which constitutional values may have an immediate effect on tort law. Throughout Europe, freedom of association is relevant in employment law to determine the legality of industrial action.[236] In other areas tort law has not yet acknowledged its constitutional dimensions,[237] for instance in respect of the scope of parental duties of care. Parental duties are currently so wide that the special protection which all European constitutions promise of the institution of the family appears to be mere rhetoric.[238] That the Spanish *Tribunal Supremo*, the supreme court of a European nation, considered it necessary to declare that giving birth to a child does not create a liability risk shows just how far we have come![239] That decision did not impress lawyers in The Netherlands, where parents remain strictly liable for their children until completion of their fourteenth year.[240] The Dutch ruling was based on both the protection of minors (under Art. 6:169 I BW parents are liable for children under the age of fourteen) and the assumption that damage will be covered by insurance. It did not occur to the legislator to compel the victim to take precautionary measures.

---

[236] More recently, Rb. Utrecht 27 March and 13 May 1992, *NedJur* 1993 no. 431 p. 1530 (union liable for collecting and keeping carrier's HGV keys during strike); BAG 8 Nov. 1988, AP no. 111 on Art. 9 GG—industrial action—note v. Bar (boycott during strike); Cass. 28 Oct. 1991, n. 11477, *Foro.it.* 1992, I, 3058 (id.); Cass. 23 July 1991, n. 8234, *Riv.Giur.Lav.* 1992 p. 429 (determining the limits of the right to take industrial action on the basis of Art. 40 Italian Constitution); TC 17 July 1981, 216/1980, BJC 5(1981) pp. 334, 345 (principle of proportionality of the means employed); Procuradoria-Geral da República 9 June 1982, *BolMinJust* 324 (1983) p. 377 (unlawful strike by doctors); Procuradoria-Geral da República 8 July 1982, *BolMinJust* 325 (1982) p. 247 (duty to carry out the *serviços necessários à segurança e manutenção do equipamento e instalações*). Cf. fns. 9 and 27 above.

[237] Heldrich, *Freiheit der Wissenschaft—Freiheit zum Irrtum?*, esp., pp. 46–58; Canaris, *JZ* 1987 pp. 993, 996; BGH 8 Feb. 1994, *WM* 1994 pp. 641, 644; OLG Karlsruhe 27 Apr. 1994, *NJW* 1994 p. 1963.

[238] RL 15 Nov. 1988, *CJ* XIII (1988–5) p. 112, held that a single mother who left her 14- and 15-year-old sons with their grandmother, exempt from liability under Arts. 486, 491 Cc for lack of contractual acceptance of the duty of care, had not fulfilled her duty. The sons should have accompanied her to the USA.

[239] TS 2 Mar. 1994, *RAJ* 1994 no. 2097 p. 2830.

[240] Art. 6:169 I BW; also no. 132 above. Liability for presumed breach of the duty to supervise only concerns children of between 14 and 16 years: Art. 6:169 II BW.

(1) Freedom of Expression, Freedom of the Press, and Freedom of Assembly

592 The influence of freedom of expression and freedom of the press on tort law is far more pervasive.[241] This is true even for English law, despite its occasional preference for protection against, rather than for, the press. The problems which would have been created by strict liability for libel under Art. 10 ECHR were resolved by sec. 4 Defamation Act 1952.[242] Since then libel has to some extent been fault-based. That 'no privilege attaches yet to a statement on a matter of public interest believed by the publisher to be true in relation to which he has exercised reasonable care'[243] is not a violation of human rights: that such privilege should be a part of English defamation law cannot be deduced from Art. 10. Besides, not only did Parliament take steps[244] in the aftermath of the *Sunday Times* case before the European Court of Human Rights[245] (concerning a contempt of court restraining order violating the ECHR)[246] but also the English courts have become more sensitive towards Art. 10 of the Convention. In 1992 the Court of Appeal held that 'a local authority had no right to sue for libel in respect of its governing or administrative reputation if no actual financial loss was pleaded or alleged. If a non-trading public authority were to have that right it would be able to stifle legitimate public criticism of its activities and thereby interfere with the right to freedom of expression enshrined in Art. 10(a) of the Convention for the Protection of Human Rights and Fundamental Freedoms.'[247] The ruling was subsequently confirmed by the House of Lords.[248] The following year the Court of Appeal reduced the award of £250,000 to £110,000 by reference to Art. 10.[249] It was considered 'excessive' to award Esther Rantzen, founder and president of the 'Childline' service, such a large sum. (The paper had accused her of protecting a private school teacher said to have abused children). That decision is interesting in that it constitutes tacit acceptance of the controversial continental prohibition against arbitrariness.

---

[241] Rigaux, *Protection de la vie privée*, nos. 147–168.

[242] (Ch. 66). Sec. 4 provides for unintentional defamation and introduces the offer of amends as a defence.   [243] *Blackshaw* v. *Lord* [1983] 2 All ER 311, 327.

[244] I.e. with the introduction of secs. 2, 3 of the Contempt of Court Act 1981 (c. 49).

[245] European Court of Human Rights 26 Apr. 1979, Série A, vol. 30, no. 66, p. 41 (*Times Newspapers* v. *United Kingdom*). Also Rigaux loc. cit. no. 169; Villinger, *Handbuch EMRK*, no. 604, Gray, [1979] *CLJ* 242–245.

[246] *Attorney General* v. *Times Newspapers Ltd.* [1974] AC 273.

[247] *Derbyshire County Council* v. *Times Newspapers Ltd. and Others* [1992] 3 All ER 65 (CA); Fleming, 109 [1993] *LQR* 12–16.

[248] *Derbyshire County Council* v. *Times Newspapers Ltd. and Others* [1992] 1 All ER 1011 (HL).

[249] *Rantzen* v. *Mirror Group Newspapers Ltd.* [1993] 3 WLR 953 (CA). Hopkins, [1994] *CLJ* 9–11.

References to basic civil rights have become so common in European Courts that it is almost impossible to distinguish between 'pure' civil law and constitutional civil law, i.e. civil law having the status of a constitutional provision. This section mentions only some of the more recent decisions in favour of press freedom rather than the protection of personal dignity. In HR 21 January 1994[250] the plaintiff was the convicted kidnapper and murderer of the industrialist *Heijn*. A photograph taken before his conviction, showing him relaxed and smoking a cigarette, was published by the defendant magazine. The photograph won a press award. The *Hoge Raad* rejected the plaintiff's claim for injunctive relief, arguing that the crime was still in the public realm when the photograph was published. Press freedom thus prevailed over the protection of the plaintiff's privacy. In the German *Lebach* ruling the BVerfG, on the basis of similar considerations, arrived at exactly the opposite conclusion.[251] Italian courts have also often found interference with a person's personal dignity by the press to be justified given the objective truth of the assertion made, the good faith of the journalist, and the existence of general interest in the publication.[252] A recent decision of the Spanish Constitutional Court bears similarities with the English defence of innocent publication.[253] The Spanish case concerned a newspaper article criticizing and naming a priest who had allegedly instigated a 'crusade' against the operators of a nudist colony. On discovering that the campaign was actually led by another priest, the paper attempted to undo any damage it had caused by publishing a clarifying article about, and an interview with, the originally named, uninvolved priest. The priest's claim for damages was upheld in all courts other than the Constitutional Court. The Tribunal Constitucional found against the priest, holding that whilst a journalist may not report untruthfully, it is not required that the information be objectively true. It suffices for journalists to examine their facts diligently and to assess their veracity. One of the few Danish tort decisions on fundamental rights concerned justification as a defence to defamation. A co-operatively run abattoir sued unsuccessfully in respect of a satirical poster criticizing the use of antibiotics in piggeries. The *Højesteret* considered this to be 'such an important issue' that freedom of

---

[250] HR 21 Jan. 1994, *RvdW* 1994 no. 36.

[251] BVerfG 5 June 1973, BVerfGE 35 pp. 202, 203 (headnote 3 b: 'The constitutional right to personal dignity does not . . . permit the television . . . to deal indefinitely with the person of the criminal and his private life'). OLG Munich 26 Jan. 1994, *NJW-RR* 1994 p. 925; KG 10 Dec. 1993, *NJW-RR* 1994 p. 926.

[252] Cass. 6 Aug. 1992, n. 9348, *Giust.civ.Mass.* 1992 p. 1278; Cass. 29 Aug. 1990, n. 8963, *Giust.civ.Mass.* 1990 p. 1640; Cass. 13 Mar. 1985, n. 1968, *Giust.civ.Mass.* 1985 p. 610. On regarding the contents and boundaries of the constitutionally guaranteed right to satire see Trib. Rome 13 Feb. 1992, *Dir.fam.pers.* 1993, I, 1119 incl. note Dogliotti, Weiss, and Lopez loc. cit. 1994, I, 170.   [253] TC 21 Dec. 1992, 240/1992, BJC 141 (1993) p. 124.

expression prevailed over the professional reputation of the plaintiff.[254]
A poster campaign was also the subject of BGH 12 October 1993: Greenpeace had in a 'satirical and sarcastic manner' named and criticized the
plaintiff chairman of the board of directors of Hoechst-AG for the company's production of CFC chemicals. In view of the public interest in the
issue, the BGH allowed freedom of expression to prevail over the protection of the plaintiff's privacy.[255] In The Netherlands the 'public interest' has even been incorporated into Art. 6:168 I BW regarding
injunctions, helping Greenpeace to succeed in yet another fight against
the producers of allegedly environmentally hazardous substances. The
organization's members blocked the railway track between the plaintiff's property and the main line. The application for an injunction was
rejected on the ground that such obstruction, if brief, might be in the
public interest.[256]

594   Whether the Greenpeace campaign should be seen as the unlawful use
of force against property, and so neither in the public interest nor protected by the freedom of assembly, is not important at this point.[257] What
is relevant here is that a constitutionally guaranteed freedom of demonstration must affect tort law. Constitutionally acceptable interpretation
of rules on participant liability is especially important where individuals
participate in large demonstrations which result in violent incidents.[258]
The German *Bundesverfassungsgericht* rightly stated that 'the freedom of
assembly which the Constitution guarantees to every citizen [must] be
maintained for all peaceful participants, even if other individuals or
minorities cause violent incidents. . . . Art. 8 GG [must to that extent]
affect the application of provisions restricting basic rights', including the
imposition of strict liability.[259] This principle has yet to be recognized in
most European countries. Even the recent Dutch BW has avoided this
issue. As admitted by the legislator,[260] its provision on the liability of
individuals in 'a group of persons' (Art. 6:166 BW)[261] was too generously drafted in view of freedom of demonstration.[262] Responsibility
thus lies with the courts, which are quite capable of dealing with such
matters, as shown in a case before the BGH in 1984.[263] During a large

---

[254] HD 29 Oct. 1980, *UfR* 1980 A p. 1038.
[255] BGH 12 Oct. 1993, *NJW* 1994 p. 124 = *JuS* 1994 p. 346 (Emmerich) = *EWiR* § 823 BGB
1/94, 133 (Nieper).   [256] Rb. Roermond 3 Nov. 1993, *KG* 1993 no. 411.
[257] OGH 25 May 1994, *SZ* 67/92 pp. 531, 534–535.   [258] Nos. 54–60 above.
[259] BVerfG 14 May 1985, *NJW* 1985 pp. 2395, 2400.
[260] *Parlementaire Geschiedenis*, vol. vi p. 664: analysis of the individual case is required
due to constitutionally guaranteed right to demonstrate.
[261] 'If a member of a group of persons unlawfully causes damage and the risk of that
damage should have prevented those persons from their collective conduct, they will be
held severally liable if the conduct can be imputed to them.' Cf. nos. 59–60 above.
[262] Asser (-Hartkamp), *Verbintenissenrecht*, vol. iii, 8th edn., no. 94.
[263] BGH 24 Jan. 1984, *BGHZ* 89 p. 383.

demonstration at the site of a prospective nuclear power station in Grohnde, police officers were injured and equipment damaged. The plaintiff *Bundesland* demanded joint and several compensation from eighteen people out of a total of 10–20,000 demonstrators. The BGH made it unambiguously clear that demonstrators not involved in the rioting could only be regarded as accessories if their 'ensuring of anonymity and utterances of sympathy . . . are intended to and capable of supporting and encouraging the perpetrators in their decisions and acts. . . . To extend civil liability for damage caused during a large demonstration to "passive" supporters is unconstitutional because it places on those exercising the right to demonstrate an incalculable and intolerable risk, thereby wrongfully restricting the right to public expression of one's opinion.'[264]

(2) General Freedom of Action and the Prohibition Against Disproportionality

The more the constitutional aspects of a delictual case are emphasized, **595** the greater is the danger of tort law becoming more than just a part of civil law. This cannot be in the interest of constitutional law. There are both procedural and substantive boundaries to such development: it cannot be in the interest of any constitution to encourage developments which push the finely balanced, continuously developed system of civil law towards superficiality. Constitutional law must restrict itself to smoothing the sharp edges; it cannot be a substitute for civil law.[265] This is particularly relevant to the question of how the basic right of freedom of action protects the individual who commits a tort at civil law from financial burden. It is equally important for the concept of the social state (*Sozialstaatsprinzip*): the right to enjoy property and the prohibition against disproportionality (*Übermaßverbot*) which derives from the rule of law.[266] The prohibition against disproportionality applies primarily in disputes between the state and the individual, such as when an innocent land owner is liable under 'police law' (*Polizeirecht*) to decontaminate the land because of activities of a previous owner.[267]

---

[264] Id. p. 395.

[265] Therefore BVerfG 19 Oct. 1993, *NJW* 1994 pp. 36, 38 is correct that it 'could not oppose a final civil judgment even if it (the BVerfG) would have decided differently had it been assessing conflicting human rights (*Grundrechtpositionen*)'.

[266] The principle of proportionality is an integral part of the European Convention on Human Rights, at least regarding relationships between state and citizen: European Court of Human Rights 7 Dec. 1976, *EugRZ* 1977 p. 38 (*Handyside* case); European Court of Human Rights 23 Sep. 1982, *EuGRZ* 1983 p. 523 (*Sporrong and Lönnroth* case; principle of economic reasonableness); Also part of European law: European Court 2 Aug. 1993, Rsen. C-259, 331, 332/91—*Allué II*—*JZ* 1994 p. 94 (official commentary no. 15). Cf. fn. 272 below.

[267] Austrian cases: VerfGH 14 Oct. 1993, VfSlg. 13.587; VwGH 20 Nov. 1984, *ZfVB* 1985 p. 331; OGH 16 Jan. 1991, *SZ* 64 I no. 3, p. 9.

Finally, it is clear that a blanket exclusion of the defence of 'mistake as to unlawfulness'[268] and a reversal of the burden of proof of fault[269] are unacceptable in criminal law, but are inoffensive (unless arbitrary) in the civil context.[270]

596   There has been intensive discussion about the effect of the prohibition against disproportionality in tort law in Germany, mainly because German law, unlike that of most other European states, has no provisions which limit damages.[271] In states with such provisions the constitutional prohibition is not a tort issue.[272] The problem here is that excessive liability may destroy a person's livelihood. German law addresses this issue only in its law on enforcement. In substantive private law it is entirely ignored, except in respect of equity. It is a moot point whether amendment is *de lege lata* constitutionally required, for example by means of the prohibition against abuse of a legal right.[273] In 1989 the OLG Celle was inclined to favour the idea regarding the liability of children.[274] However, the BGH rejected it—apparently correctly—for

---

[268] Corte Cost. 24 Mar. 1988, n. 364, *Foro.it.* 1988, I, 1385: unconstitutionality of Art. 5 CP insofar as it does not consider unavoidable errors regarding unlawfulness; the judgment is silent on whether the same conclusion may be drawn in civil law.

[269] TC 1 Apr. 1982, *La Ley* 1982 (2) p. 1066 (unconstitutionality of presumption of fault in criminal law); TS 7 Jan. 1992, *RAJ* 1992 no. 149 p. 174; and TS 25 Mar. 1991, *RAJ* 1991 no. 2443 p. 3223 (presumption of fault constitutionally unproblematic in civil law, the provisions having no punitive effect).   [270] Cf. Reinhardt, *NJW* 1994 pp. 93, 96–99.

[271] View shared by Canaris, *JZ* 1987 pp. 993, 1001; id., *JuS* 1989 pp. 161–172.

[272] Exessive liability may be reduced under rules of equity in: The Netherlands (Arts. 6: 106, 109 BW); Spain (Art. 1103 Cc, also applicable in tort: TS 11 Feb. 1993, *RAJ* 1993 no. 1457 p. 1833); Denmark (§ 24 Damages Act; *vide* VLD 19 Feb. 1993, *UfR* 1993 A p. 430); Finland (2nd Chapter, 1 § Damages Act 1974); Sweden (6th Chapter, 1 § Damages Act 1972); Norway (§ 5–3 Damages Act 1969); and Portugal (Art. 494 Cc). Cf. § 1324 ABGB, under which compensation for slight negligence is limited to special damages (*eigentliche Schadloshaltung*). Lost profits and pain and suffering are not compensated. How far the proportionality principle applies to non-contractual liability between subjects of private law has so far been left open by most European states. Current Italian law appears at least to prohibit arbitrariness (Corte Cost. 12 Apr. 1990, n. 184, *Giur.it.* 1991, I, 1, 257). Luther, *Italienische Verfassungsgerichtsbarkeit*, pp. 105–106. In Greece the principle of proportionality 'is gaining ground' (Papadimitriou, in: Battis/Mahrenholz/Tsatsos, *Grundgesetz im internationalen Wirkungszusammenhang*, pp. 117, 127). The only tort decision applying it of which this author is aware is CA Athens 5025/1990 (no. 99 above). However, that case concerned, not a limitation, but an extension of liability. The Spanish Constitutional Court has employed the principle of proportionality in relation to strike and press law (Sommermann, *Schutz der Grundrechte in Spanien*, pp. 244–245). The Portuguese constitutional court has applied it only regarding expropriation (Trib. Const. 6 Jan. 1988, *BolMinJust* 373 [1988] p. 157). The position in Germany is equally pathetic: BVerfG 24 Feb. 1971, BVerfGE 30 pp. 173, 199 expressly refused to apply any proportionality principle to tort and merely examined the case for arbitrariness. BGH 4 June 1992, BGHZ 118 pp. 312, 343, however, recently said regarding liability law that 'the principle of proportionality derived from the rule of law . . . must also be honoured in civil law'. Also BAG 12 June 1992, *NJW* 1993 pp. 1732, 1734.

[273] Cf. Canaris, *JZ* 1987 pp. 993, 1001–1002.

[274] OLG Celle 26 May 1989, *VersR* 1989 p. 709 (submission of case to BVerfG. After settlement, the decision to submit was reversed: OLG Celle 28 Nov. 1989 [4 U 53/88;

employees' third-party liability.[275] Such a deep incision into statutory tort law would require diligent legislative planning; it could not be developed from *lex lata*. Unless and until the legislator reconsiders the role of third-party insurance, the problem will be left for the civil courts to resolve. The solution will require careful analysis of employees' duties of care, courageous use of forfeiture to tackle the grotesque thirty-year, reversed burden of proof of liability for *culpa in contrahendo*,[276] and more careful use of professional uninsurable (§ 152 VVG) liability under § 826 BGB. It cannot be said that the German principle of *réparation intégrale* is unique in Europe, as it applies equally to the Romance and common law countries. Nor can it be said that German civil law ignores the prohibition against excess entirely, because the limitation of liability to the damage actually sustained, to the exclusion of punitive and exemplary damages, is an expression of the principle of commensurability in codified civil law.[277] Further, the sharp edges of the principle of restitution in kind are blunted by § 251 II s. 1 BGB.[278] Notwithstanding that the introduction of a provision limiting damages into the BGB would represent pogress, the current tort law requirement of the equivalence of damage and liability is constitutionally sufficient.

5. SEPARATION OF POWERS AND JUDGE-MADE LAW REPLACING CODIFIED LAW

a. General Overview

There is a further problem which, whilst not peculiar to tort, occurs here **597** frequently: the remarkable *'wetgevende rechtspraak'*.[279] This is judge-made law which overrides codified law. Ignoring the special case of

---

unpublished]). Scheffen, *DAR* 1991 pp. 121–126; ead., *FuR* 1993 pp. 82–89. Regarding parental power of representation BVerfG 13 May 1986, BVerfGE 72 pp. 155, 173 ruled that in execution of its guardianship under Art. 6 II s. 2 GG, the legislator must 'lay down rules which avoid an adult's gaining only an apparent freedom'. RP 3 Dec. 1987, *BolMinJust* 372 (1988) p. 466 ('*O facto de o lesante ser menor [7 anos e 8 meses à data do evento] não o exonera da obrigação indemnizatória, uma vez feita a prova de que, no caso concreto, agiu com inteligência e vontade*')('the fact that the injured party is a minor [7 years and 8 months at the date of the event] does not exonerate him from the duty to indemnify as long as it is proved that he acted with intelligence and intent') appears significantly different in tendency. However, only the headnote has been published.

[275] BGH 21 Dec. 1993, *NJW* 1994 p. 852.

[276] The Turkish Court of Cassation has recently ruled that the German thirty-year contract limitation period violates its *ordre public*: *VersRAI* 1994 p. 64 (translation into German of judgment of 15 June 1993).

[277] As stated by BGH 4 June 1992, BGHZ 118 pp. 312, 343–344. *Vide* Bungert, *VersR* 1994 pp. 15, 22–23.

[278] Essentially similar provisions in Art. 2058 II Italian Cc and Art. 566 I Portuguese Cc.

[279] Expression according to Schit, *RM-Themis* 1992 p. 353.

the *assentos* under Art. 2 Portuguese Cc,[280] only in common law systems do court rulings constitute true sources of law. The extraordinary shortness of Danish judgments is justified by the argument that it is not for the courts but for politicans to decide matters of fundamental importance for society.[281] In France and Belgium the judge actually commits a criminal offence (Arts. 127 French CP, 237 Belgian CP) if he violates the prohibition *'de prononcer par voie de disposition générale et réglementaire sur les causes qui leur sont soumises'* (Art. 5 French Cc = Art. 6 Code jud.). A corresponding provision is Art. 12 Dutch AB.[282] However, these grand words are now *lettres mortes*. Whenever the civil courts have recognized the need to create new liability law, not even the principle of the separation of powers has stopped them. They have taken this on to counterbalance the legislator's declining power to fashion legal relationships, and to open liability law up to constitutional considerations. The most prominent examples of the latter may be found in the introduction of the concept of *danno biologico* into Italian law,[283] the transformation of Art. 914 Greek Cc from a blanket provision into a general clause,[284] and the allowance of damages for pain and suffering for violations of personal dignity by the German BGH.[285] Historically, the most important example for counterbalancing the legislators' declining power is the French development of *gardien* liability under Art. 1384 I Cc.[286] Moreover, in Spain, which has long since reinterpreted its partial liability rules as providing for joint and several liability,[287] the *Tribunal Supremo* has effectively transformed liability under the delictual general clause into presumed-fault-based liability, creating an equivalent to French *gardien* liability.[288] A more recent Belgian example of reliance upon *'par voie de disposition*

---

[280] In statutorily governed cases the courts may *'fixar, por meio de assentos, doutrina com força obrigatória geral'*. Such sources of law rendering an interpretation generally binding are published in the *Diário da República*. In so far as the *assentos* merely define and specify the existing state of the law, Art. 2 Cc is considered difficult but constitutionally sound: RL 10 May 1990, *CJ* XV (1990–3) p. 117; RL 9 Feb. 1988, *CJ* XIII (1988–1) p. 129; RC 17 Feb. 1987, *CJ* XII (1987–1) p. 61.

[281] Christensen, *UfR* 1990 B pp. 73, 83. Gomard, *J* 1993 pp. 325, 335–336, however, is decisively in favour of comprehensive reasoning. Commentaries on judgments are a Danish peculiarity. Written by a member of the *Højesteret* involved, they merely reflect the author's personal view. Cf. Jensen, in: *Højesteret 1661–1986*, pp. 115, 141.

[282] Art. 12: *'Geen regter mag bij wege van algemene verordening, dispositie of reglement uitspraak doen in zaken welke aan zijn beslissing onderworpen zijn'* (No judge has the power to make general regulations when deciding cases before him).

[283] Nos. 573–574 above.   [284] No. 560 above.   [285] No. 586 above.

[286] Nos. 106–116 above. Less dramatic but still remarkable is the judicial 'implementation' of the EC Product Liability Directive into French law in Cass.civ. 17 Jan. 1995 (no. 372 and fn. 18 above).   [287] No. 52 above.

[288] Cavanillas Múgica, *Transformación*, p. 77 thus correctly comments: 'If the jurisprudence regarding the presumption of fault came into the hands of a non-lawyer he would draw the conclusion that the TS was allowed *ex novo* to create statutory presumptions. And we know this not to be the case.'

générale et réglementaire' reasoning can be found in the *ANCA* judgment of the *Cour de Cassation*. The case concerned state liability for miscarriages of justice by judges only: the court nonetheless extended the new liability scheme to cover state prosecutors.[289]

b. Developments in French and Dutch Road Traffic Third-Party Liability Law

There are a number of French and Dutch rulings on contributory negli- **598** gence in road traffic cases which exceed even the boundaries drawn by court-led developments. Although the French legislator has now reacted against that trend, the judgments are still of interest in that they obviously formed the foundation for the most recent 'measures' taken by the Dutch *Hoge Raad* on the matter. Once *gardien* liability was finally established in France by the *arrêts Jand'heur*[290] it was clear that, in cases of contributory negligence, liability under Art. 1384 I Cc was to be reduced, usually by half. In the sensational *arrêt Desmares* of 1982 the *Cour de Cassation* declared the rule void, contributory fault being irrelevant to *gardien* liability: *'Seul un événement constituant un cas de force majeure exonère le gardien de la chose, instrument du dommage, de la responsabilité par lui encourue par application de l'art. 1384 al. 1 du Code civil; ... dès lors, le comportement de la victime, s'il n'a pas été pour le gardien imprévisible et irrésistible, ne peut l'en exonérer, même partiellement.'*[291] Thus was created a wholly new principle which, while developed in respect of road traffic, was soon applied to all cases of *gardien* liability.[292] The purpose of the policy was uncomplicated: to create a more or less intolerable legal position so that the legislator would be compelled to intervene in the problematic area of road traffic accident law. The move was successful: in 1985 the *Loi Badinter*[293] (named after the Minister of Justice) was implemented, as a result of which the Cour de Cassation abandoned its 'exaggerated' approach at the first opportunity and reintroduced the traditional reduction of damages for contributory negligence under Art. 1384 I Cc.[294]

There can be no doubt that when the *Hoge Raad* adopted a similar **599** position, albeit in a slightly modified form and limited to road traffic

---

[289] Cass. 19 Dec. 1991, *RW* 1992–1993 p. 396 = *JT* 1992 p. 142.

[290] Cass.civ. 21 Feb. 1927, *D.* 1927, 1, 97 (*Jand'heur I*); and Cass.ch.réunies 13 Feb. 1930, *D.* 1930, 1, 57 (*Jand'heur II*); on both cases see no. 111 above.

[291] Cass.civ. 21 July 1982, *D.* 1982 *Jur.* 449.

[292] Cass.civ. 10 Mar. 1983, *Sem.Jur.* 1984, II, 20244 (Chabas); Cass.civ. 15 Nov. 1984, *D.* 1985 *Jur.* 20 (Carbonnier).

[293] Loi No. 85–677 of 5 July 1985 *'tendant à l'amélioration de la situation des victimes d'accidents de la circulation et à l'accélération des procédures d'indemnisation'*, JO 6 July 1985, p. 7584. [294] Cass.civ. 6 Apr. 1987, *D.* 1988 *Jur.* 32 (*arrêt Mettetal*).

third-party liability, it was merely following France's example. They too had no constitutional court to fear.[295] Under Art. 31 Dutch Road Traffic Law (repealed),[296] now Art. 185 WVW, the strict liability of the keeper (owner) of a motor vehicle is unquestionably reduced if there is contributory negligence on the part of the victim. Even before the implementation of Art. 6:101 BW (contributory negligence), with its reference to equity, the HR had already indicated its dissatisfaction with the *lex lata*.[297] Accordingly, after an accident for which the thirteen-year-old victim was at least 50% responsible, it ruled in 1991 that equity demanded that the keeper of the vehicle be wholly liable unless the child (whether pedestrian or cyclist) had been intentionally or wilfully negligent.[298] Moreover, the HR assumed legislative power to determine the age limit of thirteen years by reference to the (then draft) Art. 6:169 I BW. This age limit has been confirmed on several occasions[299] and has also been applied to mentally handicapped people aged over fourteen.[300] However, the judges had only secured the first half of the *Loi Badinter* with this restriction of children's liability. The second half was addressed in 1992 concerning a road traffic accident for which a 67–year-old pedestrian had been assessed as at least 80% responsible. The *Hoge Raad* exploited the opportunity to issue a 'Dutch *arrêt Desmares*'. Without reference to particular vulnerable persons, it held that in any accident involving a motorist and either a pedestrian or a cyclist, the motorist's liability would always amount to at least 50%. Contributory negligence on the part of the victim would affect only the remaining 50%. The court further ruled that the rule did not benefit the victim's insurer who had made payment prior to judgment: the tortfeasor's third-party liability insurer can only be required to cover payment to the extent to which the motorist actually contributed to the accident.[301] From a constitutional point of view, it would have been more appropriate to leave such developments to the legislator.

---

[295] No. 563 above.

[296] Also no. 7, fn. 34 above. The provision exonerates the tortfeasor if 'it is presumable that the collision, running into, or running over was caused by an Act of God, including cases of fault by a person for whom the owner and keeper of the vehicle are not responsible'.   [297] HR 1 June 1990, *NedJur* 1991 no. 720 p. 3125.

[298] HR 31 May 1991, *NedJur* 1991 no. 721 p. 3137.

[299] Hof 's-Gravenhage 8 Apr. 1992, *NedJur* 1993 no. 229 p. 839.

[300] HR 24 Dec. 1993, *RvdW* 1994 no. 11 (mentally handicapped girl, 14 years and 8 months; the 50% rule to be applied but may take the girl's mental condition into consideration in respect of the second 50%).

[301] HR 28 Feb. 1992, *NedJur* 1993 no. 566 p. 2117.

II. THE LAW OF DELICT AND CRIMINAL LAW

Bibliography: *Bajons, 'Schadensersatz für gesundheitliche Beeinträchtigungen nach italienischem Recht', ZVglRWiss* 92 (1993) pp. 76–114; v. Bar, 'La responsabilità del giudice nella Repubblica Federale Tedesca', *Foro.pad.* 1988, vol. ii, 131–137; Bonilini, *Il danno non patrimoniale* (Milan 1983); Buján, 'Spanien: Schadensersatzansprüche aus Verkehrsunfällen: Durchsetzung im Zivil- oder Strafverfahren?', *VersRAI* 1993 pp. 14–15; Carval, *La responsabilité civile dans sa fonction de peine privée* (Paris 1995); Chao-Duivis, 'Vergelding als schadevergoeding', *NJB* 1990 pp. 513–520; Cullen, 'The Liability of the Good Samaritan', *Jurid.Rev.* 1995 pp. 20–27; Dalcq, 'Faute civile—Faute pénale', *Ann. Louv.* 1983 pp. 73–86; van Dam, *Zorgvuldigheid en aansprakelijkheid* (Deventer 1989); Delvaux, 'Réflexions sur certains effets seconds de la dissociation entre faute pénale et faute civile', *Ann. Louv.* 1983 pp. 113–116; van Dijk/Groenhuijsen, 'Schadevergoedingsmaatregel en voeging: de civielrechtelijke invalshoek', *NJB* 1993 pp. 163–167; Dölling, 'Der Täter-Opfer-Ausgleich', *JZ* 1992 pp. 493–499; Duff, 'Criminal Injuries Compensation: Nervous Shock and Secondary Victims', *SLT* 1992 pp. 311–315; *Encyclopédie Dalloz* (-Conte), vol. viii, *Responsabilité du fait personnel* (Paris 1992); Feenstra, *Vergelding en vergoeding*, 2nd edn. (Deventer 1993); Fiebich, 'Der Begriff der groben Fahrlässigkeit im § 334 des Allgemeinen Sozialversicherungsgesetzes', *ÖJZ* 1961 pp. 141–144; Fillette, 'L'obligation de porter secours à la personne en péril', *Sem.Jur.* 1995, vol. i, 3868; Font Serra, *La acción civil en el proceso penal: Su tratamiento procesal* (Madrid 1991); Fontaine/Fagnart, 'Réflexions sur la prescription des actions en responsabilité', *RGAR* 1995 no. 12505; Franzoni, *Il danno alla persona* (Milan 1995; Il diritto privato oggi, Serie a cura di Paolo Cendon); Gallas, 'Zur Revision des § 330c StGB', *JZ* 1952 pp. 396–400; Hannequart, 'Faute civile—Faute pénale', *Ann. Louv.* 1983 pp. 87–112; Hellmann, *Die Anwendbarkeit der zivilrechtlichen Rechtfertigungsgründe im Strafrecht* (Cologne et al. 1986); Henneau/Verhaegen, *Droit pénal général* (Brussels 1991); Hopkins, 'Analysis of an Anomaly', [1993] *CLJ* 199–202; Hudson, 'Crime, Tort and Reparation: A Common Solution', *SLT* 1992 pp. 203–210; *JClCiv* (-Jourdain), 'Droit à réparation: Responsabilité fondée sur la faute', arts. 1382 to 1386, fasc. 120–1 (Paris 1987); *JClCiv* (-Espagnon), 'Rapports entre responsabilité délictuelle et contractuelle entre contractants', arts. 1146 to 1155, fasc. 16–1 (Paris 1992); Jeschek, *Lehrbuch des Strafrechts, Allgemeiner Teil*, 4th edn. (Berlin 1988); Jørgensen, 'Ersatz und Versicherung', *VersR* 1970 pp. 193–208; Kohl, 'L'action civile en dommages: intérêts résultant d'une infraction', *Rev.crit.jur.belge*

1975 pp. 372–393; Komittén om ideell skada, '*Ersättning för kränkning genom brott*' (Statens offentliga utredningar 1992: 84; Justitiedepartementet) (Stockholm 1992); Koopmann, *Bevrijdende verjaring* (Deventer 1992); Kortmann, 'Wie betaalt de rekening? Enige rechtsvergelijkende kanttekeningen naar aanleiding van het *Anca*-arrest', *NJB* 1993 pp. 921–926; Lobedanz, *Schadensausgleich bei Straftaten in Spanien und Lateinamerika* (Frankfurt/Main 1972); Mackay, 'The Resuscitation of Assythment? Reparation and the Scottish Criminal', *Jurid.Rev.* 1992 pp. 242–255; Mayer-Maly, 'Schädigung durch Unterlassung, insbesondere durch unterlassene Hilfeleistung bei Verkehrsunfällen', *ZVR* 1977 pp. 97–100; Meeus, 'Faute pénale et faute civile', *RGAR* 1992 no. 11900; Mylonopoulos, 'Greece', in: Van den Wyngaert, *Criminal procedure systems in the European Community* (London *et al.* 1993) pp. 163–183; Overeem, *Smartegeld* (Zwolle 1979); Pirovano, *Faute civile et faute pénale: Essai de contribution à l'étude des rapports entre la faute des articles 1382–1383 du c.civ. et la faute des articles 319–320 du c.pén.* (Paris 1966); Quintano Ripollés, 'Diferenciación entre la culpa civil y la culpa criminal', *An.Der.Civ.* 10 (1957) pp. 1038–1056; Ravazzoni, *La riparazione del danno non patrimoniale* (Milan 1962); v. Savigny, *Das Obligationenrecht als Teil des heutigen römischen Rechts*, vol. ii (reprint of edn. of Berlin 1853, Aalen 1981); Schöch, 'Empfehlen sich Änderungen und Ergänzungen bei den strafrechtlichen Sanktionen ohne Freiheitsentzug?', *Gutachten C für den 59. Deutschen Juristentag* (Munich 1992); Stein, 'Punitive Damages: eine Herausforderung für die Internationale Wirtschaftsschiedsgerichtsbarkeit?', *EuZW* 1994 pp. 18–25; Stolker, 'Besef als vereiste voor vergoeding van immateriële schade', *RM-Themis* 1988 pp. 3–29; Stoll, 'Schadensersatz und Strafe', in: *FS Rheinstein*, vol. ii (Tübingen 1969) pp. 569–590; Ulmer, 'Die deliktische Haftung aus der Übernahme von Handlungspflichten', *JZ* 1969 pp. 163–174; Waaben, *Strafferettens almindelige del*, 2nd edn. (Copenhagen 1989); Wahle, 'Grobe Fahrlässigkeit', *JBl* 1961 pp. 497–505; White, 'Exemplary Damages in Irish Tort Law', *ILT* 1987 pp. 60–66; Williams, 'The Effect of Penal Legislation in the Law of Tort', 23 [1960] *ModLRev.* 233–259; Zeno-Zencovich, 'Il problema della pena privata nell'ordinamento italiano: un approccio comparatistico ai "punitive damages" di "common law"', *Giur.it.* 1985, IV, 12–27.

1. PUNISHMENT WITHOUT DAMAGES

Since its separation from tort law,[302] criminal law has become **600** part of public law, by which the state attempts to prevent socially damaging conduct by suppression.[303] As a result of that separation, every European legal system includes provisions, such as those regarding criminal attempts,[304] which impose punishment for conduct which causes no damage recoverable at civil law to any individual, state,[305] or area's inhabitants.[306] Such provisions and acts are not relevant here, because tort law is a system of extra-contractual compensation for damage. The two systems therefore meet only where an act both violates the criminal law and causes damage to an individual.[307]

Where that is the case the basic rule is that both criminal and tort **601** sanctions are incurred. An offence which causes damage to another

---

[302] No. 4 above.

[303] *Inter alia:* Almeida Costa, *Obrigações* 5th ed., pp. 415–418, 421–423; Galvão Telles, *Obrigações* 6th edn., pp. 195–196; Feenstra, *Vergoeding en vergelding, passim*; Georgiades/Stathopoulos (-Georgiades), *Greek Cc* vol. iv, introduction prior to Arts. 914–938, nos. 11–17; de Ángel Yágüez, *Responsabilidad civil*, 3rd edn., pp. 49–52; Yzquierdo Tolsada, *Responsabilidad civil*, pp. 29–49; Morillas Cueva, *Consecuencias del delito*, pp. 139–140; *Encyclopédie Dalloz* (-Conte), vol. viii, *Responsabilité du fait personnel*, no. 16; Viney, *Introduction* 2nd edn., nos. 74–2 ff.; Jørgensen, *VersR* 1970 pp. 193–195; Hellner, *Skadeståndsrätt* 4th edn., pp. 22 ff., 46–50; McMahon/Binchy, *Irish Law of Torts* 2nd edn., pp. 17–18; Deutsch, *Haftungsrecht*, vol. i, pp. 89–98.

[304] So Art. 34 Port. *Código de Processo Penal* (rpld.) which coerced the granting of damages even if not claimed (last employed: RC 10 Oct. 1984, *CJ* IX [1984–4] p. 79) was an anomaly. It even led to immaterial damages being awarded in cases of attempted murder (STJ 9 Jan. 1952, *BolMinJust* 29 [1952] p. 157). Art. 19 Spanish CP (rpld.) could also be thus interpreted. Art. 116 Spanish NCP cannot: it expressly requires the presence of damage.

[305] Even after the implementation of Art. 128 Port. *Código Penal* 1982 (now Art. 129 Port. CP as amended by the Act of 15 Mar. 1995), which refers to 'civil law' in respect of criminal liability, the state sometimes had a civil cause of action against the tortfeasor under Art. 34 *Código de Processo Penal* for breach of provisions protecting the public interest (RE 29 Nov. 1983, *BolMinJust* 333 [1984] p. 543). The nature of the rule, held valid in STJ 12 Dec. 1984, *BolMinJust* 342 (1985) p. 227 (but cf. RP 4 Nov.1987, *CJ* XII (1987–5) p. 223) remained controversial until it was superseded. Art. 34 has now been replaced by Arts. 71–84 *Código de Processo Penal* 1987.

[306] Art. 18 Italian Act on the Introduction of a Ministry for the Environment, which entitles the state to claim damages for pollution, is such a bifunctional provision.

[307] Two points require mention here. First, under common law some torts which constitute offences are actionable 'without proof of special damage'. Secondly, similar concepts exist on the continent. One such is Art. 444 I Spanish CP ('persons convicted of rape, indecency, or abduction of women shall also be sentenced to compensation of the injured party'). This led TS (crim.) 29 Apr. 1995, *RAJ* 1995 no. 3082 p. 4039 to conclude that (minor) immaterial compensation must be paid even if neither material nor moral damage has been established. Otherwise, the general rule is of course that the commission of an offence does not necessarily entail the infliction of damage (TS 17 Mar. 1992, *RAJ* 1992 no. 2198 p. 2954). The rule in Art. 444 I CP is now found in Art. 193 NCP.

person usually founds an action for damages.[308] Except in cases of overwhelming contributory negligence,[309] consent exonerating private liability,[310] and exemptions from liability,[311] that will always be the case save where one applies the doctrine of envisaged risk[312] with the result that the law breached does not protect this particular plaintiff,[313] or indeed is not intended to protect individuals at all.[314] There the wrong-doer is liable in criminal law only.

Criminal failure to lend assistance is a good example.[315] Whether such failure gives rise to both criminal and civil liability is moot. Although the number of voices in favour of civil liability appears to be increasing,[316]

[308] Thus explicitly Art. 19 Spanish CP: 'Every person guilty of a delict or offence is also civilly liable': see fn. 306 above on Art. 116 Spanish NCP. Art. 185 Italian CP is the corresponding provision. Cass. 11 Feb. 1995, n. 1540, *Giust.civ.Mass.* 1995 n. 1540 p. 326 says that within the scope of Art. 2043 Cc it is necessary to distinguish in view of the term *danno ingiusto*. Criminal acts are tortious *per se* (*ingiustizia in re ipsa*), and in other cases it is crucial that the tortfeasor acted *non iure* and *contra ius*. In other legal systems violation of a criminal provision often also constitutes—*ipso iure*—a civil *faute*. Cf. Brussels 18 Mar. 1994, *RGAR* 1995 no. 12485: a piece of wood was thrown by a car onto the windscreen of a following vehicle. The act was considered to be criminal 'throwing' under Art. 557 no. 4 *Code pénal* and consequently a *faute* under Art. 1382 Cc. Whether '*un fait puisse être punissable en raison de sa seule matérialité*' is the subject of debate in Belgian and French criminal law: Henneau/Verhaegen, *Droit pénal général*, nos. 381–383.

[309] TS 3 Dec. 1982, *RAJ* 1982 no. 7376 p. 4955 (contributory negligence reduces civil liability but does not exonerate criminality). However, AP Huelva 10 July 1980, *La Ley* 1981 (1) p. 248 held that criminal but not civil liability may be reduced on causation grounds if the victim provoked the unlawful act.

[310] Walker *Delict* 2nd edn., p. 346 draws attention to such cases. To give but one example, it would be grotesque to award damages to a masochist because his sexual practices constituted an offence: *Murray* v. *Fraser* 1916 SC 623, 635.

[311] TC 18 Mar. 1992, *La Ley* 1992 (3) pp. 19, 20.   [312] Cf. nos. 30 and 306 above.

[313] STJ 28 Apr. 1993, *CJ* (ST) I (1993–2) p. 207; STJ 9 June 1993, *CJ* (ST) I (1993–2) p. 242 (criminal provisions on sexual offences against children are intended to protect children, not their mothers who therefore have no cause of action).

[314] *Biddle* v. *Truvox Engineering Co. Ltd.* [1952] 1 KB 101: breach of sec. 17(2) Factories Act 1937 by inadequately secured machine; no liability for the buyer's staff; *Newman* v. *Francis* [1953] WLR 402. That criminal non-payment of wages constitutes a breach of contract but not an unlawful act was maintained by CA Athens 1846/1971, *NoB* 19 (1971) p. 1443.

[315] Failure to lend assistance is punishable, under varying circumstances, in: Portugal (Art. 200 CP as amended by the Act of 15 Mar. 1995); Germany (§ 323c StGB); Spain (Art. 489*ter* CP [rpld.] and Art. 195 NCP); Belgium (Art. 422*bis* CP); France (Art. 63 II CP); Denmark (§§ 182, 253 Danish Criminal Code); Austria (§ 95 StGB); Greece (Art. 307 StGB); and Italy (Art. 593 II CP). It is not an offence in England (*Zoernsch* v. *Waldock* [1964] 1 WLR 675, 685 *per* Wilmer, J) or Scotland (Cullen, *Jurid.Rev.* 1995 pp. 20–27).

[316] On Austria: Mayer-Maly, *ZVR* 1977 pp. 97, 100; Koziol, *Österr. Haftpflicht*, vol. ii p. 101 (fn. 51); Belgium: Brussels 23 Oct. 1963, *Pas. belge* 1964, II, 282; Portugal: STJ 27 Jan. 1993, *CJ* (ST) I (1993–1) p. 104 (albeit *obiter* and concerning the victim of an accident left in a vulnerable position); The Netherlands: no. 92 and fn. 569 above; Greece: Litzerpopoulos, *Stoicheia Enochikou Dikaiou*, vol. ii, p. 356; France: Cass.crim. 16 Mar. 1972, *D.* 1972 *Jur.* 394 (1*ère esp.*); *Sem.Jur.* 1973, II, 17474 (2*ème esp.*); Nancy 27 Oct. 1965, *D.* 1966 *Jur.* 30; Paris 11 July 1969, *Sem.Jur.* 1970, II, 16375; Sweden: liability only for 'failure to avert a criminal act'. It arises when such failure to act constitutes an offence (2nd Chap., 5 § SKL).

many are also against.[317] The latter express the view that the offence exists to serve only the public interest, and that liability would otherwise be uncontrollable. Further, it would obviously be undesirable either to make a passive onlooker liable to the victim to the same extent as the perpetrator, or for one of several such onlookers to be liable in place of them all. The position is different where there is a special relationship of proximity between victim the wrongdoer, such as where they are married or closely related,[318] and where the defendant is independently liable at civil law for the victim's helpless position.[319]

2. DAMAGES WITHOUT PUNISHMENT

It is undisputed that civil liability may be imposed even where there is **602** no criminal liability. Cases are legion. They include cases whose cause of action constitutes no criminal offence, as in most negligence cases resulting in damage to property.[320] In Spain, civil wrongdoings follow a wholly different system from criminal offences (Art. 1092 Cc). The dual-track system[321] is not perfect, however, because it leads to numerous incongruities and contradictions.[322] Furthermore, the question of whether a tortious act may also incur criminal liability is of great practical importance in many systems, for only if a tort amounts to a crime can a civil claim be brought before a criminal court[323] which may apply

---

[317] German exponents are OLG Frankfurt/M 27 Oct. 1988, *NJW-RR* 1989 pp. 794, 795 and Ulmer, *JZ* 1969 pp. 163, 165 and fn. 29. However, cf. *BGB RGRK* (- Steffen), 12th edn., § 823 no. 136. On Denmark: Kruse, *Erstatningsretten* 5th edn. p. 116; Spain: TS 23 May 1987, *RAJ* 1987 no. 3115 p. 2888 (robbery and subsequent death: no civil liability but punishment of bystander who failed to help the deceased). Also TS 2 Nov. 1981, *La Ley* 1982 (2) p. 106: plaintiff hotelier's daughter mistook a bottle of boric acid for one containing medicine and inadvertently poisoned a hotel guest. Instead of informing the hospital of the details, the father, recognizing his daughter's mistake, exchanged the contents of the bottles to disguise her error. The guest died. The father avoided liability for failure to lend assistance because his conduct was not causative of the death. For England, see no. 288 and fn. 325 above.

[318] *R* v. *Sheppard* [1981] AC 394; *R* v. *Stone* (1977) QB 354.

[319] STJ 27 Jan. 1993 (fn. 316 above); TS 2 Nov. 1981 (fn. 317 above). Also *R* v. *Miller* [1983] 1 All ER 978; *Fagan* v. *Metropolitan Police Commissioner* [1969] 1 QB 439.

[320] Under the Spanish CP, to inflict damage on property with gross negligence (*imprudencia temeraria*) is an offence. That is also the case for simple negligence (*imprudencia simple*) if the damage is valued at an amount exceeding compulsory insurance cover: Arts. 565, 586*bis*, 600 CP; de Ángel Yágüez, *Responsabilidad civil* 3rd edn., pp. 87–90. Buján, *VersRAI* 1993 p. 14 is therefore not quite correct.

[321] Regarding its origins see (in German) Lobedanz, *Schadensausgleich bei Straftaten in Spanien*, pp. 13–34.

[322] The chaotic diversity of opinion as to when parents should be liable for their children is a particularly clear example: nos. 65, 88, 134 above.

[323] The pursuit of civil claims in the criminal court where the civil wrong also constitued an offence is common practice. For Greece: Deliyannis/Kornilakis, *Eidiko Enochiko Dikaio*,

625

rules of substantive law different from those that a civil court would apply.[324]

603 Most other unlawful acts which incur only civil liability require fault. Only criminal punishment, unlike civil liability, requires personal fault.[325] Accordingly, few systems possess regulations for the criminal punishment of legal persons and it is generally only tort law which provides for liability for others,[326] whether they have acted criminally or merely tortiously.[327] Persons incapable of fault may thus be liable at civil law although punishment is impossible. Civil responsibility commonly accrues for children at an earlier age than criminal responsibility. Further, reversals of the burden of proof of fault,[328] the blanket exclusion of defences[329] of ignorance of the law, and true strict liability are all concepts exclusive to civil law. Finally, amnesties commonly operate only to prevent punishment.[330]

604 There are many provisions under which a state may waive punishment if the wrongdoer's conduct is not gravely reprehensible and he has voluntarily redressed the results of his wrongdoing. Here one may say that compensation is substituted for punishment. An example is § 42 Austrian ABGB: a person is 'not punishable' for an offence punishable by a maximum of three years' imprisonment if his guilt is insignificant

vol. iii pp. 105–106 and Mylonopoulos, in: Van den Wyngaert, *Criminal procedure systems*, pp. 163, 170; final civil judgment need not end the plaintiff's involvement in the criminal procedures (Areopag 1213/1991, *NoB* 40 [1992] p. 324); Portugal: Art. 128 CP (now Art. 129 CP as amended by the Act of 15 Mar. 1995); RP 4 Nov. 1987, *CJ* XII (1987–5) p. 223; RC 3 Dec. 1986, *CJ* XI (1986–5) p. 103; Austria: §§ 1338 s. 2 ABGB in conjunction with §§ 4, 47, 366 StPO; The Netherlands: Art. 51a Sv; Germany: § 403 StPO.

[324] In Belgium (Cass. 26 Oct. 1990, *Rev.crit.jur.belge.* 1992 p. 497) and France (Cass.com. 17 Nov. 1987, *Sem.Jur.* 1988 II 17937; Cass.crim. 15 Jan. 1985, *D.* 1995 *Jur.* 121) the principle of *non-cumul* of contractual and delictual liability is considered only by civil courts. Criminal courts apply non-contractual liability law to allow the plaintiff 'forum shopping'. Cf. Starck (-Roland/Boyer) vol. ii, 4th edn., no. 1843. Also no. 434.

[325] No. 626 below on the effect of the principle on the definition of negligence.

[326] It may be relevant in respect of *Ordnungswidrigkeiten* (untranslatable, thank God) or, in Italy, in cases of an *atto illecito amministrativo*: Cass. 24 May 1994, n. 5063, *Dir.fam.pers.* 1995, I, p. 109: 15–year-old lit a fire in school playground which spread to the school building. Under Art. 2 II Act no. 689 of 24 Nov. 1981 *modifiche al sistema penale* (Gaz.Uff.-suppl.ord. al no. 329 of 30 Nov. 1981) his parents were fined a sum based on the cost of repairing the damage.

[327] When a principal is liable for his agent's offence, the latter remains personally criminally responsible even if the offence was committed in performance of his duties: Cour 13 June 1990, *Pas. luxemb.* 28 (1990–92) p. 45. That must not be confused with the question of whether the agent's criminal offence breaks the chain of causation in respect of the employer's liability: see nos. 204 and 348 above.

[328] TS 20 Feb. 1989, *RAJ* 1989 no. 1215 p. 1294: the presumption of innocence established by Art. 24 II Spanish constitution does not apply to Art. 1902 Cc., that provision being aimed at compensation rather than repression.

[329] Corte Cost. 24 Mar. 1988, n. 364 (no. 595 and fn. 268 above).

[330] As expressly provided in Art. 198 Italian CP. See also Conciliatore Udine 9 Mar. 1995, *NGCC* 1995, I, 784, 786.

(no. 1), if further offences are not expected of him (no. 3), and if 'the effects of the act have essentially been eliminated, repaired, or compensated in another way' (no. 2). Under § 167 I Austrian StGB sanctions against perpetrators of specified offences, including criminal damage, may be waived if they show 'active remorse'. Active remorse is presumed if the perpetrator 'has made good all the damage caused by his act prior to the authorities' learning of his wrongdoing' (§ 167 II no. 1). Other criminal systems take into account the wrongdoer's conduct after the offence and any attempts made to redress the damage in deciding on the sentence. Art. 62 in conjunction with Art. 133 Italian CP is an example.

3. DAMAGES AS PUNISHMENT

Punishment and damages are not alternatives. It is not the case that **605** punishment is imposed only by criminal law while tort regulates compensation. There are exceptions to both rules.

a. Compensation Orders

The first group of exceptions are those mechanisms which permit the **606** prosecuting authority or court to waive or withdraw from prosecution if the wrongdoer compensates the damage caused (e.g. § 153a German StPO). Sentence may also be suspended if the wrongdoer 'compensates the damage resulting from the offence' (§ 56b II 1 German StPO). The duty to compensate is a more overtly criminal sanction in the successful English and Scottish compensation orders system. Under sec. 35 Powers of Criminal Courts Act 1973 and Part IV Criminal Justice (Scotland) Act 1980 the trial judge may, instead of or as well as other punishment, order the convicted defendant to compensate the victim. The court must take account of the financial circumstances of the defendant (s. 35(4A)), and the victim may sue for any damage not covered by the order. As a rule, however, the compensation ordered is the sum recoverable in a civil action. Compensation orders are made only in relatively straightforward cases.[331] Compensation takes precedence over punishment when the defendant's means do not allow the payment of both compensation and a fine,[332] the objective being to improve the lot of victims of crime. Indeed, it would be absurd for the state rather than the victim to receive the money. A provision in Austrian law[333] allows the victim to claim against the state, but such mechanisms appear clumsy.

---

[331] *R v. Daly* [1974] 1 All ER 290.   [332] Sec. 35(4A).   [333] § 373a Austrian StPO.

607   So impressed were the Dutch by the English system that, after a trial period[334] in two first-instance courts, compensation orders were introduced generally on 1 April 1995.[335] An offender who is potentially liable for damages in a civil action may be sentenced to pay the Treasury the appropriate sum, which is forwarded to the victim. Irish criminal law also allows trial judges to order offenders to pay compensation.[336] In Germany the debate on such compensation orders has only just begun.[337] Their advantages are apparent. It is in the offender's interest to make payments diligently and the victim's chances of being compensated are not impaired by the defendant paying a fine or being imprisoned. Compensation orders are admittedly unsuited to complicated cases, but the vast majority of tort cases are neither factually nor legally complicated.

b. Punitive Damages

608   Savigny characterized tort law and the duty to compensate for damage as punishment.[338] Modern law takes a different view, although a few writers continue to see a penal element in all non-contractual liability.[339] Art. 26 Spanish CP and Art. 34 III NCP explicitly state that an obligation to compensate is not punishment if it arose from civil rather than criminal provisions.[340] In Spain and elsewhere, punitive damages are considered a peculiarity of the common law.[341] In Austria punitive damages do not even merit academic debate. In Italy, where the press can be held liable for damages for defamation as well as to an independent claim for redress,[342] it has only recently been established that the latter claim, based on the gravity of the defamation, may be pursued before a civil court:[343] in the 1960s this was thought to be a sanction 'increasing the

---

[334] Act of 23 Dec. 1992, Stb. 1993 no. 29; van Dijk/Groenhuijsen, *NJB* 1993 pp. 163–167.
[335] Art. 36f Sr.
[336] McMahon/Binchy, *Irish Law of Torts* 2nd edn., p. 18.
[337] Schöch, *Gutachten C for the 59th German Lawyers' Conference* (1992); Dölling, *JZ* 1992 pp. 493–499.
[338] von Savigny, *Das Obligationenrecht als Teil des heutigen römischen Rechts*, vol. ii (1853) pp. 295–296.   [339] Zeno-Zencovich, *Giur.it.* 1985, IV, 12, 18.
[340] TS 28 Oct. 1986 no. 5750 p. 5620.
[341] Yzquierdo Tolsada, *Responsabilidad civil*, pp. 40–41; Stein, *EuZW* 1994 p. 18. BGH 4 June 1992, BGHZ 118 pp. 312, 334–345 did not follow an American decision on exemplary damages. Punishment is within the state's exclusive jurisdiction.
[342] Art. 12 Act no. 47 of 8 Feb. 1948 on the Press (*legge sulla stampa*): 'In cases of defamation by the press, the injured party can demand an additional sum as reparation [*riparazione*] in addition to damages under Art. 185 CP. The sum is determined by reference to the severity of the insult and the circulation of the journal.'
[343] Cass.pen. 13 Apr. 1989, *Rep.Giur.it.* 1990, *voce 'stampa'*, col. 3879 no. 37; Cass.pen. 23 Apr. 1991, *Rep.Giur.it.* 1992, *voce 'stampa'*, col. 3899, no. 29.

efficacity of criminal proceedings', and which could only be imposed by criminal courts.[344]

Such development is not unusual: it accords with the general tendency   **609** of the courts to revive civil punishment for grave violations of personal dignity.[345] It would be useless to impose only compensatory damages on journals who invent scandalous interviews with real people to improve circulation: the sums awarded would be considered trifling. Accordingly, the German BGH and the Swedish Supreme Court recently decided almost simultaneously that 'the notion of prevention demands that resultant profits be taken into account in calculating the quantum of damages.'[346] The rulings clearly include elements of private punishment. The same is true of Art. 6:106 I lit. a BW, under which 'the victim is entitled to such damages as appear equitable if the tortfeasor intentionally inflicted harm of the type sustained'. Thus civil and criminal functions merge wherever the compensation of immaterial losses is intended to give the plaintiff moral satisfaction for the wrong he has suffered.[347] This is particularly apparent in Italy, as *danno morale* generally incurs compensation only if it is consequent upon criminal activity (Art. 2059 Cc with Art. 185 CP).[348] Explicit reference is made to the *funzione punitiva* of the *danno morale* which, in respect of injury to a person's dignity, is only satisfied if the anticipated or actual profit to the defendant is considered in the calculation of damages.[349] Indeed, one judgment based its compensation on the tariff set by the criminal law.[350]

Provisions with punitive characteristics, such as those in the German   **610** BGB[351] and the French *Code civil*, only operate outside the law of tort,

[344] Cass. 29 Oct. 1965, n. 2300, *Giur.it.* 1966, I, 1, 726.

[345] For a comparison of laws extending beyond European borders: Stoll, *FS Rheinstein*, vol. ii pp. 569, 570–579. For Sweden, report of the *Kommitén om ideell skada* published in 1992 (bibliography before no. 600 above).

[346] BGH 15 Nov. 1994, *NJW* 1995 p. 861 (also no. 521 and fn. 671 above). Almost identical considerations obtained in Swedish HD 16 Nov. 1994, *NJA* 1994: 115 (pp. 637, 649): the economics of press publications must also be considered; damages should be high enough to have a deterrent effect.   [347] Stoll (fn. 345) p. 579.

[348] Franzoni, *Danno alla persona*, p. 724; Bonilini, *Danno non patrimoniale*, pp. 272, 278, 291, 296; Corte cost. 14 July 1986, n. 184, *Foro.it.* 1986, I, 2053; no. 615 below.

[349] App. Rome 5 Nov. 1990, *Dir.inf.* 1991 p. 845. Cf. Trib. Monza 26 Mar. 1990, *Foro.it.* 1991, I, 2862.   [350] Pret. Monza 19 Dec. 1992, *Foro.it.* 1994, I, 2291.

[351] § 817 s. 2 BGB in particular has punitive elements. For that reason the BGH does not consider the provision suitable for analogous application. As 'a provision which is in principle unknown to civil law' it applies only to unjust enrichment, not to *negotiorum gestio*: BGH 31 Jan. 1963, BGHZ 39 pp. 87, 91. § 844 I BGB (third-party claims in fatal cases) could also have punitive properties but this has eluded German lawyers. In The Netherlands, which only introduced a similar provision in 1992 (Art. 6:108 II BW, under which the person liable must compensate the actual bearer for the funeral expenses, rather than the person who should have borne them) attention is drawn to the fact that punitive damages have been reintroduced (Feenstra, *Vergelding en vergoeding*, p. 21).

and then only in the defence of *ex turpi causa non oritur actio*.[352] Private punishment (*peine privée*) is unacceptable: *'l'indemnité ne peut être rendue plus lourde en raison de la particulière gravité de la faute.'*[353] This is because *'la responsabilité civile n'a pas de fonction pénale et la gravité de la faute ne peut donc justifier une condemnation supérieure à la valeur du dommage'*.[354] Notwithstanding this rather restrictive basis, calculation of damages, both material and immaterial, is within the judge's discretion. So, as long as the courts do not explicitly mention the intention to penalize in their reasonings, their rulings are 'cassation-proof', a fact no doubt often relied upon.[355] Indeed there have been demands that in profit-motivated violations of personal dignity profits should be forfeited, because in such cases it is essential to complement the compensatory function of tort by adding a *'fonction de prévention et de peine'*.[356] Since the first half of the nineteenth century, French courts have employed the partly punitive, partly coercive concept of *astreinte*, which has also made its way into Belgian and Luxembourgeois law.[357] A judgment debtor may be sanctioned by a fine for non-compliance with a court order. The level of the fine, independent of the damage originally caused,[358] is calculated by reference to the degree of fault of the debtor and his financial circumstances: *'[l'astreinte] présente ainsi tous les caractères d'une peine privée.'*[359]

611　　Punitive damages are therefore not unique to the common law, which merely imposes them more openly. The starting point is the House of Lords ruling in *Rookes v. Barnard*,[360] which established the distinction between aggravated and exemplary damages. The latter are imposed to set an example; whether the former are truly 'punitive' has yet to be definitively decided.[361] Exemplary damages are awarded if the defen-

---

[352] Art. 792 Cc (exclusion of claims under the law of succession) and Art. 1477 Cc (exclusion of claims under the matrimonial property regime).
[353] Cass.civ. 8 May 1964, *JCP* 1965, II, 14140.
[354] Cass.crim. 8 Feb. 1977, Bull.crim. 1977 no. 52; Paris 26 Apr. 1983, *D.* 1983 *Jur.* 376.
[355] Starck (-Roland/Boyer), *Obligations*, vol. i, 4th edn., no. 1479; Viney, *La responsabilité: effets*, no. 6; ead., *Introduction*, 2nd edn., no. 74–3.
[356] Roland/Boyer (fn. 355 above), no. 1480. Viney, *Sem.Jur.* 1993, I, 3727 no. 11; v. Bar (-Gotthardt), *DeliktsR in Europa, Frankreich*, p. 26.
[357] For more comprehensive information on France: Terré/Simler/Lequette, *Obligations*, 5th edn., nos. 1024–1031. The relevant rules of Belgian law are Arts. 1385*bis-nonies* Cod.jud. (Act of 31 Jan. 1980, Monit. belge of 20 Feb. 1980) and of Luxembourgeois law: Art. 2059 Cc.
[358] The fine is *'indépendante des dommages et intérêts'*: Art. 6 French Act No. 72–626 of 5 July 1972 *'relative à la réforme de la procédure civile'* (JO 9 July 1972, p. 7181). Confirmed by Art. 34 Act No. 91–650 of 9 July 1991 *'portant réforme des procédures civiles d'exécution'* (JO 14 July 1991 p. 9228).　　　[359] Terré/Simler/Lequette (fn. 357 above) no. 1025 (p. 779).
[360] [1964] AC 1129. Also no. 290 and fn. 340 above.
[361] The Irish Civil Liability Act 1961 refers in sec. 7(2) only to 'exemplary damages' (not to 'aggravated damages') whereas 'punitive damages' under sec. 14(4) includes both types: White, *ILT* 1987 pp. 60, 64–65. In England aggravated damages are not seen as punitive: Markesinis/Deakin, *Tort Law* 3rd edn., p. 683. Scotland recognizes only aggravated damages: Walker, *Delict* 2nd edn., p. 461.

dant's conduct violates the 'plaintiff's proper feelings of dignity and pride';[362] effectively, they compensate immaterial loss. Whether English or Irish law would describe the sum awarded by the BGH in the *Caroline von Monaco* ruling[363] as 'aggravated' or 'exemplary' is unanswerable, the boundary between them being less distinct than the theory implies.

There is no doubt that exemplary damages are punitive: 'The object of **612** exemplary damages is to punish and deter.'[364] They are applicable in English law in three[365] classes of cases.[366] Although occasionally criticized, they have often been confirmed.[367] The first class of cases involves statutory authority,[368] the second where a government authority displays 'oppressive, arbitrary or unconstitutional behaviour', and the third where the defendant calculates before acting that his profit would exceed the compensatory damages he would have to pay.[369] Exemplary damages are clearly very similar to aggravated damages, but are only awarded for torts which would have incurred exemplary damages before *Rookes* v. *Barnard*. Such cases include trespass to the person, trespass to property, and defamation. Neither negligence nor nuisance,[370] whether private or public, fall within this category.[371] Exemplary damages may be ordered for deceit, although the principle that nobody should be punished twice for the same action means that they will not be imposed if the defendant is imprisoned for the fraud.[372]

4. PUNISHMENT TO PRODUCE MORAL SATISFACTION

Given that exemplary damages are excluded by imprisonment, does it **613** not follow that imprisonment should in some cases satisfy the victim's claim to damages for 'immaterial' loss (pain and suffering)? Some Dutch[373]

---

[362] [1964] AC 1129, 1221 (*per* Lord Devlin).   [363] Fn. 346 above.
[364] Fn. 362 above.
[365] The rules in *Rookes* v. *Barnard* appear not to have become established law in Ireland: White, *ILT* 1987 pp. 60, 63–65. The case was not quoted in *Maher* v. *Collins* [1975] IR 232 (Sup. Ct.) which decided that adultery (then an offence) was no basis for awarding punitive damages.
[366] See Lord Denning in *Broom* v. *Cassell & Co. Ltd.* [1971] 2 QB 354, 380–381 (CA).
[367] Esp. in *Cassell & Co. Ltd.* v. *Broom* [1972] AC 1027 (HL).
[368] Cf. sec. 13(2) Reserve and Auxiliary Forces (Protection of Civil Interests) Act 1951 (c. 65) (special case of conversion).   [369] (Fn. 362 above) p. 1226.
[370] *AB and Others* v. *South West Water Services Ltd.* [1993] 1 All ER 609 (CA).
[371] Hopkins, [1993] *CLJ* 199, 201.
[372] Thus *Archer* v. *Brown* [1984] 2 All ER 267 (Pain, J).
[373] Hof Amsterdam 22 Oct. 1975, *NedJur* 1977 no. 282 p. 973: father threatened to commit suicide if his 18–year-old daughter did not consent to sexual intercourse; immaterial damages not awarded because the father was held criminally liable which sufficed for satisfaction; Rb. Maastricht 14 June 1990, *NedJur* 1993 no. 130 p. 390: offender sentenced to 2 years' imprisonment. Although the court accepted that his punishment did not satisfy the victim sufficiently, it was taken into consideration when assessing compensation.

and German[374] courts have taken this position, and in Greece some commentators suggest that the imprisonment of the defendant is a factor to be considered when calculating damages.[375] Debate on this issue has subsided in Germany since the BGH ruled on 29 November 1994 that in cases of liability under § 847 BGB 'a desire for moral satisfaction of the injured person may be taken into consideration but is to be distinguished from the state's right to exact punishment'. That desire is thus still a consideration even if 'the wrongdoer has been imprisoned for the action'.[376] In the interests of the harmonization of justice in Europe, it would be desirable if the *Hoge Raad*, when the question comes before it, took into account its neighbours' rulings.[377]

5. SPECIFIC REACTIONS OF TORT LAW TO CRIMINAL CONDUCT

a. Loss of Protection from Liability

614 Although the distinction between criminal and civil wrongdoing is only of great concern to Spanish tort law, other legal systems occasionally reflect the stigma attached to particular conduct. That third-party liability insurance rarely covers intentional wrongdoing is an example of this.[378] However, intentional wrongs are usually, if not always, criminal. Another typical reaction of private law to criminal conduct is to deprive the offender of certain protections from liability available to those liable only in tort. For example, when property is obtained by unlawful means:[379] if the property is damaged, the offender will be liable to the owner even for slight negligence, and sometimes in the absence of any fault other than the offence itself.[380] The liability of judges is another example: in some European systems this arises only if the judge commits a crime while acting in his judicial capacity.[381] Employers' liability insurance

---

[374] OLG Düsseldorf 12 Nov. 1993, *NJW-RR* 1994 p. 221; LG Flensburg 7 May 1992, *NJW RR* 1993 p. 351. *Contra*: OLG Celle 26 Nov. 1992, *VersR* 1993 p. 976; LG Cologne 27 Nov. 1992, *VersR* 1993 p. 980; OLG Stuttgart 28 May 1993, *NJW-RR* 1993 p. 1121. For further references: BGH 29 Nov. 1994, BGHZ 128 pp. 117, 122.

[375] Georgiades/Stathopoulos (-Georgiades), *Greek Cc*, vol. iv, Art. 932 no. 22; Deliyannis/Kornilakis, *Eidiko Enochiko Dikaio*, vol. iii p. 296.

[376] BGHZ 128 p. 117; confirmed by BGH 16 Jan. 1996, *VersR* 1996 p. 382.

[377] Nos. 403–406 above.

[378] § 152 VVG. § 19 II no. 1 Danish EAL ensures that the exclusion of liability under § 19 I EAL for damage to property covered by its owner's insurance does not apply in cases of intent and gross negligence.

[379] § 992 BGB. Art. 1099: but the Greek Cc refers only to an 'unlawful act'.

[380] No. 551 above on the owner–possessor relationship. No. 43 above on § 848 BGB and Art. 934 Greek Cc.

[381] This is the position in Italy (Art. 13 Act No. 117 of 13 Apr. 1988 on the Compensation of Damage Consequent upon the Wrongful Exercise of Judges' Powers and on Judges'

against employees' claims[382] almost invariably excludes liability for intentional wrongs[383] and criminal behaviour.[384] An intentional failure to take measures to prevent injuries, and undoing implemented measures (Art. 437 Italian CP) are examples of such criminality. In both cases the employer is also liable for damages for pain and suffering (Art. 2059 Italian Cc with Art. 185 CP).

b. Extension of the Scope of Liability

Not only are criminal offences particularly iniquitous, they often cause **615** greater harm to the victims than torts. Accordingly, some European systems allow victims of crime compensation for specific losses which is not available if the loss is caused by a mere tort. In a rule reminiscent of Art. 6:106 I lit. a BW,[385] § 1331 ABGB provides that someone whose property is damaged 'as a result of an act prohibited by criminal law is entitled to claim for its sentimental value'. Under § 335 ABGB the same applies if the wrongdoer 'came into possession [of the property] by an act prohibited by criminal law'. A person who intentionally damages something for which the owner has particular affection, such as a pet, is accordingly also liable to compensate resulting distress with immaterial damages (§ 125 Austrian StGB).

The clearest examples of the effect of criminality on the scope of civil **616** liability are found in 2nd Chap. § 4 Swedish SKL and 5th Chap. § 1 Finnish SKL, and in Art. 2059 Italian Cc in conjunction with Art. 185 Italian CP. The Swedish and Finnish provisions make purely economic losses caused 'by a criminal act' recoverable at civil law.[386] Art. 2059 Italian Cc in contrast concerns immaterial damage (*danno patrimoniale*), which 'shall only be compensated in cases specified by law'. This refers primarily to Art. 185 CP, which provides that every crime incurs liability

---

Liability); in Germany: § 839 II s. 1 BGB; v. Bar, *Foro.pad.* 1988, II, 131–137; similar in Portugal (but Art. 1083 CPC also names additional causes of action); in Austria culpable perversion of justice is a prerequisite, but extreme negligence suffices in some circumstances: OGH 23 May 1984, *JBl* 1985 p. 171. For a comparison of Dutch and Belgian judges' liability (no. 553 and fn. 2 above) see Kortmann, *NJB* 1993 pp. 921–926.

[382] Note that an employer who fails to carry out statutory precautions, and is thus criminally liable, cf. sec. 155 Factories Act 1961 (c. 34), may be subject to strict liability for breach of statutory duty. No. 307 above; Williams, 23 [1960] *ModLRev* 233–236.

[383] E.g. § 636 I RVO.

[384] E.g. Art. 10 II (Italian) Presidential Decree No. 1124 of 30 June 1965 on the unified rules on compulsory insurance for industrial injuries and diseases.

[385] No. 609 above. That provision was included in the 1992 BW, *inter alia* to regulate intentional damage to property held in particular affection: *Parlementaire Geschiedenis*, vol. vi p. 378.

[386] Nos. 244–246 and 303 above. On liability for violations of personal dignity under Swedish law, see no. 248 above.

under the 'civil provisions', and adds: 'every criminal act causing economic or non-economic loss obliges the wrongdoer and those persons liable for him in civil law to compensate [the victim]'. Another means of indemnification for non-economic loss is to compel the offender to publicize his criminal sentence at his own expense (Arts. 186, 187 CP).

617   Liability under Art. 2059 Cc with Art. 185 CP does not require that the accused be convicted. It suffices that his conduct, viewed objectively, meets the definition of an offence.[387] So the criminal act of a minor may render him and his parents liable for *danno non patrimoniale*.[388] Since the requirement is only that criminal law is contravened, whether or not the tortfeasor is found criminally responsible,[389] a civil judge may investigate *incidenter* and confirm that the conduct was criminal in the absence of a criminal conviction[390] or even an information.[391] However, if the defendant is acquitted for want of criminal negligence, the civil judge must accept that the conditions of Art. 185 CP are not fulfilled.[392] Under Art. 2059 Cc, however, the plaintiff may also recover damages for 'suffering' incurred whilst in a coma.

c. Harmonization of Civil and Criminal Limitation Periods

618   The final question is whether the criminal limitation period for an offence should be the same as the civil limitation period for the same conduct. That is not the case in the British Isles,[393] France, The Netherlands, or Germany. The state's power to punish is entirely independent of the civil right of action. In 1967 the BGH[394] even quoted approvingly a Court of Appeal ruling that 'under existing law even the most atrocious villain . . . [is] free to fend off victims with the three-year limitation period' found in § 852 I BGB.

---

[387] No claim arises under Art. 2059 Cc if no offence is committed: Cass. 5 Oct. 1994, n. 8081, *Dir.fam.pers.* 1995, I, 1352 (divorced woman retained ex-husband's name in breach of Art. 7 Cc: injunction, but no compensation). Conciliatore Udine 9 Mar. 1995, *NGCC* 1995, I, 784: no immaterial damages for owner of cat injured by a car: negligent damage to property does not constitute an offence, but compensation for *danno biologico* resulting from grief was awarded.

[388] Cass.sez.un. 6 Dec. 1982, n. 6651, *Giur.it.* 1984, I, 1, 150. See no. 83 above on whether a minor can incur liability under Arts. 2047, 2059 Cc.

[389] Bonilini, *Danno non patrimoniale*, p. 321; Ravazzoni, *La riparazione del danno non patrimoniale*, p. 105; Franzoni, *Fatti illeciti*, Art. 2059, § 7, p. 1170; App. Milan 27 Sep. 1974, *Arch.civ.* 1975 p. 236.   [390] Cass.sez.un. 6 Dec. 1982 (fn. 387 above).

[391] Cass.sez.un. 6 Dec. 1982 (fn. 387 above); App. Milan 27 Sep. 1974 (fn. 388 above).

[392] Cass. 29 Nov. 1994, n. 10201, *Riv.giur.circ.trasp.* 1995 p. 570.

[393] Neither the common law nor the Limitation Acts (no. 291 and fn. 22 above) provide for an extension of the civil period merely because the criminal period has not expired. The criminality of the conduct does not even appear to be relevant to sec. 19(A) Prescription and Limitation (Scotland) Act 1973, under which the extension of limitation periods is in the discretion of the judge.   [394] BGH 22 June 1967, BGHZ 48 pp. 125, 133–134.

This view is not shared by the Scandinavian countries, nor most of   **619** those in the Mediterranean. In all three Scandinavian EU member states, where a criminal limitation period is longer than that under private law, the civil period will be extended to equal the criminal.[395] This reflects the old concept that criminal and tort law both govern the consequences of wrongdoing.[396] Likewise, the common law is still influenced by the notion that every offence constitutes an attack on the Crown and threatens social stability. As in Scandinavia, it is also considered 'inconsistent' in Greece, Italy, and Portugal to exclude civil liability while criminal prosecution is still possible.[397]

Art. 937 II Greek Cc provides that where 'an unlawful act simulta-   **620** neously constitutes a punishable offence subject to a longer criminal limitation period, that longer period shall apply to the civil claim'. The civil period prevails if it is longer than the criminal. Thus, if the victim only discovers enough information to sue the wrongdoer twelve years after the event, at which point (under Art. 937 I Greek Cc) the five-year civil limitation period begins to run, he still enjoys the full period, although criminal liability expires three years after that date under Art. 111 II s. 2 of the Criminal Code.[398] The Italian equivalent is Art. 2947 III Italian Cc: 'whenever the (tortious) act is considered criminal by the law and is subject to a longer criminal limitation period,[399] the longer period applies to the civil action.' However, if the offender has been convicted but not yet sentenced (*condanna generica*), the ten-year period under Art. 2953 Cc applies.

Like its Italian counterpart, the Portuguese Cc provides expressly for   **621** extension of the three-year tort limitation period (Art. 498 I) if criminal prosecution is still possible (Art. 498 III Cc). After much debate, the provision is now applied even to persons severally liable in civil law but innocent of crime.[400] The longer criminal period applies in civil law even when the time limit for criminal proceedings has expired without any indictment being served.[401]

The position in Spain was until recently slightly different. Art. 117 CP   **622** referred to the Civil Code regarding limitation of claims for compensation

---

[395] Denmark: § 1 I no. 5 Act no. 274 of 22 Dec. 1908 on the Limitation of Actions (see von Eyben/Nørgaard/Vagner, *Erstatningsret* 2nd edn., p. 323); Finland: 7th Chap. 2 § 2nd sentence SKL; Sweden 3 § Limitation of Actions Act (*Preskriptionslag*, SFS 1981:130). The victim may issue proceedings up to a year after the sentence becomes binding (v. Bar [-Witte], *DeliktsR in Europa, Sweden*, p. 86).   [396] No. 4 and fn. 20 above.

[397] Georgiades/Stathopoulos (-Georgiades), *Greek Cc*, vol. iv, Art. 937 no. 44. Not wholly in favour: Filios, *Enochiko Dikaio*, vol. ii (2) 3rd edn., pp. 129–130.

[398] Deliyannis/Kornilakis, *Eidiko Enochiko Dikaio*, vol. iii p. 305.

[399] I.e. longer than the 5–year period under 2947 I Ital. Cc.

[400] STJ 6 July 1993, *CJ* (ST) I (1993–2) p. 180; STJ 22 Feb. 1994, *CJ* (ST) II (1994–1) p. 126.

[401] STJ 22 Feb. 1994 (fn. 400 above); *contra*: RC 2 Nov. 1993, *CJ* XVIII (1993–5) p. 21.

arising from an offence. However, it did not specify whether the reference was to the one-year tort period under Art. 1968 II Cc, or the general fifteen-year period for a personal claim under Art. 1964 Cc.[402] Given Art. 1968 II Cc's explicit reference to Art. 1902 Cc, the courts generally assumed the latter. Thus if the offender was convicted, the longer period applied, even though the criminal proceedings did not assess his civil liability. If the case ended any other way, including acquittal,[403] the one-year period under Art. 1968 II Cc remained applicable.[404] The NCP contains no provision similar to Art. 117 CP; how the Spanish courts will react is as yet unknown.

623   The only example of a shorter criminal limitation period reducing the civil period is Art. 26 *titre préliminaire* of the Belgian *Code de procédure pénale*.[405] This effectively puts victims of crimes in a worse position than victims of mere torts. The provision has been declared unconstitutional by the Constitutional Court.[406] Not declaring the provision void, and having no *erga omnes* effect, the ruling merely allows civil courts not to apply Art. 26.[407] Precisely which course they will pursue is unclear.

6. SAME TERMINOLOGY, DIFFERENT CONTENT?

a. General Overview

624 A final indicator of the proximity between criminal and tort law is the extent to which they share language and concepts. 'Fault', 'unlawfulness', 'causation', 'attributability', and 'damage' are central to both. A comprehensive analysis of the relationship would investigate the extent to which such expressions are defined differently in the tort and criminal systems. It would also analyse the extent to which concepts previously considered only in tort cases now play a role in criminal law. Contributory fault and set-off are obvious examples.[408] Space here allows only some brief

---

[402] Font Serra, *La acción civil en el proceso penal*, pp. 16–17.

[403] An acquittal in criminal proceedings does not necessarily free the defendant from civil liability, due to the differing burdens of proof: TS 9 Feb. 1988, *RAJ* 1988 no. 771 p. 752 (*in casu* no civil wrong was established).

[404] TS 31 Mar. 1981, *RAJ* 1981 no. 1142 p. 949; TS 7 Jan. 1982, *RAJ* 1982 no. 184 p. 124; TS 15 Nov. 1986, *RAJ* 1986 no. 6535 p. 6293.

[405] Older rulings are: Cass. 28 Dec. 1971, *Pas. belge.* 1972, I, 200, 206 (short limitation period of Penal code Art. 26 prevails over Arts. 2262, 2264 Belgian Cc limitation period, even in respect of a minor's objectively criminal conduct).

[406] Cour d'Arbitrage 21 Mar. 1995, *RW* 1994–95 p. 1324; no. 563 and fn. 55 above.

[407] Fontaine/Fagnart, *RGAR* 1995 no. 12505.

[408] Hof s'Gravenhage 17 Feb. 1993, *NedJur* 1993 no. 294 p. 1081: a convict who was later found to be innocent of one offence subsequently committed another; first prison sentence was set off against the second.

remarks on negligence (no. 626) and a warning. The term 'intent', for instance, has different meanings in tort and criminal law;[409] an act deemed causative in one area of law may not be in the other;[410] even the definition of 'damage' may be different in a civil and criminal provisions.[411]

In other fields criminal and civil provisions effect a sort of division of **625** labour. Particular defences, for instance, may only be found in one system but not the other. In such cases the rules of the one simply refer to the provisions of the other.[412] An implicit reference by tort to criminal law may also occur where the tort employs terms such as 'incitor', 'aider', 'abettor', and 'joint principal' without further definition.[413] In Italy the rules of causation under Arts. 40, 41 CP are treated as general legal principles applicable also to civil law.[414] The criminal code is even referred to for the definitions of intent (*dolo*) and negligence (*colpa*).[415]

---

[409] The German and Greek civil law definition of intent requires knowledge of the unlawfulness of the conduct. A person negligently unaware of unlawfulness is liable in civil law only for negligence even if he desires the consequences. In criminal law he is liable for intent: Deutsch, *Haftungsrecht*, vol. i p. 94; Filios, *Enochiko Dikaio*, vol. ii [2], 3rd end., p. 42; Stathopoulos, *Geniko Enochiko Dikaio*, AI, 2nd edn., pp. 91–92.

[410] TS 28 Nov. 1992; *RAJ* 1992 no. 9448 p. 9447 confirmed that a defendant acquitted in the criminal court may nonetheless be liable in civil proceedings. Cass. 23 Sep. 1974, *RGAR* 1976 no. 9659 acquitted a doctor of involuntary manslaughter because the patient's chance of survival would only have been 90 % under correct treatment. Dalcq, *Ann. Louv.* 1983 pp. 73, 75 asserts that in such cases there should be civil liability, despite the 'missing 10%'. That view is not shared by Cass. 2 Nov. 1994, *RW* 1994–95 p. 1227: criminal court found that causation was not established between the defendant's intoxication and traffic accident, whereas the civil court held otherwise. The latter decision was quashed by the Belgian Court of Cassation on the ground that it was contradictory.

[411] Paz-Ares/Díez-Picazo/Bercovitz/Salvador (-Pantaleón), *Código Civil*, vol. ii, 2nd edn., p. 1988–1992.

[412] Self-defence and necessity are mentioned in the Spanish CP but not in its Cc. In appropriate cases reference is made to the former: Santos Briz, *Responsabilidad civil*, vol. i, 6th edn., p. 35; Díez-Picazo/Gullón, *Sistema*, vol. ii, 6th edn., p. 612. The position is the same in Austria in respect of self-defence (§ 3 Austrian StGB) (Koziol, *Österr. Haftpflichtrecht*, vol. i, 2nd edn., p. 103) and in France, where the civil law refers to the criminal provisions in practically all cases of *faits justificatifs* (Flour/Aubert, *Obligations*, vol. ii, 5th edn., no. 112; v. Bar [-Gotthardt], *Deliktsrecht in Europa, Frankreich*, p. 22). The Italian Cc excludes liability in cases of self-defence (Art. 2044 Cc) but does not define self-defence; it is presumed that the Cc refers tacitly to the CP here and regarding both Art. 2045 Cc (*stato di necessità*) and all other justifications (Cass. 26 Nov. 1976, n. 4487, *Resp.Civ. e Prev.* 1977 p. 593; Cass. 16 Feb. 1978, n. 753, *Arch.civ.* 1978 p. 762; Trib. Verona 13 Dec. 1988, n. 1871, *Giur.it.* 1990, I, 2, 135). In Germany the defence of protection of legitimate interests is found only in § 193 StGB, despite its bearing on private law: 22 Dec. 1959, BGHZ 31 p. 308. The same applies to § 127 StPO (citizen's arrest): OLG Hamm 1 Aug. 1972, *NJW* 1972 p. 1826.

[413] § 830, BGH 24 Jan. 1984, *NJW* 1984 p. 1226; see no. 52 and fn. 310 above on joint and several liability in Belgian and France.

[414] Cass. 1 Feb. 1991, n. 981, *Arch.civ.* 1991 p. 541; Cass. 14 Oct. 1992, n. 11207, *Giust. civ.Mass.* 1992 no. 11207 p. 1450; Alpa/Bessone, *Atipicità*, vol. i, 2nd edn., pp. 147–148.

[415] Visintini, *Fatti illeciti*, vol. ii p. 8 correctly says that the definition of *colpa* employed by the Court of Cassation for the purposes of Art. 2043 Cc reflects the tenor and contents of Arts. 42, 43 CP. Cf. Cass. 17 Dec. 1973, n. 3420, *Giust.civ.Mass.* 1973 no. 3420 p. 1161. Also no. 28 and fn. 117 above.

This is important, given that under Art. 43 CP a *delitto* is *colposo* if it involves disregard of *'leggi, regolamenti, ordini, o discipline'*.[416] German courts have debated the extent to which criminal provisions regarding family 'relatives' and the right to initiate prosecutions for defamation of a deceased person determine who can commence such proceedings.[417] In English law many torts also constitute crimes. A criminal acquittal need not necessarily result in defeat for the tort litigant, due to the differing burdens of proof: the civil litigant need only prove his case 'on the balance of probabilites', while the criminal prosecutor must prove guilt 'beyond reasonable doubt'.

b. Negligence in Private and Criminal Law

626   The question of whether, and if so how, negligence differs in civil and in criminal law has been much debated, except with regard to English law, which in any event distinguishes between criminal recklessness[418] and civil negligence.[419] Given the relatively minor importance of the question, much of that debate was otiose. The distinction is only relevant to unskilled or inexperienced persons who have attained the age of criminal responsibility but have intellectual or physical handicaps, and cannot be blamed for their actions because the nature of the activity in which they were engaged, which should have been apparent, was beyond their understanding. In such cases it must be decided whether civil liability can be incurred independent of criminal liability. The answer to that question usually corresponds with the answer to the question of whether particular conduct may be deemed not to be criminally negligent because the defendant is not personally and subjectively guilty, although the conduct is tortious on an objective view. Personal culpability is a prerequisite of criminal punishment only.

---

[416] Cass.sez.un. 22 Oct. 1984, n. 5361, *Foro.it.* 1985, I, 2358: public health officer was obliged to retire by unlawful administrative act; liability on grounds of both *colpa generica* and *colpa specifica*. It is established practice in criminal law that an unavoidable error as to the unlawfulness of conduct exempts from punishment despite Art. 5 CP (see no. 595 and fn. 268 above). Consequently, the full force of Arts. 43 and 5 CP is only available in private law.   [417] BGH 18 Sep. 1979, *NJW* 1980 p. 45.

[418] *R* v. *Caldwell* [1982] AC 341 (*per* Lord Diplock). Recklessness may be presumed if an 'obvious risk of danger' was inherent in the conduct and if the defendant either did not consider such risk at all, or was aware of it but nonetheless acted in the manner in which he did.

[419] Recklessness closely resembles the German *Leichtfertigkeit*. A person who wrongfully underestimates a risk, or who wrongly thinks that he can reduce it, acts negligently rather than recklessly. Constructive manslaughter is developing so that its requirement of gross negligence (*R* v. *Bateman* [1925] All ER 45), which was once effectively identical to recklessness, has been relaxed: simple negligence may now suffice. See *DPP* v. *Newbury* [1977] AC 500 [HL]; *R* v. *Church* [1966] 1 QB 59 [CA].

The traditional and highly controversial[420] position in Belgian and   **627**
French law is that fault is the same in both criminal and civil law. The
principle of *identité de la faute pénale et de la faute civile d'imprudence*
prevails.[421] However, the principle seems to apply only to torts involving physical injury, and not to those damaging only property.[422] After
all, civil courts can sometimes find fault on the basis solely of damage
to property,[423] an approach which could hardly be justified in criminal
law.[424] A further practical ground for the distinction is that its absence
leads, not to subjectivizing concepts of civil fault, but to the objectivization of criminal fault.[425] This is because, where criminal judges'
findings bind the civil courts,[426] the former cannot always banish the
question of civil liability from their minds.[427] In view of the strict
liability of the *gardien* under Art. 1384 I Cc, this appears neither
sensible nor necessary.[428]

There is much to be said for distinguishing between objective civil and   **628**
subjective criminal negligence. The distinction decriminalizes tort law
without weakening it. Further, by making personal fault a precondition
of criminality, the differing purposes of criminal and private law are
better served. The distinction is an integral part of German,[429] Greek,[430]

---

[420] Various contributions by Dalcq, Hannequart, and Delvaux in *Ann. Louv.* 1983 pp. 73–
86, 87–112, and 113–116 regarding the Belgian debate. Also Henneau/Verhaegen, *Droit
pénal général*, no. 412; Kohl, *Rev.crit.jur.belge* 1975 pp. 379–393. Amongst French commentators: Pirovano, *Faute civile et faute pénale, passim*; Viney, *Introduction* 2nd edn., nos. 152–
155; Le Tourneau, *Responsabilité civile*, 3rd edn., nos. 84–87.

[421] Initiated in Cass.civ. 18 Dec. 1912, p. 1914.1.249 = *DP* 1915.1.17 and now established
practice: Cass.civ. 19 Oct. 1988, Bull.civ. 1988, II, no. 200. The fundamental Belgian decision
was Cass. 5 Oct. 1893, *Pas. belge* 1893, I, 321 and 328; recently confirmed in Cass. 13 Feb.
1988, *RW* 1988–89 p. 159 and Cass. 26 Oct. 1990, *Rev.crit.jur.belge* 1992 p. 497: *'le défaut de
prévoyance ou de précaution au sens des articles 418 et suivants du Code pénal correspond à la
négligence ou à l'imprudence visée aux articles 1382 et 1383 du Code civil.'*

[422] *JClCiv* (-Jourdain), Arts. 1382 to 1386, fasc. 120–1, no. 50 correctly states: *'l'unité des
fautes ne vaut toutefois que pour les infractions involontaires entraînant des dommages corporels,
non pour les délits d'imprudence n'entraînant que des dommages matériels.'*

[423] Cass.civ. 10 Nov. 1992, *Bull.civ.* 1992, III, no. 292.

[424] In Belgium and France, however, sentences have been passed despite no personal
fault being established: fn. 308 above.

[425] De Page, *Droit Civil Belge*, vol. ii, 3rd edn., no. 907; Mazeaud/Tunc, *Responsabilité
civile* vol. i, 6th edn., nos. 639–642.

[426] Art. 4 II French C.proc.pén.; Arts. 3, 4 Belgian C.proc.pén.

[427] *Encyclopédie Dalloz* (-Conte), vol. viii, *Responsabilité du fait personnel*, no. 63; *JClCiv* (-
Jourdain) (fn. 420 above), no. 51.

[428] Conte loc. cit. no. 66; Starck (-Roland/Boyer), *Obligations*, vol. i, 4th edn., no. 22.

[429] BGH 10 Mar. 1970, *NJW* 1970 pp. 1038, 1039 (negligence to be defined objectively
rather than subjectively); BGH 15 Nov. 1971, *NJW* 1972 pp. 150, 151 (such care is required as
'common sense demands of a careful person in that position'). See criminal court decisions
cited in Jescheck, *Strafrecht Allgemeiner Teil*, 4th edn., p. 537.

[430] Georgiades/Stathopoulos (-Stathopoulos), *Greek Cc*, vol. ii, Art. 330 nos. 31–32;
Kavkas/Kavkas, *Enochikon Dikaion*, vol. ii, 6th edn., pp. 727–728; Balis, *Genikai Archai tou
Astikou Dikaiou*, 8th edn., pp. 461–462.

Spanish,[431] Portuguese,[432] Dutch,[433] Danish,[434] and Swedish law.[435] In Austria, contrarily, where the doctrine that recklessness established by a criminal court necessarily implied gross civil negligence had long been abandoned,[436] support for a uniform definition of negligence is increasing. That an acquitted defendant[437] may be liable in civil law is disregarded, because criminal proceedings are irrelevant to civil. Contrary to the effect observed in France and Belgium, the uniform definition of negligence of Austrian law has not resulted in the objectivization of criminal negligence, but rather in the subjectivization of civil negligence.[438]

[431] Yzquierdo Tolsada, *Responsabilidad civil*, pp. 33–34, 37–40; Santos Briz, *Responsabilidad civil*, vol. i, 6th edn., pp. 71–77; Quintano Ripollés, *An.Der.Civ.* 10 (1957) pp. 1034–1050. TS 9 June 1989, *RAJ* 1989 no. 4415 p. 5100: absence of criminal negligence need not exclude civil negligence.

[432] Antunes Varela, *Obrigações em Geral*, vol. i, 7th edn., pp. 566–570; Almeida Costa, *Obrigações*, 5th edn., pp. 470–471.

[433] van Dam, *Zorgvuldigheid en aansprakelijkheid*, pp. 81–85.

[434] von Eyben/Nørgaard/Vagner, *Erstatningsret*, 2nd edn., p. 48; Waaben, *Strafferettens almindelige del*, 2nd edn., p. 136.

[435] Notwithstanding his reluctance, Hellner, *Skadeståndsrätt*, 4th edn., pp. 55–56, draws attention to 1 § I *Tarifbrottslag* (Criminal Road Traffic Act) under which slight carelessness in road traffic cannot be punished as a crime but may incur civil liability.

[436] OGH 14 Oct. 1933, *SZ* 15/214 p. 642; OGH 21 Sep. 1978, *SZ* 51/128 p. 564.

[437] As expressly stated in OGH 16 June 1954, *JBl* 1954 p. 593.

[438] Koziol, *Österr. Haftpflichtrecht*, vol. i, 2nd edn., pp. 128–129; Walch, *JBl* 1961 pp. 497–505.

Index

Index

649

Index